encyclopedia
of
urban
planning

Arnold Whittick

Editor-in-Chief

encyclopedia
of
urban
planning

McGRAW-HILL BOOK COMPANY

new york   st. louis   san francisco
düsseldorf   johannesburg
kuala lumpur   london   mexico
montreal   new delhi
panama   paris   são paulo
singapore   sydney
tokyo   toronto

Library of Congress Cataloging in Publication Data
Main entry under title:

Encyclopedia of urban planning.

   1. Cities and towns—Planning—Dictionaries.
I. Whittick, Arnold, date. ed.
HT166.E5   309.2'62'03   73-19757
ISBN 0-07-070075-3

1234567890 VHVH 7654

*The editors for this book were Daniel N. Fischel, Harold B.
Crawford, and Linda B. Hander, the designer was Naomi
Auerbach, and its production was supervised by Teresa F.
Leaden. It was set in Fotosetter Garamond by York Graphic
Services, Inc.*

Printed and bound by Von Hoffmann Press, Inc.

contents

C. F. AHLBERG *Chief Regional Planning Officer, Stockholm Region, since 1952; Professor of Town Planning, Royal Institute of Technology, Sweden, 1960–1963; and Adviser, Swedish Ministry of Physical Planning and Local Government, since 1965* [*Sweden (in part)*]

GERD ALBERS *Professor of City and Regional Planning at Munich Technical University since 1961. Formerly in municipal service as town planner in Ulm, Trier, and Darmstadt; M.S. in City Planning, I.I.T., Chicago, 1950; author of* Geistescesinichtliche Entwicklung des Stadtesbaues in Medizin und Stadtesbau (changes in the philosophies of city planning), *1957 (Baumeister, Reinhard; Fischer, Theodor; Germany, West; Hilberseimer, Ludwig)*

GABRIEL ALOMAR *Architect and city planner; author of* Teoria de la Cuidad (fundamental ideas for humanistic city planning) *and* Comunidad Planeada and Sociologia Urbanistica *(Spain)*

FRANCISCO JOSÉ ALVAREZ Y LEZAMA *Engineer and planner; President of the Mexico Committee for World Town-Planning Day (Mexico)*

ALAN ARMSTRONG *Member of Town Planning Institute of Canada; worked in Canadian government housing agency and citizen organization; Chief of Staff of Canadian Council on Urban and Regional Research (Canada)*

GIOVANNI ASTENGO *Architect and planner. Professor of Town Planning University Institute of Architecture, Venice, since 1966. Editor of* Urbanistica, *official journal of Institute Nazionale de Urbanistica 1948–52 and Director since 1952. Author of the article on town planning for the* Encyclopedia of World Art. *Author of, and consultant for, plans of several cities including Turin, Assisi, Gubbio, Soluzzo, Bastia, Bergamo, Albenga, Ankara and Mogadishu (Somalia). Member of City Council of Turin* [*Ancient Planning, Roman Empire (in part); Italy*]

IVAN AVRAMOV *Architect and planner; Senior Planning Research Officer, the Institute of Town Planning and Architecture, Sofia (Bulgaria); author for many town planning schemes* [*Bulgaria (in part)*]

vii

JOACHIM BACH   *Professor and Director of Department of City Planning and Architecture at Hochschule, Weimar (Germany, East)*

LUIS BALERDI   *Architect (Master of Architecture, University of California, Berkeley) and planner (Master of Urban and Regional Planning, University of Pittsburgh); engaged in site planning for residential projects with related community facilities [Chile (in part)]*

DARIUSH BORBOR   *Architect and planner; Associate Member of the Royal Town Planning Institute of U.K. and Member of the Swiss Society of Engineers and Architects; prepared regional plans for Abadan-Khorramshahr and Nowshahr-Chalus and for urban renewal of Mashad City Center and for the earthquake-stricken city of Khakh; Consultant to the High Planning Council and Plan Organization of Iran (Iran)*

PHILIPPE VANDEN BORRE   *Inspector General, Administration of Urban and Regional Planning of Belgian Ministry of Works; Lecturer at Ghent State University; author of* Law and Procedure, *relating to land development in Belgium (Belgium)*

DAVID BRIGGS   *(M.Sc., M.R.T.P.I.) Visiting Professor for Transportation Engineering, Federal University, Rio de Janeiro, Brazil. Formerly Lecturer on Transport, Civil Engineering Department, Imperial College, London University (1966–1973) (Airports; Air Transport; Freeways and Motorways, Transport)*

DOUGLAS BRUCE   *Chartered Engineer; Associate Fellow of the Royal Aeronautical Society; Senior Member of the Institute of Electrical and Electronics Engineers; Head of Systems Design and Commissioning Group, Telecommunications Engineering Establishment, Civil Aviation Administration, U.K. (Communications; Computers in Planning; Cost-Benefit Analysis; Electric Power Generation and Transmission)*

STANLEY BUDER   *Associate Professor of History at the City University of New York; author of* Pullman: An Experiment in Industrial Order and Community Planning *and articles on urban history in historical and planning journals (Ackerman, Frederick L.; Bellamy, Edward; Burnham, Daniel H.; Mumford, Lewis; Roosevelt, Franklin Delano; Weber, Adna)*

ALEXANDRU BUDISTEANU   *Architect; Member of the State Committee for Local Economy and Administration, Bucharest. Formerly Special Technical Adviser, Center for Housing, Building, and Planning of the United Nations, New York [Romania (in part)]*

WILFRED BURNS   *Past President of the Town Planning Institute of the U.K.; Member of the Institute of Civil Engineers; Chief Planner of the Ministry of Housing and Local Government (Shopping Centers)*

JEAN CANAUX   *Architect, engineer, and planner; Director of the Urban Research Center, Paris, since its foundation. Formerly Inspector General of Construction; Recorder-General of the Congress of Planning and Housing for Southeast Asia (New Delhi, 1954); President of the International Federation for Habitation and Development of Territories, 1958–1962. Planning Consultant for the Ottawa Regional Plan, 1965, and Tokyo Plan, 1971 (France)*

GÖSTA CARLESTAM   *Architect; Research Worker, National Swedish Institute for Building Research. Formerly Head of Research and Development Section of Regional Planning Office of the Stockholm County Council. Editor of* Plan *(Swedish Society for Town and Country Planning) [Sweden (in part)]*

E. W. CHANDLER   *Architect and planner. Since 1963, Leverhulme Research Fellow and Lecturer in the Department of Civic Design, University of Liverpool. Practice with Lord Holford & Partners and with Professor Myles Wright [United Kingdom (in part)]*

C. S. CHANDRASEKHARA   *Architect and planner; Chief Adviser on City and Regional Planning to the Government of India; Honors graduate in science and engineering, Mysore University; Masters degree in City and Regional Planning, Harvard University (Asia, Southeast, Developing Countries; India)*

F. STUART CHAPIN, JR.   *Professor of Planning and Research; Director of the Center for Urban and Regional Studies, University of North Carolina (Activity Analysis)*

MOTOSURA CHOH   *Architect and planner. Formerly with Planning Bureau, Japanese Ministry of Construction; subsequently with Tekken General Construction Co. [Japan (in part)]*

A. CIBOROWSKI   *Officer-in-Charge, Center for Housing, Building, and Planning of the United Nations (United Nations Center for Housing, Building, and Planning)*

MARION CLAWSON   *Agricultural economist (Ph.D., Harvard); twenty-five years in the U.S. Departments of Agriculture and the Interior working on land research and land administration; fifteen years with Resources for the Future; author of several books on aspects of land use and management (Agricultural Land Use; Drainage and Land Use; Irrigation and Land Use)*

KENNETH CLEMENS   *Diploma in Town and Country Planning (Manchester University); Senior Planner, County Planning Authorities; Member of Chartered Surveyors and Planning Consultants; author of* Planning Policies and Organization, *written for the 12th Congress of the Federation Internationale des Geometres (Legislation and Administration; Surveyor)*

GEORGE CONDITT   *Architect; Director of Institute of Urban Research since 1970; Director of Town and Country Planning Department, Vienna, 1963–1969; author of* Stadtplanung Wien 1963–1969 *and numerous articles on planning (Austria; Sitte, Camillo; Wagner, Otto)*

JAMES STEVENS CURL   *Architect and planner (Diploma in Architecture and Diploma in Town Planning); author of* European Cities and Society: The Influence of Political Climate on Town Design; *Chairman of Oxford Civic Society (Alberti, Leone Battista; Berlage, Hendrik Petrus; Bernini, Gian Lorenzo; Bramante, Donato; Dudok, Willem Marinus; Haussmann, Baron Georges-Eugene; L'Enfant, Pierre Charles; Le Corbusier; May, Ernst; Medieval Planning; Perret, Auguste; Renaissance Planning; Saint-Simon, C. R. De Rouvroy)*

JOHN WILLIAM DARK   *Planner and engineer; Coordinator, Administrator, and Supervisor for British Government of Hong Kong Development Plan, 1951–1955. Subsequently in Planning Department of Great London Council. Author of* Low Rent Asian Housing *(died 1971) (China)*

JACOB DASH   *Architect and planner (A.M.R.T.P.I., B. Arch., Diploma in Civic Design); Vice President of the International Federation of Housing and Planning. Formerly Senior Assistant to Sir Patrick Abercrombie, Senior Architect and Planner to the Jewish Agency. Israel Head of Planning Department, Ministry of Interior, Israel; author with Dr. E. Efrat of* Israel Physical Master Plan *(Israel)*

D. ANNE DENNIER   *(B.A., Geography) Diploma in Town Planning; Lecturer, Department of Civic Design, Liverpool University [United Kingdom (in part)]*

PETRE DERER   *Architect; Lecturer on Town Planning at the Institute of Architecture, Bucharest [Romania (in part)]*

CONSTANTINE DOXIADIS   *President of Doxiadis Associates International Co., Ltd., Consultants on Development and Ekistics, Athens; Founder and President of the Athens Center of Ekistics; Chief Town Planning Officer, Greater Athens Area, 1937–1938; Head of Department of Regional and Town Planning, Ministry of Public Works, Greece, 1939–1944; Lecturer on Town Planning, Technical University, Athens, 1939–1943; Minister and Permanent Secretary of Housing Reconstruction, Greece, 1945–1948; Minister-Coordinator of Greek Recovery Program, 1949–1951; author of plans, programs, and projects for several cities including Islamabad, the new capital of Pakistan, Tema in Ghana, Kafue in Zambia, Beida in Libya, and Detroit; author of many books on planning and related subjects, including* Ekistics: An Introduction to the Science of Human Settlements *(Ancient Planning, Greece; Dynametropolis; Dynapolis; Ecumenopolis; Ekistics; Megalopolis)*

LUIGI FALCO   *Architect and planner (degree in architecture, Turin Politechnico); Research Worker in Planning History, specializing in Roman, Baroque, and nineteenth-century planning; Contributor to* Rivista Urbanistica *[Ancient Planning, Roman Empire (in part)]*

ARTHUR H. FAWCETT, JR.   *Senior Associate with Marcou O'Leary and Associates; Member of the American Institute of Planners; Masters degree, Regional Planning, University of North Carolina. Formerly Chief of Advance Planning with the National Capital Planning Commission of Washington, D.C.; author of several plans, including those for Anne*

Arundel County, Maryland (1967), for Lynchburg, Virginia (1972), and master plans for Clarksburg, Maryland (1967) and Annandale, Virginia (1969), and the campus master plan for George Washington University (1970) (Suburbs and Suburban Growth)

DON FIELD   *Architect and planner; Lecturer on Urban Form and Planning Methodology, Department of Civil Design, University of Liverpool* [*United Kingdom (in part)*]

JOHN C. FRYE   *Geologist (M.S., D.Sc., Ph.D.); Chief of Illinois State Geological Survey (1954–   ) and Professor of Geology, University of Illinois (1963–   ). Formerly State Geologist, Kansas, Professor of Geology, Kansas University, and Geologist, United States Geological Survey (Geology and Geological Surveys for Planning)*

DAVID S. GROVE   *Bachelors degree in Architecture and Diploma in Town Planning (Auckland University); Senior Planning Officer since 1965 of Auckland Regional Authority; worked on regional plan for Auckland; practiced architecture in New Zealand, Canada, U.S.A., and Great Britain, (New Zealand)*

DAVID HALL   *Member of the Royal Town Planning Institute of U.K.; Director since 1967 of the Town and Country Planning Association (Advocacy Planning; Appeal; Blight; Campus; Cartogram; Compulsory Purchase; Conservation; Derelect Land; Goal Setting; Grey Areas; Piecemeal Development; Twilight Area)*

JORGE E. HARDOY   *Architect and Planner; Master of City Planning and Ph.D. (Harvard University); Professor of Planning (1956–1965) and Director of Institute of Urban and Regional Planning (1962–1965), Universidad del Litoral, Rosario, Argentina; Director and Researcher, Center of Urban and Regional Studies, Instituto Di Tella, Buenos Aires (1967–   ); visiting professor and researcher, Yale University, 1970; author of* Ciudades Precolombinas *(urban planning in precolumbia America) and* La Urbanizacion en America Latina *(the process of urbanization in the Americas from its beginning to the present day) (Argentina)*

HAIJA-LIISA HEINONEN   *Art Historian (M.A.); assistant and archivist at the Museum of Finnish Architecture, Helsinki (Ehrenstrom, Johan Albrecht; Engel, Johann Carl Ludwig; Saarinen, Gottlieb Eliel)*

HEIKKI VON HERTZEN   *President and Executive and Planning Director of Asuntosaatio Housing Foundation, Tapiola Garden City, since 1951; Member of the National Planning Board since 1956; Headed United Nations European Seminar on Social Aspects of Housing, 1958; Consultant to American Institute of Planners on "The Next Fifty Years, 1967–2017"; Editor-in-Chief of* Asuntopolotikka *(housing policy), 1953–1972, and* Valtakunnansuunnettelu *(town and country planning), since 1955 (Aalto, Hugo Alvar Henrik; Finland)*

EMANUEL HRUSKA   *Emeritus Professor of Town Planning, Technical University, Bratislava; President of the Central Commission of State Preservation of Momuments and Sites, Ministry of Culture, Prague; author of town and regional plans and studies for Prague, Brno, and for several regions of Moravia and Slovakia; author of many books on town planning in Czech, Slovak, Russian, and German language edited by Academy of Sciences SRR (Czechoslovakia)*

HISASHI IRISAWA   *Head of Housing, Town Planning, and Building Economy Division, Building Research Institute, Ministry of Construction; Lecturer at Chiba University, Japan* [*Japan (in part)*]

J. G. JEFFERSON   *Town Planning Consultant and Civil Engineer (M.I.C.E.); Past President of the Royal Town Planning Institute of U.K.; County Planning Officer for West Sussex, England, 1947–1965 (Civil Engineering; Harbors and Docks; Refuse Collection and Disposal; Sewerage and Sewage Disposal; Survey; Water Supply)*

R. H. KANTOROWICH   *Architect and planner; Professor and School Director of Town and Country Planning, Manchester University; Past President, South African Institute of Planners; Member of the Council of the Royal Town Planning Institute of U.K. and Chairman of the Education Committee since 1965; author of statutory plans for several towns in Cape Province, South Africa, and of plan for new town of Ashkelon, Israel, and of plan (with Lord Holford) for Central Durban (South Africa)*

SUZANNE KELLER   *Professor of Sociology at Princeton University; Fulbright Lecturer,*

Athens Center of Ekistics, 1963–1965 (Burgess, Ernest W.; Community and Community Feeling; Park, Robert E.; Social Needs and Objectives in Planning; Sociology; Urban Sociology)

ALBERT A. KLINGEBIEL   *Director, Soil Survey Interpretations, Soil Conservation Service, United States Department of Agriculture, since 1956; Fellow of the American Society of Agronomy* [Soil Classification for Agricultural and Urban Uses (in part)]

F. W. LEDGER   *Professor and Head of Department of Town and Regional Planning, University of Melbourne, Australia; Master of Town and Regional Planning (Melbourne); Member of the Royal Town Planning Institute of U.K.; Fellow of the Australian Planning Institute (Australia)*

HAROLD LEWIS   *Editor of the* Journal of the Royal Town Planning Institute *(British), 1962–1970; Member of the firm of Colin Buchanan and Partners since 1970 (Code of Professional Conduct; Competitions; Consultant; Public Participation in Planning; Public Relations)*

CARLOS LODI   *Engineer, architect, and planner; honorary corresponding member of the Royal Town Planning Institute of U.K. Formerly Director of the Town Planning Department of Prefeitura Municipal of S. Paula and member of the Bureau of the International Federation for Housing and Planning; author of* Populacao Alimentes Urbanizacao *(people, food, cities) (Brazil)*

BOLESTAN MALISZ   *Architect and planner; Member of Polish Architects Associations and of Association of Polish Town Planners; Professor of Physical Planning, 1956–1962; Director of the Research Institute for Town Planning and Architecture, 1966–1968. Head of Department of National and Regional Planning, Institute of Geography (Polish Academy of Science); author of* Threshold Analysis *and other works (Poland; Threshold Analysis)*

DEM MARONITIS   *Doctor of Classical Philology; Assistant Professor, University of Thessaloniki, 1964–1967; compiling glossary of Ekistic terms in ancient Greek, research project, "Ancient Greek Cities" (Athens Center of Ekistics) (Aristotle; Deinocrates; Hippodamus of Miletus; Plato)*

F. I. MASSER   *Lecturer on regional planning and analytical methods, since 1964; Department of Civil Design, University of Liverpool* [United Kingdom (in part)]

JAKOB MAURER   *Professor of Methodology of Planning at the Institute for National, Regional, and Local Planning of the Swiss University of Technology; Director of interdisciplinary post-diploma studies in space planning; Member of the Collegiate of Professors of the Institute for Local, Regional, and Country Planning, E.T.H., Zurich (Switzerland)*

ALBERT MAYER   *(See biographical entry on page 670) (United States of America)*

R. E. M. McCAUGHAN   [B. Arch. (Hons.), F.S.A.] *Architect, planner, and archaeologist; Lecturer in Department of Civil Design, University of Liverpool, since 1949; Town Planning Archaeologist at Pergamon for Deutschen Archaelogischen Institute since 1951* [Edward I of England; United Kingdom (in part)]

JOHN BRIAN McLOUGHLIN   *Planner; Member of the Centre for Environmental Studies, London; Lecturer at University College, London; Senior Research Fellow, University of Manchester on relevance of cybernetics to "control" in urban and regional systems, 1969–1971. Formerly Lecturer on Town and Country Planning, University of Manchester* [Ecology (in part)]

JOHN W. McMAHAN   *Urban land use economist; Founder and President of Development Research Associates; directed research in real estate development, regional economics, urban renewal, transportation, and tourism, with a view to determining the economic feasibility of housing projects, shopping centers, hotels, office buildings, industrial parks, and other urban uses; Member of NAHRO, the American Management Association, the American Economic Association, and the Urban Land Institute (Economic Considerations in Urban and Regional Planning; Industrial Sites and Locations; Research)*

MICHAEL J. MESHENBERG   *Senior Planner, American Society of Planning Officials; B.A. in Urbanism (Brooklyn College); Masters degree in City Planning (Pennsylvania) (Plans, Preparation of)*

AHMED AMIN MOKHTAR   *Architect (B. Arch.) and planning (A.M.R.T.P.L.) consultant; Professor of Planning, Al-Azhar University, Cairo; author of several papers on planning including, "An Investigation into Local Factors Influencing Planning Standards in Egypt" (Durham University), 1959, and "The Regional Plan for Maryiut" (Bagdad), 1964 (Ancient Planning, Egypt; Egypt)*

LEWIS MUMFORD   *(See biographical entry on page 707) (Theories and Ideals of Planning; Geddes, Patrick; Mackaye, Benton; Olmsted, Frederick Law; Stein, Clarence S.; Theories and Ideals of Planning; Wright, Henry)*

M. O'BRIEN   *Principal Dublin Planning Officer; Director of An Foras Forbartha Teoranta (National Institute for Physical Planning and Construction Research); prepared City of Dublin Plans, 1957; Draft Development Plans for Dublin City and County, 1968; and Dublin Development Plan, 1971 (Ireland)*

JEREMIAH D. O'LEARY, JR.   *Planner (Master of City Planning, Harvard University, and Member of the American Institute of Planners and the American Society of Planning Officials); Executive Vice President, Marcou, O'Leary; directed urban planning and renewal work in Rochester, Columbus, Springfield, and Waterbury; new town planning in Washington D.C., and historic preservation planning for the French Quarter, New Orleans; author of many articles and studies on planning, and a visiting critic at several American Universities (Systems Approach)*

SIR FREDERIC J. OSBORN   *(See biographical entry on page 769) (Abercrombie, Sir Patrick; Adams, Thomas; Country Towns Expansion; Decentralization and Dispersal; Density; De Soissons, Louis; Development Corporation; Garden City; Green Suburb; Greenbelts; Howard, Sir Ebenezer; Industrial Housing Estates; IFHP: International Federation for Housing and Planning; Land Values and Planning; More, Sir Thomas; New Towns; Owen, Robert; Pepler, Sir George Lionel; Satellite Towns; Terminology and Translations; Unwin, Sir Raymond; Utopia and Utopian Planning; Wells, H. G.; World Town-Planning Day; Wurster, Catherine Bauer)*

CHEORCHE PAVLU   *Architect; Prorector and Chairman of the Department of Town Planning, Institute of Architecture, Bucharest [Romania (in part)]*

KAROLY PERCZEL   *Architect and Planner; Deputy Director of the Hungarian Institute for Town and Regional Planning and Research; Member of the Presidium of the Hungarian Society of Urbanism; Formerly Head of the Town Planning Department, Ministry of Building (1947–1966) and Secretary-General of the Hungarian Association of Architects; author of several works on planning (Hungary)*

IVAN PETROV   *Member of Institute of Town Planning and Architecture, Sofia (Bulgaria); author of town planning schemes, projects for settlements, town centers, and housing estates in Bulgaria and of books and articles on town planning [Bulgaria (in part)]*

GILLIAN PITT   *Sociologist (B.Sc. Soc. London); Tutor in Social Science Open University (England) and Lecturer on Sociology, Brighton Polytechnic (Durkheim, Emile; Ghetto; Social Group; Social Structure; Spencer, Herbert)*

DOUGLAS R. PORTER   *Planner (M.S., Illinois University; B.S., Michigan University); Senior Associate of Marcou O'Leary and Associates, Planning Consultants; Project Administrator for neighborhood development, Metropolitan Dade County, Jacksonville, Florida, and Roanoke, Virginia; headed studies for new town near Pittsburgh and for downtown plan in Memphis, Tennessee; also responsible for downtown development plan for Schenectady, New York and several other planning and renewal schemes (Land Value and Land Ownership)*

WENDY POWELL   *Fellow of the Institute of Landscape Architects (England); Associate of Sylvia Crowe; worked as landscape architect in the new towns of Basildon, Harlow, and Hemel Hempstead and in consultants' planning teams for Washington and Warrington New Towns (Climatic Conditions and Planning; Forestry; National Parks; Parks; Parkway; Paxton, Sir Joseph)*

ENUD E. RASMUSSEN   *Architect and Chief Town Planner for Kooperativ Byggeindustri A/S Copenhagen (Denmark)*

L. W. A. RENDELL   *Planner (Dipl. T.P., F.R.T.P.I.); worked in Planning Departments of the Counties of Somerset, Wiltshire, Middlesex, Hertfordshire, and Surrey; Chairman, South East Branch of the Royal Town Planning Institute of U.K., 1970–1971 (Advertisements; Commons and Common Land; Development; Development Plan; Local Plan; Planning Inquiry; Structure Plan)*

ERWIN ROCKWELL   *Planning Officer, London Transport Executive; Member of the Institute of Transport and of the Danish Institution of Civil Engineers (Metropolitan Railways)*

ERIK ROLFSEN   *Architect and planner; Planning Officer, City of Oslo, 1948–1973. Formerly Director of Planning for war-damaged areas, 1945–1947; President of the International Federation for Housing and Planning, 1954–1958 (Norway)*

WILFRED SALTER   *Editor of* The Parthenon *(Journal of the Incorporated Association of Architects and Surveyors), 1934–1962 (died 1969) (Adam, Robert; Brown, Lancelot; Chambers, Sir William; Fourier, Francois Marie Charles; Leonardo Da Vinci; Lutyens, Sir Edwin Landseer; Michelangelo Buonarotti; Morris, William; Nash, Sir John; Palladio, Andrea; Ruskin, John; Vitruvius; Wood, John)*

RICHARD L. SANDERSON   *Founder and President of the National Academy of Code Administration (United States); Executive Director of Building Officials and Code Administrators International; author of* Codes and Code Administration: An Introduction to Building Regulations in the United States *(Building Codes of Practice; Building Regulations)*

HIDEHIKO SAZANAMI   *Senior Research Member of Town Planning Research Section, Building Research Institute (Ministry of Construction), Tokyo [Japan (in part)]*

SASA SEDLAR   *Dipl. Eng. Arch. (Dr. Sc., University of Belgrade); Professor of Town Planning and Dean of the Faculty of Architecture, Civil Engineering and Surveying, University of Ljubljana; Past President Yugoslav Town Planning Association (Yugoslavia)*

KHALID SHIBLI   *Master of City and Regional Planning and of Engineering, University of California (Berkeley), Ph.D. in Planning, Columbia University; Visiting Professor of International Regional and Urban Development, University of Pittsburgh; Member of United Nations Advisory Committee for Regional Development (Pakistan)*

MAURICIU SILIANU   *Architect; Counselor to the Central Institute for Research and Design in Urban and Regional Planning, Bucharest [Romania (in part)]*

JOHN ORSMBEE SIMONDS   *Landscape architect and planner; Past President of the American Society of Landscape Architects; author of* Landscape Architecture, the Shaping of Man's Natural Environment; *editor of* The Freeway in the City *(Landscape Architecture)*

ERLING D. SOLBERG   *Agricultural Economist; Specialist in rural and land use regulations for the Economic Research Service of the United States Department of Agriculture, Washington, D.C., and formerly engaged in the same department on economic-legal research for flood control, Arizona, New Mexico (1939–1941), land use measures and farm tenancy in Arkansas (1942–1943), and in Washington (1944–1949) other research work; author of "New Laws for New Forests: An Evaluation of Wisconsin's Forest Fire, Tax, Zoning, and Country Forest Laws in Operation" (1961), and several bulletins and papers on rural zoning and related subjects [Soil Classification for Agricultural and Urban Uses (in part)]*

ANATOLE A. SOLOW   *Architect and planner; Professor of Urban and Regional Planning at the Graduate School of Public and International Affairs, Pittsburgh University. Directed, 1970–1972, United Nations technical assistance project of municipal administration and development in Venezuela; Chief of the Division of Housing and Planning of the Pan America Union, 1948–1949. Formerly adviser on urban planning and housing to the governments of Ecuador, Costa Rica, Panama, Guatemala, Puerto Rico, and Israel [Chile (in part)]*

H. E. SPARROW   *Surveyor (A.R.I.C.S.) and Town Planner (M.R.T.P.I.) employed in the industrial field. Formerly engaged in planning in the London metropolitan area (Grid; Maps; Measurement; Models; Perspective Renderings; Projection; Scale)*

CIRUS SPIRIDE   *Doctor of Economics; Chief of Regional Planning Section, Central Institute for Research and Design in Urban and Regional Planning, Bucharest [Romania (in part)]*

VYACHESLAV K. STEPANOV *Architect and planner; Master's degree from U.S.A. Academy of Architecture; Member of the Architects Union; Head of Information Center for Civil Construction and Architecture in Moscow; author of several books and papers on architecture and town development (U.S.S.R.)*

HIROSHI TAKEBAYASHI *Senior Research Member of Town Planning Section of the Building Research Institute (Ministry of Construction), Tokyo [Japan (in part)]*

A. A. S. TRAVIS *Professor, Head and Chairman, Joint Department of Town and Country Planning, Heriot-Watt University and Edinburgh College of Art; Fellow of the Royal Town Planning Institute of U.K. Formerly Research Officer, Newcastle-upon-Tyne City Planning Dept; Senior Lecturer, Birmingham School of Planning; Senior Visiting International Research Fellow, Wayne State University, Detroit (Photography and Its Use in Urban and Regional Planning)*

JAQUELINE TYRWHITT *Editor of monthly journal of* Ekistics *(Athens) since 1955. Formerly Director of the Association for Planning and Regional Reconstruction; on the faculty of Harvard University in the Departments of City Planning and Urban Design for fourteen years; co-author or editor of a number of books on town and regional planning: the first,* Maps for the National Plan *(Lunc Humphries), 1946, and the most recent,* Human Identity in the Urban Environment *(Penguin), 1972 (Ancient Planning, Mesopotamia; City Growth and City Planning)*

JUDITH WEBSTER *(M.S.c. Design Technology) Research Officer, Housing Department, London Borough of Camden. Formerly engaged in research project on control of urban and regional systems at School of Town & Country Planning, Manchester University [Ecology (in part)]*

H. VAN DER WEIJDE *Secretary-director, Netherlands Institute for Planning and Housing; President of the European Research Institute for Regional and Urban Planning. Formerly staff member, Netherlands Institute for Planning and Housing and Secretary-General of the International Federation for Housing and Planning, 1949–1960 (The Netherlands)*

ARNOLD WHITTICK *Architectural Historian (Diploma in History of Art, London University); Member of the Council of the Town and Country Planning Association since 1948 (Executive Committee, 1958–1963); Founder (1943) and President, Beckenham Planning Group; Founder (1968) and first Chairman, Crawley Planning Group; author of* The History of European Architecture in the Twentieth Century *(2 vols.),* The Small House Today and Tomorrow, Eric Mendelsohn, *and* The New Towns—the Answer to Megalopolis *(in collaboration with Sir Frederic J. Osborn); Editor (1945–1965) of technical journals devoted to architecture, housing, and civil engineering and of this* Encyclopedia of Urban Planning *(Acropolis; Aesthetics; Agora; Air Pollution and Clean Air; Architect; Architecture; Buckingham, James Silk; Cemetery; Central Place Theory; City Region; Color; Cremation and Crematorium; Cul-De-Sac; Defense, Planning for; Disraeli, Benjamin; Earthquakes and Planning; Educational Park; Environmental Pollution; Eopolis; Flexibility in Planning; Functionalism; Furniture, Urban and Street; Gardens; Garnier, Tony; Geometric Determinism; Griffin, Walter Burley; Gropius, Walter; Growth Points and Areas; Gutkind, E. A.; Hill Towns; Industry, Distribution of; Jefferson, Thomas; Jones, Inigo; Mayer, Albert; Mendelsohn, Erich; Mobile Home Parks; Monuments and Memorials, Public; Movements and Theories of Modern Architectural Design; National Planning; Nature Reserves: Neighborhood Unit; Noise; Open Space in Urban Areas; Osborn, Sir Frederick James; Overcrowding; Place, Sense of; Playground, Children's; Population Growth and Distribution; Precinct and Precinct Planning; Preservation and Planned Change; Privacy; Processional Way; Reclamation; Recreation, Provision for; Rossetti, Biagio; Sculpture; Size of Cities, Towns, and Settlements; Trees in Urban Areas; University Campus or City; Wren, Sir Christopher; Wright, Frank Lloyd)*

TREVOR WHITTLEY *Principal Architect/Planner in the London Borough of Lambeth. Diploma in Architecture, Oxford School of Architecture, and Diploma in Civic Design, Edinburgh University (Zoning and Zoning Laws)*

ALFRED ARDEN WOOD *Architect (F.R.I.B.A.) and Planner (F.R.T.P.I.); County Planning Officer, Worcestershire, since 1972. Formerly City Planning Officer, Norwich, 1965–1971;*

Principal Housing Architect, Leeds and Glasgow; also worked as architect in Stockholm and Harlow; lectured in environmental management in numerous cities of Europe and America; author of Norwich—Draft Urban Plan, Foot Streets in Four Cities, *and of several other planning schemes (Pedestrianization)*

H. MYLES WRIGHT   *(M.S., F.R.I.B.A., M.R.T.P.I.) Lever Professor of Civic Design, University of Liverpool since 1954; Planning Consultant to the University since 1957; author of planning proposals for Cambridge and Corby New Town (with Lord Holford), 1950; Editor and contributor to* Land Use in an Urban Environment, *1961;* The Dublin Region: Preliminary and Final Reports, *1965–1967 [United Kingdom (in part)]*

FEHMI YAVUZ   *Professor of Town and Country Planning, Faculty of Political Sciences, Ankara University, since 1953; Director of Housing, Urban and Regional Planning, Ankara University; President, Turkish Society for Housing, Urban and Regional Planning; Member of American Society of Planning Officials; author of several books on planning and administration, including* Town and Country Planning Textbook *(1953),* Development of Ankara, *and* Town and Country Planning in Turkey *(1952) (Turkish) (Turkey)*

preface

Urban planning arises with the grouping of buildings that serve communities, and it dates from the dawn of civilization. Yet as a specific autonomous professional activity subject to legislation and administration, it is largely a phenomenon of the twentieth century. Up to the First World War urban planning was mainly regarded as an extension of the architect's activities—very much as architecture on a larger scale—embracing streets, open spaces, and the siting and relation of buildings.

Many factors determine the character of urban planning in history—principally religion, defense, economics, aesthetics, health, transport, communications, and social conditions; and all have played important parts at various times. Religion and defense were both very important from the time of the ancient civilizations until the late Renaissance, but they have become less so in modern times. Among the factors that contributed to modern town planning in the nineteenth century were the schemes of social reformers for improving the living conditions of industrial workers. Although utopian ideas had appeared from time to time in the course of history, they became far more frequent in the nineteenth century, being prompted by the bad living conditions in the growing towns. The schemes took the form of planned housing estates and model villages, towns, and cities. These conditions and schemes, together with the increasing public health and housing statutes, led to the first planning legislation. This occurred in Italy in 1865, with the threefold object of improving hygenic conditions, communications, and the appearance of cities. There was little further legislation in Europe until the twentieth century. In the United Kingdom the Housing and Town Planning Act of 1909, which had been preceded by several public health and housing acts, was enacted. It was after this act that the distinct profession of town planner began to emerge, with town planning as the chief purpose, and not merely an extension of the architect's work. After the 1909 act was passed, Thomas Adams promoted discussions among architects, surveyors, engineers, and lawyers —the professional people most concerned with town planning—with the aim of forming an institution devoted to the study and promotion of the art and science of town planning and "to secure the association of those engaged or interested in the practice of Town Planning" (as stated in the yearbook of the institute). As a result, the Town Planning Institute was founded at the end of 1913. A system of examinations was established, designed to provide planning qualifications for successful candidates. The first examination was held in 1920, and the town planning profession was founded.

In the United States as in Europe, city planning in the nineteenth century was an adjunct of the work of the architect, although there was perhaps a more conscious consideration of landscape architecture in the states. City planning received a great impetus with the World's Columbian Exposition at Chicago in 1893. It was not, however, until 1917 that the American City Planning Institute was established in Kansas City; one of its primary purposes "was to provide a forum for the consideration of technical details of the new 'science of city planning.'" As in the case of the British institute, an examination system was inaugurated, and the distinct profession of city planner came into existence shortly after the First World War. The institute was reorganized in 1935 with a new constitution broadening its purposes, while the changed name of American Institute of Planners was adopted in 1939.

The profession of city or town planning has greatly increased in size since the Second World War. (In 1945, the membership of the American Institute of Planners was about 240, in 1973 it had passed 5,000, and the membership of the Town Planning Institute in Britain had reached a similar number.)

By the middle of the century, city and town planning had become so complex that specialization in its various fields began. As a result, city and town planners began to work, like architects, more and more as teams. At the same time it is obvious that for successful planning there must be an overall grasp—that various needs must be seen in relation to each other. A good team works like a crew under a captain who can chart the ship and direct it accordingly. Communities suffer much from single-purpose planning, something that the good planning team seeks to avoid.

The broadening basis of the profession of urban planner involves a knowledge of many different subjects, and therefore the need for basic information in a form convenient for quick reference is becoming increasingly insistent. The purpose of this encyclopedia is to answer this need.

And, as far as we are aware, this is the first reference of its kind. It is international in scope and covers planning in forty-eight of the principal countries of the world where systems of planning legislation and administration are maintained.

Planning in each country is broadly considered, with a similar division of subjects so that comparisons of planning legislation, administration, practice, and recent history can readily be made. The division of the articles suggested to contributors was as follows:

    I. Planning legislation and administration
    II. Professional practice
    III. Education and training
    IV. Institutions (professional, educational and propagandist)
    V. Geographical and climatic conditions
    VI. *A.* Traditions of planning to the end of the nineteenth century
       B. Twentieth century
           1. New towns and communities
           2. City and town extensions
           3. Urban renewal

Most of the contributors of articles on countries followed this classification. Some, however, preferred a slightly different arrangement. A few preferred to begin with geographical and climatic conditions, one combined this with an historical survey, two inserted additional sections on demographic conditions (covered mostly under section VI by others), and one preferred the historical narrative throughout. As each contribution must be based for the best results on the way the author conceives and wishes to treat his subject, this freedom was necessarily given to contributors.

These articles on planning in different countries are supplemented by a general article on planning legislation and administration, in which some significant comparisons and contrast between countries are made. There are also articles on the various aspects of planning and on subjects closely related to it, like transportation, sociology, economics, and aesthetics. Short articles are included on well-known planners, architects, sociologists, reformers, writers, and propagandists who have contributed something original, unique, or distinctive to the art and science of urban, regional, and country planning or who have originated or have been instrumental in furthering important new planning policies. In short, there are articles on important and significant innovators or effective advocates of important innovations. There are a few exceptions in the case of planners who may not be considered as innovators but who have carried out extensive schemes with consummate ability. These criteria necessarily exclude a large number of well-known planners and architects, but this is in accordance with the design of an encyclopedia of knowledge rather than a planning *Who's Who.* Generally the selection is confined to those whose contributions to planning can be evaluated in historical perspective and who therefore belong to the past. The exceptions are a few living persons whose contributions can now be similarly evaluated.

In the compilation of the encyclopedia, some consideration has been given to definitions of terms used in planning. This has been fraught with difficulties because terms, meanings, and usage are sometimes different in the United States, Britain, and the countries of the British Commonwealth, and some terms commonly used and familiar in one country are unfamiliar in another. Also, new terms are constantly being coined—terms which, if readily used, are fairly quickly apprehended in the country of origin but which take years to become internationally understood. With increased international communication, it would be an advantage if the peoples of the English-speaking world could come to some agreement on existing terminology. There is generally one term that is logically the best. Also, as efficiency depends so heavily on good communications, it would be an advantage if terminology in urban planning could be readily understood by the layman—especially if intelligent public participation in planning is to be encouraged.

The compilation of an encyclopedia of international scope is a work of collaboration of numerous contributors, of the publisher, and of the editor. The collaboration for this encyclopedia has been a very happy one. Several of the contributors have made useful suggestions and given valuable advice. In the early, difficult stage of planning the encyclopedia, I recollect and am grateful for the valuable assistance given to me by Sir Frederic J. Osborn; Mr. Lewis Mumford; Mr. David Hall, the director of the Town and Country Planning Association; and by Mr. Harold Lewis, one-time editor of the *Journal of the Royal Town Planning Institute.* My indebtedness for encouragement and for conscientious proofreading by my wife, and for patient and efficient secretarial assistance by Mrs. Nancy Bruce, I am very happy to acknowledge. Also, I am sensible of a great many useful suggestions and of unfailing courtesy given by Mr. Daniel N. Fischel and his staff of the McGraw-Hill Book Company.

ARNOLD WHITTICK

illustration acknowledgments

An encyclopedia of planning, if it is to be comprehensive, must depend to a considerable extent on plans and photographs for the information it gives. The editor is therefore deeply grateful to those who have provided them for this encyclopedia. With most of the illustrations the source, such as a book or other publication from which they are taken, or the name of the photographer or copyright owner is given with the illustration. Many of the plans and photographs were supplied by Municipal Authorities via the contributors of the articles on planning in the various countries and it is hoped that these graphic depictures of their cities and towns will be considered in part as grateful acknowledgment. Some contributors have gone to a great deal of trouble in preparing illustrations and making drawings themselves, such as the contributor of the historical section to the article on the United Kingdom and the contributor of the article on Mediaeval and Renaissance planning, to which very grateful thanks are due. Photographs for several articles were taken by the editor.

encyclopedia
of
urban
planning

A

AALTO, HUGO ALVAR HENRIK (1898–   )   Eminent architect and planner, born in Kuortane, Finland. In 1928, at the age of thirty, he won the competition for the design of the great sanatorium in Paimio, which has since become world famous.

Aalto's first industrial plant, in 1930, was the sulphate pulp mill of Toppila. In his hands the architectonic forms of industrial smokestacks, ventilators, conveyors, processing, warehousing, and transportation elements become functional, expressive, and aesthetically effective.

Other early projects include the planning and architectural design of the Sunila factory and residential area (1936–1939). The general plan is strongly influenced by the shelving granite which naturally separates the many small groups of houses of different types standing among the ubiquitous pines. The plan itself encompasses the uncut granite of an offshore island. The intervening blue-stained waters accommodate both stored timber and Sunila's fleet of pleasure craft. Here the free, open, functional plan made its first appearance in Finland.

For the 1937 Paris International Exposition, Aalto designed the indigenous yet international Finnish Pavilion, with its undulating walls. This theme of the undulating wall had been explored by Aalto in the ceiling of the library at Viipuri, which was particularly known for its lighting.

Alvar Aalto (1898–   ).

1

This building was destroyed in 1940, during the war, but Aalto employed some of its characteristic features in later buildings, notably in the library of the National Pension Bank, Helsinki, and the library of the University of Jyväskylä.

A short distance from Jyväskylä, the urban center of middle Finland, is the small industrial town of Säynätsalo. The plan for this town was prepared in the reconstruction resettlement period of 1942 to 1946 and preceded Aalto's celebrated design for the town hall there (1950–1951). This work marked the beginning of a decade of remarkably homogeneous design.

Alvar Aalto's notable contribution to Finnish town planning includes the comprehensive plan for Rovaniemi, often called the capital of Lapland, the master plan for the Finnish Technical University at Otaniemi along Tapiola's eastern edge, and his town plan for Imatra, near the Russian border. In the Helsinki Center plan (1961–1964) he envisaged the capital as the lively and vital heart of the nation, the capital city grown into a metropolis.

The central plan for Helsinki consists of the Central Square; Hesperia Park with public buildings; the Töölö inlet, preserved and exploited as an accompaniment to the park and buildings; the Kamp area, which continues and brings to an end the present city; and some smaller parts adjacent to the main areas. An additional center is in the Pasila area, started in 1972, about 1.5 miles (2.5 kms) from the main central square.

The main entry road to the town has four or five traffic lanes in each direction. It is located above the railway, so that it provides a good general approach view of the town. This area is covered with a large, terraced, triangular plaza. There are large parking areas under the plaza, and on the western shore of the bay will be situated the monumental buildings of the Congress Hall, Concert Hall, Opera House, Art Museum, and Municipal Library. These public buildings are partly placed in the water and constitute, along with the park and reflections in the water, a unit in themselves. The Pasila area and the central swathes of lines to the present railway station in the center of Helsinki will later be joined to the plan.

Aalto was professor of architecture at the Massachusetts Institute of Technology from 1946 to 1948 and has been a member of the Finnish Academy since 1955.

Admiration for Aalto's work, in both architecture and urban planning, has steadily increased. He brought to Finland's architecture those qualities of humanism and aesthetic appeal that Finnish revolutionary architecture had lacked. He is now widely recognized as one of the outstanding architects and planners of the century.

BIBLIOGRAPHY: Frederick Gutheim, *Alvar Aalto*, New York, 1960; *Alvar Aalto*, Girsberger, Zurich, 1963; *L'opera di Alvar Aalto, Catalogo della mostra a cura di Leonardo Mosso*, Milan, 1965; *Alvar Aalto Synopsis*, Birkhauser Verlag, Basel and Stuttgart, 1970.

—HEIKKI VON HERTZEN

ABERCROMBIE, Sir (LESLIE) PATRICK (1879–1957) British architect-planner; eminent as consultant, university teacher, and writer; was born at Ashton upon Mersey. His first town planning commission was for the replanning of Dublin in 1913; his most famous work encompassed the postwar plans for the county of London (with J. H. Forshaw), 1943, for Greater London, 1944, Edinburgh, Plymouth, Hull, Warwick, Bournemouth, and the Clyde Valley and West Midlands regions. Other regions and towns for which he prepared reports and plans include Doncaster, East Kent coal field, East Suffolk, Sheffield, Cumberland, Carnarvonshire, Bath and Bristol, and Stratford on Avon; overseas, they include Hong Kong, Cyprus, and Addis Ababa. He designed (with A. C. Holliday) the new University of Ceylon.

He was professor of civic design, Liverpool University, 1915 to 1935, and professor of town planning, London University, 1935 to 1946; author of *Town and Country Planning* (Home University Library), 1933 (reissued 1959), and other books, and many articles and conference papers. He was president of the Town Planning Institute, 1925 to 1926; Royal Gold Medallist of the Royal Institute of British Architects, 1948; Gold Medallist of the American Institute of Architects, 1949; received the Howard Memorial Medal, 1943; and was knighted in 1945. Among many honorary offices he served as a member of the Royal Fine Art Commission, president of the Council for the Preservation of Rural England, and council member and vice-president of the Town and Country Planning Association.

As a member of the (Barlow) Royal Commission on the Distribution of the Industrial Population (*q.v.*), 1937 to 1940, he had much influence on its majority recommendations for decentralization and dispersal and for a national planning authority, and was one of the three signatories of its more decided minority report. In his brilliantly written and illustrated London plans of 1943 and 1944, he presented clear and far-reaching proposals based on these recommendations, including the foundation of New Towns on ten specified sites—thus preparing the way for the New Towns Act of 1946. He died at Aston Tirrold, near Didcot, where he had lived for some years.

Abercrombie had a rare combination of qualities for planning: a well-informed sociopolitical-economic philosophy, a rich academic culture, sympathetic understanding of the needs and desires of all classes of people, deep sensitivity both to natural and man-made beauty, and distinctive gifts of writing and speaking. He had tremendous and lasting influence both as a creative practitioner and as a thinker and propagandist.

—Frederic J. Osborn

ACKERMAN, FREDERICK L. (1879–1950) American architect, leading advocate of community planning and public housing in the early twentieth century. He received a degree from Cornell University in 1901 and then spent several years studying in Paris before returning to New York to begin practice. Through his reading of Thorstein Veblen, Ackerman became highly critical of capitalism and turned to planning as a means of general social reconstruction. In this respect his vision went beyond the restricted physical design principles advanced by the "city beautiful" movement. He became professionally interested in low-cost housing and in 1911 advanced the then radical—for America at least—suggestion that public housing should be the government's responsibility. In 1915 he visited Letchworth, England, and returned feeling sympathetic to the garden city movement. During the First World War he was responsible for providing several thousand units of government housing for war workers. Active in the influential Regional Planning Association in the 1920s, Ackerman was a consultant for the building of Sunnyside and Radburn. During the 1930s and 1940s, Ackerman continued his practice, served as consultant to a number of public and semipublic agencies, and wrote and lectured extensively on planning. He remained consistent in the view that physical planning could achieve only minor results unless it was accompanied by social planning and the evolution of a socialist society.

BIBLIOGRAPHY: Roy Lubove, *Community Planning in the 1920s,* Pittsburgh, 1963.
—STANLEY BUDER

ACROPOLIS   A sacred hill surmounted by temples, which formed an important part of many ancient Greek cities. It was probably originally a hill town, chosen as a site partly for religious and partly for defensive purposes, and it was generally built up, as in the case of the famous example at Athens, to form a level platform for the erection of buildings. When the city spread

The Acropolis in Athens from the Hill of Muses.

to the lower surrounding ground, its principal center became the agora (the public square and marketplace), and the acropolis became mainly a religious sanctuary for worship near its temples. In the Athenian acropolis these temples, principally the Parthenon and the Erectheum, are disposed in such a way that on entering through the Propylaea the spectator is given an impression of awe and grandeur.

The choice of the summit of a hill for a religious sanctuary was probably partly in imitation of Mount Olympus, the dwelling of the gods, or because a hill summit was nearer to the gods conceived as inhabiting the sky. Zeus was originally identified with the sky. This may have been a consideration subsequent to the construction of the acropolis as a hill town with a defensive wall, or it may have been the primary reason for the choice of site. In any event, the hilltop acropolis survived in the fully developed Greek city as a religious sanctuary. *See also* ANCIENT PLANNING—GREECE.

BIBLIOGRAPHY: A. von Gerkan, *Griechische Stadtnlagen*, Berlin, 1924; R. E. Wycherley, *How the Greeks Built Cities*, Macmillan & Co., Ltd., London, 1949.

—ARNOLD WHITTICK

ACTIVITY ANALYSIS   Activity studies are concerned with patterned ways in which households, firms, and various other institutional entities pursue their affairs in time and space. These studies classify entity systems into subsystems (for example, households into low-, middle-, and high-income households; or firms into various classes of manufacturing, wholesale, retail, and service sectors), and they identify patterns in the flow of activities or transactions of each subsystem as it evolves in time and space. Depending on whether the focus is on the person, the firm, or some other institutional entity, the time span for analysis may be the day, the week, the season, the year, or some defined life-span. The locus of these activity systems may fall largely within a single metropolitan community; but for some persons, firms, or organizations, the "activity field" may be national or even worldwide in scope.

Uses of Activity Studies   The theoretical importance which these activity patterns have for land use and its spatial organization has long been recognized. However, it has been only recently that scientific sampling procedures and modern computer capabilities have made it possible to study the dynamics of these systems in ways that would permit the linking up of human activity systems with land development processes and other environmental systems for analysis and for the conduct of simulation experiments.[1] Until this work emerges from the research and development stage, there are at least two very direct practical applications of activity studies which are useful in city planning today. One application involves the use of activity and preference patterns to make assessments of the adequacy of services and facilities—in effect, a "market analysis" for establishing levels of service and

[1] See a further discussion of this line of development in Chapin, "Activity Systems as a Source of Inputs for Land Use Models," in G. C. Hemmens (ed.), *Urban Development Models*, Highway Research Board, National Academy of Sciences, Washington, 1968.

the distribution of facilities needed with respect to the users of these services and facilities. The second kind of application has to do with the use of activity analysis in the evaluation of alternative plans. In the sense that benefit-cost analysis provides a measure of goodness primarily in terms of economic efficiency, activity analysis brings into the decision-making process a supplemental measure of goodness, one based primarily on social efficiency.[2] This approach to evaluation has particular relevance to households as opposed to firms or organizations and provides a basis for establishing values which have a social rather than an economic significance. The following discussion applies primarily to household activity systems and the use of time accounts for the analysis of human activity patterns.[3]

Historical Context   Concepts involved in household activity studies have their roots in the time and motion studies first used in factory management investigations. Systematic work in the analysis of time use in a broader framework first appeared in the twenties and thirties. S. G. Strumlin gathered daily time data on Moscow workers in 1924, and with the strong emphasis in the U.S.S.R. to measure production and worker productivity, there followed a widespread application of this work to other Soviet cities. Other efforts followed in other countries in the thirties and forties. These were principally efforts of sociologists, working with what they came to call "time budgets," a term intended to connote a broader view of human effort than what was reflected in studies economists were making and the work they were pursuing during the depression era concerned with family income, saving, and expenditure patterns. Much of this work was concerned with describing social class or cross-national differences in lifestyles. Some work drew parallels of measures of economic well-being recorded in income and savings accounts, suggesting that time accounts might provide an approach to developing social indicators of human well-being.[4]

Conceptual Basis of Activity Analysis   For planning purposes, human time accounts can be translated into a form of descriptive geometry which enables the analyst to relate human behavior to land use. This work is based on the notion that the activities of an individual can be viewed as a series of discrete episodes occurring in a sequence through some specified period of time. This sequence is seen to be a continuous stream of events where

---

[2] This application was first outlined in Richard L. Meier, "Human Time Allocation: A Basis for Social Accounts," *Journal of the American Institute of Planners,* vol. 25, no. 1, February 1959; see also Meier's *A Communications Theory of Urban Growth,* M.I.T. Press, Cambridge, Mass., 1962.

[3] For firms, activities are analyzed in terms of transactions recorded in income and product accounts. For example, see Charles L. Leven's *Theory and Method of Income and Product Accounts for Metropolitan Areas,* Center for Regional Economic Studies, Pittsburgh, 1963. For other institutional entities, activity analysis would necessarily focus on other accounting systems for recording actions for these entities.

[4] The historical background and the basic concepts which attracted sociologists to the study of time accounts is described in Alexander Szalai, "Trends in Comparative Time-Budget Research," *The American Behavioral Scientist,* vol. 9, no. 9, May 1966; see also his "Differential Evaluation of Time Budgets for Comparative Purposes," in R. L. Merritt and Stein Rokkan (eds.), *Comparing Nations,* Yale University Press, New Haven and London, 1966.

days flow into weeks; weeks into months, seasons, and years; and years into a lifetime. While most episodes are discrete to a particular day and assume significance primarily in the context of the daily cycle, some have primary significance in some other "time scale," for example, setting off on a holiday, which relates to a seasonal or yearly cycle, or getting married, which relates to the life cycle.

Under this conceptual system, activity sequences are seen to possess an essential order in the sense that certain types of episodes occur in fairly predictable cycles or routines and take place in a space of a fairly predictable locus. These are the more *obligatory* kinds of activity; for example, such activities in the daily cycle as sleep, meals, work, and housekeeping. These activities appear to serve as structuring elements to the routine in that the times and durations of these events affect the temporal and spatial characteristics of other episodes in a day's sequence—the time available for *discretionary* forms of activity.

The basic research focus in activity analysis, referred to above, seeks to draw on these distinctions in the simulation of human activity. The routinized aspects of a person's activity sequence can be represented fairly simply in probabilistic form in a set of time distributions and spatial distributions.[5] The nonroutinized aspects can be formulated in terms of choice theory, with probability distributions drawn into the simulated flow of events on the basis of appropriate preference functions for various classes of households.

Activity Analysis Format   For these and the applications noted earlier, simplifications of these concepts are needed. In place of dealing with episodes, the analyst uses broad classes of activity; and in place of developing person-specific time accounts, the analyst uses mean times for classes of individuals. Through survey research techniques, activity, time, and location data are recorded for household members in various stages of the life cycle based on a probability sample of households. The behavioral data and the data on preferences and various attitudinal dimensions are used in classifying households and individuals and assigning them to household and person types. This is done on the basis of similarities in activity patterns as defined by types of activity, durations, and the spatial loci. In much the same way that land-use surveys must be established on some kind of continuous inventory basis, it will be necessary to think of panel-type sampling studies to keep account of longitudinal changes in patterns of activity.

Essentially, then, the population of a metropolitan community is conceived in terms of archetypes, each with a distinctive set of activity patterns, distinctive patterns in time allocation, and distinctive centroid locations for neighborhood of residence and loci of out-of-home activities. As brought out above, this description of the patterned way in which people make use of their city in time and space, together with preference data on the type,

---

[5] See George C. Hemmens, *The Structure of Urban Activity Linkages,* Center for Urban and Regional Studies, Chapel Hill, N. C., September 1966; also Richard K. Brail, *Activity System Investigations: Strategy for Model Design,* a Ph.D. dissertation, University Microfilms, Ann Arbor, Mich., 1969.

timing, and location of activities, have applications as a form of "market analysis" in determining service and facility requirements and as an evaluation technique for making choices among plan alternatives. As R&D work proceeds, activity analysis can be expected to become more versatile and to provide a truly powerful tool for city planning.

BIBLIOGRAPHY: Richard L. Meier, "Human Time Allocation: A Basis for Social Accounts," *Journal of the American Institute of Planners,* vol. 25, no. 1, 1959, *A Communications Theory of Urban Growth,* The M.I.T. Press, Cambridge, Mass., 1962; Gary S. Becker, "A Theory of the Allocation of Time," *The Economic Journal,* vol. 75, September 1965; F. Stuart Chapin, Jr., *Urban Land Use Planning,* 2d ed., University of Illinois Press, Urbana, 1965; Alexander Szalai, "Trends in Comparative Time-Budget Research," *The American Behavioral Scientist,* vol. 9, no. 9, May 1966; "The Multinational Comparative Time Budget Research Project," *The American Behavioral Scientist,* vol. 9, no. 12, December 1966; F. Stuart Chapin, "Activity Systems and Urban Structure: A Working Schema," *Journal of the American Institute of Planners,* vol. 34, no. 1, January 1968; F. Stuart Chapin and Thomas H. Logan, "Patterns of Time and Space Use," in Harvey S. Perloff (ed.), *The Quality of the Urban Environment,* The Johns Hopkins Press, Baltimore, 1969.

—F. STUART CHAPIN, JR.

ADAM, ROBERT (1728–1792)   Scottish architect. One of the most versatile figures of the eighteenth century, Adam was an accomplished town planner, architect of genius, and notable designer of interior decorations. The Adam style is universally known for its elegance and dignity.

On a visit to Dalmatia in 1754, where he studied the ruined Palace of Diocletian, he seems to have imbibed indirectly the influence of Greek as well as Roman architecture and planning that was later manifest in his work.

The combined planning and architectural achievement for which he is best known was undertaken in collaboration with his four brothers, when, in 1769, they began the rebuilding of a rectangular site lying between the Thames and the Strand near Charing Cross in central London. On completion it was named in their honor by the Greek word for "brothers," The Adelphi.

The principal feature of the scheme was its southern boundary, the Terrace that overlooks the Thames. This was connected with the Strand and with a parallel street that bounds the site to the north, by short streets that run from north to south. The magnificent building that the Adams erected on the Terrace itself was demolished in the 1920s and a multistoried commercial building now occupies the site.

Robert and his brothers also planned and designed Fitzroy Square, London; the Register House and the University at Edinburgh; and the Radcliffe Observatory at Oxford. Robert alone designed the Pulteney Bridge at Bath.

Robert and James Adam published their *Works in Architecture* in 1773–1778.

Robert Adam. (National Portrait Gallery, London.)

BIBLIOGRAPHY: Reginald Blomfield, *A History of Renaissance Architecture in England,* George Bell & Sons, London, 1897; John Summerson, *Georgian London,* Pleiades Books, London, 1946.

—WILFRED SALTER

ADAMS, THOMAS (1871–1940)   British town planning consultant. In his early years a Liberal party agent, he became secretary of the Garden City Association in 1901, was the first manager of *Letchworth* (*q.v.*), 1903 to 1906, and took a leading part in the advocacy and organization of the garden city movement. In 1906 he went into private practice as a town planning consultant, and from 1909 to 1914 was town planning inspector, Local Government Board. In 1914 he founded and became first president of the Town Planning Institute, and in the same year he went to Canada as Town Planning Adviser to the Canadian government. He became well known in North America, and one of his major jobs was serving as director of the Regional Plan of New York, 1923 to 1930. Thereafter he held professorships in city planning and design at Harvard University and the Massachusetts Institute of Technology. Returning to England, he prepared numerous reports for cities and regions. He founded, in 1933, the Town and Country Planning Summer School, later taken over by the Town Planning Institute. Of his many publications the most weighty was *Recent Advances in Town Planning,* 1953.

Adams was a considerable force for the establishment and advance of the new profession of town planning. His two sons, Professor Frederick J. Adams (for many years professor of city planning at M.I.T.) and James W. R. Adams (planner for the county of Kent), became eminent in the profession and were presidents, respectively, of the American Institute of Planners and the British (now Royal) Town Planning Institute in the same year (1948–1949).

—Frederic J. Osborn

ADMINISTRATION   (*See* legislation and administration; also under countries.)

ADVERTISEMENTS   Advertisements are public announcements designed to promote a commodity or service and to communicate information to the public. In the United Kingdom they are defined as any word, letter, model, sign, placard, board (or billboard), notice, device, or representation, whether illuminated or not, employed wholly or partially for the purpose of advertisement, announcement, or direction [Town and Country Planning (Control of Advertisement) Regulations, 1969].

In Britain, comprehensive control of advertisements, mainly outside buildings and in the countryside, came into force on August 1, 1948, and practice has been governed by a series of regulations culminating in the 1969 regulations.

Ordinary Control   Many smaller advertisements, comprising primarily those used for everyday business purposes and public notices, may be displayed without express consent. Larger advertisements need the consent of the planning authority. Each case is considered on its individual merits against amenity and public safety criteria.

Areas of Special Control   These are areas where stricter standards apply. Such areas, which are chiefly county districts or "conservation areas," are selected by a local planning authority and submitted in the form of an order to the central government for approval. A public inquiry may be held to consider objections (*see* PUBLIC PARTICIPATION IN PLANNING). The powers of special control are extensive and require the removal, after a specified period, of all existing commercial advertisements of the poster type and prohibition of any new advertisements of this class. There are stricter rules governing those advertisements which would not normally require consent in an area subject to ordinary control. In 1969, over one-third of the area of England and Wales was subject to special control; and efforts are being made to extend this control to cover most of the open countryside and other places which require special protection on grounds of amenity.

Where consent is given for the display of an advertisement, it is only for a period of 5 years; and standard conditions require that displays be kept clean and tidy.

Where smaller displays, which are not subject to consent, prove to be objectionable, the planning authority may serve a notice requiring the discontinuance of the display—but the advertiser has a right of appeal. In practice, a great deal of goodwill exists between advertisers, and an Advertisers' Working Committee has produced a "clutter code" which sets out principles for advertisers to follow in those cases where consent is not required. The officers of the committee will, at the request of the planning authority, persuade advertisers to remove clutter from business premises. The Electrical Sign Manufacturers Association in Britain has also produced a code governing intensity of illuminations for rural, residential, and shopping centers.

Planning Considerations Amenity and public safety are the only criteria for controlling advertisements in Britain. The law is drafted to enable local planning authorities to decide for themselves the level of advertising they are prepared to tolerate. General principles followed by most authorities in respect to signs requiring planning consent are:

Commercial Areas. These are areas other than conservation or residential areas. The public is used to and enjoys a high level of advertising in such areas, and control is restricted to achieving a balance between advertisements relating specifically to premises on which they are displayed and commercial poster advertising. Excessive competition between these two elements results in a confused appearance, with increasing demands for greater levels of illumination and use of projecting signs and motifs, which can destroy the architectural quality of the environment. Care is taken to ensure that public traffic signs are not emulated or encroached upon by private advertising.

Conservation Areas. These are areas of special historic or architectural merit where prominence is given to character and heritage. Commercial advertising either unrelated to the premises or in an unsatisfactory style which would detract from the quality of the area is permitted only in exceptional circumstances.

Residential Areas. In these, all advertising is discouraged except on isolated business premises.

Rural Areas. No commercial advertising except that which is essential to identify commercial premises is permitted in these areas, and such advertising is kept to a minimum.

—L. W. A. RENDELL

ADVOCACY PLANNING The preparation of plans or planning proposals and their advocacy by professional planners on behalf of an organization, interest group, or community as an alternative or in opposition to plans or planning proposals prepared by an official agency. The term originated in the United States, where it is particularly used in the context of "plural planning": the planning of the same area or project by more than one agency. Thus advocacy planning is a means by which professional planning help can be given to those bodies or interest groups who claim that their interests are damaged or inadequately represented in the proposals of the official planning agency. Planners engaging in this process are said to be "advocate" (or "advocacy") planners and, in addition to carrying out the normal technical task of preparing planning proposals, they also act as proponents, or advocates, of them. Where such plans are prepared as a direct reaction to those of the official planning agency, they would contain a critique of the official proposals as well as a positive alternative (or alternatives) to them.

BIBLIOGRAPHY: Paul Davidoff, "Advocacy and Pluralism in Planning," *Journal of the American Institute of Planners*, November 1965; Edmund Burke, "Citizen Participation Strategies" *Journal of the American Institute of Planners*, September 1968; Des McConaghy, "The Limitations of Advocacy," *Journal of the Royal Institute of British Architects*, February 1972.

—DAVID HALL

AERIAL PHOTOGRAPHY (*See* PHOTOGRAPHY AND ITS USE IN URBAN PLANNING.)

AERIAL SURVEY (*See* SURVEY.)

AESTHETICS A term derived from the Greek αισθητικος, which originally meant sense perception. In the eighteenth century, Baumgarten gave a new meaning to the term as the perception and appreciation of the beautiful; and from the middle of the nineteenth century this meaning has been widely accepted by the English-speaking peoples. There is a tendency in some modern philosophical thinking to extend the term to include more than the appreciation of the beautiful; that is, to include character and power and other qualities within a comprehensive idea of beauty.

The study of aesthetics is a branch of philosophy and is concerned with one of the three Greek values of truth, beauty, and goodness. The relation and significance of these values have been discussed by philosophers since Plato and Aristotle, beauty being given less attention than the other two as being more remote from human needs; yet the effect of the beautiful on the human spirit and thus on human welfare has always been partly realized. As a preliminary to the consideration of the aesthetics of city planning and urban design, some indication of generally accepted philosophical aesthetic principles must be given.

Aesthetic appreciation is widely considered to be subjective, and the beautiful is held to be not a quality of an object irrespective of the percipient but a value that the percipient places on an object—whether it be a natural landscape, a building, a painting, a poem, or a musical composition. What is or is not beautiful is therefore a matter of opinion; yet similarities of the human mind and the tendency for people of the same civilization and similar educational bases to think alike result in similarities of aesthetic judgment, and a consensus of opinion results in what some philosophers regard as aesthetic objectivity. This is important for urban planning as will be shown later.

The sense of the beautiful in objects belongs to the initial stage of perception before their utilitarian or expressional significance is apprehended. Thus the shapes of a building are pleasing or otherwise, before the fact of its being a church or factory is apprehended; but subject and form in much of the best art, especially in poetry, music, architecture, and so-called "abstract" painting and sculpture, are so integrated that it is not easy to dissociate them, as Walter Pater emphasized (*The School of Giorgione—Studies in the Renaissance*). For aesthetic analysis and for the architect and city planner, the distinction is important.

What aesthetic principles can be formulated or at least suggested by the appreciation and enjoyment of urban design and the townscape? And what is the possible philosophic basis for legislation in the aesthetics of urban design as a public art? If a distinction can be made between the aesthetics of architecture and of town planning, it could be said that the subjects of the former are buildings, both externally and internally perceived, and integrated groups of buildings; and the subjects of urban design, in the context of city planning, are mainly the spaces for the movement of people and vehicles between large complexes of buildings. From the visual standpoint the latter is primarily design of space. The aesthetic experience of architecture is based mainly on abstract relation of forms, on the definition of space, and on the elements that contribute to making these delightful: like rhythm, color, and light and shadow. The aesthetic experience of town design and of the townscape has the same basis, but with a stronger emphasis on space, while the character of the definition of space is much more extensive.

Important in the aesthetics of urban environment, or townscape, is the mood and character of the percipient. In the appreciation of architecture a building is often isolated from its surroundings, for contemplation. The urban designer, on the other hand, thinks of the effect of an extensive sequence of buildings and spaces. The urban environment is less likely to be appreciated by the sightseer or tourist who selects special buildings for appreciation than by the conscious, or partly conscious, citizens who live in the town, who are variously aware of their surroundings, and who move in the spaces of the town every day. These citizens may be acutely conscious of this environment and may like or dislike it, or they may be merely vaguely conscious, and the liking and disliking may exist but not be clearly articulated. The citizen who is acutely conscious of his environment may enjoy certain effects, a pleasing avenue with a stately terminal feature or a pleasantly enclosed square, and he may choose to go one way rather than another because it affords more delight.

The less conscious citizen may do the same but not know why, not having analyzed the reasons for his habits. There are many other, only partly aesthetic reasons for subconscious likes and dislikes, such as those strongly present in children, who often avoid going a certain way because of slight fear of a rather forbidding building or for other similar reasons. The person who has his senses active yet who is completely indifferent to an urban environment has a doubtful existence.

Fundamental for urban design and the future appearance of cities is the validity of universally accepted aesthetic standards. Collective subjectivity results in some measure of objectivity, as previously implied. The work of visual art—building, sculpture, painting—possesses a quality or character implanted by an expressional, constructive, or aesthetic impulse which stimulates the aesthetic impulse in the percipient. The same work of art stimulates in a large degree the aesthetic impulse among those in whom it is much exercised, and standards of taste result.

Hume ("Of the Standard of Taste", *The Essays Moral, Political and Literary*), who uses the term "sentiment" to express aesthetic feelings stimulated by an object, seeks to establish universal standards of taste—"models and principles," he says, "which have been established by the uniform consent and experience of nations and ages." He speaks of prejudice corrupting our sentiment of beauty and implies that those who do not conform in their opinion to the established standards are guilty of bad taste. Kant, in *Critique of Aesthetic Judgement,* defines the beautiful as "that which, apart from a concept, pleases universally" (Meredith translation part 1, section 9), and he argues for a general consensus of opinion which he terms "subjective universal validity." Later in the same work he links aesthetic and moral values and suggests that there is some moral compulsion to like beautiful things that have won universal admiration. Hume and Kant would have had more doubts in implying a universal acceptance of aesthetic standards if they had lived in the twentieth century with its greater divergencies of considered judgments. Samuel Alexander follows a similar line (*Beauty and Other Forms of Value,* Macmillan, London, 1933, p. 172–187) and makes several claims for the impersonal character of aesthetic value and for a standard of aesthetic judgment. "The judges of aesthetic value," he says, "are those whom beauty satisfies in their aesthetic impulse or sentiment: and the beautiful is what satisfies these judges. The standard aesthetic sentiment is that of qualified persons, and those persons are qualified who possess the standard aesthetic sentiment. The standard is embodied in no one person, except so far as he is taken as representative of it."

The contentions of these three philosophers, and of others who have followed them, have in some measure been accepted by society and have influenced the little legislation on behalf of aesthetic interests that there has been in modern society. It is important that the philosophical basis for the validity of aesthetic standards should be periodically examined if legislation relating to the aesthetics of urban design is to be justified.

What constitute the essential aesthetic values of urban environment? They are essentially the patterns, shapes, color, and light and shadow, irrespective of what the buildings are, whether houses, churches, office blocks, or schools. The character of the patterns, however, is generally derived partly from the purposes of these buildings, which provide the subjects for expression. As Kant says (*Critique of Aesthetic Judgement,* part 1, section 4), concept "is not necessary to enable me to see beauty in a thing."

The perceptual stages are: first, the two-dimensional abstract pattern of colored shapes; second, the three-dimensional sense of space and of solid objects in space; and third, the symbolic reference to the purposes of these objects—churches, houses, offices, factories, and schools. The greatest degree of aesthetic experience depends on the first, a second degree on the second, and hardly any on the third. This classification presupposes an agreement with Berkeley (*New Theory of Vision,* sections 1–51), that our first visual experience is two-dimensional, like the flat plane of a picture, and we become aware of three-dimensional space and solids by our own bodily extension and touch and the habitual coordination of these with vision. William James, in refuting this (*Principles of Psychology*), contended that the perception of distance is an optical feeling, but this is difficult wholly to accept.[1]

The psychologists who say that man and animal see the world as they know it to be would probably agree with Berkeley more than with William James. The third stage comes with the reference to the labeled stock of images in the mind, very much in the sequence given by Whitehead (*Symbolism, Its Meaning and Effect,* Cambridge University Press, 1925) of presentational immediacy, causal efficacy, and conceptual analysis.

Aesthetic values according to Hutcheson, Kames, and Kant are what might be called primary and secondary. Hutcheson (*An Enquiry into the Original of Our Ideas of Beauty and Virtue*) speaks of original or absolute beauty and relative or comparative beauty; Kames (*Elements in Criticism*) speaks of intrinsic and relative beauty; and Kant (*Critique of Aesthetic Judgement*) of free beauty and dependent beauty, that is, beauty depending on concepts.

The validity of all these from an exclusively aesthetic standpoint is questionable because aesthetic pleasure based on disinterested contemplation is abstracted from what is perceived. It is really abstracted from Kant's concepts, although it is doubtful if associational disturbances of aesthetic pleasure can be entirely eliminated in perception. The first stage from which aesthetic appreciation can most easily be abstracted is a pattern of two-dimensional color shapes. The transition to the second, to the coordination of physical extension and touch with optical vision, is so rapid as to seem identical with the first in normal perception.

---

[1] James discusses this at some length in his chapter "The Perception of Space." He cites the many philosophers who agree with Berkeley—Helmholtz, Wundt, Stumpf, Hering, Lipps, and Thomas Reid—and he endeavors to disprove their contentions, but his arguments are not convincing.

Important in urban environment is the element of gravity, or weight, and its influence on our aesthetic enjoyment. A structure in the urban scene that, because of this sense of gravity, gives the feeling of insecurity disturbs our sense of order and our aesthetic enjoyment. It is based partly on experience of the capacity of materials. If the columns of the ground floor of a large building between which one perceives the landscape or townscape beyond give a sense of insecurity, our pleasure is disturbed. This is Kant's second dependent kind of beauty—the dependence on a concept of the conditions that the object should fulfill—and it is a judgment of taste "placed under a restriction" (*Critique of Aesthetic Judgement,* part 1, sections 16–25).

This aesthetic pleasure that is dependent on a concept of the capacity of materials changes with the change of concept. Hume (*Treatise of Human Nature,* volume II, part 1, section 8) says that "the rules of architecture require, that the top of a pillar should be more slender than its base, and that because such a figure conveys to us the idea of security, which is pleasant; whereas the contrary form gives us the apprehension of danger which is uneasy." The shape of the pillar mentioned by Hume gives a sense of security because of our long familiarity with the structural capacity of its material: stone. In reinforced concrete, which has a tensile strength that stone has not, a different shape has been evolved which is more functional: that of the slender column tapering toward the bottom. In the early days of the new structure these were often criticized by traditionalists as looking insecure and thus disturbing aesthetic pleasure. Greater familiarity with the structural capacities of the various systems of reinforced concrete and many developments like prestressed concrete and shell concrete will diminish the disturbing element of insecurity. It still persists until concepts are changed.

This element of gravity, the sense of stability, is the chief factor in the urban scene, where aesthetic pleasure is dependent on a concept of what a thing should be. Otherwise it is questionable whether the expression of function affects aesthetic pleasure—that a church should look like our concept of the forms of a church, and so on. Such a concept is aesthetically irrelevant. If a church looks like our concept of the shape of a factory yet it is beautiful in the abstract, so much the better for the church. This is not to say that it is not essential that the architect think as deeply as he can about the purpose of a church building, because only in that way is a beautiful building likely to result; but if that result is according to our concept more like a factory, then it may be due to the fixity of the concept.

Aesthetic principles are based on human experience of disinterested pleasure, and before any such principles can emerge in the matter of urban design it is necessary to consider the evidence of the pleasure. What in towns and cities has given pleasure and pain to sensitive percipients? Aspects useful to consider are (1) the panorama, (2) the enclosure, (3) the street, and (4) the relation of furniture to space.

The Panorama   When a city or town is planned and built or an extension is made to an existing town, it has to be fitted to a site and related to an existing landscape. The site is usually flat or undulating, and the various buildings, roads, pedestrian ways, open spaces, gardens, trees, and town furniture all have to be related to each other in an effective, functional composition. If aesthetic pleasure is also a major aim, then the composition must also be visually effective. Fundamental is the skyline, both for the town as a whole and for the various parts. In more distant prospects the skyline is part of the background to several outlines of buildings and trees seen in depth or perspective; and atmosphere is often an element, as seen in the classical landscape compositions of Poussin, Claude, and Turner. These skylines constitute a fundamental aesthetic element in the townscape. They often give much pleasure in the approach by road to a country town and in the view of a city from a prominent point.

Examples are legion. To select a few: generally the views over the central parts of Paris, Rome, and Vienna are pleasurable partly because the massing made by the various buildings is harmoniously related and the modern high-rise building does not disturb this massing, whereas in London the panorama from certain points of view is painful because of the unrelated high-rise buildings. These have often been erected in spite of the advice of the British Royal Fine Art Commission. In American cities they sometimes group well and they sometimes do not, and the impression is that either effect results more from accident than design.

High buildings in cities constitute one of the chief urban aesthetic problems of the twentieth century; and, to be practical, it is useful to ask what factors can make them pleasing, since they seem to be commercially if not socially acceptable. Much evidence could be adduced to show that attention to the principles of organic unity would yield satisfactory results. By this is meant that each part in a formal composition should by its character show its relation to the whole and to the other parts as is found in natural forms. If several multistory blocks were grouped so that they had a sequence of heights, or if being of similar height they were well spaced in relation to each other, the result might be aesthetically pleasing. But if they are unrelated and just stick up haphazardly as they do in the city of London, then the result is painful.

It is of little value to say as does Trystan Edwards (*Good and Bad Manners in Architecture,* p. 14) that "the commercial skyscraper is all wrong." It is a building commercially accepted, and this being part of the modern life of cities, it must be regarded as subject for the artist to treat as best he can. But, in the matter of urban design, his subject is the big one of the whole central area of a city, and he must, therefore, have control over the whole. If it is a small city like Bath or Welwyn Garden City, which were both the work of one supervising artist, then the result is very satisfactory; but in big historic cities like Paris, Rome, and Vienna, the overall controlling artist can be only the negative enactment of prohibiting the very high building in certain areas. In London the nearest approach to it is the Royal Fine Art Commission, whose powers are greatly limited. It has to wait to be asked, and when asked its advice is often ignored.

The Capitol, Rome. The grouping of buildings around the piazza was planned by Michelangelo in 1564 and is regarded as one of the perfect designs in the relation of buildings to the space they surround.

The central building is the Palazzo del Senatore, and flanking buildings are the Capitoline Museum and the Palazzo dei Conservatori. In the center is the ancient equestrian statue of Marcus Aurelius. The principal approach is by a ramp. (Engraving from drawing by Letarouilly, 1795–1855.)

Piazza that forms the forecourt of St. Peter's at Rome. Architect of the encircling colonnade—Giovanni Lorenzo Bernini (from an eighteenth-century engraving).

The Enclosure   The principal form of enclosure derives from the Greek agora and the Roman forum, and from the aesthetic standpoint it has most successfully evolved in the Italian medieval and Renaissance piazza. The European evolution has been traced by Camillo Sitte (see bibliography) with the purpose of deducing principles of design which have met with a considerable degree of acceptance among planners. The principal medieval and Renaissance piazzas were often either episcopal, with a church or cathedral as a dominating feature, or civic, with the town hall as a dominating feature. The piazzas were used for religious and civic assemblies and therefore the centers were generally kept clear and open, with monuments and fountains kept to the sides or corners.

In the aesthetically satisfying piazza the sense of space is pleasingly stimulated. It is sufficiently large for that purpose yet sufficiently small to give a sense of enclosure, while the enclosing architecture is agreeable with a harmonious skyline with perhaps one dominating feature. The piazzas of Perugia, Florence, Rome, Venice, Sienna, Todi, and Verona all provide good examples. They are very much large open-air halls or rooms, where the enclosure is fairly complete, with only one or at most two conspicuous entrances and exits. One glimpse beyond may sometimes be attractive, as the glimpse through the open door of a room may be, but several doors opening in all directions and giving glimpses beyond detract from the pleasure in the room. That is why Trafalgar Square in London fails as an urban space. Sitte insists that the centers of piazzas should be kept free and that they should be enclosed entities.

The dominating building at one side—the town hall or church—and flights of steps projecting into the square, giving emphasis and dignity to the building, led to interesting developments. With the symmetrical and formalizing tendencies in Renaissance design and the preoccupation with perspective both in painting and architecture, the piazza was opened at one end for an avenue approach with the principal building opposite. The classic example is, of course, Michelangelo's Piazza of the Capitol in Rome, with the principal feature of the Palazzo del Senatore at one side, with the other end open and approached by a long ramp. Another larger example is Bernini's Piazza of St. Peter, open at the end opposite the cathedral and approached since 1935 by Piacentini's avenue, the via della Conciliazione.

In England both types of square can be seen, the enclosed squares of London and Bath and the squares of Brighton open to the sea. The profusion of large trees and other greenery in many London Squares spoils the sense of space and enclosure and gives the feeling of a garden surrounded by buildings, many of which cannot be seen, rather than an urban square. It is rather like the enthusiast for indoor plants accumulating more and more without relinquishing any, so that rooms are overloaded, becoming at last like conservatories.

Selection and rejection are involved in artistic effect. In a successful urban design trees conform in scale with the buildings, and those kinds must be selected that will give the right scale. The main reason for plane trees is

Grand Canal, Venice. This has been called the finest street in the world. The skyline is varied but harmonious and the relation of the height of the buildings to the width of the canal is pleasing.

Model of new center for Bracknell, England. The tall buildings are well grouped and are not haphazard, as in the City of London.

Wren's Church of St. Vedast, Foster Lane, City of London, enclosed by tall modern buildings so that the beautiful steeple can no longer be seen against the sky.

that they survive in a smoky atmosphere; as the smoke disappears, there should be experiments of replacement with smaller trees, placed so as to emphasize the pleasing feelings of space and enclosure.

The increasing pedestrianization of town centers will make the aesthetic aspects of piazzas, places, and squares important. Of the four towns that received the R. S. Reynolds Memorial Award for Community Architecture in 1967, namely, Vallingby and Farsta near Stockholm, Tapiola near Helsinki, and Cumbernauld in Scotland, only Tapiola can be regarded as aesthetically satisfactory. The pleasant harmony of its low-level buildings surrounding the garden square on three sides and the tall block at one corner contrasts with both Vallingby and Farsta, which are a little too restless. Other good examples are the two central squares at Basildon, the upper square linked with the lower, smaller square by a ramp and steps, with a tall block of apartments on stilts and a fountain as its foot, at the point of juncture. Trees, shrubs, and a fountain with a few seats used at corners or at the sides help the overall decorative effect.

In an urban square the pleasure in the space is created by the enclosure (the parallel in architecture is the enjoyment of space in the interior of a great cathedral) and that pleasure is enhanced if the scale of the enclosing buildings appears to be well related to the space and if the enclosing buildings are harmonious with a restful skyline.

But to make aesthetically attractive squares with the modern architecture of flat curtain walls, with patterns of glass and colored panels, is difficult, as the means are much inferior to the stone architecture of the Renaissance where light and shadow in the recesses often provided a distinctive enclosing architecture.

The Street The street is a thoroughfare with walls formed by buildings, and the aesthetic interest is in the space created in the perspective or vista of the street and in the character of the enclosing buildings. Experience demonstrates that there is aesthetic pleasure if there is a good relation between the height of the flanking buildings and the width of the street. Most of the capital cities of Europe afford good and bad examples of this.

One of the best is the Grand Canal in Venice, where the general heights of the buildings relate well to the width of the canal. There is a general unity of massing in the buildings with a good deal of variety and distinctive architecture of a style that gives opportunity for the play of light and shadow. Of modern examples one of the best on a small scale is the pedestrian Lynbahn in Rotterdam. The flanking buildings are kept to two stories, which gives a sense of openness. Four or more stories for a pedestrian way would have given a closed-in feeling.

An aesthetic aspect of the street, especially in the often-discussed residential areas, is the repetition of the building unit and the extent of repetition that is possible without monotony. Trystan Edwards has dealt with this matter (*Good and Bad Manners in Architecture*) with conclusions that have met with a wide measure of agreement, which supports the notion that

Cwmbran New Town, Wales—Fairwater subcenter, 1966. Irregular yet harmonious enclosure, of a geometric sculptural character. (Architect: Gordon Redfern.)

Sishes End, Stevenage, England. Partial enclosure of a pedestrian way in a residential area of a New Town.

Town Center, Tapiola, Finland, 1960. An example of a formal shopping square with central garden enclosed on three sides, open on the fourth, and approached by a broad flight of steps. The ensemble has a classical serenity. View from the tall block at the corner of the square. (Architect: Aarne Ervi.)

LEFT: *Enclosure formed by new grouping of buildings on the South Bank, London. Festival Hall on right, Hayward Gallery on left, and Shell building in distance. The good architectural effect of the enclosure cannot be properly appreciated because of the large tree which is out of scale. In good urban design, trees conform to and enhance a desired effect.*   BELOW: *An effective composition of buildings and gardens in the town center of Hemel Hempstead, England. The tall block relates well to the long five-story block and the circular, storied car park, which form an effective visual enclosure for the gardens (1961).*

it is possible sometimes to create standards on the basis of common feeling.

If a meanly designed house is repeated in a long terrace of 20 houses, it is monotonous and dreary. If the unit is well designed but still small, the repetition is more acceptable. If it is a larger unit with portico emphasis at the entrance and well proportioned, the repetition is more pleasing, as in some of the late-Georgian terrace houses in English cities and towns. If the design of the unit is varied, or if the terrace has at either end buildings of a different but still harmonious character, the whole effect is often still more pleasing because variety is introduced into the general unity.

Varying the unit and its siting is a device employed in the residential areas of New Towns. There are architects, however, who like the long repetition of the well-designed unit, as in the Crescent at Bath, but the question arises: how far can this repetition be carried without a sense of monotony and dullness which diminishes aesthetic enjoyment? A phrase in music can often be repeated many times with good effect, as exemplified

Texture and color of houses and gardens in a pedestrian residential area of the New Town of Telford, England, with light and shadow enhancing aesthetic interest.

in Mozart, but there is a limit beyond which an element of absurdity would creep in. The same is true in architecture. It must be admitted that some architects and planners have not known when to stop. The same feeling arises with the repetition of precast concrete units in the facades of buildings. The economic asset of mass production often destroys too much.

The straight alignment of buildings along a street is a feature of the closely built central areas. Where open spaces and gardens mingle in the urban scene and in residential areas, that alignment is only partial and is varied with spaces and trees, and the composition is the subject of the landscape architect. This central avenue descends from the ancient processional way with its terminal feature, often a temple as in ancient Egypt, and the finest examples are broad thoroughfares, flanked by handsome buildings and gardens, with an impressive culminating feature.

Probably the grandest is the Champs Elysees in Paris, and the full magnificence can be appreciated by standing in the Tuileries and looking across the Place de la Concorde on to the terminal feature of the Arc de Triomphe. There are many similar examples on a smaller scale. Magnificent as it is, for some tastes it is too formal and symmetrical, and a vista with balancing masses at various distances is preferred. Examples are the classical landscapes of Claude and Turner, especially those with classical buildings flanking a view of water. The consummate example is Turner's "Dido Building Carthage," where masses on the right and left are balancing each other into the sunlit mist of the distance. These classical landscapes have probably had considerable influence on landscape architecture.

Furniture Equipment of public services that occupies the spaces in cities, like lighting standards, traffic signs, and telephone kiosks, constitutes the functional furniture; while the public monuments, fountains, trees, and gardens constitute the decorative. The aesthetic obligation of the planner is primarily the scale and placement of all the objects in the most visually pleasing manner. A good principle, mentioned by Sitte, is that the furniture should as far as possible be subordinated to the character of the space it occupies.

What further principles can be suggested? Professor Rudolf Arnheim (*Towards a Psychology of Art,* 1966) makes a serviceable classification when writing on "Order and Complexity in Landscape Design." The terms are largely variants of the old "unity and variety," but he makes a useful division of order, namely: (1) homogeneity, (2) coordination, (3) heirarchy, and (4) accident. Homogeneity he describes as the existence of a common quality in the entire pattern, thus acting as a unifying element; coordination as the balance of parts—a less satisfactory contribution; hierarchy as order with a dominant structural element with related subordinate elements; and accident as "the relationship of independence." All these are strongly apparent in the townscape. In the mid-twentieth century the last has received much attention, and it is important to consider it briefly as it is less in conformity with universal standards.

Dido Building Carthage, *by J. W. M. Turner, R. A., painted in 1815 (National Gallery, London). An example of Turner's classical period, when he aimed to emulate Claude. One of the best examples in classical landscape painting of the balancing of masses in the perspective or depth of the picture. A mass on the right is balanced by a mass on the left a little further in the depth of the picture, and so on. The balancing masses are never quite on the same plane. This type of landscape painting has had much influence on landscape architects in the designing of vistas.*

New York City. LEFT: *Midtown skylin* *The buildings are aesthetically unrelate* *and do not therefore make a satisfacto* *coordinated whole.* BELOW, LEFT: *In this view of new/old lower Manhattan the buildings do not appear to be schematically related, but some cohesion has resulted in the close grouping toward the center, probably more by accident than design. The effect is more satisfactory than in the case of the midtown skyline.*

ABOVE, RIGHT: *Chicago. In this view the buildings of various sizes and heights do not appear to be related by any aesthetically motivated scheme, with the result that the skyline is just a series of uncoordinated projections into the sky. Some degree of harmony results in the grouping on the left of the photograph, but it is less satisfactory to the right.* RIGHT: *View of Jackson Square of the Vieux Carre, the old central area of New Orleans which was planned and built in the Renaissance tradition in the first half of the eighteenth century. It is an example following Italian development of the opening of the square or piazza on one side with the principle feature opposite. Here the formal square is open on the southeast side to the Mississippi River, with the Basilica of St. Louis as the central building opposite.*

Accidental effects in the townscape resulting in the picturesque are to some extent traditional pop art. Generally there has been no urban designer; the artist is the percipient who creates the pleasurable scene according to rough ideas of coordinated pattern, color, and balance. Junk in a derelict area seen in relation to trees and modern buildings has provided accidental effects which give aesthetic pleasure; and mean cottages erected with no thought of artistic effect have sometimes resulted in something visually pleasing. There is obviously kinship here with the art of the "found object," and planning with the hope of accidental, pleasing effects could be a little disruptive of attempts to strengthen legislation of an aesthetic kind, based, as it must be, on standards.

This consideration is very important for urban design. Should scope be given for purely functional design without aesthetic considerations in the expectation that fitness for purpose results in beauty, thus giving scope for unpremeditated accidental effects? The practical answer is "yes," in a private individual art, but not in a public art like urban design, for the result is too often something very ugly.

What then can be done to ensure that aesthetic considerations have adequate influence in urban design? The artist who creates an urban environment has a much bigger physical subject than the architect of a building or group of buildings; but no real provision has been made for such an artist except in New Towns or very large-scale urban renewal. It can only be done with existing cities by the enforcement of principles and advice by a body like the British Royal Fine Art Commission, which should be given very much stronger and effective powers, and whose advice cannot be so easily overridden as it has been in the past. The wise consensus of subjective aesthetic evaluations resulting in standards for which Hume, Kant, Alexander, and others have discussed a philosophic basis are a justification for legislation, but these standards must be constantly subject to review in a changing world on an ever broadening basis of participation.

BIBLIOGRAPHY: Camillo Sitte, *Der Städtebau nach seinen kunstlerischen Grundsätzen,* Vienna, 1889, English translation by G. R. and C. C. Collins, *City Planning According to Artistic Principles,* Columbia University Press, New York, 1965; Trystan Edwards, *Good and Bad Manners in Architecture,* Philip Allan, London, 1924; Siegfried Giedion, *Space, Time, and Architecture,* Harvard University Press, Cambridge, Mass., 1941; Patrick Geddes, *Cities in Evolution,* Williams & Norgate, London, 1915 and 1949; Sir Frederick Gibberd, *Town Design,* Architectural Press, London, 1953–1967; Gordon Logie, *The Urban Scene,* Faber & Faber, London, 1954; Kevin Lynch, *The Image of the City,* Technology Press & Harvard University Press, Cambridge, Mass., 1960; John Orsmbee Simonds, *Landscape Architecture,* McGraw-Hill Book Company, New York, 1961; Ivor de Wolfe, *The Italian Townscape,* Architectural Press, London, 1963; Garrett Eckbo, *Urban Landscape Design,* McGraw-Hill Book Company, New York, 1964; Paul D. Spreiregen, *The Architecture of Towns and Cities,* McGraw-Hill Book Company, New York, 1965; Edmund N. Bacon, *Design of Cities,* Thames and Hudson, London, 1967; E. A. Gutkind, *International History of City Development,* Urban Development in Central Europe, vol. I, 1963, Urban Development in the Alpine and Scandinavian Countries, vol. II, 1965, Urban Development in Southern Europe, Spain and Portugal, vol. III, 1967, Urban Development in Southern Europe, Italy and Greece, vol. IV, 1969, Urban Development in Western Europe, The Netherlands and Great Britain, vol. VI, 1971, The Free Press, New York.

—ARNOLD WHITTICK

AFFORESTATION (*See* FORESTRY.)

AGORA The principal public place of a Greek city, which was the commercial and social center of the city. The term is derived from the Greek word ἀγορά, meaning assembly; thus it is "the place of assembly." It was the place where political meetings, religious ceremonies, and, in earlier times, dramatic performances took place; it was also the marketplace and the essential heart of the Greek city from the sixth century onward. Earlier the acropolis (*q.v.*) had been the center, but with the increase in size of the city, the agora gradually became the more important, the acropolis becoming more exclusively a religious center.

Around the agora were grouped a variety of public, commercial, and religious buildings, like the council house and law courts, temples, and stoa, a multipurpose building which served both to house stores and as a meeting place for business, often with a row of shops on the ground floor. Monuments and shrines often appeared in the agora, which up to the end of the fourth century was generally kept open in the center. In the earlier agoras, such as the famous example at Athens, the buildings were grouped irregularly around the open place; but in the later Ionian examples, such as those at Miletus and Priene, the agora was enclosed in a more regular rectangle, with stoa and other buildings forming a colonnade.

With the modern development toward the pedestrian precinct for the center of cities, there has been a revival of interest in the Greek agora. (*See also the illustrations for* ANCIENT PLANNING—GREECE.)

BIBLIOGRAPHY: R. E. Wycherley, *How the Greeks Built Cities,* Macmillan & Co., Ltd., London, 1949; "Hellenic Cities" and "Hellenistic Cities," *The Town Planning Review* 2 and 3, vol. 22, Liverpool University Press, London, 1951; Paul D. Spreiregen, *The Architecture of Towns and Cities,* McGraw-Hill Book Company, New York, 1965.

—ARNOLD WHITTICK

AGRICULTURAL LAND USE Most decisions about agricultural land use in the United States, and a great many of the decisions in Britain, are made by private landowners and land users but within a framework of governmental restraints, aids, and guidelines.

In both countries, various units of government make studies and prepare maps about the soils and the land. The soils are studied to measure their depth, the texture of the surface and deeper soils (clay, sand, loam, etc.), their topography, their natural drainage, their chemical characteristics, and other features. The soils are mapped to show these various characteristics as they actually exist in various locations. This may be done with varying degrees of detail, depending in part upon the value of the land, the need for detailed information as a basis for its use, and in part upon when the survey was made, since surveys have been made with increasing detail with the passage of time.

In both countries, the adaptability of the land for various uses is also determined and mapped. In the United States, eight land-capability classes have been established. Class I is the best crop land, with good soil structure, deep soils, nearly level, few or no limitations on crop use, and few or no special soil conservation measures required. Such nearly ideal crop land is scarce; there are fewer than 40 million acres of it in the United States. Class II land is less favorable in one or more of these characteristics than is Class I land, and Class III land is still less favorable in various ways, but both of these classes are capable of being farmed permanently if proper management precautions are taken. Class IV land has most severe limitations for crops and can be used only under special circumstances and with special practices. The other four classes are nonarable but have values for forestry, grazing, or other uses.

In Britain, the land classification is similar, with four grades of arable land rather closely similar to the four classes in the United States but with only one class of essentially nonarable land.

In both countries, government economists estimate crop acreages, yields, and demand for crops and propose land-use programs based on such estimates. The United States possesses more crop land than is needed to produce the output of crops for which there is an effective demand. For a generation, there have been federal programs aimed at reducing acreage of land used for crops. Since 1960, more than 50 million acres of land have been retired from crop production. Nearly all this land consists of relatively small parts of operating farms rather than being large acreages concentrated in few locations. The farmer chooses which land to retire, and it is generally assumed that he chooses the poorer land within his farm to retire from production. In the United States, there has been no effective program to keep urban expansion off the better agricultural lands, although there has been a good deal of talk that it would be desirable to do so. In Britain, there is more concern to keep agricultural output up and to preserve the best farm lands against urban expansion, especially the best market-garden lands nearer the larger cities, and effective programs to this end have been at least partially successful.

In both countries, the most effective public action affecting agricultural land use has generally not been called "planning," but "research." In each country, there is a rather complex agricultural research structure, primarily public although with an increasingly important private sector, especially in the United States. This research structure has produced new crop varieties; improved livestock; better and cheaper fertilizers; various chemicals and other means to control insects, weeds, and diseases; improved farm machines, including tractors; and otherwise has provided the technological basis upon which a greatly more productive agriculture could be based. In each country, government programs have provided farmers with technical assistance to install soil conservation or other measures on their land, and in each country there have been various programs of government subsidies to encourage farmers to use such soil-conserving and output-increasing measures. Thus, although comprehensive national planning for agricultural land use may not exist, especially in the United States, a great deal of agricultural land-use planning nevertheless is carried out.

BIBLIOGRAPHY: Raleigh Barlowe, *Land Resource Economics: The Political Economy of Rural and Urban Land Use,* Prentice-Hall, Inc., Englewood Cliffs, N.J., 1958; T. W. Freeman, *Geography and Planning,* University Library, London, 1958; Gerald Percy Wibberley, *Agriculture and Urban Growth: A Study of the Competition for Rural Land,* Michael Joseph, London, 1959; Marion Clawson, R. Burnell Held, and C. H. Stoddard, *Land for the Future,* Johns Hopkins Press, Baltimore, 1960; Harold G. Halcrow, Joseph Ackerman, Marshall Harris, Charles L. Stewart, and John F. Timmons, *Modern Land Policy,* University of Illinois Press, Urbana, Ill., 1960; Laurence Dudley Stamp, *The Land of Britain: Its Use and Misuse,* 3d ed., Longmans, Green & Co., Ltd., London, 1962.

—MARION CLAWSON

AIR-CONDITIONING, CENTRAL   The control of air in a building to a desired temperature and humidity, and its cleansing and circulation, obtained by means of plants designed and installed for the purpose. There are many systems of central air-conditioning, but all employ a refrigeration process and heating to the requisite temperature together with moisture infusion. Central air-conditioning is used mainly in industrial buildings, where it is necessary for certain manufacturing processes, and in public and office buildings. It has also been used in urban centers where these take the form of a covered pedestrian area, an example being the small center of Urbana, Illinois, and the large covered shopping center of the New Town of Runcorn in England opened in 1972. Air-conditioning will probably be used increasingly in covered pedestrian centers.

AIR POLLUTION AND CLEAN AIR   Pollution of the air by smoke is caused mainly by the incomplete combustion of fossil fuels which emit carbon monoxide, fine carbonaceous particles, and tarry droplets. Pollution is also caused by the discharge of sulfur dioxide from such fuel, including smokeless fuel; emissions from various industrial processes (e.g., fluorides from brick-making and aluminum smelting); dust and grit from quarries and cement works; and the fumes from chemical works, oil refineries, and motor vehicles.

Smoke and other forms of air pollution are injurious to health and damaging to vegetation, buildings, and materials. It often has serious effects on the respiratory system and can sometimes be lethal on a considerable scale when combined with certain humidity and temperature conditions to produce smog. It is estimated that about four thousand persons died from smog in London in 1952. Smoke also has an injurious effect by obscuring natural light and depriving people of sunlight. Often industrial cities are dark beneath a pall of smoke when there is bright sunlight in the surrounding country. This has inevitable psychological and social consequences. The deposit on vegetation of various chemicals is often poisonous, while it corrodes the stonework of buildings and accelerates decay.

The injurious effects of smoke have long been experienced, and smoke production has therefore been subject to restrictive legislation since the Middle Ages. London is a significant example. As early as 1273, the use of coal was prohibited in London as being prejudicial to health; in 1306 there was a royal proclamation prohibiting the use of "sea coal" for furnaces, and since then there have been a series of enactments. As a result of the rapid industrial growth in England in the nineteenth century and the increasing concentration of population in big industrial centers, the problems of smoke and its injurious effects became more insistent. To deal with them, Smoke Abatement Acts were passed from 1853 onwards; while the Public Health Acts, dating from 1875, contain sections on smoke abatement. These constituted the beginning of more comprehensive legislation, culminating in the Clean Air Acts of 1956 and 1968. These acts contain prohibitions of black smoke and give powers to local authorities to declare smokeless zones. The Alkali Act of 1963, since amended and extended, covers the emissions from various industrial processes.

Legislation has also been introduced in the United States and other countries for the control of air pollution. Research on the injurious effects of smoke, gasoline, and diesel fumes and preventive and restrictive measures is conducted on a considerable scale in many countries, and there are several associations in these countries dedicated to the purpose of developing effective improvements. Eight of these, in Argentina, Australia, France, Germany (Federal Republic), Japan, Mexico, the United Kingdom, and the United States, are members of the International Union of Air Pollution Prevention Associations, which had its first congress in London in 1966 and its second in Washington, D.C., in 1970.

BIBLIOGRAPHY: A. R. Meetham, D. W. Bottom, and S. Clayton, *Atmospheric Pollution: Its Origins and Prevention,* 3d ed., Pergamon Press, New York; National Society for Clean Air, *Clean Air Year Book,* Brighton, England, 1970–1971.

—ARNOLD WHITTICK

AIR TRANSPORT   Since 1952 world air passenger traffic has been steadily increasing at the rate of 14.5 percent annually and air freight traffic by 17.5 percent annually. This growth of air transportation has been particularly important for the effect it has had on the development of regional and national economies and in promoting international trade. The travel and tourism industries are themselves major influences in many national economies and now constitute the most valuable single item in international trade.

Types of Air Traffic   There are two major types of air traffic: they are conventionally known as "air carrier traffic" and "general aviation." The former is in effect the public sector of the air transport industry, offering air services either as regular scheduled services or on a nonscheduled or charter basis for the carriage of both international and domestic passenger and freight traffic. The second category covers all other civil aviation, serving specific private users for such diverse purposes as business and personal travel, agricultural spraying, aerial survey, and self-piloted recreational flying.

The Growth of Air Traffic   Table 1 indicates that since the year 1953 scheduled air passenger traffic has increased almost fivefold if reckoned in terms of the total number of passengers carried, or almost sevenfold if reckoned in terms of distance flown. At present the domestic flights in the United States alone account for nearly half of the total world traffic.

Although it has been estimated that air passenger traffic will increase threefold over the next 10 years, air freight traffic will possibly grow by six or eight times over the same period.

These increases in traffic have been largely brought about by successive reductions in the cost of air travel, which in turn have been made possible by progressive improvements in aircraft performance in terms of increases in payload, speed, and range.

These trends of increasing traffic and of size and performance of aircraft are presenting growing problems of airport congestion, loss of amenity, and congestion of ground transportation between airports and the major urban centers they serve. Moreover, the planning implications of the size and

TABLE 1   *Trends in Scheduled Passenger Traffic*

	Passenger kilometres, billions = 10^9			Passengers carried, millions	
	U.S. domestic	World total	Domestic	International	World total
1953	23.6	46	44	9	53
1958	40.7	85	70	18	88
1963	61.6	147	104	31	135
1968	140.1	308	208	55	263
1970	180	400	}		
1975	288	712	} Forecasts		
1980	485	1,207	}		

SOURCES: ICAO, Boeing, Lockheed, Airbus International

TABLE 2   *Trends in Demand for Air Transportation at Major Airports in the United States*

	Aircraft operations, millions	Passengers carried, millions	Air freight, million tons	General aviation, thousands based aircraft
1965	20.3	69.5	1.3	20.3
1980	74.6	370.6	19.7	50.3

SOURCE: FAA

TABLE 3   *Trends in Aircraft Size and Performance*

	Aircraft type	Maximum passenger capacity	Gross weight, lb	Cruising speed, mph
1935	Douglas DC3	28	25,200	180
1946	Douglas DC4	44	65,000	240
1952	De Havilland Comet 1	40	110,000	500
1959	Boeing 707	189	300,000	545
1969	Boeing 747	490	713,000	585

SOURCE: Horonjeff

location of major airports often go beyond this, affecting the size, location, and traffic patterns of urban and regional transportation facilities. Among the major airports, O'Hare (Chicago) currently handles over 30 million terminating passengers per year; Kennedy (New York) handles 20 million; Heathrow (London), 13 million; and Schipol (Amsterdam), 3.5 million. Additionally, a major airport is often a major feature in the local economy and therefore tends to be a strong determinant of the local land-use patterns and of the distribution of population and employment. New York's three major airports employ a total labor force of some 44,000, while some 48,000 people are directly employed at Heathrow.

Future Developments   Current problems of continued growth in air traffic and airport congestion have led to a resurgence of interest, particularly in the United States, in the development of short-takeoff-and-landing (STOL) and vertical-takeoff-and-landing (VTOL) aircraft for more widespread use by air carriers. Commercial STOL and VTOL aircraft would be smaller than the conventional short-haul aircraft and would operate on the short-haul intercity routes or as transfer services between the city airports. One idea that has been strongly canvassed is the operation of STOL and VTOL aircraft from special airports more centrally located within the city, thus reducing the amount of time spent traveling from the city center out to the major airport. It is doubtful that the adoption of STOL and VTOL could effectively reduce airport congestion without the provision of new short landing strips, air corridors, and approach paths which would be separate from those used by conventional aircraft.

At the present stage of development, STOL and VTOL operating costs are significantly higher than those of conventional air travel. Further improvements in technology should help to remove this difference in the near future, but in the more distant future the short-haul air operators will be facing increasing competition from high-speed ground transportation modes such as the tracked hovercraft, which is currently being developed.

Indications are that trends of increasing size for aircraft on medium- and long-haul services will continue.

The introduction of a nonmilitary version of the Lockheed C5A and the development of a large-capacity, medium-haul air bus should permit a slower rate of growth for aircraft movements relative to the growth in the number of passengers carried. The large aircraft now in service have provided greater capacity for the carriage of air freight. With the increasing adoption of containers and other unit-load systems for the handling of air cargos, this traffic should continue to increase.

International passenger traffic is now growing at twice the rate of domestic traffic. Although it is at present uncertain what impact the introduction of supersonic passenger services will have on the air travel market, it is probable that the nonscheduled passenger traffic will continue to grow, paralleling the increasing growth in international tourism.

BIBLIOGRAPHY: *FAA Statistical Handbook of Aviation,* Federal Aviation Administration, 1965; K. R. Sealy, *The Geography of Air Transport,* Hutchinson Publishing Group, Ltd., London,

1966; R. Miller and D. Sawers, *The Technical Development of Modern Aviation,* Routledge &
Kegan Paul, Ltd., London, 1968; *World Airports: The Way Ahead,* Institution of Civil Engineers,
London, 1970.

—David Briggs

AIRPORTS

Functions   The primary function of the airport is to provide a safe and
efficient means of interchange between air transportation and ground transportation and a means whereby passengers can transfer from one air service
to another. In addition, the airport is usually the center from which control
is exercised over air traffic on defined air routes and on the approaches to
airports. Airports differ in terms of size, in the nature of traffic handled
(whether general aviation or air carrier—*see* AIR TRANSPORT), and in the
type of air traffic control exercised (whether it is operating on instrument
flight rules or visual flight rules). In the United States the Federal Aviation
Administration (FAA) has developed a functional classification in which
major urban areas are defined as air traffic hubs according to the relative
number of passengers handled at the airport. A large hub handles more
than 1 percent of the national scheduled domestic passenger traffic, while
an airport which handles less than 0.05 percent of the total does not qualify
for hub status.

Location   The total land area required at an airport is dependent on the
nature and scale of the traffic handled and the rate at which this is expected
to grow. This factor, coupled with the physical and climatic characteristics
of the site and the performance characteristics of present and future aircraft,
determines the number, length, and configuration of runways required. There
is a group of operational factors which are important in determining
acceptable airport locations:

1. Air traffic control requirements—such as minimal interference to and
from the air traffic control operations of neighboring airports

2. Height obstructions and other navigational hazards, such as tall
buildings, smoke, or bird hazards

3. Prevalent weather conditions, including wind distribution and the
incidence of fog and snow

Planning and social factors are becoming increasingly important in airport
location problems. Perhaps the main consideration in this area is to achieve
a balance between the danger and noise disturbance created by the airport
and the requirement of providing good accessibility from the center of
population that it serves. Where travel time and costs by surface transport
are important criteria, the major airports serving large metropolitan areas
may need some form of rapid transit connection; in other cases good access
for private and public transport by highway is important.

Facilities   In planning and designing airport facilities, one of the most
important goals is to arrange for a free flow of passengers and goods. The
principle here is that there should be a balance of capacity throughout all
the facilities in the airport so as to minimize the risk of congestion in any

A passenger terminal designed on the finger concept. Terminal 1, Heathrow Airport, London. (B.A.A.)

one area—congestion that might easily impair the operating efficiency of the entire airport complex.

There are two different types of functional areas within the airport. The first, the operational areas, are sometimes referred to as the "airside" areas and include such facilities as the runways, taxiways, and aircraft holding areas. It is the design and performance of these facilities that, with the system of air traffic control, determine the operational capacity of the airport. Also included in the operational area are the servicing and maintenance areas and the airport operational buildings. The second type of areas—the terminals or "landside" areas—are the buildings and facilities which primarily

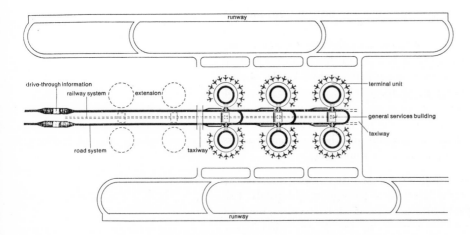

A plan for a passenger terminal designed on the unit concept. (Lufthansa.)

provide a means of interchange, for both passengers and goods, between ground transport and air transport. Design concepts have evolved from the early, simple, low-capacity terminal buildings through higher capacity "finger terminal" layouts to contemporary concepts which decentralize functions of ticketing, baggage handling, and passenger waiting and sorting areas into smaller discrete units or satellites. Other criteria which have been suggested as being important in the design of passenger terminals are convenient and efficient access to both public and private land transport, adequate parking facilities, the avoidance of long walking distances within terminals, efficient baggage handling, and smooth processing of passengers through governmental controls (customs, immigration, health). Finally, in an era of rapid technological change, a flexible layout that can accommodate change and expansion is an important requirement for most designs.

BIBLIOGRAPHY: R. Horonjeff, *Planning and Design of Airports,* McGraw-Hill Book Company, New York, 1962; *Airport Terminals,* 4th ed., International Air Transport Association, 1966; *Access to Airports—Selected References,* Biographical List No. 12, Supplement, U.S. Federal Aviation Administration, 1967; R. G. Hennes and M. Eske, *Fundamentals of Transportation Engineering,* McGraw-Hill Book Company, New York, 1969; *Manual on Airport Master Planning,* International Civil Aviation Organization, Montreal, 1969; Commission on the third London airport (various publications) H.M.S.O., London.

—DAVID BRIGGS

ALBERTI, LEONE BATTISTA (1404–1472)   Florentine humanist and architect. His best-known building is the Church of St. Andrea in Mantua, where the longitudinal barrel vault, a dominant motif of Renaissance and baroque architecture, makes one of its first appearances.

Alberti, however, is probably even more celebrated as the author of *De Re Aedificatoria,* written in the middle of the fifteenth century, in which he discusses the building of an ideal city. This work had a powerful influence, and subsequently the theme of the *città ideale* was developed by Antonio Filarete in his *Trattato d'Architettura,* written when he was in the service of the Sforzas. Alberti was thus the originator of an idea which produced Sforzinda, a star-shaped ideal city plan, and which fired the imaginations of many later thinkers such as Francesco di Giorgio di Martini, Scamozzi, and Vasari.

Alberti designed fortresses for tyrants, a significant fact considering the political climate of the day. He suggested that undulating streets should be built in ideal cities so that a journey through a town would create the impression that the place was bigger than it was in reality. He desired to segregate the nobility from the vulgar, and believed that the nobles should inhabit magnificent houses along avenues of great length. His notions came to the attention of Pope Nicholas V, who wanted to build a huge and isolated papal residence. The scheme was never realized, but designs were prepared by Alberti.

His monumental ideas are reflected in his use of the triumphal arch, as at St. Francesco in Rimini, more a monument to the glory of Sigismondo Malatesta than a church; and in the Palazzo Rucellai in Florence. It is in his use of antique *motifs* and in his theoretical writings that we find the Alberti who is both innovator and reactionary. In the Middle Ages, even in the cathedrals and churches, the sense of long centuries of growth and change is strong. Part of Alberti's conception of beauty was the idea that once something had been created, nothing could be added and nothing could be taken away without damage. The *città ideale* obeyed this view. Thus it was a static, ordered form, more symbolic of a seeking after order than capable of full life, and so—ultimately—doomed by its very perfection.

BIBLIOGRAPHY: Helen Rosenau, *The Ideal City in Its Architectural Evolution,* Routledge & Kegan Paul, Ltd., London, 1959; Sigfried Giedion, *Space, Time and Architecture,* Harvard University Press, Cambridge, Mass., and Oxford University Press, London, 1967; James Stevens Curl, *European Cities and Society,* Leonard Hill, London, 1970.

—JAMES STEVENS CURL

ALLOTMENTS   Small plots or subdivisions, within a larger area of either urban or rural land, for the cultivation of vegetables. In England allotments were originally small portions of land assigned to agricultural laborers and to artisans, either gratuitously or for a small rent, for the economical production of their own vegetables. During World War I (1914–1918), special facilities were provided for the provision of allotments to supplement supplies of food in view of the blockade, and this was repeated in World War II (1939–1945). In some planning schemes for housing estates and suburban extensions, provision is still made for space for allotments, although the demand for these is declining.

AMENITY   Originally denoting the idea of pleasantness, the term has a wide application in modern planning with some extension of meaning. It comprehends the preservation and enhancement of a pleasing and agreeable urban and rural environment, including attractive open spaces and landscape features, social and recreational provisions, and technical improvements designed to increase the pleasantness of life.

ANCIENT MONUMENTS, Protection of   In many countries ancient monuments, which include buildings, of exceptional historic or aesthetic interest are given protection and must be preserved in any development schemes, except in very special cases. In the United States monuments of historic or aesthetic interest which are scheduled for preservation by national or municipal government are called landmarks. In Great Britain protection is given by the Ancient Monuments Acts of 1913 and 1930.

ANCIENT PLANNING

Egypt   The importance of ancient Egyptian planning is not sufficiently recognized. Many of the ideas behind modern planning were already influential in ancient Egypt. In fact, the ancient Egyptians first developed the principles of town planning, zoning, site planning, and civic design.

An unusual example of ancient planning is the city which lies immediately adjacent to the eastern face of the Pyramid of Queen Khent Kawes (2900 B.C.) (see illustration). The plan shows that it was designed as a whole.

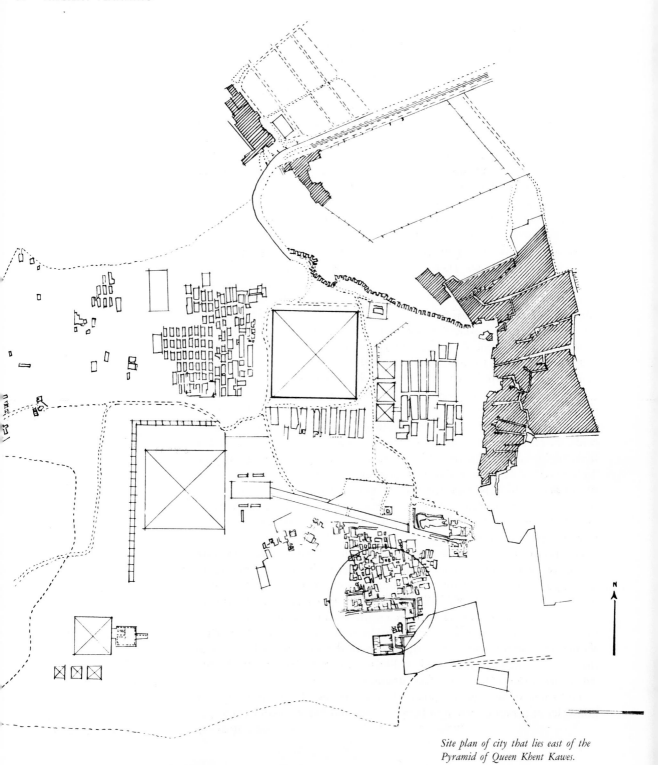

Site plan of city that lies east of the Pyramid of Queen Khent Kawes.

The streets intersect at right angles and at equal intervals. The division of the houses into groups proves that the city did not grow haphazardly.

In Upper Egypt there are the relics of the Middle and New Kingdoms with their capital at Theves. The site chosen by Akhenaton for the city called Tell el 'Amarna (see illustration) was on new ground, as he claimed in his boundary stelae. At least three of these fourteen stelae contained a first version of a proclamation concerning the founding of the city. The houses were grouped, though, in imperfect alignment along three main northern and southern streets. It is interesting to compare Akhenaton village with the town built to accommodate the officials and workmen employed on the Pyramid of Sunnsret II (1906–1888 B.C.) at El Lahun. In each case we find the great rectangular enclosure and the division into two unequal parts, an eastern and a western. The ancient Egyptians were the first to develop the gridiron principle in city planning.

Zoning   The city of Tell El 'Amarna (see illustration) was planned as a whole for different classes. There are the Royal Lodgings, the larger buildings for higher officials, storehouses and shops, and cottages for workmen. The city was divided into two main parts: the eastern zone was for high officials' houses and the western was for the workmen's cottages. This suggests that the ancient Egyptians were the first to use zoning in city planning.

Site Planning   In general, the ancient Egyptians sited their cities, villages, and great temples on the banks of the river Nile, which is the only waterway in Egypt. The pyramids, which are among the oldest monuments in stone, were the outcome of an insistent belief in future life and the belief that the preservation of the body was essential to secure the immortality of the soul. Accordingly, the sites of the pyramids were chosen on the western bank, far from the river, on high lands to protect the mummified bodies from the overflowing of the Nile. Moreover, the ancient Egyptians chose high places on which to build their defensive citadels; as, for example, the site of Semna, built by Sunnsret III (1878–1841 B.C.), near the cataract in the south of Egypt. Zemna fortress consists of three sites on both banks of the Nile and on the island of Oronarti. Evidently, these are among the first examples of site planning.

Civic Design   The Temple of Luxor and the great Temple of Karnak were connected by a paved causeway about $1\frac{1}{4}$ miles (2 kilometers) in length. The approaches to the temples were arranged on a magnificent scale. The road leading to these temples was lined with about one thousand sphinxes on both sides. Some temples were frequently rebuilt on the same ancient sites, others were enlarged and extended over many centuries. Symmetry about the main axis was most strongly marked except in such cases—as that of the temple on the island of Philae—where the nature of the site led to distortion of the customary arrangements.

The study of ancient Egyptian planning throws light on important principles of planning practiced between four and five thousand years ago.

—AHMED AMIN MOKHTAR

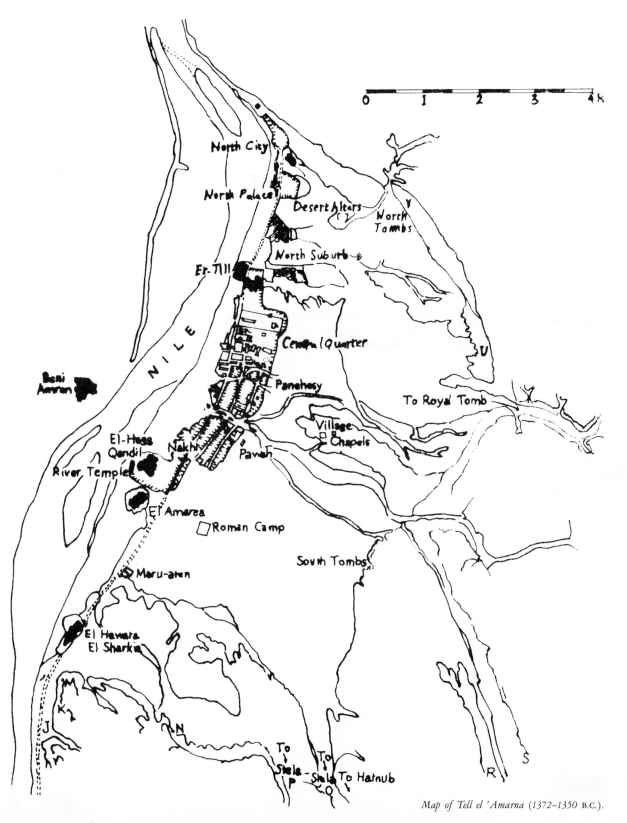

Map of Tell el 'Amarna (1372–1350 B.C.*).*

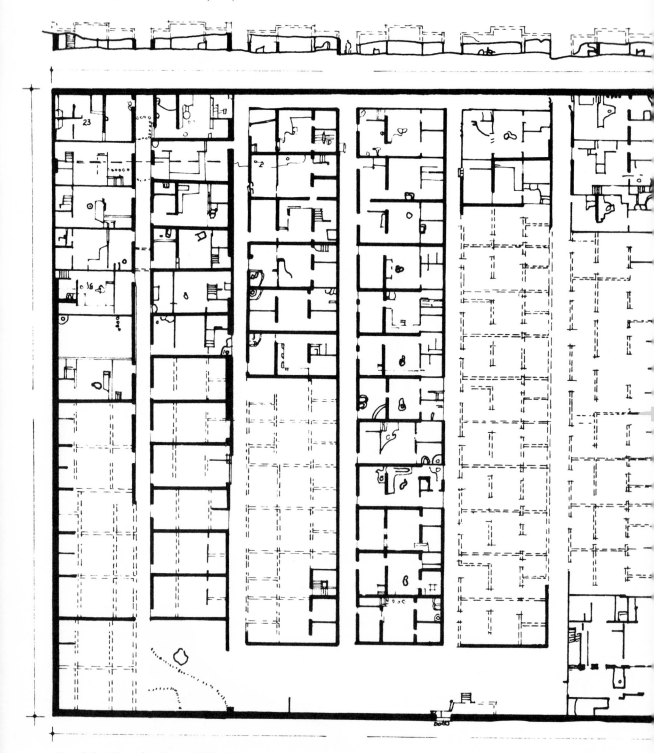

Plan of the village of workmen at Tell el 'Amarna.

Mesopotamia The world's first urban civilization almost certainly arose in the fertile area of Mesopotamia's two rivers, and it persisted there for some 2,500 years.

Although we have no records of a complete preplanning of any city of this period, the cities were certainly laid out and built according to an accepted system that allowed for orderly growth and change.

The possibility of providing for permanent concentrations of large numbers of people arose only after the development of a rural economy, based on irrigation, that could provide a surplus of foodstuffs, thus permitting the rise of specialized occupations and the evolution of an accepted system of trading goods and services. Between the fifth and the third millennia B.C., these conditions appeared in several places in the general area between the eastern Mediterranean and the Indus Valley and gave rise to a number of self-supporting rural villages.

It was the advent of the Sumerian people into the plain of the Tigris and Euphrates rivers some time before 3000 B.C. that motivated the move to an urban system of city states with a tributary countryside. No one yet knows the origins of the Sumerians. It is clear that they came from a mountainous land, and Sir Arthur Keith states that "one can still trace the ancient Sumerians eastward among the inhabitants of Afghanistan and Baluchistan."[1] The Sumerians introduced a hierarchy of priestly government with methods of taxation and record keeping (in cuneiform script upon clay tablets). Like metallurgy and many other crafts, building was a sacred activity undertaken at propitious times under the aegis of the priest-king. The only permanent buildings at first were those related to the perpetuation of the regime: temples, tombs, and storehouses. Timber and stone existed only on the fringes of the land of the two rivers and buildings were, for the most part, made of clay bricks (at first sun-dried and later kiln-baked). However, for the main buildings, "Cedar rafts like great snakes were floated down the river from the cedar mountains, pine rafts from the pine mountains . . . stones were delivered in large blocks, also bitumen in buckets and gypsum from the mountains of Magda."[2] This is part of a description of the building of a temple by Gudea, ruler of the city of Lagash.

As mass production of standardized burnt bricks proceeded, dwelling houses also became permanent structures. It is a moot point whether the standardized form of the bricks, about 1 foot square and 3 inches thick (30 centimeters square and 8 centimeters thick), or the traditional ground plan of the dwelling house exercised the greatest influence upon the town plan. In any case, from the earliest to the latest cities, the houses were always organized in compact urban blocks linked by a more or less rectangular network of alleyways. All rooms were invariably turned inward, opening off an interior court (see illustration):[3]

[1]C. W. Ceram, *Gods, Graves, and Scholars* (translated by E. B. Garside), London, 1952, p. 311.
[2]N. K. Sanders, *The Epic of Gilgamesh*, Penguin Books, Inc., Baltimore, 1960, p. 16.
[3]Sir Leonard Woolley, *Ur of the Chaldees*, Penguin Books, Inc., Baltimore, 1950, p. 127.

Through the front door of a house one passed into a tiny lobby with a drain in its floor where the visitor might wash his hands or feet, and from that into the central court. On one side rose the brick stairs leading to the upper floor, and behind the stairs was a lavatory with its terracotta drain; then came the kitchen ... a reception room ... another room might be for the servants, and yet another the domestic chapel.

Beneath the floor of this household shrine was a vaulted chamber that served as a tomb for the family members. This description by Sir Leonard Woolley of houses in the city of Ur around 2000 B.C. typifies houses found at all the other city sites over the whole period of 2,500 years. In Eshnunna, all the washrooms and latrines were ranged along the outside wall, so that

Plan and section of a typical house at Ur (circa 2000 B.C.). (Sir Leonard Woolley, Excavations at Ur, London, 1954, fig. 13.)

CROSS SECTION.

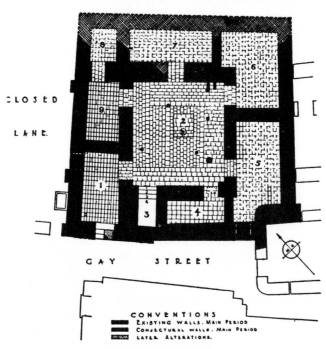

CLOSED

LANE.

GAY STREET

CONVENTIONS
EXISTING WALLS. MAIN PERIOD
CONJECTURAL WALLS. MAIN PERIOD
LATER ALTERATIONS.

they drained directly into a vaulted sewer that ran below the street. Though these streets almost always joined one another at right angles, they did not form a continuous gridiron—a fairly clear indication that there was no overall plan for the city (see illustration). The streets were narrow—only wide enough to allow for passage of a man and a donkey—and, as in their counterparts on the Greek islands today, street corners were rounded so as to facilitate turning of the laden beast.

The same type of urban plan—a rectilinear network between blank walls—and the same type of patio house—with sleeping rooms upstairs or on the roof and service rooms on the ground floor—were common to all the early civilizations, stretching from the Mediterranean across the whole of Asia. A highly systematized version was extended westward much later

Part of the residential area of Ur (circa 2000 B.C.). (Sir Leonard Woolley, Excavation at Ur, London, 1954, fig. 12.)

Reconstruction of the Ziggurat of Ur.
(Hartmut Schmökel, Ur, Assur and
Babylon, Stuttgart, 1955, Plate 57.)

by the Greek colonial settlements. The Greeks attributed this to Hippodamus, since he had elaborated the traditional system into an organized city
plan when faced with the task of reconstructing the city of Miletus in Asia
Minor around 450 B.C.

Each of the many cities from north to south of the land of the two
rivers centered upon a tall, brick-built ziggurat, or hill of heaven (see
illustration). This was a great stepped tower, its wide terraces then thickly
planted with trees. Its summit was the abode of the god of that city, and
from it the ziggurats of other cities could be seen. Even today, one can
still see the ruined ziggurats of Eridu and Al Ubaid from the ziggurat of
Ur, and their height is still immensely impressive in the flat, treeless land-

scape. The ziggurat at Ur was the height of a seven-story building, and the Tower of Babel at Babylon is said to have reached 288 feet.

At the foot of each ziggurat was an extensive rectangular temenos, or temple precinct, containing numerous offices, workshops, and storage chambers in addition to several temples, the palace of the divine king, and the residences of the priestly administrators. This temple precinct was the seat of government. It operated as the taxation center and the court of law as well as the center of trade of each city-state. The buildings in the temenos were on a grander scale than elsewhere, and they were frequently brightly colored.

Around the temenos the population of the city lived in one- and two-story patio houses varying in size and quality but very similar in plan, and the whole area of the city was surrounded by an extremely substantial and well-guarded wall (Babylon was encircled by double walls nearly 40 feet, or 12 meters, apart, each of them over 20 feet, or 6 meters, thick).

Babylon was reputedly the largest of all the cities of Mesopotamia and, at its zenith, around 600 B.C., it seems to have reached a population of a million. The city of Ur may have had a quarter of a million living at a density of about 250 to the acre (617 per hectare) according to its excavator, and Uruk is known to have been larger than Ur. Other large cities included Nineveh in the north and Nippur, Lagash, and Akkad (the still undiscovered capital of Sargon I). In addition there were numerous small provincial cities, such as Eshnunna and Khafaje, whose population Frankfort estimates at 9,000 and 12,000 respectively. The whole area was subject to constant invasion by people from the surrounding mountains, and there was frequent warfare between the cities themselves. From time to time a great conqueror would claim dominion over the whole territory, and the 2,500 years from about 3000 B.C. to the fall of Babylon in 538 B.C. included four main periods—the Sumerian, the Akkadian, the Assyrian, and the Babylonian. But, despite these turmoils, the physical organization of urban life seems to have been remarkably constant.

BIBLIOGRAPHY: H. Frankfort, "Town Planning in Ancient Mesopotamia," *Town Planning Review,* vol. 21, no. 2, July 1950, *The Birth of Civilization in the Near East,* London, 1951; V. Gordon Childe, *New Light on the Most Ancient East,* London, 1952; Sir Leonard Woolley, *Ur of the Chaldees,* Penguin Books, Inc., Baltimore, 1952, *Excavations at Ur,* London, 1954; Seton Lloyd, *Foundations in the Dust,* London, 1955; S. Giedion, "The Beginnings of Architecture," in *The Eternal Present,* vol. 2, New York, 1957; S. N. Kramer, *History Begins at Sumer,* New York, 1959.

—JAQUELINE TYRWHITT

Greece The planning of ancient Greek cities can be more fully appreciated if the notions of planning and of ancient Greek cities are clarified.

Planning may begin as a subconscious process and develop gradually into the conscious planning of a house or of any other small unit, until it becomes the conscious planning of a whole settlement. We are dealing here with the whole process of planning, from the stages of conscious concern about one unit to conscious concern about the whole settlement.

It is more difficult to define the notion of ancient Greek cities: when they were first built and how big they were. Although the city-polis was probably consciously created in the archaic era of Greek civilization (from at least as early as the seventh century B.C.), much earlier settlements could also be classified as the beginnings of urban settlements. Thermi, Poliochni, Lerna, Korakou (dating from the middle of the third millennium B.C.), or even Sesklo (fourth millennium B.C.), according to some theories, might have been early urban settlements. This suggestion may not agree with several assumptions as to what an urban settlement is. If, however, we consider that an urban settlement is a permanent settlement of people of whom a reasonable percentage are dedicated not only to agriculture and food gathering but also to other functions such as administration, handicrafts, trade, and commerce, then, on the basis of evidence given by their physical structures, the beginning of urban settlements goes back to much earlier periods.[1]

In another sense it is difficult to say exactly which types of settlements can be classified as urban. The Minoan palaces, for example, with various types of buildings and structures around them, cannot be definitely classified as rural settlements. From the social point of view, they represent theocratic centers or feudal centers with their people under autocratic administrations—not urban settlements created by the free will of the people. The question is whether we can distinguish the settlements which are purely rural, inhabited only by farmers and food gatherers, from those which begin to have functions not directly related to farming and food gathering. The Minoan palaces belong definitely to the second category.

The history of human settlements in ancient Greece is long and still not completely clarified. It lasted several thousands of years and is therefore difficult to reconstruct in the context of city planning. We do not yet know enough to be able to give a full picture of how the settlements were created and how they developed. Although we probably know more about ancient Greek settlements than about those of other ancient civilizations, we are not yet in a position to give the full picture as no systematic work has been done on the study of the overall evolution of settlements in ancient Greece.

The main reason for this is that the parts of the settlements which survive are usually their great monuments—either palaces or temples—because these were the parts of the settlements which were built with much greater care and with much better materials. These monuments were also quite often built in higher places than the other buildings, and they have therefore been covered by much less debris than the lower parts.

The second reason for the difficulty of tracing this history is that archaeology has concentrated on the monuments because they are the most conspicuous and important parts of the settlements. Although we know much about specific parts, especially about the temples and agoras, we are not yet entitled to speak with certainty about the whole settlements.

[1]C. A. Doxiadis, *Ekistics: An Introduction to the Science of Human Settlements,* Hutchinson, London, and Oxford Univeristy Press, New York, 1968.

In spite of this, enough is known to enable us to form some picture, which in some aspects is still only partial, of the whole evolution in this field. The studies now being carried out, however, have a much greater concern for the understanding of the whole settlement, and it is hoped that it will soon become possible to give a more complete picture.

Minoan Period   For the Minoan period we are obliged to study the important and monumental parts of urban settlements since these are best known. They are the famous palaces of Crete (at Knossos, Phaistos, Malia, and Zakro) and their immediate surroundings, and the settlement of Gournia, which is a Minoan provincial town of the sixteenth to fifteenth centuries B.C. The plan of the palace of Knossos (see illustration) brings to mind the ancient tradition of the labyrinth. If we look at this plan carefully, if we visit the palace and its vicinity, we will understand why any person used to simple settlements consisting of houses not connected to each other (which is how settlements always begin) could be confused by the very complex system of courtyards, inner spaces, and corridors of the Minoan palace. For the outsider—probably for the Greeks of the north who at that time were living in simple types of settlements—the image of the palace was an image of confusion; yet for anyone who lived in it and who understood it, this must have seemed a very important achievement in planning and architecture. We do not know of any other complexes of buildings in Greece, even in later periods, which could offer their inhabitants so much space of such variety as this palace: in some parts it was completely open to air and sun, in others completely enclosed. Spaces ranged from big to small, hot to cool, and light to dark. If we connect this with the climate of Crete, which varies between extremes of heat in summer and cold in winter, we will understand that the palace of Knossos, together with other palaces, exemplifies the very great ability of the Minoans to plan organized urban settlements.

Mycenaean Period   Our knowledge of urban settlements of this period is based mostly on the excavation of important fortresses and palaces, or palaces with small settlements around them. Our lack of exact knowledge leads to uncertainty as to whether the settlements around the palaces were always small. We may well find through further excavations greater extensions than had previously been suspected.

The settlement of Mycenae itself, which is a fortress with one palace, and the settlement of Nestor in Pylos, which is mostly a palace with probably several more buildings around it can be considered as typical examples of major settlements during the Mycenaean period (see illustration). The initial nucleus of Mycenae was the acropolis with its palace. Mycenae itself was not limited within its fortress, but outside the acropolis different neighborhoods were built, and with the passage of time those nearest to the acropolis were joined together. The groups of tombs give an indication both of the number of communities and of the external boundaries of the area. There are reasons to believe that other Mycenaean settlements were of a similar nature. Although many of the people living around the fortress of the palace must have been rural types, we cannot

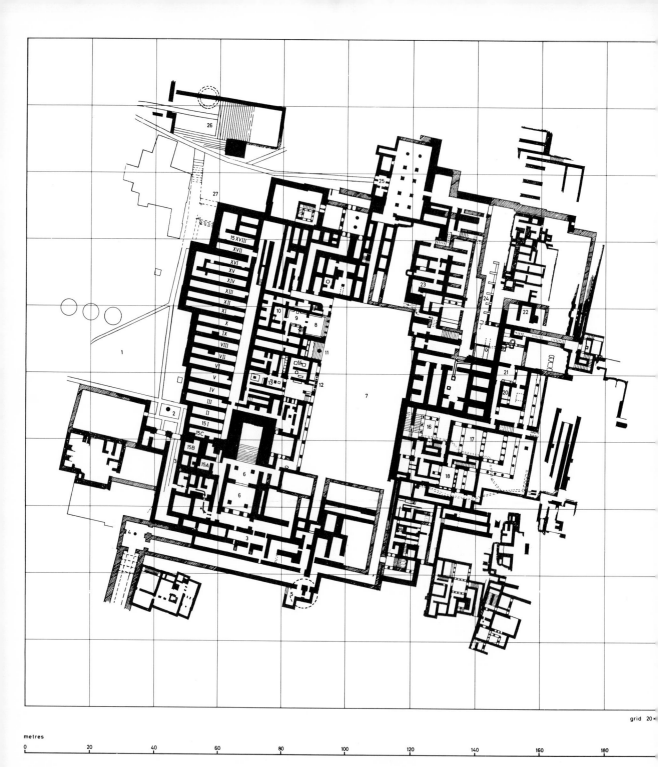

grid 20 m

metres

| 0 | 20 | 40 | 60 | 80 | 100 | 120 | 140 | 160 | 180 |

1. WEST COURT WITH WALLED PITS " KOULOURES ,
2. WEST PORCH
3. CORRIDOR OF THE PROCESSION
4. CONJECTURAL SOUTH-WEST PORCH
5. SOUTH PORCH
6. SOUTH PROPYLAEUM
7. CENTRAL COURT
8. ANTE ROOM
9. ROOM OF THE THRONE

10. INNER SHRINE
11. STAIRS UP
12. TRIPARTITE SHRINE
13. PILLAR CRYPTS
14. TEMPLE REPOSITORIES
15. A,B,C,I - XVIII WEST MAGAZINES
16. GRAND STAIRCASE
17. HALL OF THE DOUBLE AXES AND KING'S MEGARON
18. QUEEN'S MEGARON AND BATH

19. SHRINE OF THE DOUBLE AXES
20. LAPIDARY'S WORKSHOP
21. SCHOOL ROOM
22. MAGAZINES OF GREAT PITHOI
23. NORTH-EAST MAGAZINES
24. WORKSHOPS (?)
25. PROPYLON
26. STEPPED THEATRAL AREA
27. NORTH-WEST PORCH

� EXISTING PARTS
▨ PARTS WHICH PROBABLY EXISTED

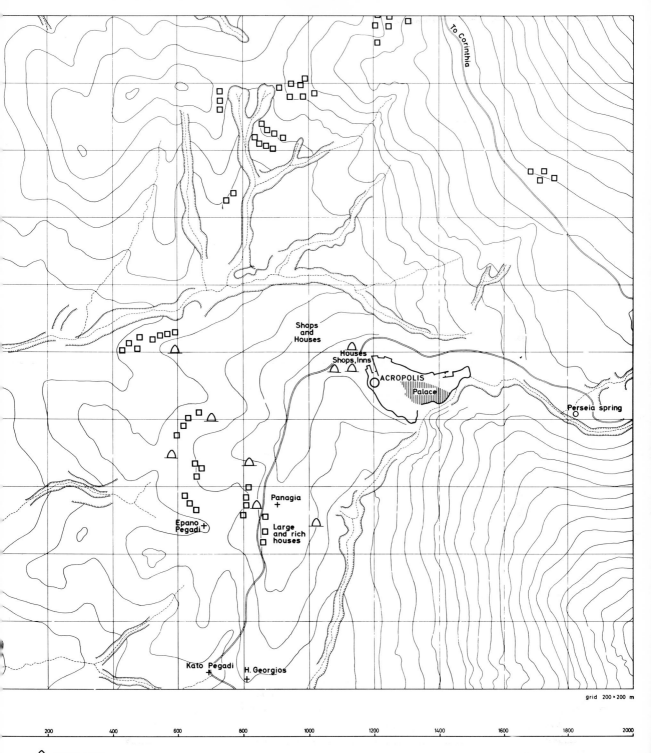

To Corinthia

Shops
and
Houses

Houses
Shops, Inns

○ ACROPOLIS
Palace

Perseia spring ○

Panagia
+

Epano +
Pegadi

Large
and rich
houses

Kato Pegadi
+   H. Georgios
              +

grid 200 × 200 m

| 200 | 400 | 600 | 800 | 1000 | 1200 | 1400 | 1600 | 1800 | 2000 |

△ VAULTED TOMBS
□ CHAMBER TOMBS
○ GRAVE CIRCLE A
+ MODERN SITES
═ ANCIENT ROADS

OPPOSITE: *Plan of the Palace of Knossos* (lower floor),
Crete (*seventeenth to fifteenth centuries* B.C.).
ABOVE: *Site plan of Mycenae* (*thirteenth century* B.C.).

exclude the possibility that many of them may also have been urban residents dealing in trade and handicrafts.

In this discussion, the term "ancient Greek cities" is used to designate cities of the archaic, classical, and Hellenistic periods. The Greeks, after the complete destruction of the Minoan civilization and probably the complete destruction of that of Mycenae, started to rebuild their systems of settlements. The physical synthesis of the city at the beginning of this period does not reflect the great skill demonstrated in the Minoan and Mycenaean palaces. It may be reasonable to assume, in explanation, that this resulted from the fact that a synthesis is much easier when there is only one authority (god or king) making decisions than when many city dwellers have an equal voice. This is the city that we all need, the city of free citizens, and this begins to take shape, slowly but systematically, after the Dorian invasion. This city is not the first urban settlement, but it is the beginning of the really human city. It is at this time that the Greeks, by uniting several settlements, started to form the city.

After studying the hundreds of examples of cities known from ancient documents and from the parts of the settlements which have been studied through archaeological excavations, we are in a position to conclude that most of the cities mentioned in history were small settlements, some of which may have had less than 1,000 inhabitants. These were probably the central places of the systems of minor rural settlements surrounding them. Several of these very small settlements have been excavated and can be seen and studied.

Some, however, had larger populations and played greater roles. We can discuss them without yet being able to calculate their exact sizes. They were fewer than the small examples, but there were certainly many of them which could have reached a population of up to 10,000 people.

Finally, there were some settlements in the classical era (479–323 B.C.) which were much larger, close to 50,000 in population, such as the city of Athens, the city of Corinth, some cities in Sicily, and some in Asia Minor. Examples like Syracuse in Sicily, under the tyrant Gelon in the fifth century B.C., should not mislead us. They had larger populations only because this was imposed on the people. It is very doubtful if any city ever exceeded them. It must be emphasized that this figure refers to the actual city, the built-up area, and not the city-state, which could comprise many more people, perhaps as many as 300,000. This is the figure probably reached by the population of the city-state of Athens. All these cities could be inscribed in a 2,000-yard (1,800-meter) square[2] and can be described as consisting of houses of relatively low quality and religious and civic monuments of much higher quality. All these cities have most of their best buildings, especially the monumental buildings, on their acropolises, and a few of the buildings, in particular the agora (marketplace), in the central place of the lower settlement.[3]

[2]C. A. Doxiadis, "Man's Movement and his City," *Science,* October 18, 1968.
[3]C. A. Doxiadis, "The Ancient Greek City and the City of the Present," *The Living Heritage of Greek Antiquity,* Mouton, Paris, 1967. See also *Ekistics,* November 1964.

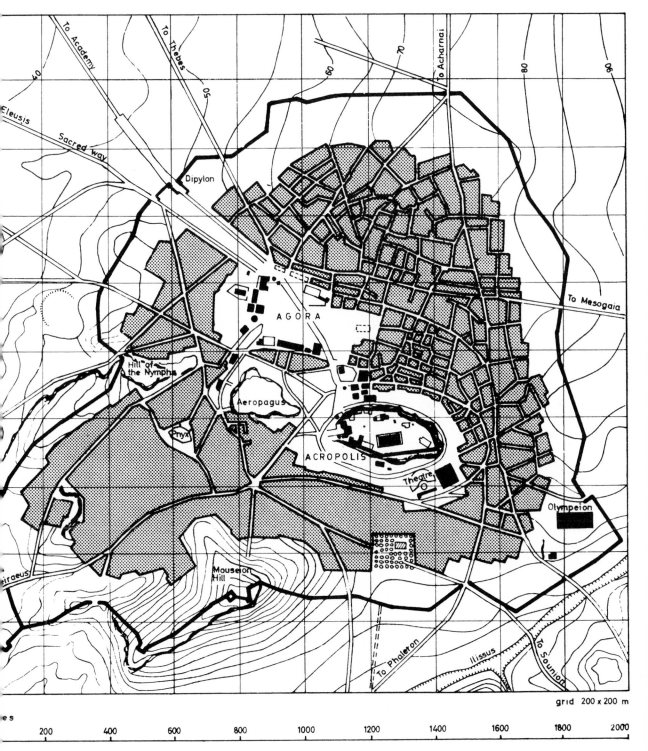

To Academy

To Thebes

To Acharnai

40

50

60

70

80

90

Eleusis

Sacred way

Dipylon

To Mesogaia

AGORA

Hill of
the Nympha

Aeropagus

Pnyx

ACROPOLIS

Theatre

Olympeion

Peiraeus

Mouseion
Hill

To Phaleron

Ilissus

To Sounion

grid   200 x 200 m

200   400   600   800   1000   1200   1400   1600   1800   2000

es

*Plan of center of Athens. The Agora
and Acropolis (fifth century* B.C.*).*

These cities can be classified, in terms of planning, into two chief categories: (1) naturally growing cities, and (2) consciously planned ones. According to Aristotle there were cities which were created in the old way (ὡς εἶχον κατά τόν ἀρχαῖον χρόνον) and the new or Hippodamian way (κατά τόν νεώτερον καί τόν Ἱπποδάμειον τρόπον).[4]

We do not have exact and complete plans of cities created in the old way, because to make such a plan it would be necessary to excavate the whole area of the ancient city and to define the date of every building. Perhaps the closest we can come to a plan of such a city is that of Athens (see illustration). It is clear that the built-up area of the city itself was not the only part of the settlement, as was very often thought, because many important functions, such as that of the Academy of Plato, were outside the built-up area. From a view of the actual city of Athens within the walls, it can be understood how the agora (the marketplace) was the nodal point of the whole city—the one fully developed area—and how the Acropolis was the monumental and religious center.

We know much more about the cities which were, according to Aristotle, designed along the lines of the method (τρόπος) conceived by Hippodamus, who was born in Miletus. He invented the division of cities into blocks and designed Piraeus. "Ὅστις τήν τῶν πόλεων διαίρεσιν εὗρε καί τόν Πειραιᾶ κατέτεμε."[5] Designs of cities were influenced by his ideas and examples, and this is why Hippodamus can be considered the father of ancient Greek city planning. Typical examples are the small city of Priene, the much larger city of Miletus in Asia Minor, the city of Rhodes in the Aegean, and the city of Cassope on the mainland (see illustrations).

The synthesis and the planning of important parts of the cities, like agoras and religious centers, have been misunderstood, and some people have spoken in terms of almost coincidental decisions about the location of the main buildings and their synthesis in space.

The location of the Parthenon on the Acropolis, and its relationship to the Erechtheum and the Propylaea, is not coincidental, as is sometimes thought. A systematic study of such monumental places has proved that their siting was very carefully studied and not at all related to the conception of gridiron planning as expressed by Hippodamus. It was thoughtfully conceived planning which could be understood only by walking into these places. The view of the complex of buildings from the Propylaea is so calculated that the angle from which every building could be seen corresponded to a sector of 30 or 36 degrees, the angle within which objects can be seen to the best advantage. The distances of the main buildings or monuments from the observer were either equal, so that he could see the main buildings at the same distance from him, or related to each other in ratios of 1:2:3, which meant that the observer could conceive them as a system of buildings in certain apparently related distances from himself.

[4] Aristotle, *Politics*, 7. 1330b. 26, 24.
[5] Aristotle, *Politics*, 2. 1267b. 22–24.

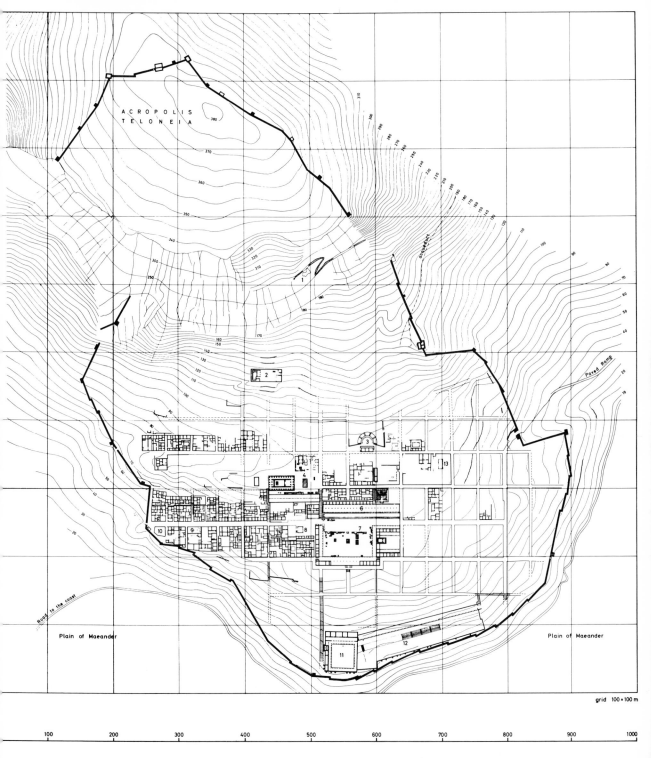

ACROPOLIS
TELONEIA

380
370
360
350
340
300
250
330
320
310
170
160
150
140
130
120
110
100
90
80
70
60
50
40
30
20

Aqueduct

310
300
290
280
270
260
250
240
230
220
210
200
190
180
170
160
150
140
130
120
110
100
90
80
70
60
50
40
30
20
10

Paved Ramp

1

2

3

4

6

7

8

9

10

11

12

13

Road to the coast

Plain of Maeander

Plain of Maeander

grid 100 × 100 m

100   200   300   400   500   600   700   800   900   1000

1. SANCTUARY
2. SANCTUARY OF DEMETER
3. THEATRE
4. SANCTUARY OF ATHENA
5. EKKLESIASTERION
6. SACRED STOA

7. AGORA
8. MARKET
9. SACRED HOUSE
10. SANCTUARY OF KYBELE
11. LOWER GYMNASIUM
12. STADIUM

13. SANCTUARY OF EGYPTIAN GODS

Plan of hill city of Priene (Asia Minor) (fourth to first centuries B.C.).

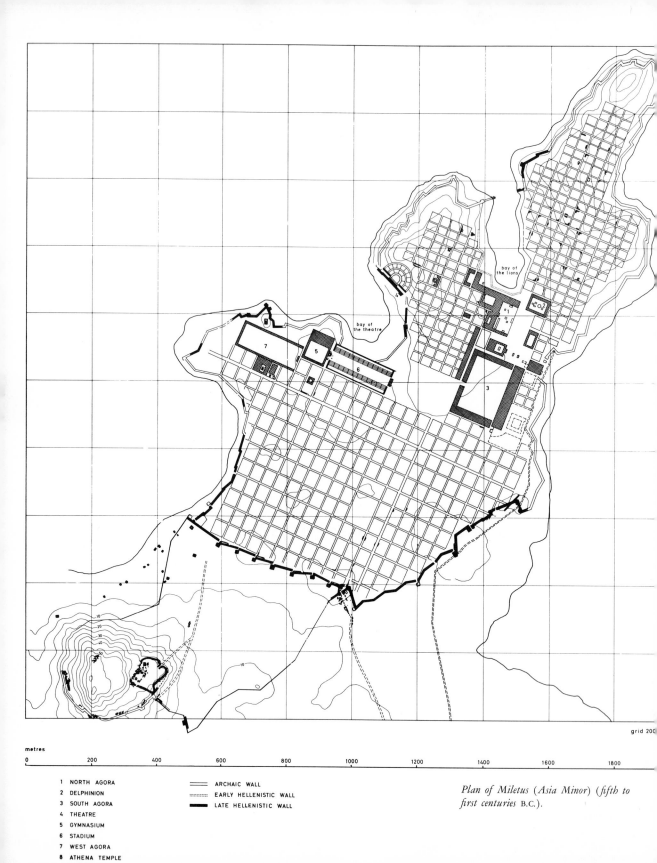

bay of
the lions

bay of
the theatre

7

5

6

3

8

1

2

4

grid 200

metres

| 0 | 200 | 400 | 600 | 800 | 1000 | 1200 | 1400 | 1600 | 1800 |

1 NORTH AGORA
2 DELPHINION
3 SOUTH AGORA
4 THEATRE
5 GYMNASIUM
6 STADIUM
7 WEST AGORA
8 ATHENA TEMPLE

ARCHAIC WALL
EARLY HELLENISTIC WALL
LATE HELLENISTIC WALL

*Plan of Miletus (Asia Minor) (fifth to
first centuries* B.C.).

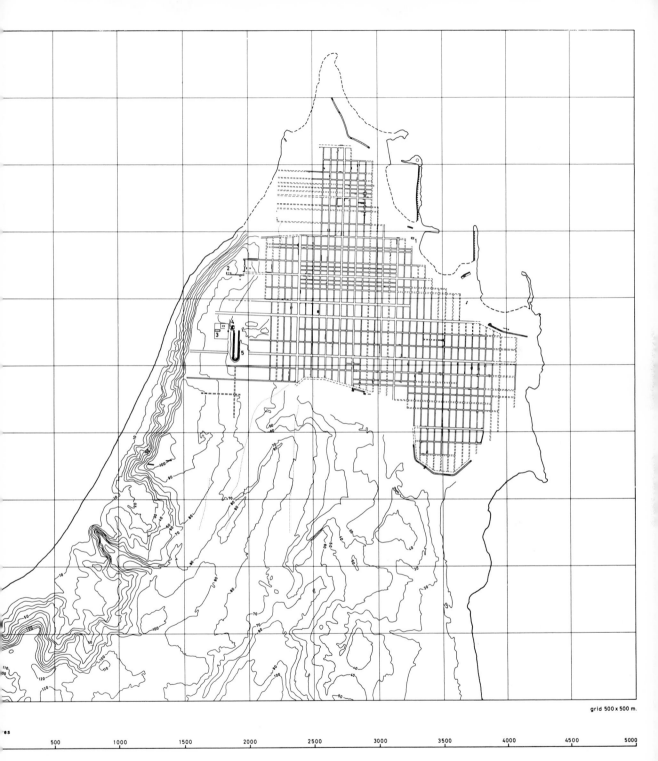

grid 500 x 500 m.

500	1000	1500	2000	2500	3000	3500	4000	4500	5000

EXCAVATED OUTER WALLS
PRESUMED OUTER WALLS
EXCAVATED ROADS
PRESUMED ROADS
EXCAVATED FOUNDATIONS OF HOUSES
PRESUMED FOUNDATIONS OF HOUSES
PATHS
HARBOUR (WHARF)

1 TEMPLE OF APHRODITE
2 TEMPLE OF ATHENA AND ZEUS POLIEUS
3 TEMPLE OF PYTHIAN APOLLO
4 THEATRE
5 STADIUM

Plan of Rhodes (fourth century B.C.).

grid 100 *

metres

0   100   200   300   400   500   600   700   800   900

1. INNER ACROPOLIS WITH CISTERNS
2. TOWER
3. CISTERN AND RETAINING WALL
4. INNER ACROPOLIS WITH CISTERNS
5. THEATRE
6. NORTH ROAD
7. WEST GATEWAY OF THE MAIN WALL-CIRCUIT
8. MAIN SOUTH ROAD

9. PRYTANEUM OR KATAGOGION (TOWN HALL)
10. EAST GATEWAY OF THE MAIN WALL-CIRCUIT
11. AGORA
12. NORTH DORIC STOA
13. SMALL THEATRE (CONCERT HALL ?) OR COUNCIL
14. WEST STOA
15. UNDERGROUND ARCHED TOMB (HEROON ?)

ABOVE: *Plan of Cassope (fourth to second centuries* B.C.).
ABOVE, RIGHT: *Plan of Acropolis, Athens (fifth century* B.C.
RIGHT: *Athens (fifth century* B.C.). *Perspective view
of a reconstruction of the Acropolis.*

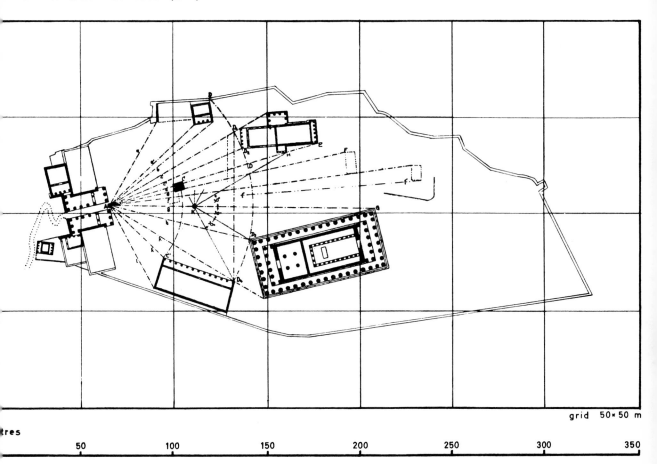

grid 50×50 m

tres

| 50 | 100 | 150 | 200 | 250 | 300 | 350 |

The example of the plan of the Acropolis of Athens and the resulting view of it show how planning in the monumental parts of the cities took place.[6]

The planning ideal for an ancient Greek city was a synthesis of organic planning developed to its best expression by its artists to transmit the image of natural relationships between buildings (although these organic relationships were very well planned in advance in the small units) and rational geometric gridiron planning for the organization of the main body of the city.

In the Hellenistic era (323–31 B.C.), cities followed the same patterns as before but with the difference that some (like Alexandria in Egypt), when they became the capitals of great kingdoms, exceeded the size and population typical of earlier times.

—CONSTANTINOS A. DOXIADIS

Roman Empire   If one has to describe urban planning in the Roman Empire, it would seem more appropriate to talk of territorial planning which, associated with the imperialistic conquest of the Mediterranean, represents its most original aspect. In fact, if the Romans can be said to be in the debt of the Greek and Etruscan civilizations with regard to the layout of cities, urban planning, and technical infrastructures, they were, on the other hand, the first to organize a state where cities and countryside could be regarded as two facets of one and the same culture. This had not come to them from either the Greeks or the Etruscans, although these had made major efforts to remodel their territories; had known the practice of integration between cities, districts, and populations with different economic standing; and had created the political and religious centers common to many cities.

Rome, born as a commercial center at the only point where the lower reaches of the Tiber could be forded, soon became a rich city, ruled by an oligarchy based on wealth, and the capital of a state of Latin towns linked by means of treaties of alliance (*foedera*). These federated towns were thus incorporated in a much larger economic system. They enjoyed Rome's political and military protection, but they were also obliged to come to Rome's defense when necessary.

Up to the beginning of the republican period in the sixth century B.C., the rising power of Rome was attacked by neighboring populations and the social organization of Rome and her allies was conditioned by a continuous state of war. After the siege of Veii (*Veio*), which is said to have lasted 10 years, there arose the social class of the military, with the citizens providing a permanent defense service. Although historians are reluctant to regard early Rome as a deliberately imperialist power, imperialism was, in fact, encouraged by the demands of the populace and by Rome's desire

[6]C. A. Doxiadis, *Raumordnung im Griechischen Städtebau,* Vowinckel, Berlin, 1937, English translation, M.I.T. Press, Cambridge, Mass.

to safeguard her conquests through the continuous expansion of her own dominions.

During the republican period, from the sixth to the first century B.C., the Romans did not exercise any direct control over their empire; and the cities, tied to the foreign policy of the Senate through pacts, preserved their autonomy. Rather than through direct rule, Rome tried to attach to herself populations with cultures not dissimilar to her own by spreading her own pattern of urban life and by conceding, without preconceived xenophobia, Roman citizenship to those cities whose civilization had been raised to her own level, i.e., "romanized."

In this way, Rome transformed the older concept of the city as a center where all the interests were focused into one of an autonomous administrative structure which created an urban *bourgeoisie* capable of imparting homogeneity to an empire composed of populations which differed greatly from each other.

Rome therefore endeavored to make all the colonies, whether newly founded or remodeled, similar to each other, and she gave them technical amenities and infrastructures previously confined to royal palaces or capital cities. These included efficient drainage; water supply even to the upper stories of the houses by means of long aqueducts; paved streets and squares; markets; public baths, gymnasia, and wrestling schools; *curiae* for the Senate; courthouses, basilicas, prisons, theaters, circuses, art galleries, auditoriums, libraries and, above all, houses instead of huts.

The settlers were generally Roman plebeians or soldiers who, as a reward for services rendered, were given some agricultural land. Loyal to Rome, they managed with their allotments to become well-to-do and even rich; and, being Roman citizens, they were able to assent to the local government.

Also resident in these cities were local persons of rank who adopted the pattern of Roman life. The forum, being the administrative, commercial, and religious center of the colony, was a lively place of economic, cultural, and artistic exchanges, and the contacts made here helped to spread the Roman language, law, and cultural heritage throughout the countries. Temples of the Roman religion were rapidly built in prominent positions and the local rites were gradually superseded by those that were imported, while theaters and amphitheaters disseminated new types of entertainment and the new literature.

Hence the importance of the numerous cities founded by the Romans and the villages transformed by them into cities; hence the drastic reshaping of their territory—a reshaping which reflected the new juridical and social conditions—and hence the need for new agrarian cultures.

Umbria was one of the first Italian regions to be remodeled by the Romans. Being adjacent to Latium, it came within the Roman orbit in 310 B.C. with the *aequissimum foedus* between the Latin city and the Etruscan cities of *Perusia* (Perugia), *Curtun* (Cortona), and *Arretium* (Arezzo).

The remodeling was based mainly on the allotment of agricultural lands, on the rationalization and integration of the preexisting Etruscan road

1. *Castrum Maiensis; Statio Maiensis* (Merano)
2. (Polpet; Ponte delle Alpi)
3. *Bellunum* (Belluno)
*4. *Tridentum* (Trento)
5. *Forum Julii* (Cividale del Friuli)
6. *Feltria* (Feltre)
*7. (Riva del Garda)
8. (Galliano)
*9. *Augusta Praetoria Salassorum* (Aosta)
*10. *Novum Comum; Comum* (Como)
11. *Acelum; Asylum* (Asolo)
*12. *Julia Concordia Sagittaria* (Portogruaro)
13. *Bergomum* (Bergamo)
14. *Opitergium* (Oderzo)
*15. *Aquileia* (Aquileia)
16. *Modicia* (Monza)
*17. *ad Aquas Gradatas* (Grado)
18. *Tergeste* (Trieste)
19. *Tarvisium* (Treviso)
20. *Eporedia* (Ivrea)
21. *Brixia* (Brescia)
22. *Novaria* (Novara)
*23. *Mediolanum* (Milan)
24. *Sirmio* (Sirmione)
25. *Vicentia* (Vicenza)
*26. *Altinum* (Altino)
*27. *Verona* (Verona)
28. (Thiene)
29. *Vercellae* (Vercelli)
*30. (Vigevano)
*31. *Patavium* (Padua)
*32. *Segusium* (Susa)
*33. *Industria* (Monteu da Po)
34. *Ticinum* (Pavia)
35. (Montagnana)
36. *Ateste* (Este)
37. *Augusta Taurinorum* (Turin)
*38. *Cremona* (Cremona)
39. (Chioggia)
40. *Carrium; Karreum Potentia* (Chieri)
*41. *Placentia* (Piacenza)
42. *Mantua* (Mantova)
*43. *Hostilia* (Ostiglia)
*44. *Clastidium* (Casteggio)
45. *Hadria* (Adria)
46. *Hasta* (Asti)
47. *Forum Fulvii* (Villa del Foro)
48. *Derthona* (Tortona)
49. *Fidentia* (Fidenza)
50. *Brixellum* (Briscello)
51. *Colonia Julia Pollentia* (Pula, Yugoslavia)
*52. *Pollentia* (Pollenzo)
53. *Alba Pompeia* (Alba)
*54. *Libarna* (Serravalle Scrivia)
55. *Aquae Statellae* (Acqui)
*56. *Parma* (Parma)
*57. *Veleia* (Velleia)
*58. *Forum Novum* (Fornovo)
*59. *Forum Lepidi; Regium Lepidi* (Reggio Emilia)
60. *Mutina* (Modena)

61. *Spina* (Comacchio)
*62. *Augusta Bagiennorum* (Benevagienna)
63. *Luceria* (S. Polo d'Enza)
*64. *Genua* (Genoa)
*65. *Bononia* (Bologna)
66. *Pedo* (Borgo S. Dalmazzo)
*67. *Ravenna* (Ravenna)
68. *Claterna*
69. *Vada Sabatia* (Vado)
*70. *Forum Cornelii* (Imola)
71. *Faventia* (Faenza)
72. *Forum Livii* (Forlí)
*73. *Forum Popilii* (Forlimpopoli)
*74. *Albium Ingaunum* (Albenga)
*75. *Luni* (Luna)
76. (Massa Marittima)
77. *Caesena* (Cesena)
78. *Ariminum* (Rimini)
79. *Albium Intemelium; Albintimilium* (Ventimiglia)
80. *Pistoriae* (Pistoia)
81. *Luca* (Lucca)
82. *Sarsina; Sassina* (Sarsina)
83. *Pisarum* (Pesaro)
84. *Faesulae* (Fiesole)
85. *Florentia* (Florence)
86. *Fanum Fortunae* (Fano)
*87. *Cemenellum* (Nice, France)
88. *Pisae* (Pisa)
89. *Urbinum Metaurense* (Urbino)
90. *Forum Sempronii* (Fossombrone)
91. *Sena Gallica* (Senigallia)
92. *Suassa Senonum* (Castelleone di Suassa)
93. *Ancona* (Ancona)
94. *Callium* (Cagli)
95. *Arretium* (Arezzo)
96. *Auximum* (Osimo)
97. *Saena* (Siena)
*98. *Tifernum; Tiberinum* (Città di Castello)
99. *Eugubium* (Gubbio)
*100. *Cortona* (Cortona)
101. *Septemdena* (San Severino Marche)
102. *Tolentinum* (Tolentino)
103. (Populonia)
*104. *Perusia* (Perugia)
105. *Sentino* (Camerino)
106. *Camerinum* (Camerino)
107. *Firmum Picenum* (Fermo)
108. *Castellum Firmanorum* (Fermo)
*109. *Asisium* (Assisi)
110. *Clusium* (Chiusi)
*111. *Urvium Hortense* (Collemancio)
*112. *Forum Flaminii* (Foligno)
*113. *Vettona* (Bettona)
*114. *Hispellum; Colonia Julia* (Spello)
*115. *Mevania* (Bevagna)
*116. *Fulginae* (Foligno)
117. *Vetulonia* (Vetulonia)
*118. *Trebiae* (Trevi)
119. (Island of Elba)

120. *Ascolum* (Ascoli Piceno)
*121. *Tuder* (Todi)
122. *Nursia* (Norcia)
*123. *Salpium* (Orvieto)
*124. *Spoletium* (Spoleto)
125. *Volsinii* (Bolsena)
126. *Interamnia Praetuttiorum* (Teramo)
127. *Carsulae* (Sangemini)
128. *Interamna Nahars* (Terni)
129. (Island of Giglio)
130. (Orbetello)
131. *Ferentium* (Ferento)
132. *Narnia* (Narni)
133. *Ansedonia* (Cosa)
134. *Tuscania; Tuscanella* (Tuscania)
135. *Vulci; Volci* (Montalto di Castro)
136. *Viterbium* (Viterbo)
137. *Ocriculum* (Otricoli)
138. *Reate* (Rieti)
139. *Amiternum* (L'Aquila)
140. *Aternum* (Pescara)
141. *Tarquinii* (Tarquinia)
142. *Falerii Veteres; Falerii Novi* (Civitacastellana)
143. *Taete Marrucinorum* (Chieti)
144. *Nepete* (Nepi)
145. *Auxanum* (Lanciano)
146. *Centumcellae* (Civitavecchia)
147. *Carsioli* (Carsoli)
148. *Alba Fucens* (Massa d'Albe)
149. *Corfinium* (Corfinio)
150. *Pyrgi* (Ceri)
151. *Sulmo* (Sulmona)
152. *Caere; Cerveteri* (Ceri)
*153. *Veio-Roma*
*154. *Tibur* (Tivoli)
155. *Marruvium* (San Benedetto dei Marsi)
156. *Sublaqueum* (Subiaco)
157. *Portus* (Ostia)
158. *Ostia* (Ostia)
159. *Tusculum* (Frascati)
*160. *Praeneste* (Palestrina)
*161. *Lavinium* (Pratica di Mare)
162. *Lanuvium* (Lanuvio)
163. *Anagnia* (Anagni)
164. *Aletrium* (Alatri)
165. (Pietrabbondante)
166. *Velitrae* (Velletri)
167. *Ferentum* (Ferento)
168. *Aufiderna* (Alfedena)
169. *Cora* (Cori)
*170. *Norba* (Norma)
171. *Aesernia* (Isernia)
*172. *Antium* (Anzio)
173. *Privergium* (Priverno)
174. *Casinum* (Cassino)
175. *Luceria* (Lucera)
176. *Saepinum* (Sepino)
177. *Fundi* (Fondi)
178. *Aecae* (Troia)
*179. *Tarracina* (Terracina)
180. *Allifae* (Alife)
181. *Herdonia* (Ordona)
*182. *Circei* (Circeo)
183. *Formia* (Formia)
184. *Minturnae* (Minturno)

*185. *Caieta* (Gaeta)
*186. *Suessa Aurunca* (Sessa Aurunca)
187. *Telesia* (Telese)
188. *Tarenum; Turenum* (Trani)
189. *Cluvia* (Buonalbergo)
190. *Forum Popilii* (Corinola)
191. *Canusium* (Canosa di Puglia)
192. *Beneventum* (Benevento)
*193. *Casilium* (Capua)
194. *Butuntum* (Bitonto)
195. *Barium* (Bari)
196. *Saticula* (Sant'Agata de' Goti)
197. *Rubi* (Ruvo di Puglia)
198. *Bonea* (Bonea)
199. *Cales Resurta* (Calvi)
*200. *Capua* (Santa Maria Capua Vetere)
201. *Caudium* (Montesarchio)
202. (Melfi)
*203. *Liternum* (Villa Literno)
204. *Venusia* (Venosa)
205. *Gnatia* (Egnazia)
206. *Nola* (Nola)
207. *Abellinum* (Avellino)
208. *Strapellum* (Rapolla)
*209. *Cumae* (Cuma)
*210. *Atella* (Atella)
*211. *Portus Julius* (Cuma)
*212. *Baiae* (Baia)
*213. *Puteoli* (Pozzuoli)
*214. *Neapolis* (Naples)
*215. *Herculaneum* (Ercolano)
216. *Aceruntia* (Acerenza)
*217. *Pompei* (Pompei)
*218. *Aenaria* (Island of Ischia)
219. *Nuceria Alfaterna* (Nocera Superiore)
220. *Irsum* (Irsina)
221. *Lupiae* (Lecce)
*222. *Stabiae* (Castellammare di Stabia)
223. *Salernum* (Salerno)
224. *Surrentum* (Sorrento)
225. *Potentia* (Potenza)
226. *Brundisium* (Brindisi)
*227. *Caprae* (Island of Capri)
228. *Bovianum Undecimanorum* (Matera)
229. *Tarentum* (Taranto)
230. *Paestum* (Capaccio)
231. (Manduria)
232. *Metapontum* (Metaponto)
233. *Grumentum* (Grumento Nova)
234. *Hydruntum* (Otranto)
235. *Sybaris* (Sibari)
236. *Braellum; Bragallum* (Altomonte)
237. *Roscianum* (Rossano)
238. *Cosentia Brutiorum* (Cosenza)
239. *Siberene* (Santa Severina)
240. *Crotona* (Crotone)
241. *Vibo Valentia* (Vibo Valentia)
242. *Caulonia* (Caulonia)

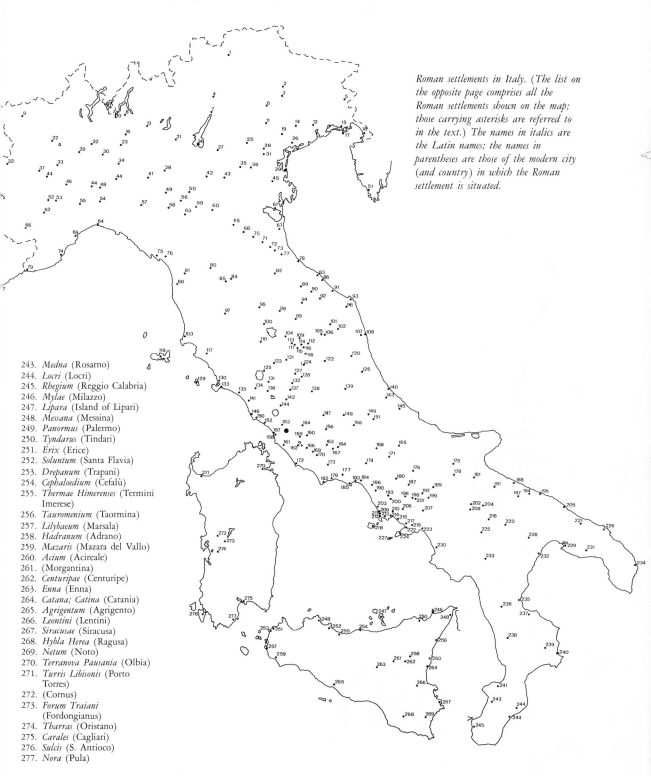

Roman settlements in Italy. (The list on the opposite page comprises all the Roman settlements shown on the map; those carrying asterisks are referred to in the text.) The names in italics are the Latin names; the names in parentheses are those of the modern city (and country) in which the Roman settlement is situated.

243. *Medna* (Rosarno)
244. *Locri* (Locri)
245. *Rhegium* (Reggio Calabria)
246. *Mylae* (Milazzo)
247. *Lipara* (Island of Lipari)
248. *Messana* (Messina)
249. *Panormus* (Palermo)
250. *Tyndarus* (Tindari)
251. *Erix* (Erice)
252. *Soluntum* (Santa Flavia)
253. *Drepanum* (Trapani)
254. *Cephaloedium* (Cefalù)
255. *Thermae Himerenses* (Termini Imerese)
256. *Tauromenium* (Taormina)
257. *Lilybaeum* (Marsala)
258. *Hadranum* (Adrano)
259. *Mazaris* (Mazara del Vallo)
260. *Acium* (Acireale)
261. (Morgantina)
262. *Centuripae* (Centuripe)
263. *Enna* (Enna)
264. *Catana; Catina* (Catania)
265. *Agrigentum* (Agrigento)
266. *Leontini* (Lentini)
267. *Siracusae* (Siracusa)
268. *Hybla Herea* (Ragusa)
269. *Netum* (Noto)
270. *Terranova Pausania* (Olbia)
271. *Turris Libisonis* (Porto Torres)
272. (Cornus)
273. *Forum Traiani* (Fordongianus)
274. *Tharras* (Oristano)
275. *Carales* (Cagliari)
276. *Sulcis* (S. Antioco)
277. *Nora* (Pula)

network, and on the development of the local government system which changed the traditional tribal bonds and caused the emergence of new social hierarchies where the tribal chiefs were superseded by the settlers, i.e., Roman citizens.

In the Clitunno Valley (the sixth of the Augustan regions), the imperial era brought the recognition as towns and colonies of *Perusia, Asisium* (Assisi), *Hispellum* (Spello), *Fulginium* (Foligno), *Forum Flaminii, Trebiae* (Trevi), *Vettona* (Bettona), *Urvium Hortense* (Collemancio), *Mevania* (Bevagna), *Spoletium* (Spoleto), and *Tuder* (Todi).

Some of these cities preserved the irregular Etruscan layout (*Perusia,*

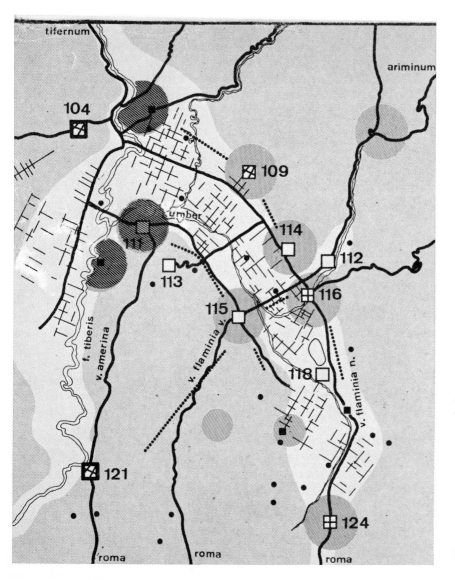

Roman territorial structure in the Clitunno Valley, and the preexisting Etruscan and Umbrian structures.

Roman main roads
Pre-Roman routes
Roman towns or colonies with regular layout
Roman towns or colonies with irregular layout
Roman towns or colonies with irregular layout which had already been Etruscan cities
Roman towns or colonies with unknown layouts
Roman villages
Minor rural centers in Roman times
Etruscan villages
Umbrian settlements
Umbrian villages
Systematically colonized fields

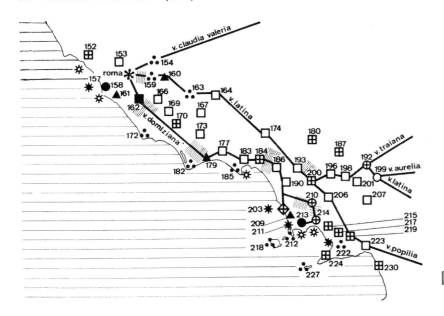

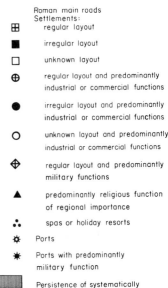

Roman main roads
Settlements:
    regular layout

    irregular layout

    unknown layout

    regular layout and predominantly
    industrial or commercial functions

    irregular layout and predominantly
    industrial or commercial functions

    unknown layout and predominantly
    industrial or commercial functions

    regular layout and predominantly
    military functions

    predominantly religious function
    of regional importance

    spas or holiday resorts

    Ports

    Ports with predominantly
    military function

    Persistence of systematically
    colonized fields

Roman territorial structure in the rural area of Latium.

Tuder, Asisium), others had a regular layout (*Fulginium* and perhaps *Spoletium*); all of them saw the construction of the forum, of temples, theaters, and public baths—buildings which physically represented Rome and its juridical, social, and religious order.

The principal colonizing activities in the Clitunno Valley took place in the first century B.C. when the road network was remodeled. The old Via Flaminia and Via Amerina [*Salpium* (Orvieto), *Tuder, Vettona*] were preserved and served as a basis for the systematic colonization of the Tiber Plain. But Roman interests spread along the *Spoletium-Perusia* axis. Here, despite the obstacles presented by *Lagus Umber* and the marshes near *Trebiae*, the land was more densely colonized and the road network enjoyed a remarkable development as a result of the new Via Flaminia. The stretch of the Tiber, made navigable as is proved by the small harbor of *Tifernum* (Città di Castello), completed the communications system.

Umbria, contained within the natural boundaries of the Apennines, was fairly similar to Latium, with preexisting Etruscan settlements and a fairly high level of urban culture. The process of romanization in Umbria was therefore more peaceful.

However, when the Romans stepped over the mountains and began the conquest of northern Italy and of Europe, they found themselves in a hostile environment, generally with a low urban culture. The first objective of romanization was the foundation of cities which were, at one and the same time, strongholds and cultural centers among *gentes* and *nationes*—cities with uncertain frontiers which could be regarded as potentially dangerous enemies.

The development of Roman imperialism was thus associated with the development of urban culture. The beginning of territorial expansion was sometimes preceded by the foundation of colonies such as *Genua* (Genoa), where the Roman city was superimposed on a Graeco-Ligurian settlement in 205 B.C.; *Luni* (Luma), founded in 177 B.C.; and *Cemenellum,* founded in 180 B.C. in the immediate vicinity of the Greek (Luna) *Nicaea* (Nice), which was accessible only by sea because of the hostility of the Ligurians.

During the second century B.C., these bridgeheads were linked with others, founded in the Po Plain, by means of roads, so that a minute network of settlements was formed. The colonies of *Cremona* and *Placentia* (Piacenza) were founded in 218 B.C. and *Mediolanum* (Milan), *Bononia* (Bologna), *Parma,* and *Forum Lepidi* (Reggio Emilia) in the first half of the second century B.C. Along the Via Emilia, constructed in 187 B.C., arose numerous colonies of similar size which gave rise to an intensive agricultural exploitation of the Po Plain, reclaimed and systematically colonized during the second century B.C.

Road construction, agricultural colonization, and land allotment were generally associated with the utilization of rivers and lakes, which became avenues of some of the commercial traffic. *Hostilia* (Ostiglia), on the river Po; *Patavium* (Padua), on the river Brenta; and *Novum Comum* (Como) had ports, while Riva del Garda was the seat of a guild of sailors. Among the ports were *Genoa, Luni, Altinum* (Altino), *Ravenna, Julia Concordia Sagittaria* (Portogruaro), *ad Aquas Gradatas* (Grado) and *Aquileia,* while military and industrial cities were situated on rivers. These cities included *Segusio* (Susa), *Augusta Praetoria Salassorum* (Aosta), *Verona, Tridentum* (Trento), *Augusta Bagiennorum* (Benevagienna), *Pollentia* (Pollenzo), *Industria, Julia Concordia Sagittaria,* and *Albium Ingaunum* (Albenga).

The roads gave rise to the accelerated development of road junctions, such as those at *Forum Novum* (Fornovo), *Libarna, Clastidium* (Casteggio), and Vigevano, and to the foundation of new cities along them—as happened, for instance, along the Via Emilia. They also gave rise to urban settlements around the forums—originally commercial centers and meeting places for rural markets in isolated positions, without housing, spread out along the roads. This was the origin of places like *Forum Cornelii* (Imola), with a regular layout, and *Forum Popilii* (Forlimpopoli), with an irregular layout. In the course of time, the process of colonization and road construction—with relay stations for the change of horses and, since Nero (54–68 A.D.), with hostelries for travelers—underwent such a development in the north that not even the most impenetrable regions were immune to romanization.

The cities, becoming standardized as the result of the experience of two centuries, had rectangular layouts, with streets intersecting at right angles, uniform street blocks, and areas ranging from 40 acres (16 hectares) at *Parma* to 121 acres (49 hectares) at *Bononia. Decumanus* and *cardo,* intersecting in the city center, were oriented toward the main points. Close to the intersection was the forum, with the buildings of the civic administration and the temple of the Capitoline Triad. At *Augusta Bagiennorum* and at *Veleia* (Velleia), the archeologists have found traces of a forum (perhaps imposed by Rome on colonized regions) which combined in a single

Roman territorial struc
in northern Italy.

(lago di costanza) (brennero)

(splugo) curia genava alpis graia illiria brigantium gallia roma roma roma roma

complex all the essential organs of public life: the temple of the Capitoline Triad, the civic premises (basilica, courthouse, curia), and the commercial buildings. Forums of the same type also exist at *Lungdunum Convernarum* (St. Bertrand-de-Comminges), *Augusta Raurica* (Augst), *Alesia,* and in about a dozen British cities.

In the course of two centuries, the romanization in northern Italy achieved the purpose of unifying the languages, cults, and cultures; and in 4 A.D., Augustus erected at *ad Tropheum* (la Turbie, Nice) a monument to commemorate the complete "pacification" of the alpine peoples. This pacification had not always taken place in a peaceful manner, and Strabo testifies that the Salassians were conquered, deported, and sold as slaves; as a result, *Augusta Praetoria Salassorum* was founded (in 25 B.C.). For the most part, however, Roman imperialism tended not to impose the Roman way of life by force; indigenous cults and primitive social orders were tolerated in the expectation that they would disappear as soon as the peasant populations had assimilated the pattern of urban life.

A remarkable episode of regional planning concerns the zone between *Roma, Neapolis* (Naples), and the Apennines. The region of Latium, rich in pre-Roman and Etruscan settlements, fertile lands, and marshes, was the

Roman main roads:
— third century B.C.
- - - second century B.C.
-·-·- first century B.C.
······· constructed at an unknown date
········ Waterways and regular sea routes

Settlements:
⊞ regular layout
■ irregular layout
□ unknown layout
⊕ regular layout and predominantly industrial or commercial functions
○ unknown layout and predominantly industrial or commercial functions
◈ regular layout and predominantly military functions
◆ irregular layout and predominantly military functions
✿ River or sea ports
▦ Persistence of systematically colonized fields

first to be overrun by republican conquest. *Norba* (Norma) in 409 B.C. and *Ostia* and *Tibur* (Tivoli) in the fourth century B.C. were the first to receive the regular layout which became the prototype of colonial practice. *Lavinium* (Practica di Mare) was, until the early centuries of Rome, a fairly important religious center for all the Latinii, together with *Tarracina* (Terracina), which came within the republican orbit during the fifth century B.C.

The rural zone in that district, densely populated, with important cities of Greek origin—*Neapolis, Cumae* (Cuma), and *Hercolaneum* (Herculaneum)—or of indigenous origin also soon came within the Roman orbit, and after the Peace of Capua (330 B.C.), the Roman state extended all the way to *Neapolis*.

Throughout the region, colonies of Latin citizens were founded and existing cities were remodeled in accordance with the new urban planning criteria taken over from the Greeks and tried out in the first Latin colonies. The great consular roads (Via Appia, Via Domiziana, Via Popilia) were constructed with grandiose engineering works (e.g., the great rock cutting at *Tarracina*) and the land was parceled out still showing traces of systematic colonization, as at *Antium* (Anzio), *Tarracina Suessa Aurunca* (Sessa Aurunca), *Capua* (S. Maria Capua Vetere), *Neapolis, Atella,* and *Casilium* (Capua). The ports—*Ostia, Caieta* (Gaeta), *Neapolis, Puteoli* (Pozzuoli)—were inserted into the system of Mediterranean communications and assumed an important commercial function, though some of them had a predominantly military function, as did *Ostia, Portus Julius* on Lake Avernus, and *Liternum*.

However, because of the proximity of Rome, the tempting beauty of the places, and the presence of thermal springs, this district became almost exclusively the preserve of capitalists resident in Rome or its environs who here built their suburban villas. Beautiful villas of this kind were erected at *Tibur, Tusculum* (Frascati), *Antium,* and *Circei* (Circeo) as well as, in very great numbers, in the vicinity of *Neapolis* and on the islands of *Caprae* (Capri) and *Aenaria* (Ischia). The thermal spas of *Caieta, Puteoli, Stabiae* (Stabia), and *Baiae* (Baia) were famous throughout the Roman world, and at *Praeneste* (Palestrina) there arose a religious complex rich in unusual and scenic spatial solutions of Hellenistic origin. Even the cities assumed, in the course of time, the appearance of country resorts, cheerful and carefree—but finally petrified by the terrible eruption of Vesuvius at *Pompei* and *Herculaneum* (79 A.D.).

From *Atella* spread the fame of the local theater and from *Cumae* that of the oracle of the Cumaean Sibyl. The *villae rusticae,* capitalistic factories with numerous slaves employed in the vineyards, olive groves, fields, and pastures, were built in great numbers, and Petronius was able to tell his guests at Trimalcione that his estates reached from the borders of Terracina to those of Tarento (*Satyricon,* 48) because, in those regions, the fortunes amounted to millions of sesterzi. But this caused the impoverishment of the old settlers, who were forced to become the founders of cities in northern Italy and in the rest of the Empire.

Partly controlled and partly uncontrolled, this episode shows the high

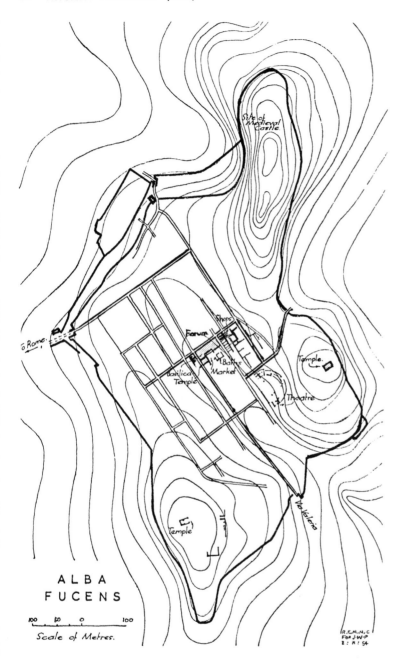

ALBA
FUCENS

100 50 0   100

Scale of Metres.

Alba Fucens, example of a regular city, founded in the fourth century, B.C., *along the Via Valeria. (Ward Perkins, T. B., Early Roman Towns in Italy, The Town Planning Review, No. 3, vol. 26, p. 142.)*

degree of integration between the city and the countryside reached by Roman urban culture. Superimposed on the planning activities of the republican era, which had developed one of the richest agricultural regions in Italy, was a dense network of amenities and equipment for the entertainment of the elite which completely changed the appearance of the region.

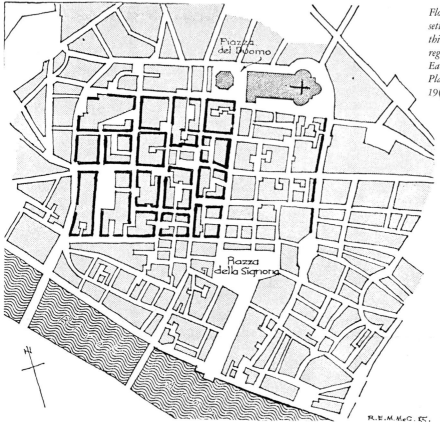

Florentia (Florence), an earlier settlement which became a city in the third or second century, B.C., *has a regular layout. (Ward Perkins, T. B., Early Roman Towns in Italy, The Town Planning Review, No. 3, vol. 26, pp. 19(a) and 162(b).)*

The main pole of this region was *Roma.* The unique city, developed from a primitive Latin settlement, reached during the imperial era a size unequalled throughout antiquity—a size which was, later, first attained by London around 1800 A.D.

The development of ancient Rome was not guided by any planning activities, but the city continued, during the republican period, to be enriched with monuments and public buildings. Its population increased from 100,000 at the time of Pyrrhus (280–272 B.C.) to 400,000 at the time of Sulla (82 B.C.). These calculations are based on a density rate of 480 persons per acre (1,200 per hectare), though Beloch's figure of 260 persons per acre (650 per hectare) appears to be more realistic.

The heart of the city consisted of the Forum Romanum, to which were later added the forums of Caesar (45 B.C.), Augustus (42 B.C.), Nerva (completed in 96 A.D.), and Trajan (98 A.D.). Though it was the capital of an empire where the cities always conformed to an overall plan reflecting the need for rapid and strict construction, Rome itself did not experience an orderly development except on three special occasions. In 45 B.C., Caesar promulgated the *lex de urbe augenda,* which contained precise guidelines for the development of the city toward the *campus Martius* and, through the diversion of the Tiber, the merging with the central zone of the eccentric *campus Vaticanus*. But realization of the plan was prevented by the Roman laws which did not recognize the public right to the land (being unable to expropriate the land, Caesar had to pay 100 million sesterci for the site of the Forum), and by Caesar's premature death.

Augustus (27 B.C.–14 A.D.) promulgated the *lex Julia de modo aedificiorum* in an attempt to achieve gradually what Caesar had tried to achieve in a single stroke. His redevelopment of the urban area and the rationalization in the field of private building construction created the conditions for the development of a zone beyond the *campus Martius* where a new urban center was created and for the construction of new road links for the city, which at that time had a population of 800,000.

Even the conflagration in Nero's time (65 A.D.) became the occasion for a great effort of urban redevelopment. The slums of 10 out of the 14 urban districts were completely destroyed and the houses were reconstructed to a better standard for a more well-to-do population, while the poorer populace was pushed out to the periphery. During the imperial period,

Augusta Praetoria Salassorum (Aosta), a military mountain town at the border of Italy, based on a layout derived from a military "castrum." The city was founded in the first century, B.C. (Ward Perkins, T. C., Early Roman Towns in Italy, The Town Planning Review, No. 3, vol. 26, Figs. 22(a) and 23(b).)

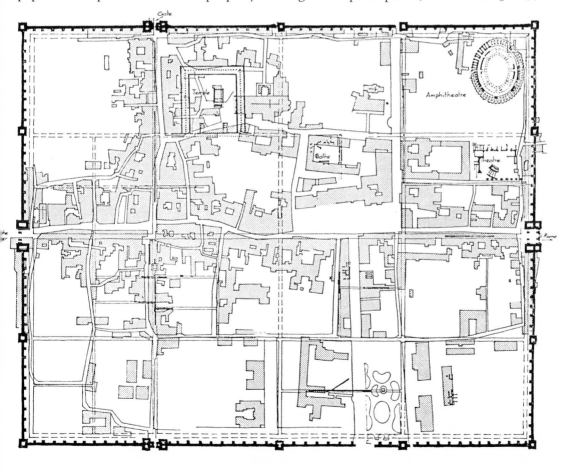

however, Rome—extended, enriched with famous monuments, and re-developed in the center—continued to be an enormous city, congested and too densely populated. The *insulae* (street blocks), with houses of five or six stories, were exploited by a class of capitalist landlords and gave shelter to a great part of the urban population under deplorable hygienic and sociological conditions. According to two documents from the time of the late Empire, the *Curiosum* by Polenius Silvius and the *Notitia* by Zacharias,

Aosta (Augusta Praetoria Salassorum). Two street blocks with standardized layout in garden setting surrounded by curtain of dwellings and shops. Time of Hadrian. (Bianchi Bandinelli, R., Roma, l'arte romana nel centro del potere [Rome, and the Roman art at the center of power]. Feltrinelli, Milan, 1969, p. 359.)

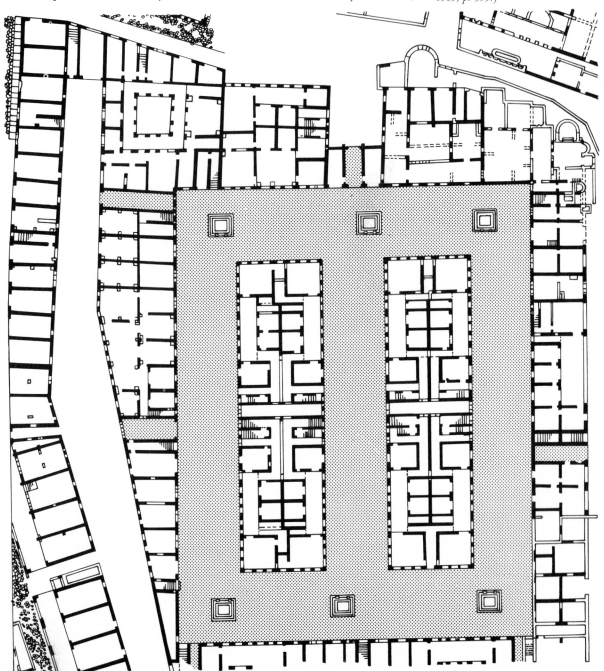

there were about 1.2 million people living in about 45,000 *insulae* and less than 2,000 *domus,* the single-story Mediterranean villas with central patio.

Throughout the Empire, the instruments of romanization consisted of the arteries of communication, of the stimulation of artisan and agricultural activities (which forced the nomads to remain in urban settlements), and of the spreading of the Latin cults, language, and way of life. The cities in Gaul, in the Iberian Peninsula, in Britain, in the Danube region, in Africa, and in Asia Minor therefore do not differ much from each other except by the type of private housing which, derived from a Hellenistic prototype, underwent regional modifications due to differences in climate, construction methods, and materials.

After northern Italy, the Roman conquest extended to the Iberian Peninsula where, apart from the Punic centers, no cities were in existence. The Iberians had settlements with mighty walls but indifferent internal organization. The Celts had fortified *oppida* on the tops of mountains and hills, with motley collections of round or rectangular huts. The *Celtiberi,* on the other hand, had already improved their cities when they came into contact with the Romans. *Numanzia,* their capital, long besieged by the legions and destroyed in 133 B.C., reveals a Hellenistic influence through the elliptical city walls and the orderly arrangement of the houses.

In the Iberian region, the Romans—attracted by the rich soil and the Punic and Greek markets—tried for two centuries to impose their empire partly by ruinous wars and partly through the foundation of cities (among the oldest were *Italica,* founded by Scipio; and *Gracchuris,* founded by the Praetor Tiberius Sempronius Gracchus), and through the transformation of the Punic cities of *Malaca* (Málaga) and *Gades* (Cádiz). With the foundation of colonies during the first century B.C., including *Tarraco* (Tarragona), *Genetiva Julia* (Urso), and *Colonia Julia Faventia Augusta* (Barcelona), the south of Spain assumed the appearance of an Italian region.

Similarly, the south of Gaul, which had already been the seat of flourishing economic enterprises established by the Greeks, was raised in the third century B.C. to a high level of urban culture as at *Massilia* (Marseilles) and *Glanon,* near St. Rémy. Although *Massilia* and the other Greek cities had made no efforts to spread their culture, the archeologists did find at Entremont, near Aix-en-Provence, an indigenous village from the second century B.C. with straight roads, regular street blocks, residential zones, and sacred enclosures of Hellenistic origin.

During the first 60 years of the Roman conquest of southern Gaul (125–61 B.C.), *Narbo Martius* (Narbonne) and *Lugdunum Convenarum* were founded. Settlers were accommodated and land was assigned to veterans, and the Greek or indigenous cities—*Tolosa* (Toulouse) and *Colonia Augusta Nemausus* (Nimes)—standing across the main traffic flows, absorbed Roman institutions and techniques. During the first century, further colonies were founded—including *Aquae Sextiae* (Aix-en-Provence) and *Colonia Julia Paterna Arelate* (Arles)—characterized by a regular layout, by fortifications, and by civic services and amenities. Originally inhabited by Italians, they attracted the families of local persons of standing and Gallic artisans and merchants. In the rural areas, on the other hand, the majority of the population continued to live in villages.

After the final conquest of Gaul by Caesar (58–51 B.C.), the Romans divided their dominion into administrative districts known as "provinces." In each province, a capital city was chosen as the seat of the representative of the Senate. *Lugdonum* (Lyons), *Tarraco, Camulodnum* (Colchester), and *Eboracum* (York) were among the most important provincial capitals. Here resided the urban *bourgeoisie,* which grew up around the provincial bureaucracy, and the tribal notables who were often entrusted with the effective government of the populations that continued to live in the rural areas and remained loyal to their ancient social conditions. Such Gallic villages as *Lutetia* (Paris) and *Samarobriva* (Amiens), commercial centers of a rich hinterland or important road junctions, provided a regular layout, romanized their ordinances, and were finally recognized as towns or colonies of Rome. And, as had happened along the Via Emilia, settlements were founded along the lines of communications by such people as traders, acrobats, actors, and the buyers who gathered at the markets. Examples are *Forum Julii* (Fréjus) and *Forum Segusiavorum* (Feurs).

The urbanization of Gaul and northern Europe was much intensified when Rome began to take a greater interest in the provinces, which were the source of wealth for the people, for the provincial governors, for the tax collectors, for the contractors, for the weapon manufacturers, and for all the hangers-on, honest or otherwise. And under the successors of Augustus, the urban pattern was deliberately favored and spread on a large scale by the central authorities, who always recognized the urban *bourgeoisie* as sturdy supporters. The cities exceeded the size of the Italian cities and were first ringed by walls during the third century, when they were first threatened by the incursions of the barbarians. It is an indication of the peace that generally prevailed during the two preceding centuries that it was possible to build, in open country at Bouchauds, some 12 miles from Angoulême, an amphitheater for the use of the dispersed agricultural villages. Nevertheless, the excavations at *Bibratte* (near Autun) and *Gergovia* show that, even during the first century, there still survived coherent and lively indigenous urban communities.

Britain, conquered from 43 A.D. onward but never completely subdued, presented a rich texture of roads linking some centers of great importance which had grown up as military and administrative cities in the southern part of the island. Among these were *Verulamium* (St. Albans), *Eboracum, Camulodunum,* and *Lindunum Colonia* (Lincoln); a certain number of indigenous Romanized towns and villages, including *Londinium* (London), *Galleva Atrebatum* (Silchester), and *Venta Silurum* (Caewert); rural villas and estates (Chedworth); and a great number of forts of various sizes including *Cilurnum* (Chester), which was the headquarters of one of the three legions. Beyond Hadrian's Wall, however, urban settlements were never established.

The Roman Empire at the time of its greatest expansion.

1. *Numanzia*
2. *Italica*
3. *Gracchuris*
4. *Malaca* (Málaga)
5. *Gades* (Cádiz)
6. *Tarraco* (Tarragona)
7. *Genetiva Julia* (Urso)
8. *Colonia Julia Faventia Augusta Barcino* (Barcelona)
9. *Massilia* (Marseilles)
10. *Glanon*
11. (Entremont)
12. *Narbo Martius* (Norbonne)
13. *Lugdunum Convenarum* (St. Bertrand-de-Comminges)
14. *Tolosa* (Toulouse)
15. *Colonia Augusta Nemausus* (Nimes)
16. *Aquae Sextiae* (Aix-en-Provence)
17. *Colonia Julia Paterna Arelate* (Arles)
18. *Lugdunum* (Lyons)
19. *Camulodnum* (Colchester)
20. *Eboracum* (York)
21. *Lutetia* (Paris)
22. *Samarobriva* (Amiens)
23. *Forum Julii* (Frejus)
24. *Forum Segusiavorum* (Feurs)
25. *Bibratte*
26. *Gergovia*
27. *Verulanium* (St. Albans)
28. *Lindunum Colonia* (Lincoln)
29. *Londinium* (London)
30. *Calleva Atrebatum* (Silchester)
31. Venta Silurum (Caerwent)
32. (Chedworth)
33. *Cilurnum* (Chester)
34. *Augusta Trevirorum* (Trier)
35. *Augusta Agrippinorum* (Cologne)
36. *Vindobona* (Vienna)
37. *Argentoratum* (Strasbourg)
38. *Colonia Ulpia Traiana* (Xanten)
39. *Regina Castra* (Regensburg)
40. *Magontiacum* (Mainz)
41. *Aquincum* (Budapest)
42. *Carnuntum* (Petronnell)
43. *Troesmis* (Iglitza)
44. *Apulum* (Alba Julia)
45. *Corinthus* (Corinth)
46. *Smyrna* (Izmir)
47. *Athenae* (Athens)
48. *Hadrianopolis* (Adrianople)
49. *Aelia Capitolina* (Jerusalem)
50. *Filippopoli*
51. *Palmyra* (Palmira)
52. *Petra*
53. *Bosra* (Busra)
54. *Damasco* (Damascus)
55. *Dura Europos* (Doura Europos)
56. *Costantinopolis* (Istanbul)
57. *Leptis Magna* (Lebda)
58. *Sabratha*
59. *Lambesis* (Lambèse)
60. *Thugga* (Dougga)
61. *Musculula* (Henchir Guergone)
62. *Thignica* (Ain Tounga)
63. *Thamugadi* (Timgad)
64. *Cuicul* (Djemila)
65. (Split)

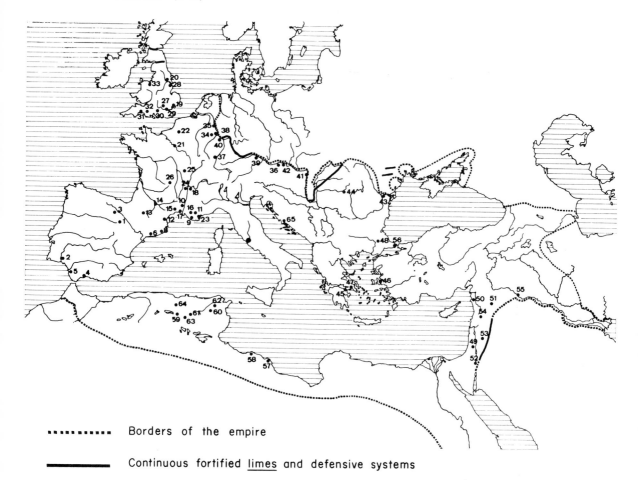

·········· Borders of the empire

━━━━━━━━━ Continuous fortified <u>limes</u> and defensive systems

Along the entire frontier or *limes* of the Empire—which extended from
the Netherlands (where two very short-lived colonies were founded) to the
Black Sea—the military camps became the nuclei of a chain of cities, some
of which became fairly important. The military camps along the *limes* were
placed at regular intervals. A large one would be manned by a legion, a
smaller one by a regiment, and an intermediate post by auxiliaries. Around
these settlements, based on the traditional layout of the *castrum,* there arose,
unaffected by the general planning principles of the Empire but in tacit
agreement with the central authorities, urban agglomerations known as
canabae which were inhabited by traders, the families of soldiers, innkeepers,
and prostitutes. They were townships devoid of any plan, without agricultural hinterland, and without recognition as cities or colonies; yet even they
were centers from which Roman culture was spread to the outermost
frontiers.

Examples of such settlements include *Augusta Trevirorum* (Trier) which,
during the late Empire, became the principal European city and which had

an area of 740 acres (300 hectares); *Augusta Agrippinorum* (Cologne) which, like *Vindobona* (Vienna) became an important commercial center; *Argentoratum* (Strasbourg); *Colonia Ulpia Traiana* (Xanten), which became a city of veterans under Trajan (98–117 A.D.); *Regina Castra* (Regensburg); *Magontiacum* (Mainz); *Aquinco* (Budapest), one of the greatest commercial centers on the Danube; *Carnuntum* (Petronell); *Troesmis* (Iglitz); and *Apulum* (Alba Julia).

Even at the frontier, the effects of romanization were profound. Thus, even after the collapse of the western Roman Empire (476 A.D.), there still survived for several centuries a strict linguistic, religious, and artistic unity despite the fact that, under the pressure of the barbarian tribes, the political cohesion had diminished.

The region of the Illyrians, Thracians, and Celts (Dalmatia, Pannonia, Mesia, Dacia, and Tracia) had never known any urban culture except along the Adriatic coast where the Greek cities had originated. As in Spain and in Provence, these became large Roman cities, and new cities were founded to counteract the Hellenization of the populations. In the hinterland, however, the primitive tribal life continued. Even so, some villages in the interior slowly became cities due to the enduring peace and a certain wealth derived from trade with the regions beyond the Danube.

The regions astride the Danube became part of the Empire at a relatively late period of time (first century B.C.), so that the rational development of the cities, villages, roads, canals, industries, systematically colonized lands, and cultures did not have sufficient time to consolidate. The cities, which offered a more diverting social life and better opportunities for trade, were completely integrated (pottery developed in the same way as in northern Italy, Gaul, or on the Rhine). In the rural areas, however, local cults, old artisan traditions, the tribal organization of society, and communal cultivation of farmlands remained more tenaciously alive.

Greece, impoverished after the Roman conquest (second century B.C.), did not experience the rise of new cities, but instead some modifications and changes were made to existing cities. Caesar effected changes at *Corinthus* (Corinth); Marcus Aurelius (161–180 A.D.) at *Smyrna;* Adrianus, when Archon of *Athenae* (Athens) tried to match his *Novae Athenae*—where he built a pantheon, a library, a gymnasium, the temple of Zeus Panhellenios, and completed the temple of Zeus Olympus—against the "Athens of Theseus" which he left, however, intact. He also transformed his native village into a city which he named *Hadrianopolis* (Adrianople).

In the Greek and Asiatic Orient, the plans of some regional arteries, the redevelopment of peripheral zones of the cities and of forum precincts with magnificent columned streets derived from Oriental traditions, the foundation of *castra stativa* along the borders, and the establishment of a few colonial cities represented marginal episodes—a patchwork on an earlier regional texture of high quality.

In these regions, the Romans attempted to assimilate the subjugated populations; but either because the urban and cultural level was already fairly high or because the Roman domination lasted a shorter time than elsewhere (from the first century to the arrival of the first barbarians in the third century), the Greek language and other national languages continued to be used and Roman artistic patterns had little influence on a highly developed local art. On the other hand, there persisted during the entire period of Roman occupation social tensions with riots, strikes, and lawlessness which, together with the tormented history of the Hebrews, certainly did not testify to a state of peace.

Hadrian founded *Aelia Capitolina* on the site where, 70 years earlier, Titus had destroyed Jerusalem (70 A.D.). Philip the Arab named his native city *Filippopoli* and made a colony of it; *Palmyra* also became a Roman colony; *Petra* and *Bosra* were trade centers, and their caravans traveled to the Far East. But the Middle East never became Roman and superimposed the new culture onto its predecessors. Hence the colonnaded streets of *Damasco* (1,640 yards long and 27.5 yards wide—1,500 meters long and 25.5 meters wide), *Apamea* (1,640 yards—1,500 meters), *Palmyra* (1,310 yards—1,200 meters long), *Bosra* (1,200 yards—1,100 meters long), and *Gerassa* (880 yards—800 meters long), the temples and buildings of *Petra* and *Dura Europos,* a Hellenistic city of the Parthian kingdom where the Greek, Aramaic and Iranian documents were, after 165 A.D., joined by inscriptions in Latin, Pahlavi, Mid-Persian, Saphaitic, Palmyric, Syriac, and Aramaic.

In the center of the Greek and middle eastern regions on the Strait of Bosporus, wealthy Byzantium changed its name, by order of Constantine in 324 A.D., to *Constantinopolis* (Constantinople). In 326 A.D., the first stone was laid for the remodeling of the city. In 330 A.D., it became the capital of the Eastern Empire.

Rich in monuments, churches, and imperial palaces, houses of officials and senators, public baths, hippodromes, triumphal arches, and commemorative columns, with a Via Triumphalis and splendid forums, the city of Constantinople represented—at a time when Roman architecture and urban planning began to decline—the birth of a new imperial art, triumphal in character, emphasized by aesthetic eclecticism, and much removed from the measured and plain art which went with the language, law, planning, and security of the vast integrated texture of the Roman Empire. Constantinople did not follow Rome in replanning the subjugated territories, and its empire faded away under the pressure first of the barbarians and then of the growing power of the Arabs. The city withdrew into itself, awaiting a fossilized death in the anachronistic repetition of styles devoid of their "imperial" significance.

Roman Egypt (first century B.C.) preserved the territorial structure of the scattered villages and the extensive and ancient urban poles just as she preserved intact—through the emperor, heir of Ptolemy—the old social structure and culture.

Even in the African regions of the Mediterranean, the pressure for romanization came, from the first century B.C. onward, from the cities. The Punic cities along the coast derived a new impulse, received large numbers of colonists who were attracted by promising agriculture, and were enlarged in accordance with regular plans which preserved the ancient Carthaginian monuments. *Leptis Magna* (Lebda) had at various times two different forums, and *Sabratha* had a colonnaded street 22.5 yards (20.5 meters) wide with 250 columns. New cities were founded and were connected with each other by a dense network of communications. In this way, the old barbarian settlements were sometimes enlarged by planned Roman extensions of military character, like *Lambaesis* (Lambessa); or of civil character, like *Thugga* (Dougga), *Musculula* (Henchir Guergour), and *Thignica* (Ain Tounga).

The cities arose within short distances of each other and were characterized by the part they played in the econimic life of the region (mines, trade, garrisons, agriculture, industry, seaports, or road junctions). Urban culture spread, together with the Roman way of life and Roman patterns, even beyond the borders of the Empire so that, even in neighboring countries, cities were founded on the model of the Roman cities. This was done by the rulers of Cyrenaica and the King of Mauretania.

Indeed, it is in Africa that the patient efforts of the archeologists have brought to light exemplary models of Roman town planning. One such example is *Thamugadi* (Timgad), founded in 100 A.D., a small town measuring 360 by 393 yards (328 by 357 meters), with perfectly regular layout and almost square street blocks, complete with all amenities and with a forum at the intersection of the main arteries. Another example is *Cuicul* (Djemile), constructed on a rocky promontory, likewise with a regular network of streets. Finally, there was the provincial capital, *Lambaesis,* where important civic buildings were erected around the *castrum.*

The Roman cities of Africa and Asia survived intact for a long time, and in many of them the Arab civilization was superimposed without causing excessive damage. In Europe, on the other hand, the need for defense during the decay of the Empire forced the inhabitants to ring their cities with walls. These walls were confined to the central part of the city. As the urban population declined, certain groups of public buildings were converted into houses, mansions, or castles (amphitheaters at Arles, Benevagienna, Aosta, and Assisi; Diocletian's Palace at Split).

While the Roman road layout survived, the architectural texture was upset. What did, however, survive more tenaciously were the interrelations between town and country as well as the public works (bridges, canals, roads, aqueducts, land reclamations, and systematic colonization) which, up to the last century, still were among the dominant features of the landscape in many parts of Europe.

BIBLIOGRAPHY:
Works of a general character
N. D. Fustel de Coulagnes, *La città antica* (the ancient city), Florence, 1924; M. Zocca, "I fori nell'urbanistica romana" (the forum in Roman town planning), *Atti del III Congresso nazionale di storia dell'architettura—Roma 1938,* pp. 277–289, Rome, 1940; G. Lugli, *Saggi di esplorazione archeologica a mezzo della fotografia aerea* (archaeological exploration by means of aerial photography), Rome, 1939, "Pomerio," *Enc. Ital.,* vol. 28, pp. 794–795; L. Piccinato, "Origini dello schema urbano circolare nel medioevo" (the origins of the circular urban

layout in the middle ages), *Palladio,* III, 1941, pp. 120–125; L. Piccinato and G. Patroni, "La citta romana" (the Roman city), *Enc. Ital.,* vol. 10, pp. 481–483; P. Fraccaro, "Agrimensura—Roma," *Enc. Ital.,* vol. 1, pp. 986–990; G. Vinaccia, "Palafitte, terramare e castra romani" (Roman dwellings and castles), *Palladio,* II, 1941, pp. 49–53; M. Rostovtzeff, *Storia economica e sociale dell'impero romano* (economic and social history of the Roman Empire), Florence, 1946; L. Homo, *Rome impériale et l'urbanisme dans l'antiquité* (Imperial Rome and town planning in antiquity), Paris, 1951; R. D'Ambrogio, *Alle origini della città* (of the origins of cities), Naples, 1954; P. Grimal, *Les villes romaines* (Roman cities), Paris, 1954; M. Coppa, "Roma senza cuore," *Architettura,* no. 2–3, 1955; F. Castagnoli, *Ippodamo da Mileto e l'urbanistica a pianta ortogonale* (Hippodamus of Miletus and the rectangular layout of cities), Rome, 1956; M. Poëte, *La città antica* (the ancient city), Turin, 1958; E. Sereni, *Storia del paesaggio agrario italiano* (history of the Italian countryside), Bari, 1961; M. Zocca, *Sommario di storia urbanistica delle città italiane dalle origini al 1860* (synopsis of the history of the planning of Italian cities from their origin to 1860), Naples, 1961; M. Morini, *Atlante di storia dell'urbanistica* (atlas of the history of town planning), Milan, 1963; L. Mumford, *The City in History,* Harcourt, Brace & World, Inc., New York, 1961 (Italian edition: *La città nella storia,* Milan, 1963); M. Pallottino, *Intoduzione all'urbanistica* (introduction to town planning), Rome, 1963; A. Grabar, *L'età d'oro di Giustiniano* (the golden age of Justinian), Milan, 1966; G. Astengo, "Urbanistica," *Enc. Univ. Arte,* vol. 14, 541–642 (American edition: *Encyclopedia of World Art,* "Town Planning," McGraw-Hill Book Company, New York, 1967); F. Franco, "Italia," *Enc. Univ. Arte,* vol. 8, 1–270; P. Grimal, *L'ellenismo e l'ascesa di Roma* (Hellenism and the rise of Rome), Milan, 1967, *La formazione dell'impero romano* (the formation of the Roman Empire), Milan, 1967; P. M. Lugli, *Storia e cultura della città italiana* (history and culture of the Italian cities), Bari, 1967; M. Coppa, *Storia dell'urbanistica, Origini* (history of town planning—origins), vol. 1, *ellenismo* (Hellenism), vol. 2, Turin, 1968; J. Hubert, J. Porcher, and W. F. Voldach, *L'Europa delle invasioni barbariche* (Europe at the time of the Barbarian Invasions), Milan, 1968; J. B. Ward Perkins, "Early Roman Towns in Italy," *Town Planning Review,* vol. 26, no. 3, pp. 126–154.

Works of specific character
T. Toutain, *Les cités romaines de la Tunisie* (Roman cities in Tunisia), Paris, 1896; P. Lavedan, *Les villes françaises* (the French towns), Paris, 1930; P. Barocelli, *Il Piemonte dalla capanna neolitica ai monumenti di Augusto,* Turin, 1933; A. De Bon, *La colonizzazione romana dal Brenta al Piave* (Roman colonization between the Brenta and Piave), Bassano del Grappa, 1933; Vitrurio, *Dell'Architettura, trad.U.Fleres,* Rome, 1933; A. Calderini, "I romani nella valle del Po" (the Romans in the Po Valley), *Lombardia Romana,* vol. 1, pp. 37–67, Milan, 1938; E. Soler, *La via Claudia Augusta Altinate,* Venice, 1938; L. Dodi, "Città romane di Lombardia" (Roman cities in Lombardy), *Atti del III Congresso nazionale di storia dell'Architettura—Roma 1938,* vol. 1, pp. 297–307, Rome, 1940; M. Bertolone, *Lombardia romana* (Roman Lombardy), vol. 2, Milan, 1939; G. Corradi, *Le strade romane dell'Italia Occidentale* (the Roman roads in western Italy), Turin, 1939; G. Mancini, "Le colonie e i municipi romani dell'Emilia orientale" (Roman colonies and cities in eastern Emilia), *Emilia romana,* pp. 73–123, Florence, 1941; F. Pellati, "Vitrurio," *Enc. Ital.,* vol. 35, pp. 493–495; L. Dal Ri and U. Tomazzoni, *Storia del trentino* (history of the Trentino), vol. 1, Rovereto, 1951; I. D. Margary, *Roman Roads in Britain,* London, 1957; S. Finocchi, "Problemi di topografia e urbanistica romana in Piemonte" (problems of topography and Roman town planning in Piedmont), *Atti del X Congresso nazionale di storia dell'Architettura—Torino 1957,* pp. 113–126, Rome, 1959; Vitrurio, *Architettura, trad.S.Ferri,* Rome, 1960; L. Dodi, *Dell'antica urbanistica romana nel Medio Oriente* (ancient Roman city planning in the Middle East), Milan, 1962; *Le formazioni urbane nel Parmense* (the formations of towns in the Parma region), Parma, 1965; J. Lasus, "Adaptation à l'Afrique de l'urbanisme romain" (adaptation of Roman town planning to Africa), *Atti dell'VIII Congrés international d'archéologie classique—Paris 1963,* pp. 245–259, Paris, 1965; V. Cabianca, "L'arcipelago eoliano" (the Aeolian Archipelago), *Urbanistica,* no. 31, pp. 53–68; M. Rotili, *Benevento e la sua provincia* (Benevento and its province), Benevento; M. Coppa, "Centri storici: la valle del Clitunno" (historic centers: the Clitunno Valley) (manuscript).
—GIOVANNI ASTENGO and LUIGI FALCO

ANNEX A supplementary or subsidiary building added to the main building, but not necessarily attached to it physically.

APARTMENT HOUSE A building, generally of several stories, containing a number of separate dwellings with a common entrance from the street and often with services like heating and lighting in common. It is called a "block of flats" in England. Some apartment houses have restaurants and recreation rooms for the tenants or owner-occupiers; such buildings are termed "service flats" in England. Dwellings in blocks of two or more stories erected for what were once called the "working classes" were often called "tenement houses" or "tenements."

APPEAL (Against Planning Decisions) A person who wishes to reverse certain types of planning decisions may, in the United Kingdom, appeal against them. The process of appealing is a formal one and covers a wide range of specific types of planning decisions. The most common form of appeal is against a planning authority's refusal of permission to carry out development under the Town and Country Planning Act of 1971; but appeals can be made against many decisions of a less specific planning nature; e.g., orders to preserve buildings or trees, orders to acquire land compulsorily, notices to enforce the carrying out of development in conformity with the development which was approved, etc. A person wishing to appeal against such decisions, orders, or notices must do so within a specified period. The procedure is initiated by his lodging an appeal with the Secretary of State for the Environment who then appoints an inspector to hear the parties to the appeal (usually the appellant himself and the planning authority), either at a public inquiry or through the submission of documents in writing. On the basis of the inspector's findings, the Secretary of State (or in certain cases the inspector himself) then finally allows or dismisses the appeal. Further appeal against the Secretary of State's decision can then only be made on a point of law as distinct from a point of planning principle. Appeals against planning decisions are distinct from objections to actual plans or proposals put forward by the planning authority for public examination.

BIBLIOGRAPHY: Robert McKown, *Comprehensive Guide to Town Planning Law,* G. Godwin Ltd., London, 1964; Desmond Heap, *An Outline of Planning Law,* 5th ed., Sweet & Maxwell, London, 1969; R. N. D. Hamilton, *A Guide to Development and Planning,* Oyez Publications, 1970; P. L. Rose and M. Barnes, *Planning Appeals and Inquiries* (2d ed.), Sweet and Maxwell, London, 1970.

—DAVID HALL

AQUEDUCT A duct or conduit for conveying water from place to place, but commonly regarded as an elevated structure carrying the duct. The main purpose is to carry water from a reservoir for supply and distribution to a city. The Romans built some very impressive arched aqueducts throughout the empire, and some are still standing. One of the most famous is the Pont du Gard near Nîmes in the south of France.

ARCADE AND ARCADING A series of arches—as distinct from lintels— supported on columns such as is seen in medieval cloisters, the interiors of basilicas and churches, and in Renaissance piazzas. It is also an arched or vaulted passage or walk, like the famous arcade in Milan or Burlington Arcade in London. The term "arcading" means a design of a series of arches supported on columns.

ARCHITECT The term "architect" derives from the Greek ἀρχιτέκτων, which is a compound of ἀρχι-, meaning "chief" or "master"; and τέκτων, meaning "carpenter," "craftsman," or "builder." The meaning of the term "architect" as "master builder" is logically very much the same today, for the architect is the person who designs a building, controls the building operations, and is the head of a team. He interprets the requirements of the client; he designs the building to suit these requirements, ensuring that the building fulfils its purpose; he superintends the erection; he ensures that the building is structurally sound; and he endeavors to make it pleasing to contemplate. In so doing he fulfils the three precepts of Vitruvius: that buildings must be erected with due consideration to *firmitas, utilitas,* and *venustas,* rendered by Morgan as "durability, convenience, and beauty," by Granger as "strength, utility, and grace" and by Wotton as "commodity, firmness, and delight." These conditions are still valid and are often quoted.

From the Italian Renaissance until the twentieth century, city planning has been assumed largely as an extension of the work of the architect, and it was conceived as architecture on a big scale comprising groups of buildings, streets, piazzas, and whole cities. Before the Italian Renaissance, however, there is no reliable evidence that city planning was mainly the work of architects, although this is often assumed. We know that Hippodamus, the first recorded city planner, was responsible for several city plans, and it is therefore sometimes assumed that he was an architect; although from Aristotle's account (*Politics,* 2-8) he appears more in the light of a politician and sociologist.

In the middle ages, city planning was so much linked with defense that it was often the work of military engineers. The bastide towns built by St. Louis of France and Edward I of England were probably designed by military engineers skilled in planning. Medieval planning seems also to have been, to some extent, the responsibility of the church and to have been the work of monastic brethren, who determined the layout of monastic buildings and often the parts of the city in the vicinity.

During the Italian Renaissance, however, when artists were at once painters, sculptors, and architects, city planning was a natural addition to their activities. An early example was Orcagna (1308-1368), whose design for the new layout of the Piazza della Signoria in Florence was accepted. Architects were often called on to plan parts of cities and the layout of streets and piazzas. The most famous examples of this include Michelangelo's plan of the piazza of the Campidoglio in Rome and, later, Bernini's plan for the colonnaded, encircled piazza in front of St. Peter's. This Italian Renaissance tradition of the architect extending his work to, and being chiefly responsible for, city planning continued up to the twentieth century; and practically all important planning schemes in both Europe and America were the work of architects. During the nineteenth century, with the increased social approach to planning, it became a much more varied and complex subject; and thus the distinct profession of city or town planner emerged in the early part of the twentieth century.

In many countries city planning is still mainly—sometimes exclusively—the work of architects, generally those who have included in their training the study of city planning. In countries like the United States, Great Britain, and Germany, where the distinct profession of city or town planner has emerged, many authorities and clients still prefer to employ a planner who is also an architect. But the complex activity of planning has become the combined work of many specialists, so that it is now largely the work of a team. Nevertheless, more often than not, it is the architect-planner who is the leader of the team. This is due partly to the traditional importance of the architect, but partly also to the belief that it is the architect who will give due consideration to aesthetic values.

BIBLIOGRAPHY: Martin S. Briggs, *The Architect in History*, Oxford University Press, Oxford, 1927; Barrington Kaye, *The Development of the Architectural Profession in Britain*, George Allen & Unwin, Ltd., London, 1960.

—ARNOLD WHITTICK

ARCHITECTURE Literally, architecture is the work of the architect (*see* ARCHITECT); but in modern times it has also been given the more specific meaning of building that has some degree of aesthetic value. Purists in the matter would deny the appellation "architecture" to a building that, for them, has no such value. This limitation on the term "architecture" has occurred mainly since the eighteenth century, when philosophers (Hegel, Lotze, Spencer, Comte, and others) classified architecture as one of the fine arts, with painting, sculpture, poetry, and music. It means that architecture is only the *venustas* of the three Vitruvian precepts for good building.

To some city planners architecture has this exclusive meaning, the term "building" being used where aesthetic qualities are not involved. This is a valid and important distinction. When the planner visualizes the architecture of a planning scheme, he is thinking of the aesthetic aspects of the urban environment as distinct from the purposes or the utilitarian aspects of the buildings. These aesthetic or architectural aspects involve primarily a consideration of the formal relations of masses, color, and light and shadow irrespective of the utilitarian functions of the buildings. (*See also* AESTHETICS)

BIBLIOGRAPHY: Geoffrey Scott, *The Architecture of Humanism*, Constable & Co., Ltd., London, 1914, 2d ed., 1924; Talbot Hamlin, *Architecture for All Men*, Columbia University Press, New York, 1947.

—ARNOLD WHITTICK

ARGENTINA

Demographic and Socioeconomic Characteristics   Argentina is a federal republic formed by 22 provinces, a national territory, and the Federal District of Buenos Aires (see illustration). In mid 1972, the population was estimated at 24,069,000. The country covers an area of 1,072,066 square miles (2,776,656 square kilometers) so that the average population density is 22.5 persons per square mile (9.0 per square kilometer). The annual rate of population increase is low and is declining. The population has tended to concentrate in the coastal provinces, along the western shores of the rivers La Plata and Paranà, forming, between the present cities of La Plata in the south and Santa Fe in the north, the greatest industrial conurbation in the country. Thus, in just over 1 percent of the national territory, there is concentrated about 50 percent of the population (see illustration). This means that if the trend should continue, Argentina would, in the year 2000, with a population of just over 35 million, form a wide empty space with a few concentrations of population. In addition to the conurbation already mentioned, which includes the metropolitan areas of Buenos Aires and Rosario, these would develop around the metropolitan areas of Córdoba, Mendoza, and Tucumán.

Argentina is one of the most urbanized countries in the world. In 1970, out of a total population of 23,364,431 persons, 18,784,000 or 80.4 percent were considered urban.[1] Its degree of urbanization is, therefore, comparable to that of the economically more developed and industrialized countries. There are also other social and economic indices which show that Argentina's situation is comparable to that of the more highly developed countries: e.g., in 1969 the degree of literacy was 92 percent; in 1967 there were 1.6 doctors and 6.2 hospital beds per thousand inhabitants; more than 1 percent of the total population is enrolled at the universities; in 1971 the birth rate was 22.0 per thousand and the mortality rate 9.0 per thousand. There are, however, other indices which clearly show that Argentina is in a less advanced state of development: in 1971, the average income per individual was $820 dollars; in 1960, the percentage of labor employed in the manufacturing sector was 24.9 percent. The annual consumption of cement, steel, and electricity per individual and the amount of meat, cereals, and their by-products exported—in terms of the trade balance—indicate an intermediate state of development.

Urbanization has preceded industrialization and, especially, the development of basic industries. Even at the time of the First World War, although the country was then still very much in the initial stage of its industrial development, more than half the population was already classified as urban.

Because of the slow growth rate of the national population (especially in the rural part of it), because of the already high percentage of the urban population, and—finally—because, in the absence of incentives, immigration from abroad is insignificant, there is little prospect of a short-term change in the population growth rates. And as there still does not exist any integrated national plan for promoting the development of regions other than the industrial conurbation along the shores of the rivers La Plata and Parana (which, although unplanned, attract investments), it is logical to assume that major geographical changes in the historic trend, already

[1] Provisional figures of the 1970 National Census of Population.

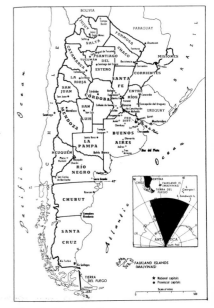

The administrative divisions.

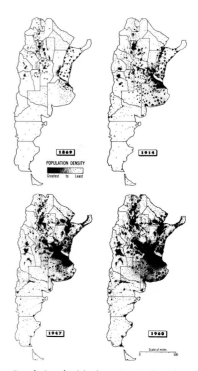

Population densities in 1869, 1914, 1947, and 1960.

discussed, are not likely to occur. Compared with nearly all the other Latin American countries, the growth of the national and urban population of Argentina is stable, and it must be expected that, during the coming decade, the urban population will increase by more than 400,000 per annum. It is expected that the rural population will decrease in absolute numbers.

There is a notorious regional imbalance between some rich and reasonably well-developed provinces such as Buenos Aires, Mendoza, Córdoba, and the center and south of Santa Fe on the one hand, and, on the other, the underdeveloped provinces in the northwest or the virtually uninhabited and unexploited provinces of Patagonia. This is reflected in the different opportunities for employment and in the differences in income between the provinces with a higher degree of industrialization and a fairly diversified and mechanized agrarian economy and those in which monoculture and antiquated systems of soil cultivation and exploitation prevail.

This pronounced difference between the center of the country and its periphery is undoubtedly due to the growing political, economic, cultural, and numerical supremacy of the city of Buenos Aires and its metropolitan area as compared with the rest of the country. Favored by its geographical position and climate; by its port, which provided a direct contact with the markets of Spain, of the rest of Europe, and of the world; and by the excellent quality of the soil in the extensive plains, the city of Buenos Aires with its immediate hinterland saw its commercial and productive prominence upheld, from the end of the eighteenth century onward, by the creation of the viceroyalty of the Rio de la Plata. The supremacy of Buenos Aires was definitely established when, in 1853, the Argentine government adopted the federal system and when, in 1880, the city of Buenos Aires was declared the federal capital. Coincident with massive migrations from Europe was the construction of the national railway network, beginning in the 1870s (see illustration), subsequent construction of the road network, the development of the industries processing the primary produce of the country for the foreign market, and the growth of the consumer goods industries for the home market. Many of the European immigrants came from Italy and Spain. Buenos Aires, Rosario, and the coastal strip in general were greatly affected by these events. The interior of the country—remote from the ports, with poor interregional communications, less favored by rainfall, and depending on precarious agrarian economies—retained many of the socioeconomic features of a colony.

The discovery and exploitation of perishable natural resources, such as petroleum and natural gas in the north of Salta, in Mendoza, in Neuquén, and in some areas of Patagonia has permitted some development, albeit highly localized, in these provinces to boost the economic standard of the region.

Argentina's development has undoubtedly been affected by the political crises and economic instability of recent decades. The result has been an economy with poor geographical and sectorial integration, and this has led to the stagnation observed since the second World War.

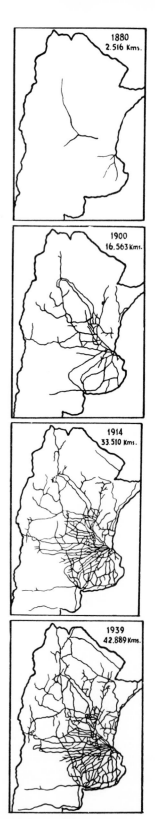

Railroad networks in 1880, 1900, 1914, and 1939.

Administration On September 30, 1966, a National System of Planning and Action for Development was set up by law (Act 16964). Prior to that date, there existed in the country a National Development Council with similar responsibilities. It had, however, been suggested on a number of occasions that there was a need for organizing an integrated planning system, and the act of 1966 was intended to define the parts and responsibilities of the various political, administrative, and technical levels of the government and of private groups. As will be seen, however, although more than 6 years have elapsed since the formal establishment of the National Planning System, it can still not be said to be functioning. It is worth mentioning that, during the Illia administration (1963–1966), the National Development Council promoted numerous studies and ended up by preparing, by 1965, a National Plan for Economic Development which was, however, never approved by the National Congress. Its authors deferred any attempt to regionalize the country and were not concerned with the social, spatial, and local aspects of development. On the other hand, their analytical assessment was valuable.

The system set up by the act of 1966 consists of the following bodies:

1. The National Development Council (CONADE), which has the task of formulating the long-term strategies and policies. It is presided over by the President of the Republic and is composed of the federal ministers, the secretaries of state, and the commanders of the armed forces. CONADE has a technical secretariat, managed by an executive secretary with the rank of Secretary of State, reporting directly to the President. Among the responsibilities of the technical secretariat are the analysis of the national problems and the preparation of the national development plan.

2. The regional development offices, which are subordinated to the President of the Republic through the CONADE secretariat. By presidential decree No. 1907, dated March 21, 1967, the country was divided into eight regions for planning and development purposes. These regions are: (*a*) Patagonia, (*b*) Comahue, (*c*) Cuyo, (*d*) Central, (*e*) Northwest, (*f*) Northeast, (*g*) Pampeana, and (*h*) the metropolitan area of Buenos Aires. The regional development offices are located in their respective regions and are concerned with regional planning and promotion in keeping with the directives laid down in the national plan.

3. The sectorial development offices, which are subordinated to the respective secretaries of state and have the responsibility for planning the activities in their respective sectors. For example, the sectors of housing, public health, community development, and social security come under the Minister of Social Welfare through the secretaries of state of each sector, and the same applies to the other ministries. The action of the sectorial offices must be coordinated by the CONADE secretariat.

4. The State Organizations for Technical Information.

5. The Organizations for Consultation and Participation, which permit the intervention of the private sector in the elaboration and evaluation of the plans at their different levels.

From the organization of the National Planning System, it should be clear that regional development has been taken into account. In their speeches, the former President of the Republic, General Ongania, and his ministers had often emphasized that the National Development Plan has "as its basic objective, the unity of the country," which should be reflected in equal opportunities for the inhabitants of all the regions of the country, or that "the Region is the operative instrument of the change to which the country is pledged," or that "the unity of the nation is in reality based on the provinces." However, a rapid assessment of the effectiveness of the system shows that its impact on the development of the country has, so far, been very small. Moreover, neither the act which created the system nor the decrees which were issued to regulate its details nor the actions of CONADE during the last few years indicated any need to promote metropolitan and urban planning. Nor has such planning in fact been promoted, apart from the formation of Region 8, which consists of the metropolitan area of Buenos Aires. In a country where about 75 percent of the population is classified as urban, this is surprising.

The state of planning in Argentina at its different levels at the middle of 1972 is as follows:

National Planning   This is essentially economic planning with little or no concern for the social and spatial aspects of development. Up to mid-1969, CONADE was content with a series of analytical studies. Finally, toward the end of 1969, a general plan for investments in public works was completed. The efforts made by CONADE to improve the coordination of the activities of the sectorial offices have resulted in very little progress. The powerful private sector of the country, especially the groups united in the Rural Association, the Commercial Exchange, and the Industrial Union, are conservative, openly biased on the side of private enterprise, and opposed to any type of government planning. Nor have the opinions of CONADE carried much weight with some of the technical ministries and workers unions. Up to a point, the efforts of CONADE have been useful in supplying the President of the Republic with information and advice; frequently, however, their action has been in conflict with the General Secretariat of the President which has greater political power. There are serious doubts concerning the possibilities of CONADE in improving sectorial coordination and promoting a national development plan on a wide basis. These arise because the planning system that exists is only an abstraction pretending to create the image of a modern, efficient state. Although CONADE is at the apex of this pyramidal organization, its influence tends to fluctuate since its prestige changes as its principal executives succeed one another. It would appear that successive governments have not known what to do with CONADE, which has not succeeded in getting planning accepted and embodied in the administrative apparatus.

Regional Planning   The regions were formed by integrating two or more provinces. The provinces are the first political and administrative subunits of the country and, in accordance with the national Constitution, the provinces should have political power and economic autonomy within the federal system. Nevertheless, due to a growing political and administrative centralization and a continuous increase in the financial dependency of the provinces on the central government, the autonomy of the provinces has diminished. Only some of the richer and better developed provinces have sufficient investment capital to implement minor programs of their own or to supplement the programs of the national government, especially in regard to education, road construction, housing, and industrial development. The political situation during the last decades, plagued by coups d'état and the suspension of constitutional rights, has enabled the national government to intervene in the provincial governments and to replace the elected governors with its nominees. This is the present situation. The administration of all the provinces is in the hands of persons appointed by the President of the Republic. Furthermore, this growing centralization and control of the provinces and local authorities by the central government has not been used to achieve a better coordination of programs.

Regional planning has been confined to attempts at coordinating certain national programs with the provincial programs and to the definition of regional objectives of a very general nature. This has been the result of annual or biannual meetings of the provincial governors of a region and their technical teams with their opposite numbers in the national government. These meetings are coordinated by the technical secretariat of CONADE. Theoretically, the governors of the provinces forming a region are jointly responsible for laying down the objectives, policies, and strategies of regional development in accordance with the directives of the National Development Plan. In order to assist the management of this plan, the governors of numerous provinces have created a group of provincial development councils (COPRODE) with a competence similar to that held by CONADE at national level.

However, CONADE has encountered numerous difficulties in pursuing its work of analysis, coordination, and advice: lack of suitable professional staff in the provinces, antiquated provincial administrations, and inadequate statistics. For these reasons and due to the lack of investment capital, it would seem that CONADE has decided to concentrate its efforts on the projects and programs of national interest with scant impact on the poorer regions.

There exist some regional development plans which have had a certain success. In general, these plans are linked with the development of agriculture through irrigation and flood control in a minor river basin such as that of the Río Dulce in the Santiago del Estero province and in the lower valley of the Río Negro in the province of Río Negro.

Metropolitan and Local Planning   Traditionally, this has been the responsibility of the local authorities. The major urban areas are formed by a number of municipalities, each with its own local authority, its own technical staff, and its own budget. But the resources of the municipalities—derived from a share in the rates, from taxes on certain services, from commercial and industrial taxes, and from other, minor sources of income—are wholly insufficient and, moreover, differ from one local authority to another in the same metropolitan area. Obviously, the resources, the deficits, the needs, and the objectives of the municipalities differ greatly, and so do the socio-economic levels of their population, the services available to them, and the use of the land which, being governed by physical conditions, does not respect the administrative boundaries. Apart from their scanty resources, the political power of the municipalities is continually dwindling. They are therefore unable to contribute basic solutions to a dynamic process like urban growth, which arises and acquires different regional and local characteristics as a result of the investments and programs of the higher levels of government and of the private sector. Even so, as a result of a delegation of duties on the part of the provincial governments, the local authorities have the responsibility of planning the land use in their areas, including zoning and the application of building bylaws.

In 1969, the local authorities of the metropolitan area of Rosario—the third-largest in the country in terms of population—intended to form a metropolitan authority with a view to coordinating their programs. This development is too recent to be appraised. On the other hand, various plans for organizing something similar in the metropolitan area of Buenos Aires have come to nought. This is an urban area covering 2,702 square miles (7,000 square kilometers) with a population of 9.5 million, where the national government, the Buenos Aires or federal district authorities, the government of the province of Buenos Aires, the governments of 18 to 22 local authorities (depending on the definition of the metropolitan area adopted), various national, provincial, and municipal authorities, and the private sector each have their own plans, programs, and investment schemes.

Nearly all the municipalities of major size have technical planning offices. In many of these offices, general development plans have been prepared, frequently with the advice of private consultants. Only exceptionally have these plans been of any use, either because they were focused on unrealistic objectives and incapable of being financed, or because the local administration was not prepared to implement even the simplest proposals, or because the previous governments or the present National Planning System has failed to take the urban problems into account.

Undoubtedly, the key to the problem is that the country lacks an integrated development plan on a national scale, and that, even if this should be prepared and approved by the President, the National Planning System exists only on paper. The "organizations for consultation and participation" have either not been created or, where they have been created, are handicapped because their members must subscribe to certain ideologies or are unrepresentative. For political and ideological reasons, the government has had neither the knowledge nor the will nor the power to make full use of fully trained specialists. In these circumstances, it is very difficult to pretend that there is a National Planning System in operation and that there are means of indicating the regional priorities. Much will have to be done in improving the coordination of the political and technical, public and private bodies involved in the planning and development process; but

CONADE must also define the parts which should be played by these bodies and the different political and administrative levels of the country, and it must then be able to make use of them. There is also a serious discrepancy between the role theoretically assigned to these levels under a federal system and the existing reality.

Professional Practice   In Argentina, the professional title of regional or urban planner does not exist, and therefore this field is not recognized as a separate discipline. In practice, there has arisen a certain division of responsibilities between the traditional professions. National planning has been in the hands of economists and engineers with some assistance from demographers and sociologists. Urban planning has been in the hands of architects and engineers with some assistance from lawyers and, to a lesser extent, from sociologists and economists. This is demonstrated by the composition of the technical teams of CONADE and the municipal authorities. Regional planning is at present (1972) almost nonexistent. There are also serious deficiencies in certain disciplines which are fundamental, such as agrarian economy, transport, ecology, demography, and public administration. Some of these disciplines have recently begun to be taught at the universities of the country. It is only since the mid-1950s that university courses in economics and sociology have begun to benefit from teaching along modern lines.

In these circumstances, it is understandable—though not excusable—that the national and local planning bodies are somewhat out of focus. The architects do not receive any training in physical planning—merely some rudimentary teaching in urban design—and their knowledge of economics, sociology, and administration is so elementary that it may well be regarded as nonexistent. The economists, in their turn, are not introduced to spatial, legal, and social problems. As a result the work of these teams tends to be out of focus, unrealistic, and difficult to integrate, giving rise to schemes that are difficult to implement.

Much more importance is attached to the preparation of the plan than to the creation of the political, administrative, financial, and legal conditions which must be met if the plan is to be realized. The general result is that planning, at whatever level it is intended to materialize, has not yet emerged from its analytical stage and has not been converted into a political and technical instrument of real practical value. The frequent administrative changes at the different levels of government, the political climate, and the low salaries, especially at provincial and local levels, have alienated numerous technicians who prefer to leave the public service and to devote themselves to private professional activities or to migrate. As a result, and also because of greater decentralization of technical studies in certain public offices, teams of private consultants have been established in recent years. These are increasingly important as advisers to the public administration.

Education and Training   For more than twenty years, the faculty of architecture at Buenos Aires University has granted a degree in town planning to architects, engineers, and surveyors who complete a 2-year graduate course on a part-time basis. This program, focused on the physical problems of the town, has never attracted any great number of professionals.

Other universities in the interior of the country have tried out better-integrated programs that require full-time attendance. Perhaps the most interesting example has been that of the Universidad del Litoral between 1962 and 1965, though this course was suspended in 1965 for reasons stemming from within the university.

A number of universities and private, nonprofit institutions have research programs on various aspects of regional and urban development. Among the universities can be mentioned the North-East University, located at Resistencia in the province of Chaco. Among the private institutions is the Di Tella Institute, whose Centre of Urban and Regional Studies concentrates the greatest number of specialists. This center has trained a fair number of young research workers by means of residential seminars, courses of lectures, and active participation in research projects.

The country undoubtedly needs numerous specialists, trained with a more integrated vision, in the fundamental disciplines concerned with national, regional, and local planning. The public and private universities have not concerned themselves with such training, and the responsible national authorities have failed to appreciate its importance. The shortage of specialists became evident in mid-1969, when CONADE intended to appoint an expert technical staff for the regional planning offices.

The responsibility of the state for the training of specialists is fundamental. If the government fails to promote the training of technical teams for service with them and to consolidate their employment, it will never be possible to create an efficient administration.

Traditions of Planning to the End of the Nineteenth Century   The basic pattern of Argentina's urban development dates back to the sixteenth century. In contrast to Mexico, Guatemala, Peru, Ecuador, and Bolivia, the indigenous population of the present territory of the Argentine was small in numbers, and a slightly higher population density was reached only in the northwestern part of the country where agricultural developments were on a reasonable scale. The Spaniards penetrated in the north (from Cuzco), in the west (from Santiago de Chile), and in the east (directly from Spain). Later, in 1553, after various setbacks, they founded the first town—Santiago del Estero—which is still in existence. At the end of the sixteenth century, most of the principal cities of the country were already in existence, among them Buenos Aires, Córdoba, Mendoza, Tucumán, Santa Fe, Salta, Jujuy, Corrientes, and San Juan, which had been founded following the pattern employed by the Spaniards in other parts of America: a chessboard of square street blocks with an open square of proportions identical to those of a street block. Around this square were placed the main church of the city, the town hall, and, in the case of Buenos Aires, the government house. The main square was always surrounded with arches. In front of the main facades of the convent churches, small piazzas were provided.

More than 250 years passed before this original pattern of settlements

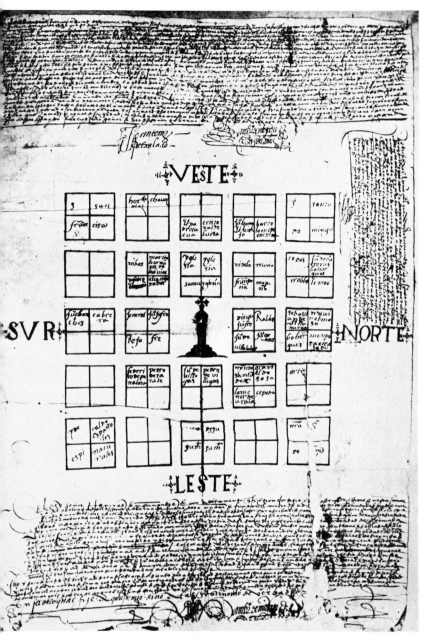

Chessboard plan of 1562 for the city of Mendoza.

was modified. More recently, from the 1860s onward, as a result of immigration from abroad, the colonization of the plains, and the construction of the national railway network, the internal frontiers were modified, Patagonia and Chaco were effectively incorporated, and the principal cities of the country were connected by modern modes of transport. In 1869, Argentina had a population of no more than 1,737,000, of whom 10 percent lived in the city of Buenos Aires (see illustration).

The second half of the nineteenth century was characterized by a rapid increase in the population of the country—of the urban population in particular—and by an accelerated increase in the production and export of meat, cereals, wool, and other products of agriculture and cattle raising. This was an age during which numerous townships were founded—some destined to become service centers for the new agricultural areas, others to become capital cities of the new territories recently incorporated into the economy of the country, and yet others to become ports. Most of these cities were connected to the rapidly expanding railway network.

La Plata, founded in 1883 to serve as the capital of the province of Buenos Aires, is undoubtedly the most interesting example. It is a unique example of a city designed in accordance with the town planning theories accepted at the time. This town is located $40\frac{1}{2}$ miles (65 kilometers) south of the city of Buenos Aires on a vast prairie which descends to a natural harbor at the mouth of the Río de la Plata. Its present population of about 350,000 spreads much beyond the original physical and administrative boundaries. In fact, because of their proximity and sprawl, the metropolitan areas of Buenos Aires and La Plata now form a single conurbation. The original design of La Plata, undoubtedly of French inspiration, is a chessboard forming a perfect $3\frac{3}{4}$-mile (6-kilometer) square (see illustration) which is intersected by two main diagonals and other minor diagonals. Its planner also tried to achieve monumental effects in the composition of some of the streets and the main square, which is flanked by the Gothic-style cathedral and the town hall. The plan provided for an extensive park to the north of the city which, together with some tree-lined boulevards, undoubtedly represent the most outstanding urban features of the town.

The French cultural influence was important up to the First World War and is clearly discernible from the residential architecture of those years. It can also be recognized in the layout of numerous parks and in the design of monumental boulevards, diagonals, and perspectives.

Twentieth-century Planning

New Towns Numerous new towns have been constructed in Argentina from the beginning of the twentieth century in connection with the development of tourism and the exploitation of new natural resources; but the reader should not be led to believe that these new towns were planned and developed in accordance with concepts similar to those adopted in Britain since the Second World War or in Holland, the Soviet Union, and other countries. They are new towns because they were built in areas and locations where no urban settlements existed before, or because they represented a considerable expansion of small existing settlements. Moreover, irrespective of the form in which they developed, they have the physical layout, density characteristics, economic functions, and administration of a town.

Some of them were developed through the initiative of the national government or some state organization connected with the exploitation of perishable national resources. This applies to Río Turbio in the province

Plan of Buenos Aires in 1867.

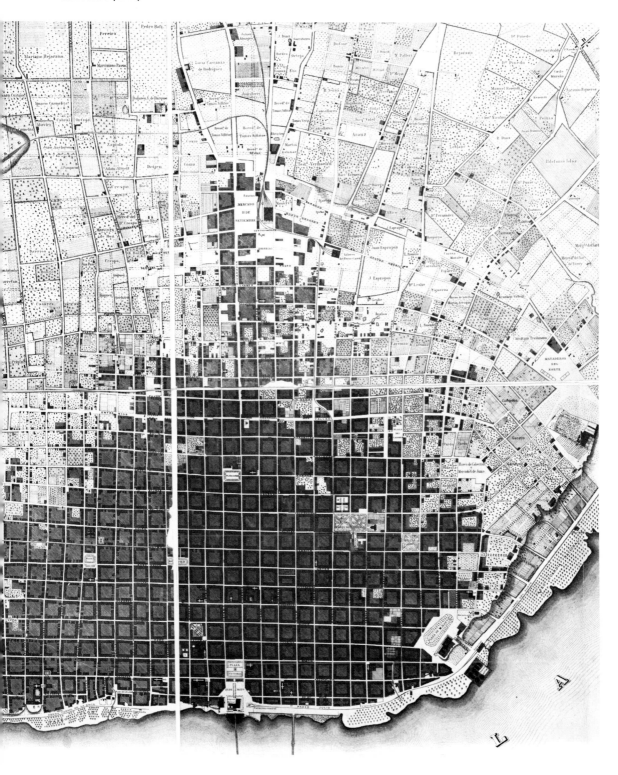

of Santa Cruz, which was built in connection with coal mining, and to Catriel in the La Pampa province, associated with the exploitation of petroleum. These are in fact encampments converted into towns, some with more diversified functions than others, the development of which was neither fully envisaged nor planned. The population of this type of center is generally below ten thousand.

Comodoro Rivadavia, on the central coast of Patagonia, did not exist at the beginning of this century. At present, its population amounts to some sixty thousand. The whole of this region was uninhabited until, in 1908, the discovery of petroleum attracted development. After the Second World War, the development of Comodoro Rivadavia proceeded more quickly, and some other industries have settled in its hinterland due to its function as a service center for other minor petroleum centers in the region.

The natural beauty of the southeastern coast of Buenos Aires and its potential as a tourist center came to be recognized after the end of the last century. A summer resort for upper-class citizens of Buenos Aires came into being, and later, during the 1930s and 1940s, the opening of a motorway converted this area into the most popular tourist center in the country. Mar del Plata is at present a metropolitan area with a population of some 250,000, the seat, *inter alia,* of the main fishing industries of the country, a naval base, the seat of a provincial university, and a service center for an extensive agricultural and cattle-raising area.

Neither Mar del Plata nor Comodoro Rivadavia were initially planned. The government surveyors and later the land speculators adopted the traditional chessboard layout without much regard for the topography and natural features of the site. When, in recent years, the local authorities intended in both cases to introduce urban development plans, the pressure of local interests and the lack of investment capital were factors too weighty to allow any substantial modification of the physical structure of these two cities and their growth trends.

Town Extensions Urban growth came about by physical expansion rather than by increasing density in districts already in existence (see illustration). The sprawl was haphazard, prompted by new and unnecessary parcelling out of good agricultural soil. The result has been the destruction of the natural landscape; continuous increases in the costs of constructing and operating the urban services; growing difficulties in providing access to the cities and, later, in providing traffic and transport facilities within the cities; the pollution of the air and rivers; and mixed and incompatible land use. These are among the evils which could have been foreseen. In the metropolitan areas with populations of 250,000 or less, these problems are not yet so evident, but very little is being done to meet them.

In Argentina, neither dwellings nor public services (water supply, drainage, electricity, and streets) nor social amenities (schools, welfare centers, parks, sports grounds, etc.) are provided on a scale that suffices to serve an urban population which is expected to increase at an average rate of more than 400,000 persons per annum between 1970 and 1985. On the other hand, the parcelling out of new areas has proliferated.

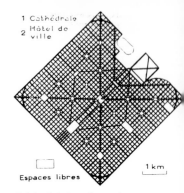

1 Cathédrale
2 Hôtel de ville

Espaces libres   1 km

Original design of La Plata forming a chessboard plan in a 3.72-mile (6-kilometer) square intersected by major and minor diagonals.

Aerial view of Buenos Aires showing haphazard city expansion, 1969.

The main problem in the urban areas is, however, the lack of adequate employment. According to the official unemployment statistics for 1969, the unemployment rate for the country as a whole has reached 4.5 percent of the labor force. The estimates for underemployment and seasonal employment are probably high and also probably show marked regional differences. This situation is reflected in an unnecessary expansion, in terms of efficient administration, of the tertiary sector and especially of the public administration and the retail trade. This results in high costs of operation, which have a bearing on the cost of living.

It is officially accepted that the national housing deficit (urban and rural) amounts to some 2.2 to 2.4 million dwelling units. This means that approximately one-third of the population lacks adequate dwellings. Although the country has one of the lowest population growth rates in the world, the number of dwellings constructed each year does not attain the level required to cope with the increase. There are no programs for rural housing. In the urban areas, the housing construction programs promoted by the national government and some provincial governments for low-income groups are totally inadequate. In these programs, the part played by the private sector is confined to that of the building contractors. The result, during the last decade, has been a sprawl of miserable huts which at present represent approximately 10 percent of all the dwelling units in the metropolitan area of Buenos Aires, approximately 15 percent of those in Rosário, and even higher percentages in some of the metropolitan areas and towns in the interior, especially those where a rapid sprawl has taken place recently. The shortcomings in public services are likewise considerable. In 1964, 32.9 percent of Argentina's urban population lacked running water, and 67.3 percent of all urban dwellings had no proper drainage facilities. Domestic electricity supplies and street lighting are considerably better.

Urban Renewal There is no legislation to promote urban renewal, nor are there special credits for this purpose. Only a few local authorities have

Aerial view of a city block near the center of Rosário showing low density and intense land use.

Aerial view of Almirante Brown Park—a modern urban development southwest of Buenos Aires.

initiated urban renewal schemes, but these are few in number, slow to progress because of insufficient financing, and they are inadequate in view of the deterioration of the oldest and worst-served districts. None of the local authorities have created a specialized agency or organization. The programming of urban renewal schemes has been the responsibility of the municipal planning offices.

Undoubtedly, the local authorities of the city of Buenos Aires have been among the most active. The area of the city of Buenos Aires amounts to 77 square miles (199.5 square kilometers) and includes large areas of publicly owned ground.

Almirante Brown Park. For this project, a special municipal office was created. The park is located in the southwestern part of the city on low-lying and unoccupied publicly owned ground, previously used as a refuse dump or partially invaded by slum shacks. The scheme covers an area of approximately 2,470 acres (1,000 hectares). Several multistory blocks have been and are being constructed for the housing of families with fairly low incomes. The scheme envisages the development of an extensive area of parks and the seat of a private university as well as various public and private sports institutes.

Catalinas Norte. This is an area of approximately 37 acres (15 hectares) northeast of the main commercial and office district of the city and closely linked with it. The site is bordered by the city's main railway station on the north and by one of the main boulevards on the west. Its position could not be better. The ground is publicly owned and was previously occupied by railway sheds. Private initiative finished in 1972 the construction of a great international hotel, and began the construction of various office blocks. The projects must comply with an overall plan for land use and building volumes prepared by the Municipal Planning Office.

Casa Amarilla. An area of approximately 100 acres (40 hectares), publicly owned, will be used for high-density housing for families with fairly low incomes. The land was previously occupied by railway sheds and marshaling yards.

Construction, which has not yet begun, is on the initiative of the cooperatives, trade unions, and nonprofit organizations. The grounds are located some 2 miles (3 kilometers) from the historic center of the city in the vicinity of lower- and middle-class districts.

There is an ambitious scheme for remodeling the center of the city of Buenos Aires. A team of private consultants has prepared the basic outline plan, which was submitted in early 1972. No decision has been taken about the implementation of the proposal.

BIBLIOGRAPHY
Economics
Alejandro Bunge, *Una Nueva Argentina,* Editorial Kraft, Buenos Aires, 1940; Miron Burgin, *Economic Aspects of Argentine Federalism,* Harvard University Press, Cambridge, Mass., 1946; Ricardo Ortiz, *Historia Económica de la Argentina, 1850–1930,* Editorial Raigal, Buenos Aires, 1955; H. S. Ferns, *Britain and Argentina in the Nineteenth Century,* London, 1960; Guido Di Tella and Manuel Zymelman, *Las Etapas del Desarrollo Económico Argentino,* Eudeba, Buenos Aires, 1967; Aldo Ferrer, *The Argentine Economy,* University of California Press, Berkeley, 1967; Gilbert W. Merx, "Political and Economic Change in Argentina from 1870 to 1966," unpublished Ph.D. dissertation, Department of Sociology, Yale University, New Haven, Conn., 1968.

Geography
Francisco de Aparicio, and Horacio A. Difrieri (eds.), *La Argentina, Summa de Geografía,* Editorial Peuser, Buenos Aires, 1958–1963.

Sociology
Carl C. Taylor, *Rural Life in Argentine,* Baton Rouge, La., 1948; José Luis Romero, *A History of Argentine Political Thought,* Stanford University Press, Palo Alto, Calif., 1963; Torcuato Di Tella, Gino Germani, and Jorge Graciarena, *Argentina, Sociedad de Masas,* Eudeba, Buenos Aires, 1965; Cesar Vapñarsky, *La población urbana Argentina,* Editorial del Instituto Di Tella, Buenos Aires, 1969.

History
James Scobie, *Argentina: A City and a Nation,* Oxford University Press, New York, 1964, *Revolution on the Pampas,* University of Texas Press, Austin, Texas, 1964; Roberto Cortes Conde and Ezequiel Gallo, *La formación de la Argentina Moderna,* Editorial Paidós, Buenos Aires, 1967; J. E. Hardoy and L. A. Romero, *La Ciudad Argentina: Documentos para una historia urbana,* Editorial del Instituto Di Tella, Buenos Aires; Tulio Halperin, *De la revolucion de la independencia a la confederación rosista* and *La democracia de masas,* Editorial Paidós, Buenos Aires, 1972; H. Gorostegui de Torres, *la organizacion social,* Editorial Paidós, Buenos Aires, 1972.

Urban and Regional Studies
Consejo Federal de Inversiones, *Bases para una política Nacional de Vivienda,* Buenos Aires, 1964; Raul O. Basaldúa, *El Control y regulación del uso de la tierra en el planeamiento urbano,* Buenos Aires, 1965; Consejo Federal de Inversiones, Instituto Di Tella, *Relevamiento de estructura regional de la economía argentina,* Buenos Aires, 1965; Cesar Vapñarsky, *Rank-Size Distribution of Cities in Argentina,* Cornell University Press, Ithaca, N.Y., 1966; A. B. Rofman et al., *Metodología para el planeamiento de la provincia De Río Negro,* Editorial del Insitituto Di Tella, Buenos Aires, 1968; Oscar Yujnousky et al., *Dessarrollo Regional del Sudeste de la Provincia*

de Buenos Aires, 1968 and 1970; J. Hardoy and C. Tobar (eds.), *La urbanización en América Latina,* Ediciones del Instituto Di Tella, Buenos Aires, 1969; J. Hardoy, *las ciudades en América Latina,* Editorial Paidós, Buenos Aires, 1972; J. L. Coraggio, *Centralizacion y concentracion en la configuracion espacial Argentina,* CONADE; Buenos Aires, 1971.

Journals
Desarrollo Económico
Revista Latinoamericana de Sociología
Revista de la Sociedad Interamericana de Planificación
Summa

—JORGE E. HARDOY

ARISTOTLE (384–322 B.C.)   Greek philosopher, born in the city of Stageiros in Chalkidice, and died in Chalkis at the age of 62. During his lifetime he was tutored by Plato; he trained a scientific team composed of his followers in Assos of Myssia and Mytilene of Lesbos; he was responsible for the education of Alexander the Great; and he established his renowned school of philosophy (the Peripatetike) in Athens. His teaching and writing embraced practically all fields of human knowledge: metaphysics, logic, ethics, rhetoric, poetry, politics, and the so-called "applied sciences"—physics, phytology, botany, medicine, astronomy, and meteorology. He is justly considered as the precursor of European science.

He differed from his teacher Plato in that his thought was more realistic and his method more empirical. He, too, like Plato, remained attached to the city-state, but his proposals for the ideal city attempted to combine theoretical demands with practical needs. The principles for the foundation and nature of the Aristotelian city-state can be found in the seventh book of his *Politics* (especially in part 1330 a and b), where the four basic conditions are stated: health, security and defense, a normal political (administrative and economic) life, and, finally, aesthetic appearance.

On the basis of Hippocrates' conditions for health, the city must be exposed to east or even to north winds; and if it does not have copious springs of drinking water, it must preserve rainwater in reservoirs. At the same time the form and location of the city must, according to Aristotle, serve the political and military life. In order to be secure from attack, both by land and by sea, and also to ensure the proper functioning of import and export trade, Aristotle proposed a site for the city that would be neither very far from nor very close to the sea. In other words, he specified a city that would have its own separate seaport.

Aristotle saw the acropolis as being directly related to the oligarchic political system; whereas—in his view—the use of plains areas was connected with democracy. He claimed that an aristocratic government, on the other hand, would prefer scattered settlements with isolated castles.

Aristotle accepted the Hippodamian system for the internal arrangement of the city, but for security reasons he modified it by mixing it with another type of city planning. The agora was placed at the foot of the acropolis and surrounded by the public buildings, the sanctuaries, and the residences of the highest magistrates. The commercial agora, however, was transferred to the outskirts of the city, though it was nonetheless on the main arteries of transportation. The city was divided into district sections, one for the priests, administrators, and warriors and one for the craftsmen, tradesmen, and farmers. The residences for the lesser administrators (city guards, market watchmen, foresters) were also located on the outskirts of the city.

BIBLIOGRAPHY: R. Martin, *L'Urbanisme dans la Grèce Antique*, Paris, 1956, pp. 21–24.

—DEM. MARONITIS

ARTESIAN WELL (*See* WATER SUPPLY.)

ASIA, SOUTHEAST, DEVELOPING COUNTRIES Southeast Asia extends over an area of 1,544,400 square miles (4 million square kilometers) with a population of over 250 million people. It covers 10 countries of varying sizes (see Table 1), some as small as Singapore, with only 2 million people, and others as big as Burma, with 25 million people. All these countries can be considered to be in the developing stage, and many have emerged as new states only recently. The area suffers from political instability, which may radically change the political configuration of the whole region.

In spite of the differences in the social, cultural, and economic structure of these countries, in the field of town and country planning they face similar problems. They all have high population growth rates, high urbanization trends, concentration of population in a few urban centers, unfavorable rural-urban ratios, low-level industrial growth, and heavy dependence on agriculture.

TABLE 1

Countries	Date of census	Area, square kilometers (square miles)	Estimated 1966 population, thousands
Burma	5/3/41*	678,033 (261,588)	25,246
Cambodia	17/4/62	181,035 (69,898)	6,320
Laos	. . .	236,800 (91,428)	2,700
Vietnam (North and South)	1/3/60	329,556 (127,241)	36,043
Indonesia	31/10/61	1,491,564 (575,744)	107,000
Malaysia	14/6/60 17/6/57	332,634 (128,397)	9,711
Thailand	25/4/60	514,000 (198,404)	31,508
Phillippines	15/2/60	300,000 (115,800)	33,477
Singapore	17/6/57	581 (224)	1,914
Total		4,064,203 (1,568,724)	253,919

*Latest census held in August 1964. Report not yet available.
SOURCE: *Demographic Year Book*, United Nations, 1966.

While the world population was growing at a rate of 1.9 percent per annum, population in these countries showed growth rates varying from 2 to 3 percent. The annual population growth rate of urban centers has ranged between 4 and 6 percent, and in some cases it has risen to 10 percent (see Table 2). In spite of the large population of 250 million, there are only 49 cities with 100,000 or more people and 8 cities with a million or more. Urban population is thus concentrated in a few major centers. Thailand is unique in that it has only one major urban agglomeration; namely, Bangkok and Thonburi.

TABLE 2 *Percentage of Urban Population and Total Population and Rate of Growth of Important Urban Centers in Southeast Asia*

Country	Year of estimate	Percentage of urban population	Name of important city	Population	Percentage growth rate	Annual growth rate, percent	Period of growth
Malaysia	1957	42.7	Kuala Lumpur	316,230	80.1	8	1947–1957
Thailand	1960	11.8	Bangkok*	1,608,305	47.5	5.9	1955–1963
Philippines	1956	35.3	Manila	1,356,000	37.8	2.2	1948–1965
Singapore	1960	62.6	Singapore	1,913.500	181.6	9.6	1947–1966
Burma	1931	10.4	Rangoon	821,800	64.21	4.0	1941–1957
Indonesia	1962	14.8	Djakarta	2,906,533	55.8	9.3	1955–1961
			Soerabaja	1,007,945	8.5	1.4	1955–1961
			Bandoeng	972,566	16.7	2.8	1955–1961
Vietnam	1960	9.5	Saigon	1,485,300	−21.8	−2.18	1955–1965
(South and North)			Hanoi	643,576	NA	NA	1960
Cambodia	1958	12.8	Pnompenh*	403,500	0.9	0.18	1957–1962
Laos			Vientiane	162,297	62.3	10.38	1956–1962

*Urban agglomerations.
SOURCE: *Demographic Year Book*, United Nations, 1960, 1962, and 1966.

A further feature of the urban centers in these countries is that not all of them were evolved by the internal needs of the land; that is, many important centers came into being as points of external contact for trade, transport, and defense. As such, many cities do not bear an organic relationship to the surrounding country and its economy. Their rapid development has often been caused more by external factors than by internal prosperity.

While the high rate of urbanization and the economic and social changes brought about by industrialization have presented development opportunities, they have also posed numerous problems, most of them concentrated in the urban areas. Town and country planning efforts in the postwar decades were concerned initially with resolving the housing shortage, resettling the refugees, and promoting industrial development through the establishment of industrial estates. Early planning at its best aimed to provide an overall framework for housing programs. In the sixties, when more settled conditions prevailed, efforts were made to tackle the problems of slum clearance and redevelopment and to prepare comprehensive development plans for the bigger cities. Examples of notable planning efforts can be found in

Southeast Asia.

Singapore, Manila, Djakarta, and Bangkok. The governments of these countries have attempted to provide, progressively, the basic legal, administrative, and financial tools for planning and plan implementation. In some of the countries attempts have been made with some success, to relate national economic planning to physical planning and to make urban and regional development programs an integral part of national development plans. A brief account of these efforts follows, with details of some of the plans.

Administration   Under the *Malaysian* constitution, town and country planning is on the concurrent list (except for the capital of Kuala Lumpur). Thus the responsibilities of town planning are shared between the federal government and state governments.

The federal Department of Town and Country Planning prepares the national plan embodying state and regional plans. It also undertakes the planning of Kuala Lumpur to take care of its rapid growth through the creation of new towns, suburban centers, and regional centers.

The Department of Town and Country Planning also undertakes the preparation of general development plans for all towns in Malaysia, the revision of existing town plans, and the location and preparation of plans for industrial estates. It also offers advice on landscape preservation and advises, assists, and prepares development plans for the Ministry of National and Rural Development with the purpose of strengthening the agricultural base and encouraging the dispersal of population.

At the state level, planning is done by state planning offices which provide technical advice on all matters concerning town and country planning to their respective state governments. They prepare layout and subdivision plans and exercise land-use and development control according to national and state policies.

At the local level, only four municipalities have their own town planners; the remainder are helped by the state town planning offices and the federal Department of Town and Country Planning.

In *Indonesia,* the National Planning Council coordinates the programs evolved by various ministries and secures their approval by the legislature. The provincial governments are responsible for coordinating local plans within the framework of national plans. In principle, town planning is initiated and performed at the local levels—subject to the approval of the provincial government. Such plans, except for public projects which involve national funds, are implemented at the local level. Physical planning at the national level is vested in the Ministry of Public Works.

Since 1945, town and regional planning has steadily increased. On the island of Java, 42 town plans have been prepared: 20 in Sumatra, 13 in Kalimantan, and 15 for the other islands. Regional plans for metropolitan Djakarta, the province of Bali, and for north Sumatra have also been prepared.

Because of the shortage of personnel, most town plans are prepared by the Central Planning Unit of the Directorate General of Planning and Construction at the instance of the local bodies; regional planning activities are also similarly organized.

Like many other developing countries in this region, the *Phillippines* are faced with basic disorder in development, with squatters living in public parks, subdividers selling plots without providing roads and utilities, prices soaring, towns and villages sprawled along the highways, and roads clogged with calesas, buses, and jeepneys. Town and city plans appear to have unrealistic goals that are unrelated to the capacities of implementing local agencies. Finance, staffing, legislation, organization, and administration have been lacking. There is no feedback, and linkages between the National Planning Commission and local governments have remained elementary.

In 1966, the Institute of Planning in the University of the Philippines was formally established, assisted by a United Nations Special Fund Project providing for:

1. The establishment of a firm basis for both national and metropolitan region framework plans, the latter to be in the four main growth areas of the Philippines

2. Supplementary to the above, the setting up of programs for demonstration action plans within the framework

3. Corollary to the above, the initiation and establishment of centers of consultation, research, and study, including in-service training programs in the growth areas

The setting up of the institute and its active role has been a major breakthrough from the uncertain and anomalous situation which the Philippines have been facing in the postwar period.

The Planning Department in *Singapore,* which is responsible for the administration of the planning ordinance, was originally set up in 1960 as a part of the Chief Minister's office. It was subsequently transferred to the Ministry of National Development (July 1964). This was done in order to secure more effective coordination by bringing within the purview of one ministry the executive and administrative functions of physical planning, public housing, and public works.

The department's main responsibilities are:

1. The maintenance of the Singapore Master Plan, including the quinquennial revision of the plan and the making of additions and alterations at any time that may be considered expedient

2. The preparation of detailed plans in interpretation of the broad proposals shown in the master plan

3. The granting of planning permissions for the use and development of land in accordance with the provisions of the master plan

4. The carrying out of enforcement actions on violations of the planning ordinance

5. The determination and collection of development charges on the granting of planning permissions in respect of certain types of development

The chief planner in the exercise of his powers under the planning ordinance is required to act in consultation with two committees known as the Master Plan Committee and the Development Control Committee:

■ The Master Plan Committee comprises seven members, all of whom are public officials under the chairmanship of the chief planner. The main function of the committee is to ensure that any action by public bodies and government departments relating to proposals for the development of land are coordinated and harmonized with the planned development of the state. The committee is also consulted on all proposals for changes to the master plan.

■ The Development Control Committee also comprises seven members under the chairmanship of the chief planner. Five of these are public officials and two are representatives of professional organizations. The committee meets fortnightly to deal with applications for development and subdivision of land from private developers.

In dealing with development proposals, the two committees must take into account the provisions of the master plan. Appeals against the decision of the competent authority may be made to the Minister for National Development.

In *Thailand,* the Department of Town Planning, established in 1962, has the responsibility of preparing plans and advising the various departments and local bodies in regard to their development programs and schemes. Its staff includes a number of city planners trained abroad and employees transferred from Bangkok and Thonburi municipalities and the Public Works Department. The Department of Town Planning is organized into eight functional and area units and is active in finding solutions to the problems of Bangkok.

Legislation   In *Indonesia,* the town planning ordinance which came into force immediately after the war provided for the town council to adopt a plan by order and detailed plans by regulations, in accordance with the standards prescribed by the government. The ordinance also provided for the review of the plan every 10 years. The Agrarian Act of 1960 introduced provisions for making planning schemes for all land, both urban and rural, and this helped to bring all land under the control of the local authorities.

New provisions have been introduced, requiring local authorities to prepare town and city plans and also enabling the setting up of joint committees of several local authorities to prepare schemes. Further, new formulations for expropriation and compensation are being evolved. The Housing Act of 1964 and Rent Regulation Act of 1963, which had attempted to freeze rents at the prewar level, have not been workable, and a revision of the Housing and Rent Control Act is being made so as to meet present-day needs.

In *Malaysia,* there are a number of legislative measures, 21 to be precise, which govern different aspects of urban and regional development. For instance, the Town Board Enactment provides for the preparation, approval, and administration of town plans by the local planning authorities; the National Land Code makes provision for the categories of land use in any alienated land; the Housing Trust Ordinance provides for housing development; and the Federal Industrial Development Authority is responsible for the promotion and coordination of industrial development in the country. There is not yet a single comprehensive law relating these various aspects of development to an overall framework.

In the *Philippines,* a comprehensive bill to provide for the establishment of a national planning, housing, and finance authority was introduced in 1964, but it did not make much progress. In 1965 an act was passed authorizing the setting up of the Institute of Planning at the University of the Philippines, which, in addition, outlined a national policy: (1) to strengthen and assist the government and local government agencies and other private organizations in the study and solution of their development problems; (2) to facilitate the realization of development proposals at all levels; (3) to improve human settlements and their environment by the integration of social and economic, physical and administrative situations; (4) to produce comprehensive and coordinated development studies and plans; and (5) to make available a group of capable professional urban and regional planners to assist in the achievement of the policy.

Planning legislation in *Singapore* starts with the Planning Ordinance of 1959, which provided the basis for the preparation of the Singapore master plan. Under the ordinance, rules have been formulated defining details of provisions to be made in the master plan and giving them the necessary legality in enforcement of development control and execution of schemes.

In *Thailand,* the history of legislation for city planning is one of long delay and inaction. The 1952 City and Town Planning Act was approved by the national government but has not been enforced. The act was found to be defective. In 1960, a draft city and regional planning bill was prepared and has been discussed at length, but it has yet to be adopted and enforced.

Education   Planning education facilities are in very short supply in the southeast Asian countries. Except for two schools, one at Bandoeng and the other, the newly established Institute of Planning, in the Philippines, there are no facilities for training town and country planners. Most countries send their students to the United Kingdom, the United States, or Australia to become qualified in town planning. For a population of over 250 million, the training facilities are woefully inadequate.

In 1970 there were only 31 planners in *Malaysia* as against an estimated requirement of 158, and by 1985 the country will probably require 266 planners. There is some dependence on planners trained either in the United Kingdom or Australia. The only course of training in town and country planning is one offered at the Technical College, Kuala Lumpur, which is of 3 years duration. A diploma is awarded. Diploma holders are recruited as technical cadets in the federal and state town planning departments as useful ancillaries to professional planners.

In *Indonesia,* the one school of planning is in the Institute of Technology at Bandoeng. It offers a 5-year program, the last 2 years being devoted to specialization in town planning. The present output is low, about five annually, but the intake—forty per year—is high, and the output is expected to increase sharply in the near future.

Most planners work in government offices. Consultants get some planning work, but the surveys preliminary to a plan are mostly handled by universities or "part-time" planners. Practically all the planners are either architects or engineers.

The Institute of Planning set up in *Manila* in 1966 has been expanding its facilities for training urban and regional planners and is an important addition to the training facilities available.

Examples of Town Planning   In Malaysia, several town planning schemes and plans for new towns have been prepared. Kuala Lumpur, the federal capital, has a draft master plan prepared in 1966 which incorporates a land-use zoning plan, a population-density control plan, and a detailed plan for the central commercial area. Earlier, in 1965, a comprehensive redevelopment scheme of a part of the central area was prepared, and this is being implemented.

Jason Bay and Shah Alam are planned as new towns. The former is a tourist resort, and the latter, which will become the capital of Selangor, is planned as a self-contained town. The construction work on Shah Alam has recently started.

Among the eight regional plans which have been prepared, that of the Penang region initiated in 1959 is comprehensive in its scope and, while recognizing constraints, relates economic objectives to physical resources. This plan is expected to spearhead the development of the Penang region. The other plans are the Johore Tenggara regional plan, Malacca master plan, Jengka triangle regional plan, southeast Pahang regional plan, Traggam regional economic plan, and Klang Valley regional schemes. Each of these regional plans has a different emphasis depending upon the resources and the role which the particular region will play in the overall national development.

Manila Plan (Philippines)   The Burnham plan for Manila, prepared in 1905, had generally adopted the principles of planning applied at the Chicago World's Fair and in Washington D.C. Major aspects emphasized were the civic center, wide radial boulevards, landscaped parks, and pleasant vistas. The main features of the Manila plan were the development of the waterfront and the location of park and parkways in such a way as to provide adequate recreational opportunities for all parts of the city, the establishment of a satisfactory street system, the location of building sites for various activities, the development of waterways for transportation, and the provision of summer resorts.

At the beginning the prospects of implementing the plan were bright, but actually nothing much was accomplished and, during the Second World War, a great portion of Manila was razed to the ground. This opportunity could have been seized to implement the Burnham plan. However, the decision to locate the capital outside Manila, in Quezon City, resulted in lack of effective control over the developments in Manila. This, coupled with the demand for commercial and speculative enterprises and the influx of refugees, caused Manila to grow in a haphazard way. The proposed ocean boulevard has become a traffic artery; shaded drives along the Pasig River have become commercial thoroughfares; the parks system has dwindled down and the areas intended for it have been used for other purposes. The Pasig River has become a traffic artery and the canals have become open sewers. New proposals leading to a comprehensive plan for the development of metropolitan Manila are being put into operation by the Institute of Planning.

Plan for Bangkok   Bangkok lies in the heart of Thailand. The characteristics and the significance of metropolitan Bangkok's form and quality reflect the natural features of the central plains of Thailand, which cover one-quarter of Thailand's total land area, with the Chao Pharaya River flowing in the center. The plain is a very flat area with an elevation at its northern extremity of only 144 feet (44 meters) above sea level. This plain slopes down to the Gulf of Thailand at a grade of approximately 0.01 percent. The city of Bangkok itself is only about 1 yard (1 meter) above the mean sea level and is located about 35 miles (56 kilometers) upstream from the Gulf of Siam on the Chao River.

Daniel H. Burnham's plan for Manila, 1905.

Bangkok's topography is characterized by low and level ground laced by a network of canals which are used for transportation and to drain off rainwater as well as sewage. Tidal actions of the river pose problems for the city because they cause continual silting of the river bed and saline encroachment from the sea during the dry season.

Bangkok became the national capital of Thailand in 1782 A.D. when King Rama I, of the present Charkri Dynasty, moved from Thonburi to Bangkok for political and military reasons. It was originally built with fortified walls and rings of city moats. Within the walls, the streets, paths, and waterways were laid out, with vertical accents provided by Buddhist temples, pagodas, gates, and forts. The inner citadel was the religious center of the country and the seat of government.

Modern Bangkok dates from 1868, when the city had grown outside the walls with a population estimated at 600,000. A communication network was developed with emphasis on road and rail systems. By 1957, Bangkok had grown to a metropolis enveloping Thonburi, a sister city on the opposite side of the river, into one great metropolitan area. The population had risen to 1,500,000, with an urbanized area extending over 24,000 acres (9,720 hectares).

The Bangkok metropolitan area now (1972) extends over 116 square miles (300 square kilometers). The urbanized or built-up area has increased to 30,000 acres (12,150 hectares), of which 30 percent has been developed over the past decade. The population has grown to 2.5 million, with 2 million living in Bangkok proper and the rest in Thonburi.

The Bangkok metropolitan area, by western standards, is a compact urban area, but it seems rather loose and sprawling to the Asian, with only small sections in the central area which are dense with buildings and inhabitants. There is little in the way of urban fringe except for strings of village settlements along the major canals and roads. Internal organization generally lacks the zonal character that is typical of many western cities. There is relatively little formal separation of industrial, commercial, and residential uses. Urban ghettos, as such, do not exist outside of the Sampeng business district, where most of the Chinese live in a cluster.

The alluvial deposits of fine silt, many hundred feet in depth, give the city poor foundation conditions and make the development of high-rise buildings expensive. Some modern buildings up to 10 stories in height (mainly offices and hotels) have recently been built in the newly developed business centers. Much of the outlying area is covered by small wooden houses in rice fields. This area also contains modern roads and housing influenced by western styles, as well as commercial structures and shops. The resulting landscape is neither rural nor urban.

In the past, practically all transportation was by foot and water and therefore parallel to the waterfront. Here also, a dense urban development laced by footpaths has taken shape, resulting in heavy traffic congestion in these areas. Traffic is a serious problem, particularly in the older parts of the city. With the advent of the automobile, the metropolitan area has extended to the north and southeast along the major roads leading out of the city. The city represents a great V with each leg having smaller lanes radiating from it. Unfortunately, there are no connecting roads between these principal roads, so that all the through traffic must reach the apex of V and hence continue from there into the central area of the city.

Bangkok has grown as an unplanned city. The first effort to create a better city through planning dates back only 30 years. The 30-year master plan for the Greater Bangkok area prepared in 1961 has as its major planning objective the future development of the city into an essentially compact, economical, and viable city of the kingdom. The plan aims at a more functional and healthy pattern of development for residential, commercial, industrial, and other areas, providing adequate facilities and eliminating the present conflict and disharmony. The plan also envisages controlled growth of population in the Greater Bangkok metropolitan area. Bangkok's target population is set to reach 4.5 million people in the next 30 years.

Along with these basic objectives, several interrelated programs have been proposed with a view to stopping the flow of migrants to the capital city from the outlying areas. These programs include planned construction of public services and facilities outside the Bangkok metropolitan area, an expanded program of decentralized economic development, and building of the essential infrastructure for industrial and agricultural development.

The master plan also provides for a sixfold expansion of urban areas in order to lessen the density in the old areas and to provide for future population increase. The anticipated urban growth will be distributed through six compact, finger-shaped development areas which follow the existing major transportation routes and spread out radially from the central area and along the river. This type of growth is believed to be most economical since the development can be made more intense along the axes leaving the areas between the "fingers" to be developed into open spaces to preserve viability and provide amenities for the whole area.

The circulation system of the metropolitan area has also been planned to encourage the development of decentralization of the central city by the creation of subcenters and the dispersal of industrial activities. The system proposed is an integrated loop and arterial roads to provide easy movement of the traffic within and around the metropolitan area and to strengthen connections to other urban centers. Expansion of the railway network, commercial airport, and seaport facilities have also been proposed.

The plan, though not yet officially approved, has had remarkable impact on the city planning in the country. In the capital city, various individual projects proposed in the plan are being implemented and initiated; for instance, the urban superhighway providing a link with the north, the transfer of rail freight operations to outlying areas in order to lessen the traffic problem in the city core, and, finally, slum clearance projects.

Singapore The island of Singapore has a population of more than 2 million people, about half of whom live in the urban area. It is a partly planned town, especially the area near the waterfront, while the rest is unplanned and rather haphazard. Before the existence of the improvement trust, control over development was largely exercised by means of building bylaws and through the imagination and initiative—or lack of it—of landowners and estate developers. After the Second World War the need to reconstruct the city together with the desire to clear the slums and rebuild them led to the establishment of a number of study groups to survey industrial development, building materials, housing needs, transportation and parking, and, most important, the rapidly growing population of the city and the island. A diagnostic survey team analyzed the data and prepared a master plan in consultation with all the agencies concerned, and this was formally approved in 1958.

This plan provided for a population of 2 million persons on the island by 1972—forecast by the census. It is estimated that the 2 million population was reached in 1967, and a reassessment of the population prospects is urgently needed.

The principles on which the plan was prepared were the limitation of the growth of Singapore city, the provision of a greenbelt surrounding the city, the construction of new towns away from the city, and the expansion of established villages in what are at present rural areas.

The object of the greenbelt was to limit the extent of the city, to provide land for open space as near as possible to those areas in greatest need of it, to provide land for agricultural and intensive market gardening use near to the consumer markets, and to provide for institutions such as hospitals, which need extensive open space.

Beyond the greenbelt it was proposed to develop a number of new towns. These are practical means of providing economic concentrations of accommodation and of services for the expanding population without adding to the problems of the main city.

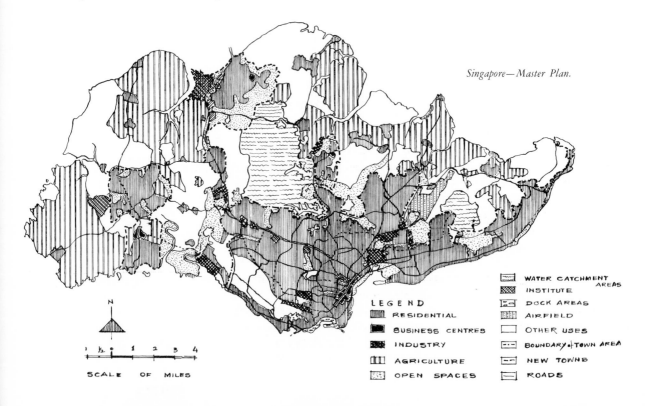

Singapore—Master Plan.

LEGEND

- RESIDENTIAL
- BUSINESS CENTRES
- INDUSTRY
- AGRICULTURE
- OPEN SPACES

- WATER CATCHMENT AREAS
- INSTITUTE
- DOCK AREAS
- AIRFIELD
- OTHER USES
- BOUNDARY OF TOWN AREA
- NEW TOWNS
- ROADS

N

SCALE OF MILES

Woodlands, a new town on the north of the island, is sited on the best building land still available and is on the main road and the railway line going northward from the city. There is also sea access to part of the site from the Straits of Johore.

The new town at Bulim on the west side of the Jurong River does not have the same positive advantages as Woodlands, but it does have first-class deepwater sea access. This may well prove an attraction for many industries which are at present finding difficulty with the already congested development on the main Singapore waterfront. A considerable area of good building land is available, and, by the construction of a new road across the Jurong River, easy access can be provided to the main dock and warehouse areas of Singapore.

The new town site for Yio Chu Kang has first-class road communications to the center and the eastern side of the city. Development of this new town is already well in hand under private enterprise and it is expected that, given reasonable conditions, the proposals of the master plan will be realized through private-sector efforts also. This new town, although it has some industries of its own, will to some extent be used for dormitory purposes in view of its close proximity to the existing urban area.

A number of villages in Singapore Island serve populations of up to 18,000 to 20,000. It is intended to rationalize the development of these villages and to provide for appropriate community facilities. In this way a considerable increase in the rural and semirural population can be catered to.

The master plan is now being revised to provide for the increased population. The revision follows the principles of the present plan described above, and it is the intention to retain as much land for agricultural and rural uses as possible despite increased demands for building sites. In general, population densities will be raised and some marginal areas will be incorporated into the town area. The satellite towns will be considerably increased in size and density and the number of villages to be expanded will be increased. In this way it will be possible to provide for 3 million people within the framework of the main proposals already approved by the government while retaining the existing community facilities.

Saigon   The urban situation in Vietnam reflects the conditions of a country weighted with a great past and torn by the ravages of more than twenty years of war and internal disturbance. Saigon (1,641,000 population), the capital of South Vietnam, has ten times the population of Danang (162,000). Saigon is a city which was formerly developed as a colony of France. It is not a city that has grown from the spontaneous evolution of the country itself. The city had only 500,000 inhabitants before 1945. It had grown to 1,641,000 by 1966, and it carries an urban population burden of 700,000 from the adjoining province. The high population growth is essentially due to refugee influx which has created the attendant problems of housing shortage and lack of sanitary services. High population densities such as 1,729 per acre (700 per hectare) exist in parts of the city where the built-up area is 95 percent of the total area.

The future plan of the city calls for the decentralization of the industrial and university functions and a parkway to surround the city, joining the auto routes of Bienhoa and Mytho. A second greenbelt about 4 miles (7 kilometers) north will join the university area, near Bienhoa highway (Tang nhoh Phu) and the Mytho Highway (An Lac), by passing the city north of Tansonnhut airport.

The Khan Hoi docks are overused. Their 3,300 yards (3,000 meters) of piers are insufficient for shipping and many vessels have to be anchored in the Saigon River. A new port is being constructed at Thanh My Tay, near the Bienhoa highway bridge, to relieve the old port of the heavy load.

BIBLIOGRAPHY: Eastern Regional Organisation for Planning and Housing, Earoph News & Notes, September 1959; German Foundation for Developing Countries, Country Reports Seminar, "Regional and physical planning within the framework of overall development," Berlin, 1968; ECAFE, Survey of facilities for education, training, and research in urban and regional planning within the ECAFE Region, Singapore, Thailand, and Republic of Viet-Nam, 1968–1969; Institute of Planning, University of the Philippines, "The Philippine Experience," Symposium on Regional Development Policy and Planning, September 1969; A. Harimen, Regional Housing Centre, Bandung, "A brief statement of town planning development in Indonesia," April 1970; Town Planning and Housing Departments, unpublished reports from the Government of Malaysia and Philippines, April 1970.

—C. S. CHANDRASEKHARA

ASSYRIAN PLANNING (*See* ANCIENT PLANNING, MESOPOTAMIA.)

ATHLETIC FIELDS (*See* RECREATION, PROVISION FOR.)

AUSTRALIA, the Commonwealth of Australia has a federal system of government and is comprised of the states of New South Wales, Queensland, South Australia, Tasmania, Victoria, and Western Australia, together with the Northern Territory and the Australian Capital Territory. Australia is also responsible for the government of the Territory of Papua and New Guinea. The population of Australia at the 1961 census was 10.5 million, which increased to 12.7 million in 1971. Between 1958 and 1971, the annual rate of increase (percent) was 2.0, compared to 1.5 percent in the United States of America and the U.S.S.R. and 0.7 percent in the United Kingdom.

Legislation and Administration Each state in the Commonwealth has its own system for the administration of town planning, and the only common feature is that the responsible minister in each state is the minister for local government.

The Northern Territory is under the jurisdiction of the Minister for the Interior. The Minister for Works is responsible for the organization of planning in Papua and New Guinea.

The planning, construction, and development of the city of Canberra, in the Australian Capital Territory which covers 910 square miles (approximately 2,300 square kilometers) and lies within the state of New South Wales, is the responsibility of the Federal Minister for the Interior. The planning work is done by a National Capital Development Commission established by act of parliament in 1957.

In each of the six states there is a clearly defined metropolitan region, and

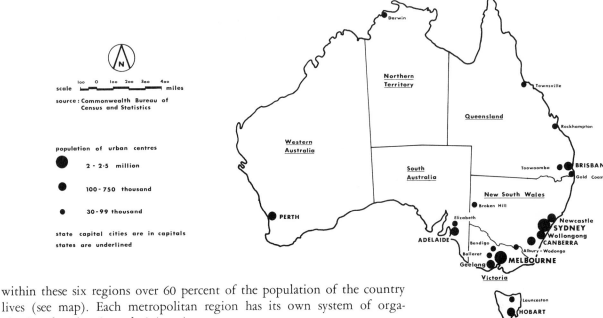

Map of Australia showing principal urban centers.

within these six regions over 60 percent of the population of the country lives (see map). Each metropolitan region has its own system of organization for planning administration.

There are varying but similar provisions in each state for the exhibition and submission of planning schemes, for the control of interim development, and for the public exhibition of plans and the hearing of objections to them. Most planning schemes in Australia have a land-use zoning map accompanied by an ordinance which sets out those developments that may be permitted, those that may be allowed with specified conditions, those over which authorities exercise discretion, and those which are specifically prohibited in the particular zones set out on the planning scheme map.

In all states there are similar but not identical procedures for the hearing of appeals against the decisions of authorities on applications for permission to develop land.

An outline of the planning system in each state and territory is set out below.

New South Wales   A State Planning Authority is responsible for advising the minister for local government on all matters relating to planning. The authority, which has 12 members, includes representatives from the state departments of main roads, transport, and local government; representatives from local government bodies in the state; one representative from the professional institutes representing architecture, surveying, or town planning; and one representative with special knowledge of public utility undertakings, rating, loans, and grants. The State Planning Authority has the power to acquire and develop land, but its primary function is to promote and coordinate town and country planning and to secure the orderly use and development of land. The bulk of its work is related to the Sydney metropolitan region, which covers an area of 4,785 square miles (approximately 12,300 square kilometers) and contains some $2\frac{3}{4}$ million people, amounting to almost 63 percent of the total population of the state. In 1968 the authority had a technical staff of 135, of whom about 50 were fully trained or in course of training as professional planners.

The State Planning Authority was created in 1963, succeeding the Cumberland County Council which had already prepared a planning scheme, approved in 1951, for the metropolitan region. The State Planning Authority began the preparation of a revised plan for the metropolitan region in 1967, using the Cumberland County Council Plan as a basis, and completed it in 1968.

Any municipal council or group of councils in the state of New South Wales may resolve to prepare a planning scheme or may be directed so to do by the State Planning Authority with the approval of the minister.

Queensland   The Local Government Department is responsible for advising the state minister for local government on matters relating to planning. The Brisbane City Council, composed of a lord mayor, who is popularly elected, and 28 ward aldermen, is responsible for the administration and enforcement of planning in the city of Brisbane, which covers an area of 375 square miles (approximately 970 square kilometers) and contains approximately 657,000 people or about 40 percent of the total population of the state. Within the city council organization there is a Department of Planning and Building which, in 1968, had a technical staff of 10, of whom 5 were qualified professional planners or in course of training. A land-use zoning plan was completed in 1961 and gazetted in 1965. In the rest of the state any local authority may resolve to prepare a planning scheme for all or any part of its area.

South Australia   A State Planning Authority is responsible for advising the minister for local government. The authority is composed of a director, who is a qualified planner and chairman of the authority, and 10 members drawn from state government departments, local government, and organizations with interests in land and development. The authority is charged with the responsibility of promoting and coordinating regional and town planning and of securing an orderly and economic development and use of land within the state. Its duties include the examination, preparation, and reporting on development plans prepared within the state. In 1968, the State Planning Office had a technical staff of 44, of whom 13 were either fully qualified professional planners or in course of training.

The Adelaide metropolitan region covers an area of 715 square miles and in 1968 contained a population of approximately 765,000, amounting to 70 percent of the total population of the state. A plan for the region was commenced in 1957, completed in 1962, and gazetted in 1963. The 1966–1967 Planning and Development Act established statutory procedures for the preparation of development plans either by the State Planning Authority or a local authority and for planning regulations by the State Planning Authority or a local authority.

Tasmania   A town planning commissioner is responsible to the minister for local government for matters relating to town and country planning.

He is also responsible for advising local authorities on the content of planning schemes, for examining and reporting on schemes, and for hearing and determining appeals against the decisions of councils relating to development applications.

The Hobart metropolitan region covers an area of 481 square miles which, in 1968, contained some 135,000 persons amounting to about 36 percent of the total population of the state. The Southern Metropolitan Master Planning Authority, which is composed of 12 members representing local authorities, is responsible for advisory outline planning in the Hobart region. The staff of the authority in 1968 amounted to five, of whom one was a fully qualified professional planner with one other in training. The plan of the authority is intended to act as a guide and policy base for individual municipalities in the region. Any local authority, group of authorities, or master planning authority may resolve, or be required by the town planning commissioner with the approval of the minister, to prepare a planning scheme.

Victoria The Town and Country Planning Board, established under the Town and Country Planning Act of 1944, is responsible for advising the minister for local government on all matters relating to town planning in the state. It is composed of a chairman and a deputy chairman, who are full-time officers, and two part-time members. The board is responsible for the examination of all planning schemes prepared in the state and in 1969 had a staff of 39, of whom 13 were qualified planners or in course of training.

Under the Town and Country Planning Amendment Act, 1968, provision was made for the preparation of statements of planning policy to serve as a basis for planning in various parts of the state. These statements may be prepared by the Town and Country Planning Board on their own initiative or at the request of the minister or by the State Planning Council. This is an advisory body of 12 members composed of the chairman of the Town and Country Planning Board, who acts as chairman of the council, and 11 other members from state departments and the Melbourne and Metropolitan Board of Works.

The Melbourne metropolitan region covers 1,995 square miles and in 1968 contained some 2,201,000 persons or a little more than 68 percent of the total population of the state.

The responsibility for the preparation of a planning scheme for this area rests with the Melbourne and Metropolitan Board of Works, an organization established in 1890 and consisting of representatives of local authorities in the region. The board was given limited planning powers in 1949 which have since been extended, and it is now the regional planning authority for metropolitan Melbourne.

A plan for a smaller, statutorily defined metropolitan area was commenced by the Melbourne and Metropolitan Board of Works in 1949 and finally gazetted in May 1968. Since that time the plan has been subjected to various amendments and is under constant review. The Planning and Highways

Branch of the Melbourne and Metropolitan Board of Works in 1968 had a total staff of 178, of whom 89 were engaged in planning. Of these, 14 were professional planners with some 6 others in training.

Outside the area of metropolitan Melbourne, municipalities or groups of them represented on regional planning authorities may prepare planning schemes. Regional planning authorities have been established in those parts of the state where development is anticipated.

Western Australia The town planning commissioner is the planning adviser to the minister for local government. Town planning procedures are prescribed for three types of planning schemes: metropolitan region scheme, local authority (within the metropolitan region) town planning schemes, and local authority (outside the metropolitan region) town planning schemes.

The Perth metropolitan region covers 2,072 square miles (approximately 5,250 square kilometers) and in 1968 contained 558,300 persons amounting to almost 67 percent of the total population of the state.

The responsible authority for planning in the Perth metropolitan region is the Metropolitan Region Planning Authority. In 1968 the Town Planning Department of the authority had a total technical staff of 54, of whom 25 were either fully qualified professional planners or in training.

Planning on a metropolitan regional basis began in Perth in 1953 with the appointment of a town planning commissioner assisted by a consultant and supported by a staff of 19. A plan for the metropolitan region of Perth and Fremantle was completed in 1962 and gazetted in 1963. The Metropolitan Region Planning Authority is composed of a chairman and 11 members representing state departments, local government, and the West Australian Chamber of Manufactures and is required to formulate, promulgate, administer, and review the metropolitan region scheme.

Australian Capital Territory Following the federation of the six Australian states in 1900, Canberra was established as the seat of federal government in 1908.

The planning, construction, and development of Canberra was the responsibility of a series of advisory committees until 1957, when the National Capital Development Commission was established. The commission, which is responsible to the Minister for the Interior, is comprised of a commissioner and two associate commissioners, and they are assisted in their work by a National Capital Planning Committee consisting of two town planners, two architects, and two engineers, each nominated by the appropriate professional institutes, and two others having special knowledge and experience in artistic or cultural matters. The commission in 1969 employed a staff of 205 including 15 town planners, 17 architects, 13 engineers, and 3 landscape architects.

Canberra in 1968 had a population in excess of 120,000 which is expected to increase to 265,000 by 1980.

Northern Territory In 1962 the Commonwealth Public Service Board on the recommendation of the Department of Territories created the position of town planning officer for the Northern Territory within the Lands branch of the Administration. Town planning legislation for the territory was enacted in 1964 and involved the setting up of a Town Planning Board which advises the administrator of the territory. The board consists of a chairman and 3 members, including a local member representing local government who changes with the location of the towns being planned. The town planning officer is based in Darwin, which in 1969 had a population of 32,000 and which is expected to grow to 50,000 by 1975. A statutory planning scheme has been prepared for Darwin and schemes for the smaller settlements in the territory are in course of preparation.

Development of Darwin and other towns has followed the Canberra pattern where Commonwealth ownership of the land allows complete development by the state to take place and control of land use to be effected by leasehold control. Leases in the Northern Territory, however, are perpetual and may be converted to freehold.

Darwin planning differs from that of other Northern Territory settlements in that the Commonwealth ownership is limited geographically to a distance of some 10 miles east from the city center, beyond which is freehold land.

Long-range planning of an urban area suitable to house a population of 200,000 is to be undertaken by consultants.

Planning for the many aboriginal settlements is being undertaken in "town" form so that the process of integration may continue to the point where these areas may become open towns.

Territory of Papua-New Guinea The territory is divided into four regions for planning purposes each under the control of a regional planning officer with a senior planner and a research officer coordinating their activities.

Development plans for a 10 to 20 year period are being prepared for all the major towns, with local plans filling in the detail. The administration purchases most land used for urban development and lets it on a 99-year-lease system.

Professional Practice Most town planning in Australia is done by planning authorities and statutory authorities at federal, state, and local government levels, but there are increasing opportunities for private practice as the awareness of the need for planning grows. Many architectural, engineering, and surveying groups are adding planners to their teams to cope with the demand. The title "town planner" is not a protected one in Australia, but in the state of New South Wales a person may not prepare a statutory planning scheme unless he has a certificate awarded after examination and issued by the Department of Local Government. In Australia a qualification in town planning has traditionally been combined with another skill in the allied professions of engineering, architecture, or surveying, or with qualifications in urban geography, sociology, or economics. This pattern still persists, but the basic profession of town planning has recently been strengthened by the establishment of undergraduate degree courses at the University of Melbourne in Victoria, the University of New South Wales, and the University of Queensland.

The growth of metropolitan regions in Australia and a general increase in urbanization is posing more complicated problems for the profession to solve, and the demand for skilled planners at all levels is growing.

Education and Training There are now facilities for training in town and country planning in each of the capital cities of the six states in Australia. The table opposite sets out the various institutions involved, the courses provided, and the student numbers in each school in 1969.

Institutions The Australian Planning Institute (Executive Secretary, Box 292 P.O., Canberra City, A.C.T. 2601) is the professional institute to which most qualified planners in Australia belong. It was created in 1951 by an amalgamation of a number of institutes previously established on a state basis. The governing body of the institute is a federal council composed of members elected by the state divisions. The institute has a code of professional conduct and a minimum scale of charges for the guidance of its members. It conducts its own intermediate and final examination, completion of which gives academic status for corporate membership. It has also granted recognition to certain courses in a number of universities and institutions of technology and accepts their examinations as equivalent to its final examination. The institute admits corporate members of the Town Planning Institute, London to its ranks and has, from time to time, recognised other overseas planning qualifications. A period of one to two years of approved practical experience, according to circumstances, is required after the completion of the examinations of the institute or a recognised examination, before corporate membership is granted. The institute membership in 1968 was 985, composed of 8 honorary fellows, 142 fellows, 328 members, 271 affiliates, and 236 students, of which all but the latter two grades are corporate members.

The Journal of the Australian Planning Institute is a high-quality production and is produced quarterly. In 1969 it had a circulation of about 2,200. Honorary corresponding editors are stationed in Burma, Fiji, Hong Kong, India, Indonesia, Iran, Malaysia, Mauritius, New Zealand, Pakistan, Philippines, Singapore, South Africa, South Korea, and Thailand.

The educational institutions involved in the teaching of town and regional planning are listed under "Education and Training."

There is an Australian Institute of Urban Studies (P.O. Box 809, Canberra City, A.C.T. 2601) which was founded in 1967. The Institute has a director and a Board of Management of 20 members selected from a Council of 100 members. Its primary function is to support, stimulate, sponsor, and undertake research into urban affairs in Australia. For this purpose it has sought and obtained funds from federal and state governments, from statutory bodies, and from private sources. Groups have been established in each state to stimulate the work of the institute.

A Planning Research Centre has been established in the University of Sydney and works under the direction of the professor in charge of the Department of Town and Country Planning.

FORMAL COURSES AND RECOGNIZED EXAMINATIONS IN TOWN PLANNING

Institution	Course	Duration	Admission requirements	Enrollments, 1969
University of Sydney	Diploma	3 years part time	Appropriate professional qualifications or recognized degree	70
	Master's degree	2 years full time	Recognized degree	31
University of New South Wales	Bachelor's degree	5 years full time and part time	Matriculation	17
University of Queensland	Master's degree	2 years full time or 4 years part time	Recognized degree	18
Queensland Institute of Technology	Introductory course	1 year part time	Matriculation	
	Diploma	3 years part time	Appropriate professional qualifications, introductory course or recognized degree	17
University of Adelaide	Master's degree	1 year full time and 1 year part time or 3 years part time	Recognized degree	15
South Australian Institute of Technology	Diploma	3 years part time	Appropriate professional qualification or recognized degree	17
	Technical certificate	3 years full time or 6 years part time	School leaving certificate (Intermediate standard only)	35
Hobart Technical College	Diploma	3 years part time	Appropriate professional qualification or recognized degree	8
University of Melbourne	Diploma	2 years full time or 3 years part time	Appropriate professional qualification or recognized degree	129
	Bachelor's degree	4 years full time	Matriculation	40
	Master's degree	1 year full time or 2 years part time	Bachelor of Town and Regional Planning or recognized degree plus Diploma of Town and Regional Planning or equivalent	5
Western Australian Institute of Technology	Associateship	3 years full time	Matriculation	54
	Diploma	5 years part time	(Intermediate standard only)	

The extent to which propaganda in favor of town and country planning occurs in Australia varies from state to state. Victoria and South Australia, for example, both have active town and country planning associations modelled on the British organization of the same name. The Victorian Town and Country Planning Association (639 Burwood Road, Hawthorn, Victoria, 3122) is particularly active and organizes meetings, seminars, and discussion groups at frequent intervals in addition to publishing a journal

Geographical and Climatic Conditions   The Commonwealth of Australia lies between 10 and 44 degrees south latitude and covers an area of almost 3 million square miles, only slightly less than the United States of America excluding Alaska, more than half as large again as Europe excluding the U.S.S.R., and about twenty-five times that of Great Britain and Ireland. Two million square miles of the country are, however, arid or semiarid. The remaining million square miles, comprising a discontinuous coastal fringe averaging 40 to 50 miles (65 to 80 kilometers) in width, is more or less well watered. It is within this fringe and particularly in the southern and eastern sections that the bulk of the population lives.

Bordering the coastal plain is the Great Dividing Range which extends from the north of Queensland to the south of New South Wales. At this point one branch sweeps westward toward the boundary of Victoria and South Australia and the other, the main branch, terminates in the island state of Tasmania. The mountains of Australia are relatively low; the highest peak, Mount Kosciusko in New South Wales, being only about 7,300 feet (2,220 meters) high. Three-quarters of the land mass of Australia lies between the 600- and 1,500-foot (180- to 450-meter) contours in the form of a huge plateau, constituting the most distinctive feature of the continent, to which most of the peculiarities of the Australian climate can be ascribed.

The country experiences a wide variation in climate ranging from tropical conditions in the north to cool, temperate weather in the south and southeast. Rainfall varies from 177 inches (4,500 millimeters) per year on parts of the east coast of Queensland to 4 to 6 inches (100 to 150 millimeters) per year around lake Eyre in South Australia. For varying periods, from late autumn in May to early spring in September, snow usually covers the ground in the Australian Alps above a level of 4,500 to 5,000 feet (approximately 1,300 to 1,500 meters) where, in both Victoria and New South Wales, ski resorts have been established. Floods occur on the shorter streams flowing from the Great Dividing Range into the Pacific Ocean along the seaboard of Queensland and New South Wales. These are sometimes particularly destructive on the densely populated coast of New South Wales.

Traditions of Planning to the End of the Nineteenth Century   The nineteenth century was a period of rapid growth of cities in Australia, and the business philosophy of laissez-faire is reflected in their present form and layout.

The first town plan in Australia was prepared for the city of Sydney in 1792 by Governor Philip. It was largely disregarded in the initial stages of growth, but a plan prepared in 1807 by James Meehan, a government surveyor working under Governor Bligh, provided the base for the present city center.

Perth was founded in Western Australia in 1829 and its first plan was published in 1838. Melbourne was established in Victoria on the shores of Port Philip Bay in 1835, and its original gridiron plan, prepared by Robert Hoddle, forms the basis for the present central area. Adelaide was founded in South Australia in 1836 and planned by Colonel Light with a continuous belt of parkland around the central-city gridiron layout. The roads planned by Colonel Light for the development of the rural hinterland also followed a gridiron pattern and still form the basis of the framework on which metropolitan Adelaide has grown. In the major cities and rural towns of Australia the rectangular pattern of layout predominates. Many plans of this type were prepared in London during the nineteenth century for use by the colonial government without regard for local topography.

Twentieth Century It was only at the beginning of the twentieth century that Australians became concerned about the form and sanitary conditions of their cities. At about the turn of the century moves began in Victoria, Queensland, and Western Australia to create authorities to plan the metropolitan areas in those states, but about 25 years passed before effective organizations were created. In 1909, following an attack of bubonic plague in Sydney, New South Wales, a Royal Commission was set up to study possible improvements to the city and its suburbs.

In 1914 the South Australian government employed an experienced town planner to advise on the planning of the metropolitan region of Adelaide.

The 1909 Housing and Town Planning Act in the United Kingdom stimulated interest in town planning, and this was fostered by the British Garden Cities and Town Planning Association which in 1914 organized a lecture tour in Australia. Since then the growth of planning legislation in all states and territories has been steady and assured.

Canberra is undoubtedly the foremost example of city planning in Australia. It is the national capital and a city of the twentieth century. The initial plan was the work of Walter Burley Griffin, a Chicago architect who won an international competition for the design of Canberra in 1912.

The site was a valley set between three hills, and the topography suggested the design. In this grand formal landscape, Parliament and the Administration were placed in the valley on the southern shore of an artificial lake to be formed by damming the Molonglo River.

The central area was contained within a large formal triangle reminiscent of the axis and radiating avenues of Washington and Versailles. Outside the formal center there were residential districts planned on garden city lines.

Griffin's plan suffered many vicissitudes before it was given statutory recognition in 1925.

Griffin had planned a city for 25,000 people which could be extended to accommodate 75,000. At the end of World War II in 1945, only 13,000 people lived in it.

In the next decade, growth accelerated, and by the mid-1950s it became evident to the government that some means of coordinating development would be necessary.

As a result of recommendations made by a Senate Select Committee which investigated the growth and potential of the city, the National Capital Development Commission was established in 1957 and began operations in 1958. One of the commission's first tasks was to review the planning of Canberra and to formulate policies for its expansion. An outline of the plans for the period 1964 to 1980 has been published in *The Future Canberra*. (Angus and Robertson). The plan provided for the completion of the original city of 75,000 and its extension by building a series of urban districts or satellite cities around it. The first of these, Belconnen, to the northwest of Canberra city, is now taking shape. (See diagrammatic layout.) The aim of the plan was to build a series of cities which would not become unwieldy in size nor be choked by the traffic which concentrated on only one or two employment centers. The traffic, instead, was dispersed by locating many centers of employment throughout the city.

The city districts are built in adjoining valleys with the intervening hilltops and ridges preserved in their natural state. This gives almost every resident of Canberra a view of tree-clad hills.

Plan of Belconnen, a satellite city of Canberra

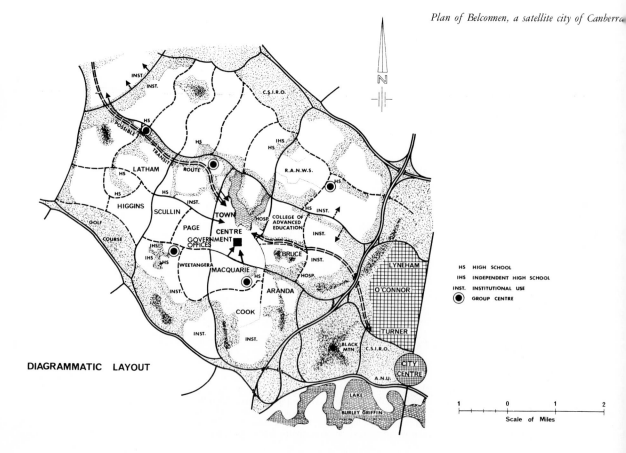

DIAGRAMMATIC LAYOUT

HS   HIGH SCHOOL
IHS   INDEPENDENT HIGH SCHOOL
INST.   INSTITUTIONAL USE
⊙   GROUP CENTRE

Scale of Miles

The population of each district is intended to be about 100,000. Although physically separated, the districts are strongly linked to the original city and to each other.

Each has its own district center and its own employment centers. Research and similar institutions are located between the districts to provide additional local job opportunities.

A traffic system has been designed to give free movement and easy access to all employment centers.

Each district is comprised of suburbs containing about 4,000 people and centering on a primary school and small shopping center. These are within walking distance of every house.

The larger shopping centers serve groups of three or four suburbs and a high school is provided for groups of about the same size.

In its plan, the commission defined the key areas of the city. These include the Parliamentary Triangle which is bisected by a $2\frac{1}{4}$-mile ($3\frac{2}{3}$-kilometer) land axis from Capitol Hill to Mount Ainslie; they also include the Australian National University campus, the city center, Lake Burley Griffin's foreshores, Anzac Park, the Russell Offices, and the Royal Military College.

The central point of these areas is the Parliamentary Triangle in which new houses of Parliament are eventually to be built. The land axis from Capital Hill to Mount Ainslie is defined by the construction of Anzac Parade, a ceremonial processional way, and by the construction of two portal buildings at its southwestern end.

At the northeastern corner of the Parliamentary Triangle there is an office complex. This is one of the many employment centers scattered throughout the city in an effort to decentralize employment and to prevent heavy concentrations of traffic in any area.

At the third corner of the Parliamentary Triangle is the hexagonal-shaped city center containing the main shops, commercial offices, cultural, recreational, and civic institutions. It is the largest employment area in Canberra, covering 300 acres, (121 hectares) and it will need parking facilities for 12,000 vechicles by 1980.

One of the main virtues of the Canberra plan is the effort that has been made to set the city into the local landscape.

The commission's present outline plan provides for a city of 250,000 accommodated in a series of clearly defined districts, each of which is relatively self-contained but which jointly support the central and other special areas in the city complex.

Transport for the foreseeable future will be based on the use of motor vehicles traveling on a network of major roads located within the parkland system, providing easy cross-city movement with a minimum of interference to the other activities within the area. Reservations have been included in the plan for a rapid-transit network should the need for this arise in the future. The general character of the city of Canberra is indicated in the accompanying illustrations.

Walter Burley Griffen's plan for Canberra.

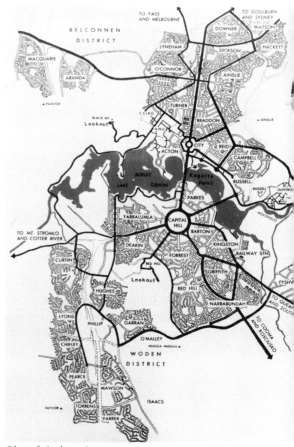

Plan of Canberra in 1970.

Aerial view of Canberra showing the Parliamentary Triangle.

Aerial view of Canberra seen from a height of 20,000 feet. Lake Burley Griffen was completed in 1964. It is 7 miles (11.26 kilometers) long and has 22 miles (35.39 kilometers) of foreshore. Other basic features of Griffen's original design can be clearly seen—the Government Triangle formed by Commonwealth (left) and King's Avenue (right) radiating northward from Capital Hill. Commonwealth Avenue terminates at Civic Centre, the main commercial and shopping area in the city, and King's Avenue stretches to the foot of Russell Hill and the Defence Secretariat. Federal Parliament House is situated within the triangle on the south side of the lake, surrounded by Government offices. The processional Anzac Parade can be seen running along Griffen's land axis to the National War Memorial nestling at the bottom of Mount Ainslie. (Photograph: W. Pedersen.)

Another notable example of twentieth-century planning in Australia is the town of Elizabeth which was established some 17 miles (30 kilometers) north of Adelaide in November 1955. It is a garden city in the English tradition, based on the neighborhood unit. It is designed to accommodate upwards of 70,000 people and has a town center on a site of 80 acres, (32 hectares), with pedestrian and vehicular separation and ample parking. Two large industrial areas totaling more than 900 acres (360 hectares) are being developed.

The major cities of Australia are reaching a stage in their growth when problems of urban renewal are beginning to be felt, but as yet no large-scale schemes have been undertaken.

BIBLIOGRAPHY: *Australia in Facts and Figures,* News and Information Bureau, Department of the Interior, Canberra A.C.T.; *Official Year Book of the Commonwealth of Australia,* no. 54, 1968, Commonwealth Bureau of Census and Statistics, Canberra; *Australia, Its Resources and Development,* National Bank of Australasia Ltd.; Brown and Sherrard, *Town and Country Planning,* Melbourne University Press; R. Kuzelka, *The Tiger's Back,* Planning Research Centre, Sydney University.

—F. W. LEDGAR

LEFT: *Aerial view of the New Town of Elizabeth.*   RIGHT: *Aerial view of the New Town of Elizabeth, with industrial area in foreground. Philip Highway is the central avenue running from the traffic circle. To the left is the General Motors Holden Ply Ltd. group of buildings, and among those to the right are Schrader-Scovill Co. Ply Ltd., Crane Copper & Aluminum Ply Ltd., and Brooks Containers SA Ply Ltd.*

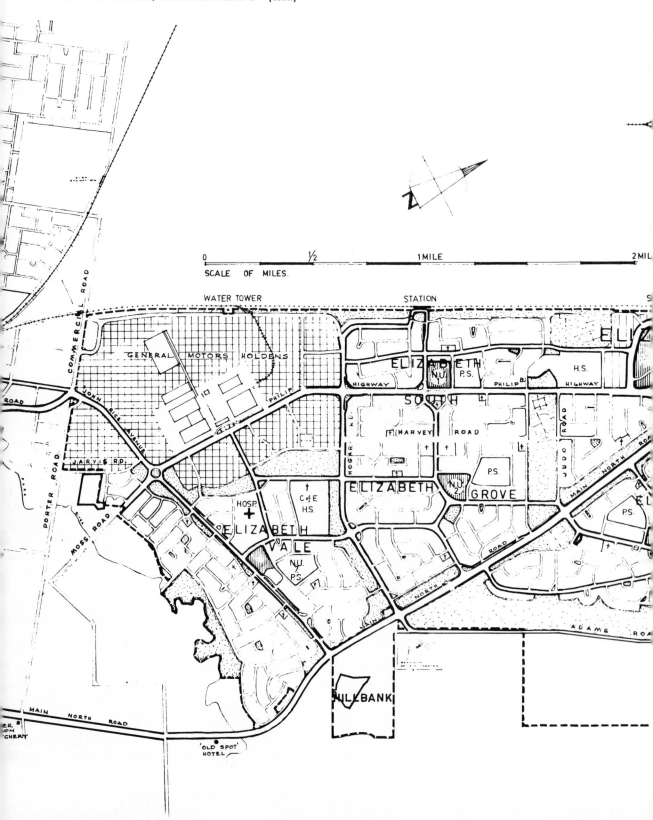

0   ½   1 MILE   2 MIL
SCALE   OF   MILES.

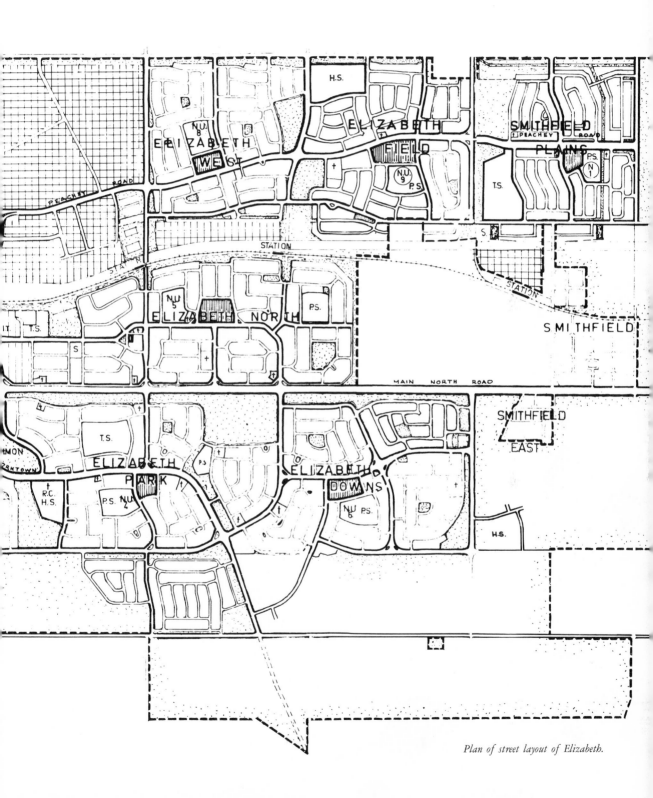

Plan of street layout of Elizabeth.

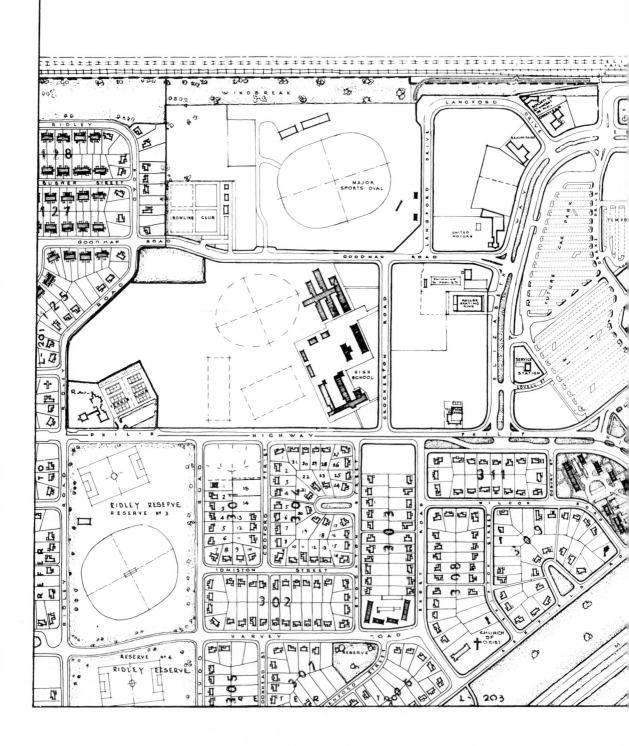

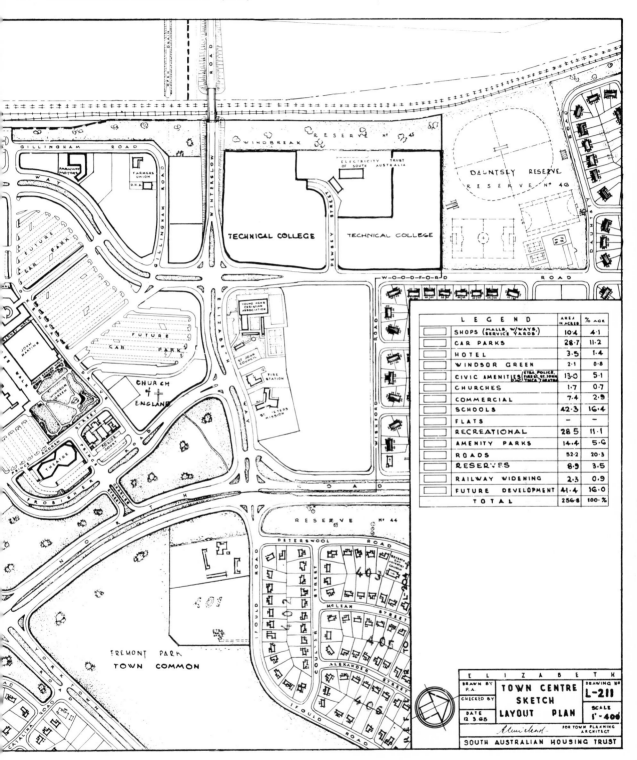

LEGEND		AREA IN ACRES	% AGE
	SHOPS (MALLS, W/WAYS, SERVICE YARDS)	10·4	4·1
	CAR PARKS	28·7	11·2
	HOTEL	3·5	1·4
	WINDSOR GREEN	2·1	0·8
	CIVIC AMENITIES (ETSA, POLICE, FIRE ST, ST JOHN D.C., YMCA, THEATRE)	13·0	5·1
	CHURCHES	1·7	0·7
	COMMERCIAL	7·4	2·9
	SCHOOLS	42·3	16·4
	FLATS	—	—
	RECREATIONAL	28·5	11·1
	AMENITY PARKS	14·4	5·6
	ROADS	52·2	20·3
	RESERVES	8·9	3·5
	RAILWAY WIDENING	2·3	0·9
	FUTURE DEVELOPMENT	41·4	16·0
	TOTAL	256·8	100·%

ELIZABETH			
DRAWN BY P.A.	TOWN CENTRE SKETCH LAYOUT PLAN	DRAWING Nº L-211	
CHECKED BY			
DATE 12·3·68		SCALE 1"-400	
		FOR TOWN PLANNING ARCHITECT	
SOUTH AUSTRALIAN HOUSING TRUST			

Elizabeth. Plan of town center.

AUSTRIA

Legislation   The legal and practical situation of town planning in Austria can be best seen against the background of the political structure of the country. Austria is a federal republic consisting of nine states (*Länder*), which are divided into 83 administrative districts. The smallest administrative unit is the municipality (community). Local authorities, states, and federal government act autonomously, each state and local authority having legislative and executive powers.

According to the Republic's constitutional provisions, the federal government has legislative and executive powers expressly provided in the constitution. It is responsible for the construction and operation of federal highways, railways, and airports. Moreover, its jurisdiction covers forestry, waterways, mining, and the preservation of historic buildings.

Legislation in the fields of planning and building comes within the competence of the states, which are also responsible for the planning of secondary roads and of nature reserves. Six of the states have their own planning laws entitling them to set up development programs either for certain regions or for the whole of their territory. These programs serve towns and local authorities as guiding schemes for their zoning and town plans.

Local authorities are entitled—in some of the provinces they are even obliged—to set up town and zoning plans in order to meet development trends. Vienna itself has a special position, being both a state and a municipality.

Legally, the competences of the regional authorities are clearly defined. Priority has to be given to federal planning, while planning and development programs of the states are binding for the municipalities. Experience shows, however, that reasonable physical planning can only be effected by a voluntary effort toward cooperation between federal government, states, and municipalities. According to the provisions of the constitution, the local authorities, in spite of existing federal and planning schemes, enjoy considerable autonomy in the fields of zoning and town planning. In Austria, as in many other countries, planning activities started in the municipalities; and they, especially the larger cities, have been pioneers in this respect. The first modern planning law was enacted in Vienna in 1929.

It was not until 1966 that the federal government started to consider questions of physical planning and not until 1971 that an organization on a national level was set up (see below).

The states themselves have only to a small extent taken advantage of the legal provisions for physical planning programs. Regional development plans exist only in a few small areas of the country, and comprehensive planning takes place mainly in the towns and cities.

Hitherto planning in Austria has generally been regarded as the task of controlling land use by restrictive regulations. Also, finance is a powerful instrument in the hands of the planning authorities. While the federal government does not have much direct planning power, it does administer the large proportion of the national budget which influences spatial development. The construction of motorways, highways, and railways; the financing of housing; and the subsidizing of agricultural and underdeveloped regions are measures of the greatest impact on the physical development of the country. Cities are affected by the financial policy of the federal government, for a considerable share of its revenue and a large proportion of its investment is devoted to the poor rural districts.

Administration In 1971 an Austrian Planning Conference was established, presided over by the federal chancellor. This conference unites all members of the cabinet (federal government) interested in planning, the governors of the nine states, and representatives of the local authorities. It has a twofold task: to draw up a Planning Concept for Austria, and to coordinate all activities, aiming at physical planning and development at national, regional, and local levels.

All states have their own planning departments. In two of them the planning offices are under the direction of the governor, in four they are under the directorate for building affairs, and two states have combined their planning office with the statistical office. In Vienna an alderman for planning affairs is responsible for this area.

The smaller communities are not in a position to employ a permanent expert staff. In smaller towns the city architect or the head of the building department is responsible for planning matters, while the larger cities have their own planning departments.

In Vienna, the only city in Austria with more than a million inhabitants, the planning administration is highly specialized. The alderman for planning affairs (his position within the city government can be compared to that of a minister in the federal government) is responsible for two planning departments, one dealing with physical planning, including transportation planning, the other with the economic development of the city. They cooperate in establishing urban cost-benefit analyses. Moreover, the alderman is the head of the department for statistics and of the surveyor's office. The common task of these four departments is to determine a development program for the city. The realization of this comprehensive program entails the working out of different plans: town and zoning plans, transportation studies, economic development plans, and medium-term investment programs.

Professional Practice In Austria, the scope of activities in physical planning in general and city planning in particular is still rather small. Planning offices will be established by the federal government only in the next few years, while the offices in the states are but slowly expanding. In some of the states the state government provides an office responsible for the supervision and coordination of municipal concepts and zoning, and sometimes prepares plans for the municipalities.

In Austria only a small number of architects have specialized in the preparation of plans for small communities which are not in a position to employ a permanent planner. Even the planning offices of the city administrations do not employ an adequate number of trained people. The training of experts (see below) has begun only in the last few years. Another difficulty arises because local authorities do not pay well enough. It is easier to raise funds for single projects than to employ a permanent expert staff. For their studies and projects, therefore, city planning offices increasingly approach research institutes, architects, and engineers.

Education and Training   Because there is no great demand for planning experts, physical planning and city planning in the technical universities of Vienna and Graz and in the academies for fine and applied arts in Vienna only ranks as one subject among the variety of other subjects included in the architect's curriculum. Lectures on planning are also held at the Vienna University for International Trade and at the University for Social and Economic Sciences in Linz. New legislation in the field of technical studies introduced in 1970 provides the opportunity of intensifying the training of planners and urbanists. In both technical universities there were only two big departments, for architecture and engineering respectively. According to the new program, planning and urbanism will be included in the second half of an architect's and engineer's studies as a main subject.

There are no provisions for postgraduate studies in Austria. Some organizations (see below) from time to time sponsor conferences dealing with questions of physical and city planning. Other training of experts is carried out in the several planning offices or in the offices of architects and engineers concerned with planning.

Institutions   Besides the planning offices of the federal ministries, the states, and the municipalities, a series of other institutions are concerned with questions of planning and research.

The Austrian Institute for Physical Planning (Österreichisehes Institut für Raumplanung) started its work in 1951 as a private working group. Now it is a semipublic body. It derives 75 percent of its income from the execution of orders on behalf of public offices—federal ministries, state governments, and the planning office of the city of Vienna—and the remainder from grants made by its sponsors. The work of the institute involves urban and regional research and planning.

The Austrian Association for Regional Planning and Applied Geography (Österreichische Gesellschaft für Raumforschung und Raumplanung) was established in 1954. Besides doing research work, the association publishes reports on physical and town planning and research and organizes lectures.

The Research Association for Housing, Construction and Planning, (Forschungsgesellschaft für Wohnen, Bauen und Plamen) founded in 1956, is engaged in fundamental and applied research. Current activity is focused upon the renewal of cities, market towns, and villages.

The Vienna Institute for Location Advice (Wiener Institut für Standortberatung) was established in 1963 by the city of Vienna and the Vienna Chamber of Commerce. Its activity chiefly relates to the determination and appraisal of location for all branches of industry. An institute of Urban Research (Institut für Stadtforschung) in Vienna was started in 1970.

Historic, Demographic, and Socioeconomic Background of Urbanization   The distribution of cities, towns, and villages in Austria is the result of a centuries-old historical development influenced by geographical conditions. The state capitals are Austria's most important cities. Vienna and Linz are situated on the Danube, Salzburg has developed at a river crossing the alpine border into the plain, Graz and Klagenfurt lie within basins in the alpine region, while Innsbruck and Bregenz are located in big alpine valleys.

More than four-fifths of the towns and villages of Austria were founded in the middle ages: only few have their origin in Celtic or Roman settlements. Hundreds of the medieval settlements perished because of their unfavorable geographical location. Those surviving showed a well-balanced settlement pattern at the time of the industrial revolution.

With the construction of railway networks and the increase of industrialization in the second half of the nineteenth century, cities began to grow rapidly. Those with a population from 10,000 to 250,000 increased their population in the period from the first modern census in 1869 until the last census before World War I in proportion to the country's whole population from 9.8 to 13.1 percent, while the proportion of communities with less than 5,000 inhabitants decreased from 65.5 to 49.5 percent. Vienna, as a capital of a great European power, increased its population in the same period from 900,000 to as much as 2.1 million.

With the fall of the Austro-Hungarian monarchy at the end of the First World War, the state territory was reduced to one-eighth and centuries-old economic bonds were broken. The trend of urban development drastically changed. Between the wars the population in urban regions decreased in proportion to the country's total. Vienna, robbed of its political role as capital of an empire encompassing 52 million people lost about 200,000 inhabitants by migration.

Nevertheless, the built-up areas of the cities continued to expand even in those hard times. As a response to unfavorable dwelling conditions in the tenement houses of the nineteenth century, the flight from the city to green areas in the suburbs continued in spite of the existing economic difficulties. The manor houses of the nobility and the prewar villas of the well-to-do were followed by one-family houses of lower-income groups. In addition, valuable building sites and recreation areas were lost, only to be occupied by "allotment gardens." The trend toward the establishment of such gardens had started before World War I; during the war their development was encouraged by the authorities because of the acute food shortage. In the postwar years, when authorities commanded little respect, uncontrolled settlements continued to spread. In the years of the world depression, so called "subsistence settlements" were created in order to provide for the unemployed. The idea was that the unemployed and their families should produce part of their means of subsistence by raising vegetables and small livestock on plots of about $\frac{1}{2}$ to $\frac{3}{4}$ acre (2,000 to 3,000 square meters).

Inflation and rent control stopped the flow of private capital into housing investments, while the average size of the households decreased considerably. The resulting housing shortage being especially bad in Vienna, the city government embarked on an ambitious public housing program.

In 1934, when parliamentary democracy terminated in Austria, this housing program was stopped.

During World War II, Austria's cities were spared significant damage until 1944. In the last year of the war, however, British and American bombers caused great destruction, above all in Vienna and other cities in the eastern part of the country.

Ten years later the scars of the catastrophe had disappeared almost completely. The reconstruction brought, however, no wholesale alteration in the former urban setup. In most cases it was faster and cheaper to reconstruct destroyed buildings than to build from scratch on a better site.

During the decade between the end of the war and the signature of the Austrian State Treaty in 1955, the same situation as that following World War I prevailed. As a result of war damage and also partly because of the influx of refugees and the exodus from the Russian occupation zone, the municipalities were confronted again with an acute housing shortage. Public housing was now acknowledged to be a national task. Most of the dwellings erected since the war have been financed or subsidized out of public funds. Among all public tasks, first priority was given to satisfying the demand for adequate housing. However, together with publicly financed housing projects, uncontrolled settlements again began to spread as during the years after World War I. This was the case mainly in those areas where the authority of Austrian public bodies was weakened by the occupying powers.

The prosperous economic development of Austria after the withdrawal of the four occupational forces, starting in 1955, was accompanied by a steady growth of the urban population. Between 1951 and 1971 population increased by 7 percent. The increase of the urban regions (towns with more than 20,000 inhabitants plus surrounding districts) was 9.5 percent; the increase in the urban regions except Vienna, however, amounted to 20 percent. Within the urban regions decentralization took place. The population within the administrative area of Vienna decreased by 0.6 percent, whereas the surrounding districts increased their population by 6.5 percent. The corresponding figures for the other urban regions are +15 percent (administrative areas) and +28.5 percent (surrounding districts).

It can be assumed that, by the end of this century, the absolute population increase will occur wholly in the urban regions and will include migration from the rural districts, meaning an increase of about 1.5 million people. Moreover, it can be assumed that this growth will be unevenly distributed, the smaller towns falling behind the population increase in medium and large towns (again except Vienna).

Without an effective national or regional planning framework, town planning is the sole responsibility of the cities, where it had started centuries ago.

Traditions of Planning to 1914   Medieval cities show a well-designed pattern in their street layout and the location of public buildings and private houses. The adaptation to local and topographical conditions is excellent. The necessity of fortification brought a clear demarcation between town and countryside. City extensions were accompanied by the extension of the

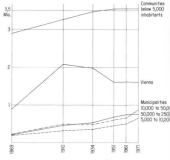

Austria. Urbanization since 1869.

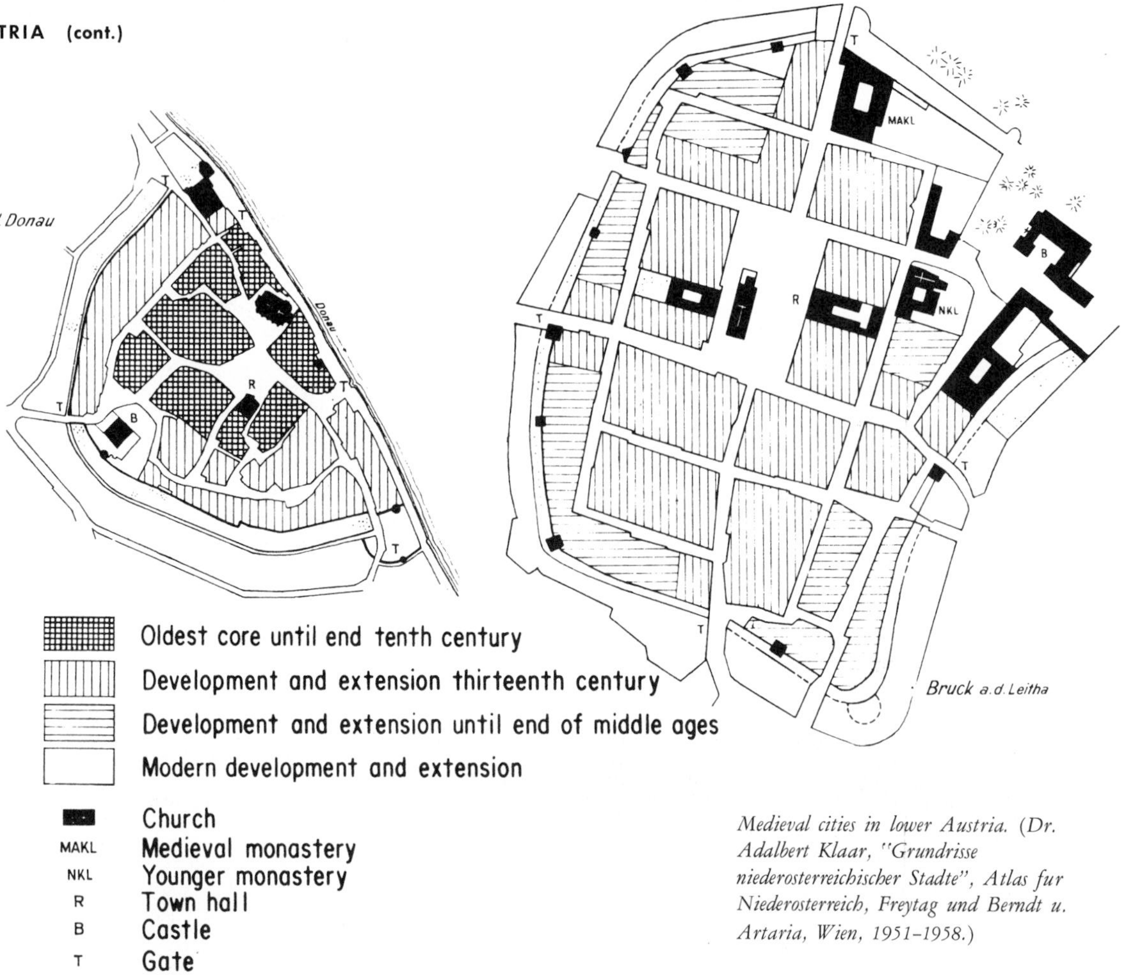

Ybbs a.d. Donau

Bruck a.d. Leitha

Oldest core until end tenth century

Development and extension thirteenth century

Development and extension until end of middle ages

Modern development and extension

■	Church
MAKL	Medieval monastery
NKL	Younger monastery
R	Town hall
B	Castle
T	Gate

Medieval cities in lower Austria. (Dr. Adalbert Klaar, "Grundrisse niederosterreichischer Stadte", Atlas fur Niederosterreich, Freytag und Berndt u. Artaria, Wien, 1951–1958.)

fortifications. In the Renaissance period cities like Salzburg and Klagenfurt were generously redeveloped and extended. In the eighteenth century, Vienna, whose suburbs were completely destroyed in the course of the Turkish sieges in the sixteenth and seventeenth centuries, was encircled by a new, large system of fortifications so generously planned that even by the middle of the nineteenth century great parts of the areas enclosed were still open or used as parks and sites for summer residences.

The dramatic growth of the cities in the nineteenth century could be controlled neither by the city governments nor by the technical experts, a fact illustrated perfectly by Vienna. After the old fortification system surrounding the medieval city had been leveled in 1857, the cleared ground was developed according to a plan which was the result of an international town planning competition. A broad, tree-lined avenue, the Ring, was constructed. Much of the newly gained land was sold to private individuals, and the proceeds were used for the construction of a series of magnificent public buildings lining the Ring. The unique opportunity offered by the demolition of the old city walls had been well used. Another great achieve-

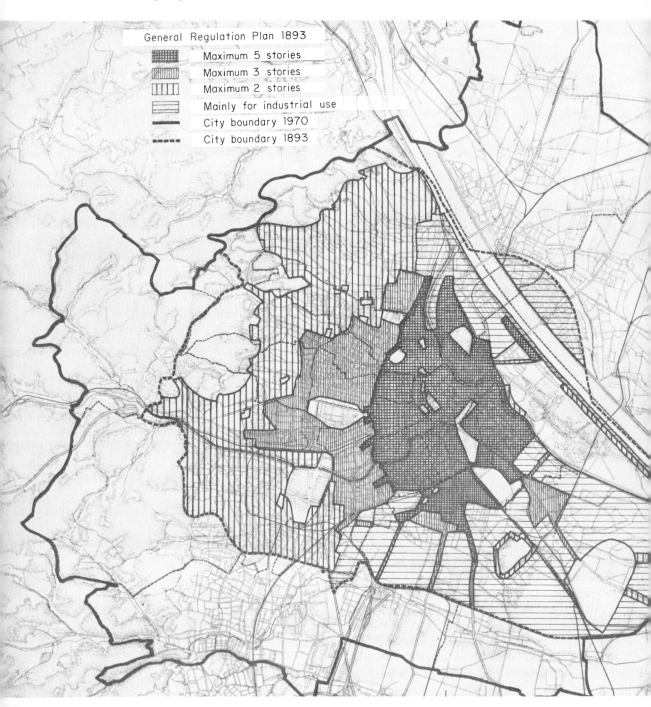

General Regulation Plan 1893

Maximum 5 stories
Maximum 3 stories
Maximum 2 stories
Mainly for industrial use
City boundary 1970
City boundary 1893

Vienna. General Regulation Plan, 1893.

M=1:75 000

Plan Nr. 37

ment was the control of the Danube, which spread out in numerous branches into the plain to the northeast of Vienna, flooding large stretches of land each year. An entirely new bed was dug, and bridges were built across it while it was still dry ground. Once the danger of flooding was eliminated, new building areas could be developed in the eastern part of the city.

What we call today the technical infrastructure was laid out for a population of 4 million. The main problem, however—the planned direction of urban growth—was not solved. The suburbs with the most rapidly increasing populations were incorporated much too late, at a time when most of their territory had already been built up or at least subdivided.

The plans for these piecemeal town extensions were influenced by degenerate Renaissance and baroque ideas. In most cases a simple gridiron pattern was adopted, aiming at maximum land exploitation regardless of the varied topography of the terrain.

It was not before 1893 that a so-called "General Regulation Plan" was established as the outcome of an international competition. It could, however, only integrate given facts and did not bring any basic changes in the shaping of the city. Even worse, this plan codified and petrified the development of the past.

The admissible height of buildings was regulated to a very simple pattern. In the core of the city, where most intensive use of space was allowed, the permitted height of buildings was greatest. In concentric zones surrounding this core, the admissible height of buildings was equally subject to uniform regulation, being graduated down to a peripheral zone reserved for low, detached houses.

Land use was regulated in an equally simple way. The whole densely built up area represented a so-called "mixed-use zone" in which the construction of tenement buildings, office-buildings, warehouses, and factories was permitted.

Vienna. Nineteenth-century mixed-use-zone development. (Polizeilichtbildstelle, Wien.)

With this plan given legal authority, town planning was reduced to a two-dimensional affair. Its main task was the delimitation of building areas and the regulation of street alignments. A last achievement before World War I came in 1905, when a "Woods and Meadows Belt" around Vienna was created by city law. This consisted of a broad circle of woodland, vineyards, and meadows—including farmland to be developed—in which no construction was allowed and in which the city had the right of expropriation. The intention of landscaping this zone was not carried out, but the open landscape has been preserved despite minor setbacks.

Twentieth-century Planning

1918 to 1955 The city government of Vienna, concentrating on public housing, planned some dwellings on the lines of English or Dutch terrace houses, but mostly the tradition of large-scale apartment houses typical of Vienna was continued. Nevertheless, the new structures are distinguished from the old ones in several important respects: where space permits, less then half—sometimes down to 20 percent—of the site is occupied. The wide courtyards are landscaped and attractively planted. Social facilities such as kindergartens, laundries, and public baths are provided.

Peripheral Development in Vienna
1. George Washington Court;
   municipal social housing between the wars
2. Municipal social housing after 1945
3. Hospital
4. Allotment gardens
5. Cemetery
6. Railway
7. Nineteenth-century development

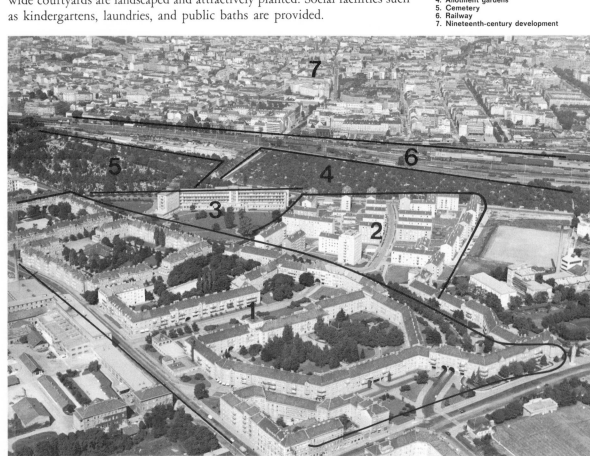

Vienna. George Washington Court; municipal social housing between the wars. (Landesbildstelle, Wien—Burgenland.)

Private housing development should have been controlled according to the General Regulation Plan. In many cases, however, this plan was amended to legalize uncontrolled sprawl. The situation was worse in rural and semirural suburban communities. In most Austrian cities the development was similar to that in Vienna.

The era of the "Third Reich" bestowed upon Austrian cities utopian plans which were never realized, nor even prepared. The actual development after 1945 was similar to that after World War I, but the attitude toward planning had changed.

During the years of 1945 to 1955, city planning was discussed widely: at first it was only by experts; later on suggestions were published and discussed publicly. The awareness that reconstruction offered a unique opportunity to correct certain shortcomings inherited from the past was not lacking during those postwar years. It must, however, be acknowledged that radically new concepts of city planning could hardly have been put across during the first 10 years after the war. Even if the experts had been able to agree on solutions and had been able to foresee future developments, such as the rapid growth of motor traffic, the mass of the population and their political representatives would hardly have been ready to make the further necessary sacrifices. The evolution of a city is so difficult for the individual to grasp, and in certain respects so slow, that a general realization that this evolution can be controlled is not to be expected. Many obvious changes in many spheres of activity must first take place before the inhabitants of a city decide to alter the familiar aspects of their everyday surroundings.

Such a turning point presented itself when full independence for Austria was achieved with the signing of the State Treaty and the subsequent withdrawal of the occupation forces. The formerly fruitless endeavors of idealistic city planners were appreciated at their full value only after 1955. At the same time two significant factors made comprehensive planning obviously necessary. One of these was the population's increasing space demands resulting from the improved standard of living. The second factor was the necessity to improve and to modernize the infrastructure of the larger Austrian cities, as this infrastructure was mainly that of the period before World War I. This in itself presented a task which could not be coped with by piecemeal planning.

Planning after 1955 As a start, town planning conquered the third dimension. Urban design got rid of the notion of large zones with a uniform height of buildings and aimed instead at a differentiated configuration and siting of buildings. Simultaneously the regulations concerning land use were further refined; the easier solution of the "mixed-use zone" being given up.

A further step was the inclusion of transportation planning within town planning, the fact being generally accepted that the traffic system constitutes an important element in town development and hence cannot be planned as an isolated item. Eventually, urbanization reaches a stage where town planning can no longer be limited to the administrative boundaries of a city. Town planning is becoming more and more the planning of urban regions. The decisive developments of city planning comprise the inclusion of a fourth dimension: time; and a fifth dimension: the cost-benefit equation.

City planning in Austria has reached a new stage. Until recently it had used, almost exclusively, the traditional means of land-use zoning, of town plans and regulations. Now it is being recognized that the development of cities cannot be guided only by restrictive plans of this kind. The most powerful means of controlling urban growth are active measures—public investments and public subsidies. This coordination of physical and economic planning in turn entails the use of mathematical methods and—what is much more important—cooperation with the social sciences. Cost-benefit analyses can be dangerously misleading if all benefits are expressed in terms of money. There are real benefits, real improvements in the living conditions of an urban population which cannot be measured in economic terms. That is to say: the most modern developments in planning technique remind us of the fact that planning derives its only justification from serving the needs of man.

Comprehensive City Planning. A good example of the planning of an urban region is the city of Linz, capital of the state of Upper Austria. It is situated nearer to the Common Market than is Vienna. While Vienna grew very rapidly in the course of the nineteenth century, the industrialization of Linz is at present in progress. The dynamic development of the central region of Upper Austria will certainly expand beyond the boundaries of the city of Linz. Three alternatives concerning the development of this region are being examined.

The optimal solution would be an integration of the whole area, the development of a regional city. South of the historic core of Linz, a new regional center would be built in order to cope with the requirements that the old city could no longer fulfill. In fact Linz would, together with the neighboring towns of Wels, Enns, and Steyr, form one single city and one labor market. This development would entail high costs for the improvement of the infrastructure.

A second pattern would be the concentric development of each of those four cities of the Upper Austrian central region. Although this pattern would involve lower costs, the advantages resulting from an integrated urban agglomeration would be lost.

Another alternative would be the establishment of small satellite towns instead of concentric peripheral development of each single city. This approach would undoubtedly enhance the residential value of each city, but it would also entail higher investments as regards infrastructure.

A decision on the political level as to the various patterns will not affect the city of Linz alone but also that part of Upper Austria in which more than 50 percent of the population lives and where over 50 percent of jobs in the secondary and tertiary sectors are concentrated. The fact that these alternatives of future development are being discussed by the authorities of the state, of the city, and of the other communities is a step forward.

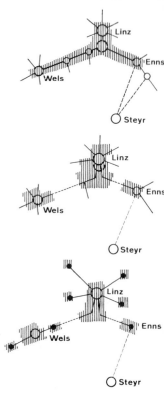

Alternatives for the development of the urban region of Linz. (Osterreichisches Institut fur Raumplanung, Oberosterreichischer Zentralraum Raumordnungsplan, Wien, 1969.)

In Vienna the point of departure differed from that in Linz. Vienna has sufficient land reserves within its boundaries to meet the increasing space requirements of its slowly growing population.

In 1958 the city of Vienna commissioned Professor Roland Rainer to prepare a development plan for the city. This was the first attempt at comprehensive planning since the competition for the drawing up of the General Regulation Plan in 1893. In 1961 the Gemeinderat, the legislative body of the city of Vienna, approved the development plan. The first two paragraphs of this concept, taking into consideration the peculiar situation of the city, read as follows:

> 1. Decongestion of the too densely built-up parts of the city. At the present time, three-quarters of Vienna's total population and nine-tenths of the total of jobs are concentrated in densely built-up areas. This fact contradicts important requirements of public health as well as economic and urbanistic needs. As a consequence, the situation has to be gradually modified, by way of developing new building areas, without encroaching westward on the Vienna Woods and other greenbelt areas. The plains in the south of the city and on the left bank of the Danube, however, offer better opportunities for an unhampered and economical development.
>
> 2. Development of the low-density peripheral zones. Unlike the districts in the center of the city, urban land use in the peripheral zones is not sufficiently compact. The exigency of breaking up the too densely built-up areas and of making more economical use of the scarce building land makes it necessary to intensify urban land use in the outskirts of the city.
>
> Economically speaking, the fragmentary and low-density development in the outlying districts fails to make the best use of building land in a big city that the general interest would require.

The most significant point made is that the situation of the densely built-up areas "has to be gradually modified by way of developing new building areas." This is in principle a kind of development program which also takes into account the time factor. At present it would be impossible to renew old parts of the city by demolishing a great number of apartments which could only be replaced by fewer dwellings on the same sites later on. From the economic point of view, the compulsory relocation of industrial plants would be equally unfeasible. The expression "by way of" means that the policy of the city administration is geared toward achieving a gradual amelioration of housing conditions and conditions of work in the densely built-up areas by bringing the city outskirts up to standard. A voluntary migration of people in search of higher standards of housing on the one hand and a voluntary migration of industrial plants wishing to expand on the other create the practical and psychological prerequisites for a comprehensive urban renewal which is to be realized to its full extent in about 10 to 20 years.

Following the approval of the development concept by the city legislature, a so-called "Land-use Balance" was prepared. It showed the number of apartment dwellers and/or the number of jobs which would have to migrate from the densely built-up areas and it simultaneously showed the size of land reserves. The next stage, carried through by Rainer's successor, Architekt Georg Conditt, was the working out of "City Models." The City Models show in a greatly simplified form the possible future distribution of residences and jobs. With regard to additional housing in the city outskirts, alternatives have been envisaged: one based mainly on multistory blocks of apartments and the other based on one-family houses. The possible alternatives for the future distribution of jobs were the preservation of the present stage of concentration in the densely built-up areas or a large-scale decentralization of working places, respectively. The combination of these alternatives has resulted in four models. The projection of these much simplified models into the city area leaves open a choice of a large variety of possible spatial structures. An equal number of apartments and commercial structures in the development areas can be designed according to various patterns.

A decision in favor of one of the many possible solutions can only be taken after considering the time factor as well as the cost-benefit factor. Consequently, a large number of alternatives relating to the development areas of Vienna are being checked and calculated. The examples of Linz and Vienna will serve for all Austrian cities. Today it is generally recognized that city planning in its broadest sense is a permanent public service.

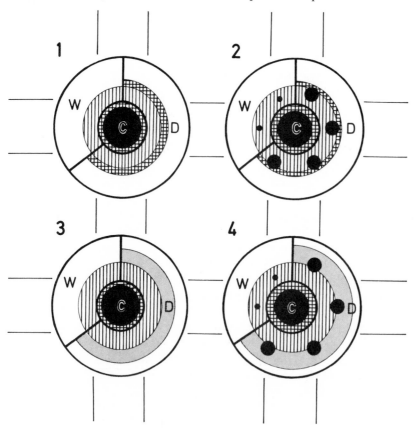

City Models for the development of Vienna. (1) and (2): Residential development in the peripheral districts at maximum density, mainly blocks of flats. (3) and (4): Residential development in the peripheral districts at medium density, mainly one-family houses. (1) and (3): Preservation of the existing concentration of workplaces in the central areas. (2) and (4): Large scale decentralization of workplaces. Key: C—Densely built-up central areas
W—Western periphery
D—Development areas

1. Residential quarter in typical "national socialist" style
2. Development after 1960

Peripheral development in Linz. ("Spektrum Linz," Osterreich in Wort und Bild, p. 31, H. Bauer-Verlag, Zeitschrift.)

Town Extensions. Town extension schemes of the twentieth century thoroughly differ from those of former epochs. In size they exceed the most important city extensions of the nineteenth century simply because building densities have become much lower. City extensions of today seldom cover virgin land, since most of the larger cities in this country are surrounded by scattered settlements. These zones comprise old villages, planned and uncontrolled settlements, residential areas sponsored by the municipality, and industrial areas with factories and dumps. In between there are still spacious areas of farmland. It would not be very reasonable to overleap these zones and build satellite towns at a distance from the central town. The task would rather be to integrate the existing settlement elements into a new development scheme. This is not a mere makeshift solution for Austria's towns. A skilled planning scheme could provide new districts offering agreeable living conditions.

Open stretches of land should be turned into high-density residential areas, at the same time being provided with good public transport communications. They could serve as focal points, surrounded by "suburbs" consisting of old villages and other existing settlements. Thus a variety could be obtained which, even in an excellent urban design, is so hard to create artificially. This type of city extension also breaks with the traditional form of a uniform growth concentrated around the city core. While formerly new residential districts only provided the minimum in the way of shopping facilities and public utilities, the bigger cities' trend is to create subcenters in the outskirts. This tendency is also favored because in these cities an increasing number of people work in the tertiary sector. The guiding

1. Future motorway
2. Future district center

Peripheral development in Vienna (blocks of prefabricated flats). (Polizeilichtbildstelle, Wien.)

Vienna. Lichtental. Urban renewal project, carried out "site after site." (International Federation for Housing and Planning.)

Stage 1: Situation in 1955

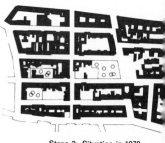

Stage 2: Situation in 1970

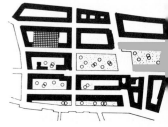

Stage 3: Future development

principle in the city extension programs in this country is to plan bigger urban units around the old city core. Moreover, the development of mere dormitory suburbs is being avoided; attempts are made to create a great variety of employment in the new areas.

Urban Renewal. Up to now the housing shortage, traffic problems, and the task of city extension has been in the foreground of public opinion and political interest. Slowly the necessity of urban renewal is being recognized.

A series of proposals and projects have been presented and some pilot projects have been completed.

In Austria there are three types of renewal areas: (1) districts of historic value; (2) districts with nineteenth-century buildings; (3) suburban districts.

The renewal of the historic parts of the city is important, especially for those Austrian cities where the old core still is the commercial and administrative center. The best-known city of this type is probably Salzburg. The

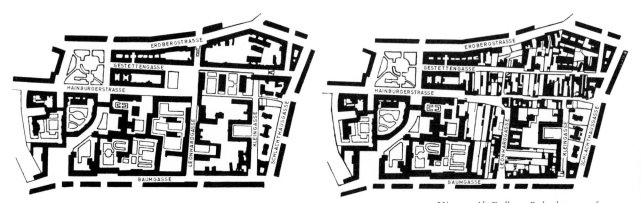

Vienna. Alt-Erdberg. Redevelopment of slum area. (Der Aufbau.)

same problem, however, is also valid for Graz, the second-largest city of this country, and it also applies to smaller cities like Krems, which is very active in the field of historic renewal. These cities owe the preservation of their historic parts to the fact that their economic development was not very significant in the past. Today, commercial enterprises threaten the survival of many old and valuable buildings. On the other hand the economic as well as the cultural value of these historic centers is well recognized. In Salzburg, in fact, a state law for the preservation of the old city was passed.

In Vienna, in the industrial boom of the nineteenth century, the medieval scene vanished. A great number of historically valuable buildings have, however, survived, which call for perservation and protection.

From the nineteenth century, Vienna and the other larger Austrian cities inherited extensive residential areas with very low housing standards. Nev-

Vienna. Grossfledsiedlung. Renewal of a former subsistence settlement.

ertheless, most of the buildings of this period are sound structurally. Therefore, it is sufficient to modernize many of these old tenement houses. Bigger flats can be divided, smaller flats can be combined, and technical facilities can be improved. To this end, the federal government and the states have been providing the necessary resources since 1970. Such modernization, however, must not interfere with urban development. Where there are old or dilapidated houses hampering new projects, the only solution is to redevelop these areas.

In the outskirts there are renewal areas with a very low building density. At present a former subsistence settlement in Vienna covering an area of 0.60 square mile (1.5 square kilometers) comprising 450 detached houses is under renewal. Of these houses, 150 will be removed, and 5,500 new apartments will be built, including a generously designed suburban center. Thus a new district will be created. There are numerous low-density settlements in the outskirts of other large Austrian cities, which could be renewed in a similar way.

BIBLIOGRAPHY: K. H. Brunner, *Stadtplanung für Wien*, Verlag für Jugend and Volk, Vienna, 1952; A. Schimka, "Die Stadt und ihr Umland in Österreich," report to the International Congress of the International Federation for Housing and Planning, Vienna, 1956, pp. 239–283; Roland Rainer, *Planungskonzept Wien*, Verlag für Jugend und Volk, Vienna, 1962; H. Bobek and E. Lichtenberger, *Wien—Bauliche Gestaltung und Entwicklung seit der Mitte des 19. Jahrhunderts*, Verlag Hermann Böhlaus Nachf., Graz-Cologne, 1966; Österreichisches Institut für Raumplanung, *Raumordnung in Österreich*, im Eigenverlag, Vienna, 1966; "Graz," *Der Aufbau*, Heft 7, 3. Jahrgang Verlag für Jugend und Volk, Vienna; Franz Seelinger, "Der Linzer Stadtgrundriß und seine Entwicklungsphasen in den letzten 100 Jahren," *Spectrum Linz*, H. Bauer-Verlag, pp. 8–32; Georg Conditt, *Stadtplanung Wien 1963–1969*, Verlag fur Jugend und Volk, Vienna, 1971; Institut fur Stadtforschung, *Der Stadtische Lebensraum in Österreich*, Verlag fur Jugend und Volk, Vienna, 1971.

—GEORG CONDITT

AUTOBAHN (*See* TRANSPORT.)

AVENUE In a city an avenue is generally a wide, straight street lined with buildings or trees, and it sometimes leads to a terminal building or feature at its end. (The word "avenue" is derived from the Latin "advenis," meaning "to come to.") An avenue is also a straight, often tree-lined road leading to a house or mansion. As an element in city planning, the avenue descends from the ancient processional way.

AXONOMETRIC (*See* PROJECTION.)

B

BABYLONIAN PLANNING (*See* ANCIENT PLANNING, MESOPOTAMIA.)

BACK-TO-BACK HOUSES Rows of terrace or attached houses backing onto and adjoining each other. This type of housing was provided in some of the industrial cities of England during the nineteenth century. The houses were mainly two-story structures, L-shaped in plan, four forming a square courtyard which provided a degree of light. This courtyard was evenly divided to provide a small yard for each dwelling.

BANGLADESH (*See* PAKISTAN.)

BASTIDE A name given to medieval fortified towns built mainly during the twelfth to fourteenth centuries in England, Wales, and Gascony. A very large number were built as the result of the enterprise of Edward I (1239–1307), who was also Duke of Gascony. Those built before Edward I, who first went to Gascony in 1254, were somewhat irregularly planned, but those built in his time, mainly from 1273 to 1307, followed a more regular grid pattern of which several examples still remain, Winchelsea in southeast England and Monpazier in the Dordogne being well-known examples. Over two hundred were built during the three centuries, a large number along the south coast of England and along the English-Welsh border. *See also* EDWARD I OF ENGLAND.

BIBLIOGRAPHY: Maurice Beresford, *New Towns of the Middle Ages—Town Plantation in England, Wales and Gascony,* Lutterworth Press, London, 1967.

BAUMEISTER, REINHARD (1833–1917) German city planner. Baumeister was born in Hamburg and studied at Hanover and Karlsruhe, where he graduated in 1853 as an engineer.

After practical work in various fields of engineering he accepted, in 1862, a chair of engineering science at the Technische Hochschule, Karlsruhe. While continuing practice, especially in railroad engineering, he devoted his first major publication to the aesthetic questions in architecture and engineering which continued to keep a prominent place in his thought. As an architect, he built a hospital at Karlsruhe around 1890. He left his first trace on the emerging field of town planning by drafting the "principles for town expansion" to be adopted in 1874 by the assembly of the Verband Deutscher Architekten-und Ingenieur-Vereine, a professional organization. Two years later, he published his main work, *Stadterweiterungen in technischer, baupolizeilicher und wirtschaftlicher Beziehung* (*Town Expansions Considered with Respect to Technology, Building Code, and Economy*). In 1906, he drafted, again for the assembly of the Verband Deutscher Architekten-und Ingenieur-Vereine, revised principles of town planning. His last publication, "Gemeinwohl und Sondernutzen," was devoted to questions of housing, real estate, and betterment. From 1872, when he won a competition in Mannheim, he produced a large number of development plans for many towns, predominantly in Baden. He died in 1917 at Karlsruhe.

In his major work (*Stadterweiterungen . . .*), Baumeister covers thoroughly all technical aspects of town planning as seen in his time but touches only lightly on aesthetics and on social aspects. The book remained unparalleled until 1889, when Sitte's work brought in new aesthetic and functional considerations, while Stübben's *Der Städtebau,* published in 1890, provided another technical handbook even more comprehensive than Baumeister's. One of Baumeister's major concerns was the improvement of building ordinances (Bauordnungen): he developed the concept of zoning which was employed for the first time in an 1891 building ordinance for Frankfurt am Main and was soon widely recognized as an important tool of planning.

Thus, as the first German to collect and to systematize the knowledge of town planning, Baumeister laid the foundations of this discipline in Germany and contributed considerably to its further development.

BIBLIOGRAPHY: *Stadterweiterungen in technischer, baupolizeilicher und wirtschaftlicher Beziehung,* Berlin, 1876; *Die Abstufung von Bauordnungen für den Stadtkern, Aussenbezirke und Vororte,* Berlin, 1892; "Die Umlegung städtischer Grundstücke und die Zonenenteignung Gemeinsam mit Classen und Stübben," *Denkschriften des Verbandes Deutscher Architekten und Ingenieurvereine,* vol. 7, Berlin, 1897; "Grundsätze des Städtebaues," *Denkschrift über Grundsätze des Städtebaues,* herausgegeben vom Verband Deutscher Architekten-und Ingenieur-Vereine, Berlin, 1907; "Bauordnung und Wohnungsfrage", *Städtebauliche Vorträge,* vol. 4, no. 3, Berlin, 1911; "Gemeinwohl und Sondernutzen im Städtebau," *Städtebauliche Vorträge,* vol. 8, no. 4, Berlin, 1918.

—GERD ALBERS

BAY A partly enclosed space with a wide opening on one side, probably derived in its building and planning application from the geographical term. In highway planning it is an enclosed space on one side of the road into which a vehicle can draw up. In building it has several meanings, the principal of which is the subdivision of a structure, often between major supports. In agricultural and industrial buildings it was often a system of measurement with a standard size of bay; and a barn was either one, two, or three bays. Another meaning is a recess, enclosed on three sides and open to the room on the fourth. This is also the internal appearance of a bay window, which externally projects from the line of the wall. It can be square, splayed, or polygonal in plan. When it is circular it is called a "bow" window.

BELGIUM

Legislation and Administration Though insufficient in many respects the decree-law of December 2, 1946, opened the way to the concept of an urban and regional planning policy in Belgium.

The organic law of March 29, 1962, provided the Administration of Urban and Regional Planning, instituted by the decree-law of May 31, 1945, with a legal instrument indispensable for the development of the country.

From this date onward, the whole of the national territory has been subject to urban planning regulations. All operations are under the control of the central government, although it is understood that the municipalities work out their own development plans and that the government takes charge of regional and district plans.

It has never been decided to prepare a national plan.

Development must be carried out by means of a sequence of plans drawn up at different levels. These plans relate to the region, the district, the total territory of a municipality, and one or several districts of this same municipality. The development plans have statutory force which can be modified only by means of a procedural revision.

The law provides for the setting up of a National Development Commission, the chairman and members of which are to be appointed by the king. The commission is required to follow current tendencies, ideas, and principles of development in order to be in a position to propose to the minister the necessary directives for the preparation and the formulation of development plans.

One of the fundamental legal dispositions concerns the way in which the development plans are to be worked out. In the Belgian system, the plan is the result of teamwork. Collaboration not only between different interested parties, but also with the public is necessary, for the law has confirmed the concept of participation.

At the regional level as well as the level of the big agglomerations and of the municipalities of more than 10,000 inhabitants, consultative commissions are set up consisting of an equal number of delegates from the public and private sectors. These delegates represent the main interests of the region.

The consultative commission collaborates in two stages of the approbation procedure:

1. During the period of the elaboration of the plan, the commission follows step by step the work of the author of the plan by making proposals and giving advice which the community council is free to accept or not. When the latter follows the commission's advice, the commission's responsibility ceases.

2. The commission gives advice on projects approved by the community council at the request of the authority invested with approbation powers. This authority still remains free to adopt the plan or not.

Regional Plans These must include information on the existing situation and the general development measures required by the economic and social needs of the region. In other words, the regional plan will be mainly a zoning or land-use plan.

If necessary, the plan may include measures for developing the network of the main routes of communication, general stipulations of an aesthetic nature, and a statement of the approximate boundaries of the sectors.

District Plans The sector corresponds to that part of a region in which there are special problems exceeding the limits of communal interests, although this particular area cannot be considered as a real region. As the district plan is only to be considered as an expansion of the regional plan, on a larger scale and more detailed, the districts are defined in the same way as the regions (see illustration).

Communal or Municipal Plans Under the law, all the municipalities must draw up development plans, whether general or detailed, and they alone are responsible for doing this. The municipality is responsible for taking the initiative in this field. But if the municipality fails to conform to the law, the king is responsible for taking the necessary measures. However, as it is considered undesirable to overburden the communes without adequate financial resources, the law permits the king—at the request of the communal council—in certain circumstances, to exempt them from the obligation of drawing up a development plan.

The General Development Plan The general development plan (or master plan)—in accordance with the principles of the law—covers the whole territory of a municipality and may modify some provisions of a plan of a higher authority, such as the district and regional plan.

Development plans may lead to expropriation and reparceling and, as such, involve restrictions on the exercise of the rights of ownership, including prohibitions on the issuing of building and parceling permits.

The Detailed Layout Plan The detailed layout plan covers only a part of the communal territory and is based on the same principles as the general development plan:

1. The plan provides detailed specifications of the district and regional plan.

2. Departures from the general development plan and from the district and the regional plans are allowed.

3. There are restrictions on the rights of ownership, including a prohibition on the issuing of building and parceling permits.

Expropriations and Compensations   Detailed layout plans are—in general—realized by means of expropriations or compulsory acquisition.

One important innovation concerns the time limit on the execution of the expropriations. In civil law, no time limit within which the public authorities must effect compulsory acquisition is laid down. This condition, disregarding the legitimate rights of the owners, could not be maintained in a law which is intended to effect development by encouraging cooperation between the public and private sectors. Therefore, a period of 10 years has been fixed for the completion of compulsory acquisition. At the end of this period, the owner may request the authority to waive its right to compulsory acquisition.

Another innovation relates to the question of compensation of servitudes imposed by public interest. The law states that no compensation is payable where restrictions are imposed on normal rights of ownership by reason of public welfare. This is derived from article 544 of the Civil Code.

In some cases, laws provided for heavy compensation in cases of this kind, but being exceptions, they do not endanger the inviolability of the principle. The legislator considered that, since the law on regional development was of a such character, in order to define the restrictions on the exercise of the rights of ownership in a more precise way, a system should be found for compensation of abnormal and excessive damage caused by town planning measures. The formula adopted has the merit of compensating for substantial damage without, however, being a deterrent to development.

In fact, the right to compensation exists only when the prohibition on building or subdivision arises as a result of a plan having binding force, and which terminates the use to which a property is put, or for which it was intended, at the date the draft plan was adopted.

A number of controlling dispositions are provided in the planning process depending on whether or not a development plan for the site on which the property is situated is approved by royal decree.

This property measure is ensured by the control of the building permit. It concerns both the building and the parceling permit.

The Building Permit   The municipality is now the sole authority responsible for the issuing of the building permits and also of permits for demolition, conversion, alterations, the setting up of depots for used vehicles and scrap, and the felling of isolated tall trees (planted in green areas and specified in a detailed layout plan approved by royal decree, as well as those growing in a duly authorized parceling scheme).

The law provides for two distinct procedures, depending on whether or not there is a detailed layout plan, approved by royal decree, for the area in which the property is situated. In the first case, before the permit is issued, the municipal authority must refer the plan for advice to the provincial town planning officer—appointed by the minister and called the "responsible officer." It might be decided to grant or to refuse a permit; or, subject to a number of conditions and to ensure proper development, to depart from existing regulations.

The permit states the conditions under which it is granted. Both the municipality and the applicant are bound to comply with the conditions. However, when favorable advice is given by the responsible officer mentioned above, the municipality, under municipal law, may still refuse to issue the permit. The reverse is not possible.

A guarantee favoring the applicant lies in the fact that a refusal to issue a permit, based solely on the grounds that the application is incompatible with a detailed layout plan, becomes null and void if this detailed layout plan is not enforced within 3 years following the refusal.

In such a case, at the request of the applicant, the original application is submitted for a new decision which can no longer be based on the foregoing grounds.

If the area in which the property is situated is subject to a detailed development plan approved by royal decree, the dossier is referred to the responsible officer, who checks the compliance with the approved layout plan and may suspend or cancel any irregular permits.

The same procedure applies to a building application within the limits of a duly authorized parceling scheme or when the detailed layout plan is subject to revision.

Parceling Permit   The law introduces permits for subdividing an area. This is an innovation. However, two restrictions should be noted:

1. The law covers only subdivision into lots for residential construction.

2. The law refers only to voluntary parceling; thus, the parceling of property resulting from the inheritance system does not come within its terms.

The Collège du Bourgmestre at Echevins (College of Mayor and Aldermen), being the executive body in the municipal government, is responsible for issuing the permits in the same form as building permits.

The municipal administration has to pay particular attention to cases where the parceling scheme provides for the opening of one or more new roads. In this case, the permit can be issued only by the college after deliberation by the municipal council concerning the alignment and the equipment of the road(s). No other approval is required.

In addition to the requirements concerning the type, the elevation, and the aesthetic appearance of the building, the parceling permit may impose on the applicant a number of other obligations, such as the construction of roads and the reservation of land for open space, public buildings, and public services.

The permit for subdividing land has importance equal to that of a detailed layout plan approved by royal decree.

Building Regulations   The king has the power to issue national building regulations. In these regulations it is not the intention to prescribe the specific details of a construction or the materials to be used but solely to revise outmoded, rigid, and empirical regulations to which municipalities must adapt their bylaws.

The general regulations, issued by royal decree, introduce the principle of the functional nature of a building to avoid empirical continuation of outmoded construction methods. Thus they facilitate the adoption of new techniques in building.

The building regulations also define the requirements of development plans (whether general or detailed layouts) which should include provisions relating to the intended land use, density, soil occupancy, and kind and volume of buildings.

The king also may request the municipalities to draw up a set of bylaws or to modify existing ones. Such regulations have to be submitted to the députation permanente (provincial government) and finally to the king for approval.

Since 1962, a number of municipalities have either worked out entirely new codes of building regulations or have modified their existing codes. A set of royally approved regulations is not yet issued. This may happen in a foreseeable future, in view of the fact that the final text is currently filed with the legislative section of the Conseil d'Etat for advice.

Penalties Compliance with the law can only be ensured by means of serious penalties in case of infringement.

As regards redress, the Urban Planning Administration is primarily concerned with reverting the property to its original state. If the violation is proved, the redress is to be officially adjudged by the Court on the request of the Planning Administration.

Another important point is that the minister no longer has the sole right to require the redress. It could be adjudged and enforced by the Court at the request of the Collège des Bourgmestre et Echevins (College of the Mayor and Aldermen) or of the injured third party.

In the case of violation of the parceling regulations, the injured party may demand the cancellation of the property title on the basis of which the parceling was issued.

Finally, there is a new section requiring the publication of the legal position of real estate, whereby persons interested in ownership or the acquisition of rights can ascertain the condition of the subdivision or construction with which they are concerned.

Regional Studies By the act of March 29, 1962, the legislature already provided a number of executive measures. Some of these measures concerning the regional plans were already taken in application of the decree-law of December 2, 1946. The study of the regional plans was started in 1954 and terminated by the publication of the last study in 1967.

From 1962 onward, the administration started preliminary studies for preparing district plans, which are more detailed and complete than the regional master plans. Executive measures have divided the country into 48 districts designated by royal order (see illustration).

The forty-eight districts of Belgium.

Generally speaking, the majority of these preparatory studies are finished. Most of these plans were legally enforced by the end of 1970.

The National Survey Atlas   Since 1946, the Urban Planning Administration has collected and presented in the form of maps, cartograms, and diagrams general data on the country, which are listed in the *National Surveys Inventory* under the following headings:

1. Climatology
2. Orography
3. Hydrography
4. Forests and Heathlands
5. Subsoil
6. Soil
7. Population
8. Agriculture
9. Hunting and Fishing
10. Energy
11. Industry and Handicrafts
12. Transport
13. Public Health
14. Water Economy
15. Leisure Activities, Tourism, Recreation Grounds, Youth Hostels, etc.
16. Protection of places of natural beauty or interest and monuments

17. Nature and Science Reserves
18. Property Development
19. Housing
20. Urban Facilities

The Urban Planning Administration also keeps the documents drawn up by the Soil Mapping Center for a large part of the national territory (agricultural land, pasture land, orchards, forests, uncultivated land, built-up land).

These documents are of real use to anyone concerned with development planning and to scientific research institutions.

Inventories of Amenities   In order to provide a common line of thinking for the administration when a parceling scheme or a construction situated in one of these amenity sites is submitted, an inventory of amenities for each province is published showing the location of the places of beauty or interest.

Special attention is given to the question of whether or not the conservation of the site is compatible with the execution of certain construction work. Quite often, the intended works are forbidden on the ground that they are incompatible with such conservation.

Other Publications   The Urban Planning Administration sponsors a number of publications such as *Les cahiers d'Urbanisme* and *STERO* for the Flemish-speaking part of the country. *STERO* is a joint venture of the Universities of Ghent and Leuven (Louvain).

The Fédération belge de l'Urbanisme et de l'Habitation, du Développement et de l'Aménagement du Territoire organizes congresses and conferences and publishes a bulletin of information. The president of the federation is Dr. Victor Bure, honorary general director of the Urban Planning Administration.

Professional Practice, Education, and Training   The urban planner in Belgium has no legal status. The urban planning degree is usually connected to another degree (e.g., architect-planner, engineer-planner) which does have a legally recognized status or to a license (equivalent to an M.A. or M.Sc. degree) in public and business administration or economics and finance which is completed by a license in urban and regional planning. The universities of Brussels, Ghent, Leuven, and Liege have organized a complete cycle of courses leading toward the "Licence en Urbanisme."

Geographical and Climatic Conditions

Situation   The area of Belgium is 13,513 square miles (30,500 square kilometers), with a population of 9,500,000 inhabitants, so that the country is one of the smallest of Europe, $\frac{1}{350}$ of Europe, with one of the highest population densities in the world. The national boundaries are artificial and rarely coincide with physical geographical phenomena, only the north sea coast of 42 miles (68 kilometers) and some parts of the Kys River and Neuce River are natural boundaries.

Northern Belgium forms a part of the great Northwestern and Northern European plain, while southern Belgium links up with the Central European region (Rhine shale plateau).

Climate Belgium is located midway between the Equator and the North Pole, in the cold moderate climate zone with four distinct seasons, but with slight temperature differences, which is attributed to the nearness to the North Sea and its favorably influencing Atlantic Drift or Gulf Stream whose climatic impact diminishes inland.

The prevailing winds are southwest, 21 percent; west, 10 percent; and south, 13 percent. The atmospheric conditions that prevail above the Atlantic Ocean account for the predominantly tepid and humid oceanic winds.

There is a relatively high degree of cloudiness (8 on the 1–10 scale) and there are a great number of rainy days. For instance, Uccle has an average of 197 rainy days a year, with an average precipitation of 33.4 inches (835 millimeters) a year.

Habitation

The Rural Settlement Pattern The rural habitat is commonest in Belgium. The population is diffused in the northern part of the country, and is more concentrated in the southern part. Consequently, the morphology of the villages in the north is different from that of the villages in the south.

The physical environment (water, climate, soil) determines, as direct cause and effect, the land tenure and the agrarian exploitation possibilities. It also determines the degree of enclosure—whether the landscape is closed (scattered homes with numerous roads) or open (pasture land, clustered homes, loose road and path networks) (see illustration).

═══	City of Brussels (Pentagon
─·─·─	Railway Yards
───	New Residential Suburbs (
─────	Forest of Soignes (FS)
W	Warande
MC	Manhattan Center
OS	Old Residential Suburbs
ind.	industry

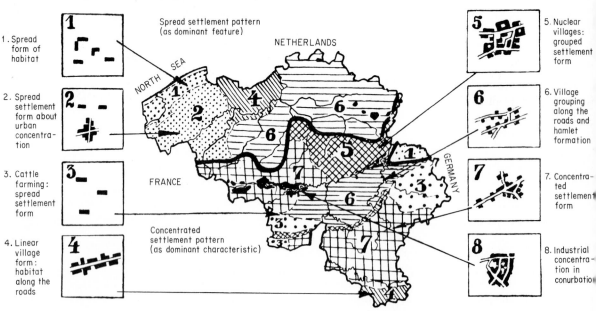

The synthesis of settlement forms.
(O. Tulippe, Cours de Geographie Humaine.

Plan of Brussels. Brussels means "dwelling place in the brooks," and, being situated on the Senne River, the city became a transit harbor for barges. In the tenth century it was a traders' center. The first fortification wall was erected in the twelfth century; the second—the present Pentagon with boulevards—dates from 1357–1379.

The agglomeration grew primarily in the nineteenth and twentieth centuries because of its central position in the country. With the eighteen suburbs, Greater Brussels has an area of 40,100 acres (16,373 hectares). The suburbs have grown at the expense of the city of Brussels (1947: 84,000 inhabitants; 1967: 55,000), and have been determined by the new labor force. The Brussels area is an important industrial center, well connected by waterways to all parts of the country.

The old residential suburbs (OS) grew simultaneously with the industries and are intermixed with them. On the aerial photograph the new residential suburbs (NS) are clearly distinguishable from the old because of their large, regular lots. The residential quarters, of a socially divergent character, spread unsystematically around the city. No general overall plan exists. Some fashionable suburbs (Ukkel-Elsene) have beautiful parks, which are lacking in the downtown area with one exception, the Warande, in front of the Parliament building (rectangular park east of the Pentagon). The forest of Soignes, of 10,070 acres (4,082 hectares), extends south of Brussels. At the time of the Brussels World Fair in 1958, an extensive system of parking garages, tunnels, and major roads to Liege, Paris, and the Ardennes was prepared, which, however, did not solve the ever-increasing traffic problems. Since 1965, an intercommunal underground of public transport has been under construction. It is expected to improve the transportation system.

The Roman influence, stronger in the south, was expressed in the "villa" and may be responsible for the present landscape arrangements.

The Urban Settlement Pattern   Belgium was always a "clearinghouse" for neighboring countries. The Belgian city has no economic contact with the soil and lives from its relationship with the outlying districts.

As a consequence, the occupations of the inhabitants determine the agglomerative urban formation. The city is a social group benefiting from a well-developed organization and occupying a rather limited area (see aerial picture of Brussels). Its importance is derived from its historic function; i.e., that of a regional or interregional market on a crossing point of rural roads and waterways (e.g., Meuse River; Roman road Cologne-Brugge).

By the end of the nineteenth century and the beginning of the twentieth, the industrial and urban evolution brought about changes in the function of many cities, including, for instance, Charleroi, which was previously a seventeenth-century fortified army town. Charleroi became the capital of the industrial basin; and Ypres, a medieval textile center, became a town of artisans and commuters.

Urban agglomerations of high density came into existence, comprising more than one-third of the entire population.

City	1880	1930	1947	December 31, 1969; agglomerative units	
				Number of suburbs	Number of inhabitants
Brussels	432,000	869,000	932,000	19	1,073,111
Antwerp	216,000	484,000	475,000	14	673,040
Liège	156,000	252,000	246,000	28	445,347
Ghent	153,000	219,000	214,000	6	228,000

Belgium: total population: 9,660,154.   2,419,498
rate of population growth for 1969: 2.93%.   or 37.5%

Source: National Institute for Statistics, Brussels.

The actual urbanizing tendency can be summarized as follows: (1) The above-mentioned economic regions became pools of labor and markets; (2) strong and fast growth extending the administrative limits of the cities, with spheres of influence reaching far outside their boundaries; (3) complex demographic migration patterns were creating specific problems in over-populated urban centers; (4) steady change of industrial agglomerations, implying important social, economic, and regional shifts (see illustration).

Control of these developments is the object of "scientific urbanism" and of a number of decrees passed by the legislative body relative to economic reconversion and to regional development planning.

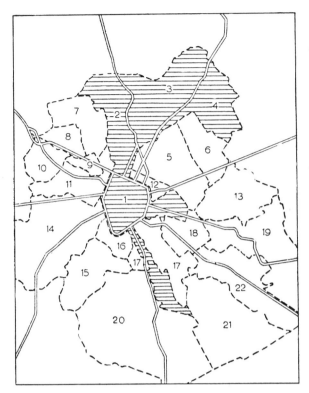

The Brussels Agglomeration: (1) The city of Brussels before 1923; (2,3,4) the former autonomous communities of Laken, Neder-over-Heembeek, and Harem, annexed to Brussels in 1923. The remaining communities have their own administrative structures and communal autonomy: (5) Schaarbeek; (6) Evere; (7) St. Pieters-Jette; (8) Ganshoren; (9) Koekelberg; (10) St. Agatha-Berchem; (11) St. Jans-Molenbeek; (12) St. Joost-ten-Node; (13) St. Lambrechts-Woluwe; (14) Anderlecht; (15) Vorst; (16) St. Gillis; (17) Elsene; (18) Etterbeek; (19) St. Pieters-Woluwe; (20) Ukkel; (21) Watermaal-Bosvoorde; (22) Oudergem.

Traditions of Planning to the End of the Nineteenth Century

Medieval Period Consequent on the Roman invasion through France and along the Rhine River, and, later on, as a result of the exploits of the Crusades, all commercial trunk roads leading from Italy to the North Sea terminated in the Low Countries. The flourishing trade gave rise to a class of wealthy merchants in the small settlements along these trade routes. The merchants founded the Hanseatic League—a trade association—which, from the twelfth century onward, supported the growth of many urban commercial centers and defended the merchants' interests. The Hanseatic cities, early nuclei of urban centers and privileged with charters, were spread as beacons of international trade and city culture along the sea road from Novgorod to London.

The population of Europe was predominantly rural, despite the existence of some great cities like Ypres (which, in the year 1300, had about 90,000 inhabitants), Antwerp (in 1567, 125,000 inhabitants), Bruges (in 1340, 70,000 inhabitants), Ghent (in 1300, 60,000 inhabitants), and Leuven (in 1300, 100,000 inhabitants). Where towns prospered, employment increased.

By the end of the sixteenth century, due to the silting up of the port of Bruges, the trade and culture were transferred to Ghent, Antwerp, and Holland. The invention of gunpowder marked the beginning of the end

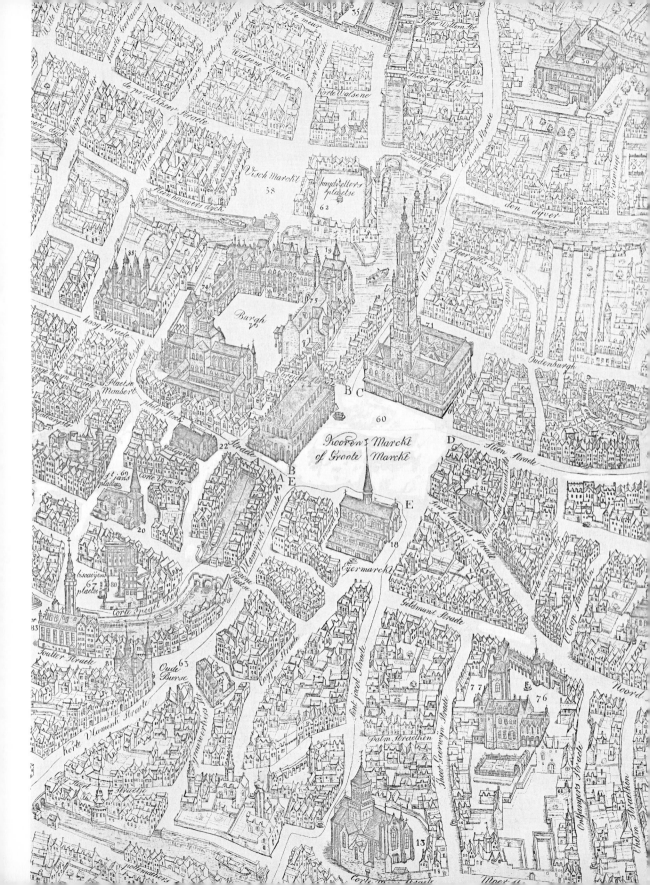

Map of Bruges of 1562 by Marcus Gheradus (1521–1604), entitled Brugae Flandrorum Urbs Et Emporium Mercatu Celebre. *The market square is surrounded by a number of smaller squares with different functions. This engraving is still architecturally up to date and provides a basis for the study of the necessary restoration and reconstruction.*   RIGHT: *Aerial view of the central market square of Bruges. The city was built in the eleventh century as a burgus in a creek system left from earlier maritime transgressions and linked with the North Sea by a widening of the existing Damme-Sluis Canal.*

of the walled town. Prior to the development of the cannon, a dry or water moat surrounded the town walls and provided adequate protection from besieging enemies.

Urban and regional planning of modern times began in the seventeenth century. During this period, the growth of technology was encouraged by France's policy of military expansion. The developments of this time must be regarded as a part of early capitalism.

The Dutch-Belgian frontier is delineated by two treaties. The first, the Treaty of Münster (1648), brought about, among many other changes, the separation of North Brabant from South Brabant (provinces of Antwerp and Brabant). It also expanded the area of the United Provinces (later the Netherlands).

In 1648 also, the left bank of the Schelde River was given to the Netherlands; thus the natural exit from Antwerp to the North Sea was blocked.

The French-Belgian frontier is very irregular: the events contributing to this layout occurred between 1668 and 1713.

Notable theoretical mathematicians (such as Simon Stevin in the Netherlands, Errard Bar-le-Duc and Daniel Speckle in France, and others) provide the basis of the geometry of military fortifications, whether in hexagonal or octagonal form. Practical strategians like Menno van Coehoren in the Netherlands and Manesson Mallet in France were outstanding military theoreticians for the seventeenth-century fortifications and made military engineering an important phase of town building. A complicated system of water moats and ramparts was devised outside the main wall of the city. These broad spaces forced the enemy into more distant positions for their cannons and attacks. The interior urban pattern was laid out according to the predominant military requirements, with open spaces in an easily controllable and accessible gridiron street system.

The French military engineer Sebastien le Prestre de Vauban (1633–1707), later Marshall of France, was a very remarkable exponent of urban and regional planning, both in detailed and in general development planning. He was the first to grasp the socioeconomic value of census statistics, which he collected privately on the occasion of the elections at Vézelay, France, in January 1696. He did this in order to obtain a better knowledge of population movement and employment patterns and to work out a more equitable system of taxation. His *Dime Royale* (1704), among other writings, shows the fertility of his ideas and the clearsightedness of his comments on population growth, on quantities of commodities, and on the characteristics of revenues from different regions. He made many suggestions for improvements.

Vauban redeveloped and expanded old existing towns around France. He "rectified" this defense belt by founding new fortress-cities after having collected socioeconomic data by means of a preliminary, careful, and minute regional survey and by additional census. Only, then did he plan his cities according to the contemporary mathematical and military concepts and scientific knowledge, with eventually new forms of government. These towns were linked by roads and water systems. They were laid out in hexagonal or octagonal urban forms, perfectly adapted to the geography of the site, with squares for regimental duties, churches, barracks, and monumental city gates. In a number of cases these towns were guarded or dominated by citadels. Flanders was the military *précarré* of France.

These patterns persisted as long as the military and strategic theories did not fundamentally change. They came to an end only with the technical and urban revolution that accompanied the Franco-Prussian War (1870–1871).

In the late eighteenth and early nineteenth centuries, long-range artillery was greatly improved and the old systems of walls, moats, and ramparts were reduced in effectiveness for military defense. As a result, the form of the city underwent drastic alterations.

The walls and ramparts were leveled, the moats were filled in, and buildings were erected in the open spaces as in the famous military boulevards encircling the original towns of Brussels, Antwerp, Ghent, and Tournai. These spaces separated the old towns from the surrounding suburbs but, as in Paris, they were gradually built up in response to the ruthless speculation of the late nineteenth century and open space disappeared from the city.

New housing quarters provided for the industrial workers, who invaded the city from the rural area, mushroomed in association with the industrial enterprises initiated in the mid-nineteenth century, especially in the years 1880 to 1890.

Government and commerce, on the other hand, established themselves in a favored place within the urban setting—sheltered from rioting mobs, from the factory noise, and from the ugliness of the workers' quarters—at the city center. Here the original crossroads of communication became the phenomenon of the *city,* where future speculation on land would find a promising site and where business would supplant residential areas.

As opposed to Britain, the European Continent was hardly affected by movements toward social reform and decent housing. There, the abuses of industrial exploitation were consistently tolerated and the status quo was maintained.

Twentieth-century Planning

Prelude: 1900 to 1945 The facts cited above do not mean that there was a total and general negation of reforms and reformers. Ebenezer Howard's book *Garden Cities of Tomorrow* was translated into French in 1917 by Louis Creplet and printed in China.

As a result, a garden city known as Floréal was built in Boitsfort (near Brussels) in 1925 and, ever since, its Japanese cherry trees have blossomed every year.

The Belgian landscape architect Louis Vander Swaelmen published in 1916, his book entitled *Preliminaries to Civic Design.* This was the first book written in French on this subject.

On the legislative level, as early as 1913, an International Conference of Cities and Communes was held in Ghent under the direction of Emile Vinck, the reporter of the conference. This conference expressed an opinion in favor of legislation in urban planning.

As a result of the destruction caused by World War I, a decree law dated August 25, 1915, was drawn up. According to this law, devastated cities had to draw up general plans, but it had no practical consequences in terms of a rational urban planning philosophy (see illustration of Ypres). One positive aspect was that the Belgian government-in-exile created a Town Planning Committee in 1916.

From 1945 Onward Only after World War II—primarily under the pressure of public opinion and a need for profound political, social, and economic change—did the city planning idea, already laid down by an advisory Commission for Urban Planning installed in 1936 by the government, take shape.

A provisional decree-law dated December 2, 1946 defined the legislative basis of urban planning, calling it a "useful instrument" of guided control for an adequate town planning act, which finally was voted as an organic law in 1962. One important feature, among many others, is the legislative provision concerning the drawing up of communal, regional, and district plans in cooperation with all public authorities.

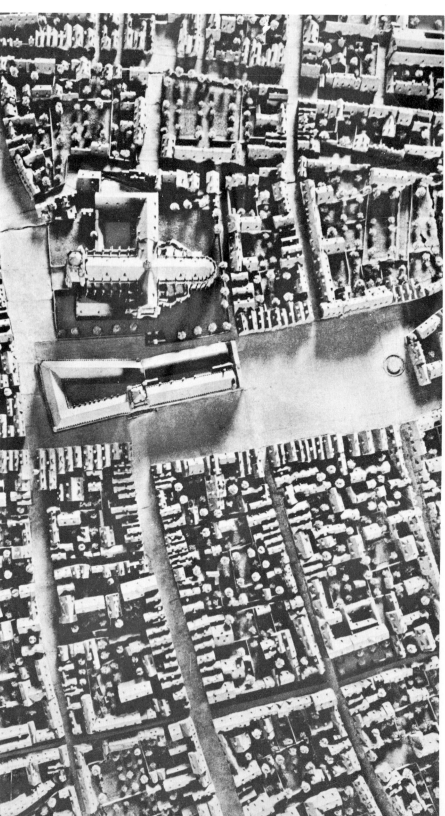

KEY
1. Cathedral of St. Martins
5. City Hall—formerly Cloth Hall
6. Market square, divided in three
   quadrangles of the same width,
   bordered on the south by the new road
   of St. James
39. New road of St. James
40. The former Cloth Market, at present the
    Merghelyackstraat
41. The former Cramynstraat, at present
    the Elisabethstraat, and, perpendicular
    to it, many parallel streets
35. Cliestraat
36. Hontstraat
38. Zuutstraat, or South Street
52. Sterrestraat
53. Boomgaaristraat, or Orchard Street,
    where once ran a tributary of the
    Ieperleet River toward the Scipleet
    Canal
Following streets lead toward the market
square:
31. The Hangwart Strate which links with
    the Menin Gate
33. The Short Torhoutstraat
51. The Diksmuidestraat

OPPOSITE PAGE: *Center of Ypres in the seventeenth century. Photograph of model in the Musee des Plan Reliefs. Hotel des Invalides, Paris. Ypres was fortified from 1678 onward. It was largely destroyed in the First World War and was rebuilt on the lines of the old seventeenth-century city.* LEFT: *Aerial view of the center of Ypres with the market square and cathedral. A comparison with the previous illustration will show how closely the rebuilding after the First World War followed the seventeenth-century city. (Photogrammetric Service of the Belgian Ministry of Public Works.)*

Replanning of the village center of Lissewege (near Zeebrugge). This center of the thirteenth century, with a beautiful Gothic church, is replanned to adapt it to the requirements of modern living. A degree of separation of vehicular and pedestrian traffic has been secured, and it will be noticed that several culs-de-sac have been introduced.

Present Trends Industrialization and the railroad had already considerably injured the urban tissue. In the twentieth century, the automobile appeared and became a new factor in the transformation process. It presented the city with a very serious problem of adaptation.

Other important elements of change are relative regression in the rate of demographic growth, increased prosperity, a higher standard of living and the concomitant increase in leisure time, the progressing phenomenon of nationalization of the country's resources, the standardization of ideas, more equal income distribution, full employment and continuous shift to the tertiary sector, and a higher demand for perishable foods combined with a lesser one for durable goods. Along with all this, an outspoken, high demand for ownership by occupiers persists.

Urban Renewal Urban renewal aims at (1) the relocation in healthy housing of those families morally and physically perishing in slums, and (2) restructuring urban centers with an architecture worthy of our era and national history.

1. The problem is all the more urgent in view of the fact that no large new town developments are being considered in Belgium, only smaller local developments.

A few major projects have been recently worked out, among which the renewal of the North Railway Center, better known as Manhattan Center, leads by the necessary coordination of juridical, public, and private means. It is a joint venture of three communities (Brussels, Saint-Josse-ten-Noode, and Schaerbeek) and is an unprecedented example of its kind in Belgium. In fact, it constitutes a superior utilization of this portion of the Brussels agglomeration in terms of land use and the communication system.

It is likewise an example of public urban renewal, where the administrative organization has to play a supervisory role in order to harmonize the interests of the economy, the needs of the urban structure, and the demands of technical progress.

Private efforts at renewal are encouraged and are—so to speak—part of the natural cyclic renewal of the patrimonial estate, either as rehabilitation or redevelopment. The common trend of urban renewal follows the economic fluctuations but is not always a positive contribution in the historic and aesthetic sense. The present Urban Planning Act does not explicitly mention urban renewal. Although the payable compensations for land acquisition are workable as a legal instrument, they certainly do not provide the minimum financial resources needed to promote a feasible and nationwide urban renewal program. The future and the viability of the city and of the central business district areas are discussed as an option to be taken in terms of a paying enterprise rather than a maximization of the net social product of land use as part of a community planning policy.

2. "The personality of a city strongly asserts itself to such an extent that this city offers a walk in the past" (Serruys).

The life of a city is an uninterrupted event materially manifested throughout the centuries, and it bestows on this city a personality taking

Louvain. The Grand Béguinage comprises primarily seventeenth century buildings. About 1230 it originated as a hospitium *near the crossing of the bifurcating Dijie River, a roman road, and an artisan's area, being the beginning of the town of Louvain. The medieval urban structure and the buildings massed around a green still exist. The facades and the Béguinage layout are harmoniously composed, with the informal organization expressed in the external appearance.*

The University of Louvain (founded by Erasmus in the early sixteenth century) acquired the Béguinage as a hostel for students, assistants, and professors. Twentieth-century life is not very different from that of the seventeenth century, for postgraduate studies are pursued far away from the hectic modern world. Married students have introduced a new aspect of university life since the Béguinage became a home for 700 married students of different disciplines. (Photograph: Cordier, 1969, University of Louvain.)

a firm root in past generations. By demystifying the notion of a historic monument, it seems desirable to introduce the museum (some Belgian cities—like Bruges—are as a whole or in part open-air museums) as an essential part of the urban life and of the townscape, instead of transforming the complete city into a museum, thus integrating the past with the present. Contemporary architecture may be the historic monument of tomorrow; and works of art of the past, as legacies and forms of civilization and of taste, are of interest to us beyond the initial intended functions.

A new veneration has to be fostered for these buildings while respecting the general character of the ensemble and developing the power to confer a new vitality on them. This is an essential factor in the urban renewal process which is purposefully worked out in a number of cases, such as the Béguinage of Louvain, now a student residential center (see illustration).

BIBLIOGRAPHY: G. Bricmont, "Aménagement du territoire et urbanisme. Commentaire de la loi organique du 29 mars 1962," *Les Recours, journal des Tribunaux,* Nov. 18, 1967; V. Bure, "Urbanisme," *Nouvelles,* vol. 4, "L'urbanisme et la propriété privée," *Cahiers d'urbanisme,* no. 52; Buttgenbach, *Droit administratif;* Delatte, "Urbanisme et aménagement du territoire," *Mouvement communal,* 1962, nos. 6, 7, 8; Delva, *Belgische Bouwwetgeving;* De Suray, "L'indemnisation des moins-values en matière d'aménagement du territoire," *J.T.,* 1966, pp. 201–204; De Tollenaere, "La loi du 29 mars 1962 organique de l'aménagement du territoire et de l'urbanisme," *R.A.,* 1962; Genot, *De la voirie publique par terre,* 3d ed., Marcotty, Bruxelles, 1964; Gilli, "Urbanisme et propriété privée," *Association Capitant,* May 1965; J. A. Gyselinck, "Le certificat d'urbanisme," *Annales du notariat et de l'enregistrement,* Nov. 1966, pp. 249–260; J. Hoeffler, "L'aménagement du territoire et le droit de propriété," *J.T.,* 1959, pp. 217–224, "L'aménagement régional de la Belgique," *Mouvement communal,* 1963, pp. 4–30, "Les effets civils du plan particulier d'aménagement et du permis de lotir," *Annales du notariat et de l'enregistrement,* 1965, pp. 11–30, "Le contentieux de la législation sur l'aménagement du territoire," "L'indemnisation des privations de jouissance," *J.T.,* 1966, pp. 89–90, "La responabilité des pouvoirs publics et notamment des communes en matière d'aménagement du territoire," *Mouvement communal,* 1966, pp. 126–139, "Faut-il modifier le livre II du Code civil?" *J.T.,* 1967, pp. 181–184, "Plans d'aménagement et permis de lotir," *Cahiers d'urbanisme,* no. 49, "La spéculation immobilière en Belgique," *Cahiers d'urbanisme,* no. 51, "La règlementation en matière d'urbanisme au point de vue des entreprises," *Faculté de Droit de Liège,* 1967, "Institut des Etudes juridiques de L'Urbanisme et de la Construction de Toulouse," *Propriété et Urbanisme,* 1968; Marty, "L'évolution du droit en fonction de la règlementation de la propriété," *Travaux conférences de L'Université libre de Bruxelles,* 1963, pp. 5–18; Mast, *Précis de droit administratif belge,* Gand; Persoons, "Les implications institutionnelles d'une politique d'aménagement du territoire," *Cahiers d'urbanisme,* no. 53; Sarot, *Revue de l'Administration,* parts 2 and 3, 1968; Senelle and Vanden Borre, "Aménagement du territoire et urbanisme," *Recueil de dispositions légales et réglementaires et d'instructions administratives et commentaire;* Wastiels, "Manuel administratif de l'aménagement du territoire et de l'urbanisme, *U.G.A.,* 1964; Wilkin, *Voirie et alignement. Urbanisme et construction,* 1964.

—VANDEN BORRE

BELLAMY, EDWARD (1850–1898)

American journalist and novelist born at Chicopee Falls, Mass., March 25, 1850. He was deeply involved in the problems of an industrial-capitalist society. In *Looking Backward* (1887) he used the vehical of a romantic novel set in the Boston of the year 2000 to try to demonstrate that a "cooperative-nationalist" society based on rational planning could end the inequities and conflicts of his own time. Of particular interest to planners is Bellamy's view of large cities as the undesirable result of uncoordinated and selfish individual behavior. He assumed a strong correlation between a society's economic system and its pattern of land use. His future society was to be characterized by a dispersed population residing in small, planned cities that were lavishly provided with well-designed parks and public buildings (including dining and cultural clubs) as keys to a community-oriented life of tranquillity and well-being. These ideas were expanded in a second novel, *Equality,* published in 1898. Bellamy's works were highly popular in reform circles in the United States and elsewhere at the century's end. Ebenezer Howard and Rexford Tugwell, the latter the sponsor in the American greenbelt towns of the 1930s, are but two who have acknowledged the importance of Bellamy's ideas on their own development. He died at the place of his birth on May 22, 1898.

BIBLIOGRAPHY: Arthur E. Morgan, *The Philosophy of Edward Bellamy,* New York, 1945; Sylvia Bowman, *The Year 2000: A Critical Biography,* New York, 1950.

—STANLEY BUDER

BERLAGE, HENDRIK PETRUS (1856–1934)

Famous as the architect of the Bourse in Amsterdam. Begun in 1898, this grand, solid brick structure owes much to both Netherlandish tradition and the nineteenth century's expressionistic use of brick to form patterns and shapes.

In town planning, Berlage's name will be remembered for his work in Amsterdam after the passing of the Housing Act in 1901, an act which required every town of 10,000 or more inhabitants to draw up detailed and general plans which had to be revised every 10 years.

Berlage prepared plans for the development of Amsterdam South in 1902. These plans were an attempt to get away from the gridiron and strongly axial approaches which had characterized town planning in the past. The works of Camillo Sitte must have had an influence on Berlage, as must some of the theories prevalent in England and America at the time, although he rejected the garden city movement. The work of Frank Lloyd Wright was known to Berlage, and the great American played some part in influencing the Dutchman. The public buildings are the dominants in Berlage's plan of 1902, but in 1915 he revised the plan, treating huge apartment blocks as the main elements in forming streets, an essentially nineteenth-century idea. Significantly, greenery and nature play a strong part in the scheme, but they are subordinated to the general form and structure of the urban matrix. This type of approach is contrasted with the more romantic attitude of Dudok at Hilversum, where individual buildings set in landscapes owe more to the garden city movement.

It might be said that Berlage's main achievement was to give the brick wall something of the integrity and repose of great monuments of the past, and later to develop this to recreate the unity of the street by means of a wider use of this technique in a refreshing and original way.

BIBLIOGRAPHY: Nikolaus Pevsner, *An Outline of European Architecture,* Penguin Books, Inc., Baltimore, 1963; Gerd Hatje (ed.), *Encyclopaedia of Modern Architecture,* Thames and Hudson, London, 1963; Sigfried Giedion, *Space, Time and Architecture,* Harvard University Press, Cambridge, Mass., and Oxford University Press, London, third edition, 1967.

—JAMES STEVENS CURL

BERNINI, GIAN LORENZO (1598–1680)   Leading architect and sculptor of the Italian baroque period. Bernini was born in Naples. His father was a Florentine sculptor of talent who moved to Rome in 1606 to work for the ambitious Borghese Pope Paul V, and he gave the young Gian Lorenzo his early training. Due to his early aptitude, the young Bernini soon came to the notice of the papal court, and commissions came thick and fast. In 1619, when he carved the *Anima Dannata,* his genius for baroque expression first became apparent. A succession of splendid works followed, including the *David* of 1623 to 1624, an astonishingly forceful work, which marks the beginning of what might be described as Bernini's *dynamic* style.

With the election of the Barberini Pope Urban VIII, Bernini's fortunes reached their zenith, for during the long pontificate of Urban, a friend of the sculptor, the genius of Bernini flowered. He started designing buildings at this time, beginning with the portico to the church of Santa Bibiena. The huge baldacchino over the altar in St. Peter's followed in 1624 to 1633, and many regal sculptures were carved, including the statue of St. Longinus and the mighty tomb of Urban VIII, both in St. Peter's.

It is necessary to understand the sculptural background to Bernini's career in order to appreciate his work as a civic designer, because his techniques of the theater and of fusing space, solid and void, into grand compositions were developed in his architectural treatments in the Church of Santa Maria della Vittoria, where his *Ecstasy of St. Teresa* can still shock. The superb theatricality of the Cathedra Petri and the diminishing perspectives of the Scala Regia heralded the design of the first large open space within a city since classical times. This was the Piazza Obliqua before St. Peter's in Rome, built in the middle of the century. This huge piazza with its colonnades stretching out from the Cathedral to embrace the city and the world embodies the grand symbolism of which Bernini was master. It is a masterpiece of civic design, perfectly suited to its function, and destined to embrace the multitudes. The surface of the space flows down to the great obelisk in its center, then rises gently in steps and terraces to the superhuman portico of Peter's church. The great piazza must be seen as a sculptural work, for the subtle flow and rise and fall of the ground to aid the theatrical effect is breathtaking. So too is the scale of the place, so grand in conception and so worthy of its creator's noble mind. It is only when we experience the hugeness of the piazza columns and the effects of the gesturing saints which crown the colonnades that we can appreciate the wonder of this design.

Later in life, Bernini submitted plans for the completion of the Louvre in Paris and carved a magnificent bust of Louis XIV. His later works are personal in style, though still highly baroque. Full of pathos, his *Truth,* in the Galleria Borghese, and the statues in Siena Cathedral testify to his study of Hellenistic sculptures and especially the *Laocoön,* while the angels on the Ponte Sant' Angelo are almost Bavarian rococo in their lightness and elegance.

Bernini died after he had completed a *Salvator Mundi* for Queen Christina of Sweden and had carried out a restoration of the Palazzo della Cancellaria. His death occurred in Rome during the pontificate of Innocent XI, the eighth Pope he had served.

BIBLIOGRAPHY: Howard Hibbard, *Bernini,* Penguin Books, Inc., Baltimore, 1965; Sigfried Giedion, *Space, Time and Architecture,* Harvard University Press, Cambridge, Mass., and Oxford University Press, London, 1967; James Stevens Curl, *European Cities and Society,* Leonard Hill, London, 1970.

—JAMES STEVENS CURL

BETTERMENT   (*See* LAND VALUES AND PLANNING.)

BIOTECHNIC   This and other similar terms (paleotechnic, neotechnic, and eotechnic; explained under the separate headings) were coined by Patrick Geddes. All the terms apply to modern technology and its effect on economic and social life. The biotechnic phase is that in which the biological sciences excerise a dominant influence. This term and the others mentioned are defined and extensively used by Lewis Mumford in *Technics and Civilization* and *The Culture of Cities.*

BIRD SANCTUARIES   (*See* NATURE RESERVES.)

BLIGHT   Sometimes called "planning blight," but among planners often referred to simply as "blight." It stems from depreciation in the value of land or buildings as the result of planning proposals or planned development. Blight may occur in two ways:

1. As the result of the putting forward of alternative planning proposals for public discussion. In such a situation, until a single and final proposal

is decided upon, there is uncertainty about the future development of all land affected by each proposal. As the practice of putting forward alternative planning proposals for public discussion increases, there is likely to be an increase in this form of blight.

2. Where a specific, confirmed proposal, or a development actually carried out (e.g., a new road), so affects the value of the properties in the vicinity that they cannot be sold at the market value they had before the development was proposed or took place. At present this is the more common form of blight.

Blight can thus be regarded as the opposite of "betterment"; in a sense, therefore, as "worsenment." Whereas in some countries there is provision for the community to collect all or part of betterment value, there is little statutory provision for property owners to be compensated for blight.

BIBLIOGRAPHY: Desmond Heap, *An Outline of Planning Law,* 5th ed., Sweet & Maxwell, London, 1969; R. N. D. Hamilton, *A Guide to Development and Planning,* Oyez Publications, 1970.

—DAVID HALL

BOULEVARD   The word "boulevard" originally designated the broad, horizontal surface of the rampart of a city wall. Later, the term was applied to the wide thoroughfares that took the place of the city walls of Paris. The first such boulevard was opened in 1670 on the site of the ancient walls extending from Port Saint-Denis to the Bastille. The term has since been used to typify any broad, handsome avenue.

BRAMANTE, DONATO (1444–1514)   Celebrated architect and town planner of the Italian Renaissance. Bramante laid out the line for one of the first new streets of the Rome of the Renaissance, the Strada Giulia, at the command of Pope Julius II, who called Raphael to Rome at the same time as Bramante.

A native of Urbino, he grew up in a creative atmosphere where Piero della Francesca was painting; Laurana was working at the Ducal Palace; and Francesco di Giorgio was writing his great treatise following those of Alberti and Filarete. Bramante was one of the first Renaissance architects to treat the monumental stairway as a dominant motif in the design of formal elements to capture the grandeur of the period. In 1506 he was given the task of linking the Vatican with the Belvedere to form a grand architectural unity. The *Cortile del Belvedere* was the agency which he used to mold the two elements into a whole. The stairway became the model for the stunning *Scala di Spagna* and many other splendid monuments of the baroque age long after Bramante's death.

Bramante employed other means to achieve effects, including theatrical illusions such as those in the choir in the Church of Santa Maria presso San Satiro (1479–1514) in Milan. This is only a small space, but is painted to give the appearance of great depth and size. The church itself is similar to Alberti's St. Andrea in Mantua.

He was greatly interested in the theories of centrally organized space, and he produced many designs showing great domed structures with radiating chapels, very much a microcosm of the *città ideale*. That he learned much from Alberti while at Urbino and more from Leonardo da Vinci while at Milan cannot be doubted, but his characteristic works date from his call to Rome in 1499. There, his individualistic strength of forms and austerity of detail first appear in the cloister of St. Maria della Pace and in the Tempietto of St. Pietro in Montorio of 1502. His most important commission, however, was in 1506, when Julius II appointed him to rebuild St. Peter's in a style more suited to the period of humanism and of the Renaissance. His design was a huge Greek cross, completely symmetrical, which created a precedent for boldly modeled masonry and nobility of scale. For Bramante, the order of the Renaissance was complete in this astonishing plan. The magnificent simplicity, however, was never to be realized, for humanist order, like the architecture it favored, was to give way to the wordly splendor of the age of baroque.

BIBLIOGRAPHY: Nikolaus Pevsner, *An Outline of European Architecture,* Penguin Books, Inc., Baltimore, 1963; Sigfried Giedion, *Space, Time and Architecture,* Harvard University Press, Cambridge, Mass., and Oxford University Press, London, 1967; Arnaldo Bruschi, *Bramante Architette,* Editori Laterza, Bari, 1969; Sir Banister Fletcher, *A History of Architecture on the Comparative Method,* Athlone Press, seventeenth edition, London, 1961.

—JAMES STEVENS CURL

BRAZIL

Geographical, Climatic and Economic Conditions   Brazil can be compared with a continent, its huge size—over $3\frac{1}{4}$ million square miles ($8\frac{1}{2}$ million square kilometers)—spreading from 5 degrees north latitude southward through equatorial and tropical zones to 34 degrees south latitude, an almost temperate zone. It can be roughly divided into three regions, different in climate, geography, population, and development. The north is the rainy, wet Amazon River basin. It includes Maranhão and the region north of Goias and Mato Grosso—about 2 million square miles (5 million square kilometers)—with a population of 8 million (1967), about four inhabitants per square mile. Human settlements are small and largely scattered, with only three cities above 100,000 population: Belem (540,000), Manáus (200,000), and São Luis (190,000). A few more exceed 30,000. The population is part Indian. The economy is based mostly on mining and tropical agriculture, with some cattle raising.

In the northeast is the generally arid region of the São Francisco River basin and vicinities, including the areas north of Minas Gerais: it is heavily populated by old European stock strongly mixed with Indians and Africans. The main occupations are agriculture and cattle raising, with some manufacturing industry. Most of the industry has been established only recently because of the limited availability of capital. The region is over $\frac{1}{2}$ million square miles (1.35 million square kilometers) in area with a population of about 24.5 million, giving almost 50 persons per square mile. There are a dozen towns with more than 100,000 inhabitants and a score that have between 50,000 and 100,000. The main cities are Recife (1,050,000), Salvador (880,000), and Fortaleza (790,000).

In the south is the most populated and developed third region, in the basins of the Paraná and Uruguay Rivers, including, in the northwest, a tropical and mostly wet section (Mato Grosso and Goias). The coastal band, nearly 375 miles (600 kilometers) deep, has a semiwet climate in the north and a temperate one in the Uruguay basin. This band is the more advanced and populated part of Brazil, having profited from strong waves of recent immigrants. Since the middle of last century Italians (1,300,000 from 1876 to 1925), Portuguese, Germans, Spaniards, Poles, Syrians, Japanese, and natives of the northeast region entered this southern region. In its extent of 800,000 square miles (nearly 2.15 million square kilometers) there were, in 1967, 55 million people, at a density of almost 70 per square mile, rising to about 200 in the state of São Paulo, the most populated and advanced of the country. The two great metropolitan areas of Brazil rise here, 218 miles (350 kilometers) apart: São Paulo (with a population of more than 6 million) and Rio de Janeiro (more than 5 million). Large cities are Belo Horizonte (1,100,000), Pôrto Alegre (880,000), and Curitiba (580,000). There are nine towns of about 200,000 inhabitants and nearly sixty from 50,000 to 200,000 inhabitants.

Most kinds of agricultural, breeding, and mineral products are developed here, while Santos and Rio de Janeiro are the largest ports in Brazil. The money required for imports comes mostly from coffee, reaching about 45 percent in value of the total Brazilian exports. In this region, mostly in the zone of the Rio São Paulo axis, is the largest concentration of industries in Latin America, benefiting from one of the most powerful groups of hydroelectric power stations in the world, now (1972) being built on the River Paraná (Urubupunga power stations, 4.6 million kilowatts).

Where these three regions of Brazil join together in the hinterland, about 560 miles (900 kilometers) from the coast, the new federal capital Brasília (1960) has been established, over 3,280 feet (1,000 meters) above sea level. In 1968 its population was 350,000.

Urbanization is mostly in a coastal strip over 2,000 miles (3,500 kilometers) long from Ceará to Rio Grande do Sul and about 300 miles (500 kilometers) wide; nearly three-fourths of all the towns and five-sixths of the people in Brazil are found here, in a fifth of the country. The average rate of population growth of Brazil was 3.66 percent a year from 1950 to 1960 and it is estimated now at about 3 percent.

Legislation and Administration   Brazil is a federal republic with a presidential government, established on a federal constitution (that of 1967, largely amended in 1969, being more centralized than the former, of 1946). Each state of the Federation is ruled by an elected governor and has its own constitution and assembly. The whole country is divided into municipalities (*municipios*), whose autonomy is assured, being generally ruled by an elected mayor (*prefeito*) who is accountable to an elected town council. The mayors of the capital cities of states are appointed by the governors; the mayor of the federal capital (Brasília) by the President. Hence, city planning rests on three legislative degrees: federal, state, and municipal laws—the last providing the main machinery of the planning process. All plans, improvements, and regulations are proposed and approved by the municipal administration on the basis of the constitutional provisions, laws, and regulations of states and Federation.

The Federation has very recently passed an act providing powers for the preparation of 4 years' national or regional general development planning for the establishment of total, sectional, or local goals and policies. It can also initiate specific regional plans.

By a decree of 1956 the Federation established a financial fund to support city planning for homogeneous areas with more than 50,000 inhabitants, cities interested in credits being obliged to submit their programs with applications for funds. The Federation wishes to ensure the prompt completion of development plans for communities all over the country by the concentration of all public means; the final goal being to reach a general homogenous planning process and to give it a permanent character.

Most of the states also, by their organic law of municipalities, connect the granting of financial support to cities with the approval, by the city councils, of an integrated development plan comprehending territorial, economic, social, and administrative aspects.

Major cities have their own building and allotment laws, generally the codes of capital cities (São Paulo, 1934; Rio, 1937) being taken as models. Some states also issue planning regulations for minor communities, mostly starting from the enactments of the Federal Service for Housing and Planning (SERFHAU), responsible, in connection with the National Housing Bank (BHN), for the national housing and planning policy, which is intended to provide cities with the technical and financial resources for their planning and housing. The Federation is authorized by its constitution to establish metropolitan regions, linking cities for the benefit of common services.

Large cities could always cope reasonably well with their planning problems because they have their own laws and revenue. Their principal problems are public services and city extension, the latter being almost entirely undertaken by private enterprise, the control of which is frequently a very difficult task.

Municipal laws generally establish rate of land occupancy, distance from boundaries, and height and bulk of buildings as well as their illumination, ventilation, and use. Zoning regulations are generally inadequate or too rigid in some zones occupied only by single-family dwellings. Special laws are, however, improving some of the worse conditions.

Local laws regulate also the width and grade of roads and the need of open spaces in new allocations, a very useful provision being the right of cities to establish in private plans, within a legal limit, the main road connections and the open spaces that the communities consider are needed. In this way an adequate provision of thoroughfares and open spaces is ensured, although most of the improvements required are a drain on public expenditure. The above provisions were particularly helpful to the state capitals, which, however, do not have a reasonable share of public revenues to help solve their many urban problems. They are forced to depend on the benevolence of state and Federation for special credits. Only Rio is exempt from this difficulty, having once been the Federal capital and being now constituted in the State of Guanabara (about 524 square miles, or 1,356 square kilometers).

The financial problem was difficult for São Paulo, the largest metropolis in Brazil and one of the quickest growing in the world. It could not establish the subway system it needed nor the necessary large-scale improvements for its increasing population; but recently, by a new constitutional amendment, things have changed. The subway is under construction, a wide program of public works has started, and planning prospects have improved because of affluence. The most striking example of expansion is represented by the increase in the general income of the municipality of São Paulo since 1950. The following table shows this increase—about sevenfold in 18 years—as well as the growth of taxation per capita, about 3.5 times in 3 years.

Year	General income (millions)	Population (millions)	Per capita income
1950	$ 32.4	2.2	$14.75
1960	46.7	3.8	12.30
1965	53.9	5.0	10.80
1966	99.2	5.25	18.90
1967	192.0	5.5	34.95
1968	216.4	5.8	37.30

Professional Practice, Education and Training, and Institutions At the end of last century and in the first quarter of the present one, city planning was looked at from a hygienic point of view, mostly because of the need for protecting developing communities from tropical diseases such as yellow fever and malaria (Recife, Rio de Janeiro, Santos). From the aesthetic aspect, there was the need to make new capital cities suitable for their important civic functions (Rio de Janeiro, São Paulo, and Belo Horizonte). Lastly, with increasing traffic problems, it was necessary to provide cities with straight and large thoroughfares, first for trolley cars, then for buses and automobiles. New trends appeared slowly. First, engineers, architects, and surveyors were the sole professionals devoted to planning, and they still prevail today in planning practice. Planning was hence a subject dealt with in schools of engineering and architecture. It was first established as a course in the sanitation programs for civil engineers and of general design for architects. At a later stage, distinct departments of city planning were established in the universities.

A postgraduate course of two years has been established, for architects and engineers, leading to the title of city planner (Pôrto Alegre, Belo Horizonte, Rio de Janeiro). Up to 1965, 185 planners, most of them architects, had graduated from these three schools.

Because of the increase of planning practice, especially due to the new financial legislation, large professional groups of planners have been established which include in their teams geographers, sociologists, and economists. Sometimes these are associated with similar foreign groups (United States, West Germany, France, and Greece).

Town and country planning is studied today in the schools of engineering of São Paulo (Escola Politécnica, Mackenzie) and São Carlos, and in the schools of architecture of São Paulo (Faculdade de Arquitetura e Urbanismo Mackenzie), Pôrto Alegre, Belo Horizonte, and Rio de Janeiro.

Planners freely group themselves within the professional associations of engineers (Instituto de Engenharia, São Paulo; Clube de Engenharia, Rio de Janeiro) or in the Instituto de Arquitetos do Brazil. Some of these institutions, and also some official local bureaus devoted to planning problems, publish reviews with articles on planning.

Special issues on planning problems are prepared by institutions such as the SERFHAU, Rio de Janeiro; the Centre of Studies and Researches on Municipal Administration (CEPAM), São Paulo; and the Brazilian Institute of Municipal Administration (IBAM), Rio de Janeiro.

Propaganda and education in planning is accomplished by articles in the press, in radio talks, and in television programs. Both professional institutions and public offices, separately or together, promote conferences, exhibitions, meetings, seminars, discussions on specific or general planning problems, specially in correlation with the World Town Planning Day commemorations, founded in 1949 by Carlos Maria della Paolera of the University of Buenos Aires. A special issue of postage stamps was produced by Brazil in 1952, when São Paulo was that year's host city of Town Planning Day.

Traditions of Planning to the End of the Nineteenth Century   When, in 1889, Brazil was transformed from an empire into a republic, planning had been mostly an inheritance of colonial times and a result of imported practice from Europe. Not having a stable pattern to follow, as Spanish territories had in the "Laws of Indias," cities developed freely, conforming to the natural conditions of the site, although some chessboard planning was employed in some of the principal settlements, even on sloping ground. This occurred throughout the country until recently. Later the model of Parisian planning (boulevards and traffic circles) was followed for principal streets and squares, and an eclectic style was adopted for buildings. Planning was therefore limited to street design, sometimes associated with canal projects to improve marshy soils.

The French pattern was largely followed also in plans for such new large cities as Belo Horizonte (1897) and Rio de Janeiro in 1927, and later, in 1937, for Goiania, a new capital city with the same type of plan as Belo Horizonte. These plans, as also that for the recent Brasília, were produced by single planners. New trends became fully apparent only in the forties and more strongly in the fifties. The lack of general systematic planning up to the thirties was responsible for the haphazard growth of towns.

Because of changing economic conditions from colonial agriculture to industrial development mostly in the southern part of the country, the present century shows the decay of large northern cities—all Brazilian cities having begun as ports—and the quick growth of those in the southern zone (Rio de Janeiro having been always the largest city until it was recently surpassed by São Paulo). Manáus, on the Rio Negro (Amazon), was developed because of rubber. It has very fine public buildings and a floating port to follow the great floods of its rivers, but it later declined. The same happened to São Luis (Maranhão), at one time a very important commercial city which is now very much a memory. Some northern cities such as Recife and Salvador, because their population spread inland and because of the influx of some industry, continued to develop reasonably well.

Those Brazilian cities which, in the past, were mainly the meeting places of rural undertakers and the seats of local government cannot be expected to grow beyond a certain size and structure. Industrial settlements are the cause of recent increases. But many urban increases are due more to desertion from the fields.

Twentieth-century Planning

City and Town Extensions   *Rio de Janeiro* is still the leading and the finest city in Brazil, endowed with the noble legacy of two centuries as the nation's capital and enjoying a wonderful site. At the start of the century very important works were planned, including the demolition of local hills to permit downtown expansion; the improvement of the coastal marshes; and

LEFT: Rio de Janeiro. Master plan of 1960 showing main thoroughfares. In the middle, near the bay, is the main central area. South of the center are the long tunnels through the mountain range. (Secretaria de Obras—Estado da Guanabara.) BELOW: Master plan for the year 2000. Compare with the illustration at left. The two large empty zones represent wooded mountains. Thoroughfares are clearly indicated. Cedug-Doxiadis; FAU, São Paulo, 1965).

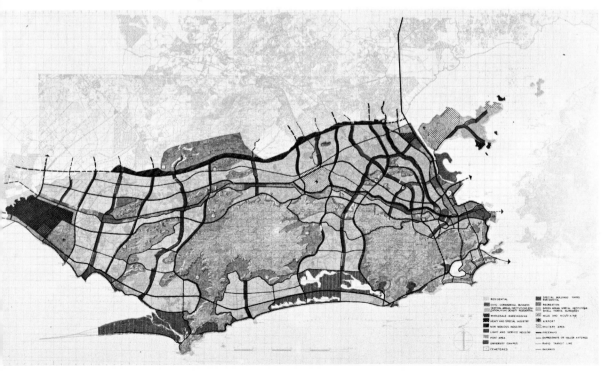

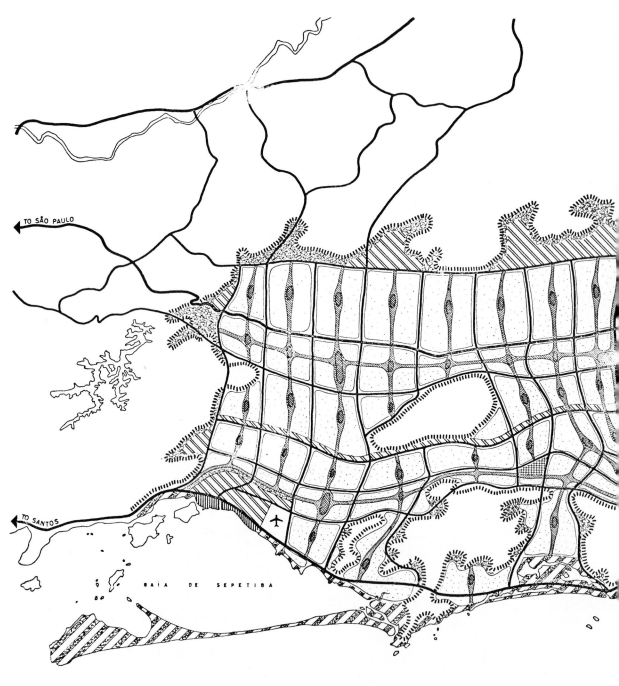

TO SÃO PAULO

TO SANTOS

BAÍA   DE   SEPETIBA

OCEANO   ATLANTIC

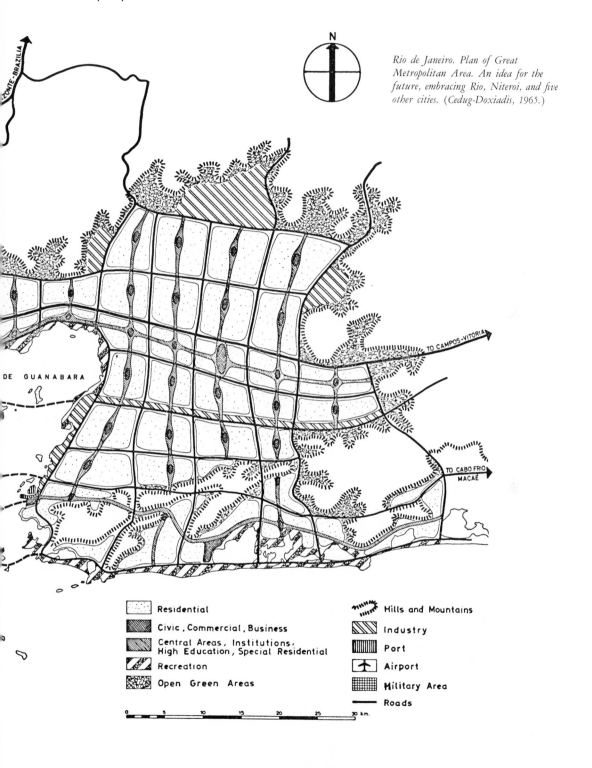

N

Rio de Janeiro. Plan of Great Metropolitan Area. An idea for the future, embracing Rio, Niteroi, and five other cities. (Cedug-Doxiadis, 1965.)

TO CAMPOS-VITORIA

TO CABO FRIO
MACAÉ

DE GUANABARA

Residential

Civic, Commercial, Business

Central Areas, Institutions,
High Education, Special Residential

Recreation

Open Green Areas

Hills and Mountains

Industry

Port

Airport

Military Area

Roads

0 5 10 15 20 25 30 km.

the establishment of beautiful parks and wide avenues on the sea front of the bay for better connections with growing residential districts like Copacabana. To connect this coastal system with north and west, the wide and fine Rio Branco Avenue was opened, cutting through the gridiron pattern of old, narrow central streets. In recent decades a new central hill was demolished, new roads were improved, and a large one was opened— Presidente Vargas Avenue, almost 90 yards (80 meters) wide—transverse to Rio Branco Avenue, running westward toward residential districts and to the Maracaña Stadium. Connections with the southern and northern zones were facilitated not only by widening the coastal parkway system on reclaimed land and encircling the city center with elevated expressways, but also by piercing the mountains to the south with large new tunnels that made it possible to bypass the downtown area. The first two tunnels to be opened to traffic were Catumbí-Laranjeiras, about 1,500 yards (1,357 meters) long and about 19 yards (17.5 meters) wide; and Rio Comprido-Lagôa, about 3,000 yards (2,720 meters) in total length.

To improve mass transportation, now provided by buses and trains, a subway is being built. The building of a great bridge across the bay has also been begun. It is to connect Rio with the opposite cities of Niterói and São Gonzalo.

Important measures have been taken to redevelop or improve the nearly two hundred *favelas* (slums), comprising more than seventy thousand dwellings (430,000 inhabitants), which have arisen mostly as a result of mass transportation difficulties.

Very recently the local government offices, with the help of foreign consultants, have made general proposals for a wide network of freeways and a thorough decentralization of urban functions throughout a wider area, scattering industrial zones on the periphery of the town, with workers' residential centers beyond them (see illustrations).

São Paulo. The growth of São Paulo, the main industrial city of Brazil, deserves special consideration because this city is one of the most impressive examples of urban development in the world, having risen to its present great size in less than half a century.

In 1881 São Paulo, with 40,000 inhabitants, was a quiet colonial town with a rural background and with only *one* large factory (weaving). Buildings were mostly one- and two-story houses. In 1930, the city, with 900,000 inhabitants, occupied an area 55 times larger, high buildings being common. By 1967 the big metropolis of 5 million people displayed a panorama of skyscrapers, the highest being about 490 feet (nearly 150 meters) tall. The skyscrapers are generally too closely spaced, creating numerous problems.

Planning in recent times has been a very difficult task because of insufficient financial support (see "Legislation") and of tremendous pressure of private development. In the fifties an outline of a decentralized road system was adopted and generally followed with some necessary adjustments. A wide highway ring was also planned to connect all roads and thoroughfares and is now under construction. The large underground system recently started has 4 lines about 40 miles (66 kilometers) long. A general survey

Rio de Janeiro. The extensive downtown areas reclaimed from the bay, with shores, gardens, public buildings, and monuments. The development is crossed by a speedway. (Mercator, São Paulo.)

São Paulo, 1967. City center looking south. The wide thoroughfare (left of center) is crossed by several bridges. (Mercator, São Paulo.)

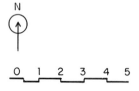

N

0 1 2 3 4 5

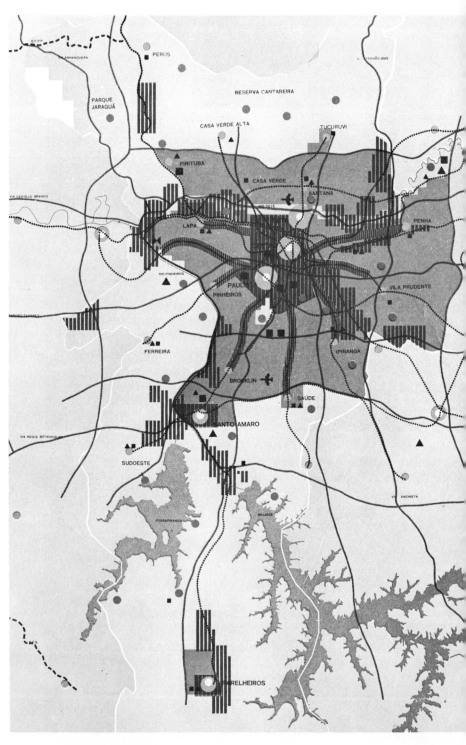

Low density
Medium density
High density
Industrial area
Rural area
Waterways
Area of multiple
  activities
Metropolitan center
Suburban center
Secondary center
Subway
Expressway
Airport
University
School
District park
Main hospital
District emergency
  hospital
Supply center
City limits

LEFT: *São Paulo. Proposals for the urban structure in 1990, based on a general survey of present conditions and problems. (Prefeitura Municipal de São Paulo.)*   BELOW: *The great metropolitan constellation of Rio-São Paulo, 1969. The map shows the metropolitan areas of Rio de Janeiro and São Paulo, a conurbation along the valley of the Paraiba River, running diagonally between the coastal mountain range and the high Mantiqueira Range. (H.M.D.—FAU, São Paulo.)*

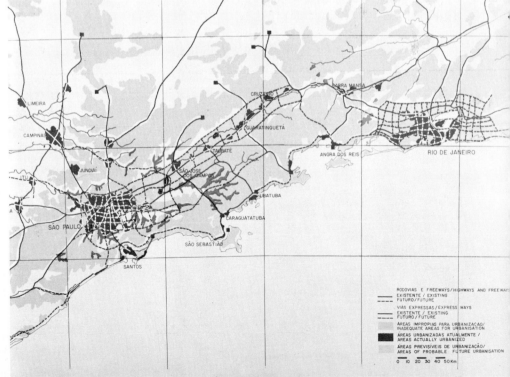

RODOVIAS E FREEWAYS/HIGHWAYS AND FREEWAYS
EXISTENTE / EXISTING
FUTURO / FUTURE
VIAS EXPRESSAS/EXPRESS WAYS
EXISTENTE / EXISTING
FUTURO / FUTURE
AREAS IMPROPIAS PARA URBANIZAÇÃO/
INADEQUATE AREAS FOR URBANISATION
AREAS URBANIZADAS ATUALMENTE /
AREAS ACTUALLY URBANIZED
ÁREAS PREVISÍVEIS DE URBANIZAÇÃO/
AREAS OF PROBABLE FUTURE URBANISATION

0 10 20 30 40 50Km

Brasília. General Plan, 1963. Each side of the quadrates of the checkerboard gridiron on the map is 3.1 miles (5 kilometers). The government center with the Parliament Building, Presidency, Supreme Court, and ministries is on the main straight east-west axis. (I.B.G.E.)

of the present metropolitan conditions has been made, and this has led to the drafting of the planning principles that the city must follow in the next decades together with the other cities of the greater São Paulo area. The idea of a large gridiron pattern of expressways, superimposed on the present general road system, is one of the developments that these general propositions suggest.

A very important element in planning in all large Brazilian cities is the settlement of garden suburbs, with dwellings in green areas, affording a peaceful home environment.

Brasília. The new federal capital inaugurated in 1960, was established on a general plan drawn from a national competition in 1956. It was planned as the capital as well as the political and cultural center of half a million people. It displays a formal pattern, based on two axes crossing at right angles, the east-west being the principal one (parliament; presidential palace; high court; ministries; religious, cultural, business, and traffic centers). Brasília's other main avenue, which is curved, is occupied by dwellings (apartments and houses grouped in neighborhood units, with local commerce and schools), businesses, and professional premises. At the southern end are embassies and legations.

Individual dwellings rise around the artificial lake, and suburbs are scattered in different directions, Nucleo Bandeirantes and Taguatinga being the larger ones, with some local commerce and industry. A substantial section of the population in this area is made up of poorer people who live in underdeveloped areas, for which the original plans made no provisions.

There are several different sorts of roads depending on the type of traffic, the main arteries being wide expressways. The large blocks are served by secondary roads (see illustration).

Brasília. General aerial view showing the curved axis, with the residential area including apartment complexes and two-story terrace housing. In the distance are the buildings of the ministries and the twin towers of the Parliament Building. (Mercator, São Paulo.)

Other Large Cities. Reference has been made to the plans of Belo Horizonte, which is well situated and established as the capital of Minas Gerais in place of the old, monumental Ouro Prêto, which was unfit to evolve to a great city because of its hilly site. Belo Horizonte is primarily developing vertically in the area of the former plan, while extending beyond the disordered districts out of the planned zone to develop good modern areas, as that of Pampulha.

Recife (Pernambuco), although having a difficult problem with housing because of slums, has a good .commercial center on the islands; some new planning ideas having been introduced, mostly in the road plan, as is also the case with Salvador (Baía), famous for its historic and yet active city center. Pôrto Alegre (Rio Grande do Sul) followed a general road and zoning plan from 1938 to 1959, with some good projects. Curitiba (Paraná), developed mostly for government and private employees, has a regional plan of 1965 which includes some decentralization of urban activities in four regional centers, one of which includes industry and technical schools. Santos, with a great port and heavy industries in the vicinity is, with the cities of São Vicente and Guarujá nearby, an important seashore resort. A special authority has been established to improve the coastal region. This authority is also working on the improvement of industrial facilities. The plan for Santos is closely related to the metropolitan plan of São Paulo, about 35 miles away, the high ground of the coastal range being the sole but strong obstacle to the fusion of these two clusters of cities.

Some large regional plans have also been made with a view to economic development, the most interesting one being the basin of Paraná-Uruguay rivers survey, with a section devoted to the state of São Paulo (1954) and some topical reference to the main problems of the state capital (see illustrations).

New Towns—Communities—Urban Renewal   No New Towns have been established to decentralize population from large cities except partially in Curitiba's plan; yet new towns arise all over the country because of the expansion of settlements in free lands. They are established mostly on a gridiron pattern, with some scattered squares or rows of squares for public, religious, or recreational purposes. Some of these new towns have been built to serve agricultural and industrial needs. Following are some examples: Volta Redonda (100,000 inhabitants, Rio de Janeiro) was founded during the Second World War around a great steel plant, being established on a traditional pattern. As a center to meet the needs of a dispersed population in a wild mining zone north of the Amazon River's mouth is the new establishment of Vila Amazonas. In the northeast region new industrial districts near the main cities have been planned, the largest being Aratu, near Salvador, that offers employment in several factories, including heavy industry. It conforms somewhat to the New Towns as a means of decentralization. Industrial complexes are rising everywhere in the vicinities of south Brazilian cities, as isolated establishments or grouped ones, sometimes with dwellings.

Salvador. Aerial view of the capital of Bahia showing the port on the bay front. (Mercator, São Paulo.)

Goiania. Aerial view of the center of the Goias capital with government buildings on the circular place and straight avenues radiating from it, on the French model. (O Estado de São Paulo.)

One typical example in the agricultural field is Blumenau (Santa Catarina) with 85,000 inhabitants, founded as a settlement for German farmers at the end of last century. It is now a very interesting industrial town of European character in a tropical zone, spread in a long, narrow valley. It has a curiously high number of bicycles—nearly one to every two persons—used by the workers at the more than five hundred factories. Another example is Londrina (Paraná) with nearly 200,000 inhabitants, founded by English enterprise in 1929 within an expanding agricultural region. It is one of the more important cities of the state, controlling the coffee growing, commerce, and finance. Established on a gridiron plan, it is now crowded in the center by very high buildings of twenty or more stories, as in other progressive towns in Brazil. Although no space problem is alleged, it is fighting with the problem of slums.

A new town is now rising near a great dam of the Urubupungá system on the Paraná River (São Paulo): Ilha Solteira (50,000 inhabitants) close to a very important water-power plant under construction. This town is intended first to serve as a general camp for the workers during the construction, but the plan is to continue its urban functions when the work is completed and to use the electrical energy for the industries of the town. It is built to a modern design, each urban area being disposed like the teeth of a comb along its green central axis, comprehending educational, commercial, recreational, and social activities.

Self-supporting urban communities have been constructed elsewhere in Brazil, the most interesting being in Rio de Janeiro. There is the old one of the Bangú factory: the Conjunto Residential Pedregulho, with a large curved block of apartments and good community services; and the more recent communities of Parque Proletário Gávea and Deodoro, also with very large curved blocks of apartments. A very fine example is the one built in Laranjeiras, overlooking a good park. An unusual example of housing is in Osasco, near São Paulo, which with urban improvements and facilities, is for the employees of a big bank situated just within the community.

BIBLIOGRAPHY: Antonio Bezerra Baltar, *Diretrizes de um plano regional para o Recife*, Recife, 1951; *Problemas de desenvolvimento—Necessidades e possibilidades do Estado de São Paulo*, Comissão Interestadual da Bacia Paraná-Uruguai, vol. I, São Paulo, 1954; *Delta do Jacuí-Plano Piloto*, Prefeitura Municipal de Pôrto Alegre, Pôrto Alegre, 1958; *Planejamento*, Prefeitura do Município de São Paulo, São Paulo, 1961; *Plano Diretor de Pôrto Alegre*, Prefeitura Municipal, Pôrto Alegre, 1964; *Guanabara, a plan for urban development*, Comissão Executivo para o Desenvolvimento Urbano-Doxiadis Associated, Consultants on Development and Ekistics, Athens, 1965; *Plano Diretor da Região de Curitiba*, Companhia de Urbanização e Saneamento de Curitiba, Curitiba, 1965; *Areas metropolitanas e deselvonimento integrado no Brasil*, Serviço Federal de Habitação e Urbanismo, Serviço Nacional dos Municípios, Rio de Janeiro, 1967; Nestor Goulart Reis Filho, *Evolução urbana no Brasil*, Pioneira São Paulo, 1968; Juarez Rubens Brandão Lopez, *Desenvolvimento e Mudança social*, Cia Editora Nacional, São Paulo, 1968; *Sistema nacional de desenvolvimento urbano e local no Brasil*, Serviço Federal de Habitação e Urbanismo, Rio de Janeiro, 1968; *Plano diretor de desenvolvimento integrado*, Secretaria do Interior, CEPAM, São Paulo, 1969; *Plano urbanistico básico de São Paulo*, Prefeitura do Município de São Paulo, São Paulo, 1969.

—CARLOS LODI

BROWN, LANCELOT (1715–1783)   English architect and landscape gardener, known as "Capability" Brown. By the sheer scale and number of his achievements he became and has remained the most famous exponent of the "natural" style of garden layout.

Until the eighteenth century, gardens of any size and pretention were almost invariably designed on formal, architectural lines. Symmetry and highly conscious patterns were obtained by imposing on the natural landscape a maximum of regularity.

A reaction to this conception—largely inspired by the writers Pope and Addison—produced in England a new class of designer, the landscape gardener, or "landscape architect" as he is known today. The new ideal was to cooperate with nature rather than to subjugate it; to reproduce in parks and gardens the visual variety, the apparent spontaneity, and the element of surprise offered by the natural landscape at its best.

In the attainment of this goal, the early landscape gardeners made considerable use of artifice as well as art. Artificial lakes, streams, and ruins were common features; also meandering paths and circuitous roads that often served no practical purpose.

Lancelot Brown, known as "Capability Brown." Portrait by Nathaniel Danep. (National Portrait Gallery, London.)

Brown was a follower of the English pioneer in landscape gardening, William Kent, the painter and architect who designed among others, Richmond Park in Surrey. Brown, however, surpassed his master, remodeling what are probably the greatest landscape gardens, those of Blenheim Palace, seat of the Duke of Marlborough in Oxfordshire. The famous gardens of Longleat and Wilton are among his many works, and he also took a hand in the extension and remodeling of Kew Gardens.

BIBLIOGRAPHY: Reginald and Thomas I. Blomfield, *The Formal Garden of England*, London, 1892.

—WILFRED SALTER

BUCKINGHAM, JAMES SILK (1786–1855)   Author, journalist, traveler, and planning theorist, born near Falmouth in Cornwall on August 25, 1786. He spent much of his early life at sea. In his twenties he turned his attention to writing and in 1818 established the *Calcutta Journal*. Because of his outspoken criticism of the government in India, the paper was suppressed and he was expelled from the country. However, he was later given a pension by the British government as compensation for the unjust treatment he had received. He founded *The Athenaeum* in 1828, but several other journals that he started were short lived. He was Member of Parliament for Sheffield from 1832 to 1837. He wrote numerous travel books and late in life, in 1849, he wrote *National Evils and Practical Remedies,* in which he spoke of the many defects of existing towns and of the desirability of building them on much better principles. He outlined the kind of town that he thought should be built—a town which he appropriately called Victoria and which he described in detail.

Buckingham's ideal town was to occupy 1,000 acres (405 hectares) in the center of a country area of 10,000 acres (4,050 hectares), and it was to have a population of 10,000. It was planned in the form of a square, the houses being aligned along the sides and graduated according to social class. The richest people were to live in the largest houses with the largest gardens round the central square, and the other homes were graduated outward to the poorest, near the outskirts of the town, where also were the factories. The public and administrative buildings were arranged in a formal and symmetrical manner near the center. The rows of houses were to have colonnades in a sequence of styles from Gothic for the outer rows to Doric, Ionic, Corinthian, and lastly Composite for the houses in the center, and they were to be built of iron so as to mingle tradition with industrial progress. The land and buildings were to be in the sole ownership of a limited-liability stock company, and all the residents were to have shares in the company.

Although Buckingham's Victoria was never built, it had considerable influence on subsequent planning theorists. Its value was that it was a planned town, it was conceived as a community, it was limited in size, and it was surrounded by a country belt. Ebenezer Howard recognized its contribution to planning and spoke of its similarities to his own conception of a garden city, although there were also obvious differences.

—ARNOLD WHITTICK

BUILDING BYLAWS   (*See* BUILDING REGULATIONS.)

BUILDING CODES OF PRACTICE   A building code is a legal document which sets forth requirements to protect the public health, safety, and general welfare as they relate to the construction and occupancy of buildings and structures. This is accomplished by establishing the minimum acceptable conditions for matters found to be in need of regulation. Topics generally covered are exits, fire protection, structural design, sanitary facilities, light, and ventilation.

Types of Codes   Building codes are commonly classified as being specification codes or performance codes. The specification code describes in detail exactly what materials are to be used, the size and spacing of units, and the methods of assembly.

The performance code prescribes the objective to be accomplished and allows broad leeway to the designers in selecting the materials and methods that will achieve the required results.

As a practical matter, a pure performance code would be impossible to enforce because the only proof of inadequate design or poor construction would be the failure of the building. What is important about a performance code is that where specifications are used, provisions are made for the substitution of alternate systems and materials that can be proved adequate by tests or engineering calculations.

All four model building codes used in the United States today are considered by the publishing organizations to be performance codes. Actually, they are all a judicious combination of standard specifications and performance requirements. Although these codes establish performance requirements that the designers must satisfy, the quality of the materials selected and the manner in which they are used is governed by material standards and accepted engineering design criteria, which are specification documents. The proof of performance of the methods and materials selected by the designer is governed by nationally recognized and accepted test standards.

Model Codes The nationally recognized model codes and their publishers are the Basic Building Code, Building Officials Conference of America; the National Building Code, American Insurance Association; the Southern Standard Building Code, Southern Building Code Congress; and the Uniform Building Code, International Conference of Building Officials.

Major cities generally have developed their own building codes based on the provisions of one or more of the model codes.

—Richard L. Sanderson

In Great Britain codes of practice in building are given in a series of publications issued by the British Standards Institution. These recommend what are considered to be good standards of practice in building. Each code of practice is prepared by experts from the particular section of the industry. They are influential, but unlike the codes of practice in the United States, they have no statutory authority.   *Editor*

BUILDING LINE An agreed-upon boundary line for the area occupied by a building. It is also a line, usually determined by the local authority, indicating the limit of a building near the public highway.

BUILDING REGULATIONS The typical building code regulates the construction, alterations, maintenance, repair, and demolition of buildings and structures. It may or may not regulate the installation and maintenance of mechanical systems and equipment within or appurtenant to buildings and structures. Many experts look upon the entire complex of regulatory codes—including electricity, plumbing, heating, boilers, pressure vessels, air pollution, air conditioning, refrigeration, elevators, and flammable liquids—as integral parts of the comprehensive building code. Those holding this view use the term "big B building code" to indicate that it is all-encompassing.

Housing codes are basically maintenance codes which also regulate the environmental factors of residential buildings and, in the case of rental property, the facilities that must be supplied by the landlord. Housing codes are frequently a chapter in the building codes of major cities, but there is a trend today to separate the housing code from the building code.

Laymen frequently confuse zoning ordinances and subdivision requirements with the building code. The confusion arises because the zoning ordinance is usually enforced by the same agency that enforces the building code. Subdivision regulations, although generally not enforced by the code enforcement agency, do have a direct effect on the ultimate cost of buildings, and, therefore, are mistakenly placed in the same category as codes.

The scope of the requirements in the big B building code reflects its broad objectives.

The Requirements   Although the bases for modern code requirements are a mystery to the layman and to many building officials, most of them are based on the natural scientific laws, known properties of materials, and the inherent hazards of uses or occupancies.

Adequate records have been kept of fires, building failures, panics, and natural disasters such as earthquakes, hurricanes, and floods to establish minimum criteria for the design of buildings.

It is a combination of the natural scientific laws and the compiled and evaluated statistics of disasters that form the basis for code requirements.

Fire Protection   Since the first building regulations in the United States were enacted because of disastrous fires and the first model building code was published by the National Board of Fire Underwriters, it is not surprising that building codes devote considerable attention to fire safety requirements. For example, all the model building codes provide for the establishment of fire limits within which only buildings of certain types of construction may be erected. The object of establishing fire limits is to restrict the spread of fire to limited areas within a city.

Another fire safety requirement is the limitation of the maximum heights and areas of buildings depending on the type of construction and occupancy.

Occupancy or use classifications are established according to the inherent hazards of the use. The number of people, the conditions of occupancy or confined spaces, the amounts and kinds of materials, and the equipment are all factors that must be considered. Uses having similar characteristics are grouped together to minimize the number of classifications that must be considered.

Safety   The most important life safety requirements in a building code are those covering building exits. Like the height and area requirements, the determination of safe exit requirements is based on research and observation of past conditions and experiences. It is far from an exact science.

Structural Design   The structural design requirements in building codes are based on nationally recognized standards developed and maintained by accredited, authoritative agencies in the fields involved.

Environmental Requirements   Requirements covering natural and artificial light and ventilation, room sizes, ceiling heights, and sanitary facilities are generally found in building codes.

—RICHARD L. SANDERSON

In England and Wales building regulations were adopted in 1965 (Statutory Instrument No. 1373) and came into operation on February 1, 1966 (Revised and reissued in 1972). These superseded local building bylaws. They cover such matters as the erection of buildings, the fitness of materials used, resistance to moisture, structural stability, fire resistance, thermal and sound insulation, stairways and balustrades, ventilation and height of rooms, chimneys and fireplaces, heating appliances, and drainage. A formula adopted in several of these regulations is that a certain material or construction, etc., shall be "deemed to satisfy" if it fulfils the requirements stated. In Scotland similar regulations were adopted in 1964.   *Editor*

BUILDING SOCIETY   An association formed for the purpose of enabling persons to acquire landed property (real estate) by providing a fund for making advances upon the security of that property, either "freehold, copyhold or leasehold estate by way of mortgage" as stated in the Building Societies Act, 1874. Funds are obtained for the purpose by members investing money in shares. A building society is, therefore, a combination of investors and borrowers designed partly to encourage house ownership and operating under the control of the Registrar of Friendly Societies. The difference between the interest paid by a society to investors and that paid by borrowers to the society is determined by the amount necessary to defray administrative and operational costs and to earn a surplus to maintain a specified reserve. This difference rarely amounts to more than 1 or 2 percent.

The first building society was established in Birmingham, England, in 1781. The movement expanded slowly during the nineteenth century and, with the great increase in house ownership, rapidly during the mid-twentieth century.

In the United States, the first building society, called the Provident Building Association, was established in 1831 on similar lines to the British societies. According to their location in the United States these organizations are variously called building associations, building and loan associations, cooperative banks, homestead associations, and savings and loan associations. They are all devoted mainly to the encouragement of home ownership and are responsible for nearly half the mortgages for dwellings in the United States.

In some other countries the term "building society" has a different meaning. For example, in Germany, a *Bautrager* is a contractor or corporation that is commissioned to build for a government, municipal authority, or other organization.

BUILT-UP AREA   An area, mainly occupied by buildings, where a system of street lighting is required. In modern usage the term is broadly synonomous with "urban" in its physical sense.

BULGARIA   Town planning in Bulgaria has two basic periods of development. The first one includes the period from the liberation from Ottoman rule in 1878 to the Socialist Revolution of 1944, and the second from September 1944 onwards.

During the first period, town planning was influenced by efforts to overcome the country's backwardness due to the 500-year Ottoman rule and the slow industrialization of the country. During the second period, Bulgarian town planning reflects the new social and economic conditions corresponding to the social order established in this country and represents an integral part of state economic planning.

Legislation and Administration   The first government act in the field of town planning was the issue of Regulations for Private Urban Buildings published in 1881, prompted by the urgent need for reconstruction and modernization of towns. The regulations gave instructions in planning and building.

Town planning legislation began in 1897, when the Law for Development of Settlements came into force, defining the order for preparing town plans, procedure for approval, the technical qualifications of the authors, and giving a 10-year period for the planning of all towns and county centers. In 1941 the law was supplemented with special provisions treating specific town planning problems in the light of modern developments.

During the second period, in 1948, the fundamental changes in the social, political, and economic life of the country were reflected in the new Law for Planned Development of Settlements. A number of amendments were made to provide a joint town planning code that reflected the new conditions of life in the country. These new provisions were to assist in solving problems closely related to space planning, utility services, the transport network, and open spaces as well as various architectural-aesthetic problems.

The closer interrelation between urban planning, on the one hand, and the general settlement network and the whole territory of the country, on the other, will be provided by the Law for Space Organization and Development of Settlements sanctioned by the National Assembly in 1970.

During the first period (1878–1944), administration and management in town planning was the function of the Ministry of Public Buildings. Road networks and utility services were administered through the agency of the Ministry's District Technical Offices. From 1948 to 1958, town planning policy in Bulgaria was carried out by the Ministry of Communal Economy and Public Works. This was taken over by the State Committee of Building and Architecture and the present Ministry of Construction and Architecture. The Ministry excercises managing, sanctioning, and control functions over all the town planning activity in the country. These functions consist of assigning town plans and providing directions for their elaboration, approval, and realization control; the drafting of regulations, decrees, and rates for professional practice; as well as the organization and financing of town planning research.

The chief architects of the district and town councils and the Architecture and Public Works Departments carry out the town planning policy of the Ministry and are in charge of the implementation of the town plans.

Planning Practice   During the first period mentioned, town planning was confined to the working out of cadastral surveys and town plans. At the beginning of the period (1878–1897), this was carried out by foreign technicians, employees, or contractors. These first town plans are confined to improvements of existing conditions; i.e., improvements in the street network, designation of plots for new public buildings, and their regulation according to housing requirements.

Typical of the middle of the period is the improved quality of the cadastral surveys and town plans. The credit for urban development in this period is due to Georgi Nenov, architect, author of nearly seventy town plans within the years 1890 to 1925.

At the end of this period (1936–1944), the drafting of new town plans began, corresponding in content and scope to contemporary ideas (for example the town plans of Sofia, Plovdiv, Bourgas, Kyustendil, and Peshtera). These plans were prepared by specialists from Bulgaria and abroad on a free agreement basis (Professor Hermann Janzen, Professor Adolf Mussmann, Architect Lyuben Tonev, and Architect Deltscho Sougarev).

During the second period (after 1944), town planning in Bulgaria was placed on an obligatory basis for the building of settlements. Since 1948, city plans are prepared only by the state design organizations in close cooperation with the economic development of the country.

In this period plans are developed in the following phases:

1. General town plans, dealing with the land use, location of main and secondary centers, transport network, recreation grounds, and application of labor in full conformity with the trends in the economic, demographic, and space development of the town and in close connection with its environs. Implementation is on the basis of a program, set up in advance, defining the development of the town for a period of 15 to 20 years.

2. Detailed plans, defining the ways and means for town development; i.e., space composition.

3. Detailed plans for the development of separate town units and areas.

The town plans are prepared by a team of specialists in different fields under the leading role of the architect-town planner. Competitions for building and planning schemes are frequently organized both on a national and international basis.

Education and Training   During the first period (up to 1944), specialists in town planning obtained their education exclusively abroad—in Germany, Czechoslovakia, France, and Italy. In 1942 the Higher Technical School was founded in Sofia, developing consecutively into the State Polytechnic and the Higher Institute of Civil Engineering. Town planning specialists are trained at the Faculty of Architecture, which includes a Chair of Town Planning. Specialization of the architects-town planners is effected in the last stage of their training and further by practice and specialization courses both in the country and abroad. Other specialists working in the same field, such as geodesists and specialists in urban traffic and transport, obtain their training at the same institute. Specialists in urban economy and regional planning are trained at the Higher Institute of National Economy in the town of Varna; in economic geography, sociology, and demography at the State University, Sofia; and in landscaping of urban settlements at the Institute of Forestry and Landscaping, Sofia.

Institutions   The Union of Bulgarian Architects includes a section in town and regional planning, and the Scientific-Technical Unions in Bulgaria include sections on urban traffic and transport. The basic aim of these institutions is the raising of the standard of qualifications and broadening of the interests of their members.

Research and design activity in town planning is carried out by:

1. The Institute of Town Planning and Architecture, Sofia, in the field of urban science and practice

2. The Bulgarian Academy of Sciences in the theory and history of town planning and architecture

3. The Institute for Regional Planning, Sofia, in preparing regional plans for given districts and the whole country

4. "Glavproect," Sofia, institute for investigation and designing of urban projects on a national scale

5. "Sofproect," institute for investigation and drafting Sofia town plans

6. The district design organizations (12 in number), drafting town plans of settlements in given parts of the country

The achievements in the field of town planning as well as the results of the research work are published in the journals of the different institutes or in the periodical *Architectura*—the organ of the Ministry of Construction and Architecture and of the Union of Bulgarian Architects.

Geographic and Climatic Conditions   Bulgaria lies in the southeast part of the Balkan Peninsula. It has an area of 43,000 square miles (110,990 square kilometers, much of which is of a hilly-mountainous character. The Balkan Range divides the country into two parts—North Bulgaria and South Bulgaria. Along the Danube, the Black Sea coast, and partly in South Bulgaria there are flat lands, while the most southern and western parts of the country are occupied by mountain ranges.

Bulgaria is situated in an area of transitional continental climate. The Black Sea coastline and the greater part of the Rhodope Mountains along the southern boundary of the country are influenced by the Mediterranean climate. The annual mean temperature varies between 48 and 55°F and the average annual precipitation amounts to 422 gallons per square mile (650 liters per square kilometer). The greater part of Bulgaria lies in the seismic zone. The big towns of the country are spread on flat terrain, while a number of the middle-sized and small towns are situated in the hilly-mountainous regions. These circumstances control their plan structure and development.

Traditions of Planning to the End of the Nineteenth Century   Till the liberation of Bulgaria from Ottoman rule (1878) and at the beginning of the first period, the Bulgarian towns developed predominantly under the traditions of the Bulgarian national revival (from the end of the eighteenth century to the middle of the nineteenth) and are characterized by an informal layout and street network structure that conforms to the terrain and develops along the main thoroughfares leading from town centers toward the neighboring settlements. The town and its elements—squares, streets, shops, public buildings, and housing—are of small scale and create an atmosphere of coziness and intimacy.

The beginning of the first period shows tendencies toward sharp modification of the layout and composition of the bigger and rapidly developing towns expressed in geometric street systems and in new squares and spaces for public needs. These were planned by foreign experts who were badly acquainted with the local conditions. Striking examples in this respect are the plans of the towns of Stara Sagora, Nova Zagora, and Sofia developed in the years 1880 to 1885.

More realistic tendencies with a better approach to the problems of town planning appear at the end of the nineteenth century, resulting from the efforts of Bulgarian architects, among them Georgi Nenov, Yordan Milanov, and Petko Momchilov. These tendencies find expression in the Law for Development of the Settlements (1897), requiring the satisfactory relation of town planning to existing local conditions, as well as the preservation and further development, in harmony with the specific nature and pattern, of the towns, as in the examples of Koprivshtiza, Bansko, Elena, and Lovech.

Twentieth-century Planning Town planning traditions so far established continued and developed further in the first two decades of the twentieth century. The years after World War I and the ensuing economic crisis affected the development of almost all big towns, whose territories expanded considerably in order to absorb those leaving the villages and to shelter the great number of refugees from Macedonia and Aegean Thrace. The new conditions provided sharp contrasts between town center and outskirts in their development, utility services, and public amenities.

The development plans of a number of towns—Sofia, Plovdiv, Kyustendil, and Peshtera—prepared in the 1936 to 1944 period remain unrealized, in spite of their positive qualities and new ideas, because of the political and economic situation of the country.

The rapid economic progress of the country and her transformation from a backward agrarian and poorly industrialized country into one with highly developed industry and intensive and mechanized agriculture has been

Town of Veliko Turnovo. General view of the town, 1944; shows the specific manner of development, imposed by the relief of the terrain and the density of development.

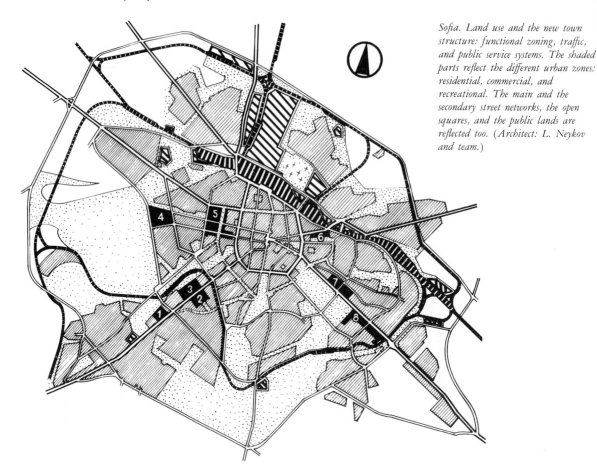

Sofia. Land use and the new town structure: functional zoning, traffic, and public service systems. The shaded parts reflect the different urban zones: residential, commercial, and recreational. The main and the secondary street networks, the open squares, and the public lands are reflected too. (Architect: L. Neykov and team.)

accompanied by extensive urbanization. The urban population, representing 24.1 percent of the total population in 1944, increased to 33.6 percent in 1956, to 46.5 percent in 1965, and reached 51.6 percent in 1969. The urbanization process is most strongly apparent in the big towns having from 100,000 to 350,000 inhabitants. Nearly 38 percent of the total urban population lives in such towns—Sofia, Plovdiv, Varna, Rousse, and Bourgas—while the rest of the urban population inhabits the middle-sized towns with 25,000 to 100,000 population and small towns with under 25,000 population, which together number 163. Several will soon pass from the lower into the higher population category. The new social-political setting after the socialist revolution and the continuous economic advance and urbanization create favorable conditions for rapid town planning developments.

At the beginning of the period 1945 to 1950, a number of competitions were conducted for drafting the town plans of Sofia, Vidin, Yambol, Sliven, and the town centers of Sofia and Varna. These competitions make for the clarification of trends of socialist town planning in Bulgaria and for the intensification of the architects' efforts in this field.

Due to the existing dense settlement network, only a few new towns are being developed, situated near rich ore deposits and new, large industrial areas. Such are the towns of Dimitrovgrad, Madan, Roudozem, and Bobov Dol. In the years 1950 to 1955, the new towns developed at an accelerated rate and became interesting examples of the standard of town planning and architecture at this period.

The rapid urbanization of the country (with an urban population two or three times greater than that in 1944) demanded urgent reconstruction and renewal. In the big and middle-sized towns where nearly 20 percent

Sofia. Development plan of Zapaden Park Housing Estate, 1958. (Architect: K. Bossev.)

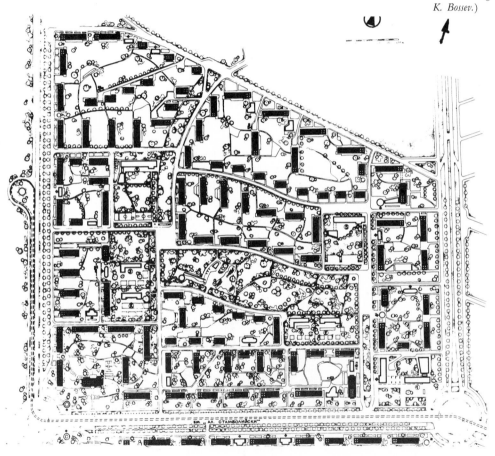

■ — Housing

▭ — Educational and children facilities

▨ — Recreational areas (green spaces)

◆ — Shopping and service buildings

▲ — Garages

of the manpower is engaged, new industrial zones were developed. In existing towns and on their outskirts a great deal of new housing is in progress. The development of new sites is accomplished mainly by using industrialized methods of building with a general increase of the height—eight stories on the average—on the basis of differentiated residential districts and neighborhood units, with higher general standards of utility services, public amenities, and landscaping.

Housing estates of improved standards of design that have been built in the last 10 years include Zapaden Park, Krasno Selo, Gara Iskar, Hipodroma in Sofia; Kamenitza I, Kamenitza II, Gagarin, Hristo Botev, and Mladejki Halm in the town of Plovdiv; Tolboukhin, Izgrev, and P. R. Slaveykov in the town of Bourgas; and the Roupite District in the town of Varna.

Urban reconstruction involves especially the town centers, where the new public, cultural, and business buildings are concentrated. For the designs for these centers both home and international competitions were held, including those for Sofia, Varna, Plovdiv, Rousse, and Bourgas. Since 1960, as a result of this activity, the town centers of Mikhailovgrad, Targovishte, Silistra, and Pernik were completed. In these new urban plans, the higher level of public services, the rapidly increasing motorization, and other factors are reflected. All industrial and resort towns have new town plans prepared in the last 10 to 15 years. Significant achievements are the plans for Plovdiv

Sofia. Model of new hous *estate, 1969. (Architects:* *Tomalevsky and A. Antono*

Town of Rousse (above 100,0 *population). Competition pro* *for the town center, 19* *Contemporary tendency is* *opening the square space towa* *the natural distinc* *feature—the river Danube—wh* *offers compromise solution of* *transport in the town cent* *Average height of the n* *housing: eight stor.* *(Architects: I. Avramov,* *Toplyiski, I. Petrov, P. Evre*

Town of Varna. Renewal of *town territory, 1965.*

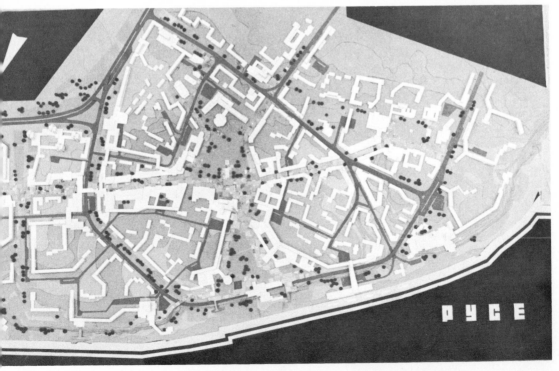

ABOVE: *Village of Bounovo. Experimental project, 1968. (Institute of Town Planning and Architecture, Sofia.)*   LEFT: *Part of the resort Zlatni Pyassatsi near Varna, 1965.*

by Architect Ivan Popov and team, Varna by Architect K. Boychev and team, and Veliko Turnovo by Architect N. Nikolov and team. As in the case of other new towns, the urban structure is based on a differentiation of residential districts and neighborhood units and groups, yet all are supplied with the necessary public services.

Characteristic of contemporary town planning in Bulgaria are the different methods of approach when solving the problems arising from the diverse specifications of the different settlement categories. Another achievement of Bulgarian town planners is the physical organization and development of the Bulgarian village, realized in conformity with the new management of agricultural production in terms of its cooperation and mechanization, which has led to the renewal of over 60 percent of the village public and residential stock of buildings during the last 15 years.

Since 1955, town planning in Bulgaria marks significant achievements with the successful planning and realization of a number of resort settlements along the Black Sea coast and in some mountainous regions for home and international tourism. Among them are: Zlatni Pyasatzi, Slunchev Bryag, the International Youth Camp at Primorsko, Albena, and Roussalka. The planning and development of the resorts is accomplished on the basis of a general recreation and tourism development plan. The layout and space compositions of each of these resorts has an individual character and pattern

Part of the resort of Albena.
(*Architect: N. Nenov and team.*)

achieved through preservation of the local landscape while providing the necessary recreational facilities.

The contemporary trend in Bulgarian urban planning is to base it as scientifically as possible on the study of the social, economic, and technical conditions of the country.

BIBLIOGRAPHY: A. Stoichkov, "Possibilities for Reorganization of Residential Districts in the Centre of Sofia," *Bulletin of the Institute for Town Planning and Architecture,* vols. 5–6, Sofia, 1953; T. Zlatev, *The Bulgarian Town during the National Revival Period,* "Nauka i Izkustvo," Publishing House, Sofia, 1955; Ivan Avramov, "Planning of the Settlements in Bulgaria from the National Liberation till September 9th 1944," *Bulletin of the Institute of Town Planning and Architecture,* vol. 10–11, Sofia, 1957; A. Stoichkov, "Street Traffic in Sofia and the Solution of Some Transport Problems," *Bulletin of Institute for Town Planning and Architecture,* vol. 13, Sofia, 1959; L. Tonev, St. Stanev, and D. Bakalov, *Town Planning Technical Economical Indices and Rates for the Big Towns in Bulgaria,* Bulgarian Academy of Sciences Press, Sofia, 1959; R. Robev, Ivan Gloukharov, and assoc., *The Neighbourhood Unit Problem in Bulgaria,* Bulgarian Academy of Sciences Press, Sofia, 1960; St. Staney, *Planning of the Middle-sized Towns in Bulgaria,* Bulgarian Academy of Sciences Press, Sofia, 1962; R. Robev, and Ivan Gloukharov, *The Children's Playgrounds,* "Technika" Publishing House, Sofia, 1965; *Short History of Bulgarian Architecture,* Bulgarian Academy of Sciences Press, Sofia, 1965; St. Stanev, Ivan Gloukharov, and assoc., "Planning Villages in Bulgaria," *Bulletin of the Institute for Town Planning and Architecture,* vol. 20, book 2, Sofia, 1966; Ivan Avramov, Ivan Petrov, and assoc., "Planning of the Urban Industrial Zones in Bulgaria, *Bulletin of the Institute of Town Planning and Architecture,* vol. 20, book 2, Sofia, 1967; L. Tonev, "the Sofia City Centre Problem," *Bulletin of the Section for Theory and History of Architecture at the Bulgarian Academy of Sciences,* vol. 20, Sofia, 1968; N. Kamenov, "On Some Problems of the Renewal of the Residential Territories," *Bulletin of the Section for Theory and History of Town Planning at the Bulgarian Academy of Sciences,* vol. 21, Sofia, 1968; St. Stanev, and N. Kamenov, "On the Problem of the Optimum Size of the Towns in Bulgaria," *Bulletin of the Section for Theory and History of Architecture at the Bulgarian Academy of Sciences,* vol. 21, Sofia, 1968; Ivan Avramov, Ivan Petrov, and assoc., *Planning of the Small Towns.*

—IVAN AVRAMOV AND IVAN PETROV

BULK ZONING   (*See* ZONING AND ZONING LAWS.)

BURGESS, ERNEST W. (1886–1966)   A luminary of the "Chicago School" of sociology associated with the empirical study of the city in the United States as well as with studies of the family and of aging. Planners will be most interested in what has come to be known as his "Concentric Zone Theory" (or hypothesis). This theory, first suggested in 1923, has had tremendous appeal, especially for those seeking some synthesis in the sprawling field known as "urbanism" and "urban sociology."

In substance, the theory proposes that cities assume a definite form and grow in patterned ways which reflect fundamental properties of a so-cial-ecological interchange. In this view, everything starts from the center and grows out from there in the form of broad belts or zones. Each of these zones contains a distinctive population and distinctive mixes of activities, forged out of complementary yet antagonistic processes of con-centration and dispersion. Among these zones we find the following: first, a downtown center in which is focused the economic, political, and cul-tural life of the city; and a second zone, known as the "zone of transi-tion," which is both areawise and populationwise an area in limbo. Im-mediately adjacent to the central business district (the form assumed by the center in industrial cities) is an area that may be slated for expansion if business is good, hence land and properties are held for speculative purposes. This inherent instability attracts a population similarly in transition—newly arrived immigrants from abroad, rural migrants, and transients of various kinds including those who seek to escape the long arm of the law. It is an area of rooms for rent and rooming houses, where one pays in advance and no one ever stays for very long. Beyond the zone of transition are more settled zones of stable working-class and immigrant groups, the little Italys and other ethnic enclaves. Further out still are the residential commuting zones for people wealthy enough to afford larger homes and open spaces.

The description and even the stipulated number of these zones varies according to the context in which the theory is discussed, but its underlying principles remain consistent. Its central idea is that the activity or function which commands the greatest interest enjoys the central position in space and is established via the competitive process. The forces which determine the shape and size of the center reverberate throughout the entire city, including the outlying residential areas. New functions in the community as well as demographic growth or decline provide the chief impetus to these changing ecological and demographic configurations. Nor are the residential zones fixed permanently. A similar shifting of populations and functions occurs within each of them and realignments via "invasion and succession" processes occur continually. Each zone thus assumes a certain value in the city as a whole which is determined by its accessibility to the center, calculated in terms of time-cost, and the nature of its inhabitants.

Burgess believed that the circular zone tendency exists unless topography or factors like discrimination block it. Later work, however, suggests that this model of how cities grow and become internally structured is probably most applicable to new, rapidly growing, industrial cities.

Burgess's work has been supplemented by other "theories" of city growth, most notably by Galpin's Axial theory, Hoyt's Sector theory, and Harris and Ullman's Multiple Nucleii theory. Quite apart from the continuing substantive merits of his own theory, Burgess deserves credit for giving a major impetus to these later contributions.

BIBLIOGRAPHY: Ernest W. Burgess, "The Growth of the City: An Introduction to a Research Project"; Robert E. Park and Ernest W. Burgess, *Introduction to the Science of Sociology,* Chicago, 1921.

—SUZANNE KELLER

BURIAL GROUNDS (*See* CEMETERIES.)

BURMA (*See* ASIA, SOUTHEAST, DEVELOPING COUNTRIES.)

BURNHAM, DANIEL H. (1846–1912) American architect and planner born at Henderson, N.Y., September 4, 1846. His professional career was closely associated with Chicago's rapid rise in population, wealth, and prominence. He came to this city in his childhood, and in his late teens served a brief apprenticeship with the firm of Lorring and Jenner. In 1870, Burnham and the more architecturally imaginative and talented John W. Root formed a partnership. By the 1880s they were among the city's leading firms, playing a prominent role in the "Chicago school," which pioneered in the use of steel skeletal construction in skyscraper buildings. In 1891 Root died and Burnham was given charge of the planning and construction of the Chicago Columbian Exposition of 1893. Burnham was always adept at working with the business community, and with their support he embarked on an ambitious program. Frederick Olmsted, selected to prepare the site, and the participating architects agreed to coordinate their work to a general plan. The resulting Court of Honors of the fair was widely publicized as an example of rational and unified aesthetic design. The view, however, that the fair marked the birth of the "city beautiful" movement and hence of modern American planning overlooks the earlier and more complex roots of the movement. In 1899 Burnham was appointed to the McMillan Commission created by Congress to prepare a plan for central Washington, D.C. In the following years he prepared plans for San Francisco, Cleveland, and Manila. His most ambitious and important undertaking, though, was the Chicago plan (1909). It attracted national acclaim and considerable local enthusiasm with many of its features, especially those related to the lakefront, which were realized during the next two decades. At the time of his death, at Heidelberg, Germany, on June 1, 1912, Burnham was internationally recognized as the principal spokesman for American city planning, then largely identified with the "city beautiful" movement. His ideas and approach, however, met with increasing criticism. To social reformers and the younger planners who were sympathetic to their cause, Burnham was too preoccupied with parks, boulevards, and civic centers while ignoring the planner's potential role in housing reform and community planning. For other critics, Burnham and the "city beautiful" movement were guilty of an exaggerated concern with art and architecture at the expense of the engineering and transportation problems basic to urban functioning. In the decade after Burnham's death, the "city beautiful" movement gave way to the "city efficient" as the guiding force in American city planning.

BIBLIOGRAPHY: Charles Moore, *Daniel H. Burnham,* Boston, 1921; Mel Scott, *American City Planning Since 1890,* Berkeley, Calif., 1969.

—STANLEY BUDER

BYLAW, BUILDING   The regulations controlling the construction and erection of buildings in England and Wales were formerly bylaws administered by local authorities on the basis of model bylaws provided by the Ministry of Housing and Local Government, which, however, permitted local variations. These were superseded in 1966 by National Building Regulations administered by the Minister of Public Buildings and Works and since 1971 by the Secretary of State for the Environment. In the United States, the term "Building Codes" (*q.v.*) is used.

BYPASS   A road which passes by a built-up area, in order to expedite traffic movement and to minimize its nuisance in a town. Generally it takes the form of a loop joined to a major road in order to skirt a town, thus avoiding congestion in a city caused by through traffic.

C

CAMBODIA (*See* ASIA, SOUTHEAST, DEVELOPING COUNTRIES.)

CAMPUS A term—from the Latin *campus,* meaning field—used to describe the land and buildings that make up a university, college, or other large institute of higher education. The whole land area and buildings of a new university on a single site would thus be called "the campus." Occasionally, where the parts of a university are on separate sites, the main site alone is called the campus. The word has acquired this meaning in the United States, where it was first used at Princeton University.

—DAVID HALL

CANADA
Geographical and Climatic Conditions Canada extends from the latitude of Rome almost to the North Pole. The settlements where most of her 21 million people live are near her southern edge, in a band reaching half around the Western Hemisphere. So large a land mass presents a range of features that can be sketched but briefly here.

The eastern shores are rocky and indented by many inlets of the Atlantic and the mouths of great rivers. The temperate maritime climate makes for productive farming in the areas where the soil is favorable; fishing and forestry are more widespread. The four Atlantic provinces are peopled by about 2 million Canadians, of whom the urban 50 percent live typically

211

in seaports and administrative centers. The largest of these are Halifax, Saint-Jean, Sydney, and St. John's.

The St. Lawrence valley, carrying the flow from the Great Lakes, offers another typical landscape: rolling slopes with deeper soil cover than on the east coast, and in their original state largely covered with mixed deciduous and conifer forests. The St. Lawrence basin has heavy snowfall in winter; but warm summers and rich soils make possible (between Niagara and the head of Lake Erie) the growing of grapes, peaches, and tobacco. The region drained by this great lake and river system is the most populous part of Canada, it contains the two largest cities (Montreal and Toronto) plus 10 urban centers of 100,000 or more. The central provinces of Quebec and Ontario lead the country in trade and commerce; nearly two-thirds of all Canadians live in the St. Lawrence basin.

The headwaters of the St. Lawrence system rise in Precambrian formations rich in minerals and clothed with evergreen forests that are worked for pulp and paper. To the west, the prairie grasslands have a truly continental climate with extremes of heat and cold; few places are free of frost for more than four months of the year. Settlements in the prairie provinces are scattered very widely, serving the large and highly mechanized farms growing grains. Petroleum and natural gas deposits are abundant. The largest prairie cities (Winnipeg and Edmonton) are also provincial capitals and bases for development of the Northwest Territories. About 3½ million people live in the prairie provinces.

Most of Canada north of 60 degrees north latitude is administered by the federal government, with limited authority delegated to the very sparse resident population. The greater part of these vast territories, including the whole of the Arctic Archipelago, is a treeless tundra with subsoils that are permanently frozen. Exploration for minerals and oil has led to the establishment of a few small settlements, which with defense and weather outposts are served mainly by air transport. The whole population of the northern territories numbers about 50,000 people.

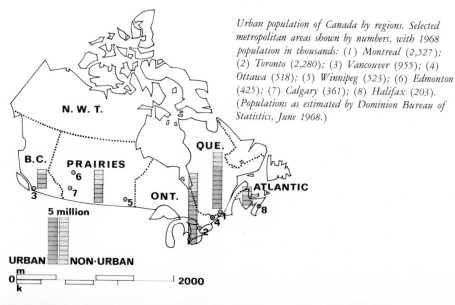

Urban population of Canada by regions. Selected metropolitan areas shown by numbers, with 1968 population in thousands: (1) Montreal (2,527); (2) Toronto (2,280); (3) Vancouver (955); (4) Ottawa (518); (5) Winnipeg (523); (6) Edmonton (425); (7) Calgary (361); (8) Halifax (203). (Populations as estimated by Dominion Bureau of Statistics, June 1968.)

The Pacific coast is separated from the great plains by the Rocky Mountains, with ridges rising more than 12,000 feet (3,600 meters) above sea level. The western slopes of these mountains are clothed in evergreen forests of great size and age growing in the mildest and dampest climate in Canada. Fully 60 percent of the 2 million people in the coastal province of British Columbia live in its southwest corner, in the metropolitan areas of Vancouver and Victoria.

Legislation and Administration The legal framework for planning in Canada varies from province to province. Details will be found in provincial statutes and documents. Only the major provisions can be dealt with here. In general, the legislation prescribes on four matters:

1. Comprehensive development plan
2. General regulation of owner's use of land (zoning)
3. Consent to major projects on their specific merits
4. Terms on which a holding may be divided and parts sold (subdivision)

Comprehensive Development Plan The chief task given to local bodies by provincial planning laws is the preparation of a plan for the physical development of the designated area which may be a single municipality or several adjoining municipalities. The multimunicipal planning area may correspond with that governed by an upper-tier regional government (as in Toronto, Winnipeg, Ottawa), or it may be used for limited administrative functions (as in Vancouver), or it may serve for planning purposes only.

The content of the plan is usually specified to include the general disposition of areas according to use, with indication of the thoroughfares, open spaces, and public facilities needed. Procedures are prescribed for the review and adoption of a draft plan by the local authorities affected. In some provinces the adoption is by the municipal councils in the designated area, in others by the provincial minister. The official plan binds the local council against carrying out major works or passing bylaws inconsistent with it. The official plan is conventionally made for a period of up to 20 years, with provision for its amendment like that for its original adoption.

Faced with rapid urban development since the war, Canadian local governments that intended to prepare comprehensive plans have often been too preoccupied with detailed, private development applications to do so. Indeed, the vigorous dynamics of urban growth and change have raised the question of whether a fixed and formal town plan is still useful. In a mixed economy, one alternative would resemble a military operation—where strategic goals are pursued by tactics adapted to events as they occur in the field.

Although the formal adoption of an official plan requires action by the elected municipal council, that plan may be drafted by an appointed planning commission. This is a peculiarly North American institution, invented early in this century when belief in planning was high but confidence in municipal politicians was low. The typical planning board is a small group of public-spirited and prominent citizens charged with the oversight of planning. They may rely upon municipal officers for advice or may be given funds with which to engage their own permanent and consultant staff.

The metropolitan conurbations that have emerged in Canada have in some cases (Toronto, Winnipeg) been given a two-tier form of government. Comprehensive development planning can become a function of the metropolitan council; or, as in Toronto, planning at the regional level may relate specifically to given metropolitan responsibilities (as trunk roads, major parks, bulk water supply) with metropolitan review of the planning proposals of the constituent borough councils.

Land-use Regulation   Early municipal councils were, from the mid-nineteenth century, given authority by colonial governors to rule on the location of such local nuisances as slaughterhouses. By 1914 these municipal powers were extended, so that councils can now regulate generally the uses of all private lands within their jurisdiction by what are called "zoning bylaws." The council has to set limits on the population and activities allowed in a specific zone and to determine the capacities of those works (roads, schools, etc.) required of the municipality for that zone.

Hardships may be imposed on particular owners by a zoning bylaw, because it is bound to enlarge or reduce the future values of properties. In most provinces the payment or collection of money by the council on this account is ruled out. Councillors may for this reason be reluctant to use a power that can inflict injuries upon specific owners for the sake of assumed general benefits.

Development Permits   The usual local building code deals with the structural and mechanical safety of the single building. Officials in charge of these codes in larger cities may be confronted with applications to build large urban complexes. Any one of these may propose hotels, shops, offices, and apartments integrated with parking structures and open spaces on a large and valuable downtown site. The municipality may have to respond on short notice to a compound development proposal of which the economic and social impact equals that of a whole new town. The council is likely to ask its planning officers for advice on the specific terms of the development consent to be given.

Enterprise on this large scale will have expert professionals at its command who will have kept their own counsel about current market demand for space and momentary financial opportunities. Neither the city's long-term "official plan" nor the general zoning bylaws may fit the particular composition of uses, densities, and traffic resulting from these private calculations. Private intent and public interest in this type of planning application can be resolved by a legal agreement, between the municipality and the development enterprise, setting out the terms on which a comprehensive development permit is issued. Major departures from previously adopted plans for the area may have to be ratified by the municipal council, or even by the provincial minister; less important modifications may be left to the discretion of a committee of council or to its planning officers.

Approval of Plans of Subdivision   Historically, those charged with colonizing North America had quickly to parcel out great territories for agricultural settlement. Often the tract to be allocated was forested and could not be fully surveyed. The simplest way for a hard-pressed land agent to assign holdings to settlers was to divide his territory into farm-plots forming a rectangular grid on his rudimentary map. In English-speaking Canada, the unit of land later urbanized was commonly the oblong farm section of 160 acres (65 hectares). In regions originally settled by French farmers, the typical land holding was a long, narrow rectangle; the house and outbuildings were near the frontage on a waterway (as main travel route), with fields running up the slopes to a wooded area at the rear of the plot.

As the pace of urbanization accelerated, the land unit put to urban development at any one time became larger. This allowed for greater freedom in layout and more intricate forms of planning. Legislation was passed to require municipal approval of the division of land for urban use (shown on plans of subdivision) before legal ownership of parcels could be transferred from the vendor of the large development tract to buyers of small urban plots within it. Advice as to this approval is given by the municipal planning staff.

Whereas only one-twentieth or less of the land in agricultural use was in municipal care, the ratio of public land in urban areas might quickly rise to as much as 40 percent. Although the law on municipal approval of subdivision did not usually contain financial provisions, local governments commonly made payment of development charges a condition of subdivision approval. This practice has two effects:

1. The quality of street services is agreed to before people come to live in the area and may be set so high as to preclude any but prosperous buyers.

2. These off-site services are financed as private mortgage debt of the new landowners rather than as public debt of the local government.

Education and Training   Only after World War II did the majority of Canadians congregate in cities ranging in size from 20,000 to over 1 million persons. For most of its first century, Canadian local government was thus carried on with very small permanent staffs; as late as 1940 it was an unusual city that employed a qualified town planning officer. The census of 1946 revealed to Canadians that they had become one of the most urbanized of nations. Official documents pointed to the urgent need for people with thorough knowledge of urban planning; the new federal housing agency (Central Mortgage and Housing Corporation) took the lead, both in support of Canadian courses of instruction and in sponsoring the transfer to Canada of those already qualified elsewhere.

The first teaching program in physical planning was instituted in 1947 at McGill University in Montreal; candidates from a variety of disciplines proceeded to the master's degree in their own field, through courses supervised by an interfaculty committee. During the early 1950s, graduate programs were established at the universities of British Columbia, Manitoba, and Toronto. At that period, one of the schools of planning required a previous degree in architecture or engineering for admission, and a high proportion of all planning candidates came from these two disciplines.

These initial courses of instruction in urban planning have broadened in content to include urban analysis and administration; they have also widened their terms of entry, so that in recent years candidates for planning degrees are often from the social sciences. By 1960, professional education in French was arranged at the University of Montreal, where there is now one of the larger Canadian schools. More recently a graduate program in planning has been instituted at the University of Waterloo in Ontario.

Faculty appointments and the subject matter of instruction have been influenced by the analytical preoccupations of professionals in the United States and by the nature of professional practice and research now carried on in Canada.

At present there are some 150 students enrolled in the six graduate schools of planning in Canada. Of nearly 700 qualified practitioners, over 300 have received degrees or diplomas from Canadian professional schools between 1948 and 1966. Students who have entered the schools to date number well over 500. It is likely that these schools have now caught up with current new demand for qualified men and women in Canada. Total demand doubles in each decade. Of present practitioners about 40 percent began in architecture or engineering and about 40 percent have degrees in the social sciences or humanities.

During the 1960s a few technical teaching institutions have offered courses of instruction to prepare candidates for supporting positions in large planning offices. Those who complete these courses are expected to relieve senior members in their offices from routine tasks.

The Canadian Council on Urban and Regional Research was founded in 1962 to promote the conduct and use of systematic studies of urban affairs. The council's 60 members include planners; and its bibliographic and other information services, as well as its programming and funding of original research on urbanization, provide resources for continuing education in this rapidly developing profession.

Institutions By 1900, Americans were becoming aware that the habitable land was largely taken up. Concern for depletion of natural resources led in Canada to formation of the Commission of Conservation in 1909. That body advocated city planning by advisory committees of distinguished citizens as early as 1912. In 1913 the commission invited Thomas Adams (of the British Local Government Board) to come as Adviser on Town Planning. By 1917 he was presiding over the first meetings of what was to become the Town Planning Institute of Canada, incorporated a few years later.

Early members of the Institute included the administrators of the planning legislation adopted by most provinces prior to 1920; these men were usually surveyors, engineers, or architects. The institute also welcomed lay enthusiasts for planning as members. It published a bimonthly journal during the 1920s.

Economic depression after 1930 affected urban building in Canada more severely than in Britain or the United States, and the institute was unable to continue its activities. Concern for the quality of reconstruction after

World War II led to formation of the lay Community Planning Association of Canada; by 1949, the Town Planning Institute of Canada had been reconstituted as a body limited to professional practitioners and teachers. In addition to its prewar members, the institute admitted many newcomers to Canada who had gained professional qualifications in Britain, the United States, or elsewhere.

Courses recognized by the institute now include those offered at six Canadian universities. Only in the 1960s did professionals educated in Canada come to form the majority in the Institute, of which the total membership is now nearly one thousand. It has published a quarterly journal, *Plan Canada,* since 1959.

In Canada, statutes governing professional qualification and practice (as well as the law of property and local government) fall within provincial jurisdiction. Most of those who practice planning are therefore organized within a provincewide or regional association. These bodies have all been formed since the national institute came into being, and most of them agree with it on rules for admission and practice.

To encourage active expression of nonprofessional viewpoints in the planning process, the Community Planning Association of Canada was founded in 1946. Through bilingual publications and annual conferences, it conducts a broadly educational program; while provincial and local units of the association sponsor meetings and bulletins on topical questions. This citizen body has been supported by federal and other governments and has attained a membership of some six thousand individuals and of local and regional organizations.

Professional Practice Belief in comprehensive city planning sprang in Canada mainly from the practice of architecture. Civic design was seen as an extension of building design and the early essays in planning were often made by architects. They conceived the needs of citizens as those of upper-middle-class architectural clients writ large; and their plan was often a bold and simple urban composition dominated by fine public and institutional structures set out in impressive boulevards and squares.

These "set-pieces" of planning excited public interest early in this century; there followed disappointment when it was found that the authors of great plans had little idea of the public and private investments involved, still less of the intricate economic processes reflected in the bustling city around them. The reaction in Canada, as in the United States and elsewhere, was to devote new attention to the behavior of land markets, to the rising demands of automobile traffic, and to the diverse life-styles of distinctive social groups within the major North American city. Critics of more recent and "realistic" plans contend that they are in no sense plans for change but merely statistical verifications of current trends. Emphasis on observation of social behavior has, however, produced greater professional use of empirical data and systematic urban analysis.

Planning practice in Canada varies among jurisdictions and also among individual offices. The legal framework makes for fewer court tests than occur in the United States; while the division of administrative oversight among provinces results in less central guidance by way of circulars than a British office receives. Studies of slum conditions and schemes for rehabilitation or clearance and redevelopment are more uniform throughout the country, probably because much of the cost of this work is met under the urban renewal provisions of the National Housing Act. As in the United States, draft urban renewal programs have taken their place with draft comprehensive plans, land use plans, and plans of subdivision among the major documents produced by planning offices.

A recent survey of practice by the Town Planning Institute of Canada (TPIC) makes three points. On public *support* for planning activity, the TPIC report indicates adequate local government belief in routine jobs (zoning amendments, development permits, subdivision control) but political hesitancy about fundamental innovations. Professional help to the local offices from provincial capitals has been uneven; in several, the legislature is rural-dominated and urban concerns tend to be neglected.

On the *scope* of the profession's mandate, there is sometimes positive linkage (as in Alberta or Nova Scotia) between local-regional and provincial plans and budgets; the same is becoming true where (as in Ontario or British Columbia) regional units of government are being set up.

On the *impact* of planning activity, the institute report says that a shift from the "fixed end-state" type of official plan (often by an external consultant) toward continuous and adaptive development planning is proving effective; all but the smallest cities have had permanent planning staff long enough to reduce obvious evils (like ribbon development) and to achieve occasional triumphs. Professionals are employed in some two hundred planning offices, of which about half are public agencies and one quarter are consulting firms. On the average there may be in a larger office, for each four planners, one other professional (engineer, architect, or social scientist) and five or six supporting staff. Planning professionals are engaged across the country in these proportions by type of office: municipal, 35 percent; regional or provincial, 18 percent; private consulting, 29 percent; universities, central government, research, and not specified, 18 percent. There is marked variation as to kind of employer from one part of the country to another. In the Atlantic region fully two-thirds of all professionals work for the provincial or federal government, while in Quebec only one in six is so employed and over half the planners are in private firms. In British Columbia, about half of all planners are in local government. Both private development corporations and public authorities turn to private consultants as and when needed; there are few public development corporations.

Most Canadian municipal councils depend on property taxation for the greater part of their revenues; the costs of installing and carrying on the services they must perform (under provincial law) have outgrown their revenue sources. Councils are therefore liable to be tempted by the prospect of immediate tax income from a private development proposal without a close look at all its other implications, including the effect on the city's appearance. Professionals in planning, with longer-term obligations to society as a whole, find in Canada one of their most severe challenges in meeting this situation.

Traditions of Planning to the End of the Nineteenth Century   The eastern seaboard of Canada was the first part to be developed. On this rugged topography with relatively sparse vegetation, the practical mariner-settlers built their towns to fit the irregular sites around natural harbors: St. John's (Newfoundland), founded in the sixteenth century, is a good example. On the St. Lawrence, the villages of the French regime assumed a more regular form: houses facing across the principal street (*chemin du roi*) close to the river, with the dominant church set further from the shore to leave an open place near the center of activity. A notable exception is Charlesbourg, founded by the Jesuit order in the first half of the seventeenth century, some miles inland from Quebec city: the houses and church were grouped in a ring at the center, with triangular tilled fields radiating outward in all directions.

British army surveyors in the nineteenth century brought another tradition: straight streets laid out to form rectangular blocks, of which one at the center and one in each quarter of the town were set aside for public parks. The compact, oblong townsite was often surrounded by straight ranks of larger plots for agriculture (the "liberties"). Charlottetown (Prince Edward Island) and Brockville (Ontario) are two of many examples.

Also in the nineteenth century the Colonial Office gave extensive grants of land to private colonization companies whose officers sometimes hoped to plan new utopias in Canada; for these they might impose arbitrary plans, of which those for Goderich and Guelph in Ontario are well known. The former has eight equal streets radiating from the central, octagonal public space; while Guelph has the shape of a halfwheel. Both towns were laid out in the 1820s by the Canada Land Company on notions traceable to Edinburgh.

The constituent form of early prairie towns derives from the dominance of the transcontinental railway and the division of farmland into quarter-mile squares. Where a north-south road crossed the east-west railway, a regular pattern of station, hotel, postoffice, storage buildings, and shops would emerge, with houses spreading outward from this focal point. The late nineteenth century also saw many villages built quickly to serve remote timber or mining operations; these settlements were incidental to the sponsors' main purpose. The same period saw some deliberate town design under railway auspices, for their terminals required a skilled labor supply, and the abundant lands given them by governments had to be settled if railway traffic was to prosper. The town of Mount Royal on the edge of Montreal was an early example of an urban extension planned to exploit daily "commuting" by rail. The city of Prince Rupert on the Pacific coast was laid out at the very close of the century, by Messrs. Brett and Hall of Boston, as the terminus of the Grand Trunk Pacific Railway.

Twentieth-century Planning

New Towns In a newly-settled country most towns are "new"; the oldest residents of some western metropolitan cities in Canada can still recall the first settlers, who sometimes brought a townsite plan with them. By now, automobile ownership in these cities is so general that smaller urban places within an hour's drive of the main center are subsidiary to it; the self-sufficient "new town" at that distance (as conceived in 1946 in Britain) does not occur. In this century, the deliberately planned, freestanding urban place characteristic of Canada is the "single-enterprise community" created for the extraction of minerals, forest products, or hydroelectric power. There are about two hundred such towns in Canada, most of them very remote from main urban centers. Many of these frontier towns have been created hastily, as unwelcome preliminaries to primary operations, and they are of uneven environmental quality. Corporations with long experience and elaborate on-site workings (as in paper making, aluminum refining, or nuclear power) have fashioned a few remote towns with greater care. Kitimat in British Columbia is an example.

To produce aluminum requires a fairly common ore plus a great amount of electricity: a ton of aluminum takes about 4 tons of bauxite and nearly 22,000 kilowatthours of power. The metal can be refined where cheap bulk transport and abundant energy supplies meet. Surveys of hydroelectric potential near the Pacific coast led the government of British Columbia in 1948 to invite this sort of development. Within 6 years the Aluminum Co. of Canada delivered its first ingots from the new town of Kitimat, some 400 miles (650 kilometers) north of Vancouver. In that time, the company had reversed the flow of a powerful river, built a generating station

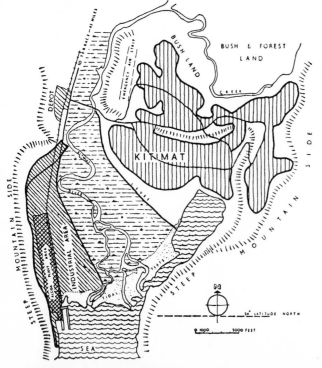

Kitimat, British Columbia. Key plan showing aluminum smelter location at the head of an arm of the Pacific at 54 degrees north latitude, with the rest of the town across the Kitimat River on terraces at the head of the fjord. Each neighborhood planned to consist of mixed dwelling types grouped around a central space for common facilities, with sidewalk circulation in the Radburn manner. (Plan conceived by Clarence Stein and carried out by Mayer & Whittlesey, architects, with Milton Glass.

On this dramatic site housing had to be built quickly, and the available types were those devised for disposition on conventional suburban streets, to this degree contradicting the plan. (Central Mortgage and Housing Corp.)

inside a mountain, constructed a harbor and smelter, and planned a new town for a population of up to 50,000 persons on rugged land at the head of a fjord. The town design, conceived by Clarence Stein and carried out under Mayer and Whittlesey of New York, is made up of residential districts of irregular shape fitted to terraces on the site. A stable and well-paid work force was assumed, so major shopping and recreation areas are reached by car. Detached houses typical of a metropolitan suburb were built; but the original plan disposes them between the roads and the independent sidewalk system, in the manner pioneered at Radburn and the greenbelt towns of the United States. Heavy winter snowfall and use of orthodox house plans (not affording the needed privacy at both front and rear) have worked against full realization of the planners' intent as to the use of open space for travel on foot.

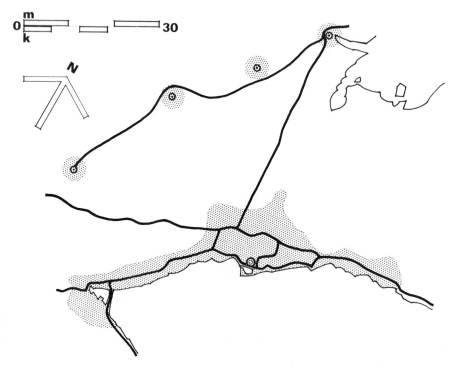

Possible pattern of urbanization in central Ontario. A conurbation extends around the west end of Lake Ontario, centered on Toronto; its population may well double in a generation. The governments of Ontario and metropolitan Toronto, with the national railways, have set out four "goal plans" for this growth, of which the most radical is shown here. Four "arc cities," located an hour away from the metropolis and linked by truck routes, would take most of the new growth. (Based by Albert Prisner on Metropolitan Toronto and Region Transportation Study.)

City Extensions The capital of Ontario and hub of activity in the densely settled southern portion of the province is in metropolitan Toronto, with a population of over 2 million. Here were planned many of Canada's early railways, a deep-water harbor in the St. Lawrence system, a publicly owned regional power grid, Canada's first underground rapid transit, and a notable regional government. Growing problems of water supply, waste disposal, and traffic management, with shrinkage of food-growing and recreational lands, led the province and the metropolitan government in 1962 to mount a major study of the future of the region with special emphasis on transportation. In 1967 the study group reported, recommending that the province shape growth policies for metropolitan regions and offering four possible futures for this one. With a minimum of public intervention, the metropolis would continue to spread outward, demanding and then following expensive transportation corridors. The most deliberate of the four solutions, lying within provincial but not local government powers, would direct metropolitan growth to four substantial "arc cities" linked by a high-speed transport network while enjoying considerable freedom from the hazards anticipated with uninterrupted sprawl. This fourth "goal plan" is illustrated.

Montreal, Canada's largest metropolis, is governed by numerous local councils and has now a general-purpose regional government. The city of Montreal had to provide major arterial routes and a rapid transit system to deal with the influx of visitors to the 1967 Exposition. For the building of these regional facilities the city received provincial and federal financial aid but assumed the physical planning responsibility. The city was convinced that a fully satisfactory regional plan could be made only under the aegis of a regional government; and to demonstrate what benefits this governmental reform might achieve, the city prepared in 1967 an outline plan known as "Montreal Horizon 2000." Arterial routes, satellite towns, a hierarchy of work and cultural centers, and a regional park system were features of this outline plan for the Montreal region.

Urban Renewal In recent years, federal and provincial legislatures have provided aid in the rehabilitation as well as the replacement of obsolete urban areas. Sensitivity is developing in the fashioning of these schemes according to the essential social and architectural character of the local areas to which they are addressed.

The strong nineteenth-century flavor of an area fronting on the harbor of Victoria has been reinforced in the careful resuscitation of Bastion Square. (Planned by Roderick Clack, City Architect.)

Renewal in British Columbia's capital. The city architect of Victoria has been persuasive in giving new life and use to nineteenth-century buildings between the City Hall and the harbor. Shown here is Bastion Square, a pedestrian precinct flanked by the Maritime Museum and other refurbished properties. (Central Mortgage and Housing Corp.)

At the other extremity of Canada, a difficult slope overlooking Halifax harbor and formerly a military site has been newly developed in a mixture of terraces and flats for families of low income; it retains the name Mulgrave Park. (Planned by Ian Maclennan, Chief Architect, Central Mortgage and Housing Corporation.)

Modern housing in a maritime tradition. A sloping site overlooking Halifax harbor, once used for storage of defense gear, has been given to housing sponsored on a partnership of governments. Rents are charged according to incomes earned and the local building vernacular has been respected by the federal architects. (Central Mortgage and Housing Corp.)

Low-rental housing near central Vancouver. Flats and terraces were built with public funds on a neglected open space to accommodate families from adjacent slums. These slums could then be cleared according to an ambitious plan of redevelopment. (Central Mortgage and Housing Corp.)

The remarkable series of office towers, hotels, and institutions of commerce and the arts that have arisen in central Montreal in the 1960s are being linked below street level by pedestrian routes sheltered from the weather and lined with gay shops and cafés.

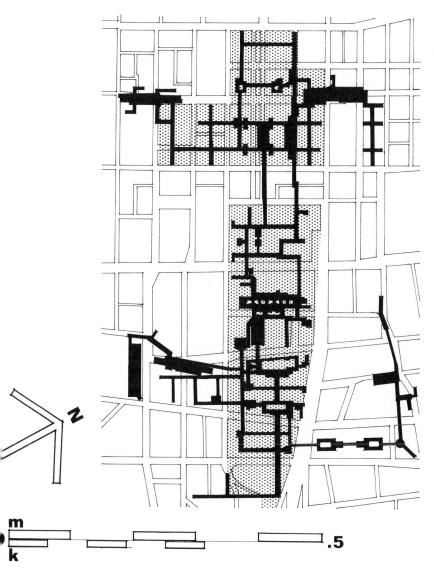

Off-street pedestrian circulation in downtown Montreal. Underground passages (black) are developing to connect rapid transit stations with much of the central commercial, shopping, theater, and hotel district (shaded). Punctuated with plazas, restaurants, and boutiques, this network makes possible a host of urban activities, out of sight of motor vehicles. (City Planning Department.)

Changing transport technology has released much of Toronto's waterfront from the rail marshaling yards that have dominated it for a century. A private consortium of interests, including the main railways, propose the reuse of this vital area for an intermodal passenger transport terminus, broadcasting and communication headquarters, luxury hotels and apartments, and related

Redevelopment of Toronto waterfront. Like many North American cities, Toronto is located on a natural harbor, equipped for ships plying the Great Lakes and the world's sea-lanes. In the railway age, the harbor front was covered with marshaling yards. Transport technology is releasing much of the land for new uses: entertainment, telecommunications, commercial display, and luxury housing. Municipal and harbor authorities, with the railway companies and private developers, have prepared a bold redevelopment plan. (Metro Centre Ltd.)

functions. Separate indoor pedestrian circulation is intended throughout this complex, linking it with adjoining major structures. The scheme, known as Metro Centre, has been worked out by collaboration of the railways, the Toronto Harbour Commission, the city, the metropolitan government, the province of Ontario, and federal transport authorities with private development enterprise.

BIBLIOGRAPHY

Geographical and Climatic Conditions
M. K. Thomas, (comp.) *Climatological Atlas of Canada*, Queen's Printer, Ottawa, 1953, *Atlas of Canada*, Queen's Printer, Ottawa, 1958; Donald G. G. Kerr (ed.), *A Historical Atlas of Canada*, Nelson, Toronto, 1961.

Legislation and Administration
James B. Milner (ed.), *Community Planning: a Casebook on Law and Administration*, University

of Toronto Press, Toronto, 1963; R. M. Bryden, *Saskatchewan Planning Legislation Study,* Department of Municipal Affairs, Regina, 1968 (Includes brief accounts of planning legislation in 9 provinces); *Rapport de la commission provinciale d'urbanisme,* L'Imprimeur de la Reine, Québec, 1968.

Education and Training
John Willis, *Education for Town Planning in Canada,* Town Planning Institute of Canada, Toronto, 1964.

Professional Practice
"Community Planning," in *Encyclopedia Canadiana,* vol. 3, p. 58, Canadiana Co., Ottawa, 1958; Leonard O. Gertler (ed.), *Planning the Canadian Environment,* Harvest House, Montreal, 1968.

Twentieth-century Planning
Canadian Council on Urban and Regional Research, *Urban & regional REFERENCES urbaines & régionales* (bibliography), the Council, Ottawa, 1964– ; Leroy O. Stone, *Urban Development in Canada,* Queen's Printer, Ottawa, 1967; Lithwick and Paquet (eds.), *Urban Studies: A Canadian Perspective,* Methuen, Toronto, 1968; *Bibliography: Resource Frontier Communities,* 2 vols., Center for Settlement Studies, University of Manitoba, Winnipeg, 1969.

—ALAN ARMSTRONG

CANALS (*See* WATER.)

CAPITAL CITY The chief city or town of a country, generally the seat of government. Sometimes a country is thought of as having two capitals: that which is the seat of government and that which is the commercial center. Thus, The Hague is the capital of the Netherlands, but Amsterdam is the commercial center and is often referred to as the commercial capital. The same applies to Bern and Zurich in Switzerland, and a few other countries can offer parallels.

CARAVANSARY In the East, an inn consisting of a large quadrangular building enclosing a court to accommodate caravans.

CARAVAN SITING (*See* MOBILE HOME PARKS.)

CARDO The two main streets of a typical Roman city or town were the central east-west street called the *decumanus* and the street crossing it from north to south, usually nearer one end, called the *cardo.* In some plans they crossed at the forum. These streets were principal features in a general checkerboard plan.

CAR PARKS (*See* SHOPPING CENTERS.)

CARTOGRAM A graphic method of showing statistical data about an area on the map of the area itself. Thus it was at one time required by development plan regulations pertaining to the presentation of town maps under the United Kingdom Town and Country Planning Act of 1947 that areas on the map proposed primarily for residential use should have the three features of area in acres, proposed population, and proposed gross density shown in a box on that part of the map to which they related. Thus an area of proposed residential use with such a cartogram was sometimes referred to as a "cartogram area."

—DAVID HALL

CARTOGRAPHY   (*See* MAPS.)

CATCHMENT AREA   An area of country, often hilly, from which water drains to a river, canal, or reservoir either naturally or artificially. In planning and sociology the term is sometimes used analogously to indicate an area from which institutions draw their members, and shopping, cultural, social, and recreational centers draw their customers.

CELLULAR GROWTH   A conception of urban growth derived from organic cellular growth, where organisms expand as cells reproduce themselves. In planning, cellular growth means the approximate repetition of existing cells in the city structure. Cellular growth thus implies a degree of planning, such as the planned addition of new neighborhoods to existing towns. Expansion of a city by cellular growth as distinct from expansion by satellite communities is that the former consists of additions on the periphery of the city, whereas the latter generally implies areas of open country between the city and the new communities. Cellular growth also means a little more than haphazard suburban growth. The latter may mean only the addition of more residential areas on the outskirts, whereas cellular growth involves some conception of the cell as a unit of planning.

CEMETERY   In planning a new settlement or community or a major urban extension, provision has to be made for space for a cemetery, usually on the outskirts of the development. The amount of space required for a cemetery is small and rarely reaches as much as 1 percent of the total area, even in small countries with large populations like Great Britain. A rough calculation will demonstrate this. With 1,500 burials to the acre, which is a fair average, and at the current death rate in Great Britain, not more than 400 acres would be required a year. Allowing for an increasing number of deaths with growing population, this would not mean more than 50,000 acres in a hundred years, which is about 0.1 percent of the total area of 56,803,840 acres. But the land would probably be reused for this or another purpose at least every 300 years.

In ancient Greece and Rome cemeteries were provided outside the city walls, often along particular roads; the ancient cemetery of the Ceramacus at Athens and the Appian Way at Rome are famous examples. In these cemeteries the graves and monuments lined the roadways.

In the early centuries of Christianity burial often took place within a sacred structure, sometimes in catacombs and later within basilicas and churches. A burial ground was often formed around the church and sometimes around a sacred preaching station marked by a cross, and a church often was built later on the site. Thus evolved the well-known churchyards of Europe. From the seventeenth century onward, when burials within churches

Street of Tombs, Pompeii (first century B.C.*).*

became crowded, churchyards were more commonly used for burial purposes. The churchyards were controlled and administered by the church. Churchyards are also a feature of New England in the United States, but these more often had secular administration, which is also often the case with later extensions of those in England.

During the eighteenth century churchyards in large cities were becoming overcrowded and unsanitary, and cemeteries began to be provided on the outskirts. An early example of this is Paris, where churchyards in the center were closed in 1765 and cemeteries began to be provided on the periphery. Among the earliest of these were Père Lachaise, where many famous Frenchmen were buried, Montmartre, and Montparnasse.

This movement was followed in London in the first half of the nineteenth century when Kensal Green, Norwood, and Highgate cemeteries were opened in 1833, 1838, and 1839, to be quickly followed by several others. Many of these cemeteries have effective landscaping and interesting monuments, but later, when burials increased in the late-nineteenth century, the general appearance often became monotonous and dreary. Good landscaping also characterized some of the early cemeteries in the United States, where more spacious setting of monuments often obtained. One of the notable early examples is Mount Auburn Cemetery in Boston, planned by Frederick Law Olmsted.

Twentieth-century Europe presents the spectacle of the extremes in the appearance of cemeteries, from the very beautiful to the ugly and dreary. Some of the most notable are to be found in Switzerland, the Scandinavian countries, and Germany, where there have been developments in effective and sometimes beautiful landscaping. In Germany, there are many cemeteries with forest areas. These are planted mainly with conifers, and graves and monuments are placed within small clearings in the forest. Sometimes other parts of the cemeteries are for cremated remains, with smaller-scale monuments.

In Switzerland cemeteries are carefully designed, with effective use of natural features and planned distribution of trees, shrubs, and flowers in relation to graves and monuments. Often evergreen shrubs are employed as backgrounds to memorials. The cemetery of Enzenbühl in Zurich, opened in 1902, is a notable yet typical example and can serve to indicate what is possible in cemetery landscape planning. It is situated on hilly ground with many pleasant features like streams and pools, which have been partly formalized and partly left in their natural condition. One part on the highest ground has been leveled to form a small plateau, and here are a broad central avenue and transverse paths, lined with some of the larger monuments set among shrubs and trees. At the lower levels, reached in many places by steps, are more open areas where sloping lawns and pools of water and dark fir trees compose the landscape. A formalized treatment is given to one expanse of water, and near the edge is a large, bronze, recumbent figure which adds a focal point to the composition and reflects into the pool. The sloping ground is terraced, and memorials are placed along the terraces

Stokes Poges, churchyard, England. The churchyard that inspired Grey's Elegy.

Kensal Green Cemetery. The first in London, opened in 1833. The monuments seen in this photograph are typical of the grandiose memorials of the mid-Victorian period.

Part of the cemetery of east Zurich (opened in 1902), showing decorative landscaping.

Meuse-Argonne American Military Cemetery, one of the principal ones in France. It is an effective example of symmetrical formal planning, with a circular pool in foreground and chapel in distance.

among trees, shrubs, and plants. The control of monuments allows for a pleasing variety, so that figure sculptures mingle with inscribed slabs often of distinctive artistic merit.

Among the examples of modern cemetery planning are the military cemeteries of the two world wars. It must suffice to note those of the United States and the British Commonwealth. Both are located near the battlefields in many countries. In both each soldier is buried in a separate grave. In the American cemeteries each grave is marked with a white marble cross, a six-pointed star, or a shield of David. In the British cemeteries the graves are marked with uniform headstones, each incised with a cross for a Christian and a shield of David for a Jew. (In some cemeteries in the East where those commemorated are of different religions, graves are marked with recumbent stones.) Many of the dead were not found, and these are commemorated by monuments near the battlefields or incorporated as parts of the cemeteries. The names of the missing are recorded on these monuments.

Most of the memorials are arranged formally in rows a little like soldiers on parade; yet because of the very effective landscaping, the disposition of trees and shrubs, and the well-kept lawns and flowers near the memorials, they often impress visitors as very beautiful and as a contrast to the rather dreary city cemeteries that they know. The effectiveness of these military cemeteries has prompted local authorities to introduce something similar in the civil cemeteries, with rows of small memorials, strictly limited in size, and extensive lawns. The question arises, however, whether the regimentation apparent in the military cemetery, beautiful as the effect often is, is really applicable to the civil cemetery, and whether the beautiful cemeteries of Switzerland, Germany, and Scandinavia are not better examples to follow.

What are known as "national cemeteries" in the United States are those inaugurated shortly after the American Civil War for members of the United States Armed Forces and their families. There are 98 of these national cemeteries, and in some of them, such as Arlington National Cemetery in Washington, many of the most distinguished Americans have been buried and commemorated.

—ARNOLD WHITTICK

Taiping British War Cemetery, Malaya (1939–1945).

Irregular yet effective landscaping in Arlington Cemetery, Washington.

CENTRAL PLACE THEORY In the original formulation of the theory by Walter Cristaller in his book, *Die Zentralen Orte in Suddeutschland,* published in Jena in 1933 (see bibliography) central place is the source of goods and services to the surroundings beyond its own area. Implicit in the theory is the complementary relation of the two areas and the conditions governing the spatial distribution of central places and their hierarchical arrangement. The theory was formulated to provide answers to the questions why cities, towns, and villages are distributed as they are, and why there are the degrees of size. The theory was foreshadowed by several previous German writers, especially Robert Gradmann, and by a few others, but Cristaller was the first to fortify the theory with extensive and detailed analysis.

Cristaller claims that the theory is organically based for, he says (Baskin's translation), "The crystallization of mass around a nucleus is, in inorganic as well as organic nature, an elementary form of the order of things which belong together—a centralistic order. This order is not only a human mode of thinking, existing in the human world of imagination and developed because people demand order: it in fact exists out of the inherent pattern of matter."

The increasing or decreasing centrality of a place depends on the extent to which it functions for the surrounding region. Cristaller gives a simple mathematical explanation. If the town has an aggregate importance of B, of which Bz represents the town's population, then $B - Bz =$ the surplus of importance for the surrounding region, and it is this, the magnitude of the surplus, that shows the degree to which the town is a central place.

Important in Christaller's theory is the hierarchy of central places which he elaborates on a mathematical basis from the smallest—the village or dwarf town—to the largest—the metropolitan city. Their importance as central places is not invariably related to population but to numerous factors.

Among those which have been variously classified in the voluminous literature on the subject are (1) the supply of goods to the population of surrounding areas, (2) provision of resort amenities, (3) nodes on transportation networks, (4) the provision of banking and commercial facilities, (5) the provision of educational and cultural facilities, and (6) governmental and other administrative functions. The growth of a central place is also dependent on numerous factors such as (1) the amount of support that is required for a particular function called threshold population, (2) spacial competition, and (3) the choice of a particular central place for the location of new functions.

In the choice and growth of a central place Christaller places main emphasis on its servicing function for surrounding areas, and it is questionable whether he gives sufficient importance to other factors such as climatic and geographical conditions, location of raw materials for power and manufacture.

In applying his theory to the cities and towns of southern Germany, Christaller diagrammatically employed, not the circle, as this leaves some areas uncovered, but the hexagram which covers the area completely.

How is it possible to measure the centrality of a place and its importance as such? Christaller stated that centrality "is equal to the relative importance of the place in regard to a region belonging to it." He suggested that the best method of determining the importance of a place as a center is, not by the size of the population, but by the number of telephone connections. This may have been true in southern Germany at the time Christaller wrote, but it could not be true of America in 1973, because of the extensive domestic use of the telephone. This has prompted subsequent writers to speculate on more reliable measures of centrality. Professor Edward Ullman suggested some, such as "the average number of customers required to support certain specialized functions in various regions," and, "the excess of these functions over the normal required for the urban population." Another suggestion is the number of automobiles entering a town excluding those from the suburbs. If census questionnaires could include data pertinent to the causes of centrality this would probably answer the questions most satisfactorily.

The many questions relating to central place analysis are important to surveys preceding the preparations of plans, but there is still a good deal of research necessary before satisfactory answers can be found to the many questions the theory poses. Progressive steps have been taken by many economists and geographers and others in the United States, among them J. L. Berry and William L. Garrison (see bibliography), who have suggested that the theory is more understandable and more viable when formulated in a series of simple concepts, such as that of the range of a good,[1] and of threshold. Such concepts make possible a hierarchical structure which could be used by planners.

BIBLIOGRAPHY: Robert Gradmann, "Das landliche Siedlungswesen des Konigreichs Wurttemberg," in *Forschungen zur deutschen Landes-und Volkskunde,* 21, part 1, Stuttgart, 1926; Mark Jefferson, "Distribution of the World's City Folks," *Geographical Review,* vol. 21, 1931; Walter Christaller, "Die Zentralen Orte in Suddeutschland," Jena, 1933 (English translation by Carlisle W. Baskin entitled *Central Places in Southern Germany,* Prentice-Hall, Inc., New Jersey, 1966); August Losch, *Economics of Location* (English translation by Wolfgang F. Stolper, Yale University Press, New Haven, 1954); Krystyne Szumeluk, *Central Place Theory,* Centre for Environmental Studies, London, 1968; John Urquhart Marshall, *The Location of Service Towns—an approach to the analysis of central place systems,* University of Toronto Press, Toronto, 1969; William H. Leahy, David L. McKee, and Robert D. Dean (editors), *Urban Economics— Theory, Development and Planning,* Part II, The Free Press, New York, 1970. Central Place Theory consisting of Edward L. Ullman, *A Theory of Location for Cities,* although published in 1941, was included as it gives an excellent background for central place theory. Brian J. L. Berry and William L. Garrison, *Recent Developments of Central Place Theory;* Leslie Curry, *Central Places in the Random Spatial Economy;* Brian J. L. Berry, *Cities as Systems within Cities;* Gunnar Olsson, *Central Place Systems, Spatial Interaction and Stochastic Processes.*

—ARNOLD WHITTICK

CHAMBERS, SIR WILLIAM (1726–1796) English architect and planner prominent in the reign of George III.

At Kew, near Richmond, in Surrey, where a well-known herbal garden had existed from the sixteenth century, Chambers designed the Royal Botanic Garden, founded by the Dowager Princess of Wales in 1759. At the time Kew House—an established center of botany and horticulture—had become a royal palace, and with the grounds it occupied a site of 11 acres (4.45 hectares).

In 1840, Queen Victoria assigned the gardens to the nation, and later they were greatly enlarged and extended in scope until eventually they attained their present area of nearly 300 acres (121.5 hectares).

---

[1] Singular of the more customary plural: "goods." The singular form has been revived by central place theorists as having a slightly different application from the plural form.

Chambers designed his gardens on formal lines, introducing into them a number of temples in the Roman style and a Chinese pagoda that reflected the influence of his travels in the East.

His principal work in London was Somerset House (1776–1786), a building of great dignity, with a frontage on the Thames of over 600 feet (181.5 meters), one of the finest river facades in the world.

Chambers was an exponent of the Palladian school of architecture and the author of a number of books, including *A Treatise of Civil Architecture, Designs for Chinese Buildings,* and *A Dissertation on Oriental Gardening.*

BIBLIOGRAPHY: Reginald Blomfield, *A History of Renaissance Architecture in England,* George Bell & Sons, London, 1897.

—WILFRED SALTER

CHESSBOARD PLAN (also called checkerboard and gridiron)   An urban plan divided into approximately square building blocks formed by the street pattern. This system of planning can be traced back to ancient Egypt and Mesopotamia and was prominent in much Greek and Roman planning and in modern planning following such traditions. The planning of American cities in this way was influenced by the system of laying out lands for settlement, and gridiron plans characterize the layout of some entirely new towns and cities in the present century.

CHILE

Geographical and Climatic Conditions   Chile stretches approximately 2,630 miles (3,908 kilometers) along the Pacific Coast, from Tacua (17 degrees south latitude) on the Peruvian border southward to Cape Horn (56 degrees south latitude) on the southernmost tip of the South American continent.[1] It occupies 292,268 square miles (759,897 square kilometers) excluding the Antartic Territory. Its average width is only 110 miles (176 kilometers), and in certain parts no more than 50 miles (80 kilometers). Approximately one-fourth of Chile's territory is made up of islands.[2]

Major Geographic Characteristics   Chile begins in the north as a desert rich in nitrate and other minerals, followed by a transitional zone of mining and agriculture. Farther south there is the fertile central valley, followed by a colder, rainy, heavily wooded area of varied topography. The southern end consists of an almost uninhabited wilderness of islands, foggy channels, rocks, glaciers, and fjords. The Andes Mountains occupy the entire eastern portion of continental Chile, leaving the country with flatlands equal to only about one-fifth of its total land area.

Climate   The country, pressed between the ocean and the mountains, presents marked climatic contrasts. The north is practically rainless, the center enjoys a Mediterranean climate, and the south is drenched in heavy rains.

[1]Fundación "Pedro Aguirre Cerda," *Geografía Económica de Chile.* Corporación de Fomento de la Producción, Santiago, Chile, 1965, p. 1.
[2]UCLA, Latin American Center, *Statistical Abstract of Latin America 1967,* University of California, Los Angeles, 1968, table 1, p. 48.

Accordingly, temperatures from north to south range from tropic heat to sub-Antarctic cold.

Chile has frequently been affected by earthquakes, and many towns have been destroyed. There are many active volcanoes in the country. The threat of earthquakes is always imminent; the earthquake of 1939 killed as many as sixty thousand persons. In 1960 a series of earthquakes devastated southern Chile from Concepción to Puerto Montt, and, as a result, new mountains, islands, and lakes came into existence while other islands and some coastal areas disappeared into the sea. At least five thousand persons were killed.[3]

Demographic and Socioeconomic Background of Urbanization

Population Growth and Trends Chile's urbanization is rapid and continuous. Over the last three decades a major internal rearrangement occurred in the distribution of its population: the rural sector declined to less than one-third of the total as the urban sector increased proportionately to over two-thirds of the country's population. The total population has increased steadily, from 3,714,887 in 1920 to 7,374,115 in 1960 (most recent census of population).[4] The 1960 census indicated that 63.7 percent of the total population was considered urban and 36.3 percent rural.[5] The annual rate of population increase is approximately 2.4 percent (1965).[6] The annual rate of urban population growth in 1965 was 5.9 percent, whereas the rural population decreased by 0.2 percent.[7] By midyear, 1970, the total population of the country was estimated at 9,636,000 inhabitants, of which 6,850,000 or 71.1 percent represent the urban population and 2,786,000 or 28.9 percent represent the rural areas.[8]

Geographic Distribution Most of Chile's population is concentrated in the central valley, which contains the largest urban centers of the country. The 19 central provinces have only 32 percent of Chile's total area, but they are inhabited by about 91 percent of the total population.[9] According to the 1960 census, 48.7 percent of the total population lived in cities with 20,000 or more inhabitants, and 68.2 percent in cities over 5,000.[10] The 1960 census included 9 cities with a population of between 20,000 and 50,000; 12 cities between 50,000 and 100,000; and 2 cities between 100,000 and 500,000.[11]

---

[3]Charles Paul May, *Chile, Progress on Trial,* Thomas Nelson & Sons, Camden, N.J., 1968, pp. 22–23.

[4]UCLA, Latin American Center, *op. cit.,* table 6, p. 59.

[5]U.N., Economic Commission for Latin America, *Boletín Estadístico de América Latina,* vol. 4, no. 1, 1965, table 4, p. 9.

[6]UCLA, Latin American Center, *op. cit.,* table 14, p. 77.

[7]U.N., Economic Commission for Latin America, *Economic Survey of Latin America,* United Nations, New York, 1967, table 30, p. 15.

[8]U.N., Economic Commission for Latin America, *Boletín Estadístico de América Latina, op. cit.,* table 4, p. 9.

[9]K. H. Silvert, *Chile, Yesterday and Today,* Holt, Rinehart and Winston, Inc., New York, 1965, p. 26.

[10]John Friedman (ed.), *Chile: la Década del 70,* Fundación Ford, Santiago, Chile, 1969, p. 3.

[11]*Ibid.*

Santiago, the capital, had a population of 2,248,378 in 1965.[12] Greater Santiago comprises the *comunas* or townships of Barracudas, Conchali, La Cisterna, La Florida, La Granja, Los Condes, Maipú, Nuñoa, Providencia, Quilicura, Quinta Normal, Renca, San Bernardo, and San Miguel. The metropolitan area has been growing almost twice as fast as the rest of the country. In the same year Valparaíso, the second-largest city, had a population of 276,000, followed by Concepción (174,000), Viña del Mar (135,000), Talcahuano (102,000), and Antofagasta (112,000).[13] If the adjacent townships are included, the metropolitan population of these cities increases considerably.

Density   The pattern of population distribution is highly uneven. The national population density in 1965 was 30.6 persons per square mile (12 per square kilometer).[14] However, the northern desert contains a density of 2.6 persons per square mile (1 per square kilometer), the southern extreme has a density of 2 persons per square mile (0.74 per square kilometer), whereas Chile's center has a density of 58 persons per square mile (23 per square kilometer).

Age Composition   Of the Chilean population, 39.6 percent are in the 0- to 14-year group; 56.1 percent in the 15- to 64-year group; and 4.3 percent in the 65-and-over category (1965).[15] These figures, compared to previous statistics, show a decline in the death rate and an increase in the percentage of population under 15. The birth rate is 34 to 36 per thousand of population.[16] The average life expectancy is about 51 years.[17]

Migration Trends   Internal migration is fairly high: in 1963, estimates indicated that migrants constituted 37 percent of the population of Greater Santiago. At the same time, of a labor force of 778,000 workers, more than half (53 percent) were migrants.[18] Demographic trends have tended to magnify the dominance of the central region and its urban centers to the detriment of the rural areas. Whereas the highly urban areas generally maintain their populations or increase them, there are some exceptions in the far north (Tarapacá, Antofagasta, and Atacama) and in the far south (Valdivia, Osorno, and Llanquihué). In the former case, northern people abandon their mining towns, pushed by cyclical economic factors as well as by conditions of the labor market in the nitrate industry, and move to the more attractive central valley. The southern agricultural areas, with stable populations, are comparatively prosperous.

Socioeconomic Characteristics   During colonial times and long after independence, Chile had a fairly rigid two-class society—a landowning aristocracy

---

[12] UCLA, Latin American Center, *op. cit.*, table 9, p. 65.

[13] *Ibid.*, table 10, p. 67.

[14] *Ibid.*, table 15, p. 78.

[15] U.N., Department of Economic and Social Affairs, *1967 Report on the World Social Situation*, United Nations, New York, 1969, table 1, p. 126.

[16] U.N., Economic Commission for Latin America, *Boletín Estadístico de América Latina*, vol. 4, no. 1, table 12, p. 27, 1967.

[17] *Ibid.*, 1960–1965.

[18] Bruce H. Herrick, *Urban Migration and Economic Development in Chile*, The M.I.T. Press, Cambridge, Mass., 1965, p. 46.

and a lower class formed by a large mass of peasants. The Indians lived as a nation apart. As race mixture proceeded, large numbers of mestizos (mixed bloods) appeared, some of whom acquired education and rose to occupy a middle position. In the latter part of the nineteenth century, this middle category gradually enlarged, its ranks swelled from many sources. Stimulated by the growth of the population, which was accompanied by the trend toward urbanization and by general economic and educational development, this emerging middle group became, in less than a century and a half, one of the largest segments of Chilean society, estimated in 1949 at roughly one-fifth of the total population. In 1960, Indians and mestizos (who lead the same type of life) constituted 31.8 percent of the total population.[19]

Chilean overall economic growth in recent years has failed to keep up with an expanding population. For example, the per capita income was no higher in 1961 than it was in 1953,[20] yet the Chilean population, which had grown steadily at a rate of 1.8 percent annually between 1942 and 1952, has maintained a growth rate of 2.5 percent per annum since 1953.[21] This has put additional stress on an economy that must increase more rapidly to hold its own. In 1966 Chile's per capita gross national product was $588 (United States dollars).[22] The economically active population in 1960 was 32.4 percent,[23] of whom approximately 23 percent were employed in services.[24] Chile has been beset by inflationary problems for more than eighty years. The inflationary rate was 60 percent between 1953 and 1956, and 25 percent between 1956 and 1960.[25]

Minerals are among the most important resources of Chile, to the extent that for most of its modern history the nation's economic existence has depended primarily on their exploitation. The mining extractive industry furnishes nearly 80 percent of the country's exports, and approximately one-fourth of the fiscal revenues derive from mining. Nitrate and copper are the chief minerals, and they have been found in northern and central Chile.

The origins of Chile's industry can be traced to before 1914, but its greatest acceleration occurred after the 1930s. Chile's industrialization process has been occurring while the country has been transforming itself from a rural into an urban country. After becoming stagnant in 1956 and 1957, Chilean industry has shown a very low rate of growth. Per capita domestic income generated in the manufacturing sector grew only 1.3 percent during the 1950s, as against an annual rate of 6.5 percent during the 1940s.[26] During the period 1953 to 1959 the annual increase in industrial production was

[19]UCLA, Latin American Center, *op. cit.*, table 19, p. 89.

[20]*La Economía de Chile en el Período 1953–63*, Tomo II Instituto de Economía, University of Chile, Santiago, Chile, 1963, Cuadro no. 1, p. 2.

[21]*Ibid.*, Tomo I, Cuadro no. 2, p. 3.

[22]UCLA, Latin American Center, *op. cit.*, table 74, p. 181.

[23]*Ibid.*, table 20, p. 91.

[24]*Ibid.*, table 22, p. 95.

[25]Herrick, *op. cit.*, p. 4.

[26]*Ibid.*, p. 8.

0.9 percent per capita. The average annual growth rate of manufacturing during the past 15 years was 4.3 percent.[27] In 1960, manufacturing absorbed 17.2 percent of the total population. The great bulk of Chile's manufacturing industry is located in the Santiago-Valparaíso region, with a subsidiary center in the south at Concepción.

Agriculture contributes only about 12 percent of the gross national product, although it employs more than 27 percent of the labor force. Two-thirds of Chile's total area is wasteland. The usable area is more than 56 percent forest lands; 20 percent is actually cultivated. In recent years, while the population has been increasing by about 2.5 percent annually, agricultural production has risen only 1.6 percent. The income per person active in agriculture is estimated at slightly more than half of that found in industry and approximately one-third of that shown in mining. Over 50 percent of the farms in the country are in about 2.8 percent of the arable land. In contrast, about 13,000 farms (8.5 percent) hold over 68 percent of Chile's arable land.[28]

Urbanization and National Development   The country's regions are economic units rather than organic-historic-cultural entities, and they enjoy little political expression of their own. The 25 provinces are administrative subdivisions patterned after the French prefectorial system. Chilean cities are highly dependent on the national government. Municipal budgets, as an average, run to less than $10 per annum on a per capita basis. The central government administers 97.9 percent of national expenditures, leaving only 2.1 percent to municipal governments for their most essential needs.[29]

There is heavy demographic and economic concentration in Santiago. The capital city and its region, which includes the central macrozone of Santiago, Valparaíso, Aconcagua, O'Higgins, and Colchagua, absorbs approximately 49 percent of the country's population, 59 percent of the active population, 70 percent of the industrial labor sector, and 53 percent of the gross national product.[30]

Migration to the cities has exceeded the capability of the economic system to integrate the immigrants successfully at full and productive levels of employment. As a result, a growing proportion of the population in the cities has been unable to rise out of a condition of nearly total economic dependency, the urban subproletariat or *marginados*. Extensive shantytowns or *poblaciones callampas* have mushroomed on the periphery of most urban centers. The economic dependency of the marginal population is manifested by an extreme poverty, high rates of unemployment (or disguised unemployment), and lack of public services. Since urbanization has not been accompanied by a proportional increase in industrial jobs, a large segment of the working population has been absorbed into unskilled services, and a large proportion of the urban labor force remains unemployed. The cost of urban expansion has been very high. Nearly the totality of public

[27]Fundación "Pedro Aguirre Cerda," *op. cit.*, p. 399.
[28]*Ibid.*, Tomo III, Cuadro no. 38, p. 68.
[29]Friedman, *op. cit.*, p. 56.
[30]*Ibid.*

investment in cities has been financed from the national budget, since neither provinces nor cities have sufficient resources of their own. It is estimated that the proportion of urban investment in housing and infrastructure amounts to between 35 and 40 percent of all public outlays.[31]

Legislation and Administration Chile was one of the first Latin American countries to establish a national system of regional development planning articulated within the context of a national plan. However, Chile's political structure is unitary and its governmental and administrative organization is highly centralized, which renders the implementation of regional planning difficult. Although important advances have been made recently, regional planning in Chile is still carried out in an advisory capacity. An organizational chart displaying Chile's economic policy and programming system for urban and regional development is illustrated.

[31]John Friedman, "Planning as Innovation: the Chilean Case," *Journal of the American Institute of Planners,* vol. 32, no. 4, p. 198, 1966.

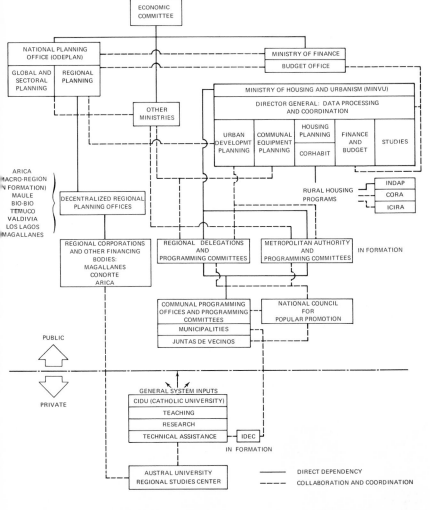

Chile's economic policy and programming for urban and regional development, 1969. (John Friedman, Urban and Regional Development in Chile, Ford Foundation, Santiago, 1969, p. 77; URDAPIC, Annual Report 1967/68, Ford Foundation, Santiago, 1968, p. 7.)

National Planning Office (Oficina Nacional de Planificación—ODEPLAN) The core of Chile's planning system is in Santiago. Regional planning is carried out through one of the two subdirectorates of ODEPLAN, the regional planning subdirectorate (the other being for global and sectoral planning). ODEPLAN is directly under the authority of the President of the republic and was legally recognized on July 15, 1967.[32] It is a policy-making and advisory body and has no executive authority or investment resources of its own. Its main responsibility is to allocate public investments (about 75 percent of total investments) in geographic space as well as according to the traditional sectors of governmental activity.

The country has been divided into development regions for the purpose of decentralizing governmental decision-making powers. These regions, representing various combinations of the existing 25 provinces, are:[33]

ZM—Metropolitan Zone (Santiago)

1. Tarapacá
2. Antofagasta
3. Atacama-Coquimbo
4. Aconcagua-Valparaíso
5. O'Higgins-Colchagua
6. Curicó-Talca-Maule-Linares
7. Ñuble-Concepción-Arauco-Bío Bío-Malleco
8. Cautín
9. Valdivia-Osorno
10. Llanquihué-Chiloé-Aysén
11. Magallanes

This regionalization of the country's territory is related to a series of administrative changes of great significance: the appointment of regional governors or *intendentes*, the creation of regional advisory councils (consejos administrativos regionales), and the establishment of technical planning offices at the regional level (ORPLANs).

There are ORPLANs, dependent on ODEPLAN, in the following cities within the regions mentioned above (1969): Bío Bío (7), Maule (6), Los Canales (10), Magallanes (11), and Los Lagos (9). There is also a technical secretariat in Cautín. In addition, development advisory services are provided under contract by ODEPLAN to the financing agency for development in the north (CONORTE), comprising the Tarapacá, Antofagasta, and Co-quimbo regions, and to the Development Junta for Arica. An additional ORPLAN is under consideration (1969), which will include the provinces of Santiago, Valparaíso, O'Higgins, Colchagua, and Aconcagua.

This ORPLAN structure was established with a series of important aims and functions in relation to national planning. These consist basically of (1) the preparation of planning strategies for each development region (2) the guidance of national investment policies according to specific locational

[32] ODEPLAN, *Política de Dessarollo Nacional—Directivas Nacionales y Regionales*, Editorial Universitaria, S.A., Santiago, Chile, 1969, p. 142.
[33] *Ibid.*, p. 149.

criteria; (3) the preparation of a regionalized investment budget for the nation (which is not submitted to the National Congress for approval); (4) the evaluation of government investment policy in the regions according to the yardstick established in the development strategy of the area; (5) the achievement of improved coordination of government programs in the regions; and (6) the promotion of local development by the private sector. These activities are supported by the analysis of regional resources and economic activities throughout the country.

The ORPLANs maintain close contact with the *intendentes* (prefects) of the respective provinces, serving as their technical secretariat. The *intendentes* represent the President of the republic in the provinces and have ample powers of coordination and guidance.

All the ORPLANs are also participating in an effort to regionalize the national capital budget that, until 1968, was presented only along the traditional lines of sectoral investment without regard to location or spatial interrelationships. Projects are supposed to originate in the regions, where they are costed out and related to each other within the format of a program that not only considers the phasing for implementation but also locates projects in geographic space. National policy guidelines for this exercise are prepared jointly by ODEPLAN and the Ministry of Finance (budget bureau). The draft programs are then studied and revised at the central office in Santiago, with the participation of local ORPLAN chiefs.

Both the regional subdirectorate of ODEPLAN and the ORPLANs have been staffed by professionals. Information has become available on the development characteristics of different regions. National statistical programs are now being coordinated through ORPLAN to provide more relevant planning data at provincial and regional levels. In general, the regional Sub-Directorate of ODEPLAN has become a central point of information, counsel, and policy decision affecting the peripheral economies of Chile. The ORPLANs are playing a similar role. Support comes from provincial prefects and community leaders.[34] Many professionals from the staff of ODEPLAN and ORPLAN's, who work only part time for these agencies, also work for private consultant firms that are engaged in preinvestment studies for urban areas. This unofficial collaboration is considered to strengthen the relations between urban governments and ODEPLAN.

Ministry of Housing and Urbanism (Ministerio de la Vivienda y Urbanismo— MINVU) The Ministry of Housing and Urbanism was officially created by law on December 16, 1965.[35] It has a staff of approximately five thousand (1969), and it is responsible for one-fifth of the national investment budget.[36] MINVU is legally in charge of orienting and coordinating the total public investment effort in urban development and of managing the country's housing program. Planning and finance are handled by the General

[34] John Friedman, *Urban and Regional Development in Chile,* Ford Foundation, Santiago, Chile, pp. 58–60.
[35] MINVU, *Ley 16, 391,* December 16, 1965, Título I, Párrafo 1°, Artículo 1°, p. 23.
[36] Friedman, *Urban and Regional Development in Chile, op. cit.,* p. 133.

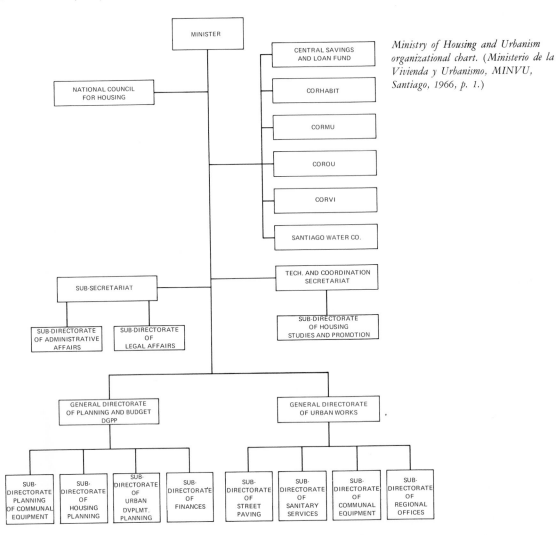

Ministry of Housing and Urbanism organizational chart. (Ministerio de la Vivienda y Urbanismo, MINVU, Santiago, 1966, p. 1.)

Directorate of Planning and Budget (DGPP), while the functions of execution are the responsibility of a series of semiautonomous corporations. The Ministry took over a number of functions that had been scattered among various government agencies, and it is attempting to merge these into integrated programs for housing and urban development within the context of national policies.

By the same law (article 5), the activities of the following semiautonomous institutions were coordinated under MINVU.[37]

1. Central Savings and Loan Fund (Caja Central de Ahorro y Préstamos)
2. Housing Services Corporation (Corporación de Servicios Habitacionales—CORHABIT)

[37]MINVU, *op. cit.*, Título I, Párrafo 1°, Artículo 5°, p. 25.

3. Urban Improvement Corporation (Corporación de Mejoramiento Urbano—CORMU)

4. Housing Corporation (Corporación de la Vivienda—CORVI)

5. Santiago Water Company (Empresa de Agua Potable de Santiago)

6. Municipal Sewage Company of Valparaíso and Viña del Mar (Empresa Municipal de Desagües de Valparaíso y Viña del Mar)

7. The remaining water companies in the country

The organizational structure of MINVU (1969) is shown in the chart. The Ministry's branches[38] and functions, summarized, are:

1. The *Sub-Secretariat,* which is responsible for the Ministry's legal and administrative matters and for the coordination of the various regional committees within the Ministry.

2. The *General Directorate of Planning and Budget* (Dirección General de Planificación y Presupuesto—DGPP), which includes four subdirectorates:

a. Sub-Directorate of Urban Development Planning (Dirección de Planificación del Desarrollo Urbano—DPDU). Guides the growth of cities through the provision and enforcement of regulatory controls. In practice, this is accomplished through the control of sales and purchases of land and by assisting the municipalities in the implementation of their master plans. By law, municipalities are responsible for producing a physical master plan for the development of their urban areas. In the case of metropolitan areas (Santiago, Valparaíso, and Concepción), the responsibility for producing the master plan lies with DPDU, which must approve all master plans proposed by municipalities.

The municipalities are assisted by *programadores* or programmers, who are discussion leaders and technical advisers for *comités de programación* (programming committees) made up of local officials. These committees are responsible for budgeting nationally allocated funds to their local areas. The committees allocate funds and designate projects for all sectors of urban development: housing, industrial parks, utilities, and community facilities. Membership is made up of mayors, *intendentes,* representatives from *Promoción Popular* (Popular Promotion), and the local officials in charge of water, sewage, and housing.

This subdirectorate has over the past years contracted a number of preinvestments studies for each of the principal cities of Chile. These studies sometimes include recommendations for the development of new *poblaciones,* or communities. The DPDU is also planning a model cities program in Concepción, which will be administered by an ad hoc agency in which the community will have a high degree of participation.

b. Sub-Directorate of Finances (Dirección de Finanzas). Prepares and supervises the operating and capital budgets of the Ministry and subordinated agencies.

c. Sub-Directorate of Planning and Communal Equipment (Dirección de Planificación del Equipamiento Comunitario). Programs the Ministry's

[38] *Ibid.,* pp. 25–54.

investments in communal equipment including urban works, and it directly executes public equipment works in incorporated localities. Its operations are related to those of CORVI, CORHABIT, and COROU.

d. Sub-Directorate of Housing Planning (Dirección de Planificación Habitacional). Programs housing investments at the national, regional, community, and institutional levels. Its operations relate it to CORVI, CORHABIT, CORMU, and the Central Savings and Loan Fund.

3. *The Sub-Directorate of Housing Studies and Promotion* (Estudios y Fomento Habitacional), which advises the Directorate of Planning and Budget in the coordination of the agencies related to the Ministry as well as in the Ministry's dealings with those institutions—national or international, public or private—having to do with housing, urbanism, and communal equipment.

4. *Technical and Coordination Secretariat* (Secretaría Técnia y de Coordinación), which is in charge of providing technical assistance to CORVI. It also handles the revision of all housing investment programs and the establishment of priorities of such programs.

5. *Semi-Autonomous Corporations Coordinated by MINVU.*

a. CORMU (Corporación de Mejoramiento Urbano—Urban Improvement Corporation). Has two main functions: the purchase of land to be developed—publicly or privately—for housing, and the promotion of mixed public and private societies. These societies have largely been formed to undertake urban renewal programs.

b. CORVI (Corporación de la Vivienda—Housing Corporation). Is in charge of directly executing government-financed housing projects, through contracts with private companies and public bids. CORVI, established in 1953, draws its funds from annual budgetary appropriations, 5 percent of the net profit of industrial, mining, commercial, and agricultural enterprises and an annual percentage of the surpluses of the social security service and welfare institutions. Banks, insurance companies, corporations, and semi-governmental institutions must set aside for low-cost housing construction a minimum of 20 percent of the portion of their capital reserves invested in property to be leased. CORVI's construction effort amounts to approximately 60 percent of all the new housing built in Chile (1965).[39]

c. CORHABIT (Corporación de Servicios Habitacionales—Housing Services Corporation). Administers the Popular Savings Plan (PAP—Plan de Ahorro Popular); extends credit for housing and housing facilities and collects savings and dividends from its investments.

d. Central Savings and Loan Fund (Caja Central de Ahorro y Préstamos). Controls, on a national scale, the National System of Savings and Loans (Sistema Nacional de Ahorro y Préstamo—SINAP), which includes local savings and loan funds throughout the country. These local funds receive savings from private individuals and, in accordance with central fund regulations, grant these individuals credit for the construction of low-income housing.

---

[39] Friedman, "Planning as Innovation: the Chilean Case," *op. cit.,* p. 199.

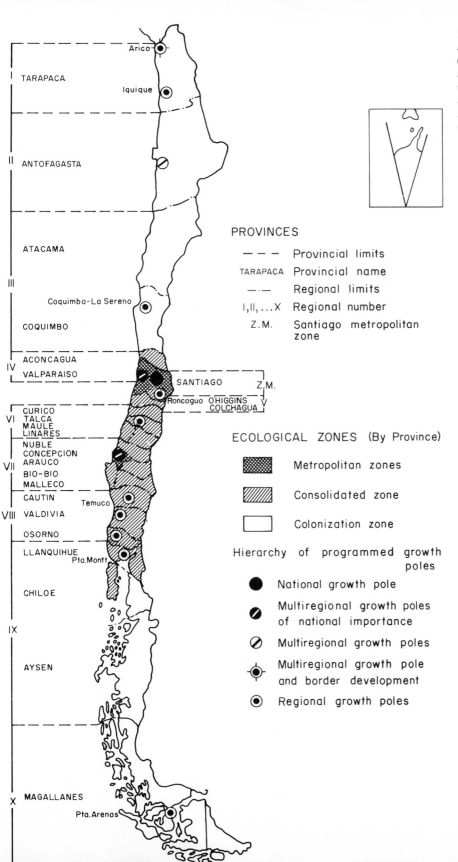

The planning regions of Chile according to the National Planning Office, Santiago, Chile. (Lower-case names are those of growth poles whose names do not coincide with that of the Province. Only Chiloe Province has been divided into its Continental and Island Territories.)

PROVINCES

— — — Provincial limits

TARAPACA Provincial name

— · — Regional limits

I,II,...X Regional number

Z.M. Santiago metropolitan zone

ECOLOGICAL ZONES (By Province)

Metropolitan zones

Consolidated zone

Colonization zone

Hierarchy of programmed growth poles

● National growth pole

◉ Multiregional growth poles of national importance

⊘ Multiregional growth poles

⊙ Multiregional growth pole and border development

◉ Regional growth poles

I TARAPACA
Arico
Iquique

II ANTOFAGASTA

III ATACAMA
COQUIMBO
Coquimbo-La Sereno

IV ACONCAGUA
VALPARAISO
SANTIAGO Z.M.
Roncoguo O'HIGGINS COLCHAGUA

VI CURICO
TALCA
MAULE
LINARES
NUBLE
CONCEPCION
ARAUCO
VII BIO-BIO
MALLECO
CAUTIN
Temuco
VIII VALDIVIA
OSORNO
LLANQUIHUE
Pta.Montt
CHILOE

IX AYSEN

X MAGALLANES
Pta.Arenas

e. COROU (Corporación de Obras Urbanas—Urban Works Corporation). Has recently been established to formulate and execute urban public work programs in accordance with MINVU's goals; it approves urbanization projects, including public utilities.

Housing Policy   With the exception of high-income housing, scarcely any housing unit is built in Chile without some form of public assistance. In recent years MINVU's housing policy has evolved beyond the simple provision of physical shelter toward becoming a tool for community and national development. Present housing policies consist of a series of related but separable housing services including land, water supply, sewage disposal, electric light, roads, transportation to other parts of the city, schools, community halls, shops, sports fields, health clinics, nursery schools, and police and fire stations. A dwelling unit is also included, but the quality of the shelter depends on the family's ability to save. What is designated as a *module* includes the aforementioned elements. An aggregation of modules, in turn, constitute a housing estate or *población,* and a cluster of housing estates forms a new urban district or *barrio.* At the *barrio* level workplaces and certain higher-order services are added as additional elements to the original housing module.

CORVI estimates have indicated that the Chilean housing shortage was approximately 550,000 units (1960).[40] This deficit was expected to increase in the following years at the rate of 38,000 units per annum. In 1962, more than 42,000 new dwellings were completed, mostly for the lower middle-income groups.[41] Recently, MINVU undertook a major reform in housing policies, creating a system of popular savings as a condition for receiving public assistance. This new plan, generally known as PAP (Plan de Ahorro Popular), is currently (1969) being applied on a national scale. The 10-year development plan prepared in 1961 contemplates devoting to housing approximately 20 percent of all public investment from 1961 through 1970.[42]

Rural Housing   In recent years rural housing has involved, for the most part, linking the government action agencies in the area of agricultural development and agrarian reform to MINVU. In January 1968, an agreement was signed between the National Institute for Agricultural and Livestock Development (INDAP) and the Housing Services Corporation (COR-HABIT) which provides for the construction of approximately 1400 rural houses and related community facilities through loans to farmers' organizations participating in the INDAP programs for agricultural development. INDAP is in charge of the promotion of the program, with CORHABIT providing the financing and required technical assistance. The most recent trend has been for the Agrarian Reform Corporation (Corporación de Reforma Agraria—CORA) to incorporate rural housing activities,

[40] Federico G. Gil and Charles J. Parrish, *The Chilean Presidential Election of September 4, 1964,* Operations and Policy Research, Inc., Washington, D.C., 1965, p. 184.
[41] *Ibid.,* p. 185.
[42] URDAPIC, *Annual Report 1967/68,* Ford Foundation, Santiago, Chile, 1968, p. 34.

formerly handled by MINVU and other agencies, into its overall agrarian reform program.

A Rural Housing Committee has been established within the newly formed Social Development Council at the Ministerial level. The Committee is to produce support for programs related to the improvement of rural living conditions.

National Council for Popular Promotion (Consejo Nacional de Promoción Popular—CNNP)   This institution was established soon after the Frei government took office in November 1964 as the agency for integrating the poor (the marginal population) within the larger society. It was to work primarily at the level of the local community, where it would assist the population to organize themselves in the promotion and defense of their own interests. This agency does not have a budget of its own.

Programming and Budget Systems   At present Chile has a rather rudimentary system of programming and budgeting for the development of cities and regions. The system is implemented through two institutions: MINVU for coordinated urban development, and ODEPLAN for regional development. Limited coordination exists between the regional programs prepared by ODEPLAN (in collaboration with its decentralized regional offices) and MINVU's programs. Nearly thirty community programming offices have been established throughout the country by agreement with the municipalities concerned, including all the more important cities outside the major metropolitan areas.[43] In contrast to urban programming, regional planners have not yet evolved an institutionalized pattern of local participation. Consequently, regional programs largely reflect the thinking of the central government and very little participation of private organized interests.

Municipal Planning   Chilean municipalities are extremely dependent on the central government. They are reduced to playing a minor role in the development of the physical environment. Their functions include little more than garbage collection, street lighting, and public gardens, while central government policies are of overriding importance in providing housing. Specifically, municipal programming offices are responsible for four broad functions: (1) the programming of municipal expenditures; (2) the programming of all urban and housing investments within the municipalities; (3) the detailed elaboration of a master plan and supervision of zoning; and (4) ad hoc technical advice and assistance, such as that given to local housing cooperatives.[44]

Metropolitan Planning   Chile has three major metropolitan areas, each one containing several townships. Santiago is the largest, followed by Valparaíso and Concepción with about a half million each. These three areas account for nearly 60 percent of the urban population in Chile and for larger percentages of industrial employment and essential services. Attempts have been made to coordinate the efforts of public agencies through metropolitan plans prepared by special offices that depend on MINVU. The creation of

[43] Friedman, *Urban and Regional Development in Chile, op. cit.,* p. 64.
[44] URDAPIC, *op. cit.,* p. 28.

an ORPLAN for the metropolitan regions is under study by MINVU, with the assistance of the Ford Foundation Advisory Mission to Chile and ODEPLAN. The effort aims at creating closer collaboration between the national agencies in their metropolitan-level decisions, to encourage greater participation on the part of the constituent townships, and to attain more unified direction of the process from the central-national level. The plan of 1969 was still in its preliminary stages.

Education, Training, and Research Traditionally, architects and engineers in Chile have functioned as physical planners. Architectural schools tend to stress the role of physical design and esthetic values. Schools of economics tend to stress economic factors. Teaching in Chile in the field of urban-regional development consists of: (1) university training for undergraduates at various faculties with interest in development planning, (2) a graduate program offered by the Interdisciplinary Center for Urban and Regional Development (CIDU), (3) short extension courses for personnel intending to operate at the local level.

Institutions Related to Education and Research in Planning At the *Univeristy of Chile,* undergraduate courses in a variety of subjects related to planning are offered within the faculties of architecture (instruction on large-scale design and land-use master planning), physical sciences and mathematics (including engineering), economics, and philosophy and education (including sociology and geography). Research programs are conducted through the institutes of urbanism, economics, business administration, sociology, and geography. Limited postgraduate instruction and research are offered through the centers of planning within the faculties of engineering (Planning Center) and economics (ESCOLATINA, a Latin American postgraduate school, and the Economic Planning Center). The University of Chile includes an Institute of Housing, Urbanism, and Planning (IVUPLAN).

At *Catholic University,* undergraduate instruction relevant to planning is offered within the faculties of architecture, engineering, economics, and philosophy and education. Research and postgraduate work are conducted through the Interdisciplinary Center for Urban and Regional Development (CIDU) and the Center of Economic Studies.[45]

CIDU (Centro Interdisciplinario de Desarrollo Urbano y Regional). The Interdisciplinary Center for Urban and Regional Development was created and began operations in January 1966 with the support of the Ford Foundation Mission to Chile. At present CIDU is the interdisciplinary center at Catholic University offering graduate and specialized training courses, doing both basic and applied research, and providing technical assistance services to public institutions. During 1969, CIDU's budget (approximately $250,000) has been supported to the extent of about 33 percent by the University, 49 percent by the Ford Foundation, and 18 percent from other sources (MINVU, ODEPLAN, and various municipalities).[46]

---

[45] John Parker, *Post-Graduate Planning Education in Chile,* USAID/Chile, Santiago, Chile, 1962, p. B-3.

[46] Friedman, *Urban and Regional Development in Chile, op. cit.,* p. 71.

CIDU is providing certain specialized services to MINVU and ODE-PLAN, mostly in the form of intensive training courses (a course of municipal programming for staff of local offices established by MINVU, another on program budgeting for regional planners) and research. Recently, MINVU provided a grant to CIDU under a special agreement to sustain a flow of technical services to the Ministry. During 1968, CIDU offered a specialized training course to municipal officials from metropolitan communities. This course was entirely financed by the municipalities.

The center's program is composed of (1) the equivalent of one semester of undergraduate work which is part of the regular program of the various schools, (2) a 1-year graduate program in urban and regional development planning, and (3) a thesis, which is submitted 6 months after course work is completed. The curriculum includes a minimum of 16 courses (besides workshop and the thesis): four introductory courses at the undergraduate level, plus eight basic and four specialized courses at the graduate level.[47]

CIDU has made metropolitan policy one of its two major lines of research activity, and a number of relevant courses have been introduced into the basic curriculum. The center has made an agreement with three adjoining municipalities in the Santiago area which have formed an InterUrban Council for developing joint projects. The center is to study development possibilities, programs, and projects in the municipalities mentioned.

At *Austral University* in Valdivia, a Regional Studies Center has been created with the cooperation of the Ford Foundation Mission to Chile and Catholic University through CIDU, which is providing training and assistance. The Regional Studies Center is attempting to establish close working relationships between the university and the local ORPLAN.

IDEC (Instituto de Desarrollo Comunal—Institute of Community Development). The Ministry of Housing signed an agreement in 1969 with CIDU, backed by a small grant of $25,000, for initiating this institute, which will extend technical assistance to the municipalities, particularly in the areas of public administration, municipal services, and programming. IDEC is, in the future, expected to be financed by the municipalities themselves.[48]

In addition to the aforementioned university programs and research centers, Santiago is the home of several international institutions such as: CLACSO (Latin American Social Science Research Council), which offers advanced instruction in sociology and is developing a program in public administration; CEPAL (U.N. Economic Commission for Latin America), which conducts a planning institute; and FAO (International Food and Agriculture Organization).[49]

Institutions and Professional Societies   The Chilean Planning Society (Sociedad Chilena de Planificación y Desarrollo—PLANDES) is the official society

---

[47] Guillermo Geisse, "La enseñanza en el campo del desarrollo urbano-regional en Chile: un nuevo enfoque," *Revista de la Sociedad Interamericana de Planificación,* vol. 1, no. 2, pp. 30–35, 1967.

[48] Friedman, *Urban and Regional Development in Chile, op. cit.,* p. 64.

[49] Parker, *op. cit.,* p. B-4.

that represents the planning profession in Chile. The society comprises primarily professionals with background in architecture and engineering, but it also includes lawyers, agricultural engineers, and a number of public officials professionally related to planning. PLANDES was founded in 1962 at the time of the third Interamerican Planning Congress. Official recognition of its existence was published in the *Diario Oficial* of October 2, 1963. It has (1970) three chapters with the following approximate membership: Santiago, 300; Valparaíso, 100; and Concepción, 100.

In addition to its regular publication (*Boletín Informativo*), PLANDES also publishes special reports and studies concerned with urban and regional planning. (Address: Sociedad Chilena de Planificación y Desarrollo, Moneda 973, Santiago, Chile.

BIBLIOGRAPHY: Municipalidad de Santiago, Departamento de Obras, Planificación y Estudios, *Informe preliminar sobre metodología y organización del plan general urbano de la comuna de Santiago,* Departamento de Obras Municipales de Santiago, Santiago, Chile, 1960; John Parker, *Post-Graduate Planning Education in Chile,* USAID/Chile, Santiago, Chile, 1962; *La economía de Chile en el período 1953-63,* Tomo II, Instituto de Economía, University of Chile, Santiago, Chile, 1963; George Pendle, *The Land and People of Chile,* The Macmillan Company, New York, 1964; J. P. Cole, *Latin America, An Economic and Social Geography,* Butterworths, Washington, D.C., 1965; Fundación "Pedro Aguirre Cerda," *Geografía económica de Chile,* Corporación de Fomento de la Producción, Santiago, Chile, 1965; Federico Gil, and Charles J. Parrish, *The Chilean Presidential Election of September 4, 1964,* Operations and Policy Research, Inc., Washington, D.C., 1965; Bruce H. Herrick, *Urban Migration and Economic Development in Chile,* The M.I.T. Press, Cambridge, Mass., 1965; Markos Mamalakis and Clark Winton Reynolds, *Essays on the Chilean Economy,* Richard D. Irwin, Inc., Homewood, Ill., 1965; MINVU, *La investigación tecnológica, la información especializada y la coordinación en el Ministerio de la Vivienda y Urbanismo a través de la labor de la Secretaría Técnica y de Coordinación,* Ministerio de la Vivienda y Urbanismo, Santiago, Chile, 1965; MINVU, *Ley 16, 391,* Ministerio de la Vivienda y Urbanismo, Santiago, Chile, 1965; K. H. Silvert, *Chile, Yesterday and Today,* Holt, Rinehart and Winston, Inc., New York, 1965; Francisco Frías, *Manual de Geografía de Chile,* Editorial Nascimiento, Santiago, Chile, 1966; John Friedman, "Planning as Innovation: the Chilean Case," *Journal of the American Institute of Planners,* vol. 32, no. 4, 1966; Federico Gil, *The Political System of Chile,* Houghton Mifflin Company, Boston, Mass., 1966; Walter Krause (ed.), *The Economy of Latin America,* The University of Iowa, Iowa City, Iowa, 1966; MINVU, *Ministerio de la Vivienda y Urbanismo,* Ministerio de la Vivienda y Urbanismo, Santiago, Chile, 1966; United Nations, *Boletín estadístico de América Latina,* vol. 4, no. 1, 1965; Boletín Informativo PLANDES, *Programación de vivienda y desarrollo comunitario en Chile,* Sociedad Chilena de Planificación y Desarrollo, Santiago, Chile, 1967; John Friedman and Thomas Lackington, *La hiperurbanización en Chile: algunas hipótesis,* Universidad Católica, Santiago, Chile, 1967; Guillermo Geisse, "La enseñanza en el campo del desarrollo urbano-regional en Chile: un nuevo enfoque," *Revista de la Sociedad Interamericana de Planificación,* vol. 1, no. 2, 1967; MINVU, Secretaría Técnica y de Coordinación, *Versión ordenada y actualizada de la Ordenanza General de Construcciones y Urbanización,* Ministerio de la Vivienda y Urbanismo, Santiago, Chile, 1967; *El Ministerio de la Vivienda y Urbanismo, instrumento de la política habitacional,* Ministerio de la Vivienda y Urbanismo, Santiago, Chile, 1967; Walter Stöhr, "El caso de Chile," *Revista de la Sociedad Interamericana de Planificación,* vol. 1, no. 4, 1967; United Nations, Economic Commission for Latin America, *Boletín estadístico de América Latina,* vol. 4, no. 1, 1967; United Nations, *Economic Survey of Latin America—1967,* United Nations, New York, 1969; CIDU, *Comité Interdisciplinario de Desarrollo Urbano—Programa 1968,* Universidad Católica, Santiago, Chile, 1968; Guillermo Geisse, "El caso de Chile," *Revista de la Sociedad Interamericana de Planificación,* vol. 2, no. 5, 1968; Charles Paul May, *Chile, Progress on Trial,* Thomas Nelson & Sons, Camden, N.J., 1968; UCLA Latin American Center, *Statistical Abstract of Latin America—1967,* University of California, Los Angeles, Calif., 1968; URDAPIC, *Annual Report 1967/68,* Ford Foundation, Santiago, Chile, 1968; Charles A. Frankenhoff, *Hacia una política habitacional popular: el caso de Chile,* CIDU, Santiago, Chile, 1969; John Friedman (ed.), *Urban and Regional Development in Chile,* Ford Foundation, Santiago, Chile, 1969; *Chile: la década del 70,* Ford Foundation, Santiago, Chile, 1969; MINVU, Dirección de Plani-

ficación del Desarrollo Urbano, *Prehipótesis de estructuración y crecimiento para el área metropolitana de Santiago,* Ministerio de la Vivienda y Urbanismo, Santiago, Chile, 1969; Oficina Nacional de Planificación (ODEPLAN), *Política de desarrollo nacional—Directivas nacionales y regionales,* Editorial Universitaria, S.A., Santiago, Chile, 1969; United Nations, Department of Economic and Social Affairs, *1967 Report on the World Social Situation,* United Nations, New York, 1969.
—ANATOLE SOLOW AND LUIS BALERDI

CHINA China is a subcontinent with ill-defined boundaries ranging from Tibet to the Pacific Ocean, from Mongolia to Vietnam, populated by about 750 million people of diverse races, languages, customs, and physiques. It is at present ruled by a Communist committee under Chairman Mao Tse-tung whose famous thoughts, the *Little Red Book,* embody its national aims.

Too often Westerners think of China in terms of a European state with traditions of Roman law including regional and urban planning in the legal context. To the Chinese however, China (*Chung Kwok,* or the Middle Kingdom) is the center of a beneficent culture which, since 2500 B.C., has extended its philosophy through numerous bordering kingdoms that, in return for the gift of inclusion within China's benevolent empire, rendered tribute.

Planning as a separate art and social service in the Western sense does not exist in China. It is part and parcel of this ancient culture, interspersed within its tradition, more especially in the classics of Confucius (550–478 B.C.) and his most famous disciple, Mencius (372–289 B.C.). Precisely because Chinese planning, like Chinese painting, is primarily a philosophical exercise, its influence has accompanied the spread of Chinese culture. This is the fundamental difference between Chinese and Western techniques.

A Western planner will quite happily plan a house, a district, or a city on any convenient axis (or none at all) provided legal requirements are satisfied. On the other hand, a classical Chinese planner would feel inadequate, indeed guilty, if he planned other than on a north-south axis with the front facing south. Two thousand years of tradition, experience, and instinct prove to him that this axis inevitably brings longevity, good luck, and happiness. To him geomancy (*fung-shui*—wind water, and *shan-shui*—mountain water) are far superior to planning legislation and administration, if indeed he is minded to recognize the latter. It is difficult to grasp the full significance of this attitude without some appreciation of Chinese history.

The Historical Background Starting with the unification of small states situated on the lower reaches of the Yellow River and the Yangtze, the empire expanded over 2,000 years by successive conquests and dynasties, each having its origin in widespread peasant revolts. The 10 major rebellions during this time exhibit the same cycle of events, although they may have been centuries apart:

1. The declining dynasty loses the "mandate of heaven" through undue corruption and exploitation.

2. A new dynasty supported by the peasants ousts the old.

3. Peasant production and population increase. The economy expands. Massive public works, neglected by the old dynasty, are put in train. China adjusts itself to increase of population.

4. Landowners, gentry, and merchants emerge in combinations to exploit the peasantry. The emerging middle class (*bourgeoisie*) turn to land owning as a classic means of exploiting the lower classes.

5. In desperation the peasantry revolts against the corruption of officials and the oppression of landowners, thus producing the next dynasty.

Unlike European peasant revolts, the *bourgeoisie* in China has never emerged from these revolts as a dominant class. It has always become part of the landowning gentry, changing its function from trading to peasant exploitation. This oft-recurring process is governed by two factors. The first, an economic factor, is the shortage of metals relative to the size of the empire. The Chinese have succumbed to those groups which disposed of substantial metal stocks for armaments and ploughshares—Turks, Mongols, Manchus, Japanese—but they have always outlived and absorbed their conquerors. The second, a cultural factor, is Chinese calligraphy, important and distinctive script in which whole words are represented by ideographs (pictorial characters) instead of being composed of alphabetic and phonetic symbols. These ideographs stand outside the numerous dialects or spoken languages as a complete system of communication, but they are readily translated into the spoken languages.

These two factors produced and maintained an empire ruled by each dynasty, with an imperial court supported by landed gentry from which its officials, scholars, merchants, and magistrates were drawn. Under this middle stratum, the poorly educated peasantry toiled at subsistence levels to maintain this social superstructure. The existence of this system for 2,000 years and its expansion over 10 major upheavals and innumerable revolts, with their inherent tendency to disruption and discontinuity, could not have been a random process. It sprang from conscious planning, the result of trial and error based upon standardized concepts elaborated, distilled, and codified by countless scholars analyzing the opposing philosophies of Confucius and Lao-Tze; the former standing for rigid social order, the latter for the spirit of individual anarchy. These two complementary philosophies are intertwined in the Chinese character and culture, the male and female, the *yin* and *yan*. In success the Chinese is Confucian; in failure he finds solace in Lao-Tze. In planning cities, the emphasis is on Confucian order; when planning a garden, the subtle anarchy of Taoism is supreme. Each philosophy balances the other and provides an infinite variety of mood, expression, and beauty.

Legislation and Administration   In this context planning could not be isolated as a separate function of imperial administration. Its basic principles were known and practiced by every educated Chinese, who would instinctively and customarily seek advice on any building project from the *fung shui* geomancer who was invariably ready with apt quotations from the classics. As the same principles governed the planning of a city, a house, and a farm, argument could only center on details of craftsmanship and implementation. Outside these areas, the garden and the artificial landscape were planned solely by the cultured taste of the client subject only to the approbation and criticism of respected friends and scholars. Since his design would be an expression of his personality, the client's self respect was involved and acted as powerful deterrent to ugliness.

The great public works—cities, walls, canals, bridges, roads—were conceived in outline by the emperor and drawn up by the high officials of the court. They were implemented by the regional governors, mandarins, and magistrates, all of whom were classical scholars and graduates of the classical examinations.

The actual work was controlled by skilled craftsmen, not educated in the formal sense but imbued with the traditions of centuries. This system provided a wide variety of effects and freedom of expression within a strong unity of principles. Timber and masonry predominated; brick was used to a lesser degree due to the shortage of fuel for brick making. The disadvantage of strong tradition was that it discouraged experimentation with concrete, steel, and other modern techniques.

Instead of employing architects and design draftsmen to prepare detailed drawings and specifications, emperors would ask artists to paint the imperial concepts on long scrolls, conveying impressions. As the works were carried out by conscript labor, the prime responsibility of the Mandarinate was to get the work done and not to argue over costs. An impressive result enhanced the glory of the emperor and a poor effort was an insult; therefore the projects tended toward monumentality. Chinese history abounds with monuments to each dynasty; e.g., the Great Wall, the imperial canals, Peking itself, and the West Lake at Hangchow.

Professional Practice All art forms attract professionals, and Chinese planning is no exception; but little is known of these practitioners as their work is invariably ascribed to the ruling dynasty. Undoubtedly there were masterminds, like Europe's Michelangelo, whose genius embraced painting, sculpture, architecture, and fortifications; but like many of the medieval cathedral builders, their names are lost in generations of communal effort.

For houses, the craftsman and client cooperated in design. For public and official buildings, the master craftsman was guided by regional practice and the local mandarins. For the grand projects, an inspector of the imperial ministry of works with supporting staff was directly responsible to the court. To achieve this high position, an official was expected to write authoritative books, as did Li Ming Chung, author of *ying tsao fa shih,* a detailed technical work on building.

While the imperial court decreed the siting of cities, dikes, canals, bridges, roads, and similar major projects, local planning was left very much to local gentry; advised by the local *fung shui* expert (professional geomancer). He was invariably an old man respected for his long experience of the local vagaries of climate, natural disasters, agrarian practice, and customs. Unlike Western planners, this *fung shui* "doctor" never left his practice or his district, never explained his reasoning, and wrapped his opinions in romantic descriptions of hills as dragons, rivers as snakes, and unsuitable terrain as tigers waiting to devour the misguided builder.

As a means of ensuring that local land-use knowledge was readily available at relatively low cost, this system has much to commend it; chiefly in that the adviser could not afford to make mistakes or evade the consequences of poor advice. When the family residence absorbed a high proportion of family wealth, its siting called for the deepest consideration. The principles of *fung-shui* can only be acquired by long study of landscape scrolls hanging the full height of a wall. This strange discipline ensures that the planner becomes completely involved within the depicted landscape in a three-dimensional continuum of space, visualizing the proposed site from every direction.

When Chinese silently meditate for hours before these scrolls, very often they have the practical object of investing in some sort of development.

Education and Training   The architect is foreign to Chinese tradition, but nevertheless the disciplines of the classics, history, and philosophy were essential for any official aspiring to build. The key to these disciplines is Chinese calligraphy, to which painting is closely allied and which holds the secret of the permanence of Chinese planning concepts. Unlike English, this is very difficult to memorize and its 40,000 characters are absorbed at an early age by children in class chanting each word in their own dialect as the teacher exhibits each character. Although innumerable dialects are spoken in the subcontinent, the idea expressed by each ideograph or character is universally understood and subtly conditions the pupil to accept the common cultural base and ethos. It also provided a means of escape from rural drudgery by way of the official examinations. A family would sponsor the tuition of a bright boy to become a member of the official mandarinate in the confident hope that success would bring many benefits through his influence. Thus the court was continually vitalized with fresh peasant blood. Alien dynasties may have conquered the empire, but Chinese culture and classical philosophy remained.

Institutions   From the foregoing comments, it will be seen that under the imperial dynasties planning institutions had no place. Under the Communist regime, planning institutions have no separate existence apart from the political aims of the government. In a revolutionary period, all institutions must serve, and be subject to, national policy.

Geographical and Climatic Conditions   China extends from Peking (40 degrees north latitude) to Hanoi (20 degrees north latitude) on the Gulf of Tonkin, and from the central mountain mass of Tibet to the Pacific Ocean. The snows of Tibet drain eastward by several large rivers; namely, the Yellow River to the Gulf of Tientsin in the north, by the Yangtze to Shanghai in mid-China, by the Si-kiang to Canton, by the Red River to Hanoi in the south, and by many smaller rivers and tributaries. The original heartland of the Chinese people is found in low-lying, flat silt lands of the Yellow River and the Yangtze. South China is more broken and elevated, the hills becoming higher as they merge into the ranges and gorges of West China and the mountains of the Himalayas.

The great rivers provide vast areas of fertile land, improved by generations of flood control. The climate ranges from the warm, rainy summers with crisp, dry winters of Peking to the humid heat of the South, broken by typhoons. The climate in the mountains of West China is more temperate, becoming cooler as the land rises to the Tibetan sources of the great rivers.

Climatic differences are reflected in the physiques of the people, varying from the tall, big-boned Mongolians of the north to the wiry, seemingly delicate Indochinese of Southeast Asia. Generations of immigrants have, however, intermingled these types.

Traditions of planning to the end of the Nineteenth Century.

Rural Areas *Mencius, 3d Century* B.C. Some three hundred years after Confucius, Mencius, one of his growing number of followers, devoted himself to the practical administration of state and land. A native of Tsow in Lu of the department of Yen Chow in Shantung, he recognized that the growth of population demanded reduction of taxation and an acceptable system of land use involving proper subdivision and security of tenure. He therefore stressed the "rectification of boundaries" just as Confucius advocated the "rectification of names (things)."

Mencian thought is expressed in the following extract:[1]

> Duke Wan of T'ang sent Peih-Chen to consult Mencius about his *Nine Squares System* of dividing land among families. Mencius said to him "Since your prince has put you into this employment ... the first thing you must do ... is to lay down boundaries. If the boundaries are not defined correctly, the division of land into squares will not be equal to the population. The produce will not be evenly distributed and available for salaries. . . .
>
> "In the remoter districts you should reserve one out of the Nine Squares for cultivation by *Mutual Aid* for the payment of officials. In the more central parts (urban areas) the people must pay a tithe or tenth of their production.
>
> "From the highest to the lowest officials, each must have his Sacred Square of 50 *mow*. Each supernumerary male official must have 25 *mow*. Families who belong to the same Nine Squares should render mutual aid and friendly offices to one another, keeping the watch and sustaining each other in sickness. Thus the people are brought together in harmony and affection."

An interesting parallel is the Anglo-Saxon "Tens and Hundreds" in England around 800-1000 A.D.

Later he writes:

> A square *le* covers nine squares each of 100 *mow*. The center square is the Sacred or Public Field and the adjoining eight family squares may not presume to attend to their private land until the cultivation of the Sacred Square is finished. (*Works of Mencius,* Book III, Part I).

Rural Housing Each rural square was allowed not more than 3 *mow* for housing and a further 3 *mow* in the nearby village, totaling 6 *mow* for housing. The *mow* was not a fixed area. It varied from district to district depending on the fertility of soil and the pressure of population. It was supposed to be a square having 100 paces on each side. On richer soil the pace was made smaller. If the pace was 15 inches in Mencian days, the *mow* would be about 1,740 square yards or 1,455 square meters. The family square of 100 *mow* would be about 36 acres.

Increasing population through the centuries reduced the *mow* to less than half its original area. The basic layout of countryside and village remained the same, the latter containing one square for shops and crafts, one square for official use, and the remaining squares devoted to housing. This close linkage between farm and village housing was highly successful in settling regions and maintaining soil fertility through human excrement. The interest of officials lay in keeping the farmers satisfied enough not to evade cultivation of the Sacred Square.

Sericulture Silkworms subsist on mulberry trees, and the silk industry in general in South China in the Shang Dynasty (1450 B.C.) is a typical example of planning technique. By imperial decree each family square had to have

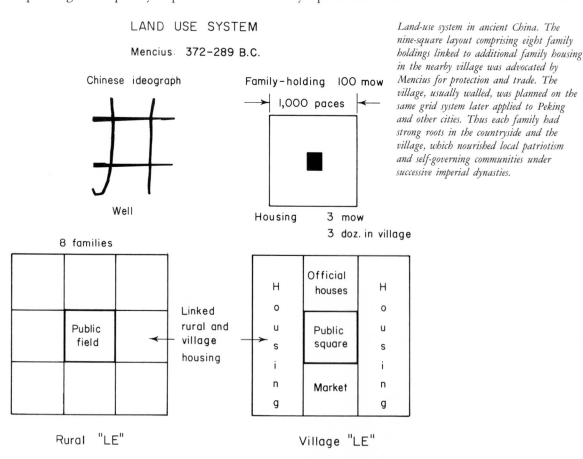

LAND USE SYSTEM

Mencius: 372–289 B.C.

Chinese ideograph

Well

8 families

Rural "LE"

Family-holding 100 mow

1,000 paces

Housing   3 mow
3 doz. in village

Linked rural and village housing

Village "LE"

Land-use system in ancient China. The nine-square layout comprising eight family holdings linked to additional family housing in the nearby village was advocated by Mencius for protection and trade. The village, usually walled, was planned on the same grid system later applied to Peking and other cities. Thus each family had strong roots in the countryside and the village, which nourished local patriotism and self-governing communities under successive imperial dynasties.

a specified number of mulberry trees, providing both shade and food for silkworms. The profitable nature of this cultivation was not lost on Chinese women. By this simple device an immensely valuable silk industry was established and flourished until the recent invention of artificial silk. The peculiar charm of Peking, Nanking, and other cities with their uptiled roofs punctuating the green foliage of mulberry trees was remarked by Marco Polo.

Urban Planning Confucian regularity and order dictated the form of Chinese cities, of which Peking is the archetype. In the same latitude as Madrid and Istanbul, Peking has a continuous history since 2400 B.C., being a state capital when the English nation was formed in 878 A.D. and becoming the imperial capital under the Ming Emperor Yung Lo in 1403 A.D. Like all cities in China, it was built from the defensive walls inward. It consists of the Forbidden City, containing the imperial Throne Halls, protected on the north, east, and west sides by the Tartar City, and with the larger Chinese City on the south, all held together about a wide north-south axis comprising a series of monumental climaxes. Whereas the anarchic principles of Mao-Tze were given full scope in the pleasure gardens and private courtyards, Confucian order and the Mencian square control the city layout.

City planning was founded on the following simple principles:

1. The enclosing wall (the word for "wall" and "city" is the same, *cheng*), with huge forts over the gates and at the corners

2. The rectangle with a north-south main axis in the middle (*chung* ⟂⟁)

3. The grid layout with straight avenues linking the city gates

4. Numerous square family courtyards with open space within the grid layout

5. Low buildings and many trees, the skyline punctuated by pagodas, temples, and palaces seemingly at random

6. Orientation facing south for climatic and religious reasons

7. Monumentality befitting an ancient imperial culture

The Enclosing Wall. Unlike European cities where cathedrals, monuments, opera houses, and railway stations serve as focal points, the Chinese city is dominated by the wall. Every important group of buildings with attached courtyards within the city wall has its walled enclosure within which a labyrinth of even smaller enclosures, each facing south, is contained. The principle is illustrated within Peking by the Throne Halls in the Forbidden City, the moated walls of which rise 30 or 40 feet from a width at base of some 50 feet. This city is contained in the *inner city* or Tartar City. The *outer* or Chinese City lying on the south side has similar walls. The Forbidden City is surrounded by the Imperial City. Great towers or forts surmount the corners and gates.

Boulevards 70 to 150 feet wide link opposite gates, symmetrically placed in the length of the walls. These gates are more than entrances, being massive towers originally designed to house garrisons, customs, and city officials. They form watchtowers commanding a view of the boulevards. Originally built for defense, they now are used as the headquarters for internal "law and order," and the numerous markets, schools, and warehouses are administered from them.

The Rectangular Grid and Axis. The grid layout can be broken down into smaller squares or consolidated to form larger squares. This latter facility provides the open space necessary for a proper visual appreciation of palaces and large buildings. The feeling of serenity, dear to the Chinese, is exemplified by the *Tianmen* (Gate of Heavenly Peace), 80 feet high, with a depth through the city wall of some 80 feet on the main city axis and approached from the south by an avenue that is a half-mile long. This avenue leads through a courtyard capable of holding at least 100,000 people.

This open space is entered from the *Chien Men,* the main gate in the south wall of the inner city. It is 125 feet high, 80 feet deep, and has a southern facade 165 feet wide. A sense of grandeur is induced by the approach to the main gates along the central axis of Peking, an approach relieved only by vistas through the arches below the superstructure which provide irresistible invitations to one's progress to the next monumental climax.

Orientation and Monumentality. The ubiquitous southern orientation of large buildings holds two major benefits. Climatically, the enclosure of the north, east, and west sides makes a sun-trap and gives protection from cold winds. Aesthetically, generations of craftsmen have been able to accumulate subtle methods of catching infinite variations of light on the different materials and patterns used.

Versailles, built by the Sun King of France, is a monumental work of an absolute monarchy; but it is dwarfed by the concept of the Imperial City of Peking. With the Great Wall of China in mind, the emperors of successive dynasties regarded monumentality as a natural expression of the imperial power, whether this was expressed in canals, palaces, the artificial lakes and hills (e.g., Coal Hill) of Peking, or the West Lake at the pleasure capital of Hanchow. The permanence, prestige, and power of the emperor were subtly emphasized by thronging these public works with ordinary people so that the sense of being part of and participating in works of art gave the public sentimental pride in the achievements of empire.

The City Landscape. The strong, rigid lines and delicate curves of Chinese calligraphy, the unity of opposites, find expression in the axial order of Peking and in the imperial pleasure gardens of the inner city to the west of the main axis. Swampland was drained by artificial lakes and canals, thus also replenishing local supplies of well water. Pollution of waterways by human waste was forbidden, the night soil being collected from the east and west sides of the walled enclosures and transported to the countryside for fertilizer.

Taoist freedom is applied, as always, in the public gardens of the capital. Zigzag bridges, covered walkways, intriguing islands, surprise views, curious rocks, intimate pools, screens of rare shrubs, grottoes, all with the qualities of color and seclusion, abound.

The Traditional Courtyard House. The internal planning of houses follows the external, rectangular city layout. The important rooms lined the north side facing the central courtyard and main gate of the southern wall. Lesser rooms lined the other three sides, overlooking the courtyard and presenting a blank wall to the public road—a system opposed to the Western practice of making all houses face the public road regardless of the road's orientation.

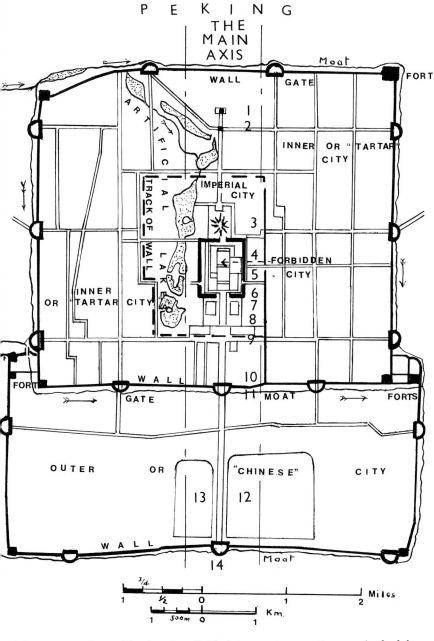

PEKING
THE MAIN AXIS

The walls of the Forbidden City within the Imperial City. The Inner City and the Outer City are moated. The walls of the Imperial City no longer exist. The main axis is a series of architectural climaxes, some of which are: (1) the bell tower; (2) the drum tower; (3) Coal or Prospect Hill—an artificial hill 300 feet (9.15 meters) high, with five pavilions and planted with rare trees; (4) the inner court; (5) the throne halls; (6) Gate and Hall of Supreme Harmony—the main ceremonial hall; (7) Meridian Gate (Wu Men)—entrance to the Forbidden or Palace City; (8) Tuan Men; (9) Tien An Men (Gate of Heavenly Peace) north of Tien An Square; (10) Chung Hua Men; (11) Chien Men—main gate of the south wall of the Inner City; (12) Temple of Heaven and triple circular Altars of Heaven; (13) Temple of Agriculture, a popular park; and (14) Yung Ting Men—main gate in the south wall of the Outer City.

The courtyard would often be divided into minor patios overlooked by the verandahs of living quarters. Rolls of oiled paper served as windows in winter. Space heating was quite primitive, being supplied by bowls of glowing charcoal prepared in the courtyard and brought into the rooms by servants. A wealthy family might have a raised dais under which heated air from an outside source would be circulated. Typical Chinese clothing of padded quilt gowns and thick felt shoes kept the residents warm.

Chimneys and bathrooms were rare. Baths were taken in tubs brought into the rooms by servants and emptied after use around the shrubs in the courtyard. Each residence had its well. By these means cities remained healthy and enjoyed clean air despite the absence of piped water supplies and sewerage disposal plants. However, the lack of paving and drainage made muddy tracks of the roads after rain.

In time single-family residences would become multioccupied; but even so, a high degree of privacy was ensured by strict control of entry at the courtyard gate. By these living habits Peking and other cities could provide housing for millions of people for generations without social breakdown.

Transportation. The survival of millions of people in innumerable cities of the empire required elaborate communications. *Roads* were regarded mainly as a means of personal transit on foot or on horseback, primarily for the imperial post. Riders and runners relayed imperial decrees in short stages at full speed to all parts. Mule trains and, even more commonly, long lines of coolies carrying heavy burdens used these tracks. The cost of constructing and maintaining paved roads suitable for the clumsy, heavy-wheeled vehicles of the period was prohibitive.

Canals and *waterways* were the predominant means of transporting bulk supplies to the main centers. The abundance of conscript labor, the numerous rivers, and the vital necessity of flood control coupled with irrigation for rice growing and fish farming impelled each dynasty to cut canals. The classic example is the great canal era of Emperor Yang Ti of the Sui dynasty, of about 600 A.D. This Emperor started the Imperial Canal linking the Yellow River and the Yangtze. He decreed the cutting of many other canals to take barges of 800 tons, chiefly to supply his new capital of Loyang in the wheat belt of east China.

After the collapse of the Mongol Dynasty in 1386 A.D., the Mings made Nanking a secondary capital to Peking and, as a countermeasure to incessant raids on coastal shipping by Japanese pirates, put in train a large program of canal works completed in 1410 A.D. Henceforth commerce relied on some 200,000 miles of inland waterways which carried a floating population of many millions.

Railways are a very recent event in Chinese history. The stubborn conservatism and ignorance of the Manchu Dowager Empress delayed the coming of railways. The first railway was built in 1876 from Wu-Sang to Shanghai, but it was destroyed by the Chinese official Li Hung-chang who, by curious chance, was the first Chinese to build a permanent line, from his coal mines in Kai-ping to the port of Tientsin. By the Treaty of Tientsin 1860 a number of ports (in addition to Shanghai) were thrown open to foreign traders and railways were routed from the interior to such ports, cutting across the traditional north-south trading routes. Railways were a Western, not a Chinese, concept.

Twentieth-century Planning The collapse of the Manchu Dynasty after the death of the Dowager Empress ("Old Buddha") plunged China into a century of international and civil war. The old planning philosophies have been superseded by Communist doctrine. The landed gentry and merchant class has been discredited by the peasant revolution of Mao Tse-tung, himself a Confucian scholar, whose theory of "Permanent Revolution" is basically a statement that China cannot revert to its former agrarian policy but must struggle forward at all costs to the creation of an industrial society firmly based on a more advanced agricultural production. Western revolutions have always seen the *bourgeoisie* emerge as the dominant class in an industrial society. Chairman Mao rejects this class and believes that state officials and peasants, with industrial workers, can dispense with *bourgeois* elements in an industrialized China.

New Towns and Communities   More than 70 years of war have necessarily absorbed the vast amounts of capital resources needed for new towns. The age-old threat from Mongolia and Russia must still be countered. Population growth demands new towns to replace those wrecked in war. Undoubtedly towns are being built around the new industrial plants, but their precise locations are uncertain because strategical considerations have necessarily some influence in their siting.

City and Town Extensions   In 1937 the Japanese judged that the civil war between the landed gentry (led by Chiang Kai-shek) and the peasantry (led by Mao Tse-tung) had laid China open to Japanese invasion from their bases in Manchuria. By 1941 their "Greater East Asia Policy" had swept aside resistance from Peking to Singapore and southward to the East Indies. The Communists were contained in mountainous Shensi, close to the Great Wall in the north; Chiang Kai-shek fled from the coastal plains to Chungking in Szechwan in the mountainous southwest. With immense effort and sacrifice small industries were set up in West China and small towns expanded to house the refugees, but with little hope of return. In 1945 Hiroshima and the collapse of Japan brought a dramatic change. The atom bomb removed the immediate menace, but the civil war recommenced, culminating in the complete success of the Communists on the mainland in 1949. By then, however, the Korean war was raging and the Vietnam war was escalating to destroy the food supply of Southeast Asia.

In the circumstances of these wars, for sheer survival, extensions to towns and cities, though much needed, were not planned except in the crudest manner.

Urban Renewal   China is faced with increasing population, soil exhaustion, loss of food supplies from Southeast Asia, wrecked towns, roads, railways, and canals, not to mention the need to rehabilitate internal and foreign trade. The need for industrialization is recognized, but the Chinese people feel they are menaced by American forces in the south and Korea and by the Mongols and Russians in the north. The recent "Cultural Revolution" is a phase in the revolutionary turmoil following the Manchu collapse in 1911. Former revolutions had the main object of replacing a corrupt dynasty by a new set of rulers. The dynasty and its officials changed but the toiling masses still remained exploited by the landed gentry. This present revolution, however, strives to graft an industrial society into the former agrarian economy. Its leaders demonstrated their determination in the Long March of 1934, whereby the socialist state of Kiangsi in the heart of the Yangtze basin moved its people and artifacts 6,000 miles through western China to Yenan in Shensi, fighting a rearguard action daily for 368 days.

Beginning as a military escape from encirclement, this epic march developed into the essential first step toward a form of land-use planning new to China. The power of the landed gentry was declared superfluous to the economy and broken. From Shensi this process has spread throughout the whole empire, now called a "republic." The break with the past is irrevocable and will absorb China's total energies for 100 years. In such social conditions, urban renewal is unlikely to have any priority until the new society feels confident of its future.

The Future Town and country planning is a reflection of the aspirations of the dominant culture. For over 2,000 years the aims of the landed gentry in China have been dominant despite changing dynasties. Events of the past 100 years have rudely shattered these aims, and a modus vivendi must be found between age-old traditions and the demands of a modern industrial society. Planning is by trial and error, subordinated to the exigencies of survival. Much depends on the distortions of the economy resulting from foreign military threats.

Removal of trade restrictions on Chinese products (despite the obvious difficulties of style, type, and quality), thus increasing foreign trade, would have a beneficial effect on town and country planning by providing the necessary funds for the purpose. In this event, a new form of planning may emerge in which the Chinese love of poetic and delicate imagery would combine with Confucian principles adapted to modern needs. The products of 2,000 years of continuous history cannot be ignored, and if but a fraction of the charm and beauty of past planning infuses the new China, the world would be entranced and enriched.

BIBLIOGRAPHY: E. A. Gutkind, *Revolution of Environment*, Routledge & Kegan Paul, London, 1946 (The second and major section of the book is devoted to growth and planning, mainly in China and Russia); Wolfrain Eberhard, *A History of China*, Routledge & Kegan Paul, London, 1950; J. W. Dark, *Low Rent Asian Housing*, Hong Kong, 1952; Andrew Boyd, "Planning Principles and the Chinese City," in *Chinese Architecture and Town Planning, 1500 B.C.—1911 A.D.* Alec Tiranti, London, 1962; Lin Yütang, *Imperial Peking*, Elek Books.

—J. W. DARK

CHURCHYARD (*See* CEMETERY.)

CIRCUS (from the Greek *kipkos*—kirkos—meaning circle) The name often given to a circular urban open space or place, such as Oxford Circus in London.

In ancient Rome the circus was a long narrow structure for chariot races, succeeding the hippodrome in ancient Greece. It was enclosed by tiered seats and was semicircular at one end. The Circus Maximus in Rome, built in the first century B.C., was among the most famous. The character of the structure has given its name to a popular entertainment with acrobats, clowns, and animals which usually takes place in a circular arena.

CITY In the United States, a municipality governed by a mayor and corporation is called a "city." In Great Britain a city is traditionally the seat of a bishop and contains a cathedral church, and in such instances this title by long custom continues to be used. In modern times other towns in Britain have acquired the title of "city" by special grant or by being so described in their charter. From the early days of professional planning in the United States, "city planning" was the term employed, and the American Institute of Planners was founded in 1917 under the name of American City Planning Institute. It was changed to its present name in 1939.

In Great Britain, "town" had traditionally been preferred to "city" as the adjective for planning (*see* TOWN). In some countries the choice of which term to employ does not arise as there is the one term for both, as *citta* in Italian and *stadt* in German.

CITY GROWTH AND CITY PLANNING A planned city is one in which the site and the main street pattern (locations and widths of major roads) have been predetermined, as have also, usually, the locations of major public buildings, public open spaces, and the frontage sizes of the residential plots. In the absence of some well-organized system of continued implementation of the plan, the street pattern of a planned town is usually a rectangular or square grid. This is not only the simplest system of partitioning land but it also enables work to be undertaken simultaneously in different areas with a reasonable expectation of creating an operational and orderly whole. Sometimes some diagonal roads are incorporated in the original plan, sometimes they are cut through at a later date; but plans that start off with a geometrically radial pattern seldom hold to it as they expand. Leningrad, under a very powerful and centralized system of planning controls, may be cited as an exception.

An organic town is one in which accretions are made slowly, piece by piece, around a small original core settlement or agglomeration consisting of a few dwellings, workshops, or an institution. The additions usually border established lines of communication between the core settlement and its farming area or its neighboring settlements. These lines of communication are directly influenced by the local topography and follow the most convenient route for whatever transportation system is employed. They are seldom related to one another in a regular geometrical system.

Planned Cities Planned cities have existed alongside organic cities almost since the dawn of man's development as an urbanizing creature; that is, ever since he developed an organized social hierarchy. At first they were established by the decree of priest-kings, usually as centers of government. Later they became tools of political or military colonial settlement. Still later they were organized by landowning institutions, corporations, or individuals as a profitable way of disposing of parcels of land to prospective settlers. These three types of planned cities have persisted through the centuries and specific examples of each are described in other sections of this encyclopedia.

Examples of new government cities date from very early days, especially in the East (Mesopotamia, India, China, Japan, etc.), and most of the Western new towns of the Renaissance fall into this category, from Ludwigsberg and Karlsruhe to Versailles and Washington. In the postwar period of the fifties the world saw another period of new government centers being built for the developing countries, the most notable being Chandigarh, Brasilía, and Islamabad. (*See* INDIA, BRAZIL, *and* PAKISTAN.)

Planned colonial settlements could take the form of military outposts, such as the Roman *castra* throughout much of Europe in the first centuries of the Christian era or English settlements on the Welsh borders in the thirteenth century (see illustration); or they could be trading centers, like the Greek colonies around the coast of the Mediterranean and most of the early colonial settlements of the New World (see illustration) by the Spanish, Portuguese, Dutch, and French, or like British colonial settlements in Africa and India.

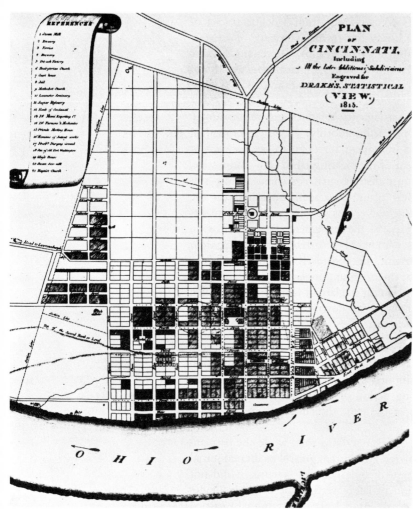

PLAN
of
CINCINNATI.
Including
all the later Additions & Subdivisions
Engraved for
DRAKE'S STATISTICAL
(VIEW.)
1815.

The third type of planned settlement, organized as a way of opening up new tracts of land, has occurred in all periods of rapid population expansion. It was particularly prevalent in Europe in the expansionist period between the Dark Ages and the Black Death. Of the 618 settlements existing in England and Wales just before the Black Death of the fourteenth century took a heavy toll of the population, more than a third were new towns, "planted" by royal decree—and only a few of these had any military significance. In Gascony, 33 new bastides had been built as market centers by both the French and the English, compared with thirty local organic towns.[1] But the heyday of this kind of settlement was in the New World during the nineteenth century (see plan of Cincinnati) rising to a peak in the early railway period of the United States.[2]

[1]Maurice Beresford, *New Towns of the Middle Ages,* London, 1967.
[2]John W. Reps, *The Making of Urban America,* Princeton, 1965.

Organic Cities   Organic settlements do not result from a deliberate act of will on the part of someone in authority but from a sequence of separate actions on the part of individuals or small groups. Successful organic settlements have almost invariably been situated at places convenient for the exchange of goods; i.e., places where different communication systems come together.[3]

As the growth of these organic settlements has not been programmed, their orderly operation can only proceed smoothly when the individual accretions are sufficiently small and infrequent for them to be absorbed or digested with very little readjustment of the existing fabric. Any large-scale, sudden accretion of population must disrupt such a system. Ideally this emergency would be met by a new planning scheme instituted for the immigrants, coupled with complementary plans for necessary adjustments to the older and now congested parts of the settlement. Such a situation is rare. Usually, the new inhabitants, who have been attracted by the apparent economic advantages of the settlement, are considerably poorer and have fewer marketable skills than most of the existing population. They therefore gravitate to the cheapest living quarters near the largest markets for unskilled labor, thus creating the well nigh universal downtown slums as well as outlying shantytowns accessible to industrial estates.[4]

Rapid Growth   Preplanned settlements are almost always better able to absorb a large new influx of population than organic towns, even if the immigration exceeds the target population envisioned in their original plan. But if the new influx occurs only after a long period of stagnation, the absorption of the newcomers encounters almost the same difficulties as are met with in the organic town.

Also, particularly in the United States, one finds that, while the preplanning of an arbitrary and undifferentiated grid system greatly facilitated initial land acquisition and the organization of orderly street systems, it did not contribute to an orderly distribution of land uses for the best advantages of the city's inhabitants, taken as a whole. An absence of communally owned land, crowded slums, and a general makeshift appearance very detrimental to civic pride characterize all but the wealthiest areas of United States cities.

Size and Scale   Among the most important influences upon the future well-being of a new town or a remodeled area of an old town is the size of the mesh of its traffic network, for it is these meshes—the areas between major transportation routes—that constitute the positive elements of a city.

We talk of a network of traffic "arteries" (the word implying an insistent need of fresh new blood pumping through the body), but the traffic system is perhaps better likened to the body's process of elimination, extending from small veins to the intestines and bowels. As every transportation engineer knows, traffic is caused by matter being in the wrong place:

[3]Griffith Taylor, *Urban Geography*, London and New York, 1951. R. E. Dickinson, *The West European City*, London, 1951.

[4]Beckinsale and Houston (eds.), *Urbanization and its Problems*, Oxford, 1968.

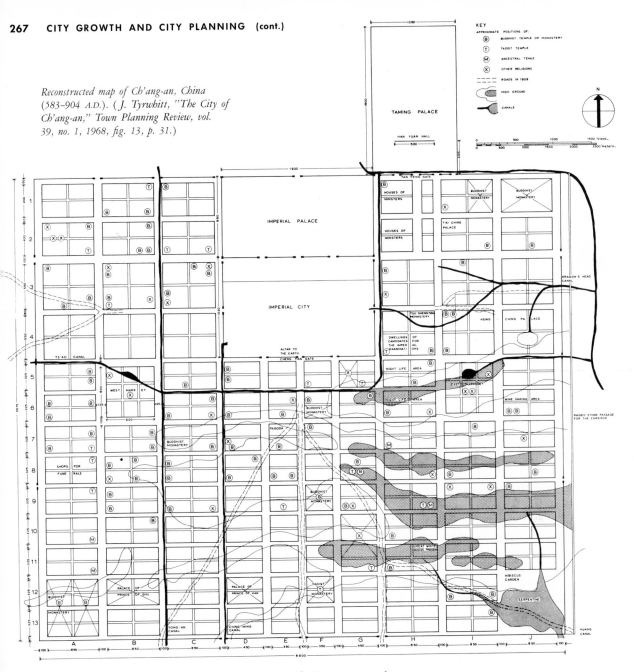

Reconstructed map of Ch'ang-an, China (583–904 A.D.). (J. Tyrwhitt, "The City of Ch'ang-an," Town Planning Review, vol. 39, no. 1, 1968, fig. 13, p. 31.)

movement is a corrective action, not a good in itself. However, no human society can function without constant communication between its human components, and the variations in the size of the meshes of urban grids should be a reflection of the locally available means of communication and the scale of the total urban enterprise.

One of the most revealing early examples of this relation between scale and function can be seen in Chang-an (see map), the very systematically organized capital city of T'ang China (583–904 A.D.). Here a grid of very wide avenues divided a huge city of a million or more people into regular precincts of approximately 1,050 by 525 yards (960 by 480 meters), almost the size of Le Corbusier's divisions of Chandigarh a thousand years later. These wide avenues allowed for swift horseback and horse-drawn communication between the administrative center (the Imperial City, or CBD) and all other parts of the metropolis, as well as to all parts of the far flung T'ang Empire, whose road system was as good as that of the Roman Empire in Europe. The large size of the urban mesh allowed concentrations of urban land uses—markets, colleges, entertainment areas, monasteries, etc.—to operate without interrupting the main through traffic routes by frequent crossings of local traffic. Additions to the city took the form of new or more intensely developed precincts.[5]

In strong contrast, the *insulae* of the center of the Roman Empire, developed at a time of high population pressure, were seldom larger than 165 by 66 yards (150 by 60 meters) usually comprising a grouping of apartment houses with some facilities used in common, such as public baths and shops.[6] Rome thus suffered from an overall penetration of heavy wheeled traffic throughout the city. There were so many complaints of the resulting noise and disturbance that market traffic was permitted to enter the city only between certain hours.[7]

The divisions or meshes of the Hippodamian grid for Miletus (fourth century B.C.) ranged from 77 by 66 yards to 192 by 110 yards (70 by 60 meters to 175 by 100 meters). They normally operated like building blocks, with no internal traffic, and the meshes of other Greek cities did not differ greatly from these dimensions, though they became somewhat larger in the later cities.[8] However, the main public areas of most Greek cities were usually directly approachable by sea or by a wider access route which could accomodate the passage of people from outside who came to attend the city's major festivals; and as the total population of these cities seldom rose above forty thousand (approximately the size of one of the precincts of Chang-an) there was no reason to make special provision for fast through traffic.

The population of medieval European towns, whether organic or planned, was no larger; and the size of their mesh was equally small or smaller. Sometimes there was a wider access to the open market square, but often not. Differentiation of roadways was introduced in most of the planned Renaissance towns, with wider traffic routes leading directly to the seat of power. Along these the new light-wheeled vehicles could travel at high speed. However, the idea of building up a city from an orderly series of large superblocks or precincts, with a slow-moving internal traffic system, was not rediscovered until the present century (see illustration).

[5]Arthur F. Wright, "Changan," in Arnold Toynbee (ed.), *Cities of Destiny*, Thames & Hudson, London, 1967, McGraw-Hill Book Company, New York, 1967.
[6]Siegfried Giedion, *Architecture and the Phenomena of Transition*, Cambridge, Mass., 1970.
[7]Lewis Mumford, *The City in History*, New York and London, 1961.
[8]R. E. Wycherley, *How the Greeks Built Cities*, London, 1962.

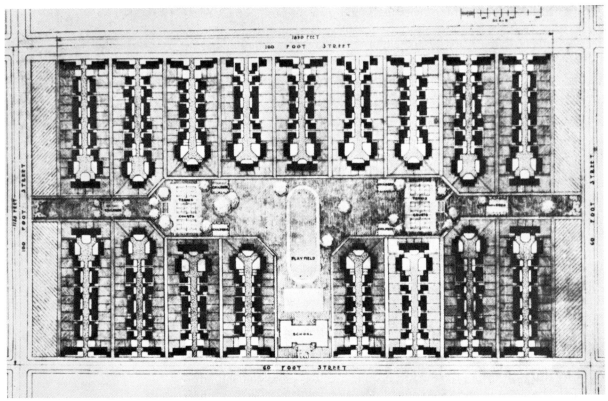

Study of superblock (1928) (Clarence S. Stein, Toward New Towns for America, *New York, 1957, fig. 17, p. 38.)*

Unforeseen Growth Except in the case of a powerful imperial regime with highly organized systems of transportation and communication, the response to rapid population growth in earlier times had inevitably entailed founding new settlements. Man was dependent on food grown near at hand, and a large city exhausted local food supplies.

The many Greek colonial settlements all around the Mediterranean, the Roman settlements along the trade routes across Europe, and the numerous new medieval towns of the eleventh and twelfth centuries were all related to periods of rapid population expansion.

However, the next great wave of population expansion was accompanied by three "revolutions": in agricultural production, in transportation, and in industrialization. This meant that people could follow the trends into the industrial cities and still be fed by the increased yields of local agriculture as well as foodstuffs transported from much further away.

Most cities of the nineteenth century were totally unprepared for this great influx, and Engels's well-known descriptions of the conditions of living in Manchester in 1845 depict conditions as bad as those in Calcutta more than a century later.[9]

[9]F. Engels, *Condition of the Working Classes in England in 1844,* London, 1844, reprinted 1952; Leonardo Benevolo, *The Origins of Modern Town Planning,* London, 1967.

First the idealists and the "reformers," and then the businessmen, recognized a need for powerful controls of land use to maintain reasonable standards of living space for the population. Except for a few important but small-scale experiments, action in the nineteenth century was confined to the regulation of street widths and housing conditions. It was not until after the first impetus of the industrial revolution had spent its force in Europe and after the waves of immigration to the New World had subsided that the first town planning acts started to come into the statute books of the Western countries.[10]

These early town planning acts were timid affairs, mainly designed for the prevention of abuses worse than those that had already occurred and for the preservation of the health, safety, and welfare of the urban population. They were born of fear and anxiety and bore little or no relation to the major problems posed by new technologies and new population expansions in the immediate future.

A summarized version of the sequence of concepts and action in Britain may perhaps be used to illustrate a general trend. New self-contained industrial settlements were advocated in Britain from 1816 onward, the notion gradually becoming more formalized following several pioneering experiments. Then, in 1946—four generations later—the New Towns Act gave official sanction to a concept that was by then obsolete in terms of its scale and its ideas of self-containment in relation to the actual problems of the country at that moment in time.[11]

By that time town planning had become a serious profession and urban studies had been admitted into other fields, such as urban geography, urban sociology, and public administration. There was a growing consensus of opinion that a considerable bulk of population was necessary to provide an urban milieu able to respond to contemporary economic and social needs. The figures being suggested generally hovered around the 300,000 mark— sometimes higher, sometimes lower, but all several times the size of the nineteenth-century notion of self-contained settlements.

Only after a number of "Mark One" New Towns had been built in Britain did these "Mark Three" ideas begin to attract public attention—perhaps two generations after they were first advocated—and the 1960s saw several plans (still on paper) for new "counter-magnet" cities of 250,000 to 500,000 people.

But the rate of change is still accelerating, and all indications point to an era of "megalopolitan" growth before the world can—hopefully—steady itself at a level of several times its present population—the "ecumenopolis" of Doxiadis. A handful of new cities of half a million are likely to make no more impact upon this rapid urban expansion than the early garden cities exerted upon the square miles of interwar suburban sprawl.

[10]T. H. Hughes and E. A. G. Lamborn, *Towns and Town Planning,* Oxford, 1923.

[11]For a different point of view, see the article on New Towns in this encyclopedia by Frederick Osborn, a stalwart follower of Ebenezer Howard and lifelong advocate of garden cities.

The desperate need for the last decades of this century is to establish some easily understandable and easily implementable techniques for handling very large-scale developments of industrially produced housing; education and entertainment centers; dangerous and noise-producing transporation routes; and large tracts of industrial plants. This can only be done by the acceptance of a new unitary scale of operations. This means increasing the size of the individual meshes in the main transportation network from the obsolete "block" of dwellings facing outward upon traffic streets to the inturned "precinct" or "human community" approximately as large as the whole of most ancient and medieval cities. The physical dimensions of this precinct must continue to be conditioned by human movement, but the number of its inhabitants—its density—would reflect existing levels of technology and life styles. Signs of such a change of attitude are all around us, from the large regional pedestrian shopping centers in the United States to the great tracts of industrialized housing in the U.S.S.R. But its lessons have not yet been absorbed into our thinking of the organization and reorganization of urban areas; though some metropolitan plans—notably Colin Buchanan's plan for South Hampshire, 1966 (see illustration) and almost all the work of C. A. Doxiadis—operate with an extendable grid system. South Hampshire has a rectangular mesh of 1.5 by 0.6 miles (2.4 by 1 kilometers)[12] and Doxiadis' plans usually have a square mesh (1.25 miles square—2 kilometers—in the case of Islamabad, 1961; and 1 mile square —1.6 kilometers—in the case of Detroit, 1967). We may note that these contemporary urban sectors are roughly equivalent to four of the Chang-an and Chandigarh precincts.

Each of these new urban sectors operates to some extent as an independent town, with its own local services, schools, and recreation facilities near at hand. But each is attached to the transportation system of the whole metropolitan region; and the aim of Doxiadis's plan for Detroit is that the home of every inhabitant should be less than half an hour's travel from any other point within the metropolitan area.[13] This can be achieved by a rigid separation of the lines of fast-moving traffic (whether on the ground, above it, or below it) from the slow-moving traffic at the "human scale" of the residential precinct.

The intention of all planners working in this direction is to return a much greater freedom of movement, action, and decision-making to the individual man (and woman and child) within the ambiance of his home environment and yet enable them to operate as citizens of the metropolis, the megalopolis, and the world. The possibility of creating a number of semi-independent and hostile urban ghettos is rendered unlikely by the large size of the individual sectors and the great freedom of movement between them. Cities throughout the ages have been confronted with the problem of enabling people with different cultural and economic backgrounds to

A grid of routes of various categories.

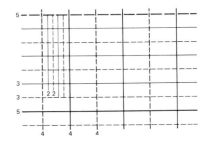

The facilities are grouped along the routes termed 'red'; the alternate or 'green' routes provide for through or random movement.

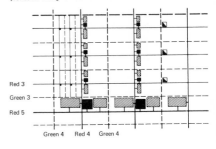

A basic arrangement showing the relationship of facilities to residential areas.

■ Retail and office centers

▨ Industry

■ Residential

▨ Open space

◪ Schools

○ Office centers

An urban structure for southern England proposed by Colin Buchanan. (MOHLG, The South Hampshire Study, London, 1966, figs. 6 and 7, pp. 100 and 101.)

[12]Ministry of Housing and Local Government, *The South Hampshire Study*, London, 1966.
[13]C. A. Doxiadis, *Emergence and Growth of an Urban Region; the Developing Urban Detroit Area*, vol. 2, Detroit, 1967.

live peaceably together. It is clear that this aim is not automatically achieved by the organization of the physical environment; but it is equally clear that an inimical physical environment can exacerbate conditions that lead to friction. As far as we know, human beings develop more fully as individuals and also develop more friendly relations with others if they have considerable freedom and privacy in their private life, if they feel themselves useful members of a local society, and if they have easy access to a much more varied "outside world" to which they consciously feel themselves to belong as citizens. The aim of modern planning is to facilitate the functioning of these human needs within the framework of a rapidly urbanizing world.

BIBLIOGRAPHY: F. Engels, *Condition of the Working Classes in England in 1844,* London, 1844, reprinted 1952; Patrick Geddes, *Cities in Evolution,* London, 1915, reprinted 1969; S. Giedion, *Space, Time, and Architecture,* Cambridge, Mass., 1941, 5th ed., 1968; F. J. Osborn, *Green Belt Cities,* London, 1946, new ed., 1969; Griffith Taylor, *Urban Geography,* London and New York, 1951; R. E. Dickinson, *The West European City,* London, 1951; Patrick Abercrombie, *Town and Country Planning,* 3d ed., London, 1959; Coleman Woodbury (ed.), *The Future of Cities & Urban Redevelopment,* Chicago, 1953; Lewis Mumford, *The City in History,* New York and London, 1961; R. E. Wycherley, *How the Greeks Built Cities,* London, 1962; John W. Reps, *The Making of Urban America,* Princeton, N.J., 1965; C. R. Collins and C. C. Collins, *Camillo Sitte and the Birth of Modern City Planning,* New York, 1965; Walter L. Creese, *The Search for Environment,* New Haven, 1966; Ministry of Housing and Local Government, *The South Hampshire Study,* London, 1966; Arthur F. Wright, "Changan," in Arnold Toynbee (ed.), *Cities of Destiny,* Thames & Hudson, London, McGraw-Hill Book Company, New York, 1967; Maurice Beresford, *New Towns of the Middle Ages,* London, 1967; Leonardo Benevolo, *The Origins of Modern Town Planning,* London, 1967; C. A. Doxiadis, *Emergence and Growth of an Urban Region; the Developing Urban Detroit Area,* vol. 2, Detroit, 1967; S. Giedion, *Architecture and the Phenomena of Transition,* Cambridge, Mass., 1970.

—JAQUELINE TYRWHITT

CITY REGION

CITY REGION   A region can be defined as an area which has a considerable degree of unity because of associated conditions of the land, the people, agriculture, industry, and commerce. Lewis Mumford has commented that "in conceiving a region it is necessary to take an area large enough to embrace a sufficient range of interests and small enough to keep these interests in focus and to make them a subject of direct collective concern."[1]

Regions held together by common interests have often grown in population round a city center, resulting in conurbations such as those which evolved in industrial England. The disadvantage of these is an increasing pressure on space near the center, resulting in congestion, poor living and working conditions, and overloaded, congested transport, while continued growth results in more and more suburban spread and increased separation of homes and workplaces—which generally remain in or near the center.

One theory to counteract these disadvantages is the development of the city region, which means several centers instead of concentration round one center, with lower population densities and partly open country between the centers. Modern transport and communications make this possible, and as a result activities that were formerly concentrated in one place can be dispersed to several centers. In such an evolution there still remains a chief

[1] *Culture of Cities,* London and New York, 1938, p. 314.

center—the mother city of the region—but its growth can be restricted by the dispersal of many functions to the various centers within the region. It is possible to see in London an evolution of this kind, where several commercial centers are being developed on a bigger scale than hitherto within the Greater London region. Croydon is perhaps the most highly developed regional center of this kind. It now has many firms and organizations which would formerly have been in or near the heart of London.

The city region can obviously be most successful if the areas between the centers are kept fairly open, with considerable stretches of parkland and even rural areas, because it is important that further development of the conurbation in its original sense be avoided.

The city region is a conception of the mid-twentieth century, but it has evolved from earlier ideas. Some credit Patrick Geddes in his famous book *Cities in Evolution* (1915) with thinking on these lines. Although Geddes deals with the growth of conurbations (a word that he coined) and speaks of city regions, he makes no real distinction between the two. A conurbation is as much a collection of towns gradually joining, as the Manchester or

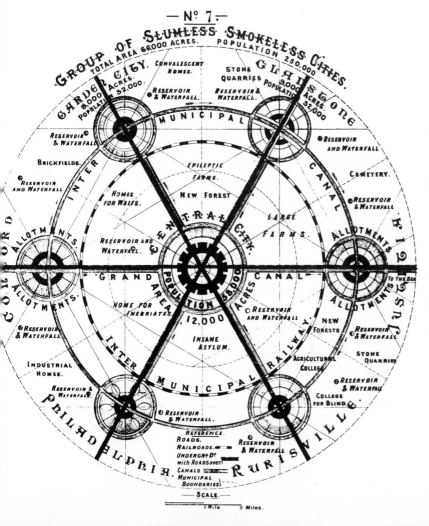

Ebenezer Howard's "Cluster City." Diagram no. 7 in To-morrow, *1898, omitted in second edition of 1902* (Garden Cities of To-morrow), *in which Howard also revised his chapter on social cities. His original text is of great interest in view of the modern concept of city clusters. "The idea of a carefully-planned town lends itself readily to the idea of a carefully-planned cluster of towns, so designed that each dweller in a town of comparatively small population is afforded . . . the enjoyment of easy, rapid, and cheap communication with a large aggregate of the population, so that the advantages which a large city presents in the higher forms of corporate life may be within the reach of all, and yet each citizen . . . may dwell in a region of pure air and be within a very few minutes' walk of the country."*
"The reader is asked not to suppose that the design is put forward as one likely to be strictly carried out in the form thus presented; for any well-planned town, and still more any well-planned cluster of towns, must be carefully designed in relation to the site it is to occupy. With this understanding, however, such a diagram as I have here sketched may be useful, as showing some of the broad principles which should be followed."

Tyneside areas, as the spread of a larger city, and in referring to the evolution in the United States, Geddes speaks of cities "flowing together" (*Cities in Evolution,* p. 48).

Much nearer in principle, if not in magnitude, to the modern conception of a city region was Ebenezer Howard's idea of garden city clusters,[2] an idea which was suggested by the building of North Adelaide, in Australia, a little way from the main city and separated by parklands. From this he evolved the idea of the garden city growing beyond its maximum planned size by establishing "another city some little distance beyond its own zone of country." "The inhabitants of the one," he continues, "could reach the other in a very few minutes; for rapid transit would be specially provided for, and thus the people of the two towns would in reality represent one community." This would ultimately lead to a cluster of cities grouped round a central city and "each inhabitant of the whole group, though in one sense living in a town of small size, would be in reality living in, and would enjoy all the advantages of, a great and most beautiful city," yet the country would be within a very few minutes' walk or ride.

The perhaps unforeseen developments of road transport, and the possession by the majority of a motor vehicle, have much enlarged the scale of Howard's conception, but the principle is the same and can be applied. It foreshadows the best modern conceptions of the city region.

BIBLIOGRAPHY: Raymond Vernon, *The Myth and Reality of Our Urban Problems,* Harvard University Press, Cambridge, Mass., 1966; Sam Warner (ed.), *Planning for a Nation of Cities,* The M.I.T. Press, Cambridge, Mass., 1966; Robert Dickinson, *The City Region in Western Europe,* Routledge & Kegan Paul, Ltd., London, 1967.

—ARNOLD WHITTICK

CIVIC CENTER   Primarily that part of a town or city center with buildings for civic administration, such as the town hall, administrative offices, law courts, and sometimes also buildings for recreational and cultural purposes. The term may be applied to a building complex combining a number of these. Such centers are often handsomely and spaciously planned to express civic dignity.

Traditionally, the center of a European city can roughly be divided into three sections: (1) the religious center; (2) the market, shopping, and commercial center; and (3) the civic center. In small medieval towns the three are often integrated into one; in larger cities the separation is apparent. In ancient Greek cities, where the tradition originated, the acropolis was the religious center while the civic and commercial centers were generally combined in the agora, although even here a temple was often introduced.

In modern towns and cities which are not too large to lose the identity of distinct communities with a definite center, the civic center and shopping centers are often adjacent yet distinct. Examples can be seen in several of the British New Towns like Basildon, Hemel Hempstead, Harlow, Newton Aycliffe, and Corby.

[1]*Garden Cities of Tomorrow,* chap. 12, "Social Cities," 1902.

CIVIL ENGINEERING Important branches of civil engineering which affect land-use planning are transportation (i.e., roads and bridges), sewerage and sewage disposal, and drainage and water supply. The civil engineer is also concerned with the design and construction of airports, docks and harbors, sea defense works, and the provision of such services as electricity, gas, telecommunications, and the disposal of refuse. These subjects are dealt with under separate headings.

The initial studies which are undertaken in relation to any land-use project, whether it be a new town, a housing estate, an industrial development, or an airport, will include an assessment of the cost and feasibility of the civil engineering works involved—e.g., the bearing capacity of the ground, the contours of the site in relation to its surroundings, and such questions as whether drainage can be by gravity or whether pumping will be necessary, whether the area is liable to flooding, and whether the proposed development will increase the risk of flooding.

The estimated cost of the civil engineering work involved is weighed against the merits or demerits of the alternatives. For example, the enormous expense of land reclamation work in The Netherlands has been balanced against the alternatives of building on good agricultural land or increasing building densities which are already high.

Civil engineering has been defined as "the art of directing the great sources of power in nature for the use and convenience of man"; but in relation to town planning the very act of directing these sources of power often results in a conflict with amenity.

The reservoir, the power station, the cement works, the coal mine, the motor road, the oil refinery, the refuse disposal plant, or the sewage works—none of these can be built without some loss of amenity; and usually that loss can be reduced substantially only at very great expense. Occasionally, however, as in hydroelectric schemes involving the construction of reservoirs and dams, scenic beauty can be improved, as has been the case in Scotland.

The skill of the civil engineer lies in finding ways of carrying out projects such as these at a reasonable cost and in a manner which is acceptable in their environment.

Up to about 1940, urban planning in the United Kingdom was carried out by the borough engineers of the cities and towns. These municipal engineers were, in the main, chartered civil engineers.

Today the authorities responsible for this work are the county councils and the county borough councils, and most of them have appointed planning officers who are usually chartered town planners and who have on their staffs representatives of other professions, including civil engineers, to advise on those matters which specially concern them.

In town and country planning it is impossible to make a clear distinction between the work of the architect, the structural engineer, the civil engineer, and the urban planner; and in recent years most of the plans, whether regional plans, development plans, structure plans, plans for new towns or for areas of redevelopment, have been prepared by teams working under the direction of a town or city planner.

BIBLIOGRAPHY: J. W. Henderson, "Planning and Engineering," *Journal of the Town Planning Institute,* vol. 37, no. 2, London, 1951; F. G. Hill, "Public Health Engineering," *Journal of the Town Planning Institute,* vol. 38, no. 5.

—JOHN G. JEFFERSON

CLEAN AIR   (*See* AIR POLLUTION AND CLEAN AIR.)

CLIMATIC CONDITIONS AND PLANNING   Climate comprises certain conditions of temperature, wind, rainfall, sunshine, frost, and fog. Climate, soil, and vegetation are interacting elements, and therefore must all be given equal importance when considering the influencing factors in planning.

There are many world climatic types with varying conditions. The British Isles are said to have an oceanic climate within which regional or subclimates can be distinguished. Information on the general conditions within the four regional climates can easily be obtained. However, the regions do not have definitive boundaries but tend to merge into one another, sometimes by imperceptible transitions or by a marked physiographical feature such as a hill or mountain range. There are many variations within the regions and information on a particular area can be collected from nearby meterological stations whose location is similar in elevation and exposure to a proposed area of development. Some interpolation and adjustment should be made to relate the details to the site.

Study of the local climate within the regions is essential in understanding the existing land and settlement patterns and any changes which may occur in the course of planning.

The configuration of the land, its height, and its degree of exposure affect wind velocities and temperatures. A valley may be open to warm airflows and protected from cold winds. Another valley may lie so that the wind is constantly funneled through, making the valley's prevailing temperatures low. Land form can produce major local climatic contrasts where climatic conditions in some areas differ greatly from the general climate of the surrounding region.

Microclimate is the small-scale aspect of climate; that is, the climatic conditions that exist in an area that may be only a few feet square. It is of great significance in an area of space between buildings or above small undulations in the ground. Microclimate concerns temperature; heat reflection; air turbulence; areas exposed to or sheltered from wind, frost, or fog; and wind funnels. Consideration of these details is essential in the practical planning of small areas, such as courtyards, piazzas, and open spaces, as local topography is likely to cause severe climatic variations over small distances.

The influence of climatic conditions has been recognized in the early planning of settlements. In hot climates, houses were grouped close together, with high walls to give shade from the sun and protection from the wind. Individual dwellings with gardens were enclosed by walls, and the gardens were thickly planted with trees providing not only shade in the hot desert and a lowering of the temperature but also a source of food supply. Water was also introduced to help the plants to grow, to reduce the temperature in the area immediately near the pools, and to provide psychological relief from the oppressive heat and dust of the surrounding land.

Climate affects not only the broad aspect of planning, with regional and local variations relating to the proposed position and pattern of development, but also the detailed planning of smaller spaces within the towns. A town is not sited on a cold, windy hilltop if it can be positioned on warm, gently sloping land or in a warm valley.

Certain climatic conditions may be serious restraints to planning on a certain site and may make development impossible. Careful studies should be made in the preplanning stages, for a factor which appears to be a restraint may be counteracted by careful design. In some instances, by preventing a site problem from being accentuated in some form and by the type of new development, it may be possible to take positive steps to control site conditions and ameliorate adverse climate.

If the data collected shows that a proposed site is in a frost or fog pocket with lower than average temperatures and a higher rainfall than surrounding areas, a different location should be examined. If all other conditions prove acceptable to development except the temperature, which shows the site to be subject to cold conditions, the examination of local and microclimatic factors together with topographic variations may prove that a site only a small distance away would be more suitable.

The climatic information collected may be based on yearly, 5-yearly, or 20-year readings and would include details of direction of prevailing winds and temperature. The winds may prevail from one direction, but there may be certain shorter periods of time when the winds are from another direction and colder, thus reducing the temperature. These variations should be taken into account in the detailed planning.

Development should preferably be planned on a warm, sheltered slope and not on a windy, cold hillside. Closely knit grouping of the elements will help eliminate windy open spaces. Thickly planted shelter belts can give protection, reduce wind velocity, and generally improve site conditions. Shelter belts can also, if planted obliquely to the direction of the maximum slope of the ground, prevent the ponding of cold air.

Climate influences the siting and form of development and the proportions of the parts of the development. The needs of people for sun, shade, and shelter must be met. The small, shaded spaces so desirable in hot, sunny climates are unwelcome and unused by people in cool climates with high rainfall.

Planning is for people whose practical and spiritual needs should be satisfied. Climate is a known factor whose variations should be fully examined, with other elements, in the design process.

—WENDY POWELL

CODE OF PROFESSIONAL CONDUCT   Professional bodies require their members to adhere to a code, or set of standards and rules, of conduct. The code is a statement of the ethics of a profession; its purpose is to define the responsibilities that are imposed on members by considerations of personal integrity, the public interest, and professional status. Certain elements derived from a general concept of "professionalism" are common to most codes of conduct; e.g., warnings about conflicts of interest and the prohibition of advertising for work and competing on the basis of fees. Other aspects arise from the case law of the profession or relate to specific circumstances in which the individual practitioner may benefit from guidance.

The Royal Town Planning Institute of the United Kingdom introduced its present Code of Professional Conduct in January 1968. The code is prefaced by a positive statement of principle:

> Every member or student is to conduct himself in such a manner as to uphold the reputation of the Institute, and in no way to prejudice his own professional status as one who provides services related primarily to his professional training and experience for remuneration related strictly to those services in accordance with personal integrity.

Some general precepts of professionalism are expressed in clauses that prohibit a member from holding or accepting a position in which his interest conflicts with his professional duty; from forming or joining a limited liability company for the purpose of practicing as a chartered town planner; from receiving discounts, gifts, commissions, or any form of remuneration other than his professional fees or salary; from making statements that are contrary to his professional opinion; and from soliciting work by commercial advertising.

Other clauses in the RTPI Code relate to specific areas of practice in which previous case law has shown that conflicts of interest may occur or in which a planner must take care to avoid any appearance of subordinating objectivity to self-interest.

For example, the position of planners employed in local government is defined with regard to dealings in land and private practice, and consultants who act for local authorities as well as for other clients are warned that they must not advise on the granting or refusal of their own applications for planning permission. One special clause of the code allows members in private practice to disseminate information about the extent and availability of their services by the use of "practice information forms" provided by the institute.

Further provisions of the RTPI Code require members to uphold and apply the institute's scale of professional fees; to take care, when stating their general views on any matter, not to seem to be speaking on behalf of the institute or any of its branches; and to comply with the institute's competition regulations. The code also includes a clause that outlines the procedure adopted by the institute's Board for the Code of Conduct and Discipline and by its council in investigating any alleged breach of the code's provisions or other unprofessional conduct.

One salient feature of this code is the precision of its phrasing, which reflects the concern of the institute that its members should have a clear and unambiguous guide to conduct and one that relates firmly to practical issues.

The same spirit informs the Code of Professional Responsibility which the American Institute of Planners published in May 1970. The AIP's code is in two parts—Canons and Rules of Discipline. The former state established standards of professionalism in general terms; the latter indicate the minimum level of conduct below which no member may fall without being subject to disciplinary action. The code has as its complement a detailed set of rules and a procedure for treating allegations of misconduct.

The code states that

> The ultimate objective of the planning profession is the coordination, for the general welfare, of that use and development of community resources that are best designed to fulfill human needs and purposes. . . . In view of this objective the professional endeavors of the planner demand the highest values of social consciousness and professional conduct.

The five Canons are as follows:

> (a) A planner serves the public interest primarily. He shall accept or continue employment only when he can insure accommodation of the client's or employer's interest with the public interest.
> (b) A planner shall exercise independent professional judgment on behalf of his client or employer and shall serve him in a competent manner.
> (c) A planner shall preserve the secrets and confidences of a client or employer.
> (d) A planner shall assist in maintaining the integrity and competence of the planning profession.
> (e) A planner shall avoid even the appearance of improper professional conduct.

These principles are exemplified in the 15 rules of discipline. Planners are precluded *inter alia* from seeking personal publicity; from advertising in "self-laudatory language calculated to attract clients"; from giving any form of consideration to secure employment or as a reward for favors; from accepting any gift or other consideration made for the purpose of influencing their actions as public officials or employees; from taking up employment if the exercise of their professional judgment on behalf of a client or employer may be adversely affected by personal or other interests; from undertaking planning services which they are not competent to perform; from using public office or employment to gain any special advantage; and from competing on the basis of fee or attempting to supplant another member.

Under both RTPI and AIP codes a member who is found to have acted unprofessionally may be warned as to his future conduct, censured, suspended from membership for a specific period, or expelled.

—HAROLD LEWIS

COLOR The visual effect of the urban environment depends on a wide variety of factors such as space, mass, light and shadow, color, and on innumerable conditions and associations. The effects of color in the urban scene depend on climate and light and are associated with texture. Furthermore, different individuals perceive these effects in varying degrees. The acutely sensitive visitor, for instance, will be more aware of them than will the half-aware everyday percipient. Color effects are not, therefore, easy to measure, yet they are probably more important to the human spirit than many architectural and planning practitioners have recognized. Color can contribute strongly to making an urban scene harsh or harmonious, gay or dismal, and it is therefore very much the concern of the architect, urban designer, and planner. When buildings were mainly of stone or brick, general color harmony was less difficult to obtain than it is with the great varieties of facing materials in modern building. But even with stone or brick, harsh contrasts instead of pleasant harmonies have often been perpetuated, as in the introduction of violent red brick or polished red granite in a town with predominately pale limestone buildings.

With new materials like colored glass or enamel panels in curtain walling, the task becomes more difficult and harsh effects more jarring—partly because polished surfaces are more obtrusive than mat surfaces. With colored reflecting surfaces, positive colors may be destructive of a pleasant, quiet urban environment; yet for publicity reasons buildings are often made obtrusive by the use of strong colors.

The effects of color have some relation to texture. Various shades of red in a highly vitreous surface may be unpleasant, but as an exposed granite aggregate they may be agreeable.

Although good color effects are matters of opinion and personal preference, there is yet some measure of agreement among sensitive percipients which suggest certain general principles that could be followed by architects and urban designers. Some persons have a natural color sense and are very successful in making good color arrangements; others are far less skilled in this matter. For the less gifted, a few principles are useful, since the architect or planner is very rarely chosen for his color sense.

When seen in an open landscape, colors appear weaker in intensity and grayer the further away they are. Contrast also lessens with distance. The more positive colors appear in the foreground and seem to come forward. Most conspicuous among these are the hues at the red end of the spectrum, while the less prominent, receding colors are at the violet end of the spectrum. A field of ripe corn in the foreground is yellow, orange, or gold; in the far distance it is softened with an atmospheric overlay of blue or violet often with a mixture of gray. Distant hues are associated with and conduce to a sense of space. The softer hues, especially if they have a mixture of gray, are background colors, while the more positive colors are foreground colors and come forward. This visual experience suggests a basis of harmonious color dispositions in the urban scene. It is in this sense that Renaissance artists thought of art as an imitation of nature, not—as they are commonly misunderstood to have done—in the sense of copying the exact forms and colors of nature. Color schemes that follow principles derived from natural coloring are generally satisfying.

Applying such principles to an urban square, it will be appreciated that where the buildings are all of stone, as in the city of Bath, a harmony is apparent; and if there is also a unity of massing and style, a sense of peace and dignity is secured. Also, with the buildings all a soft, gray, receding hue, the square looks its full size. If, however, modern buildings are introduced into the square, curtain-walled with colored glass or enamel panels of a strong red or orange, they will be obtrusive and the whole harmonious effect of the square will be disturbed. If modern buildings of this kind are introduced, then their colors should be harmonious with the rest of the square. In a totally new square with modern buildings, many strong, positive colors, all clamoring for attention, may be good modern publicity, but the result may be an ugly and vulgar urban scene. It would be better to obtain some measure of agreement among the various property owners to secure harmonious coloring. Highly colored façades can be beautiful and effective, as the colored marble encrustations of Venetian architecture demonstrate, but they should be subjected to a general harmony which is, or should be, the province of the urban designer. While the façade of a building may resemble, in some respects, a geometric abstract painting, it should harmonize with the buildings that surround it. That is, a building should not, like one of the very individual paintings in an exhibition, clamor for the viewer's attention regardless of its neighbors. Rather these buildings, like pictures carefully chosen and arranged to be seen together as a group, should complement one another to make one "picture" or urban scene. It may be that brightly colored, curtain-walled buildings in a modern square, related to an overall harmonious color scheme, could have both a stimulating and agreeable effect. Much depends on climate. Dark buildings in a northern city, where sunlight is at a premium, can be depressing, as they are or were in the smoke-grimed industrial cities of northern England; but as smoke is reduced and buildings are cleaned, cities become brighter, with incalculable effects on the human spirit. The introduction of white marble facing in northern cities, as, for example, in a recent building by Alvar Aalto in Helsinki, is enlivening. Generally pale or bright coloring in northern cities, where there is little sunlight in the winter, is desirable, and it is a question whether the dark grays and blacks that predominate in one housing estate in a New Town in northern England were the happiest choice. In Mediterranean towns, where sunlight is plentiful, cool color schemes appear appropriate. Examples include some of the small towns on the island of Rhodes.

Inharmonious color notes are sometimes produced by street furniture, such as traffic signs which have to be quickly and easily seen and are thus often made a prominent red or yellow. These, because of their function, must be conspicuous. Also, parked motor vehicles are rarely visually attractive, but with the increase of pedestrian urban areas and of underground and multistory car parks, there are prospects that the urban scene may become more agreeable.

Guidance in the effective harmonious and contrasting disposition of colors can be obtained from the color classifications made by Newton, Young,

Helmholtz, Oswald, Munsell, and others and from their applications by various artists.

BIBLIOGRAPHY: *Munsell Book of Color,* 1915; Egbert Jacobson (ed.) et al., *Color Harmony Manual* (based on the Oswald system). For color designations in the United States see National Bureau of Standards, *Method of Designating Color* and *A Dictionary of Color Names.*

—ARNOLD WHITTICK

COMMONS AND COMMON LAND   These are areas of land which are generally privately owned but which groups of people or the population at large have certain specified legal rights to use or exploit. These rights can be one or all of the following:

- The right of common pasture, being the right to graze one's animals over the herbage.
- The right to gather wood as a source of fuel (estovers).
- The right to dig turf for use as a fuel or for roofing purposes (turbary).
- The right to fish from common waters (piscary).
- The right to collect or cut bracken for cattle bedding or fuel.
- Finally, there is the more general right which may apply to or be granted to the local population; that is, the right to use the land for recreation purposes described as "air and exercise."

The origins of common land go back to the Saxon open-field system of farming where land was held communally for use by parishioners. The common rights basically relate to the privilege endowed by the crown, in whom all land vests, to the lord of the manor and thence to peasants in order that they may be provided with the essentials for living; namely food, fuel, and water.

Common land has been the subject of a bitter dispute when any effort has been made by government or lords of manors to reduce or eliminate the rights of the commoners. In the twelfth and thirteenth centuries, many powerful lords of manors permitted common land to be used for new towns and be enclosed for farming purposes, with the result that essential pasture necessary for the survival of villagers' animals became seriously diminished. The Statute of Merton in 1236 A.D. was intended to protect an adequate acreage of land for the free tenants of villages, and the manorial courts were empowered to protect their rights.

This statute permitted the lord to enclose or otherwise to improve the wastes and commons only if he left sufficient common pasture for his free tenants. It is chiefly important because it marks the first interference by the state in the problem of common lands.

Nevertheless, court records show that the impoverished commoners were often bitter and took concerted action to break down fences, "steal" wood, and produce from what they considered to be their land. At Doningsby, Yorkshire, a hundred villagers drove their cattle over corn growing on enclosed common land.

The demand to enclose commons arose because, up to the time of the black death (1349), the growing population in the towns required more food and the demand at market town centers needed to be satisfied. A means of limiting the use of common land and therefore releasing more land for arable purposes was achieved by specifying the number of animals to be grazed on the land, and this was described as "stinting." Local laws enforced this principle, known as "*couchant* and *levant.*" The overall effect of these measures during this period was to reduce the area of good land available to the peasants and lower their standard of living. However, essential food was produced for the growing town, thus enabling a more complex and advanced economy to develop.

Throughout the seventeenth century, open fields and their apportionment meadows and common pastures were enclosed, parish by parish, by means of private agreements between lords of manors and their tenants.

This troubled process of enclosure continued by encroachment or agreement until the "agrarian revolution" in the eighteenth century.

The period from 1700 to 1845 is known as "the age of parliamentary enclosure."

A more scientific approach to farming was introduced by Messrs. Coke, Tull, Townsend, and Bakewell. A combination of their ideas resulted in improved farm management; mechanized ploughing; rotation of crops; use of the root crop, turnip, for storage for winter fodder; and selective breeding of cattle. Productivity on farms became much greater due to the higher yielding crops and elimination of the necessity to slaughter cattle in the autumn. The introduction of these methods required amalgamation of lands into larger holdings and fencing. It was obvious that the three-field system had become obsolete, and parliamentary pressure was exerted to accelerate and achieve by legal means the enclosure of common land. Consequently food production was increased for the rapidly growing towns and the foundation laid for the British industrial revolution. The transformation of the agricultural system clearly gave rise to considerable social and economic hardship to commoners and small farmers, who found it necessary to leave the countryside for the towns.

With the increasing importance of imported corn from North America and the invention of refrigerated ships for meat in the latter part of the nineteenth century, pressure for more land decreased.

By the 1830s, some of the social disadvantages of the enclosure of commons were apparent, not least because the country now had twice as many people as it had in 1700.

With the spread of literacy, opposition to enclosure became more effective and social conscience was aroused.

As a result, enclosure came to be controlled by the General Inclosure Act 1845 on the principle that the consent of one third of the commoners was necessary and that, where commons were situated within 5 miles of towns of a population of 10,000 or more, the expediency of the proposed enclosure had to be proved and allotments had to be made for recreation and for field gardens.

Between 1845 and 1864 over 614,000 acres (248,670 hectares) of commons were enclosed, yet a total of only 4,000 acres (1,620 hectares) was allotted for recreation or for the benefit of the poor.

As the population grew, commons began to have enormous intrinsic value as building sites, and commons around London were threatened by building. For this reason they became, in the 1860s, a subject of concern to Parliament. The threat to build on Putney Heath was the immediate cause of a government committee (called the 1865 Committee) being set up to inquire into the best means of preserving, for the use of the public, the commons in the immediate neighborhood of London.

The committee adopted the views of Lord Eversley, founder in 1865 of the Commons Preservation Society, and it led to the Metropolitan Commons Act (1866), which made the enclosure of London commons practically impossible. There followed the Commons Acts of 1876 and 1899, but it was not until the Law of Property Act (1925) that the right of the general public to air and exercise was recognized. Section 193 gave the public legal right of access to all urban commons and to such rural commons as the owners, by deed, applied the section to.

There are at the present time some 1.5 million acres (607,500 hectares) of common land in England and Wales. The various classes of common can be summarized as follows:

1. Land with common rights permanently or for specific periods during any one year

2. Town and village green, such as manorial waste and roadside land which may not have specific common rights but which is publicly used

3. Allotments granted under enclosure acts as compensation to provide fuel, food, or exercise and recreation

Due to the difficulty of management and the marginal agricultural quality of most commons, many have taken on a wild appearance or have been adapted for recreational use. With a more sophisticated society and modern methods of agriculture and also because of the new management problems that entail, the original common rights associated with the basic requirements of man have become irrelevant in the twentieth century. In an effort to clarify the situation, the Commons Act, 1965 requires the registration of common rights, common land, and town and village greens as a first step in making a more realistic appraisal of such land.

Many public authorities are already purchasing commons and improving their appearance and accessibility in order to satisfy the growing demand for recreation areas. They are frequently sanctuaries for rare species of wildlife and plants which could not otherwise survive.

It is virtually impossible for the freeholder of common land to build upon or develop it; and even for such public purposes as roads, a suitable piece of land must be attached to the common as a replacement. Consequently common land has been protected from the rapid expansion of towns, and in many cases such lands are important open spaces which are vital to the well-being of citizens. Notable examples in London are Blackheath, Wimbledon, Hampstead Heath, and Epping Forest; and elsewhere in the country there are Walton Downs, Surrey; the New Forest, Hampshire; and Dartmoor, Devon, Somerset, and the Langdales in the Lake District.

—L. W. A. RENDELL

COMMUNICATIONS Perhaps the greatest single factor upon which the success of human organizations depends is the ability to communicate. The revolution brought about by the development of the telegraph, telephone, and radio has had a profound effect upon human society. These have made possible greatly increased centralization in business and government. They have stretched the vision of communities and amalgamated cultures, arts, and techniques. Indeed, it is upon the quality of its communications system that the efficiency of any enterprise ultimately depends.

In city planning there is a tendency, as with other national endeavors, to draw upon national and regional communications facilities without much regard to a systems approach. The national and regional authorities and enterprises cooperate with city planners to provide the components of what is, after all, to be the city's nervous system. There is evidence, nevertheless, that these elements are often regarded as adjuncts to, rather than integral parts of, the urban plan.

The rapidity of development in the communications field is well known. The demands arise from the ever-increasing scope of interests which depend upon communication in one form or another for their very existence. The growing application of computer utilization, the increased participation of television in education (an example is the part television plays in the British Open University scheme), and the demand for leisure-time entertainment— which increases as working hours are shortened—all add up to a phenomenal growth rate.

While rising demand in certain aspects of communications is not too difficult to satisfy (for example, in line telephony), physical laws place ultimate boundaries upon the extent of demand in other cases. In broadcast radio and television, the bandwidth/frequency relationship places limits upon the number of services which can ultimately be provided within the frequency spectra available. Indeed, in highly developed nations, radio frequency spectrum allocations must be regarded as one of the most valuable of national assets. Evidence that this fact has long been officially realized in the United States is to be found in President John F. Kennedy's Executive Order 10995 of 1962, in which he stated that "the radio spectrum is a critical natural resource which requires . . . efficient and prudent management in the national interest."

Television frequency allocations in many countries are already inadequate in certain bands. Heavy interference between adjacent systems in the VHF bands are already commonplace. The UHF band is being exploited and the band space fast eaten up. Land mobile communications, an area where there is greatly increasing growth of demand, is already forcing itself into frequency bands formerly reserved for other uses. The United States Federal Communications Commission has recently permitted land mobile users to share in the UHF 800- to 900-megahertz band, formerly intended only for television. Indeed the commission has forecast a doubling of the land mobile communications demand within the present decade.

Consideration of this brief outline will indicate that a serious and growing problem is already forcing itself to general attention and that radical solutions must be planned and acted upon if national and urban organisms are not to suffer through atrophy of those "nerve" systems upon which their prosperity and well-being so much depend.

It has been mentioned that the growth of telephone systems can be more easily accommodated since communication can be confined to cable systems not constrained by these considerations which so much affect radio, television, and land mobile communications. While alternatives which can satisfy the latter cannot easily be found by abandoning radio propagation methods, the same is not true in respect of radio and television services. For example, each television channel requires about 10 megahertz of bandwidth. Although more channels can be provided when the higher frequencies are used, there is here (apart from the band space limitation which must eventually be reached) the problem of increasing atmospheric propagation loss as the carrier frequency increases.

Houses with television aerials.

These higher frequencies fortunately lend themselves to propagation within the confines of wave guides when losses decrease with increase of frequency. Networks of wave guides offer an attractive alternative. Design and construction poses electronic and civil engineering problems of some magnitude but not incapable of solution. Television and telephone traffic could be accommodated within great trunk systems of long-distance wave guide laid underground and linking centers of population, with supply directly to the urban users.

Intercity communication by wave guide, capable of satisfying the enormous increases in demand which are foreseen for telephone, television, and computer data traffic, will be a reality in Britain before the end of the present decade. A wave guide system 18.6 miles (30 kilometers) in length is at present under construction between the British Post Office research station at Martlesham, Suffolk, England, and a repeater Station on the existing microwave radio-relay route. A 0.62-mile (1-kilometer) test route has already been publicly demonstrated, carrying transmission of two two-way color television channels plus telephone conversations and other data. Digital transmission in which pictures, conversations, and other data are converted to binary digits transmitted at a rate of several millions of pulses per second is employed. This pulse-code technique is already well known to communications engineers. Trials of the 18.6-mile (30-kilometer) system are planned to be complete by 1976 and intercity installation will begin in 1977 or 1978.

It will be seen that intercity networks are realizable. However, wave guides in these terms do not offer a complete answer to the problem of distribution to users within the city complex, since they do not lend themselves easily to departure from straight or gently curving routes. To solve the problem of urban distribution, it is necessary to look for a solution to particular design problems the solution of which is necessary to permit exploitation of the optical transmission possibilities offered by the invention of the laser. A breakthrough in this field of research has been achieved by the Standard

Telecommunications Laboratories at Harlow New Town in England. This organization is part of the vast I.T.T. Corporation.

In September of 1970, this laboratory announced the successful development of a solid-state laser of the pinhead size required for light transmission down hair-thin glass fiber and (most importantly) capable of adequate continuous output of light while operating at room temperatures. The device, about 0.02 inch (0.50 millimeter) long, is a double heterostructure of gallium arsenide sandwiched between layers of gallium aluminium arsenide. It is sufficient for the purpose of this article to state that, from the technical data available, the device should be relatively cheap to produce and be capable of efficient performance in its role.

In company with this laser development, the same laboratory has successfully fabricated a single-mode optical wave guide fiber ideal for very-wide-band communications. Hair-thin fibers have been successfully processed through a plastic extruder for assembly into a complete cable. The Corning Glass Company, which produces the essential glass fibers, indicates that fiber losses as low as 20 decibels per 0.62 mile (kilometer) can be obtained while retaining the fiber geometry required.

These developments, together with the achievements of both S.T.L. and Bell Laboratories in producing the laser light source capable of operating at room temperatures, mean that practical optical fiber communications systems are likely to be in production by 1975.

The benefits from the urban planning viewpoint would be considerable. The aesthetic endeavors of architects and city planners would no longer be defeated by the inevitable forest of television antennas which sprout from the rooftops of otherwise pleasing homes (see illustration). Accessible common duct systems to carry radio, television, telephone, power and other utilities could be designed and built into the urban structure from the outset, with national, urban, and domestic networks feeding one to the other.

Wired broadcasting systems, for both audio and video services, have already reached considerable stages of development in both the United States and Great Britain; and powerful arguments, both economic and aesthetic, have been made in favor of greater exploitation of these systems. For example, in the Crawley, England, New Town development, an attempt has been made to encourage a form of "piped" television. This service, although not based upon a system as sophisticated as that outlined above for the longer term, does point in the right direction. Here, in a limited scheme, homes are connected to an underground distribution network fed from a centrally and carefully sited television receiver station (see illustration). The benefits can be twofold, both aesthetic and in quality of service, especially when the town is in an area of fringe reception.

That solutions to the radio frequency allocation problem must be found is self-evident. That suggested in this brief survey would remove from the problem a considerable and growing element, leaving scarce band space for those types of international, national, regional, and urban communications

The television mast and station in a high wood at Sussex, England.

which must continue for the foreseeable future to depend upon propagation through the atmosphere.

BIBLIOGRAPHY: *Radio Frequency Handbook,* appendix I, Federal Aviation Agency, Washington, D.C.; A. H. W. Beck, *Words and Waves,* World University Library, Weidenfeld and Nicholson, London, 1967; R. P. Gabriel, "Wired Broadcasting in Great Britain," I.E.E.E. *Spectrum,* April, 1967; S.T. Laboratories, Harlow, England, *Press Releases* 1130 and 1132, September 15, 1970.

—DOUGLAS C. BRUCE

COMMUNITY AND COMMUNITY FEELING   Definitions of community vary almost as much as their proponents. In the past, it is generally agreed, the territorial aspect was most pronounced. According to MacIver, for example, a community implies a delimited territory within which individuals could, if they wished, satisfy their basic needs and live out their round of life (MacIver, 1927). Today, with the rise of nonterritorial networks, created by greater and more varied symbolic exchanges and contacts among men, such a definition no longer suffices or satisfies. It is now possible for individuals to travel throughout the globe without ever leaving home, while others are at home wherever they set foot. Expanding spiritual and physical horizons have severed the original link between place and community. This has led to a number of conceptual innovations, as, for example, the idea of the "non place realm" (Webber, 1967), or of dual spatial-social orders (Greer, 1962) reminiscent of earlier discussions by Durkeim, among others, of interest communities that transcend national or ethnic boundaries.

If, as is increasingly thought, the stable, permanent communities of the past represent but one class of communities, what criteria are there for differentiating other types? One common method is to classify communities according to the predominant activities and attributes of their members, which in conjunction with such factors as size, wealth, and heterogeneity of the population leads to hierarchical rankings of cities or to typologies of centers according to principal purpose or functions. Accordingly, we find cities divided into vacation, resort, university, or production centers; or by size into small, medium, and large cities; or by tradition into the familiar villages, small towns, metropolises, and megalopolises. Innumerable gradations and variations are possible and the typology developed and used will depend upon one's purposes.

For planners the discrepancy between locale and community poses special problems. Once physical and social boundaries cease to coincide, which community is one to plan for? When does one have a community? Where do communities begin and end? Once upon a time it was easy to answer these questions because communities were small, isolated, relatively self-sufficient, and long established. But now, common traditions, loyalties, and life-ways are eroding as mobility, diversity, and multiple interests pull individuals in a myriad of directions. Once the symbolic environment begins to transcend the physical environment, the erstwhile unity between man and space has been irrevocably altered.

This development is captured by such familiar conceptual distinctions as mechanical versus organic solidarity (Durkheim), *Gemeinschaft* versus

Gesellschaft (Toennies), folk versus secular society (Redfield), and the standard rural-urban dichotomy. With the advance of the division of labor, the links between individuals become indirect and specialized. Hence, in modern urban communities, men are bound to each other less by the common space they share than by the different services and products they exchange. This means that the physical community is not necessarily, and certainly not automatically, a social community, which poses some important questions for everyone and perhaps most especially for planners. In particular, it compels us to examine the various possible bases for communal life and to choose the most feasible or relevant.

This split between physical and social community is not equally true for everyone. Some groups and individuals are far more mobile than others, notably the younger and wealthier inhabitants; while others, such as the poor, the aged, and infants plus their caretakers are more spatially confined. Also, the community of consumption is more confined than the community of production. And in this as in most other areas, one's social class and ethnic affiliations play an important role, focusing one's loyalties to particular localities.

By and large, planners tend to overemphasize the physical features of social communities. As a result, they are disappointed when their efforts to provide soundly planned spaces and dwellings are not appreciated. One of the most difficult lessons for them to learn, in fact, is that even soundly planned spatial arrangements may not and often do not engender the sense of mutual awareness and common destiny usually associated with community sentiment. Indeed, if we had to pick one area where the professional perspectives of planners and sociologists stand most clearly revealed, their respective definitions of community would surely be it. Planners start with space and then incorporate collective activity and purpose, whereas sociologists start with purpose and only incidentally consider space.

In the most general sense, community refers to the arena of collective experience and endeavor as this is shaped by communication and communion. These determine the extent of a collectivity's reach and its sense of sentimental and functional interdependence. The physical features can help to bind and give definition to communities existing on other grounds, but they cannot create communities from scratch. No community will be everyone's ideal, nor will a single yardstick—density, street layout, type of services—enable us to formulate such an ideal. Many splendored and multidimensional communities are created by people acting with, for, and against each other in particular settings. To the extent that individuals will become more self-sufficient and resourceful in the future, comprehensive and all-embracing communities may be expected to diminish and more partial fragmentary structures to take their places. If planners wish to keep pace with human needs, they will have to keep pace with these developments and anticipate them.

BIBLIOGRAPHY: Robert E. Park, *Collected Papers*, Human Communities, the City and Human Ecology, vol. 2, 1916–1939; Robert Redfield, "The Folk Society", *American Journal of Sociology*, vol. 2, January 1947; Emile Durkheim, *The Division of Labor in Society*, The Free Press, Glencoe,

Ill., 1947; Scott Greer, *Governing the Metropolis,* John Wiley & Sons, Inc., New York, 1962; Roland L. Warren, *The Community in America,* Chicago, 1963; Melvin M. Webber, "The Urban Place and the Non Place Realm" in Webber et al. (eds.), *Explorations in Urban Structure,* University of Pennsylvania Press, Philadelphia, 1967; Herbert J. Gans, *The Levittowners,* Random House Inc., New York, 1967; Robert Mills French (ed.), *The Community, a Comparative Perspective,* F. E. Peacock, 1969; Robert M. MacIver, *Community.*

—SUZANNE KELLER

COMMUNITY CENTERS   Provide meeting places for people with similar interests but often of varying social, religious, and political backgrounds, who come to play, to learn, or to work together for personal satisfaction and/or community improvements.

The impulses which brought about the establishment of community centers are similar to those which led to the founding of social and university settlements in England from 1884 and in the United States from 1886. These initially sprang from the concern of educational, business, and professional people (often individuals) and a wish to alleviate drab living and working conditions, particularly in the congested areas of large cities. Community centers, however, often resulted from the urge of neighborhoods to do something for themselves.

Centers are sometimes self-supporting, but usually some public moneys (municipal funds) need to be invested if the group which organizes the activities is not to be unduly deterred by the effort to raise funds to cover the running costs of the premises.

In Chicago and Los Angeles, recreation centers for year-round use were opened in 1905. In Great Britain, community centers have been provided in many municipal housing estates since 1937.

Premises must satisfy the need for a wide diversity of uses in an age of increasing leisure for all workers, and though good work has been carried out in makeshift premises and converted houses, it is generally accepted that these facilities should be designed specifically as community centers. A hall which will accommodate a fair proportion of the population of the area it serves—for special social occasions, weddings, concerts, dramatic performances (amateur or professional), lectures, and exhibitions—is desirable; also committee and craft rooms with adequate storage space and a kitchen where food can be prepared. There is also, often, considerable demand for a room with top lighting, suitable for art exhibitions and sports contests.

Considerable ingenuity has been shown by architects in designing multipurpose rooms so that an operatic or choir group may have acoustics which give a fair notion of the sound it is producing while offering other users the most adequate conditions.

Organization and management is often, and most suitably, carried out by an elected group of representatives of users and other interested persons, a group that is often responsible to a central body (in Great Britain, often a Council of Social Service). Sometimes a full- or part-time warden is appointed whose task it is to foster community spirit and endeavor to supply the community's needs.

BIBLIOGRAPHY: National Council of Social Service, *Our Neighbourhood: a handbook of information for community centres and associations,* Revised edition, London, 1955; National Federation of Community Associations, *Building a Community Centre,* London, 1969.

COMMUTING The process of traveling between homes in one district or town and to places of work in another. Most commuting occurs around big cities and in metropolitan regions where places of work are in or near the city centers and the homes are in the suburbs and beyond. The gradual extension of commuting distances that occurs as commercial and industrial concentrations increase and the growth of urban sprawl create major transport problems in modern planning.

COMPENSATION AND BETTERMENT (*See* LAND VALUES AND PLANNING.)

COMPETITIONS (Town Planning) Instead of placing a direct commission with a planning consultant, a client, whether public authority or private developer, may prefer to promote a competition in order to obtain the design that best suits the purpose of the development. The competition system in planning, as in architecture and other related professions, offers a client certain distinct advantages. It gives him the chance to draw on a wider range of professional skills and expertise than might otherwise be accessible to him, and it provides an opportunity to stimulate fresh talent and original ideas as well as to demonstrate concern for good design and environmental quality.

Competitions can take several forms. They can be open to the general public (often as "ideas" competitions held as part of a participation program) or to all members of the appropriate professional institute; or they may be limited to a selected number of planners who are invited to compete. They may be held in one stage, for straightforward projects, or in two stages when a small number of competitors are selected to work out their proposals in greater detail for the final assessment.

Competitions are judged by "assessors," whose decision on the submitted designs is regarded as final. The assessors draw up the conditions of entry, which specify the form in which designs are to be submitted and other criteria. It is their task to award the premiums in accordance with the conditions and, where it is appropriate, to satisfy themselves that the winning competitor has the resources to carry out the work efficiently.

The Royal Town Planning Institute of the United Kingdom has made a comprehensive set of regulations for the guidance of promotors and competitors; its members are not permitted to enter any planning competition in the United Kingdom unless the conditions are based on the institute's regulations and have been approved by it. The regulations cover the promotion of competitions, the appointment and duties of assessors, deposits, entries, notification of result, exhibition of entries, premiums and honoraria, copyright, and the modification of designs. International planning competitions are controlled by the International Union of Architects and are adjudicated by international juries.

The financial outlay incurred by a competition promoter will not be appreciably more than for a direct commission, since the first premium is counted as payment of fees for work done up to the time of the competition result; the only additional costs are the second and third premiums (and/or honoraria), assessors' fees, and administrative costs. Consequently, the prize money can be made very attractive. The preparation of entries can involve competitors in considerable expense, and the scale of premiums and honoraria that are offered is expected to take account of the value of that effort.

Frequent subjects of planning competitions include residential layouts, community and neighborhood development, commercial and recreation centers, and urban parks. Work on the larger scale, such as regional plans and New Town proposals, are not generally regarded as suitable for the competition procedure in view of the heavy demands that the preparation of entries would entail on staff and resources and the range of complex data that would be required.

—HAROLD LEWIS

COMPLEX A term often used in planning to denote an aggregation or group of related and interconnected buildings or installations planned for the same purpose (e.g., industrial complex, school complex, hospital complex).

COMPULSORY PURCHASE In a planning context "compulsory purchase" refers to the compulsory purchase of land (including usually the buildings on it). In most countries the various official agencies of central and local government and the statutory undertakings (e.g., water supply agencies, national railway undertakings, etc.) have powers to compel landowners to sell their land so that it can be used for purposes relating to the functions of those agencies; i.e., public purposes. In the United States this compulsory purchase power is known as the power of "eminent domain," and appropriate public bodies acquire property by what are known as "involuntary condemnation proceedings." Occasionally the power of eminent domain is delegated to privately owned organizations to enable them to fulfill a public purpose. The public purposes for which land may be compulsorily purchased in this way vary widely from country to country and according to the type of agency. The assessment of compensation also varies widely from country to country but is commonly based on the market value of the land either in the proposed or the existing use, though it may also take account of any consequential losses or benefits to the owner other than the actual loss of his property.

BIBLIOGRAPHY: Desmond Heap, *An Outline of Planning Law,* 5th ed., Sweet & Maxwell, London, 1969; Robert McKown, *Comprehensive Guide to Town Planning Law,* G. Godwin, Ltd., London, 1964; R. N. D. Hamilton, *A Guide to Development and Planning,* Oyez Publications, 1970; Mary McLean (ed.), *Local Planning Administration,* International City Managers' Association, Chicago, 1959; Lewis Keeble, *Principles and Practice of Town and Country Planning,* Estates Gazette, Ltd., London, 1969 (includes comprehensive bibliography).

DAVID HALL

COMPUTERS IN PLANNING The digital computer offers the planner the opportunity to apply techniques which formerly would have been impossible because of the enormous volume of mathematical work they would have involved. Although it is no substitute for human reason, the computer, with its high-speed arithmetical ability, can allow rapid comparison of alternative courses of action.

While the writing of computer programs is in itself time consuming, virtually all the techniques which the planner can employ are based upon programs already written and available from the many organizations which offer digital computer capability for sale or hire.

The objectives of the plan having been clearly defined, alternative schemes to satisfy these can be devised. Such schemes can be tested with computer aid in terms of circumscribing considerations (e.g., sociological, cost-benefit, and finance). Systems analysis and statistical examination can be applied and a model solution derived. This can be further tested by examination in the light of any statistics available on similar projects already in existence.

The model solution having been decided upon, translation into a schedule of work can follow, this ranging from legislation, through acquisition of real estate, drainage, sewage, power and water supply provisions, to the complex of contracts and constructions involved in bringing the plan to finality.

Once scheduling is complete, activity/event networks for all levels of execution can be constructed with regard to logical sequence, each activity having estimates of time allocated to it.

A computer program is then written (or adapted) for the networks. Printouts will reveal the critical path (the sequence of interdependent activities and events which fixes the minimum time to completion). As work proceeds, progress is reviewed and revised data are fed to the computer. Subsequent printouts will indicate shifts in the critical path due either to optimism or pessimism in prior estimating. The plan can by these means be "managed by exception."

It will be seen from this brief resume that a great deal of computation is necessary to the operation of critical path analysis and its sophisticated developments, such as PERT (Project Evaluation and Review Technique), PERT/COST, and RAMPS (Resource Allocation Multi-Project Scheduling).

Except in the most elementary projects, with less than, say, 200 activities involved, operation without the digital computer would be impractical.

Without these techniques, every contributor to the project is usually driven to work at maximum pressure, usually with excessive or untimely commitment of resources. Further, at the stage where the plan is first evolved, the mass of mathematical work which arises from systems analysis, cost/benefit examinations, discounted cash flow application, and the general sifting of existing statistics can be executed—where formerly time and labor considerations would have deprived the planner of these invaluable aids.

—Douglas C. Bruce

CONCENTRIC PLAN   A plan where the roads and other dispositions are planned in rings round a center. It is usually combined with a radial plan, but whereas radial development is a natural evolution of settlements on either side of radiating roads, concentric development is often employed as a corrective to some of the disadvantages of radial development and is designed to improve communications between the communities that have grown on the radiating roads.

Basic diagrams for new or ideal cities are generally designed concentrically; Renaissance and baroque planning abounds in examples. It was also the basis of Howard's garden city concept.

CONSERVATION   The word "conservation" is used in two senses. In the broadest sense, it means the wise use and management of all our resources, both natural and man-made, and the careful planning of those resources to meet our future needs. The need to ensure a continuity in the supply of the natural resources so used and managed is often embraced by this definition. This is the sense in which the term is used in "European Conservation Year."

Conservation Areas   In its other sense "conservation" has a narrower meaning and refers to the conservation of buildings or groups of buildings and their surroundings. In this sense "conservation" means improvement, protection, or enhancement. In the United Kingdom Civic Amenities Act of 1967, provision was made for areas of good architectural quality or important historic significance to be defined as conservation areas, and the act made it the duty of the local authorities to identify and protect such areas. Such areas may comprise a whole village or even a small town, or they may be part of a town or city such as a street, a market square, buildings grouped around a cathedral or church, a great urban estate, or simply a unified terrace or crescent of buildings.

BIBLIOGRAPHY: Robert Arvill, *Man and Environment,* Penguin Books, Inc., Baltimore, 1969 (includes comprehensive bibliography); Her Majesty's Stationery Office, "Civic Amenities Act 1967," London, 1967, "Historic Towns: Preservation and Change," London, 1967.
—DAVID HALL

CONSULTANT   In the context of planning, the terms "consultant" and "planning consultant" denote, in their strictest sense, a qualified planner who has set up in private practice, as a principal or partner in a firm, to provide professional advice to clients on a fee-earning basis. Both terms are also used loosely to include practitioners in related fields who may contribute to various stages of the planning process.

There are an estimated 600 firms of planning consultants in the United States and 350 firms in the United Kingdom. Some 50 percent of these firms are consultants working on their own or with a few assistants, and most offer architectural as well as planning services. The trend in consultancy is toward larger practices with several partners, employing up to 50 qualified assistants together with other specialists. Small firms often collaborate in "group practices" or form consortia with specialist consultants to enable them to undertake large-scale commissions. Certain consultants prefer to concentrate their skills on specific aspects of planning, such as transportation or economic appraisals.

Three main fields of consultant activity are: (1) advising on planning procedures and the implications of planning proposals; (2) assisting local authorities to prepare development plans; and (3) for the larger firms, producing feasibility studies and strategies for development on the regional and New Town scale commissioned by government and other official agencies. In the United States, some consultants have adopted the role of "advocacy planners," representing specifically, on planning and social issues, the interests of underprivileged and inarticulate groups in the community.

—HAROLD LEWIS

CONURBATION A term coined by Patrick Geddes to describe a large concentration of urban communities. Planners in Britain speak of "the London conurbation," "the Tyneside conurbation," and so on.

COST-BENEFIT ANALYSIS In urban and regional planning, administrations are frequently faced with a number of alternatives. The technique of cost-benefit analysis can provide a comprehensive basis for comparison and enable objective judgment to be made. Although it is not a substitute for administrative decision making, the technique of cost-benefit analysis does provide quantitative terms upon which to judge, thus limiting the dangers of intuition and prejudice.

Methodology varies according to the nature of the problem, but in general it involves the following: (1) an identification of factors attracting cost and benefit, (2) evaluation of the significance of the factors, and (3) expression in value terms of both costs and benefits. This done, aggregates—all expressed in real money terms—of the costs and the benefits due to the different factors can be isolated.

In practice, costs of material factors present few problems. When nonmaterial factors are considered, the answers are not so straightforward. For instance, there is the value that is lost to the inhabitants of a rural environment when urban development takes place. This is difficult to estimate, as is the value "lost" by those who suffer industrial noise or pollution where formerly there was none. Although difficult, it is not impossible to place a money value on such factors. Things, conditions, environments, must surely be worth what people are prepared to pay for their retention. Valuation in money terms of such nonmaterial considerations may seem unfamiliar and even unreal, but it is nevertheless possible, and can be useful to the planner.

In new city development, considerable value can be apportioned to the benefits afforded by well-planned living conditions and the close proximity of places of work. In the presentation of analysis, it is important to define who is receiving benefit and who is paying cost and to consider, in so doing, the wider aspects of the problem. A state-supported new city venture may place the burden of cost on the population as a whole, while benefit may appear to accrue only to the city inhabitants. A broader view will reveal that the social benefits of planning policy are reflected on the state and national levels.

Costs and benefits can be set at different values according to the time scale of the plan. It is self-evident that a given sum spent now represents more expense than the same sum spent in 5 years' time since the money, invested in the interim, would bring in a return. Conversely, benefits derived now can be reckoned worth more now than in 5 years' time. A process of appropriate discounting of cost and benefit values must, therefore, be applied, and at the same rate of interest. As far as the individual is concerned, the time-preference rate of discount is a measure of the value which is put upon cost or benefit now as opposed to cost or benefit deferred—or, that discount rate r which makes the individual equally satisfied with $\$(1 + r)^n$ worth of income in any future year n as compared with \$1 at present. In the case of the community, a social time preference rate must be derived. This rate is not necessarily an average of individuals' rates but must also take account of political factors not usually considered by the individual. The choice of this social time preference rate falls to the administration and not to the cost-benefit analyst.

The analyst can advise upon the suitability of any scheme for application of the technique; he can enumerate the costs and benefits and place these in order of remoteness. But the administrator alone must decide which aspects are too remote to come into the account and he must determine both financial limits set by policy and the social time preference rate to be used. Finally, having regard to the criteria revealed by the analysis, the administrator must make the final decision.

BIBLIOGRAPHY: *Report of the Commission on Third London Airport,* vol. VII, H.M.S.O., London; Walsh and Williams, *Current Issues in Cost/Benefit Analysis,* H.M.S.O., London, 1970.
—DOUGLAS BRUCE

COUNTRY TOWNS EXPANSION   New towns (*q.v.*) in a populous country like Britain usually have to be based on existing villages or small towns. Where these are very small, a development corporation under the New Towns Acts is employed for each. For places that are already large enough to have a competent local authority, an alternative method of expansion was instituted through the Town Development Act of 1952. By this the authorities of great cities are empowered to make agreements with those of small boroughs or urban and rural district councils for the reception of some of their "overspill" population and industry, and to provide or make contributions to the cost of housing, factories, and community buildings, with financial aid also from the government and/or county councils. Though not now regarded as a full substitute for the New Towns Acts procedure, the Town Development Acts have proved a substantial supplement. Up to June 1971, agreements had been made by 10 authorities of the major conurbations, including London, Birmingham, Liverpool,

Manchester, Tyneside, Bristol, and Glasgow, with 115 expanding towns, for schemes for 191,200 dwellings. Of these, over 102,000 had been completed, housing about 340,000 persons, and new factories and workplaces had been provided in proportion. From London, for example, over 620 firms had moved into factories totaling nearly 24 million square feet.

—Frederic J. Osborn

CREMATION AND CREMATORIUM Although cremation was widely practiced among ancient civilizations, the traditional Christian method of the disposal of the dead was until the twentieth century, by body burial (inhumation).

In the late-nineteenth century cremation was revived (the first cremation was in Wales in 1883) and at first made very slow progress. During the middle of the present century, however, the progress has been much more rapid, particularly in Great Britain, the British Commonwealth countries, and the Scandinavian countries. In 1968 the cremations in terms of percentages of deaths were 51.22 percent in Great Britain, 37.2 percent in New Zealand, 35.8 percent in Australia, 37.9 percent in Denmark, 36.3 percent in Sweden, and 24.85 percent in Norway.[1] In the United States and West Germany, the spread of cremation has been much less marked. In West Germany in 1968 the cremations in terms of percentage of deaths were 12.59 percent, while the percentage figure for the United States and Canada in 1965 was 4.26 percent.[2] In France, Belgium, Italy, and Spain, the number of cremations is negligible.

The provision of crematoria has an effect on the number of cremations, and there can be little doubt that as these increase the percentage of the dead that are cremated will increase accordingly, but there still persists much religious opposition to cremation and it is doubtful whether this procedure will increase greatly in the Roman Catholic countries at least in the next few years. The advocates of cremation often say that it saves land for other purposes, but the amount of land used by cemeteries is so small (*see* CEMETERY) that it is not a valid reason.

Crematoria are either built in existing cemeteries or on new sites. Ashes are usually placed in urns and placed in a niche of a columbarium, or buried in a grave sometimes with a monument, or the ashes are scattered in a garden. For these purposes, therefore, provision generally has to be made for ground surrounding the crematorium, and this gives scope for effective and appropriate landscaping.

—Arnold Whittick

CUL-DE-SAC A street closed at one end, also called in residential areas a "close." Other expressions used are "blind alley" and "dead end," but these are not terms used in a purposeful planning sense.

Cul-de-sac planning has been very widely employed in residential areas

---

[1] These figures are taken from the International Cremation Survey published in *Pharos*, no. 3, vol. 35, August 1969.
[2] This appears to be the last year for which a figure is available.

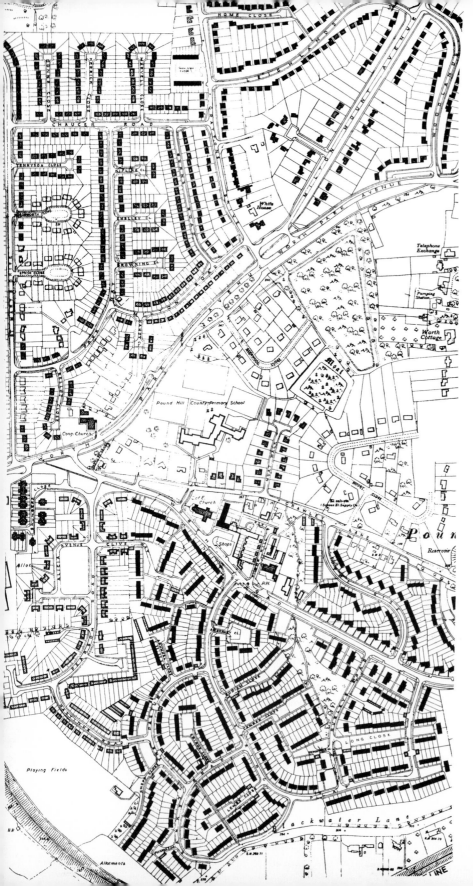

LEFT: *Examples of varied cul-de-sac planning in the neighborhood of Pound Hill, Crawley, England (1953–1956). The formal culs-de-sac in the northern part are mainly private development. The more irregular ones are in the southern part, by the Crawley Development Corporation.* RIGHT: *Cul-de-sac planning in Wildriding, Bracknell, England, where roads branch from a peripheral road to garages at the backs of houses while walks branch from a main central sidewalk.*

SENIOR PLAYING FIELDS

ENNERDALE

JUNIOR PLAYING FIELD

CAR PARK | PROPOSED CHURCH SITE

DEEPDALE

RESERVE SITE

CAR PARK

PROPOSED NURSERY SCHOOL SITE

NETHERTON

PEDESTRIAN
PASS

SITE FOR COUNTY COUNCIL
OLD PERSONS HOME.

RESERVE SITE

NEIGHBOURHOOD CENTRE

INFANTS

JUNIOR

CROSS FELL

PRIMARY SCHOOL

OXENHOPE

OLD CROSSWAITE ROAD

BISHOP DALE

PICKERING

N

ARNCLIFFE

ROSEDALE

JUNIOR PLAYING FIELD

JUNIOR PLAY AREA

during the mid-twentieth century because the cul-de-sac affords the advantage of residential seclusion and freedom from the noise and vibration of traffic while economically it compares satisfactorily with other forms of layout.[1]

A very wide variety of designs of *culs-de-sac* have been employed in residential planning, and these figure prominently in their many varieties in much residential development in Europe and the United States. *Culs-de-sac* branch either from a main or minor road and are either straight or curved, long or short, with a variety of terminations. *Culs-de-sac* may be T-shaped, circular, square, hexagonal, elliptical, rectangular, or other geometric shapes; and they may be of various sizes. Sometimes they are terminated with a fairly large place or square with small garden or parking area, and the terminal area may be linked with another by a walkway.

Variations on the *cul-de-sac* theme can be seen in most of the British New Towns and in many town extensions. One method is arranging houses round a plot, with a *cul-de-sac* or close running into the center and terminating in a square or irregular plot of grass with shrubs and trees onto which the houses face. Another method employs *culs-de-sac* branching in series from the residential or main road, a method which can be likened to tree branches from a main stem. This method is susceptible to many variations, one of which is the use of secondary branches.

Another variation, which is coupled with the purpose of segregation of vehicles and pedestrians in residential areas, is the layout, based on the plan for Radburn, a suburban development in New Jersey, made in 1929 by Henry Wright and Clarence Stein. In this plan *culs-de-sac* or service lanes run off a principal road and give direct access to the garages and backs of houses, the fronts of which face onto walkways and gardens. This Radburn layout is world-famous. It was followed in the planning of several of the British New Towns and has been the subject of many ingenious variations. One is a residential neighborhood area encircled by a road, through the center of which runs a walkway. Branching from the peripheral road are service *culs-de-sac* to the garages grouped around squares at the backs of the houses, while branching from the main central walkways are paths to the fronts of the houses. An approximation to this is in Wildridings, one of the most recently built neighborhoods of Bracknell, England.

BIBLIOGRAPHY: Clarence Stein, *Towards New Towns for America*, Cambridge, Mass., 1966; Frederic J. Osborn and Arnold Whittick, *The New Towns: The Answer to Megalopolis*, 2d ed., Leonard Hill, London, 1969.

—ARNOLD WHITTICK

CURTILAGE The land between a building and the boundary of the plot of land on which it stands. Sometimes the term also includes the land on which the building stands.

---

[1] See Barry Parker, "Economy in Estate Development," *Journal of the Town Planning Institute*, no. 8, vol. 14, London, 1928. Also Lewis Keeble, *Principles and Practice of Town and Country Planning*, 3rd ed., The Estates Gazette, Ltd., London, 1964, pp. 339–340.

CZECHOSLOVAKIA The Czechoslovak Republic was founded in the year 1918 after the disintegration of the Austro-Hungarian monarchy, when Central Europe was separated into a number of ethnic states of democratic constitution. Czechoslovakia inherited the largest industrial potential, for almost 85 percent of the industry of the former monarchy was concentrated in Bohemia and Moravia. It has further developed in a rapidly urbanizing environment. The pattern of settlements in Czechoslovakia was relatively dense and of medieval origin, which counteracted the process of urbanization. After World War II an intensive industrialization of economically backward Slovakia was started, and the integration of Czechoslovakia into a block of socialist states grouped on the periphery of the U.S.S.R. has been followed by the adoption of a system of planning—directive management—in economy, social politics, and development of settlements. In 1968 the political structure of the country was changed by the creation of a federation of the Czech and the Slovak Republics.

The area of the Czechoslovak Republic is about 50,000 square miles (129,000 square kilometers) with a population of about 15 million in about 12,000 communities. This means that the structure of settlements is relatively dense, the average distance between them being about $1\frac{1}{2}$ miles ($2\frac{1}{4}$ kilometers). The capital of the country, Prague, exceeded a million population several years ago. The capital of Slovakia, Bratislava, is undergoing very rapid growth, having recently exceeded a population of $\frac{1}{4}$ million. Only a few cities may be classed in this category: Brno, the capital of Moravia, and the industrial centers of Ostrava and Pløzen. Only nine cities have more than 50,000 population. The urban distribution is in industrial regions, such as the Silesian coal district with its metallurgical industry, the North Bohemian coal fields with chemical industries, and the East Slovakian combined steel works in a number of city regions.

Geographical and Climatic Conditions Czechoslovakia lies in that area of Central Europe where some of the most important rivers have their source. In Bohemia the Labe is an important waterway flowing into the North Sea at Hamburg, the Odra River rises in Moravia and flows into the Baltic Sea at Szczecin, and the Morava River discharges into the Danube near Bratislava. In its short stretch in Slovakia the Danube is fed by a number of tributaries from all parts of Slovakia.

The Czech basin is surrounded by sharply distinguished mountain ranges at the center of which lies Prague. Since prehistoric times Moravia has served as a gateway into the Danubian plain. Slovakia's northern boundary is defined by the distinct arch of the Carpathian mountain range with its characteristic High Tatra and Low Tatra ridges.

Climatically Czechoslovakia lies in the transition zone between the Atlantic and continental climate of middle Europe and enjoys excellent conditions for agriculture as well as for settlements distributed in the range of 650 to 1,650 feet (200 to 500 meters) above sea level. The only areas unsuitable for development are in the regions of the high mountains, which are, however, suitable for recreation. The High Tatra range attains a height of about 8,200 feet (2,500 meters).

Under these natural conditions the thousand-year history of urbanization in Czechoslovakia has left a system of settlements situated mostly in river basins, beyond the inundation areas and avoiding areas of sharp climatic changes. Whereas the first town formations evolved in the tenth century along the transport arteries or on their crossings, the town dispersals in the thirteenth century covered the whole territory with a network of commercial and trade centers. For this reason practically every town and almost every village has its historic center substantially influencing the urban development.

Examples of Regional Planning   In the feudal era many feudal lords pursued a colonization or dispersal policy in connection with economic and technological reorganization of their estates, including the foundation of villages and towns. Land-use planning in the modern sense in Czechoslovakia dates from the late eighteenth century. In this period the origin and growth of modern manufacturing industries produced concentrations of the population in the new industrial centers and a shift of the medieval residential centers to new communities, mainly locations of the textile industry. In this way the North Bohemian industrial belt developed which, later in the nineteenth century, was transformed into a zone of chemical industry as a consequence of the developing extraction of lignite.

Nineteenth-century industrialization created a new structure of settlements oriented toward the sources of raw materials, to the areas of the processing industries, and to new business and administration centers. In Bohemia and Moravia it was the growing metallurgical and mechanical industries as well as the food production industry that brought these changes, whereas Slovakia kept its agricultural and feudal character and structure. This period gave birth to some interesting industrial housing developments; e.g., that of the Ringhofer Company in Prague-Smichov in the second half of the nineteenth century. Most of these schemes are of inferior quality. Towns and cities grew as the result of suburban residential extensions, mostly in the form of apartment blocks or flats. The aim of these developments was the creation not of suitable human environments but of profit for the owners. This, of course, was a worldwide phenomenon.

Urbanization was intensified after 1948, when mechanization and collectivization of agriculture was started and when the population surplus from the regions of primary production came to towns and cities as providing the best opportunities for employment in the developing secondary production. The industrialization of Slovakia became an item of the political program, and it is there that the most important urbanization schemes have been carried out. Cities grow by means of individual "settlements," which are not "satellites" but suburban developments on the outskirts of cities. These are growths from the existing city core, creating functional and aesthetic disproportion which must be coped with in the next phase of planning.

The flow of labor from the primary into the secondary sphere of production and further on to the tertiary sphere[1] is occurring thanks to automation. For the time being it is still industry which absorbs labor, but this process is supposed to culminate in 1975 when labor employed in the secondary sphere will start to be released in favor of the tertiary sphere. This process emphasizes the urgency of reconstruction of central areas of our cities, the centers of tertiary activities. The question of the preservation of historic cores of cities, which constitute a valuable cultural legacy and which are menaced by this process, is important. The process of reconstruction of central areas of cities cannot be stopped, but it must be carefully examined in the light of every interest.

In Czechoslovakia a dense network of settlements has evolved. Hence, there is no need, in the complex process of urbanization, to concentrate on the introduction of further satellites, because any new developments crystallize around existing centers, which results in scattered settlements in areas which are perhaps suitable from the point of view of landscape, but which engender increased demands on transport into the places where jobs are concentrated. For this reason the concentration of settlements and the simplification of their structure is felt as an urgent need, because only larger units may be satisfactorily provided with services and city amenities.

Today about 50 percent of the population is in towns or cities, although regionally dispersed. Czechoslovak towns and cities melt into city regions; town planning is identified with regional planning and with the creation of a living environment of complex territorial wholes involving the main functions of city life, including housing, production, culture, and recreation. The intensive urbanization process in Czechoslovakia involves the necessity of national planning.

The creation of new cities is exceptional. The bulk of the urbanization process lies in the extension of cities, in addition to the urgent task of reconstructing central areas as well as preserving and reviving historic cores.

Legislation and Administration   Before the birth of the Czechoslovak Republic, the legislative and administrative patterns of the Austro-Hungarian monarchy included "building codes," eventually "municipal statutes," specifying among other items the height of cornices, the width of streets, vaguely the aesthetic aspects, but paying no attention to town planning as a specific subject. In the period of 1918 to 1945, including the period of German occupation, much work was done on the theory of town planning. Connecting links with economic management were sought, but the time was not ripe for legislation relating to modern town planning. It was only in 1948, when the country was integrated into the Soviet economic and political system and when Soviet planning patterns were accepted, that the

[1]Primary: agriculture; secondary: industry; tertiary: service (classification by the economists Colin Clark and Jean Fourastié).

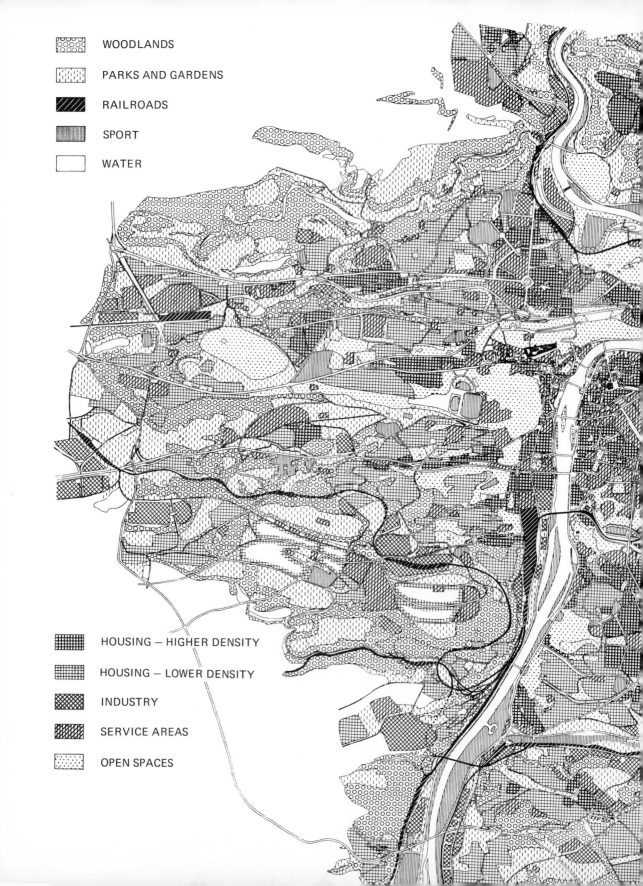

WOODLANDS

PARKS AND GARDENS

RAILROADS

SPORT

WATER

HOUSING – HIGHER DENSITY

HOUSING – LOWER DENSITY

INDUSTRY

SERVICE AREAS

OPEN SPACES

Urban and regional scheme for Prague, 1965. (Also see sketch plans on next page.)

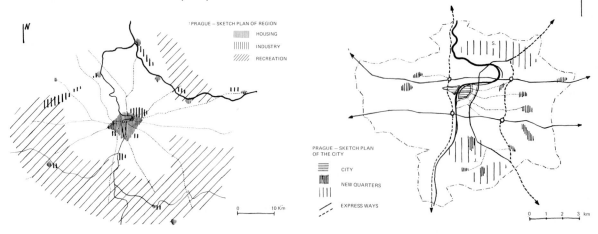

first land-use planning act was passed. It was restricted, however, to the problems of town planning, leaving the problems of the regions to be solved by economists. To make the matter clear: in the initial stage of economic planning it was believed that these economic planners were capable of solving problems of the territorial distribution of production, but even in the Soviet Union it became evident that there must be a "Gosplan"—economic planning—treating economic problems side by side with a "Gosstroy," which would solve the problems of physical planning. After 10 years of experience it became clear that an amendment of the act was necessary. This implied the introduction of "regional planning," which by that time had already proved its value.

In paragraph 1 of the amended land-use planning act of 1958, land-use planning is defined as a systematic activity concerned with the arrangement in space of all functions and factors of social life in accordance with the tasks of economic planning and on the basis of detailed investigations and surveys in the fields of anthropology and physical geography, culture, economics, sociology, and technology. The aim of land-use planning is to create organic spaces capable of further development in which a logical coordination is secured of workplaces, residences, leisure and cultural needs, allied to an efficient transport network. Land-use planning is concerned with coordination of investments with long-term operational economic planning. Paragraph 4 defines three levels of land-use planning, the highest of which is logically linked with economic planning and the lowest with engineering schemes.

Whereas the earlier act divided land-use plans according to their national and regional scope, an amendment to the act, which was adopted in 1970, does not define the planning stages in terms of territorial criteria but in terms of time, distinguishing (1) short-term plans of operational character, thus covering actual building schemes; (2) plans of long-term territorial developments for 15 to 20 years ahead; and (3) forecasts of territorial development for periods of 50 years and more as a fundamental guide to future development.

RIGHT AND BELOW: *Suburb*
Housing in Kolin, Bohem
(Architects: Zdenek Kuna a
Zdenek Stupk

Extension and rebuilding of Ml. Boleslav, Bohemia. (Architects: Osvald Dobert, Jaroslav Kosik, and Frantisek Rezac.)

New suburb in Brno, capital of Moravia. (Architects: Zounek and Associates.)

Extension of Ziar in central Slovakia.
(Architects: Ruzicka and Associates.)

A new feature in this act is the legalization regarding these "forecasts," the conception of which has already proved its justification in this country, in the highest level of time-performance of territorial plans. The main provisions for work, housing, cultivation of mind and body, and transport remain in force, although their consistent segregation cannot be emphasized any more, as required earlier.

The executive agencies of physical planning are the government ministries, while in Bohemia there are also county planning authorities. Larger cities have their own architects' departments responsible for the problems of land-use planning in the city region.

Education and Professional Practice Land-use planning is the proper domain of architects, but it is largely a matter of teamwork. The creative functions of the team are carried out by an architect/town and country planner, who is a graduate of the faculties of architecture and civil engineering from the technical universities of either Prague, Bratislava, or Brno. The planning teams include geographers, economists, natural scientists, and sociologists who cooperate in providing the foundations for regional plans. Whereas architect-planners play the leading part in preparing plans of settlements and constructional work, the higher levels of regional planning are dominated by planners of wider and more complex fields of interest comprehending other branches of knowledge, including various sciences which allow an objective approach to problems and who have attended special postgraduate courses organized by the faculty of architecture and civil engineering in Brno. They may be graduates of several university faculties which have some relationship to territorial planning.

Town and regional plans are worked out by the state's design offices or specialized design offices, by the county ("county" is used as English

Three views of Kosice, new subu
east Slovakia. (Architects: Horn
Kurca and Associa

equivalent for *kraj,* an administrative unit of about 4,000 square miles or 10,000 square kilometers area and 1 million inhabitants) design offices, (*Stavoprojekt*), or by institutes for regional planning in Prague and Bratislava and eventually by the state institute for reconstruction of historic cities, such as the Prague institute for planning of historical areas or by nonspecialized offices.

Institutions Architects—town and country planners working in the fields of land-use planning—are organized by the Union of Czech Architects and by the Union of Slovak Architects. The general secretariat of the former is in Prague 1, Letenska 5, that of the latter in Bratislava, Nalepkova ulica 15. These unions are collective members of the UIA, IFHP, and other international organizations. The other professions taking part in territorial planning are mostly organized by scientific and technical associations and are trying to found independent organizations of territorial planners.

The scientific and research institutions in the field of physical planning are the Research Institute of Building and Architecture in Prague, Bratislava, and Brno; the State Institute for Regional Planning, which is also concerned with theoretical problems of national and regional planning; the Institute of Construction and Architecture of the Slovak Academy of Sciences in Bratislava (Dubravska costa); the Institute for Environmental Studies of the Czechoslovak Academy of Sciences in Prague; the Department of Economic Geography, affiliated to the Geographic Institute of the Czecho-

slovak Academy of Sciences in Brno; and some other research units in Prague, Bratislava, and Brno affiliated to applied research institutes.

BIBLIOGRAPHY: In recent years, since 1960, a number of works on town planning have been published, mainly by the publishing departments of the Czechoslovak and Slovak Academy of Sciences. Among them are: B. Fuchs, *New Zoning;* E. Hruska, *Problems of Contemporary Town Planning;* J. Hruza, *Theory of the City;* O. Novy, *Decay of Large Cities.* Works by J. Stvan, T. Zalcik, P. Zibrin (Slovakia), V. Matousek, and V. Lorenc deal mostly with the problems of structure of settlements.

The monthly review *Architecture of CSSR,* published by the Union of Czech Architects, and the monthly, *The Project,* published by the Union of Slovak Architects in Bratislava, are both concerned with town planning. In addition, town-planning problems are discussed in the weekly *The Czechoslovak Architect,* published by the Union of Czechoslovak Architects in Prague.

Scientific problems of territorial planning are treated by the quarterly *Architecture and Town-Planning,* published by the Institute of Construction and Architecture of the Slovak Academy of Sciences in Bratislava. The bimonthly *Town and Territorial Planning,* containing general information of the town-planning department of the Research Institute of Construction and Architecture in Brno, has a very good standard. The *Terplan Information* as well as bulletins of other institutions concerned with the problems of town and territorial planning are issued at varying intervals.

—EMANUEL HRUSKA

D

DAYLIGHT IN BUILDINGS The amount of daylight admitted to buildings is one of the controlling factors in residential or other layouts. The required amount of daylight in a room for functional use is a percentage of the total light available outdoors under an unobstructed sky. This total outdoor light is known as the "daylight factor" (d.f.).[1] The area of a room nearest to the window would have the highest daylight factor, and this would lessen as the distance from the window increased. A good daylight factor for a room would be above a minimum of 2 percent d.f. for half the area, but what is considered good varies with the purpose of the room. If it is a laboratory that is planned to depend for certain periods on daylight, then the d.f. should be high, preferably 3 percent for the areas of primary use; but for a bedroom it could be as low as about 0.5 percent.

Daylight penetration depends on the measure of obstruction from neighboring buildings and trees. For good natural lighting indoors, windows should be large and the angle of light from outside should be as low as possible. In many closely built-up areas the angle of light is, of course, much too high for good natural lighting. The task for the planner in cities is often to provide the maximum accommodation while preserving a low

[1] See *The Lighting of Buildings,* Lighting Committee of the Building Research Board, H.M.S.O., London, 1944.

angle of light, generally not much above 30 degrees. It will be found, for example, that a bigger population can be accommodated in a certain area in tall blocks of flats with the same angle of light than in low blocks of flats or in two-story family dwellings.[2]

DEAD END (*See* CUL-DE-SAC.)

DECENTRALIZATION AND DISPERSAL "Decentralization" is a general term for several types of outward movement: (1) of persons from homes in inner urban areas to fringes of the same town or conurbation; (2) of industries and businesses from centers to such fringes; or (3) of both population and industry from inner areas to new towns or smaller towns, detached and at some distance from the built-up continuum. It is convenient to name type 1 "suburban expansion" and type 2 "subcentralization." For type 3, the term "dispersal" is now widely used. For the scattered spread of population and development at large over rural regions predicted by H. G. Wells in *Anticipations* (1902) and advocated by some theorists, the term "diffusion" would seem appropriate (*see* NEW TOWNS).

In the course of the industrial revolution of about 1750 to 1850, which began in Britain and spread later to Western Europe and the United States, population greatly increased and people flocked to the manufacturing towns. Closer and closer building resulted in a high concentration of dwellings, factories, and commerical premises. The need for housing greatly outstripped provision, and families crowded into dwellings without adequate water supply or sanitation, leading to a serious degradation in living conditions. As stated in the Report of the (Barlow) Royal Commission on the Distribution of the Industrial Population (London, 1940) this "concentration of population in the great towns . . . has been marked by a disastrous harvest of slums, sickness, stunted population and human misery."

The Barlow report reviewed the social, economic, and strategic disadvantages of these unhealthy concentrations and suggested as remedial measures redevelopment of the congested areas on more spacious lines together with "decentralization or dispersal" from such areas to garden cities, satellite towns, small towns, or other places (*see* NEW TOWNS).

Revulsion from the industrial towns—indeed from the industrial system itself—had prompted schemes for model communities in the country (*see* UTOPIA), most of which were never realized. A number of good housing projects, however, were founded in the nineteenth century by individual industrialists such as Robert Owen at New Lanark, Sir Titus Salt at Saltaire, the Cadburys at Bournville, and Lord Leverhulme at Port Sunlight. Elsewhere, there were Krupp's in the Ruhr, Goransson in Sweden, and several projects in Western Europe. Planned decentralization in the national sense began with the garden cities concept of Ebenezer Howard (*q.q.v.*).

---

[2] See Walter Gropius, *The New Architecture and the Bauhaus,* Museum of Modern Art, New York, 1936, pp. 72 and 73; 2d ed., London, 1965, pp. 104, 105.

Unplanned and haphazard suburban decentralization has, however, occurred in most big cities in the last hundred years. As central areas became more congested, smoky, squalid, and unhealthy, the middle classes escaped to the outskirts where there was more space, the air was cleaner, and the pleasures of the country were more accessible. This process was continually repeated, so that it was a kind of successive leapfrogging, transforming outer suburbs to inner. This has occurred in many of the big European and American cities. London is a particularly conspicuous example because there was much more horizontal than vertical extension, whereas in such cities as Paris and Berlin there has been a greater degree of vertical extension by means of tall apartment blocks.

Unplanned and haphazard decentralization in the form of suburban sprawl is not true decentralization, since it is accompanied by a further centralization of industry and business. It is motivated by the quest for desirable homes but is not related to the location of workplaces, and it has resulted in an increasing separation of these along with an extension of daily commuting, with its many economic and social disadvantages. It produces an intractable transit and traffic congestion problem and further divides the residents of central areas from the open country. Nevertheless, where a city is not outrageously large, planned suburbs of an open character can be added to it with advantage, up to a point. The trouble is that the process is carried much too far. Suburbs must have a stop (*see* GREENBELTS).

Planned decentralization, apart from the small industrial communities mentioned, began to emerge as a policy of planning at the beginning of the century. The two principal methods which have been advocated and been the subjects of vigorous propaganda involve (1) planned continuous urban extension and (2) New Towns or new communities well separated by open country from central congested areas. The former can be of many kinds. It is really planned suburban development which avoids making the suburb too much a dormitory by dispersing a degree of industry with the population. Each extension is a small community with its own shopping center, and there are numerous examples in Europe and America. Some of the best planned are Vallingby and Farsta on the outskirts of Stockholm. Such developments have sometimes been confused with that of satellite towns or New Towns. Another method often advocated, and sometimes partly realized, is extension in the form of a star pattern with green wedges coming near the center; while another is linear development in the form of a series of communities, each with its own center, in planned relation to industry and all linked together near main traffic arteries.

Decentralization by means of New Towns has generally been the most favored and satisfactory method. It has been applied most completely in Great Britain but also to an extent in many other countries including the United States, Germany, France, and the Soviet Union. As previously mentioned, it began with the ideas of Ebenezer Howard, which led to the building of Letchworth, commenced in 1903, the first "garden city," and the model for successive New Towns.

In addition to social and economic reasons, decentralization has sometimes taken place for strategic reasons, which have provided a further reason for the policy. In France, strategic decentralization has been adopted for the aircraft industry; and in the United States for nuclear armaments.

Decentralization that includes employment as well as population involves the migration of industrial and commercial businesses from overcrowded cities to other places. Since each business has its own special requirements, such as sources of materials, markets, premises, and classes of workers, relocation cannot be simply dictated, at any rate in free enterprise states. The methods employed, for example in Britain, are therefore (1) planning restrictions on settlement or expansion in overconcentrated places, and (2) inducements to go to a choice of places, New Towns or suitable towns in regions where more development is nationally desired. These inducements may be the provision of factories or office buildings, or sites for these, housing for workers, rail and road communications, and good shopping, educational, recreational and other amenities. In Britain there are also capital grants to firms settling in regions suffering a high percentage of unemployment or the decline of older industries. These measures have varied over the years, and are the subject of constant political and local pressures and controversy. Though not completely successful, they have had substantial effects.

—FREDERIC J. OSBORN

DECUMANUS The principal straight street of a Roman town, generally running east-west and crossed toward one end by the *cardo* (*q.v.*).

DEFENSE, PLANNING FOR The great changes that have taken place in methods of warfare during the twentieth century have greatly affected urban planning for defense. From ancient times to the early-nineteenth century, many cities and towns in Europe were surrounded by defensive walls. Great Britain dispensed with these defensive walls centuries earlier because, being isolated by the sea and not having been invaded for many centuries, the British enjoyed an unusual sense of security. With the development of air warfare, a different kind of defense arose. It was necessary to provide protection and shelter from air attack, while, from the standpoint of planning, defense required the dispersal of population and industry rather than their concentration in large cities. The widespread vulnerability to nuclear war, however, has prompted doubts as to whether dispersal is effective defense, especially in small countries, and in consequence it must be admitted that defense considerations do not figure largely in present planning policies. Yet it must be acknowledged that large regional concentrations of population alongside very large areas that are sparsely populated, a situation that obtains in many countries, makes a country more vulnerable in modern warfare than if the population and industry were more widely and evenly distributed.

—ARNOLD WHITTICK

DEINOCRATES A Rhodian or, according to less reliable sources, a Macedonian architect in the time of Alexander the Great.

Ancient sources do not agree on his exact name. Vitruvius refers to him as Deinocrates; Plutarch as Stassicrates; while Strabo confuses him with Cheirocrates, another fellow architect. Plutarch (*De Alexandri magni fortuna ant virtute,* II, 335c) and Vitruvius (*De architectura,* II, preface) give details (mixing facts with fiction) of the handsome looks, honesty, and generally imposing aspect of the architect.

The contribution of Deinocrates in the construction of Alexandria in 331 B.C. is now considered as certain. He is responsible for the planning and architectural appearance of the new city. The large dimensions of the Hippodamian system which Deinocrates applied in the street layout of the new city are noteworthy: while in Miletus, for example, the main thoroughfares are not more than 23 feet (7 meters) in width, in Alexandria the two main vertical arterial axes have a width of 98 feet (30 meters). These large dimensions, together with the impressive monuments and the parks, must be attributed to the advanced conceptions of Deinocrates.

Strabo's presumption that Deinocrates rebuilt the burned temple of Artemis at Ephesus is now considered erroneous and is attributable to the confusion of the name of Deinocrates with the name of Cheirocrates (see Fabricius, *Real Encyclopaedie,* vol. IV, 2, col. 2393).

Deinocrates became famous for his fanciful plan to transform Mount Athos into a gigantic figure of Alexander the Great. This figure, whose base would be washed by the waves of the sea, would have held in one hand a walled city of 10,000 inhabitants, while in the other, inside a huge bowl, it would collect the waters from all the rivers of the region and let them fall majestically into the sea. According to ancient evidence, Alexander admired but finally rejected this plan because, according to Vitruvius, it was impracticable, and according to Plutarch because he considered it impious and provocative. The same wild imagination is shown in another anecdote concerning Deinocrates told by Plutarch (*Alexander,* 72): Deinocrates is presented as the instigator for the construction of an extremely expensive and grandiose pyre for Alexander to honor the memory of Hephaestion, his general.

Deinocrates, however, seems to be identified with the new tendencies in architecture and ekistics as they emerged in the Greek, metropolitan, and peripheral world at the end of the fourth century B.C. During this period, under the Asiatic and Egyptian influence, a group of Greek architects demonstrated their technical ability by showing preference for large and even colossal constructions which would develop and transform the natural scenery. Thus the boundaries between sculpture and architecture were abolished, and the way was left open for Hellenistic and Roman art on the one hand and on the other for the baroque art of the Renaissance.

BIBLIOGRAPHY: W. Körte, "Deinokrates und die baroche Phantasie," *ANTIKE,* vol. 13, pp. 289–312, 1937; R. Martin, *L'Urbanisme dans la Grèce Antique,* Paris, 1956, pp. 24–29.
—DEM. MARONITIS

DEMOGRAPHY (a compound of δρμos—people—and γραφn—graphe)   The collection of vital economic and social statistics and of related matters concerned with the racial makeup, growth, density, and distribution of a national, regional, or city population. Demographic studies are essential preliminaries of large-scale regional and urban planning and are an important part of the survey preceeding the plan.

DENMARK

Legislation and Administration   Local planning in Denmark is based on the Town Planning Act of 1938, according to which the communes are obliged to prepare town plans for all urban settlements with more than 1,000 inhabitants. In practice, the communes have primarily prepared "disposition plans" (master plans), which are not based on any law and are not binding on the landowners. On the other hand, after the approval of a master plan by the ministry, the commune is bound to observe the provisions of the plan. Town-planning bylaws, binding on the landowners, are usually prepared by the communes for small areas when special problems arise. By the Building Act of 1960 (not covering Copenhagen), a third type of planning was introduced whereby communes with urban settlements of more than 1,000 inhabitants can fix details in built-up areas through building bylaws which have to be approved by the Ministry of Housing.

The above-mentioned types of plans are primarily restrictive land-use plans in the sense that they delimit zones for various purposes (residential, industrial, recreational, agricultural, mixed, etc.) and allow various building heights and intensities. They also reserve areas for roads and public institutions. They do not, per se, indicate when the various projects are to be executed. However, the master plans are now, in the most advanced cases, combined with a long-term communal economic and investment plan.

According to administrative practice, the commune is almost sovereign as regards its town planning policy. The approval procedure in the Ministry of Housing deals primarily with formal questions. The 1970 communal reform has amalgamated the previous 1,400 communes to about 275, and it is generally expected that these bigger communes will be able to cover the country with town plans of a satisfactory standard.

A special Act on the Planning of the Køgen Bay Area was passed in 1961 for the planning of eight small communes southwest of Copenhagen. In this area the planning responsibility has been delegated to a committee with representatives from the state and the communes in question. The committee has prepared a master plan which, because it indicates a sequence of stages in which the development will take place, is unique in Denmark.

From 1949, The Regulation of Built-up Areas Act authorized the Ministry of Housing to appoint town development committees for regions where there is a need to control the growth of built-up areas. The committee consists of representatives of the communes involved. Its task is to prepare a town development plan dividing the area into an inner zone, where building is allowed; an intermediate waiting zone; and an outer zone where building is forbidden except for farming purposes.

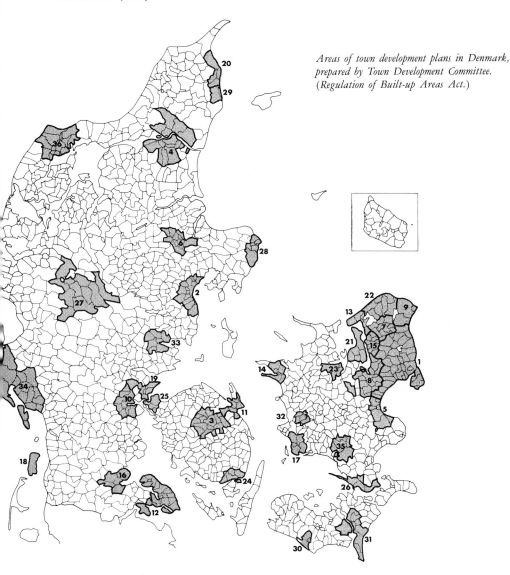

Areas of town development plans in Denmark, prepared by Town Development Committee. (Regulation of Built-up Areas Act.)

In 1970, this legislation was superseded by an Urban and Rural Zones Act, according to which the total area of Denmark was to be divided into urban and rural zones binding on the landowners.

The Preservation of Nature Act of 1937, amended several times, contains a number of provisions aiming at preserving the natural environment and making it accessible to the public. This legislation falls within the competence of the Ministry of Cultural Affairs. By an ammendment in 1959, regional preservation planning committees were introduced. These committees have prepared landscape analyses which have formed the basis for final preservation and for the designation of summer-house zones by virtue of the planning legislation.

There is no legislation for regional planning in Denmark. However, in some cases regional planning has been carried out through voluntary co-operation between the communes and counties of a region. In recent years, the Ministry of Housing has subsidized such work up to a third of the costs.

In the Copenhagen region, regional planning took place on private initiative just after World War II, resulting in the 1947 Finger Plan. The city development plan for the Copenhagen region was based on its principles. A new regional plan was presented in 1960, but it was not possible to obtain general agreement on the proposals, and through the sixties only a provisional first-stage plan existed as a guideline. In 1967, a new regional council was set up by the local authorities, and a new regional plan is in preparation.

Around some of the major provincial towns, similar planning work has been done in the sixties, notably in the Aarhus, Odense, and Esbjerg regions. In northern Jutland, a much larger area consisting of three counties has established a regional planning scheme.

It is expected that some legislation for regional planning will be passed after 1970, as the 22 former counties outside the Copenhagen region have been amalgamated into 11 new ones. National planning was started in 1961 by a government decision. A National Planning Committee was established, consisting of representatives on chief section level from the various ministries.

Only in two cases has the committee prepared reports on main policy issues, namely on an overall land-use policy (in the 1962 Zoning Plan) and on the division of Denmark into planning regions. The committee has done little coordination work and has not had any meeting since 1966, when the government set up a committee of ministers to study a reorganization of the planning work. After the change of government in 1968, the new government appointed a planning committee of ministers, and later in the year it launched a so-called "perspective planning" program (long-term economic planning). According to this, all ministries are to prepare plans for their activities up to 1985. A small steering group consisting of the directors-general of the Treasury, the Ministries of Economic Affairs and of Housing, and the Prime Minister's office supplies general guidelines, gross national product and population forecasts, and coordinates the work of the sector ministries.

In 1959 a new Slum Clearance Act was passed, revising the law in this field for the first time since 1938. The act authorized municipalities to prepare plans for the clearance of unhealthy areas or areas with high fire risks. If the plans were approved by the Ministry of Housing, the local authorities had the right to expropriate the buildings within the area and receive economic aid from the government to carry out the slum clearance program. Government aid is still given to compensate for half the losses resulting from the clearance, the other half being covered by the municipality.

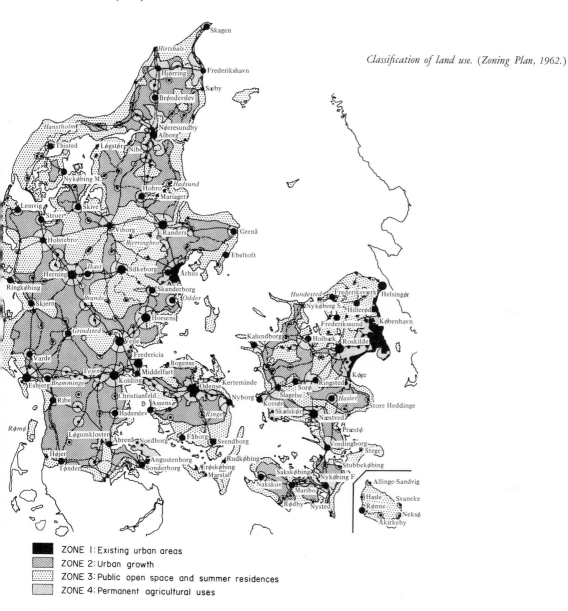

Classification of land use. (Zoning Plan, 1962.)

ZONE 1: Existing urban areas
ZONE 2: Urban growth
ZONE 3: Public open space and summer residences
ZONE 4: Permanent agricultural uses

As the resulting slum clearance had been very limited, a new revision of the law was passed in 1969. According to this, not only municipalities but also authorized slum-clearance societies can prepare plans and obtain government aid.

Professional Practice The planning profession in Denmark, as defined by membership in the Association of Town Planners, consisted of 524 persons in 1969. Of these, 218 were architects, 138 engineers, 58 surveyors, 36 economists, 21 were educated in other social sciences, and 63 were listed as "others" (including some politicians and other nonprofessionals).

There are no statistics available on their jobs. Many work on a local level with the preparation of site plans for private and semiofficial building companies. This is primarily architects' work. The majority may be working on the preparation of town plans for the communes. In small communes, this job is generally performed under contract by a local consulting surveyor or architect or with assistance of the county road office. In middle-sized towns, the city engineer prepares the plans, in many cases with the assistance of a bigger, specialized planning-consultant firm. About ten such firms exist in Denmark, most of them in Copenhagen. The majority are staffed by architects, a few by traffic engineers or economists. The largest cities have their own town planning office attached to the city engineer's or the city architect's office or—as in Copenhagen since 1968—forming a department of its own.

Of 450 master plans submitted for approval to the Ministry of Housing up to 1966, 161 were prepared by engineers, 82 by architects, 88 by surveyors, and the rest by mixed teams. The town development committees usually have their plans prepared by the county road office or the county architect; in one case a committee has established its own secretariat. The regional preservation-of-nature planning committees have established secretariats or are assisted by the county architects. The voluntary regional planning committees have in some cases hired private consultant firms to prepare the plans. In other cases, as in the Copenhagen region, they have established their own secretariats which are staffed by mixed teams. On the national level, the Ministry of Housing, for the approval procedure of local plans, is assisted by its technical consulting office staffed by architects, engineers, and surveyors. The secretariat of the National Planning Committee has a mixed staff of economists, geographers, sociologists, engineers, and architects, whereas the planning prepared in the Treasury and the Ministry of Economic Affairs is mainly by economists.

In some sector departments, special offices are already doing planning work; in others, planning may require the establishment of such offices. The staff-members will usually have normal training for the sector administration in question.

Education and Training Traditionally, until long after the first planning acts, the administration of the various physical aspects of town planning was taken care of by architects and engineers without special education.

The town planning institute 'Dansk Byplanlaboratorium' was founded in 1921, and its main purpose was to promote the study of town planning, to assist institutions and persons interested in town planning, and to inform the public on town planning questions. This institution has organized courses for town planners and for many years offered the only instruction available. In recent years the courses have been especially for staff members without academic training, the re-education of academic planners having been taken over by their own organizations. Dansk Byplanlaboratorium has established a library which has an excellent basic collection, although it has only to a limited degree been able to keep pace with the recent growth in urban planning literature.

In the 1950s, the students at the Academy of Fine Arts (architects), at the Polytechnic High School (engineers), at the Agricultural High School (surveyors), and at the University of Copenhagen (geographers and economists), on their own initiative, formed an annual common course in town planning. The purpose of the course was to create better understanding and cooperation between the groups involved. Town planning in these schools and faculties was only a secondary subject. A separate department for town planning was established at the School of Architecture in 1960. Since then, the subject has become more important at the various high schools and faculties, and new specialization has become involved.

It has often been discussed whether or not a school devoted primarily to town planning should be established in Denmark; but the decision has always been that, in order to become a valuable town planner, the student should obtain a basic education as a specialist and be trained in cooperative group work with other specialists.

Therefore, re-education has become a very important factor in the training of town planners. In recent years the professional organizations have arranged a large number of re-education courses which are open to all planners.

Institutions The oldest planning institution in Denmark, the Dansk Byplanlaboratorium (Danish Society for the Promotion of Town Planning), already mentioned, is governed by a body of representatives of the ministries involved in planning, of the organizations of the communes, of the professional organizations, and of societies in related disciplines. It organizes big national conferences for politicians and planning staff members and smaller seminars on special problems. It has, on several occasions, taken the initiative in planning (e.g., work in the Copenhagen region in 1945 and planning research at the State Building Research Institute in 1962). However, its freedom to maneuver has been limited by the fact that it is governed by representatives of many powerful institutions with, in some cases, conflicting policies.

In 1948, the review *Byplan* was started as a forum for urban, regional, and national planning as a joint Danish-Norwegian venture. After some years, it has become a purely Danish enterprise.

Research in planning has for some time been carried out at the university and other educational institutions mentioned under "Education and Training." Some of the bigger administrative offices as well as the Institute for Center Planning occasionally do research work. An institution with research as its only purpose was set up in 1962, when a government grant was made available for this purpose. It was organized as a town planning department under the State Building Research Institute, but with its own governing body, the Town Planning Research Committee, which also coordinates the research at the various institutions mentioned.

Planners in Denmark belong to various professional associations according to their education and functions: associations of architects, engineers, surveyors, and economists. Some of these have special sections or committees for town planning. Feeling that none of the existing institutions gave sufficient opportunities for professional debate on urban planning and development, some young planners in 1960 started a series of discussion meetings. On the basis of this initiative, the Association of Town Planners was founded in 1963. Membership is open to all interested persons and in 1970 was about five hundred.

Geographical and Climatic Conditions Denmark is situated on the northwestern side of the European continent, at 55 to 57 degrees north latitude and 8 to 12 degrees east longitude. The climate is temperate with a high degree of maritime influence, giving winter and summer temperatures of about 32 and 62 degrees Fahrenheit (0 and 17 degrees centigrade) and abundant rainfall the whole year round. The country has an area of 16,500 square miles (43,000 square kilometers) and consists of the peninsula of Jutland and several hundred islands, of which Zealand is the biggest. The landscape is undulating or flat, formed by moraines and water deposits from the ice age. The intricate and almost omnipresent coast is a unique feature in the landscape.

The population of Denmark is about five million (1971) and is growing at an annual rate of 0.6 to 0.8 percent. This corresponds to the birth surplus, whereas the international net migration is negligible. The average population density is thus 300 persons per square mile (115 per square kilometer); however, there are marked regional variations from the highly urbanized eastern and central parts of the country to western Jutland, where densities amount to less than a third of the average. For the country as a whole, the degree of urbanization, as measured by the share of the population living in urban settlements with more than 1,000 inhabitants, is about 70 percent. If the dispersed population in suburbanized zones is added, the figure reaches 75 percent, and it is rapidly increasing. The dominating metropolis is Copenhagen, which with its contiguous suburbs has 1,400,000 inhabitants. If the total commuting zone within a radius of more than 30 miles (50 kilometers) is included, the Copenhagen region has 1,700,000 inhabitants or 35 percent of the total population of Denmark. Other major cities are Aarhus (250,000 inhabitants), Odense (175,000), Aalborg (150,000), and Esbjerg (75,000).

The economic structure of Denmark is illustrated by the fact that, in 1969, 12 percent of the active population was working in primary occupations (agriculture and fisheries), 38 percent in secondary activities (manufacturing and construction), and 50 percent in the tertiary sector (trade, transport, private and public services). Agriculture was, until recently, a main economic sector, accounting for the major part of Denmark's exports. However, in the 1960s, employment in agriculture and its share of the national export has been rapidly decreasing. In manufacturing industries, production and export are increasing, and employment is relatively stable

Growth of population in Denmark, 1960 to 1965. Urban growth is concentrated mainly in the Copenhagen region and around the larger provincial towns of Aalberg, Aarhus-Sil-Keborg-Herning-Holstebro, Esbjerg, and Odense.

OVER +12%

+8 – +12%

+4 – + 8%

0 – + 4%

+4 –   0%

UNDER +4%

in the country as a whole. There is increasing employment in manufacturing in middle-sized towns and small towns and a decrease in the major cities. Employment in the tertiary sector is growing rapidly everywhere; this is particularly true of specialized services in the metropolitan areas.

Traditions of Planning to the End of the Nineteenth Century   Almost all Danish towns of any importance existed at the end of the Middle Ages. From 1660 onward, the development of the provincial towns was deliberately restrained for about 200 years by the absolute monarchy, which found it necessary to concentrate the growth on Copenhagen. Not until the second half of the nineteenth century did the provincial towns develop, mainly due to a change from agriculture to cattle farming but also because of the railways that were being constructed after 1860. The 200 years of absolute monarchy had a great influence on the development of Danish towns. Except for the nationwide construction of royal roads in the eighteenth century and the building of royal castles and estates around the country, there was no overall physical planning outside Copenhagen and North Zealand during these centuries.

Copenhagen was a fortified town at about A.D. 1200, but its real growth and development dates from the middle of the seventeenth century. King Christian IV wanted to make Copenhagen a city which, in scale and wealth, would rank with Amsterdam and other important Continental cities of the time.

Among many other enterprises, Christian IV transformed Copenhagen from a little mediaeval town to a city with fortifications large enough to contain the development in the following two centuries. Within these fortifications, in the middle of the eighteenth century, a new town called Frederiksstaden was built next to the old one. This new town was based on a grid network of streets around Amalienborg, the new royal estate.

The population of Copenhagen grew in these two centuries from about 40,000 to 130,000. The city became tightly packed and, as the fortifications had lost their military value, the town spread over the neighboring open land. Before the turn of the century—within about 40 years—the land up to 2 miles (3.2 kilometers) around the old city became packed almost as tight with housing and industrial areas as the old city itself. This development occurred without planning, and this was also the case with all other Danish towns during the same periods.

Twentieth-century Planning   Even though the growth in urban population has been relatively rapid toward the middle of the twentieth century, it has not been possible to plan completely new towns and communities. As big areas of heath were cultivated in the inland of Jutland, Herning grew up rapidly around a road intersection and became an important town and a center of the textile industry. The structural change in Danish farming developed the need for an export harbor on the North Sea coast, and this need led to the development of Esbjerg, which today is one of the bigger towns in Denmark. These towns developed without preparatory town planning.

Growth in urban areas has taken the form of extensions to existing towns. Planned growth first took place in Copenhagen after the Second World War. In 1947 the so-called "Finger Plan" was published, in which the idea was to concentrate growth in neighborhood units along railways and roads in fingers from the old city, mainly toward the west and north.

The previously mentioned Act on the Planning of the Kogen Bay Area

(1961) made possible detailed planning along one of these fingers. The plan contains a segregated traffic system throughout the whole area, linking industrial areas and residential neighborhood units with their related facilities such as shopping centers, schools, and nurseries. Many of these areas are now (1973) under construction.

Along the other finger to the west, less coordinated plans were made, commune by commune, as here there were already existing, unplanned settlements. However, the plan of Albertslund built in the mid-sixties, is notable for its time. It contains about 3,000 dwellings consisting of atrium houses, two-story row houses, and apartment blocks. There is a shopping center near the railway station, and there are two schools as well as several institutions for smaller children. Here also is a segregated traffic system.

Between and around these fingers, detailed plans for extensive recreational areas have been worked out in recent years. However, the existing development to the north was so haphazard that it did not allow for large-scale, coordinated planning.

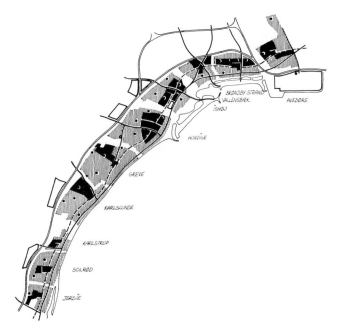

Master plan for the Köge Bay Area, 1961. Adopted 1966. Based on the structure of the Fingerplan, 1947. New Towns are planned along the coast around the railway stations of a new line to Copenhagen.

In the early sixties, pressure from the unexpectedly large growth in population and traffic did not allow for a continuation of the single-centered structure. Plans were developed for concentrating a large number of employment areas and central functions in two new centers to the north and the west of the region in order to relax the pressure on the old city. The necessary agreements were lacking, due to the fact that authority in the Copenhagen region is divided up into about a hundred local communes and three counties beside the various state authorities.

There are many notable examples of good physical planning on a small scale in Denmark, but regional coordination is lacking, making it almost impossible to carry through any planning in the existing, inner parts of the bigger towns, especially in Copenhagen.

In the sixties, town planning became an important factor in many provincial towns and has, together with economic planning, become a tool for the local politicians. This, together with a reform in the administrative pattern, has made it possible to plan for town development to a greater extent and with more certainty.

Project for a large new regional center west of Copenhagen in Hoge Tostrup, which will serve the new residential areas in the region.

BIBLIOGRAPHY: Steen Eiler Rasmussen, *Town and Buildings,* Danish Edition, 1949, English edition: Liverpool University Press, 1951; *Slum Clearance Act of June 5th, 1959; The Regulation of Built-Up-Areas Act of March, 1959,* (English and German editions); Bibliography of selected literature on town planning and housing in Denmark, in languages other than Danish, or with a summary in languages other than Danish, August 1961; *Introduction to the National Zoning of Denmark,* National Planning Committee, Copenhagen, 1962; *Town Planning Act of April, 1962,* (English and German editions); *Report of the Technical Committee Appointed to Examine the Preliminary Outline Plan for the Copenhagen Metropolitan Region,* Copenhagen Regional Planning Office, Copenhagen, 1964; W. R. Simonsen, *Long Term Programmes of the City of Copenhagen,* 1964; *Survey of Danish Planning Legislation,* The Secretariat of the National Planning Committee, Copenhagen, 1965 (English and German editions); Vagn Rud Nielsen, *Problems of Land Use Planning,* Ministry of Housing, Copenhagen, November 1965; *Long-term Planning and Industrialization of Housebuilding in Denmark,* Ministry of Housing, Copenhagen, 1965 (English and French editions); *Danish Town Planning,* Ministry of Housing, Copenhagen, 1966; *Planning Regions in Denmark,* The Secretariat of the National Planning Committee, Copenhagen, 1966; *La Legislation de la construction, les plans urbains et regionaux,* Ministere de l'Habitation, Copenhagen, February 1966.

—KNUD EJVIND RASMUSSEN

DENSITY   In planning usage, "density" means the ratio of persons, households, or volume of building or development to some unit of land area. Thus, population density is the number of persons per square mile or square kilometer in a country, or state, or region (see POPULATION). Residential or housing density is variously expressed in numbers of dwellings, households, habitable rooms, or persons per acre or hectare. The prescription of maximum housing densities is an important tool of planning control for preventing overcrowding and for safeguarding environmental amenities. In Great Britain for example, from 1919 onward, housing laws imposed a normal maximum density in new urban housing of 12 dwellings an acre and in rural districts of 8 an acre, though somewhat higher densities were permitted in large towns. Later, much higher densities were allowed for multistory dwellings: under the London plans of 1944 to 1945, densities of 136 persons an acre, and in certain central areas 200 an acre, were conceded. In some other countries, very much higher permitted densities prevail.

Raymond Unwin's famous maximum of 12 dwellings per acre was related to the net area of the house plots only. With access roads, the equivalent density was about 10 dwellings per acre. It is the latter calculation that is now known as "net residential density"; and in the British New Towns the usual maximum for small, low-price houses ranges between 12 and 18 dwellings an acre with a few exceptions up to 24 an acre, which of course

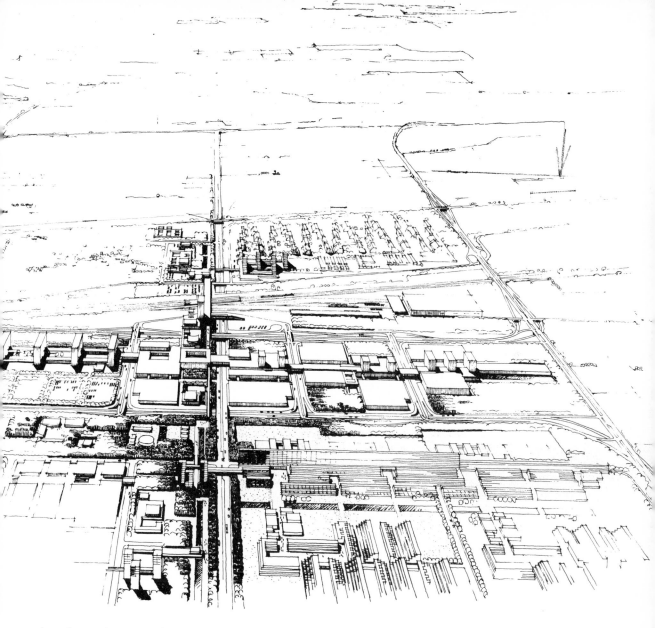

much reduces the size of private gardens. In suburban (largely owner-occupied) districts in Britain, the United States, and many other countries, residential densities are commonly much lower, varying from 8, 6, or 4 dwellings an acre to 1, 2, or more acres a dwelling. The question of maximum (and minimum) density standards is one of intense controversy, affected by popular demand, pressures on space, and, it should be added, professional theories and fashions of dubious validity.

Business density is measured in various ways: by floor space or number of employees per acre or hectare of plot area (floor-space index). Here again national and local planning standards vary very widely.

Neighborhood density (in Great Britain and United States) is that of a local, mainly residential section of a town, including its dwellings, access roads, shops, schools, churches, community buildings, and minor open spaces. Overall town density is the population per acre or hectare in the whole built-up area of a city or town.

BIBLIOGRAPHY: J. B. Cullingworth, *Housing Needs and Planning Policy,* 1960; Kevin Lynch, *Site Planning,* 1962; Ministry of Housing & Local Government, *Density of Residential Areas,* 1962; Robin H. Best, *Land for New Towns: A Study of Land-Use Densities and Agricultural Displacement,* 1964; Frederic J. Osborn and Arnold Whittick, *The New Towns: The Answer to Megalopolis,* 1969.

—FREDERIC J. OSBORN

DERELICT LAND The Department of the Environment in the United Kingdom precisely defines derelict land as "land so damaged by industrial or other development that it is incapable of beneficial use without treatment." By this definition it is essentially land that has been damaged by man's intervention and not land that has simply been neglected. However, land which is neglected or unsightly, be it due to man's intervention or not, and which cannot be put to beneficial use without treatment is usually included in the general meaning of the term. Thus there is a wide range of specific types of derelict land: spoil heaps and holes arising from all forms of mineral extraction, bombed sites in built-up areas, land covered by industrial effluents, demolished or semidemolished buildings, land formerly used for development or agriculture and now overgrown, and disused military camps or aircraft runways. Land that is unused by virtue of its natural characteristics, e.g., desert or jungle, is not termed derelict. In developed countries the most common form of derelict land is that caused by mineral extraction and industrial activity, and such land is often the aftermath of industrialization. In the United Kingdom two-thirds of the derelict land is designated as such because of either spoil heaps or holes. In spite of official measures to treat derelict land in developed countries, it is thought that its extent is increasing, particularly as the result of continuous mineral extraction.

BIBLIOGRAPHY: Robert Arvill, *Man and Environment,* Penguin Books, Inc., Baltimore, 1969 (includes comprehensive bibliography).

—DAVID HALL

DE SOISSONS, LOUIS (1890–1962) British architect-planner of French ancestry, son of Count de Soissons; born in Montreal and educated at R. A. Schools, London, and Ecole des Beaux Arts, Paris; Tite Prizewinner, 1912; Jarvis Rome Scholar, 1913. After distinguished war service in Italy 1914 to 1919, he was appointed architect-planner for Welwyn Garden City, the design of which was his chief life work through 42 years. Among his many other works were housing schemes, schools, factories, offices, public buildings, British war graves in Italy, and the George VI memorial in London. He was on the Royal Fine Arts Commission 1949 to 1961, was elected a Royal Academician in 1953, and received the honor of C.V.O. in 1956. He was also a Fellow of the Royal Institute of British Architects and member of the Town Planning Institute.

As architect-planner of Welwyn Garden City he expressed the fundamental concept in an ensemble that was an advance on any previous whole-town plan. With his first partner, A. W. Kenyon, F.R.I.B.A., M.T.P.I. (1884–1969) and later partners, he was also responsible for very many buildings in the new town and impressed upon it the combination of aesthetic quality, economic efficiency, and good living conditions that made it internationally famous and influential. The architectural style he adopted for Welwyn was a refreshed and modernized version of the local Hertfordshire tradition and had much influence on the Georgian revival of the period between the two World Wars. Louis de Soissons also developed with immense resourcefulness the varied and richly landscaped type of layout pioneered by Unwin (*q.v.*) and Parker at Letchworth and Hampstead, and he achieved a standard of overall harmony never before reached in a complete industrial town.

In the control of designs by other architects, he was very ably assisted by A. W. Kenyon as resident architect of the town. It is not without importance to mention that de Soissons and his wife lived and brought up their family in the town and took an active part in its social life for over 30 years. He died in London in 1962.

BIBLIOGRAPHY: L. De Soissons and A. W. Kenyon, *Site Planning in Practice*, 1927.

—FREDERIC J. OSBORN

DETACHED HOUSE Generally, a single-family house that stands apart from others and that is surrounded by land on all sides. (*See also* SEMIDETACHED HOUSES AND TERRACE.)

DEVELOPING COUNTRIES (*See* ASIA, SOUTHEAST, DEVELOPING COUNTRIES.)

DEVELOPMENT For statutory planning purposes in England and Wales, this term has a very wide meaning. It is used primarily to define projects of the sort that require planning permission. With certain exceptions defined by the Town and Country Planning Act of 1971 [S.22,23], all "development" is subject to planning control, known as "development control," and requires planning permission. "Development" is defined by that act as the carrying out of building, engineering, mining, or other operations in, on, over, or under land or the making of any material change in the use of any buildings or other land. Among the operations and uses not constituting development are certain works for the maintenance of buildings, roads, and services and changes of use within classes specified by an order (the use classes order).

Planning permission for development is required before a project is carried out, but certain block planning permissions have been granted by a general development order which permits small extensions to houses, factories, new farm buildings, and routine operations of public authorities. The block permission given by the order may be withdrawn, wholly or in part, with the approval of central government, and planning permission is again necessary for this form of development. This procedure is only invoked in exceptional circumstances where harm could result if development takes place. An official ruling from a local planning authority to determine if a specific project constitutes development and whether planning permission is or is not required can be obtained by an intending developer.

Where planning permission is required for development, an application must be submitted to the local planning authority which has 2 months (or sometimes 3 months) in which to make a decision.

An application may be permitted with or without conditions, or it may be refused. Most applications are determined by local planning authorities or their agents, the district councils. Central government may make the decision in some exceptional circumstances and adjudicates on all appeals against conditions or refusals of permission which are not acceptable to the applicant. In such cases a public inquiry may be held by an officer of central government to assist in finding facts and determining the correct decision (*see* PUBLIC PARTICIPATION IN PLANNING). Most planning permissions are valid only for a limited time—three years for an outline approval, five years for detailed permission. (Permissions for mineral extraction are granted for longer periods.)   —L. W. A. RENDELL

DEVELOPMENT CORPORATION   Body of persons legally constituted to undertake the development of land for a town, part of a town, or a region. In Britain the term was adopted in 1946 for bodies appointed by the government to develop New Towns (*q.v.*). Analogous public agencies, known as "boards," "commissions," "trusts" or by other titles, have in Britain been set up for industrial estates, transport, coal mining, gas, electricity, and other public services. The public corporation is a mechanism of enterprise and administration of wide utility for many purposes and is increasingly employed in large-scale land development.

DEVELOPMENT PLAN   A development plan comprises written statements, maps, and diagrams prepared by an authority responsible for planning in town and country. It is based upon a survey and analysis and ideally should be revised periodically from trends observed in the monitoring of survey information.

In England and Wales the Town and Country Planning Act of 1971 requires the preparation of a structure plan and local plans which, together, form the development plan for a specified area. The plans will gradually supersede those which are in force and have been prepared under the 1962 act. Both types of plans are the responsibility of the local planning authority but are subject to the approval of the government in respect of major policy.

The object of development plans is to satisfy the social and economic desires of the community by creating an effective plan for the physical structure of an area and by encouraging measures to create a pleasant environment while reconciling conflicting land-use claims. A good plan provides the matrix for the day-to-day planning decisions; it is a firm statement of policy for action in the short and long term. It provides the public, developers, and government with proposals for future land use and community requirements. The survey and analysis, which is the essential prerequisite of the preparation of a development plan, is designed to identify the problems and characteristics of the area and be capable of continuous review, which is known as "monitoring." The survey includes physical and economic characteristics—including land use, size, composition, and distribution of population and employment—together with an analysis of the system of communication. It also includes an examination of all trends, including technological metamorphosis. Alteration to structure or local plans then follow if necessary.

Consultations take place with other government and public agencies during the preparation of the plan, and an opportunity is given for the public to participate at all stages of the plan-making process. There is a legal right to object to the provisions of the plan at a public inquiry.

The implementation of the plan depends upon statutes governing development and development control and the interpretation of the plan by the local planning authority. If the objectives of a plan are well understood and represent a balanced and reasonable solution to community problems, developers will be more inclined to conform to the plan for the common good. (*See* LOCAL PLAN and STRUCTURE PLAN.)   —L. W. A. RENDELL

DISPERSAL   (*See* DECENTRALIZATION AND DISPERSAL.)

DISRAELI, BENJAMIN (*Earl of Beaconsfield*) (1804–1881)   English statesman and novelist, born in London on December 21, 1804. He was twice Prime Minister, for 9 months in 1868 and from 1874 to 1880. His best-known novels are the political trilogy of *Coningsby, or the Younger Generation* (1844), *Sybil, or the Two Nations* (1845), and *Tancred, or the New Crusade* (1847). In the first two he outlined schemes for industrial housing estates which had considerable influence.

In *Coningsby* (Book IV, Chapter 3), the industrialist Mr. Millbank built a village near his factory or mill which was

> ... remarkable for the neatness and even picturesque character of its architecture, and the gay gardens that surrounded it. On a sunny knoll in the background rose a church in the best style of Christian architecture, and near it was a clerical residence and a school-house of similar design. The village, too, could boast of another public building: an Institute where there were a library and a lecture-room, and a reading-hall.

The houses and cottages were built with gardens and a new system of ventilation. In *Sybil* (Book III, Chapter 8), a similar provision for his workpeople was made by the industrialist Mr. Trafford, who built a village which included a well in every street, public baths, and schools. It should perhaps be remarked that a well in every street may seem very primitive in the mid-twentieth century, but it was a great advance in the mid-nineteenth century. The tremendous factory built by Mr. Trafford consisted of a "single room, spreading over nearly two acres and holding more than two thousand workpeople. The roof of groined arches, lighted by ventilating domes at the height of eighteen feet, was supported by hollow cast-iron columns, through which the drainage of the roof was effected."

These ideas had a great influence on Sir Titus Salt (1803–1876), a manufacturer of alpaca cloth, who had a great admiration for Disraeli and who put his ideas into practice by building in 1850 to 1853 the small community of Saltaire, a few miles from Bradford, Yorkshire, near his factory. This factory was on somewhat similar lines to Mr. Trafford's, with iron construction, and was claimed to be, at that time, the largest in the world. The three-bedroom houses at Saltaire—with parlor, kitchen, and scullery, built of stone lined with brick—represent a considerable advance in industrial housing, and the community includes public baths, a church, library, philosophical institute with museum and lecture hall, and, near the river, a park with cricket ground and bowling greens. The community still exists very much as Salt built it.

Saltaire was the first industrial housing estate to be built in England. It was followed by many others, and there can be little doubt that the rough preliminary sketches in Disraeli's *Coningsby* and *Sybil* were contributory factors in this progress.

Disraeli died at Beaconsfield on April 9, 1881.

BIBLIOGRAPHY: A recent assessment of Disraeli's influence in the building of Saltaire is given by Robert K. Dewhirst in his article on "Saltaire," *Town Planning Review,* vol. 23, Liverpool, 1960–61.

—ARNOLD WHITTICK

DISTRIBUTION OF POPULATION (*See* POPULATION GROWTH AND DISTRIBUTION.)

DISTRICT HEATING A method of providing space heating and hot water to buildings, houses, apartment blocks, offices, and industrial premises in an urban area by conducting hot water or steam from a central source, as, for example, an installation using the waste heat of an electric power station. It is widely employed in the United States and the U.S.S.R. but only to a very limited extent in Great Britain.

DOCKS (*See* HARBORS AND DOCKS.)

DORMITORY AREA A residential area from which a high percentage of persons travel to work in another locality. Typical examples are the suburbs of a big city where people live and from which they commute to their offices and factories in the central areas.

DOWNTOWN Used in the United States to denote the business or lower part of a city or town. Its use in this sense is beginning to spread to other countries.

DRAINAGE AND LAND USE Drainage has several similarities with irrigation. Irrigation is putting water onto land which is naturally lacking an adequate supply in order ot permit crop production. Drainage is removing excess water from the land. The excess water may have come from heavy precipitation on the land in question, by flooding from streams or overflow from other land, or from the irrigation itself. The drained land may be used, after successful drainage, for various urban or rural uses.

Drainage requires channels to carry the excess water off the land into a natural channel or water body or onto other land. These channels may be open ditches, dug to an adequate depth, with sloping sides and sufficient gradient to permit the water to flow; or they may be covered pipes, usually clay tile but sometimes plastic, into which the excess water can seep and be carried off. More important than the drainage channels is the matter of internal soil drainage; some soils permit ready movement of water, but others do not. In many naturally swampy areas, it is not difficult to build the conduits, on the surface or underground, but internal soil drainage is so poor that the excess water cannot be carried away from the land and drainage is a partial or total failure.

Drainage planning requires data about the physical situation: the volumes of water that are likely to require removal, sometimes data on the salt content of the water, soil character, land slope, character of the channels into which the drainage water will be discharged, and sometimes other matters. Obviously if drainage is to remove unwanted water, the physical works must be adequate to do the job. Drainage planning also requires economic data: construction cost of the drains, maintenance costs, effect of drainage on land productivity, and hence the benefit-cost ratio of the proposed drainage project. In many countries of the world, drains are installed as part of a major construction job, often financed by a government agency, and then they are inadequately maintained; as a result, they soon do not perform satisfactorily and they have a shortened life. Open drains can often be constructed more easily and cheaply than tile drains, but they require more maintenance at more frequent intervals if they are to operate satisfactorily.

Drainage planning also requires attention to administrative arrangements: what organization is going to construct the drains, which one is going to maintain them, and how the costs are to be repaid. Frequently, some agency of some unit of government constructs the drains, directly or by contract with private firms; sometimes the same agency is responsible for their maintenance, but often not. In the United States, special drainage districts have frequently been formed, or irrigation districts have also undertaken drainage activities. The districts may or may not construct the drains, they are usually responsible for their maintenance, it is through them that the costs involved are repaid. Drainage districts typically have legal powers to levy taxes of assessments, sometimes in proportion to estimated benefit to the land in question, sometimes on a general or flat basis throughout the district.

BIBLIOGRAPHY: H. B. Roe and Q. C. Ayres, *Engineering for Agricultural Drainage,* McGraw Hill Book Co., New York, 1954; R. B. Thorn (ed.), Design of Land Drainage Works, Butterworth and Co., Toronto, 1959; J. B. Luthin, *Drainage Engineering,* John Wiley & Sons, Inc., New York, 1966.
(*See also bibliography under* IRRIGATION AND LAND USE.)   —MARION CLAWSON

DRIVE-IN   A facility provided by a shop, restaurant, bank, cinema, or other retail establishment into which customers can drive and be served or entertained while remaining in their cars.

DUDOK, WILLEM MARINUS (1884–   )   Dutch architect and town planner, born in Amsterdam. Trained as a military engineer, he afterward (1912–1913) practiced with J. J. P. Oud in Leiden. Early in his career he accepted a post in the municipality of Hilversum and designed a considerable number of buildings as town architect-engineer while in his early thirties. His work derives from the school of Amsterdam, of which the best-known member was Hendrik Petrus Berlage. The De Stijl influences are clearly detectable in Dudok's work, but many observers, including Hitchcock, refer to him as an individualist rather than as a wholehearted convert to the dominant architectural mode of his generation. His organization of crisp, cubic, brick-constructed elements reflects his contact with De Stijl, and this aspect of his work has been widely influential outside the Netherlands. His compositions are simple and direct, and he developed a clean, dignified, and essentially horizontal architecture with contrasting elements. He emphasized with restraint, but always with integrity and grace, and he avoided excess. His acceptance of the brick wall with windows enabled him to experiment with proportion and detail, and it is in the feeling for the craftsmanship of his own country that he is most convincing.

His work is seen as having its successful beginnings with the early schools at Hilversum, but he achieved international renown with his Town Hall at Hilversum. His own house, at 71 Utrechtscheweg, is a charming example of his basic design philosophy, but on a smaller scale. In both the house and the Town Hall, the fine qualities of workmanship for which the Netherlands and Flemish brick traditions are famed are emphasized. A massive interlocking of brick blocks with a delicate decoration introduced at crucial points are characteristic of Dudok's work and link it with the vernacular traditions of the Netherlands as well as with the tenuous ramifications of De Stijl. The proportioning of mass against mass and the interpenetration of cubic forms is where Dudok excelled. The Town Hall at Hilversum is a fluent essay in the juxtaposition of masses. The preliminary studies for this tour de force may be found in the schools, where window patterns, huge areas of brick, and the play of solid against void are tried again and again. In the Town Hall the trials are over and an assured composition takes shape: a triumph, a fugue of cubic elements. Dating from 1928 to 1930, it is still a timeless building.

It is essential to understand the roots of Dudok's creations in order to grasp the essentials of his work in town planning. When he took over the responsibilities of planning Hilversum, he found a star-shaped town, with ribbon development along the main roads, and a beautiful heathland in danger of being destroyed by buildings. All along he insisted that preservation of the heath and the containment of the town, together with a respect for nature, should be among the prime considerations of his conception.

He filled in the spaces between the points of the star so that the town was made regular and roughly square. Beyond it, the heathland was planted with trees which are now growing to maturity.

Hilversum was described by E. V. Lucas as "the Chislehurst of Holland—a discreet and wealthy suburb." It gains its character from the Arcadian qualities of its landscaping and the large ponds which are in fact basins for rainwater, as well as from the distinguished architecture of its villas, schools, and major buildings. The bosky villadom which surrounds the Town Hall is very much of the garden city ideal, belonging at the same time to the settings and traditions of Dutch suburbia, with prosperous villas and well-kept gardens. The delightful corners of Hilversum, so dominated by nature, are poetic and inspired and are as deliberately composed as Dudok's architecture, which is, of course, part of the composition. His earlier works, classics of their time, seem romantic and deeply satisfying, with closed views, short vistas, and complex patterns. Later developments have a simplicity which the earlier plans do not possess, and spatially the new areas are more open, with nature beyond as the visual stops, so that in composition larger blocks are used to frame views of the corset of greenery beyond the town. As an example of the ultrasimplicity of Dudok's later period, the broad vistas of the southern cemetery at Hilversum serves to illustrate his outward-looking approach, now less romantic and much more open.

Dudok used the filling-in technique when he drew up plans for the Hague-Scheveningen complex. The latter is a coastal resort and also a dormitory suburb of the Hague. Dudok united the two in a cohesive pattern which simply developed the existing organic pattern. His town planning might thus be described as consciously controlling the natural process of development without altering the organic growth. The Hague scheme strengthened and rationalized the existing pattern of communications between the city and the coastal suburb.

It is significant that it was Dudok's design which completed the Zuider Zee dike, and his dynamic monument in the center of the barrage is an eloquent expression of the work of this deeply humane and brilliant man.

BIBLIOGRAPHY: *W. M. Dudok, Übersicht über sein Werk,* Amsterdam, 1954; W. M. Dudok, "Forty Years of Hilversum," *Town and Country Planning,* London, November, 1955; James Stevens Curl, "Dudok and the Modern Movement," *Country Life Annual,* 1972.

—JAMES STEVENS CURL

DURKHEIM, EMILE (1858–1917) Sociologist, born into an important Jewish family in Epinal, Lorraine (France). He received a stimulating education culminating at the Ecole Normale Superieure, followed by studies in Germany and teaching experience which led to his appointment as lecturer in education and social science at Bordeaux University in 1887. In 1896 he became the first professor of social science in France at this university and in 1902 he became professor of education (and sociology from 1913) at the Sorbonne, a position he held until his death.

A pioneer in the scientific study of society, he has a dominant position as one of the founders of modern sociological theory. He maintained that the specific task of sociology is to study social facts which are external to and exert constraint on the individual. The relation between the individual and society was his continuing concern and found expression particularly in his two major works, *The Division of Labor* (1893) and *Suicide* (1897). In *The Division of Labor* he was primarily concerned with the forms of social solidarity which integrate members of society. He distinguishes two extreme forms. Mechanical solidarity, based on likeness and the integration of parts through common tasks, values, and beliefs; and organic solidarity, a more complex form produced by the division of labor and arising with specialization and consequent interdependence of the parts. Although posited as polar types, Durkheim also sees them as "two aspects of one and the same reality."

The concept of anomie developed in his two major works is of central importance in social science. Anomie is a feature of social disorganization and occurs at times of crises or rapid social change to which the norms, values, and goals of society can only adjust more slowly. The individual is cut adrift from the restraints normally exerted by society and is left without a sense of purpose or clear goals and aspirations. This is a pathological state, a cause of suicide and dislocation in the pattern of social relations.

Durkheim's pioneer work is of enormous significance in the social aspects of urban planning.

BIBLIOGRAPHY: E. Durkheim, *The Division of Labor,* The Free Press, Glencoe, Ill., 1947, *Suicide,* Glencoe Free Press, New York, 1951.

—GILLIAN PITT

DWELLINGS (*See* HOUSE.)

DYNAMETROPOLIS In the same way in which humanity moved from city to dynapolis (*q.v.*), it has moved from metropolis to dynametropolis. The basic difference is that where the dynapolis has one center and the solution is usually a parabolic system, the dynamic metropolis has many more centers than one. The solution for its rational growth is not as simple as for the one-center city. Actually, there is no uniform solution that is valid for dynametropolises in general, as every metropolis is different. Each metropolis has a different system of centers with different values for each one, and when it turns into a dynametropolis it has to be analyzed so that we can find the answer for every specific case. As one example we can mention a three-center dynametropolis which is on the sea (see illustration) and which is the schematic solution given to the dynametropolis of Accra-Tema in Ghana (see C. A. Doxiadis, *Ekistics: An Introduction to the Science of Human Settlements,* p. 475, fig. 460).

There is also one more difference between city, dynapolis, and dynametropolis, and this is that though there have been many thousands of cities which turned into dynapolises, there have been very few metropolises which were static. The most characteristic one is Peking, which for a few

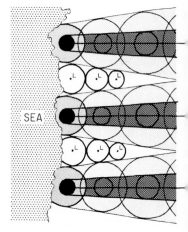

A three-center dynametropolis.

centuries after its creation was a static metropolis and which, together with all other metropolises, has by now turned into a dynametropolis.

BIBLIOGRAPHY: C. A. Doxiadis, *Ekistics: An Introduction to the Science of Human Settlements,* Hutchinson, London, 1968, Oxford University Press, New York, 1968, pp. 101, 371–374.
—CONSTANTINOS A. DOXIADIS

DYNAPOLIS The dynamic polis or the dynamic city. All cities up to the seventeenth century, some of which may have been dynamic for only a very short period of their life, were static and were often surrounded by walls. Later cities started growing in a dynamic way, and today they are almost all dynamic. Humanity did not understand this, and this is one basic reason why so many mistakes have been made in our cities and why we are suffering so much today. It is necessary to classify the cities of the present era, which grow under the impact of many new forces, in a different category from the static cities of the past. This is why we need to understand that from the city-polis we have moved to the dynamic city, to dynapolis.

The ideal solution for a one-center static city that grows into a dynamic one is a center expanding in one direction, so that the city turns into a parabolic system of growth (see illustration), which thus does not choke the existing center to death, as is done in our cities today.

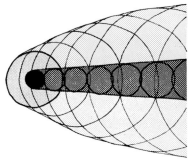

Ideal one-center dynapolis.

BIBLIOGRAPHY: C. A. Doxiadis, *Ekistics: An Introduction to the Science of Human Settlements,* Hutchinson, London, 1968, Oxford University Press, New York, 1968, pp. 101, 371–374.
—CONSTANTINOS A. DOXIADIS

E

EARTHQUAKES AND PLANNING It is calculated that about 120 earthquakes of a fair magnitude (above 6) occur every year, of which probably less than 20 are of a size to cause much destruction; while several thousand small shocks (magnitude 3 and 4) also occur every year. The few big earthquakes often cause extensive destruction and loss of life, and these generally occur in the known earthquake regions of the world. The loss of life, however, is caused mainly by falling buildings and fire. N. C. Heck in his book on earthquakes says that "if the buildings survive there will be little loss of life. Accordingly the safety of buildings and other structures is one of the principal aims of earthquake investigation." G. A. Eiby in his book on the same subject says, "Most injuries and loss of life in earthquakes have been caused by the collapse of man-made structures." It is a wise precaution, therefore, for the authorities—together with architects, planners, structural engineers, surveyors, and others in urban areas situated in earthquake zones—to know the kind of destruction that occurs and the risks involved and to employ methods of construction and siting that will minimize the destructive effects. The cooperation of seismologists is valuable.

It is still not possible to predict the occurrence of an earthquake, even one of great magnitude. Therefore it is not possible to organize any dispersal of population from an area. The most that can be done is to predict that in an earthquake zone there will probably be several more or less severe shocks in the next 50 years. Research is proceeding on the possibilities of predicting earthquakes, and experiments are being conducted with a view to controlling them. One method is actually to trigger them off in geologically dangerous sites, either by underground explosions or by great water pressure or other means; but as the movement causing an earthquake may be very deep—as much as 400 miles (644 kilometers)—the difficulties are obviously considerable. Meanwhile the most practical approach is to minimize the destructive effects of earthquakes by constructing buildings in the vulnerable zones by methods that give the maximum resistance and by building in areas or on sites that provide the most stable conditions.

Ever since the effects of earthquakes have been recorded it has been observed that poorly constructed buildings collapsed and caused loss of life while well-constructed buildings often withstood the shocks. When Goethe visited Messina a year after the earthquake of 1786 in which 12,000 people were killed, he noticed that "most of the buildings had collapsed and the cracked walls of the rest made them unsafe," but that "the few buildings which were solidly constructed survived. The Jesuit College and Church, which were built of quarried stone, are still intact" (*Travels in Italy*). Similar observations have been made after numerous earthquakes, but there are, of course, many exceptions. A few tentative principles are, however, possible, although there is always the liability of error.

Experience indicates that a building that has some measure of resilience in its construction and is at the same time monolithic, or in one piece, is more likely to withstand earthquake shocks than a building constructed— for instance—of bricks with roof tiling which collapses easily, especially if the walls are not very thick and the mortar is not very strong. Among constructions having a fair degree of resilience are timber-framed buildings, steel-frame constructions, and reinforced or prestressed concrete; and if the parts are firmly linked, then they all sway together and the building remains intact, although it may tilt, especially if the foundations are not substantial—as was the experience in the Niigata (Japan) earthquake of 1964.

The height of buildings may have something to do with their resistance, because it has been observed that in some areas earthquake shocks are more strongly felt in the upper parts of tall buildings than in the lower parts. It can be appreciated that here again some degree of resilience is important.

The planner, however, is particularly concerned with the areas and sites of urban development in earthquake zones. Available evidence indicates that buildings erected on deep alluvium are particularly vulnerable and that those built on solid rock are much safer. It was observed, for example, in the San Francisco earthquake of 1906, that the damage to buildings on the alluvial land was very much greater than that to those built on the rock a short distance away. Heck pointed out, however, that deep alluvium may act as a kind of cushion to a rigidly constructed building, and G. A. Eiby mentions that "a foundation of alluvium has the effect of absorbing small earthquakes, but it amplifies the vibrations of larger ones." It would appear, therefore, that a building on solid rock will be less vulnerable if it has some degree of resilience in its construction and is in one piece.

In an earthquake, land over a considerable area may rise or fall. One of the most spectacular quakes of this kind was the Hawkes Bay earthquake of 1931, when the ground rose 5 feet (1.52 meters) out of the sea and added about five square miles (13 square kilometers) to New Zealand territory. The extent to which deep rock, as opposed to deep alluvium, would resist such a movement is still problematical.

In earthquake regions a system of seismic zoning, based on the earthquakes of the past, is obviously a practical step. It is necessarily speculative. Any resulting building regulations determining degrees of earthquake resistance would probably have some degree of flexibility, would vary with the type of building, and would be more stringent for halls of assembly than for warehouses. Although these are matters more for the seismological engineer than the urban planner, it is important for the latter to be aware of them and to seek the advice of the former when planning in earthquake regions.

BIBLIOGRAPHY: There are a large number of books on seismology. The following include references to the behavior of buildings and the selection of sites for building.

J. R. Freeman, *Earthquake Damage and Earthquake Insurance,* McGraw-Hill Book Company, New York, 1932; Nicholas Hunter Heck, *Earthquakes,* Hafner Publishing Company, Inc., New York and London, 1936 and 1965; G. A. Eiby, *Earthquakes,* Frederick Muller, London, 1957, fully revised edition, 1967; D. F. Richter, *Elementary Seismology,* W. H. Freeman & Company, San Francisco, 1958.

—ARNOLD WHITTICK

ECOLOGY   The science of ecology was born at the beginning of the present century and can be defined as the study of the relations of all living organisms to each other and to their environment. A fundamental concept is the *ecosystem,* which the originator, Tansley, interpreted as the *biome* ("the whole complex of organisms, both animals and plants, naturally living together as sociological units") and its habitat. "All parts of such an ecosystem, organic and inorganic, biome and habitat, may be regarded as interacting factors which, in a mature ecosystem, are in approximate equilibrium; it is through their interactions that the whole system is maintained."

To understand ecosystems, special techniques, quantitative as well as qualitative, and procedures have been developed. They rely on (1) detailed observation of internal structure and processes (*dominance* of a particular species and their *influence* on others, their combined *productivity,* interspecies *competition,* and their degree of *symbiosis*) over a period of time (*succession* of communities); (2) measurement and evaluation of the physical factors (such as weather, soil conditions, influence of other organisms) which determine distribution; and (3) quantification of *transfers* within the ecosystem and between it and the environment (materials and energy).

However, once man is introduced into the systems, the problems of analysis inevitably become more complex since the relevant environment is no longer simply the physical and biological but also "the culture of his [man's] own creating." Identification of system elements is difficult and interactions consist not only of food and energy but also values, sanctions, money, etc. Such problems are not the responsibility of ecologists alone since their needs converge with those of many other disciplines, all of which contribute to urban and regional sciences and planning.

The interpretation of human settlement patterns and their evolution by analogy with ecological processes dates back to at least the 1920s. In 1926 the British ecologist Charles Elton compared the species in ecosystems with the occupations of humans in an urban community which usually possesses a basic economic activity (originally determined by energy and materials sources) and a variety of other job types. Increases in population result in increased diversity of occupations. Since then there have been repeated attempts to "humanize" ecology. One method is to add to the normal ecological feedback mechanisms of starvation, predation, disease, migration, and competition those attributes that are unique to man; i.e., public opinion, punishment and rewards, wealth, taxation, supply and demand, cooperation, and the democratic process.

The influence of organic and ecological concepts in geography has been profound, particularly on methodology. In 1921 a group of urban sociologists in Chicago coined the phrase "human ecology." Their theory was directly based on concepts derived from animal and plant ecology. Some geographers recognized the attraction of such an approach, but in general, its essentially biological standpoint prevented the formation of a substantial following. It was the concept of ecosystem proposed by Tansley in 1935 which provided the basis for important recent work by geographers. Its potential as a framework for model building (the bridge between observation and theory) lies in the fact that it requires the explicit elucidation of the structure and functions of a community and its environment, with the ultimate aim of quantifying the links between components. Present trends are moving beyond the simple concept of ecosystem toward recognition of its general systems qualities and the study of *geosystems*.

In urban analysis, as in geography, awareness of dynamic complexity was bound to raise the question of the "organic" analogy. Without accurate definition, however, it was likely to be abused and thus discredited for lack of rigour, but the "ecological" analogy shows more promise. Important supports for it are the common features of exchanges of energy and materials between elements and *the competition for space and locational relationships.* Other arguments put forward refer to the unit of study—the community. An urban community, like a natural ecosystem, is readily identifiable. Within its boundaries are particular social and physical characteristics, of which an important one is the symbiotic nature of the relationships between members of the population. Like the ecologist, the urban analyst seeks to understand the forces which influence the structural pattern and evolution of the community.

Critics of the ecological approach point out that it is only a "partial" theory: that it results only in a static description of an urban system at one point in time while planners need to be concerned with the prediction and design of future states. Even the deeper understanding that this description may bring does not tell the planner how to design the environment.

However, taking into account these criticisms, the usefulness of ecosystem science in planning can be summarized as follows:

1. It is a comprehensive approach which includes man, plants, animals, and their environment(s) in a single framework within which interactions between elements can be observed and analyzed. One result of this is the provision of a common language for a number of disciplines engaged in such studies.

2. The structure of an ecosystem is both rational and functional (i.e., containing movement of energy and matter). Thus identification and quantification of interchanges should, in most cases, be possible.

3. A most important characteristic of an ecosystem is that it can be regarded as a kind of general system and has, therefore, a sound theoretical and methodological backing in general systems theory together with the mathematical techniques of cybernetics, information, and communication theory. Such a property is of importance to the urban model builder for it forces him to attempt quantification of all the interaction processes present in the urban system, thereby exposing his theories to empirical testing.

BIBLIOGRAPHY: T. Howard Odum and W. C. Allee, "A Note on the Stable Point of Population Showing Both Intraspecific Co-operation and Disoperation," *Ecology,* vol. 35, pp. 95–97, 1954; J. Roger Bray, "Notes towards an Ecologic Theory," *Ecology* (journal of the Ecological Society of America), vol. 39, pp. 770–776, Duke University Press, Durham, N.C., 1958; Ramon D. Margalef, "Information theory in ecology," *General Systems,* vol. 3, pp. 36–71, 1958; Howard T. Odum, John E. Cantlon, and Louis S. Kornicker, "An Organisational Hierarchy Postulate for the Interpretation of Species-individual Distributions, Species Entropy, Ecosystem Evolution and the Meaning of a Species-variety Index," *Ecology,* vol. 41, pp. 395–399, 1960; J. S. Rowe, The Level of Integration Concept and Ecology," *Ecology,* vol. 42, pp. 420–427, 1961; David Garfinckel and Richard Sack, "Digital Computer Simulation of an Integral System Based on a Modified Mass-action Law," *Ecology,* vol. 45, pp. 502–507, 1964; W. B. Morgan and R. P. Moss, "Geography and Ecology: The Concept of the Community and its Relationship to Environment," *Annals of the Association of American Geographers,* vol. 55, pp. 339–351, 1965; E. Max Nicholson, "Ecology and Conservation as a Scientific Basis of Landscape Design," *Journal of the Institute of Landscape Architects,* vol. 69, pp. 10–12, 1965; Timothy O'Riordan, "Planning to Improve Environmental Capacity: A Case Study of Broadland," *Town Planning Review,* vol. 40, pp. 39–58, Liverpool University Press, 1967; F. Fraser-Darling, "A Wider Environment of Ecology and Conservation," *Daedalus,* vol. 96, pp. 1003–1019, American Academy of Arts and Sciences, Boston; S. Dillon Ripley and Helmut K. Buechner, "Ecosystem Science as a Point of Synthesis," *Daedalus,* vol. 96, pp. 1192–1199, 1967; Harold J. Morowitz, *Energy Flows in Biology,* John Wiley & Sons, Inc., New York, 1968; Maurice H. Braverman and Robert G. Schrandt, "Colony Development of a Polymorphic Hydroid as a Problem in Pattern Formation," *General Systems* (yearbook of the Society for the Advancement of General Systems Theory), vol. 12, pp. 39–51.

—J. B. McLoughlin and Judith N. Webster

ECONOMIC CONSIDERATIONS IN URBAN AND REGIONAL PLANNING A planner tries to direct and control the effects of past and present causes to achieve his goals. Urban and country planners aim at the creation of a better environment—an object which is many goals in one. The elements involved in realizing such a complex ambition are so numerous and so intricately related that a team of planners is needed to bring order and direction to them. Architects, engineers, urban designers, city planners, and economists all make unique contributions to the overall plan. It is with the contributions and techniques of the economist that this article deals.

The economist is not a seer who exactly describes the shape of the future; he is a specialist trained to identify the problems and opportunities inherent in economic trends and resources and to evaluate alternative ways of capitalizing on the opportunities and circumventing the problems. Throughout the planning process, his findings are screened and interpreted through collective experience.

A typical economic analysis begins with a data-gathering work phase during which the economist develops a current economic profile of the area under study, evaluates the economic base which sustains the area, and performs research of development opportunities. He then reviews his results with the team to incorporate their insights into his subsequent efforts. Finally, specific actions which could alleviate problems, resolve issues, or capture opportunities are identified and an implementation program is developed for the team's consideration and use.

The level of economic planning affects the scope of an economist's effort, although not necessarily his basic approach or techniques. It is helpful to envision the economic effort as a series of concentric circles, broadening in diameter to include larger geographical areas at each level of planning. The most sharply focused level, of course, would be planning for a *single site;* the next level would be *neighborhood* planning. *Community* planning would be much broader. *Regional* planning would encompass extremely widespread forces. Each of these planning levels shares the need to channel existing resources and infuse new ones to bring about desired results. *New Town* planning is a special situation. In breadth of effort, it falls between community and regional planning; in depth, perhaps, it is greater than any, since it permits and obliges the planner to build an economically mature community unshaped and unburdened by its past.

While each community or planning region is unique, most share certain problems which result from nationwide or worldwide trends. Since planning involves problem solving, it is appropriate to begin our survey of economic considerations in urban and country planning with a review of recurring problems.

Problems Fundamentally, economic problems result from a pace of change which outstrips resources and services, creating stresses in society. Perhaps the most powerful agents of normal change are population growth and technological advance, which are bursting the structures and institutions that accommodated them in the past and creating needs faster than society can fulfill them.

Because of the lag between the creation of a problem and its solution, "hot spots" recur throughout urban society. Just a few of these are depletion of urban land and open space, shortages of low-income housing, shortages of funds for services such as education, increased crime rates, transportation and circulation problems, air and waste pollution, subtle ecological changes, and the loss of a sense of meaningful involvement with government—which creates the well-known "credibility gap" and makes the tasks of government planners immeasurably more difficult.

In analyzing the factors described below, the planner looks for opportunities to begin solving some of these problems.

Economic Profile The scope of this article precludes discussion of all the features of an area's profile (which include population size, demographic characteristics, and many other items). One feature is selected which is basic to planning: land use—the raw material of a city.

The largest part of a city's land is apportioned to residential uses. The rest is divided among commercial and office uses; community, cultural, and health institutions; open space and recreation; and streets, utilities, and parking. The economist's task involves determining the presence of balance or imbalance in land use, the opportunities for bringing about more desirable uses or patterns of use, the practicality of introducing a new development to the city, and the costs of fulfilling (or ignoring) land-use needs. As a result of many studies, economists have developed quantitative standards and ratios for arriving at present and projected requirements. These are tools which can be used in the planning process.

Change brings new trends in land use, some of which are identified below and some of which, it is hoped, the economist will be able to predict. Recent apparent trends include (1) clustering—of retail facilities in shopping centers, of industry or offices in parks, of residential dwelling units, and even of single interests, such as automotive services; (2) the migration of certain types of business, such as furniture stores, to the sides of highways; (3) the decline of central business districts and the parallel suburbanization of industry, offices, and people; and (4) the dispersal of major regional headquarters across the country due to rapid air transport.

Economic Base The primary object of economic base studies is to determine the sources of principal economic effort, especially those elements of the economy which attract "new money"—income from outside the local community.

A second purpose is to define the different areas within an urban complex which, in effect, have their own economies. A large area tends toward a balanced economy; but smaller areas within the urban mass (e.g., ghettos) may suffer a high degree of imbalance.

A third object is to investigate the time variable and its effect on economic projections and base analyses. Population projections may be expressed in two ways: (1) by saying that in 1990 population will range from 190,000 to 210,000, or (2) that the population will reach 200,000 between 1985 and 1995. In urban planning, it is generally more important to plan for a given population, irrespective of date, than for a range of people at a given date.

Market Research In urban and country planning, it is important to identify market potentials for new uses or developments. It must be recognized, however, that *qualitative* variables affect the reliability of *quantitative* projections. Market-demand estimates, therefore, are not absolute; they are only indicators of maximum potentials.

Demand, for instance, may be latent rather than attainable. If a strong demand for low-cost housing cannot be met without massive public assistance, it is latent; its inclusion in demand estimates would be misleading to the planner.

Demand is also affected by competition and timing. For instance, demand for a regional shopping center does not focus on one site. Planners might wish it to be built so as to generate jobs in a depressed area; but if a fast-moving developer introduces one into a wealthy suburb, its presence will drain demand from the site preferred by the planners.

Other variables affecting demand include quality and location. On paper, the supply of office space may equal the demand; but if an office development can offer outstanding features, it can attract demand away from less desired space.

Since all these variables affect market predictions, planners must be able to assess their probable impact on the plan on the basis of experience, judgment, and intuition, using quantitative predictions as a provisional framework of decision.

Other Considerations   Clearly, the successful implementation of any development or plan depends on its financing. Municipal and government economics are often the key to development of city and country, since some form of public assistance is frequently needed. The economist must therefore analyze the capacity of the appropriate government agency to provide assistance. The level of government under consideration must be defined. Some plans have purely local impact; others have regional implications. This often involves cost-benefit studies to determine the economic impact of a development on the governmental unit.

Similarly, if private developers are involved in the plan, their financial returns must be considered. Return on investment may have to exceed 10 percent per year to be considered adequate.

Implementation   With all these problems and prospects in mind, the economist and his fellow team members approach the implementation phase in which information is channeled toward action. The economist examines *vehicles* for implementation, which include parking districts, beautification districts, promotional districts, redevelopment projects, and municipal provision of key services and facilities. In choosing one or more of these vehicles, the economist analyzes the relative costs and benefits of each one to discover which vehicle would produce the greatest benefits at the least cost. Since benefits may be intangible, this calculation is not hard and fast. The economist must balance his figures with some subjective sensitivity and compassion for unquantifiable human needs.

—John W. McMahan

ECUMENOPOLIS The term "ecumenopolis" expresses, in the theories of Doxiadis, the universal city toward which the cities of mankind are developing. The same forces that turn the city into a dynapolis and the metropolis into a dynametropolis gradually lead to urban systems—to megalopolises—which will again be interconnected as they become dynamegalopolises. Probably from the middle of the next century on, they will lead toward a universal system of cities which could be called a "universal city" or "ecumenopolis."

The forces which will form ecumenopolis are the same as those which form the dynamic cities of the present, but they are multiplied, interconnected, and lead to more complex systems. When they have all formed one universal system, this will become static. Ecumenopolis will have to find a balance between people and their habitat, the same type of balance that existed between the ancient city and the city-state or the feudal castle and its area.

BIBLIOGRAPHY: C. A. Doxiadis, "Ecumenopolis: Tomorrow's City," in *Britannica Book of the Year, 1968,* Encyclopedia Britannica Inc., 1968, *Ekistics: An Introduction to the Science of Human Settlements,* Hutchinson, London, 1968, Oxford University Press, New York, 1968, pp. 376–380.

—Constantinos A. Doxiadis

EDUCATIONAL BUILDINGS Provision in any extensive planning development is made for educational buildings which include nursery and elementary schools, various kinds of secondary schools, colleges, and specialized schools of various sorts. The elementary schools are closely related to the residential areas they serve, and distance from home to school for the very young is a paramount planning consideration. With secondary schools and older pupils the intimate physical relation of school and home is less important, and schools can be related more to transport accessibility, which is also the case with colleges and universities. Thus it may be said that primary and junior schools are intimately related to the residential areas of neighborhoods, secondary schools to the larger areas of a town or city, and universities to large urban centers or regions.

While planning must concern itself with the location of schools in relation to the residential areas they serve, the educational buildings themselves may sometimes have an important influence on the general plan. In many British New Towns, for instance, the size of the neighborhood unit is controlled by the population necessary to support one-, two-, or three-stream[1] primary schools. In such towns secondary schools are located in relation to the town as a whole, with some habitual use of transport being taken for granted,while colleges and other advanced educational institutions are usually in town centers. For the location of universities and university building complexes, *see* UNIVERSITY CAMPUS OR CITY.

—Arnold Whittick

EDUCATIONAL PARK An educational park consists of a number of schools

[1]Children of the same age group divided into two or three classes.

situated in a park and grouped round a central core which provides facilities that can be shared by the schools. One of its purposes is to provide common access to facilities for different kinds of schools and for children coming from different strata of society. It is in some measure an antidote to segregation. As such, a campus would be large, possibly for as many as 4,000 or 5,000 pupils. It would mean a degree of centralization and would replace the neighborhood school related to local residence. The concept has been evolved in the United States and has evoked widespread interest. About a hundred American cities are planning educational parks of some sort. An interesting example is the plan for educational parks in Syracuse, N.Y., where eight schools of about 500 pupils each are grouped round a central core.

The facilities provided in the central core would consist of a library; a health center; a multipurpose hall for theater, concerts, etc.; facilities for the study and enjoyment of the arts and for physical recreation and training, and so on. This sort of development involves, of course, the possibility that its facilities may be enjoyed by the community as a whole.

So far (1972) there do not appear to be any approximations to the educational park planned in Great Britain. The nearest approach to it is the comprehensive school, which is a more limited concept. The educational park may well be the next stage.

BIBLIOGRAPHY: Max Wolff, Esther Rothman, and Leopold Berman, "The Case for Educational Parks," *Architectural Record,* 1966; Max Wolff, "Educational Park Development in the United States," Center for Urban Education, New York, 1967, "The Education Park Picture Book," Center for Urban Education, New York, 1967; Christopher Abel, "Educational Parks," *Royal Institute of British Architects Journal,* vol. 11, no. 2, February, 1970.

—ARNOLD WHITTICK

EDWARD I OF ENGLAND (1239–1307) Edward I, the first king after the Conquest to bear an English name, was born at Westminster in 1239 and died in 1307 at Burgh-on-Sands. His reign saw the emergence of the English people as a nation and the early development of parliament and the courts of justice. In 1254 he succeeded Simon de Montfort as Lieutenant of Gascony. After his return from the Holy Land in 1274 he was crowned King of England.

His reign was marked by a legislative and administrative program that earned him the title "The English Justinian." In 1275 the Statute of Westminster the First corrected the abuses in royal administration. The same year saw the compilation of the Hundred Rolls, the greatest survey since Domesday. It was followed by the Statute of Gloucester and the Quo Warranto Inquiry in 1278 and by the Statute of Mortmain in 1279. In 1283 the Parliament of Shrewsbury met and the Statute of Acton Burnell, governing the development of trade and commerce, was enacted. The statute of Westminster the Third, the celebrated Quia Emptores was enacted in 1290. In 1295 the Model Parliament established a firm basis for government by consent. Just as important was Edward's implementation of Henry of Bratton's legal reforms, which had preceded Edward's accession to the throne.

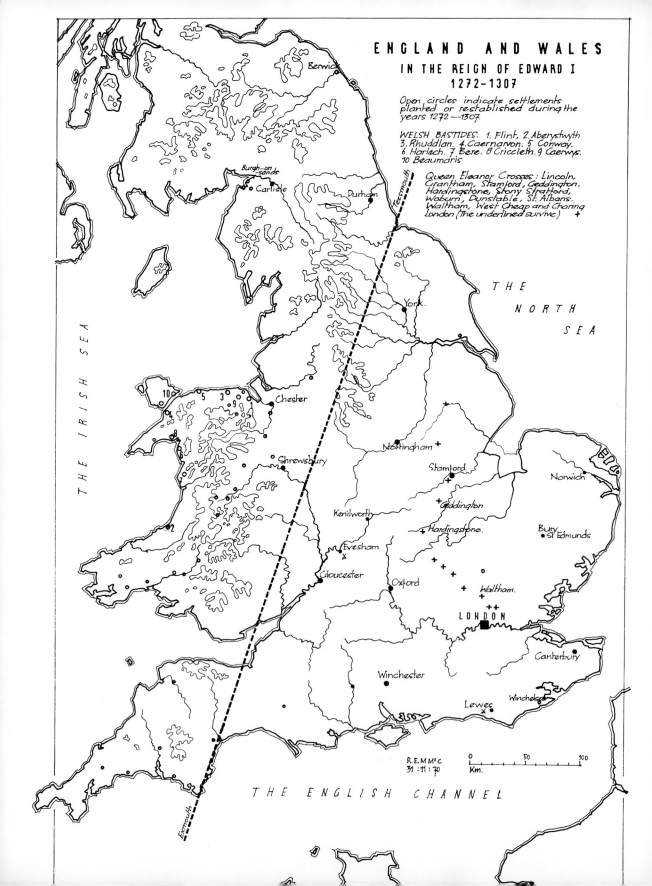

ENGLAND AND WALES
IN THE REIGN OF EDWARD I
1272–1307

Open circles indicate settlements
planted or restablished during the
years 1272–1307.

WELSH BASTIDES. 1. Flint, 2. Aberystwyth
3. Rhuddlan. 4. Caernarvon. 5. Conway.
6. Harlech. 7. Bere. 8 Criccieth. 9. Caerwys.
10. Beaumaris

Queen Eleanor Crosses: Lincoln,
Grantham, Stamford, Geddington,
Hardingstone, Stony Stratford,
Woburn, Dunstable, St. Albans.
Waltham, West Cheap and Charing
London (The underlined survive) +

THE
NORTH
SEA

THE IRISH SEA

THE ENGLISH CHANNEL

Berwick

Burgh-on-sands
Carlisle
Durham
Teesmouth

York

Chester
Shrewsbury
Nottingham
Stamford
Norwich
Geddington
Kenilworth
Hardingstone
Bury St Edmunds
Evesham
Gloucester
Oxford
Waltham
LONDON
Canterbury
Winchester
Lewes
Winchelsea

Exmouth

R.E.M MᶜC
31 : 11 : 70

0   50   100
Km.

After the settlement of Wales in 1284, Edward continued the planning of military settlements, drawing, no doubt, on his experience in Gascony and the Holy Land. Earlier settlements at Flint, Aberystwyth (1277), and Rhuddlan (1278) were followed by Caernarvon, Conway, and Harlech (1283), Bere and Criccieth (1284), Caerys (1290), and Beaumaris (1295). Caernarvon is the best surviving example of an Edwardian town. It is situated on the Menai Straits and is enclosed by a defensive wall linked with the famous castle at the further side from the sea. The regular plan of Caernarvon today, with its insulae or *placeae,* preserves the layout of mediaeval settlements. A well-known example in the southeast of England where this gridiron plan is still strongly apparent is Winchelsea, which Edward built in 1287.

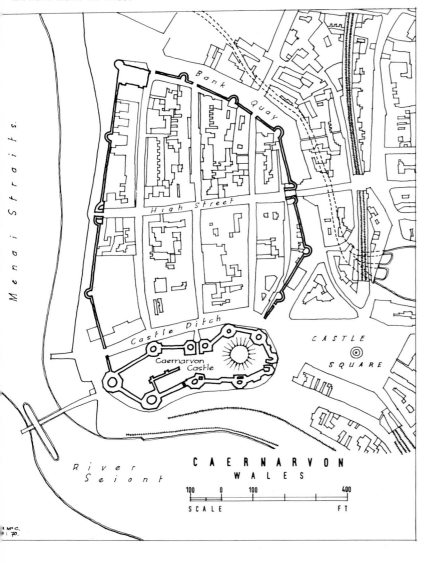

OPPOSITE PAGE: *Planted settlements in England and Wales 1272–1307. The most important plantations were the bastides planted by the King in North Wales. (Making use of inter alia Maurice Beresford, New Towns in the Middle Ages, London, 1967.)* LEFT: *Plan of Caernarvon, Wales. Planted by King Edward I in 1283. The castle situated on the south of the settlement was erected between 1283 and 1327. (Ministry of Works pamphlet on Caernarvon—Crown Copyright.)*

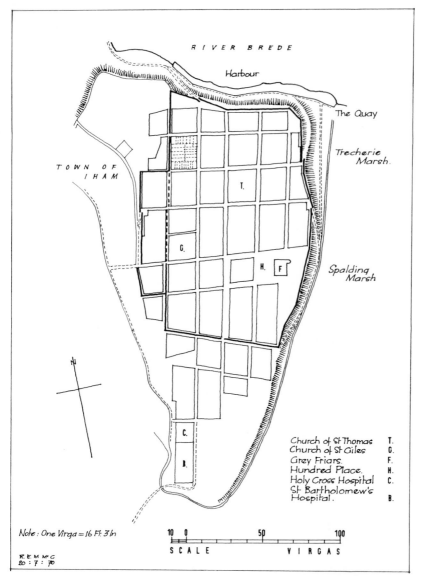

RIVER BREDE

Harbour

The Quay

Trecherie
Marsh.

T O W N   O F
I H A M

T.

G.

H. F

Spalding
Marsh.

C.

B.

Church of St Thomas   T.
Church of St Giles   G.
Grey Friars.   F.
Hundred Place.   H.
Holy Cross Hospital   C.
St Bartholomew's
Hospital.   B.

Note: One Virga = 16 Ft 3 In

R.E M McC
20 : 7 : 70

10   0   50   100
S C A L E   V I R G A S

*Plan of New Winchelsea, Sussex. New
Winchelsea was planted by Edward I
in 1288 to replace the older settlement
which had been eroded by the
encroaching sea. The gridiron plan
recalls that of Salisbury, planted in
1219 after the abandonment of the
cramped site of Old Sarum. (W. M. L.
Homan, The Founding of New
Winchelsea, Sussex Arch. Coll.
LXXXVIII, 1949, 22–41.)*

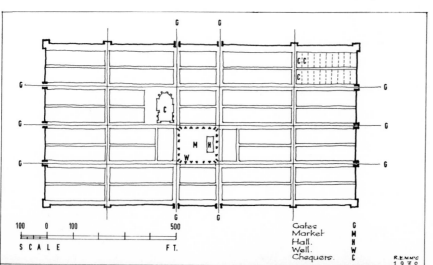

G   G

C C

C

G

C

G

M H
W

G

G

G   G

100   0   100   500
S C A L E   F T.

Gates   G
Market   M
Hall.   H
Well.   W
Chequers.   C

R.E MMcC
1 9 7 0

*Plan of Montpazier. Planted by the
King in 1285. An almost symmetrical
plan compared with that of Old
Winchelsea.*

Reconstruction of Beaumaris, Anglesey. The settlement was planted by Edward I in 1295 and the castle erected between 1295 and 1330. (Reconstruction by Alan Sorrell in Alan Phillips Beaumaris Castle. H. M. Stat. Office, London, 1961.)

In 1293, Wyke-on-Hull was acquired by Edward and developed as Kingston-on-Hull. Here he introduced a new road system to facilitate the movement of merchandise to the port, and he extended the outskirts of the town in the gridiron manner.

During his reign, over 70 bastides were erected in Gascony, the most famous being Monpazier (1285), the classic example of a medieval grid-iron-planned settlement, where the *placeae* are a fairly regular series of rectangles.

After the Parliament of Bury St. Edmunds in 1296, Edward summoned experienced burghers from London and 20 other English towns to rebuild Berwick-on-Tweed in a manner similar to the Welsh bastides. Apart from the walls, little survives of the Edwardian reconstruction.

Edward died on July 7, 1307, at Burgh-on-Sands on the Solway during the renewed war with Scotland. His body was taken south and buried at Westminster. Above his tomb is the proud epitaph *EDWARDUS PRIMUS SCOTORUM MALLEUS HIC EST 1308 PACTUM SERVA* ("Here lies Edward the First, Hammer of the Scots, 1308. Keep Troth"). So died Edward Plantagenet, the most illustrious of England's kings: warrior and statesman, legislator and administrator, and the greatest builder of towns since the Age of Alexander and his successors, the Seleucid kings.

BIBLIOGRAPHY: E. A. Lewis, *The Medieval Boroughs of Snowdonia*, London, 1903; Edward Jenks, *Edward Plantagenet, the English Justinian, or the Making of the Common Law*, London, 1923; T. F. Tout, *Medieval Town Planning*, Manchester, 1934; J. E. Lloyd, *A History of Wales from Earliest Times to the Edwardian Conquest*, London, 1938; J. Goronwy Edwards, *Edward I's Castle Building in Wales*, Sir John Rhys Memorial Lecture, British Academy, 1944, London, 1944; F. M. Powicke, *The Thirteenth Century 1216–1307*, second edition, Oxford, 1952; Maurice Beresford, *New Towns of the Middle Ages*, Lutterworth Press, London, 1967.

—R. E. M. McCaughan

EGYPT, ARAB REPUBLIC OF

Legislation and Administration Hitherto there has been no comprehensive town and country planning act in Egypt, but further legislation has been under consideration. Egypt has regulated the physical development in construction and building activities by a number of acts, and their amendments signify evolution resulting from experience. National comprehensive planning and regional planning are recognized. The task of drafting legislation is entrusted to the Ministry of Housing and Public Works and the Ministry of Local Government.

The object of the present acts is to ensure adequate minimum standards of health, sanitation, and safety by enforcing proper land use. Also, these acts have been used in directing renewal activities. Among the acts most related to planning are the following:

The Building Restrictions Act, 1889, which enables local authorities to enforce building lines with a view to developing and widening local streets so as to ensure the civic value of the cities.

The Building Act, No. 52/1940, which is mainly concerned with the subdivision of land for building purposes. The main objectives are to ensure proper development and to regulate the expansion of cities. (1) The act requires that any subdivision of land within the city boundaries should be approved by local authorities before implementation. (2) The act fixes the width and the proper design of the intersection of roads. (3) The act requires that the developer should provide proper utilities at his own expense. (4) It regulates housing densities by permitting only 60 percent of a building site to be developed, plus 10 percent of the built-up area for balconies and stairs. (5) The act controls the height and design of buildings. (6) The act regularizes methods of approval and determines penalties when regulations are ignored.

The Industrial Areas Act, No. 28/1947, which enables local authorities to locate industrial areas within the cities and outside their boundaries and to prohibit the establishment of industry in certain areas.

The Public Housing Act, No. 206/1951, which encourages public, nonprofit, and private organizations to carry out public housing projects for low-income groups with different types of government assistance.

The Property Acquisition for Public Improvement Act, No. 577/1954, which gives power to public authorities for the compulsory purchase of land and buildings for the purpose of redeveloping, widening streets, or providing open spaces.

The Slum Clearance and Redevelopment Act, No. 27/1956, which enables local authorities to acquire slum districts for clearance and redevelopment purposes and provides for the payment of compensation to the owners, either in kind or in cash, with a chance to share profits gained from the redevelopment.

The Subdivision Act, No. 52/1960, which controls street width, ratio of built-up area, the provision of public open space, and the installation of necessary utilities before the sale of the lots.

The Building Restrictions Act, No. 45/1962, which provides local authorities with facilities for urban renewal and power to impose planning restrictions for zoning, densities, and other related purposes.

Planning administration is regulated by the above-mentioned acts and the Local Authorities Act, No. 124/1960, and Presidential Decree 1119/1968, which entrust to the local authorities the tasks of planning and administration. Despite the recognition of community and neighboring analysis as two basic tools towards project planning and programming, this succession of systematic procedure usually requires high technical competence, continuous administration and coordination, as well as patience for the length of time required for the preparation and implementation of renewal programs. These requirements have been handicapped by the lack, so far, of sufficient planners and specialized professional personnel. An attempt at solving this problem has been made by encouraging the cooperation of local and foreign consultants, and by the direction of centralized planning staff located in the Ministry of Housing and Public Utilities, which is now the responsibility of the General Organization of Housing and Development. These parties have helped in concentrating efforts toward the preparation of community planning and neighborhood analysis for many cities and towns. In the case of specially important areas such as Cairo, Alexandria, and Aswân, independent planning bodies are carrying out the studies necessary for the master plans of these areas.

Professional Practice The professional practice of planning is not fully recognized in Egypt and is considered part of the architectural profession. Therefore, the regulations and bylaws of the architecture section in the Egyptian Institute of Engineers are applicable to the planning field. This is because the majority of practicing planners have architecture as a basic qualification and planning as a secondary one. Also, they are very few in number. Egyptian planners are trying to establish a separate section within the Egyptian Institute of Engineers.

Town planning has been governed by regulations for buildings and town planning since March 12, 1881. These regulations require prior permission from "local authorities" before building or demolishing can be done with a view to improving the existing conditions of cities. Planning was carried out only by local authorities. Since 1950 a few projects on a limited scale have been carried out by Egyptian architect/planners in a private capacity. Since 1960 work has been done by a few planners in private practice, in the fields of both city and regional planning, notably in the new reclaimed areas at the New Valley (Western Desert), Maryût Project (south of Alexandria), and the East of Canal Project.

The administration of planning acts is entrusted to the Ministry of Housing and Public Utilities. The planning department at this ministry implements master plans for a large number of Egyptian cities.

According to the Local Administration Act, the responsibility for planning was entrusted to the local governors of the different administrative districts. The governors were forced to ask the help of the Ministry of

Housing and Public Utilities to prepare town master plans and other planning projects because of the lack of qualified planners at the local level. Some governors appointed private planning firms to carry out planning work within their districts. The first planning competition in Egypt was for a new tourist city in the vicinity of the Giza pyramids, sponsored by the governor of Giza in 1964.

In 1968 the Ministry of Local Government was entrusted with the task of preparing regional planning projects. Accordingly, the ministry divided the country into ten different regions, and six different planning boards were appointed to carry out the regional studies. It is hoped that national comprehensive planning will be under way in the near future.

Major planning projects are carried out by well-qualified planners. The fees for the different planning projects so far have been a matter of private agreement.

Education and Training The education and training of planners should be based on the different targets to be attained by planning. There are two aims to achieve in planning: (1) The determination of policies—social, economic, and physical; and (2) The preparation and carrying through of a plan for the use and development of land in conformity with these policies.

It is important to note in considering the training and education of planners that aesthetic quality is only one of the numerous different elements of value which have to be taken into account to provide the best environment for living.

In the first period, before 1964, planning was taught only in the third and fourth years of an architecture course. Instruction (6 hours weekly) consisted mainly of planning history and a brief study of land-use planning.

The second phase, after 1964, was very important in planning education. This was enhanced by the belief in the importance of planning in developing the country. One of the first university planning departments in the Middle East was established, in 1964, at El-Azhar University in Cairo. The main course is a 5-year study leading to a B.Sc. (planning). Besides, there are postgraduate studies for 2 years leading to an M.Sc. (planning) and another 2 years for a Ph.D. (planning). The courses, which are under constant revision, are carried out according to experience gained in application. They have been prepared with special emphasis on planning in different Arab countries. Generally speaking, they are similar to those given at English and American universities, with modifications to suit local conditions, but stress has been laid on the study of national comprehensive planning and regional planning. The first graduates were awarded the B.Sc. (planning) in June 1969 and the first M.Sc. (planning) in May 1968. Meanwhile, the study of town planning in architectural departments has been raised from 6 to 10 hours weekly. Besides, postgraduate diploma courses leading to an M.C.D. (planning) have started in most of these departments.

Institutions The Egyptian Institute of Engineers is the professional body in Egypt which is responsible for the engineering profession. This Institute is divided into different sections such as architecture and mechanical, electrical, chemical, and civil engineering. All graduates from the Egyptian faculties of engineering and persons with equivalent qualifications can apply for the membership in the institute. There have been efforts to establish a planning section within the institute, but that was postponed till the number of planners reaches 50, according to the institute bylaws. The planners, therefore, for the time being are affiliated with the architecture section.

Education in Egypt is supervised and controlled by the government. Education in planning, so far, is the responsibility of the universities. Moreover, different short planning courses are organized by the Ministry of Housing and Public Utilities and by local government. These are designed as refresher courses for planners working at these ministries. Moreover, the Society of Engineers, an independent body, has established a section for planners and organizes public lectures in planning.

According to the Egyptian planning acts, all master plans of towns and cities and all major planning schemes should be exhibited and explained to the public, which has the right to put forward its opinions. Planning bodies should, therefore, consult public opinion before the Ministry is asked to approve the plans.

Geographical and Climatic Conditions   Egypt comprises not only Egypt proper but also the Sinai Peninsula and a number of uninhabited islands in the Red Sea. It is situated in the northeastern corner of Africa, between 22 and 32 degrees north latitude, and occupies nearly one-thirtieth of the total area of the African continent. It is bounded on the north by the Mediterranean Sea, on the south by the Republic of Sudan, on the west by the Republic of Libya, and on the east by Israel, the Gulf of Aquaba, and the Red Sea. The total area of Egypt is almost 386,110 square miles (about a million square kilometers) with a maximum length of 667 miles (1,073 kilometers) from north to south, and a maximum width of 762 miles (1,226 kilometers) from east to west. Its area considerably exceeds that of any European country except Russia.

It is noticeable that, in addition to being directly accessible by sea from all the countries of southern and western Europe, Egypt lies about halfway along the sea route from Britain to India via the Suez Canal.

Egypt may be divided geographically into the following seven main parts (Map 1):

1. The valley and delta of the Nile. The Nile is more than 4,160 miles (6,695 kilometers) long from its source to its mouth, but only the terminal 951 miles (1,530 kilometers) or so lie within the borders of Egypt, where the Nile does not receive a single tributary. The width of the cultivable land gradually increases from Aswân to a certain extent for about 584 miles (940 kilometers) to Cairo, where the valley opens out into the delta. The average width of the flat alluvial floor of the Nile valley between Aswân and Cairo is about 6 miles (10 kilometers).

The river flows in a northwesterly direction for some 12 miles (20 kilometers), and its two main branches discharge into the Mediterranean

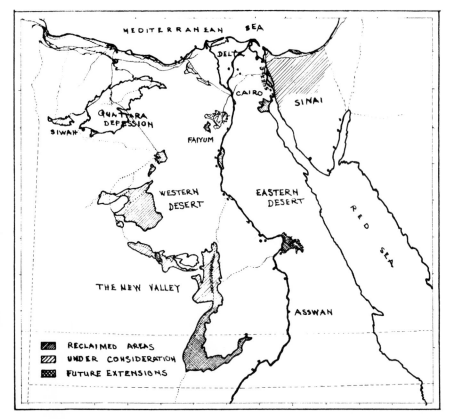

MEDITERRANEAN SEA

DELTA

CAIRO

SINAI

QUATTARA DEPRESSION

SIWAH

FAIYUM

WESTERN DESERT

EASTERN DESERT

RED SEA

THE NEW VALLEY

ASSWAN

RECLAIMED AREAS
UNDER CONSIDERATION
FUTURE EXTENSIONS

The seven main regions of Egypt: (1) the valley and delta of the Nile, (2) Faiyûm Province, (3) the Suez Canal, (4) the Western Desert, (5) the Eastern Desert, (6) the Sinai Peninsula, (7) the islands of the Red Sea.

Sea at Rosetta and at Damietta, to the east, so ie 3.75 miles (6 kilometers) further along. The Nile delta has an area of about 8,494 square miles (22,000 square kilometers), about half of which is cultivated.

2. Faiyûm province. The Faiyûm is a deep depression in the desert about 100 miles (60 kilometers) southwest of Cairo and is connected with Cairo by a narrow opening through the desert hills. The province consists of 77 square miles (200 square kilometers) of shallow, brackish lake called Birket Quârûn and 656 square miles (1,700 square kilometers) of the depression area, of which 502 square miles (1,300 square kilometers) are cultivated, being irrigated by canals from the Nile.

3. The Suez Canal. Having a total length of 106 miles (171 kilometers), it separates Egypt proper from the Sinai Peninsula. The zone consists of a narrow strip of land running along the length of the canal with nearly all the settlements on the western side of the waterway.

4. The Western Desert. The Western Desert area, exclusive of Faiyûm, is more than two thirds of the whole of Egypt, and is one of the most arid regions in the world.

The mountains are only seen in the extreme southwestern corner. In the northern and central parts, the plateau surface is broken at intervals by great depressions; some of these depressions are habitable and called "oases," using artesian water for agricultural purposes. The five principal ones are Siwa, Baharîya, Farafra, Dakhla, and Khârga; the other depressions contain only salt lakes and salt marshes and are consequently uninhabitable. The largest and deepest is the Quattara depression.

5. The Eastern Desert. This region of Egypt extends from the Nile Valley to the Suez Canal and the Red Sea and has an area of about 86,000 square miles (223,000 square kilometers). The Eastern Desert consists essentially of a great backbone of high mountains running roughly parallel to the Red Sea, at a comparatively short distance inland from the coast, flanked on the west and north by a highly dissected lower plateau. The water sources consist only of springs and rock pools in the mountains and of wells sunk in the wadi floors in the lower country. Nowhere in the Eastern Desert are there any artesian water supplies; consequently, it is only in a very few spots that agriculture can be practiced.

6. The Sinai Peninsula. The Sinai Peninsula has a total area of 23,500 square miles (61,000 square kilometers). The southern part is formed of a complex of high mountains (the highest, Gebel Katherina, is about 8,658 feet or 2,639 meters tall). The mountainous tract in the south is intensely dissected by canyonlike wadis draining on the one hand to the Gulf of Suez and on the other to the Gulf of Aqaba. The northern two-thirds of the peninsula is a great plateau sloping downward to the Mediterranean Sea (Wadi El Arîsh).

7. The islands of the Red Sea. The Egyptian islands in the Red Sea are of little importance except to navigators, being barren of all vegetation and devoid of natural water resources. Most of the islands are situated in the neighborhood of the Strait of Jubal, at the southern end of the Gulf of Suez.

Climate The Egyptian climate is extremely dry and stable most of the year. Rainfall decreases steadily from north to south. Alexandria, on the Mediterranean Sea, has 7.24 inches (184 millimeters) annually, whilst Ghardaka on the Red Sea has just 0.12 inch (3 millimeters). Damietta, at the northeastern corner of the delta, has 4 inches (102 millimeters); Cairo, at the apex of the delta, has 1 inch (26 millimeters); Assiut, halfway up the Nile Valley, has only 0.28 inch (7 millimeters); and Aswân, at the extreme south of Upper Egypt, has 0.04 inch (1 millimeter) annually.

Humidity is extremely low in the desert, but the proximity of the Nile adds considerable moisture to the air of the valley and the delta. Consequently, humidity is higher in autumn, attaining an average of over 80 percent in the delta during December, while it is lower in May and June when the average is less than 25 percent in Nubia.

The lowest atmospheric pressure in Egypt occurs during the summer (July and August) and the highest during winter (January). The general distribution of pressures during the summer shows pressures to be higher on the western side of the country as a consequence of the high-pressure zone which persists over the Azores. However, pressure variations and consequent climatic changes are much more marked during the winter than the summer.

A representative cross section of temperature conditions in Egypt is taken from Alexandria in the north, to Tanta in the delta, to Cairo, and to Aswân in the south. The lowest temperature recorded was 43°F (6.3°C) at Tanta in January and the highest was 107°F (41.7°C) at Aswân in June.

Egypt is affected by two main winds, the "trade winds," which have a moderating effect all year round, and the "khamsin winds," which blow mainly from the southeast, south, and southwest. The khamsin winds carry hot sand and dust from the desert, especially during April and May. There is a very marked difference in the wind velocities at the above-mentioned cities. The velocity is very much higher at Alexandria, averaging 9 miles (14.4 kilometers) per hour, compared with the annual mean velocities of 0.93, 1.36, and 1.05 miles (1.5, 2.2, and 1.7 kilometers) per hour at Tanta, Cairo, and Aswân respectively.

The cloudiest time of the year is December and January. The cloudiest part of Egypt is in the vicinity of Alexandria, where during these months it is very cloudy but much less so at Aswân. Generally, the cloud decreases to a minimum during June and July. Generally, the sun shines in Egypt all the year round and accordingly the intensity of light is very strong.

Traditions of Planning to the End of the Nineteenth Century   The history of the Egyptian city goes back 6,000 years, the age of the ancient Egyptian culture which flourished along the Nile Valley. Two periods are considered to be most characteristic in the history of the Egyptian city:

1. The ancient Egyptian city (5000–332 B.C.), which could be broken down into two phases: The first phase (5000–3315 B.C.), where provincial towns functioned as central administrative towns or as centers of trade and commerce within the surrounding agricultural land. Towns in this respect were centers for 20 regions in the delta area and 22 other regions in Upper Egypt; examples are Heliopolis and Kift. The second phase (3315–332 B.C.) is considered to be that of the capital city. Thebes and Memphis, for example, were capital cities for the whole united regions of Egypt. The site of the ancient Egyptian city was usually at the far end of the Nile Valley, higher than the lower areas near to the river banks; the city pattern was a gridiron, directed to the cardinal lines; it usually had a congregation court near to the main entrance gate and not specially in the middle of the city; the city was surrounded by high walls and was usually divided into two sectors: the royal residential sector including the houses of the nobles, and the workers' sectors where the people lived.

2. The Egyptian Islamic city (641–1800 A.D.). The Fustât city is the first Islamic city founded by the Arabs (641 A.D.). It was succeeded by cities like El-Aksûr, El Katayeh, and Cairo. In the Islamic city (a) the site was usually chosen with a natural protective backing of hills or rivers and was artificially protected by city walls, fortresses, and castles; (b) the mosque, as the religious center, dominated the city buildings as well as the city plan; and (c) the structure of the Islamic city was based upon the clearly democratic strata of the community. The larger residential unit was the El Hayy

quarter. The city was composed of many quarters, each of which was inhabited by a particular tribe or groups of relatives. These groups were virtually self-contained families. Their houses adjoined one another and comprised a kind of communal residential cell. The neighborhood of some residential blocks composed a "Hara," which was the second residential unit in the Islamic city structure. Each block was designed to accommodate 10 to 20 houses. These opened on a private square, with sharp angles in the inlets and outlets of the housing block to keep it visually isolated from the neighboring block.

To enter the neighborhood from the main street, the visitor had to pass along a sharply angled road (Atfa), thus assuring privacy for this cell-like community. The neighborhood square (El Saha) served a variety of social functions; i.e., wedding parties or religious ceremonies, which played an important role in the life of the square. The dwelling, the smallest unit in the city structure, was usually a patio-type house with special quarters for men and women (Salamlek and Haramlek).

Twentieth-century Planning The Egyptian population nearly doubled from 1917 to 1960 (183 percent). The total area of agricultural land has remained in the neighborhood of 6 million acres in spite of the steadily increasing population. This expansion in population resulted in sudden city and town expansions as well as in the founding of new towns and communities.

New Towns and Communities New towns and communities are numerous, occasioned by several projects, the principal of which are the following:

The High Dam Emigration Project. The lake behind the dam flooded the Nubian region south of Aswân, where 33 villages disappeared under water permanently. The inhabitants of these villages had to be evacuated.

The extension area where emigration villages are chosen has to support a population of 98,609 emigrants: 25,328 families in 33 villages and a central town where all the services (educational, social, and administrative) have been concentrated. The villages vary in size between 500 and 3500 inhabitants with an average of 1,650.

The Gourna Village near Luxor. The aim of this experiment was to restore to the peasant population its heritage of vigorous, locally inspired building traditions and a native art which is common to the region between Nubia and Lower Egypt. The total gross area of the village is 50 acres planned for a population of 7,000, giving an overall density of about 140 inhabitants per acre.

Maryût Regional Plan and New Towns. The project is on 80,000 acres of reclaimed desert area about 25 miles (40 kilometers) southwest of Alexandria, bounded by the desert road from Cario to Alexandria on the east and the railway from Alexandria to Matrûh to the north. The project includes 30 villages, 7 subcenters, and a capital city (see illustrations). A thorough survey formed the basis of a series of maps to isolate the areas least suitable for cultivation and to be earmarked for other purposes—in particular as sites for villages.

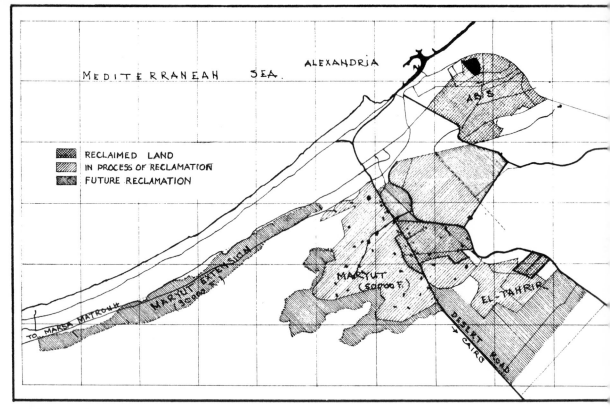

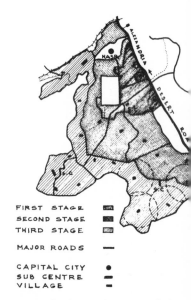

The Capital City of Maryût. The site of the capital city is selected on land not suitable for cultivation. It is located to the northeast near the main desert road and railway. The city design was based on the gridiron principle. It consists of two major neighborhood units, each subdivided into 4 precincts and each with a local center. Its population is expected to reach 16,000 inhabitants in the next 20 years. The gross density is expected to be 31.1 persons per acre and the net density 45 persons per acre.

Heliopolis Town. The town was founded in 1906 to the northeast of Cairo and reached a population of 120,000 and 200,000 in 1960 and 1967 respectively, with a population density of 60 people per acre. It started as a suburb connected to Cairo by means of an electric train. Heliopolis is now an independent town which attracts other adjacent suburbs into its circle of influence.

All Egyptian cities and towns are expanding both horizontally and vertically, and there are very many extension projects all over the country. The scale of the efforts can be appreciated by the examples of Nasr New City and Maady Town.

Nasr New City, situated to the northeast of Cairo and south of Heliopolis, was established by a republican decree in 1959. The city area is about 600 acres. It has an agreeable climate and is close to Cairo, of which it is mainly a residential extension. The most important landmarks in the city are Cairo Stadium, the International Market and Amusement Park, El-Azhar University, and the government institutions.

The progress of desert reclamation in the vicinity of the Maryût Region Project.

Project for the Maryût Region which includes 30 villages, 7 subcenters, and a capital city.

The planning of the residential areas was based on the neighborhood-unit principle (see illustration), with an average population in each neighborhood of not more than 10,000. The residential density varies between a minimum of 100 and a maximum of 200 persons per acre. The neighborhood units are a mixture of three- or four-story blocks and large blocks of apartments of 7, 10, or 14 stories. The neighborhood units have the necessary services and facilities.

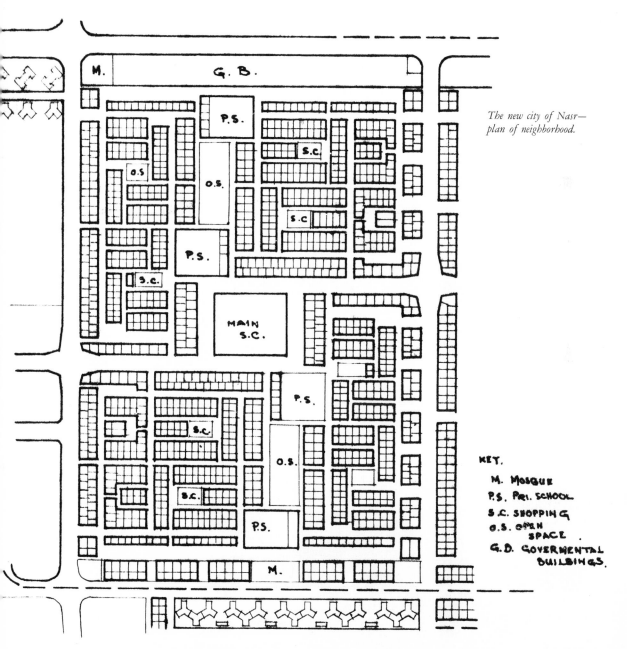

The new city of Nasr—plan of neighborhood.

KEY.

M. MOSQUE
P.S. PRI. SCHOOL
S.C. SHOPPING
O.S. OPEN SPACE
G.B. GOVERMENTAL BUILDINGS.

Maady Town was planned in 1905 as a garden city based on the gridiron pattern. The built-up area covers 15 percent of the total gross area, which is 1,400 acres and has a population of 60,000. Maady is connected to the central area of Cairo (6 miles or 10 kilometers) by an electric railway. Although the town has adequate educational and recreational services, it is dependent on Cairo for other services. There is a project to extend the area of the community by 1,000 acres in a northern direction.

Urban Renewal The renewal program in Egyptian cities aims to deal effectively with the problem of urban slums and to promote and preserve

A central area of Cairo—Midan (Place) al Tahrir le Caire.

The Nile at Cairo with some of the modern buildings and the embankment road. An underpass is in the foreground.

a healthy community with adequate community facilities. The program covers most of the Egyptian cities, but the following are the major projects:

1. Recent developments in Cairo, which has a long history of more than 1,000 years and has now reached a population of about 4.5 million inhabitants, are according to Cairo Master Plan of 1955. These developments were specifically concerned with: (*a*) Conservation of historic areas; i.e., the redevelopment of the Fatimid Cairo. (*b*) Redevelopment of the central city

Stanley Bay Beach, Alexandria.

El-Charnish, Alexandria.

area; i.e., redevelopment of the Fawala, Maarouf, and Maspiro areas. (*c*) Slum clearance in neglected poor areas providing for new housing facilities; i.e., Zienhum, El-Seera, and Shubra areas. (*d*) Improvements of roads and traffic systems. As a result of such improvements, three main arteries have been planned and constructed. Moreover, the Nile Cornish Road was built in 1954. It is 43 miles (70 kilometers) long. Five new bridges along the Nile have been constructed in the last 15 years linking the eastern and the western parts of Cairo. The city entrances were cleared and replanned, connecting the city directly with the regional pattern of main highways and roads to the delta and to Upper Egypt.

2. Reconstruction of Port Said, a city of about a quarter of a million, took place as a result of the war damage in 1956. The bombed site west of the Suez Canal together with reclaimed land (part of Manzala Lake) which covers 250 acres constitute the project area. The plan was based on neighborhood criteria. The population of the project area reached 30,000 people (5,500 families) housed in multistory blocks. This gives an average density of 120 persons per acre.

BIBLIOGRAPHY: M. R. Raid, *Alexandria: Its Town Planning Development,* The Town Planning Review, the Dept. of Civic Design, University of Liverpool, vol. 15, No. 4, December 1933; B. Snah, *Egyptian Architecture as Cultural Expression,* New York and London, 1938; Maxwell Fry and Jane Drew, *Tropical Architecture,* London, 1946; A. Badawy, *A History of Egyptian Architecture,* vol. 1, Giza, 1954; Ministry of Housing and Municipalities, *Report on Gourna,* Housing and Town Planning Department, Cairo, May 1956; Smith W. Stevenson, *The Art and Architecture of Ancient Egypt,* Penguin Books, London, 1958; Ahmed Amin Mokhtar, *An*

Investigation into Local Factors Influencing Planning Standards in Egypt, Durham University, England, 1959; E. T. H. Zurick, *The Development of Urban and Rural Housing in Egypt,* Azzam O. A., 1960. Ministry of Housing and Municipalities, *Handbook of Basic Statistics,* U.A.R. Dept. of Public Mobilisation & Statistics, October 1963, *Planning & Housing for the Egyptian Rural Village,* presented to Afro-Asian Housing Conference, Cairo, December 1963, *Report on the Execution Organisation of the Nubian Emigration Project,* Ministry of Social Affairs, Kom Ombo, 1964, *Urban & Rural Renewal in U.A.R.,* Ministry of Local Administration in Collaboration with the Ministry of Housing & Public Utilities, Cairo, 1965; Ahmed Amin Mokhtar, *The Regional Plan for Maryût,* paper presented at the 9th Congress of Arab Engineers, Baghdad, 1964, *Planning Education,* paper presented to the 9th Congress of Arab Engineers, Baghdad-Iraq, 1964, *The Effect of Education,* paper presented to the First Congress of the Organization of Arab Cities, Beirut-Lebanon, July 1968; Hussein Shafei, *Housing Project for the Resettlement of the Nubian Population in the Region of Kom Ombo,* Afro-Asian Housing Organization, Singapore, 1967; Heliopolis Company for Housing and Construction, *Heliopolis its Past and Future,* Arabic Cairo, 1969; Nasr New Town Company for Housing & Construction, *Nasr New City.*

Geographical and Climatic Conditions:
H. J. L. Beadnell, *An Egyptian Oases,* London, 1909; Hume & Hraghes, *The Soil and Water Supply of the Maryût District,* Cairo, 1921; W. F. Hume, *Geology of Egypt,* Cairo, 1923; J. Ball, *Contribution to Geography of Egypt,* Cairo, 1939; Hurst, Black and Simaika, *The Nile Basin, the Future Conservation of the Nile,* vol. 3, reprint 1951; A. Rakeeb, *A Report published on the 25th December 1958 by A. Rakeeb, Permanent Secretary of Public Works,* Cairo.

—AHMED AMIN MOKHTAR

EGYPTIAN PLANNING, ANCIENT   (*See* ANCIENT PLANNING, EGYPT.)

EHRENSTROM, JOHAN ALBRECHT (1762–1847)   Politician and diplomat who made historic contributions to the planning of the Finnish capital, born in Helsinki, August 28, 1762. Helsinki was destroyed by fire in 1808, and in 1810 Ehrenstrom prepared a new plan for the city which was put forward by the committee appointed to supervise the reconstruction of Helsinki. Ehrenstrom submitted his plan in the name of the finishing draftsman, Lieutenant Anders Kocke. When, in 1812, Helsinki became the capital of Finland, Ehrenstrom was appointed chairman of the committee, remaining at this post until 1825, when the committee was disbanded. Ehrenstrom's plan gradually emerged in stages, by successive versions of 1812, 1814, 1815, and 1817, but all the fundamental planning principles already existed in the first project. A new grid plan was created in place of the old street network, a plan based on blocks of varying sizes and a strongly differentiated townscape.

Johan Albrecht Ehrenstrom (1762–1847). (*Finnish National Museum.*)

In 1816, at Ehrenstrom's initiative, the German-born architect Carl Ludvig Engel (*q.v.*) was called from St. Petersburg to be architect to the development committee. Under Ehrenstrom and Engel, Helsinki's Empire-style center and its numerous buildings were planned and built.

In 1824, Ehrenstrom made a new plan for the town of Oulu, which also had been destroyed by fire.

Ehrenstrom died in Helsinki, on April 15, 1847.

BIBLIOGRAPHY: Yrjo Blomstedt, *Johan Albrecht Ehrenstrom,* Helsinki, 1963.

—RAIJA-LIISA HEINONEN

EKISTICS   The name given by Constantinos A. Doxiadis to the science of human settlements.

The scope of the science can be elucidated as follows: Planners are concerned with all types of human settlements from the isolated and nomadic hut—which is in some way repeated today by people using caravans and trailers—to the organized farmhouse, village, small town, city, metropolis, megalopolis, and future major urban systems. They, not merely the traditional town or city, are all the concern of society and the subject of study by planners. This means a completely different discipline from the methods that were developed by traditional schools of architecture and planning.

Ekistics evolved as the result of the realization that it was impossible to deal comprehensibly with problems if planners were restricted to using only the knowledge given by architecture, engineering, and planning—the fields in which they were trained. There is the need to collaborate with economists, social scientists, geographers, and gradually with many more professions—including administrators, lawyers, and mathematicians—in order to form the complete team that could deal with the complex problems of human settlements.

Thus the need for "interdisciplinary" effort arose. This is meaningful in ekistics only in the sense that an orchestra is a multi-instrumental team that strives toward a good interpretation of a given composition. But can an orchestra perform without its conductor? No, and in the same way ekistics cannot be the result of an interdisciplinary effort without a leader. There must be an ekistician, a person whose discipline is the synthesis of all parts into one whole.

On the basis of a belief in these ideas, an effort was made in the Greek underground movement during the Second World War to study the reconstruction of Greece. This led, during the postwar period, to the creation of the Greek Ministry of Reconstruction and Housing which was responsible for Greece's successful reconstruction. Later Doxiadis Associates, an office providing consultation in development and ekistics, was created. The office covered more than thirty countries and many types of projects, from the very small to the very large. These projects ranged from a small neighborhood or the campus of a small college to cities; from old structures that were to be remodeled to new ones that were yet to be created.

The work of Doxiadis Associates can be seen in projects such as the building of new cities or the remodeling of old ones; projects in urban renewal or regional development, and others.

Examples among new cities are: Islamabad, the new capital of Pakistan; Kafue, the new industrial city of Zambia; Tema, the new harbor and industrial city of Ghana; and Beida, the new administrative center of Libya; remodeling of old cities: Athens, Baghdad, Homs, Khartoum, Lusaka, Rio de Janeiro, Riyadh, Skoplje, and Tobruk; urban renewal plans: Eastwick in Philadelphia; Hampton, Virginia; Louisville, Kentucky; Malden, Massachusetts; Miami, Florida; Washington, D.C.; and regional plans: the urban Detroit area, the Great Lakes megalopolis, and the Rio de la Plata Basin.

It was early recognized that the effort could not be fully developed without one special organization dedicated to research and education in this field. The Athens Technological Organization, a nonprofit organization, was thus created in 1958, and in 1963 it gave birth to the Athens Center of Ekistics, which exists to foster a concerted program of research, education, documentation, and international cooperation in all major fields related to the development of human settlements.

The Athens Center of Ekistics has five divisions:

1. Research. Large-scale basic research into the development of human settlements under a wide range of conditions. Current major projects are entitled "The City of the Future," "The Capital of Greece," "The Human Community," and "Ancient Greek cities."

2. Education. Advanced educational and training programs in ekistics.

3. International Programs. Worldwide contacts and collaboration; international meetings; the Athens Ekistics Month; and secretarial services to the World Society for Ekistics.

4. Documentation. Collection, classification, and dissemination of information related to ekistics.

5. Administration.   —CONSTANTINOS A. DOXIADIS

ELECTRIC POWER GENERATION AND TRANSMISSION   The demand for electric power by the industrial nations has grown rapidly as their development has advanced. In general terms the worldwide requirements have doubled every 10 years. In the United States alone the consumption of 258 million megawatthours in 1947 had grown to 1,057 million in 1965. By 1980 it is expected to exceed 2,500 million.

Since, from the point of view of a nation's economy, cheap power enhances its competitive position, planners support a cheap power policy. Therefore increasing attention is being given not only to production costs but also to tariff arrangements. The earlier tendency to weight tariffs in favor of domestic consumers is being abandoned, and more attention is being given to the adjustment of existing systems to give weight to the claims of industry for cheaper power.

The rapid growth of demand for electric power has brought with it many aesthetic problems. The widespread invasion of the countryside by the installations and internetworks of electricity generating sources has prompted reactions. Ill-planned and ill-conceived schemes are not only sometimes visually offensive but also contribute to the pollution of the environment. In this latter respect the outcry has now assumed global proportions. New chapters in the history of power development remain to be written, and there is an exciting challenge to shape and control this development. Well designed and well planned, these edifices can be made to harmonize with their natural surroundings so as to adorn rather than despoil. The planner, by securing harmonious collaboration from scientists, engineers, architects, and landscape architects, has an important role in achieving a systems approach in these developments.

Of these, the role of the landscape architect will be increasingly important. The pace of demand for long-distance overhead transmission systems will continue to increase, at least until the late 1980s. There will, at the same time, be corresponding reaction to this development because of the effect of wires and pylons upon the beauty of the landscape. Application of the landscape architect's skill to the siting and routing of the systems can do much to overcome these objections. Lines can often be sited so that they do not intrude upon the skyline but merge into the background. The engineer and architect can do much to ensure that their pylons and edifices are as free as possible from intrinsic ugliness. The landscape architect can advise upon route and location, so that there is the best possible proportion and composition with the natural surroundings.

Power Generation There are three prime sources of energy for the generation of electric power:
  1. The fossil fuels (coal, oil, natural gas, shale)
  2. Water power
  3. Nuclear fuels

The fossil fuel sources at present contribute the greater proportion toward the general demand. In the United States in 1965, about 75 percent of the total was derived from these fuels. Hydroelectric power provided for the major part of the remainder. Nuclear fuels accounted for the small balance. Estimates for 1980, taking account of planned investment programs, indicate a much accelerated growth rate for the use of nuclear power, and it is in this field that major developments in the generating of electric power are likely to take place. However, because of the long-term, high-value nature of generating-plant investment programs, fossil fuels will continue to play a major albeit decreasing role for the remainder of the twentieth century.

The primary costs of production and delivery of electric power are three: cost of fuel, cost of transmission and distribution, and cost of administration and real estate. Of these, only the first comes into the consideration of making nuclear energy competitive with hydroelectric power and fossil fuels. With recent developments in high-voltage transmission over great distances, the building of plants close to sources of fossil fuel or hydroelectric power is more feasible. It is unlikely, therefore, that nuclear sources will be *less* expensive than conventional fuel sources, since the cost of the latter can be much reduced by removing the expensive transportation element when there is a long distance between the fuel source and the generating plant. This factor does not justify lack of enterprise in the continued development of nuclear power generating techniques. Fossil fuel sources are fast being eaten up, even allowing for possible payoff from nuclear mining techniques. Considerable developments have already been undertaken in much larger nuclear powered units. The increased efficiency of high-temperature gas-cooled reactors and the possibility by the mid seventies of fast breeder reactor plants, planned for both Sweden and Britain, are important in assessing the growing importance of nuclear power generation in the years ahead. Further, conventional power sources are coming increasingly under pressure of legislation because of air pollution, although the effect upon marine and fluvial ecology of cooling-system water discharge from certain nuclear-plant designs must not be overlooked.

Methods of Generation   Electricity is generated by converting the prime fuel source to drive turbines which in turn drive the generators. With fossil fuel there is combustion of the fuel to produce steam for this purpose. With atomic fuel, heat from a reactor produces the necessary steam by an arrangement of heat exchangers. First-generation plants achieve this by using pressurized liquid to cool the reactor. Second-generation developments have led to nonpressurized sodium coolants. The third-generation involves the use of high-temperature gas to cool the reactor. This last arrangement uses helium as the cooling gas. Latest designs of this type have the gas leaving the reactor at temperatures of the order of 800°C, and they make it possible to use the gas itself to drive a gas turbine, thus eliminating the use of boilers and steam. In all these cases, uranium fuels, graphite-moderated, are used. Development on a large scale is being undertaken on the fast breeder reactor concept. If it can be carried to success, a facility of much interest to urban planners will emerge. This would lead to the possibility of obtaining nuclear energy from a reactor set underground in a steel vessel, capable of providing all the power required by a given area with a minimum of labor expenditure. This system would also be capable of producing, from its own waste, fuel to sustain its efforts.

Despite these developments, generation by water power will continue to have claims to consideration for many decades. Here the stream or head of water is directed into water turbines to drive electric generators. Here the fuel cost is nil. Nevertheless, high maintenance and high investment costs can make unit cost of production high as compared with other methods. If the system is designed to combat peak demands, there can be loss due to the production of unwanted power in "off peak" times. This disadvantage can be offset by "pumped storage" techniques, whereby unwanted power is used to pump water back to higher-level storage reservoirs for release when peak demands arise. With this arrangement generating capacity is set at a lower overall level but still meets maximum demand. Also, hydroelectric systems are generally connected to interties with adjacent power sources. Then the problems of peak demand can be dealt with over the system as a whole.

With hydroelectric schemes, as with overhead transmission systems, there will be increasing objection to the damming of streams and the flooding of valleys. Here, however, the aesthetic objections are not so well founded. Water reservoirs are, for the most part, a contribution to the landscape, always provided that they are created so as to lie naturally within the contours of the surrounding land, with the dams in harmonious proportion to the surrounding country. The photographs of Loch Monar Dam, part of the Scottish Strathfarrar scheme, show these principles put to practical effect. It must be remembered that the construction of water dams is not required only for power generation; the long-term aims of flood control,

Strathfarrar hydroelectric scheme, Scotland. View of Loch Monar. By the building of the two dams, this loch was enlarged from 4 to 8 miles (6.4 to 12.9 kilometers) in length and the level of the water raised by 75 feet (22.9 meters). Despite this, the water lies in relation to the land contours and headlands as though it were a natural consequence.

Strathfarrar hydroelectric scheme, Scotland. Loch Monar dam. The elegant design of the structure, together with the preservation of existing trees in the foreground, produces a pleasing effect.

irrigation, and water supply come into consideration. However, each hydro-electric scheme brings with it a requirement for overhead transmission-line systems, and it is against these that the outcry will be greatest. As atomic energy plants in or close to urban areas become more feasible, they will gradually meet more and more of the expanding demands for power during the remainder of the twentieth century. It is, therefore, unlikely that major hydroelectric schemes will be constructed in the century to come. Existing plants will continue in use beyond 2000 A.D., but they will be making an ever-decreasing contribution to the global power demand.

Power Transmission   If electric power could be generated at any location for the same unit cost, the problems of transmission would not arise. Although future developments in nuclear power may one day make this practical, present conditions demand transmission of power, often over great distances. The larger the generating plant, the lower is the unit cost. Ideally, these large plants should be located at the epicenter of demand. However, this is seldom possible because of fuel availability, real estate values, and water supply.

Electric power is the product of the current flow in the circuit and the electromotive force applied to the circuit to maintain this flow. In the direct-current case, the power (in watts) is the product of the rate of current flow (in amperes) and the electrical pressure (in volts). In the alternating-current case, any inductance or capacitance present in the circuit has a reactive effect upon the phase relationship of the voltage and current elements. Any "out of phase" component must be taken into account in the calculation of average power in an ac circuit. Only that proportion of the current which is in phase with the voltage provides the average power. The proportion of voltage effective in terms of power is 0.707 of the peak voltage (the root mean square). Nonetheless, it is the peak voltage level which is to be reckoned with in transmission-line insulation and support designs. Transmission of power over transmission lines and distribution systems cannot be achieved without loss. The principle element of loss is due to the resistance of the conductors. This resistance depends upon the cross section of the conductor and the amplitude of the current which it carries. Ohm's law (current = voltage/resistance) indicates that for the transmission of a given amount of energy, any increase in voltage will permit of a decrease in current. Also, assuming a given loss, higher voltages permit the use of conductor wires of smaller cross section. It follows that, within the compass of what is permissible from the point of view of insulation, electric power should be transmitted at the highest possible voltage levels. Unfortunately, the high voltages preferred for transmission are much above those at which generator apparatus can be operated in practice. Trans-formation is therefore necessary, and fortunately alternating current lends itself to this. This, in fact, is the main reason for the emergence of alternating current as the principal mode of generation.

The usual power system achieves distribution by ac generation in the power station, transformation to high voltage, and transfer to the transmission line. It is then conveyed to a substation close to the load. It is here transformed to lower voltage and fed into a distribution network which conveys the supply to the customer's premises.

It will be seen that there is advantage in the transmission of direct current. However, the advantages of alternating current in respect of voltage-level transformation, the existence of ac generating plant, and the universality of ac motors and other electrical devices makes this impossible unless some compromise can be arranged. Great improvement in the design of ac/dc conversion apparatus now offers a solution. In many countries where long transmission distances are involved, power is generated as alternating current, transformed to high voltage, converted to direct current, and transmitted on lines to the destination. There, it is reconverted to alternating current, transformed, and distributed to customers. In the United States, planned for completion in the early 1970s, are two 800-kilovolt dc lines of 1,500 kilovoltamperes capacity, to be part of the giant Pacific Northwest and Southwest transmission grid system. There exist shorter, lower-voltage dc lines in the United States and Sweden. Others are in use in Europe and the Soviet Union. The Franco/British Power Exchange line under the English Channel is an interesting example which exploits the different social and domestic patterns of the two countries. The Soviet Union is proceeding with studies for an all-union power grid system in which dc transmission will play an important part. Claims that they intend to use lines with voltages as high as 2,000 kilovolts are made, although this would present formidable problems in respect of the corona discharge phenomenon caused by ionization of the air surrounding the conductors.

The satisfactory design of transmission systems presents many problems. To solve these it is necessary to achieve a satisfactory relationship between voltage level, wire size, insulation complexity, support-tower design, and access for maintenance. All these factors, moreover, are related to unit cost of delivered power and the reliability of the system.

The effects of resistance and, in the case of alternating current, of inductance and capacitance of the lines have been mentioned. These factors cause the voltage at the end of the line remote from the generator to vary with the load. These variations can be combatted by voltage-regulation devices. However, in large and complex intertie systems, reaction to load variation must be rapid if it is to be effective. The effect upon communities of the failure of electricity supply is well known. The experience of such occurrences as the United States Northeast blackout of 1965 has caused the federal authorities concern. The United States Federal Power Commission Report following the 1965 incident stressed the need for coordinated automatic load shedding, but at the same time it defined load shedding as an "insurance program" and not a substitute for good system control with adequate transmission generation and intertie exchange ability. It is now generally accepted that, in large systems, human reaction time is inadequate and computer capability is necessary to assist the operatives in their task.

BIBLIOGRAPHY: Sylvia Crowe, *Tomorrow's Landscape,* Architectural Press, 1956, *Landscape of Power,* Architectural Press, 1958; Fitzgerald, Higginbotham, and Crabei, *Basic Electrical Engineering,* McGraw-Hill Book Co., Inc., New York, 1967; E. J. Cory (ed.), *High Voltage Direct Current Converters and Systems,* Macdonald, London, 1970.   —DOUGLAS C. BRUCE

ENGEL, JOHANN CARL LUDWIG (1778–1840)   Architect and town planner, born in Berlin, Germany, on July 3, 1778. Engel qualified as an architect in 1804 at the Berlin Academy of Art, where he had been taught by Friedrich Gilly, the great master of neoclassicism. From 1809 to 1814 Engel worked as city architect in Tallin, Estonia, and from 1815 to 1816 in St. Petersburg. J. A. Ehrenstrom, (*q.v.*), chairman of the Helsinki development committee, invited Engel to Finland in 1816 as architect to the committee. Between 1824 and 1840 Engel was Controller of Public Works and shared in the planning of Helsinki, newly elevated as the capital city. He designed most of the Empire-style buildings in the center, his main undertaking being the Senate Square and the monumental buildings around it.

Johann Carl Ludwig Engel (1778–1840). (Helsinki City Museum.)

Engel also produced plans for other towns, including Turku (1827–1828), the new part of Porvoo (1832), and Mikkeli (1837). He designed a regular grid plan for Turku, though he took the topography of the town more into account than had been the custom in earlier regularized plans. The blocks were mainly divided into four or sometimes six plots, with a row of one-plot blocks along the edges of the town. For fire safety reasons, the blocks were split by internal greenbelts and the street structure was made wider and lower, with larger open areas. The environs of the medieval cathedral were partly left as a park.

Engel's architectural design closely approached that of the St. Petersburg Empire style, though dating from a later period. In the 1820s and 1830s particularly, and up to the middle of the century, his influence on Finnish architecture was very great. This is especially evident in the wooden-built Empire style to be found—though decreasingly now—in Finland's small towns, which represents one of the most imteresting stages in the history of Finnish architecture.

Engel died in Helsinki on May 14, 1840.

BIBLIOGRAPHY: Carl Meissner, *Carl Ludwig Engel,* Berlin, 1937; Nils Erik Wickberg, *Carl Ludwig Engel,* Berlin, 1970.

—RAIJA-LIISA HEINONEN

ENGLAND   (*See* UNITED KINGDOM.)

ENVIRONMENTAL POLLUTION   In this context environment is understood to be all external and physical conditions that affect the well-being of man and other life, both animal and vegetable, on which man depends and for which he cares. The well-being of man in such a context involves his health, comfort, and aesthetic susceptibilities.

The great increase in population during the last hundred years and improvements in the standard of living have meant greater use of natural resources to supply human needs and to meet the requirements of industry. However, this increase in production and consumption has created pollution on an increasing scale. Its injurious effects have prompted governments to give the matter increasing attention and to foster research into the nature and causes of pollution with a view to proposing and applying controls and remedies. While much has already been done, much more remains to be done, and the constant vigilance of governments is required if pollution is not to endanger the well-being of mankind.

Pollution can be broadly classified as affecting the air, the land, fresh water, and the sea and beaches. There is also pollution by noise and by radioactivity. This classification is adopted by the British government in its white paper of May 1970 entitled *The Protection of the Environment—the Fight against Pollution.*

Air pollution and pollution by noise are considered in separate articles. Fresh-water pollution is partly considered under sewage disposal and sewerage, and one aspect of land pollution is considered under derelict land. The other forms of pollution of chief interest to the planner are briefly considered here.

The principal forms of land pollution in urban and industrial areas is from various kinds of dereliction but chiefly from mineral waste tips, especially in coal mining and iron ore extraction districts. The heaps thus formed are often prominent and extensive, as in the coal mining areas in the north of England, and government assistance has been given toward clearing such derelict regions. Fortunately much of the waste from colliery shale tips can be utilized for road construction and as concrete aggregates. From the standpoint of planning and development they represent obstacles, although in some cases ingenious planners use these heaps as embryo landscape features.

Another form of land pollution of importance to agriculture and wildlife is the increasing use of some forms of pesticides which have the effect of destroying life other than that which they are intended to control, and it is clear that the effects of such pesticides must be constantly watched.

The principal cause of the pollution of fresh water is the discharge of sewage and industrial waste into rivers, a practice which is common in most countries. Many of these are aware of the dangers and have taken measures, with varying success. Both sewage and industrial effluents will increase with increase of population and the expansion of industry, and measures of control have some degree of urgency. Fortunately, as the result of measures that have been taken in recent years, conditions have improved in some countries, as, for example, in the rivers of Great Britain. Among the methods employed to deal with this kind of pollution is the treatment by the industry of its own waste and the discharge of industrial wastes into the public sewers and thence to sewage treatment works. These measures are taken on the assumption that gradually all sewage will be treated before it is discharged into rivers. Until that is accomplished, it is desirable that the flow of rivers and streams should be maintained and stagnant water avoided (*see* SEWERAGE AND SEWAGE DISPOSAL).

Untreated sewage with industrial waste is either carried by rivers or discharged directly into the sea where, it is assumed, it is ultimately diluted and purified; but it may be damaging to fisheries in the process and it is sometimes washed back onto beaches, as occurs, according to reports, in New Jersey in the United States and on parts of the Norwegian coast. The most satisfactory remedy is obviously the treatment of industrial waste and sewage before it reaches rivers or the sea.

Another serious form of sea pollution is the accidental discharge of oil, either from tankers or in the course of exploration work, and governments are discussing the best methods of dealing with this.

Pollution from radioactivity is comparatively recent and results from the testing of nuclear weapons and from nuclear power stations. The former is much reduced since the Partial Test Ban of 1963. The United Kingdom has probably made the greatest progress in the development of nuclear power. Some of the methods employed include the storing of radioactive wastes in tanks underground, while in other cases they are piped into rivers or the sea under strict control. Solid waste is placed in canisters and dumped on the ocean bed. As pollution from radioactivity is comparatively recent, measures to deal with it have developed simultaneously.

As many forms of pollution extend beyond national boundaries and as almost all forms present the same problem, environmental pollution can best be dealt with internationally. There are obvious advantages to doing research by international cooperation and to international agreement on standards and measures of control. Some steps have already been taken and a move toward further cooperation was made during European Conservation Year 1970, sponsored by the Council of Europe. A further step was the United Nations Conference on the Environment, which was held in Stockholm in 1972.

BIBLIOGRAPHY: W. L. Thomas (ed.), *Man's Role in Changing the Face of the Earth*, University of Chicago Press, Chicago, 1956; Robert Arvill, *Man and Environment*, Pelican Books, Penguin Books, Inc., Baltimore, 1969; British white paper on *The Protection of the Environment—The Fight against Pollution*, H.M.S.O., London, 1970; Papers given at the European Conservation Conference, 1970, R. J. Benthem, "Urban Conglomerations," R. Passino, "Industry," M. E. Maldague, "Agriculture and Forestry," R. J. S. Hookway, "Leisure," in *The Management of the Environment in Tomorrow's Europe*.

—ARNOLD WHITTICK

EOPOLIS In the cycle of development and deterioration of cities Lewis Mumford gives six stages, which represent an amplification of an earlier classification by Patrick Geddes. These stages are: (1) eopolis, (2) polis, (3) metropolis, (4) megalopolis, (5) tyrannopolis, and (6) nekropolis. By eopolis (from the Greek ἠως-εος—meaning dawn and πολις, polis, meaning city) is meant the first small community, settlement, or village and the systematic agricultural development in the surroundings. "The agricultural village, not the market, is the prototype of the city," says Mumford. The second stage, polis, is "an association of villages or blood-groups having a common site that lends itself to defense against depredation." Many of the cities of the world have resulted from a congregation of villages. The third stage, metropolis, is, according to Mumford, attained when one city within a region "emerges from the less differentiated groups of villages and country towns" and becomes the metropolis or "mother city." The fourth stage, megalopolis, arises when "the city under the influence of a capitalistic mythos concentrates upon bigness and power." This stage marks the beginning of the decline. The fifth stage, tyrannopolis, arrives when the city becomes subject to all the abuses of commercialism, aggrandizement, and irresponsibility and crime becomes common. The sixth and final stage, when the physical towns become mere shells, is called nekropolis. It spells the death of the city and marks the point at which the city has become a graveyard.

History offers, in various ways, numerous examples of this cycle.

BIBLIOGRAPHY: Lewis Mumford, *The Culture of Cities,* Secker and Warsburg, London, 1938.
—ARNOLD WHITTICK

EOTECHNIC   Following the terminology of Patrick Geddes, who coined the terms "paleotechnic" and "neotechnic" (*q.v.*) to signify the early and later periods of the industrial age, Lewis Mumford coined the term "eotechnic" to define the important period of preparation when all the key inventions were either introduced or foreshadowed.[1]

EXCESS CONDEMNATION   (*See* EXPROPRIATION.)

EXPROPRIATION   The dispossession of an owner of his property for some public or social development such as municipal housing or the provision of public services like transport, electricity generation, or the implementation of planning schemes. (*See also* COMPULSORY PURCHASE.)

EXTRACTIVE INDUSTRIES   Minerals are extracted from the earth by various methods under a wide variety of geological and climatic conditions. In the context of land use the types of extraction can be classified mainly as mining and quarrying.

Mining is extraction by means of subterranean passages or tunnels, and various methods are employed according to geological conditions, depth of mine, and mineral extracted. Open-cut or open-cast mining is extraction by removing the overburden, which is often deep, instead of tunneling. This method has been used for mineral extraction, including that of iron and coal, in the United States for over 150 years. In Great Britain open-cut mining has been used for iron extraction for a long period, but only in the last 30 years has it been employed for coal extraction. Even with an overburden of 100 feet (30.5 meters), it has often proved more economical than mining by tunneling.

Quarrying has generally been associated with the extraction of stone in its various forms—granite, limestone, sandstone, quartzite, slate, sand, and gravel—which generally lies near the surface.

[1]Lewis Mumford, *Technics and Civilization,* Harcourt, Brace & Co., New York, 1934, George Routledge & Sons, Ltd., London, 1934, p. 109.

The use of land for mineral extraction must, in planning, be related to other land uses. Mining and quarrying is necessarily a temporary use of land. This use is of very varied duration, from about 5 years—as often with open-cast coal working and sometimes with sand and gravel workings—to several hundred years as with building-stone quarries. The workings take place mainly in country districts; and if these districts have contiguous populations, open-cast workings and quarrying necessarily affect many interests. This prompts such questions as what effect the workings will have on nearby urban areas, how noise and dust will be felt, and whether and in what ways agriculture, forestry, landscape amenities, wildlife, and features of archaeological or scientific interest will be affected. It is certain that some of these questions will be raised when any area is considered as a site for new mineral extraction. Where the number of sites from which a given mineral can be extracted is severely limited, then there is often no alternative; but the operation should be conducted with the least damage to other interests. Where the mineral is plentiful, scope is, of course, given in the choice of sites, and a site may be so chosen that there will be the least possible adverse effect on the general well-being of the area.

Much can be done in open-cast workings and quarrying to minimize the unsightly effects of the operations. In the case of hillside quarrying, entrances can be sited in relation to contours for the purpose of concealment, while existing and planted trees can be utilized for screening.

Restoration of land and the landscape after mining and quarrying is one of the most important questions in country planning. It is now, fortunately, receiving much more attention, and in some countries it is the subject of legislation. Mining and quarrying of the past have often left scars on the landscape, have produced derelict land, and have left great slag heaps in industrial areas. The process of removal and conversion to the more visually acceptable is necessarily slow, but with new workings restoration can be visualized and planned from the outset. Sometimes open-cast workings and quarrying may result in changes in the landscape—in the outlines of hills and the disposition of trees—and in some cases this may be an actual improvement. The important thing is that the whole undertaking—the open-cast working or quarrying and restoration of the site to its former or other desired use—should be imaginatively planned before operations begin.

Mining by subterranean passages is generally of a more permanent character, but it involves surface equipment that should be sited as far as possible in such a way as to harmonize with other interests. Also, mining will affect surface urban development, and it is often necessary in such cases to have cooperative plans, one for the mining and one for the surface development, as in the New Town of Peterlee, which is built over a coal mine in England.

BIBLIOGRAPHY: Sylvia Crowe, *Tomorrow's Landscape,* Architectural Press, London, 1956, *The Landscape of Power,* Architectural Press, London, 1958; H. E. Bracey, *Industry and the Countryside,* Faber & Faber, Ltd., London, 1963; J. Oxenham, *Reclaiming Derelict Land,* Faber & Faber, Ltd., London, 1966; Brenda Colvin, *Land and Landscape—Evolution, Design & Control,* John Murray (Publishers) Ltd., London, 1947, second enlarged edition, 1970.

—ARNOLD WHITTICK

F

FACTORIES (*See* INDUSTRIAL SITES AND LOCATIONS.)

FAMILY UNIT The family is the smallest and, by tradition, the basic collective unity of society. Its dwelling place should, therefore, logically form the unit of physical planning. This may appear obvious, but it is only recently, with the emphasis on the social aspects of planning, that it has been generally accepted. Up to the middle of the present century, many planning theorists based their ideas on the assumption that the street, or square, derived from the marketplace, was the unit of planning, and that the siting of dwelling houses must conform to the layout of streets and squares, as has been done for centuries. In the last half century, however, it has been increasingly believed that planning must start with the family and the house, and that streets, squares, and other urban configurations should be designed to conform to the best siting of family dwellings. The precept that the sun should determine the orientation of houses, not the street, is being more widely accepted, although tradition dies hard.

FARMING (*See* AGRICULTURAL LAND USE *and* SOIL CLASSIFICATION.)

FENCING (*See* FURNITURE.)

FINLAND Municipalities (towns, market towns, and rural communes) in Finland are practically self-governing. They collect taxes, and the 13 to 77 members of the town or communal councils are elected by direct elections. The councils appoint the town or communal boards that are responsible for the development of the towns and rural communes and the planning work carried out with regard to them. There are 78 towns (49 towns and 29 townships) and 428 rural communes in Finland.

Planning Legislation Urban planning is essentially regulated by the Building Act of 1958. This act, which has undergone several adjustments in the last few years, regulates physical planning as well as management and control of building activities. It contains stipulations on regional planning, master plans, town plans, and shore plans.

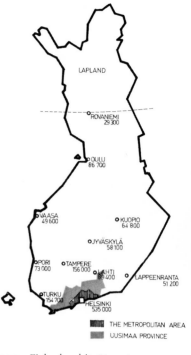

ABOVE: *Finland and its 11 most important cities.* LEFT: *The structure of social planning at the national level.*

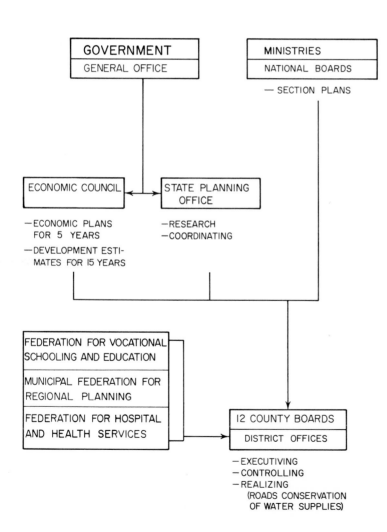

The Ministry of the Interior gives the order for a regional plan, and the preparation is made by the association for regional planning, the members of which are the towns and rural communes of the region in question. The draft for the regional plan is prepared by the board of the association with the help of specialists. The plan will then have to be approved by the council of the association for regional planning and ratified by the Ministry of the Interior and in certain cases by the Cabinet. The preparation of a regional plan is by stages: the first step is to make an outline structural plan, and after this has been approved, the actual regional plan is prepared and presented for ratification. Even though a regional plan is meant essentially as a physical plan, it requires extensive and specified functional and economic research and section plans. The highest population of a planning region is 800,000 and the lowest 30,000. In 1969, expenditure for regional planning for the whole country totalled $1,700,000. Regional planning has gained momentum in the last few years.

According to an adjustment in the building law made in 1968, every town must have a master plan. Prepared by the town board and approved by the town council, it is submitted to the Ministry of the Interior for ratification. In the 1950s and 1960s, master plans were drawn up for most towns, and the work of bringing these plans up to date in accordance with the new stipulations of the building law is either beginning or already going on. It is possible to draw up a master plan also for rural communes.

The main purpose of regional and master plans is to give guidance in preparing *town plans,* the procedure for which is similar to that for a master plan. Generally, the scale of a town plan is 1:2,000. In a town plan, certain areas can be stipulated to be used for certain purposes. Under certain conditions, a town has the right to buy off areas stipulated for general purposes in the town plan and to take possession of part of the street areas, and it can be granted the right to buy off building lots. The town can also obtain remuneration from the owners of building lots for road and sewage work. Permission to build houses and industrial and business premises is granted by the Board of Magistrates. A town plan is obligatory also for the densely populated areas of the rural communes, but for them a simplified version will suffice and, generally speaking, its juridical effects are less than those of a plan for a town or city. Town plans for rural communes are usually ratified by county boards and in certain cases by the Ministry of the Interior.

All towns and rural communes have a *building ordinance* with detailed regulations for building. That for a town is ratified by the Ministry of the Interior, and that for a rural commune by the county board.

Towns and rural communes have an exclusive right to prepare a master plan and a town plan, while landowners, according to an adjustment in the building law made in 1969, have been given the right to prepare a *shore plan*, which is the newest type of planning. A landowner must have a plan prepared for his shore area should the area be expected to attract densely built holiday houses or if the town or rural commune in question wishes to secure adequate free areas for its inhabitants. A shore plan for a town is ratified by the Ministry of the Interior, that for a rural commune by the county board.

Among other acts affecting the planning of a town, the most important ones are the Housing Production Act, the Waterways Act, the Highway Act, and the act for underdeveloped areas. The Housing Production Act that was given in 1966 stipulates that all towns and rural communes with population of at least 10,000 must have an up-to-date program for housing production for a period of the next 5 years. The Waterways Act obliges public institutions, for instance, to draw up plans for clearing their waste within a certain time.

Professional Practice   The basic structural and target alternatives are twice submitted to the consideration of the representatives of the city and, if necessary, also to the public and other interested parties. One will be selected

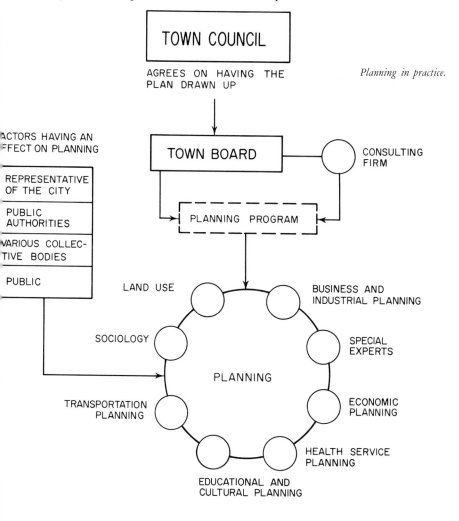

Planning in practice.

as the basis of the final plan and accepted by the town board. The plan will then be exhibited to the landowners, after which it will be approved by the town council and ratified by the Ministry of the Interior.

The work for *regional plans* is mainly carried out by the staffs of the associations for regional planning. Consultants are engaged for special tasks. The preparation of *master plans* is usually given to consulting engineers and architects, but in this case the technical officials of the town take part in the planning work. *Town plans* are generally prepared by specialized architects employed by the town, but using the assistance of outside experts, especially when the planning work is extensive. Consulting offices or the General Survey Office of Finland prepare town plans for rural communes. *Shore planning* is carried out by consultants.

Governmental institutions do their planning mainly with their own staffs. Only the National Board of Public Roads and Waterways and the National Board of Agriculture use consultants.

Land development programs have been realized in Finland only to a certain extent, especially in Helsinki and its surroundings. The first scheme of land development, the new town of Tapiola, serves as a good example. The planning and realization of Tapiola was carried out by one corporation, the Housing Foundation Asuntosäätiö.

Education, Training, and Institutions Most planners of land use in Finland have studied at the Helsinki Technological University, particularly in the department of architecture; while the department of surveying in the same university gives instruction in certain fields of planning. The planning of transportation has, in the last few years, occupied a significant position in the curriculum of the department of civil engineering.

Students at the Helsinki Technological University have to be high-school graduates. Qualified architects and engineers can pursue postgraduate studies in all departments on the licenciate and doctoral level.

The Helsinki Technological University has founded another institute in Tampere, operating for the time being as a branch of the mother institute. Plans for an institute of technology in Lappeenranta are also taking shape. There is a government-supported university in Oulu, where planning can also be studied, mainly in the department of architecture.

To a certain extent, basic academic studies in community planning can be pursued at the University of Helsinki, the biggest and oldest of the Finnish universities (about 25,000 students in 1969). The teaching of geography has in the last few years been extended to include social sciences and particularly community structures. Social sciences and other studies serving community planning can be taken in the faculty of political science at the University of Helsinki. Students in sociology, national economy, social politics, and statistics can take courses associated with community planning, and these subjects are also included in the curriculum of the faculty of agriculture and forestry.

In connection with the teaching of geography and social politics, some training for the tasks of community planning is given at the private University of Turku.

Åbo Akademi is another private university in Turku, where all teaching is in Swedish (about 7 percent of the population has Swedish as its mother tongue, and Finland is officially a bilingual country). In Åbo Akademi, students can include community planning in their programs, especially in connection with studies of geography and sociology.

The University of Tampere, formerly called the School of Social Sciences, is a private institute where the education of community planners has been linked with the study of sociology, social politics, economics, and municipal policy. In addition, there is a separate chair for regional planning. In this subject, special emphasis is given to matters relating to interaction within the community.

In addition, there are four commercial institutes at the university level in Finland (the Helsinki School of Economics and Business Administration, the Swedish School of Economics in Finland, the Turku School of Economics, and the Vaasa School of Economics). In these, studies in regional planning with an emphasis on commercial-geographical viewpoints can be pursued.

The state gives financial support to the private universities also. Thus, they are not dependent on private industry and commerce in the way that is common in, for instance the United States. The university council and the department for universities under the Ministry of Education take care of university planning for the state.

Postgraduate education in community planning is proposed. This would be carried out by the existing universities and institutes and would be available for university graduates (engineers, architects, and masters of arts and sciences). Parallel to preparing and starting this postgraduate education, organizations of people working in the planning field have for several years striven to provide further education for planners active in their own circles by means of special courses. The following organizations should be mentioned: the Society for Community Planning, the Finnish Architects' Association (SAFA), the Educational Center of the Engineers' Associations, and Suomalaisuuden Liitto.

Certain other enterprises, specializing in further education of persons employed by business and industry (Rastor, Ekono), have included courses in community planning in their programs. Two other organizations, the Union of Finnish Towns and the Finnish Union of Rural Communes, have arranged courses serving regional planning purposes.

The question of the need for education in community planning was taken up in the Nordic countries in the early 1960s. The Nordic Council appointed a committee to study the question, and in 1968, this led to the founding of the Nordic Institute for Community Planning in Stockholm. The institute accepts university graduates working in the field of planning in the Nordic countries (Denmark, Finland, Iceland, Norway, and Sweden).

Studies in community planning can be pursued on the licenciate and doctoral levels. The costs of the institute are covered by the Nordic countries.

The Nordic Council also agreed that a similar, separate institute for postgraduate education in community planning should be founded in Finland. The council came to an agreement that Finnish planners could study as well as teach either in the institute in Stockholm or in their own country (the academic requirements are similar in all Nordic countries).

As a result of these decisions, the Finnish Ministry of the Interior requested that the Helsinki Technological University, together with the other universities and institutes, should study the possibilities for training in regional planning.

Since 1968, Helsinki Technological University has given opportunities for postgraduate studies in community planning. These studies have been organized in close cooperation with the Nordic institute. In both, the courses take one year. The education program has been arranged into periods of concentrated courses involving individual study and absorption of the material as well as team work. The branches of study include subjects associated with social sciences, hygienies, limnology, health service, administration, transportation technics, physical planning, and automatic data processing.

In Finland, there were 35 students in the University course and 39 in the Nordic Institute course, all graduates of one of the above-mentioned institutes and universities, but students with technical degrees were in the majority.

Finland still lacks experts in regional planning and in physical and functional planning. A committee was therefore appointed to study this inadequacy. According to the report of the committee (1969) the number of students in the postgraduate courses for community planners in Finland should be doubled. In addition, the various institutes are preparing to increase the range of subjects associated with regional and community planning in their curricula.

Authorities have taken the problems of regional planning and the education in the field seriously. They have given considerable financial support to the various organizations pursuing these subjects. The state, the municipal communes, and the institutions stipulated by the law, that is, the associations for regional planning, customarily send their planners and administrators to courses arranged by the Helsinki Technological University, the Nordic Institute, and various other organizations.

Geographical and Climatic Conditions   Significant for the Finnish geographical and climatic conditions is the country's northern position between the fifty-ninth and seventh parallels; i.e., Finland is on the same latitude with northern Siberia and the southern part of Greenland. Together with Iceland, Finland is thus the northernmost country in the world. The Baltic Sea, the Gulf of Finland, and the Gulf of Bothnia form natural boundaries, but in the east and in the north the country has land boundaries. The climate is far more favorable than is normal in these latitudes, mainly because of the closeness of the Gulf Stream and the Atlantic Ocean. In the coldest regions, the average temperature of the year is about 29°F (less than -1°C), and in the warmest region (Ahvenanmaa), over 40°F (+5°C). The agricultural growing season (the period with temperatures of more than 40°F) is, at its shortest, less than 120 days and, at its longest, more than 180 days. The period of the lasting cover of snow is less than 4 months in the southwest and about 7 months in the north. In northern Finland, the long period of darkness in the winter is a further handicap, and the freezing of seaways causes great difficulties for navigation.

The topography, the bedrock, and the soil are suitable for building. The differences in height levels are not significant. Finland belongs to the Precambrian bedrock area, with a low and even topography. The bedrock is covered by loose soil, and this gives the country its character of small-featured ruggedness. Finnish scenery is characterized by low hills and numerous rivers, small lakes, and islands. The configuration is mostly the result of the effects of the glacial period.

Finland can be divided roughly into three parts: coastal regions, Inner Finland, and Virgin Finland. Population and also business and industry are mostly concentrated in the coastal areas, where the climatic and economic conditions are most favorable. Inner Finland is characterized by a great number of lakes that have to a certain degree hindered the formation of densely populated areas. Virgin Finland, as the name suggests, consists of virgin country with evergreen forests and swamps and marshland dominating the scenery. Only the upland areas in the northernmost fjeld district are barren of trees.

From about the beginning of the Christian era, Finns are known to have migrated into the area now called Finland. A union with Sweden, lasting for 600 years, began in the twelfth century. In the sixteenth century, settled population could only be found in the southern part of the country and on a narrow strip of land on the coast of the Gulf of Bothnia. In 1640, Finland's first university was founded in Turku, then the national capital. In 1950, 42 percent of the total population got their main livelihood from agriculture and forestry. The corresponding figure for 1960 was 31 percent, and for 1970 it is estimated to be about 22 percent, with 45 percent of the total population urban. This means that Finland is rapidly turning into a modern industrial country whose position between eastern and western Europe provides great possibilities for trade. In 1967, the total population of Finland was 4,678,500. In the 1960s, the yearly growth of population has been about 30,000.

In 1969, there were 79 towns and market towns in Finland. These two types of town differ in their administrative systems, but both are urban in character. The oldest towns are Turku, Pori, Porvoo, and Rauma, which have sprung up at old market places. These towns were granted their rights as corporate towns in the fourteenth and fifteenth centuries. The biggest cities are Helsinki, the capital of Finland, with a population of 535,000 (Greater Helsinki about 638,000); Tampere, 156,000; Turku, 154,000 (1969); and Espoo, 103,000 (1972). There are no other towns with populations of more than 100,000, but some, especially Lahti and Oulu, have shown a rapid rate of growth in the last few years and are quickly approaching 100,000.

Most of Finnish towns are situated on the coast and are therefore ports. The Saimaa Canal, completed in 1968, has brought many inland towns into contact with the sea. Finnish towns are mostly commercial and administrative centers, characterized generally by their service facilities. Very few towns originate as industrial centers. The most important industrial town is Tampere, but even this town is a center of services for the surrounding area.

The Finnish economy is a market economy. Its basic element is private enterprise, but there is room in this also for public activities. Finland has a position among the first 15 nations in terms of national income per capita. The following statistics give a picture of economic development during the 1960s.

	1968		1960	Annual growth in volume 1960–68, percent
Gross domestic product	Marks (millions)	Percent	Percent	
Agriculture and forestry	4 578	15.4	19.8	+0.5
Industry and building	11 524	38.9	39.7	+4.9
Services	13 527	45.7	40.5	+4.5
Total	29 629	100.0	100.0	+3.9

	1968		1960	Annual growth 1960–68, percent
Labor force	Man-years (thousands)	Percent	Percent	
Agriculture and forestry	465.5	23.9	31.4	−2.9
Industry and building	683.8	35.2	34.1	+0.9
Services	796.2	40.9	34.5	+2.7
Total	1 945.5	100.0	100.0	+0.5

Traditions of Planning The origin of the urban concept in Finland can be traced back to the seventeenth century, when Sweden-Finland was a superpower. Then, 15 of the present 78 towns had been either founded or were being planned. Those old town plans were outlined in accordance with the planning ideals of the Renaissance. Attempts were made to change the plans of the seven already existing towns according to the same principles, their structure having been the result of natural growth. As the towns were built of wood, frequent fires gave opportunities for extensive revisions of town plans.

A town plan was given the shape of a long rectangle, divided by a network of roads into building blocks of equal size. The necessary squares and free areas for public buildings were created by simply leaving some

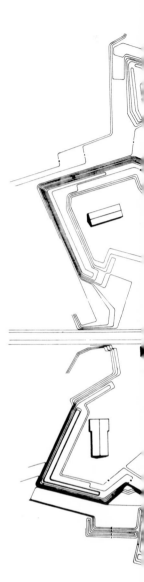

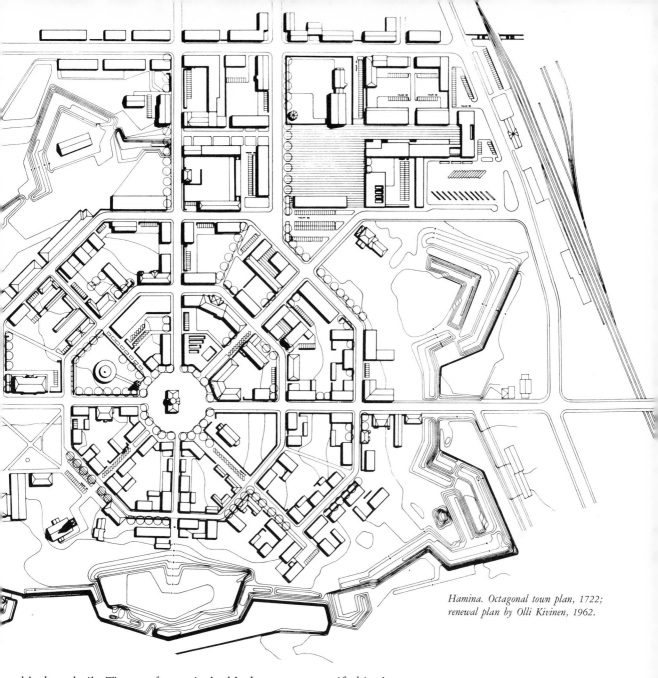

Hamina. Octagonal town plan, 1722; renewal plan by Olli Kivinen, 1962.

blocks unbuilt. The uses for particular blocks were not specified in the town plan. Until the end of the nineteenth century, entrance into a house was from the yard. The law stipulated that selling and buying might be done in the marketplace only, therefore shops did not appear on the street scene until the end of the nineteenth century.

In the eighteenth century, urban development was negligible. The main achievements of this period were the Viapori fortress and the unusual star-shaped town plan of the border town Hamina, both designed for defense purposes.

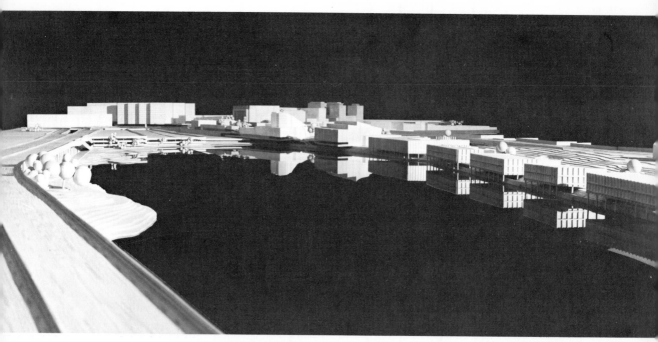

Töölö inlet from the east and public buildings along the shore, by Alvar Aalto (miniature model).

Owing to frequent fires, fire protection became increasingly important in the nineteenth century. Orders were issued that alleys should be left inside blocks for checking the spread of fires, and the fire ordinance given in 1856 stipulated that towns be divided into fire zones by means of wide avenues. By the end of the nineteenth century, Finnish urban tradition had developed into an original and sophisticated environmental culture. Avenues, gardens within blocks, the uniform empire style in architecture, and blind fences joining the houses to one another created a compact and green milieu that formed a very pleasant townscape. In accordance with neoclassical ideals, public buildings were placed in parklike open areas with a lot of free space around them. The town-planning models published in Sweden in the 1860s show that Finnish urban planning was considered exemplary.

From the architectural point of view, town planning did not exist at the end of the nineteenth century. The coming of the railways into towns often broke up the unity of the structure. In bigger towns, the German model of speculative tenement-house building gained ground and the old garden-city milieu of the empire period was gradually replaced by multistory brick houses with their unhealthy and dark, built-in courtyards.

Shortly before the turn of the century, Camillo Sitte's teachings inspired a reaction in Finland. With a medieval town as an ideal, the planners strove to create picturesque townscapes by means of organic placing and asymmetrical setting of the buildings, and by using closed-in plazas. The competition for the Töölö (Helsinki) city plan in 1899, demanded by young architects headed by Lars Sonck, meant a breakthrough of new ideals in Finland.

Twentieth-century Planning   Romanticism prevailed for about 50 years. Following this, the aim at the "monumental" in architecture was also to be seen in town planning. The villa districts of Eira and Kulosaari, with their homogenous milieus, were built in Helsinki in accordance with the principles of Art Nouveau. Before World War II, the garden-city ideal of Ebenezer Howard had an influence in Finland. An important application of it was the Munkkiniemi-Haaga plan made by Eliel Saarinen in 1915.

Eliel Saarinen was also a key figure in the development of modern master planning and decentralization. During the years 1911 to 1915 he programmed the master planning of Budapest, won the competiton for the master plan of Tallinn, and prepared, together with B. Jung, a scheme for the master plan of Helsinki based on carefully studied development estimates. In 1918 Saarinen finished an amended version of this master plan for Helsinki. By applying the principle of the garden city consistently and allowing for traffic and population growth as well as social development based on estimates, Saarinen created one of the models of modern master planning, which is also the basis of the present structure of Helsinki, but instead of the independent garden-city units that he visualized, only neighborhood units have been built, Tapiola forming the only exception, while his plan for rail traffic has not been realized. Among Saarinen's later works in the field of urban planning is his project for the shore districts of Chicago, completed in 1923, in which the farsighted solution of traffic problems called for several levels. Saarinen also wrote *The City*, an important book on the theory of town planning.

The greatest achievements of the neoclassical style are in the field of housing. Efforts to create healthy housing and the simplified architectural style prevailing at the time anticipated the breakthrough of functionalism at the end of the decade. By stipulating internal building limits for the blocks, unhealthy buildings in dark courtyards were avoided. Architects strove to apply the Carré principle: a peaceful courtyard was surrounded by a closed circle of buildings. The most significant achievement in the urban planning of the period was the building of the Käpylä garden suburb in Helsinki during the period of 1921 to 1924, a project partly financed by the city. This area, a typical example of public housing as well as of flexible standardization, can be regarded as one of the best urban milieus in Helsinki. The demolition plans suggested in the 1960s have been strongly opposed.

Functionalism arrived in Finland around 1930, but, because of the economic depression of the time, it was not much realized in urban planning. The most important projects that were carried out, the housing area of the Sunila factories by Alvar Aalto (1936) and the Olympic Village for the Olympic Games of 1940 (by architects H. Ekelund and M. Välikangas), partly reflect the softened idea of a milieu of the following period.

Regional planning saw its first beginnings in Finland in the 1940s. The first example was the project for the Kokemäki River valley by Alvar Aalto, completed in 1943. The problems of rebuilding after the war caused a lot of intensive research work. Alvar Aalto acted as a central figure in activities leading to the foundation of planning and standardization institutes. Work in town planning gathered momentum in the 1950s, and several towns obtained master plans from Alvar Aalto (Imatra in 1951), Otto-I. Meurman (Oulu in 1951), and Olli Kivinen (Lappeenranta in 1956 and Hämeenlinna in 1957), among others. However, it has been necessary to amend these plans since, as the growth in motor traffic had not been sufficiently anticipated.

Development in town planning since 1945 can best be seen in Helsinki proper and its metropolitan area. There are two main trends: on the one hand the creation of Tapiola Garden City, which can be regarded as the only realization of the New Town principle in Finland, and, on the other hand, the general tendency in the remaining areas that can be described as production of scattered dormitory neighborhoods and continuation of the urban sprawl. The complete separation of functions has led to an impoverishment of the environment and to increasingly difficult traffic problems in the city proper. An underground railway system has been considered as the only solution for the problem of transport and a decision about the building of the first stage was made in 1969. Tapiola corresponds to the conception of an independent garden city planned by Eliel Saarinen in 1918, but it differs greatly in its working possibilities and various services from the neighborhood units mentioned above.

Tapiola Garden City   Tapiola is a New Town sited on the Gulf of Finland about 7 miles (11 kilometers) west of Helsinki. It is designed for a population of about 17,000 which in turn will be the nucleus for a city of 80,000.

The way in which Tapiola came into being is unique. It has been created by a private nonprofit enterprise, the Housing Foundation Asuntosäätiö, established in 1951 and backed by six social and trade organizations (the Family Welfare League Väestöliitto, the Confederation of Finnish Trade Unions, the Federation of Civil Servants, the Central Association of Tenants, the Mannerheim League, and the Finnish Association of Disabled Civilians and Servicemen).

The aim of the founders was not only to provide housing but to create a society. Tapiola is planned as a largely self-sufficient core city. In relation to its 4,575 residential units, 6,000 jobs are planned in all categories except heavy industry. The town-center retailing functions will serve an ultimate market of 80,000 persons. The commuting involved is handled by an expressway system and by buses for mass transit.

Based on gross cubic measure, 50 percent of completed construction is in high-rise apartments, 15 percent in row housing and single-family houses, and 35 percent in schools, industrial plants, a town center, churches, shops, and services. Tapiola is divided into a town center and three neighborhoods: east, west, and north. Limited areas are set aside for light industry, such as a large, modern printing plant.

Among the social and physical objectives are:

General view of Tapiola center to the northwest.

1. A community that is balanced, economically (45 percent of residents from the low- to middle-income economic levels, 55 percent from middle to upper) and socially (artists, professionals, industrial workers, and executives).

2. A variety of housing types consistent with the social and economic objectives. These include large and small detached dwellings, townhouses, atrium houses, garden apartments, and walk-up and high-rise apartments. Costs (including land and public improvements) range from $6,000 for a

ABOVE: *Two of the leading planning principles of Tapiola are illustrated in this picture. It shows one-family houses, row-houses, walkups, and high-rises as components of the same neighborhood unit. More expensive houses face the same street as low-cost garden apartments. On the horizon, the skyline of Helsinki.*

LEFT: *High-rise apartments in Tapiola garden city environment. Under the roof constructions, club and other facilities and saunas. Concrete yards have been replaced by common gardens.*

two-room unit with kitchenette to $18,500 for a five-room unit with full kitchen (1972).

Efforts have been made to link the disciplines of urban design, urban sociology, and urban economics. The planners of Tapiola were convinced that no one professional group could solve the manifold problems of modern community planning. A one-sided architectural approach was rejected, and the same applies to one-sided economic or technical ways of thinking. Planning had to be highly skilled and strictly directed teamwork at all levels. Tapiola is the result of close teamwork in the fields of architecture, civil engineering, landscape gardening, sociology, domestic science, and child and youth welfare. This work has been led by Heikki von Hertzen, the Executive Director of the Housing Foundation, who is responsible for its planning work.

In 1953 a competition was held for the town center. The winning design by Aarne Ervi has received considerable praise for its clarity of plan, its unified architectural expression, and for the sensitivity of its execution.

A general view of the model of Tapiola center to the southwest. Buildings on the left: church and the international hotel. On the opposite side to the right: indoor/outdoor swimming pool, theater, library and college of music, central administrative tower and, behind it, Heikintori department store, sports hall, health center, and office buildings.

An artificial lake has been formed in the site of an old quarry. The central administrative tower—the landmark of Tapiola—with its restaurant and roof-cafe, dominates the town center. Another focal point of the area is Heikintori, a combined department store, consisting of 65 specialty shops and a social center. It is, in fact, a covered shopping street which also offers numerous facilities for day and evening activities.

Tapiola. Main entrance to the town center.

Around the lake stand the church with its parish hall and youth center, the swimming pool with its ancillary outdoor facilities, the health center with doctors' surgeries, clinics, and laboratories, as well as the sports hall with its bowling alley and "Keep-Fit School." A theater, concert hall, library, a college of music, and an exhibition hall have been planned.

The social and economic mixture of population was carefully structured in advance of the planning. Beyond the social plan and the physical plan that articulates it, there has been a program of implementation involving careful selection and education of potential homeowners, a full program of cultural and recreational activities, and a complement of physical facilities to accommodate this program. These include a full range of school facilities, nursery facilities, youth centers, an outdoor amphitheater, a children's village, ski trails, gardens and garden allotments, and a marina.

The message of Tapiola is clearly that of a well-designed city, as originally proposed by Ebenezer Howard, father of the British New Towns movement, can be built today with private financing for a broad cross section of the community.

The Helsinki Region and the Uusimaa Province   The significance of Tapiola is that it was an experiment on two fronts. It was a test of a prototype of

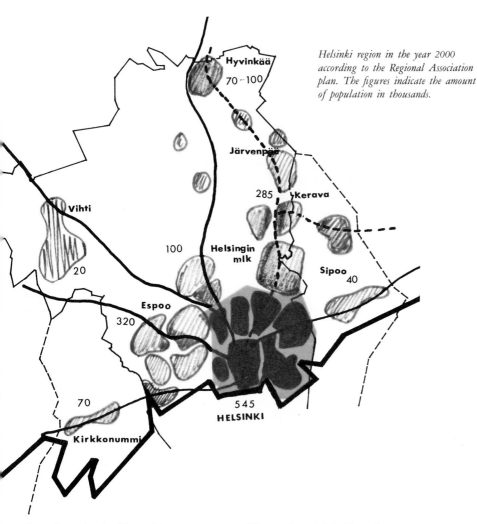

Helsinki region in the year 2000 according to the Regional Association plan. The figures indicate the amount of population in thousands.

Hyvinkää
70 - 100

Järvenpää

285 Kerava

Vihti

100 Helsingin mlk

20

Sipoo
40

Espoo
320

70

545
HELSINKI

Kirkkonummi

urban form in itself, and it was a test of how the Helsinki region as a whole might be urbanized.

The larger Tapiola (80,000 inhabitants) is one of the seven cities proposed by Heikki von Hertzen in 1962 to accommodate the population growth of the Helsinki region (in Uusimaa province). This plan assumes varying degrees of self-sufficiency in the seven new cities as well as varying sizes (from 50,000 to 200,000) in terms of population. It further assumes a limit of about 600,000 upon the population within the Helsinki Peninsula itself.

These seven cities would be partly new and built on virgin ground where modern planning principles could be realized according to economic and social criteria without the opposition of site owners. Some other communities would be placed in existing centers, assuming that the surveying of the land and site ownership of these centers will make for sound development of the community.

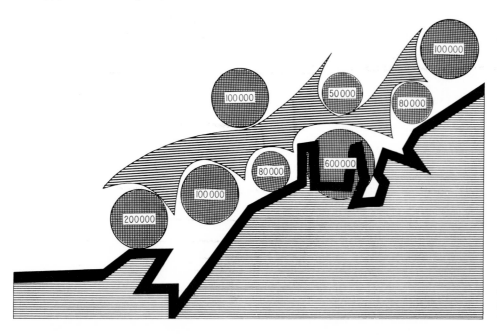

The plan of the Seven Cities (von Hertzen, 1962) to accommodate the population growth of the Helsinki region (in Uusimaa Province).

Preliminary investigations had shown that the locations of the bigger communities in the west would be in the regions of Espoo Bay and Porkkala, in central Uusimaa in the regions of Lohja and Riihimäki-Hyvinkää, and in eastern Uusimaa in the regions of Porvoo and Loviisa.

Large, uniform areas would remain between these communities, representing approximately 90 percent of the total area of Uusimaa, and they should be placed under the protection of the law and kept as agricultural, forestry, and recreational areas. These extensive greenbelts would have well-kept forests, cultivated land, and miniature communities where old traditions could still be fostered. Town dwellers would thus also be able to enjoy vital and valuable recreational areas.

Von Hertzen's Seven Cities plan would create a genuine metropolitan area with its focus on Helsinki for central government and commercial and cultural functions, while allowing those activities that are not essentially central to disperse. What the proposal means is building New Towns on a region wide scale. The seven new or expanded towns together with central Helsinki would form a metropolitan city of 1.3 million, envisaged for the year 2000 and beyond. This solution would combine human-scale living with urbanity and effective administration with good services.

A precise study along these lines was initiated in 1964 by The Housing Foundation Asuntosäätiö. A working group of eight experts with the most varied experience, led by Lassi Iharvaara, M.Tech.Sc., completed 2 years later the study *Uusimaa 2010* (that—2010—being the target year)[1].

[1] *Uusimaa 2010* (Uusimaa Plan), Oy Tilgman Ab, Helsinki, 1967. The book includes an English summary.

It corroborated von Hertzen's 1962 proposal in all essentials while making several modifications and refinements.

The Seven Cities regional plan is proposed as a substitute for the official Regional Association plan for Helsinki. The latter assumes an accomodation of 1.5 million people by 1990 (a regional population, growth of 600,000 from 1960) in Greater Helsinki. This population is to be accommodated both within the old city and within new dormitory neighborhoods in suburban greenbelts along arterial radials serving Helsinki.

Both the Seven Cities plan and the Uusimaa plan assume renewal of the inner-city core (already under development based on Aalto's Lakeside plan).

More New Towns The Seven Cities plan is now being implemented by the Asuntosäätiö, which has acquired the land and is developing plans for the second and third of these cities—Espoo Bay and Porkkala seaside town—both on the Gulf of Finland to the west of Tapiola.

Competing with the school represented by the planners of Tapiola, another school has made itself felt in the 1960s. The latter advocates "the rational approach." Koivukylä, a new town project in a Helsinki rural commune by architects Salonen, Savela, and Riihelä, represents the rational and technical approach influenced by the densely built towns of the railway age. The main goal of the planners is to produce "an economic environment." There are the rectilinear grid pattern, disregard of nature, and strong architectural order. The planners admit, however, that they do not know how this kind of urban pattern will affect future city dwellers.

The planners of Tapiola stress that one of the great dangers in urban planning of today is monotony and uniformity. They are for a wide range of various urban patterns—the garden-city conception being by no means the only one. These different urban patterns should be tried out and realized in practice. But, whichever the pattern chosen, the starting point should be the family and biological, sociological, and pollution problems. These are of primary importance. The planners of Tapiola continue to warn their colleagues of "the misuse of technology to subordinate people instead of serving them."

City Extensions and Urban Renewal Urban renewal in Finland is mostly associated with efforts to alter existing urban structures to make them correspond with the demands of circulation and a new kind of sociological approach. In most Finnish cities and towns, their centers have been renewed as a result of planning competitions held in the 1960s. Thus, the regular urban structure favored by the Renaissance and Empire has shown its great flexibility with regard to structural alterations.

Some of the more interesting subjects of urban renewal are the "Amuri" and "Pispala" projects in Tampere and "Puu-Käpylä" in Helsinki.

With the growth of the city, the existing center of Helsinki has developed away from the original center planned by C. L. Engel and J. A. Ehrenström and built mainly between 1820 and 1880. It was around 1910 that Eliel Saarinen prepared a plan for the center of Helsinki according to which the central railway station should be moved from its present location

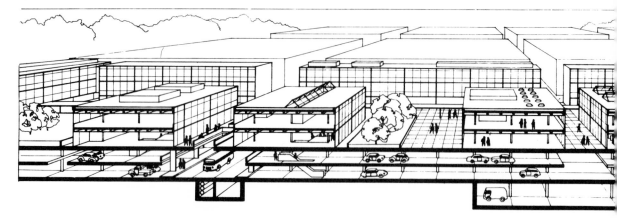

to Pasila, about 3 miles further north, and the Bay of Töölö should be filled up. Neither Saarinen's plan nor other plans which were amendments of the original ever materialized. In 1954, Yrjö Lindgren and Etik Kråkström completed a draft plan.

In 1958, the city board of Helsinki appointed a committee to develop the plan for a new city center. After a preparatory phase of work, the city board commissioned Alvar Aalto to make this plan under the direction and supervision of the committee.

Aalto's plan is based on a space composition around the Bay of Töölö and forms a wide, fan-shaped plaza (the Terrace Place). There is a row of official buildings and a road connecting the city center with the planned subcenter of Pasila, a point where the roads from the east, north, and west will link up and join Vapaudenkatu, the street leading into the city center.

The plan for the Terrace Place includes a concert and congress hall. Aalto's idea is that the next building north of the concert hall should be an opera house with an art gallery and four other public buildings behind it. The lower part of the buildings will form a free continuation of the green area in the form of colonnades of various kinds in direct contact with open greenery. The Terrace Place will also be a gathering point for traffic. At a point which links the main incoming traffic arteries with the point where they split off into the city area, a parking center will be provided for about 3,500 cars.

The Helsinki city area will have to be expanded, even if city-type business groupings are established in the Pasila area. An additional commercial district will be created in the Kamppi as an extension to the city center with parking for 8,000 vehicles.

In 1961 the city council approved Aalto's proposal as a basis for the further development of the new center of Helsinki. The first phase of the construction, the concert and congress hall, was started in 1968.

BIBLIOGRAPHY: Bertel Jung, *Pro Helsingfors: Entwurf zu einem Stadtplan für "Gross-Helsingfors,"* worked out by Eliel Saarinen and others, Helsingfors, 1918; Heikki von Hertzen, *Koti vai kasarmi lapsillemme* (homes or barracks), W.S.O.Y., Helsinki, 1946; O.-I. Meurman, *Asemakaavaoppi* (study on master planning), Helsinki, 1947; Eduard and Claudia

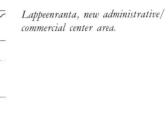

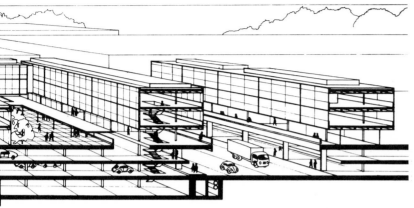

Lappeenranta, new administrative/ commercial center area.

Neuenschwander, *Finische Bauten, Batiments finnois, Finnish Buildings,* Atelier Alvar Aalto, 1950, 1951, Erlenbach-Zurich, 1954; Gerhard Eimer, *Die Stadtplanung im Schwedischen Osteereich, 1600–1715,* Stockholm, 1961; Skyttä, *Muuttuva Maaseutu* (changing countryside); Helsinki, 1962; Sigfried Giedion, *Space, Time and Architecture: The Growth of a New Tradition,* Cambridge, Mass., 1962; Alvar Aalto, *Band I, 1922–1962,* Zurich, 1963; Alvar Aalto, *Helsingin keskusta-suunnitelma—Helsinki Central Plan,* Helsinki, 1965; *Yleiskaava—generalplan,* Nordisk planmöte, 1965, Helsinki, 1965; *Städtebau in Finnland* (exhibition catalogue), Stuttgart, 1966; *Porkkalan merikaupunki* (Porkkala seaside town), Helsinki, 1966; *Uusimaa 2010* (the Province of Uusimaa in 2010), Asuntosaatio, Helsinki, 1967; Sipponen, *Päätöksenteko kansanvallassa* (decision in democracy); Helsinki, 1967; *Seminar on Finnish Architecture and Urban Planning, 1968,* Helsinki, 1968; *Koivukylä: 1, Koivukylän suunnittelutyöryhmä* (The Village of Koivukylä: 1, The Planning Team of Koivukylä), Helsinki, 1968; Lagerstedt Sipponen, *Yhteiskuntasuunnittelu* (Community Planning), Helsinki, 1968; Waris, *Muuttuva suomalainen yhteiskunta* (The Changing Finnish Community), Helsinki, 1968; Kuntasuunnittelu, *Toiminnan, talouden ja maankäytön kokonais-valtainen suunnittelu erityisesti kaupungeissa ja kauppaloissa* (Administrative, economic, and land-use planning on the Urban and Communal Level), Suomen Kaupunkiliitto (The Association of Finnish Towns), Helsinki, 1968; Olof Stenius, *Helsingfors stadsplanehistoriska atlas,* Helsingfors, 1969; *Seminar on Finnish Architecture and Urban Planning, 1969,* Helsinki, 1969; Carl Ludwig Engel, *Berlin, 1970* (exhibition catalogue); Heikki von Hertzen and Paul D. Spreiregen, *Building a New Town: Finland's New Garden City, Tapiola,* The M.I.T. Press, Cambridge, Mass., 1971.

—HEIKKI VON HERTZEN

with the assistance of LASSI IHARVAARA, LAURI HAUTAMÄKI, ILKKA SUMU, KIRMO MIKKOLA

FISCHER, THEODOR (1862–1938) German architect and town planner. Fischer was born at Schweinfurt, studied architecture in Munich between 1880 and 1885, joined Paul Wallot's office—then occupied with the construction of the Reichstag building in Berlin—and after some years' practice as an architect in Dresden and Munich was appointed head of the newly established Stadterweiterungsamt at Munich in 1893. After 8 fruitful years as one of the first planning officials in Germany, he was appointed professor of architecture at the Stuttgart Technische Hochschule, where he shaped the principles of what came to be known as the "Stuttgart School."

In 1908, he accepted an invitation from the Munich Technische Hochschule, where he worked for 20 more years as professor of architecture and town planning. After his retirement he remained active for some years in research and in lecturing.

Fisher's *oeuvre* as an architect and town planner is rich and varied: it consists of schools and churches, bridges and monuments, residential and communal buildings (predominantly in southern Germany), as well as of a large number of development plans and master plans for virtually all Bavarian and many other cities. His written work, although not voluminous, is of a high quality and shows his profound insight into the situations and problems of his time, his modesty, and his clarity and firm adherence to principles. Though a conservative by disposition, he was interested in future needs and searched continuously for new ground. His concise *Sechs Vorträge über Stadtbaukunst* (*Six Lectures on the Art of Town Planning*) contains his basic philosophy as a planner and reflects the combination of skilled craftsmanship, artistic sensitivity, and strong moral involvement which is so characteristic of the town-planning pioneers of this period. Among their German representatives, Theodor Fischer, together with Fritz Schumacher, stands out as one of the key figures in the first third of this century.

BIBLIOGRAPHY: *Sechs Vorträge über Stadtbaukunst*, Munich and Berlin, 1920 and 1922; *Die Stadt*, Sonderdruck 1928 der Freunde der TH, Munich; *Gegenwartsfragen künstlerischer Kultur*, Augsburg, 1931.
—GERD ALBERS

FLAT   The British name for a dwelling on one floor in a storied building generally containing other such dwellings, it corresponds to the term "apartment" in United States and most European countries. An apartment house or block is called in Great Britain a "block of flats."

The term "flat" is derived from *flet,* an old Friesian word meaning story, used mainly in Scotland since the thirteenth century but changed to its present form in the early-nineteenth century.

FLATTED FACTORY   A factory on one floor in a storied building with other such factories. These may be leased to firms either in the same or different industries.

FLEXIBILITY IN PLANNING   When a plan is prepared for a large area and population, such as a New Town or a major extension—a plan that is likely to take 10 to 20 years fully to implement, the question of the degree of flexibility that would have to be allowed in preparing the plan has to be considered. Ideas and needs change over the years, and some of these changes are unforseen. It is therefore important not to make a plan so rigid that changes with changing needs are difficult. One factor in making it possible for a plan to be changed according to needs is the provision of more space than is required for intitial needs, but this is sometimes difficult for economic reasons. Some of the plans of the earlier New Towns in Great Britain designated between 1946 and 1950 have been criticized for being too rigid and for not giving scope for changes with changing needs. One example is the inadequate provision for domestic garages. When these towns were planned, the great growth in the use of the motorcar was unforseen and only one garage for about five houses was provided. When, 20 years later, there was the need for at least one garage for each house, there was inadequate space to provide them. Another example is provided by the centers of New Towns and communities, many of which were originally planned in the late forties and early fifties with through traffic roads but which have since been changed and converted to pedestrian precincts. These conversions have been most successfully, easily, and economically accomplished where a degree of looseness or flexibility existed in the original plan. Additional space may be required for other unforeseen developments such as the greater provision of educational and recreational facilities. In plans that will take many years to implement there should be the greatest possible flexibility to allow for adaptation to change. This consideration has given a pliant structure to many plans of the sixties and seventies.   —ARNOLD WHITTICK

FLOOR SPACE STANDARDS A measure of the standard of provision of accommodation—e.g., domestic or educational—expressed in terms of floor space per person. In Britain a "floor space index" has been used by town planners to give a comparative measure of the amount of accommodation on different sites. The floor space index is, broadly speaking, the total floor space in a building or proposed building divided by the area of the site.

FOOTPATH (*See* SIDEWALK.)

FOOTSTREET (*See* PEDESTRIANIZATION.)

FORESTRY A forest originally is wild land covered mainly by tree growths, and forestry is the science and art of managing forests for the production of timber.

Climate, soil, and vegetation are interacting factors. Vegetation forms under favorable conditions of soil and climate, and the most suitable conditions allow the formation of trees, the highest order of vegetation. Plant geography shows that there are worldwide vegetation patterns.

There are no natural forests in Britain. In the postglacial climatic periods, various types of plants were introduced. The first species were birch, Scots pine, yew, and juniper. Broad-leaved trees successfully established included oaks, alder, ash, hazel, hawthorn, and holly. Slower to adapt were beech, hornbeam, whitebeam, and field maple.

The type of vegetation found depends on the prevailing climatic and soil conditions and the influences on the use of the land by the activities of man and animals.

In early centuries a high proportion of the land was covered by forests. As man's activities increased, the trees were used for various purposes including fuel, building, furniture, and implements, and forests were cleared to permit the grazing of livestock and the growing of crops. In 1662, John Evelyn, in his book *Sylva,* sounded the warning that Britain's forests were rapidly disappearing. Many of the landowners, heeding Evelyn's words and encouraged by the economic benefits and hunting and shooting provisions, began to replant forests in the late-seventeenth and early eighteenth centuries. At this time came enclosures, changes in agricultural methods, and the interest in designed landscapes. A great deal of capital investment was made in forests, and foresters were being trained to manage them.

In the United States up to the end of the nineteenth century, there was almost uncontrolled exploitation of forests. In the present century, however, the federal government has purchased forest lands for watershed protection, and large areas are reserved and controlled for timber production. Much research has been done in later years in good forestry practice.

After the First World War, the woods in Britain had again become exhausted. An act of Parliament in 1919 established the Forestry Commission, which was to purchase land to grow trees for industry. It was realized that forestry was a valuable resource and that it required long-term planning.

The commission now has 1,750,000 acres (708,750 hectares) in timber production. The work includes replanting old woodland; the afforestation of poor-quality upland areas where other cultivation or grazing is impossible; planting to stabilize poor coastal soils; planting on old spoil heaps in industrial areas; and planting to form shelter belts to farmland, recreation areas, and towns.

Another important aspect of forestry which the Commission considers is recognizing the landscape character of the areas to be afforested. The groups of conifers and broad-leaved species are designed to give scale and pattern and to fit the forest into and not upon the existing configuration of the landscape. Felling and replanting programs are planned to guard against damage to the trees remaining and to provide a view that does not show a scarred landscape.

Timber crops are the prime concern in forestry, but as the foresters realize, there is a responsibility for the conservation of natural resources. This includes allowing wildlife habitats to be established and preserved and allowing the public some use of the forests for recreation. Several national forest parks have been established for this purpose. In Britain the Forest Nature Reserves and Forest Trails which have been created are interesting and worthwhile, as their popularity proves. Also, Forest Centers giving information about the natural history are useful.

The encouragement of the multipurpose use of the forests will help man to understand his heritage and responsibility for conservation and the contribution forestry makes towards the total environment.

BIBLIOGRAPHY: Sylvia Crowe, *Forestry in the Landscape,* Forestry Commission Booklet no. 18, H.M.S.O., London, 1966; R. F. Wood and I. A. Anderson (compilers), *Forestry in the British Scene,* Forestry Commission Booklet no. 24, H.M.S.O., London, 1966.

—WENDY POWELL

FORTIFICATION (*See* ANCIENT PLANNING *and* DEFENSE, PLANNING FOR.)

FORUM In ancient Rome the central open space or square of a city used for assemblies, public meetings, ceremonies, business transactions, and as the marketplace. It corresponded to the Greek agora. In smaller cities there was usually only one forum, but in larger cities there were sometimes several. In central Rome, for example, there were five. The first was the Forum Romanum, which at the time of the Empire was surrounded by handsome and dignified buildings. Later additions were the forums of Caesar, Augustus, Trajan, and Vespasian, all surrounded by public buildings and temples. The Greek agora and the Roman forum are the ancestors of the Italian piazza, the Spanish plaza, the German *platz*, the French *place*, and the English open square.

FOUNTAINS   (*See* MONUMENTS AND MEMORIALS, PUBLIC.)

FOURIER, FRANCOIS MARIE CHARLES (1772–1837)   French philosopher and sociologist who, after suffering in the French Revolution, conceived a scheme for the reorganization of society in planned communities.

He advocated that society should be divided into sections of from 1,600 to 1,800 persons, each section to be lodged in a common building or *phelanstere*, surrounded by 3 square miles of arable land. Each was to be self-governing, though federation between the sections should be optional. Work was to be undertaken by the members on an alternating basis, a minimum wage paid to each, and the surplus wealth divided into shares apportioned to labor, capital, and individual talent.

Fourier's ideas, which were not unlike those of Robert Owen, his English contemporary (*q.v.*), attracted considerable attention in the nineteenth century and several experiments based on them were made in England and America. None survived, however, as self-contained economic communities, probably because they were too rigid and paternalistic in conception and made no allowance for individual enterprise.

Fourier expounded his system in a number of volumes of which *Le Nouveau Monde Industrial et Societaire* (1829) is perhaps the best known. His disciple, Victor Consideraut, also published in 1845 an *Exposition abregee du Systeme de Fourier*, which is discussed by John Stuart Mill in his *Political Economy*.

—WILFRED SALTER

FRANCE

Legislation and Administration   There are two main periods in the administrative history of French town planning. The 20 years between the two world wars saw its birth and early growth. The next 20 years brought it to maturity.

Planning was a new discipline embracing the artistic, scientific, and technical aspects of both urban and rural development. It was first given official status and a legal framework by the act of March 14, 1919. The scope of this act was broadened by a later measure passed on July 19, 1924. However, when the promoters of this legislation began to put it into practice, certain shortcomings became apparent. Most notable of these was failure to provide for cases where planning affected more than one local authority. The necessity for planning on a regional scale was quickly appreciated, and nowhere more so than in the conurbation of Paris.

Planners encountered a problem of a different kind when they began to apply the legislation of 1919 and 1924 to the reconstruction of areas devastated during the First World War. This was the almost total indifference of public opinion to the issues and possibilities raised by planning. The population which had suffered wanted only to rebuild their homes on the same primitive lines which had existed before. Such plans were rudimentary. The work was carried out in feverish haste. Scarcely anyone realized that reconstruction could mean urban renewal, that it provided a test bench on which to apply the fundamental principles of planning. (It is worth noting that the same hasty spirit was to prevail again, though there were some exceptions, in the period of reconstruction after the Second World War.) The attitude of local authorities toward the new legislation was unenthusiastic. It made the cost of preparing development plans their obligation. The expense seemed disproportionate, particularly in view of the opposition that publication of a plan was likely to arouse among local people. More serious still was the critical state of national finances at the time, which was such that even if a plan were adopted, it stood little chance of being implemented. Finally, the extreme shortage of persons qualified in the new discipline put a further brake on the formulation of the "development, amenity and expansion plans" envisaged by the acts of 1919 and 1924. As a result, by 1939, of 2,300 local authorities which should have benefited from planning, only about 600 had plans approved or in preparation. Of these, only 273 were given official sanction.

Confirmation of the inadequacies of the early planning legislation came throughout the 1930s at planners' congresses and from numerous other bodies as well. Technicians, administrators, responsible politicians—all those, in fact, who "believed in planning" and who understood the importance of its postulates—wanted it to assume its rightful place in the minds of those who formed government policy. Government was thus faced with the task of revising its procedures in this sphere and in particular with the creation of specialized services whose function was the preparation and implementation of plans. The years 1940 to 1944 proved to be a suitable time for reflection and for the elaboration of projects "to be undertaken after the war." It was during this period that the urgently needed reform was made. The Delegation Generale a l'Equipement National (DGEN—Commission for National Supply) was set up in 1944. Within this commission was a Direction de l'Urbanisme et de la Construction Immobiliere (Board of Planning and Building). This board drafted the text which became the planning act of June 15, 1943.

Technically speaking, the new act was chiefly concerned with codifying previous legislation but without altering its general drift. Rather, it was in the field of administrative practice that the main innovations occurred. In the first place, regional planning services were instituted to work beside the central administrative machinery for planning, described in the previous paragraph. These regional services would be responsible, at the state's expense, for working out development projects. Next, the new act made it possible to set up *groupements d'urbanisme* ("groupings for planning purposes"). Thus several local authorities having common interests were enabled to undertake joint development in their areas. It was in this way that the notion of regional planning was recognized officially. Finally, the new act brought into use an indispensable formality for the correct implementation of plans—the building permit.

In 1944, two sets of specialized services—those of the DGEN and those which had been functioning since 1940 at the Commissariat a la Reconstruction Immobiliere (Commission for Reconstruction)—were reorganized and amalgamated under the Minister of Reconstruction and Planning. Thus, for the first time, planning was represented in the Cabinet. Since then, while the name of the ministry has changed from time to time, these services have worked both at the level of central government and at the county level to apply planning legislation and improve it. They have, it should be stressed, had to adapt themselves to new government practices, notably since 1945, and to the evolving pattern of economic and social planning which extended progressively and which, in 1963, eventually combined all development of land under political control. Today these services function under the Ministere de l'Equipement et du Logement (Ministry of Supply and Housing), which amalgamated them in 1966 with the former Ministere des Travaux Publics (Ministry of Works).

Apart from two obligatory provisions relating to drinking water supply and drainage, the acts of 1919 and 1943 define a development project (whether submitted by a single local authority or a group) as consisting of two documents: (1) the plan itself, a document showing all the topographical detail; and (2) the development program or building schedule, a document setting out the phasing and control of implementation. The value of this arrangement was that implementation could generally be carried out fairly quickly. It was reasonably effective between 1945 and 1950, when towns damaged or destroyed during the war were reconstructed. The comparatively short time this work took is also explained by the fact that it was financed from public funds. However, the procedure was less satisfactory when applied to towns which had not been damaged but which were expanding and which contained a high proportion of private development. Another important factor at this stage was the acute housing shortage. It was such that land originally scheduled for, say, roads was taken for houses. Towns spread beyond their boundaries to encroach on rural areas. Thus plans had to be redrawn, with all the administrative delay and formality that this involved. That is why in 1958 the legal requirements were modified. A statutory distinction was made between outline plans and detailed plans. The former fixed the main lines of future development but without making any provisions which ran the risk of proving inapplicable. It was left to the latter to state, when appropriate, precisely which parts of the area covered by the outline plan were to be utilized. This modification of the law had become necessary with the framing of decrees affecting urban renewal and *zones a urbaniser par propriete* (ZUP—areas designated for private development). These decrees embodied the notion of operational planning as opposed to the strictly regulated planning conceived by the acts of 1919 and 1943. It was sometimes hard to draw the line between "detailed plans," "ZUP plans," and "renewal plans."

However, since 1960, the economic and social planning of the Commissariat General du Plan de Modernisation et de Productivite (General Commission for Planning Modernization and Productivity) has included programs for the modernization and reequipment of urban areas. With these programs a new concept of planning has emerged. It was found necessary, and has become possible, to fix much more accurately than in the past the timing of the implementation of projects. This has led to a rapid increase of projects such as the extension and restructuring of towns and cities, the restoration of their historic parts, and the establishment of new towns. The land-use act of December 30, 1967, now provides for three kinds of documents to regulate such development. The documents differ mainly by the extent to which each anticipates the future. First there is the "master plan for development and town planning." This states the capacity of sites and defines the possible long-term uses of land. Next there are "plans for the use of land in particular areas." These plans define zones and the type of use to which the various sectors of these zones may be put. While these plans normally set the pattern of evolution for a period of roughly 10 years, they can be adapted at any time to take account of unforeseen changes. Finally, there are the "operational plans" which are drawn up as and when they are needed, in particular to implement modernization and reequipment projects. At the big-city level, operational plans are the instruments of the economic and social planning of the Commissariat General du Plan.

The progressive integration of town planning with economic and social programs is leading toward a situation where planning is a dynamic and all-embracing process. It is dynamic because it is seeking to distinguish between projects realizable in the short or medium term and projects which, although desirable, cannot be considered at the present time. It is all-embracing because it fuses the aims of land development with those of economic and social development.

The new concept of development planning is tending to balance supply and demand in the market for the various types of building land. This is helping those who struggle to check the abuses of speculation in property. Associated with this is a trend toward greater public interest in the framing and implementation of plans. The better the possible repercussions of planning are understood, especially by the purchasers and vendors of land, the less will planning risk being the cause of "one-way" losses and profits.

Professional Practice   Hitherto, the preparatory planning stage has been the province of a single practitioner, normally a person with qualifications in architecture. Now this work is being taken over more and more by a team comprising several disciplines—a group of specialists working together to resolve the problems of planning, using techniques that are in large part those of operational research.

When economic and social planning reaches the big-city level, the Ministere de l'Equipement et du Logement takes over the work of the state planning services. Clearly, by setting up this machinery, government regards all-embracing or "global" planning as a matter of political concern.

Planning seeks to define land use and to organize human institutions in relation to the land. On a global scale it involves forecasting future needs and making territorial development studies. These things are beyond the capacity of a single individual. They presuppose teamwork—the participation of various specialists, each contributing different knowledge. Thus, if planning is to retain its specific nature and its unity of outlook, it is desirable that all involved should adopt a common approach and a common vocabulary.

Government has recognized that planning is a blend of long-term vision and patient, painstaking, day-to-day work, and that it requires the support of permanent administrative and technical services. When planning is undertaken for one or two local authorities or for whole counties, it must, regardless of its extent, have offices and other facilities to carry out its work.

However, such permanent study groups do not cover the whole country, nor will they for a long time to come. Present priorities dictate that urban sprawl is planning's first concern. On the other hand, much of the detailed planning, particularly in large-scale developments, is left to the local authorities. Civil servants and other officials employed by the state tend to respect as far as possible the principles of local autonomy. During the immediate postwar period of reconstruction and development, local authorities and the state planning services jointly adopted the system of appointing an independent practitioner to draw up plans. It seems inevitable that this system will continue. However, these "free-ranging practioners of the art of planning" will increasingly have to adapt themselves to the requirements of the established procedures of official planning departments. Instead of employing a planner to do a particular job in a given time, there will be a full-time planning consultant who is bound by contract to regular work. In place of remuneration by means of fees, there will be remuneration by salary.

Training and Research   Until the recent changes in professional practice took place, qualification as a planner consisted of a diploma in architecture and a two-year course at the University of Paris Institute of Planning, the only establishment devoted exclusively to this field. It was a method of training that left people notoriously illprepared, for planning is learned by experience, through daily contact with real problems.

Developments in territorial planning have affected all levels of regional and urban government and have increased the need for specialist planning staff—not only in quantity but also in quality. Planning is becoming more sophisticated, extending its range further and further into the future, making ever greater use of operational research techniques. As a result of this evolution in the methods of planning and territorial development studies, the single practioner is being replaced by a team representing a number of disciplines. Planning departments and planning groups are being created. In order to prepare students to join such teams, introductory courses in planning and territorial development are now given both in schools of architecture and engineering and in faculties of law, the humanities, and economic, social, and political science.

Following the establishment of public planning services in almost all countries, it has been suggested on numerous occasions that professional training in planning should be specific and autonomous, that a planner should first be trained as such, only later to specialize in one of the particular aspects of the discipline—surveys, economics, sociology, demography, health, the preparation of plans, and so forth. With this procedure there is always the risk of incurring severe criticism from the pure specialist; nevertheless, in both North and South America some progress toward these aims has been made. In France, to date at least, planning has no such official status. It is preferred to take the various technicians and specialists who contribute to development planning and give them training to complement their previously acquired qualifications, thus fitting them to work among the various other specialists on planning teams. They need to know the fundamental principles of planning and territorial development, and they need training in the methods used for the survey and study of plans. They must know not only what their own discipline has to contribute and how that contribution can be made, but they must also be fully aware of the contributions of the other disciplines. These are the basic elements of the "common vocabulary" enabling all involved to understand each other. In addition, they must have knowledge of planning legislation and the regulations governing land use. They must be familiar with the organization of the services administering economic and territorial planning. They must possess a thorough knowledge of how the different kinds of development plans are drawn up, approved, and implemented, how such plans complement or overlap each other, what they contain, and what they prescribe.

Training in planning is thus given to students already possessing basic qualifications in architecture, agronomy, civil and construction engineering, economics, geography, sociology, and administration. It provides complementary knowledge, the purpose of which is to teach the common vocabulary necessary if such people are to work together. Even so, no one can foresee with any accuracy what the real professional value of any student will be, for planning—like medicine, for instance—is above all a matter of practice and experience. It is only when he sets to work that one can recognize the talent of a planner for finding good solutions. To select a suitable person to head a planning team is often very problematical.

Until recently the Institute of Planning of the University of Paris was the only school giving this specialized instruction. At one stage it was criticized for failing to keep up with the evolution of professional practice, but it has undergone major reforms which place it at the highest level of advanced teaching. In October, 1969, at Grenoble and Aix-en-Provence, two other institutes of planning and development were formed. The teaching in these university departments covers all aspects of planning practice in principle. In addition, at certain important centers of higher education which give training in the various disciplines contributing to planning, there are

often seminars and courses of specialized study to introduce students to
the problems of planning. Such centers include the Atelier et Séminaire
Tony Garnier of the Ecole Nationale Supérieure des Beaux Arts de Paris,
the Cycle d'Études Spécialisés of the Institut des Etudes Politiques de Paris,
and seminars in advanced planning studies at various universities, notably
Paris (Sorbonne and Vincennes), Montpellier, and Toulouse.

Such then are the principle means whereby French technicians and
specialists in urban and rural development acquire a grounding in planning
and familiarity with its structure. Nevertheless, they still appear inadequate—
particularly as regards developing in students the ability to synthesize, in
space and time, a multiplicity of varied and often contradictory data. This
ability is the essence of a good planner. The authorities are endeavoring
to correct certain deficiencies in this field and to rationalize the approach
to training.

Research has seen some important advances in recent years. To satisfy
the requirements of both territorial planning and economic and social
programs, specialized units have been created and methodological studies
ordered at planning offices.

The units engaged in fundamental research—theoretical and methodological—in the fields of planning and urban programming are as follows:

- The Integrated Research Group at the Direction de l'Amenagement
Foncier et de l'Urbanisme (Planning and Development) of the Ministry
of Supply and Housing

- The Centre de Recherche d'Urbanisme (CRU—Planning Research
Center), a private association set up under the aegis of the Ministry of Supply
and Housing and the Ministry of Education

- The Centre d'Etudes et de Recherches sur l'Amenagement Urbain
(CERAU—Center for Study and Research in Urban Development), a
private firm whose shareholders are public or semipublic bodies

- The Institut d'Amenagement et d'Urbanisme de la Region Parisienne
(IAURP—Institute for Development and Planning in the Paris Region),
which has undertaken many interesting general studies in connection with
its more specific work

- The Institut de Recherche des Transports (IRT—Institute for Research
into Transport), which, in the field of road transport particularly, is engaged
upon important theoretical and methodological studies

To these different units must be added a number of research departments
belonging either to the University of France or to the National Center for
Scientific Research. These departments, particularly in the social sciences,
are participating in work on the phenomenon of urbanization.

In the main, studies carried out hitherto, most often on behalf of the
General Planning Commission or the Ministry of Supply and Housing, have
been inspired more by the needs of economic and social programming than
the rational and harmonious apportioning of land for all the various human
uses. In this respect, however, attention should be drawn to the theoretical
research carried out by the CRU on models of towns and to the methodo-

logical research of the IRT, which has made urban transport systems more coherent.

It became clear that coordination was needed in the field of urban research in order to avoid overlapping of studies and errors in method. The Delegation Generale a la Recherche Scientifique et Technique (General Commission for Scientific and Technical Research), set up in 1967, has taken the first steps in this direction. A special working party has drawn up a program of concerted action to tackle planning problems. To implement this program a number of study contracts have been awarded to public and private organizations. This experience has shown that coordination in research should be confined within narrower limits. For this purpose a Committee for Further Research and a research unit have been established to work in association with the Minister of Supply and Housing and the Minister of Transport. Their terms of reference are to direct and stimulate research in areas where both ministries have interests; to coordinate the activities of the public and private organizations engaged in research projects; and to control the way in which this work is carried out in terms of optimum utility.

In the field of quantitative studies, much has been done, with the result that calculations involving such measurable elements of urban planning as population, density, area, and movements are much more accurate than in the past. Comparisons can now be more fruitful. In the same way urban sociology has advanced considerably. Thus the elements of a true "urbanology" are beginning to emerge. In the qualitative field, a number of methods have recently been elaborated for tackling a variety of different problems. The technique of working in a multidisciplinary team, for example, is now well established. Insofar as we regard planning as the discipline which exists to apply the principles of urban science, it belongs to the quantitative field. Finally, fundamental research in France has been concerned with problems arising from the analysis of theoretical models for the development of towns and urban communication networks and also with the ways in which information related to planning is used.

Institutions, Education, and Public Participation   By the turn of the century, the terms "public art" and "civic art" were in current use to describe the concept of rational urban development. The protagonists of these new arts were not slow to organize in order that their ideas should be more effective. In 1907 a public health section was established at the Musée Social, which itself had been founded only 12 years earlier. This section quickly set about drawing up planning legislation similar to that which had already, for some 20 years, been in operation in Sweden, the Netherlands, and Britain. In 1911 the Société Francaise des Urbanistes (SFU) was founded—a professional association which was to draw together the practitioners of the new discipline. It owed its inception to certain members of the public health section, notably the architects Agache, Aubertin, Berard, Hebrard, Jaussely, and Prost, men who had distinguished themselves in numerous town planning competitions of the period (Antwerp, Barcelona, Canberra, Guayaquil). Other societies like that for the Protection des Sites et Paysages (Protection of the Environment) were equally concerned with these problems, putting more emphasis on the social, economic, or aesthetic aspect of the development of towns and villages. Contacts were made with the International Federation of Garden Cities, founded in 1913. Finally, at the height of the First World War, a movement pressing for specialized training for planners began. The influence of the Musée Social was responsible in 1915 for the founding of a School of Public Art. Many eminent specialists, both technicians and administrators, were to teach there. The school was later to become the Planning Institute of the University of Paris. During the same period, Marcel Poete, at the Paris Institute of History, Geography and Urban Economy, undertook a documentation embracing the various aspects of urban art (evolution of towns, technical, demographic, and morphological data). In association with activity abroad, this movement helped to promote a number of planning exhibitions. There was, for instance, the International Exhibition at Nancy (1913), and there were several exhibitions in Paris between 1907 and 1913 on the theme of the "evolution of Paris and urban art." As a result of the destruction caused by the war, an exhibition was held in 1916 entitled "The City Reconstituted."

Between the two world wars the application of the first legislation on "development, amenity and expansion planning" slowly got under way. At the same time the process of informing the public was also being pursued. The SFU organized France's first planning congress in 1923 at Strasbourg. From time to time during the interwar period it also held exhibitions under the name "Salon des Urbanistes." It made sure that planning was represented at the international exhibitions of 1925 and 1937 and the Colonial Exhibition of 1931. This same year, 1931, was to see the birth of the magazine *L'Architecture d'Aujourd'hui*. By adopting the ideas of Le Corbusier and of the CIAM (Congrès Internationaux d'Architecture Moderne, founded in 1928) this magazine made an important contribution to the diffusion of a resolutely progressive theory of planning, adapted to the demands of our machine-based society. In 1932, the first number of the magazine *Urbanisme* appeared. Its character was closer to daily realities—it showed greater awareness of administrative practices and proved to be more evolutionary than revolutionary. Finally, from 1930 onward, the French Association for Planning and Housing was to ensure professional representation at the congress and in the work of the International Federation of Housing and Planning. In this, Henri Sellier, Mayor of Suresnes, general councillor of the Department of the Seine and founder of the Paris Institute of Planning, played an important role.

After the Second World War, with the establishment of state planning services, the authorities tended more and more to make use of public relations techniques. They adopted the practice of renting stands at big exhibitions such as the "Arts Menagers" (Ideal Home) and at festivals both in Paris and in regional centers. Leading members of the Société Francaise des Urbanistes entered the new administrative services. National conferences on planning and housing became annual events. World Planning Day, celebrated every November 8 since 1950, has had increasing impact both in Paris and the provinces. French participation at meetings of the International Federation of Housing and Planning (FIHUAP) has become very active. The numbers of French delegates attending have risen, and France has twice acted as host country for annual congresses—in Bordeaux in 1955 and in Paris in 1962. On the latter occasion the congress was marked by a full-scale planning exhibition. In 1958 a French planner—Jean Canaux—became president of the FIHUAP.

As far as the press, both daily and periodical, is concerned, planning problems are more and more being treated as news. Along with such pioneer publications as *Urbanisme* and *L'Architecture d'Aujourd'hui,* a large number of newspapers and magazines with varying degrees of specialization are discussing the evolution of planning, criticizing mistakes and publicizing successes. The old-established *Moniteur des Travaux Publics et du Batiment* is an unsurpassed source of information for everybody concerned with the subject. Finally, publishers are now producing an increasing range of books, particularly paperbacks, on planning and development.

Over recent years, too, the growth of urban sociology has provided the public with more information about planning studies and long-term urban redevelopment. More participation by the public in the formulation of plans has resulted. Associations like ADELS (for local social democracy and education) or GAM (Municipal Action Groups) are becoming more numerous and influential. Often working in liaison with planning offices and agencies, they seek to unite the more militant elements of the forces of goodwill. At the departmental level, the notion of concerted action has been institutionalized. The land act of December 30, 1967, has made it possible for state or local authorities to combine with private interests in the implementation of planning and development projects.

Geographical and Climatic Conditions   Insofar as its administrative and authoritative functions are concerned, French planning has scarcely been touched by the variety France presents in terms of both geography and climate. The strongly centralized administration leads to uniformity of practice throughout the country. The egalitarian mood of public opinion condemns all differences which might be introduced into laws and regulations to allow for climatic variations. However, as far as building is concerned, regulations are generally adapted to local conditions by manipulation of plans whose provisions might differ from those of the "regulation types" prepared by the central administration. This applies particularly in the designation of building land and the regulations controlling light, the height of buildings, and the use of materials. Normally certain materials are stipulated to conform to local traditions, and these, of course, almost always owe their character to the demands of the climate.

Geographical considerations—both human and physical—have led to the formulation of a distinction between "regional groupings with administrative responsibilities" and "regional land development units." The "groupings" number 21 (excluding Corsica), and each comprises several counties. They are headed by a regional prefect assisted by a regional development committee. The question of endowing the regions with elected assemblies having the status of autonomous public collectives has been under discussion for some years. The "units" are defined as the "action cadres" of various public and semipublic concerns created especially to implement the development policy of the area in question. Best-known of these are the National Company for the Development of the Lower Rhone and the Languedoc, the Interministerial Scheme for Coastal Development in Languedoc-Roussillon, and OREAM (Organizations for the Development of Metropolitan Areas). These last have the task of planning the development of eight great cities destined to counterbalance the Paris region.

National development policy is strongly influenced by such factors as present populations densities, differences in patterns of industrialization, and the economic and social conditions prevailing in France today. The principal features of this policy are given in the act of December 22, 1964, and are related to the options possible under the fifth modernization plan. They may be summarized as follows:

- Rapid modernization of present regional agricultural patterns in order that they may be better adapted to varying soil types, climatic conditions, and demand, both domestic and from abroad.

- Industrialization of the regions of the west. Development of light industries for which transport costs are a relatively small factor. Development of certain heavy port installations and ancillary services required by these developments.

- Engineering projects in the east on an economic axis extending from the Mediterranean to the North Sea, using natural features, such as river systems and relief, in ways leading progressively towards logical concentration of industry and population.

- Modernization of the Paris region with a view to satisfying the needs of its inhabitants and permitting the capital to play its national and international role in conditions comparable with the other great capitals of Europe.

- Specific action in certain localized areas where problems of modernization or adaptation have become acute.

- Development and renewal of housing and major installations in collective use, to be carried out within the framework of an urban organization giving order and rhythm to the process of planning, reconciling the demands of the economy to the preferences of man.

- Overall plan for a modern communications network, comprising land routes (highways and high-speed railways), domestic air services, and telecommunications.

- Pursuit and strengthening of a coherent policy covering all aspects of the water problem.

To all this should be added the French government's response to international pressures when in 1970 it expressed willingness to promote active measures to protect the atmosphere and the human environment.

Traditions of Planning to the End of the Nineteenth Century   In a sense, the origins of French planning belong to the first half of the nineteenth century. Ideas which provide the subjects of planning were generated from concern over public health, the denunciation of poverty by such men as Guepin of Nantes and Villerme of Lille, and the agitation of Fourier, Godin, Proud'hon, and Saint-Simon for social and economic reforms. One result of their theoretical work was the establishment of an experimental industrial community known as the Familistere de Guise. However, it was to aesthetics that planning owed its main inspiration. Contemplation and study of the ruins of ancient cities provided the basic research material from which urban art was developed. Significant in the early stages of this process were the contributions made by students of the École des Beaux Arts who had been sent on scholarships to Rome. As a result of this approach, French planners enjoyed remarkable successes in competitions during the early years of this century. The only exception to the aesthetic tradition of the time was the "industrial city" of Garnier. This was a vision of a complete city—derived as much from social and economic considerations as from architectural ones. (Ledoux in the eighteenth century, with his project for the town of La Saline de Chaux, had foreshadowed Garnier.) After the First World War, Le Corbusier, with his "plastic" conception of cities and his concept of the "machine civilization," contributed a number of revolutionary ideas. At the same time, Poete was bringing to planning the important idea that above all a town is a "social being" whose movements dictate the architectural form, that a town is a place where "being" and "form" interact reciprocally.

Twentieth-century Planning   The first planning act came into force just after the war, in 1919. At the time much effort was being devoted to reconstruction, which posed special problems demanding special solutions. Nevertheless, planning in general continued to develop as an exercise in aesthetics, with planners conceiving their work in architectural or geometrical terms. Over the next 25 years, however, planning absorbed new ideas, most notably the idea of "urban functionalism." Le Corbusier and the "Athens Charta" of the CIAM paved the way. The extent to which planning had changed became particularly apparent after the Second World War, with the development of the planned economy. Planners say that functionalism is achieved by so devising an organism that the best possible quality of service is achieved at the least possible building and running costs. Progressively, principles of scientific organization as propounded by the Taylor-Fayol School began to be adopted by the various different municipal services. Later they were applied to the "organism" of the whole city and even to the surrounding region as well. In 1946, the General Planning Commission was established to promote economic and social planning. In response to the commission's needs, groups of researchers—notably those inspired by Berger—began to work on methods of long-term forecasting.

When planners and administrators began to examine the present organization of collective life, they criticized the enormous waste in terms of

CITÉ INDUSTRIELLE
PLAN GÉNÉRAL

ABOVE: *Project for an industrial city, by Tony Garnier (1901–1904).* LEFT: *Model of the Voisin Plan for the center of Paris, by Le Corbusier and P. Jeanneret (1925).*

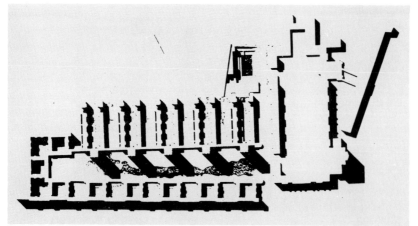

fatigue, time, and money caused by poor siting of installations. In both urban and rural areas maximum efficiency could be achieved only by applying the principles of scientific organization. Thus they proposed certain norms, such as the stipulation for commerical projects of their optimum volume of business and the extent of territory over which they would operate. The means of implementing plans, and particularly of financing them, are provided for under the Urban Modernization Program. This makes possible the progressive reorganization of conurbations, adapting them to the needs of the end of this century insofar as these needs can be foreseen.

Most estimates agree that the population of France will increase by about a quarter—or 12 million people—between 1970 and 2000. The population of urban areas is likely to increase by 15 million. This forecast anticipates a trebling of population in the eight regional metropolitan cities chosen to counterbalance Paris, while the towns of the Paris Basin itself (Amiens, Orléans, Reims, Rouen, and Troyes) will probably double in size. Thus over 60 percent of the urban population will be accommodated in cities and towns of more than 100,000 inhabitants.

The majority of existing dwellings in France were built before 1914. Many need replacement. To provide for this and for the population increase, France must build 12 million new dwellings between 1970 and 2000; that is, 400,000 per year. Modern construction consumes a great deal of space for roads, parking, service installations, and factories. Thus in new urban areas, average population densities are lower than in old. Using an average of

Drancy la Muette (1932–1934). Group of low-cost dwellings. (Architects: E. Beaudouin and M. Lods; L'urbanisme en France, vol. 1., Paris, 1933.)

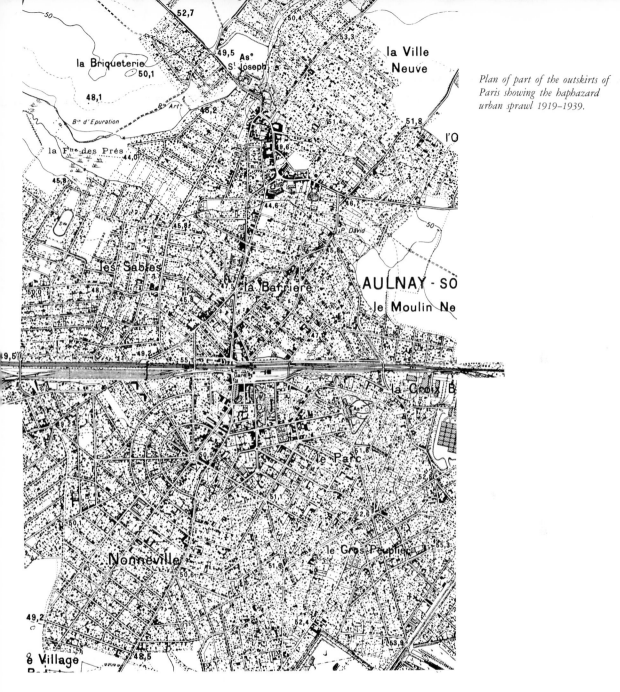

Plan of part of the outskirts of Paris showing the haphazard urban sprawl 1919–1939.

16 dwellings to the acre (40 per hectare), requirements of building land during the 30-year period will amount to 750,000 acres (303,750 hectares), or, in any one year, 25,000 acres (10,125 hectares). While these figures allow for the normal shared amenities accompanying housing development and for the normal infrastructure and superstructure of urban life, they do not include land for activity centers, notably those of industry. For this, the General Planning Commission has scheduled some 3,000 extra acres (1,215 hectares) to be developed annually. Two-thirds of this area will accommodate

new industries, while the remainder will be used to relocate factories transferred from within existing cities.

Installations such as warehousing, power stations, refineries, and smelting and foundry complexes are considered as separate from the normal industry of urban areas. Land required for them is not included in the estimates of the previous paragraph.

In most urban areas services are already saturated and renovation work is often difficult. Nevertheless, over the next 30 years France faces the task of doubling (if not trebling) her cities. The quickest and cheapest way of doing this would seem to be by designating overspill areas and even new towns. But clearly urban development cannot always follow a uniform pattern. In certain cases expansion will mean high-density building, thus "polarizing" land use over a particular area. The same process of polarizing will be used in the renovation of existing sectors of cities. On the other hand, there will also be residential areas consisting of single-family houses or small blocks of flats set in ample green space. Thus, according to the various local, geographical, and human factors involved, densities will vary from 28 to 32 dwellings per acre (70 to 80 per hectare) in central districts down to 10 to 12 (25 to 30) or even fewer in outlying suburbs.

Development on such a scale cannot simply be left to private initiative. Such a course would invite anarchy. If human life and institutions are to be organized within a framework allowing for maximum functional efficiency, if the process is to be controlled and land preserved for ecological, agricultural, and recreational purposes, if the expansion of human activity is to be reconciled with environmental realities, then planning should take its place as a major preoccupation of government.

Urban Extensions Efforts to cope with the housing problem in Paris and the other large cities of France led quickly to research into industrial

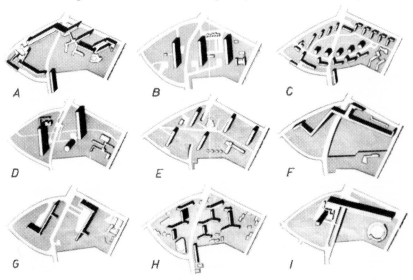

Competition for the Cité Rotterdam a Strasbourg—development for 800 dwellings. The aims of this competition were to obtain the maximum density as economically as possible consistent with good standards of development, and to secure rapid completion by employing modern methods of construction. (A) First prize and commission for the work— E. Beaudouin; (B) Second prize— B. Zehrfuss and J. Sebag; (C) Third prize—J. Fayeton, F. Herrenschmidt, and O. La Halle; (D) Fourth prize —Le Corbusier and A. Wogensky; (E) Commended—H. Colboc and G. Philippe; (F) Commended—J. Dubuisson and P. La Mache; (G) Commended—J. de Mailly; (H) Commended—P. Vago, Dunoyer de Segonzac, and Dupre; (I) Commended —O'Zavaroni and collaborators.

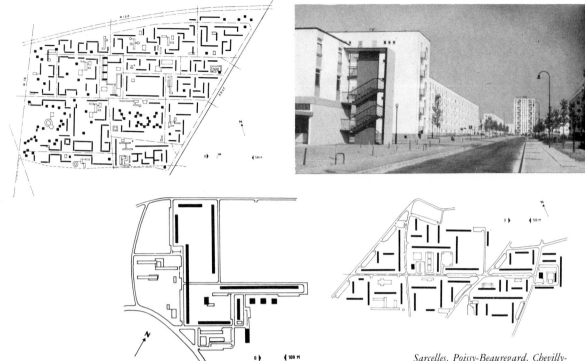

solutions. As a result, the notion of operational planning emerged and began to be applied to the construction of new estates comprising hundreds, sometimes thousands of homes and their shared services.

This activity created an enormous demand for building land. In consequence the doctrines governing expropriation of land had to be modified. In 1953 an act was passed enabling public authorities to make compulsory purchases of land required for housing or industry. At this stage, the pattern of development could be described as a systematic filling up of vacant land in urban areas. The year 1958 saw a new step in the definition of priority development areas (ZUP). This procedure is designed to create complete new urban areas by concentrating all available resources, public and private, toward implementation.

Development of new housing areas and new sectors of economic activity demands strict control. In the past, big projects have often encountered difficulties from such things as inadequate coordination in programming (causing, for instance, delay in occupation of housing because some essential service was lacking) or from unfavorable local conditions (a supply of housing not matched to demand, speculation in property, divided administrative responsibility). In 1967 the Orientation Act was passed to encourage growth of a coherent and effective strategy for land use, both at national and urban levels. Under this act, authorities can acquire reserves of land, and new revenue arrangements make the provision of public services easier.

Sarcelles, Poissy-Beauregard, Chevilly-Larue, 1953–1955. A search for maximum productivity in the construction of large-scale housing in the Paris region. Massive use of "industrialized" construction techniques in order to build fast, at minimum cost. The result has been high density housing, dotting large plots of land, at the urban periphery; buildings with uniform façades standing in geometrically rigid arrays, creating an environment both dull and oppressive—and much deplored by most of the local dwellers. Future trends will lead to the design of smaller housing projects, better integrated in the existing urban network; or else in the creation of true "new towns".

RIGHT AND OPPOSITE PAGE:
*Marly-les-Grandes Terres—1,500
dwellings in 27 apartment blocks of
medium height (1955) in the Paris
region. This is an attempt to
rehumanize urban environment.
(A,B,C.) center; (D) service station;
(E) school; (F) central heating plant.
(Architect-in-Chief: M. Lods with
J. Honegger and Brothers Arsene-Henay.)*

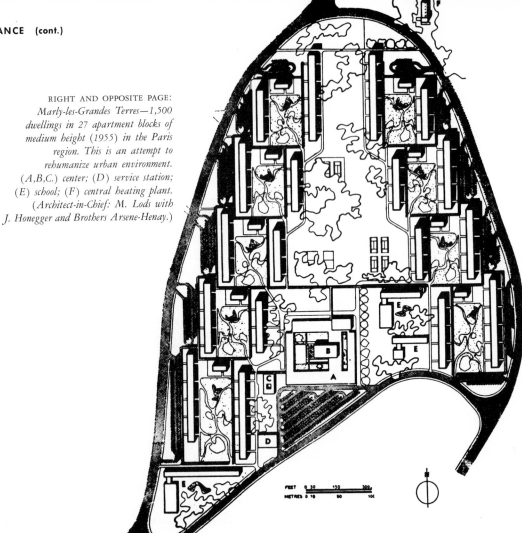

It also provides for joint development areas (ZAC) in which private interests can associate in the financing and building of public projects. This practice is becoming more and more widespread. However, it is important that only schemes conceived within the framework of general social and economic planning and regional development planning should receive financial assistance. In the case of urban development schemes, it is important that a careful study of the inhabitants' needs and existing public services should always precede action.

From the technical and aesthetic points of view, large-scale urban development in France closely resembles that in other industrially advanced countries. The size of the demand for housing, coupled with the shortage of suitable building land, has led to high population densities in big blocks of flats. Such architecture reflects the rigidity of government building specifications which are concerned with avoiding waste and ensuring full

use of housing grants. Time and cost considerations have led to prefabrication systems and other industrialized building techniques. The result has often been monotonous, uniform facades geometrically arranged. Inhabitants of flats have sometimes suffered from the absence of services regarded as indispensable to daily life. However, latest developments do show that progress in this direction has been made. Cooperation between the different administrative departments concerned has improved. The latest programs and plans provide for more single-family houses, more green spaces, research in to landscaping, wider separation of the pedestrian from the vehicle, more parking space, and more land for cultural and sporting activities, shopping centers, and schools. It is regrettable, however, that the enormous financial burden of providing housing means that the authorities cannot provide new districts with more services and amenities. New housing estates are often situated far from existing places of work, which aggravates rush-hour traffic congestion in many towns. Speculation in property tends to be encouraged.

New Towns and Communities   The centers of big cities suffer from more or less permanent congestion, while their suburbs often have insufficient

Pantin-les Courtillieres—1955. 1,650 dwellings in 16 tower blocks of 13 stories and 9 long 5-story buildings. Construction by industrial methods does not prevent the creation of new urban landscape. (Architect: E. Ailland.)

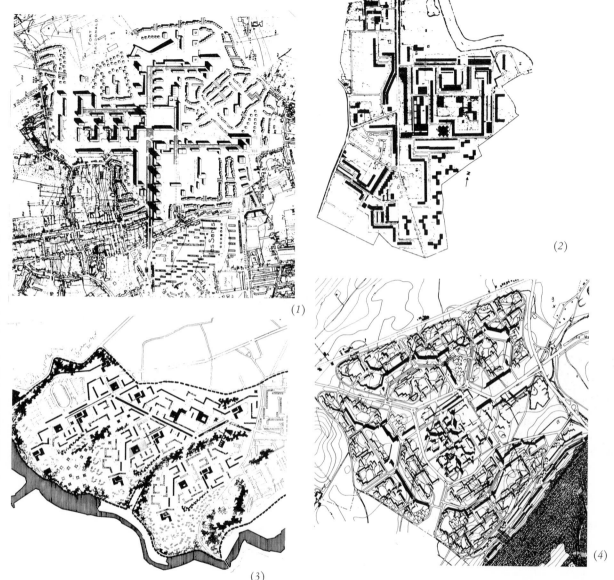

(1)

(2)

(3)

(4)

services—sometimes none at all. There would seem to be two types of solution—either restructuring of the city or dispersal of its population by creating completely new and self-contained urban areas.

Hitherto, cities have spread by means of dormitory suburbs. The new urban areas will differ in that they will encompass not only housing but also sufficient employment for their inhabitants. This raises delicate problems of programming and finance, administration, and leadership. To make possible the solution of these problems, various legal and financial arrangements have been made.

Priority Urbanization Zones (Z.U.P.)— 1958. Discipline of urban development— creation of new urban extension in which public participation is encouraged together with research into new forms of construction and new urban landscapes.

(1) Z.U.P. de Mons-en-Baroeul (Architect and planner: G. Perpere); (2) Z.U.P. d'Allones au Mans (Architect and planner: J. Le Couteur); (3) Z.U.P. de Brest (Architect and planner: H. Auffret); (4) Z.U.P. de Besancon (Architect and planner: M. Novarina).

An act of July, 10, 1970, lays down the procedure governing the creation and development of a certain number of new urban areas. These will complete the number of new developments to be launched under the Fifth Economic and Social Development Plan. Having fixed their minimum size at 10,000 dwellings and having stated that their building will be authorized by the decree of the Council of State after consultation with interested local authorities, the act makes it possible for them to be built as autonomous towns. Following the period spent in construction, their autonomy will be assured by a special body known as the ensemble urbain. This body will possess the same moral authority and be administered by a council subject to the same regulations as an ordinary municipal council. At first the new council will have nine members appointed by a special assembly of municipal councils and the county council. Membership of the new council will then be made up in three stages by three members elected by the inhabitants—the first after 2,000 dwellings have been occupied, the second and third following at two-year intervals. The council then elects from its members a president and vice-president who fulfill the functions normally carried out by the mayor and his deputies.

Three years, at the latest, after completion of the elections described above, an order is made conferring the common-law status of commune on the ensemble urbain. Attached to the order is a map on which the new commune's boundaries are drawn. Thus it is finally separated from the original commune or communes.

Finally, the act provides a grant (as opposed to a loan) of capital to be made to each new ensemble urbain. Such grants are made as part of the investment program of the Fifth Economic and Social Development Plan. There are also special provisions in the national budget for credit to finance services and amenities. In 1970, nine new towns were due to receive aid under the arrangements. Five are in the Paris region (Evry, Pontoise-Cergy, Trappes, Vallée de la Marne, Melun-Sénart) and four are in the provinces (Lille-Est, L'Isle-d'Abeau near Lyon, Le Vaudreuil near Rouen, L'Etang de Berre near Marseilles).

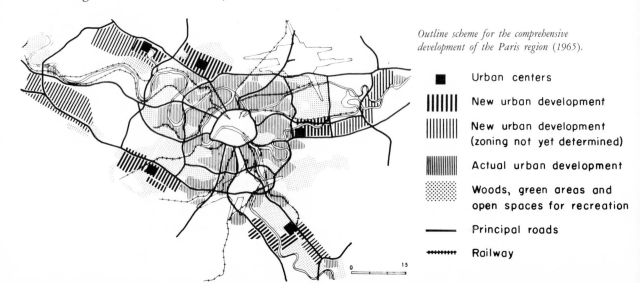

Outline scheme for the comprehensive development of the Paris region (1965).

■ Urban centers

▥ New urban development

▦ New urban development (zoning not yet determined)

▨ Actual urban development

░ Woods, green areas and open spaces for recreation

── Principal roads

┅┅ Railway

0   15

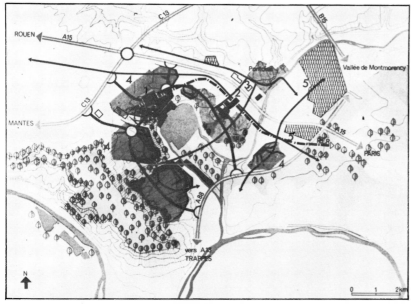

ABOVE: *Grigny (Paris region) "La
Grande Borne." Model of development.
Part was implemented in 1968.
(Architect: E. Aillaud; Photograph:
Leni Iselin.)*

LEFT: *New Town of Cergy-Pontoise:
(1) shopping and commercial center;
(2) civic center; (3) service industry;
(4) housing; (5) industrial areas.*

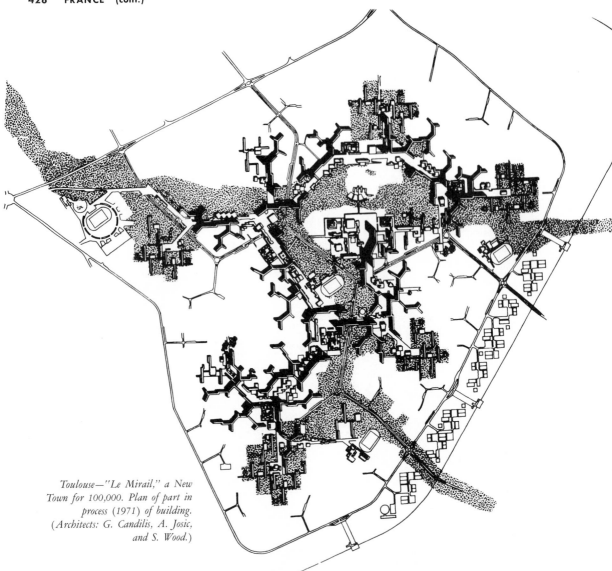

Toulouse—"Le Mirail," a New Town for 100,000. Plan of part in process (1971) of building. (Architects: G. Candilis, A. Josic, and S. Wood.)

Urban Renewal Planning authorities are not solely concerned with new development in the form of extension areas of cities and new towns. Legislation and regulations introduced in 1958 and 1962 concerning the improvement of the older parts of towns gave impetus to policies of urban renewal and restoration.

For this purpose, administrative, legal, and financial machinery was set up. The aims of the urban renewal policy may be summarized thus: to bring back sunlight and fresh air to the centers of old towns; to remedy the tendency of high-density building to create slums; to combat the poverty and social segregation associated with slums by moving the inhabitants and rehousing them in decent conditions; to restructure town centers so that they will be better able to satisfy new and future needs; to safeguard and preserve historic buildings and areas of interest to tourists; and to permit "classified urban sites" to continue taking an active part in the life of the city.

The task of urban renewal is difficult, whether it is undertaken entirely by a public body (often a "mixed economy" communal development agency) or whether it is planned in circumstances involving private interests (landowners' associations, building combines, and private landowners). The choice of procedure and its management demand great perseverance and continuity of vision. Considerable detailed prior study is needed to resolve the complex of interrelated problems surrounding urban renewal. Private ownership raises legal questions of compulsory purchase, the constitutions of associations, and the lot-by-lot acquisition of property. The eviction and rehousing of inhabitants, in most cases people with small economic resources, pose social problems. Upheavals cause concern of a different kind

"La Defense" development, Paris. Model of zone A in course of construction in 1971.

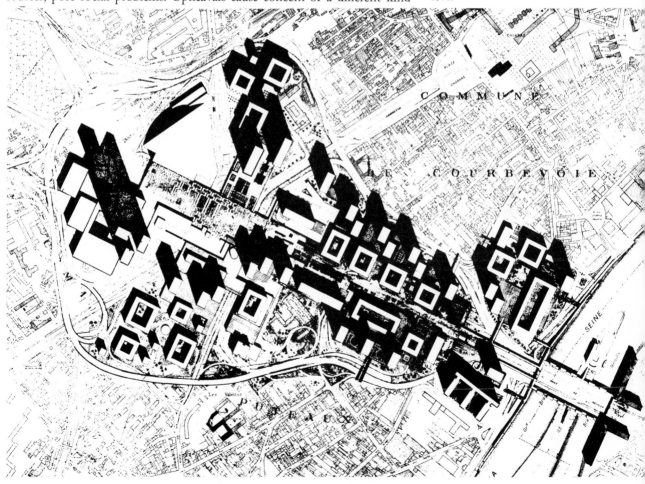

to commercial interests. From a financial point of view, numerous arrangements have to be made for state subsidies, municipal borrowing, and participation of owners and builders. Administratively, urban renewal is an exercise in coordinating the activities of a large number of public services, contractors, and individuals. In strict planning terms, these things represent only the "operational" aspect of implementation. When it comes to programming them, the overriding factor is the town's general policy which might include, for example, creation of a tertiary center or some public open space. Wherever renewal reduces the population density of an urban area, extra land must be found to accommodate the people dislodged. This has repercussions on the general process of restructuring and extension.

Thus urban renewal is slow and painful. Land in old districts, "liberated" in this way for new building, becomes very expensive. So much so that in some cases public funds suffer losses. This is why, at the end of 1969, there was a large backlog of renewal scheduled under the fifth plan. Only 50 such projects had been finished, while 200 are being studied or are in course of implementation.

BIBLIOGRAPHY: Eugene Henard, *Etudes sur la transformation de Paris,* Paris, 1907; Le Corbusier, *Urbanisme,* Paris, Cres, 1925 (new edition by Vincent-Freal, Paris, 1966); Marcel Poete, *Introduction a l'urbanisme,* Paris, Boivin, 1929 (new edition by Antropos, Paris, 1967); Le Corbusier, "La ville radieuse," *l'Architecture d'Aujourd'hui,* Paris, 1935 (new edition by Vincent-Freal, Paris, 1964); CIAM, *La Charte d'Athenes,* Plon, Paris, 1941; Gaston Bardet, *Problemes d'urbanisme,* Dunod, Paris, 1941; ASCORAL *Les trois etablissements humains,* Denoel, Paris, 1946 (Editions de Minuit, 1959); Le Corbusier, "Maniere de penser l'urbanisme," *l'Architecture d'Aujourd'hui,* Paris, 1947 (new edition by Ed. Gonthier, Paris, 1963); Gaston Bardet, *Le nouvel urbanisme,* Vincent-Freal, Paris, 1948, *Mission de l'urbanisme,* Editions Ouvrieres, Paris, 1949; Robert Auzelle and Ivan Jankovic, *Encyclopedie de l'urbanisme* (par fascicules, 30 parus depuis 1947), Vincent-Freal, Paris; Maurice F. Rouge, *Introduction a un urbanisme experimental,* Librairie generale Droit et Jurisprudence, Paris, 1950; Pierre Lavedan, *Histoire de l'urbanisme* (3 volumes), Paris, ed. Laurens, 1926-1941-1952; Robert Auzelle, *Technique de l'urbanisme,* P.U.F., Paris, 1953 (new edition 1970), *Plaidoyer pour une organisation consciente de l'espace,* Vincent-Freal, Paris, 1962; Andre Gutton, *L'urbanisme au service de l'Homme* volume 6 of *Conversations sur l'architecture,* Vincent-Freal, Paris, 1962; Robert Leroux, *Ecologie humaine—science de l'habitat,* Paris, ed. Eyrolles, 1963; Robert Auzelle in collaboration with J. Gohier and P. Vetter, *323 citations sur l'urbanisme,* Vincent-Freal, Paris, 1964; Centre de Recherche d'urbanisme, "L'urbanisation Francaise," Paris, 1964; Francoise Choay, *L'urbanisme—utopie et realites—une anthologie,* Editions du Seuil, Paris, 1965; Jean Gohier, "L'evolution de l'urbanisme en France—suivie d'un repertoire chronologique des faits marquants," *Etudes et Essais,* Centre de Recherche d'Urbanisme, Paris, 1965; Rene Magnan, "Art urbain evolutif," *Urbanisme* no. 94, Paris, 1966; Robert Auzelle, *Cours d'urbanisme* Vincent-Freal, Paris, 1967; Christian Pawlowski, *Tony Garnier et les debuts de l'urbanisme fonctionnel en France,* Centre de Recherche d'Urbanisme, Paris, 1967; Georges Meyer-Heine, *Au-dela de l'urbanisme,* Centre de Recherche d'Urbanisme, Paris, 1968; Waclaw Ostrowski, *L'urbanisme contemporain* (volume I, Des origines a la Charte d'Athenes; volume 2, Tendances actuelles Paris), Centre de Recherche d'Urbanisme, 1968–1970 (English translation—*Contemporary Town Planning*—The International Federation for Housing and Planning at The Hague); Georges Meyer-Heine, *A Human Approach to Urban Planning,* The International Federation for Housing and Planning at the Hague 1968; Peter Wolf, *Eugene Henard and the Beginning of Urbanism in Paris 1900-1914,* The International Federation for Housing and Planning at the Hague 1968; "Urbanisation and Planning in France," The International Federation for Housing and Planning at the Hague 1968; Paul Dufournet, *Les plans d'organisation de l'espace* (3 volumes), Centre de Recherche d'Urbanisme, Paris, 1969; Henri Prost, *Oeuvres d'architecture et d'urbanisme,* edited by the Academie d'Architecture, Paris, 1960.

—JEAN CANAUX

FREEWAYS AND MOTORWAYS The freeways of North America, the motorways of the United Kingdom, and the *Autobahnen, autostrada,* or *autoroutes* of continental Europe are all very similar types of highway. Each is designed to carry motor traffic exclusively and is constructed with two roadways physically separated by a central reservation or median strip. Access to the highway is controlled along its whole length; the road intersects with only certain other public roads and does so by means of grade-separated interchanges.

In the United States the freeway is but one of a family of access-controlled highways which are designed to offer a higher level of service to traffic than is obtained on the normal street network. The control of access in each case restricts the rights of property owners and occupiers to obtain access to the abutting highway. The *expressway* is a highway predominantly

Urban Freeway Interchange, San Francisco, Calif. In this case the medium strip is being utilized as right of way for a new rapid transit facility.

for through traffic and generally only partial control of access is enforced, so that on certain lengths there may be some lateral connections to adjoining properties and some at-grade intersections with other roads. The *parkway* is a special type of either expressway or freeway. Goods vehicles are usually excluded from this type of highway, which is located either within a park or within a broad right-of-way which has been landscaped to give a parklike appearance. The *turnpike* is a freeway on which a toll is payable. Many of the freeways in countries such as France, Italy, Spain, and Greece operate as toll roads.

Regional freeway systems were first developed in Italy and Germany, and prior to 1940 there were 2,300 miles (3,700 kilometers) of freeway in Germany alone and many hundreds of miles in Italy and North Africa. In North America the first purpose-designed controlled-access highway of any significance was the Bronx River Parkway in New York, which had been completed by the mid-1920s. Subsequently, there was considerable development of expressways and freeways, largely in the form of turnpike roads, and by 1940 there were some 160 miles (257 kilometers) of urban expressway and parkway. The bulk of freeway and motorway development has, however, occurred within the past 15 years. In 1944 the United States Congress designated a new 40,000-mile (64,360-kilometer) system of inter-state highways, but implementation of the plan did not begin in earnest until the 1955 Federal Aid Highway Act removed the burden of financing the program from the states to the federal government. The interstate and defense highway system, when completed in the mid-1970s, will have incorporated into its 41,000 miles (66,000 kilometers) of freeway some 2,500 miles (4,022 kilometers) of existing turnpikes, bridges, and tunnels and will have over 6,000 miles (9,654 kilometers) of urban freeway. In the United Kingdom the Special Roads Act of 1949 enabled the construction of limited-access motorways, but the first short section of the national motor-way system was not opened until 1958. Current plans are to have a 1,000-mile (1,600-kilometer) system linking the major conurbations completed by the early 1970s.

Standards for geometric design and layout for freeways and motorways are now very similar from one country to another, designed with a defined optimum safe operating speed for traffic, which, in turn, determines the maximum amount of horizontal and vertical curvature in alignment and profile within the range 60 to 90 miles (96 to 145 kilometers) per hour for rural areas and 40 to 60 miles (64 to 96 kilometers) per hour for urban areas.

The freeway offers many advantages to traffic compared with conditions normally prevailing on urban streets; advantages include a relatively un-interrupted traffic flow, the opportunity to travel at a sustained higher speed, and a comparatively low accident rate. However, the urban freeway is increasingly being recognized as a disruptive feature. The right-of-way tends to become a barrier to movement within local communities, and although attempts are made to minimize these problems of local accessibility by constructing either elevated or depressed roadways, the elevated highways in particular tend to be visually intrusive and broadcast the traffic noise over a wider area. The right-of-way for the urban freeway, and in particular the land for the interchanges, can often be obtained only at the expense of extensive demolition and clearance. In recent years there have been many proposals to resolve these difficulties by adopting an interdisciplinary design approach, by redeveloping the entire "corridor" within which the freeway is located (rather than appropriating only the minimum width of land needed for the right-of-way), and by attaching greater weight to community preferences and participation.

BIBLIOGRAPHY: *A Policy on Geometric Design of Rural Highways,* American Association of State Highway Officials, Washington, 1954; *A Policy on Arterial Highways in Urban Areas,* American Association of State Highway Officials, Washington, 1957; C. Oglesby and L. I. Hewes, *Highway Engineering,* John Wiley & Sons, Inc., New York, 1963; *Highway Capacity Manual,* Bureau of Public Roads, Washington, 1965; *Roads in Urban Areas,* Ministry of Transport, H.M.S.O., London, 1966; C. O'Flaherty, *Highway Engineering,* Edward Arnold (Publishers) Ltd., London, 1967; L. K. Bridwell, *Highway Research Record,* no. 220, pp. 1–4, Washington, 1968; J. Drake, H. Yeadon, and D. Evans, *Motorways,* Faber & Faber, Ltd., London, 1969.

—DAVID BRIGGS

FRONTAGE The direction in which a building faces and the side on which there is the main entrance, usually that facing a street, road, footway, place, or expanse of water. A building occupying an island site or open to a street on more than one side can have two or more frontages which are usually designated. The term also applies to that boundary of a site which adjoins a street.

FUNCTIONALISM Theoretically, functionalism means designing an object, building, or urban space for the function or purpose it has to serve. This should always be a principal aim in the design of anything of a utilitarian character. Functionalism, however, admits of some differences of interpretation which should be briefly examined.

Although functionalism is of fundamental importance in architecture and city planning, it has received particular emphasis and attention and has exercised a greater influence in some periods than in others. It has been one of the dominating creeds of modern architecture, the genesis of which can be traced to the middle of the nineteenth century in the ideas of Henri Labrouste and Viollet-le-Duc in France and William Morris and Philip Webb in England, to develop with particular vigor in Germany during the first three decades of the twentieth century.

The interpretations of functionalist theory vary from that of designing logically according to physical requirements, sometimes accompanied by the utmost expression of structure, to the inclusion of spiritual, social and aesthetic values.

These extreme interpretations, with many stages in between, have been variously held by the many architects and planners actuated by functionalism in their designs. It is helpful to clarify with examples.

The actual physical and material requirements of a church, town hall, or head office of an industrial organization are that they must be structurally sound; they must afford protection from the weather; they must be well lighted, heated, and ventilated; and the different parts must be in the most convenient relation or sequence—in brief, they must conduce to the utmost efficiency and comfort. These are the main physical and material purposes of the buildings, and if these are satisfied, then the buildings are functional.

There are some who contend that if a structure is perfectly fitted for its purpose then it will automatically be beautiful, a belief which gives rise to the view that architecture, which can be taken to mean building that has some degree of aesthetic value, automatically results from successful functional design. There are those who say also that the structural elements of a building should be fully apparent and expressed, because good construction—the functional relation of the various parts—gives aesthetic pleasure. Carried to its logical conclusion, this theory would mean that the church, town hall, or head office should be structurally and serviceably efficient, and that this is enough. There are others however, who contend that this is a far too narrow and exclusive view of functionalism, and that spiritual, civic, social, and aesthetic values should be comprehended as definite purposes in functional design. In the case of the church, there should not be thought only of the physical conditions of worship and meeting, comfort and convenience, but there should be some expression of religious atmosphere to actuate religious emotion. In the case of the town hall, there should be some expression of civic pride and dignity; and in the case of the head office of a large industrial organization, the building should symbolize pride in achievement and commercial status. That the meaning of functionalism should comprehend these values was widely held by some of the most noted architects of the great age of functionalism between the wars.

The application of these interpretations of functionalism to urban planning and civic design is simple. For instance, the center of a medium-size city or town of about eighty thousand population would comprise shops, offices, a town hall, entertainment centers, and religious buildings. It would thus be a place where people could congregate for many purposes, and the study of its functions would spell certain conditions of design. Citizens should be able to get as close as possible to the center by public or private transport, but there should be no facilities for through traffic as this would have an adverse effect on the efficient functioning of the center. A visit to the center by a resident may be designed to include visits to various shops, to an office, to the library, or to the town hall, and the center serving the convenience of citizens is therefore functionally designed if these different locations are within convenient walking distance, which spells a degree of compactness in the overall design.

A city center could be physically very convenient, but, in spite of the views of those who hold that fitness for purpose results in the beautiful, it may have an unpleasant or even ugly appearance while still being functional. To those who hold the wider interpretation of functionalism, it is important, therefore, if a city center is to be completely functional, for it to give an impression of civic dignity and harmonious composition so as to prompt some feeling of pride and satisfaction among the inhabitants of the city. That these feelings are sometimes partly subconscious and not always expressed makes them none the less real, as the storm of protest that arises with the threatened destruction of some much-liked familiar monument will demonstrate.

BIBLIOGRAPHY: Arnold Whittick, *European Architecture in the Twentieth Century,* vol. I, 1950, vol. II, 1953—The second volume comprises Part III, *The Era of Functionalism* (Crosby Lockwood); E. R. de Zurko, *Origins of Functionalist Theory,* Columbia University Press, New York, 1957.

—ARNOLD WHITTICK

FURNITURE, URBAN AND STREET   The provision of services and their equipment in urban development is a matter of prime concern to the planner. It involves the economic installation and the best functional location of such equipment and its effective and harmonious disposition in the urban scene. This street furniture, as it is generally called, serves the functions performed by the lighting, transport, telephone, postal, protective, and other services and includes various forms of lighting equipment such as lighting masts, columns, standards, wall brackets, and other fittings; the wide variety of traffic signs, telephone kiosks, post- or mailboxes, guardrails and fences, litter and storage bins, bus shelters, outdoor seats, poster display units, and several others. These are generally provided by the various service undertakings who also decide their best functional location, thus making general effective coordination by the planner difficult. Planning is further complicated by the fact that the various service organizations often act independently of each other in the placing of street furniture. Sometimes, however, there is some degree of cooperation, especially in the building of a New Town or town extensions, with a view to more effective functioning and in the interest of good overall appearance.

Much attention has been given to the improved design of street furniture and some good effective shapes have been evolved, especially in lighting columns with arms, which often look effective in a sequence. Good designs in a variety of materials have also been introduced for litter bins, kiosks, and other objects; but too often urban furniture, which consists of good, well-designed, individual pieces, does not coordinate in a good general harmony because design ends with the individual piece. This has prompted much criticism of the hodge-podge of street furniture. Where there has been some overall design or control, as in the building of a New Town by a development corporation, the general effect is better. With the installation of furniture in existing towns, good overall appearance consistent with efficient functioning could best be served by reference to a coordinating planning authority if and when such exists.

Other prominent features in the urbans scene, not strictly furniture as their purpose is mainly decorative (like the pictures and ornaments in a room), are monuments, sculpture, clock towers, trees, flower tubs, and other such decorative elements. These are often large objects and, because they are mainly decorative and have not exigencies of function, more consideration is generally given to their location—yet not always with the best results. (*See* AESTHETICS and MONUMENTS and MEMORIALS.) Whereas in furniture size and scale are generally determined by function, the scale of monuments and trees can be controlled in some degree by their setting. Trees, for example, although desirable, are best when they not only give a sense of refreshment but serve to enhance the effectiveness of the overall architecture. They should not, therefore, be so large as to blot out fine architectural effects, as they so often do in the London squares. Trees, as well as clock towers, monuments, fountains, and sculptures, should be in scale with their surroundings.

BIBLIOGRAPHY: Harold Lewis Malt, *Furnishing the City,* McGraw-Hill Book Company, New York, 1970; Council of Industrial Design (London), *Street furniture from design index,* 1970/71.

—ARNOLD WHITTICK

G

GARDEN CITY Though the description "garden city" was claimed by various towns in the past, in pride of their verdant character or surroundings, its use in the town-planning context dates from the proposal of Ebenezer Howard (*q.v.*) in his famous book of 1898 suggesting the creation of new moderate-sized towns in place of the continued growth of over-large and congested cities. Such towns, Howard said, would not only be healthy, efficient, and pleasant in themselves but would enable existing cities, through dispersal of some of their excess population and industry, to be redeveloped satisfactorily. He coupled this physical arrangement with a system of land tenure that would make possible considered town planning and the use of rising land values for urban facilities and other community benefits.

The concept was briefly defined in 1919 by the Garden City Association in agreement with Howard: "A Garden City is a Town designed for healthy living and industry; of a size that makes possible a full measure of social life, but not larger; surrounded by a rural belt; the whole of the land being in public ownership or held in trust for the community."

Howard, in his book, describes the concept as "an unique combination of proposals" that had never been united before. Among these proposals were those of E. G. Wakefield (1849) and of Professor Alfred Marshall (1884) for organized migratory movements of population (the former to

437

overseas colonies and the latter to the home countryside) with a balance
of industrial and agricultural employment; those of Thomas Spence (1775)
and Herbert Spencer (about 1845) for systems of land ownership that would
capture increments of value for public purposes; and that of J. S. Buckingham (1849) for a model town in rural surroundings, so planned as to
have all the advantages of town and country without the disadvantages of
either.

Howard's proposal was at first widely regarded as just another of the
numerous projects for self-sufficient ideal communities (*see* UTOPIA AND
UTOPIAN PLANNING). But in fact it was a new conception in that it was
not to be paternalistic, collectivist, or economically "closed." While the
ownership of the whole site was to be unified and permanently held by
a single quasipublic agency (and ultimately by an elected municipality),
sites for the various uses within the town were to be granted to industrial,
commercial, cooperative, and other enterprises as well as to individuals, on
long leases, at ground rents rising as population grew. Thus the industry
and trade of the town would not in any way be insulated from the economy
of the nation or the world. Whatever future changes might occur in the
ownership and management of industry and business, through nationalization, municipalization, or cooperation, the economy of the town would
remain part of the general economy, yet the inhabitants would still have
the advantages of nearness to work and the countryside, good houses with
gardens, healthy and pleasant environments, and modern urban services. Such
a proposal, made at a time when opinion was divided between sectarian
beliefs in private enterprise and nationalization, may be said to qualify
Howard as a prophet of the "mixed economy" toward which opinion in
all parties has since moved.

Not less important than Howard's proposed physical arrangement and
economic structure of New Towns was his invention of a practical machinery
by which they could be created. His quasipublic trust or company, at the
experimental stage, had to be financed by risk-taking shareholders, content
with a limit on dividends. This, though general skepticism made capital
difficult to raise and a sufficient site was difficult to assemble in the absence
of compulsory powers, did prove an excellent mechanism, and can now
be seen as the prototype of the Development Corporation (*q.v.*) which,
with public finance and powers of land acquisition, has become a most
useful type of agency, not only for establishing entirely new towns but
for the redevelopment of old towns and many other large-scale enterprises.

In 1899 Howard founded the Garden City Association (now the Town
and Country Planning Association) to promote the aims of his book of
1898, and in 1903 he founded a joint stock company. This company, First
Garden City Ltd., acquired by private treaty a site of 3,822 acres (later
increased to 4,598 acres) at Letchworth, 35 miles north of London, for
£160,000, and set out to build the first experimental model for a population
of about 33,000. The company's shares were entitled to a maximum dividend
of 5 percent per annum and a maximum bonus of 10 percent on winding

up, all surpluses to be used for the benefit of the town and its inhabitants, and on completion the whole freehold estate was to be passed into local public ownership. Capital being difficult to obtain on these terms, the progress of development was slow, but after many vicissitudes the town was established, and by 1961 it had a population of 25,000, a wide variety of prosperous industries, and a lively social life. By then its financial success was such that, owing to a regrettable abandonment by the shareholders of their profit limits, the company became vulnerable to a commercial takeover. Widespread national indignation was aroused, and Parliament passed by overwhelming all-party majorities the Letchworth Garden City Corporation Act (1962) under which the estate became public property as originally intended. Though the shareholders, instead of the inhabitants, benefited by the increment of land value up to 1961 (£2.5 m.) the financial soundness of Howard's principle of unified freehold ownership of a town estate was vindicated, and future gains in value will benefit the town.

The plan of Letchworth by Raymond Unwin (*q.v.*) and Barry Parker, with its houses and gardens for all income classes, architectural control, variety of informal grouping, and rich landscaping, has had a profound and permanent international influence. But the essential garden city principle was for long misunderstood and neglected (*see* NEW TOWNS).

In 1918 the garden city movement was revived by Howard and a small group of Letchworth associates, and in 1919 Howard initiated the second garden city project at Welwyn, 20 miles from London, which, again after many difficulties, including the same shortage of capital, was successfully established, and by the end of 1969 attained a population of about 43,000 of its target of 50,000. Benefiting by Letchworth experience, Welwyn Garden City made impressive advances in design, architectural control, and the finance of commercial buildings. Its plan, by Louis de Soissons, R.A., F.R.I.B.A. (*q.v.*), is regarded as a masterpiece. Welwyn Garden City was taken over in 1948 by a development corporation under the New Towns Act (1946)—an act to which its own example had historically led.

Both Letchworth and Welwyn are complete industrial towns in which the majority of occupied residents work. There is a natural interchange of employment with places within 5 to 10 miles, but they are not dormitory suburbs. In 1966 (census report) the occupied persons commuting to London from Letchworth were only about $2\frac{1}{2}$ percent and from Welwyn Garden City about $6\frac{1}{2}$ percent.

BIBLIOGRAPHY: E. Howard, *Garden Cities of Tomorrow* (1898), 1965 ed.; C. B. Purdom, *The Garden City*, 1913, *The Building of Satellite Towns*, 1949, and *The Letchworth Achievement*, 1963; F. J. Osborn, *New Towns After the War*, 1918 and 1942, and *Green-Belt Cities* (1946), 1969 ed.; the periodical, *The Garden City* (later *Town and Country Planning*), monthly and quarterly, 1904 to date. (*See also* bibliographies *under* EBENEZER HOWARD *and* NEW TOWNS.)

—FREDERIC J. OSBORN

GARDEN SUBURB   Term used in English for an extension or offshoot of a town, planned at low or moderate density, having gardens and open spaces and being essentially residential; i.e., without local industry. It should be distinguished from "garden city," which is a quite different concept, though in other languages (*Gartenstadt, Cité-Jardin, Tuinstad, Citta-Giardins, Ciudad-Jardin,* etc.) the terms have been confused or homologated. Hampstead Garden Suburb, an English masterpiece in this form, had great influence on residential planning all over the world. (*See* EBENEZER HOWARD; GARDEN CITY; NEW TOWNS.)

GARDENS The provision of gardens in urban areas is in answer to widespread human wishes, for, as Bacon said, a garden "is the purest of human pleasures; it is the greatest refreshment to the spirits of man, without which buildings and palaces are but gross handiworks." (*Essays*)

The planner makes provision for both public and private gardens. The former vary from little wayside or corner spaces off the street or road with lawns, flower beds, trees, seats, and perhaps a pool, fountain, or sculpture to much larger gardens which are synonymous with parks; or the gardens may be the more cultivated sections of larger parks (*see* PARKS). Often the difference is merely in the name, as in the case of Hyde Park and Kensington Gardens in London.

Private gardens are mainly of two kinds: the garden of the family dwelling house, enjoyed exclusively by the family and their visitors, and the communal garden of an apartment house or block of flats available to all the families that occupy the building. Overwhelming evidence indicates that the majority of families would like a private garden of their own. Pressure on space in many urban areas makes this only a dream.

In a residential development mainly of one-, two-, and three-story family dwellings, the planner may sometimes be confronted with the alternative of providing very small private gardens and fairly large public gardens or parks, or larger private gardens with correspondingly smaller public gardens. Available evidence again indicates that the preference would always be for the former, and if the planner has doubts it is a matter that he can usually test for himself. Where high-density development occurs by means of apartment blocks, the alternative may be low blocks of four stories or high blocks of eight stories, the latter giving more spacious gardens at the same density with a greater amount of sunlight.

The great value of the private garden (even if it is small) adjoining the family house is that it provides, in summer, an open-air room which can be enjoyed irrespective of any particular interest in gardening. If there is this interest, it is an added delight; if not, then the garden is maintained as attractively as possible in the same way as one does necessary housework. A garden can be a great solace to the human spirit. It is one of the urban values to which the planner should give full consideration.

—ARNOLD WHITTICK

GARNIER, TONY (1869–1948) Architect and planner, was born in Lyons in 1869. He was notable as one of the pioneers in the design of reinforced concrete construction and is remembered for the ideas he incorporated in his plan for an industrial city. The outline plan for this was made in 1901 and the details were worked out by 1904, but it was not until 1917 that it was published under the title *Une cite industrielle—Etude pour la construction des villes.* Thus it was conceived a few years after the publication of Ebenezer Howard's idea for a garden city (*q.v.*). It has many features similar to Howard's conception, but there are also important differences. Garnier's industrial city is planned for a population of 35,000. It is situated on the north bank of a river from which the ground rises gently. The residential area is a long rectangular shape, broken in the middle to form the city center. This center includes public buildings for culture and recreation, assembly halls, a museum, a library, exhibition galleries, two theaters (one open-air) a high school, and a sports ground. To the north, higher up on the slopes,, is a health center, with hospital, sanatorium, and convalescent home, separated from the residential area by a strip of open space. Beyond another open space to the southeast is a large industrial area complete with a goods railway station, and wharves are provided so as to utilize the river for goods transport. In the residential areas the houses are arranged in plots, the majority with tree-lined sidewalk access and a minority facing the roads. Garnier illustrated his plan with a remarkable series of drawings of various imagined views of the town and of the many buildings. They are all designed in the new constructional medium of ferroconcrete, with flat roofs and plain walls. Classic restraint with an artistically calculated balance of verticals and horizontals generally characterizes the designs. Perhaps the most outstanding building is the railway station, which has mushroom roofs and a tall, framed clock tower.

The inevitable question that arises is what provision shall be made for the increasing population when the city reaches its planned maximum size. Garnier, unlike Howard, who proposes the city cluster, gives no adequate answer. Garnier may have intended to let growth take place linearly along transport routes. This, however, would not mean the extension of his planned city, as that would destroy its character, rather but its repetition in the form of other similar cities, possibly separated by open country.

Garnier's Cité Industrielle was never realized; it remained but an idea. However, it has undoubtedly had an influence on later planners, while some of its architecture is reflected in many of the buildings erected from Garnier's designs at Lyons. Among the most notable of these were the Hôpital de Grange Blanche (1912–1930), the Sports Stadium (1910–1914), and also in the pleasingly proportioned Town Hall of Boulogne-sur-Seine (1931–1934), where classical feeling is combined with modern ferroconcrete construction. Tony Garnier died at La Bedoule in 1948.

BIBLIOGRAPHY: Tony Garnier, *Une cité industrielle—Etude pour la construction des villes,* Vincent, Paris, 1917; Giulia Veronesi, *Tony Garnier,* Il Balcone, Milan, 1948; Christopher Pawlowski, *Tony Garnier and the Beginning of Functional Planning in France,* Centre de Recherche d'Urbanisme, Paris, 1967; Dora Wiebenson, *Tony Garnier: The Cité Industrielle,* George Braziller, Inc., New York, 1969, and Studio Vista, London, 1970. —ARNOLD WHITTICK

GEDDES, PATRICK (1854–1932) Born in Ballater, Scotland, Geddes studied biology under T. H. Huxley at the University of London. He became interested in sociology and city planning, partly through coming in contact with the thought of Frederic Le Play, partly through taking up residence in one of the old tenements on Castle Hill, Edinburgh. Nearby, in the Outlook Tower, he established a new type of sociological museum as a center for new sociological, civic, and regional studies. From 1891 on he pioneered in organizing a series of 14 collegiate summer meetings, the forerunner of later university summer schools. While only a lad of fifteen, his initiation as a geographer and regionalist began with a walking tour of 200 miles, in company with his father, through the river valleys of Scotland.

Geddes's constructive planning activities began in Edinburgh with slum rehabilitation, the redemption of small open spaces as public gardens cared for by volunteers, and the building through private investment of a series of student hostels, which the university then lacked. Geddes's first public opportunity as planner and landscape architect came in a competition arranged by the Carnegie Trust for the improvement of the parks and cultural institutes of Dumfermline. Though his elaborate, detailed analysis and his bold imaginative proposals did not gain him the award, it helped to lay the ground for his later work: his design (with Frank Mears) of the Edinburgh Zoo, his once-unique Town Planning Exhibition, his series of plans and reports on Indian cities (1915–1924), and his plans for Tel-Aviv and for the University of Jerusalem (from 1920 on). In his earlier proposals for the social, agricultural, and economic rehabilitation of Cyprus, Geddes again led the way in making a comprehensive ecological diagnosis of problems usually treated in specialized compartments. Not the least witness to his sagacity as a sociologist was his diagnosis in 1911 of the likelihood of a European War by 1915, and his planning, with Victor Branford, of the *Making of the Future* series, which sought to guide thought in the postwar period.

As professor of botany at Dundee till 1919, as a lecturer in sociology at the University of London, and as professor of civics and sociology at the University of Bombay (1919–1924), Geddes's academic activity went hand in hand with his practical planning. But because of his wide intellectual range it was only after his death that his ideas, his methods, and his proposals began to attract the attention they deserved. As a lifelong student of cities, Geddes was the first scholar in the English-speaking world to recognize the city as an essential organ in the development of civilization: and a whole generation before Toynbee introduced his concept of "withdrawal and return," Geddes analyzed the function of the "cloister"—in the modern form of laboratory, studio, library—as necessary for raising the creative potential of the city; while in his advocacy of "the University Militant," he anticipated the current concern of university students to make the university play a responsible, dynamic part in the improvement of urban and regional life.

By preference an oral teacher and only reluctantly a writer, Geddes published all too little, except under pressure of his own planning work. For all that, in the early *Sociological Papers* of The Sociological Society and his *University Extension Syllabuses,* along with his *Cities in Evolution* (1915), landmarks in urban thinking are to be found. The quintessence of his wisdom as planner was assembled by Jacqueline Tyrwhitt in *Patrick Geddes in India.* Geddes had a direct influence on planners like Unwin and Abercrombie in Britain, and upon Stein, Wright, and MacKaye in the United States. Indirectly, the Land Utilization Survey of Britain and the Tennessee Valley Authority's regional planning stem from Geddes's teaching.

Geddes was the first to understand the organic interdependence of city and region as the basic geographic and historic structure underlying the complex interaction of place, work, people, and of educational, aesthetic, and political activities. Though preceded by Charles Booth's monumental but overdetailed *Survey of London,* Geddes was the most effective proponent of the idea that a systematic firsthand survey should precede all planning; and in such a survey he regarded personal experience, through walking and talking and contemplative absorption, utilizing all the senses, as no less important than the systematic gathering of geographic, climatic, demographic, and economic data: indeed more important, since only by this means could the mind embrace urban needs and functions as a dynamic, unified whole.

Significantly, it was Geddes's original training as a biologist that brought home to those who grasped his thought the immense biological and social complexity of the city as it develops both in space and time. As against authoritarian formalism and technocratic planning, Patrick Geddes stands preeminently as the exponent of organic planning, through which all the functions and purposes of the city may be cumulatively realized in appropriate structures, conserved, renewed, or when necessary replaced and creatively enlarged through the city's continued self-metamorphosis.

BIBLIOGRAPHY : Patrick Geddes, *City Development: A Study of Parks, Gardens, and Culture Institutes,* Edinburgh, 1904; "Civics as Applied Sociology," *Sociological Papers,* London, 1905–1906; "A Suggested Plan for a Civic Museum (or Civic Exhibition)," *Sociological Papers,* London, 1907; "City Deterioration and the Need of City Survey," *Annals of the American Academy of Political and Social Science,* July 1909; *Cities in Evolution,* London, 1915, reissued, London and New York, 1968; *Town Planning Toward City Development: A Report to the Durbar of Indore,* 2 vols., Indore, 1918; *Town Planning in Patiala State and City,* Lucknow, 1922; Jacqueline Tyrwhitt (ed.), *Patrick Geddes in India,* London, 1947.

—LEWIS MUMFORD

GEOLOGY AND GEOLOGICAL SURVEYS FOR PLANNING Planning, to be meaningful, must be placed in the context of a physical setting. The physical setting of any urban area includes the shape of the terrain, the character of the materials that occur below the surface, the fluids that flow over and through these surface materials, and the air above the surface. Clearly, the first three of these four factors are the subject matter of geologists, or, if one is in Europe, of physical geographers. It seems reasonable that the planning function should start with an analysis of the terrain and its "underpinning" and of the hydrologic system of the region. For this reason, geologists—usually available from the government-supported geological surveys—should be brought into the activity at the very beginning.

The guidance that can be obtained from geologists and publicly supported geological surveys falls into four broad categories:

First—information about the physical character of the terrain itself. This includes, in addition to the shape or form of the surface, information about the properties of the earth materials from the standpoint of construction; earth moving; installations of structures on, above, and below the surface—sometimes to considerable depths; stability of slopes; probability of earth tremors; and underground openings that may have significant implications for potential uses.

Second—geologic evaluations relating to problems of waste management and disposal. As the increasing volumes of waste make it less feasible to render substances harmless by diluting them in water or air, the containment of wastes in the sediments and rocks of the earth's crust has become a necessary method of operation. As these waste materials range from liquids that are subject to natural purification to almost indestructible solids including nonconvertible chemicals and long-lived radionuclides, the methods of management and disposal are indeed many faceted. Here again, geologic counsel should be called upon in the early stages of planning to ensure that costly mistakes, or potentially hazardous conditions, may be avoided. Even in the problems of air pollution, many of the pollutants originate as mineral materials, and proper planning and research can greatly alleviate the problems.

Third—appraisal of groundwater conditions and potential water resources. Water supplies are an essential item in all planning. Hydrogeologists can provide information on movement of water through the soils and rocks below the surface. This is an important factor where underground water sources are to be used, and it is also an essential item in planning for surface impoundments. Surface and underground water, in most regions, are a continuum, and one cannot be properly evaluated without adequate knowledge of the other.

Fourth—delineation of the rock and mineral resources essential to the proper development of an urban area. This is perhaps the least understood area of geologic input. Here, the economic geologist is the source of data for the farsighted planner. Bulk construction materials—stone, sand, and gravel; clay and shale for ceramic products; cement; fill material—are essential to the development of any modern city. Generally, these commodities must be available within a reasonable distance. Furthermore, there are specialized mineral and rock raw materials needed for the industries of the city. Although these will range widely from one community to another, virtually all will need some. If the mining of such substances is zoned out of development, urban areas cannot properly attain the level sought in intelligent planning.

Although these four areas of geologic input to the early stages of planning are listed as separate categories, it should be emphasized that they merge with one another. The planning of an area as reserve for construction-materials supply must be done while also considering the terrain characteristics of the area and its hydrogeologic features. Also, the use to which the area could be put after the construction materials are produced should be determined before it is reserved for such a purpose. Likewise, waste management and water-supply planning must be coordinated.

Public geological surveys are the most widespread source of geologic data for the planner. However, there is a wide range of these organizations from one governmental unit to another. State and province geological surveys, as well as national surveys, generally exist in the United States, West Germany, Australia, and Canada. In most other countries they operate as national organizations. Within the United States, although only two states are without geological surveys, their size, and types of available data, range widely from state to state. In addition to the governmental surveys there are geological consulting firms in many cities that are equipped to supply some of the specialized services listed, and some university faculties are available for this type of work.

Below are selected references to illustrate the type of geologic data available to the planner.

BIBLIOGRAPHY: Clifford A. Kaye, "Geology of the San Juan Metropolitan Area, Puerto Rico," U.S. Geological Survey Professional Paper 317-A; E. Dobrovolny and R. H. Harris, "Map Showing Foundation and Excavation Conditions in the Burtonville Quadrangle, Kentucky," U.S. Geological Survey Miscellaneous Geologic Investigations Map I-460, 1965; P. T. Flawn et al, "Urban Geology of Greater Waco (Texas)," Department of Geology, Baylor University, Waco, Texas, 1965; C. F. Withington, "Distribution of Gravel in the Patuxent Formation in the Beltsville Quadrangle, Prince Georges and Montgomery Counties, Maryland," U.S. Geological Survey Professional Paper 525-B, p. B439–B442, 1965; R. F. Yerkes et al., "Geology of the Los Angeles Basin, California—An Introduction," U.S. Geological Survey Professional Paper 420-A, 1965; J. C. Frye, "Geological Information for Managing the Environment," Illinois State Geological Survey Environmental Geology Note 18, 1967; G. M. Hughes, "Selection of refuse disposal sites in northeastern Illinois," Illinois State Geological Survey Environmental Geology Note 17, 1967; D. H. Radbruch, "Approximate Location of Fault Traces and Historic Surface Ruptures within the Hayward Fault Zone between San Pablo and Warm Springs, California," U.S. Geological Survey Miscellaneous Geologic Investigations Map I-522, 1967; H. E. Risser and R. L. Major, "Urban Expansion—An Opportunity and a Challenge to Industrial Mineral Producers," Illinois State Geological Survey Environmental Geology Note 16, 1967; J. E. Hackett, "Geologic Factors in Community Development at Naperville, Illinois," Illinois State Geological Survey Environmental Geology Note 22, 1968; E. E. Lutzen, "Engineering Geology of the Maxville Quadrangle, Jefferson and St. Louis Counties, Missouri," Missouri Geological Survey, Engineering Geology Series No. 1, 1968; M. R. McComas, "Geology Related to Land Use in the Hennepin Region," Illinois State Geological Survey Circular 422, 1968; J. E. Hackett and M. R. McComas, "Geology for Planning in McHenry County, Illinois," State Geological Survey Circular 438, 1969.

—JOHN C. FRYE

GEOMETRIC DETERMINISM   The belief that natural phenomena are governed by mathematical laws has existed since the time of the mathematicians and philosophers of ancient Greece. It has led artists, architects, and others to seek mathematical principles in organic structures and natural appearances. Thus geometric forms and their relations have often provided the basis for architectural proportion and have often formed the starting point of architectural design, especially during periods of classical revival like the Italian Renaissance. Initial planning schemes were generally expressed by geometric diagrams; and plans of ideal cities were conceived geometrically, such as the central circle with radiating and concentric streets. Often these formal patterns of the Renaissance tradition have been realized on irregular sites, as many European and American cities demonstrate. This tradition of geometric architectural design and planning continues into the twentieth century, not only among architects of the classical school but among exponents of the modern new architecture. There are, for example, strong elements of geometric determinism in the work of Sir Edwin Lutyens, Walter Burley Griffin, and Le Corbusier. The famous facades of Lutyens were partially controlled in their designs by geometric forms, and such designing was carried to his very formal plans for Delhi and London. Griffin's plan for Canberra is, to some extent, a geometric pattern imposed on the site which, however, is cleverly combined with natural features and with the creation of an irregularly shaped stretch of water. Much of Le Corbusier's designing is influenced by geometric principles and by such figures as the "golden section." In his book *Vers une Architecture,* he sought to demonstrate how many famous buildings of history conform to geometric principles and shapes, ideas which he carried to the field of urban planning. Many would see in these lines of thought religious determinism in design and planning.

BIBLIOGRAPHY: For the basis of the "golden section," Euclid, Book II, proposition XI, and Book VI, proposition XXX; Vitruvius, especially Book III; Leon Battista Alberti, *Ten Books on Architecture,* English translation by James Leoni (1726, 1729, and 1755), reprinted by Tiranti, London, 1955.

Le Corbusier, *Vers une Architecture,* Paris, 1923, English translation by Frederick Etchells, London, 1927; Christopher Hussey and A. S. G. Butler, "The Life and Work of Sir Edwin Lutyens," *Country Life,* London, 1948.

—ARNOLD WHITTICK

GERMANY, EAST (German Democratic Republic)

Geographical and Climatic Conditions   The territory of the German Democratic Republic (G.D.R.) extends over 41,766 square miles (108,174 square kilometers) stretching from the Baltic Sea to the Erzgebirge and Thuringian forest range of mountains in the south. The largest part of the country is flat, and only in a few places do the mountains exceed 3,280 feet (1,000 meters). With the exception of the hilly regions in the south, a relatively mild climate prevails, influenced by the maritime weather conditions of northwestern Europe. The annual mean temperature is between 45.8 and 48.6° F (7.8 and 9.2° C), and the annual rainfall is between 24 and 32 inches (600 and 800 millimeters). To the east is Poland; to the southeast, Czechoslovakia; and to the west and southwest, the German Federal Republic.

The population of the German Democratic Republic was 17,079,654 at the end of 1966, of which 7,683,807 persons were employed. The age structure of the population still clearly shows the effects of the war and so influences the demographic development.

Although the average population density is 409 per square mile (158 per square kilometer), the population is very unevenly distributed. In the largely agricultural districts of the north the density is below 260 persons per square mile (100 per square kilometer). In district Neubrandenburg for instance, the figure is about 150 per square mile (59 per square kilometer). In the highly industrialized areas of the south, on the other hand, it is about 780 per square mile (300 per square kilometer). District Karl-Marx-Stadt, for instance, has a population density of about 896 per square

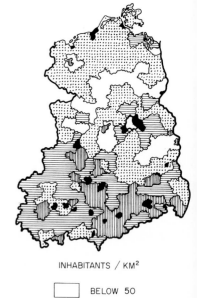

INHABITANTS / KM²

☐	BELOW 50
▦	51 – 100
▤	101 – 200
▥	201 – 1000
■	1001 AND ABOVE

Habitation density of the territory of the German Democratic Republic.

mile (346 per square kilometer). The distribution of population reflects the historic origin of the territorial structure (see illustration).

When, in 1949, the G.D.R. was founded on the German territory occupied by troops of the U.S.S.R. in the Second World War, there was hardly any concentration of industry in this area except in the region of Saxony, in the districts of Leipzig, Halle, and Magdeburg, and in Berlin. The only natural deposit is lignite, which is the chief source of energy and is used by the chemical industries. Since the Second World War, the aim of economic policy, apart from measures for the reconstruction of heavy industry, has been the development of a highly valued manufacturing industry, which depends to a great extent on imports of raw material and semimanufactured goods from the socialist countries. Today the G.D.R. ranks among the first ten industrial countries of the world.

Having overcome the immediate effects of the war, the territorial structure policy, as an economic basis for regional and town planning, has followed two long-term purposes:

1. The completion of the existing industrial centers.
2. The gradual industrialization of the agricultural northern and eastern territories in order to make full use of the labor-force reserves, which are becoming available with the industrialization of agriculture and the growth in population in those areas. It is intended in this way to compensate for a historically created balance (see illustration).

The settlement structure as a historical basis for regional and town planning consists of 9,150 communities, of which 8,000 rural communities have less than 2,000 inhabitants each. There are 220 towns with populations of more than 10,000 each, of which only 25 have more than 50,000 inhabitants. Of these 25, only 11 towns have populations of 100,000 or above. Most of the towns are therefore small or medium-sized. The largest cities in the G.D.R. are Berlin, the capital, with a population of 1,880,726; Leipzig, with 594,099; and Dresden, with 505,188.

This characteristic settlement structure influences the main present and future trends in town planning development as follows:

■ The large towns will grow relatively slowly, but the surrounding agglomeration spaces will be developed and drastic measures of urban reconstruction will be carried out.

■ The urbanization process will be concentrated on towns which have between 20,000 and 100,000 inhabitants and particularly on some 50 to 60 towns in this category with special industrial expansion potential.

■ The development of rural settlements will concentrate on some 500 to 600 main centers which will be developed primarily to serve as the core of an industrialized agricultural and food products industry as well as cultural and service centers. At the same time a systematic redevelopment and modernization of the technical infrastructure will take place.

Legislation and Administration   On the basis of the socialist society existing in the G.D.R., regional and town planning are part of the homogeneous socialist planned economy. In this way conditions are created which enable

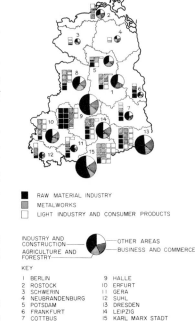

RAW MATERIAL INDUSTRY
METALWORKS
LIGHT INDUSTRY AND CONSUMER PRODUCTS

INDUSTRY AND CONSTRUCTION ———— OTHER AREAS
AGRICULTURE AND ———— BUSINESS AND COMMERCE
FORESTRY

KEY
1 BERLIN   9 HALLE
2 ROSTOCK   10 ERFURT
3 SCHWERIN   11 GERA
4 NEUBRANDENBURG   12 SUHL
5 POTSDAM   13 DRESDEN
6 FRANKFURT   14 LEIPZIG
7 COTTBUS   15 KARL MARX STADT
8 MAGDEBURG

Regional divisions of industrial production in the German Democratic Republic.

regional planners to work out plans for the optimal organization of the whole territory, to base the redevelopment of towns on predictions of the total social development, and to achieve this step by step within the framework of the economic plans of the country. Part of this program is the complex rationalization of the regional manufacturing structure, the rearrangement of interlacing relations, and the development of large-scale settlement systems as well as the redevelopment of town and country settlements.

For administrative purposes the territory of the G.D.R. is arranged into 14 districts (excluding the capital, Berlin) and these again into 215 counties, 24 of which are urban areas. The main responsibility for town and regional planning lies with the council of districts, counties, and cities. The district councils are provided with offices for territorial planning, which work out the regional analysis and plans, as well as with offices for the tasks of town and village planning. Larger towns have city or chief architects who have their own planning offices. Apart from these there exist traffic planning offices in the districts and large towns.

Administrative tasks concerned with the preparation and execution of town planning are within the scope of construction offices of the districts, counties, and towns. As a matter of fundamental principle, the confirmation of town planning proposals is made only after the people's representatives have discussed the plans. There are a number of state-issued laws, regulations, and guidelines covering town planning. Here the law covering the construction of towns—enacted in 1950—ranks first. In this law uniform principles for the reconstruction of destroyed towns were formulated for the first time in conformity with modern ideas of function and design. These provisions make it possible to declare cities, parishes, or parts of these as regions for redevelopment. It serves to regulate the takeover of estates for town planning purposes, including the necessary restriction or expropriation of private property and associated compensation. In recent times two most important codes of law affecting town planning have been published: (1) the law for the protection of the countryside and natural living conditions, and (2) the act of the Staatsrat which regulates, among other matters, the planning tasks of the local state authorities and the future organization of regional and town planning.

For working out town planning schemes, there are legal bases within the framework of a uniform system of technical standards.

Professional Practice   The uniform organization of regional and city planning made possible the development of a coordinated system of planning institutions. Working together, according to their professional specialization, are architects, civil and traffic engineers, economists, landscape architects, surveyors, and representatives of other disciplines. All these specialists have received university or specialized technical training and are involved in various systems of postgraduate training. The planning offices are financed by the state and are not tied to any commercial interests. Through their close contact with the organs of state economic directorates, they have an important influence on the preparation of economic and communal political decisions concerning the coordination of investments, the choice of sites, and town reconstruction.

Education and Training   So far there has been no special professional training of experts in urban planning. Town planners have emerged from among the graduates of architectural and civil engineering faculties of the Technical University of Dresden and the College of Architecture and Building at Weimar. There have been certain modifications within the framework of specialized studies. Specialists are also trained at the College of Economics in Berlin, the University of Halle (regional economics), the College for Communications in Dresden (planning of traffic), at the Humboldt University in Berlin (garden and landscape architecture), and at various specialized technical schools.

In 1969 a section of regional and urban planning was established at the College of Architecture and Building at Weimar. It provides a 2-year specialized course on urban design and technical regional and urban planning which follows the basic training for architects and civil engineers. It awards a degree in regional and urban planning (*Diplomingenieur*). At the same college there is an institute for the postgraduate training of executives in town planning and architecture.

The specialized study of regional and town planning, in addition to the fundamental subjects of architecture and engineering, embraces urban planning, urban design, regional planning, settlement development, regional economics, garden and landscape architecture, town redevelopment, traffic planning, and water and power supply as well as Marxist social science, sociology, operational research data processing, cartography, and statistics. In the next few years the number of students will be considerably increased. The postgraduate training of architects and engineers engaged in town planning is carried out both institutionally in the framework of the regional planning offices and through the professional organization of the Association of German Architects and the Chamber of Technology with their specialist groupings. The colleges hold seminars and maintain a system for candidates in these subjects and other postgraduate studies.

Institutions   The German Academy of Building (Deutsche Bauakademie) in Berlin is a state research institution for all branches of building. Problems of town planning are covered in the first place by the Institute of Urbanism and Architecture (IUA), but special subjects are also dealt with in other institutes (e.g., industrial planning, rural planning, statistical prediction, science organization). The Association of German Architects (Bund Deutscher Architekten) is the professional organization of architects and urbanists of the G.D.R. It is a member of the IUA and has its headquarters in Berlin.

There are three educational institutions: (1) the College of Architecture and Building at Weimar, divided into departments of regional planning and urban planning, architecture, and an institute for postgraduate training; (2) the Technical University at Dresden with its departments of architecture and civil engineering, and (3) the Berlin School of Fine Arts.

There are the following periodicals and organs of information:

Under the title *Deutsche Bauinformation,* the German Academy of Building in Berlin publishes a series of works on building, among them a special series on town planning and architecture. *Deutsche Architektur* is the monthly journal for architecture and town planning (published by VEB Verlag für Bauwesen, Berlin). There are two other periodicals—*Deutsche Gartenarchitektur,* the monthly journal of the landscape architects of the G.D.R. (published by the Deutscher Landwirtschaftsverlag, Berlin), and *Die Straße,* a journal for traffic planning and traffic technology published by VEB Verlag Transpress, Berlin).

Development of Urban Planning Since 1945   The development of urban planning in the G.D.R. began with the reconstruction of war-damaged cities, some of which suffered from catastrophic devastation. In Berlin, for example, 32 percent of all dwellings, 86 percent of all classrooms, 79 percent of hospital beds, as well as extensive transport and city installations were destroyed. In Leipzig, 44,000 dwellings and 40 percent of all official buildings were either destroyed or badly damaged. In Dresden 75,000 dwellings suffered total destruction and 200,000 were heavily damaged; 85 percent of the built-up area, including the entire city center of 5.8 square miles (15 square kilometers), with its world-famous art and cultural monuments, sixty-nine schools, three hospitals, and numerous theaters, was destroyed (see illustrations). In Magdeburg, 41,000 out of 106,000 dwellings were destroyed and 9,000 were badly damaged.

Apart from the large cities, many medium-sized and small towns were destroyed, among them Halberstadt, Nordhausen, Frankfurt/Oder, Prenzlau, Pasewalk, Anklam, Neubrandenburg, Potsdam, Plauen, and Karl-Marx-Stadt (Chemnitz). During the developments of the last 25 years, three stages have become apparent: The years 1950 to 1955 were spent trying to overcome the worst war damage. However, simultaneously, a modern development was introduced, based on the "sixteen fundamental principles of town planning," whose significance lies particularly in the creation, for the first time, of large connected complexes—an expression of the new social system. In fifteen towns, new road networks, squares, and extensive residential areas based on master plans (renewal plans) were created. The first New Town, Eisenhüttenstadt, was built on the river Oder.

Great sacrifices were made in order to rebuild the world-famous Dresdener Zwinger and Berliner Forum complexes. The second period, from 1955 to 1966, was marked by the introduction of large-scale industrialized methods of building which resulted in new features in urban design. The necessity for clear shapes, disciplined design, and adaptation to the conditions of a modern technology led to new structures and functional solutions; this also fostered the criticism that the design of the new structures was monotonous. Typical of this period is the complete setting up of new residential areas—with all the social provisions required—and their combination and concentration in complex centers. It began with the building of large industrial

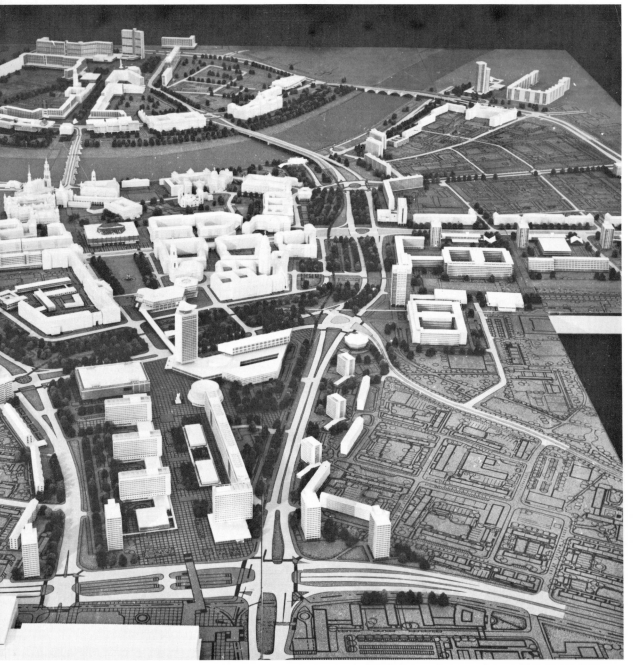

The rebuilt town center of Dresden (the model corresponds roughly to the present stage of rebuilding).

complexes and a number of New Towns, such as Schwarze Pumpe of the lignite combine and the dormitory town of Hoyerswerda (planned population: 95,000). Other examples include the dormitory town of Schwedt on the Oder (60,000), associated with the Schwedt oil refinery, Leuna II, and Halle-Neustadt (110,000). The third period, beginning in 1967, was oriented toward thorough renewal of the towns, the completion of the rebuilding of the town centers, and the adaptation of their structures to the conditions arising from social changes and the scientific-technological revolution. Fundamental changes in the system of settlements are beginning to take place. Some towns are growing rapidly, in the agricultural areas settlement centers are beginning to form, and there is considerable investment in the reconstruction and renewal of the technical infrastructure. It is anticipated that this period will be a long one. In the first place, there is the need for the renewal of old dwellings. Of approximately 5.8 million dwellings in 1965, about 60 percent were built before 1918. In the case of 2.3 to 2.4 million dwellings, modernization is considered possible. Some 1.5 million dwellings have to be replaced (see illustration). Altogether, about 3 million dwellings are expected to be built by the year 2000. Urban planning is concerned with long-term forecasts of the future requirements resulting from social and technological evolution.

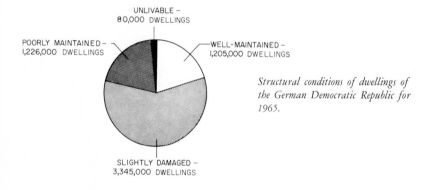

UNLIVABLE –
80,000 DWELLINGS

POORLY MAINTAINED –
1,226,000 DWELLINGS

WELL-MAINTAINED –
1,205,000 DWELLINGS

SLIGHTLY DAMAGED –
3,345,000 DWELLINGS

Structural conditions of dwellings of the German Democratic Republic for 1965.

New Towns

Halle-Neustadt. Halle-Neustadt, the building of which began in 1964, is not a classical example of a New Town. Nevertheless, it should be considered here because it is the latest and most extensive new foundation of an urban structure in the German Democratic Republic. To the town of Halle (almost 1,000 years old, with a present population of 275,000), which is the center of a significant industrial concentration (chemicals) and a university, has been added a twin town for a population of about 110,000 (see illustrations). Construction is entirely of prefabricated building elements. About 3,000 dwellings are erected annually, together with nursery schools, schools, and social centers. About 4,000 to 6,000 dwellings form a complex with its own center. A main center common to the whole town comprises social, cultural, administrative, and educational establishments as well as

Halle-Neustadt, overall model for first stage of building (70,000 inhabitants).

scientific institutions. Fast rail connections link the city center to the main places of work—large chemical enterprises situated about 6 to 12 miles (8 to 20 kilometers) away—around which no further building can take place. Between both towns is a river valley which forms a large recreational area. With the building of the new town, extensive measures of reconstruction have had to be undertaken, in particular with regard to the transport system of the old town.

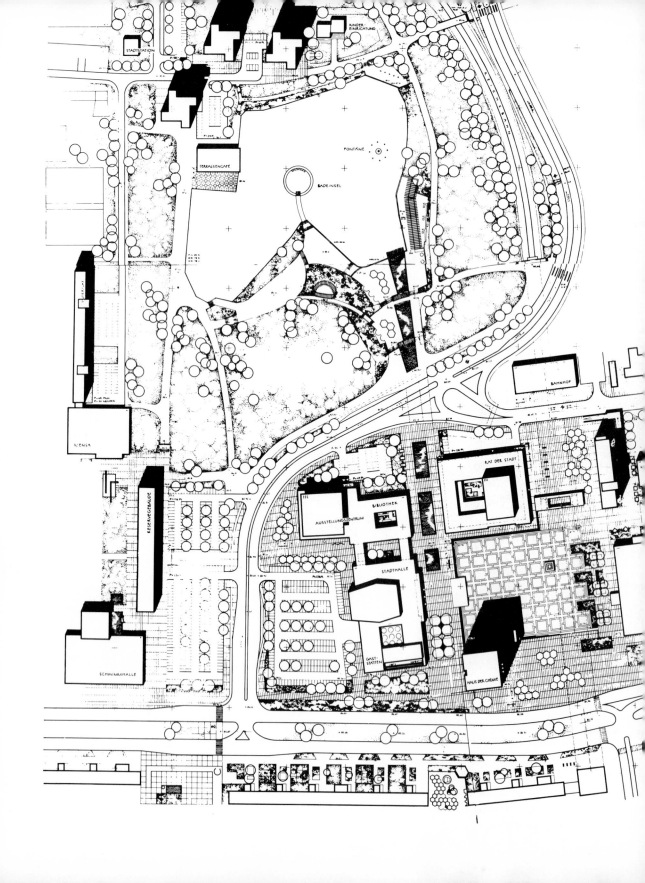

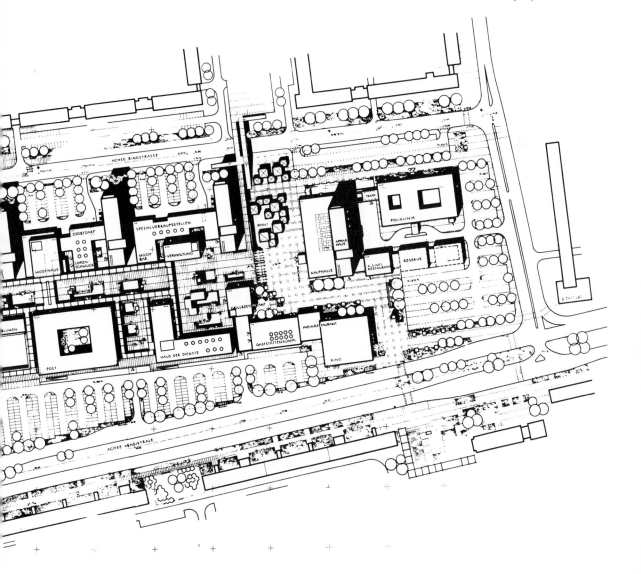

Plan of city center, Halle-Neustaa

Land-use plans of Halle and Halle-
Neustadt (schematical).

Town expansion

Rostock. Rostock is the most important port in the G.D.R. as well as
being a university town and an industrial center. Due to the building of
a new harbor for ocean-going vessels and the development of an extensive
shipbuilding and machine manufacturing industry, the growth of the town
has been considerable (see illustration). During the Second World War the
town was badly damaged. The population, which stood at 100,000 at the
end of the war, had almost doubled by 1969. New residential areas for 20,000
people in the northwest of the town and for 21,000 in the south sprang
up. Between Rostock and the town of Warnemünde, the community of

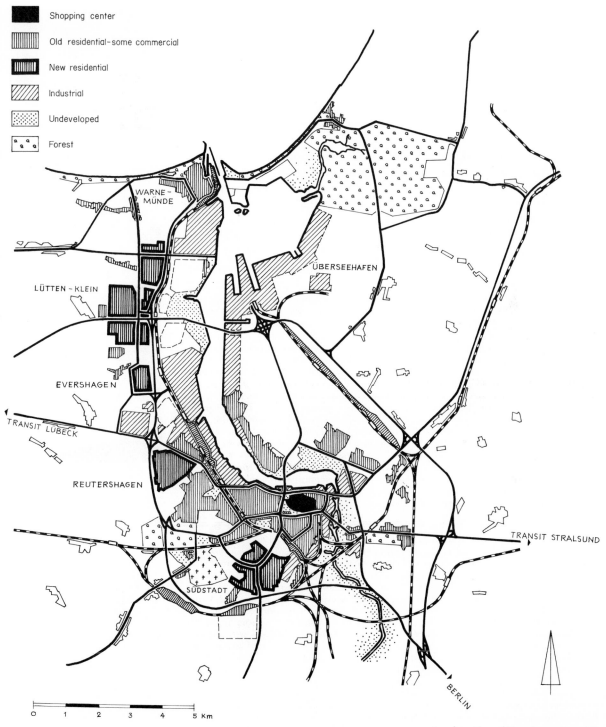

Shopping center

Old residential-some commercial

New residential

Industrial

Undeveloped

Forest

WARNE-MÜNDE

ÜBERSEEHAFEN

LÜTTEN-KLEIN

EVERSHAGEN

TRANSIT LÜBECK

REUTERSHAGEN

TRANSIT STRALSUND

SÜDSTADT

BERLIN

0   1   2   3   4   5 Km

Land-use plan of Rostock, together with the extension regions in the south, west, and north and the new harbor.

Lütten Klein with a population of 60,000 is being developed. Parallel with this the basic renewal of the old town center is taking place. By 1980 the expected population of Rostock is about 270,000 inhabitants.

Urban Renewal

Erfurt. Erfurt is one of the oldest German towns and was mentioned in a document dating back to 742 A.D. In the early Middle Ages it was one of the largest German towns, with a population of 20,000. Today the figure is nearly 200,000, and by the year 2000 the number will have grown from 250,000 to 300,000. Important industrial activities in Erfurt include the data processing and office equipment manufacturing industry as well as horticulture, especially seed cultivation. Of all the buildings, 52 percent are more than 50 years old, and large parts of the extensive old town center are under preservation orders. The town was practically undamaged during the war. Reconstruction is concentrated in the ring surrounding the old town center. Inside this ring the main task to be carried out has been the reconstruction and modernization of historic old buildings. At the same time the town is spreading toward the north in new industrial and residential areas (see illustration).

BIBLIOGRAPHY: Works on regional and urban planning published in the German Democratic Republic during 1968–1969. *Architektur und Städtebau in der DDR,* Hrsg. Deutsche Bauakademie, Inst. Stadtebau und Architektur (*Architecture and Urban Development in the G.D.R.,* published by the German Academy of Architecture, Institute of Urban Development and Architecture), Leipzig, 1969; Andrä, Scholz, and others, "Stadtzentren—Beitrage zu Planung und Umgestaltung," *Deutsche Bauenzyklopadie* (Town Centers—Contributions to Planning and Redevelopment, *German Encyclopedia of Architecture*) series STA, issue no. 6. Andrä, Scheibel, and Kirchherr, *Stadtzentren—Kennziffern, stadtebauliche Varianten* (*Town Centers—Code Numbers, Variants of Urban Development*); Autorenkollektiv, "Umgestaltung der Wohngebiete," *Deutsche Bauenzyklopädie* (Collaboration of several authors, "Redevelopment of Residential Areas," *German Encyclopedia of Architecture*), series STA, issue no. 13; Autorenkollektiv, "Dorfplanung in der DDR," *Deutsche Bauenzyklopadie* (Collaboration of several authors, "Rural Development Village Planning in the GDR," *German Encyclopedia of Architecture*), series STA, issue no. 9; Autorenkollektiv, *Planung der Volkswirtschaft in der DDR* (Collaboration of authors, *Economic Planning in the G.D.R.*), Berlin, 1969; "Mathematische Methoden in Stadtebau," *Deutsche Bauenzyklopadie* ("Mathematical Methods Used in Urban Development," *German Encyclopedia of Architecture*), series STA, issue no. 21; *Die Stadt—ihre Stellung in der Deutschen Geschichte* (*The Town—Its Place in German history*), Leipzig, 1969; *Jahrbuch fur Regionalgeschichte,* Bd. III, Hrsg. Institut fur Deutsche Geschichte an der Karl-Marx-Universitat, Leipzig (*Yearbook for Regional History,* vol. III, published by the Institute of German History at the Karl-Marx University, Leipzig), Weimar, 1968; Lanig, Linke, Rietdorf, Wessel, *Strassen und Plätze—Beispiel zur Gestaltung städtebaulicher Räume Streets and Squares—Examples for* (*Creating Spaces in Urban Development*), Berlin, 1968; Lindenau, "Der gebietswirtschaftliche Aufwand," *Schriftenreihe Planung und Leitung der Volkswirtschaft* ("Regional Economic Expenditure," *Series for Planning and Direction of Economy*), issue no. 22, Berlin, 1968; Mucke, Immerschied, "Untersuchunger zur Umgestaltung von Klein- und Mittelstädten: Riesa," *Deutsche Bauenzyklopadie* ("Investigations into Changing Small and Medium-Sized towns: Riesa," *German Encyclopedia of Architecture*), series STA, issue no. 18; Müller, Reissing, *Wirtschaftswunder DDR; Zur Geschichte der Okonomischen Politik der SED* (*Economic Miracle G.D.R.: Contribution to the History of the Political Economy of the SED*) Berlin, 1968; Schmidt, Lanig, *et al.,* "Funktion und Komposition der Stadtzentren," *Deutsche Bauenzyklopadie* ("Function and Compositions of Town Centers," *German Encyclopedia of Architecture*), series STA, issue no. 4; *Stadte und Stadtzentren in der DDR* (*Towns and Town Centers in the G.D.R.*), Krenz, Stiebitz, Weidner, Berlin, 1969; "Territorialokonomie in Theorie und Praxis," ("Regional Economy in Theory and Practice"), *Wiss, Zeitschrift der Martin-Luther-Universitat Halle,* Borgmeier and Reuscher, 1969, vol. 18, series C.

—JOACHIM BACH

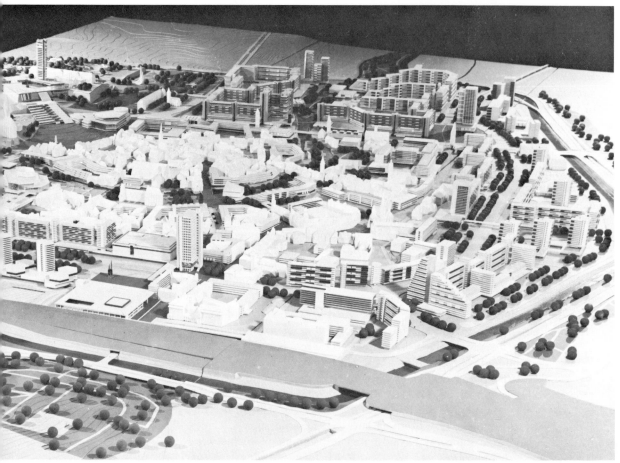

Model for the transformation of the city center of Erfurt.

GERMANY, WEST (Federal Republic)

Legislation and Administration Planning legislation in the proper sense of the word—disregarding building regulations of preindustrial times—can be traced back to the year 1868, marking the first *Fluchtliniengesetz* (building-lines act) in the Grand Duchy of Baden, to be followed by similar laws in other German states. These regulations enabled local authorities at the city and community level to fix building lines and thus to guide an important part of their physical development: the division of streets and building lots, then generally coinciding with public and private land. Consequently, street systems were the first object of planning theory, and it was not before the last decade of the nineteenth century that steps were taken to control the use of land, if only in some broad categories. This was done by local zoning ordinances (*Staffelbauordnungen*) which had come to be an accepted branch of planning by the turn of the century. At about the same time the need became apparent for a plan which was to be more comprehensive in spatial terms as well as more flexible in legal terms than the statutory plan showing building lines and land-use regulations, then called *Fluchtlinienplan, Baulinienplan,* or *Bebauungsplan.* Thus the concept of a general land-use plan was born, similar to the "master plan" idea but with different forms of realization and different names—*Flächenaufteilungsplan, Generalbebauungsplan, Wirtschaftsplan* and others. Of them, the term *Flächennutzungsplan* has persisted and found its way into the present nomenclature of planning.

While all this, by state enabling legislation, had come to be a matter of local responsibility, the density of land use—lot coverage, floor-space index, distance between buildings—remained for a long time part of the state building ordinances (*staatliche Bauordnungen*). These regulations allowed, during most of the nineteenth century, a very high degree of exploitation—up to densities of more than 400 inhabitants per acre (more than 1,000 per hectare). From the eighties of last century, however, these upper limits were gradually reduced in the different states by amendments of building ordinances, mainly for hygienic and social reasons. In the twenties of this century and more so after the 1939 to 1945 war, the control of land use was covered partly by local statutory plans, with the consequence of an uneasy dualism of local and state powers.

To increase difficulties, another dualism existed between state and Reich (later federal) powers to control the legal framework of town planning. Since planning legislation for a long time had been considered as an outgrowth of building legislation, it was vested originally in the states and was handled with varying degrees of efficiency; the most coordinated and progressive legislation of its time was that of Saxony (then a kingdom) of 1900. In the twenties, the Reich as well as some of the states, especially Prussia, tried to formulate new planning laws, but without success. Under national-socialist rule some of the most urgent planning problems were covered by Reich ordinances, but work on Reich town-planning law was not completed.

In the first years after World War II, there was not only a profound mistrust of planning, with its undertone of regimentation and rigid control characteristic of the dictatorship just experienced, but also a serious lack of legal machinery. To fill the gap, most of the postwar *Länder* (the majority newly created) enacted reconstruction laws (*Aufbaugesetze*) around 1949, which were basically similar in taking account of postwar conditions but leaning heavily on prewar experiences. They were all superseded in 1960 by the Federal Building Act (*Bundesbaugesetz*), which has a misleading name since it refers to town and country planning rather than to building. The first draft had been under discussion 10 years earlier, but it seemed necessary to get the opinion of the supreme court on constitutional questions (*Bundesverfassungsgericht*) as to the competence of *Bund* and *Länder* to pass laws on planning matters, since the constitution of 1949 (*Grundgesetz*) was not entirely clear on this point. The court ruled that the Federation had the right to regulate by law matters of national physical planning (*Bundesraumornung*) and local authority planning (*Städtebau*), whereas the states had the right to pass laws on state physical planning (*Landesplanung*) and on all matters of building, including design regulations in town-planning schemes.

The main points of the present legal situation according to the *Bundesbaugesetz* can be summed up as follows: All local authorities at community level (*Gemeinden*)—which include cities of around a million inhabitants down to villages with a few hundred—are entitled and if necessary required to guide their spatial development by plans. As a rule, two kinds of plans are necessary: the preparatory or land-use plan (*vorbereitender Bauleitplan, Flächennutzungsplan*), which indicates the main features of the envisaged future development in broad categories like major land uses, communication lines, and open space reserves; and the legally binding plan (*Verbindlicher Bauleitplan, Bebauungsplan*), which shows in detail the site, the delimitation of public and private land, kind and density of land use, the land which may be built upon and that which must be kept free from buildings. If necessary, more details may be indicated including the arrangement of parking areas on the lots or the planting of trees. Both sorts of plans are decided upon by the community council and are available to the public for a month for the purpose of making suggestions and objections which the municipality is bound to consider. Both sorts of plans need confirmation by an intermediate state authority (*Regierungspräsidium*), but whereas the *Flächennutzungsplan* obliges only public authorities which have been consulted during its preparation and have not objected, the *Bebauungsplan* has the character of a local statute and is legally enforceable.

While preparing a plan for a given area, the municipality may delay all building activity for at most 4 years without compensation if it is anticipated that it is not in keeping with the future plan. Conditions for compulsory purchase (*Enteignung*) and for public preemption (*Vorkaufsrecht*) are stipulated, public benefit being the basic criterion. The rules for the repartition of lots for building purposes (*Umlegung*) as well as for minor adjustments of lot boundaries (*Grenzregelung*) constitute another important part of the law. The legal instrument of such a repartition had been proposed before the turn of the century by the then lord mayor of Frankfurt, Adickes, but did not pass the Prussian legislature before 1909, and then in a rather mutilated condition. In 1918 it was adopted generally by Prussia, with some other states following suit, and it was in some form or other part of all *Aufbaugesetze* after 1949.

Other parts of the law cover the payment for streets and public utilities, the establishment of land assessment committees in order to make market conditions clear, and a number of minor aspects. The levy of a special tax on lots with unused development rights, designed to promote the concentration of building activities in areas properly developed, had been part of the law but was cancelled a few years later for political reasons.

A major point in which the law falls short of needs, which has been apparent for years, is that there is no provision for compensation and betterment, although the first draft of a measure did contain a scheme not unlike that of the 1947 act in Britain (since partly repealed). Administrative and legal difficulties, political expediency, failure to recognize the scope of the problem, and the futile hope of keeping down land prices by other means all worked together toward avoiding this issue. In the meantime, public interest in the matter has considerably increased, so that some legislation in the future may be expected.

The first attempt in this direction is a bill concerning urban renewal (*Gesetz zur Sanierung und Entwicklung von Gemeinden; Städtebauförderungsgesetz*) which after several unsuccessful attempts between 1965 and 1969, finally won parliamentary approval and was enacted in 1971. The act is aimed at facilitating urban renewal and large-scale development, like town expansions or New Towns, by providing a suitable institutional framework with the necessary powers for realization, by offering federal grants for this purpose, and by excluding gains based solely on the expectation of renewal or development. The 1969 Bundestag will have to decide again on this issue.

Two ordinances based on the *Bundesbaugesetz* remain to be mentioned: one concerning signatures for plans, the other, more important, fixing the kinds of land uses and the limits of their density to be embodied in statutory plans, thereby putting an end to the aforementioned dualism and making this matter finally part of planning law. The first version of 1962 had fixed maximum floor-space indices for new development at 1.0 for dwellings and at 2.0 for offices; its amendment of 1969 raised this ceiling by 20 percent and provided a wider scope for the discretion of local authorities in granting exemptions for special cases.

In view of the fact that West Germany had in 1968 more than 24,000 communities (this number has since been reduced due to local government reforms in some of the states), it is obvious that no planning system based on the relative autonomy of such administrative units can be adequate in our time with its many interlocal interdependencies. The *Bundesbaugesetz* tried to overcome this difficulty by requiring that all plans should conform to the aims of state and national physical planning (*Landesplanung und Raumordnung*) and by providing some legal instruments for closely connected communities: a common land-use plan and a joint planning authority. So far, this machinery has rarely been used; coordination has normally come about by other channels if it was achieved at all.

Interlocal cooperation in planning dates back to the years around 1910 when special authorities were established both for greater Berlin (later to be consolidated into a single community) and for the Ruhr area; from the latter sprang in 1920 the *Siedlungsverband Ruhrkohlenbezirk,* which is still active as the earliest German regional planning authority. In the twenties, similar organizations were established in some of the more densely settled and politically diversified areas; under Hitler the tendencies toward centralization of national planning were strengthened by the establishment of the *Reichstelle für Raumordnung* but found no expression in law.

In the fifties, most states of the Federal Republic enacted state planning laws (*Landesplanungsgesetze*), thus creating a basis for large-scale planning measures, especially for a framework to which local planning objectives could be related. In that time, however, *Landesplanung* was more characterized by observation and reaction to outside events than by initial action. The laws fix the procedures of state planning, normally by requiring a state development program (*Landesentwicklungsprogramm*) to be adopted by the state legislature and by providing the statutory framework for safeguarding certain plans or measures of regional importance.

In 1965, the Bundestag legislated for national physical planning (*Raumordnungsgesetz*), which established as the goal of spatial organization the development of the Federal Republic in a manner "which serves the free unfolding of the personality within the community in the best possible way." The law fixes some principles concerning the material objectives of planning; e.g., for densely settled areas and for areas lagging behind the general level of development, and obliges the states to establish a framework of regional planning in which the communities concerned are entitled to participate. Some of the *Landesplanungsgesetze* have been amended in the meantime to conform to these requirements.

Regional planning is still in its early phases; although in most states there have been district offices of the *Landesplanung* for a long time, neither their powers nor the somewhat haphazard limiting of their administrative area (*Regierungsbezirk*) allowed them to fulfill genuine regional planning tasks. There is, however, a considerable number of regional planning agencies of recent origin, especially in areas where people and jobs concentrate, but usually still loosely organized and without much power of their own. Only in a single case—the Hanover metropolitan area—has a regional planning authority has been created by law; in some other cases local government reforms presently under way may ease the situation. But there are areas in need of regional policy which cut across state borders and for which administrative solutions are rather difficult. It is therefore probably not unreasonable to say that there is still much to be done before regional planning is established firmly enough to play its proper role of mediation between state and local planning.

Professional Practice Since planning is basically considered to be a responsibility of local and state authorities, it has come to be an established staff function both of state governments and of the administration of all cities and towns above about 30,000 inhabitants. All these authorities employ professional planners; a recent survey shows that the number of staff in municipal planning departments corresponds roughly to one person per 10,000 inhabitants; of these staff members, about a third are likely to be academically trained in a field related to planning (see "Education and Training"). Normally, the planning department in a city of 100,000 or more inhabitants is one of thirty to forty departments and is grouped with related departments like engineering, surveying, and building inspection under the responsibility of a chief technical officer who may have public service status or be an official elected by the council for 6 to 12 years. In recent years, planners are more likely to be selected to fill this post than architects or engineers, but there is also a growing tendency to consider it more as a managerial job and to turn it over to administrators with a background of training in law.

Smaller towns and villages often entrust the preparation of plans to private consultants; some of the states provide offices staffed with planning personnel which are available to such local authorities for the same purpose. The activity of consultants is faced with some difficulties, among them the unsatisfactory condition of regulations for professional fees and the fact that in many cases the work of the planning consultant is still seen as the preparation of a plan within a given time limit, whereas planning today requires a long-term advisory activity and entails a host of subtle interactions. The number of private consultant's offices fully equipped to comply with such requirements is as yet relatively small; in larger cities, therefore, consultants are frequently called in for limited tasks; long-term planning considerations and routine work being the function of the permanent staff. As a means of inviting private contributions to planning, the town-planning competition has a long tradition in Germany, but recently criticism has been strong. The ideal situation for a competition—precise conditions, data, programs; clearly defined task without interdependencies with other fields—is very rarely given in planning problems, and much of the thinking which goes into planning cannot be adequately expressed by a plan or a design even with explanatory notes. Moreover, the usual competition does not provide the opportunity for discussion and feedback of information necessary for the development of a realistic plan. It is therefore likely to be superseded by forms which allow gradual elaboration and revision.

The situation concerning professional practice in state and regional planning is similar, with a difference in degree: in state planning the planning consultant is even more of an exception than in regional and local planning. The state planning offices are attached to the state administration in various ways—either integrated into one of the ministries like interior or economic affairs or else immediately responsible to the prime minister. The background of state planning officers varies from architecture and engineering to economics, geography, and law. The same holds true for the staff of regional planning offices, although with a somewhat larger proportion of technically trained planners.

Education and Training   Planning education in the proper sense of the word has been established only very recently; planners in Germany have normally received their academic education in a related field covering some aspects of planning. Urban design or site planning (*Städtebau*) has held for a long time an important place in architectural education, just as streets and sewerage engineering (*Stadtbauwesen*) has played a prominent part in engineering studies. The first attempt to integrate these elements into some sort of planning education in the later phases of academic studies for architects, engineers, and surveyors dates back to about 1910 at the Technische Hochschule Berlin-Charlottenburg; a similar effort was made in the twenties at the Technische Hochschule Dresden, but both were short-lived and without marked institutional consequences.

After World War II the lack of an adequate planning education was felt more acutely, and a postgraduate education was advocated. As a first step, the Technische Hochschule Aachen established in the fifties a new system—postgraduate training in cooperation with selected planning offices. In the late sixties, full-time postgraduate courses were offered by the Technische Hochschule at Karlsruhe and Munich, undergraduate courses in close connection with the department of architecture were developed by the Technische Universität Berlin and Technische Hochschule Aachen, and the newly founded Universität Dortmund offers an undergraduate education in planning with an interdisciplinary faculty and without any institutional ties to a traditional discipline.

At the same time, architectural and engineering curricula have been readjusted as a consequence of the steadily rising requirements of factual knowledge, and they now offer a greater variety of options emphasizing a number of special fields. Among them, normally, is the urban design aspect for architects and the traffic and sanitary engineering aspects for civil engineers.

Besides the institutions at university level (Universität, Technische Universität, Technische Hochschule) there are technical colleges (Ingenieurschulen) which offer training in building and engineering on the basis of a 3-year curriculum. Here, too, the technical side of planning has received more attention recently, and this may lead to the development of a planning technician.

More important still is the provision of educational opportunities for practicing planners. There are some institutes which devote their activities to this end, notably those of the Deutsche Akademie für Städtebau und Landesplanung in Berlin and Munich. A special characteristic of German education remains to be mentioned: the 30-month training of applicants for public service in technical fields by the states, which is offered after the completion of studies and includes at present a 3-month period of theoretical education for planners, probably to be extended to 6 months in the near future.

Little or no provision is as yet available for the training of planners in the nonphysical field of state and national planning, although some steps in this direction are under discussion. Social sciences and geography tend to make up an increasing share of university courses and more research on questions relating to planning is being done.

Institutions   Institutions concerned with town and regional planning exist in West Germany at different levels. There are two academies, the Deutsche Akademie für Städtebau und Landesplanung, which is limited to 300 members and comprises practically all prominent planners together with a considerable number of persons tied to the field of planning by research or other activities. They elect their president and other officers to 3-year terms; most of their work is accomplished in regional groups roughly coinciding with the major *Länder*. The academy has many corresponding members in other countries. The other academy, Akademie für Raumforschung und Landesplanung, is of a different character; it is primarily concerned with research on questions of state and national planning; its membership of 55 is mainly composed of scientists, with practicing planners in the minority. Both academies supplement each other in the general character of their activities and have therefore entered into formal cooperation. An institution with a similarly scientific character is the Gesellschaft für Regionalwissenschaft, the German branch of the Regional Science Association, in which the emphasis is more on economic than on physical aspects of planning. A professional organization exclusively for planners with the representation of the profession's interests as one of its major objectives was founded only in 1969 under the name of Vereinigung der Stadt-Regional-und Landesplaner.

Another important institution with a somewhat broader field of activity is the Deutscher Verband für Wohnungswesen, Städtebau und Raumplanung, which includes the wide field of housing in its objectives. Unlike other organizations, it has not only individuals as members but also a considerable number of corporate members: state and local authorities as well as building societies and associations which constitute the bulk of housing investors and operators in West Germany.

Geographical and Climatic Conditions   West Germany, with an area of about 95,000 square miles (about 245,000 square kilometers) extends roughly from 47 degrees 30 minutes to 55 degrees north latitude and from 6 to 14 degrees east longitude. Altitudes rise from sea level to the Zugspitze, about 9,700 feet (2,963 meters) high, with the highest metropolitan area (Munich) slightly above 1,640 feet (500 meters) on the Oberdeutsche Hochebene. North of the Danube, mountainous areas of heights between nearly 5,000 feet (1,500 meters) (Schwarzwald and Böhmerwald peaks) and less than 1,640 feet or 500 meters (at the northern rim) fill most of the area up to the Norddeutsche Tiefebene. This plain, with an average elevation of not more than 160 feet (50 meters), occupies the northern part of the Federal Republic. The Rhine, Danube, Weser, and Elbe are the main rivers; for transportation, they are supplemented by a network of canals.

Climatic conditions vary between a rather mild maritime climate in the northwest and along the Rhine Valley and an intermediate climate with continental influences in the southeast. Similarly, precipitation varies between below 20 inches (500 millimeters) in a few places and more than 80 inches (2,000 millimeters) in the Alps, with an average of 27.6 inches (690 millimeters). Temperature over the year averages 48°F (9°C), with considerable variations between different parts of the country. Duration of sunshine reaches in most regions roughly 30 to 40 percent of the astronomically possible.

Population density over the whole of the Federal Republic reached 626 inhabitants per square mile (242 per square kilometer) in 1968; among the states—excluding city states—North-Rhine/Westphalia has the highest density with 1,285 inhabitants per square mile (496 per square kilometer), Bavaria the lowest with 378 inhabitants per square mile (146 per square kilometer).

The general settlement pattern is characterized by a continuous population concentration along the Rhine Valley, with a smaller axis branching off at the Ruhr area and extending toward Hanover and on to Berlin. Within these axes, four of the nine major conurbations are situated: Rhine/Ruhr, Rhine/Main, Rhine/Neckar, and Hanover. The others are the city regions (metropolitan areas) of Hamburg, Bremen, Stuttgart, Munich, and Nuremberg; with more than 23 million inhabitants, these contained in 1961, 43 percent of the population of the Federal Republic (without Berlin). Of the 1967 population, 32.5 percent lived in cities of 100,000 or more, 34.8 percent in towns between 5,000 and 10,000, and the remaining 32.7 percent in communities of smaller size. Present local government reforms are continually changing these proportions.

Traditions of Planning in the Nineteenth Century until World War I   In the planning traditions of the nineteenth-century Germany has several roots. First the impact of industrialization and the unprecedented growth of cities led—a few decades later than in Britain—to technical demands especially in the field of engineering. Street improvements, installation of sewerage, and provision of gas and water were the first answers, along with the attempt to develop street patterns suitable to the aims of town expansion—to create new dwellings and to facilitate traffic—as they were formulated by Germany's first author on town planning, R. Baumeister (1876). Some ambitions for plans of a formal character occurred, mostly influenced by Haussmann's replanning of Paris, but these proved hardly satisfactory. Moreover, opposition rose against social conditions in these growing cities, and thus two sources fed the movement toward reforms of the physical environment: Social reformers criticized living conditions in the cities—notably overcrowded dwellings and lack of open space—while architects rebelled against the ugliness of the industrial city, the soulless straight streets, the lack of aesthetic interest in the urban scene. In a way, all this entered into the planning literature of the nineteenth century: the efforts of the sanitary engineer and the building inspector toward technical efficiency and order, the ambitions of the architect who wanted to make the city a work of art, and the stimulus of the social reformer who sought primarily to improve the dwelling conditions of the lower classes but who basically aimed at bettering society by changing its environment. All these components contributed to form the type of the town planner as he emerged at the beginning of the new century.

The nineteenth century saw few realizations of planning which stood the test of time—among them a number of low-cost housing projects for workers in the wake of the more famous English examples. But there had been some promising beginnings of a new way of thinking: Camillo Sitte's book on the art of town planning had found many followers in Germany, Munich had invited designs for its future expansion by a competition in

1893, and Theodor Fritsch had published in 1896 a book on the city of the future which anticipated some of Howard's ideas, although with much less response. All this did not come to fruition, however, before the first decade of the new century. A new periodical, *Der Städtebau,* was founded in 1904 by Sitte and Goecke; a first "cities exhibition" was held in 1903 at Leipzig which, incidentally, provided the opportunity for the publication of Simmel's famous essay entitled "Die Großstädte und das Geistesleben"; a German branch of the garden-city movement was created by H. Kampff- meyer; and a competition for Greater Berlin was held whose winning design was published under a heading which contained, for the first time in a book title, the word *Planung.* This phase culminated in the town-planning exhibition of Berlin in 1911, aptly reported and commented upon by W. Hegemann. The garden-city movement, in spite of the support of many progressive men, did not result in more than a few garden suburbs, none of which could claim to approach a "self-contained community for work and living." Among its most notable achievements in the field of low-cost housing was the Krupp housing estate, Margarethenhöhe, at Essen. Metzen- dorf's design betrays the influence of English garden cities and suburbs.

Between World Wars   With the twenties, town planning in Germany entered into a new phase: the end of World War I, the newly created republic, the promise of a new beginning—all this created an atmosphere of hope and enthusiasm which even contained some utopian elements. The Weimar Republic did much to promote a progressive housing policy, and the achievements in this field won a worldwide reputation. It has been correctly said that although manifestations of modern tendencies in architecture, housing, and planning were present in many countries, Germany at that time was the only one to accept and promote them officially.

Berlin was of course one of the major centers of building activity, and among the many progressive developments of that time at least the "Hufeisensiedlung" Britz—with a building of a horseshoe ground plan as its focal point—by Bruno Taut, and the Siemensstadt housing estate by Gropius, Forbat, Scharoun, and others deserve special mention. Of com- parable importance are some housing developments at Frankfurt/Main initiated by the city's chief technical officer (*Stadtbaurat*) Ernst May. Römerstadt, Praunheim, and Westhausen are well-known and typical exam- ples of low-cost housing with a strong imprint of modern aesthetics. It was no accident that the International Congresses of Modern Architecture (CIAM) held their 1931 assembly in Frankfurt under the heading of "the dwelling for minimum existence" which dealt extensively with new forms of building arrangements in parallel rows (*Zeilenbau*), with new floor plans for dwellings with regard to function and orientation, and with more economical means of access by footpath (*Wohnwegerschließung*), all of which was practiced in Germany at that time. At Hamburg, the most important developments were town expansions for residential purposes, notably northeast of the center (Barmbeck, Dulsberg). Here, the Zeilenbau was applied less rigidly, without sacrificing its main advantages. Of similar importance was the execution of some urban renewal projects near the city center partly for residential, partly for office construction. Hamburg's outstanding personality in planning was at that time—between 1909 and 1933—Fritz Schumacher, city architect and planner, who made a unique contribution to the development of planning thought and practice.

One of his most important achievements was the initiation of a joint planning authority for the city and the surrounding local government areas of Prussia which persisted until 1937, when most of the area concerned was consolidated into the city-state of Hamburg. In this emerging field of regional planning, the earliest organization with lasting influence was the Siedlungsverband Ruhrkohlenbezirk (Joint Settlement Authority for the Ruhr Coal District), which has been active for over half a century, as a steering and coordinating element in this densely settled and administratively divided region.

Planning achievements of the National Socialist era are ambiguous and difficult to assess due to many divergent elements. There were some pompous redevelopment schemes for cities aiming at an impressive "grand design" in the language of an arid and monumental classicism. But there were also some reasonable housing developments, although mostly somewhat formalistic and/or influenced by a romanticist "blood and soil" ideology. National planning in the sense of coordinated space allocation made considerable headway by the establishment of the Reichsstelle für Raumordnung (Reich Office for National Physical Planning) which was called into being mainly to deal with space demands for military purposes but came to serve more general aims also.

After World War II After the war, shortages of materials and lack of any long-range perspective hampered planning and development for the first few years. Yet in most cities planners endeavored to turn the disaster into an opportunity—with varying degrees of success. Most of the rebuilding started by following the lines developed before 1933, embodying the tenets of the Athens Charter, and it was not much before 1960 that a reevaluation of these principles took place. By that time, the main lines for reconstruction of city centers and other built-up areas had been fixed, and many additional developments on virgin ground had been added at the outskirts of the cities. It is, of course, difficult to assess the degree of success in various plans, and there is a sizeable number of remarkable achievements in cities and towns, considering the restraints of the situation. For an outstanding example, mention should be made of Hanover. Its reconstruction as well as its overall planning and development have been directed continuously since 1948 by R. Hillebrecht as chief technical officer (*Stadtbaurat*). In particular, the Kreuzkirche redevelopment, as one of the first postwar schemes in a destroyed central area; the "Constructa block" built in connection with a first large exhibition of reconstruction in 1951; and some later city extensions, notably that of Hemmingen-Westerfeld, deserve mention. West Berlin's most noteworthy development is the Hansaviertel, subject of the 1957 international building exhibition, which is more appealing, however, as a collection of good buildings by a large number of world-famous architects than as a success in integrated urban design. Of more recent developments, the residential quarters of the Märkisches Viertel in the north and of Britz-Buckow-Rudow in the southeast are of particular importance. Hamburg has some remarkable residential schemes in war-devastated areas, especially the early Grindelberg development of 12 slab blocks between 8 and 14 stories. A more recent feature is the erection of a new administrative center 4 miles north of the city core to relieve pressure on the latter. In Munich, in Essen, and in Bremen, large areas of the city centers are open to pedestrians only; similar developments of a considerable scale exist in Cologne and Kassel, while many other cities are preparing or have established smaller pedestrian schemes. Some good examples of the integration of motorized traffic into cities in terms of both urban structure and urban design, a difficult and urgent problem, are offered by Bremen, Düsseldorf, and Hanover.

Aerial view of Geschäftsstadt Nord, Hamburg.

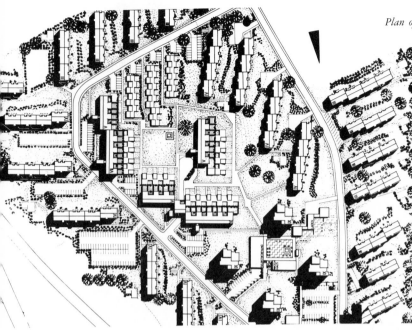

Plan of Bebauung Holsteiner Chaussee, Hamburg.

View of housing at Holsteiner Chaussee, Hamburg.

OPPOSITE PAGE: *Plan of Buckow-Rudow in the southeast of West Berlin. It is sometimes called Gropius City, as it was planned by Walter Gropius and built in the sixties. The residential areas consist of tall tower and slab apartment blocks, with a generous provision of open space and many variously designed one-family houses. The principal communal installations are numbered as follows: (1) Multipurpose buildings; (2) sports area with covered and open swimming pools; (3) playing fields and running tracks; (4) schools; (5) day nurseries; (6) old people's homes; (7) churches and community centers; (P) parking areas.* LEFT: *Old people's home and view beyond at Buckow-Rudow in the southeast of West Berlin.*

Model of Olympic Village, Munich, for the Olympic Games of 1972. (Design by Heinle, Wischer and Associates.)

ABOVE: *Aerial view of Mannheim Vogelstang, a development for a population of 20,000 (1960–1969). The density of the dwellings diminishes from the center outward—from tower blocks to two-story houses. The multilevel pedestrian shopping center has an electric rail service passing through it at the lowest level.* LEFT: *View of multilevel pedestrian shopping center of Mannheim Vogelstang.*

Hemmingen-Westerfeld near Hannover, residential development, built by Niedersächsische Heimstätte, F. Dellemann, architect, in 1958 to 1959. Wohnen in Neuen Siedlungen, Kramer, 1965, Stuttgart.)

KREITHWINKEL

KÖLLNDRINKWEG

WEIDENKAMP

RATHAUSPLATZ

GREIFFENBERGER STRASSE

IRCHDAMM

BOBERWEG

LÖWENBERGER STRASSE

LINSBERGER WEG

KÖLLNDRINKWEG

KATZBACHWEG

GLATZER WEG

WESTERFELDWEG

| 1-2 stories |
| 3 stories |
| 8 stories |

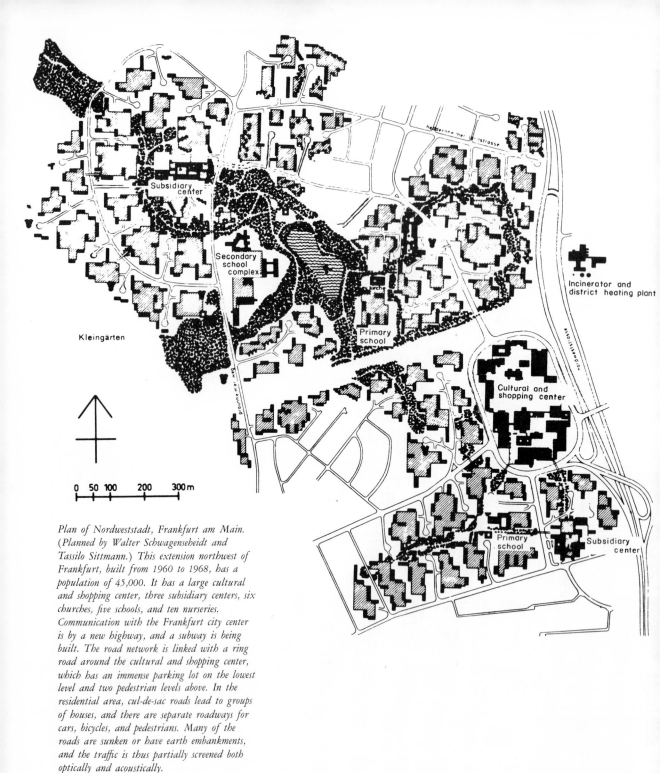

Plan of Nordweststadt, Frankfurt am Main.
(Planned by Walter Schwagenseheidt and
Tassilo Sittmann.) This extension northwest of
Frankfurt, built from 1960 to 1968, has a
population of 45,000. It has a large cultural
and shopping center, three subsidiary centers, six
churches, five schools, and ten nurseries.
Communication with the Frankfurt city center
is by a new highway, and a subway is being
built. The road network is linked with a ring
road around the cultural and shopping center,
which has an immense parking lot on the lowest
level and two pedestrian levels above. In the
residential area, cul-de-sac roads lead to groups
of houses, and there are separate roadways for
cars, bicycles, and pedestrians. Many of the
roads are sunken or have earth embankments,
and the traffic is thus partially screened both
optically and acoustically.

View showing two levels of the three-level pedestrian shopping and cultural center of the Frankfurt northwest development. A large parking lot on the lowest level extends the whole area of the center.

Aerial view of the first section of the New Town of Wulfen, planned for a population of 50,000, to serve the needs of workers in a coal mine near the Ruhr district. The plan won the first prize in a competition. As will be seen, the housing is mainly one, three, and eight stories. (Planner: Fritz Eggeling, Berlin.)

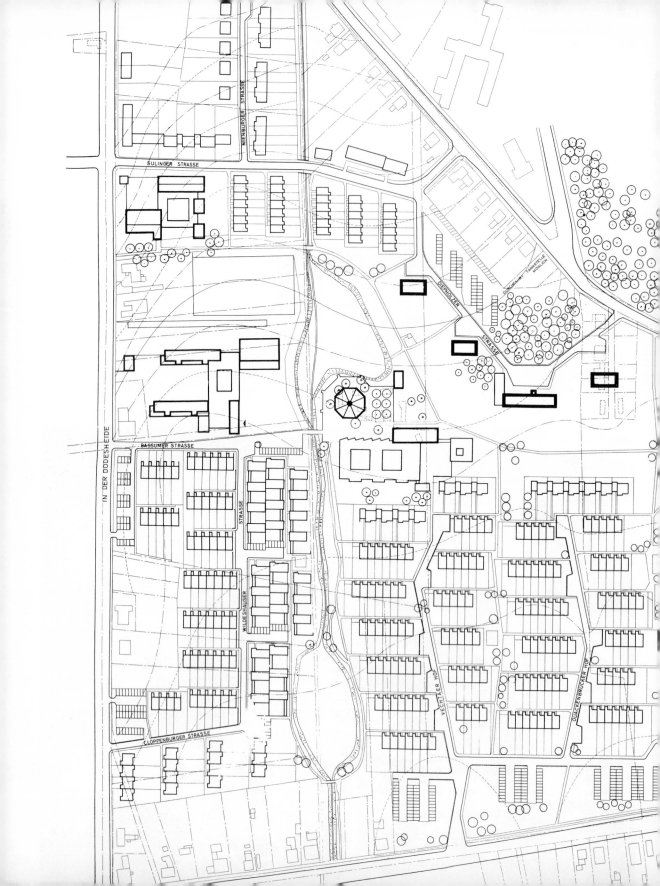

OSNABRÜCK, DEN 25. JANUAR 1960

☐ 12-story buildings

▭ 3-story buildings

▬ 8-story buildings

▥ Garages

☐ Existing buildings

▤ Open green areas

○ Existing trees

Osnabrück. Am Dodeshaus, new neighborhood (1955–1971) with an area of 91.5 acres (37 hectares) for a population of about 3,000. The residential area consists of one-and-a-half-, three-, and eight-story dwellings with shopping center, school, two churches, old people's homes, and nurseries. The plan provides for a sidewalk system with cul-de-sac roads in the residential areas.

LÖHNER HOF

STEINFELDER HOF

DAMMER HOF

HASTER WEG

Düsseldorf. Aerial view of the new urban district of Garath, taken in 1970, when it was nearing completion.

New Towns New Towns in the proper sense of the word have been built only in a few cases. The earliest and so far most successful example is Wolfsburg, city of the Volkswagen factory, founded under national socialist rule with very high ambitions and changed subsequently according to more modest plans. Its population numbered 84,600 in 1966, with the Volkswagen factory providing the overwhelmingly dominant source of employment and municipal taxes. The city owns virtually all its built-up area; it endeavors to make up for its lack of historic interest by entrusting its main buildings to famous architects (cultural center by Aalto).

A foundation of the same age is Salzgitter, started as the first part of a much larger project destined to house workers for low-grade ore works and after the war adapted to the new situation.

A few postwar foundations of new towns were more or less accidental, based usually on converted military establishments, like Traunreut or Espelkamp; none of them has achieved particular importance. Some other new towns have been planned in the regional context of larger centers to relieve population pressure or to serve special tasks; their development was in the hands of development corporations constructed mainly along the lines of the British precedent. The earliest and most advanced is Sennestadt near Bielefeld, with its master plan by H. B. Reichow, followed by Wulfen, on the northern rim of the Ruhr agglomeration, planned by F. Eggeling. Similar developments that are closer to their regional centers are Hochdahl near Düsseldorf and Meckenheim-Merl near Bonn, still in their early stages.

Urban Renewal Urban renewal as a specific concern dates back to the turn of the century and has been practiced up to the Second World War on a limited scale with fair success in the old city centers—partly in the form of rehabilitating buildings of historic interest, as at Frankfurt, partly as wholesale clearance of preindustrial unsanitary buildings for new development, as at Hamburg. After the Second World War, such clearance was held back for a long time due to the shortage of dwellings; in a way, of course, most postwar rebuilding could be classified as renewal, since it departed from former street patterns, building lines, and lot borders. Renewal beyond the removal of war damage is presently in preparation and under way in a considerable number of cities, although little has been finished or even seriously started because legal powers, until recently insufficient, have just been secured by new legislation (see "Legislation and Administration"). As examples could be mentioned renewal projects and processes at Berlin-Wedding, Hamburg/Neu-Altona, and Dortmund-Nord, all rather large scale; and the small, picturesque rehabilitation area of Bremen/Schnoorviertel. A very special and urgent problem is posed by middle-sized towns with a large share of historically valuable buildings in their central areas. Many of these centers are threatened by economic decay unless they are adapted to modern needs, which endanger in turn the historic buildings; Regensburg is a pertinent example.

BIBLIOGRAPHY: A. v. Dohna-Poninski Arminius, *Die Großstädte in ihrer Wohnungsnot und die Grundlagen einer durchgreifenden Abhilfe,* Leipzig, 1874; R. Baumeister, *Stadterweiterungen in technischer, baupolizeilicher und wirtschaftlicher Beziehung,* Berlin, 1876; C. Sitte, *Der Städte-Bau nach seinen künstlerischen Grundsätzen,* Vienna, 1889 (Austrian, included in view of its strong impact on German planning); J. Stübben, *Der Städtebau,* Darmstadt, 1890; Th. Fritsch, *Die Stadt der Zukunft,* Leipzig, 1896; K. Henrici, *Beiträge zur praktischen Ästhetik im Städtebau,* Munich; L. Hercher, *Großstadterweiterungen,* Göttingen, 1904; R. Eberstadt, *Handbuch des Wohnungswesens,* Berlin, 1909/1917; P. Schultze-Naumburg, *Kulturarbeiten,* Bd. IV, *Städtebau,* Munich, 1909; W. Hegemann, *Der Städtebau nach den Ergebnissen der allgemeinen Städtebau-Ausstellung in Berlin,* Berlin, 1911, 2. Bd., 1913; R. Schmidt, *Denkschrift betr. Grundsätze zur Aufstellung eines Generalsiedlungsplanes für den Regierungsbezirk Düsseldorf,* Essen, 1912; F. Schumacher, *Kulturpolitik,* Jena, 1920; C. Gurlitt, *Handbuch des Städtebaues,* Berlin, 1920; Th. Fischer, *Sechs Vorträge über Stadtbaukunst,* Munich, 1920; O. Schilling, *Innere Stadterweiterung,* Berlin, 1921; R. Heiligenthal, *Deutscher Städtebau,* Heidelberg, 1921; K. A. Hoepfner, *Grundbegriffe des Städtebaues,* Berlin, 1921, 2. Bd., 1928; H. Ehlgötz, *Städtebaukunst,* Leipzig, 1921; H. L. Sierks, *Wirtschaftlicher Städtebau und angewandte kommunale Verkehrswissenschaft,* Dresden, 1926; W. Hegemann, *Das steinerne Berlin,* Berlin, 1930; F. Kneller, *Die Sammeltangente,* Berlin, 1931; Internationale Kongresse für Neues Bauen (CIAM), *Rationelle Bebauungsweisen,* Stuttgart, 1931; O. Blum, *Städtebau,* Berlin, 1937; G. Feder, *Die neue Stadt,* Berlin, 1939; F. Schumacher, *Probleme der Großstadt,* Cologne, 1940; H. Wetzel, *Wandlungen im Städtebau,* Stuttgart, 1942.

The following are Federal Republic only: H. B. Reichow, *Organische Stadtbaukunst,* Braunschweig, 1948; R. Rainer, *Städtebauliche Prosa,* Tübingen, 1948; W. Schwagenscheidt, *Die Raumstadt,* Heidelberg, 1948; F. Schumacher, *Vom Städtebau zur Landesplanung und Fragen städtebaulicher Gestaltung,* Tübingen, 1951; J. Umlauf, *Vom Wesen der Stadt und der Stadtplanung,* Düsseldorf, 1951; M. Wagner, *Wirtschaftlicher Städtebau,* Stuttgart, 1951; K. Gruber, *Die Gestalt der deutschen Stadt,* Munich, 1952; J. Göderitz, R. Rainer, and H. Hoffmann, *Die gegliederte und aufgelockerte Stadt,* Tübingen, 1957; P. Vogler and E. Kühn (ed.), Medizin und Städtebau, Munich, Berlin, Vienna, 1957; J. Umlauf, *Wesen und Organisation der Landesplanung,* Essen, 1958; H. P. Bahrdt, *Die moderne Großstadt,* Reinbek b. Hamburg, 1961; Sachverständigenausschuß für Raumordnung, *Die Raumordnung in der Bundesrepublik Deutschland,* Stuttgart, 1961; K. Müller-Ibold, and R. Hillebrecht, *Städte verändern ihr Gesicht,* Stuttgart, 1962; J. Göderitz, *Stadterneuerung, Organisation, rechtliche und wirtschaftliche Voraussetzungen für die Sanierung ungesunder Wohngebiete,* Wiesbaden, 1962; Deutsche Akademie für Städtebau und Landesplanung (ed.), *Beiträge zum neuen Städtebau und Städtebaurecht,* Tübingen, o. J., 1962; K. Meyer, *Ordnung im ländlichen Raum,* Stuttgart, 1964; H. G. Niemeier and G. Müller, *Raumplanung als Verwaltungsaufgabe,* Hannover, 1964; Akademie für Raumforschung und Landesplanung, *Handwörterbuch der Raumforschung und Raumordnung,* Hannover, 1966; H. P. Bahrdt, *Humaner Städtebau,* Hamburg, 1968; Deutsche Akademie für Städtebau und Landesplanung (ed.), *Deutscher Städtebau 1968, Übersicht über die städtebauliche Entwicklung und Planung sowie regionale Verflechtung von 70 deutschen Städten verschiedener Größenordnung,* Essen, 1969; W. Pflug, and A. Boettger (eds.), *Stadt und Landschaft, Raum und Zeit,* Cologne, 1969.

—GERD ALBERS

OPPOSITE PAGE: ABOVE: *Model of plan for the community of Langwasser, southeast of Nürnberg, for 60,000. Plan awarded first prize in 1956. Work commenced in 1961. (Architect: Franz Reidel.)* BELOW: *Aerial view (1968) of Langwasser, southeast of Nürnberg.*

GHETTO Originally that part of a city in which Jews were required to live, the name probably derives from the first segregation of the Jews in Venice (1517), in the vicinity of the Iron Foundry (*getto*). Following a papal edict of 1555, ghettos were established throughout Italy and in many other cities in Europe until the nineteenth century. Some, notably the Warsaw ghetto, were reestablished under the Nazi regime. Ghettos were also found in cities in Islamic countries until recent times.

In modern usage the term is applied to any area where a minority, or deprived, group is compelled to live. Today this compulsion arises from social and economic pressures rather than political, legal, or religious sanctions, and in many countries legislation is designed to mitigate the effects of social and economic forces and to prevent rather than promote ghettos. The term is frequently applied to the areas of large cities in America where the Negro population lives. These ghettos are maintained by segregation and poverty, the basic ingredients of many of the urban social problems which have become the focus for attention of planners and administrators. (*See also* SOCIOLOGY.)

BIBLIOGRAPHY: Louis Wirth, *The Ghetto,* University of Chicago Press, 1928; Gilbert Osofsky, *Harlem: The Making of a Ghetto,* Harper & Row, Publishers, Incorporated, New York, 1966.

—GILLIAN PITT

GOAL SETTING   The process of defining goals for a plan. Goals have been defined as "statements of directions in which planning or action is aimed." They are thus "set" or formulated at the earliest stage of the planning process, though they need to be modified later to resolve the differences between conflicting goals. Goals should be distinguished from objectives. These emerge *from* the process of goal setting and are "specific steps toward the attainment of a goal." The goals of a plan thus tend to be general value statements representing an ideal end which the community wishes to attain. The process of setting them should be carried out democratically and with the widest possible consensus.

BIBLIOGRAPHY: N. Lichfield, *Goals in Planning,* Town & Country Planning Summer School, (Manchester, 1968) Royal Town Planning Institute, London, 1968; Her Majesty's Stationery Office, "The Intermediate Areas," (report of a committee under the chairmanship of Sir Joseph Hunt), London, 1969.

—DAVID HALL

GREAT BRITAIN   (*See* UNITED KINGDOM.)

GREEK PLANNING, ANCIENT   (*See* ANCIENT PLANNING, GREECE.)

GREENBELTS   Permanently reserved zones of unbuilt-on land around and between cities, to limit the cities' overgrowth and to prevent their merging into each other. Greenbelts were an integral part of Ebenezer Howard's proposal for garden cities (*q.v.*). They had many historical foreshadowings; for example, in the "pasture lands" of the Levitical cities (thirteenth century B.C.); the plans of Ezekiel (sixth century B.C.) and Nehemiah (fifth century B.C.) for the rebuilding of Jerusalem; of Lycurgus of Sparta (ninth century B.C.), Solon of Athens (seventh century B.C.), Plato (fifth century B.C.), and Aristotle (fourth century B.C.); and of Sir Thomas More in his *Utopia* (*q.v.*). Ancient Roman cities often had a consecrated unbuilt-on *pomoerium* surrounding their walls, which on a necessary expansion of population had to be solemnly deconsecrated. Howard quoted as a precedent the "park lands" surrounding Adelaide in South Australia (founded 1837), for which there were a number of forerunners in British colonial planning. There is much other evidence that the concept of a permanent country belt around a town answers to a universal human desire (see bibliography).

In Great Britain the greenbelt principle as part of a national planning policy was governmentally accepted in 1955. Many suggestions had been made earlier for such a belt round London, and this concept became specific with the ministerial support of Neville Chamberlain in 1927 and Raymond Unwin's recommendations in the Greater London Planning reports of 1929 to 1933. The London County Council initiated its own greenbelt scheme in 1935, which led to the Green Belt Act of 1938, under which the council in association with adjoining counties acquired a girdle of park spaces of about 26,000 acres for public use, to the cost of which it contributed over £1 million. This admirable project, however, made no pretense to be an agricultural belt in Howard's sense. That was definitely envisaged in Abercrombie's Greater London Plan of 1944, which proposed a massive decentralization of population and industry from the congested center of London to New Towns and other places beyond a metropolitan greenbelt of 5 miles or more in depth. A belt 7 to 10 miles deep has, in fact, since been reserved from building development under planning schemes, with some permitted "infilling" within existing villages and small towns.

The generalization of the principle was announced in 1955 by the then Minister of Housing Mr. Duncan Sandys, who required all planning authorities in England and Wales "to consider establishing a greenbelt wherever this is desirable in order: (1) to check the further growth of a large built-up area; (2) to prevent neighboring towns from merging into one another; or (3) to preserve the special character of a town." He added: "Whenever practicable a greenbelt should be several miles wide, so as to ensure an appreciable rural zone all round the built-up area concerned."

Since 1955 the British greenbelt policy has been further evolved both in theory and practice. The concept is changing from that of inviolate rings of rural land around particular towns to that of planning consideration of the placing of any extensions of urban development anywhere in the existing countryside. The arrangement to be desired is broadly that of Raymond Unwin's "towns on a background of open country," but the actual shape of the green reservations will not necessarily always be in quasigeometrical "rings"; rather, they will depend on regional topography, the location of existing development, and the strength of the impulse to population and industrial growth in the region. Considerable administrative problems arise from the conflict between the general desire to have access to the countryside and the individual desire to reside in it. But the necessity of a strong planning control to decide where building is permitted or prohibited is now accepted in Britain. Proposals for development, for industry, for airports, for public or private housing, even for planned New Towns, are often vigorously opposed by local interests, by the well-organized Councils for the Preservation of Rural England, Wales, and Scotland, and by the National Farmers Union, and in many cases such proposals are modified by the suzerain ministries after public inquiries. The official Countryside Commission now exercises useful influence in the general planning policy, still in a state of evolution.

In other countries suffering from metropolitan overgrowth and congestion, the concept of the greenbelt or rural reservation is now increasingly entertained as an element in planning policy. (*See* COUNTRY TOWNS EXPANSION, GARDEN CITY, and NEW TOWNS.)

BIBLIOGRAPHY: Frederic J. Osborn, *Green Belt Cities,* Faber & Faber, London, 1946 (second edition: Evelyn Adams & Mackay, London, 1969); London County Council, *Green Belt around*

London, L.C.C., 1956; D. R. Mandelker, *Green Belts and Urban Growth*, University of Wisconsin Press, 1962; Ministry of Housing & Local Government, *The Green Belts*, H.M.S.O., London, 1964.

—Frederic J. Osborn

GREEN WEDGE   A tongue of open land extending from the country into a city or urban area. The land may be used for agriculture, recreation, cemeteries, or the grounds of institutions. If a system of green wedges is applied completely to a city, an approximation to an urban star results.

GREY AREAS   This is the colloquial term used to describe the "intermediate areas" of Great Britain, which were the subject of a report entitled *The Intermediate Areas* prepared by a committee under the chairmanship of Sir Joseph Hunt (published by Her Majesty's Stationery Office, London, April 1969). In the context of the report, such areas were those where the rate of economic growth gave cause for concern; where, although economic growth was taking place, it was progressing at a rate too slow to make full use of the area's resources. Such areas are "intermediate" in the sense that, on a scale of economic growth rates, they lie between those where there is a decline or very little growth and those where economic growth is substantial.

—David Hall

GRID   A checkerboard network of intersecting streets and avenues forming the basic layout of a city or town. Just as in architecture a system of proportions, related to a basic dimension or module, has sometimes been used to facilitate construction and serve functional needs, so the elements of a town may be arranged with reference to a set of related dimensions. Grids were employed in the ancient planning of Egypt, Mesopotamia, and Greece. The Greeks' Hippodamian planning was based on the most conveniently sized residential blocks or insulae.

Dimensions are based on the living patterns of the communities forming the town and on circulation needs. The size of a local housing area will be conditioned by convenient access to local shops and schools, while the grouping of such areas will be conditioned by transport facilities and the location of employment areas and the main center. The application of such a formalized concept is practicable only in the case of a new settlement or of an extensive renewal project. Some of the plans in the second generation of British New Towns offer examples. The plan of the New Town of Washington in England is based on a grid of primary roads of approximately 1-mile (1.6-kilometer) squares and that of Milton Keynes on a grid of primary roads of 1-kilometer (0.62-mile) squares.

Another significant example is the plan of the new city of Chandigarh in India. Here the basic plan is a gridiron arrangement of roads dividing the city into blocks generally measuring ¾ mile by ½ mile (1.2 by 0.8 kilometer). The civic center occupies a block approximately at the center of the city, and this can be conveniently reached from each of the "neighborhood" blocks grouped around it. The size of each neighborhood block is appropriate and convenient for the daily life of the local community it accommodates. Its dimensions were purposefully chosen and are related to the wider dimensions of the city, so as to give a coherent and functional structure to the plan as a whole.   —H. E. SPARROW

GRIDIRON PLAN   (*See* CHESSBOARD PLAN.)

GRIFFIN, WALTER BURLEY (1876–1937)   Architect and planner, born in Maywood, a suburb of Chicago, in 1876. Griffin received his training in the department of architecture of the University of Illinois from 1895 to 1899, graduating with a B.Sc. degree in architecture. In his last year Griffin also took courses in horticulture and forestry, which were useful to him later in landscape architecture. He began his professional career as a draftsman in the office of Dwight Perkins. From 1902 to 1907 he worked with Frank Lloyd Wright at Wright's Oak Park Studio, and from 1907 he worked independently, designing mainly houses and the Stinson Memorial Library at Anna, Ill. (1912–1914). His early architecture—with its massive character and horizontal emphasis—shows the influence of Frank Lloyd Wright. In 1910 he ventured into the field of community planning. He planned a group of 20 houses on a 16-acre (6.48-hectare) site at Rock Glen, Mason City, Iowa, and although only eight houses were built, the project gave him his first opportunity to exercise his talents as a landscape architect. A little later he planned New Trier Neighborhood, in which many of the houses faced away from the road onto an internal park area—an original scheme for the time. He also prepared a scheme along formal lines for the small town of Idalia in Lee County, Fla., and, in 1913, another more interesting scheme for Mossmain, Mont., a town of 25,000 planned, partly on garden city principles, concentrically round a railway terminal. This had been called America's first garden city, but because of lack of funds it was never realized.

The great event of Griffin's life was his winning of the competition for the design of Australia's new capital city of Canberra in 1912. His success was probably helped by the beautiful series of drawings prepared by his wife who, as Marion Mahony, was a colleague in the Oak Ridge Studio and whom he married in 1910.

In his planning Griffin was to some extent a follower of Daniel H. Burnham and the Beaux Arts tradition of formal geometric schemes of dignity and grandeur. He was, at the same time, a landscape architect who delighted in the introduction of natural effects—of trees and lawns and sheets of water—into the urban scene. He was also a follower of the garden city movement that originated with Ebenzer Howard. In his plan for Canberra there is a combination of all these elements. On a site which he likened to a vast amphitheater with its background of mountains, he placed his formal geometric plan. He took as the axis a line from Mount Bimberi 25 miles (40 kilometers) to the south to Mount Ainslie immediately to the north, and he made the basis of his plan an equilateral triangle with one point south of the Molonglo River to form the government center. Then the two sides crossing the river led to the two points of the municipal center and the market center. Straight avenues were to continue from these centers to other centers in accordance with a zoning system. The Molonglo River was to be dammed to make a formal ornamental reflecting pool in the center flanked by irregularly shaped lakes. (*See plan*—AUSTRALIA.) The city was envisaged as having a maximum population of about 100,000 (although it will probably reach a quarter of a million by 1985). The residential areas, planned on garden city lines, involve houses and gardens with some degree of separation from roads.

Although Griffin was given the appointment of Federal Capital Director of Design and Construction so that he might supervise planning and building operation, the path was not easy. There was much political interference, and he resigned in 1920. In essential outline, however, Canberra is today very much as Griffin had planned it, although it varies in several details.

In addition to his work at Canberra, Griffin carried on a practice as architect and planner in Australia. Among his important buildings are Leonard House and the Capitol Theatre in Melbourne. Later he went to India, where he died in the Prince Edward Hospital at Lucknow on December 11, 1937.

BIBLIOGRAPHY: Mark L. Peisch, *The Chicago School of Architecture*, Phaidon Press, London, 1964, Random House, New York, 1965. In this history Walter Burley Griffin is the principal figure.

—ARNOLD WHITTICK

GROPIUS, WALTER (1883–1969)   Architect, planner, sociologist, and teacher, born in Berlin, Germany, on May 18, 1883. He was the son of an architect, and his great uncle Martin Gropius (1824–1880) was principal of the Arts and Crafts School in Berlin and architect of the new Gewandhauz in Leipzig.

After attending courses in architecture at Munich and Berlin (1903–1907), Walter Gropius worked in the office of Peter Behrens for three years. Then, in 1910 he began practice as an architect and industrial designer. His first important buildings, the Fagus shoelace factory at Alfeld-an-der-Leine (1911) and the administrative office building for the Deutsche Werkbund Exhibition at Cologne (1914), both in collaboration with Adolf Meyer, were notable contributions to the modern architecture of steel and glass. After serving in the German Army during the First World War, he was appointed director of the Gross herzogliche—Sachsische Kunstge-werbeschule and the Gross herzogliche—Sachsische Hochschule fur Bilden Kunst at Weimar. In 1919 he combined the two under the name of Das Staatliche Bauhaus, so as to integrate as closely as possible design and craft. In 1925 the Bauhaus was transferred to Dessau, where Gropius designed the world-famous group of school buildings. He resigned in 1928 and was succeeded as director by Mies van der Rohe. While director he had continued his practice as an architect. He studied the best ways of building in accordance with people's needs and of obtaining the best living conditions in cities. He aimed to build dwellings with the maximum sunlight in accordance with required densities and with the maximum amount of trees and lawns. To obtain this he evolved his theory that this is best achieved by tall slab blocks extending from north to south, with broad stretches of garden, open at both ends, between the blocks. He showed that with high blocks of ten stories there is more space and the angle of light is less than with lower blocks for the same densities. He was able to realize his theories in part in two housing estates at Dammerstock near Karlsruhe, erected in 1927 to 1928, and at Siemensstadt, Berlin, in 1929 to 1931. In both Gropius was the supervising architect with several collaborating architects. The estate at Siemensstadt consists of a considerable number of long, five-story slab blocks placed north-south, with generous provision of open space between them. This layout has had considerable influence on later schemes.

With the increasing power of National Socialism in Germany, so damaging to the spirit of free enterprise, Gropius went to England in 1934 and became the partner of E. Maxwell Fry. In 1937 he came to the United States to become professor of architecture at Harvard University, becoming chairman of the department of architecture in the following year.

From 1937 to 1943 he was in partnership with Marcel Breuer, and a notable planning work of this period was the wartime Aluminum City housing estate near Pittsburg, Kansas. In this plan a principal road winds through a hilly site, with irregularly placed sun-oriented dwellings reached by winding walks. This plan was unusual at the time and excited attention and controversy.

Gropius's most notable contribution to city planning in later life was the plan that he made for Buckow-Rudow in the southeast portion of West Berlin, sometimes called Gropius City, built during the sixties. The residential areas consist mainly of tall tower and slab apartment blocks and numerous, variously designed one-family houses. Both are sited mainly in the islands of open space formed by roads, with footpath access. There is a generous provision of communal installations. It was in this city that Gropius was able to realize many of his planning ideas, and it merits careful study by the student of planning.

Gropius died in Boston, Mass., on July 5, 1969.

BIBLIOGRAPHY: Walter Gropius, *The New Architecture and the Bauhaus,* Faber and Faber, London, 1935; Sigfried Giedion, *Walter Gropius: Work and Teamwork,* Architectural Press, London, 1954; James Marston Fitch, *Walter Gropius,* George Braziller, Inc., New York, 1960.

—ARNOLD WHITTICK

GROWTH POINTS AND AREAS   Points and areas that hold the potential for successful development. Sometimes such areas have begun to attract industry and population for a wide variety of reasons, and it is considered by governments and planning authorities that the development would be assisted and best directed in the public interest by some measure of control and governmental incentive. Mr. W. L. Taylor, the chairman of Livingston Development Corporation, said that:[1]

> At its most significant [a growth area] involves an assessment of the relative economic and physical planning merits of alternative locations; it involves

[1]W. L. Taylor, "Growth Area Philosophy," *Town and Country Planning,* vol. 35, no. 6, 1967.

sponsored growth; it involves the fostering of growth at a location capable of becoming the focal point of a region. The inference is that the area is capable of growing more significantly than the surrounding areas not selected. The implication is that the public authorities must give the area special priority and attention by way of public investment. But finally and most importantly it is predicated upon growth—not just growth of the selected area but overall growth of the region of which it is but one part.

Growth areas and points are most valuable to planning when the growth has only just begun or when it is seen as a good potential. This gives scope for creative planning. But areas which are already well populated and showing rapid increases of population are sometimes selected as growth points, and the encouragment of further development by public investment in these may contribute to the growth of the conurbations that modern planning wishes to avoid.

GUTKIND, E. A. (1896–1968)   Architect and urban historian, born in Berlin in 1896. He studied architecture, city planning, sociology, and the history of art at Berlin University, receiving a doctorate in city planning. He began practice as an architect and designed several large apartment blocks in the suburban areas of Berlin. At the beginning of the National Socialist regime in Germany in 1933 he went to London, and in 1940 he was in charge of the Demographic Survey and Plan under the Ministry of Town and Country Planning.

While in England Dr. Gutkind wrote several books on planning, among them a two-volume work entitled *Creative Demobilisation* (1944), the first subtitled *Principles* and the second *Case Studies of National Planning*. This was followed by *Revolution in Environment* (1946), which contains one of the best surveys in English of the history of planning in China.

Dr. Gutkind moved to the United States in 1956 and embarked on a ten-volume *International History of City Development,* probably the most ambitious work of its kind ever planned. Dr. Gutkind completed eight volumes before he died on August 9, 1968. These are devoted to urban development in (1) Central Europe, (2) the Alpine and Scandinavian Countries, (3) Spain and Portugal, (4) Italy and Ancient Greece, (5) France and Belgium, (6) The Netherlands and Great Britain, (7) Poland, Czechoslovakia, and Hungary, and (8) Romania, Bulgaria, and the U.S.S.R. The ninth volume dealing with China and Japan was only partly completed at the time of his death. The survey concentrates on the history of city development to the mid-nineteenth century, and the most typical examples of each civilization are selected. In the completed volumes, Dr. Gutkind probably gave as full a picture of the evolution of cities as has so far been presented. Evaluation of trends and examples is accompanied by critical appraisal from both the social and aesthetic aspects. Dr. Gutkind had intended a final volume dealing with modern planning, on which he had very decided views. He was a strong believer in the decentralization and dispersal of cities, because he felt "that urbanization in all parts of the world has resulted in a general decrease of the individuality of cities."

—Arnold Whittick

HARBORS AND DOCKS The economic planning of any region is largely dependent on the availability of commercial docks and harbors in the area, since these are essential to the importation of raw materials and food and for the export of finished products. In a report on major ports in Great Britain (1962), the need for more deepwater berths was stressed, particularly dry-cargo berths for the discharge of iron ore. Modern vessels are steadily increasing in size, and ore-importing ports should be capable of taking ships of at least 45,000 deadweight tons (44,290 metric tons).

Even greater demands are made by oil cargo, and this is the main reason for the phenomonal expansion of the port of Rotterdam, which is now the largest in the world. After the Rotterdam docks and harbors were rebuilt following the Second World War, it was soon realized that accommodation would have to be provided for larger ships, especially oil tankers that were likely to exceed 100,000 tons (98,421 metric tons) and the development of Europoort as a western extension of the harbors has been made with this purpose. At the western extremity it involved the construction of a new polder with harbors out to sea. It should be mentioned, however, that the need for such large harbors, necessitated chiefly by large oil tankers, may be only a temporary phase, because by the end of the century the transport of oil throughout the world may be largely by pipeline.

491

The inland transport system contributes greatly to port efficiency, as it is important that arrangements for the delivery of exports to and the collection of imports from the docks should be as efficient as possible. The shift from rail to road transport in recent years often necessitates adjustments, while the planner must be constantly alive to possibilities of the reversal of these trends. Also, land-use potentials around port estuaries can be usefully assessed with a view to the utilization of the sites to the best economic advantage.

Among the principal recent problems for planners is that which arises from the greatly increased demand for yacht harbors and marinas. This demand stems from four factors: the increase in the population, the growing popularity of boating, the increasing amount of leisure time, and the need to make more efficient use of sheltered water by providing mooring facilities clear of the areas available for navigation. This last mentioned is akin to the demand for off-street parking for motor vehicles.

But the provision of a new yacht basin almost always gives rise to objections. These may not be directed to the harbor itself but to the indispensable ancilliaries—the cranes, storage or repair sheds, the restaurant, the clubhouse, the parking lot, possibly some dwelling accommodation, and new access roads. These are the features which may intrude adversely into a rural setting.

The method of access to the basin from deep water—e.g., free flow, over a sill, or through a lock—will depend on the range of tide and the depth of water in the approach channel; and the arrangements for mooring may depend on the amount of shelter afforded by the surroundings and the degree of sophistication required. A common arrangement is to moor to floating pontoons with water and electricity laid on to each berth.

In recent years the scale of development of this kind has been considerable. An example on the south coast of France, in the Languedoc-Rousillon region, are the arrangements to accommodate over 10,000 small craft in new yacht harbors.

BIBLIOGRAPHY: Lord Rochdale, chairman, *Report of the Committee of Inquiry into the Major Ports of Great Britain*, H.M.S.O., London, 1962; West Sussex County Council, *The Chichester Harbour Study*, Chichester, Eng., 1968; H. F. Cornick, *Dock and Harbour Engineering*, 4 vols., Charles Griffin & Co., London, 1960–1969; American Society of Civil Engineers, *Report on Small Craft Harbors*, 1969.

—J. G. JEFFERSON

HAUSSMANN, BARON GEORGES-EUGÈNE (1809–1891)   Préfet de la Seine under the Emperor Napoleon III. What Napoleon I and the Commission of Artists started in making Paris a grand city on a splendid scale as a setting for imperial power, Napoleon III and Haussmann completed. Persigny described Haussmann as having a "backbone of iron," and it was he who had the audacity and ruthlessness necessary to drive the enormous boulevards and monumental avenues through the jungle of old Paris.

Since the days of the first Emperor, when the transformation of Paris was begun, the pattern was continued under the restored Bourbons and under Louis Philippe. It was due to Haussmann's dynamic personality, however, that the progress became rapid, and vast sums were expended on an unprecedented scale in relatively modern times on construction and demolition.

Undoubtedly Haussmann's scheme, partly dictated by a fear of street fighting, was intended not only to ensure easy progress of troops and artillery but also to simplify the clearing of areas round palaces and larger public buildings to make them easily defensible. The traffic bottlenecks in the narrow streets had to be removed as well, and improvements were necessary in order to provide decent sanitary conditions by letting light and air into the high apartments and narrow courts. Unfortunately, the fine new avenues simply cut their way through the urban squalor, leaving the warrens behind the grand façades.

On the credit side, Haussmann created several large and popular parks out of derelict land. He foresaw the development of the Paris of 1900, and it is his basic plan which provides the skeleton of the main thoroughfares of modern Paris. Without his Avenue de l'Opéra, much of the circulation of Paris would have stopped. It is this street and the magnificent opera house which must be seen as Haussmann's chief monument.

Of particular interest to us today is Haussmann's ruthless manipulation of finances to obtain his goals and his refusal to compromise when faced with the problem of having to demolish costly *new* buildings in order to achieve the realization of his plan. It was such demolition of the houses of the wealthy and influential Parisians which helped to undermine Haussmann's power.

His insistence on transplanting mature trees to transform the boulevards might well provide lessons for us today, for the new streets he created were never allowed to look raw. Nature was brought in at the beginning, using special machines, and the townscape was made agreeable and humane at once.

The scale and splendor of Haussmann's achievement is staggering when we see how near he is to our own time. The man had vision, ruthlessness, conviction in the rightness of the empire he served, and sensibility as well. These qualities he possessed to a remarkable degree. The Paris of today that is remembered and which people go to see is largely his creation.

BIBLIOGRAPHY: Cecil Stewart, *A Prospect of Cities,* Longmans, Green & Co., Ltd., London, 1952; Sigfried Giedion, *Space, Time and Architecture,* Harvard University Press, Cambridge, Mass., and Oxford University Press, London, 1967; James Stevens Curl, *European Cities and Society,* Leonard Hill, London, 1970.

—JAMES STEVENS CURL

HEIGHT ZONING The application of maximum height limits for buildings in selected areas of a town. Such a control is usually applied for aesthetic reasons. In Great Britain town planners use a system of height control to secure good daylighting standards for buildings. Different standards are laid down for various zones, but the system does not lay down maximum heights for buildings. Instead it relates control over height to the spacing between buildings in particular instances.

HILBERSEIMER, LUDWIG (1885–1967) German city planner, studied architecture at Karlsruhe Technische Hochschule and practiced as an architect in Germany from 1910 until his emigration to the United States in 1938. From 1928, he taught housing and city planning at the Bauhaus, at Dessau, until its closure in 1933. In 1938, he became professor of city planning at the Illinois Institute of Technology, Chicago, where he remained active in teaching and writing until his death.

Hilberseimer was an early proponent of modern architecture (*"neues bauen"*) and designed one of the houses for the renowned Weissenhofsiedlung, Stuttgart, in 1927 as well as some other dwellings and office buildings in Berlin. In his first publication on city planning, he advocated a tightly integrated city of high density with workshops and offices on the lower floors and dwellings above. Later he turned to a spatial separation of functions and to much lower densities. He expounded the idea of the linear city and developed it further into regional settlement patterns.

One of Hilberseimer's main concerns was the arrangement of settlements so as to minimize the effects of air pollution; another was the integration of agriculture into the regional framework. His critical mind and his uncompromising approach to planning won him esteem, but no commissions. His influence on planning thought is stronger than one might surmise on the basis of his only executed work in the United States, the Gratiot project, Detroit, carried out in cooperation with Mies van der Rohe.

BIBLIOGRAPHY: Ludwig Hilberseimer, *Internationale neue Baukunst,* Stuttgart, 1927; *Großstadtarchitektur,* Stuttgart, 1927; *The New City,* Chicago, 1944; *The New Regional Pattern,* Chicago, 1949; *The Nature of Cities,* Chicago, 1955; *Entfaltung einer Planungsidee,* Berlin-Frankfurt-Wien, 1963.

—GERD ALBERS

HILL TOWNS There has always been an impulse to build a city on a hill, from the early days of Mesopotamia and ancient Greece to mid-twentieth-century Scotland. Evidence suggests that there are three main reasons for this: religion, defense, and health. The desire to build temples and other religious edifices as near as possible to the sky where the gods dwelt, with the houses built round the temples, obtained in many early settlements, including those of Mesopotamia and Greece (*see* ACROPOLIS). These were often developed for defense later on, and in later medieval times a hill is frequently the site of a castle with walls surrounding it, the walls often being of sufficient extent to enclose a village or small town. As the town grew from this nucleus, further, more extensive walls were built around a larger area.

Hill towns abound in Mediterranean countries, and it can be appreciated that they would be far healthier than the mosquito-infested marshlands on the plains below. In a good warm climate where the winds are not too strong, a hill can be an excellent site for a town, and some of the most favored residential areas of large cities are on the surrounding hills. But a hill exposed to strong cold winds is a doubtful site for a town, although some modern towns have been built on such sites. Cumbernauld in Scotland is an example.

—ARNOLD WHITTICK

HIPPODAMUS OF MILETUS Son of Euryphon, born circa 500 B.C., became famous in ancient times mainly for his preeminent role in the planning of Piraeus, at the invitation of Themistocles, immediately after the Persian Wars. With this reconstruction of Piraeus, it seems that Hippodamus introduced the Ionian innovation in urban planning to mainland Greece; though it had been applied some years earlier in Miletus. This new urban planning method, which soon took Hippodamus's name, thereafter became the model for all the cities which were built or rebuilt in the classical and early Hellenistic period (Olynthos, Priene, Thourioi, Magnesia, etc.).

It is probable that Hippodamus participated in the planning of the Panhellenic colony of Thourioi (444–443 B.C.); Hesychius records that Hippodamus moved to Thourioi, but Diodorus Siculus (XII, 10) in his description of the new town does not mention the Milesian architect. Modern research has rejected Strabo's (XIV, 654) statement that Rhodes was built in 408 to 407 under the personal supervision of Hippodamus. It has also refuted the identification of Hippodamus with a man of the same name, the father of Archiptolemus, in Aristophanes's play *The Knights* (line 327).

We owe to Aristotle (*Politics,* 1267b, 22) a portrait of Hippodamus describing the scientific, political, and social ideas which interested the Milesian philosopher and pointing out the roots of the harmonious geometric conception that he applied in his method of urban planning. In this portrait the most interesting information concerns his radical ideas about the ideal city-state: that it would have about 10,000 citizens, that the citizen body and the usable land would be divided into three parts, that it would have a triple legislative system, that its courts of arbitration would operate on the basis of a secret vote, and that its archons would be elected.

All modern researchers do not agree on the nature of the contributions made by Hippodamus to city planning, or on how his ideas were first applied. Erdmann (1884) and Cultera (1923) supported the imaginative but not provable theory that the Hippodamian system was, from its earliest application, a circle or half circle; that it introduced a radial street network; and, besides the radial street plan, that it presented monumental constructions and eventually perspective arrangement of buildings. However, ancient tradition and the evidence provided by the inscriptions and the excavations render more probable the view put forward by Fabricius, Gerkan, Martin, and Castagnoli. According to this view the Hippodamian method is basically a gridiron system, it provides a eurithmic and functional organization of the built-up area in bigger urban areas (which are bounded by the intersecting main arterial streets) and in smaller built-up blocks (which are formed in each section by the intersecting orthogonal secondary streets and constitute the basic urban units).

Within this geometric but not inflexible and monotonous frame, the system provided suitable land for public areas whose site and boundaries were laid out from the beginning (harbors, docks, markets, cemeteries) in such a way that they constituted the nodal points of the areas intended for private habitation.

Thus Hippodamus remains a town builder and not an architect in the sense of a constructor of public buildings. Martin even denies that Hippodamus was responsible for the construction of the agora of Piraeus, which according to the lexicographers bore his name in ancient times.

BIBLIOGRAPHY: The best presentation and criticism of the Hippodamian system is in R. Martin, *L'Urbanisme dans la Grèce Antique,* Paris, 1956, pp. 15–16, 101–108 (it also contains the complete bibliography). See also the relevant articles by E. Fabricius in the *Real Encyclopaedie,* vol. VIII, 1913, under "Hippodamus," and vol. III, A₂, 1929, under "Städtebau der Griechen." An informative article with a bibliography is Castagnoli's article on Hippodamus in the *Enciclopedia Dell'Arte Antica,* vol. IV, pp. 183–184.

—DEM. MARONITIS

HISTORIC AREAS The value of areas of particular historic interest in cities and towns is that they are part of the cultural heritage, from which we also often receive aesthetic delight, for time is a harmonizing and sometimes a beautifying influence. There is also the desirable preservation of distinctive achievement in urban planning and architectural design which is not only valuable for its own sake but as a guide to future work. And further, some places are considered of special interest for their associations with famous historical persons and events. Historic areas are thus often preserved and maintained in good condition, with as little alterations as possible, for the reasons indicated. In some countries the value of such conservation is acknowledged by legislation. In Great Britain, for example, the Civic Amenities Act, 1967, gives to local planning authorities the power to determine which parts of their areas are of special historic or architectural interest, making it desirable to maintain and preserve their character and appearance. Such areas are designated as conservation areas and have special claims to protection.

Often when development—which is usually claimed as much needed—is proposed in an area of historical or architectural interest, especially development which would involve some measure of destruction, there is conflict between the advocates of development and the advocates of preservation. Decision requires a careful estimate of respective values. The decisions never satisfy everybody. (For discussion of the factors that are considered in such decisions, *see* PRESERVATION AND PLANNED CHANGE).

HISTORIC MONUMENTS   (*See* MONUMENTS AND MEMORIALS, PUBLIC.)

HOLLAND   (*See* NETHERLANDS.)

HOUSE In the context of planning, "house" means a building for human habitation. It can take many forms, from a mud hut or cave with a single room to a palace with 500 rooms. For modern planning the majority of houses are either one-, two-, or three-story single-family dwellings and are either detached, semidetached (that is, in pairs structurally joined side by side), or terraced (that is, structurally joined in rows of three or more). Except in housing statistics, the term is not usually applied to single-floor dwellings in multistory buildings; these are called "apartments" in the United States and most European countries and "flats" in Great Britain.

HOUSEHOLD　A household is one or a group of persons that is domestically autonomous. It has also been defined as a group of persons who habitually both eat at the same table and sleep under the same roof. A household is different from a dwelling as two or more households can occupy one dwelling (house, apartment, or flat) or one household can occupy or possess two or more dwellings. Thus, in census statistics, households and dwellings are distinct.

HOWARD, Sir EBENEZER (1850–1928)　Founder of the garden city movement. Born in the city of London, where his parents were small shopkeepers, he left school at 15 and was an officeboy and junior clerk until he reached the age of 21, when he emigrated to America and took up 160 acres in Nebraska. Finding himself not adapted to farming, he moved, within a year, to Chicago, where he resumed office employment and became an expert shorthand reporter. Returning to London at 26, he supported himself and his family by that arduous profession for the rest of his life. A typical Victorian in his interest in scientific and mechanical progress, he spent much of his spare time in invention, especially in attempts to improve the typewriter and to develop a shorthand-writing machine, but these cost him more money than he ever gained from them. Another spare-time preoccupation in his early years was the anxious concern of his period with reconciling the conflict of religion and science. Later he became deeply interested in the social problems of "poverty in the midst of wealth," with its corollaries of urban degradation and squalor. He attended to the multifarious proposals of radicals, socialists, nationalizers, single-taxers, and other reformers and revolutionists, but he was unable to accept any of them as at once beneficial, humane in application, and politically feasible.

Sir Ebenezer Howard.

After much patient thought he worked out his own concept of the garden city (*q.v.*), discussed it from 1893 onward in private and public meetings, and in 1898 published at his own expense his famous book *To-morrow: a Peaceful Path to Real Reform* (revised and reissued in 1902 as *Garden Cities of Tomorrow*). This was widely reviewed and aroused much interest, and in 1899 Howard started the Garden City Association (later the Garden Cities and Town Planning Association and now the Town and Country Planning Association) to advocate his proposal. Being an eloquent speaker with remarkable persuasive powers, he gained the support of a very able group of public-spirited persons, including powerful industrialists like the Cadburys, Rowntrees, T. W. Idris, Aneurin Williams, W. H. Lever (Lord Leverhulme), and newspaper proprietors like the Harmsworths. With them he acquired a large area of land at Letchworth, 35 miles north of London, on which the First garden city was begun by a private limited-dividend company in 1903.

The experiment of founding a New Town on new planning principles in an old country produced an immense international impression. But its essential principle, that of a complete planned town with local employment, was for many years generally misunderstood, being confused with the quite different concept of the garden suburb (*q.v.*). First Garden City Ltd. was undercapitalized from the start and grew far less rapidly than Howard had expected. It did prove Howard's case, but it did not lead to the widespread emulation for which he had hoped. In 1919, at the age of 69, Howard, on his own initiative and without any money except £5,000 borrowed from a few wealthy supporters, acquired at an auction sale the site for a second garden city at Welwyn, 20 miles from London, and formed another limited-dividend company to develop it. Again the project was undercapitalized and encountered daunting difficulties. But it was successfully established, and as a result of experience made advances on its predecessor. It has come to be regarded as a planning masterpiece, clinching the world impression that Letchworth had created.

This second demonstration had a vital influence on the governmental acceptance of the dispersal and New Towns policy and the passing of the New Towns Act of 1946. Howard did not live to see this decisive success of his invention. But he was internationally honored for his great idea and beloved for his sincere, benevolent, and modest personality. He was the first president of the International Garden Cities and Town Planning Association (now the International Federation for Housing and Planning) from its foundation in 1913 till his death at Welwyn Garden City in 1928. He was knighted in 1927. There are memorials to him in Howard Park, Letchworth, and Howardsgate, Welwyn Garden City.

BIBLIOGRAPHY: E. Howard, *Garden Cities of Tomorrow* (with historical biographical introductions by F. J. Osborn and Lewis Mumford), Faber & Faber, 1945, MIT Press, 1965 (translations available in French, German, Italian, Spanish and Japanese); Dugald Macfadyen, *Sir E. Howard and the Town Planning Movement,* Manchester University Press, 1933; reprinted M.U.P. and MIT Press, 1971; F. J. Osborn, "Ebenezer Howard, The Evolution of His Ideas," *Town Planning Review,* October 1950; Stanley Buder, "Ebenezer Howard: The Genesis of the Town Planning Movement," *Journal of the American Institute of Planners,* November 1969.

—FREDERIC J. OSBORN

HUNGARY

Legislation and Administration Hungarian building regulations were administered by the town councils during the nineteenth century and special committees were appointed for their implementation. The most significant of these was the Council of Metropolitan Public Works in compliance with the Act of 1870.

Town planning legislation began between the two world wars and was administered by the Ministry of Industry.

The task and scope of town planning were for the first time codified at a national level by the Act of 1937. The act calls for the obligatory preparation of town development plans under the Ministry of Industry within a period of 6 years. The act regulated the procedure of replotting and empowered public institutions to do this. It also specified town planning conditions for the formation of plots and made possible the expropriation of real estate for urban planning purposes. Under the act plans were collated and accepted by each town and then submitted to the Ministry of Industry for confirmation. They were prepared by private planners commissioned for the purpose.

After the Second World War a Government Comissariat for Reconstruction was formed. The Act of 1946 provided for the establishment of the Ministry of Building and Public Works, and in 1947 the Ministry issued national building regulations. These regulations extended the most important provisions of the Town Planning Act to the entire country. On the basis of the decree concerning the abolition of the system of large estates and providing land for the people, 2,800 building plot plans were made in order to provide 400,000 building plots.

The institute for Regional Planning was set up by the ministry, and in 1949 regional plans covering the whole country were prepared.

After the Ministry of Building and Public Works ceased to exist, town development became temporarily decentralized. In principle administration was by the National Building Bureau, the management of town development by the Ministry of Building, and the management of councils carrying out town development by the Ministry of Town and Community Management.

Town development was centralized again in 1957, and administration became the responsibility of the Ministry of Building which, in 1967 became the Ministry of Building and Town Development.

The most recent comprehensive regulation for town development was made by the Act of 1964, which codified the basic principles of town and regional planning. This codification made it possible for the development plans of the settlement network to form—in addition to the sectoral concepts—one of the bases of the development of the economy.

The act of Parliament—similar to that of 1937—provides for the obligatory drawing up of the development concepts of the master and specified development plans of the settlements. It determines the objectives, the content, and the types of plans as well as the order of the approval. It provides for the designation of plots, for the preservation of historic monuments, and for planning responsibility.

Town planning provisions are contained in the National Building Regulations published in 1960. They determine the methods of zoning and include specifications for the assignment and use of areas for different purposes. They regulate in detail the planning of building plots and blocks and conditions of the location and establishment of public supply institutions and plants. They forbid activities contrary to the good appearance of towns and landscape, provide for nature conservation, and contain provisions for the preservation of health and holiday resorts and of historic monuments.

Expropriation is regulated by a separate decree which makes possible the acquisition, in the public interest, of real estate and makes provision for appropriate compensation.

Planning directives and indices issued by the Minister of Building are available for both the master and specified town development plans. The instructions of the Minister of Building and Town Planning issued in 1969 regulate the work of the organizations responsible for drawing up town and community development plans.

The building act gives the building departments of the executive committees of councils, as their special administrative organizations, powers to grant permits and administer controls. In order to facilitate the work of the building authority, the act specifies that standing building committees should be established in the communities.

In 1955, a new situation was created which transferred the control of town planning to the Minister of Building. Collation was performed again by the councils, while the authority for the approval of plans—depending on the significance of the settlement—came within the competence of the Council of Ministers and the Minister of Building, respectively. Since that time, obligatory methodologies and directives for planning have been given by the minister. The state planning organ is responsible for the quality of the plans, and the planner is responsible to his institution.

The institutional elaboration of plan operations of regional planning began in the 1930s. Especially with regard to Greater Budapest and a few counties, regional studies substantiating administrative decisions were made by the Hungarian Institute for Administration Science with the cooperation of the Council of Metropolitan Public Works. After 1945, it became the task of the Institute for Regional Planning to elaborate the studies of regions serving to substantiate plans of the national economy, mainly for regions to be developed. The instructions for the preparation of the plans and for the pursuance of studies were given by the Minister of Building, in some instances by the President of the National Planning Bureau and by the leaders of certain industrial departments.

A government resolution of 1958 finally decreed complex regional investigations and then the preparation of plans concerning the whole area of the country. A single state planning body, the Scientific and Design Institute for Town Construction, is authorized to prepare regional plans. The authorization is given by the Minister of Building and Town Development in agreement with the President of the National Planning Bureau. The approval of more important plans is the task of the government, that of the less important ones is the task of the councils. The planning body makes a proposal for the directives and methodology of regional planning, and it is approved by the ministry. The plans are collated by the councils, by the Minister of Building, and by the leaders of the departments concerned.

From the point of view of the coordination of regional plans, it is of paramount importance that the general plan for the Development of the Settlement Network is being approved by the government.

Administration of urban planning falls within the competence of the Ministry of Building and Town Planning. The chief forum of scientific activity in this field is the Committee for Settlement Science functioning within the framework of the technical section of the Hungarian Academy of Sciences.

A department of regional planning has been established in the Ministry of Building and Town Planning to perform these duties. The central institute of town planning is the Scientific and Design Institute for Town Con-

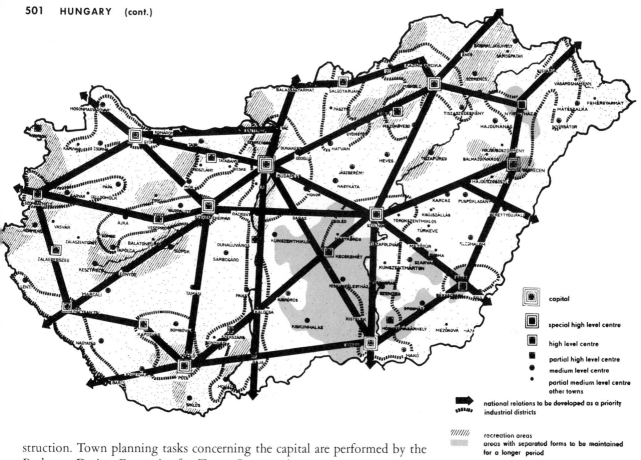

capital

special high level centre

high level centre

partial high level centre

medium level centre

partial medium level centre
other towns

national relations to be developed as a priority
industrial districts

recreation areas
areas with separated forms to be maintained
for a longer period

*Development scheme of the National
Settlement Network. (Planners: Karoly
Perczel, Klara Kormendi.)*

struction. Town planning tasks concerning the capital are performed by the
Budapest Design Enterprise for Town Construction.

In addition, five major provincial planning bureaus prepare master plans
and 19 planning bureaus directed by county councils deal with the town
planning of minor settlements. Building plot plans are made by the land
surveying organizations. Some of the planning bureaus designing buildings
and edifices have recently been concerned with the preparation of specified
town development plans. Among these are the bureaus carrying out the
planning of residential, public, and industrial buildings.

The official tasks of building administration connected with town planning are performed by the sections of the executive committees of the county
councils, councils of towns of county rank, and district councils.

Education and Training The teaching of engineering was included as early
as the middle of the eighteenth century at universities of arts and sciences.
Economics and engineering sciences were taught at the Collegium
Oeconomioum, Tata, from 1763 to 1780. The Institutum Geometrico-
Hidrotechnikum was organized in 1782. In 1856, the Jozsef University was
organized from the Jozsef Industrial School, where a section for building
engineers also functioned since 1871. In 1952, the University of Building
and Transport Engineering was separated from the Budapest Technical

University, together with the Faculty of Building Engineers. Then the two universities were united again under the name of Technical University of Budapest, where the subject of town planning is taught at the Faculty of Building Engineers.

The object of the faculty is to train building engineers for the designing, construction, and maintenance of residential, public, industrial, and agricultural buildings as well as for urban construction and settlement planning—individuals who are to be well versed in both architecture and engineering. It is possible to apply for the day section of the faculty after obtaining the certificate of the final examination of the secondary school. The faculty does not train specialists within the framework of ordinary teaching. The certificated building engineers—after proper professional practice—become specialists by studying with specialized engineers at the university or through self-education and postgraduate lectures. Specialized engineers are trained at the faculty in the subject of town construction and town economics.

The sciences of town construction and urbanistics are taught by the department of town construction. Included are the history of town construction, the fundamental concepts of settlement science, and the principles serving as a basis for the preparation of town and community construction and development plans. The faculty seeks to stimulate the ideas, thinking, imagination, and taste necessary for planning. The teaching is partly of central and partly of seminary character, and it is supplemented by planning practice. The students have an opportunity to prepare their diploma work at the Faculty of Town Construction. Supplementary studies under the department of building construction include organization, management, and the coordination of complex building operations in time and space.

The Postgraduate Training Institute of Engineers of the Technical University of Budapest organizes courses every year in which the requirements of institutions concerned with planning, administration, and construction, essential to the tasks of planning, are fully considered and taken into account. Lectures are delivered by the most knowledgeable members of the profession.

The reviews, lectures, and debates on club days in the Hungarian Urbanistic Society and in the Association of Hungarian Architects are of the highest importance.

The teaching of engineers trained for the performance of the tasks of town planning takes place within the framework of the Technical University of Budapest. The documentation department of the Scientific and Design Institute for Town Construction provides a national information service. The publicity given by councils has recently increased.

The profession of planning is represented by three voluntary associations of engineers and technicians: on questions of town architecture by the Association of Hungarian Architects, on questions of town construction by the Scientific Society of Building, and on special questions of town development by the Hungarian Urbanistic Society.

Geographical and Climatic Conditions Hungary is a country situated far from the seas. Its area constitutes the basin of the Carpathian Mountains, portions of which extend into the northern and southern parts of Hungary. Two thirds of the area is a plain less than 650 feet (200 meters) above sea level. The hilly region occupies nearly one-third, and the area made up of mountains above 1,312 feet (400 meters) in height is only 772 square miles (2,000 square kilometers) in area. The mountain range is of medium height, not exceeding 1,640 feet (500 meters).

It has six large, varied topographical areas. The 17,375 square miles (45,000 square kilometers) of the Great Hungarian Plain, varying from 259 feet (79 meters) to 597 feet (182 meters) in elevation, is situated in the vicinity of the Danube, the Northern Medium Mountain Range, and the frontier. Its flat central area is situated in the Jaszbereny-Szeged-Sarkad-Tokuj region. Its surface is varied by a large number of drift hillocks, loess table lands, lowland soils divided into clods, and by the surface forms of sand. Its sediment layers, several thousand meters in depth, contain artesian water, natural gas, and mineral oil. Its geothermal gradient is extremely favorable; for this reason, it has a large number of hot-water and medicinal springs. The plain in northwestern Hungary is situated in the Danube region, at the base of the Alps and the Transdanubian Medium Mountain Range, contains the detrital cone of the Danube having a radius of 100 kilometers (62 miles). It is on the western frontier of the country, along the slopes of the eastern Alps. It is a richly articulated and varied region. The mountains of Sopron and of Koszeg are important for tourism because of the beauty of their landscape and their interesting flora. The first coal mine of the country operated here in 1765. Its steatite and limestone quarries are significant. Here is a rich region in the hilly country of Transdanubia, with an area of 16,000 square kilometers (6,178 square miles). Its main parts are the area extending from the river Mura through the axis of the Lake Balaton as far as Budapest, the hilly country of counties Zala, Somogy, and Tolna, and the island hills of county Baranya.

Its mineral oil and natural gas layers, coal mines, sulphurous and radioactive medicinal waters, and limey and loamy rocks suitable for the manufacture of cement are important. The Medium Mountain Range of Transdanubia, extending from Keszthely to Visegrad, is 200 kilometers (124 miles) long and 20 to 50 kilometers (12 to 31 miles) wide, the part of the former forest land which has remained in the most contiguous form. Several areas of the range are excellent wine-growing regions. Its thermal waters, karst springs, caverns, bauxite layers, and stone quarries are famous. The Tihany Peninsula, which was declared a conservation area because of its natural rarities, protrudes into the basin of the Lake Balaton. The Northern Medium Mountain Range extends from the Danube to the Bodrog and includes Borzsony, Cserhat, Matra, and Bukk. The two last mentioned are recreational areas. Its mineral and natural resources are coal, building materials, ores, mineral oil, and thermal waters. There are also caves and human remains from the Stone Age. Its wine-growing region is Tokaj.

It could be said that geographically Hungary links western, eastern, and southeastern Europe. It belongs to the catchment area of the Danube, its secondary catchment area being the river Tisza. Initially, both played a dividing role, with characteristic fords and shipping junctions; in recent development, however, both rivers contribute to settlement agglomerations, industrial development, water transport, and water supply. The rivers are of great significance in the planning and construction of several settlements at Budapest, Szeged, Gyor, and Szolnok.

The climate is characterized by rapid changes where east-European continental, west-European oceanic, and south-European subtropic-Mediterranean air streams converge.

The natural vegetation has remained only in 10 to 15 percent of the area. Among the plant communities, the characteristic varieties of each surrounding large region can be found. This richness is expressed in the vegetation of the green areas of the settlements.

With the spreading of the humanized landscape, very little has remained of the country's original zoogeography. The fauna of the mountains and of the considerable flood areas of the rivers have been maintained where there are game reserves. It is significant from the point of view of zoogeography that these places, which are actually preserves, are visited by both the northern and southern migratory birds.

Traditions of Planning to the End of the Nineteenth Century Systematic town planning activity began with the Romans. The first towns—Savaria, Szombathely, Scarabantia, and Soprona—were established in Transdanubia in the eighth and ninth centuries B.C., coming under Roman jurisdiction later on. Fortified towns along the line of the Danube were built. Pannonia was organized by Claudius into a province possessing a dense settlement network and road system.

Hungarians coming with the great migrations 986 A.D. did not at first settle in the Roman towns, but King Istvan I (1001–1038) pursued a settlement policy similar to that of the Romans. The focal points of the new settlement network of the country were the royal capital city of Szekesfeherver and the episcopal sees of Pecs, Gyor, Eger, Esztergom, Veszprem, and Kalocsa, which are connected with the foundations of the monastic orders and with the network of fortresses. King Bela III (1173–1196) built the new capital of Esztergom. After the Mongolian invasion (1241–1242), a further network of fortresses was established, the most important being Buda. The medieval network of towns took a final form in the fifteenth century.

During the Turkish occupation (1526–1686), the majority of the villages were destroyed and the towns degenerated. Two different kinds of settlement evolved in the eighteenth and nineteenth centuries. In one, of European character, the components were the town and the agrarian village. The other was a specific Hungarian form of settlement: the market town uniting the urban and rural in its functions.

During the first years of the nineteenth century, several Hungarian towns

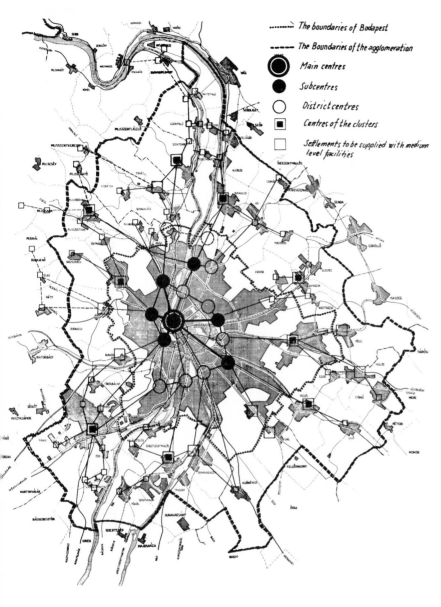

The boundaries of Budapest

The Boundaries of the agglomeration

Main centres

Subcentres

District centres

Centres of the clusters

Settlements to be supplied with medium level facilities

Hierarchy network of the subcenters of the Budapest agglomeration.

prepared development plans. The most significant among these is the master plan of Budapest made by the architect Janos Hild (1776–1811).

The prominent figure of the age, Istvan Szechenyi (1791–1860) elaborated a transportation, river regulation, and shipping concept. His name is connected with the construction of the Chain Bridge (1839–1843) joining Buda and Pest.

After the middle of the nineteenth century, the former logical structure of towns in process of industrialization disintegrated. More favorable phenomena appeared only during the last decades of the century, such as the building of several monumental thoroughfares which united Buda and Pest into a capital, Budapest, and the reconstruction of the flood-stricken Szeged (1879) on the basis of the plans of Lajos Lechner. Some theoretical works on planning were published at that time, such as Gyula Ehen's *The Modern Town* (1897).

Twentieth-century Planning   The theoretical acceptance of town planning took place between the two world wars. The Council of Metropolitan Public Works was organized to support the technical administration of the capital and its environment functions on a European level. The effects of its work are manifest in the activities of the chief engineers of several country towns: Szeged, Debrecen, Szekesfehervar, and Pecs. The Hungarian Institute for Administration Science is concerned with the technical and administrative questions of towns and urban agglomerations and takes the first steps in the preparation of regional development plans. There is extensive activity in the field of special literature; various disciplines concern themselves with the problems of the town. Some plans are notable, such as *The Town Development Programme of Budapest,* published in 1940, and the town development programs of Szeged and Szekesfehervar. The master plans of Vac and Eger are also prominent examples.

After the liberation of the country (1945–1948), reconstruction and repair of war damage took place. In some zones inhabited by workers, three- to four-storied modern residential building blocks were constructed (Budapest, Elmunkas Square, and Csepel) with up-to-date, spacious accommodation. At the beginning of the 1950s, several New Towns were established in connection with the large-scale development of industry. This led to the study of the science of settlements, dynamic town planning activity, and the creation of norms and methodologies. In 1953, an independent planning bureau was established for the national tasks of urban planning. Owing to the development of industry, the establishment of universities and colleges, the increase of the administrative functions of towns, tourism, and in several cases, the housing shortage, several considerable extensions of existing towns were undertaken. The construction of new housing estates of the size of a town district became general in Budapest and in other country towns in this period. Master plans and specified development plans were prepared for all the important towns and for several villages; still in a sense with a schematic, academic concept. More modern town planning practice began with the construction of 10,000 dwellings for miners in 1957. This policy became even more vigorous after the promulgation of government decrees concerning residential and recreational areas. Thereafter a rapid development of building technologies took place. From 1960 onward, the increasing pace of housing, the development of industry, and the expansion of agriculture imposed further tasks on urban planners. Development plans were revised for most of the settlements, and recent regional planning concepts and modern guiding principles of planning were taken into consideration, including their application to the reconstruction of the inner areas. Master plans of more than 600 settlements have been completed. The

Eger, with approximately 40,000 inhabitants (1973). First master plan of the town, prepared in 1928. (Planner: Professor Laszlo Wargha.)

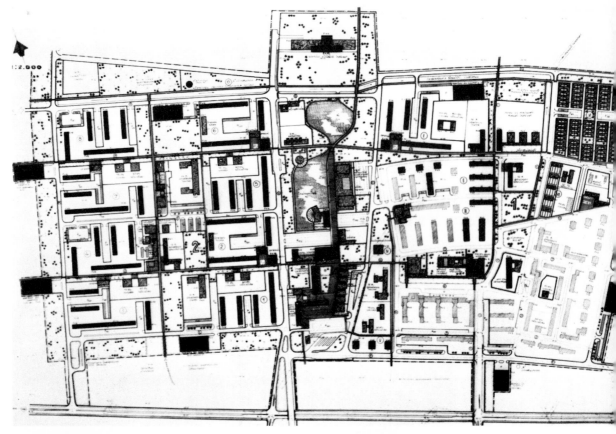

ABOVE: *Master plan of new industrial town of Leninvaros for a population of 60,000. First phase. New buildings—dark tints; existing buildings—light tints. (Planner: Lajos Fule.)* LEFT: *Dunaujvaros. A New Town for the iron industry on the Danube for a population of about 45,000. (Planner: Tibor Weiner.)*

number of plans prepared for minor settlements and parts of settlements
is more than 2,500. It can be expected that by 1975, the proportion of
the total buildings erected after the liberation will exceed 50 percent.

New Towns The establishment of Dunaujvaros resulted from the creation
of a combine of the iron industry. It was located by the Danube partly
because of the convenient water transport and partly because of the high
water requirements of the plant. The town is built to comply with the
conditions of the loess terrace and to the valleys dividing it. Its climate
is that of the towns of the Great Hungarian Plain.

Kazincbarcika is a base of the chemical industry, built in the Sajo Valley
for the sake of the coal supply. The placing of the residential area west
of the industrial buildings on the terrace of one of the side valleys of the
Sajo Valley is determined by the direction of the wind. The structure of
the town accords with the natural conditions. The arrangement conduces
to quiet, is harmonious, intimate, and friendly yet spacious.

Tiszaszederkeny is a uniform, up-to-date town whose economy is based
on one of the largest chemical plants in the country. Because of the
organization of its residential area and its uniform expression of form, it
is one of the most successful towns.

Komlo is developing from a mining village into an important town
situated in the coal basin of Pecs. The hilly conditions of the town have
determined the layout of the residential areas, giving a vertical articulation.

Szazhalombatta, the newest town, is being built at one of the important
key points of the international oil pipeline. The aim in the plan is to achieve
an urban effect by a bold building-in, in accordance with the conditions
of the terrain.

Developed Towns Budapest, a metropolis of 2 million inhabitants, has
doubled in size since the liberation. This has come about through the
annexation of the satellite towns and through large-scale development. Its

*Budapest. Reconstruction in the
historical sites of Obuda. (Planner:
Lajos Mezo.)*

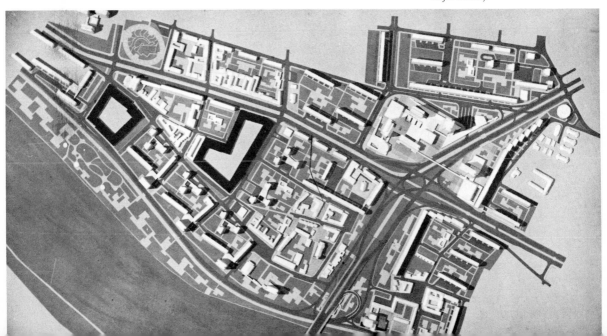

Model of plan for Budapest north by the Danube. (Planner: Dezso Papp.)

rapid development is due to the expansion of industry and of public services and institutions (among them hospitals, ambulatory clinics, vocational schools, three universities, and sports grounds—including a stadium for 100,000 people), by the construction of several extensive housing estates and numerous subcenters, and by the reconstruction of the historic monuments and the Castle. The implementation of its master plan in the next 25 years is in progress.

From four villages in 1949, the mining town of Tatabanya is expanding to a planned population of eighty to ninety thousand inhabitants. The new town center is centrally situated with an extensive, longitudinal arrangement corresponding to the terrain.

Budapest. Proposal for the reconstruction of a central sector. (Planner: Laszlo E. Kiss.)

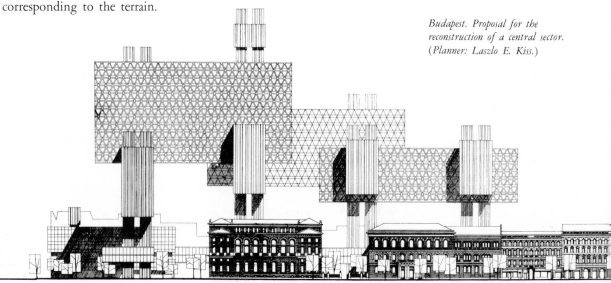

Varpalota, the traditionally idyllic town partly because of its romantic setting, is developing into one of the centers of lignite production. It is the first settlement where development started with the reconstruction of the town center. A characteristic feature of this town is the castle dating back to the early 1400s.

The rapid development of the town of Veszprem, which takes pride in the only medieval castle of the country which has remained intact, is due to the siting near it of the Chemical University, the Research Institute of the Heavy Chemical Industry, and the Institute for Natural Gas Research. These involved the construction of two new districts. With the modernization of its traffic system and with its new town center, it is one of the most successful combinations of historic preservation and modern town planning.

Several other medium- and small-sized towns are being developed on modern lines in answer to the increasing needs of industry, recreation, and administration. Examples include Miskolc, Szekesfehervar, Debrecen, Pecs, Szeged, and Nagykanizsa.

Miskolc. Regional center, inhabitants today approximately 180,000. Site plan of the area around the medieval castle.

Medium-sized semiindustrial town of Szolnok with a population of about 65,000. The four residential areas, each with its center, are numbered. The town center is in the foreground. (Planner: Attila Molnar.)

Urban Renewal   An outstanding town reconstruction project is in progress at Salgotarjan. The apartment blocks are mostly of medium height, and the town center is one of the most visually effective in the country.

The reconstruction of Szolnok is combined with the linking of the hitherto separated districts of the town and in the construction of the town center. Large-scale reconstruction work and modernization of the town center of Gyor is in progress, together with the restoration of the historic monuments of large districts of the town.

The population of Zalaegerszeg, a county seat, has doubled in 24 years. Several districts of the town are being rebuilt. Existing buildings of two to three stories and the new buildings of medium height achieve a harmonious appearance.

Among town centers notable for their historic monuments, Sopron's is of first significance. Here, the reconstruction work following wartime damages provided an opportunity for the uncovering of several medieval buildings. In the center of Koszeg, the historic appearance of the town has been completely restored.

The centers of 13 historic towns have been declared historic monuments and are thus being preserved. In most towns like Vac, Szentendre, Eger, and Gyor measures are taken for the preservation of their traditional appearance and historic monuments.

BIBLIOGRAPHY: J. Rados, *Budapest varosepiteszetenek tortenete* (History of the city planning of Budapest), Budapest, 1928; Endre Palffy-Budinszky and Viktor Hergar (editors), "Szeged varosepitesi problemai" (Town planning problems of Szeged), *Prometheus Nyomda*, Szeged, 1934; Karoly Martonffy (editor), "Varosfejlesztes, varosrendezes, varosepites" (Urban development, town planning, urban architecture), *Magyar Kiralyi Allami Nyomda*, Budapest, 1940; P. Granasztoi Rihmer, *Varosok a multban es a jovoben. Varosepitesi tanulmanyok* (Towns in the past and in the future. Studies in town planning), Budapest, 1942; Egyetemi Nyomda, *A varosrendezesrol es az epitesugyrol szolo 1937: VI.t.c. es a kapcsolatos rendeletek* (The 1937: VI Act about town planning and building and the orders related to it), *Kokai Lajos Kiadoja,* Budapest, 1942; F. Erdei, *Magyar Varos* (Hungarian town), *Athenaeum,* Budapest, 1946; F. Pogany, *A varosszepseg problemai* (Problems of the beauty of towns), *Mernoki Tovabbkepzo Intezet,* Budapest, 1948; D. Szabo, *Varosi Kozlekedes* (Urban traffic), *Tankonyvkiado,* Budapest, 1952; F. Pogany, *Terek es utcak muveszete* (Art of squares and streets), *Epitesugyi K.,* Budapest, 1954; L. Gero, *Magyar varoskepek* (Hungarian townscapes), Budapest, 1954; M. Major, *Epiteszettortenet* (History of architecture), *Epitesugyi K.,* Budapest, 1954; I. Perenyi, *Telepulestervezes. Varosepitestan* (Settlement planning. Science of town planning), *Tankonyvkiado,* Budapest, 1958; B. Borsos, A. Sodor, M. Zador, "Budapest epiteszettortenete, varoskepei es muemlekei" (The history of architecture, townscapes, and historic monuments of Budapest), *Muszaki Konyvkiado,* Budapest, 1959; I. Genthon, "Magyarorszag muveszeti emlekei" (Art monuments of Hungary), *Kepzomuveszeti Kiado,* Budapest, 1959; P. Granasztoi, "Varos es epiteszet" (Town and architecture), *Muszaki Konyvkiado,* Budapest, 1960; G. Preisich, "Budapest Varosepitestortenete" (History of town planning of Budapest), *Muszaki Konyvkiado,* Budapest, 1960; J. Borsos and I. Vallo, "Videki varosaink" (Our towns in the provinces), *Kozg. es Jogi Kiado,* Budapest, 1961; I. Perenyi, "A varosepites tortenete" (The history of town planning), *Tankonyvkiado,* Budapest, 1961; I. Perenyi, K. Farago, J. Major, "Mezogazdasag es telepulestervezes" (Agriculture and settlement planning), *Muszaki Konyvkiado,* Budapest, 1962; E. Lettrich, "Urbanizalodas Magyaroszagon" (Urbanization in Hungary), *Akademiai Kiado* (Geographical Studies, 5.), Budapest, 1965; F. Dallos, E. Szabady (editors), "Magyar varosok. Szerk: Dallos Ferenc-Szabady Egon" (Hungarian towns), *Kozg. es Jogi Kiado,* Budapest, 1966; K. Perczel, Gy. Gerle, "Regionalis tervezes es a magyar telepuleshalozat" (Regional planning and the Hungarian settlement-network), *Akademiai Kiado,* Budapest, 1966; F. Vidor, "Tudomanyos eljarasok a varosrendezesben a merhetoseg es prognosztika kiterjesztesi lehetosegei egy atfogo telepulestudomanyi rendszerben" (Scientific methods in town planning. Application of measurability to forecasting within a comprehensive system of settlement science), *Felsooktatasi Jegyzetellato* (Mernoki Tovabbkepzo Intezet eloadassorozatabol, 4401), Budapest, 1966; I. Perenyi, "A korszeru varos. Gondolatok a varostervezes multjarol es jovojerol" (Up-to-date town. Conceptions about the past and future of town planning), *Muszaki Kiado,* Budapest, 1967; I. Szelenyi and Gy. Konrad, "Az uj lakotelepek szociologiai problemai" (Sociological problems of new housing estates), *Adademiai Kiado,* Budapest, 1969; G. Preisich, "Budapest varosepitesenek tortenete, 1919–1969-ig" (History of town planning of Budapest 1919–1969), *Muszaki Kiado,* Budapest, 1969; I. Perenyi, "A varos kozpontja. Tervezes es rekonstrukcio" (The center of the town. Planning and redevelopment), *Muszaki Kiado,* Budapest, 1970; J. Korodi and Gy. Koszegfalfi, "Varosfejlesztes Magyarorszagon" (Urban development in Hungary), *Kossuth,* Budapest, 1971; F. Erdei, "Varos es videke" (Town and its surroundings), *Szepirodalmi Kiado,* Budapest, 1971; T. Madarasz, "Varosigazgatas es urbanizacio" (Administrations of towns and urbanization), *Kozg. es Jogi Kiado,* Budapest, 1971.

—Karoly Perczel

HYDROELECTRIC DEVELOPMENT   (*See* ELECTRIC POWER GENERATION AND TRANSMISSION.)

I

IDEAL CITY CONCEPTIONS (*See* CITY GROWTH AND CITY PLANNING; THEORIES AND IDEALS OF PLANNING; *and* UTOPIA AND UTOPIAN PLANNING.)

INDIA

Geographical and Climatic Conditions With an area of 1.13 million square miles (about 2.93 million square kilometers) and a population of about 550 million, India is marked by a great diversity of physical features and land forms. It may be divided into three distinct physical areas which are dissimilar in geological history, surface configuration, and potential utilization. These are the mountain wall of the Himalayas and other encircling ranges; the lowland plains drained by the Indus, Ganges, and Brahmaputra rivers; and the dissected plateau in the peninsula to the south, including the coastal belt.

    Physiography The Himalayas, extending over a distance of 1,550 miles (2,500 kilometers) and covering an area of about 193,000 square miles (500,000 square kilometers), are composed of a group of very young folded mountains, in three nearly parallel ranges interspersed with large plateaus and valleys. The three ranges are the Siwalik foothills or the Outer Himalayas; the Lesser or Middle Himalayas; and the Greater or Inner Himalayas. In the Inner Himalayas are the high, snow-clad peaks like Everest,

Kanchenjunga, K^2 or Godwin Austen, Nanda Devi, Kedarnath, Kamet, and others, their average elevation being more than 16,452 feet (6,000 meters). To the south of them lie the Middle Himalayas with a mean elevation of about 13,710 feet (about 5,000 meters), and in this range are found the famous hill stations of north India—Simla, Naini Tal, Mussoorie, and Darjeeling. The Outer Himalayas or the Siwalik Hills, with an average elevation of 2,742 feet (1,000 meters), are not a continuous range like the other two but are foothills created by the sediments brought down by the great rivers originating in the Himalayas. These are heavily forested, in some parts ill-drained, and till recently malaria-ridden; e.g., the Terai and the Duars.

The Himalayas are rich in forest wealth. The flora is of three altitudinal zones—tropical, temperate, and alpine—most of which constitutes an untapped resource for the country. The Himalayan region also abounds with possibilities of large-scale hydroelectric power development. The belt along the Himalayas from the Sutlej to the Brahmaputra has nearly half the country's aggregate hydroelectric potential, most of it concentrated in the eastern part.

The Indo-Gangetic plain, 1,500 miles long and 150 to 200 miles wide (2,414 kilometers long and 241 to 321 kilometers wide), is a featureless alluvial plain, remarkably homogeneous in character and formed by the three distinct river systems, the Indus, the Ganges, and the Brahmaputra. Geologically, it is a geosyncline; i.e., a sag in the earth's crust formed during the buckling of the mountains. The thickness of the alluvial deposits is considerable everywhere in the plains, in some areas being as much as 6,500 to 9,800 feet (2,000 to 3,000 meters). The Indo-Gangetic plain may be divided into two units: the "Bhangar" lands comprising the old alluvium occurring as slightly elevated terraces generally above the flood level, the rivers having cut through it, and the "Khaddar" lands or the new alluvium cut out of the Bhangar by the rivers and liable to inundation in times of flood. The rainfall in the plain decreases from east to west, and this is also reflected in the agricultural land use, which varies from rice and jute in the delta lands to rice, sugar cane, and wheat in the interior. The entire plain is densely populated.

The peninsular plateau is marked off from the Indo-Gangetic plain by a mass of mountain and hill ranges varying from 1,502 to 4,000 feet (458 to 1,220 meters) in height. The more prominent among these are the Aravalli, Vindhya, Satpura, Maikala, and Ajanta ranges. It is also flanked on one side by the Eastern Ghats (average elevation, 2,000 feet or 610 meters) and on the other by the Western Ghats (elevation between 3,000 and 4,000 feet or 915 and 1,220 meters), which meet near the hill block of the Nilgiri Hills (Blue Mountains).

The plateau is highest in the south and gently inclined from southwest to northeast, and has considerable variety mainly based on relief, soil, and climate. The southern Deccan consists of the plateaus of Telengana and Karnataka and is of the red soil group. The western Deccan is formed of basaltic lava which extends to a thickness varying from 1,970 to 4,920 feet (600 to 1,500 meters) and which on weathering has given rise to the black cotton soil. The northeastern Deccan consists of the rich mineralized plateau of Chota Nagpur, the valleys of the rivers Damodar, Subarnarekha, and Mahanadi, and the forested hills of Dandakaranya. The northwestern border of the Deccan is a wide belt of hilly country bordered on the west by the oldest tectonic mountains of India, the Aravalli ranges, and on the east by the Vindhyan escarpment.

Surrounding the peninsular plateau of the Deccan are two coastal plains—a narrow western coastal belt and a slightly broader coastal plain to the east. These coastal belts are distinct from the plateau both in environmental and human associations. They also differ in rainfall distribution, cropping pattern, settlement pattern, and the way of life of the people. In their development and cultural evolution, they have been considerably influenced by maritime traditions distinctly different from those of northern India, where historic influences have played a dominant role.

Climate Climatically India is a monsoon country with a pronounced seasonal rhythm of rainfall which has influenced all human activities. Within the country, however, there is a striking variety of meteorological conditions. There are four broad rainfall regions. The whole of Assam and the west coast of India are areas of very heavy rainfall. In contrast, the Rajasthan desert extending to Kutch and the high Ladakh plateau of Kashmir extending westward to Gilgit are regions of low precipitation. Between these extremes are two areas of moderately high and low rainfall respectively. The first area consists of a broad belt in the eastern part of the peninsula merging northward with the north India plains and southward with the coastal plains. The second area comprises a belt extending from the Punjab plains across the Vindhya mountains into the western part of the Deccan, widening considerably in the Mysore plateau. Four principal seasons have been recognized during the year: cold-weather season; December to February; hot-weather season; March to May; southwest monsoon season; June to September; and retreating monsoon season; October to November.

Resource Structure Agricultural areas are widely distributed. The interaction of the various physical elements such as relief, soil, and climate has resulted in distinct cropping patterns in the different parts of the country, such as the rice-coconut economy of the western coastal plains; the cotton-maize economy of the western Deccan, rice predominance in the river deltas of the Ganges, Mahanadi, Godavari, Krishna, and Cauvery; the wheat-sugarcane association in the upper Ganges plain, tea cultivation in Darjeeling and the hills of Assam, and coffee cultivation in Coorg (Mysore).

While agricultural areas are widely distributed, some natural resources like forests, minerals, and hydroelectric power are concentrated in certain areas. Nearly 80 percent of the coal occurs in the Gondwana coal fields situated in southern Bihar, in eastern Madhya Pradesh, and in Orissa, an area where there is also a concentration of iron ore. This is emerging as the leading industrial region of India because of the iron, steel, and associated industries. In some parts of the four southern states there are smaller areas rich in iron ore, manganese, limestone, and mica. The oil fields of Gujarat and Assam have provided the base for petrochemical complexes. The pattern of distribution and variations in resource structure of the country have largely influenced the pattern of regional economic development and at the same time created problems of regional imbalance.

Population Distribution and Settlement Patterns   The population of India was 439 million in 1961 and is currently estimated at over 550 million, living in 507,000 villages and 2,700 towns. The growth rate of population was 2.4 percent per annum during 1961 to 1971. The urban population in 1971 was 109 million (20 percent of the total population) and urban areas have grown at rates varying from 3 to 10 percent per annum. The population distribution is very uneven, nearly one-third being concentrated in about one-tenth of the land area, living mainly in high-density areas of over 750 persons per square mile (290 per square kilometer). The areas of high concentration are:

1. The Indo-Gangetic plain from Punjab in the northwest to the Ganges delta in the east, an extensive and contiguous belt of high density, somewhat narrow in the northwest but broader in Uttar Pradesh, Bihar, and West Bengal.

2. Areas to the south of the line connecting Madras and Mangalore; here the Kerala coastal plains have relatively higher densities.

3. The Gujarat Plain from Surat to Ahmedabad.

4. The coastal delta plains of the Krishna, Godavari, and Cauvery rivers.

The plateau area, excepting in the tracts mentioned above, has lower densities and is mostly below the national average.

The concentrations of urban population follow closely the pattern of distribution described, the high-density areas having multiple urban clusters and a high degree of urban scatter. The settlement pattern and the growth of urban centers reflect the different physical controls such as local relief, availability of water, drainage conditions, soil fertility, forest coverings, and transport facilities.

In the Gangetic plains, the population is distributed in small, compact villages spaced evenly across the landscape, often seemingly independent of surface water. In the Ganges delta, however, settlements are strung in lines along slight elevations resembling levees, which give protection from seasonal floods. In the Deccan, where the availability of water is of great importance, settlements generally follow the river valleys (almost hugging their sides, as in river valleys of Godavari, Krishna, and Periyar) or around natural water reservoirs as in southeast Tamilnadu.

The location of urban centers follows the same pattern. In the Indus and upper Gangetic plains, the major urban clusters are at river junctions, which had defense facilities and also offered strategic positions for controlling the plains. Such centers as Pataliputra (present Patna), Allahabad, and Taxila functioned as focuses of power for centuries. In other parts of the country, urban centers have developed as nodes in the network of railways, being either junctions on routes traversing Deccan, or linking the plains to the ports of Bombay or Calcutta. Elsewhere, the contact zones between the hills and the alluvium seem to have attracted towns by the presence of a higher water table and a defensive site (e.g., Gwalior, Jaipur, and Udaipur). In the coastal plains, the delta heads have become important town sites.

Early Urban Planning Current knowledge of urban planning in India commences with the towns and cities of the Indus Valley civilization, the best known of which are Harappa and Mohenjo-Daro. Mohenjo-Daro on the Indus River in Sind, and Harappa on the Ravi River, a tributary of the Indus, were large cities, upwards of three miles in circumference, which appear to have conformed to certain distinctive and evolved principles of planning.

Laid out to a common ground plan, each with its protected citadel towering above the rest of the city, together they functioned as twin capitals of a kingdom which had a centralized government, adequate communications provided by natural waterways, a common script, and a system of weights and measures. The citadel contained a carefully constructed bath or tank, a granary, pillared halls, and the residence of a high official—a high priest or the ruler. Below the citadel, the town stretched in orderly array to the river, showing a remarkable regularity constituting, perhaps, the oldest example of systematic town planning. Broad streets about 45 feet wide from south to north were crossed by others at right angles, and the blocks thus formed, each about 400 by 200 yards, were subdivided by narrow lanes parallel or at right angles to the arterial streets.

The houses, often substantial and sometimes of appreciable size, consisted typically of rooms around a courtyard. They contained stairs to an upper story as well as a bathroom, sometimes a well, and occasionally a privy on the ground or upper floor. The houses were of different sizes indicating different levels of income and social status. A feature of the houses was their windowless outer walls; the doors opened onto the narrow lanes rather than onto the main streets. Throughout, the streets and buildings are marked by the brick drains with their trim inspection holes, laid most elaborately, which are characteristic of the Indus Valley civilization. There were no decorative features to relieve the blank cubes of rooms or the monotony of the unvarying facades.

After the Indus Valley civilization, the first information of ancient Indian town planning is from the Vedic texts and early treatises describing a well-developed science of village planning (*Grama-Sannivesa*) and town planning (*Nagara Sannivesa*). Ancient treatises such as *Viswakarma Vastushastra, Manasara, Mayamatam,* all dating from before 3000 B.C., and *Artha Sastra* of Kautilya (third century B.C.), contain clear directions regarding the location and planning of villages, towns, and cities as a part of general town administration. The directions are as detailed for the village and the town as they are for the individual building, be it a palace, a temple, a market, or a sacrificial altar. The science of town planning had been developed systematically to an advanced stage to meet the needs of the

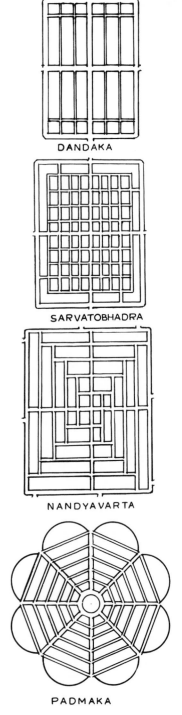

DANDAKA

SARVATOBHADRA

NANDYAVARTA

PADMAKA

terrain, defense, religious congregations, and other social and economic conditions of the times.

The plan of an Indo-Aryan town fairly reproduces the plan of an Indo-Aryan village, which in turn corresponds to the plan of a temple. In all these, there are two central crossroads and the *Mangalavithi,* or the road surrounding the village or the city; the same division of the ground into wards by a chessboard system of roads; the same method of distribution of wards to people according to their profession and status in the social scale; the same type of communal temples, tanks, or wells; and towers over the gates at the four cardinal points with smaller doorways in the corners, all enclosed by a massive wall surrounded by a moat. This similarity in the plan facilitated the development and extension of a village into a town and the town into a city. The Indo-Aryan town or city was a collection of villages, each of which could be likened to the present-day municipal ward. According to their shape, method of street planning, folk planning, and temple planning, the villages were classified differently by different writers. The better-known classification is by Manasara, who describes eight types of villages (see illustration).

The Indo-Aryan civilization was predominantly agricultural, and the villages and towns were based upon an agrarian social structure strongly bound by religious traditions and worship. While in the north of India, owing to the frequent invasions from the northwest, towns built according to the Indo-Aryan traditions were either destroyed or built over when new influences were followed, in the south Indian towns (e.g., Madurai and Srirangam) the planning concept according to the Vedic tradition is still perceptible in the older parts, in and around the temples and palaces. In the Indo-Gangetic plains, owing to the periodic invasions from outside and frequently changing rulers, each of whom attempted to extend his territories, town development was confined chiefly to the construction of strongly fortified capital cities. The rulers of Magadha built a fortress in the plains beside the rivers Ganges and Son where the straggling town of Patna now stands. This fortress of Patali was later enlarged into the splendid capital city of Pataliputra by Chandragupta Maurya, the first Mauryan emperor, in 320 B.C. Information about Pataliputra derives mainly from the records of visitors to Pataliputra; for instance, Megasthenes, the envoy of Seleucus to the Mauryan Court, describes the fortifications of a moat and a timber palisade as well as a splendid palace and garden complex, planned in the Persian style, eclipsing contemporary capitals like Susa and Ekbatana.

During the same period, the spread of the Buddhist philosophy led to the establishment of several university towns, like Nalanda, managed by monasteries. Located 6 miles from Rajgriha and conceived as a university town giving education in Buddhism, Nalanda was located a little away from the city, on a site with good climate, shady trees, and adequate water supply. The plan of Nalanda shows a series of cells for students around courtyards with temples, platforms for religious observances, and accommodation for the monastic order.

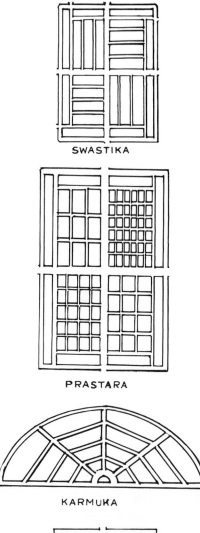

SWASTIKA

PRASTARA

KARMUKA

CHATURMUKHA

OPPOSITE PAGE AND ABOVE: *Eight types of villages described by Manasara.*

Jaisalmer. Plan of the walled town and extended area.

The history of India after the Mauryan and Gupta empires (sixth century A.D.) up to the time of the Moghuls (sixteenth century A.D.) is one of successive invasions and endless strife between the different rulers, each trying to establish his suzerainty with the assistance of invaders establishing themselves as rulers. The kingdoms established by Harsha, Kanishka, Mohammed of Gazni, and Mohammed of Ghori were followed by a series of Muslim dynastic rulers in the north. During these times urban development was confined mainly to the establishment of well-fortified capital cities. These fortresses, many of which were impregnable, secured the safety of the rulers and their accumulated wealth.

Each of these fortress towns had a citadel where the residence of the ruler, his place of worship, administrative offices, treasury, and arsenal were located and well guarded; the townspeople lived partly inside the fortress or just outside and were protected by the ruler to whom they owed allegiance. The splendor of the kingdom was reflected in the palaces, the temples, and other public buildings which also reflected the art and culture of the times.

There are a number of such fortress towns; Jaisalmer in Rajasthan and Golconda in the Deccan are good examples. Jaisalmer (see illustrations), founded in the twelfth century by Maharawal Jaisel Singh, a Bhatti Rajput king, stands on a sand hill named Trikut (three-sided) 350 feet high and protected by a range of sand hills all around. Its location was based upon natural defense advantages and the availability of water. The town flourished both as a capital and a center of commerce and trade for the caravan routes passing through the desert territory.

Jaisalmer has two lines of fortifications: the outer wall encompassing the town and the fort and the inner wall around the fort on the hill. The walled town covers an area of about 2 square miles (about 5 square kilometers) and the fort covers about a quarter square mile (0.7 square kilometer). The massive stone walls of rubble masonry are strengthened at intervals by bastions and corner towers. The main entry to the town is through the gates called Amar Sagar Prol. The main road runs east-west along the northern foothill of Trikut. Close to the main gate there are town squares, later called Gandhi Chowk, used for the resting of camels as the caravans enter the town. Typical of a medieval town, the main road, narrow and paved with stone blocks, takes twists and turns and opens into a series of squares—Junadi Chowk and Gopa Chowk—as it negotiates the contours of Trikut. It descends to the Ghatse Lake, then from the Akai gate, it ascends steeply, passes through a series of gates, and leads to the palace square in front of the palace, or Raj Mahal.

Because of the development of trade and commerce, a number of market squares or *chowks* came into existence within the walled town and each

Fort wall of Jaisalmer.

specialized in a particular trade such as jewelery, grain, or cloth. The palace square is used for religious and public functions. Important landmarks within the walled town are the Haveli, the residences of ministers or wealthy traders, built in a style indicating the social status of the owner. The settlement of population within the walled town was mostly on the basis of occupation, according to which the different sections of the town were designated as Padas: e.g., Sashi Pada for priests and teachers (Brahmin); Oswala Pada for rich traders, mostly Jains; and Tibba Padda for soldiers.

Golconda (see illustrations), founded as a capital by Sultan Quli in 1518, stands on a boulder-strewn hill in the Deccan peninsula commanding extensive views of the surrounding countryside and enclosed by an elaborate system of fortifications, walls, and moats. There are three lines of fort walls; the outer wall encompassing the town; the second, a double wall, is within the first and surrounds the citadel; and the third, higher and within the second, protects the King's palace. The eight gates that lead into these fortresses are massive in structure, with winding approaches, outer and inner doors, and ample guardhouses between the doors.

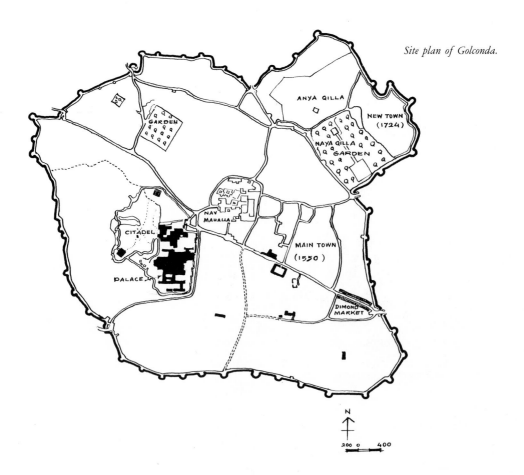

Site plan of Golconda.

The Citadel, Golconda.

The citadel, called Bala Hissar, houses the armory, the garrison, and official buildings. At the top of the hill stands the King's palace; the assembly hall or Baradari; and the seraglio containing the harem, palaces, extensive arcades, large halls, vaulted chambers, balconies, baths in the Turkish style, fountains, and flower gardens, all now in ruins. The entire fort was well supplied with drinking water by a system of lift wells, channels, and storage tanks.

The notable features of Golconda fort are the concentration of government in the palace; the straight and wide processional route from the main gate up to the Baradari for the grand procession of the King and his ministers, nobles, and soldiers on elephants, horses, and on foot (the processional street received every attention and was impressive in contrast to the other streets in the town); and the mosques, palaces, and rest houses, all in Persian style, indicating the frequent and dominant Moghul influence on Golconda.

The Moghul period of Indian history, starting from the sixteenth century and lasting over 300 years, brought a comparatively settled period to the country when city development covered not only capitals but also defense outposts, trading extablishments near ports, and military cantonments. Many rulers who were vassals to the Moghul emperor built splendid cities and gardens for their people, and these indicate the influence of the French and Italian Renaissance. Shahjahanabad (Delhi), built by Shahjahan in 1648, and Jaipur, established by Raja Sawai Jaisingh II in 1728, are good examples.

The city of Shahjahanabad—founded by Shahjahan, the Moghul emperor, on the banks of the Yamuna River (see illustration)—was protected by

Plan of Shahajanabad in 1700.

massive fortifications and was approached by seven gates from north, south, and west, with the river on the east. The royal palace, called the Red Fort, was located to the northeast inside the walled city. In Chandni Chowk, the great bazaar of the Orient, there used to flow a beautiful canal ending against the eastern entrance of Fatehpuri mosque, west of the main entrance to the palace. Shahjahan also built the great Jama Masjid. His design of the city had wide roads, gracious parks, and nobles' houses with large courtyards. Residential streets were kept narrow to protect people from the scorching summer sun and the biting winds of the winter. Quiet streets meander past the houses, which were closely built and not more than two stories high. Jaipur (see illustration), located about 200 miles north of Delhi, was planned and built by Maharaja Sawai Jaisingh II in 1728 to serve as his new capital. Amber, the previous capital located just north of Jaipur in an inaccessible tract of the Aravalli Hills, was eminently defensible but unsuitable for its growing population and activities. With the decline of the Moghul empire and the growing safety from enemy attack, the capital was moved to a flat site nearby having adequate drinking water, good drainage, and abundant building stone.

The town is bounded on the north and east by rugged hills crowned with forts. Jaisingh, being well versed in astrology and astronomy, had the capital designed according to the *prastara* type of layout with emphasis on the cardinal directions. Thus the central axis of the town was laid from east to west between the gates of the sun (*Surajpol*) and the moon (*Chandpol*), and this was crossed by three roads at right angles dividing the town into nine blocks which were further subdivided by lanes and alleys. The palace buildings covered two blocks, the town six, and the remaining ninth block was not usable on account of the steep hills. The town has around it a masonry wall 25 feet (7.6 meters) high and 9 feet (2.5 meters) thick, with eight gates; the palace buildings are surrounded by a similar wall, the two walls acting as successive defense lines. The main activities of the town are located along the central axis which links them and the palace complex. On the main streets strict control was exercised on the street facade, along which were located shops and arcades one story in height; but beyond the frontage the buildings could be of any height or any shape, some built with flat roofs and others with traditional chatries.

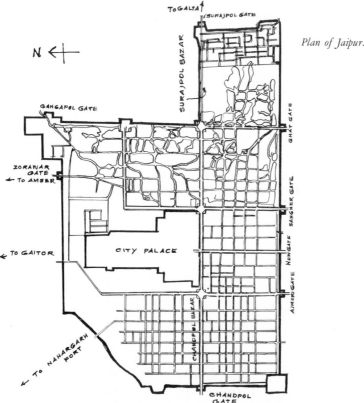

Plan of Jaipur.

The residential areas were planned with internal courtyards which provided access to the streets. At street intersections spacious squares were elaborately designed with domed buildings or spired temples flanking them. The entire city was built in pink sandstone and has therefore been known as "the pink city."

With the British regime in India came three types of towns: cantonments, hill stations, and provincial capitals. The provincial capitals were located mostly at ports such as Calcutta, Bombay, and Madras. The capitals of inland provinces were located mostly on the trunk routes like Allahabad, Lahore, and Nagpur. These were administrative and commercial centers which subsequently developed into industrial centers also. In these towns, the residential areas for the white population were clearly separated from those for the native population, and the areas reserved for white population were distinctly better in regard to the layout, amenities, entertainment, and commercial activities. The native areas were allowed to grow without much direction, under the supervision of the local bodies as they had existed before, without any provision for legislation, taxation, or policing.

Cantonment towns were established along the main routes in all parts of the country and at strategic places. These were permanent army camps with small civil populations to serve them. The cantonments were planned with wide roads in a gridiron pattern, with low-density housing—laid out strictly according to ranks—the parade grounds, and the mall where shops and entertainment were located for the use of the army personnel.

Hill stations were developed both in the north and south, examples being Simla, Dalhousie, Nainital, Darjeeling, Ootacamund, and Kodaikanal. These stations were primarily places where the governors of provinces, the administration, and the white population could spend their summer months away from the hot plains, and they developed into centers of social activities. These picturesque hill stations were laid out with spacious bungalows, parks, and wide roads and avenues. The residential areas for the native population were at the lower levels, generally crowded, with narrow streets and little or nothing in the way of sanitary facilities. Hospitals, recreation centers, and—in one or two cases—important ammunition factories were established in such centers. Most hill centers did not have any continual activity and during the winter months they languished. They have now become tourist resorts during summer.

Town Planning in Nineteenth and Twentieth Centuries The first efforts in modern town planning in India began with the appointment of the sanitary commissions in 1864 in the three presidencies of Madras, Bengal, and Bombay under directions from the Royal Sanitary Commission nominated by the British Parliament in 1859. The sanitary commissions were required *inter alia* "to give advice and assistance in all matters relating to public health and sanitation, to advise on the sanitary improvement of native towns and prevention and mitigation of epidemic diseases." The work of the sanitary commissions was gradually taken over by the sanitary engineering and health departments of the states under the direction of special committees or boards constituted for the purpose.

In the early part of the twentieth century, town planning was considered and accepted as a routine municipal function and the problems in town improvement were such, both in their scope and complexity, that the average municipal administration could handle them satisfactorily with its resources. Town improvement then comprised mainly such matters as the improvement of sanitary facilities, the digging of a well or a pond to provide drinking water, and the imposition of health measures in the event of an epidemic. Where a town was growing, it meant construction of a few new roads; and the question of inadequacy of existing services and amenities hardly arose. As these problems grew in size and went beyond the capacity of the municipal bodies to handle them, improvement trusts were created. They were entrusted with town improvement and expansion schemes and the provision of services and amenities. The improvement trusts were also given powers to raise funds for their programs through special measures not normally available to the municipal administration.

The first improvement trust to be constituted in India was in Bombay in 1898. It was soon followed by others for Mysore (1903) and Calcutta (1911). The United Provinces Town Improvement Act in 1919 led to the constitution of improvement trusts for Lucknow (1919) and Allahabad (1920). Punjab followed with its own Town Improvement Act in 1922; but the first in undivided Punjab, namely the Lahore Improvement Trust, was not set up until 1936. The trust for Nagpur was created in 1937 under the Nagpur Improvement Trust Act of 1937.

The Delhi Improvement Trust was also constituted in the same year by the extension of the United Provinces Town Improvement Act of 1919 to develop on proper lines the government lands transferred to its charge. Improvement trusts for the cities of Bangalore and Madras were set up as late as 1945 and 1946. The Hyderabad Improvement Trust, constituted in 1912, was on a footing different from those mentioned earlier. This trust came into existence by a firman issued by the Nizam of Hyderabad to improve the sanitation and the general conditions of the city of Hyderabad. This board had jurisdiction not only over the city but also 2 miles beyond the municipal limits.

The improvement trusts were very active in the beginning and had to their credit many town improvement and housing schemes as well as the construction of new roads. During the 35 years of its existence, the Bombay Improvement Trust launched 71 improvement schemes, acquired properties, cleared slums, built hutments, constructed roads, reclaimed lands, and laid out plots, leasing or selling them with restrictions regarding open spaces, heights of floors, and architectural features. The activities of the Mysore Improvement Trust Board earned for that city the name "Garden City of the South." The Calcutta Improvement Trust, with its ample financial resources and good liaison between itself and the Calcutta Corporation, has done extremely useful work.

Some of the trusts ran into difficulties and they were merged either with the corporations or with newly created authorities with wider powers. The Bombay Improvement Trust, which met with financial difficulties due to land transactions in the twenties, was merged in 1933 with the Bombay Municipal Corporation. The Kanpur and Delhi Improvement Trusts have been replaced by the Kanpur Development Board and the Delhi Development Authority.

The activities of the trusts have not always been satisfactory. As new bodies such as housing boards, cooperative housing societies, and planning authorities under town planning acts came into existence, the utility of the trusts has been questioned. A parallel agency having functions similar to or in some cases the same as the municipal functions created unhealthy rivalry between the municipal bodies and the improvement trusts. This gave rise to political strife, as the trusts were nominated bodies while the municipal bodies were elected.

The improvement trusts, by virtue of their constitution and method of operation, limited themselves to those schemes which were remunerative in preference to those for which subsidies would have to be obtained from government. Thus, the trusts concentrated on the development of new areas which would give them adequate returns, in some cases extraordinarily good returns, and the money so realized was not always spent on subsidizing other needy schemes. Thus, the older parts of the city suffered neglect while the town or the city expanded outward. This called for extension of the physical services and social amenities for which the municipal body, with its limited resources, had to seek financial aid from the state government or face public criticism. The municipal bodies gradually came to consider improvement trusts as infringing on their own field of operations and to some extent as being obstructions to their programs for development. Added to this, the magnitude and complexity of problems increased the number of factors that required an overall approach to the development of the city as a whole. Such problems should be handled by an agency not with parallel powers but with concurrent or overriding powers.

As far as town planning was concerned, very few improvement trusts could undertake the preparation of a development plan for a whole city or a town, and their efforts were mostly directed toward particular parts of urban areas. Thus the contribution of improvement trusts to general town planning was not very significant, though as implementing agencies they have been quite effective and useful.

The visit of Patrick Geddes to India in 1915 to advise the Governor of Madras on the replanning and redevelopment of some of the old towns helped to establish town planning as not only the planning of streets and houses but also the planning for the people who lived in them, to meet their economic, social, and aesthetic needs and aspirations. Dr. Geddes made it clear that replanning of any area had to be considered from a much wider angle; i.e., on a regional basis rather than as a mere local problem, and he gave to town planning its basic sociological approach. The relation "Folk-Place-Work" expressed, in his view, the true objectives of any town improvement schemes, and replanning meant restoring certain old values which the townspeople had lost as a result of deterioration in the environmental conditions. Mere widening of streets or provision of some parks would not restore these values; in fact, indiscriminate improvements might even destroy the social cohesion and the economic interdependence of communities, endangering their very existence.

Following Patrick Geddes's visit and because of the interest which he evoked in modern town planning by a series of lectures delivered in the different cities of India, the government of India appointed a Town Planning Adviser; and some of the states, particularly Madras and Bombay, passed town planning acts on the lines of the United Kingdom's Housing and Town Planning Act of 1909. The progress in town planning, however, was sluggish both in the twenties and early thirties. The establishment of a number of basic industries in the beginning of the century and the construction by these industries of labor colonies led to the planned development of a few industrial towns such as Jamshedpur (see illustration). The

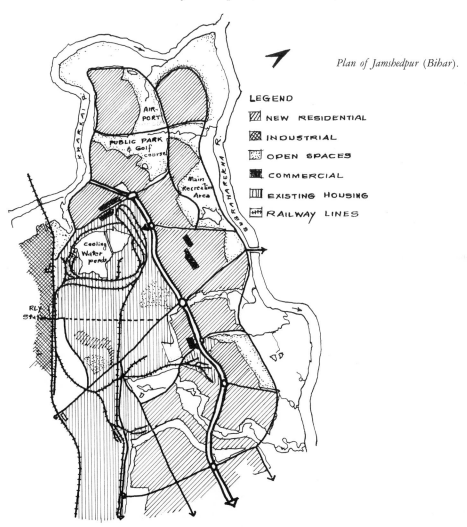

Plan of Jamshedpur (Bihar).

LEGEND

NEW RESIDENTIAL

INDUSTRIAL

OPEN SPACES

COMMERCIAL

EXISTING HOUSING

RAILWAY LINES

town planning acts in the presidencies of Madras and Bombay resulted in a larger number of town improvement schemes being undertaken by the local bodies with assistance given by state governments. A number of large towns like Bombay, Poona, Hyderabad, Nagpur, Calcutta, Kanpur, and Delhi benefited from these schemes. During this period, the new capital of India, New Delhi, was planned and its construction was started.

The Second World War practically put a stop to town improvement activities, and it was not until postwar planning started that the problem of urban improvement was given any serious thought. In the early forties, motivated by the large expansions necessitated by the demands of the war, industrial towns like Jamshedpur and Bhadravathi and metropolitan cities like Bombay and Madras started planning on a scientific basis. The foundation for the newly planned capital of Orissa, Bhuvaneshwar, was also laid in the late forties.

The postwar planning activities of the government of India led to the setting up of the Health Survey and Development Committee under the chairmanship of Sir Joseph Bhore. The report of the committee, published in 1946, is notable for its very progressive thinking and anticipation of developments far ahead of the period. The committee comprehended not only public health and medical facilities in the country but also environmental hygiene, under which town planning and village planning were specifically considered. The recommendations of this committee on village and town planning set the line of thinking at government level, both central and state, in dealing with regional and urban planning and development in the postwar years.

The postwar years saw vastly increased activity in town planning resulting from (1) the partition of the country and the resettlement of displaced persons arising therefrom, (2) the large-scale industrial development sponsored within the framework of national plans, and (3) the rapid urbanization due to industrialization and heavy migration to urban centers. The task of meeting the needs of resettlement, of large industrial plants for iron and steel, fertilizers, petroleum products, and the expansion of urban centers, especially the metropolitan cities to accommodate the migrants, led to the establishment of a number of self-contained towns, like Nilokheri and Faridabad, for refugees; the founding of new industrial towns like Bhilai, Rourkela, Sindri, Durgapur, and Nangal; and the planned expansion of large cities and metropolitan areas like Delhi, Bombay, and Calcutta. In addition to these, the birth of new states gave rise to the development of new state capitals, among which can be mentioned Bhuvaneshwar, capital of Orissa; Chandigarh, capital of Punjab; and Gandhinagar, capital of Gujarat. Examples of these planning enterprises are described.

Faridabad (see diagrammatic plan) lies on the Delhi-Muttra-Agra trunk road and on the Delhi-Bombay railway line about 16 miles from Delhi. Originally Faridabad was intended to be developed as a self-contained town with industry, commerce, and other activities for rehabilitating the refugees. On account of its proximity to the national capital of Delhi and as a consequence of the restrictions imposed on the growth of industries in the

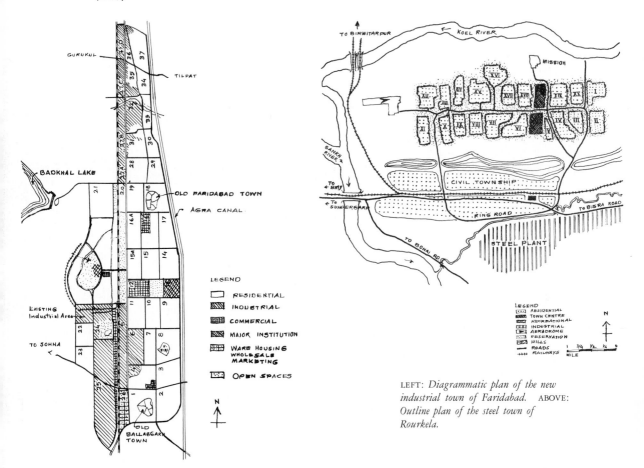

LEGEND
☐ RESIDENTIAL
▨ INDUSTRIAL
▦ COMMERCIAL
▨ MAJOR INSTITUTION
▦ WAREHOUSING WHOLESALE MARKETING
▦ OPEN SPACES

LEGEND
▦ RESIDENTIAL
▦ TOWN CENTRE
▦ RECREATIONAL
▦ INDUSTRIAL
▣ AERODROME
▦ RESERVATION
▦ HILLS
— ROADS
+++ RAILWAYS

LEFT: *Diagrammatic plan of the new industrial town of Faridabad.* ABOVE: *Outline plan of the steel town of Rourkela.*

national capital, Faridabad has grown as a big industrial complex enveloping adjacent small towns and villages. The potential of Faridabad for being developed into a second-order town to Delhi has been recognized and it is now planned for a population of 300,000 by 1981. The plan for the national capital region, which includes Faridabad, provides for the development of Faridabad as a ring town and for moving into it some of the activities of the national capital such as central government offices and large manufacturing industries. The town extends over nearly 10,000 acres (4,047 hectares) and provides good civic facilities. Faridabad is a good example of a refugee town which has established its own place in the regional economy.

Rourkela, the steel town, built for the workers of the steel plant of Ms. Hindustan Steel Ltd., lies on the main Bombay-Calcutta railway line. The plant is located to the south of the railway line, while the town is to the north of the line, separated by a range of hills running alongside the railway. These hills serve as excellent buffers between the town and the steel plant, keeping away noise, dust, and smoke arising from manufacturing activity. The general plan of the town (see illustration) indicates a number of

View of housing at Rourkela.

self-contained neighborhoods served by a ring road, centrally located community services, and a town center. The ring road, which is the main spine, links the steel plant and the railway station. The neighborhoods are located on both sides and all the facilities are located along it. Each neighborhood is provided with nursery and primary schools, local shops, parks, and playgrounds, and a neighborhood community center. The town extends over an area of 3,500 acres (1,416 hectares) and is designed for a population of 150,000; but it can be expanded to accommodate double this population.

Chandigarh, originally established as a capital to compensate East Punjab for the loss of Lahore, is located on a beautiful site on the gently sloping terrain of the foothills of the Himalayas. Chandigarh may be said to have started a new movement in the planning of towns, public buildings, and residential quarters in India. Designed by the famous architect Le Corbusier, Chandigarh (see illustrations) is based on a seven-level hierarchial road system, VI-V7 starting from a housing street to a high-speed, dual-carriage, grade-separated arterial road and well-knit residential neighborhood planning. The city is planned for an ultimate total population of 500,000. The government complex, called "the capitol," is placed to the east of the town against the backdrop of the Himalaya Hills and dominates the entire city.

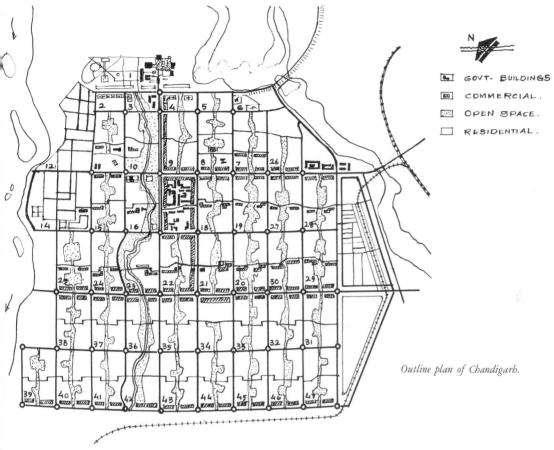

N

GOVT. BUILDINGS
COMMERCIAL.
OPEN SPACE.
RESIDENTIAL.

Outline plan of Chandigarh.

Chandigarh. City center under construction.

Group of ministerial buildings in Chandigar

Chandigarh. Secretariat complex.

The town center is located along the leisure valley which extends from the capitol toward the west in the heart of the town. The town center has been developed with strict architectural controls of the facades and of building densities.

The industrial area is located to the south of the city. While initially dust-free and light industries were intended to be developed, Chandigarh is attracting all types and has exceeded its target of industrial development. The residential area is divided into a number of neighborhoods fully self-contained with nursery and primary schools, shops, playgrounds, and open spaces. An efficient separation of pedestrian and vehicular traffic has been achieved. Several experiments have been made in the layout of the neighborhoods which will provide useful comparative data for future work.

The capitol complex consisting of the central Secretariat, a multistory building, the High Court, and the Legislature has been designed in a unique way by Le Corbusier and has attracted worldwide attention. The two torrential streams to the east of the town have been dammed and a lake has been created, providing a delightful environment for the capitol complex as well as the whole city.

Delhi saw unprecedented growth in the post-independence era, owing first to the flood of new refugees, second to its importance as a national capital, and third because of the expansion of government as well as commercial and industrial activities. The problems created by this rapid and haphazard expansion demanded that a master plan be drawn up, and such a plan was started in 1956 and completed in 1961. The Master Plan for Delhi (see illustration), which is strictly enforced today, envisages its growth to a city of 5 million and provides for different functions such as the national government and a metropolitan government, the housing of a large number of government employees, extensive industrial and commercial activity, and a wide range of social and cultural activities—all of which, as the national capital, Delhi will have to sponsor and nourish. There is also a separate area for the diplomatic corps, well laid out with avenues, parks, and other amenities. The growth of Delhi in the sixties has been phenomenal, and almost the entire area projected to be developed by 1981 has already been assigned to various purposes.

The continued rapid growth of Delhi has resulted in promoting parallel development of secondary urban centers, such as Meerut, Faridabad, Ballabhgarh, and Sonepat, within a distance of 40 miles (64 kilometers) from Delhi. Such development would reduce the pressure on the growth of Delhi. While Delhi would continue to be a metropolitan center of the area and the national capital, the development of second- and third-order towns within the region of Delhi and well-connected to Delhi by rapid transport would lead to a lessening of the pressures on the main city itself and help in distributing the economic activities over a much larger area.

The Master Plan for Delhi provides for the traditional pattern of concentric arterial ring roads along which work centers have been located. The ring roads connect the existing residential neighborhoods and also those

delhi urba

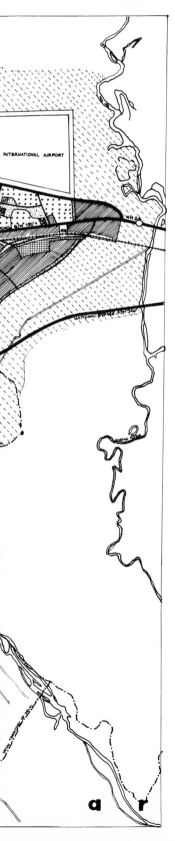

Delhi. Land-use plan.

	DENSITY UPTO 150 PERSONS PER ACRE
	DENSITY FROM 150 TO 250 PERSONS PER ACRE
	COMMERCIAL
	INDUSTRIAL
	GOVERNMENTAL
	RECREATIONAL
	EDUCATIONAL, RESEARCH, SOCIAL AND CULTURAL INSTITUTIONS
	COMMUNITY FACILITIES

    H HOSPITALS
    P POLICE HQS. & STATIONS
    PT GENERAL POST & TELEGRAPH OFFICES
    F FIRE HEADQUARTERS

	PUBLIC UTILITIES

    W WATERWORKS
    ST SEWAGE TREATMENT PLANTS
    E ELECTRIC POWER HOUSES

	GREEN BELT

INTERNATIONAL AIRPORT

NATIONAL & WEST ROAD

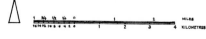

a r e q

MILES
KILOMETRES

planned to be developed hereafter. A unique feature of Delhi is its vast central space wherein the capitol complex is located, surrounded by a low-density residential development. Unlike most capital cities, where the central core is heavily built up and building densities lessen as we go toward the periphery, Delhi is planned with a central low-density area surrounded by high-density areas for residential and other uses. This is expected to provide a more economical, rational, and satisfactory transport network and at the same time to elimate the traffic bottlenecks that build up around highly centralized cores of cities.

The process of implementing the national economic development plans at the regional and state levels has given rise to resource regional planning both on a statewide and an interstatewide basis. Efforts toward economic

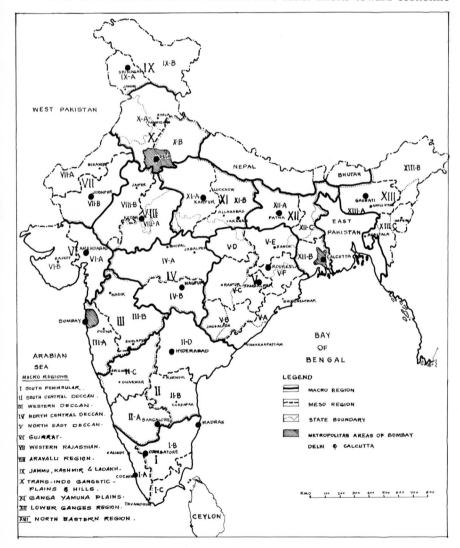

Map of India showing planning regions. (Note: In 1972 East Pakistan became the Republic of Bangladesh.)

regionalization in order to achieve balanced regional development have led to the evolution of a set of planning regions in the country based upon economic viability and a degree of ecological balance. The preparation of plans for the different regions within the national framework will ultimately lead to a national physical plan as a counterpart of the national economic and social development plans.

Legislation and Administration   The Indian Constitution, which is federal in structure, provides for land legislation both by the central government and the state governments within their respective jurisdictions. Town and country planning law which refers basically to land is therefore largely state-administered and the legislative and administrative patterns have been developed at the state level, the central government exercising chiefly a supervisory and advisory role.

Planning legislation in India had its beginning in the town planning and improvement trust acts of the states which enabled the setting up of improvement trusts to undertake town improvement schemes which the municipal administrations found difficult to handle. After World War II the Bhore committee recommended planning legislation on a uniform basis throughout the country and suggested that a model law for town and country planning be evolved for that purpose. The first model law prepared by the Institute of Town Planners of India was subsequently revised by the Central Town and Country Planning Organization in the light of experience and requirements for legal acceptance. The revised model law has been currently guiding the state governments and other agencies in enacting comprehensive town and country planning laws for different parts of the country.

In the model law, planning and implementation are recognized as separate functions, the latter being carried out by a large number of statutory, executive, financial, and other bodies. For planning, the law establishes area planning authorities, appointed by the state and having overriding planning powers over local and regional agencies. The model law provides for a statutory planning authority, preparation of outline and comprehensive plans for areas, planning of schemes within these frameworks; and enforcement of the schemes. Local bodies may be planning authorities if they are found suitable. Penalties for contravention of the plans and schemes are prescribed, and provision is made for removal of nonconforming uses and for reservation of land for public purposes.

State laws concerned with town development and regional planning are listed at the end of this section. Some of the acts deal directly with town planning; others do so indirectly on account of the powers for controlling land use and development included in them.

City planning administration started with improvement trusts, which were staffed initially by general administrators and engineers. With the planning laws in the presidency states came the town planning departments, which were initially staffed largely by general administrators, engineers, and architects. The Bhore committee's recommendations to establish at the federal level a town planning adviser's office and the increasing importance given to overall economic planning has led to the recognition of the need for properly staffed town and country planning departments at the state and central levels to undertake physical planning within the framework provided by economic plans.

Town planning administration is organized at three levels: federal or central, state, and local. At the central level, the Town and Country Planning Organization plays an advisory role and formulates policies and programs at the national level as an integral part of the national five-year economic development plans. It also advises and assists central ministries, state departments, governmental and semigovernmental agencies, and others in all matters concerning urban and regional planning and development. It is also largely, though not legally, responsible for the Delhi Master Plan. Recently, it has taken the responsibility for preparing interstate regional plans to bridge the gap between state planning and national planning, and also to obtain maximum coordination in development programs within a framework of resource-based spatial planning.

Each state has a town planning department with appropriate town planning and other staff forming multidisciplinary teams. The chief town planner or the director of town planning in a number of states (i.e., Madras, Maharashtra, Gujarat, Andhra Pradesh, Bihar, Orissa, Assam, Madhya Pradesh, and Mysore) is a statutory officer and his advice is legally binding on the state governments. The state town planning departments are generally organized into a central office at the state capital and a number of area units, the areas being groups of districts called "divisions." Divisional town planners have responsibility for both rural and urban planning and development in their respective areas.

Planning administration is yet to emerge as a distinct part of the local administration. In the case of metropolitan cities like Bombay, Calcutta, Madras, and Delhi, town planning departments have been in existence for some time and have played important roles in the planning and implementation of developmental programs. They have also been responsible, with the help of central and state organizations, for preparing comprehensive plans for the metropolitan areas and the regions in their immediate vicinity and for advising the state governments and the local bodies in these regions with regard to development control. A similar setup is gradually being introduced in other large cities such as Baroda, Bangalore, and Hyderabad.

The role of local town planning departments will always be subsidiary. As legislative powers for planning and plan implementation are derived from the state acts, the powers which local town planning administrations can exercise are limited. For instance, compulsory land acquisition for public purposes, taxation, and levies can be imposed only by the state. Comprehensive planning laws, however, increasingly enable the state to vest adequate powers with the local planning authorities.

ACTS

1. Andhra Pradesh	(1) Andhra Pradesh Municipalities Act, 1965; (2) Andhra Area Town Planning Act, 1920; (3) The Andhra Pradesh (Andhra Area) Public Health Act, 1939; (4) Cinema Regulations Act, 1955. *Rules:* (1) Revised Building Rules, 1942 (Under District Municipalities Act, 1965); (2) Town Planning Rules, 1933 (as amended from time to time under the Town Planning Act, 1920); (3) (*a*) Lodging House Rules, 1940; (*b*) Madras Improvement Rules, 1943; (*c*) Private Sanitary Conveniences Rules of 1941 (under Public Health Act); (*d*) The Andhra Pradesh Cinema Regulations Rules, 1962 (under Cinema Regulation Act, 1955).
2. Assam	(1) Assam Town and Country Planning Act, 1959; (2) Assam Slum Areas (Improvement and Clearance) Act, 1959.
3. Bihar	(1) Bihar Town Planning and Improvement Trust Act, 1951; (2) Bihar Restriction of Uses of Land Act, 1948; (3) Bihar and Orissa Municipal Act, 1922; (4) Patna Municipal Corporation Act, 1951; (5) Bihar Panchayat Sanitaries and Zila Parishad Act, 1961.
4. Gujarat	(1) Bombay Town Planning Act, 1954; (2) Saurashtra Town Planning Act, 1955; (3) Bombay Provincial Municipal Corporations Act, 1949; (4) Gujarat Municipalities Act, 1963; (5) Gujarat Housing Board Act, 1961.
5. Haryana	The acts currently in force in Punjab have also been extended to the state of Haryana.
6. Jammu and Kashmir	(1) Jammu and Kashmir, State Town Planning Act, 1963.
7. Kerala	(1) Madras Town Planning Act, 1920; (2) Travancore Town Planning Regulations, 1932; (3) Travancore Town and Country Planning Act, 1945.
8. Madhya Pradesh	(1) M.P. Town Planning Act, 1948; (2) M.P. Regulation of Uses of Land Act, 1948; (3) M.P. Towns (Periphery) Control Act, 1960; (4) M.P. Town Improvement Trusts Act, 1960; (5) M.P. Slum Improvement (Acquisition of Land) Act, 1956; (6) M.P. Land Revenue Code, 1959; (7) M.P. Municipalities Act, 1961; (8) M.P. Municipal Corporation Act, 1956; (9) M.P. Town Planning Rules, 1960; (10) M.P. Diversion of Land Rules, 1962; (11) M.P. Town and Country Planning (Amendment) Act, 1969.
9. Tamil Nadu	(1) Madras Town Planning Act, 1920; (2) Madras District Municipalities Act, 1920; (3) Madras City Municipal Corporation Act, 1919; (4) Madras Panchayats Act, 1958; (5) Madras District Development Council Act, 1960; (6) Madras Public Health Act, 1939; (7) Madras Land Improvement Scheme Act, 1950; (8) Madras Land Improvement Schemes Act, 1959; (9) Madras Town Nuisance Act, 1889; (10) Madras Parks, Playfields, and Open Spaces

(Preservation and Regulation) Act, 1959; (11) Madras Housing Board Act, 1961; (12) Madras Slum Improvement (Acquisition of Land) Act, 1954.

10. Maharashtra   (1) Maharashtra Regional and Town Planning Act, 1966.

11. Mysore   (1) Mysore Town and Country Planning Act, 1961 (as amended in 1964); (2) Mysore Slum Areas (Improvement and Clearance) Act, 1958; (3) Mysore Housing Board Act, 1962; (4) Mysore Municipalities Act, 1964; (5) Mysore Village Panchayats and Local Bodies Act, 1959; (6) City of Bangalore Improvement Act, 1945; (7) City of Mysore Improvement Act, 1903; (8) City of Bangalore Municipal Corporation Act, 1949; (9) Hubli Dharwar Corporation Act, 1962; (10) Mysore Highways Act, 1964; (11) Mysore Industrial Area Development Act, 1966.

12. Orissa   (1) Orissa Town Planning and Improvement Trust Act, 1956.

13. Punjab (including Haryana)   (1) Punjab Town Improvement Act, 1922; (2) Punjab Development of Damaged Areas Act, 1951; (3) Punjab New Capital (Periphery) Control Act, 1952; (4) East Punjab Refugees and Building Sites Act, 1948; (5) Punjab Urban Estates (Development and Regulations) Act, 1964; (6) Punjab Slum Areas (Improvement and Clearance) Act, 1961; (7) Punjab Municipal Act, 1911; (8) Punjab Scheduled Roads and Controlled Area Restriction of Unregulated Development Act, 1963; (9) Punjab District Boards Act, 1883; (10) Pepsu Towns and Suburban Area Development Act, 1952; (11) Punjab New Mandi Townships (Development Regulation) Act, 1960.

14. Rajasthan   (1) Rajasthan Urban Improvement Trust Act, 1959; (2) Municipal Act, 1959; (3) Rajasthan Urban Land Tax Act, 1964.

15. Uttar Pradesh   (1) U.P. Town Improvement Act, 1919; (2) U.P. Municipalities Act, 1916; (3) U.P. Regulation of Building Operations Act, 1958; (4) U.P. Nagar Mahapalika Adhiniyam, 1959; (5) U.P. Slum Areas (Improvement and Clearance) Act, 1962.

16. West Bengal   (1) Calcutta Metropolitan Planning Area (Use and Development of Land) Control Act, 1965; (2) Durgapur (Development and Control of Building Operations) Act, 1958; (3) Howrah Improvement Act, 1956; (4) Calcutta Improvement Act, 1911.

Education and Training Prior to 1955 town planning and civic design were being taught as a part of the civil engineering course, and Calcutta University gave a part-time undergraduate course in town and regional planning. Formal education in town and country planning was started in 1956 with the establishment of an independent school for instruction in town and country planning in Delhi—the first of its kind—sponsored jointly by the government of India and the Institute of Town Planners, India. At the same time the department of architecture of the Indian Institute of

Technology at Kharagpur (West Bengal) started a course in urban and regional planning for graduates in architecture, engineering, and social sciences.

With the growing demand for town planners for the state town planning departments, metropolitan cities, and various large industrial undertakings, a program of education in town planning was evolved and is now being implemented. In addition to the two already established, three more institutions at Madras, Poona, and Bombay are offering part-time courses in town and regional planning at the postgraduate level; the course at the Bengal Engineering College, Calcutta, is being upgraded into a full time postgraduate course. New courses of planning have also been contemplated in the schools of architecture at Ahmedabad and Chandigarh. By 1971, India was producing annually about a hundred qualified planners.

The annual intake and the number of graduates expected to be produced annually by the different institutes is given in the table below. In addition to the above, the Institute of Town Planners, India, holds an examination for those who seek to study privately and qualify in town and country planning. The scheme of examination is comprehensive and can be completed in parts, leading to the associateship of the institute, which is recognized for official purposes as being equivalent to a degree from a university. About 10 to 15 planners qualify each year.

Institute	Qualification awarded	Duration of course	Intake
School of Planning and Architecture, Delhi	Diploma in town and country planning	2 years	30
Indian Institute of Technology, Kharagpur, dept. of architecture & regional planning	M.C.P. (architecture) M.R.P. (social sciences)	2 years	20
University of Madras, dept. of architecture and planning	Master's degree in town and country planning	2 years	20
University of Poona, College of Engineering	M.E. (civil town planning)	2 years full time	20
University of Bombay, J. J. School of Architecture	M.E. (civil town planning)	3 years part time	20

The courses in these institutions are based upon minimum instruction approved by the Board of Technical studies in Architecture and Regional Planning of the government of India with variations dependent on specialization offered and entry qualifications. The Delhi School of Planning and Architecture offers a postgraduate course in town and country planning both as a general course and with specialization in traffic and transportation planning and housing and community planning. The course is of 2 years' duration. The general course is integrated with the specialized courses in the first year, and the second year is devoted to specialization in the respective fields.

The Indian Institute of Technology, Kharagpur, offers two courses of 2 years' duration: one for architects and engineers for the master's degree in city planning with emphasis on urban design and development, and the other a master's degree in regional planning for geographers and social science students with emphasis on regional development.

The course offered by the department of architecture and regional planning of Madras University is of 2 years' duration for a master's degree in city planning. No specialization is offered at the university and the course has a comprehensive planning curriculum with a broad outlook toward regional and city development.

The College of Engineering, Poona, gives a 2-year course for a master's degree in engineering (civil, town planning) for graduates in architecture and civil engineering. It is a general one following broadly the curriculum recommended by the government of India.

The J. J. School of Architecture, Bombay, gives a 3-year part-time course for a diploma in town planning open to graduates in architecture and in social sciences. The curriculum is similar to the course followed by the Poona Engineering College.

Institutions   Institutions concerned with town and country planning arose in the recent postwar period. On the professional plane, an Indian Board of Town Planners was formed in 1949 and became incorporated as the Institute of Town Planners, India, in 1951, with nine qualified planners as its founding members. It has grown since, and it had over two hundred members in 1970. The institute is both a professional and a propagandist organization. It admits qualified town and country planners into its professional membership, conducts an examination recognized officially as equivalent to a degree of the university, and publishes a quarterly journal. The institute has successfully organized annual planning seminars with large participation from official and nonofficial organizations, and it has also established professional alliances with the Town Planning Institute, London, and other Commonwealth professional bodies. The institute has its headquarters in Delhi and has lately established regional chapters at Madras, Bangalore, Bombay, Trivandrum, and Chandigarh.

The Town and Country Planning Association at Bombay, started by the All India Local Self-Government Institute, has a nonprofessional status and conducts courses in town and country planning at a junior level. This helps to provide supporting staff in town planning departments in the country. The association publishes a journal and brings out monographs periodically. The Eastern Regional Organization for Planning and Housing, the regional chapter of the International Federation for Housing and Planning (IFHP), is also located in Delhi and promotes town and country planning and housing activities in association with national bodies like the Institute of Town Planners, India, and it undertakes propagandist activities such as the publication of newsletters and the holding of international congresses and seminars.

Professional Practice   The profession of town planning in India has yet to emerge. There was no profession of town planning in actual practice prior to World War II. Town planning was done mostly by local bodies and improvement trusts under the advice of the state government and with the help of engineering staff. A few of the firms of architects established during the British days acted as consultants to the large industrial concerns in providing labor colonies, establishing new factory towns, and planning extensions. New Delhi—the capital of India—and some of the other state capitals were planned by Sir Edward Lutyens and Sir Herbert Baker with other architects who came from England.

Postwar reconstruction led to the recognition of city and regional planning as one of the specific fields in which Indian architects and engineers should be trained to meet the needs of the country, and a large number of students were sent abroad on government scholarships for training in the field. With the cessation of hostilities and the beginning of reconstruction work, a large number of programs were undertaken; but these were handled mostly by government agencies and the professional town planner was not much in demand. The establishment of the Institute of Town Planners, India, in 1951, and its promotion of the profession of town planning in India served as a stimulus to a large number of people seeking to become trained in the field and to start professional practice.

The number of qualified planners in the country grew slowly initially, from 9 in 1949 to 65 in 1957. Later, with the establishment of schools of planning, the number has steadily increased, about 60 being added every year. The number of planners in professional practice in the country is little more than 20, and these practice both as architects and town planners. As most planning work in the country is done by government agencies and will so continue, it is likely that the profession in practice will grow rather slowly. However, specific tasks—specially those sponsored by industrial undertakings, metropolitan cities, and large towns—are being increasingly entrusted to professional planners.

Institutions teaching planning are also taking up professional work with the dual object of providing professional experience to qualified people in the teaching profession and of giving practical experience to students. Such a step has helped to extend the availability of professional people in the country for various jobs and has also brought teaching close to practical field experience.

The prospects for the town planning profession—in view of the tremendous amount of planning and regional development that is being generated by the increasing urbanization and rapid industrialization of modern India—promise to be bright and expanding.

BIBLIOGRAPHY: B. B. Dutt, *Town Planning in Ancient India,* Thacker, Spink & Co., Calcutta, 1925; *Report of the Committee on Environmental Health,* Government of India, Publications Division, New Delhi, 1948; Stuart Piggot, *Prehistoric India,* Pelican Books, Penguin Books, Inc., Baltimore, 1950; Otto H. Koenigsberger, "New Towns of India," *Town Planning Review,* vol. 23, no. 2, July 1952, University of Liverpool, Liverpool, England; *Viśwakarma Vastuśāstram* (with commentary), T. M. S. S. M. Library, Tanjore, India, 1958; Stamp L. Dudley, *Asia: A Regional* and Economic Geography, 10th ed., Methuen & Co., Ltd., London, 1959; K. M. Panikkar, *A Survey of Indian History*, rev. ed., Asia Publishing House, Bombay, 1962; *Town and Country Planning in India*, Town and Country Planning Organization, Government of India, New Delhi, 1962; George B. Cressey, *Asia's Lands and Peoples*, McGraw Hill Book Company, New York, 1963; *Gazetteer of India*, vol. 1, Government of India, Publications Division, New Delhi, 1965; Mortimer Wheeler (ed.), *Splendours of the East, Temples, Tombs, Palaces, and Fortresses of Asia*, Asia Publishing House, Bombay, 1965; *Civilization of the Indus Valley and Beyond*, Thames and Hudson, London, 1966; T. C. K. Reddy, *Study of Historical Towns—Golconda*, School of Planning and Architecture, New Delhi, 1966; P. R. Shrivastava, *Study of Historic Towns—Nalanda*, New Delhi School of Planning and Architecture, New Delhi, 1966; Bijit Ghosh, "Jaisalmer, Urban Form and Pattern of Medieval Town," *Urban and Rural Planning Thought*, vol. 11, no. 1, New Delhi, January 1968; *India, 1968, A Reference Annual*, Government of India, Publications Division, New Delhi, 1968; O. H. K. Spate and A. T. A. Learmonth, *India and Pakistan*, rev. ed., E. P. Dutton & Co., Inc., New York, 1968; Amita Ray, *Villages, Towns and Secular Buildings in Ancient India, C. 150 B.C.—350 A.D.*, (Dirma K. L. Mukhopadhyay), Calcutta.

—C. S. Chandrasekhara

INDONESIA (*See* ASIA, SOUTHEAST, DEVELOPING COUNTRIES.)

INDUSTRIAL EFFLUENTS (*See* ENVIRONMENTAL POLLUTION.)

INDUSTRIAL HOUSING ESTATES The vast movements of population from rural to urban areas during the Industrial Revolution (in Britain between 1750–1850) led to overcrowding and shocking social conditions in rapidly growing towns. Many employers had to provide dwellings for their workers, and in general these were mean back-to-back types huddled together in narrow streets and courts, like those provided by commercial builders and speculators. A number of the more benevolent and imaginative manufacturers, however, built housing schemes of somewhat better quality, in "model villages" for their own employees. Among these the most notable were those of Robert Owen (*q.v.*), Edward Akroyd (at Copley, 1844–1853), Sir Titus Salt (Saltaire, 1853–1863), and the Crossley family (West Hill Park, 1863–1864). Some British railway companies and mining, steel, and iron industries also provided for their workers' housing schemes on better standards than generally prevailed in the early nineteenth century, and their precedent probably inspired the famous fourteen Krupp housing colonies in Germany (1859–1902) and the admirable Goransson steelworks village in Sandviken, Sweden, (about 1860.). Parallel schemes appeared in other European countries; for instance the formally planned housing estate of Charles Godin at Guise in France (about 1850). These were in essence business enterprises ancillary to manufacture; though some which had partially a paternalistic or moralistic character are, in the literature of the subject, classed (mistakenly) with the many "utopian" or communitarian projects of the period (See UTOPIA AND UTOPIAN PLANNING).

Further advances of major planning importance were made in the factory villages of Port Sunlight, near Liverpool (Lord Leverhulme, 1889), Bournville, Birmingham (the Cadbury family, 1895), and New Earswick (the Rowntree family, 1902), all designed by architects and effectively landscaped, with houses and gardens, civic buildings, churches, and a good if modest range of cultural and recreational facilities. These three villages played a considerable part in the modern revolution in housing design and planning layout.

In the United States in the nineteenth and early twentieth centuries many industrial firms provided housing for their workers, and some of these were on the scale of complete towns. Well known among these "one-industry towns" are Gary, Indiana, founded by the U.S. Steel Corporation in 1906; Chicopee, Georgia; Kingsport, Tennessee, with a good plan by John Nolen; Kohler, Wisconsin; Longview, Washington; and Forest Hills Gardens, New York, planned by F. L. Olmstead, Jr., and Grosvenor Atterbury (1911). And tragically famous is Pullman, Illinois, founded on the most imaginative lines by the inventor of the Pullman railroad car. Owing to a great strike and social dissatisfaction this experiment was a failure, and permanently discredited the concept of a single-industry community with a strong element of paternalism.

These experiments, however, influenced modern urban development and planning in many ways, and were partial anticipations of the Garden City or New Towns movement initiated by Ebenezer Howard (*q.q.v.*).

BIBLIOGRAPHY: Budgett Meakin, *Model Factories and Villages*, London, 1905; "Guide to the Workmen's Colonies, Essen, Ruhr," compiled for the Garden Cities and Town Planning Association, London, 1911; "Sixty Years of Planning: The Bournville Experiment," Bournville, 1939; Arnold Whittick, *European Architecture in the Twentieth Century*, vol. 1, Crosby Lockwood, London, 1950; William Ashworth, *Genesis of Modern British Town Planning*, Routledge and Kegan Paul, London, 1954; J. W. Reps, *Making of Urban America*, Princeton University Press, 1965.

FREDERIC J. OSBORN

INDUSTRIAL SITES AND LOCATIONS The choice of a location for an industrial concern—for the first plant, for a branch, or for a relocation—is a kind of rite of passage. Rarely does the same generation of management of a firm have to make this decision more than once; but then the decision becomes a determinant of the future of the business. Locational decisions, therefore, must be carefully and knowledgeably weighted.

The purpose of this discussion is to isolate some of the common elements in choices of industrial location and to frame them in a planning context. The geographical area in which a planner works is not a passive partner in the locational decision. Through its public representatives, it may actively solicit industry to expand job opportunities and promote economic growth. Or, through its private voices, it may seek to ban some or many types of additional industry because its residents feel increased concern for the quality of life and have questioned the traditional definitions of progress.

Types of Locational Decisions The locational decision can occur at three points in the life of an industry: when a new company opens its first plant, when an established company decides to relocate, and when an industry branches to one or more additional locations.

A new plant is usually indigenous to an area; its concept, its management, and its resources develop where the founder lives. It is not the new plant, therefore, but the relocating plant or industrial branches which are significant to this discussion; they are the signs of a viable industry with the economic freedom to make reasoned choices. Locational decisions for new branches and for relocations share many common elements.

Why Do Firms Move?   An industrial firm may move because it is pushed or because it is pulled. Lack of room for expansion may force a plant either to open a branch elsewhere or to move bag and baggage to a new location. The choice of the new site may reflect new directions in the firm or it may simply denote that with growing prosperity the firm can now afford to find a more profitable or economical location. In the latter instance, elements of dissatisfaction with the original site may include the level of taxation, inadequacies in transport systems for goods or employees, deteriorating surroundings, or deficiencies in the local labor force.

On the other hand, the firm may be attracted to a new location by a shift in its markets, by changing requirements for skills or materials, or by the attraction of environmental amenities. The economic lure of the new site may include lower taxes, decreased costs, and the absence of labor unions. If the locational decision applies only to a branch plant, it may be that the branch is a new "face" of the parent company, with different needs from those of the main plant.

What Does a Firm Look for in a Location?   Different firms look for different things in a new or branch location. The weight given to each factor varies depending on the type of industry involved and the kind of people it employs. The most commonly mentioned features of a desirable location include availability of a labor force with appropriate skills and numbers, accessibility of markets or resources, and environmental amenities for the employees of the firm.

Experts on the subject of industrial site location enumerate categories of industry in which different factors weigh more or less heavily in locational decisions. The number of categories varies. Four large, inclusive categories are pertinent.

Distribution and Warehousing   Industrial firms involved in distribution and warehousing are basically market-oriented. They tend to locate near the market for their goods or where the transportation systems make the markets most accessible at the least cost. They also require proximity to an appropriate labor supply; therefore, as clean industries, they may locate in industrial parks in or near large metropolitan areas. They are not incompatible with residential and commercial development.

Heavy Manufacturing   Heavy industry, such as the manufacture of steel or cement, tends to be resource-oriented. Its locations are near the cheapest source of supply of raw materials. Because of the demand for labor, such industry must be near people; but because of its nature, it cannot be too near residential development. Good public transportation and highways become important in attracting and holding a labor force; but residential areas, with their necessary schools and services, must also be acceptable in quality and be located at not too great a commuting distance from the plant.

Light Manufacturing   Light manufacturing often specializes in more sophisticated products, such as electronic components. It requires skilled labor, often of a highly educated and salaried professional type. Accessible markets are important in the locational decision, but management must also consider the ability of the chosen area to satisfy and hold a mobile staff. The amenities of the surrounding environment in terms of housing, schools, leisure activities, open space, and clean air become important in the decision-making process.

"Footloose" Industry   Some industries are big enough or specialized enough to be independent of their markets. Some of the large electronic data processing and research and development organizations are of this type. Because of their independence, they can create their own environments by choosing a new location for the desirability of its setting. Locations away from congested metropolitan areas, with environmental amenities and aesthetic attractions, can be the key to holding the operating necessity of these industries: their highly educated and independent professionals.

The Impact of Locational Decisions   The area in which a plant or branch plant is located absorbs the impact of the locational decision, which may be desirable economic growth—or increased air, water, and noise pollution, congestion, and unsightliness.

Economic growth is generated first by the construction of the new plant; then by the increased business to local suppliers of goods and services; and finally by the increased number and diversity of suppliers of goods and services in the market area. The growth of the size and number of businesses attracts an influx of population, which in turn expands the labor pool. In the course of time, the introduction of one or more significant new plants into an area can change the economic structure and environment of an area by enlarging the labor pool, catalyzing diversification of local business and industry, and providing opportunities for entrepreneurs to initiate plants in the local economy, thereby enhancing the attractiveness of the area to new industry and to labor.

The Planner's Perspective   To a certain point, industrial growth and new formations in an economy are a catalyst to progress of a desirable kind. However, as the growth takes hold, new demands are made on housing, on public services, and on the land and resources of the area. To prevent unchecked and undisciplined growth, which may tend toward environmental catastrophe, the planner in a developing area must begin as early as possible to survey the directions of growth and to attempt to channel it as seems most desirable for the area.

This kind of planning is usually regional in nature; industrial growth is rarely confined for long by political boundaries. The planning is more than purely economic; it involves the use of the land and space and also, therefore, the local public concept of what the landscape of its life is to be. This in turn requires the establishment of controls over the use of land through such mechanisms as zoning (preferably in the context of regional master plans.) On the economic side, it involves planning for healthy diversity and stability in the economic base.

Planning must take into account the increasingly vocal position that economic and industrial growth, in and of itself, is not necessarily progress. This counters the traditional western view of progress and national purpose. Isolated counties and cities, however, now believe that if the price of industrial growth is the disappearance of open space, the pollution of the air and water, and population congestion, it is too high. They demand a stabilization of industry at a level to support what they consider to be the optimum level of population, thus allowing local governments to concentrate on improving the services and amenities offered to just the number of residents that housing, public, and natural resources can comfortably support.

Progress has always been measured largely in numbers. Many planners desire that in the future it will be measured not by the calculator or the census enumerator but by the quality of life that the area's residents enjoy. As this attitude takes hold, it will introduce new considerations into the process of making locational decisions. These will include such questions whether the locality is receptive to a given type of industry; whether the industry can offer the area something positive in terms of growth; and whether management is willing to make concessions to the standards set by the residents of the area for the development of their environment.

—JOHN W. McMAHAN

INDUSTRY, DISTRIBUTION OF The reasons for the distribution of industry are multifarious, complex, and constantly changing, but they are obviously very important to the planner in their economic, social, and geographical connotations. No more than a brief summary of the reasons can be attempted here, but sources of fuller information are indicated in the bibliography.

At the beginning of modern industrial expansion, in the early years of the industrial revolution in the late eighteenth century, the bulk of industry was located near the sources of raw materials and power. Power at that time was mainly water power, so that industries were often sited near rivers. With the change to steam power and the introduction of more and larger machinery, industries developed near the coal fields, which resulted in considerable industrial concentrations in these regions. This was particularly the case before railway transport had been developed. Once rail transport became available, industry tended to be more widely distributed. This can be seen by considering the industrial concentration in Great Britain before the advent of railways as contrasted with the more widely spread industrial development in northwestern Europe—in northern France, Belgium, The Netherlands, and Germany—which arose mainly after the development of rail transport.

Good transport is a vital and increasingly powerful factor in the location of industry because it not only brings raw materials and fuel to the place of manufacture and generation of power but also carries the manufactured goods to the markets. Concentrations of industry from what are called "natural causes" continue for man-made or artificial reasons. Industry located near the raw material and source of fuel draws labor to these centers, frequently from surrounding rural areas, a process that began in the eighteenth century and has continued increasingly throughout the world ever since. Increases in population resulting from industrial concentration create pools of labor as well as markets, and they thus beget other industries in the area. These other industries are often thus located because of their relation to kindred industries in the area—making further components for finished products or supplying machinery or equipment to existing industries. These influences operate in addition to those of the availability of labor and proximity to markets in the concentration. The main reasons for the location of industry could be broadly summarized as:

1. Proximity of raw materials for the manufactured goods
2. Proximity of the sources of power—water and coal
3. Availability of good transport
4. Proximity to markets, or, in the case of exports, to other countries; proximity to means of access to markets, like sea and river ports and airports
5. Availability of labor, including pools of skilled labor which would attract industries where such skills could be employed
6. Proximity to other related or linked industries
7. Fortuitous reasons
8. Diversification of industry in the interests of stable employment
9. By dispersal to secure a socially, economically, and strategically satisfactory distribution of population

In the case of (1), proximity to raw materials, this has been a less and less decisive factor with the improvement of all forms of transport, particularly road and rail. A determining factor as suggested by Alfred Weber (see bibliography) is the proportion of the cost of raw material in the ultimate cost of the finished product. If it is large, as in the case of bricks, then there are economic advantages to locating the manufacture as near as possible to the source of the raw material. If it is small, as in the case of watches, then the proportionate cost of the principal raw material is so little as to allow the location to be determined by other factors. Thus plants manufacturing bricks (made of cement using lime, clay, and sand) or synthetic boards (using timber) are generally located near the sources of the raw materials.

In the case of (2), the generation of power has changed from the direct use of coal and coke to electricity and gas, which gives flexibility in the location of industry; while in the case of power stations using coal it is obviously necessary to transport the fuel to the power station sited in its area of electricity distribution. Nuclear power stations, on the other hand, must be sited where large quantities of water are available, generally near the seacoast.

There are, of course, numerous fortuitous reasons such as climate and the amenities and recreational facilities of one area compared with another; some of these may occasionally be trivial.

The first seven reasons result very much from the natural course of events and the last two are measures of government control, introduced in the interest of the welfare of a community. The aim of diversification of industry in a particular area, as in an industrial estate forming part of a new town or community, is to stabilize employment, so that if one industry suffers a decline there will be other industries, some perhaps expanding in the same area, in which the workers can seek employment.

The last reason, (9), comes into play when government endeavors to introduce some measure of inducement by financial assistance and some degree of control in the location of industry in the interests of a satisfactory distribution of population. At the time of the great economic depression of the early thirties there was, in several countries, a migration of workers from the more severely depressed industrial areas to the areas that were less seriously affected. Thus the various governments embarked on a policy of supporting the revival of the depressed industrial areas.

In 1964, McGraw-Hill conducted a plant site survey in which 2,000 firms participated. The firms were asked which of 30 considerations would be of importance in selecting an area or site for their new plant. The greatest number (76 percent) gave trucking as important. Other important considerations were reasonable cost of property (67 percent), reasonable or low taxes (65 percent), ample area for expansion (63 percent), favorable labor climate (62 percent), nearness to existing sales area (56 percent), favorable climate for personnel (50 percent), availability of labor skills (48 percent), access to utilities (43 percent), and near source of raw materials (42 percent). Pleasant living conditions were of some importance (39 percent), as were educational facilities (32 percent) and recreational and cultural facilities (25 percent). The replies would, of course, be conditioned by the types of goods manufactured. If these were heavy, bulky goods, there would be a major interest in transport such as rail (35 percent); and if a good proportion of specialist skilled labor and professional personnel were involved, educational and recreational facilities would be important. Fortuitous reasons, although not listed, were apparent in the survey. A company president requested data on the pollen count, as his wife suffered from hay fever. When that was obtained, the projected relocation was canceled.

At the beginning of the industrial revolution, the location of industry was determined by natural factors and limitations of transport, which were restricting factors. In the mid-twentieth century the majority of industries can be located in a wide variety of places without serious detriment to their interests. This allows governments to apply inducements and controls in the interests of the people as a whole. The impression that in the nineteenth century people existed chiefly for the sake of industrial prosperity is certainly supported by the history of that period. Enlightened governments in the mid-twentieth century, however, are moving toward the view that industry exists for the people as a whole, and where and how people live is a major consideration. Wide choice in the location of most industries makes possible a more planned distribution in the interests of a community.

BIBLIOGRAPHY: Alfred Weber, *Uber den Standort der Industrien,* Berlin, 1909, tr. by C. J. Friedrich as *Theory of the Location of Industries,* Chicago, 1929; Montague Barlow, chairman, *Report of the Royal Commission on the Distribution of the Industrial Population,* H.M.S.O., London, 1939; Edgar M. Hoover, *The Location of Economic Activity,* McGraw-Hill Book Company, New York, 1948; N. J. G. Pounds, *An Introduction to Economic Geography,* John Murray (Publishers), Ltd., London, 1970; R. C. Estall and R. Ogilvie Buchanan, *Industrial Activity and Economic Geography,* Hutchinson Publishing Group, Ltd., London, 1961; Richard S. Thoman, *The Geography of Economic Activity,* McGraw-Hill Book Company, New York, 1962; T. E. McMillan, "Why Manufacturers Choose Plant Locations vs. Determinants of Plant Location," *Land Economics,* vol. 41, no. 3, 1965, based on The McGraw-Hill Plant Site Survey, 1964.

—ARNOLD WHITTICK

INFRASTRUCTURE   A term, widely used in planning, denoting the services and facilities which are an integral part of the life of an urban community. In a healthy urban community such an infrastructure is geared to expanding economic and social life. It comprehends transport facilities and communications, power, shopping facilities, housing, schools, and recreational facilities.

IFHP: INTERNATIONAL FEDERATION FOR HOUSING AND PLANNING   Founded in 1913 as the International Garden Cities and Town Planning Association by the British association of the same name, the federation has taken a leading part in the advocacy of better housing and of town and regional planning through world congresses and regional conferences in many countries. It maintains active contacts with governmental, professional, and public-interest organizations in at least 65 countries and is financed by subscriptions of corporate and individual members and grants from a number of national and city governments. It has "consultative status" with the United Nations Economic and Social Council (ECOSOC) and the World Health Organization (WHO), maintains specialist standing committees on various aspects of housing and planning, and issues important *Congress Reports* and a periodical *Bulletin.* Address: Wassenaarseweg 43, The Hague, Netherlands.

INTERNATIONAL STYLE   (*See* MOVEMENTS AND THEORIES OF MODERN ARCHITECTURAL DESIGN.)

IRAN

Legislation and Administration   The town planning legislation of Iran consists mainly of the Municipal Act of 1955 with its 1965 amendments and the Urban Renewal Act of 1968.

The Municipal Act presents in detail the general setup with regard to the duties and election of mayors and the organization of municipal councils and municipalities. It also provides regulations for new development, slum clearance, development control, and a number of town planning recommendations. All development within towns must adhere to the guidelines set by the master plans. These must be prepared by either the municipal technical bureaus or recognized consultants. The municipal bureaus must prepare and implement the necessary bylaws to be approved by the municipal councils. They must issue building permits, and they may serve notice and expropriate or demolish property in accordance with the law and subject to the approval of the municipal council.

Urban renewal corporations are run on commercial lines by the municipalities for buying, selling, and rebuilding according to plans which must have the prior approval of the municipal council and the Ministry of Interior.

The Urban Renewal Act sets out, in detail, methods of compensation and betterment, land-use control, and the control of height and facade of buildings. Its main object, however, is the levying of 0.5 percent tax on all property to be used solely for town improvement schemes and urban renewal projects, and the definition of methods of expropriating land and property for development purposes.

The land value is based on a price established for each zone, and the building value is determined by qualified appraisers in accordance with a number of guidelines. These values are revised every 5 years.

The Town and Country Department of the Plan Organization of Iran has up to now supplied the funds and initiated the programs for the preparation of master plans and regional plans.

The plans are usually prepared by private firms of recognized plan organization consultants under special contracts. A number of regional plans, master plans for all major cities, and plans for some minor towns have already been prepared in this way.

These plans are submitted to the Technical Committee of the High Planning Council which is responsible for the coordination and approval of all the country's town planning schemes, including regional plans, master plans, urban renewals, housing, and other development projects. The final decisions and sanctions are made at the ministerial level. The Ministers represented on the High Planning Council are the Ministers of Development and Housing, Interior, Economy, Health, Education, Culture and Arts, Water and Power, and War; others not on the ministerial level include the heads of the Plan and Tourist Organizations, the mayor of Teheran, the head of Teheran University Social Research Institute, and the deputy to the Minister of Justice.

After the final sanction of the High Planning Council, the approved plans are submitted to the Ministry of Interior to send to the appropriate municipal councils for local approval, after which they are ready to be implemented by the technical bureaus of the municipalities. The technical bureaus are responsible for planning control, building permits, and the day-to-day technical problems of the towns.

Professional Practice A professional town planner in Iran has three essential choices: private practice, employment in private practice, or employment in any of the government bodies concerned with planning.

The government bodies concerned in some way with city planning include the technical departments of the Ministries of Interior and of Development and Housing, the Technical Committee of the High Planning Council, the

Town and Country Department of the Plan Organization, and the municipal technical bureaus. The profession of town planner in Iran is not yet officially dissociated from that of architect or engineer.

Education and Training   The only school of town planning in Iran is a department of the Faculty of Fine Arts of Teheran University School of Architecture, which provides an extension in town planning to the course in architecture. This department was founded in 1965, and it offers the equivalent of a Ph.D. in civic design after a 3-year course which includes a thesis.

There are no town planning institutions in Iran.

Geographical and Climatic Conditions   Iran has an area of about 618,000 square miles (1,600,000 square kilometers). It lies between 25 and 40 degrees north latitude and 44 and 64 degrees east longitude. Consequently it experiences vast climatic differences which are due partly to its geographical position and partly to its varied topography.

Iran can be divided into four major geographic-planning regions:

1. The Elburz and Zagros mountain ranges, in the form of a reversed U
2. A high plateau within the U
3. The low-lying plain of Khuzistan
4. The Caspian Sea coast, which is below sea level in many parts

Over 50 percent of the total land surface of Iran is mountainous and rough. Some of the factors that determine the major climatic conditions of the country are the Caucasus Mountains on the northern border and the Persian Gulf and the Sea of Oman at the southern boundaries. Apart from the Caspian coast with annual rainfall ranging between 39 and 79 inches (1,000 and 2,000 millimeters), the major portion of the country is arid or semiarid. On the plateau, the average annual rainfall may be as little as $4\frac{3}{4}$ inches (120 millimeters). Snow is common at heights above 4,300 feet (1,300 meters).

Vegetation varies according to climate and soil cover, ranging from the conifers of the Caspian coast highlands to the palm trees of the oasis on the Khuzistan plain in the south. In these major geographical and climatic sections, there are great variations in geology, soil cover, vegetation, and microclimate. These geographical and climatic factors have influenced the inhabitants' way of life throughout the ages: their dwellings, their clothes, and their staple foods, which change from one region to another.

The above variations, plus the influence of a number of industrial and economic factors, have resulted in an extremely uneven distribution of population.

Teheran and its immediate surroundings contain over 3 million of the total 30 million population. The city's growth is estimated at about 7 percent annually. The rest of Iran's population is spread over a vast surface, and well over two-thirds of the country is unpopulated. The population density is highest in the western provinces bordering the Caspian Sea and in the central province (because of the heavy concentration of population in Teheran). The average density for this central province is 52 to 65 persons per square mile (20 to 25 persons per square kilometer). The least densely populated provinces are those within or around the vast deserts of east, southeast, and central Iran. The average density in these areas falls below 13 persons per square mile (5 persons per square kilometer). Densities of even less than 3 persons per square mile (1 person per square kilometer) are found in the areas around Na'in and Tabbas.

According to the 1966 national census, Teheran has the highest population density of 630 persons per square mile (243 per square kilometer), followed by Bandar Pahlevi, 536 (207); Abadan, 443 (171); and Khorramshahr, 414 (160). Even the highest population densities in Iran fall well below high densities in other parts of the world. The size of the cities, towns, villages, and smaller settlements varies from 10 cities of more than 100,000 population to nearly 2,000 settlements with populations of less than 10,000 persons.

The average size of household in Iran is approximately 4.4 persons. The households in northern and western Iran, where living conditions are better, tend to be slightly above the national average; while in eastern Iran the size of households averages between 3.9 and 4 persons. Apart from the Teheran province, all other provinces have a much greater rural than urban population.

The above factors combined with some other national and local matters have given rise to vast differences in size, character, and layout of different cities of Iran.

Traditions of Planning to the End of the Nineteenth Century   It is maintained by some that the Caspians of northern Iran, the land of the Aryans, were the first agriculturalists. This is important in view of the fact that it was cultivation alone which allowed the wandering nomads to settle and to multiply to the point where the formation of communities and towns became possible. Some historians believe that the fertile river valleys were the original birthplace of agriculture; this appears unlikely because of the artificial irrigation needed in those regions. It is more likely that the upland farming areas, with an extensive variety of natural vegetation due to favorable soil and climatic conditions, were the cradles of the first agriculturalists. It can be reasonably assumed that agriculture was discovered long before 5000 B.C. on the Caspian highlands, and that from there it began to spread to the surrounding alluvial plains of Mesopotamia and the Indus.

The view that the Caspians were the original metallurgists as well as the first agriculturalists is supported by the wealth of metal objects distributed throughout the Bronze Age (3000 B.C. to the first millenium), and it is important when considering that the gradual change from village to town life came about from the beginnings of the Copper Age. Thus, an outline of changes from the Stone Age to the Iron Age and the important step from village to urban life first found in Man, the "Minni" of the Bible, can be traced.

Even at the end of the Neolithic period a sedentary population was living in large villages in southern Iran; the marking of property by sealing was known long before the discovery of script in Sumer; and sea trade as far away as the Mediterranean and the Indian Ocean led to the development of famous ports, such as Magan on the Persian Gulf, as far back as 3000 B.C.

Whereas at the end of the Stone Age and in the early Copper Age the highland cultures were further advanced than those of the plains, the relation was reversed at the end of the Copper Age. The important step from the village to real city life had been taken during the fourth millennium.

With the Aryan immigration from the highlands to the plains came great changes in Iranian history. Although most of the plateau had remained at the village-life stage, except in Man and later Atropatene, ever since the Stone Age, with the immigration came large, highly sophisticated, and carefully planned cities: first Ecbatana; then Pasargadae and Persepolis; then Rhagae, near Teheran; Tausa, near Mashad; and others. Thus not only had civilization brought a major change by introducing city life but, within a short period of some 150 years, an empire was established which under Cyrus and Darius comprised the whole of the civilized world, marking the beginnings of administration and planning on regional and global scales.

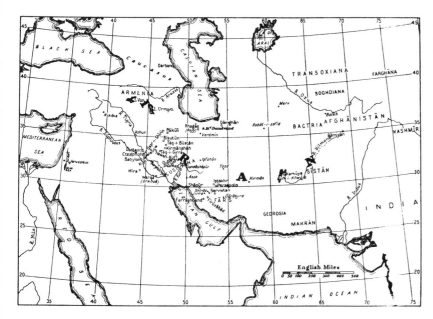

Map of Iran at the time of the Sassanian Empire (241–628 A.D.).(A Survey of Persian Art.)

The cities of Iran, even from ancient times, took a variety of forms. The outer limits and the centers of the old Iranian cities, however, were always well defined. The outer limits consisted of fortifications and the center was marked either by a fortress or an open square with the major buildings situated around it. While the gathering of communities within a fortification goes back to prehistoric times in Iran, the town with an open square as its focal point appears at least as far back as the Parthian period.

Where the focal point of the city was the square, that square usually contained the Friday mosque, the bazaar, and the palace of the king (if a capital) or the governor's residence (if a provincial town). Other features included a caravansary, bathhouse, hostel, prison, pavilion, and even very high view towers whenever the city had a particularly impressive surrounding countryside.

The defensive walls were very often surrounded with a large, deep moat; and the entrance to the city was approached across viaducts with single, double, or even triple rows of arches, a typical architectural feature already established at the Parthian period. The citadel was often surrounded by its own walls, then by the city, and finally by the city's surrounding walls. When population increased, there was an overspill that clustered around the outer walls for protection, thus creating a kind of suburb. The houses were usually very closely built for defense purposes and did not always follow a logical plan; they were often eventually made part of the city.

The garden wall was and still is a major feature of Iranian towns. These walls were built not only for defensive purposes but also for the sake of privacy, which plays an important role in those major portions of Iran where people live, eat, receive guests, swim, and even sleep out of doors for about 6 months of the year.

Beyond the city walls there were often extensive plantations, not only supplying the cities with fresh fruit, vegetables, and staple food but also acting as a greenbelt. In the dry, rainless climate of Iran, these greenbelts required artificial irrigation and thus the siting of the towns was an important factor. Many of them were situated at the foothills of the mountains in order to take advantage of the running streams which were often brought into cities by means of *ghanats* or underground canals in order to prevent evaporation and water contamination.

Gardens have always played an important role in city planning, and the plan forms of the famous Persian gardens, which have very ancient origins, are the forerunners of the formal gardens of Europe. They have also influenced the city plans which were often laid out in the garden form of Chahar-Bagh or the four quadrants. The culmination of these "garden cities" were Samarkand and Isfahan of the Shah Abbas period.

The first city of Iran, Istakhr, is accredited by legendary history to Gayumarth, the original King of Iran. The earliest known prehistoric settlement of the plateau was discovered at the site where this city is said to have stood.

Four major plan types have dominated the city plans of Iran throughout history: the circular, the rectangular, the elongated cross, and, very much later, the open-plan form. Although the Greeks set out their towns geometrically, the idea of circular towns appears to have an Iranian origin. Towns older than those of the Median period in Azerbaijan and Elam are represented in Assyrian sculptures with one or more battlements crenellated and closely set with towers. The gates to many of these were staggered to make a tortuous entry in time of siege.

Round cities with single or double fortifications are known from the

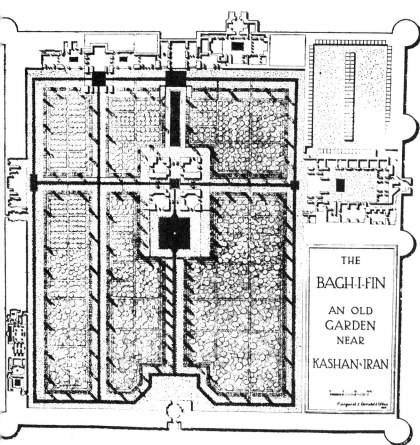

THE
BAGH·I·FIN
AN OLD
GARDEN
NEAR
KASHAN·IRAN

Kashan, Bagh-i-Fin—plan (1799–1834 A.D.). (Donald N. Wilber, Persian Gardens and Garden Pavilions.)

Parthian period, the most interesting being the city of Darabjird where the battlements and the moat form an exact circle and the diameter of the citadel is equal to the radius to the outer wall. The existence of eight evenly spread gates probably suggests a radial street layout. It is possible that the circular city plans of the Parthians were originally taken from circular encampments common in the ancient East, and it is quite probable that these plans were the protoypes of Mansur's famous "Round City" of Baghdad.

Ghazvin's ancient circular walls are attributed to Harun-al-Rashid. But perhaps the perfect example of the concentric "four quadrant" plan is that of Herat. Its plan was interesting in that the central square was the shopping and commercial center, and this was connected to the city gates by two rows of shops, thus creating a commercial core in the form of a cross with four great avenues of shops. Each quarter or neighborhood had its own similar but smaller marketplace and avenues of shops.

The city of Balkh originally had three concentric walls which must have been very ancient. Concentric cities continued to be common throughout the Middle Ages, and a town to one side of the earlier Isfahan had three concentric walls in the late Middle Ages. The circular road or the *ringstrasse* was a common feature of many of the circular towns.

General view of Imperial Shah Square, Isfahan.

The Sassanian principles of city planning probably followed those of the Parthians. Oval or circular plans continued as well as the square and the rectangular. Nishapur was laid out, apparently by Shapur I, in a checkerboard with 16 divisions. Isfahan of the tenth and fourteenth centuries was later laid out in similar forms.

The Sassanians sometimes laid out their cities in the form of an animal or other object. Shushtar was originally laid out by Ardeshir in the form of a horse.

The elongated-cross plan was often formed by a large avenue which connected the palace to the main congregational mosque. This avenue with its line of shops and long vistas became the focal point of the city and is well exemplified by Qazvin of the twelfth century.

As security increased and the need for defense diminished, the open garden-city plan began to develop, and its culmination was Tabriz of the fifteenth century and Isfahan as reconstructed by Shah Abbas. The city created by Shah Abbas was especially laid out in the open fields to the south of the then-existing Isfahan in order not to be hampered by existing development.

The huge Imperial Shah Square was the focus of the whole layout with the Royal Pavilion, two magnificent mosques, and the bazaar on it. From the southeast corner ran a continuous covered street which crossed the river Zayand by the famous Khajou bridge. Another covered street went from the northeast corner of the square through the vast bazaar and its complex of caravansaries, hostels, mosques, and schools all the way to the city gate. Thus, people and horsemen could travel from one side of the city to the other under cover.

West of the Imperial Square was the majestic avenue of Chahar-Bagh, constructed with its separate lanes for pedestrian and vehicular traffic and lined with magnificent plane trees, water channels, fountains, pools, and jasmins. On either side of this prodigious thoroughfare were the houses of the nobility and the ministerial palaces, all set back a considerable distance and landscaped with formal gardens.

The grouping of buildings, or civic planning, played a major role in Iran throughout its history. Persepolis was neither a capital nor a simple palace but an outstanding Achaemenid civic center. A huge raised terrace served as the base to the successive structures which were approached by wide, shallow steps which could be used by both men and horses. The relationship of the various buildings at right angles to one another, their varying levels, different heights, and spatial relationships remain an outstanding example of civic layout to this day.

One of the most outstanding works of civic design in the world is undoubtedly the complex of buildings which constitute the Shrine of Imam Reza in the city center of Mashad. The biggest center of pilgrimage for the Shi'ite sect of Islam, it has had a continuous development from about the ninth century.

A series of mosques, caravansaries, bazaars, oratories, schools, libraries, museums, and a series of interconnected squares make this complex, one of the finest and most colorful pieces of civic design in the world. A broad avenue built by Shah Abbas I makes an impressive entrance to the huge old square of the shrine, thus the main entrance to the shrine is placed at right angles to this, and this famous esplanade, which had a running stream in the middle, connected the shrine buildings to the two main gates of the town.

Neighborhood planning and the segregation of different trades and shops has been an ancient custom in Iran. Susa had its distinct zones: the Acropolis, the Apadana, the Royal, and the Artisan. Ardabil of the tenth century was divided into neighborhoods with their own shopping and civic facilities.

It has been for long a tradition in bazaars to have the different trades separated and each section of the bazaar named after the product which is sold; the coppersmiths' bazaar, the ironsmiths' bazaar, or the shoemakers' bazaar are only a few examples of the different departments of a bazaar complex. Another important and ancient feature of Iranian cities is the

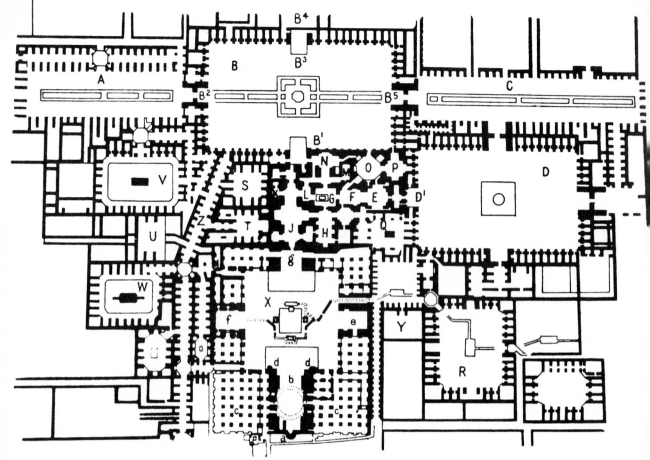

A. Bālā Khiyābān (Upper Esplanade).
B. Ṣaḥn-i-Kuhna (the Old Court).
B1. The gold īvān (Īvān-i-Ṭalā) of 'Alī Shīr Nawā'ī (now called the Īvān-i-Ṭalā-i-Nādirī).
B2. Entrance from Upper Esplanade of Shāh 'Abbās I.
B3. Īvān of Shāh 'Abbās II.
B4. Minaret of Shāh Ṭahmāsp.
B5. Entrance from Lower Esplanade.
C. Pā'īn Khiyābān (Lower Esplanade).
D. Ṣaḥn-i-Naw (the New Court).
D1. The gold īvān of Fatḥ 'Alī Shāh.
E. Dār as-Sa'āda (Chamber of Felicity).
F. Dome chamber of Ḥātim Khān.

G. Ẓariḥ-i-Ḥaẓrat (the Tomb Chamber).
H. Dār al-Ḥuffāẓ (Chamber of the Guardians).
J. Dār as-Siyāda (Chamber of the Nobility).
K. Bālā-Sar (Above the Head (a)).
L. Bālā-Sar (Above the Head (b)).
M. Mosque of the Ladies.
N. Tawḥīd Khāna (Chamber of Mono-theism).
O. Dome chamber of Allāhverdī Khān.
P. Dār aẓ-Ẓiyāfa (Chamber of Hospitality).
Q. Madrasa of 'Alī Naqī Mīrzā.
R. Madrasa-i-Pā'īn-i-Pā (Madrasa Below the Feet).
S. Madrasa-i-Bālā-Sar (Madrasa Above the Head).

T. Madrasa-i-Parīzād.
U. Madrasa Do-Dar (Madrasa of Tw Doors).
V. Caravanserai Vazīr-i-Niẓām.
W. Caravanserai Nāsirī.
X. Masjid-i-Gawhar Shād.
    a. Miḥrāb.
    b. Sanctuary īvān (Īvān-i-maqṣūra).
    c. Oratory (Shabistān).
    d. Minaret.
    e. Īvān of Ḥājjī Hasan.
    f. The water īvān (Īvān-i-āb).
    g. Īvān of the Nobility (Īvān-as-Siyāda).

Scale of Metres
0 10 20 30 40 50

interrelationship between the mosque, bazaar, bath house, school, caravansary, and the highly sophisticated planning features of each in relation to one another.

Iran's contribution to city planning has been extensive and varied from prehistoric times to the nineteenth century. Many of the West's twentieth-century city planning ideas can be traced back to Eastern origins.

Twentieth-century Planning

New Towns and Communities The biggest and the most important of the twentieth-century towns is the industrial town of Abadan with a population

ABOVE: *Mashad, Shrine of Imam Reza—plan.* OPPOSITE, ABOVE: *Plan of the modern industrial town of Abadan built in connection with the large oil refinery.* OPPOSITE: *Aerial view of Abadan showing the palm trees, some of the housing with the tank farm, and the oil refinery in the distance.*

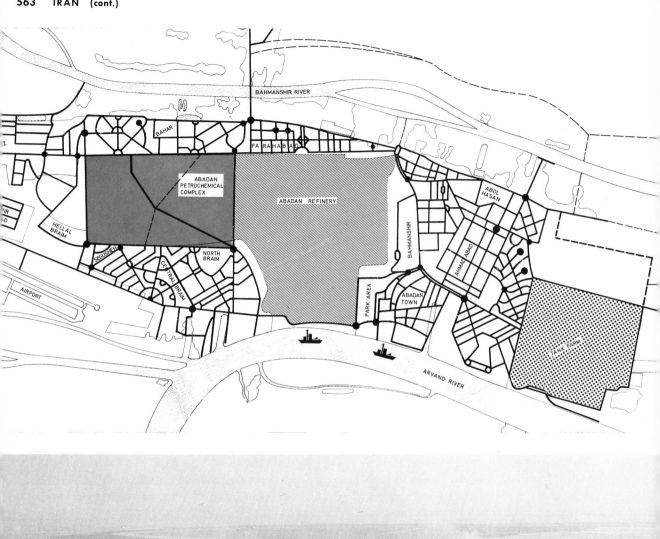

of 300,000. It was designed to serve the huge oil refinery and the oil exporting facilities in the early decades of the century. It is laid out as a garden city. The overall relationship of the vertical elements of the refinery and the new petrochemical plants, with the low-lying, flat development around them, surrounded on two sides with rivers and palm groves, is quite impressive.

The most important new town under construction is the steel mill satellite town near Isfahan with an eventual population of 300,000. Another projected town is a satellite of Arak to serve the new aluminium industry. Some small communities have been built in southern Iran to serve the highly automated exporting ports and the petrochemical industries.

The general trend in recent years has been toward the dispersal of mining and industry in order to discourage concentration of population in Teheran and the revitalization of other cities.

Urban Renewal   There are three important urban renewal projects. Two of these are in Teheran and include a new city center and the rebuilding of an old neighborhood near the bazaar.

Model of Steel Mill satellite town near Isfahan. It shows an axial central core of offices with housing on either side.

The most important urban renewal, however, was designed by Dariush Borbor for the historic city center of Mashad. This follows a traditional idea of circular planning and includes a multilevel development for the whole of the area surrounding the shrine buildings. When completed, this project will turn Mashad into the most interesting of Islamic religious and pilgrimage centers.

BIBLIOGRAPHY: G. Le Strange, *The Lands of Eastern Caliphate,* Cambridge, 1930; E. Beaudouin, "Ispahan sous les Grands Chahs, XVIIᵉ Siècle," *Urbanisme,* vol. 2, pp. 8–48, Paris, 1933; E. Herzfeld, *Archaeological History of Iran,* London, 1935; A. Pope and P. Ackerman (eds.), *A Survey of Persian Art,* vols. I, II, III, Oxford, 1964; D. Borbor, "The Influence of Persian Gardens on Islamic Decoration," *Architecture Forms and Functions,* no. 14, pp. 84–91, Lausanne, 1968.

—DARIUSH BORBOR

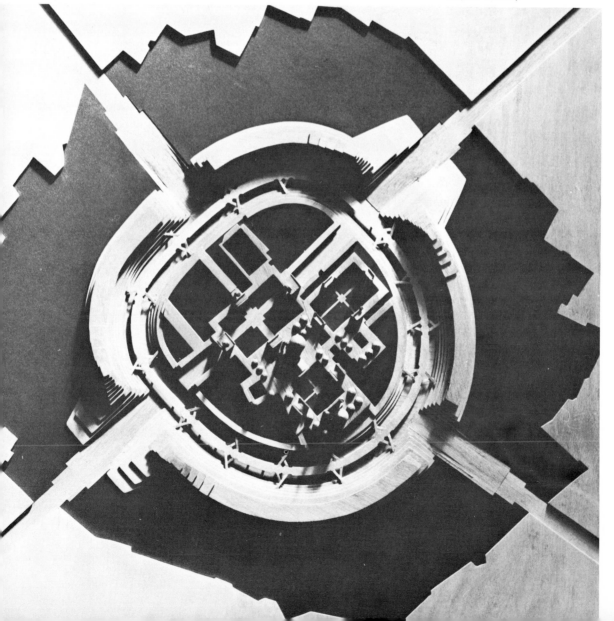

Approved model of the reconstruction of Mashad City Center. The shrine buildings are seen in the middle. There is a green area between the proposed buildings and the rest of the city. Air view. (Architect and Planner: Dariush Borbor.)

Reconstruction of Mashad City Center.
(Architect and Planner: Dariush Borbor)
ABOVE: *Ground level view of model.*   BELOW:
Vertical section through building complex.
RIGHT: *Air view of model.*

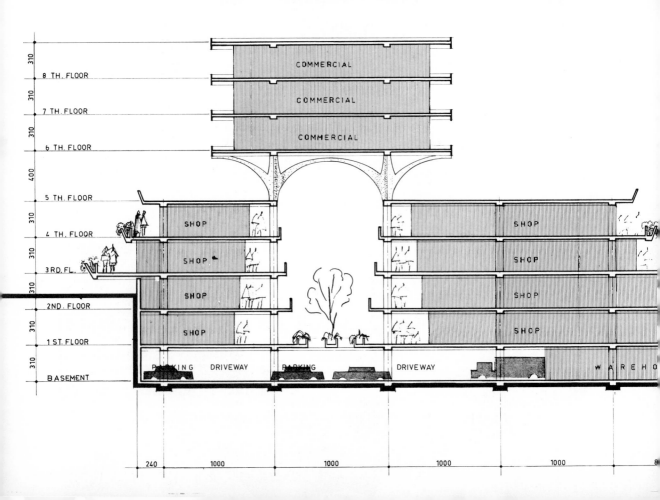

8 TH. FLOOR	COMMERCIAL
7 TH. FLOOR	COMMERCIAL
6 TH. FLOOR	COMMERCIAL
5 TH. FLOOR	
4 TH. FLOOR	SHOP
3RD. FL.	SHOP
2ND. FLOOR	SHOP
1 ST. FLOOR	SHOP
BASEMENT	PARKING DRIVEWAY PARKING DRIVEWAY WAREHO

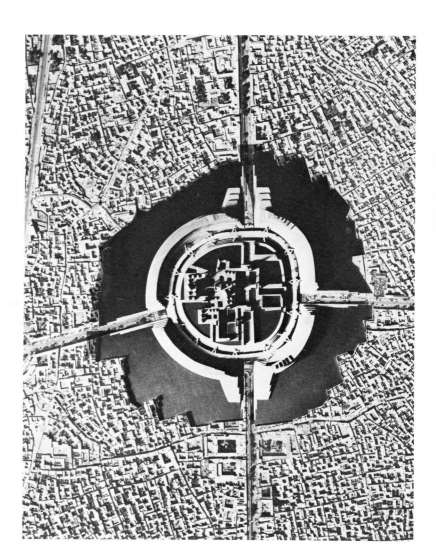

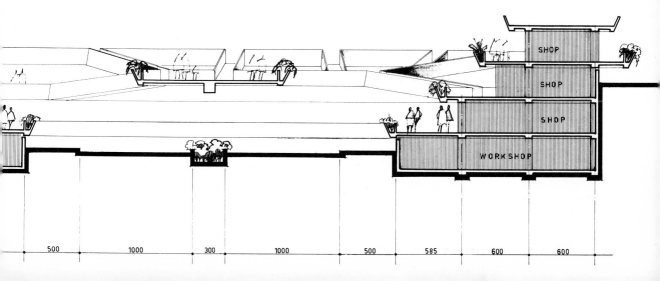

| SHOP |
| SHOP |
| SHOP |
| WORKSHOP |

500   1000   300   1000   500   585   600   600

IRELAND Situated in the northwest of the continent of Europe, between $51\frac{1}{2}$ and $55\frac{1}{2}$ degrees north latitude and $5\frac{1}{2}$ and 10 degrees west longitude, this island has a total area of 32,595 square miles (84,421 square kilometers). The part under the jurisdiction of the government of the Republic of Ireland, comprising 26 out of a total of 32 counties, is 27,136 square miles (70,282 square kilometers). The population of the whole of Ireland in 1966 was 4,368,772 and that of the Republic of Ireland just under 3 million.

Legislation and Administration The Local Government (Planning and Development) Act, 1963, controls the main planning legislation in Ireland. Previously there was an act known as the Town and Regional Planning Act, 1934, which was amended in 1939. These older acts proved cumbersome and restrictive and failed to stimulate positive planning. The only scheme of planning in accordance with the 1934 act was made by Dublin Corporation in 1957.

In the early part of the 1960s it became apparent that a new approach to physical planning was required to meet the conditions which were emerging. The government had embarked on comprehensive economic programming at the national level. This, in turn, called for large-scale expansion in industry and tourism and for intensified investment in the building and construction fields. The growth of traffic made it obligatory to call for improved communications. There was also the question of obsolescence and congestion in larger urban areas and inadequate means of dealing with it on a comprehensive basis. There was a demand for more building land and services to keep pace with the industrial and housing programs in the larger urban areas. In the rural areas tourism was bringing economic opportunity and planning problems, thus bringing to light conflict of needs between development and conservation in regard to land use.

From these considerations sprang the need for a planning system which would enable decisions, both in the public and private sectors, to be correlated with the most effective use of limited capital resources.

The government, when publishing in 1964 its second program for economic expansion, included a statement of physical planning policy. Three specific objectives were emphasized:

1. Renewal and redevelopment in towns and cities
2. The identification of economic and social growth
3. The preservation and development of amenities

The program also provided that all major development would be carried out within a comprehensive physical planning framework.

The Local Government (Planning and Development) Act, 1963, which came into force on October 1, 1964, provided the necessary legislation to deal with the physical planning aspects of major development. The planning authorities were given three years from October, 1964, to prepare draft development plans for their areas. The first development plans under this act constitute the framework at county and town level. They contain policy statements for the use and development of land and for the creation of new conditions which would be an incentive to private enterprise. For example, the technical background of the plan for the city of Dublin and its surrounding areas is contained in a series of subject studies covering many facets of life in Dublin city and surrounding areas. These studies are not part of the plan but contain a summary of conclusions indicating problems facing the planning authorities. These problems relate to deficiencies in the current situation and to those emerging problems which will have to be faced over the next 20 years or more. It is toward their solution that policies must be adopted by the planning authority; hence these policies are related to actual and emerging situations.

The objectives include provision for the allocation of land for development and for the promotion of public programs in housing, sanitary services, and communications and for such special incentives to development as the provision of serviced sites for industry. In some instances development plans indicate proposals to enhance the viability and attractiveness of the area by urban renewal and amenity development. Generally the purpose is to improve living conditions by advances in community services and in social and recreational facilities. The plan is intended to be a complete statement of the physical planning measures envisaged to advance the local economy.

There are some 87 separate local planning authorities in the country. The act provides a system to achieve coordination between the planning objectives of these authorities. The coordinating authority is the Minister for Local Government. He is empowered to require planning authorities to work together on their plans and may, if necessary, vary their plan, to resolve local conflicts so as to achieve consistency on the regional scale. If planning authorities are to operate effectively in the promotion of social and economic development in their areas, there should be a means of communication and interaction between the local statutory planning and national economic planning. The local plans must be consistent with the employment and population objectives in the national program and with the projections of capital availability. Regional planning has, as part of its task, to provide the means by which local plans may be geared to national and regional objectives.

The government has engaged consultants to advise on the nine regions which have been formed for planning purposes. One of the purposes of the current regional planning studies is to identify the opportunities and the obstacles which exist in the translation of social and economic objectives into building and other forms of land use. These opportunities may take different forms depending on their location and advantages in relation to markets or communications, extra provision in manpower or services, special education or training facilities, untapped amenity capacity, or evidence in population and employment trends of special development aptitude or capacity for regional functions.

On the other hand the obstacles may be equally varied, such as the physical and economic limitations on expansion, inadequate social and community equipment, bad communication, or deterrent effects of dereliction in town or country. There would be a feedback of information to the national level on regional conditions. It is the task of the regional

The Republic of Ireland showing planning regions.

donegal

NORTHERN IRELAND

sligo

leitrim

monaghan

mayo

cavan

louth

roscommon

longford

westmeath

meath

DUBLIN

galway

offaly

kildare

GALWAY

laoighis

wicklow

ENNIS

SHANNON

carlow

kilkenny

LIMERICK

tipperary

wexford

limerick

WATERFORD

kerry

cork

waterford

CORK

— Boundaries of Planning Regions

County Boundaries

● Development Centre

▢ Model Development Plan in Progress

Regional Studies Completed

Model Amenity – Tourism Study Completed

Studies in seven regions in progress

0 miles 50

planner to advise on the exploitation of opportunities and on the overcoming of obstacles. The purpose is to discover a regional development strategy which will inform and guide as well as serve the national economic policy, especially in relation to undeveloped areas.

In 1965 the government issued a policy statement favoring the principle of development centers, with industrial estates, as a means of promoting further expansion of economic activity. One of the objectives of the regional studies was to try to identify these growth points, and the program was given an immediate impetus by the establishment of state-sponsored industrial estates at Galway and Waterford.

It is desired to develop a new urban strength in the region, featuring expansion in all forms of urban employment and services and providing support for the specialist as well as social facilities which are an effective incentive to private enterprise. With the existence of improved employment opportunities, the surrounding areas will benefit, especially those which are within commuting distance from the advanced educational, training, and social outlets associated with the new centers. There is also the expectation of increased demand for agricultural products and a general rise in the tempo of economic activity.

The development of subsidiary employment, shopping, and social centers is envisaged to serve the rural areas. The normal financial incentives to encourage the establishment of industries in underdeveloped areas will continue to apply.

The government has set up a regional development committee representing all state departments concerned with development. The objective is to assess the various aspects of regional planning policy. These studies have been formed under the aegis of the Minister for Local Government. The studies have been completed and advisory and regional plans prepared in outline by consultants in the nine regions covering the entire country.

An Foras Forbartha (The National Institute for Physical Planning and Construction Research) is an important body in physical planning in Ireland. It was set up in 1964 to carry out research and training in physical planning, building, road traffic, and road safety and to advance knowledge in these subjects.

The institute operates under the supervision of the Minister for Local Government and is being assisted by the United Nations in its initial years. Many of its projects in planning are designed to assist planning authorities in practical ways, with special emphasis on urban and amenity planning. The institute has produced model plans of different kinds and has undertaken various pilot projects, including a study of development potential in the Irish-speaking areas on the western seaboard where there are special values in the cultural life of the country.

The institute is administered by a board of 16 directors who, between them, comprise responsibilities, skills, experience, and geographical coverage which reflect the activities of the institute. The work of An Foras Forbartha is greatly increased and enriched by the assistance received in advisory committees and working parties from representatives of the many professional and vocational bodies concerned with environmental matters. The institute collaborates with other major research institutes in the country, such as The Institute for Industrial Research and Standards and the Economic and Social Research Institute. There is close collaboration with other bodies, including the Tourist Board (Bord Failte); The National Trust (An Taisce); the Industrial Development Authority; Department of the Gaeltacht; and the Federation of Builders, Contractors, and Allied Employers of Ireland.

Professional Practice   In the Republic of Ireland there are about fifty chartered town planners (members of the Town Planning Institute). About twenty are engaged as professional planners employed by local authorities or by the central government and other government agencies. The local authority planners are concerned mainly with the preparation of development plans and development control in accordance with the terms of the Local Government (Planning and Development) Act, 1963. Some are also engaged on positive planning projects and development by local planning authorities. Others are engaged by semigovernmental bodies and by the universities. The remaining members are in private practice and are mainly in association with consultant architectural and engineering firms. Some of the planners in private practice are also engaged as consultants by local authorities and others on various planning matters.

Education and Training   Before the 1960s planning education of any sort was practically nonexistent in Ireland, the reason being lack of demand and opportunities for planners due to the absence of any appreciation of the need for comprehensive planning. Ultimately, new legislation was introduced into Parliament; this act, known as the Local Government (Planning and Development) Act, 1963, has made clear the importance which the government attaches to the proper planning of developments.

The matter of increasing the facilities for education and training was considered by a committee set up by the National Institute for Physical Planning and Construction Research (An Foras Forbartha). This committee comprised a number of professional and administrative personnel who were closely connected with the planning and allied professions. They confirmed the view that a shortage of physical planning personnel existed in the country, and they reported that 200 qualified planners were immediately required in the public-services sector. They recommended that arrangements should be considered to provide courses in physical planning, the estimated output of the requirements being 25 qualified persons per annum over a period of 10 years.

At the request of the Minister for Local Government, discussions took place between the board (An Foras Forbartha), the universities, and the vocational bodies in Dublin with a view to having courses in planning education formulated. The College of Technology, administered by the Vocational Education Committee of the City of Dublin, established part-time courses in town planning in 1963. These courses were designed to prepare students for the examinations of the Town Planning Institute.

The situation in 1969 was as follows:

University College Dublin   In 1966 University College Dublin inaugurated a part-time course extending over 3 years and leading to a diploma in town planning from the National University of Ireland. In 1969 the college added to its program a 2-year full-time course. The introduction of degree courses remains for the future.

College of Technology   The planning course has now been reorganized and has developed from a part-time course into a full-time diploma course extending over 2 years, the second year of which may be part time. The course is related generally, but not specifically, to the final examination of the Town Planning Institute. Recognition of the diploma has been sought from the government through the Department of Local Government. The new course commenced in 1967 and the first diplomas were recently awarded to six students.

Future Development   Higher education in Ireland is now going through a process of rationalization and reorganization.

Many people now consider that the two existing planning courses should, because of the scarcity of resources—both teaching and financial—be merged into a single more viable school of planning to produce planners of a high caliber.

Institutions   Apart from the work of the National Institute for Physical Planning and Construction Research, there are other bodies that assist in educational and propagandist fields. These include the Royal Town Planning Institute (Irish Branch), the Royal Institute of the Architects of Ireland, and The National Trust (An Taisce). These bodies collaborate with each other and assist in arranging seminars, lectures, and other forms of educational and propagandist work with the object of stimulating an interest in physical planning.

The Civics Institute of Ireland is probably the oldest established body in the country to assist in the propaganda of planning. This body, in 1912, promoted an international competition for a plan for Dublin. This competition attracted many well-known planners from abroad, the premiated design being that of Patrick Abercrombie & Kelly of England. The Civics Institute published this plan and report, together with extracts from other proposals, in a book entitled *Dublin of the Future,* which had a wide circulation in the early 1920s. The Civics Institute also produced, in 1925, the *Civic Survey of Dublin 1924,* which was prepared under the supervision of H. T. O'Rourke, the city architect; they also published a *Civic Survey of Cork.* The firm of Abercrombie & Kelly was subsequently appointed as planning consultants to the Dublin Corporation and they produced the Dublin Sketch Development Plan in 1939. They were also consultants for the Statutory Planning Scheme prepared in 1957 by the Dublin Corporation.

Geographical and Climatic Conditions   Ireland consists of a broad central lowland diversified by a number of hills and surrounded by a discontinuous rim of mountains. Many lakes are scattered over the surface; and the coastline, especially in the west, is so deeply indented that no part of the island is more than 70 miles (113 kilometers) from the sea.

The most significant feature of Ireland's geology is the central lowland bounded by a series of mountain chains. Underlain mostly by carboniferous rocks and ranging from 200 to 400 feet (61 to 122 meters) above sea level, it is covered by a deep coating of glacial deposits and provides almost all the good agricultural land of the country.

The mountain chains are related to the main eras of European mountain building. The ancient Caledonian Mountains of Donegal, Mayo, and Connemara are composed of granite and quartzite and are related to the mountains of Scotland and Scandinavia. These mountains give Ireland its most rugged scenery and topography. The Caledonian Mountains of the southeast are more molded and subdued, but the Amorican folds of the south and southwest give Ireland its highest mountains. In more recent times, intense volcanic activity gave rise to the basalt hills of Ulster.

During the ice age, glaciers were centered on the western and northern hills and, having scoured these, deposited the till over the lowlands in the form of drumlins, moraines, and outwash plains. As a result Ireland's river system was to be influenced more by the effects of the ice age than by solid geology.

The climate and weather of Ireland is largely controlled by the passage of depressions which move eastward across the Atlantic Ocean between 50 and 65 degrees north latitude. These depressions, more numerous in winter, draw in winds which are predominantly westerly. Because these winds blow across the warm ocean waters of the Atlantic before reaching land, they are relatively warm and moist in winter, hence Ireland has mild, damp winters followed by cool, cloudy summers.

There is a close correspondence between areas of heavy rainfall and the relief of the land—the greatest precipitation occurring on the seaward-facing hills of Kerry, Galway, and Donegal. While parts of Kerry have an average annual total rainfall of 94 inches (239 centimeters), most of the central lowlands and the eastern part of the country have 30 to 50 inches (75 to 127 centimeters) on average. Dublin, the capital, has an average rainfall of only 26 inches (66 centimeters) per year. Though rainfall is greatest in the winter months, there is no prolonged dry season.

Proximity to the sea gives Ireland a very low range of temperatures. The annual average at Valentia is only 46°F (8°C) and 50°F (10°C) at Dublin. In winter months the average temperature is 45°F (7°C) in the southwest and 41°F (5°C) in the east. July temperatures are 59°F (15°C) to 61°F (16°C) in the south and about 55°F (13°C) in Donegal on the average. May and June are the sunniest months, and the most favored part of the country in this respect is the southwest.

The outstanding feature of Irish weather is its changeability, with consequent problems for agriculture.

Traditions of Planning to the End of the Nineteenth Century Because of the unsettled conditions which prevailed throughout Ireland during much of its history, there is little evidence of formal planning to be seen in its towns. Many were too small to provide scope for the styles of planning which may be seen in many Western European towns. There are few buildings dating from before the seventeenth century. In general these older buildings do not constitute important features in the townscapes of Ireland. The tradition of planning which is to be seen on large estates in other countries is absent; many of those mansions built as country seats were destroyed during the fight for independence. Outstanding examples of planning, or provision for amenity, may be seen in Dublin in the Phoenix Park (1,760 acres) and the small park of St. Stephen's Green. This latter was laid out some time after the middle of the seventeenth century.

The eighteenth century saw considerable improvement in the economic conditions in the country and as a consequence extensive developments were carried out in the larger towns. As might be expected, Dublin, as the center of administration for the entire island, saw the most advanced forms of this.

Urban development had commenced north of the Liffey and spread rapidly from what is now Grattan Bridge through Capel Street, Henrietta Street, Dominick Street, and Mountjoy Square to create the massive Georgian residential areas which have, during the ensuing centuries, deteriorated to such an extent as to create a serious problem for the authority responsible for their maintenance and preservation or redevelopment. In or about the same time the Wide Streets Commissioners commenced the replanning of the road network of the city. These commissioners were set up by acts of 1757 to improve access to the Castle and to bring about the general improvement of the development of the city. They appear to have acted to some extent as a planning authority, particularly in relation to the development carried out on the Pembroke Estate south of the Old Town.

This development, which is the best-preserved and most attractive of the Georgian type of building in the city, is seen at its best in the vicinity of Fitzwilliam Square, Fitzwilliam Street, and Merrion Square. Much of this

View of the east side of Merrion Square, Dublin, showing the Georgian houses which are a characteristic feature of the early-nineteenth-century city.

area is scheduled for preservation by the Planning Authority in its Draft Development Plan.

A fortunate consequence of the example set by the Wide Streets Commissioners and the estates which were developed under their control or influence is the absence of the very large and dreary expanse of bylaw development which is so noticeable in many English towns. There is some such development, but fortunately not a great deal of it.

Other influences of the Wide Streets Commissioners and of some of the more enlightened of the viceroys is shown in the quays which line the River Liffey for its entire length from Heuston Bridge to the Customs House. Much of the building which fronts to these quays, now up to 200 years old, has passed its useful life and may, unfortunately, have to be replaced. It will not be easy for the citizens and the authorities to create an environment as humane and attractive as that left them by their forefathers.

Twentieth-century Planning Among the last of the viceroys sent to this country by the occupying power was one, the Marquis of Aberdeen, who, in 1912, inaugurated a competition for a town plan for Dublin. Fortunately for Dublin, this competition was won by Patrick Abercrombie and his partners, who proposed the replanning of the city in the grand manner which was prevalent at that time. However, the usefulness of the plan was apparent, and when eventually planning legislation was enacted by the Irish government, Abercrombie was employed by the city authorities to assist in the preparation of a plan for the urban area.

War and changing times overtook Abercrombie's proposals, and though the maps of Dublin of today show, in a number of major items, the lines of Abercrombie's proposals, the rate of change has rendered obsolete the type of planning in fashion both at the early quarter of the century and even immediately after the end of World War II. After a number of false starts, the planning legislation of 1963 was put on the statute book.

Urban renewal has always been in progress in the cities. For many years this took the form of slum clearance and flat (or apartment) building for the less well off elements of the community. In doing this work the Corporation of the City of Dublin were fortified by effective powers of compulsory purchase (eminent domain). Some examples of urban renewal date from the last century when the South City Market was erected under the provisions of a special act of Parliament. Another instance, and of much greater public value, was the creation of St. Patrick's Park, adjoining St. Patrick's Cathedral. The city is indebted to the Guinness family—of brewery fame—for this valuable amenity on what was a slum area.

The new planning law enables authorities to redevelop obsolete and dilapidated areas on a much more comprehensive scale. They are no longer confined to acquiring land for housing purposes but may acquire and redevelop land which, because of its bad layout or poor condition, has become obsolete and redevelop it for a wide variety of purposes. The first major attempt to use these new powers has been opposed unsuccessfully in the High Court.

Unlike the Act of 1934, the new law has produced positive results—not merely because its terms are appropriate to the times but also because of energetic action by the Department of Local Government in ensuring that the various planning authorities do, in fact, discharge the duties laid upon them by the act.

A new climate of public opinion has been created by the passing of this legislation and by the insistence that the various authorities throughout the country not only prepare the relevant plans but that the public be made aware of the development which has been going on and of their opportunities of intervening. The entire public has become planning conscious. It does not follow from that the entire public is in favor of planning; but even those who unwisely or selfishly would sacrifice public or long-term interests for immediate gain have come to recognize that the policies of planning authorities cannot be entirely disregarded. Particular problems have to be faced in the delicate balance to be held between tourist development and preservation of the scenic areas and the seacoast. Tourism cannot develop in the absence of facilities, but the facilities must not, in their provision, destroy the amenity which they are to exploit.

The pressure to create new towns has not been felt in the Republic of Ireland because of the continuing fall in the population. However, with the aim of consolidating the national investment in Shannon Airport and its duty-free industrial estate, the state, though an agency created specifically for this purpose, has developed a new town between Shannon Airport and the river estuary. This town, with a population of around 3,000, is growing rapidly and developing to form an intermediate point of growth between Ennis and Limerick, which is scheduled to expand over three times its present population. A third local institution of higher education is to be located there to meet some of the technological needs of the Limerick area.

The regional planning policies of the government can, perhaps, be illustrated by examples of operations already under way. The outstanding example of this is the constitution of a regional planning or development agency for the Limerick region. Instead of creating an ad hoc body, the government has directed the highly efficient corporation, which has developed Shannon's new town and the industrial estate, to undertake the function of a regional development authority.

Waterford County borough, which has been designated a growth point in the southeast, is the location of an industrial estate now being developed by the state. Galway has been selected as the major growth point on the western seaboard. Its university has been recommended for major expansion by the Higher Education Authority.

The natural growth points in Dublin and Cork can be expected to expand as a result of their physical location and size and the advantages which

they can offer to private enterprise. Both cities have attracted industry and service developments in spite of a continuing state policy of favoring, by grant and taxation, concessions to industrial developments in the less endowed parts of the country.

An aerial view of the New Town at Shannon, incorporating the industrial and housing estates.

BIBLIOGRAPHY: *Traffic Planning for Smaller Towns*, An Foras Forbartha, Dublin, 1966; Nathaniel Lichfield & Associates, *Report and Advisory Outline Plan for the Limerick Region*, for the Department of Local Government, Government Publications Office, Dublin, 1966; *Industrial Development and the Development Plan*, An Foras Forbartha, Dublin, 1967; Joseph Newman, *New Dimensions in Regional Planning—A Case Study of Ireland*, An Foras Forbartha, Dublin, 1967; H. Myles Wright, *Dublin Region—Advisory Plan and Final Report, parts I and II*, Government Publications Office, Dublin, 1967; Colin Buchanan & Partners in Association with Economic Consultants, *Regional Studies in Ireland*, Commissioned by the United Nations on behalf of the Government of Ireland, An Foras Forbartha, Dublin, 1968; *Seven Seminars— An Appraisal of Regional Planning in Ireland*, An Foras Forbartha, Dublin, 1970; *Planning for Amenity, Recreation and Tourism*, vol. 2, parts 1, 2, and 3, An Foras Forbartha, Dublin, 1970.

—MICHAEL O'BRIEN

IRELAND, NORTHERN (*See* UNITED KINGDOM.)

IRRIGATION AND LAND USE In large areas of the world, annual precipitation is low or is poorly distributed seasonally. In some of these areas, successful crop production is possible only with irrigation; in others, irrigation can greatly increase crop yields. Irrigation is ancient, having been practiced for thousands of years in some parts of the world, but it has expanded greatly in modern times and is likely to expand further over the next few generations. Where irrigation is extended onto lands previously not cultivated, opportunities for the settlement of additional people may be provided.

Planning for irrigation involves several essential steps, of which the following are the major ones:

1. Planning for a water supply, either from streams or from wells. This requires hydrological and engineering planning to increase the usable water supply, to—usually—conduct the water from its location to the land to be irrigated, and to ensure the wise use of the water once it reaches the land.

2. Land surveys and plans (*see* LAND VALUES AND PLANNING). This requires various surveys and investigations and also projections of the probable yields and cropping patterns on land not now in crop use. The provision of irrigation water opens up new opportunities for land use which did not previously exist; but it also requires the estimation of crop responses where there is no direct experience on which to base them.

3. Drainage is extremely important for irrigated land. A desert area may have no drainage problem before irrigation simply because its water supply is so low. But when this land is irrigated, water accumulates in some areas, some soils become waterlogged, or harmful concentrations of salts arise unless adequate drainage is provided. The world is littered with wrecks of irrigation projects which failed largely because of inadequate soil drainage.

4. The economics of the irrigation enterprise should be calculated with great care. It is physically possible to irrigate large areas where the costs would be excessive in relation to the benefits. In addition to calculating the overall costs and benefits, such planning should consider who is going to pay for the costs and whether they will in fact be able to do so. Farmers frequently experience difficulty in paying for the full costs of the irrigation; the other costs of developing their land may absorb all their capital and income above living and production costs. In many countries, irrigation has been heavily subsidized by the government.

5. Frequently irrigation permits additional settlement, and this requires special planning. Roads and towns must be laid out, public services of all kinds provided for, and the settlers must be given consideration and frequently public help in coping with the difficult problems of developing a productive farm.

In the United States, a substantial program of irrigation development has been undertaken by the federal government during the twentieth century; small programs have been undertaken by some states; but most of the total irrigated acreage has been privately developed, especially where the water supply was from wells which could be drilled and operated by the farmer. There is almost no irrigation in Britain, since its climate makes irrigation unnecessary except for special crops in special circumstances. There is a great deal of irrigation throughout Asia. There, largely by means of new rice and other crop varieties developed through agricultural research, crop production can be increased greatly in the future. In the more tropical areas, such as the Philippines and much of India, a succession of crops can be grown throughout the whole year when irrigation is available, and thus the same area of land can be made to give a very large output.

BIBLIOGRAPHY: Alfred R. Golze, *Reclamation in the United States,* McGraw-Hill Book Company, New York, 1952; Roy E. Huffman, *Irrigation Development and Public Water Policy,* Ronald Press, New York, 1953; Wynne Thorne (ed.), *Land and Water Use,* American Association for the Advancement of Science, Washington, 1963; Vernon W. Ruttan, *The Economic Demand for Irrigated Acreage,* Johns Hopkins Press, Baltimore, 1965.

—MARION CLAWSON

ISOMETRIC PROJECTION   (*See* PROJECTION.)

ISRAEL

Legislation and Administration   Comprehensive planning legislation enacted by the Knesset, the Israel parliament, came into effect in February 1966 with a new Planning and Building Law. This law, which introduced the concept of countrywide overall planning, replaced the former Mandatory Town Planning Ordinance of 1936. Thus a national outline scheme may be drawn up for the entire country.

There are three levels of planning administration; national, district, and local. The state of Israel is divided into six administrative districts, and in each district a planning commission is established. The National Planning Board consists of 10 representatives of government ministries, 6 representatives of Local Government (among them the mayors of the 3 largest cities in Israel), 6 representatives of public and professional organizations—among them 1 representative of a Women's Organization—to make a total of 22 in all.

The National Planning Board prepares the national outline scheme, approves district outline schemes, and advises the government in all matters of planning and building in Israel. The national outline scheme also provides for a forecast of the changes in the distribution of the population within the state; the stages in the development of such distribution and their desirable timing; the estimated future size of existing settlements; the siting and size of new settlements and their location, classification, and size.

The National Planning Board must submit the scheme prepared in accordance with directions, together with the comments of the district commissions, to the government for approval.

A Committee for the Protection of Agricultural Land, of 11 members, was established with the National Planning Board. Each of the six district planning and building commissions is composed of 15 members, 9 of whom are government officials, 5 representatives recommended by local authorities in the district, and 1 an expert in planning and building.

The most important function of the district planning commissions is the approval of local outline schemes, local detailed plans, and the drawing up of a district outline scheme. The whole area of the state is divided into town planning areas. Within each area planning is administered by the local planning and building commission. In the case of a local planning area which includes the area of only one local authority, the council of that local authority is also the local planning commission, which establishes a planning and building subcommission; the town planning functions being divided between them.

The law specifies the composition of the commission in the case of a local planning area in which there is more than one local authority.

The main task of the local planning commissions includes the preparation of local schemes, allocation of lots, and issuing building permits. Unlike the former Town Planning Ordinance, the new law requires the state to have its plans and buildings approved by planning commissions. On the other hand, the law recognizes that in certain parts of the country almost all the building is carried out by the government, therefore provision is made for special planning commissions in which government representatives have a large majority.

The special planning commission will act, with certain restrictions, as a local and district commission. The Minister of the Interior may, upon the recommendation of the Minister of Housing, declare by order that any area situated within one district shall be a special planning area. Every special planning area shall have a special planning and building commission.

The Minister of the Interior, after consultation with the National Planning Board and the planning agencies concerned, may by order establish a joint planning and building commission for more than one district or more than one planning area. The Minister of the Interior shall prescribe the composition of a joint commission and shall appoint its members upon the recommendation of the planning agencies concerned. Within a prescribed area, a joint commission shall have all such powers and duties of a district or local commission (as the case may be) as are assigned to it by the order of the Minister of the Interior. The local commission may expropriate immovable property intended for public purposes under any scheme. It may, at any time after the coming into force of a local outline scheme or a detailed scheme, expropriate such property within the area of the scheme. Four-tenths of a plot intended for either roads, parks, sports and recreation areas, or for buildings serving educational, cultural, religious, and health purposes can be expropriated without paying compensation; but, no part of a plot shall be expropriated, whether with or without payment, if the value of the remainder of the plot is reduced as a result of the expropriation.

The law enumerates several planning requirements which are deemed not to affect land injuriously provided that the requirements do not go beyond what is reasonable in the circumstances of the case. It is not equitable to pay compensation to any person aggrieved if these provisions are complied with. Other provisions include repartition, partition, and combination of land; licensing; defense installations and flight obstructions; nonconforming use; and offenses and penalties.

The first schedule deals with the composition and duties of the Committee for the Protection of Agricultural Land, the second with the composition and duties of the Territorial Waters Committee.

The Minister of the Interior is charged with the implementation of the law and may make regulations after consultation with the National Planning Board as to anything relating to the implementation of the law.

Other legislation particularly important for physical planning includes the National Parks and Nature Reserves Law, promulgated in 1963, which establishes a National Council for Parks and Nature Reserves and two executive authorities—one for national parks and the other for nature reserves. The Urban Renewal and Slum Clearance Law of 1965 sets up the Slum Clearance and Urban Renewal Authority.

The following ministries have powers relating to economic, physical, and development planning:

1. The Prime Minister's office is responsible for the National Parks Authority.

2. The Ministry of Finance is responsible for the Economic Planning Authority, the function of which is to prepare long- and medium-term programs, dovetail major ministerial projects, determine social policy, and balance overall regional development, all involving research, forecasting, and the following of economic progress.

3. The Ministry of Interior is responsible for general administration and control of local government. It includes the Department for Town and Country Planning, responsible for physical planning on national, regional, and local levels, planning legislation, and general control over building activities, development, and land use.

4. The Ministry of Education and Culture is responsible for the department of antiquities.

5. The Ministry of Agriculture is responsible for agricultural and rural development, water economy and irrigation projects, soil mapping, and soil conservation. The Land Management Board in the Ministry administers 93 percent of the total area of Israel (rural, undeveloped, and urban) owned by the government and the Jewish National Fund.

6. The Public Works Department is within the Ministry of Labour and its functions include road construction and government buildings.

7. The Ministry of Communication and Transport is responsible for the management and detailed planning of railways, harbors, and airports; and the Road Safety Authority within this Ministry employs consultants on economics, planning, and research.

8. The Ministry of Housing is responsible for state-financed housing projects (50 to 60 percent of the whole building industry of the country), slum clearance, new town projects, and generally detailed urban planning

connected with government-sponsored housing and building activities and research. The Authority for Building and Clearing Rehabilitation Areas is within this Ministry, which also includes the departments of physical planning, of rural building, and The Planning and Development Institute, which has prepared many schemes for developing countries.

9. The Ministry of Immigrant Absorption is responsible for the absorption of immigrants in Israel. It cares for their housing, employment, and social absorption.

Working in close cooperation with the government are:

1. The Jewish Agency—responsible for Jewish immigration, outside Israel and rural settlement in Israel.

2. The National Fund (Keren Kayemet Leisrael)—responsible for forestry and land reclamation.

Professional Practice

Local Authorities In all the municipalities there are technical departments and engineering services which may include town planning, architecture, and civil engineering.

Not all local councils have engineering departments which include all the above activities, for, in planning, they usually engage a planning consultant.

Rural councils join together to prepare outline schemes within the framework of a local town planning commission.

The Planning Consultant Such consultants are widely engaged in Israel. Fees are paid according to a scale prepared and approved by the professional bodies and employees, based on the size and area of the scheme. Architectural competitions for public buildings and housing schemes are widely employed in Israel as a basis for awarding contracts.

Education and Training One of the academic institutions which plays an important role in the training of specialists in the field of physical planning is the Faculty of Architecture and Town Planning of the Technion of Haifa (Israel Institute of Technology). The faculty gives a 5-year undergraduate course leading to the degree of bachelor of architecture and town planning, giving the student a background of basic applied sciences and the technical knowledge concerned with architectural design, environmental design, environmental engineering, municipal engineering, community planning and industrial design, data processing in planning, town planning, landscape design, legislation, traffic engineering, and the computer in arts and town planning. During the fifth year, among the obligatory subjects is a course in regional planning. This faculty also gives two parallel courses leading to degree of master of science in architecture and town planning and master of science in urban and regional studies. These courses are open also to graduates of subjects other than architecture and town planning, such as engineering, social sciences, and geography. For the degree of master of sciences in environmental studies, a student is required to submit a thesis on an environmental problem related to his undergraduate discipline of study.

The syllabi for the graduate courses include different specialized courses concerning comprehensive regional planning, urban and architectural geography, quantitative methods in planning, ecology, the theory of location, theories and values in planning, and transportation planning.

Faculty of Agricultural Engineering   The two main courses given at this faculty are at the undergraduate level, each lasting 4 years and leading to the B.Sc. degree. One course is on problems in agricultural development and comprises technical and nontechnical subjects; the other, a technical course, is on water resources and systems engineering. Of interest is a one-semester course at the graduate level dealing with the planning of development projects.

Urban and Rural Settlement Study Centre Rehovot   The center is sponsored by the Settlement Department of the Jewish Agency; the Ministries of Agriculture, Labor, Housing, and Interior; the Department for International Cooperation of the Ministry for Foreign Affairs; and the Economic Planning Authority. The center serves as a research and teaching institute in regional planning and development. It offers a 2-year course in comprehensive rural planning to train development project leaders. A second course is designed to train team leaders for Israeli technical assistance programs.

Institutions   The Association of Engineers and Architects in Israel, founded in 1921, is organized in professional sections of architecture and planning and civil, mechanical, electrical, hydraulic, municipal, and chemical engineering. It has initiated numerous activities and founded a number of institutions, which include The Engineering Council, founded in 1960 with the aim of studying public policy, including the economic aspects with regard to technological projects and development and The Central Competitions Committee, which directs public competitions for building and town planning projects. Symposia and lectures on professional and scientific subjects are held frequently, and tours and visits to engineering works and industrial enterprises are organized.

Codes of practice and scales of fees for professional services are periodically drafted and published by the association. Engineers' clubs provide platforms from which ministers of the state, heads of government, and public institutions as well as leading members of the engineering profession review activities and programs of their ministries and institutions and discuss problems of interest to the engineering profession.

An International Technical Cooperation Centre (I.T.C.C.) for furthering technological advancement in developing countries was initiated by the association in December 1967. Periodicals published by the association include:

1. *Handasa W' Adrikalut* (*Engineering and Architecture*), a bimonthly journal of the association published in Hebrew, with English synopses

2. A monthly bulletin published in Hebrew, providing members with current information of the activities of the association

3. *Technical Progress in Israel,* a monthly bulletin published in English

4. Publications of the Building Centre—sheets of documentation and bibliographical publications on building planning and construction in Israel.

The Association for Environmental Planning is an organization established by professionals of various backgrounds concerned with environmental planning. Membership is open to those with appropriate professional training and/or those who are engaged in environmental planning. The aims of the association are to initiate environmental planning in Israel and to improve its standard; to create "meeting platforms" for cooperation of the various professions engaged in environmental planning; to establish platforms for expression and discussion of problems concerned with environmental planning, for the widening of the professional knowledge of members of the association, to distribute knowledge of environmental planning among laymen; and to hold symposia for members and guests. The association publishes the quarterly *Environmental Planning*.

Geographical and Climatic Conditions   Israel is situated in the eastern Mediterranean basin and constitutes a meeting point between the continents of Asia, Africa, and Europe. It is bordered by Lebanon in the north, Syria in the east and northeast, Jordan in the east, and Egypt in the south and southwest.

The country is divided into three main longitudinal strips: the coastal plain, the mountains, and the Jordan Valley. The coastline is generally straight, with one major promontory at Haifa Bay. Most of the population lives in the coastal plain, which contains the largest, most populated cities and is endowed with the best agricultural soil. A chain of mountain ranges forms the backbone of the country, bisecting it from north to south.

The mountains rise to a maximum height of 3,962 feet (1,208 meters) in upper Galilee and to an altitude of 3,280 feet (1,000 meters) in the Negev. Most of the mountains in Israel are limestone formations, built of dolomitic rock. In Galilee and in Samaria they are highly dissected, but less so in Judaea. The western slopes are moderate, whereas the eastern slopes are very steep and cut by canyons.

East of the central mountain ranges, the Jordan Valley extends from north to south, beginning at the sources of the Jordan at the northern frontier of the country. It passes through the Sea of Galilee and the Bet Shean Valley down to the Dead Sea. From a height of 656 feet (200 meters) above sea level, it falls to a depth of 695 feet (212 meters) below sea level at the Sea of Galilee and from there descends to 1,286 feet (392 meters) below sea level at the Dead Sea, the lowest place on earth. From there the Arava continues to the Red Sea.

The climate of Israel is distinctly Mediterranean, with a typical summer season of 7 to 8 months and a moderate cold season lasting 4 to 5 months per year. Hot, dry spells continuing several days at a time and known as "khamsins" occur in the transition periods between winter and summer and vice versa. On the coastal plain the heat is generally tempered by a cool breeze from the sea, while in the hills the heat is dry with a relatively low humidity. The Jordan Valley is very hot in summer, with a temperate climate in winter. The Negev and the Arava are the hottest regions in the country with the highest range of daily temperatures. In Jerusalem the minimum and maximum average daily temperatures in August are 69 to 87°F (20.8 to 30.6°C) and in Eilat 78 to 105°F (25.6 to 40.3°C).

The rainy season lasts about 5 months, from November to March, with some rainfall also in October and in April. The coldest and rainiest months of the year are January and February. The number of rainy days per year in the northern part of the country averages from 40 to 70 and in the Negev from 10 to 30.

Only 20 percent of the land is suitable for cultivation. An additional 16 percent can be afforested. The sand dunes along the Mediterranean are unsuitable for cultivation, but the coastal plain inland of the dunes has sandy red soil ideal for citrus culture. The eastern edge of the coastal plain has black soil. This soil is excellent for vegetables and noncitrus fruits. The red loam of the mountains is of very good quality for fruit trees, grapes, olives, tobacco, and grain, but much of the mountain area is badly eroded and the Negev portion is too dry.

The main pipeline of the National Water Conduit runs from the Sea of Galilee south to a point near Beersheba, and supplemental pipelines reach out to settled areas as far as Eilat.

Traditions of Planning to the End of the Nineteenth Century

The Old City of Jerusalem   Sir Patrick Abercrombie described the old city of Jerusalem as[1]

> One of these inextricable palimpsests of planning: what exists to-day (apart from David's city and the temple topography) is probably Roman in origin; but a fusion of Roman, Crusader Gothic and Islamic design has produced one of the finest cumulative civic effects in the world; the narrow vaulted approach, shot with beams of light, through continuous suks (or bazaars), the sudden vast, open, golden-hued sunlit esplanade, the central Dome of the Rock (one of the five domes of the world) and the grey Mount of Olives as background—beyond this human magnificence using a background of austere nature can no further go.

Akko   A comprehensive survey revealed the structure of the medieval town as a unique crusader city, the capital of the "Kingdom of Jerusalem" composed by quarters of the Venetian, Genovese, and Pisan states and the fortresses of the military-religious orders: the Templars, Hospitallers, and Teutons.

Jaffa   Jaffa is one of the oldest ports of the eastern coast of the Mediterranean, inhabited from Biblical times to the present day. Built on a hill overlooking the harbor, this picturesque town has become a tourist attraction. The existing buildings in old Jaffa date mainly from the early nineteenth century and were mostly built by Italian craftsmen.

Under Turkish rule, Palestine had no planning legislation as such. Town planning in a most rudimentary and limited form did, however, take place under an Ottoman law of 1877 which gave the municipalities powers with regard to the arrangement of streets and the erection of buildings and a law of 1891 concerning the construction and alignment of streets.

According to Ottoman land laws, lands set aside for charitable purposes

---

[1] *Town and Country Planning,* London, 1933, p. 38.

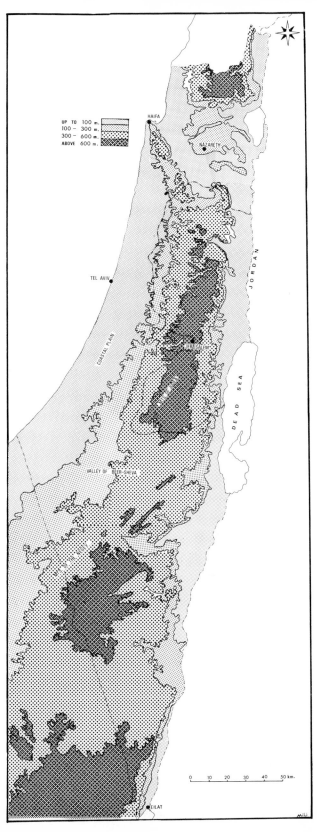

Topographical regions.

UP TO 100 m.
100 – 300 m.
300 – 600 m.
ABOVE 600 m.

HAIFA

NAZARETH

TEL AVIV

JERUSALEM

COASTAL PLAIN

JORDAN

DEAD SEA

VALLEY OF BEER-SHEVA

0 10 20 30 40 50 km.

EILAT

could not be expropriated, and as a result the old areas abound in religious preserves.

Twentieth-century Planning

New Towns and Communities   Soon after the capture of Palestine from the Turks, the British set up a territorial administration, and in April 1918, a military proclamation was issued forbidding building in the neighborhood of Jerusalem without a permit. The British introduced a new system of land registration and advanced legislation in the sphere of town planning and construction. During this period there were considerable achievements in the planning of rural settlements, such as the kibbutz and the *kvutzah*.

The greatest challenge for overall planning came with the vast mass immigration after the establishment of the State of Israel in 1948.

Distribution of Population Plan. A physical national plan was prepared by the planning department of the Ministry of the Interior envisaging a network of regional urban centers the size of which would differ in accordance with their function. A hierarchy of urban centers was proposed, beginning with small district urban centers serving populations of 30,000 to 50,000, extending to towns with populations of 80,000 to 150,000, and culminating in big cities. The distribution of population plan served as a guide to the siting of new urban centers; the expansion of existing centers; the siting of new industries; the siting of institutions, parks, and recreation areas; and the planning of the road network.

Regions of Priorities for Directed Development. The division of the country into regions of priorities was a measure to implement the policy for a balanced distribution of population and development. Six regions were proposed. That of top priority was given the maximum incentives for development. Such aid was given in many ways; i.e., priority in erection of immigrant housing, grants, exemption from taxes, building of roads and services, establishing industries, encouraging private investments, allocating land, low valuation of leases and land prices, priority in erection of public buildings and schools.

The National Road Network. The plan shows the layout of the existing and proposed roads and their classification as regional, national, express, and secondary roads. Some express roads are shown in the coastal strip. As far as possible, good agricultural land is preserved. Landscape considerations played a predominant part in the layout and construction of roads. Scenery and panoramic roads are shown in the plan.

National Parks and Nature Reserves. Since 1948, preliminary national plans for parks and nature reserves have been prepared. The first step taken was the surveying of antiquities; historic sites; holy places; places of zoological, geological or geomorphological interest; and woodlands. The survey served as a basis for formulating preliminary proposals for a national plan of parks and nature reserves.

Other national plans prepared include a master plan for development of tourism and a plan for siting of regional and national institutions.

The Lakhish regional plan with Qiryat-Gat as its urban center is an Israeli example of an integrated regional project.

LEFT: *Distribution of population, 1*
FAR LEFT: *Distribution of population, 1*

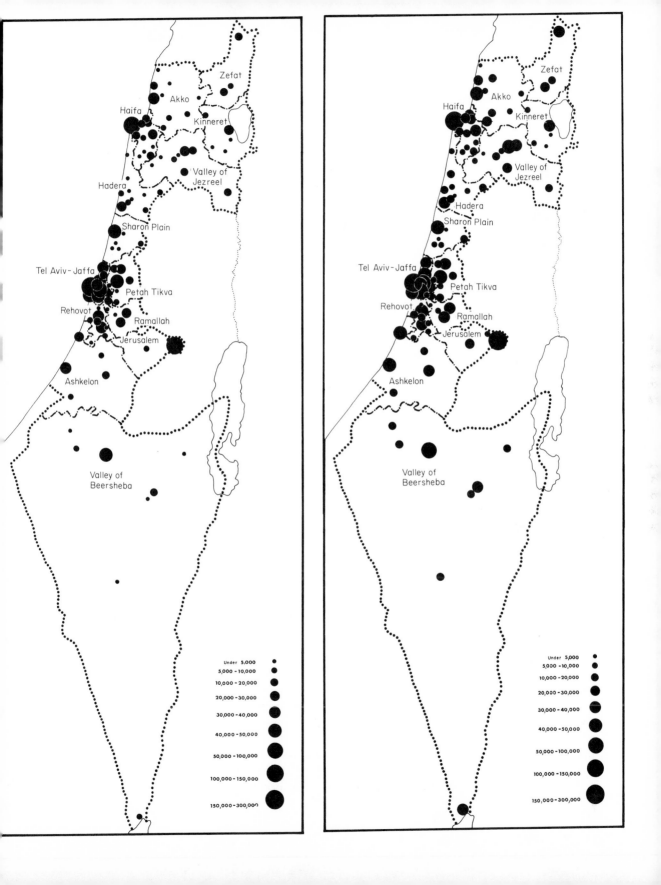

Left map		Right map	
	Under 5,000		Under 5,000
	5,000 –10,000		5,000 –10,000
	10,000 –20,000		10,000 –20,000
	20,000 –30,000		20,000 –30,000
	30,000 –40,000		30,000 –40,000
	40,000 –50,000		40,000 –50,000
	50,000 –100,000		50,000 –100,000
	100,000 –150,000		100,000 –150,000
	150,000 –300,000		150,000 –300,000

Zefat

Akko

Haifa

Kinneret

Valley of
Jezreel

Hadera

Sharon Plain

Tel Aviv–Jaffa

Petah Tikva

Rehovot

Ramallah

Jerusalem

Ashkelon

Valley of
Beersheba

Agricultural areas were planned with small urban nuclei to provide services such as schools, repair shops, garages, agricultural implements, and the like for a cluster of three to five agricultural settlements surrounding them.

Twenty-eight new towns have been established since the foundation of the state. They were predominantly sited in the Negev, western Galilee, and in northern, Upper Galilee. Immigrants were engaged first in building their own houses and on agricultural work in the vicinity. Only in the later stages did the Ministry of Industries and Commerce make efforts to bring industries to the new towns.

Some new towns are emerging into full urban status. One such is Beersheba, which served at all periods as an important station for travelers to the south and is known as the City of the Patriarchs. After the establishment of the state, it developed rapidly. Six neighborhood units were sited southeast of the town. The outline scheme was based on a population target of 250,000 persons. The new town of Ashdod was an important achievement in urban development in Israel. With Israel's second deep-water harbor, it is sited in the south on the dunes of the Mediterranean coast to save agricultural land and speed up the development of southern Israel. Eilat is a new port town on the Red Sea. The latest new towns are Arad on the western cliff overlooking the Dead Sea and Garmiel in the north.

City and Town Extension Some new towns are built around existing ancient and medieval nuclei such as Zefat, Tiberias, Akko, Bethshean, Nazareth, Ashkelon, and others, with special care given to the old sites.

The Jerusalem Outline Scheme. The topography of Jerusalem is of special significance and affects the entire character of the city. There is practically no flat land within the entire confines of the city, which is made up exclusively of valleys and hills. In accordance with the topographical structure, the mountains and mountain slopes were selected for building purposes and the valleys left as open public areas. The built-up hills constitute compact neighborhood units.

Each neighborhood unit has cultural and commercial centers, a special zone for artisans and craftsmen, and the most essential services.

Stone buildings are characteristic of Jerusalem. This form of building, in addition to its beauty, enhances stability and saves maintenance costs.

A special team of experts was set up by the Ministry of the Interior and the municipality to prepare plans for the historical and religious parts of Jerusalem including the old city, Mount of Olives, and adjacent areas. The old city was given special attention; very strict regulations were designed to assure the preservation of its character.

Nazareth has become the largest Arab center in the country. A comprehensive outline scheme was prepared, its object being to ensure protection of the holy sites and the preservation of the character of the old city. New Jewish and Arab quarters were planned on the outskirts of the existing ancient Arab town.

Ashkelon, one of the most ancient cities on the Mediterranean coast,

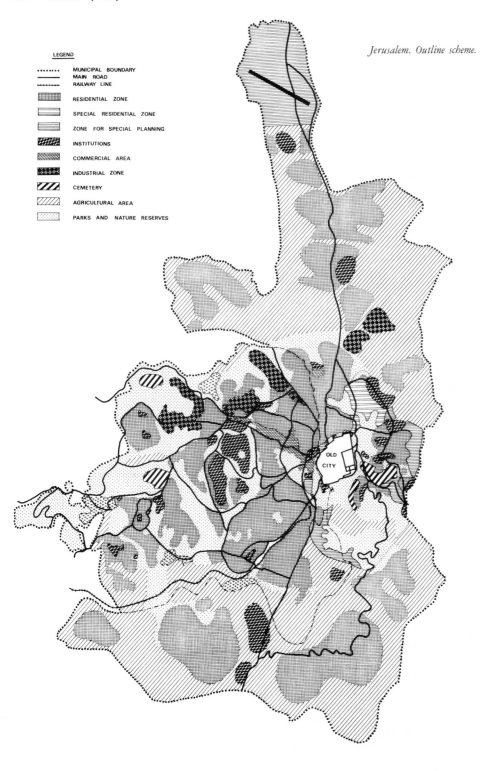

Jerusalem. Outline scheme.

LEGEND

.... MUNICIPAL BOUNDARY
_____ MAIN ROAD
+++++++++ RAILWAY LINE

RESIDENTIAL ZONE

SPECIAL RESIDENTIAL ZONE

ZONE FOR SPECIAL PLANNING

INSTITUTIONS

COMMERCIAL AREA

INDUSTRIAL ZONE

CEMETERY

AGRICULTURAL AREA

PARKS AND NATURE RESERVES

OLD CITY

Plan Boundary

Special Residential Zone

Residential Zone

Residential Zone

Residential Zone

Institutions

Hotels and Recreations

Public Buildings

Commercial Zone

Public and Private Open Space

Cemetery

Proposed Road

City Wall

Plan for the historical area of Jerusalem.

OLD CITY

0   1 km.

was reestablished and inhabited mainly by new immigrants. Ancient sites were carefully preserved within a national park.

In the old city of Akko problems of decay and neglect were pressing. A company consisting of the central government and the local authority undertook to prepare a survey and to undertake research work, to identify the historical sites, and to reconstruct the entire city. The new town of Akko was built north of the crusader town.

Urban Renewal The constant immigration which has enlarged the population on an unprecedented scale within a short period considerably expanded the scope of urban renewal. Quarters and old city centers, which were never planned to serve anything like modern requirements, are due for reconstruction.

The big cities jointly with the government have been engaged in urban renewal activities since 1961, when special slum clearance companies were established. Their objective was to clear the area assigned for renewal of all structures.

In August 1965 the Knesset (the Israel parliament) adopted the Urban Renewal and Slum Clearance Law, under which the statutory Slum Clearance and Urban Renewal Authority was set up to deal with areas declared as "renewal regions." When a region is so declared, all land transactions and building activities within that area cease, the land is requisitioned by the government, and a general plan for reconstruction is prepared by the authority.

Tel-Aviv. Aerial view of Dizengoff Circus.

Nahalal. Aerial view of agricultural settlement.

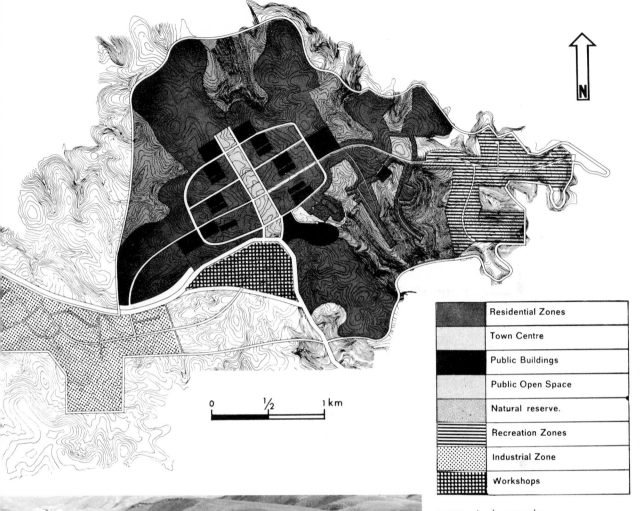

	Residential Zones
	Town Centre
	Public Buildings
	Public Open Space
	Natural reserve.
	Recreation Zones
	Industrial Zone
	Workshops

ABOVE: *Arad master plan.*
LEFT: *Aerial view of Arad.*

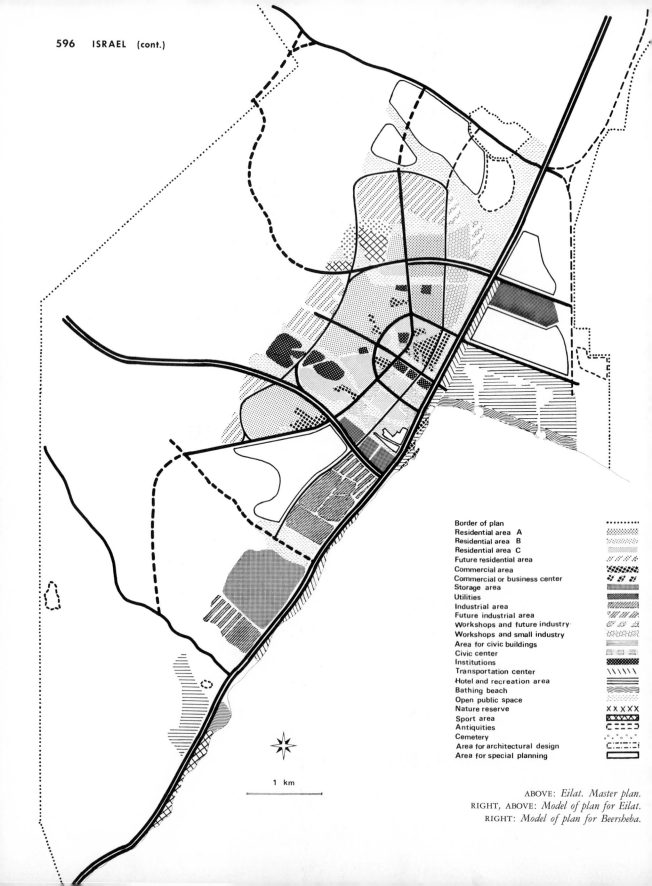

Border of plan
Residential area A
Residential area B
Residential area C
Future residential area
Commercial area
Commercial or business center
Storage area
Utilities
Industrial area
Future industrial area
Workshops and future industry
Workshops and small industry
Area for civic buildings
Civic center
Institutions
Transportation center
Hotel and recreation area
Bathing beach
Open public space
Nature reserve
Sport area
Antiquities
Cemetery
Area for architectural design
Area for special planning

1 km

ABOVE: *Eilat. Master plan.*
RIGHT, ABOVE: *Model of plan for Eilat.*
RIGHT: *Model of plan for Beersheba.*

The authority is empowered to move occupants from a renewal region on condition that other suitable premises are provided and that they are not located in some other prospective renewal region.

In 1967 a general survey of slum areas was carried out. The data of this survey enabled the authority to apply a scheme of priorities. Areas in Tel Aviv, Jaffa, Zafat, and Jerusalem were approved by the government as renewal zones. The most important steps taken to rebuild and redevelop Tel Aviv are directed towards the Manshieh Quarter. A redevelopment company was founded jointly by the government and the municipality to carry out this Tel Aviv/Jaffa Central Area Redevelopment Project. It included a reclamation scheme approximately 328 yards (300 meters) out to sea. The area is planned for 4,000 apartments, commercial offices, public buildings, hotels, retail business premises, recreation, entertainment, and public open spaces.

Problems similar to those in Tel Aviv exist in Haifa. Renewal in Haifa is concentrated mainly in the old city district, where old structures are no longer fit to be inhabited.

In Jerusalem plans were prepared for the reconstruction of the central business area. Jerusalem has a number of old quarters which do not satisfy present-day requirements of density of population and hygienic conditions and therefore had to be reconstructed.

The rebuilding of the old city Jewish quarter is an important urban renewal project in an historical site adjacent to the Wailing Wall and the Temple site. A government company was formed to prepare detailed reconstruction plans and to carry out the building operations.

BIBLIOGRAPHY: A. Sharon, *Physical Planning in Israel,* Jerusalem, 1951 (Hebrew, with English summary); A. Glikson, *Regional Planning in Israel,* Leiden, 1955; E. Brutzkus, *Physical Planning in Israel, Problems and Achievements,* Jerusalem, 1964; J. Dash and E. Efrat, *The Israel Physical Master Plan,* Ministry of the Interior, Jerusalem, 1964; *National Planning for the Redistribution of Population and the Establishment of New Towns in Israel,* report for the 27th World Congress for Housing and Planning, Jerusalem, 1964; M. D. Gouldman, *Legal Aspects of Town Planning in Israel,* Jerusalem, 1966; E. Spiegel, *New Towns in Israel,* Bern, 1966; J. Dash, *National Physical Planning in Israel,* 1st World Congress of Engineers and Architects in Israel, 1967.

—JACOB DASH

ITALY

Traditions of Planning to the First World War   In Italy, as in other European countries, nineteenth-century industrialization and its effects on the cities led to the disintegration of the baroque townscapes and, after a period of instability, to the birth of modern urban planning.

In Italy the process of deterioration came relatively late, as it was only after the consolidation of a single national state (1861) that industrialization of the country began. But the effects were at once serious and considerable, as the instability affected a very extensive fabric of cities and rural territories which had been planned over a period of centuries, a heritage of rare urban environments, rich in exceptional artistic monuments which are among the finest on the European continent.

■ Measures relating to the entire municipal
    area: development and expansion plans,
    variants to plans and zoning.
● Measures relating to parts of the municipal
    area: plans for new districts, for the
    central areas of cities, for industrial zones
    and slum clearance.
▲ Measures of a modest scale within the
    conurbation: creation of new roads and
    piazzas and construction of retaining walls.

*Geographical distribution of urban
planning in Italy between 1861 and
1918. (Yearbook of the Italian Cities,
INU, Rome, 1934.)*

milano
venezia
bologna
genova
firenze
ancona
perugia
l'aquila
roma
bari
napoli
potenza
cagliari
palermo
reggio
calabria

In the nineteenth century, the effects of neoclassicism and the Haussmann treatment on the fabric of the Italian cities were confined to a few alterations such as the diagonal cuts of the Via Pietro Micca in Turin, the Via Nazionale in Rome, and the Via Indipendenza in Bologna which, being based on detailed rather than overall plans, left the baroque tradition of urban growth virtually unchanged.

The first major urban planning problems arose from the successive transfer of the capital of the new nation first to Florence (1864) and then to Rome (1871), and from the terrible epidemic which struck Naples in 1885.

The development plan for Florence as the intended capital city was entrusted to Poggi, who was to prepare the city to welcome the new residents who were to be transferred as a result of the removal of the court and the ministries; but the transfer from Turin took place within a mere six months, and the plan was not carried out until after the final transfer of the royal capital to Rome had taken place. In this way, Florence assumed the highly respectable aspect of a serene, middle-class city.

On the alignment of the demolished medieval walls, a ring of roads was constructed which linked the parks of the Boboli Gardens, the Cascine, and the public gardens outside the Porta S. Gallo. Beyond this ring, residential districts of regular layout were rapidly built up, creating a bastion around the old city and surrounding it almost completely, so that any possible organic development was blocked. Moreover, notable parts of the historic town center, one of the most precious and intact medieval centers, were demolished. Poggi thus damaged the medieval fabric of old Florence; the problems of the relationship with the historic buildings and environments were not solved, while those arising from the construction of a modern and functional city were not faced.

Similarly, the preparation of a master plan for the new capital, Rome, met with the sort of difficulties that have ever since confronted planning in Italian cities: building speculation and the impotence of the local authorities responsible for urban development. There also emerged at that time certain fundamental requirements for correct urban planning which were, however, not met in practice. These requirements included that of forming a municipal authority capable of directing the development of the towns in accordance with priority principles, and that of not leaving primary development of the expansion zones to the authorities alone.

Rome did not possess a development plan because that of 1873—"mutilated and monstrous" according to those officials who had debated it—was not adopted while the one examined in 1883 and subsequently enacted in fact merely sanctioned the existing development pattern as well as the buildings and drab districts desired by the great national banks, by the Roman building contractors, and by the descendants of the papal aristocracy. This approach lacked coherence and failed to reflect any clear ideas about urban development.

It was at Naples that the first slum clearance plan for a population center was prepared. Already in 1865, a national law had been passed which permitted the expropriation of properties by the government and by the provincial and local authorities for the public good and which laid down standards for the preparation of building regulations and development plans. It was in Naples that, at the behest of General Garibaldi in his capacity as royal commissioner for the south, programs for "healthy houses" were prepared which were, however, not followed up, as they had no adequate financial backing. In 1885, a disastrous cholera epidemic struck the city, which was overpopulated and contained slums in which the hygienic conditions were deplorable. As a result, the act of 1865 was supplemented by a special act, known as the Naples Act, which permitted the compulsory acquisition of slum districts for redevelopment in the public interest. On the strength of this act, some of the most miserable zones in the town center were demolished and a new wide road, the Rettifilo, was built (1888–1894), which linked up with the railway station and was studded with respectable mansions in the style of the late nineteenth century.

These laws, which were among the first of their kind in Europe (the Belgian law was passed in 1867, and the French laws were enacted between 1902 and 1912), are still legally in force and could have been used in Italy with advantage on a number of occasions but for the universal opposition of the property owners.

The most complete episode of urban planning in nineteenth-century Italy concerned Milan. After Lombardy was annexed to the Kingdom of Italy, Milan developed at an accelerated rate which was associated with the industrial development of the north. The first measure, dictated by sentimental reasons and undertaken on the initiative of Mengoni, was the redevelopment of the Piazza del Duomo. The construction of the central station and of the market station at the Porta Garibaldi gave rise to major successive measures affecting the urban road network. In 1884 and again in 1889, Beruto, the chief municipal engineer, prepared two master plans, but only the second plan received the ministerial approval required for making it operative. The plan, influenced by foreign examples (Beruto himself mentioned the Belle Alliance Platz in Berlin and Haussmann's star-shaped piazzas in Paris), envisaged the city's great expansion to the north. This expansion encircled the old city, and the concentric development was emphasized by the construction of radial roads linked by successive ring roads.

There also appeared the concept of zoning, defined in a rather timid and summary fashion for the San Siro district and for the lower part of the Corso Indipendenza. Another new concept was of a time limitation for the plan (fixed at 30 years for Milan).

However, these four episodes did not represent the whole urban planning experience up to the First World War; encompassed in a new and enlarged territorial reality, the cities continued to expand by means of development plans of the nineteenth-century type which merely laid down the road alignments and building densities without considering the social composition of the districts which had been constructed and without providing the services and location plans for industrial plants. The latter were, as a result, inserted in the residential fabric in a disorderly fashion.

Between 1861 and 1918 general development plans were adopted by 106 cities great and small, including Turin, Imperia, San Remo, Biella, Vercelli, Como, Brescia, Carrara, Bologna, Ancona, Foggia, and nearly all the local authorities on the island of Ischia, Catania, and Messina. Fifty towns had partial instruments (expansion plans or plans for specific districts); in addition, slum clearance plans were in operation in ten cities including Naples, Mantua, and Turin. Finally, there were a fair number of minor redevelopment works within the urban fabric, such as the opening up of new roads or piazzas. The geographical distribution of this urban planning was peculiar: in some regions, such as Puglia, Piedmont, Lombardy, and Liguria, it was fairly intensive; in other regions, such as Veneto and Umbria, it was virtually nonexistent. These territorial differences, largely independent of the wealth of the region concerned, can probably be explained only by the influence of the prefects (the representatives of the central government in the provinces), or that of the influential deputies. There is not adequate knowledge to judge these plans, and their social and cultural background still calls for further investigation.

Knowledge is confined to a few cases, such as that of Turin, which, following the baroque tradition, was enlarged by means of a few localized plans which were carried out with some delay and which provided for residential districts and amenities (churches, markets, schools). Being concentrated on certain important axes and their avenues, these amenities finally predetermined the model of urban development within large isolated rectangles. In Genoa, on the other hand, some hundred specific plans prepared between 1850 and 1920 were realized by means of restrictive land acquisition and public development, followed by assignments of the areas thus developed. Owing to these plans of limited extent, the city grew in orderly fashion and in accordance with an urban design of high quality as, for example, the Circonvallazione a Monte.

Contrary to this trend was the master plan for Palermo by Felice Gianrusso (1885) which, on the lines of the baroque tradition that had given rise to the Quattro Canti (1609–1631) in accordance with the Haussmann technique, provided for wide cuts of rectangular streets superimposed on the delicate and time-honored warren of streets. Behind these measures were valid reasons for slum clearance, yet only slow progress was made with the demolitions while futile public works designed for the urban bourgeoisie—two theaters, including one extolled as the "third in Europe"— were realized quickly.

In Venice, which was kept in a condition of misery and economic scarcity by the Austrian government (1798–1805 and 1814–1866), radical measures which had a profound influence on the unique configuration of the lagoon city (see illustration) were carried out in the nineteenth century. The railway link with the mainland was built (1846) and, on areas reclaimed either from the urban fabric or from the lagoon itself, a new dock near the arsenal,

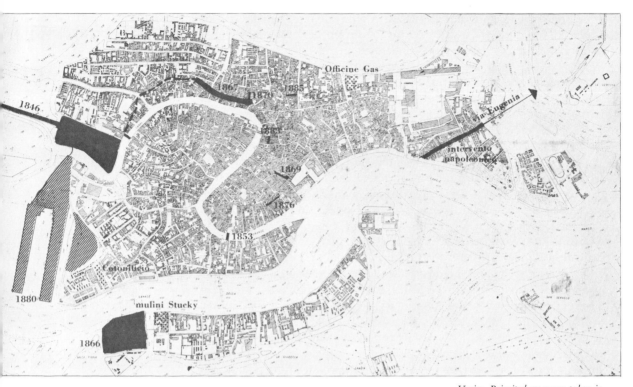

industrial plants such as the Stucky cotton mill, the gas works, and the commercial port with the new harbor station (1880) were built.

An attempt was made to remedy the very poor hygienic conditions of the old dwellings by means of the slum clearance scheme of 1891. This, however, suffered from the fact that it was limited to the solution of road access and hygienic slum clearance problems.

After the terrible earthquake of 1908, Messina was largely rebuilt without a master plan until a legislative basis was created on July 26, 1910; and it was only in 1914 that, by royal decree, the zone for industrial development was designated.

In some cities, the time-limited plans of earlier eras were still in operation; in the majority of cases, however, these plans were allowed to lapse and no steps were taken to bring them up to date although, in many towns, the development limits originally fixed had already been exceeded.

The activities of the united state of Italy in the sphere of public works were more effective in the countryside than in the cities; but these activities were of a casual nature, not integrated with land improvement projects, too much biased in favor of northern and central Italy, and sometimes even contradictory. For instance, although 953,420 acres (386,000 hectares) of marshland were reclaimed between 1861 and 1876, no attempt was made before 1890 to halt the destruction (denounced by Engels) of 4,940,000 acres (2 million hectares) of woodlands, mainly in the Alpine region, which

Venice. Principal measures taken in the city prior to the first slum clearance plan of 1891. Hatched areas indicate reclamation areas, framed areas industrial plants. (Urbanistica, No. 52, 1968, p. 84.)

caused the disappearance of a specialized Alpine economic activity and of a balanced hydrogeological situation. To counteract the devastations caused by natural calamities (heavy floods in Sardinia in 1892, the earthquakes in Reggio Calabria, Cantanzaro, and Messina in 1894, the further earthquakes in Messina in 1908 and Lazio in 1898, and floods and inundations in 1898 and 1899), public works of considerable magnitude were carried out; but no reafforestation or river training works were undertaken.

Of a more orderly and consistent character was the construction of roads and railways. The latter increased from 1,347 miles (2,173 kilometers) in 1860 to 11,182 miles (18,036 kilometers) in 1914. Canals were opened, ports reconstructed, the shipyard industry increased and, with the introduction of electric power, the location of industries soon began to become independent of the location of natural sources of power. Moreover, with the construction of the great Alpine railway tunnels (Mont Cenis, 1857 to 1871; Gotthard, 1872 to 1882; and Simplon, 1898 to 1906), the Italian railway network was integrated with the principal European traffic flows.

In the past, the population density—expressed by the ratio of population and rooms[1]—was particularly high in the south. The first population censuses of the kingdom revealed a density of 2.32 persons per room in Calabria, yet fairly satisfactory densities in the north (e.g., in Liguria, where the ratio was approximately 1.16 persons per room). But the significance of these regional averages is merely relative; a parliamentary inquiry conducted in 1879 revealed a population density of no fewer than 10 persons per room in the working class districts of Rome—and many of the rooms covered by the census were nothing but squalid, uninhabitable hovels.

It was in the large cities—which were bursting under the weight of industrialization, immigration from the countryside, and the consolidation of the state bureaucracy—that the living and housing conditions were worst.

Toward the end of the century, under the pressure of the Marxist parties of the left and of the trade unions (which had consolidated after the popular reaction to the events in Milan in 1898), there arose a greater awareness of the problem of working-class housing. The book by Friedrich Engels, on the condition of the working class in England according to an inquiry directly based on authentic sources, originally published in 1845, became available in an Italian edition in 1899; and through the agency of enlightened intellectuals, a knowledge of the English models of garden cities soon began to spread.

In 1910, the "garden suburb" of Milanino was built 5 miles (8 kilometers) from Milan. It consisted of 150 cottages with kitchen gardens, front gardens, and wide access roads. The garden city was built to demonstrate the solution of the housing problem for workers and artisans, but it was in fact occupied predominantly by intellectuals. Milanino was linked to the city by the railway and by steam tramways which were later electrified. In the same

---

[1]This does not correspond to the generally accepted definition of density in planning usage, which is the ratio of persons to land area. The ratio of persons to rooms relates more to space standards in housing and to definitions of overcrowding.—*Editor*

year the First Italian Congress for Low-rent Housing was held, and during the proceedings information was made available on a working-class estate built in La Spezia for 1,000 families of dockyard workers. This project was made possible by the new laws on social housing enacted between 1903 and 1908.

These laws (Act No. 254 of March 31, 1903 and the royal decree of February 27, 1908) were designed to determine the character of social housing destined for a population mainly composed of wage earners, small traders, artisans, and lower ranking employees, and to make possible either low rents or economical small-house ownership backed by bank loans at modest interest rates. The loans were, by preference, granted to the local authorities and the assistance boards, but the industrial undertakings and great landowners were also able to benefit from them. The planning aspect of this legislation was, however, hardly of great importance, and a plot ratio of four fifths of the area, fairly close to that normally adopted by private speculation, was permitted.

Under the pressure of the legislation and of the needs of the less well-to-do classes, numerous measures were taken in the Italian cities. In Turin, which was already about to become one of the European capitals of the automobile industry (at the beginning of the century there were some twenty factories in Turin, including Fiat and Lancia), 2,454 dwelling units were built by the Istituto Autonomo Case Popolari (IACP) between 1907 and 1918, while the population of the city rose from 335,651 in 1901 to 502,274 in 1921.

Ebenezer Howard's ideas, which very largely prompted this initiative, were applied only superficially, and the cities upset by industrialization did not bring their planning tools up to date but were content to apply some sectorial modifications, producing the squalid peripheral districts which even today are a dominant feature of the Italian urban scene.

The increase in mobility brought about first of all by the development of the railway network and then, after the turn of the century, by the introduction of motor vehicles on the roads favored in various zones of Italy the emergence and consolidation of tourism. Tourism, at that time a pleasure enjoyed only by the higher social classes and not yet very widespread, gave rise—at first—to some dignified modifications of the environment such as large hotels with extensive parks along the lake shores and at the thermal spas as well as in a few centers of the Ligurian Riviera. Later, however, this development assumed more and more extensive, aggressive, and disfiguring aspects, which, with the extension of seasonal tourism, caused a gradual and progressively worsening deterioration of the most attractive and spectacular sea and mountain scenery of the peninsula. It was only in Liguria that some coastal regions, albeit small, adopted development plans through which they were able to control the requirements of seasonal tourist accommodation. San Remo, Ventimiglia, Sestri Nervi, Santa Margherita, and Rapallo, among the oldest tourist centers of the Riviera, had development plans. On the other hand, the coasts in the vicinity of Naples and the Aosta Valley, which had already in the nineteenth century attracted Italian and international tourists, had no such plans.

Twentieth-century Development after the First World War   After the First World War, Italy was dragged into a totalitarian political adventure and was upset by a world economic crisis which left little opportunity for town planning. On the one hand, Italian culture was eager for a "classic" experience; this is the lesson of "la Ronda" in literature and of "Valori plastici" in the figurative arts. On the other hand—due either to the requirements of the new European capitalism which needed the reconversion of capital previously employed in the war industries, or to the threat of worldwide inflation, or to the real eagerness of the administrations and governments to stem the increase in unemployment caused by the influx of poorly qualified manual labor demobilized from the armed forces—investment capital was redirected toward the construction of low-price dwellings for the less well-to-do. An orientation similar to that experienced in the Netherlands, France, and Vienna was also encountered in Milan, where the socialist municipal administration was responsible for a vast housing program. This resulted in a number of garden cities such as Campo dei Fiori, Baravalle, Gran Sasso, Tiepolo, and Breda, but there was little scope for town planners in these schemes, which were hastily carried out in Milan and other Italian cities.

In 1928, the last traces of representative government were eliminated by Fascism which, with its March on Rome in 1922, had begun its ascent to power. And with the final establishment of the dictatorship, a government-inspired planning mentality was imposed.

The 1926 contest for a Milan development plan provided perhaps the first opportunity for urban planners to apply their own ideas to a complex organism which contained all the planning problems of a great city: transformations of the town center, dictated by the rise in car ownership and by the need for slum clearance, and the construction of a subway system. The first prize project by Portaluppi and Semenza took a purely technological view of the city and envisaged such demolitions that the historic town center would have completely vanished.

The second prize was awarded to the Club of Milanese Town Planners (linked to the Milanese group of 1900), consisting of Alpago Novello, Buzzi, Cabiati, De Finetti, Ferrazza, Gadola, Lancia, Marelli, Muzio, Palumbo, Ponti, and Reggiori. They believed in proceeding by means of microoperations designed to improve the old and inadequate road networks. In contrast, the Roman town planners (led by Aschieri and Limongelli) inaugurated a vision of the city inspired by Piranesi, which was devoid of scientific coherence but sustained by the dictatorial regime which regarded it as a valid means of glorification and saw in it a tie (nonexistent in fact) with ancient Rome (and Fascism always had a Rome complex).

Limongelli's school was joined by Marcello Piacentini who, early in his professional career, had followed the classifying simplification of Olbricht's methods and who, in 1926, had completed the construction of a new town center for the lower part of Bergamo—having won a first contest in 1906 and a second, together with Quaroni, in 1907.

Around 1930, Marcello Piacentini's planning and building activities included the reconstruction of the town center of Brescia, the University City in Rome (which, though redeemed by some rationalistic buildings, suffers from a showpiece monumentalism in the general arrangement), the "E 42," the demolition of the Spina dei Borghi (which had provided a correct access to Bernini's Piazza San Pietro in Rome), and the construction of the Via della Conciliazione.

To monumentalize the country, ill-advised demolition and irreparable destruction were imposed on the fabric of nearly all the Italian cities, large and small. Avellino, Milan, Catanzaro, Palermo, Bergamo, Cremona, Lecce, Genoa, Naples, Como, Triest, Brunico, Ferrara, Lucca, Viterbo, Sassari, Benevento, Mantua, Pesaro (where, as in other cities, the ghetto was eliminated—not without good justification), Alessandria, Taranto, and Rome witnessed the disappearance under the pickaxe of their oldest and most jealously guarded neighborhoods in order to make room for the rhetorical edifices of Fascism, for civic centers rich in travertine and marble, for wide and straight avenues which upset the minute and balanced fabric of streets. Such avenues were designed partly to permit the exposure of anonymous remnants of Roman culture which, however, thus isolated and displayed, lost their attraction and their beauty.

Opposed to the trend initiated by Piacentini—a trend which had become the fashion and was supported by the official representatives of culture and by the Fascist Union of Architects—were Pagano, editor of the journal *Casabella,* and some young architects united in the defense of rationalist architecture, in the desire to overcome the narrow bounds of national culture imposed by the cultural autarchy of Fascism. These young architects aimed at a more scientific and up-to-date approach to the problem of the city.

To this school belonged the proposal by Pagano, Levi, Cuzzi, Aloisio, and Sottsass for the Via Roma in Turin (which was eventually built in "miniature baroque" because of a misunderstanding of the principles governing the insertion of new structures into a historic environment) and the construction of some urban centers for agricultural units created afresh by the regime where a certain modesty, or rather a subdued rhetoric, was tolerated.

The scheme for the reclamation of the Pontine Marshes was an unusual example of regional planning, proving, as it did, to be unique as a realization, complete, and very extensive.

In the political context of the "battle of the grain" (for self-sufficiency in the agricultural sector) and of the "demographical battle" (to increase rather than restrict the population of the country), the Fascist state had launched a program of "complete reclamation" of the entire national territory. The Pontine Marshes, vainly tackled first by the popes and then by the unified state, had remained for a long time a vast, unproductive territory covering an area of 197,720 acres (80,000 hectares), owned by a few landlords, and inhabited by very few shepherds and woodcutters (18 inhabitants per square mile or 7 per square kilometer).

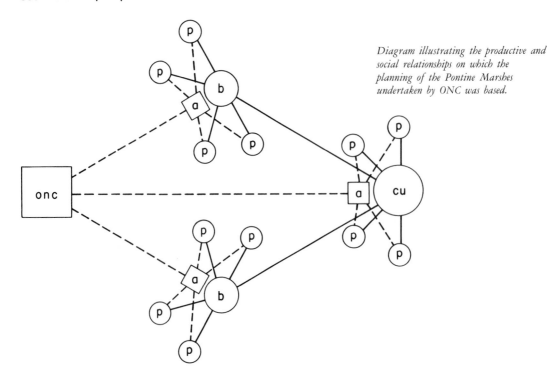

Diagram illustrating the productive and social relationships on which the planning of the Pontine Marshes undertaken by ONC was based.

onc = Opera Nazionale Combattenti (National Works for War Veterans), Rome headquarters.

cu = centro urbano (urban center), main center for social functions.

b = borghi agricoli (agricultural villages).

p = poderi sparsi (scattered small-holdings).

a = azienda agricola (agricultural agency, ONC branch office).

_____ = relationships of social type.

----- = relationships of productive type.

The Opera Nazionale Combattenti (ONC) undertook the task of making this zone one of the richest agricultural provinces of the nation. The land was expropriated and, by 1926, ONC had already completed the construction of dikes, canals, and embankments. The year 1930 saw the construction of roads, deforestation, property transfer, and necessary initial cultivation. The year 1934 saw the creation of the province of Littoria (now known as Latina), comprising the whole zone of the lowland and a ribbon of hilly country in the background formerly belonging to the province of Rome. In 1939, the objectives which ONC had adopted were attained. In 10 years, there were constructed 1,240 miles (2,000 kilometers) of canals, 6,200 miles (10,000 kilometers) of drains, 124 miles (200 kilometers) of roads, 4,000

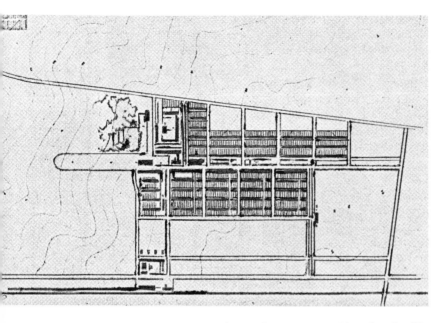

Aprilia. Contest for the master plan, 1936. The project (not awarded a prize) reproduces on a smaller scale than at Sabaudia the themes of European rationalism which had little bearing on the architectural and urban planning culture of the country during the Fascist era. (Architects: Quaroni, Tdeschi, and Montuori.)

houses for settlers, 20 villages, and 5 urban centers—Littoria, Aprilia, Sabaudia, Ponezia, and Pontinia.

As part of the general plan for this territory, the national park on Monte Circeo was created. Unfortunately this was confined to a mere 4 square miles (10 square kilometers). By 1936, the population density of the area had risen to 98 inhabitants per square mile (38 inhabitants per square kilometer). The figure reached 194 per square mile (75 per square kilometer) by 1951 and 342 per square mile (132 per square kilometer) by 1965.

From a technical point of view, the reclamation was a large-scale operation carried out on the basis of thorough engineering studies; but from an urban planning point of view, it had more negative than positive aspects. The forecasts of population growth were inaccurate, so that out of the five "towns," only Littoria (a provincial capital and industrial center of some importance) and Aprilia (completely destroyed during the Allied landings at Anzio) reached or exceeded the predicted figures. It was, therefore, necessary, in the postwar period, to revise the master plans. The other towns, however, failed to reach the predicted maximum limits of their development. The forecasts for the development of productivity were imposed on the rigid assumption that, with the exception of Littoria, the region would assume an essentially agricultural character. This premise, made immutable by the static character of the plans, still weighs on the provincial economy. Even the small agricultural landholder, whose livelihood depends upon time-honored patterns of agrarian organization, has been unable to adjust to postwar technological developments or to the emergence of new social values (mobility, urbanization, new requirements of agricultural workers).

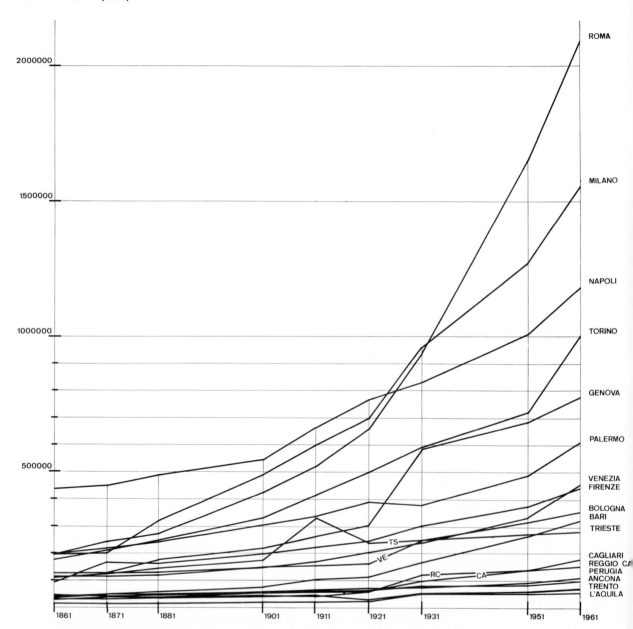

Increase in the resident population in the regional capitals between 1861 and 1961. (ISTAT data.)

On the other hand, concrete and extensive experiments were made with the concepts of zoning and standards (20 prototype buildings for small landholders were developed, as well as numerous prototypes for urban dwellings based on a housing standard of one room per person and 344 square feet or 30 square meters per room); a beginning was made to solve the traffic problem in a rational manner and, most important of all, the concept of regional planning was introduced for the first time.

The small landholding, conceived as a social, economic, and planning unit, was the basic element in regional planning. The small holdings contained within a radius of $2\frac{1}{2}$ to 3 miles (4 to 5 kilometers) had a first center in the *borgo* or village—a functional rather than an administrative unit which, apart from the houses of the ONC officials, comprised the essential services. The *borghi* were in direct contact with the ONC headquarters in Rome as far as questions of productivity were concerned and with the local *città* or city as far as administrative and political relations were concerned. The *città* was the seat of the administrative, political, trade union, educational, assistance, commercial, leisure time, religious, and military authorities and of the commercial agencies.

This scheme of simple relationships provided the theoretical framework for the plan of Sabaudia (Cancellotti, Montuori, Piccinato, and Scalpelli)—in deliberate contradiction to the nineteenth-century concept of the static city and as a means of resolving the dualism of town and country.

In 1931, Alberto Sartoris suggested a city of the "belt" type, thus transferring to the orbit of Italian culture the themes which, in earlier years, had been suggested by Le Corbusier. In 1940, Diotallevi, Marescotti, and Pagano designed the horizontal city with detached houses and amenities concentrated in the center and a density of about 100 persons per acre (250 per hectare). In 1938, the architects Albini, Gardella, Minoletti, Pagano, Palanti, Prevadal, and Romano presented a plan for a Milan district known as Milano Verde (Green Milan). This redevelopment, which assigned to each district the usual scenographic features and the usual purposes, represented a new approach and incorporated correct orientation of the dwellings (never previously heeded in Milan), abolition of the backyards and use of all the open spaces for green zones (of which the city was almost totally devoid), tidy differentiation between roads of varying importance, and careful zoning with emphasis on district centers.

A similar scheme was actually realized by Sartoris and Terragni in Como (1938) with the satellite city for workers at Rebbio (never completed).

These urban planners, young at that time, who strove to renew urban culture in Italy and to enable it to overcome narrow national bounds, did not succeed in finding allies for their struggle either in the colleges or in the National Town Planning Institute.

The latter, founded in 1929 following the Twelfth International Town Planning Congress and promoted in Rome by the International Federation for Housing and Town Planning, was dominated by Italian academicians such as Giovannoni and Ojetti and by the very active Piacentini, Foschini, Del Debbio, and Morpurgo. The Faculty of Architecture, founded after 1919 from conflicting elements of the engineering colleges and the academies of art, was likewise the undisputed domain of professors who had lost interest in European architectural culture and had, for a long time, excluded the teaching of town planning, just barely tolerating it if it conformed to building regulations.

Only the journals took up the struggle between the two opposite cultural positions; but the lack of mutual understanding, the difference in substance and even in terminology made agreement between the two opposing viewpoints impossible. The periodicals of that time were, on the one hand, *Architettura* (1932–1943), edited by Piacentini, which had taken the place of *Architettura ed Arti decorative* (1921–1931), edited by Giovannoni and Piacentini; and, on the other hand, *Casabella* (1928–1943), edited by Pagano until 1936 and by Persico until the journal had to cease publication by order of the Ministry for Popular Culture. There followed *Rassegna di architettura* (1929–1940); *Quadrante* (1933–1936); *Domus* (1928–   ) edited by Gio Ponti on principles of impartiality with regard to the two tendencies; *Poligono* (1923–1931); *Colosseo* (1933–1934); *Colonna* (1943); *Vetrina,* which had the cooperation of Raffaello Giolli; and finally *Urbanistica,* organ of the Piedmontese section of INU Instituto Nazionale di Urbanistica (1932) and later of the National Town Planning Institute (1933–1945) under the editorship of Betta and di Melis.

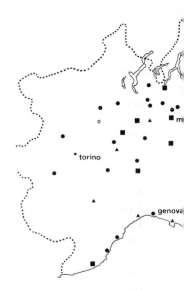

Although modern urban planning aligned with modern experience abroad had little opportunity to assert itself in the cultural and political context of Fascism—generally given to improvising, being nationalistic in culture and reactionary in politics—the Italian cities underwent during the Fascist period a considerable development which was also due in part to the increasing rhythm of industrial production and a relative rise in the average income. Between 1921 and 1931, among the cities which at the latter date had more than 100,000 inhabitants, La Spezia, Genoa, Reggio Calabria, Bari, and Cagliari—all being coastal cities with ports—had a high growth rate; the same applied to the industrial cities of Milan and Verona as well as to Venice, where the economic standard rose as the town again became the market for the newly acquired eastern provinces. Rome, center of the government, also grew. The only decline in population occurred in the southern cities of Palermo and Catania, while the other cities of industrial or tertiary character, mostly in the interior of the country, experienced moderate increases in population. The virtually general increase was due to the abrupt stoppage of emigration imposed by the United States and by many European and other American countries, to the boom of the industries protected by the autarchic government policy, and to the anti-Malthusian battle directed toward an increase in population—which was taken to represent the "virility" of the country. The building industry of traditional type was required to produce dwellings which slightly improved the nineteenth-century ratio of persons per room which continued, however, to remain more favorable in the north as compared with the south, with peaks of overcrowding in Calabria and Puglia.

The activities of the official town planners, supported by the journals and by the single government party, continued to be moderate and, between 1919 and 1934 (see illustration), approval was given to numerous plans of which those of the provincial capitals are enumerated, 15 master plans (l'Aquila, Chieti, Cremona, Foggia, Gorizia, Lecce, Milan, Pesaro, Pescara, Rome, Salerno, Treviso, Triest), 9 plans for town centers (Bari, Forli,

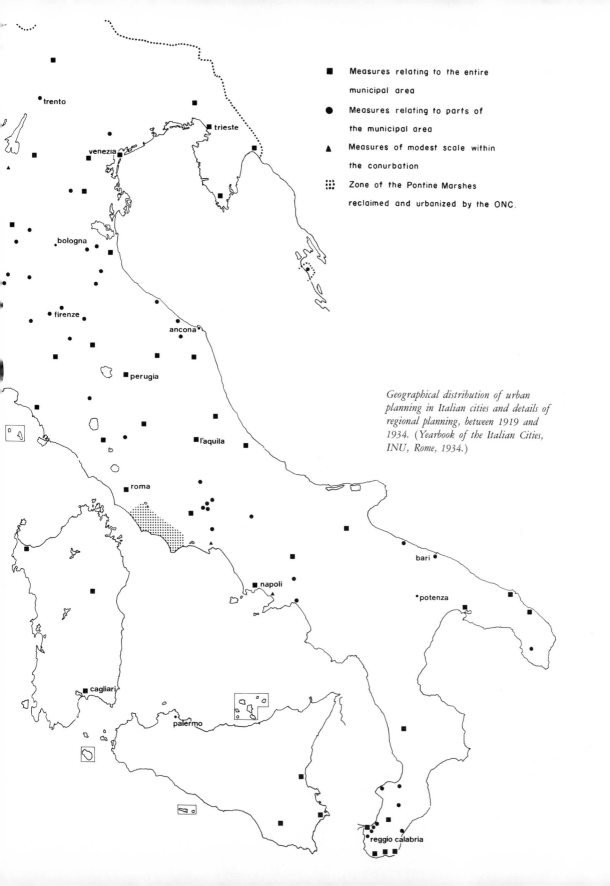

Measures relating to the entire municipal area

Measures relating to parts of the municipal area

Measures of modest scale within the conurbation

Zone of the Pontine Marshes reclaimed and urbanized by the ONC.

Geographical distribution of urban planning in Italian cities and details of regional planning, between 1919 and 1934. (Yearbook of the Italian Cities, INU, Rome, 1934.)

trento

trieste

venezia

bologna

firenze

ancona

perugia

l'aquila

roma

napoli

bari

potenza

cagliari

palermo

reggio calabria

Modena, Terni, Venice), 4 slum clearance plans (Ancona, Parma), 1 general development plan, 45 expansion plans (Alessandria, Asti, Florence, Ragusa), and 6 localized development plans for noncentral zones (Bergamo, Venice, Massa, Reggio Calabria).

In 1934, 16 general plans were in the course of being approved (Arezzo, Benevento, Brindisi, Grosseto, Leghorn, Perugia, Reggio Emilia, Rovigo, Sassari, Siena, Vercelli, Viterbo). Six were being prepared by winners of national contests (Bolzano, Brescia, Cagliari, Catania, Como, Genoa), and 8 by planners entrusted with the work without contests (Avellino, Bari, Frosinone, La Spezia, Lucca, Macerata, Padua). In 36 cities, the development was still governed by prewar plans which had not yet lapsed (Cosenza, Cuneo, Fiume, Messina, Palermo, Reggio Calabria). But although the principle that a plan could not have an unlimited period of validity was already accepted in practice, Bologna and Turin, whose plans had been approved in 1889 and 1910 respectively, should have expanded in accordance with directives, principles, and standards laid down in the old plans which were supposed to be valid for 65 and 55 years respectively, i.e., until 1954 and 1965. In spite of this, many provincial capitals and many important industrial and tourist centers continued to be without any plan.

The Fascist era saw the beginning of highway construction, which had, from the outset, a considerable bearing on planning developments and territorial changes. The most important autostradas were those connecting Milan with Turin and with the lakes which were superimposed on an already extensive development of infrastructures (railways, roads, and urban developments). They intensified the industrial and commercial development in the Po Plain and marked the beginning of new standards of living and the use of leisure time (the popularity of the weekend cottage and the holiday flight from the city). Other autostradas were constructed from Florence to the coast, from Rome to Ostia, and from Naples to Pompeii, and they became the first sections of the vast network of highways which now permits rapid connections all over the peninsula despite its rather unfavorable geographical and geomorphological characteristics.

Apart from the highways, then still confined mainly to the north, reference must be made to the increasing importance of the southern ports as a result of the colonial and imperialistic policy of the regime and to the networks of aqueducts and hydraulic works in the south, designed first of all to promote the industrialization of the regions with the lowest industrial development and, secondly, to make the agricultural economy in the most arid zones of the country competitive.

The Second World War led to the collapse of Nazism and Fascism and, through the resistance movement and the liberation struggle, to a democracy in Italy. The war period, however, witnessed the first town planning legislation, promoted by the Fascist government (1942). This act remained wholly inoperative because of the wartime conditions; but it could have become, in peacetime, an effective means of urban planning despite its narrow base and unavoidable imperfections. Moreover, if it had been adapted to the new constitutional regime, to the need for regional planning, and to the practice of organic and integrated urban planning, it could have become the essential instrument of an orderly reconstruction of the country.

Twentieth Century: 1945 to 1970   It has been difficult to talk about urban planning in Italy between 1865 and 1945 because of the absence of legislation permitting a comparison between specific measures, because of the scarcity of information about planning, and because of the absence of official data and of important town planning examples. It is, however, even more difficult to talk of urban planning during the 25 years from 1945 to 1970 because of the great variety of the development that has taken place during this period.

Two great projects, begun in secret and both coming into the open in the spring of 1945, marked the beginning of a new modern urban planning culture: these were the AR Plan for Milan and the Regional Plan for the Piedmont, the first being designed to produce a geographically differentiated reconstruction of the greatest economic concentration in the country, and the second intended to form a general guide for a thorough restructuring and development of the industrial region focused on Turin. The first of these plans is associated with the names of Albini, Bottoni, and Gardella, the second is part of the experience of the writer.

The AR Plan gave rise to the official studies for the General Development Plan of Milan; but, with the involvement of persons and ideas in a bureaucratic machine of plethoric size, the persons became exhausted and the ideas were dispersed. The first public encounter between the various forces at

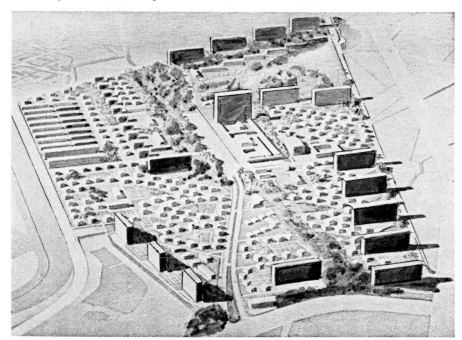

Milan. Model of a project for the Q T 8, 1947. In the democratic revival after 1945, new initiatives were taken in the sphere of urban planning. Among them was the revision of the Milan Master Plan which would have included the Q T 8—the district developed by the Milan Triennial. (Architects: Bottoni, Cerutti, Gandolfi, Morini, Pollini, Putelli, and Pucci.)

work took place at the First National Reconstruction Congress (1945) and did not, in fact, leave much scope for the introduction of new ideas into the planning and building practice of Italy's ruling class.

The studies carried out by the group comprising Astengo, Bianco, Renacco, and Rizzotti were communicated to the Milan Congress, submitted to the Mayor of Turin (February 1946) publicly displayed at the Research Council, published in *Metron*, (February 1947) and displayed in Paris (August 1947) at the International Exhibition of Housing and Town Planning. These are matters of planning history. The commission set up by the Ministry of Public Works in 1948 for the preparation of the first regional plan was unable to succeed because of the lack of political support and because of the existence, even at that time, of the sort of creeping bureaucratic paralysis which has undermined—in the two following decades—all planning attempts of a nonconformist sort.

In June 1948, the first postwar National Town Planning Congress took place under the sponsorship of the INU which had, by that time, been democratically reconstituted. The themes and resolutions of that congress gave rise to a highly topical debate on the need for, and principles of, a profound revision of the urban planning legislation which had seen the light of day in 1942 and had to be adapted to the new republican constitution, the new requirements, and the new role of the administration which, at all levels, had to preside over an orderly postwar reconstruction.

The rebirth, in a new form, of the journal *Urbanistica* during the early months of 1949 and the first introduction of the new cultural forces into the universities complete the picture of that first organizational period. But the weight and statutory authority of this new urban planning culture was soon found to be rather weak.

In the postwar period the case of Turin was symptomatic.

With the liberation, the democratic administration was reconstituted. Numerous requests for the preparation of a new master plan were voiced in many quarters, and the climate also seemed to be favorable because the city was, for the first time, governed by a popular front formed by the parties of the left. It was unfortunately necessary to wait until the end of 1947, as the City Council decided to hold a nationwide contest for the project of the master plan. The contest, adjudicated at the end of November 1949, ended with the award of two first prizes of equal merit, one to a project prepared by a team of Milanese architects, Dodi, Morini, and Vigliano, the other to a project by a team consisting of Astengo, Renacco, and Rizzotti.

The two projects, both rich in ideas, had a number of points in common. The second project provided for the complete integration of the plan with the regional development model which had emerged from the regional studies conducted by the same team over a number of years. It would therefore have been easy to combine forces and to proceed rapidly with the preparation of the plan; but nothing of the kind happened.

Rather similar was the case of Milan, although it must be acknowledged that, in that city, the building episodes and municipal measures were undoubtedly of higher quality. And yet, these were the two cities which, in the immediate postwar period, appeared to be most ripe for advanced urban planning due to the presence of lively cultural and political forces and a genuine tradition of correct urban administration. The situation in the rest of the country was much less encouraging.

This was the reason why, during the whole decade of the 1950s, the town planners were embroiled in a largely theoretical debate. There were, however, a few concrete cases of plan studies which served as a cultural test bench for exemplary projects. The plans for Padua and Siena prepared by Luigi Piccinato, date back to 1954 and 1955, respectively; the plan for Rome prepared by the Piccinato-Quaroni team was ready in 1956; and Astengo's plan for Assisi was ready in 1957. But none of these was implemented.

The plans for Padua and Siena were approved—but they were continually watered down in a manner that tended to destroy their vitality. The plan for Rome was deferred in order to gain time and to permit free interpretations and successive variants until, 10 years after the already belated approval, a considerably distorted plan was introduced. But the most notorious case was that of Assisi (see illustration). The master plan was unanimously approved in 1958; a few months later, the plan was repudiated by the same city council, only to be readopted later. Completely revised in 1966, the plan has recently been under examination by the central authorities. Meanwhile, factories, houses, convents, and roads have been built around the historic city of Assisi without any plan.

On the other hand, certain other plans had fairly easy successes. These were the cases where the plans happened to agree completely with the interests of the pressure groups which were in power or had an influence on the local and central authorities. The master plan for Genoa, approved in 1959, envisaged a conurbation of 7 million people and was clearly based on unattainable growth estimates. It represents an extreme case among the large cities but has found its counterparts in the overinflated growth estimates formulated and codified in the plans for small and medium-sized cities. An example is Andora, a town on the Ligurian coast with a population of 10,000, for which the plan envisaged a population of some 400,000.

Such plans are easily passed at the local level and attain ministerial approval, while other important and highly dynamic towns have remained without plans for years; one example is Naples, where a master plan was adopted only in 1970.

Over a period of 15 years, another 20 million rooms have been constructed either in the absence of plans, in defiance of the restrictions laid down in prudent and cautious plans, or spreading at will between the wide meshes of imprudent and incautious plans. Private building activities and many public projects (which, in Italy, have been greatly reduced, accounting for hardly 6 percent of the total) have followed their own transitory logic and have been sited at the fringes of the historic, thick network of infrastructures

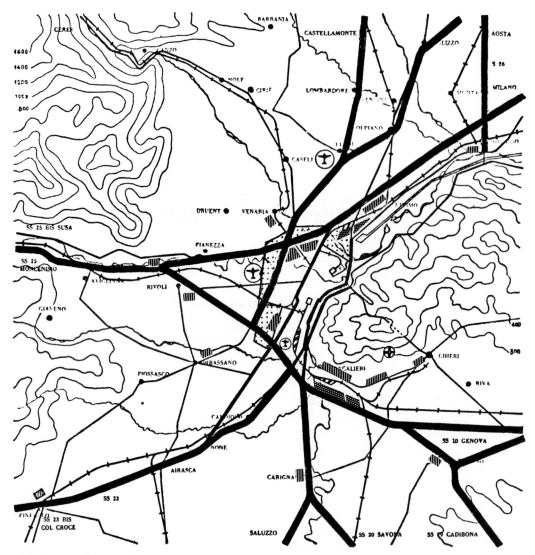

without regard to the final result or the well-being of the urban environment as a whole.

This progressive degeneration of the urban development system has prompted a reaction on the part of the most active representatives of Italian town planning.

In 1955, at Florence, the INU called for a substantial reform of town planning legislation and, in 1959, the institute formulated an alternative text to the existing law which permits and favors discontinuous and sectorial planning, imposes on the plans an unlimited period of validity, does not insist on the need for interlinkage of geographical units at different levels, eludes the operative and practical aspects, and ends by exempting the public administrations from the need to observe the already weak prescriptions of the plan.

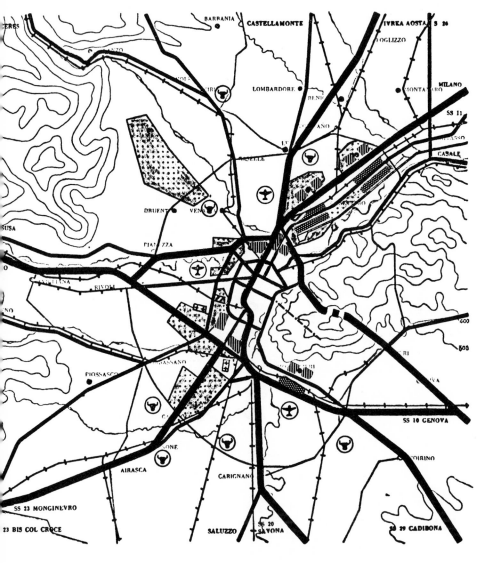

Turin. Master Plan Contest, 1947. Two First Prize projects.
(Urbanistica, No. 1, 1949, pp. 34 and 36.)
OPPOSITE PAGE: *"Piemonte '48." (Architects: Dodi, Morini, and*
Vigliano.) The project, comprising the road network within the regional
context, envisages the decentralization of the industrial plants and a
residential development, both in Turin and in the minor centers, balanced
and managed by means of self-contained units. Special solutions for the
historic town center and the north-south road artery across the
city. ABOVE: *"Nord-Sud." (Architects: Astengo, Renacco, and Rizzotti.)*
The project combines flexibility (outlines serving as a framework for
development) with a positive outlook. The main problems are the
reorganization of the industrial areas, of the residential districts, and of
the communications infrastructures.

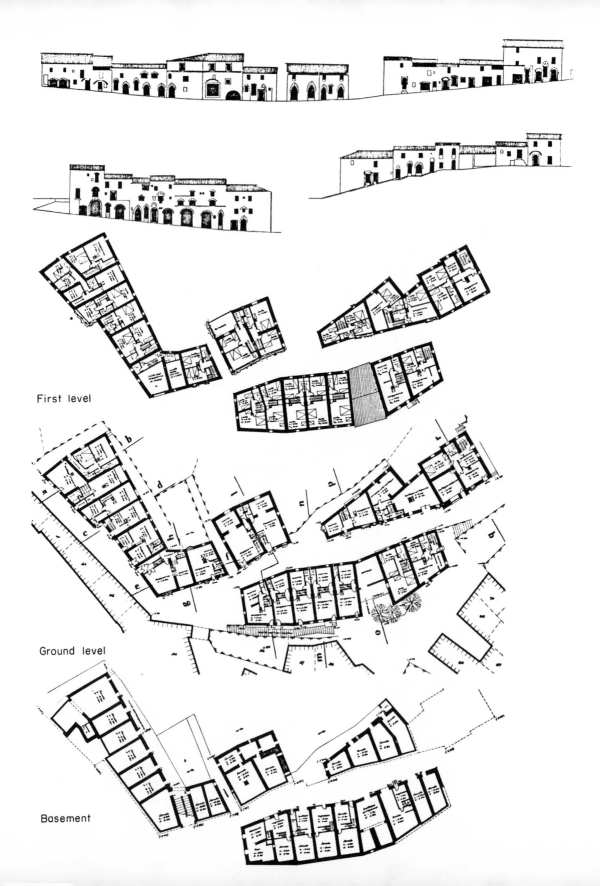

First level

Ground level

Basement

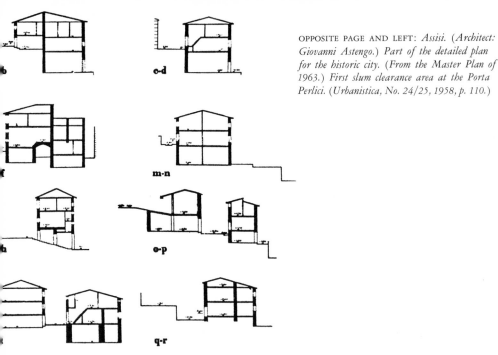

OPPOSITE PAGE AND LEFT: *Assisi. (Architect: Giovanni Astengo.) Part of the detailed plan for the historic city. (From the Master Plan of 1963.) First slum clearance area at the Porta Perlici. (Urbanistica, No. 24/25, 1958, p. 110.)*

The entire spirit of that law and of a tendentiously developed jurisprudence should have been reversed. The plans should have been capable of becoming largely operative and, as such, should have been subjected to time limits and finalized. The options should have been made more democratic, though not in the sense of giving full rein to the opposition of private persons but rather by conferring on the democratic institutions at all levels real decision-making powers and freeing the options from any form of pressure. Urban planning could have been integrated with economic programming; the plans could have been effective *erga omnes;* the costs of urban development could have been equitably spread, and parasitic profits could have been eliminated.

To the achievement of these objectives, which were extremely clear to all those who actively participated at the INU in formulating the reform proposals, years of intensive effort have been dedicated. At its Rome congress in December 1960, the INU presented a draft for a general law on urban planning. In 1961, three representatives of the institute—Piccinato, Samona, and Astengo—were called in successively by Minister Zaccagnini for a study of a ministerial project for an organic reform of the law. In 1962, when Signor Sullo succeeded to the Ministry of Public Works, the committee—still consisting of the same three representatives of the institute—were asked to draft the new bill which, published in the financial press, was immediately attacked and met with bitter opposition.

Meanwhile the ideas progressed and the key points of the urban planning reform penetrated so far that they became, in November 1963, an integral part of the agreements within the first center-left government with the socialists in a position of responsibility and majority. They constituted a substantial element in a policy of overall structural reforms.

A new committee, set up by Minister Pieraccini, still had the collaboration of the three representatives of the institute and, in April 1964, the bill was ready. Of all the projects put forward up to that time, it was the most organic scheme, with a clear definition of the interrelations between urban planning and economic programming to which the government and Parliament were at that time fully committed. The road toward the planning policy initiated by the center-left government thus seemed finally open. From April to June 1964, the bill was the subject of impassioned public debates. Suddenly, with the political crisis of June 1964, all this enormous effort of five years collapsed. Time passed and the bill was removed from the political scene.

Builders, house owners, and landowners joined forces against the bill, which was opposed as being ruinous to private property and stifling the freedom of initiative.

Then, on July 19, 1967, the landslide of Agrigento occurred. The report of the investigating committee set up by the Minister and produced in less than 2 months, on October 8, is destined to remain inscribed in the annals of public life in Italy. This report examines the history of 20 years of unsatisfactory local government which permitted irregularities and disregard of building legislation and which contributed to the serious effects of the disaster.

Some Recent Legislation   The landslide of Agrigento had one beneficial effect: the absence of plans, standards, and control was suddenly revealed. It seemed that this shock might generate pressure for new town planning legislation or at least for some urgent measures. But the urgent measures,

Agrigento. Illustrations prepared for the Ministerial Report on the landslide of Agrigento. The drawings below illustrate, in typical sections through the historic town center, the degree of obstruction of the central part of the city and the violent intrusion of recent buildings; on the opposite page, top, are two typical sections through the zone of the landslide with the recent buildings and the presumed line of the natural escarpment; the third group of drawings opposite page, below, shows some cases where the laws and regulations have been infringed. (Urbanistica, No. 48, 1966, pp. 65, 96, 97.)

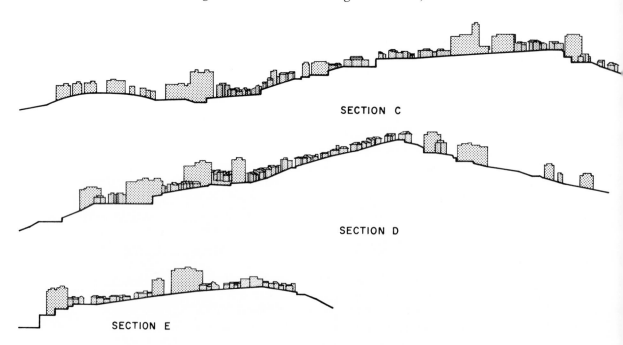

SECTION C

SECTION D

SECTION E

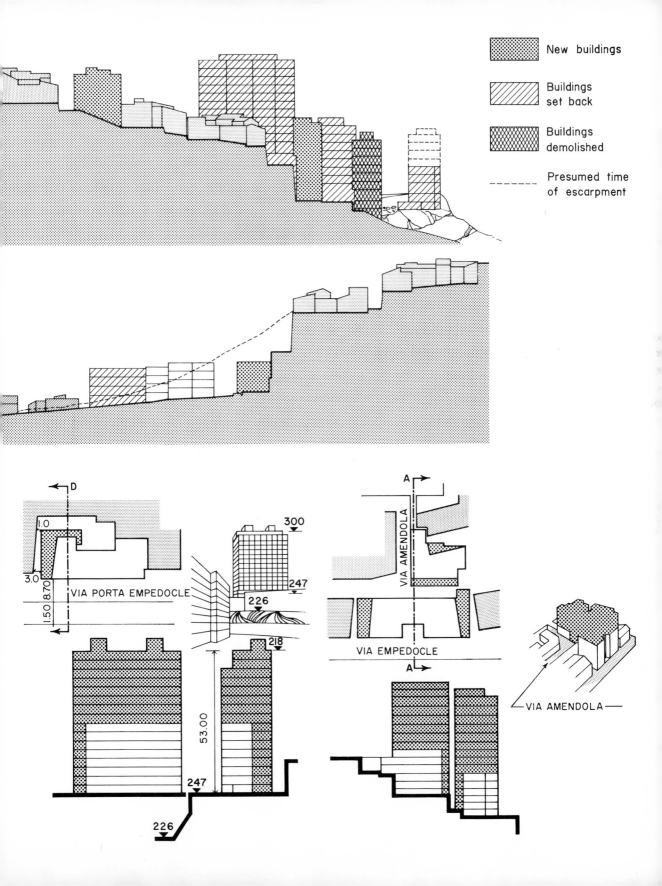

New buildings

Buildings set back

Buildings demolished

Presumed time of escarpment

VIA PORTA EMPEDOCLE

300

247

226

218

53.00

247

226

10

3.0

8.70

1.50

D

A

A

VIA AMENDOLA

VIA EMPEDOCLE

VIA AMENDOLA

soon submitted by Minister Mancini to the government and by the government to Parliament, were deferred from month to month, and the only result was the passing of the Bridging Act of 1967 which introduced some new rules for parcelling out whereby the costs of such developments must be wholly borne by the developers with the risk of being refused a license in the absence of development works and in which certain general building standards are laid down. However, by a strange legal concession, the same act permitted the construction of approximately 8 million rooms during the moratorium period of 1 year, obtained by the contractors, before the act became effective. This caused an artificial boom in the building industry which, together with the evasion of the law itself, led to the maximum exploitation of any piece of land still available for building, with predictable effects on the degree of overcrowding in the already overcrowded and badly served cities of Italy. But the Bridging Act also had a few, albeit belated, positive effects. In 1968, two ministerial decrees were issued which laid down certain minimum planning standards with an obligatory minimum of 193 square feet (18 square meters) per inhabitant for urban amenities at the local level, 48 square feet (4.5 square meters) for schools, 22 square feet (2 square meters) for general amenities at the local level, 97 square feet (9 square meters) for open spaces for recreation, games, and sport, and 27 square feet (2.5 square meters) for parks, as well as another 188 square feet (17.5 square meters) for amenities at the district level to serve as parameters to be observed in the preparation of new statutory instruments for urban development.

These represent a fairly solid advance in quality as the present provisions at the local level are generally no more than 54 square feet (5 square meters) per person and the public open spaces are nearly everywhere on the order of only 11 to 22 square feet (1 to 2 square meters) per person.

The immediate effects have, however, been scanty as the local authorities are not obliged to revise their development plans on the basis of the new standards, which are applied merely on a voluntary basis. A case in point is the new plan for Bergamo (prepared between 1965 and 1969 by Astengo and Dodi with the collaboration of Faranda and Spalla), where experiments have also been made with new scientific methodologies to ensure the coherence between urban development and economic development and between infrastructures and housing densities.

As a result of this situation, it can be estimated that there exists, in 1970, a reservoir of approximately 20 million rooms for which building or development licenses have already been granted. If all these licenses were to be used, the remaining open spaces in the cities would disappear and vast stretches of land would be used for urban developments still governed by the logic of individual choice and profit. However, these developments are now being strongly opposed.

In fact, quite recently, new circumstances have arisen in the sphere of Italian urban culture. That which for a long time had remained the aim of a few small groups which, repelled by existing conditions, resorted to civilized protestations and demands for a more humane city, adequate amenities, open spaces, the preservation of the historic, artistic, and natural heritage—this aim has now been incorporated as one of the main planks in the platforms of the trade unions, of the student movement, and of the voluntary local organizations.

The protest has been transferred from the halls of congress and from the pages of the technical press to a wider public opinion which is now also concerned with urban planning problems. It may well be that, in future, something really new will emerge for the Italian cities under pressure from the people.

A second gleam of hope arises in the academic world: From the year 1970 to 1971 onward, a first Italian course in town planning, with specific diploma, will be initiated at the Istituto Universitario di Architettura, Venice, on an experimental basis.

City planners used to be architects who had completed some fairly limited town planning studies during their educational careers and who, in many cases, alternated eclectically between urban and regional planning on the one hand and architectural, industrial, and interior design on the other with little depth of knowledge in any of these. It may be assumed that the urban planner, prepared by a course of specialized studies in which all the disciplines connected with the problem of the city and region are combined, might emerge as a completely new professional figure who will be equal to the tasks with which he will be entrusted.

In 1970, "regions" were set up in fulfillment of the republican constitution which holds specific legislative and administrative powers in the field of urban planning. The regions are placed at an intermediate political level between the local authorities and the national government as well as being organisms responsible for economic programming and regional planning. A profound restructuring is now possible, so that the archaic governmental structures can be adapted to the new requirements of a complex and composite country which, despite its high standards of technological and industrial development, still contains pockets of misery not only in the south but also in the more developed regions—a country whose intellectual vitality and working capacity merit a more humane standard of housing.

BIBLIOGRAPHY: Istituto Nazionale di Urbanistica, *Annuario delle citta italiane* (National Town Planning Institute, yearbook of the italian cities), urbanistica (vol. 1), statistica (vol. 2), Rome, 1934; F. I. Mauro, *L'ubicazione degli impianti industriali* (The location of industrial plant), Rome, 1936; G. Rigotti, *Piani regolatori in Italia* (Development plans in Italy), Rome, 1937; F. Mauro, *Terotismi dell'industria* (Monstrosities of industry), Milan, 1942, *Industrie e ubicazioni* (Industries and locations), Milan, 1945; G. Astengo, "I piani urbanistici" (Urban development plans), *Urbanistica e edilizia in Italia*, pp. 37–88, Rome, 1948; A. Sartoris, *Introduzione alla architettura moderna* (Introduction to modern architecture), Milan, 1949; B. Zevi, *Storia dell'architettura moderna* (History of modern architecture), Turin, 1950; G. Russo and C. Cocchia, *La citta di Napoli dalle origini al 1860* (The city of Naples from its origin to 1860), vol. 1, *Il risanamento e l'ampliamento delle citta di Napoli* (The redevelopment and expansion of the city of Naples), vol. 2, *L'edilizia a Napoli dal 1918 al 1958* (Building in Naples from 1918 to 1958), vol. 3, Naples, 1958; E. Howard, *L'idea della citta giardino* (The idea of the garden city), ed. it. a cura di Giordani, P. L., Bologna, 1962; L. Benevolo, *Le origini dell'urbanistica moderna* (The origins of modern town planning), Bari, 1963; a.a.v.v., "Il novecento e l'architettura" (The twentieth century and architecture), *Edilizia Moderna*,

December 1963; L. Benevolo, *Storia dell'architettura moderna* (History of modern architecture), 2d ed., Bari, 1964; G. Astengo, "I piani urbanistici vanno rifatti" (The urban development plans are being revised), *Fascicolo XVIII delle Conferenze dell'A.C.I.,* Rome, 1965–1966; Istituto Autonomo per le Case Popolari della Provincia di Torino—1907–1967 (Autonomous Institute for Popular Housing in the Turin Province), Turin, 1967; G. Astengo, "Urbanistica," *Enciclopedia Universale dell'Arte* ("Town Planning," *Encyclopedia of World Art,* English translation, McGraw-Hill Book Company, New York, 1967) vol. 14, 541–642; *Commissione d'indagine su Agrigento* (Report of the Investigating Committee into Agrigento), *Urbanistica,* no. 48, pp. 31–160 and I–LI; G. Astengo, "Venti anni di urbanistica in Italia" (Twenty years of town planning in Italy), lecture held February 18, 1968, at the IUAV; L. Benevolo, *L'architettura delle citta nell'Italia contemporanea* (The architecture of the cities in contemporary Italy), Bari, 1968; R. A. C. Parker, *Il XX secolo: Europa 1918–1945* (The twentieth century), Milan, 1969; R. Gabetti and L. Re, "Via Roma nouva a Torino" (The new Via Roma in Turin), *Torino,* no. 4/5, pp. 28–44, 1969; F. Tentori, "Ordine per le coste italiane" (Orderliness for the Italian coasts), *Casabella,* no. 283–284, pp. 5–18; G. Canella and V. Vercelloni, "Cronache di dieci triennali" (Chronicles of ten triennials), *Communita,* no. 38, 44–52; I. Insolera, "Gli sventramenti di Firenze" (The demolitions in Florence), *Comunita,* no. 103, pp. 58–77; R. Orefice, "Standards urbanistici" (Town planning standards), *Comunita,* no. 136, pp. 34–51; G. Roisecco, "Problemi dell'universita: le facolta di architettura" (University problems: the faculties of architecture), *Comunita,* no. 97, pp. 39–43; A. Samona, "Il dibattito architettonico e urbanistico oggi in Italia" (Today's architectural and planning debate in Italy), *Comunita,* no. 115, pp. 60–71; G. Astengo, "Studi, esperienze e problemi attuali dei centri storici in Italia" (Studies, experiences, and typical problems of historic centers in Italy), *Urbanistica,* no. 42–43, pp. 50–53; R. Chirivi, "Venezia: eventi urbanistici dal 1846 al 1962" (Venice: town planning events from 1846 to 1962), *Urbanistica,* no. 52, pp. 84, 113; "Convegno di Dichiarazione finale del Convegno di Gubbio" (Final declaration of the Gubbio Convention), *Urbanistica,* no. 32, pp. 66–68; L. Dodi, "L'urbanistica milanese dal 1860 al 1945" (Milanese town planning from 1860 to 1945), *Urbanistica,* no. 18–19, pp. 24–39; E. Edallo, "Formazione e attuazione del nuovo P.R.G. di Milano" (Preparation and realization of the new development plan for Milan), *Urbanistica,* no. 18–19, pp. 40–156; I. Insolera, "La capitale in espansione" (The Capital in expansion), *Urbanistica,* no. 28–29, pp. 6–90, "Storia del piano regolatore di Roma" (History of general development plan for Rome), *Urbanistica,* no. 27, pp. 74–94; *Introduzione e Titolo IV del documento conclusivo della Commissione d'indagine per la tutela e la valorizzazione del patrimonio storico, archeologico, artistico e del paesaggio* (Introduction and Part IV of the final document of the Investigating Committee for the protection and evaluation of the historic, archeological, artistic, and rural heritage), *Urbanistica,* no. 46–47; G. Michelucci and E. Migliorini, "Firenze: storia dello sviluppo urbanistico" (History of town planning development), *Urbanistica,* no. 12, pp. 5–28; D. Rodella, "Aspetti giuridico-legislativi del risanamento" (Juridicial-legislative aspects of slum clearance), *Urbanistica,* no. 32, pp. 74–77; G. Samona, "I centri storici delle citta italiane" (The historic centers of the Italian cities), *Urbanistica,* no. 35, pp. 73–80; A. Schiavi, "Industrialismo ed urbanesimo" (Industrialism and town planning), *Urbanistica,* no. 13, pp. 47–55; E. Trincanato, "Venezia nella storia urbana" (Venice in urban history), *Urbanistica,* no. 52, pp. 7, 70; G. Astengo, "Le nostre tigri di carta" (Our paper tigers), *Il Ponte,* December 1968, pp. 1493–1510, "Town and regional planning in Italy," *The Town Planning Review,* pp. 166–181, Liverpool, July 1952.

—GIOVANNI ASTENGO

J

JAPAN

Legislation and Administration   The fundamental enactment for urban planning in Japan is the City Planning Law of 1919, amended in 1968. It was amended because of the difficulties caused by the accelerated expansion of urban areas through the rapid increase of the urban population and the expansion of industry. These difficulties include the following:

1. Conspicuous urban sprawl which is partly the result of the rise in land prices. The areas surrounding cities are rapidly becoming new urban districts of low density that still include large areas of agricultural land.

2. The areas in which public facilities such as roads and sewerage are required have expanded so quickly that public investment cannot catch up with needs.

3. Rapidly changing conditions make it difficult to establish a plan.

4. As the urban extensions are beyond existing local administrative areas, no uniformity in planning can be maintained by individual municipalities.

The amended City Planning Law of 1968, which is designed to solve these problems, may be summarized as follows:

1. An area may be designated to be planned as an integral part of the central urban area, and it need not be limited to the area belonging to city, town, or village.

2. The city planning area is divided into two sections: an urbanization advancement area and an urbanization control area. The former will be urbanized systematically within approximately 10 years, with public investment concentrated in this area. Urbanization in the latter area will be limited.

3. In the urbanization advancement area, specific land use is designated in accordance with the control provided in the Buildings Standard Law.

4. Decisions on urban planning are made in principle by the governor of the prefecture; but where the planning covers two or more prefectures it is done by the central government. In small urban facilities, decisions are left to the city, town, or village.

5. When a draft plan is prepared, it is made public, and when necessary a public hearing is held. Thereafter decisions are made by the local council of urban planning of the prefecture concerned.

6. In urban planning, the matters to be decided are the special provisions and areas for residential, commercial, industrial, and quasi-industrial uses; density potentials; educational, cultural, and social facilities; transport; open spaces; landscaping; and aesthetic standards.

7. The approval of planning by the governor of the prefecture is required for development, and in an urbanization control area no permission is given except for enterprises concerned with agriculture and fisheries.

8. An enterprise carrying out large-scale development is required to construct the necessary public facilities and transfer them to the city, town, or village authority concerned.

9. In general, a thorough study is made initially and a review of the plan is carried out every 5 years.

10. The Ministry of Construction is responsible for the central administration of urban planning.

National and Regional Development Plans   Parallel with a national economic plan, a comprehensive national development plan is prepared by the Economic Planning Agency on the basis of the National Land Comprehensive Development Law, 1950. The most recent plan, made in 1969, aims at integrating various plans and laying the foundation for the comprehensive plans of prefectures. The law does not control urban planning directly, but it does give the political orientation.

The procedures for comprehensive planning in the three big urban areas of Tokyo, Osaka, and Nagoya are regulated by the Capital Region Development Law of 1956, the Kinki Region Development Law of 1963, and the Chubu Region Development Law of 1966. They also control the implementation of recommendations; adjustment between various organizations concerned; zoning; the designation of existing central and suburban areas and development, and reservation areas; limitation of industrial locations in existing urban areas; and financial assistance by the state for development enterprises.

Law Governing the Plans for Specific Areas   In order to transfer large industrial complexes to places other than the existing big cities, to bring about the focussing of public and private investments, and to strengthen the bases of regional development, two laws were promulgated: the Law for the Promotion of Construction of New Industrial Cities of 1962 and the Law for Promotion of Special Industrial Area Development of 1964. The former aims at dispersing industries from big cities, and designates fourteen areas as New Industrial Cities. Some of these designated areas are already showing very favorable results. The second law aims at developing powerful industrial zones at locations chosen for optimum investment efficiency. This development is confined to six areas on the southern shores of Honshu (the Japanese mainland). Each of these districts is contributing considerably to the rapid economic growth of Japan.

Measures of Development and Control The Building Standards Law of 1950, which is closely related to the City Planning Law, provides for a minimum standard in the construction of individual buildings and at the same time defines detailed limitations in zoning. Besides providing overall control in the zoning of specific urban blocks, such a method may serve to regulate the total density and height of buildings on each street block.

For the redevelopment of existing urban areas, such laws as the Land Lot Adjustment Law of 1954 and the Urban Redevelopment Law of 1969 were enacted. The former includes provisions for reducing the size of a building site and of acquiring part of it for road space or other purposes without the purchase thereof. The landowners, in turn, are given the benefit of high land prices resulting from environmental improvement, and thereby the loss sustained by the reduced land area is offset. The latter law makes provisions for redevelopment by the participation of private associations and by city, town, and village authorities as well as by the Japanese Housing Corporation. In order to develop new urban areas, the New Residential Town Development Law of 1963 regulates the procedures in regard to development of urban areas on a large scale and provides standards for the acquisition and disposal of land, for public facilities, for financing, and for rebuilding for those who sold their land. The Land Lot Adjustment Law mentioned above serves very usefully also for the new development.

The necessary sites for urban planning works (private residential building and building for industry are excepted) may be obtained by the exercise of compulsory expropriation on the basis of the Land Expropriation Law of 1956. In this law, the property right of landowners is strongly protected. It is seldom exercised on account of the traditional public feeling against compulsory purchase and also because of the cumbersome procedures involved.

Housing The housing situation was still acute in 1973 owing to increasing concentrations of population and the increase in the number of households. These developments are due to the reduced size of the household unit and to the rise in land prices, costs of construction labor, and utilization of natural resources. Such conditions continue, although recovery from the effects of the Second World War has been completed. For those with lower incomes, local public bodies provide dwellings at low rent, with subsidy from the state, on the basis of the law of 1952 governing publicly operated housing. In major cities, the Japanese Housing Corporation supplies houses for both sale and rental, while the local housing supply corporations and private entrepreneurs get loans from the Housing Financing Corporation. Further, under the Residential Area Improvement Law of 1960, the improvement of slum areas is being carried on. Such projects may be undertaken in combination with projects based upon the laws controlling new development and redevelopment of urban areas.

Execution of Works   After approval is given by the governor and by the city, town, or village authorities, the state or the prefectures either carry out the work themselves or works may be undertaken by others with the approval of the governors of prefectures concerned. For these works, a state subsidy or a loan may be given based on the appropriate law.

The governor of the prefecture, being the head of the local self-governing body, has, at the same time, authority as the representative of the state to supervise the city, town, or villages under his jurisdiction. When the city, town, or village is in need of subsidy, the governor requests aid by applying to the appropriate ministry of the central government. Besides the subsidy for each enterprise, the prefecture and city, town, and village receive a local delivery tax from the state. When the standard financial revenue of each local body, fixed in law, is less than the standard financial demand, the deficit is paid. There are several items to be defrayed by the state in its duty to local bodies, such as the expenses for compulsory education and the expenses for public enterprise legally sanctioned. Those items which a local body carries out in the exercise of its minimum duty amount to only 30 percent of total financial expenditure.

Professional Practice   Most persons engaged in the practice of urban planning in Japan are public officials. Almost all of them are university graduates in civil engineering, architecture, or landscape architecture.

The departments in colleges and universities specializing in urban planning are still few. In recent times, graduates with M.A. degrees have gradually increased. Some of them have an educational background in geography, sociology, and economics. As the number of those who have been trained in urban planning and practice is few, in-service training in urban planning is widely adopted.

Planners usually work in central government offices, prefectures, public housing corporations, and big cities. A few take jobs in smaller cities, towns, and villages. This is because the smaller municipalities cannot afford to employ professional planners and because they have few senior planners from whom training in urban planning may be obtained. In the central government (Ministry of Construction), prefectures, and public corporations, the exchange of officials is common and this practice helps planners to acquire diversified experience.

Although urban planning is done chiefly at the prefectural level, each city, town, and village has ideas and demands of its own. The prefectural office—having a more powerful planning staff than any particular city, town, or village—in ordinary cases drafts a plan taking into consideration the demand of each city, town, or village and is in communication with other prefectures on such matters. When a city, town, or village tries to shape its own policies into draft form or when prefectures attempt to prepare draft planning, they may find their planning staffs inadequate. In such cases, the works are entrusted to private consultants, nonprofit corporations, architectural offices, universities, or the national institutions. The organization to which such work is entrusted may ask for assistance as needed from other organizations or private experts.

The central government (Ministry of Construction), besides drafting laws and regulations and formulating standards, often gives advice.

The determination of urban planning is primarily the role of administrative offices throughout the state at the local level, but, the local assembly, besides having the right of resolving fundamental policies, customarily obtains explanations and consults informally upon individual planning projects.

The specializing departments in the central government, while exercising authority in the matters under their jurisdication, prepare work programs and projects of their own. The functions of the planning branch include drafting the total framework and integrating the plans and works of different branches. Thereafter, each branch fixes the details and enforces them.

In Japan, the rapid economic growth of the 1960s resulted in an increase in the number of secondary and tertiary industrial workers. Parallel with this growth, urban and regional development works have been undertaken on a large scale. This tendency is expected to continue for some time; therefore, the demand for experts in urban and regional planning is increasing year by year.

According to the 1966 survey, the number of physical planners in active service is as follows: private consultants, 165; in the Ministry of Construction, 105; in other central government offices, 30; in prefectures, 460; in city offices, 560; and in universities, 50, making a total of 1,370. There are also a considerable number of private architects who are actively engaged in urban planning.

Education and Training   In Japan, there are few organizations or schools in which urban planning is systematically taught. The following are university departments related to urban planning: the urban engineering department of Tokyo University, started in 1962; the social engineering department, established in 1967, of the Tokyo Institute of Technology; and the formative art department of Kyushu University, established in 1968. Besides these, urban planning courses are provided in the departments of civil engineering and architecture in some twenty national, public, and private universities, where general lectures on town planning are given to students of civil engineering and architecture. These lectures in many cases cover a term of 6 months or a year and the lecture of $1\frac{1}{2}$ to 2 hours is given once a week. The lectures cover an outline of urban planning, residential community planning, urban traffic, urban facilities planning, and regional and national comprehensive planning. Courses in the design of housing, in community and town planning, and in the technique of field surveys of traffic and housing are given under the guidance of professors in charge to students studying urban planning.

The demand for physical planners is great in Japan. At present, a program to increase university departments of physical planning is being studied at the Fifth Section of the Japan Science Council. National universities send (1973) about 140 graduates to 20 courses on physical planning annually. It is intended to expand this number in future to 80 courses with 500 students. As the first step, an increase to 30 departments is being studied.

Besides the education and training of Japanese students, international cooperation in regional development is progressing. The importance of regional development research and training was recognized in the session of United Nations Economic and Social Council held in July, 1965.

In answer to requests, the United Nations Secretariat proposed a detailed training and research plan and recommended the setting up of several training and research centers. In response, the Japanese government established, in September, 1968, in Nagoya, the Chubu Center of Study and Training for the United Nations Regional Development Program.

The first collective training course sponsored by the center lasted for 3 months, from January to April of 1969. Ceylon, India, Indonesia, Iran, Malaysia, Singapore, Thailand, Vietnam, and Brazil sent students. One trainee from each country, nine in all, participated in the course, and one observer from Japan also took part. The majority of these trainees were leaders in regional development administration in their respective countries and were senior officials in administration or professors in universities. The substance of the lectures was primarily based upon actual cases of regional development in the Chubu Region and was organized as follows:

1. General consideration of regional development
2. Detailed consideration of regional development
3. Case study
4. International exercise
5. Individual exercise
6. Study trip (Kansai and Kanto districts)

The second collective training course in regional development took place for 4 months from January to May, 1970. In the first training course, a fellowship from the Japanese government was provided to all the members. In the second training course, in which 20 members participated, 11 members received the Japanese fellowship and the other 9 the fellowship of the United Nations.

Institutions There is a specialized department in the Building Research Institute in the Ministry of Construction which studies urban planning, urban traffic, land problems, housing schemes, and building economy for the research organizations of urban and regional planning. In the Public Works Research Institute of the Ministry of Construction as well as in the

National Geographical Institute of the same ministry, the study of urban traffic, urban geography, and photogrammetry is being advanced.

Among institutions related to this field in academic circles are the Urban Planning Institute, the Urban Affairs Institute, the Japanese Center for Regional Science, the urban planning department of Japanese Architectural Institute, and the urban planning department of the Japanese Civil Engineering Institute. Study is also carried on by privately sponsored institutions such as the Urban Planning Association, the Japanese Housing Association, the Japanese Residential Land Development Association, the Japanese Center for Regional Development Research, the Japanese Industrial Location Center, the Japanese Real Estate Institute, and the National Land Development Association.

Of international interest are such organizations as the Japanese Chapter of IFHP, the Japanese Society for Planning and Housing (JASOPH), the Japanese Chapter of the Eastern Regional Organization for Public Administration (EROPA), and the Japanese Chapter of the East Asia Regional Oranization for Planning and Housing (EAROPH), which are engaged in such activities as the sponsoring of international conferences and seminars, and overseas study groups, or exchanging information on urban and regional development among the countries concerned.

Steps have been taken recently to study urban and regional planning quantatively and scientifically and to use electronic computers for urban analysis. The study project has also been gradually augmented. For example, a traffic analysis for an area of 31 miles (50 kilometers) radius around Tokyo was undertaken by the Urban Planning Section of the Construction Ministry in cooperation with the Building Research Institute of that ministry and the prefectures of Tokyo, Chiba, Saitama, and Kanagawa. A plan is now being advanced to make current traffic studies and future forecasts based upon personal trips at a cost of approximately 1,000 million yen in total for a period covering 3 to 4 years. Also, the redevelopment program of the Koto district in Tokyo, with the prevention of accidents as one of its objects, has been successively carried on for several years. It is expected that redevelopment work on a large scale will be undertaken on the basis of such a program.

The Overseas Technical Cooperation Agency, at the request of various developing countries, offers active international cooperation by sending research groups composed of experts in the various branches of urban and regional planning to countries in Southeast Asia, the Middle and Near East, and Latin America.

Geographical and Climatic Conditions Japan is a chain-formed archipelago extending along the eastern coast of the Asiatic continent from the southwest to the northeast, with the Pacific Ocean along the south and east coasts. The latitude, compared with that in the United States, ranges from that of the southern tip of Florida to that just to the north of Boston. Japan is 1,860 miles (3,000 kilometers) long but only 186 miles (300 kilometers) wide at its widest point. The total area is 142,857 square miles (370,000 square kilometers). The chief area is the island of Honshu, which makes up 87,630 square miles (228,000 square kilometers).

Topography   Mountain ranges of 3,200 to 9,800 feet (1,000 to 3,000 meters) traverse the center portion with many steep hills, and the level ground occupies only 24 percent of the entire area. The major portion is the alluvial plain and diluvial plateau. The rivers are short; they run rapidly and the ratio of maximum and minimum discharge is considerable. Japan is located on the circumpacific earthquake zone and is subject to big earthquakes and the calamities they cause in great cities.

Atmospheric Phenomena   Japan has a rather cold climate for its latitude. The average atmospheric temperature in Tokyo, located at 36 degrees north latitude, is at its height in August, being 79.5°F (26.4°C), and at its lowest is in January, being 42.2°F (5.7°C). The seasonal changes are considerable. In general, Japan has a high atmospheric temperature and high humidity in summer. On the Pacific Ocean side there is much rain at the beginning of summer, monthly precipitation amounts to 8 to 12 inches (200 to 300 millimeters); while on the opposite seacoast much snow falls in winter. During August to October, Japan is attacked by typhoons which are accompanied by violent storms, rain, and wind. As a result of these heavy rains, the turbulent rivers cause brief but heavy flooding which often damages the urban areas. The annual precipitation amounts to twice that characteristic of European countries and the United States, but as the population density is high, the water resources per person are approximately equal to those of the European countries. The entire population amounted to 103 million in 1972, and nearly half of this is concentrated in the urban areas.

On the Pacific side, there are three great urban regions: the Capital Region with Tokyo and Yokohama as its center, the Chukyo Region with Nagoya as its center, and the Hanshin Region with Osaka, Kyoto, and Kobe as the center. In these three regions, 44 percent of the entire national population is concentrated. In the past century, the ratio of primary industry workers to total workers fell from 90 to 10 percent and, at the same time, industrialization and the migration of population into urban areas progressed. This tendency was particularly marked after the Second World War, especially in the three urban regions. This rapid development and the highest land-use density in the world—that is, the high production per acre of land—caused a sharp rise in land prices, and the rise in average land values in the three big urban regions has already exceeded 10 percent annually.

The big cities with populations of 500,000 or more and the major industrial developing areas are situated on or near the southern coast of Honshu, with the greatest industrial concentrations in the area between Tokyo and Kobe. This area is called the Tokaido megalopolis, and many cities both large and small are located therein, linked together by the expressways and the New Tokaido Line, which runs throughout the area, serving these cities at an average speed of 105 miles (170 kilometers) per hour.

Cities of Japan.

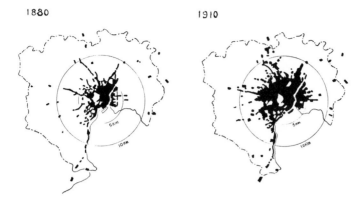

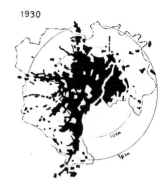

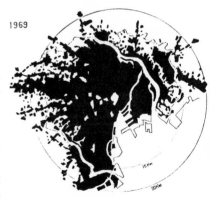

Expansion of Tokyo—1880, 1910, 1930, 1950, and 1969.

Traditions of Planning to the End of the Nineteenth Century At the beginning of the nineteenth century, Japan was a feudal country governed by the stable feudal government which had lasted for over three centuries. Through the policy of seclusion, Japan had no contact and no diplomatic relations with western countries and her social condition remained peaceful, at least superficially.

Therefore, neither social nor economic change affected the majority of towns and cities at that time; these centers of politics and commercial markets were old towns, each dominated by the feudal castle at its center. The castle was surrounded by an urban area and, for military reasons and because of the absence of carriages, streets were narrow and wound into L- or T-shaped turnings. There was also a zoning system, clearly dividing the urban area into military, commercial, and religious quarters. Furthermore, living space was fixed according to a person's social standing and occupation.

The feudal system, which had continued for over 300 years, ended in 1868, and a new government based on the constitutional monarchy was established. The new government began to assimilate the characteristics of advanced western civilization as it tried to modernize itself. The shapes of old cities began to be affected by this transition. First of all, in the capital city of Tokyo (the population was then about 1 million), a reconstruction of the urban area was carried out. Roads were widened, European-style parks were laid out, and commercial streets were designated. In order to establish a system under which such urban reconstruction might be advanced, the Street Amendment Ordinance of 1888 (an ordinance governing the improvement of streets) was promulgated. Thus, by degrees, the reconstruction of streets and general urban development began in Tokyo and in other big cities.

Twentieth Century

New Towns and Communities The cities in Hokkaido, located in the northernmost part of Japan, may be mentioned as cities that were built schematically and that have some historical background. The new Meiji government, which advocated the development of a modern state at the end of the nineteenth century, tried to develop the relatively backward Hokkaido

NEW TOWNS OF JAPAN

Name	Mother city	Commencing date	Population	Area (ha)	City function
Senri	Osaka	1961	150,000	1,150	Residential
Senboku	Osaka	1964	188,000	1,520	Residential
Kozoji	Nagoya	1965	68,000	702	Residential
Kohoku	Tokyo Yokohama	1968	220,000	2,530	Residential
Tama	Tokyo	1968	400,000	3,061	Residential
Tama Denen	Tokyo	1963	400,000	4,290	Residential
Kitachiba	Tokyo Chiba	1966	360,000	3,300	Residential
Narita	. . .	1969	60,000	487	Airport
Tsukuba	. . .	1965	120,000	2,700	Research and university
Kashima	. . .	1963	300,000	10,000	Industrial

region. It began by building, at strategic locations, hamlets which were to be the foundation of Hokkaido's development and were to receive the new population. The roads in the hamlets, as in the surrounding agricultural land, formed a lattice or checkerboard pattern. The cities of Sapporo (population 800,000 in 1965) and Asahikawa (population 250,000 in 1965) show this lattice pattern, which is like that of cities in the United States. On the island of Honshu, which is the principal part of Japan, there are many cities and city groups, and as these develop and absorb population and industry, the residential areas around them expand correspondingly. Only recently, in the past 10 years, have full-scale new cities been built. As the result of the disorderly expansion of big, high-density cities and on account of the high price of land, houses became narrow and small and the public facilities were far from sufficient. To solve this problem, the building of large-scale cities by public enterprise, aiming chiefly at the provision of residences upon low-price land in the suburban areas of big cities, is being carried out. The majority of these new cities are connected with the parent city by newly built railways, and most residents there commute to their offices in the parent city. Some of the plans provide workplaces in the new cities. (see table)

As examples of specialized types of new cities, the research and university city, and the industrial city may be mentioned. An example of the former is Tsukuba, 60 miles (96 kilometers) northeast of Tokyo, which consists of laboratories and colleges and will become a city inhabited mainly by students of the sciences. It will have a population of about 150,000. The industrial city will form a port on the coast of Kashima facing the Pacific Ocean, some 37 miles (60 kilometers) to the east-northeast of Tokyo. It is designed as a city with a population of about 300,000, and modern industry will be located there. Both these plans are already being implemented.

City and Town Extensions   Large-scale industrialization in Japan began be-

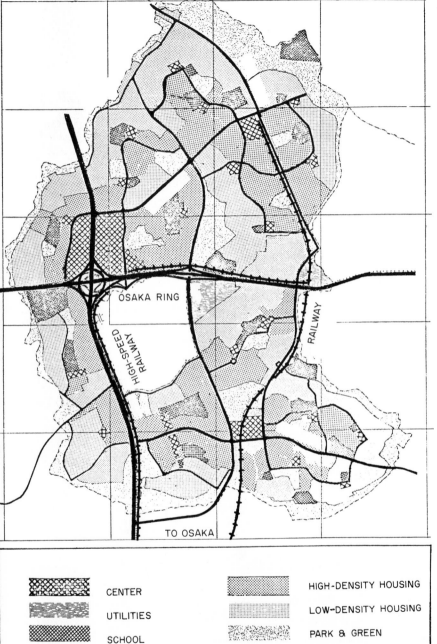

Plan of the New Town of Senri.

OSAKA RING

HIGH-SPEED RAILWAY

RAILWAY

TO OSAKA

CENTER	HIGH-DENSITY HOUSING
UTILITIES	LOW-DENSITY HOUSING
SCHOOL	PARK & GREEN

tween 1920 and 1930. This came later than the corresponding development in Europe, and in consequence city development in Japan was rapid. Population and industry were at first concentrated in the existing big cities such as Tokyo and Osaka, which continued to expand. At that time, the motor

Aerial view of the New Town of Senri.

vehicle was still in its infancy, and the presence of factories did not threaten the well-being of the general public. Also, land prices were still low, and there was little warning of the coming urban sprawl.

After about 1955, when Japan had recovered from the calamities of the Second World War, her economy began to expand rapidly. Tokyo, with a central population of about 9 million, and Osaka, with about 3.2 million, commenced spreading into the suburbs beyond their administrative areas. The progress of tertiary industry and the concentration of poplation brought about urban sprawl, and housing and traffic problems arose. Besides, rapid motorization in suburban areas with small road ratios resulted in the rapid increase of traffic accidents, air pollution, and smog from the exhaust of motor vehicles. Smoke and fumes from factories and boilers are aggravating the environmental situation in big cities.

Japan's industrialization brought about a rapid decrease in the number of people engaged in primary industry and a rapid increase in the number of those in secondary and tertiary industries. As a result, prefectural capitals and other industrial cities have grown very rapidly. On the other hand, agricultural areas and the towns within them are losing population. The Urban Planning Law of 1968 is designed to cope with the very rapid growth of cities, which has resulted in urban sprawl and the insufficient provision of urban facilities.

Urban Renewal About 120 cities, including Tokyo and Osaka, were partly destroyed by air raids in the Second World War. Taking advantage of this opportunity, the reconstruction plans were designed to reorganize the old city patterns which had developed from castle towns, increasing road widths and calling for the construction of new roads. However, because of custom and for natural and economic reasons, the majority of buildings were low storied and of wood; the land was not efficiently used, and the danger of fire remained ever-present.

The economic necessity of making good use of the land in big cities while also retaining open spaces, increasing building volume capacity, and reducing fire risks has led to the construction of high-rise, fireproof buildings. Such construction has gained momentum since about 1955, along with the provision of parks and roads. This redevelopment by high-rise structures is being carried out mainly in individual small blocks, but it is rarely attempted on a large districtwide scale. This redevelopment on a small scale has been undertaken in the commercial areas of great cities or in the central commercial districts of smaller cities. In the late sixties, the partial redevelopment of residential districts in the big cities was undertaken. This involves the construction of high-rise apartment houses with parks which are to be laid out in space vacated by large factories which have been removed to other areas.

The best example of urban redevelopment is the Shinjuku Project, for a subcity center at the pivot point of traffic in the Yamate area, some 5 miles (8 kilometers) to the west of the center of Tokyo. This is a plan to build an office town of high-rise buildings on lots vacated by the

Yodobashi Water Purification Pond Plant. The space of each block is approximately 2½ acres (1 hectare), and roads are crossed at different levels by pedestrian footways.

—Hisashi Irisawa, Hidehiko Sazanami, Hiroshi Takebayashi, and Mototsura Choh

JEFFERSON, THOMAS (1743–1826)   The third president of the United States, an apostle of democracy, architect and innovator in university planning, was born at Shadwell on April 13, 1743. His father was a civil engineer, which possibly generated an interest in the son in building and planning. After studying law, followed by seven years of practice, Jefferson entered public life as a justice of the peace and in 1775 became a member of the Virginia legislature, and Governor of Virginia in 1779.

Jefferson's early work as an architect included the design of his own house, called Monticello, built on the summit of a hill on his estate in Albemarle. It was designed in a formal symmetrical manner in the Renaissance style, showing the influence particularly of Palladio and Gibbs. He also planned the grounds with their decorative structures in the manner of the English Romantic School.

The seat of the government of Virginia was removed in 1780 from Williamsburg to Richmond, and in anticipation of this Jefferson had introduced a bill which included provisions for the new capital. He proposed six squares appropriated to public buildings, with separate structures for the various functions of government—legislative, judicial, executive, etc.—which at that time was an innovation, for the functions of governments in Europe and elsewhere had hitherto, with few exceptions, been concentrated in single buildings such as remodelled palaces.

From 1784 to 1789 Jefferson was Minister in France and his interests prompted him at this time to further his studies of Renaissance architecture in Europe.

Shortly after his return to the United States he became Secretary of State (1789–1793) and one of the four members of Washington's first cabinet. The government was at that time in Philadelphia and considerations were being given to the building of a capital city. Jefferson exerted a major influence in formulating plans for the capital city, producing a memorandum on the requirements and preparing a sketch plan of the central part of the city. Washington transmitted Jefferson's ideas and sketch to L'Enfant, the official planner, and thus many of the features of the city originated with Jefferson.

After his two terms as President, the major activity of his life was the founding of the University of Virginia and his project for its buildings and layout, which constituted his chief innovative work in planning and architecture. Early plans were submitted in 1814 and 1817 and consisted of a central square open at one end and surrounded by a series of small buildings, each with a large classroom with two professor's rooms above, together with a students' building, the units linked together by a covered way and sited in a verdant area of grass and trees. It was somewhat in the nature of a small village—a departure from the traditional planning of university buildings (*q.v.*) in Europe—and had considerable influence on later university campus planning. Jefferson's plans were implemented with the assistance and modifications of William Thornton.

Jefferson died at his home in Albemarle on July 4, 1826, the fiftieth anniversary of the Declaration of American Independence of which he was the author.

BIBLIOGRAPHY: There are a very large number of biographies of Jefferson. One that gives much information of his manifold activities and sometimes regarded as the standard work is H. S. Randall's *Life of Thomas Jefferson* (New York, 1853). For his work as architect and planner see W. A. Lambeth and W. H. Manning, *Thomas Jefferson as Architect and Designer of Landscape,* Boston, 1913; Fiske Kimball, *Thomas Jefferson, Architect—Original Designs in the Coolidge Collection of the Massachusetts Historical Society with Essay and Notes,* Da Capo Press, New York, 1968.

—ARNOLD WHITTICK

JOINT PLANNING BOARD A board or committee formed of representatives of a number of planning bodies to deal with matters and problems in their common interest.

JONES, INIGO (1573–1652) English architect, planner, and stage designer born in Smithfield, London, on July 15, 1573. He was the first to introduce the complete Italian Renaissance style of architecture into England.

In his late twenties he was sent to Italy to study painting, to which he had early served an apprenticeship. After about 5 years there, he returned to England in 1605, when he designed scenery for court masques. In 1610 he was appointed surveyor to Henry, Prince of Wales. In 1613 he paid a second visit to Italy, this time in the suite of the Earl of Arundel. While in Italy he was converted to the practice of architecture by his admiration for the buildings of Palladio, whose *Four Books on Architecture* he introduced to England and of whom he remained an ardent disciple throughout his life. In 1615, shortly after his return from his second Italian visit, he was appointed surveyor of the king's works. Among his notable buildings are Queen's House, Greenwich Park (1617–1635); the Banqueting House as part of an extensive royal palace in Westminster (1619–1922); and St. Paul's, Covent Garden. His work as a city planner is distinguished mainly for the layout of Lincoln's Inn Fields and the piazza of Covent Garden.

While in Italy, Jones was impressed not only with the stately Renaissance architecture, particularly that of Palladio's Vicenza, but also with the spacious formal layout of cities of which the piazza was a conspicuous feature. When he was appointed, in 1618, one of the commissioners to lay out Lincoln's Inn Fields, he was also instructed to prepare a plan for a large square surrounded by stately houses in the Renaissance style, with the fields or gardens in the center of the square. Several of the houses on the west side were designed by Jones himself.

In 1631, Jones was employed by the Earl of Bedford, possibly at the instigation of Charles I, to plan the Church of St. Paul's, Covent Garden,

Inigo Jones. (Van Dyck—National Portrait Gallery, London.)

and the large piazza to the east of it. The piazza was planned as a large rectangular space with arcaded ways beneath large houses on the north and east sides, a dignified treatment that Jones had seen in Italy. On the south side was a wall that separated the large square garden of Bedford House.

The layout of Lincoln's Inn Fields and the magnificent Covent Garden piazza were something entirely new to London, and they formed the prototypes of the many beautiful residential squares which are perhaps the most attractive feature of London planning. Unfortunately, the fifth Earl of Bedford was accorded permission to establish a market in the piazza in 1670. As this grew to become the principal vegetable market in England, the magnificent piazza disappeared.

Jones died in London on June 21, 1652, and was buried in the Church of St. Bennet, Paul's Wharf. The distinguished architectural historian Sir Reginald Blomfield considered Inigo Jones England's greatest architect.

BIBLIOGRAPHY: Reginald Blomfield, *A History of Renaissance Architecture in England,* 2 vols., G. Bell & Sons, Ltd., London, 1897; John Summerson, *Inigo Jones,* Penguin Books, Inc., Baltimore, 1966; Ronald Webber, *Covent Garden Mud-salad Market,* J. M. Dent & Sons, London, 1969; Survey of London (Greater London Council), vol. xxxvi, *The Parish of St. Paul,* Covent Garden, Athlone Press of the University of London, 1970.

—ARNOLD WHITTICK

L

LAISSEZ-FAIRE A term often applied to the habit of letting things evolve in social and economic life in an apparently natural manner and allowing development to remain in the hands of commercial interests. It is the reverse of planning by the state and represents the minimum of interference by government. Those who justify this policy contend that it is a natural and inevitable evolution resulting from commercial enterprise; those who oppose it claim that it represents the sacrifice of the many for the few and encourages the development of social evils like slums. Sir Patrick Abercrombie began his history of town and country planning with a significant contrast of the laissez-faire and planning approaches.

LAND CLASSIFICATION (*See* AGRICULTURAL LAND USE.)

LAND SURVEY (*See* SURVEY.)

LAND VALUE AND LAND OWNERSHIP The value of land, and hence its attraction for ownership, arises from its potential utility and from the scarcity of the potential utility in comparison with other land. In turn, the utility of land derives in large part, especially in urban areas, from the nature of its extrinsic relationships—the uniqueness of its proximity to activities which confer value.

Thus economic and cultural forces which affect the locational advantages of land are instrumental in expanding or restricting the utility of land and consequently its value.

The effects of such forces on land tenure and value are only vaguely understood and partly recognized. Certainly governmental policies, which are one major expression of economic and cultural forces, are usually based only on an intuitive understanding of their implications for land value and ownership. In fact, far more is known about the reverse implication—the ways in which land value and ownership patterns affect public policies. This situation leaves the appraiser of land value, for instance, to draw conclusions from half-understood trends and inadequate information.

Determining the Value of Land   Land is distinctive as the essential source of wealth. In fact, landholding, whether communal or individual, is one of the oldest methods of acquiring wealth. Land increases in value as its intrinsic characteristics—slope, soil and subsoil conditions, shape—and as its extrinsic relationships—accessibility, environment, regulatory requirements—are able to satisfy economic and social demands. As the pressures for land utilization grow, the extrinsic relationships outweigh the intrinsic characteristics of land. Land values are due more to external factors than they are to activities of the owner of the land.

The evaluation of these external factors, therefore, becomes the central problem in determining land value. Such an evaluation is not simple. In the first place, each tract of land, being fixed in space, has a unique set of external factors and thus a unique capacity to satisfy demands for land. Furthermore, the measures taken to make land productive (constructing buildings in urban areas) fix the use of the land for a relatively long time. Most important, the basis of present value is the future worth of land, which requires a forecast of future external factors. Economic and social demands change with time, as do the accessibility, environment, and other relationships of the land to external activities. Because land is a permanent commodity, its value must be measured by its relative utility and scarcity over several decades at least. Also, the measure of future worth should account for short-term fluctuations in value. This highly imperfect market situation makes the determination of value a difficult enterprise.

In practice, land value is normally ascertained by estimating the potential value of property at specific points in time and subtracting the value of any improvements. The three common methods of evaluating property are a calculation of the capitalization of estimated long-term income, an estimate of replacement costs, and a comparison with values of similar properties. All these methods are more concerned with obtaining a value for improvements; land is treated as a residual value, in part because the value of improvements on the land can be more readily calculated than the flow of value to land alone. Open land is valued by assuming a use and capitalizing long-term income from it or by comparison with established values of similar land. None of these methods is totally satisfactory.

Land Values and Public Policy   The external forces which give value to land are molded by public policies, either those formalized in regulations and public works or those reflecting cultural attitudes. Land values are limited or expanded, for instance, by public regulation of building, by construction of highways, schools, and parks, and by containment of population groups to certain areas. Because accessibility is essential to land value, the construction of a new highway or rapid transit line will confer new values on land which it affects. Further, the slums and ghettos of cities throughout the world attest to political and social effects on land value.

In recent years the implications for land values in formulations of public policy have had some attention. Henry George's "single tax," which was based on taxation of land as the most basic indicator of economic value, was a notable forerunner of modern concern. An increasing interest in accessibility models and in the land development process has led to a number of research studies which have constructed analytical models for examining the influence of public action on land values and for exploring their determinants. Kaiser and Weiss, for example, have demonstrated the links between land characteristics, the physical, social, and economic context of the land, and the landowner's characteristics as they affect a decision to sell or to hold land. Brigham has attempted to fix the determinants of residential land values.

The use of cost-benefit measures, an emerging trend in the decision-making process for determining public policies, holds promise for recognizing land values as a factor in development. Among other possibilities, cost-benefit analyses could enable a balancing of the public desire for an optimum use of land, which sometimes imposes a lesser value on the land, and a private owner's plans, which may emphasize short-term values.

Aspects of Land Ownership   The value of land flows from the rights attached to its ownership, rights which historically have been controlled or abridged by governments. The rights of land tenure in primitive societies are usually dependent on the form of food supply: land is held communally, for instance, in order to permit periodic shifts of cultivation and pasturage. Pressures of urbanization and competition for space bring individual ownership and fixed boundaries, both subject to sovereign rights. In the Britain of William the Conqueror, land was held by one individual from another in return for payment of dues or services. The system of land grants carried over to British colonies, where immense areas were given by the Crown in return for settlement.

Land ownership takes many forms based on the conception of ownership as the holding of all or some of the rights to its use. "Fee simple" ownership, for instance, confers all rights to use subject to certain governmental restrictions. Further limitations on ownership may involve the leasing of development rights, mineral rights, or air rights, or the granting of easements for passage.

Public ownership of land traditionally has fallen into two categories: (1)

outright ownership of all rights, and (2) easements over an indefinite time for a particular purpose, as for streets. Often the public easement reverts to private ownership on cessation of its public use. Acquisition of land for public ownership always has recourse to the ultimate eminent domain rights of the state, in which the public sovereignty is invoked in the public interest.

In recent years there has been much interest in acquiring partial rights of ownership to carry out public policy; for instance, to preserve open space around urban areas. This practice has been extended to include land in the developing urban fringe in order to postpone its development or to control development more fully.

Air and ground rights to property use have also figured more and more in public and private plans for land development. The utilization of air space over railroads in densely built urban areas is precedent for similar development over urban highways. The use of these types of rights sometimes responds more to environmental and social problems created by highways than to an established economic need. In New York City, however, an apartment building has been constructed over a new school in order to reduce land costs.

The conception of splitting ownership rights—whether separated by physical or functional, vertical or horizontal means—undoubtedly will be expanded as urban land values increase and as ownership is increasingly viewed as segmented rather than total. Furthermore, it is increasingly apparent that the influence of public action on the use, value, and ownership of land should be employed more constructively and systematically.

—Douglas R. Porter

LAND VALUES AND PLANNING   The growth of population, especially in towns, is inevitably accompanied by increases in the rental and capital values of land. The produce and rents of privately owned land have historically been taxed in various ways, usually on an area or percentage basis. In modern times many reformers, regarding the enormous increases of rents and values in growing towns as results of the collective activities of the population rather than of the enterprise of landowners, have proposed the social appropriation of the "unearned increments"; and there have been strong movements for the nationalization or municipalization of land or, alternatively, for systems of taxation, such as the single tax proposed by Henry George (1810–1897), that would appropriate all rent for public purposes.

Modern town planning—the governmental control of the use of land—can have a considerable effect on land values. Restrictions on the future use of a piece of land often reduce its value but may increase the value of other land in the same or in different ownership. Under prewar planning laws in Britain, compensation was generally payable for any such loss in value, but a claim could be made by the local authority for payment of any increase in value (betterment). In practice, however, it was found that little or no betterment could be proved and collected, whereas compensation for losses always had to be paid in full.

As the necessity for planning became recognized and its powers advanced and its two-way effect on values became evident, much study was given to the possibility of collecting increases in value in order to balance the compensation claims. The classic document on the subject is the Uthwatt report (*Report of the Expert Committee on Compensation & Betterment,* 1942) which concluded that no local balancing arrangements were possible. They therefore recommended that all development values should be transferred to the state with a once-for-all payment by way of compensation. The British Town and Country Planning Act of 1947 gave effect to this recommendation, a global fund of £300 million being set up to compensate owners for their loss of such development value as had accrued by 1947. The act then enabled a "development charge" of 100 percent to be levied on increases of land value arising from permissions to develop or to change the use of land, and the price paid for land on compulsory purchase was limited to "existing use value." Private sales were expected to take place at or about the same price.

This sweeping solution, in principle logical, broke down in practice, though many think it would have been successful if the charge had been fixed at some rate less than 100 percent to leave a sufficient inducement for the disposal of land for development. In 1952, however, the development charge was abolished and compensation for the loss of development values by refusal of planning permission to develop was limited to the amount (if any) of the 1947 development value. For a time the same formula applied to the price paid on compulsory acquisition, but in 1959 this was abolished and thereafter full market value, including prospective development value, was again paid on the compulsory purchase of any land. The compensation on refusal of permission to develop was still limited, however, to the 1947 level of development value (if any). As a result, land could be kept in agricultural use or reserved against development in order to maintain a greenbelt without any payment of compensation. In 1967 the Land Commission Act imposed a betterment levy of 40 percent (which might later be raised to 50 percent) on any increases in the development value of land realized by way of sale, development, or change of use. The Land Commission also had powers to buy land compulsorily if necessary, at market value less the amount of the levy, and to make it available for desirable development in accordance with official plans.

The then British system thus accorded with the principle expounded by the Uthwatt committee (see above)—a principle that broadly applies also in the United States and certain other countries with similar traditions—that at common law the state has a right to regulate the use of land for the common good without having to pay compensation, but that the state must pay fair compensation if actual rights in the property are compulsorily acquired (in the United States, "condemned") and the owner is dispossessed. The Land Commission and betterment levy, however, was abolished in 1971. Capital profits on loaned transactions are subject to the same "gains tax" as on transactions in stocks and shares (in 1972, 30 percent).

In communist states, on the other hand, land has been nationalized without compensation, though in some of them much nonurban land remains in private ownership and compensation is paid for compulsory acquisition for public purposes. On the allocation of land to meet the needs of the national economy—e.g., on setting up collective farms or factories—leases are granted to the operating agencies, which may be regarded as a revival of the feudal conception that rights in land are granted by the state in return for services, and that the land can be repossessed if the services fail or are no longer needed.

BIBLIOGRAPHY: Ministry of Works and Buildings, *Report of Expert Committee on Compensation & Betterment* (Uthwatt Report), London, 1941 and 1942.

—FREDERIC J. OSBORN

LANDSCAPE ARCHITECTURE The practice of landscape architecture comprises those professional activities relating to the planning of land areas, the arrangement of structures and objects upon the land, the design of out-of-door places and spaces, and thus the continuing development of a safer, healthier, and more stimulating environment for mankind.

The art and science of landscape planning was practiced by the ancients and brought by them to a high level of proficiency. As an example, the

The Hanging Gardens of Babylon.

fabled Hanging Gardens of Babylon were created in 572 B.C. as a new garden landscape for Nebuchadnezzar's queen, who longed for the luxuriant tree-covered slopes of her native Median hills. Concurrently, the Egyptians expanded the concept of landscape planning to embrace the meticulous reshaping of much of the Nile River Valley for agricultural, military, and religious purposes. A unique feature of Egyptian planning was its lineal quality, for sequential movement along a ceremonial way was for the people of the Nile a deep-rooted philosophic and religious compulsion. Reflecting the authoritarian power of their king-priests, they constructed great processional avenues that progressed in dignified cadence from imposing palace courtyard to the innermost temple shrine. Absolute symmetry prevailed.

In contrast, the Greeks, with their passion for free and individual expression, planned their cities asymmetrically with a refreshing directness of purpose. Streets were winding, the marketplaces were casual, and homes were grouped informally about their central courts. In Athens, a looming stone outcrop was transformed into the Acropolis or dwelling place of the gods. This great upthrust of white marble temples against the blue sky could be viewed from all parts of the city by the Athenians, to dominate their thinking and their lives. Still considered one of the site-planning wonders of the world, the Acropolis was a masterful arrangement of structures and open spaces composed with great skill to provide to the utmost the pre-planned experiences of worship.

By 1264 A.D., in China, landscape planners had come to attempt the creation of an entire metropolis, Peking, the capital of Kublai Khan's vast empire, as a huge, all-embracing park. Its reservoirs were formed as canals and lakes; its temples and civic buildings were placed atop wooded hills shaped from the excavation of the moats and waterways. Homes were placed along the water edges and amidst groves of rare trees brought from all parts of the world. This magnificent old city was perhaps the first to be planned "in harmony with nature" and with a comprehensive effort toward environmental planning.

The Japanese too, with their Taoist and Zen Buddhist teachings, sought a way of life in harmony with nature. Over a span of 3,000 years they developed most of their national landscape as a beautiful garden park. Stone, wood, water, and plant materials were used with reverence. In their treatment of mountainsides, valleys, and even views, they sought to align their roadways and to contrive their structures so as to reveal and express the highest qualities of the design components.

Meanwhile, in Europe, medieval man had become so preoccupied with his survival and his fortifications that there was little time for parks or pleasure gardens. Even his church stormed against such "frivolities." But with the coming of the Renaissance, men, with expanding intellectual powers, discarded the notion of suffering through an earthly existence in the hopes of achieving a heavenly paradise after death. They set about, instead, to create a paradise upon this earth; and in many aspects of their culture, as in architecture, literature, and the fine arts, they succeeded.

Hiroshima, Japan. In this beautiful town on the Inland Sea, asymmetry prevails except in the central temple, where discipline, ceremony, and the implied presence of the Supreme Being demand symmetrical order.

In their landscape planning the Renaissance designers strove for *geometric* perfection. As in ancient Egypt, nature was reordered and subjected to a rigid discipline of form. Large areas of existing cities were razed and picturesque sweeps of the natural landscape were leveled, terraced, and walled as palace grounds and boulevards. Streams and rivers were diverted to supply the water basins and fountains. Palace grounds and princely villas were furnished with ornate pavilions, sculpture, and parterres. The results were impressive in their grandeur but sterile and boring in their total effect. This drive to express the power of wealth culminated at Versailles, the vast summer palace of Louis XIV. Under the hand of Le Nôtre, the landscape planner, the grand axis of the palace grounds was extended to the very horizon by expansive terraces, architectural water basins, and bosques.

While rebellion against such excesses was to spur the French Revolution, a revolt against the grandiose and formalistic landscape treatment itself was to come from England. Here a return to a more naturalistic approach was urged by the distinguished landscape designer Humphrey Repton and by John Claudius Loudon, a popular author of the time. Their influence soon spread to America through the writings and work of Andrew Jackson Downing and later through the estate, park, and town planning of Federick Law Olmsted, Sr. It was he, the codesigner of New York's Central Park, who was the first to use the title "landscape architect" and who is generally acknowledged to be the father of the profession in its present form.

Landscape architecture, today, is being widely taught and practiced as a systematic body of knowledge which embraces the timeless principles of

Arc de Triomphe de l'Étoile, at the head of the Champs Élysées, Paris. Central Park, New York. Its effect on real estate values, its inestimable value to the city, its ineffable meaning to all who see and sense and use it, hold many lessons for the urban planner.

land planning and correlates them with emerging social, political, and economic factors.

Historically, landscape designers have had as their patrons kings and emperors. In a free society the client of the landscape architect has become society itself. Within the past century, for example, landscape architects have developed the plans for most of American national, state, and city parks and parkways, for most of the better communities, university campuses, athletic fields, golf courses, fair grounds and public gardens, and a large share of the more notable institutional grounds, industrial parks, and urban squares and plazas. In a preponderance of those places where men, women, and children find themselves refreshed, inspired, and truly in harmony with their natural and man-made environment, the landscape architect has been at work.

BELOW: *Mellon Square, Pittsburgh. This plaza has changed the city's center of gravity and created a refreshing oasis in the urban desert of asphalt and masonry.* RIGHT: *View from the office tower of the 3½-acre (1.41-hectare) Kaiser Center Roof Garden, Oakland, California. Five stories above the street and designed to support plants on a concrete roof, the garden provides a visual relief from the acres of parking lots and typical rooftops.* RIGHT, BELOW: *Model of the proposed town center for Miami Lakes New Town in Florida.*

The role of the landscape architect in society is changing and ranges now from concern with the treatment of a specific parcel of land to concern with the development of vast and complex systems of land areas and their uses. Leading educators and practitioners believe that it is not enough simply to build recreation areas and public gardens within communities and plazas within cities and towns. Rather, as in the planning of the older oriental dynasties, they believe that each community must be designed in itself as a total garden and that whole nations must be planned as wide, spacious parks, with residential neighborhoods, factories, institutions, agricultural lands, and forests beautifully interspersed.

The profession of the landscape architect should not be considered as separate from or competitive with that of the *architect, planner,* and *engineer;* indeed the four are usually closely allied. The four fields together are concerned with environmental design: *planning* principally with the broader issues of programming and policy formulation, *landscape architecture* with area and land design, *architecture* primarily with the design of buildings and groups of buildings, and *engineering* with mechanical systems and structures. City planning, and environmental study on even the most modest scale, requires a *team* approach. Each project needs the collaborative consideration of a group of experts working together, a group in which each man brings his specialized training and knowledge to bear on the problems.

In the training and work of the landscape architect, special emphasis is given to the ecological basis of life and to the natural sciences. It has been said that to this profession, above all others, history and precedent have delegated the "stewardship of the landscape." In the natural and man-made surroundings the landscape architect is uniquely trained to join in and guide the creative process of conserving, shaping, and reshaping for mankind a more livable and expressive environment.

BIBLIOGRAPHY: G. A. Jellicoe, *Motopia: A Study in Evolution of Urban Landscape,* Frederick A. Praeger, Inc., New York, 1961; John O. Simonds, *Landscape Architecture, the Shaping of Man's Natural Environment,* McGraw-Hill Book Company, New York, 1961; Lawrence Halprin, *Cities,* Reinhold Publishing Corporation, New York, 1963; Christopher Tunnard and Boris Pushkarev, *Man-made America: Chaos or Control?* Yale University Press, New Haven, Conn., 1963; Garrett Eckbo, *Urban Landscape Design,* McGraw-Hill Book Company, New York, 1964; *Beauty for America, Proceedings of the White House Conference on Natural Beauty,* Washington, 1965; Urban Advisors to the Federal Highway Administrator, *The Freeway in the City,* Washington, 1965; Albert Fein, *Landscape into Cityscape,* Frederick Law Olmsted's Plans for a Greater New York City (Historical), Cornell University Press, Ithaca, N.Y., 1968; Ian L. McHarg, *Design with Nature,* The Natural History Press, Garden City, N.Y., 1969; American Society of Landscape Architects, *Landscape Architecture,* a quarterly magazine, 2013 Eye Street, N.W., Washington, D.C.; *Institute of Landscape Architects,* monthly journal, London.

—JOHN ORMSBEE SIMONDS

LAOS   (*See* ASIA, SOUTHEAST, DEVELOPING COUNTRIES.)

LE CORBUSIER (CHARLES-EDOUARD JEANNERET) (1887–1965)   Swiss architect and planner who had a profound influence on later generations of architects and others concerned with the physical environment.

He settled in France early in his career and worked with Perret, whose early ideas and experiments with reinforced concrete had a considerable effect on Le Corbusier's later development. He published a number of books, including *Vers une architecture* and *L'Art decoratif d'aujourd'hui,* in which he gave strong and forceful accounts of his ideas. In his early houses he insisted on the reduction of all buildings to the essential basic structure and form, thus leaving space free for easy adaptation for any needs.

With his *unité d'habitation* blocks, Le Corbusier translated the utopian schemes of Godin, Fourier, and others into modern terms. He placed shopping "streets" inside the blocks on the central floor with a central walkway, and he also provided many other facilities within each structure. He visualized in his Ville Radieuse and Ville Contemporaine of the twenties and thirties dominant motifs of large blocks set amid greenery. In both schemes attention is paid to transport problems and to the zoning of activities, and both are notable for their axes, for their symmetry and for their geometrical construction. La Ville Contemporaine even had triumphal arches. Unfortunately, the placing of large numbers of people in tall blocks in natural surroundings requires huge areas on the ground for servicing, roads, and recreation. The "natural" areas quickly become overused and are no longer gardens of calm and peace but windswept deserts. The model which Le Corbusier made became fashionable after the war, and the new eclectics quickly adopted the superficial forms which Le Corbusier had designed. Slab blocks of flats, purely residential, with an exterior resemblance to the *unités* because of the use of "pilotis," balconies, lift towers, and concrete finishes, have become commonplace. They are not themselves products of the social imagination which created the originals. The parodies of Le Corbusier's ideas are fast becoming the new slums and new wastelands of the urban environment.

Among the most extraordinary achievements of Le Corbusier are the Church of Notre Dame du Haut at Ronchamps, a completely sculptural work which treats concrete as a plastic material with no concessions to previous architectural forms; the Dominican Priory at La Tourette near Lyons; and the plan for the capital at Chandigarh in India. The last mentioned is conceived on a huge scale at the foot of the Himalayas, the powerful concrete forms deriving extra strength from the strong shadows cast by the southern sun.

Le Corbusier was a painter and sculptor as well as a writer, architect, and planner. His work in a sense symbolizes the age in which he lived. We trace the sophisticated forms of the twenties with their crisp, factorylike, clinical lines through a metamorphosis of disenchantment with early hopes. Then there is the almost baroque attempt to force order back into the world in the projects for the *Ville Radieuse* and the *Ville Comtemporaine.* At the end, after the war, there is a desperate striving after plastic form and huge monolithic shapes, as at Ronchamps and La Tourette. Utopian idealism lies behind the *Unités.*

He was both artist and fighter. He desperately tried to force men to envision the possibilities of the contemporary environment. He tried to give the world new languages of expression to replace the old traditional forms.

It is unfortunate that his own work has tended to produce yet more eclecticism in a world already weary with confusion.

BIBLIOGRAPHY: S. Giedion, *Le Corbusier et l'architecture contemporaine,* Paris, 1930; Le Corbusier, *Oeuvre Complète,* Zürich, 1929, 1934, 1938, 1949, 1953, 1957, 1965; Sigfried Giedion, *Space, Time and Architecture,* Harvard University Press, Cambridge, Mass., and Oxford University Press, London, 1967.

—JAMES STEVENS CURL

LEGISLATION AND ADMINISTRATION   A detailed comparative analysis of planning legislation and administration across the whole international field is not only a formidable task but might prove of little practical value, particularly as planning is, by its very nature, a dynamic and not a static process.

In general terms, land-use planning has as its objective the utilization of land to its maximum advantage commensurate with the political, ethical, and economic characteristics of the country concerned, and with its social goals.

In some countries, the roots of planning are deep and stem from a long history of land and property legislation. In others, and particularly those in which the necessity for planning has only comparatively recently been recognized, the root formation is quite different. Indeed, as the natural flora of a country is largely determined by its climatic characteristics and has adapted itself to prevailing conditions, so too has planning legislation and administration developed and been adapted to the prevailing way of life of the country concerned. The time cycle of changes, and in particular of changes in the sociopolitical climate, tends to be considerably more rapid than changes in natural climatic conditions.

It is possible, however, to detect three strands which have, over the years, been woven to form the fabric of present-day planning—planning which is sometimes crude and imperfect, sometimes elaborate and overornate.

The three strands may be described as:

1. Good neighborliness
2. Civic design
3. Resource allocation

Carrying the analogy a stage further, the strands of good neighborliness and civic design form the warp and the strand of resource allocation the weft of the fabric. If planning legislation is the loom on which the fabric is woven, then administration must be the salesman; and if the fabric is shoddy and ill designed, then the product will, sooner or later, prove to be unacceptable to the public.

Good Neighborliness   It has often been asserted that this is fundamental to effective planning. While this is largely true, the principle extends far beyond the original concept that individuals have both rights and obligations, a right to do what they like with their property except insofar as their action would be harmful to their neighbor.

The principle also applies to the wider aspects of the setting and achievement of social objectives and, in turn, the needs of the public, which are not infrequently in conflict with the wishes of the individual. These conflicts have become greater with the changes in planning from a mainly negative or control function to the point where planning authorities are enabled to act in a positive manner so as to promote development.

Despite the wide differences in planning policies and their administration, there is, in almost every planning system, a strong motivation toward the achievement of higher standards in environment and housing conditions. The preambles to planning legislation in countries of widely differing political character have a surprising similarity in their objectives. For example, "A decent home and a suitable living environment for every American family . . ." (United States Urban Renewal Federal Legislation, 1949), and "In order to provide the inhabitants with the best possible conditions of work, rest, recreation and a many sided social life . . ." (Romanian National Plan).

The constitutional basis of a country has an indirect but important effect on the efficiency of its planning system. It is apparent that, in general, federal constitutions tend to less efficient systems—particularly in the formulation and application of national policies—as each state has considerable autonomy. Thus, federal planning legislation in the United States, Canada, and Austria, for example, "enables" provinces to undertake planning, but the real power stems from state legislation, which may vary considerably between individual states.

In Switzerland the constitution has created practical obstacles to efficient and comprehensive planning because of the principle of free choice of residence, which is guaranteed by the federal constitution. In that country planning legislation is, in the main, based on cantonal building laws.

Conversely, in countries such as Germany, which, although having a federal constitution, also have long histories of local building codes and ordinances in the principal cities and towns, the public has accepted rather more readily the advent of planning legislation and more rigid, definitive, and precise forms of control. The land-use plan (*Flächennutzung Plan*), although making general land allocations for various uses, has itself no legal force, but the building plan (*Bebaungsplan*), which is a very precise and detailed planning instrument, is prepared within the framework of the land-use plan and gains its legal force by adoption as a local bylaw. At the other end of the scale, the new development plans in the United Kingdom, which are initiated under the Town and Country Planning Act of 1968, are very flexible and rely more on policy statements than precisely defined land allocations. There is, too, a considerably higher degree of local autonomy in the preparation and implementation of local plans than had been available under earlier legislation.

The response of law to changing social conditions and objectives tends to be slower in the more liberal democracies than under authoritarian forms of government, although the factors which generate the need for change are usually very similar. These factors include changes in the economic base from, say, an agricultural economy to a more industrialized economy, rapid population growth, imbalances in employment opportunities, traffic growth, and urban obsolescence.

The period immediately following the Second World War saw an intense preoccupation with new planning legislation and administrative systems; and most European countries, both Western and Eastern, enacted sweeping planning laws. There were attempts at monolothic systems, as, for example, in Poland, with strong emphasis on central government direction, to an extent that national policy provided a land development plan as well as an economic plan. The relationship of physical planning and economic planning is referred to later under the strand of resource allocation.

In the 10 years after the Second World War, there was also a significant change from the concept of planning as an instrument of control (i. e., the so called "negative" aspects of planning—the original and formalized recognition of the principle of good neighborliness) to a more "positive" role, enabling authorities to promote development and redevelopment and to extend good neighborliness to the setting and achievement of social objectives.

The widening scope and powers of planning legislation during the latter part of the period and in the early 1960s also brought recognition of the need for regional planning. In some countries, particularly in Eastern Europe, the development of regional planning has been a logical sequence downward from national planning; in others it has tended to spring upward from local plans, as, for example, in the Netherlands and Sweden. In others, such as the United Kingdom, it has developed from existing but rudimentary measures for the coordination of local plans. In Denmark, particular emphasis has been placed on regional planning, and the National Planning Board conducted an extensive study to determine the most effective regional framework. This now forms the basis of their planning system.

The more complex and cumbersome the planning system, the less is the principle of good neighborliness apparent, even though the social objectives may be laudable and in strict accord with that principle.

It is the apparent submergence of this principle which, in certain countries, has caused more reaction against planning than almost any other single factor and has engendered the demands for greater public participation in planning which have, in turn, caused the emergence of the so-called "advocate planner" in the United States and the celebrated Skeffington Report in the United Kingdom.

It is the strand of good neighborliness which, properly utilized, can give strength with flexibility to the fabric, but if ineptly woven or even worse, omitted, can cause the greatest weakness.

Civic Design While the strand of good neighborliness provides the bulk in the planning fabric, the strand of civic design can be said to provide the color, the visual interest, and the texture of the fabric.

If one discounts early tribal codes of social conduct as the basis of good neighborliness, civic design has been one of the oldest facets of planning with the objective of visual beauty. The earliest motivations were rarely social. They were more usually self-aggrandizement, or religious fervor, or a mixture of these combined with attempts at achieving some form of immortality, of which particular examples are the pyramids and temples of a town in a harmonious whole."

The strategic needs of military conquerors have been one of the main elements in the establishment of planned new towns. Alexander's strategic and logistic needs gave rise to the building of Alexandria, Miletus, Nicaea, Pergamum, and Ephesus. According to Aristotle, Hippodamus of Miletus (ca. 450 B.C.) ". . . introduced the principle of wide, straight streets and, first of all architects, made provision for the proper grouping of dwelling houses and also paid special heed to the combination of the different parts of a town in a harmonious whole."

The Greeks prescribed a multitude of rules and regulations on urban planning, and builders and occupants were subject to stringent bylaws relating to light, air, water, and structural design. This local planning legislation was, apparently, readily accepted by the community, which thereby assumed responsibility for the control of its environment rather than allowing it to be dictated by a free market.

Most examples of earlier comprehensive planned development sprang from a combination of, on the one hand, wealthy, enlightened patrons who owned extensive areas of land, and, on the other, architects of broad vision and organizational ability. It was therefore in countries where wealth and land ownership was concentrated in the hands of relatively few individuals or social groups that the civic design thread was first spun. In particular, the cities of Paris and Vienna, parts of Rome, London, Edinburgh, and Bath owe much to the foresight of these patrons and architects.

In the eighteenth and nineteenth centuries, with the trend toward more diffuse patterns of ownership, the opportunities for comprehensive development and redevelopment became less and planning legislation was mainly in the form of building codes.

It is therefore something of a paradox that the prerequisite of effective civic design and, to quote again the precepts of Hippodamus, "The combination of the different parts of a town in a harmonious whole," have had a significant influence on the generation of legislation directed to the assembly of diffuse ownerships into one unified whole for the purposes of development and redevelopment.

In countries such as the United States, where powers of compulsory purchase of land (eminent domain) are less readily accepted than in Europe, planners have difficulty in implementing comprehensive planning schemes of a size that would allow the precepts of civic design to be effectively followed.

It is of interest that in France, where planning thought is still much influenced by the concepts of civic design, recent legislation has laid down special procedures for dealing with areas of comprehensive development. This legislation provides measures for the prevention of land speculation by establishing ZADs (*Zones d'Amenagement Differe*) in which a special government agency (the Agence Fonciere) may oppose any private sale of land and can buy the land itself at a value corresponding to the price current one year before the issue of the decrees. This procedure usually has the effect of "freezing" the land. When the area is ready to be developed, it is defined as a ZUP (*Zone a Urbanisme en Priorite*), and compulsory powers can be invoked to acquire the land at the prescribed price.

The strand of civic design has therefore had effect both at the macro level, by emphasizing the need for powers to assemble land into adequate parcels, and at micro level, by calling for power to control both the detailed design of buildings and their spatial relationship.

The principle of civic design can be dangerously eroded or stifled by legislation that is too doctrinaire or administration that is too rigorous and chauvinistic. In such a field administration flexibility and adaptation to change are important.

Resource Allocation Planning legislation and its administration enables authorities both to prohibit and to initiate development. Development requires the resources of money, land, materials, and labor, and it is apparent therefore that any planning decision to prohibit, approve, or initiate development is, in essence, a decision on resource allocation.

It is an aspect of planning which is increasingly important and with regard to which significant changes in planning legislation and administration have taken place over the past decade. Predictably perhaps, the Eastern European countries have achieved a very close integration of economic planning with physical planning.

In general, the Eastern European countries have initiated national plans which are largely economic plans and which are used as the main instruments for developing and directing the national economy and setting up programs for investment and other fiscal policies. National plans of this type are often directed toward the rectification of economic and/or population imbalances, for the speedy exploitation of natural resources, or for some other special purpose.

The effective synthesis between economic and physical planning is usually at the regional level, and the example of the comprehensive national and regional planning systems of Poland is particularly significant. There, the responsibility for overall planning rests with the Planning Commission of the Council of Ministers under the Long Term Plan for the National Economy, which originally covered the years from 1961 to 1970 and has now been extended to 1985.

At the regional level, the plans are prepared under the direction of the provincial economic planning commissions, and plans have been prepared for the economic and physical development of special areas for the exploitation of minerals and other natural resources. Examples include the mining and power complex of Konin and Leczyca and other areas scheduled for rapid development, such as, for example, the petrochemical and associated industries in the Plock region of the Vistula.

In the Western European countries the need for the coordination of physical and economic planning has not been so readily accepted, nor has such planning been achieved. There are, nevertheless, an increasing number of examples of regional planning being used as vehicles for the implementation of national economic policies.

The economic imbalance between the northern and southern parts of Italy was the subject, in 1957, of special planning legislation which provided for the establishment of new industrial development areas of southern Italy.

In the Netherlands the problems and opportunities of the western parts of the country (the Randstad) directed attention to the need for comprehensive economic and physical planning. Coordinated programs for public-sector investment and physical development have been promulgated, and rapid but controlled development is taking place in the area.

Regionalization and resource allocation planning was initiated in France within the framework of the National Five-year Economic, Social, and Physical Development Plans under the Commissionaire General du Plan d'Equipment et de la Productivite. Responsibility for the implementation of government policy relating to economic development and physical planning rests with the prefect of the region assisted by an advisory regional administrative conference.

It appears therefore that the efficient coordination of resource allocation (economic) planning with physical planning has been achieved most effectively either from a system of strong national plans, as in the Eastern European countries, or where there has traditionally been a strong regional administration, as in France and latterly in Italy.

Despite the difficulties which have generally been experienced in the United States in securing coordinated planning between a number of state authorities, one of the largest and, in modern times, one of the earliest comprehensive economic and physical planning schemes is that of the Tennessee Valley Authority—"a multipurpose long-term development agency" set up (1933) by the federal government to produce and implement a coordinated plan to restore prosperity to an area of about 42,000 square miles (109,680 square kilometers).

In the last 10 years, other examples of coordinated planning of extensive urban and semiurban areas have been prepared in the United States, particularly for metropolitan Los Angeles and the San Francisco Bay area, schemes which have derived their basis from California state legislation.

It seems reasonable to assume that the demands of social objectives will always outstrip the resources available for their satisfaction and hence that planning legislation will respond increasingly to this situation. Despite the considerable history of planning legislation in the United Kingdom and a planning system which is probably more comprehensive, as far as physical planning is concerned, than that of any country in the world, it is only since the 1968 act that planning authorities have been statutorily required to have regard in their surveys to the economic as well as the physical characteristics of the area and, in the preparation of schemes, to have regard to "the resources available."

It would seem, too, that the implications of resource allocation planning will increasingly challenge the pure and financially untrammelled thinking of the old concepts of civic design and prove to be the strand that dominates the future fabric of planning.

—K. CLEMENS

L'ENFANT, PIERRE CHARLES (1754–1825)   French military engineer who arrived in America in 1777 with the colonial troops in the Continental army. He became a captain in the engineers in 1778 and promoted major in 1783. His work as an expert in fortification was much admired by George Washington. In 1791 he was employed to plan and direct the work of building the new capital city of Washington, D.C.

Essentially, the plan is a design of two axes intersecting at right angles, each with its own focus—the White House and the Capitol. Diagonal boulevards accentuate these focuses, and a background of gridiron pattern is superimposed over the whole. The diagonals cut through this pattern, providing star-shaped points from which boulevards radiate. The rectangular plots and gridiron plan were undoubtedly for convenience, but precedents had been formed in the layouts made by Jefferson and others. The plan of Washington may well express the combination of late baroque planning on the French model (which to contemporaries would have suggested liberty, equality, and fraternity rather than absolutism) with the urbane, colonial, Georgian manner of the civilized Jefferson. Although the combination of gridiron and diagonals is unfortunate, causing a number of impossible sites at awkward junctions, the plan of Washington symbolizes the aspirations of the new republic admirably. On the main axis is the Capitol and on the secondary axis is the White House, the two great buildings of the principal political powers of the state. L'Enfant made the president's house the center of seven radiating boulevards, but as Hegemann points out in his *Civic Art,* this was probably as much to "serve the pleasure of the president himself" as for the enjoyment of the public. An egocentric plan to us smacks of absolutism, but in the political climate of the late-eighteenth century such a device, stemming from revolutionary France, would have savored of the promised land of democracy.

In 1792, however, L'Enfant withdrew his labor. Having failed to achieve recognition or remuneration on an adequate scale, he died poor and disappointed. In 1909, his body was reburied in Arlington National Cemetery, a belated recognition on the part of the young republic he had served so well.

BIBLIOGRAPHY: Werner Hegemann and Elbert Peets, *The American Vitruvius: An Architects' Handbook of Civic Art,* New York, 1922; John W. Reps, *Monumental Washington, The Planning and Development of the Capital Center,* Princeton University Press, Princeton, N.J., 1967; Arnold Toynbee (ed.), *Cities of Destiny,* Thames and Hudson, London, McGraw-Hill, New York, 1967.

—JAMES STEVENS CURL

LEONARDO DA VINCI (1452–1519)   Italian artist and scientist and one of the most remarkable many-sided intellects in history, born at Vinci, a hill village near Florence, in 1452 (the month and day are not known).

As a child he was fascinated by natural phenomena and made numerous drawings of animals and plants. His ability to represent appearances, combined with his insight into the organic structure of natural objects, formed the basis of his later activities. "Go to nature for your teacher" was the maxim that he constantly observed in both his creative work and analytical studies.

Simultaneously with his work as a painter, Leonardo was engaged in designing military fortifications, water engineering plants, engines of war, dams, and flying machines.

In 1482, Leonardo joined the court of the Duke of Milan—not as a painter but as a musician and as a sculptor who would work on the equestrian statue of the Duke's father, Francesco Sforza. He remained in Milan for 17 years, variously engaged in his many pursuits but holding the official title of designer of festivals and processions. It was during this period that he made his chief contributions to city planning. As in so much else, his work foreshadowed subsequent developments.

The mind of the artist veers instinctively to order, and confronted with what has been described by Lewis Mumford as "the clotted disorder of fifteenth-century Milan," Leonardo turned his inventive powers to the task of replanning the city. In place of the congested urban mass that Milan had become, Leonardo proposed that the population be distributed into 10 new cities of 30,000 inhabitants each. The proposal did not materialize, but it is of interest in the history of city planning as an early adumbration of the principle of delimiting large cities and the creation of new towns.

Leonardo made a proposal for a two-level city, the upper level for pedestrians and the lower level for vehicles and the transportation of goods. The city design also incorporates a system of sewers. Connection between the two levels is by means of spiral staircases. The high-level roads begin outside the gates of the city, and when the gates are reached the upper level is 6 *braccia* high (12 feet). Leonardo mentions that the site should be near the sea or some large river, so that the city's water-borne sewage may be carried far away. He illustrated this scheme by a drawing which shows a section of the city.

Leonardo also made notes on ideas for laying out a water garden and on plans for churches, castles, and fortifications.

Leonardo spent the last 3 years of his life in France in the service of Francis I. He lived in the Castle of Cloux near Amboise, where he died on May 2, 1519.

BIBLIOGRAPHY: Leonardo da Vinci, *Notebooks,* arranged and rendered into English and introduced by Edward MacCurdy. Jonathan Cape, London, 1938.

—WILFRED SALTER

LEVEL CROSSING An intersection of road and railway on the same level, with hand-operated or automatic gates. Such crossings are gradually being replaced by road bridges. In the United States this is called a "grade crossing."

LINEAR CITY A city designed on the principle that transport routes should be the main determinant of the form of plan for the city and in which the development is arranged in a long, narrow belt on either side of a central spine road. Such a city can be extended along the spine road without upsetting its balance as a whole, and all its parts have ready access to the countryside. The idea was developed by Don Arturo Soria y Mata in 1882 for a Ciudad Lineal near Madrid. One development of the theory proposed the linking of existing towns by a series of linear towns along routes joining them.

LOCAL PLAN   Any plan, subject to an approved structure plan, adopted by a local planning authority for part or all of an area. In Great Britain there are three different kinds of local plans:

1. District plans. These relate to: (a) all or part of a town for which an urban structure plan has been approved, (b) entire towns and other urban areas in a county for which a county structure plan has been approved, and (c) rural parts of such a county. District plans apply the strategy of the structure plan, provide a detailed basis for development control and the coordination of development, and bring before the public local and detailed planning issues. They comprise a proposal map, a written statement, a district diagram, and a separate report of survey.

2. Action area plans. These relate to the comprehensive planning of areas indicated in the structure plan for improvement, redevelopment, or new development, or combinations of these actions starting with a period of 10 years. They are concerned with intensive change and represent a concentration of investment and other resources. City centers; district centers; old and new residential areas; industrial, civic, commercial, shopping, or recreational areas in small towns; villages and other focal points in the countryside may be the subject of such plans. An action area plan comprises a proposals map and other illustrations and a written statement which explains: (a) present conditions, problems and prospects of the action area, (b) the structure plan proposals, (c) proposals of the plan, (d) phasing of related proposals, and (e) method of implementation including finance.

3. Subject plans. These deal with particular aspects in advance of the preparation of a comprehensive plan, or they may serve where a comprehensive plan is not needed. A subject plan comprises maps, diagrams, and statements of policies and proposals. Sample topics are recreation in a river valley, restoration of derelict land, and landscaping of a motorway corridor. (See DEVELOPMENT PLAN.)   —L. W. A. RENDELL

LUTYENS, Sir EDWIN LANDSEER (1869–1944)   English architect and planner.

Generally accounted the consummate stylist of the English architects of his period, Lutyens in his civic and larger commercial buildings was influenced by the architecture of the later Renaissance and especially by the work of Sir Christopher Wren.

In the many country houses for which he was responsible, Lutyens was less formal in style, adapting his designs to the site, the adjacent gardens, and the environing landscape.

His greatest achievement in combined architecture and planning is undoubtedly the complex of buildings designed for the British government at New Delhi, India, and completed in 1930. Planned in the main on formal, symmetrical lines with ornamental open spaces and numerous vistas, this new city has an axis running east to west, 2 miles in length, that terminates in its principal monument, the Viceroy's House.

For sheer magnificence, both in the conception of its layout and in the aesthetic quality of its buildings, New Delhi is a notable example of planning on formal classical lines. The whole represents a subtle blend of Western classical architecture with Indian motifs, domes, and minarets. The English architect Sir Herbert Baker contributed the designs of some of the buildings, notably the Council Chamber and the two secretariats.

In the late thirties Lutyens collaborated with Sir Charles Bressey in the Highway Development Survey for London, and he prepared plans in which he introduced the spacious and formal elements of Renaissance planning designed to give impressive visual effects to the city and open up development so as to give views of monumental buildings. Among these projects was the enlargement of the precincts of St. Paul's Cathedral with a southward vista to the River Thames, another was the opening of approaches to the British Museum. Wide avenues, terminal features, and greater spaciousness everywhere were characteristic of the plan.

Later, during the Second World War, Lutyens was appointed joint consultant with Sir Patrick Abercrombie for the planning and reconstruction of Hull.

BIBLIOGRAPHY: A. S. G. Butler, Christopher Hussey, and George Stewart, *The Life and Architecture of Sir Edwin Lutyens,* Country Life, London, 1951.

—WILFRED SALTER

M

MACKAYE, BENTON (1879–   )   Forester, geotect, and regional planner. MacKaye was born in Stamford, Connecticut, but his family moved when he was nine to Shirley Center, Mass. Though he did not meet Patrick Geddes until 1923, he began the practice of regional exploration as a youth in his own rural neighborhood and made systematic notes on his expeditions, culminating in a grand view of his region in *Expedition Nine.* As a student at Harvard, he came under the influence of two outstanding geographers, Nathaniel Southgate Shaler and William Morris Davis; but he chose forestry as his profession and from 1905 to 1917 served in the U.S. Forest Service, at first under Gifford Pinchot. In 1921 he published his proposal for the Appalachian Trail, a 1,500-mile mountain walking trail from Maine to Georgia. This proposal incited local groups to lay out and mark the entire trail, section by section within the next 30 years, by voluntary effort and without any government aid. In 1923 he became one of the founders of the Regional Planning Association of America; and he was coeditor of the regional planning number of the *Survey Graphic* (May 1925), which first introduced the idea of the region as the essential framework for modern urban development. In this same decade, MacKaye did a series of studies for the New York State Housing and Regional Planning Commission (a prelude to later planning studies for the U.S. Indian Service, 1933) the

Tennessee Valley Authority, 1934 to 1936; and the U.S. Rural Electrification Administration, 1942 to 1945. His chief book, *The New Exploration,* 1928, was an original analysis of the geographic habitat in terms of natural resources, energy and commodity flow, and human settlements. A full generation before MacKaye's prognosis was justified by the urban congestion, traffic jams, deaths and injuries, and environmental pollution that have become a threat to survival, he demonstrated both the need for public control over all these areas and outlined the means for canalizing and containing the population flood. MacKaye's next foresighted planning proposal was for the townless highway. Published first in 1930, and developed further in later articles, this was the first coherent plan for major highway design on the lines only later followed by "expressways," "throughways," and "*autostradas*": a road system as insulated from settlement as a railroad, with access for feeder roads limited to intervals of a dozen miles or so. Unfortunately the most essential part of this plan, the strict avoidance of congested areas, bypassing towns and even villages, has been flouted by highway engineers. As a geotect and exponent of regional planning, MacKaye's influence is nevertheless slowly permeating American thought in these fields and has won public recognition. Though his final opus, *Geotechnics of North America,* still awaits publication, a collection of essays entitled *Geography to Geotechnics,* and a little book, *Expedition Nine,* a resurvey of the same home acres he had first explored as a boy, marked his ninetieth birthday in 1969.

BIBLIOGRAPHY: Benton MacKaye, *Employment and Natural Resources,* Washington, 1918, *The New Exploration: A Philosophy of Regional Planning,* New York, 1928, "Regional Planning," *Encyclopedia Britannica,* 14th ed; Benton MacKaye and Lewis Mumford, "Townless Highways for the Motorist," *Harper's Magazine,* August, 1931; Benton MacKaye, *From Geography to Geotechnics,* Urbana, Ill., 1968, *Expedition Nine,* Washington, 1969, *The Geotechnics of North America,* unpublished manuscript, 1969.

—LEWIS MUMFORD

MAPS   A survey for the purposes of preparing a plan means the collection and processing of a mass of information under many different headings as necessary for delineating the situation the planner is faced with and for the formulation of the proposals in the plan. For these purposes it is necessary to organize the volume of detail amassed so that its main features can be comprehended readily. For most subjects this can be done most effectively in map form. In some cases, such as a survey of land use, published physical maps of the area are used at the stage of collection of the data as well as for a base map for the final presentation of the survey material. In the interests of clarity and to facilitate cross-comparison of the results of the subject surveys, outline maps are sometimes prepared. These are based on published maps, and on them survey results are presented in diagrammatic form. This is done where the survey results would not lend themselves to clear expression by notations applied to various areas. Examples of such specialized maps include growth diagrams of population and employment.

For a large-scale regional survey, many maps would be prepared, including:

1. A land-use survey

2. Maps showing the physical features of the area, such as its topography, its geology, areas of high landscape value, and obstacles to development like subsidence or flooding risks

3. Maps giving economic information—the industrial structure, mineral workings and resources, agriculture and the classification of farmlands, and public utilities and services

4. Maps illustrating the social makeup—the distribution of population and population trends, the location of employment and employment trends, and the existing shopping provision

5. Maps showing communications

In a survey of a town area, the survey maps would be different in some respects and would include such subjects as population density, age and condition of buildings, buildings of interest, and traffic studies.

A plan of proposed development, once prepared, is presented in the form of a master plan or basic plan usually partnered by another map showing the stages by which it is intended the plan should be realized. These will be accompanied by a number of subject plans, such as one dealing with transport proposals, and often plans of parts of the area where the proposals are worked out in greater detail (e.g., where comprehensive redevelopment of part of an existing town is practicable).

In Britain the content of planning surveys and the form of presentation of surveys and plans by planning authorities is codified in considerable detail by the central administration.

For surveys and the preparation of plans, developments are in hand to exploit the capacity of computers to handle rapidly and efficiently vast amounts of information. It is technically possible to store mappable information on magnetic tape from which maps can be produced automatically on a plotting device linked to the computer. Conversely, information on a map can be converted to data in digital form on a magnetic tape.

Computers can sort and analyze information at great speed. Thus maps could be produced showing any factor or combination of factors specified, giving a rapid and efficient cross-comparison of survey results.

—H. E. SPARROW

MARKETPLACE An open area in the center of a village, town, or city to which goods are brought and where they are sold. The origin of the marketplace is described in Plato's *Republic* (book 2), and the needs which create the marketplace also create the town, city, and state. In the conception of Hippodamus, according to Aristotle, the town is a grouping of houses and other buildings round a central marketplace. As, with the growing needs of civilization, cities grew and became more complex, the marketplace was often combined with the civic or religious center, but in larger cities these were sometimes separate. The marketplace was in some measure, if not entirely, the origin of the Greek agora, the Roman forum, the Italian piazza, and their counterparts in other countries. In medieval towns and cities, the marketplace formed the center, often adjacent to the parish church or cathedral. In numerous country towns it still functions as such.

In many modern towns and cities provision is still made for a marketplace—as, for example, in several of the British New Towns, such as Harlow, Hemel Hempstead, and Hatfield—and in many other places covered markets are provided. Some planners think, however, that the provision of a marketplace is an anachronism as its function is served by the main shopping center. Shops are the modern equivalent of market stalls, and even in ancient Greece shops were gradually superseding the function of the marketplace.

MAY, ERNST (1886–1970) German architect and town planner, born in Frankfurt am Main. He studied in Munich and in England and was very much interested in the work of Ebenezer Howard and Sir Raymond Unwin and in the early garden cities. He was a lifelong seeker after a wholeness where all facets of life could be combined instead of being separated from each other, and he tried to integrate urban and rural life, enhancing the best qualities of both.

He became city architect of Frankfurt in the twenties and built celebrated housing estates there at Römerstadt, where parallel rows of houses were unbroken by traffic streets and both high and low blocks contributed to an interesting and varied townscape. The streets and spaces of Römerstadt are pleasant and mellow places today, embodying some of the best English and continental ideas of the time. Basically municipal low-income housing, they nevertheless were planned with small gardens and with something of the individual qualities of English garden city ideals, yet the architecture was much more avant-garde than that of Welwyn Garden City, owing more to the models of such postwar German architects as Walter Gropius and his circle. Römerstadt is a successful essay in community design that is essentially urban, not suburban.

In the late twenties, May was invited to the Soviet Union to advise on town planning. He led teams responsible for the planning of Tirgan and for the drafting of the Moscow Regional Plan, but after 3 years of bureaucratic restriction on his activities, he left Russia for East Africa, where he worked as a planning adviser.

As a pioneer of low-cost housing, he became consultant to the Neue Heimat housing combine after the Second World War. He specialized in planning for the renewal of the shattered German towns and cities. In later years he became increasingly concerned with the deterioration of the environment and the growing dehumanization of planning due to the complexities of modern technology and materialism. Just as Soviet Russia did not live up to his expectations, so postwar reconstruction in a new era of peace also failed him. A great humanitarian, May saw the dangers in modern society, especially in the growing power of the planner to make an environment so lacking in human qualities that it becomes the equivalent of an Auschwitz of the spirit.

He was primarily a creative artist and visionary who never lost sight of the need to plan for *people,* providing them with an environment worthy of their humanity. That he was able to do this with low-cost housing—using the dominant architectural styles of the twenties, crisply cubic buildings, and landscaping where nature was respected—is a tribute to his professional standards. His greatest works are undoubtedly the Römerstadt and other developments at Frankfurt, where the environments are conducive to collective and individual activities and where the social advantages of the town are found together with the humanizing advantages of nature.

BIBLIOGRAPHY: Berthold Lubetkin, "Town and Landscape Planning in Soviet Russia," *Journal of the Architectural Association,* 1933, p. 186; J. Hoffmann, *Die Wohnung für das Existenzminimum,* Stuttgart, 1930; Arthur Korn, *History Builds the Town,* Lund Humphries, London, 1953.   —JAMES STEVENS CURL

MAYER, ALBERT (1897–   )   Architect and planner, was born in New York City on December 29, 1897. The early years of his professional career were devoted mainly to the practice of architecture and civil engineering, but since the New Deal days in 1933, and especially since the Second World War, his activities have been concerned more with large-scale urban and regional planning, prompted to some extent by his experience in India during and after the Second World War. His contribution to planning has combined design and execution of specific undertakings of innovative technical and social grasp, and pioneering introduction (1946) of new dimensions in the form of involvement and self-development of the people, later called "community development."

His demand for and actual introduction of new ideas was epitomized in the phrase "Trend is not Destiny," which he coined. A new tyranny of the twentieth century he found to be research, and especially statistics. He noted that statistics are very often the record of actual but undesired conditions, which must not simply be extrapolated. We can bend or change trend and must constantly be alert to the possibility.

An advocate and designer of self-contained New Towns, he however emphasizes that their benefits are not fully realized when they are placed in the already ecologically over-developed areas and continuously over-developing regions. They still contribute to regional ecological total overloading. To fulfill the national destiny, many need to be located in the comparatively undeveloped "New Regions" with plenty of room, with the surrounding verdant areas and land available at low cost.

Another of his significant concepts is "Decentralization of Excellence." Observing the continuing accretion to the major urban centers which contribute to the self-image and self-interest of the rich and the powerful, he has preached decentralization of excellence by directing resources to city subcenters as sources of local enjoyment and pride (later expanded to the concept of functional subcities); and to smaller cities. He has been able to design and produce several of these, in recognition of which a number of public awards have been made to him.

As the result of his life and experience in India, he became interested in its future development. He felt that it could benefit greatly from Western experience—of both successes and mistakes. Following Gandhi's insistence that India lives in her villages, Albert Mayer suggested to Pandit Nehru that with the introduction of more scientific methods of agriculture and industry villages should be built that could act as prototypes. In the Spring of 1946, Mayer went to India and started planning and building these villages in the district of Etawah about 190 miles southeast of Delhi. The project gradually expanded to include 300 villages in the region. The work was done in close collaboration with the people themselves. Mayer's early community development work helped to channel the assistance that the United States could give to India. In the words of Taya Zinkin, "Albert Mayer, more than any single individual, has provided the Government with the combination of techniques that has made it possible for them not to forget Gandhi's priorities."[1]

In 1949, Mayer prepared a master plan for Chandigarh, the new capital city of the province of Punjab, in which he enjoyed the collaboration of a brilliant young Polish architect, Matthew Nowicki, who designed many buildings for the city. On a site between two rivers Mayer prepared a fan-shaped master plan. Two large parks stretch east-west through the city, which is divided into neighborhoods, each consisting of three superblocks, each for about 1,150 families with a small central park, a shopping area, and schools. The plan for a city of 150,000 was influenced by the garden city concept and aimed at an integration of town and country. It is one of the notable plans of the century.

Mayer's project was later superseded by a plan produced by Le Corbusier in collaboration with Maxwell Fry and Jane Drew. The reasons for the change are explained by Norma Evenson in her book on Chandigarh.[2] Much of Mayer's plan was, however, retained in the actual development.

Among Mayer's other Indian work was a master plan for Bombay and a regional plan for New Delhi. He also made a plan for Ashdod, a seaport city for 150,000 in Israel. Among Mayer's many planning and housing schemes in the Western hemisphere is the plan for Kitimat, a city of 50,000 in British Columbia, prepared and implemented in collaboration with Clarence Stein (*see* CANADA); plans for Greenbelt Towns for the United States Resettlement Administration; plan for Maumelle, a new city of 40,000 in Arkansas; schemes for urban redevelopment in several cities including Washington, St. Louis, and Cleveland; and many large-scale housing and community projects. Mayer's triple qualifications of architect (Fellow of the American Institute of Architects), civil engineer (Member of the American Society of Civil Engineers), and planner (Member of the American Institute of Planners) have been a great asset in a comprehensive understanding of the numerous problems that arise. He is also keenly interested in the social aspect of planning, some evidence of which is perhaps indicated by his honorary Fellowship of the Society for Applied Anthropology.

[1] Taya Zinkin, *India Changes,* Oxford University Press, New York 1958.
[2] Norma Evenson, *Chandigarh,* University of California Press 1966 (pp. 25–28).

Mayer has received many tributes and recognitions of his contributions to civic design and planning. Two may be mentioned. One, of 1964, was an appreciation by the National Association of Housing and Redevelopment Officials of Mayer's creative ability, comprehensive thinking, and social vision, which has made possible a new opportunity for public housing; the other in 1965 was a tribute by the Citizens' Union of the City of New York for promoting the city's aesthetic interests in its submerged subcity areas. Singled out for special appreciation are his notable design of the East Harlem Plaza at Jefferson Houses, this creation of a festive atmosphere in the design of Franklin Plaza, his revision of the playground area at James Weldon Johnson Houses, and his concept of the plazas in the Park Avenue Market.

BIBLIOGRAPHY: Albert Mayer, *Pilot Project India,* University of California Press, 1963, *The Urgent Future—People—Housing—City—Region,* McGraw-Hill Book Company, New York, 1967, "It's Not Just Cities," *Architectural Record,* 1969–1970.

—ARNOLD WHITTICK

MEASUREMENT   Human societies have developed their systems of measurement in forms convenient to them and to the practical situation. The basic measurements were related to the human body and its physical capacities, e.g., the "foot," and "ell" or arm's length, and the "pace." Understandably, differences of degree in these customary units occurred not only between countries but between regions and even trades in a particular country. In 1878, in the United Kingdom, an act was passed to consolidate weights and measures, and so far as length, surface measurement, and measurements of volume were concerned, the authorized units became the following:

Length   inch, foot, yard, fathom, pole, chain, furlong, mile
Surface   square inch, square foot, square yard, square pole, rod or perch, acre, square mile
Volume   cubic inch, cubic foot, cubic yard

In Europe, as international commerce grew, the need to standardize led to the introduction of the metric system, which discarded the old units and selected new basic units, all other measures being multiples or subdivisions of those units. The meter, which became the basic unit for linear measurement, was planned to be one-ten-millionth of the distance from the North Pole to the Equator, although it now has a much more sophisticated scientific definition.

The use of the metric system has expanded and most people live in countries that use it. The United States has studied increased use of the system, and the United Kingdom is in course of converting to metric, the intention being to complete the transfer by 1975. The United Kingdom will be one of the countries adopting the Systeme International d'Unités ("S.I. Units") as the only legal system of measurement. For measurements of length, area, or volume under this system, the units which the professions concerned with land use are most likely to employ are as follows:

Length	the millimeter (one thousandth part of a meter), the meter and the kilometer (1,000 meters)
Area	the square millimeter, the square meter, the hectare (10,000 square meters), the square kilometer
Volume	the milliliter, the liter (or cubic decimeter), the cubic meter

The ordinance sheets published in the United Kingdom are already metric to the extent that they are based on a metric national grid, and the margins of all sheets based on the grid are subdivided into meters or multiples of meters according to scale. It will be many years before all sheets are converted to metric form, but the 6-inch-to-1-mile series (1 : 10, 560) will be gradually replaced by a 1 : 10,000 scale. On new and revised sheets of the 1 : 2,500 and 1 : 1,250 series, levels are shown metric; and on the former, areas are shown in hectares as well as acres.

The scales used by draftsmen for drawing plans of buildings will be replaced by the nearest metric scale. For example, $\frac{1}{8}$-inch-to-1-foot scale (1 : 96) will be replaced by a 1-millimeter-to-0.1-meter scale (1 : 100).

—H. E. SPARROW

MEDIEVAL PLANNING Between the collapse of the Western Roman Empire and the eighth century, there was a period of social, political, and urban breakdown. The old Roman towns declined, fell into disrepair, and any sense of political organization disappeared. Invaders occupied the vacuum left by the fall of the Empire.

It was only through the rise of the influence and power of the Church, especially in the Ostrogothic and Frankish kingdoms, that towns and cities once more came into their own. Roman settlements were revived gradually, and with the organization of the spheres of influence of the church into bishoprics, many towns grew in importance politically and commercially, especially those which were seats of monastic learning, of bishops, of pilgrimage, and of trade. In many cases, cities grew again because of the siting of a bishopric within an earlier settlement, such as a *castrum* or old Roman *civitas*. Centralization of power and external threat from hostile peoples coagulated settlements into larger units, and older foundations were rehabilitated. Roman walls were restored and walls were erected around monastic buildings.

Medieval society was centered on the church. The original church of a town often became the "town church" and in Germany the "market church," since the markets were held under its walls. The church was the great landowner of the Middle Ages. It was responsible for building much, including houses for the poor, and it played an important part in furthering the growth of towns by encouraging commercial enterprise, building, and the arts. The church was the focus for worship, for pageantry, for education, for entertainment, and for art.

Religious buildings were of enormous significance, and round them the urban center developed. Ecclesiastical buildings were the nuclei of many towns, and the establishment of bishoprics gave rise to cities developing on the earlier foundation. In Germany, cathedrals were built on dominant walled sites, so that the city with its wall grew in turn round the central ecclesiastical stronghold. The church was a citadel, and *Kloster* and *Burg* took on literal and symbolic meanings. In some cases, ecclesiastical and secular power were united, as at Salzburg, where the prince-bishop ruled from his fortress. In England, the cathedral was usually of monastic origin and had cloisters, but it was always near an urban settlement.

Parallel with the rise of the Church was the growth of an aristocracy, or secular ruling class, in charge of armaments and defense. This class originally was responsible for the formation of camps or defensive forts, but it later developed castles. The settlements then huddled round the castle for protection, and the town fortifications themselves were often in the control of the castle authorities. Protection of the town was assured, but so was the political dominance of the authorities in the castle. In due course, the growing power of town groups tended to make them resent the castle, which in many cases had become the oppressor. Often, the castle was destroyed because it symbolized the power of the nobility. Various groups would form alliances at various times in order to challenge power or to seek it, and these expressed themselves in the dominant features of the medieval town: the church, above all; the town hall; the guild houses; the marketplace; the walls; and the castle. The walls, in a way, symbolized the inviolability of the medieval town, and when the first guns battered them down, the ethos of the town was lost and medieval society was doomed with it. The walls were the protectors of the town from the hostile barbarian countryside without.

Medieval towns had a sense of order and continuity which may be seen from the orientation of the religious buildings and the spaces associated with communal activity such as fairs, markets, and religious observance. Homogeneity was attained by the use of natural materials, indigenous to the area, while craftsmanship and the universal architectural manners of the time ensured that there was no jarring note.

From the beginning of the Middle Ages, a regular type of plan developed at the same time as the cluster pattern around castle, church, or natural eminence. This regularity preceded both the time of colonization and the growth of modern capitalism. There were, of course, Roman prototypes, but there may also have been cosmological significance in such plans as well as the obvious advantages of easy subdivision into plots. The market-place and church together formed what might be likened to agora and acropolis, the profane and the sacred, united in the urban nucleus. Many market foundations were given to the church rather than to the towns, and so the orders and bishoprics grew in importance.

Bastide towns were formed in France and in Wales. These were originally fortresses, but the term came to mean a colonial town. The first bastide towns were those built by Louis IX after he had conquered the Albigensian heretics, but the most celebrated ones are those built by Edward I of England

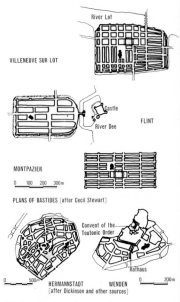

Medieval colonial town plans.

to consolidate his own power in France and in Wales. They were laid out on a regular plan like the Roman insulae. Large rectangles were kept clear for the market, town hall, and church, which might itself be fortified. Similar towns were laid out in the eastern marks of Germany, in virgin territory. A different type of town was the Baltic port, built to encourage trade. This had a less formal layout combined with a spectacular three-dimensional form, a vivid forest of brick towers, copper spires, and gabled houses. Lübeck is a superb example of this type, with its powerful red brick Gothic architecture and strangely Venetian imagery; very proud, very nautical, and highly original, as one would expect a free city to be.

Many towns and cities, such as Venice, were important because they were on the trade routes to the east and especially to Constantinople, capital of the Eastern Roman Empire. When the Turks took Constantinople in 1453, other routes to the Indies had to be found. The explorers who found the New World were looking for India, and the discovery changed the face of Europe. The Atlantic Ocean replaced the Baltic and Mediterranean as the sea of commerce. Seats of the rulers of nation-states, such as Paris and London, grew in importance.

After the sixteenth century, many medieval towns lost the dynamism which might have carried them on to develop. The better the walls were preserved, the more this expressed the decline of importance. The medieval

CLOCKWISE, FROM TOP LEFT:
*Salzburg. The castle of the
Prince-Bishop dominates the town.
Haarlem. The town center—the church
dominates.   Solbad Hall. The narrow
medieval street is dominated by the tower
of the church.*

town was distinguished from the countryside, but changing methods of warfare and changing attitudes to rural life lessened the distinction. Towns were no longer safe, for the walls were no protection, and the rise of the nation-states hastened the decline of many cities, bringing, at the same time, security to the country. Institutions became enfeebled, for the new monopolies were invested in individuals, and even the church was taken over by the families of commerce.

The Black Death had ravaged Europe, and superstition was rampant. Religion became polytheistic and cults grew. The light of the Renaissance had dawned at the time of Dante and Giotto, but the plague arrested development, causing social and political chaos and the suppression of intellectual freedom. From those dark days came fear and witch-hunting, which were not to be halted until the Enlightenment.

Corruption within and the influence of Protestantism from without lessened the church's importance as the prime inspiration of daily human life, and so its expression in building became less. When we think of the hundreds of churches and chapels that once stood in the square mile of the City of London alone, we can have only an inkling of the immense influence of the church on the design of towns. As the old order died, however, so did its symbols, and with the rise of a new society, new dominants appeared. The monumental road, the buildings of commerce, the princely churches, and, above all, the palaces show us that the world of Hans Sachs had vanished, to be replaced by that of *Le Roi Soleil*.

BIBLIOGRAPHY: Lewis Mumford, *The Culture of Cities,* Martin Seeker & Warburg, Ltd., London, 1938; R. E. Dickinson, *The West European City,* Routledge & Kegan Paul, Ltd., London, 1951; Cecil Stewart, *A Prospect of Cities,* Longmans, Green & Co., Ltd., London, 1952; Arthur Korn, *History Builds the Town,* Lund Humphies, London, 1953; Helen Rosenau, *The Ideal City in Its Architectural Evolution,* Routledge & Kegan Paul, Ltd., London, 1959; Camillo Sitte, *City Planning according to Artistic Principles,* G. R. Collins and C. C. Collins (translators), Phaidon Press, Ltd., London, and Random House, Inc., New York, 1965; James Stevens Curl, *European Cities and Society,* Leonard Hill, London, 1970.

—JAMES STEVENS CURL

MEGALOPOLIS   In Greek, "the big city." "Megalopolis" is a word coined by the ancient Greeks when they decided to connect many small cities of Arcadia into a big city which could be used as their major administrative and cultural center. To distinguish it from the small cities, it was called Megalopolis. It was created in 371 B.C. by Epaminondas of Thebes.

In modern times "megalopolis" has been used by Jean Gottmann, the geographer, to indicate the multiple and complex urban system which comprises many metropolises on the eastern coast of the United States, from Boston to New York, Philadelphia, Baltimore, and Washington. Another megalopolis, the Great Lakes megalopolis, is now under study by the Developing Great Lakes Megalopolis Inc. and by Doxiadis Associates. Many more (a total of 14, located all over the world) are now under study by the Athens Center of Ekistics.

BIBLIOGRAPHY: Jean Gottmann, *Megalopolis, the Urbanized Northeastern Seaboard of the United States,* The M.I.T. Press, Cambridge, Mass., 1961; C. A. Doxiadis, *Ekistics: An Introduction to the Science of Human Settlements,* Hutchinson Publishing Group, Ltd., London, 1968, Oxford University Press, New York, 1968, pp. 101, 374–376.

—Constantinos A. Doxiadis

MENDELSOHN, ERICH (1887–1953)   German architect and urban designer, born in Allenstein, in East Prussia, on March 21, 1887. Among his works of urban design was a cul-de-sac off Kurfurstendamm (1928), for the Woga Company, which consisted of a cinema at one corner, a cafe-restaurant and cabaret-theater on the opposite corner, a row of shops, blocks of flats, and a six-story bachelor hotel to terminate the street. The interesting feature of the scheme was the unified architectural conception on the theme of long horizontals related to curved and semicircular motifs. When building his famous Columbus Haus (1931), since destroyed, he prepared a scheme for the replanning of Potsdammer Platz which included a garden court. Another scheme of about the same time, for Alexander-Platz, included a tall, circular block bridging the radiating streets and designed with the purpose of completely encircling the Platz.

Because of the Nazi regime, Mendelsohn left his native land in 1933 never to return. He went to England and for the next 7 years divided his practice between England and Palestine. In the former country his principal planning scheme, made in 1935 in collaboration with his partner, Serge Chermayeff, was the White City Housing Project and Exhibition Center, on a site of 80 acres (32.5 hectares). This plan centered upon long, curved, eight-story parallel blocks of about two thousand apartments oriented approximately north-south. At the southern end was a series of five tower blocks. Several amenities were introduced—among them a cinema, swimming pool, shops, and a restaurant for a thousand people—designed, of course, partly for the exhibition buildings which were to occupy the southern section of the site and were to include an exhibition hall larger than any in London. An alternative scheme eliminated the exhibition buildings and continued the long curved blocks of flats in the southern area. This was one of the earliest schemes of apartment blocks in England in which the courtyard layout was abandoned. The generous spacing of the eight-story apartment blocks with extensive gardens between, thus obtaining good lighting in the flats at all levels, was in line with Gropius's Siemensstadt development. The scheme was never carried out.

Of the many notable buildings by Mendelsohn in Palestine, the Hadassah Medical Center (1937–1939) which formed part of the Hebrew University on Mount Scopus, Jerusalem, involved a planned conception of university buildings extending along a distance of over 1,000 yards (900 meters) along the mountain ridge, with the medical center group at the northwestern end. A notable circumstance about the buildings is that they appear as very much an integral part of the site.

In 1940 Mendelsohn went to America. He practiced in San Francisco from 1945 until his death on September 15, 1953. During this last period he prepared an interesting scheme for the Pittsburgh Golden Triangle.

Apart from his distinctive contribution to the architecture of the twentieth century, a notable feature of Mendelsohn's work was the integration of his buildings with their sites and settings. Where the buildings were on hilly ground with open surroundings, their relation to the contours of the site was carefully studied. This is particularly apparent in the Hadassah Medical Center on Mount Scopus and in the Temple and Community Center at Cleveland, Ohio (1946–1950), where the contours seemed to influence the character and disposition of the buildings.

Mendelsohn gave many lectures on architecture and planning, always viewing these subjects in their broadest and most human aspects. He had an ability to say things pithily, as in the lecture entitled "Architecture in a Rebuilt World," in which he says, "isolated planning by one-track experts must be replaced by an all-round plan" and "financial instability is caused by an insane passion for big and bigger cities and for mechanical monuments." He believed that planning should attempt to give human beings the opportunity to enjoy contact with the soil and the natural world, "with nature's seedtime, growth and decay."

BIBLIOGRAPHY: Mario Frederico Roggero, *Il contributo di Mendelsohn alla evoluzione dell'architettura moderna,* Libreria Editrice Politecnica Tamburini, Milan, 1952; Arnold Whittick, *Eric Mendelsohn,* Leonard Hill, London, 1956, F. W. Dodge, New York, 1956; Wolf Von Echardt, *Eric Mendelsohn,* George Braziller, New York, 1960, Bruno Zevi, *Erich Mendelsohn,* Elas Kompass, Milan, 1970.   —ARNOLD WHITTICK

METROPOLITAN RAILWAYS   Urban rail transport has played an important role and will continue to play a vital part in creating and sustaining the cities of today and tomorrow.

The term "metropolitan railways" covers a great variety of facilities. They are primarily rapid transit facilities of a railway or similar type, generally with self-contained rights-of-way and stations at, below, or above ground level. They are primarily designed to handle relatively heavy volumes of inner-urban and suburban traffic over medium distances, where the advantage of the higher overall speed ("commercial speed"), compared with public transport on often congested roads, begins to outweigh the disadvantage of the longer walks to and from the stations.

But the dividing lines between metropolitan railways proper—variously known as Subway, Underground, Métro, Metropolitano, U-Bahn, Tunnelbahn—and other modes of transport have tended to become blurred. In particular, this applies in relation to (1) the faster urban railways generally associated with main-line suburban railways (e.g., S-Bahn, Réseau Express Régional); (2) the slower modes more akin to streetcars (e.g., underground streetcars, Pré-Métro, U-Strassenbahn); and (3) nontypical modes such as funicular and rack railways, monorails, etc., which have, in some cases, come to be regarded as inner-urban rapid transit facilities.

A brief indication of these three contiguous minority groups will provide the necessary background to an appreciation of the modern developments of metropolitan railways.

S-Bahn Systems   The German term S-Bahn, originally derived from Berlin's Stadt-, Ring-, und Vorortbahnen ("City, Circle, and Suburban Railways")

but later also attributed to other derivations, may serve as a convenient generic term to denote those railways which, in contrast to metropolitan railways proper, originated from and are still associated with the suburban sections of the main lines. Having themselves been instrumental in promoting the growth of the conurbations, these suburban lines have, in the course of time, built up a considerable volume of suburban commuter traffic along the radial lines to the central area so that it became, first of all, necessary to achieve a measure of physical segregation between the suburban and long-distance services. Where these services terminated at the fringe of the central area, they were in some cases subsequently projected beyond the in-town terminal across the central area, perhaps to link up with similar services on the opposite side, so that suburban commuters were able to reach their in-town destinations without having to change. Not surprisingly, such cross links have often also assumed purely inner-urban transport functions rather similar to those of underground-type lines, though they usually have more widely spaced stations and, therefore, a higher commercial speed.

Among cross-link systems of this type are the long-established S-Bahnen in Berlin (two links) and Hamburg (second link under construction), the Junction Line in Brussels, the Copenhagen S-Bane, the Vienna Schnellbahn, the Blue Trains in Glasgow, and the new S-Bahn in Munich. The first cross link of the Réseau Express Régional is at present (March 1973) in partial operation, and one Frankfurt S-Bahn is in an advanced stage of construction. Similar schemes are well advanced, e.g., in the Ruhr region of Germany, Stuttgart, Manchester, Liverpool, and Melbourne.

Underground Streetcars At the other end of the speed and capacity scales, the dividing line between subways and streetcars has been blurred by the promotion of underground streetcars where in-town tunnel sections are used for the operation, with or without automatic signaling systems, of short trains of the streetcar type which are sometimes extended as conventional streetcars along surface roads. Underground streetcars have been in operation for many years—for example, in Boston, Philadelphia, Pittsburgh, Oslo (Majorstua Line), and Vienna (the old Stadtbahn).

In recent years, in spite of a marked general decline in streetcar operations throughout the world, the construction of comparatively short in-town sections of streetcar tunnels has again occurred mainly in Germany (U-Strassenbahnen) and Belgium (Pré-Métro). Such schemes are mainly intended to serve as an intermediate stage to a full-fledged subway, the general argument being that—provided that alignments and tunnels are designed for this purpose from the outset—the transitional stage will permit an easier phasing of expenditure on infrastructure and rolling stock. Streetcar tunnels are in operation or under construction in, for example, Kassel, Hanover, Stuttgart, Essen, Dortmund, and especially Cologne (where subsequent conversion might be difficult), Antwerp, and also in Frankfurt and Brussels (where it should be easy). Other cities which originally intended to have underground streetcars have changed to high-capacity underground railways (e.g., Munich, Nuremberg, Prague).

Nontypical Modes   In relatively few cases urban transport demands are, for geographical or topographical reasons, mainly met by nontypical modes. Among prominent existing examples are the long-established Schwebebahn above the river at Wuppertal, the funicular railways in Haifa and Istanbul, and the rack railway Lausanne-Ouchy. This list will no doubt be extended by the advent of new or revived modes of transport such as monorails of various types, hover trains, etc.

Subways   It is in the vast field vaguely marked out by these "fringe" modes that the great majority of subways or rapid-transit railways can be found.

As the cities began to spread and the streets became increasingly congested, the need arose for faster, unencumbered in-town railways which were primarily designed to cope with heavy volumes of inner-urban traffic and which, being taken across heavily built-up areas, generally had to be placed below or above ground. In many cases, these in-town subway or elevated lines were later extended into the suburbs—often as surface railways and sometimes by taking over preexisting branches of suburban lines—so that in the suburbs, too, the differences between "centrifugally developed" underground lines and "centripetally developed" lines of the S-Bahn type have tended to diminish.

While such rapid-transit facilities were originally confined to metropolitan cities, the growth of traffic congestion in the streets has induced an increasing number even of smaller cities to have subways, especially where, owing to geographical or topographical conditions, commuter traffic is concentrated on a few "corridors" (as in Stockholm or Helsinki).

It is now generally recognized that rapid-transit facilities are the most efficient means of moving great numbers of people safely and quickly through congested urban areas. It is also increasingly recognized that rapid-transit facilities are not only of direct benefit to the passengers using them but are also of vital importance to the community at large in that they help to alleviate street congestion, promote the mobility of labor, and generally revitalize the central business districts which are otherwise in danger of being stifled by congestion and pollution. The construction—and sometimes even the operation—of rapid-transit facilities has therefore increasingly come to be regarded as a task incumbent on the public authorities as part of a concerted transport and planning policy without insisting on commercial viability which—with the high interest rates on the steeply rising capital costs of facilities that are fully used during short peak periods only—can no longer be expected.

It is against this background that the present worldwide boom in the construction of rapid-transit facilities should be seen.

The first subways, dating back to 1863 (London), were steam-operated; but electrification followed soon and is now the universal mode of traction. There have been progressive improvements in all technical respects. Tunnelling methods have been greatly improved for all kinds of tunnels— deep-level, cut-and-cover, rock; rolling stock and performance have been greatly improved (though some innovations, such as rubber-tired traction, are not universally regarded as major improvements); and signaling and telecommunications have been revolutionized by the advent of modern electronics, leading to highly sophisticated automatic train operation and fares collection (e.g., on London's Victoria Line). Track capacities are usually quoted as forty trains per hour (though, for greater reliability, lower maximum frequencies of thirty to thirty-six trains per hour are often preferred). Train capacities vary greatly with the design and number of the cars; crush load capacities of 1,500 passengers per train and more are sometimes quoted but can hardly be regarded as tolerable loads; moreover, such theoretical capacities are hardly ever fully utilized during a full peak hour. Commercial speeds–which depend on station spacings, rolling stock, performance, etc.—generally range from about 15 to 25 miles per hour (22 to 40 kilometers per hour).

In March 1973 rapid-transit facilities of the subway type were in operation in the following thirty-eight cities: Athens, Baku, Barcelona, Berlin (West and East), Boston, Budapest, Buenos Aires, Chicago, Cleveland, Glasgow, Hamburg, Kiev, Leningrad, Lisbon, London, Madrid, Mexico City, Milan, Montreal, Moscow, Munich, Nagoya, Nurenberg, New York, Osaka, Oslo, Paris, Peking, Philadelphia, Rome, Rotterdam, San Francisco, Sappero, Stockholm, Tbilisi, Tokyo, Toronto, and Yokohama.

In most of the cities, further lines or extensions are under construction or planned. In addition, new rapid-transit lines of the subway type are at present under construction or in an advanced state of planning in the following twenty-eight cities: Amsterdam, Atlanta, Baltimore, Bombay, Brussels, Calcutta, Caracas, Copenhagen, Helsinki, Hong Kong, Johannesburg, Kharkov, Los Angeles, Lyons, Marseilles, Prague, the Rhine-Ruhr region, Santiago, São Paulo, Seoul, Seville, Singapore, Tashkent, Turin, Vienna, Warsaw, Washington, and Zurich.

Finally, plans for rapid transit facilities are under consideration in at least twenty other cities.

Among existing systems, London has the greatest route length (over 250 miles or 400 kilometers), Moscow the largest number of passengers (approximately 1,500 millions per annum); and New York the greatest number of stations (nearly 500), vehicles (over 7,000), and staff (27,000). But statistical comparisons can be misleading and ought to be appraised in the light of different local circumstances.

BIBLIOGRAPHY: There are numerous books and periodical articles dealing with rapid transit. Particularly useful for reference purposes are the "Statistics of Urban Public Transport" issued by the U.I.T.P. (International Union of Public Transport, Brussels); the publication entitled *Metropolitan Railways in the World,* prepared annually by the Régie Autonome des Transports Parisiens (Paris) on behalf of the International Metropolitan Railways Committee of the U.I.T.P.; the special chapter on "Rapid Transit Underground and Surface Railways" included in Jane's *World Railways;* and the rapid-transit section of the annual *Railway Directory and Year Book.*
—ERWIN ROCKWELL

METROPOLITAN REGION The metropolis is the chief or capital city of a country or state. The metropolitan region includes the surrounding area which experiences the direct influence of the capital, has interests within the same focus as the metropolis, and shares the capital's economic and social activities. As the capital city grows, so the metropolitan region extends. The extent of such regions is vaguely or precisely defined, an example of the latter being the London metropolitan region, which in recent planning maps concerned with developments in the southeast is clearly marked. (*See also* CITY REGION.)

In the United States, the term "metropolitan region" has come to mean any agglomeration around a city (not necessarily the capital of a state), which has a total population of 200,000 or more. In the census for the decade 1940 to 1950, a standard metropolitan area is defined as a country or a group of contiguous countries socially and economically integrated with a central city of at least 50,000 inhabitants. There were then 168 standard metropolitan regions conforming to this description, and by 1971 there were probably nearer 200, more than 30 of which had regional populations of over a million.

To the planner, metropolitan regions are likely to be more and more comprehended as regional planning areas to be seen and planned as a whole.

MEXICO

Physical Features   The country of Mexico consists mainly of a high plateau with a general elevation of about 8,000 feet (2,440 meters). Lowlands are along the coasts and cover the peninsula of Yucatán in the Gulf of Mexico. The long, narrow, mountainous peninsula of Lower California, on the Pacific side, is a continuation of the Coast Range of the United States. The Sierra Madre Occidental mountain range runs north and south near the Pacific coast, and the Sierra Madre Oriental, a continuation of the Rocky Mountain system, runs down on the eastern side nearly to Veracruz. The tallest of the volcanic peaks is the beautiful Orizaba, which is 18,564 feet (5,662 meters) high. Both it and Popocatepetl—another huge, snow-covered cone which is 17,543 feet (5,350 meters) high—stand in a range that crosses the highest part of the plateau. On the gulf side, the mouths of the rivers are closed by sand bars, and the good harbors are artificial. The Pánuco River has been improved by means of jetties to aid the commerce of Tampico, and the Coatzacoalcos has been improved to help the commerce of the town of Coatzacoalcos (formerly Puerto Mexico). The forests produce spruce, pine, mahogany, logwood, and rosewood. From the guayule bush, which flourishes in arid regions, rubber is made. In mineral resources, Mexico is one of the richest countries in the world, with deposits of gold, silver, lead, zinc, tin, tungsten, mercury, iron, coal, and petroleum.

Geographical and Climatic Conditions   Mexico extends from 32 to 14 degrees north latitude and from 86 to 117 degrees west longitude.

Mexico has a highly varied climate. The lowlands along the coasts are very hot, and on the gulf side they are unhealthy and subject to a heavy rainfall. On the Pacific side, where the mean annual temperature gets as high as 105 or 110°F (40 or 43°C)—and even 119°F (48°C) at Guaymas—irrigation is necessary, as it is in the interior, for the trade winds lose their moisture across the eastern mountains. In the foothills is a subtropical zone, with a mean annual temperature of 75°F (25°C). On the vast high plateau of

Mexico the average temperature is 63°F (18°C), and there is never extreme heat or cold. Only south of 28 degrees north latitude are there wet and dry seasons. In Mexico City the coldest months are December and January, the warmest, April and May. Eternal snow lies on the country's highest mountains.

Historical Background   Before Cortez arrived in Mexico, Anahuac was the most powerful empire of the American continent; and during the colonial period, Mexico City was considered to be the most important capital of America. It was only after Mexico achieved independence that its importance gradually decreased. At present, it is one of the five most populous cities of America and among the ten most densely populated cities in the world.

The valley of Mexico, which covers an area of 3,148 square miles (8,153 square kilometers), is a politically integrated region which includes the Federal District (711 square miles or 1,843 square kilometers), which represents 4.9 percent of Mexico's total area, and the states of Mexico (58.9 percent), Hidalgo (20 percent) and Tlaxcala (4.9 percent). The Federal District includes Mexico City, which is the heart of the country and which contains the principal political, economic, and cultural institutions. It has a population of more than 3 million in an area of 54 square miles (140.45 square kilometers).

Population   Mexico has a population of more than 40 million, and its average annual growth rate is 3.01 percent. Some 6 million live in the Federal District area, where the annual growth rate is above the national average and was nearer 4.6 percent for the decade 1950 to 1960.

The increased population of the Federal District is the result of internal migration from country districts and other towns. This internal migration, which is due to socioeconomic factors, is resulting in the enormous growth of an area where the only limitations are lack of water and the inadequate housing facilities of the city. Everything leads to the conclusion that if the socioeconomic conditions of Mexico are not changed and if the development of the provinces is not encouraged and pressed forward in accordance with current government intentions, the population will continue to migrate to the Federal District.

The growth rate of the state of Jalisco, one of the most important of the nation, with an approximate population of $2\frac{1}{2}$ million inhabitants, was only 3.33 percent in 1950 to 1960. Nuevo León, which is another center of development, had a growth rate of 3.7 percent per annum; Veracruz, 2.9 percent; Puebla, 1.8 percent; the state of Mexico, 3 percent; Michoacán, 2.6 percent; Sinaloa, 2.8 percent; and Tamaulipas, 3.4 percent. Only Sonora has had a population growth rate of more than 4 percent.

A phenomenon which has many explanations is the rural exodus, as a consequence of which chaos, resulting from the impact of human masses which invade them, is to be observed in the cities.

Agriculture and cattle raising are affected by the abandonment of land, causing economic problems beyond those brought about by the explosive growth of the population.

Human Groups   The various forms of social organization demand considerable attention because of the complexity of the situation. The smallest
is the patriarchal group of 5 to 15 biologically linked couples. The environmental difficulties accentuate the struggle for survival, which engenders
group solidarity and cooperation between members. In 1960 such groupings
consisted of 1,568,268 people widely dispersed in 51,555 localities and
representing 4.4 percent of the national population.

The domestic group is more important and is characterized by specific
geographical and economic conditions. It is the first properly urban element
and supports the more complex groups. It is a small community composed
of 50 to 150 families. In 1960, 10,664,079 people (30 percent of the total
population) lived in these groups in 33,250 localities.

When the domestic group grows it becomes a real neighborhood, establishing monuments and public buildings that exercise an influence on the
area. This grouping is called the vicinal unit or neighborhood, which
comprises 500 to 1,500 families or groups of approximately 2,500 to
7,500 inhabitants.

If we consider only such groups of less than 5,000 inhabitants, we may
observe that in Mexico they account for 7,955,124 individuals (1960 census
data) or 22 percent of the national population in 4,207 localities.

To the type of group described above we must add those which constitute
cities, which very often and almost without exception have grown without
order and lack good or at least acceptable municipal services.

Among these larger bodies the following groups may be mentioned:

1. Those composed of agglomerations of 100,000 to 250,000 inhabitants,
which represents somewhat more than 5 percent of the national population
and reside in 12 localities.

2. Population in five other localities of more than 250,000 inhabitants,
which comprehend at present approximately 20 percent of the national
population.

Legislation and Administration   When a nation has adequate machinery for
urban legislation and administration and exercises it efficiently, it is possible
to reach a desired goal; but when legislation is defective or does not exist,
the difficulties of regional and national urban development are great. Such,
to some degree, is the state of affairs in Mexico.

At a national level there is no legislation referring to urbanism, and there
are still several persons with political power who believe it should not exist.
The same could be said at regional and local levels.

In spite of this, some progress has been made, as when, for example,
in July 1930, an enactment entitled Law about General Planning of the
Republic was approved. This enactment, however, has not been implemented.

In the provinces there is some difference. The most prominent example
of the acceptance of the need for planning is that in the state of Nuevo
León, in recent years the most important industrial center of the nation.
In the private and public sector recognition of the importance of planning
prompted approval of the Planning Law of 1952. This was revised in 1968,

when the Planning and Urbanization Law of Nuevo León State was approved.

The preoccupation of this century has been principally with creating regulations of an engineering character—excluding architecture. Every city in the country has construction, water supply, and sewerage regulations.

There are a few technicians assigned to implementing these regulations, but their interpretations are not always followed, not even by the authorities. Generally speaking, the situation in Mexico in this respect is precarious, notwithstanding the fact that there seems to be some renewed activity resulting from the new laws and administration. Following are some of the measures introduced to rectify deficiencies:

1. The Sixth Law of Planning for the state of Veracruz was passed on March 17, 1958, and augmented and renewed December 27, 1967. It partly changed the system of the first law and was named the Municipal Cooperation and Planning Law of Veracruz.

2. The state of San Luis Potosi adopted a Planning and Urbanization Board in 1968.

3. The state of Jalisco adopted the Planning and Urbanization State Law of Jalisco (state law of *Fraccionamientos*), on August 12, 1959.

4. In the state of Colima, the Planification and Urbanization State Law was adopted on March 4, 1969.

Most of the urban designs of Mexican cities had been controlled by the Laws of Indias.

Professional Practice Mexico has little experience of professional planning owing to the small number of qualified practitioners, for there have been only about 50 persons with a professional education prepared to deal with the subject.

There are, however, a lot of professionals working in planning, especially engineers, architects, economists, and geographers—all of them autodidacts or improvisers.

Education and Training There are no schools of planning in Mexico. The few persons that have made specialized studies at foreign institutions or by independent study are from such schools as the Superior and International Institute of Applied Planning of Brussels, Paris University, Chicago Technological College, The University of California at Berkeley, London University, and some schools and universities in Germany and South America.

Several architectural and engineering schools devote part of their courses to urban planning, and recently there have been postgraduate courses in engineering, architecture, and economics which grant the master's degree in planning; but compared with specialized schools in other countries, they are very limited partly because of the lack of teachers and the little time devoted to the subject.

Planning Institutions Among the institutions concerned with planning are the Permanent Committee for the World Township Day in Mexico, the

Mexican Institute of Social Planning, and the Mexican Society of Planning.

Members of the last mentioned are mostly amateurs with some interest in contemporary, national, or regional planning who have not yet begun any formal studies of these subjects.

Traditions of Planning to the End of the Nineteenth Century   The rules established by the Laws of Indias provided the principal lead in Mexican planning for several centuries. But in the nineteenth century the conceptions of Georges Eugene Haussmann (1853) were followed—not in their functional aspects but only in some characteristics of the boulevards (form and section), as can be observed in the Paseo de la Reforma in Mexico City and in the Paseo Montejo in Mérida, Yucatán.

The buildings and integration of the neighborhoods show some influence of French concepts of the second half of the nineteenth century.

The checkerboard plan was characteristic of the nineteenth century, but earlier centuries also provide good examples of it, as can be observed in the capital cities of Puebla and Yucatán. The concepts of diagonal avenues and *damero* terraces were scarcely used, even though they were conceived in Mexico City. Public parks, gardens, and open spaces of the nineteenth century show French and English influence, in their value, good localization, and form.

The so called "utopians," especially the English, did not have a significant influence, and idealists like Robert Owen and John Silk Buckingham were unknown in Mexico, although there is some coincidence between their efforts and those of Mexico to solve housing problems. The ideas of Patrick Geddes, however, were known by professionals in Mexico or coincided with their thinking. Other conceptions, such as Soria and Mata's linear city (1883) and the garden city of Ebenezer Howard (1898) were known, but there are no examples.

At the end of the nineteenth century public works increased in Mexico. All the state capitals and most of the municipalities built government palaces, most still existing, and provided theaters, public buildings, avenues, transportation, water supply, sanitation, and railroads. As a consequence, by 1910, in the Centenary of the Independence of Mexico, the capital city had become a great urban center and one of the most important cities in the world.

In Yucatán, Oaxaca and Mexico State are important monuments of the era before Cortez—invaluable jewels of the American continent. In the Federal District are the most important monuments, buildings, and temples of the nation. In religious art the Federal District is the most important of the American continent, and its artistic treasures are among the greatest in the world. Perhaps this is why the capital city received the name of the City of the Palaces and also why it was the center of the greatest American empire before the arrival of the Spaniards. Afterwards it became the enormous viceroyalty of Nueva España ("New Spain"). One of the first universities of the continent was in Mexico, and one of the first printing presses in America was located here.

Twentieth-century Planning The European movement projected in America at the beginning of this century did not reach Mexico very early. During the Socialist Revolution in Mexico in 1909, the United States of America had its first National Urban Planning Congress. In 1911 the National Association of Housing and Planning was founded, and in 1913 eighteen cities of the American Union had planning commissions.

At the end of the First World War the new thesis of planning was introduced by the planner and architect Carlos Contreras, who lived in New

Plan of Queretaro with the checkerboard layout of streets of the sixteenth century.

York (1818–1925) and who, on his return to Mexico, worked in collaboration with the civil engineer Javier Sanchez Mejorada. An indication of progress was the interest shown in 1933 by the Minister of the Treasury Department in the formulation of the planning and zoning law of the Federal District and of the Baja California territories.

In 1938, the Sixteenth International Congress of Housing and Planning was organized by Carlos Contreras and the civil engineer Jose A. Cuevas. Since then, interest in planning studies has decreased and only short-lived small groups have been established. The so-called "planning committees" did some work from 1938 to 1947 in Mexico City, but there was no continuity, nor interest from the authorities.

In 1957, the Permanent Committee for the World's Day Township in Mexico cited Carlos Contreras, Jose A. Cuevas, Federico Mariscal, and Guillermo Zarraga y Carlos Obregon Santacilia as the pioneers of planning in Mexico in the twentieth century.

Some studies were begun in 1949 in the state of Mexico, and these were used in the 1951 to 1953 period. In 1952, architect Carlos Lazo became a cabinet member for communications and public works of Mexico and gave much encouragement to planning ideas.

In 1953 during the second Congress of Civil Engineering in Guadalajara city, the formation of the National Institute of Planning was proposed. Later, in 1955, a memorandum was presented to the Geographical and Statistics Society proposing the inclusion of planning studies as regular activities of the society. This was supported at the Fifth National Sociology Congress in Guanajuato city, at the Seventh Sociology Congress in Monterrey city, at the Third Civil Engineering Congress in Mérida city, and in hundreds of articles, papers, and conferences. On January 16, 1957, the Mexican Institute of Social Planning was founded. Other institutions are the Mexican Society of Urbanism and the Mexican Society of Planning. In 1964 the Fifth International Congress of Planning was held in Mexico City.

There has also been interest in planning in the provinces, principally in Monterrey in 1926. After investigations by the lawyers Saenz and Benitez and by Carlos Contreras, the Planning Board and the Improvements Board were established. In 1931 Antonio L. Rodriguez, accompanied by the architect Diez de Bonilla, continued these studies, and in 1933 they engaged the assistance of the civil engineer Armando Diaz. In 1941 the Coordinating Commission of Planning was created. By 1945 the urbanist Kurt A. Mumm, from Harvard University, continued with the plan of Monterrey, and worked on it until 1955. After a period of recess the state government engaged the collaboration of the planner Guillermo Cortes Melo, who had studied at the Superior School of Applied Urbanism in Brussels and was a member of the Permanent Committee for World's Town Planning Day.

Characteristic of government action generally is that instead of solving the main problems, concern has been with minimum details without a general plan, analysis, or synthesis. This increased the problems and created

A central area of Mexico City. In the foreground is the Secretariat of Foreign Relations.

National Museum of Anthropology, with dramatic use of modern roof construction.

others. It can be seen in the capital city with its regulator plan, archaic even in its name, and in efforts to resolve the problems as they occur, but without deep studies of the Federal District and much less of the metropolitan areas of Mexico.

Since about 1955 the several developments in Mexico City have been influenced more by political interests than by efforts to solve problems. Several neighborhoods called Unidades Habitacionales appeared, some of them well planned but generally very expensive. The most acceptable is the so-called Unidad Independencia, and the most costly is Tlatelolco, which is poorly situated and the design is questionable.

Aerial view of stadium and approach roads, Mexico City.

MASTER PLAN
LOMAS VERDES
MEXICO

LEFT: *Master plan of Lomas Verdes,
northeast of Mexico City.* BELOW:
*Model of the Urban Center of Lomas
Verdes.*

Since 1965 efforts to correct mistakes have been redoubled, but the fact is that everything in the Federal District has yet to be done and that it requires technicians dedicated to the task.

The following are some provincial planning schemes:

Jalisco State In the surroundings of Guadalajara there are more than two hundred cities, several surrounding the Jalisco capital city, principally Ocotlán, Tepatitlán, and Puerto Vallarta.

In the first years of our century, the San Juan de Dios River was the scene of extensive public works, including the construction of Independence Avenue and the installation of the electric train service in 1907. Some years later, in the period of Governor Lic. Gonzalez Gallo, there was an ambitious plan to change Guadalajara, and since then successive governments have continued its implementation. Guadalajara and Puerto Vallarta are growing rapidly; there should soon be considerable signs of progress, and the beauty of Puerto Vallarta offers good conditions for new development.

Nuevo León State Monterrey continued its demographic expansion on the original orthogonal lines during the first quarter of this century; but squares and green areas were missing.

During the 1925 to 1940 period, there were no new designs of zones or neighborhoods, called *colonias,* even though the authorities were asked to donate areas for schools, public parks, and squares. The great majority of these *colonias* were built near factories and were occupied principally by artisans and their families.

From 1940 to 1955, luxurious neighborhoods arose for rich families, with spacious axial planning and gardens, and near them green areas and schools were provided. Rotundas, the first diagonals, and monuments appeared.

The big industries developed, and land was allocated almost exclusively to the housing of industrial employees and the necessary services, including recreational and civic centers. The popular land partitions were developed in a traditional orthogonal way. From 1955 onward, better partitioning appeared, with English influence, irregular streets, and a better integration of the public areas. The neighborhoods increased in popularity with these better services.

Since 1960, the problem of industrial slums has emerged as the result of the lack of any technical control or planning studies. The city has allowed its new modern misery belt to form—a characteristic of the great Latin American cities.

In 1964, for the first time, a group of communal buildings were developed near the city center and new industrial partitions appeared.

If the actual plans of Monterrey are implemented, new prospects will emerge for this industrial city.

Veracruz State The century began with several works in the capital city of Jalapa; in 1901 two schools were inaugurated—the Colegio Preparatorio and another industrial school. Members of the Geographical and Exploration Commission continued working until 1914.

In 1925 the Jalapa Stadium was built and new avenues were constructed.

Monterrey—perspective sketch of suggested central street development.

Santa Rosalia—view from the harbor, 1969.

Aerial view (1969) of Mexicali, capital city of the state of Baja California. In the foreground is the Government Palace.

Piped water supply was introduced in 1943 for a population of 5,000 inhabitants. Since then, buildings, monuments, streets, libraries, and schools have been built without any specific urban plan. Jalapa and the port of Veracruz—the principal port in the country—and other urban centers in the state need immediate attention.

San Luis Potosí State   The City of San Luis Potosí, the state capital, was of great importance at the end of the last century and the beginning of the present century, but the many social and political problems in the state, especially in the capital city, prevented progress and urban development. A few years ago, however, a study and analysis of these problems was begun. Governor Lic. Antonio Rocha Cordero has realized the importance of planning studies as a way to satisfy the needs of the population. New land partitions have appeared in all the urban centers in spite of the political and economic problems. San Luis Potosí is at the stage of preparation for development. Its situation in the country has many advantages.

Baja California State   The capital city, Mexicali, with no planning tradition, was founded in 1903. New cities in the state are: Tijuana, Tecate, Enseñada, Ciudad Morelos, and Guadalupe Victoria. Seven first-class land partitions—five of social interest and two public—became the principal planning work of the state. Its development, however, has been without order.

Baja California Territory   The capital city of the southern territory of Baja California is La Paz, and in this century nine cities or small urban centers have arisen.

There have been some recent planning developments, but the small population and specific locale of this area requires more comprehensive study. Efforts in this direction have been made by Governor Lic. Hugo Cervantes del Rio.

Mexican Coast Development In this century urban centers on the coast have grown gradually. The study of demographic conditions shows that in the next 30 years they will be much changed. The rapid growth of these centers and the public needs demonstrate the big problems facing Mexico. It has scarcely had time to adopt comprehensive regional planning to protect its coasts, to facilitate urban development, and to satisfy the exigencies of its population. In some regions this population is growing at a rate of 9 percent a year.   —FRANCISCO JOSE ALVAREZ Y LEZAMA

MICHELANGELO BUONAROTTI (1475–1564) Sculptor, painter, architect, and poet, born in Florence, Italy, on March 6, 1475. His chief contribution to civic design was his redevelopment of the ancient Capitol in Rome. Traditionally the most sacred of the city's sites, the hill had been the center of Roman religion and government and of the twenty-seven Roman temples that stood on the slopes with the temple of Jupiter on the summit. When, in 1536, Pope Paul III commissioned Michelangelo to redesign the Capitol, it had been for many years in a ruined state, together with two dilapidated neighboring buildings, the Palazzo del Senatore and the Palazzo dei Conservatori.

The two objects of the project were to link up the surrounding districts and to provide a memorial to the continuous glory of eternal Rome. To serve these ends, Michelangelo created a piazza, trapezoidal in plan and approached by a specially designed stairway. It is a remarkable design, one of the finest ever made, and it grew partly out of the relative siting of the existing palazzi. Michelangelo took as the main axis of his design the line through the center of the Palazzo del Senatore (southeast to northwest) and repeated the angle (of about 85°) of the front of the Palazzo dei Conservatori with another building symmetrically placed on the other side of the axis. In the center, the ancient Roman equestrian statue of Marcus Aurelius was placed, and the facades of the two existing palazzi were rebuilt to Michelangelo's designs. The circumstance that the piazza is only partially enclosed by stately buildings, that there is a glimpse beyond, in one corner, to the landscape of Rome, and—finally—that the approach side is open rather enhances its subtle beauty. It is one of the rarely perfect compositions in urban design.

When, in 1534, Michelangelo, at the request of the Pope, completed Antonio da Sangallo's Palazzo Farnese with a magnificent cornice and with the addition of two stories facing the court, he continued the sequence of piazza, courts, and palazzo garden along an axis to a bridge over the Tiber and to the villa and garden of the Farnese on the other bank, so that, to quote Vasari, "from the principal door of the Campo di Fiore one looked straight through the court fountain, Strada Julia, the bridge, and the other beautiful garden right to the other door into the Strada di Trastevere, a rare thing worthy of the Pope, and of the genius, judgment, and design of Michelangelo."

He died in Rome on February 17, 1564.

BIBLIOGRAPHY: Giorgio Vasari, "Michelangelo Buonarotti," in *Le vite de piu eccellenti architetti, pittori, et scultori italiani da Cimabue insino a tempi nostri,* Florence, 1551, first complete English edition by Mrs. J. Foster, 1850; Edmund N. Bacon, *Design of Cities,* Thames & Hudson, London, 1967; E. A. Gutkind, *International History of City Development,* Urban Development in Southern Europe, Italy and Greece, vol. IV, The Free Press, New York, 1969.   —WILFRED SALTER

MIGRATIONS OF POPULATION   (*See* POPULATION GROWTH AND DISTRIBUTION.)

MINING AND MINING AREAS   (*See* EXTRACTIVE INDUSTRIES.)

MOBILE HOME   A vehicle equipped like a small house, which is either designed to be towed by a car or is itself a specially adapted motor vehicle. In Great Britain the term is "caravan" (originally, in Eastern and North African countries, a company of persons, including pilgrims and merchants, traveling together for security; later, the vehicles in which they traveled). They are used for vacations and, with the housing shortage, as permanent dwellings, usually on sites provided with water supply, drainage, and other services. The use of land for this purpose, or for the stationing of vacation trailers and equipping of sites is controlled by legislation. (*See* MOBILE HOME PARKS.)

MOBILE HOME PARKS   The residential use of trailers or caravans—as distinct from short-period and holiday use—has greatly increased since the Second World War in the United States, Great Britain, and several other countries. In the United States, trailers used as residences are increasingly being called "mobile homes," and this term is beginning to be used in Great Britain.

At least 3 percent of all families in the United States live in mobile homes, a proportion that rises greatly with lower-cost dwellings of less than $20,000. In Great Britain the number living in caravans is nearly 100,000, or about 0.5 percent of the total.

Most of the owners of mobile houses rent the sites; comparatively few own them. The increase in this kind of residence has necessitated legislation to regulate the use of sites for this purpose. Both in the United States and Great Britain the developer of a site for this purpose has to obtain planning permission or a license. Mobile-home parks must comply with the zoning, controlled in the United States by planning and zoning boards. Such is the growing demand for mobile homes that requests can be made for changes of zoning for development of a site as a mobile-home park provided that a sufficiently strong case can be presented.

In Great Britain the development and regulation of mobile-home sites and the granting of licenses for the purpose is controlled chiefly by two acts of Parliament: the Caravan Sites and Control of Development Act of

1962, Part I, and the Town and Country Planning Act of 1962, Part IV, which supersedes and repeals Part II of the 1960 act. The Caravan Sites Act of 1968 gives additional protection to caravan residents.

BIBLIOGRAPHY: Hodes and Robertson, *The Law of Mobile Homes*, 2d ed., 1964; Frederick H. Bair, *Local Regulation of Mobile Home Parks, Travel Trailer Parks and Related Facilities*, 1965; Desmond Heap, "Control over Caravans," chap. 10 in *An Outline of Planning Law*, 5th ed., Sweet & Maxwell, London, 1969.   —ARNOLD WHITTICK

MODELS   When a planning scheme or urban design such as the redevelopment of a central area or the formation of a new residential neighborhood is conceived in three-dimensional form, some clear impression of the effect in three dimensions is needed, particularly when, as is usually the case, the proposals have to be presented for approval or comment to others, some of whom may be laymen unfamiliar with the interpretation of plans. Artists' impressions or perspective renderings only illustrate one viewpoint and some of the detail, while the careful casting of shadows on a plan to illustrate height variations is often difficult for someone who is not an experienced draftsman to interpret. A model of such schemes, however simply assembled, gives a better interpretation than any map, as all perspectives can be tested.

Architectural models of individual buildings or groups of buildings can be very complicated and costly, giving a highly realistic impression not only of the massing of the subject but also of details of design and even surface finishes. They are sometimes prepared in sectional form to illustrate variations in plan or circulation at different levels. However, very simple models—made, for example, from balsa wood or even stiff cardboard—can convey the desired impression very effectively, although it will usually be desirable to add a little elevational detail or some additional details such as model trees to convey the impression of scale.

Variations in ground level are sometimes crucial to the interpretation of a design; and in new development or redevelopment proposals covering a wide area, variations of level will usually be present. Quite clear gradients on the ground would be imperceptible at model scale, and for this reason they are exaggerated on the model, a larger scale being used for determining the surface levels than for the plan measurements. The gradient can be built up by using layers of cardboard, wood, or similar material cut to follow the successive contours. Plaster of paris or some moldable material can then be spread over the model, forming the ground surface to receive the scale models of the buildings, trees, etc. Sometimes this stage is omitted and the models of the buildings are arranged directly on the stepped contour layers. In the latter case the contour layers are often left uncolored, are painted in a neutral color, or the base map or plan may be cut and stuck to the respective layers. Where a smooth ground surface is simulated, ground color and textures can be applied to illustrate roads, grass, and pavings. Several models are shown in the illustrations of this encyclopedia.

—H. E. SPARROW

MODULE   (*See* GRID.)

MONORAIL SYSTEMS (*See* TRANSPORT.)

MONASTERIES (*See* RELIGIOUS INFLUENCES IN PLANNING.)

MONUMENTS AND MEMORIALS, PUBLIC The purpose of a public monument is to commemorate a famous person or persons, a notable event such as a military victory or sacrifice in war, or an important cause. Public monuments have been erected in cities, towns, villages, and at places in country districts since ancient times, and notable examples of most periods survive from the times of ancient Egypt, Greece, and Rome.

The function of the planner in connection with public monuments is in the matter of their siting—their satisfactory setting in relation to their surroundings—and it is useful to be aware of some of the best examples of such siting. The satisfactory setting for a monument depends to a considerable extent on its type, character, and size. Public monuments may take many forms: the standing or seated figure on a pedestal, an equestrian statue, a symbolic sculptural group, a fountain, large-scale monuments like the tall column or triumphal arch, or a purely commemorative building like the Lincoln and Jefferson memorials in Washington. If the planner is asked advice on the best setting for a memorial, he must be aware of its type and proposed size, and he must be equipped to suggest modifications in its design if it is to accord satisfactorily with a particular setting.

Capital cities, especially Rome, Vienna, Paris, Stockholm, and Washington, all offer good examples of the siting of monuments. The many fountains of Rome and Stockholm are generally well sited and of a scale to harmonize with their surroundings. Rome offers good examples of ancient, Renaissance, and modern monuments that are well sited and in scale with their surroundings—with the notorious exception of the Vittorio Emmanuele Monument erected in 1870 to the design of Sacconi. This immense classical Renaissance structure (about 400 feet wide and 200 feet high) at the end of the Corso Umberto is altogether out of scale with its surroundings and is one of the few monuments that does not take its place gracefully in this beautiful city.

The siting of public monuments depends very much on the character of the urban plan. If it is a formal, regular, geometric plan, as in the magnificent sequence of the Louvre and the Tuileries, Place de la Concorde, Avenue des Champs Elysees, and the Place de l'Etoile in Paris, with their monuments—the Arc de Triomphe, the obelisk, the statuary on pedestals, and the Arch of Constantine—all set as centerpieces or otherwise symmetrically arranged, then to be successful the monuments must be of the right scale in relation to the surrounding space and the surrounding buildings and trees, as they are in this central Parisian scene. This whole formal symetrical composition, one of the finest in the world, is greatly assisted by the slight ascent of the Avenue des Champs Elysees to the culminating and impressive mass of the Arc de Triomphe. Washington presents a similar effect of formal grandeur with the sequence of the Capitol, the long wide

Mall, the tremendous marble Washington obelisk, the long straight reflecting pool, and the classical Lincoln memorial. In several north Italian cities, monuments, particularly memorial fountains, are sited less formally rather to the side or corner of a piazza the center of which is left open as a much-valued space for various civic, commercial, and recreational purposes, but which is also valuable just as a space. This type of siting was admired and recommended by Camillo Sitte. Another very attractive siting is in gardens that flank an important highway, avenue, or boulevard, as those bordering the Champs Elysees in Paris and the gardens of Vienna, with

Air view of Washington showing the formal geometric plan and the placing of monuments. In the foreground is the Capitol, from which runs the long straight avenue of the Mall. Rising in the middle distance is the tall marble obelisk of the Washington Monument. Beyond is West Potomac Park and the classical building forming the Lincoln Memorial in line with the obelisk and the Capitol. To the left, in the distance, can be seen the Jefferson Memorial on the shore of the Potomac River.

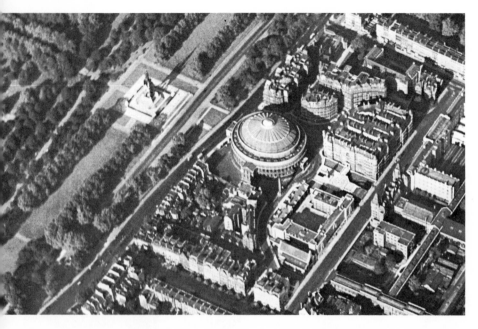

Albert Memorial, Kensington Gardens, London. Set in gardens bordering a main highway, the memorial is excellently sited, being near the hub of life in a capital city yet situated to allow contemplative appreciation. It is placed on the axis with the Albert Hall to which it is happily related in scale. (Aerofilms Ltd.)

their monuments to musicians, bordering The Ring. Siting monuments in gardens is generally attractive because the setting of lawns, shrubs, and trees shows sculpture to the best advantage, while a garden is also just the place to appreciate a monument. One of the best-sited large monuments is the much-abused Albert Memorial in Kensington Gardens, London. It is a very large, Gothic, canopied structure designed by Sir Gilbert Scott in 1863 (completed 1872). Also, though large, it appears to be right in scale opposite the mass of the Albert Hall. The adverse criticism of it, strongly prevalent between the two world wars, has died down as many eminent architects and critics have had the temerity to admire it.

Less satisfactory siting of public monuments is in the centers of streets and at the junctions of roads. Examples are legion, especially in London, where several have had to be removed because of traffic requirements. With the increase of traffic, these monuments become more and more remote and can only be seen from a distance unless the pedestrian risks his life to look at them. If a committee suggests a monument site in the center of a road, however wide, or at a road crossing, the planner should ask if there is not a public garden just off the highway that could be used instead.

Modern traffic planning often results in traffic islands (spaces of various size surrounded by roads), and monuments sometimes either survive on these islands or are placed on them. The monument closely surrounded by traffic is really remote, whereas its purpose requires that it should be seen and appreciated. Thus a prime requisite in the siting of a public monument is that it be so placed that it can be seen at leisure, if possible with some degree of peace and quiet, yet that it be sufficiently close to the hub of things to be part of the city life. The monuments to musicians in Vienna

Memorial to the ruined city of Rotterdam, in an open paved place near the old dock of Leuvehaven, erected in 1953. The figure is the work of Ossip Zadkine and depicts a giant figure in agony with its heart severed from its body.

Memorial Amphitheater and tomb of the unknown soldier in the Arlington National Cemetery, Washington. The impressiveness of this design depends partly on its effective siting and landscape setting.

are ideally sited in this respect. The monument must also be right in scale and be as eloquent in its setting and design as possible, and it is not beyond the province of the planner sometimes to say that pale stone has a clarity which is less often apparent in bronze in the urban scene.

BIBLIOGRAPHY: Camillo Sitte, *Der Städtebau nach seinen Künstlenischen Grundsatzen,* Vienna, 1889, English translation by G. R. and C. C. Collins, *City Planning According to Artistic Principles,* Columbia University Press, New York, 1965; Sir Lawrence Weaver, *Memorials and Monuments,* Country Life, London, 1915; S. D. Adshead, "Monumental Memorials and Town Planning," *Journal of the Town Planning Institute,* vol. 3, no. 5, London, 1917; Arnold Whittick, *War Memorials,* Country Life, London, 1946.

—ARNOLD WHITTICK

MORE, Sir THOMAS (1478–1535)   English scholar, theologian, statesman, and saint associated in Reformation thought with Erasmus (1466–1536) and Colet (ca. 1468–1519). He was a member of Parliament, Speaker of the House of Commons, and from 1518 Privy Councillor and 1529 to 1532 Lord Chancellor to Henry VIII. Refusing to condone Henry VIII's divorce from Catherine of Aragon and his breach with the Papacy, he was executed in 1535. More is world famous as the author of *Utopia*, first published in Latin in 1516 and in English in 1551; an account of an ideal state in which the population was distributed in fifty-four cities of about 4 square miles (10 square kilometers) each, 20 miles (32 kilometers) apart, with access to open country and the combination of urban and agricultural occupations: the nearest historical anticipation of Howard's garden city and greenbelt principles.

BIBLIOGRAPHY: There are many editions of *Utopia* and several lives of More and bibliographies of his works. For the planning pattern in *Utopia*, see F. J. Osbern, *Green-Belt Cities*, London and New York, 1969.

—FREDERIC J. OSBORN

Portrait of Sir Thomas More. (After Holbein, in the National Portrait Gallery, London.)

MORRIS, WILLIAM (1834–1896)   English designer, medievalist, poet, and reformer.

In every field of design—building, town planning, household art and decor, typography, and book illustration—Morris was one of the great reformers of the nineteenth century, seeking, along with Ruskin, to counter through the arts and crafts movement of the period, the widespread visual decadence that was a legacy of the industrial revolution.

Trained in architecture, though never himself a professional practitioner, Morris inspired and activated a new concept of domestic building and suburban planning which, together with the garden city, remains the most important contribution that England has made to resolving the planning problems of modern times.

In 1859 Morris, with his architect, Philip Webb, built for himself the Red House, at Bexley, Kent, and marked thereby a new epoch in domestic architecture. It was a new example of comprehensiveness in design. Not only were house and garden viewed as complementary, but the exterior and interior of the house—together with its furniture, fittings, and decorations—were conceived as a single unit, determined throughout by considerations of comfort and utility—"nothing that you do not know to be useful and believe to be beautiful."

The principles underlying the Red House were carried into communal dimensions when the English architect Norman Shaw designed a colony of small houses, completed in 1880, at the London suburb of Bedford Park. Comprising detached, semidetached, and terraced houses intermingled, the buildings reverted in style to an indigenous, pre-Renaissance spontaneity; while the layout of streets and gardens, though aspiring to symmetry, respected the natural character of the terrain—its contours, trees, and other existing features. In this, Morris and his associates followed the example of the English landscape gardeners.

William Morris, by George Frederick Watts. (National Portrait Gallery, London.)

The "cottage style" of architecture and planning (as it was sometimes known) was an important element of Morris's dream of recapturing and renewing the largely unconscious creative processes of the Middle Ages. It proved immediately practical and influenced architects of the next generation in the persons of Edwin Lutyens (in his country houses particularly), C. F. A. Voysey, Baillie Scott, and C. R. Mackintosh. It continues to attract the attention of planners and sociologists in many parts of the world.

BIBLIOGRAPHY: J. W. Mackail, *Life and Letters of William Morris,* London, 1908; P. Henderson, *William Morris: His Life, Work, and Friends,* McGraw-Hill Book Company, New York, 1967.

—WILFRED SALTER

MOTORWAYS (*See* FREEWAYS.)

MOVEMENTS AND THEORIES OF MODERN ARCHITECTURAL DESIGN
Some knowledge of the many movements in modern architecture and of theories of architectural design may occasionally prove useful to the planner, as they are among the determinants of the visual character of the urban scene. During the twentieth century the theories and movements which have had the greatest influence (with indication by dates of the periods when they were chiefly in vogue) are art nouveau (1890–1915), expressionism (1905–1925), organic unity (1910–1940), functionalism (1910–1940), constructivism (1920–1940), de stijl (1920–1940), neoclassicism (1925–1940), the international style (1925–1950), and brutalism (1955–1965). There have been more recent revivals of interest in several of these.

With the possible exception of the first, these all belong to modern architecture, from which most of the contemporary idioms have descended. Two factors, common to all, bring them into the category of modern architecture as distinct from traditional architecture. First, in all of these, modern methods of construction and cladding and the use of steel, concrete, glass, and synthetics are accepted as being more subject to precise calculation than natural material. Second, they all represent a departure from the decorative character of traditional styles.

Art nouveau originated in Belgium with the work and theories of Henri van de Velde and Victor Horta. It was part of the general effort to develop a decorative character independent of historical styles. It was manifested as an art of linear rhythms and appeared in many forms of decorative art, from book illustration to architecture. Although mainly concerned with decorative effects, van de Velde tried to associate linear rhythm with structure and lines of force, an approach exemplified, to some extent, in the theatre that he designed for the Cologne Exhibition of 1914. He also, with others, linked the linear rhythms with lines of growth seen in the paintings of Van Gogh, and this led to the idea of organic unity which he developed. It had some kinship with expressionism, which also, in many of its manifestations, was an art of linear rhythms closely associated with organic growth.

The origin of expressionism, however, was the desire of some German painters—among whom the group called Die Brücke ("the bridge"), founded in 1905, was the most important—to express the essential character

and inner significance of things. The name of the group refers to the bridge
from the world of the senses to the world of the essential and often hidden
significance of things. The movement was influenced by Freud's theories
of the unconscious and led to the later movement of surrealism. It had
considerable influence on architecture, and among the well-known architects
whose work shows this influence were Hans Poelzig, Max Berg, Henri van
de Velde, Erich Mendelsohn, and Hans Scharoun, although the influence
may not always have been consciously felt by these architects. Perhaps the
three outstanding modern European buildings that show most dramatically
the influence of expressionism are the Observatory at Potsdam by Erich
Mendelsohn (1920–1921), the Goetheanum at Basel by Rudolf Steiner
(1925–1928), and the Chapel at Romchanp by Le Corbusier (1951–1954).

Related to both art nouveau and expressionism is the architectural theory
of organic unity, a creed strongly held by Louis H. Sullivan and Frank Lloyd
Wright in the United States and by Henri van de Velde and Erich
Mendelsohn in Europe. The theory of organic building must be distinguished from the theory of organic architecture. The former is a type of
functional building according to social needs, where a house or other
building, for example, is provided in stages according to growing and
changing needs. The theory of organic unity in architecture originates with
ancient Greek and Roman precepts that the proportions of buildings should
be derived from the proportions of the human figure and that our bodily
existence and bodily feelings are the measure of the world around us—a
theory revived and applied again during the Renaissance and systematized
in modern German philosophy by Lipps in the theory of *Einfühlung*,
sometimes rendered into English as "empathy."

Organic unity can be briefly defined in modern practice as the integration
of the parts with the whole, so that the design of the whole controls the
design of the subordinate parts. In its relation to functionalism it could
be further defined as a structure integrated into a harmonious whole which,
together with its various parts, is determined in form by the functions to
be performed. An analogy may be made to the conditioning of the parts
of an organism by the work they and it are created to perform.

The theory of functionalism has a long tradition, but it became, possibly,
the most important of all modern movements in architecture in the period
between the two world wars. Its influence was particularly powerful in
Germany and France in the second and third decades of the century, in
the United States in the third and fourth decades, and in Great Britain
in the fourth decade. The dicta of "fitness for purpose" and "appropriateness
of form to function" have been widely accepted by the many practitioners
of functionalism, but they have been differently interpreted, from the stark
fulfillment of bare material purpose to the inclusion of civic and spiritual
values—as explained in the article in this encyclopedia (*see* FUNCTIONAL-
ISM).

Constructivism originated in Moscow in 1920 with the *Realistic Manifesto*
of the sculptor brothers Naum Gabo and Antoine Pevsner, who have

remained for over 40 years its principal exponents. It had a considerable following among European architects and is really more akin to architecture than to traditional sculpture. Naum Gabo always preferred to call his works constructions rather than sculptures. One purpose of the movement was to express in symbolic forms the conceptions of life and the universe prompted by modern science. It was associated with other early movements of the twentieth century, especially cubism and functionalism, and much constructivist work aimed at exhibiting the relations of geometric forms to which, it was claimed, natural forms could be reduced. Broadly stated, it could be typified as symbolic construction; and in architecture, construction in all its aspects was emphasized, all traditional ornamental accessories were discarded, and aesthetic effect depended on the formal relations of mass and space emanating from the most efficient construction. This, if well designed, expresses a unity symbolic of the universe. Among architects who show either the influence of or kinship with constructivism are the Russians Vladimir Tatlin and El Lissitzky and the Dutch architects Theo van Doesburg and Thomas Rietveld, while Le Corbusier and Marcel Breuer both worked for a time on parallel lines. The excesses of constructivism might be called constructional exhibitionism—suggesting in some instances construction for construction's sake. There is a distinct probability that a new monumentality in architecture to succeed the traditional monumentality, which depended on the grandeurs of traditional classical architecture—Greek, Roman, and Renaissance—will take the form of impressive monumental constructions.

The De Stijl group of artists and architects was founded in Leiden, Netherlands, in 1917. Its aims were much influenced by cubism. The cube was regarded as a basic unit of design capable of extension in all directions, while space as an element in design and as material for expression was of the first importance. Forms in their maximum visual purity, with plain surfaces and flat, unbroken primary colors as well as white, black, and grey, constituted a primary aim. Among the notable architects of the group were J. J. P. Oud, Theo van Doesburg, and Thomas Rietveld.

Neoclassicism is the adoption of the essential forms, masses, and proportions of Greek and Roman architecture with the traditional ornamentation and other decorative embellishments minimized. Buildings are designed in a bare and eloquent simplicity, the aesthetic effect depending on pure formal relations of volumes and plain surfaces. Neoclassicism had many varied manifestations and is apparent in the architecture of most countries of the western world, particularly from about 1925 to 1940. It varied from the mere discarding of ornament—Greek columns, capitals, and bases becoming merely plain shafts (as in much of the official architecture of Italy, Germany and the U.S.S.R.)—to the application of classical principles of proportion, massing, and restraint most notably seen in the work of Le Corbusier, Walter Gropius, and Mies van der Rohe.

The term "international style" probably appeared first in the catalogue for the exhibition of modern architecture at the Museum of Modern Art in

New York in 1932, having been used by Henry-Russell Hitchcock and Philip Johnson at the suggestion of Alfred Barr, the museum director. What, however, is embraced by the international style begins much earlier, about the time of the modern applications of the theories of functionalism, of which it is an important phase. The international style denotes a functional building with dependence for aesthetic effect on masses and their relation and integration, on plain surfaces and the discarding of ornament and decoration, with a preference for flat roofs and a full use of the devices made possible by modern construction—such as cantilevering. It has some kinship with, and includes in part other movements such as functionalism, constructivism, and neoclassicism. The international style, as its name implies, was worldwide in its manifestations, although this could be said of most of the modern movements in architecture. Among its most notable practitioners were Walter Gropius, Le Corbusier, Mies van der Rohe, Richard Neutra, and Philip Johnson.

Brutalism emanated largely from a discontent with architectural trends felt in Britain by such architects as Alison and Peter Smithson. It dates from 1954. The aim of the movement—the uncompromising presentation of the structure and materials of functional building—is seen in the work of such architects as Le Corbusier and Mies van der Rohe; but the members of the movement went further and exposed not only the bare structure and the structural materials but even the service ducts. It is a phase of functionalism and clearly has kinship with constructivism.

It will be appreciated that the various aims and the work of these modern movements in architecture are both stimulating and fruitful of ideas to the urban designer and planner.

BIBLIOGRAPHY: H. R. Hitchcock and P. C. Johnson, *The International Style,* Museum of Modern Art, New York, 1932; Arnold Whittick, *European Architecture in the Twentieth Century,* Crosby Lockwood, London, vol. I, 1950, vol. II, 1953; Bruni Zevi, *Towards an Organic Architecture,* Faber & Faber, Ltd., London, 1950; Jurgen Joedicke, *A History of Modern Architecture,* The Architectural Press, London 1959; Cranston Jones, *Architecture Today and Tomorrow,* McGraw-Hill Book Company, New York, 1961; G. E. Kidder Smith, *The New Architecture of Europe,* World Publishing Co., New York, 1961, Penguin Books, Ltd., London, 1962; Gerd Hatje (ed.), *Encyclopedia of Modern Architecture,* Thames and Hudson, London, 1963; Rayner Banham, "Brutalism" and "Neoclassicism," Peter Blake, "Functionalism," Robert L. Delevoy, "Art Nouveau," Vittorio Gregotti, "Expressionism," Henry-Russell Hitchcock, "International Style," Arnold Whittick, "Constructivism" and "Organic Architecture."

—ARNOLD WHITTICK

MULTILEVEL CAR PARKS AND GARAGES   (*See* PARKING.)

MULTILEVEL DEVELOPMENT   A pattern of urban design that has, during the mid-twentieth century, become a familiar feature of city and town centers. It is introduced into modern urban planning for the purposes of compactness, convenience, space saving, and in order to segregate pedestrians and vehicles. Notable modern examples are the Penn Center and East Market Street in Philadelphia; Cumbernauld town center in Scotland, which has seven levels, with pedestrian areas on the upper five and vehicular traffic

on the lowest two levels; and the New North West Town of Frankfurt, which has two very extensive pedestrian levels above a car park.

Two-level urban planning, apart from that within buildings, began in ancient Greece with the stoa, usually a long, multipurpose building for storage, offices, and shops which, as in the case of the building in Athens, was often on two levels. The custom of having shops on two levels was continued during the Middle Ages and Renaissance. Some examples survive today, a famous one being at Chester, in England.

The idea for a two-level city appears to have originated with Leonardo da Vinci (*q.v.*), who proposed an upper level for pedestrians and a lower level for vehicles and a sewerage system. The idea was further developed by Le Corbusier, but in practice the arrangement of two levels or more has never extended beyond the city or town center. A considerable number of multilevel town centers have, however, been constructed between 1955 and 1972.

MULTILEVEL SHOPPING CENTERS   (*See* SHOPPING CENTERS.)

MUMFORD, LEWIS (1895–   )   Born in Flushing, Long Island, on October 19, 1895, and educated at The City College of New York and Columbia University. In 1914, while studying biology, he became acquainted with the work of Patrick Geddes (*q.v.*). Under Geddes's direct influence, Mumford began a systematic study of New York and its region, surveying every part of it on foot. In this he followed Geddes's lead in his report on Dunfermline (1904) and in *Cities of Evolution* (1915). This sociological and ecological approach to the city, pursued in many cities large and small from Honolulu to Athens, is what distinguishes Mumford's work. Through his first article in the *Journal of the American Institute of Architects* entitled "The Heritage of the Cities Movement in America" (1918), Mumford came into contact with Clarence Stein, Benton MacKaye, and Henry Wright (*q.v.*), and he took an active part, from 1923 on, not only in the Regional Planning Association of America but in the New York State Housing and Regional Planning Commission. The final report of this commission, in 1926, laid the basis for the national and state planning projects, including the TVA and the greenbelt towns, that were furthered by the Roosevelt administration. Under Mumford's editorship, the regional planning number of the *Survey Graphic* (May 1925) brought this approach to urban planning on a regional basis to a wider public more than a generation before these ideas began to filter into professional courses on urban planning. Mumford's critical contributions to contemporary planning, published mainly in the *Architectural Record* and *The New Yorker,* form the core of four books: *City Development: Disintegration and Renewal* (1945), *From the Ground Up* (1956), *The Highway and the City* (1962), and *The Urban Prospect* (1968). But his central works on cities are his two original surveys entitled *The Culture of Cities* (1938) and *The City in History* (1961). Though by profession neither an urban planner nor an architect, Mumford served as consultant to the

Lewis Mumford.

Park Board of Honolulu in 1938 (*see* "Whither Honolulu" in his *City Development*), to Stanford University (1947), and to Christ Church College, Oxford (1965). From 1951 to 1961, he was Professor of City and Regional Planning at the University of Pennsylvania and Visiting Bemis Professor of the Massachusetts Institute of Technology. He received in 1957 the Gold Medal of the British (now Royal) Town Planning Institute and in 1961 the Royal Gold Medal of the Royal Institute of British Architects.

Though no single book sums up Mumford's contributions, his essential ideas on contemporary planning are best expressed, perhaps, in *The Urban Prospect,* particularly in his paper entitled "Planning for the Phases of Life."

BIBLIOGRAPHY: The principal works on planning by Lewis Mumford are *The Culture of Cities,* New York, 1938, paperbook edition with new introduction, 1970, *City Development: Studies in Disintegration and Renewal,* New York, 1945, "The Modern City," in Hamlin, Talbor (ed.), *Forms and Functions of Twentieth-Century Architecture,* New York, 1952, "The Natural History of Urbanization," in Thomas, William L. (ed.), *Man's Role in Changing the Face of the Earth,* Chicago, 1956, *The City in History,* New York, 1961, *The Highway and the City,* New York, 1962, *The Urban Prospect,* New York, 1968.

—STANLEY BUDER

N

NASH, Sir JOHN (1752–1835) English architect and planner. A leading architect of his period, Nash in his scheme for Regent Street and Park was the author of the most extensive piece of continuous city planning ever carried out in London.

The Prince Regent, later George IV, proposed to build himself a villa in the park, which he required to be connected by means of a direct road to his Westminster residence of Carlton House, nearly 2 miles south.

Embarking on a scheme unprecedented in scale, Nash designed the park with provision for the villa, which in the event was never built, and combined with it a primary road that now comprises Park Crescent, Portland Place, Upper Regent Street, and Regent Street itself. The original terminus, Carlton House, was demolished in 1827, the Duke of York's Column and Carlton House Terrace being later erected on the site.

Nash's sensitive and imaginative treatment of the scheme was an advance on Renaissance planning principles—his long arterial road, for example, avoids the monotony of being perfectly straight. He provided it with traffic places and, with his architectural solution of the whole, demonstrated his ability both as planner and architect to comprehend development on a major scale.

His many works included the conversion of Buckingham House into

Buckingham Palace and the planning and architectural design, also for the Prince Regent, of the Royal Pavilion at Brighton.

BIBLIOGRAPHY: John Summerson, *John Nash*, George Allen & Unwin Ltd., London, 1935.

—WILFRED SALTER

NATIONAL PARKS Areas of outstanding natural beauty which are reserved for public use and enjoyment. Such areas are usually administered by a special body, and the land may be owned either by the state or privately.

The world's first national park was established in 1872 in Wyoming in the United States and is known as Yellowstone. As other areas of outstanding scenic magnificence were established, an act of Congress in 1916 set up a National Park Service to act under the Department of the Interior as trustee for all the national parks in the United States. The act states that the service shall "promote and regulate the use of the federal areas known as national parks and reservations . . . to conserve the scenery and the natural and historic objects and the wild life therein, and to provide for the enjoyment of the same in such manner and by such means as will leave them unimpaired for the enjoyment of future generations." Today the service administers approximately 25 million acres (10 million hectares).

The parks consist primarily of natural landscape and are kept in their original state. The lands are owned by the federal government. The parks are recreational areas and concessions have been granted to allow the establishment of hotels and shops. Provision is also made for camping, horseback riding, boating, fishing, hiking, and, where suitable, skiing.

The roads and all other routes and stopping places are designed by the National Park Service to fit into the landscape. Many of the parkways are spectacular and rank among the most superbly designed roads in the world.

In Britain the national parks were designated under the National Parks and Access to the Countryside Act of 1949, by the National Parks Commission (now the Countryside Commission). There are ten national parks in England and Wales comprising a total area of 5,258 square miles (13,618 square kilometers).

The commission's purpose in designating an area is to ensure the proper control of development and the continued preservation of natural beauty.

The commission does not own land or directly administer the park; it is an advisory body only. Executive powers are vested in joint planning boards or park planning committees which control development within the park. Control is exercised through the planning acts, ensuring that special attention is given to the preservation of natural beauty and to finding ways in which public enjoyment may be enhanced and extended.

The normal work of the countryside continues within the park area. The careful management of the land and development secures the perpetuation of the landscape's beauty. Also, positive measures are encouraged to promote enjoyment by the public. The government makes grants of 75 percent available toward the costs of approved works.

Inhabitants and visitors may enjoy the scenic beauty in any way they prefer—riding by car, pony, or horse; climbing; hiking; picnicking; or camping.

National parks similar to those in the United States and Britain have been established in other countries. —WENDY POWELL

NATIONAL PLANNING Although national economic and industrial planning has been undertaken by many countries and national economic development is guided by period plans, national land-use planning has rarely been undertaken with the same completeness. Regional land-use planning, on the other hand, is fairly common, and many countries—including Belgium, Chile, Denmark, India, the United Kingdom, and others—have planning regions for which plans have been prepared. But as yet these plans have not been coordinated into positive programs of national physical planning, despite the fact that the advantage of national planning, as forming a framework into which regional and local planning can fit, is recognized by planners and is often advocated by them. It is at the same time understood that the planning framework must be flexible and must change with changing conditions.

A national plan would logically follow the planning technique of survey-plan-implementation that has been evolved in practice. Survey would comprehend matters of climate, physical features, distribution of population and industry—indeed, all conceivable conditions and trends that are likely to have a bearing on physical planning. Among the most important matters in a national survey of this kind, which is also generally included in economic surveys, is the existing distribution of population and industry (*q.v.*), why this has developed in the way that it has, and what are likely to be the future trends. The survey would thus classify the prosperous and less prosperous areas, the areas more vulnerable to periods of economic depressions, the areas of comparative expanding and declining industries and of comparatively stable industry, the comparative rates of industrial growth of different regions, the likely developments in the future and the effects these would have on the living conditions of the population. Also included in a national survey would be all necessary demographic statistics, the possible consequences of an increase and intensification of congested areas, and the possibilities of development in sparsely populated areas. A national survey is most valuable when it is not merely static but is to some extent creative in spirit, made with a view to possibilities of development.

The objects of a national physical plan would be mainly (1) to maintain and improve conditions of living and all the amenities that contribute to this, and (2) to assist in the distribution of population and industry and of communications and transport so as to ensure the utmost prosperity. These closely related objects are best pursued together, but too often in the past the former has been sacrificed to the latter.

The first stage, which is an important factor in economic planning, is a system of controls and inducements in the location of industry. This was a feature in the National Plan for the United Kingdom for 1964–1970. In this plan a program was adumbrated for reducing congestion in overcrowded areas, of encouraging the growth of less populated areas, and of developing new sites for housing and industry. Three objectives were indicated: (1) public investment programs to modernize the infrastructure of the older and less prosperous industrial regions and to reduce the congestion of large cities; (2) measures to influence the distribution of population by facilitating movements such as accommodating urban overspill and providing for population growth to facilitate "national economic growth and the provision of pleasant human environment"; and (3) stimulating "growth in the less prosperous regions by influencing the geographical pattern of employment and economic activity." One method by which these objectives could be substantially achieved is the large-scale establishment of New Towns in areas of declining or stationary population or in sparsely populated areas.

This first stage (and the National Plan for the United Kingdom did not go much beyond this) is toward effecting an improved distribution of population by control and inducements in the location of industry. In reaching the desired objectives, however, it would be necessary for a national plan to go further. There is the likely trend in the distribution of population and industry which a national survey would reveal, and there is a desirable trend based on a conception of national well-being, good general standards of living, and national prosperity. One purpose of a national plan would be, therefore, to endeavor to form a picture of a satisfactory distribution of population at a particular time in the future, a picture that might form a goal for national land-use planning over a certain period. The character of that goal would be susceptible to change with changing conditions. It is questionable whether satisfactory planning of national transport in all its various forms is possible until some picture is formed of where people are likely to be.

National planning is of greatest value if it goes beyond the consideration of the potentials of growth areas. It is useful planning if encouragement is given to these areas, but in addition most countries (the exceptions are a few small, densely populated countries) have very sparsely populated areas which have not yet been considered for development or which have, because of their physical characteristics, been dismissed as too unpromising or too costly to develop. Studies of such regions with a view to possible development can usefully be included in national planning. An outstanding example of such national enterprise is the Tennessee Valley scheme inaugurated by President Franklin D. Roosevelt.

National planning can more easily be accomplished in small countries like Denmark and the Netherlands than in large countries like Brazil and the United States. Yet even in large countries, in the preparation of regional plans it is invaluable to have something bigger to which a regional scheme can be related. A very large number of countries have prepared, are preparing, or will prepare regional plans. If a national plan or picture of some kind is already in existence, then the regional plans can be related to this; and when they are all completed and considered together, the formal national plan can be modified with the possibility of national guidance emerging that will at least provide some vision for the future in every field. Such a procedure would prevent developments without plans and the sort of single-purpose planning from which most countries have suffered.

A further stage is land-use planning on an international basis, and there are signs that this is influencing the thought of planners. Already, planning in relation to international concentrations of industry and trade, such as that in northwest Europe, is becoming increasingly important.

BIBLIOGRAPHY: British Department of Economic Affairs, *The National Plan*, H.M.S.O., London, 1965; Albert Mayer, *The Urgent Future*, McGraw-Hill Book Company, New York, 1967 (indirectly provides some of the arguments for national planning); William Lean, "Economics of Land Use Planning: Urban and Regional," *Estates Gazette*, London, 1969 (especially chap. 13, "National, Regional and Land Use Planning").

—ARNOLD WHITTICK

NATURE RESERVES   Areas where flora, fauna, and land forms are protected in their natural environment for the purpose of scientific study and human enjoyment. Thus, in civilized communities, they constitute important claims on the use of land. Areas with distinctive and unique examples of flora, fauna, and land forms have very strong claims for protection as nature reserves.

The movement to conserve areas of exceptionally interesting natural phenomena began in the United States, and the first such area to receive protection, in 1832, is at Hot Springs, Arkansas. At first the movement toward the protection of further areas was very gradual. Another important stage was the acquisition by the state of California, in 1864, of the Yosemite Valley and the Mariposa grove of *Sequoia gigantea* which became part of the Yosemite National Park in 1890. A very important nature reserve was that which formed Yellowstone National Park, established in 1872 as the first national park following the inauguration of national parks under federal ownership in 1870 (*see* NATIONAL PARKS). Yellowstone is also the largest (3,348 square miles or 8,671 square kilometers), containing remarkable geysers and waterfalls and extensive wild-bird and animal preserves— including buffalo, antelope, deer, elk, and bear. Although there is thus identity of nature reserves and national parks, which are for the edification and enjoyment of the public, certain restraints of access are necessary to allow animals, birds, trees, and plants to develop fully in their natural environment. By the year 1970 there were about 230 national parks in the United States covering about 28,000,000 acres (11,340,000 hectares).

Whereas in the United States nature reserves are integral to the national parks, in Great Britain they are entirely separate areas. The ten national parks are regions of outstanding natural beauty for public enjoyment and recreation. National nature reserves, of which there are 130 in Great Britain, are mostly comparatively small areas which are protected so as to maintain examples of important kinds of vegetation, bird and animal life, and land forms. The largest is Cairngorms in Scotland (64,118 acres or 25,968 hectares), which has among its animals and birds the wildcat, red and roe deer, ptarmigan, dotterel, crested tit, Scottish crossbill, and golden eagle. Several nature reserves in England comprise only a few acres. Many are wholly or partly in private ownership. In most cases there is public access with restraints. They are administered by the Nature Conservancy, established under the Countryside Act of 1949, which, in 1965, became a component body of the Natural Environment Research Council (NERC). In addition to the 130 nature reserves, there are over two thousand areas of special interest for their flora or fauna or for their geological features. Planning authorities are informed of these by the NERC, and in the case of proposed development, the NERC must be notified so that its views can be considered. The claims of development and conservation are then adjudicated.

—ARNOLD WHITTICK

NEIGHBORHOOD UNIT An integrated, planned, urban area related to the larger community of which it is a part and consisting of residential districts, a school or schools, shopping facilities, religious buildings, open spaces, and perhaps a degree of service industry. An early exponent of the neighborhood theory was Clarence Arthur Perry, who contributed a memorandum on the neighborhood unit to volume VII of the *Regional Survey of New York and its Environs* (New York, 1929). Among the features of this scheme was the provision of an elementary school and other institutions required by the residents; the provision of one or more shopping districts on the periphery of the unit, preferably near traffic junctions and adjacent to shops in other neighborhoods; a street system designed to facilitate circulation within the unit but to discourage through traffic; and arterial roads at the boundaries to facilitate bypassing of the unit.

These principles influenced the preparation of plans for cities and towns during and immediately after the Second World War. Sir Patrick Abercrombie and J. H. Forshaw, in their *County of London Plan,* 1943, advocated the neighborhood as a valuable unit in the planning of communities, and they decided that:

> The elementary school should be the determining factor in the size and organisation of the subsidiary or neighbourhood units and those communities in which large-scale reconstruction is proposed. The desirable scholar capacity of the elementary school and the desirability of fixing a maximum walking distance from home to school, make the latter the one suitable building on which to base the size and arrangement of the neighbourhood units [paragraph 106].

This gives, according to the authors, a population for neighborhood units of between 6,000 and 10,000 persons, although it was found in practice, in the extensive use of the neighborhood unit in the plans of the British New Towns, that a primary school served a population of nearer 6,000 and that the larger figure would mean two schools. It was the intention that children living in these neighborhoods should not have to cross a main road. Each neighborhood would have a center, preferably near the school, as well as local shops, community buildings, and smaller amenity open spaces. In his subsequent Greater London Plan of 1944, Abercrombie prepared a plan for the new satellite town of Ongar with a population of 60,000. This town was planned with six neighborhoods of between 8,200 and 11,750 population and an industrial area grouped around a center, a plan which, although not implemented for Ongar, had a tremendous influence on the planning of British New Towns. The idea was recommended by the New Towns Committee which, in 1946, stated that "the neighbourhood is a natural and useful conception, but it should not be thought of as a self-contained community of which the inhabitants are more conscious than they are of the town as whole." Ten thousand is considered a convenient size subject to wide variations, and "in each neighbourhood there should be a centre with adequate provision of shops, places of recreation and refreshment, and a grouping of buildings containing a public hall and meeting rooms for various purposes."

The neighborhood unit has formed the basis of the planning and building of most of the first generation of British New Towns (1946–1950). In some, like Crawley, Cwmbran, Bracknell, Peterlee, and Corby, the neighborhoods are generally small, between 5,000 and 8,000 (with a few a little larger). Others, such as Stevenage and East Kilbride, have larger neighborhoods, which has meant two and sometimes three primary schools and longer distances to the neighborhood centers. In Harlow the principle has been followed, but with considerable variation. In this plan there are four main groupings around a center, and these have been subdivided to make fourteen residential areas. The original plan of Basildon (1951) had fairly large neighborhoods with populations of 5,000 to 20,000, but in the new outline plan (1967) for a bigger population, the neighborhoods are much smaller, some of the original ones being subdivided.

With the plan for Cumbernauld in Scotland (1958), the neighborhood system was abandoned, but with the second generation of New Towns (1961–1967) there was a general return to the principle of neighborhood planning, although there seemed to be a general anxiety among the planners to call the units anything but "neighborhoods." Such terms as "residential communities" (Runcorn), "districts" (Redditch), or "villages" (Washington) were preferred. In the plan for Milton Keynes (1969), the town is divided by primary roads into grid squares of about 0.4 square mile (1 square kilometer) each. Within the squares thus formed will be residential areas for about 5,000 persons. Estate roads branch from the grid to serve the residential areas, while a system of pedestrian routes traverses the whole town, crossing the primary roads generally by underpasses. At these points of crossing, shops and schools and other facilities will be concentrated. Thus, in this recent plan, there is in principle some return to Clarence Arthur Perry's New York plan of 1929, a plan in which the shops are placed on the periphery of the neighborhood unit, adjacent to those of other neighborhoods.

It will be seen that the neighborhood unit is a persistent theme of modern urban planning—a theme subject to many variations that provide a rewarding field of study.

BIBLIOGRAPHY: Clarence Arthur Perry, *Regional Plan of New York and its Environs,* vol. VII, *The Neighborhood Unit,* Russell Sage Foundation, New York, 1929; J. H. Forshaw and Patrick Abercrombie, *County of London Plan,* Macmillan & Co., Ltd., London, 1943; National Council of Social Service, *The Size and Social Structure of a Town,* George Allen & Unwin, Ltd., London, 1943; Patrick Abercrombie, *Greater London Plan,* H.M.S.O., London, 1944; Dudley Report,

Design of Dwellings, H.M.S.O., London, 1944; *New Towns Committee Final Report,* H.M.S.O., London, 1946; *Housing Manual,* H.M.S.O., London, 1949; James W. R. Adams, *Modern Town and Country Planning,* J. & A. Churchill, London, 1952; Lewis Keeble, *Principles and Practice of Town and Country Planning,* 3d ed., Estates Gazette, 1964; Sir Frederick Gibberd, *Town Design,* 5th ed., Architectural Press, London, 1967; Sir Frederic J. Osborn and Arnold Whittick, *The New Towns: The Answer to Megalopolis,* 2d ed., Leonard Hill, London, 1969.

—ARNOLD WHITTICK

NEOCLASSICISM   (*See* MOVEMENTS AND THEORIES OF MODERN ARCHITEC-TURAL DESIGN.)

NEOTECHNIC   A term coined by Patrick Geddes, following Lubbock's typification of the epochs of prehistoric archaeology, to describe the later and more highly developed stage of the industrial age.[1] (*See also* BIOTECHNIC, EOTECHNIC, PALEOTECHNIC.)

NETHERLANDS

Legislation and Administration   Town and country planning in the Netherlands rests chiefly on one act (some exceptions are mentioned below)—the Physical Planning Act (Wet op de ruimtelijke ordening)—which became operative on August 1, 1965. Before that date local planning was based on the Housing Act of 1901, subsequently revised on more than one occasion, whereas regional and national planning was based on a specific act of a provisional nature, maintaining in substance a decree on this matter from the war period. The present act keeps to a three-tier system in physical planning—local, provincial (regional), and national—which is in accord with the traditional administrative setup of the country. One of the main characteristics of the present act in comparison with its predecessors is the wish to bring about a new type of planning, less rigid and more easily adaptable to evolving ideas and circumstances, without causing the responsible authorities to lose their firm grip on all relevant forms of development. The only plan which now has the force of law is the local development plan. Previously, regional plans were binding on the local authorities in the region in that they had to bring their development plans into line with the regional plan. Similarly, a national plan under the old regime, should it have been completed and passed, would have had the force of law in regard to all regional plans.

The local development plan is obligatory for all local authorities insofar as the area outside the existing towns and villages is concerned. For the built-up area, however, the local authorities are empowered to draw up a development plan. The plans are passed by the local council after having been made available for public inspection. They need the approval of the provincial authorities, and in both instances anyone may object to the plan. If the provincial authorities do not accept the validity of their objections, there is a right of appeal to the Crown. The local authorities also have a right of appeal in case the provincial authorities should withhold their approval.

Another type of local plan mentioned in the act is the structure plan,

[1] Patrick Geddes, *Cities in Evolution,* Williams & Norgate, Ltd., London, 1915.

which does not schedule the land for various purposes and does not bind anyone. It is, rather, a program and does not need the approval of higher authorities.

At the provincial level the main instrument of planning is the regional plan. As a rule it covers a fairly limited part of the area of a whole province. It has to be passed by a body of the Provincial State elected by the citizens.

At the national level, the idea of an all-embracing plan has disappeared. For special facets of national planning, however, the government still has the right to pass a plan. Apart from this, the act speaks of a national planning policy, the preparation of which is entrusted to one minister (at present the Minister of Housing and Planning). The act does not specify how this policy is to be laid down and made known. In 1966 the government proceeded to the publication of a report in which they gave a deliberate account of their physical planning policy, a policy which was discussed in Parliament and subsequently confirmed in essence by the following government.

As stated before, the enforcement of planning is restricted to the local level. The local development plan has the force of law in that building licenses may not be granted unless the relevant project is in accordance with the development plan. Moreover, the plan itself may stipulate that, for specific forms of development of any other kind (with some restrictions) in the area of the plan or special parts thereof, a license from the local authorities is mandatory and that this license is to be refused when the proposed development does not tally with the development plan.

Regional plans have no similar protection. The local authorities, when drawing up their plans, are free to deviate from the regional plan, but they have to take into account the fact that any lack of conformity with the latter will be a matter of special concern to the provincial authorities when they consider the local plan for approval. Besides this, the provincial authorities have been given an instrument of enforcing their view on the local authorities in advance by promulgating a directive, based on a regional plan, which the latter authorities are bound to follow.

The same power is vested in the Minister of Housing and Planning with reference to regional plans, and in a directive of this type the Minister may order the provincial authorities to pass his directive on to the local authorities concerned. It should be noted that, until now, the Minister has only four times availed himself of this power.

An important aspect of the implementation of a plan is the extent to which it is followed by the authorities themselves in carrying out projects. Locally and provincially, serious questions are not likely to arise in this context owing to the unity of the local or the provincial administration. But on the national level a number of ministers, who are largely autonomous, are responsible for various types of development which may run counter to the national planning policy. However, the act provides for a national planning committee consisting of representatives of many ministries. It stipulates that all measures and projects that are relevant to the national planning policy, apart from a few exceptions for special fields of action where similar coordinating committees already existed, shall be placed before this committee. If agreement is not reached on any issue, it is to be referred to the Cabinet.

Questions of compensation are not likely to arise from any plan except the local development plan, this being the only one which may restrict the owner in his choice of future forms of development. Anyone who feels he is adversely affected by a local development plan may apply to the local council for compensation, which is to be granted if there is damage which in reason cannot be left to the private owner. If he does not concur with the council's decision, he has the right of appeal to the Crown. The compensation is at the expense of the local authorities, but in case it is the result of a directive from a higher authority, the Crown may decide that the whole or part of it and, in general, additional costs resulting from such a directive shall be borne by the public bodies responsible for the interests that were served by the directive.

The old Housing Act contained important provisions furthering the implementation of development plans by means of compulsory purchase. This matter is now solely dealt with in the Compulsory Purchase Act. It enables local authorities to acquire compulsorily any land or buildings in the interest of the implementation of a development plan or to ensure that a situation which is in accordance with such a plan be preserved. The acquisition is made by a decision of the local council subject to the approval of the Crown.

The Planning Act also deals with departments and committees in the realm of planning. At the local level everything is left to the authorities concerned, which is probably due to the fact that the size of many municipalities does not admit of special departments for this work.

Each province, however, is expected to set up a provincial planning department and a provincial committee. At the governmental level the act provides for a national planning department which, apart from some inspectors of planning representing the department in an area comprising from two to four provinces, is mainly centralized. Secondly, there is a national planning committee, as mentioned above; and thirdly, there is a Council of Advice on Physical Planning, which consists mainly of representatives of a large number of private organizations and a number of experts. This council is an important link between the government and organized public opinion.

Some forms of regional and local planning in the Netherlands are being prepared and adopted outside the legal system as described above. This applies to the plans for the Zuider Zee polders and in general to the planning of newly reclaimed land. Plans of this type are very much like regional plans with one important reservation: there are no responsible provincial and local authorities on whom it could be incumbent to prepare and implement those plans. It is the Minister of Traffic and Waterworks who is responsible for them. The same holds good of the more detailed plans for new towns and villages in these areas, at least until this task can be transferred to a public body for the new polder, which becomes the forerunner of a future local authority.

Another type of regional planning has developed out of the agricultural reallotment schemes. At present such schemes have a multipurpose character, covering the general improvement of the area concerned (roads, recreation, slums, etc.). Such plans need the consent of the landowners in the area and are prepared by a special government service.

Professional Practice   When modern town planning started under the influence of the Housing Act of 1901, there were no professional town planners. The preparation of the plans prescribed by that act was mostly in the hands of civil engineers in the local departments of public works. Occasionally, private architects were called upon to serve as consultants, and some of them showed a special competence in this field. It was only in the twenties that the first departments of town planning were set up in the largest cities, either as separate departments (Rotterdam), as a part of the Department of Public Works (Amsterdam), or combined with the Housing Department (the Hague). On their staffs not only civil engineers and architects but also some economists and landscape architects were employed, so that the first attempts at teamwork could be made. At the same time a growing number of private architects began to specialize in town planning without giving up their architectural practice. Their services were available to medium-sized and small towns, where it was increasingly felt that the local departments were unable to handle the job properly. The slogan "Survey before plan" was advocated at the same time in the Netherlands, but only where a full-fledged town planning department had been set up could it be put into practice.

At the end of the thirties the first geographers entered this field. After 1945, representatives of other branches of knowledge were added to the town planning departments as well as to the new regional and national planning departments: sociologists, traffic engineers, economists specializing in traffic problems, and others. At the same time towns of medium size set up special town planning departments or sections and several firms of private town planing consultants began to enlist a more diversified staff, including research workers and lawyers. More often, however, planning research work for the smaller municipalities is being done by institutes for economic or social research, sometimes of a public character, sometimes private firms working on a purely commercial basis. The Netherlands Union of Local Authorities, which is a strong body whose membership includes all local authorities in the country, has also set up a research section whose services are available to the members.

Education and Training   As mentioned above, the first town planners had, apart from some elementary instruction in the course of their architectural schooling, not been trained specifically for their task. Gradually, however, in particular after the appointment of the architect-planner Granpré Molière as professor in the Technical University at Delft (1924), town planning began to rank higher in the architects' training and, step by step, opportunities were offered of specializing earlier and more thoroughly in this direction. A similar training is now open to students working toward a degree in civil engineering. Students in one of the social sciences are now in a position, at most universities, to specialize in planning by taking "planology," the theory of planning, as a main subject or a subsidiary subject when preparing for their doctoral examinations in geography, sociology, etc. The idea of a doctoral examination in planning based on a 3-year study in one of the social sciences is now being put into practice. At the agricultural university of Wageningen, which also covers sociology, landscape architecture, and home economics, there are opportunities of specializing in town and country planning.

Practitioners having an architectural background who wish to study planning in their spare time can take a course at the Amsterdam Academy of Architecture. Some training on a nonacademic level is given at the higher technical colleges at Tilburg, Zwolle, and the Hague (a 1-year course on the basis of a diploma in architecture or civil engineering granted by a similar college).

Planning research assistants can prepare for an examination organized by the Netherlands Institute for Planning and Housing by taking a 3-year course on Saturdays.

Institutions   In 1918 a private society covering the whole field of housing, including town planning, was set up. It was called the Netherlands Institute for Housing, now the Netherlands Institute for Planning and Housing. Its membership includes, on the one hand, local authorities, housing societies, and other bodies working in this field, and, on the other hand, professionals and people merely interested in housing or town planning.

In 1923, this organization instituted a town planning council which developed into a center of propaganda for better town and country planning. A special professional organization of planners (mainly architect-planners) was set up in 1936. Its membership is restricted to planners who have qualified as such. Planning research workers are organized in a section of the Netherlands Institute for Planning and Housing, as are specialists in planning law.

Institutes for planning research are attached to several of the Dutch universities, under the leadership of professors of planning. Their work is closely related to the tuition programs of the universities. In 1971 a planning study center was instituted as part of the strong, semipublic organization INO for applied scientific research. This center is expected to fill the gap between purely practical and purely academic research work in physical planning.

Geographical and Climatic Conditions   The area of the Netherlands is 13,000 square miles (33,000 square kilometers), with 13 million inhabitants. There is a marked concentration of the population in the western part of the country, in particular in the provinces of North Holland (Amsterdam) and South Holland (Rotterdam and the Hague). The area between these cities is already largely urbanized, and this process continues, owing to the attractiveness of this region for shipping, industries, and for the tertiary sector.

The soil consists almost entirely of alluvial and diluvial sedimentary deposits. The eastern part of the country is mainly covered with sand deposited by the great rivers after the glacial period. In the northeast, considerable areas were covered by peat moors, but this has been dug off to a large extent. Along the rivers wide strips of river clay are to be found. Peat alternates with marine clay in the western part of the country except along the coast of the North Sea, where the sand dunes are situated, interrupted by some tidal inlets. The entire western part of the country is below or barely above the level of the sea. The eastern part, which is above sea level, shows little variation in height apart from the south of Limburg and some push moraines in other areas. The country is not rich in minerals: coal, some oil, salt, and a considerable amount of natural gas are present. The climate is of the marine type, with much rain and little difference between summer and winter.

Traditions of Planning to the End of the Nineteenth Century In the course of the nineteenth century the last vestiges of a tradition of town planning dating from previous centuries disappeared. A marked process of urbanization occurred, especially after 1870, but layout of the new quarters was left mainly to private developers, whose objective was the highest possible degree of land utilization without regard to hygienic requirements and amenities. In some instances, the city authorities felt the necessity of general town plans; but these plans, even if they were adopted by the town council, had no force of law and were often rapidly abandoned.

About the turn of the century, the first symptoms of a revival of town planning became evident. The housing movement, which rapidly gained momentum at the time, inscribed town planning in its program as a prerequisite of good housing. Thus the Housing Act of 1901, reflecting the main ideas of the housing reformers of the time, contained a town planning section which imposed on the local authorities of rapidly growing towns and villages above a certain size the obligation to draw up and pass a local plan.

Twentieth Century

New Towns and Communities The ideas underlying the garden city movement in Great Britain and other countries did not pass unnoticed in the Netherlands. As the towns in this country were of a moderate size and were often surrounded by attractive rural or semirural communities, the urge to build New Towns was weaker than in Great Britain. However, several garden villages, which were strongly influenced by the British examples, came into being, sometimes owing to private initiative (e.g., Vreewijk near Rotterdam) and sometimes owing to public action (e.g., Amsterdam).

In the twenties, a plan emanating from an Amsterdam alderman, aiming at a full-fledged garden city in the Gooi region not far from Hilversum, was quickly rejected. Apart from the difficulty of finding a suitable location without inflicting irretrievable damage to natural scenery and without being too close to existing towns, the idea of building New Towns was given up in the light of the population estimates of the time, which predicted a stationary population for the near future. As a matter of fact, entirely new villages were created in the Zuider Zee polders, the first of which, the Wieringermeer, was reclaimed in 1929. After the Second World War the population estimates had to be thoroughly reconsidered in the light of the high postwar birthrates. Owing to this and to the continuing concentration of industry in the urban regions, in particular the western part of the country, a situation arose in which the creation of New Towns as an alternative to an unhampered growth of existing towns received renewed attention. Thus, in the area of the Hague, the New Town of Zoetermeer was planned for about 100,000 inhabitants. Similarly, near Amsterdam the Bijlmermeer is being developed. This is not a New Town proper but rather something in between a new quarter and a New Town.

In the Ijsselmeer polders the New Town of Lelystad is being built with a target population of 100,000. This is the only example of a New Town not closely connected, economically speaking, with an existing town. Several other New Towns are in the planning stage.

It is to be noted that, apart from the Zuider Zee polders, where a government department is responsible for the development of New Towns and villages, the local authorities of the area are responsible for the planning and the building of a New Town. This may create serious problems when the existing municipality is considerably smaller than the proposed development and is thus confronted with problems of a scale hitherto unknown in the area. Sometimes they obtain the help of the technical departments of their "big brothers" in the neighborhood. In the case of Bijlmermeer, the area to be developed was temporarily added to the territory of Amsterdam in order to ensure that the apparatus and the experience of this city could be fully utilized and that a complete coordination with urban renewal in the central city could be established.

City and Town Extensions The first attempts at planning town extension on the basis of the Housing Act of 1901 did not cover more than a single quarter. The plans of this period do not rest on any scientific study. The main considerations of the time were proper hygienic conditions in the residential areas and the provision of a suitable network of roads as well as some green spaces. The extensions of that time are monotonous, the building density is very high, and the street system is entirely inadequate for motor traffic.

Occasionally, overall plans for the extension of a town were prepared, often bearing the personal stamp of the architect-designer and showing the influence of famous examples of nineteenth-century town planning in other countries.

After World War I, the influence of the English garden city made itself felt. Several new quarters, even in the largest cities, were laid out on garden city lines.

In the thirties, new tendencies appeared. Master plans for entire towns were prepared on the basis of survey and research. The utmost concentration of future building development around the existing town or village was the watchword of the time. It was increasingly realized that the plans for new housing development should provide for various types of houses or

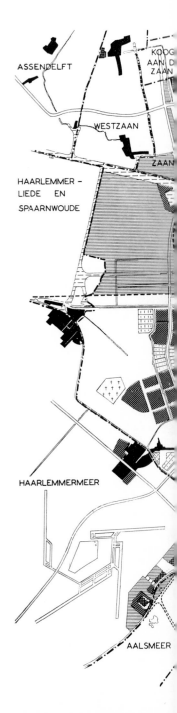

flats and for diversity in the new quarter. Some of the ideas advocated by the CIAM (Congrès Internationaux d'Architecture Moderne) movement were being put into practice (e.g., strips of building embedded in green instead of the traditional closed block of flats). The highlight of town planning in this period is undoubtedly the Master Plan of 1935 for Amster-

Master plan of Amsterdam (1935), with subsequent additions.

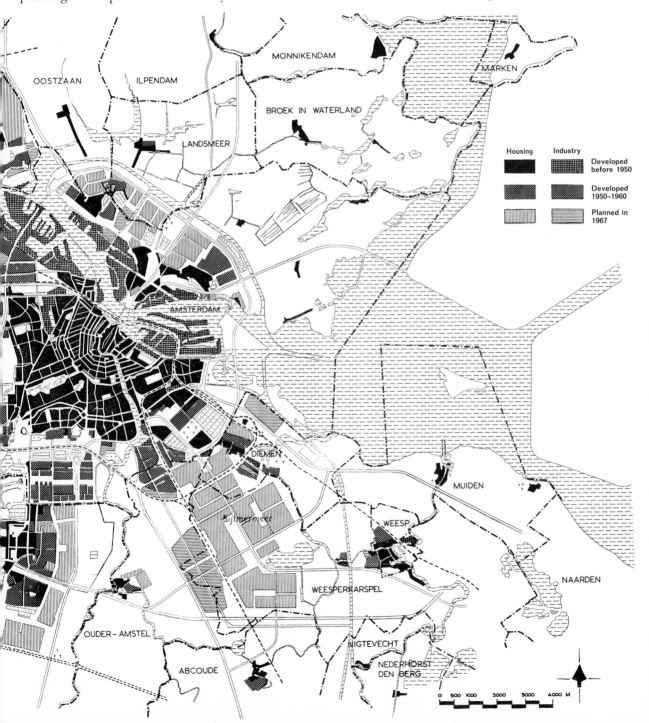

Housing	Industry	
		Developed before 1950
		Developed 1950–1960
		Planned in 1967

OOSTZAAN ILPENDAM MONNIKENDAM MARKEN

BROEK IN WATERLAND

LANDSMEER

AMSTERDAM

DIEMEN

MUIDEN

Bijlmermeer

WEESP

NAARDEN

WEESPERKARSPEL

OUDER - AMSTEL

NIGTEVECHT

ABCOUDE

NEDERHORST DEN BERG

0 500 1000 2000 3000 4000 M

dam, which was the embodiment of the new ideas of the time, resting as it did on a sound and variegated survey and taking into full account the whole gamut of future city life. It kept to the principle of a concentric city development, though green spaces were interspersed among the built-up areas. The plan represented a compromise between the garden city principle and traditional town extension. It was passed and approved, thus constituting a firm basis for the town planning policy of the city authorities in subsequent years.

In the years after World War II, the neighborhood principle gained more support. It was soon found, however, that the adherents of this idea exaggerated the importance of the neighborhood as a social unit and that a rigorous application of the neighborhood principle would counteract the efficiency of many services and hamper the inhabitants' freedom of choice. Another feature of the postwar planning of town extensions was the increase in high-rise building for residential purposes. Several factors furthered this development: the government policy favoring industrialized building techniques, the necessity of increasing building density for reasons of economy, and also a wish to bring about a more urban atmosphere and to avoid the monotony of neighborhoods consisting solely of low-rise buildings. The question arises, however, whether a proper balance between houses and flats of various types has been established. At present, in view of the patent preference of many householders for the one-family house, there is a considerable uncertainty on this point among local authorities.

Lijnbaan shopping center, Rotterdam.

Not only in this respect, however, but in several others the layout of postwar housing estates is the subject of much criticism on the part of the inhabitants, as they feel it is not in accordance with their needs and wishes. Many spokesmen for the inhabitants insist on a more democratic method of preparing plans, leaving ample opportunities for the present or future inhabitants to express their views, so that their preferences can be fully integrated in the plans.

Turning to the credit side of postwar urban planning in the Netherlands, there is a certain consensus of opinion that, during the second half of the period of reconstruction of war-damaged towns and villages, positive results were achieved. The first attempts at replanning heavily damaged areas were too much inspired by a strong wish to reconstruct or imitate the old buildings and styles. Gradually, the idea of planning for the future came to the fore. The present central district of Rotterdam, of which the now famous Lijnbaan shopping center is an important feature, is a product of modern town planning on a high level.

As a prerequisite of any development, planning has been accepted more generally than before. Village planning had become as common as town planning, in the strict sense of the word, even before the present planning act made planning obligatory regardless of the size or type of the local area. The plan for the village of Vries in the province of Drenthe is an example of simple postwar village planning.

Another tendency of postwar town planning has been the acceptance of structure plans and undetailed development plans, which are the expression of a more realistic attitude. Planners are increasingly aware of the impossibility of looking far into the future without making fundamental mistakes. Thus they often prefer to restrict themselves to the near future and to the allocation of land in very broad outline, leaving many decisions to their successors, who will be better equipped for a proper choice. The structure plan for the town of Zwolle is a recent example of this type of planning, which is quite different from the old type in which, particularly in this country, the element of architectural design was prominent from the beginning. With regard to the more detailed plans for new residential areas, the large-scale dimensions, both in the buildings and in the surrounding areas, are noteworthy. An illustration, derived from the plan for the New Town of Zoetermeer, is shown as an example of this tendency.

Another characteristic is the provision in the plans for a wide range of those amenities and services which are deemed to be indispensable in modern urban life. In this respect, much care is being taken to ensure the proper allocation of land and an efficient concentration and distribution of the relevant elements. Still another feature is the impact of traffic on the planning of residential areas. Earlier postwar plans showed considerable inadequacy in the capacity of roads and in the parking areas, but now much is being done to catch up by providing for public transport (sometimes underground, as in Rotterdam and Amsterdam) and for an integrated network of roads of various functions, sometimes on different levels, aimed

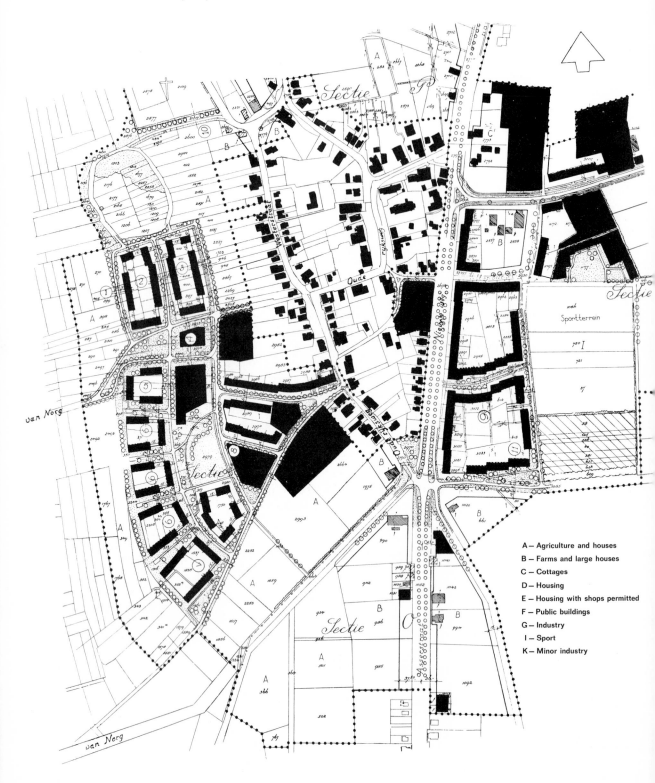

A — Agriculture and houses
B — Farms and large houses
C — Cottages
D — Housing
E — Housing with shops permitted
F — Public buildings
G — Industry
I — Sport
K — Minor industry

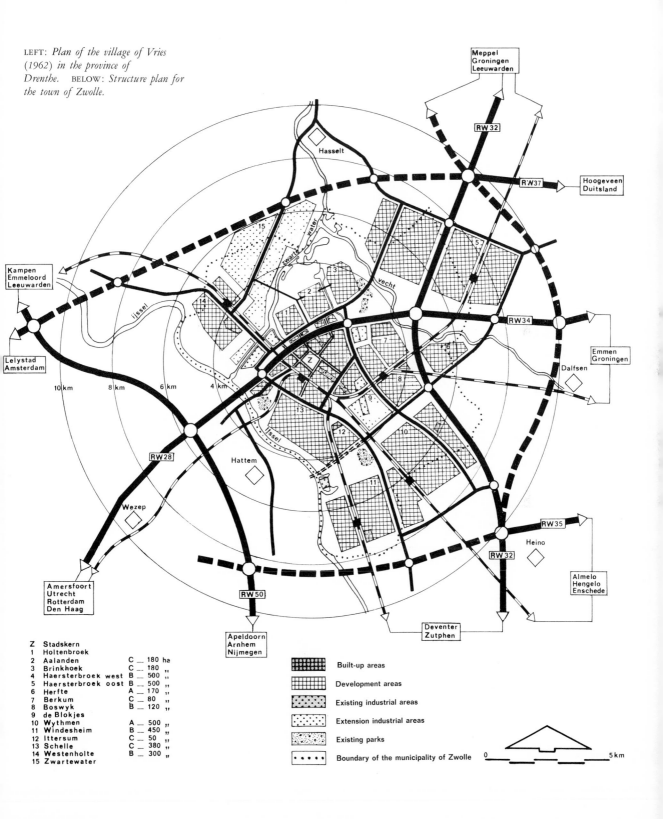

LEFT: *Plan of the village of Vries (1962) in the province of Drenthe.* BELOW: *Structure plan for the town of Zwolle.*

Meppel
Groningen
Leeuwarden

RW 32

RW 37 — Hoogeveen
Duitsland

Hasselt

Kampen
Emmeloord
Leeuwarden

RW 34 — Emmen
Groningen

Dalfsen

Lelystad
Amsterdam

10 km   8 km   6 km   4 km

RW 28

Hattem

Wezep

RW 35

Heino

RW 32

Almelo
Hengelo
Enschede

Amersfoort
Utrecht
Rotterdam
Den Haag

RW 50

Apeldoorn
Arnhem
Nijmegen

Deventer
Zutphen

Z	Stadskern		
1	Holtenbroek		
2	Aalanden	C _	180 ha
3	Brinkhoek	C _	180 ,,
4	Haersterbroek west	B _	500 ,,
5	Haersterbroek oost	B _	500 ,,
6	Herfte	A _	170 ,,
7	Berkum	C _	80 ,,
8	Boswyk	B _	120 ,,
9	de Blokjes		
10	Wythmen	A _	500 ,,
11	Windesheim	B _	450 ,,
12	Ittersum	C _	50 ,,
13	Schelle	C _	380 ,,
14	Westenholte	B _	300 ,,
15	Zwartewater		

Built-up areas

Development areas

Existing industrial areas

Extension industrial areas

Existing parks

Boundary of the municipality of Zwolle

0   5 km

View of Zuidwijk, southern suburb of Rotterdam. An example of the decorative use of water in a housing area.

Model of part of the plan for the New Town of Zoetermeer.

at a separation of various types of traffic, and also by allotting sufficient areas for parking. The pedestrian receives renewed attention in this context, as in a plan for the urban area named Malburgen, designed to be the twin of Arnhem, south of the river Rhine, where a Radburn-like unit has been introduced.

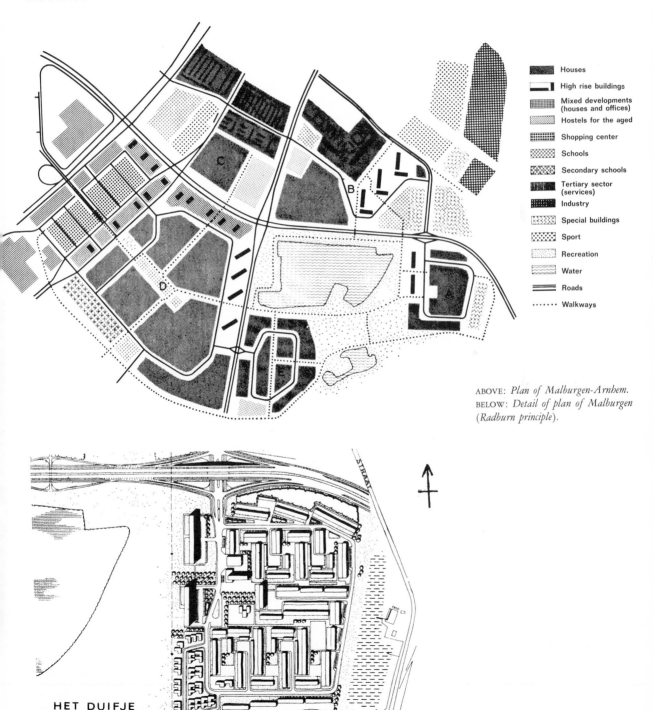

▓	Houses
▭	High rise buildings
▦	Mixed developments (houses and offices)
▨	Hostels for the aged
▦	Shopping center
▦	Schools
▩	Secondary schools
▓	Tertiary sector (services)
▓	Industry
▨	Special buildings
▨	Sport
░	Recreation
▤	Water
═	Roads
⋯	Walkways

ABOVE: *Plan of Malburgen-Arnhem.*
BELOW: *Detail of plan of Malburgen (Radburn principle).*

HET DUIFJE

Finally, because every town is part of an urbanizing region, it is evident that the major problems of town planning can no longer be dealt with by individual local authorities. A striking instance of this is the development of the port of Rotterdam, which now covers a whole region (Rijnmond, for which a special public body has been set up) and which is one of the key points of national planning policy and even of international discussion. There are also numerous instances of voluntary cooperation of local authorities toward the preparation and implementation of structure plans for an entire agglomeration. A bill aiming at the creation of a new type of regional authority is under consideration.

Urban Renewal The Housing Act of 1901 did not provide for urban renewal in a form that is now acceptable. Urban renewal was primarily looked upon from the housing angle and could only be effected by combining various measures based on the act. Before World War II, there were only a few instances of large-scale slum clearance and urban renewal. The economic crisis of the thirties, the devastation of the war years, and the ensuing housing shortage—which has not yet been overcome—led to a complete standstill in the field of urban renewal.

Today, many towns are faced with serious problems of obsolescence and are preparing plans for urban renewal. As yet, there is very little experience in completing plans of this kind for large quarters with clashing interests, and still less in carrying them out. Many town authorities and their advisers are trying to reconcile the urgent need for improving housing conditions, correcting the lack of amenities, and improving the usually poor traffic situation with the preservation of monuments of historic value in central areas and the adjoining old quarters.

Here again the active participation of the population in the preparation of the plans is demanded. In some cases the authorities are negotiating with private developers who offer to carry out the entire operation of urban renewal in a specific area. The first and most outstanding example of an agreement of this type between a city and a private developer concerns a part of the city Utrecht on both sides of the central railway station.

The problem is how to utilize the merits of private enterprise in this field without compromising a well-balanced urban renewal policy.

BIBLIOGRAPHY: G. L. Burke, *The Making of Dutch Towns* (A study in urban development from the tenth to seventeenth century), London, 1956; "Second Report on Physical Planning in the Netherlands" (condensed edition of a report in Dutch), The Hague, 1966; G. L. Burke, *Greenheart Metropolis. Planning the Western Netherlands,* London, 1967; J. Bommer, *Housing and Planning Legislation in the Netherlands,* Rotterdam, The Hague, 1967; "Brief Summary of the Physical Planning Act," Ministry of Housing and Physical Planning, The Hague, 1967; P. Heywood, "Regional Planning in the Netherlands and England and Wales," *Journal of the Town Planning Institute,* December 1970; A. Rogers, "Changing Land-use Patterns in the Dutch Polders," *Journal of the Royal Town Planning Institute,* London, June 1971; H. McClintock and M. Fox, "The Bylmermeer Development and the Expansion of Amsterdam," *Journal of the Royal Town Planning Institute,* London, July/August 1971; Periodicals: *Stedebouw and Volkshuisvesting,* The Hague, *Bouw,* Rotterdam, *Plan,* Amsterdam.

—H. VAN DER WEIJDE

NEW TOWNS New urban settlements have come into being all over the world throughout human history, many spontaneously by the "organic" growth of villages and many by deliberate "plantation." The latter class, especially the colonies of ancient Greece and the Roman Empire and the numerous foundations of the Middle Ages in Europe, have been much studied and have considerable town planning interest.

The New Towns movement here described began with Ebenezer Howard's proposal for garden cities (*q.v.*) and the establishment in England of Letchworth (1903) and Welwyn Garden City (1919). Its primary purpose is to provide an alternative to the overgrowth, congestion, and suburban sprawl of cities by creating new moderate-sized towns in which people can have good homes in healthy and pleasant surroundings near their places of work, with urban services and cultural facilities and access to the open countryside. Ownership of the whole site of a town by a public or quasipublic agency enables it to be preplanned and its development intelligently guided; it allows the increase of land value to be conserved for public benefit; and it makes possible the setting of a limit on growth, in extent and population, by the reservation around the town of a greenbelt (*q.v.*).

Though the two pioneer garden cities proved the practicability of Howard's concept, they grew very slowly, and his hope that they would soon be widely copied was not fulfilled. There were a few partial applications of the concept in other countries; e.g., in Germany (Hellerau, 1908), the Netherlands (Hilversum, 1912), Australia (Canberra, 1911), and the United States (Radburn, 1928, and the Tennesee Valley and Greenbelt Towns, 1933). But it was not until after World War II that a state policy of limitation of metropolitan overgrowth and dispersal to new towns was anywhere adopted. Persistent advocacy by Howard's Garden City Association (now the Town and Country Planning Association) had led to the setting up in Britain of a series of official committees whose reports were favorable but failed to inspire action. Among those influenced, however, was Neville Chamberlain who, when Prime Minister in 1937, appointed the (Barlow) Royal Commission on the Distribution of the Industrial Population. This commission's report (1940) recommended a national policy of "decentralization and dispersal" and a central planning authority. This was accepted by the government in principle, and after the reports by the New Towns Committee, 1945 to 1946 (chairman Lord Reith), the then Minister of Town and Country Planning, Lewis (Lord) Silkin, introduced the New Towns Act 1946, which was passed with all-party support.

Between 1947 and 1955 the first 15 New Towns were started: 8 for dispersal of excess population and employment from London; 4 in other parts of England and Wales for coal mining, steel, and engineering industries; and 3 in Scotland. They were originally planned for populations of 25,000 to 60,000 each, but some of their targets have been enlarged, and they are now planned for a total population of about 1.1 million, averaging about 75,000 each. By 1972 these 15 had reached a total of 775,000.

Between 1950 and 1960 only one New Town (Cumbernauld in Scotland) was founded, the government of the day preferring the expansion of existing country towns (*q.v.*), under the Town Development Act, 1952, under which many dispersal schemes have been undertaken by agreements between the authorities of great cities and small towns, with financial aid by the government and county councils.

Since 1961 the designation of projects has been resumed, and up to 1970 more than thirty were in progress in various regions of Great Britain and Northern Ireland, some of them for "new cities" or groups of New Towns with target populations of up to 250,000 or even more. The total capacity of the towns already commissioned may well exceed 2 million people. This is an impressive program, but in view of the anticipated increase of the British population by the end of the century it is certain to be greatly expanded. The siting of further new towns is therefore a major factor in the regional planning policy now rapidly developing.

For each New Town a site is chosen by the appropriate ministry in consultation with the local planning authority, and a designation order is made. If there are local objections, a public inquiry is held, after which the order is confirmed, usually with some modifications of the area. The ministry then appoints a development corporation (*q.v.*) of up to nine members empowered to acquire land (by agreement or if necessary by compulsory purchase at market value), to prepare a town plan for the ministry's approval, and to undertake the construction of roads and basic public services. It also has powers to provide housing, industrial and commercial buildings and social facilities, and to lease sites for buildings provided by private enterprise at market ground rents, retaining the freehold estate as a whole intact. Under the Leasehold Reform Act of 1967, owner-occupiers have certain rights to acquire the freehold of residential properties, but this right does not extend to sites for business purposes. Most of the larger factories have been provided by the firms themselves on sites held on 99-year leases; but many of the smaller ones, and almost all the retail shops, have been built by the development corporations and let to the traders on occupation leases at rents revisable periodically as the population grows—a system of cardinal importance in the finance of New Towns.

The capital for the land purchase and development is advanced by the government at current rates of interest on public loans, repayable over 60 years. At the end of 1971 the government investment was about £842 million, of which £576 million was for housing by the corporations. Comparable sums must have been spent by private enterprise on factory buildings and equipment; by county and district councils on schools and public works; and by other agencies on gas, electricity, water, postal and telephone services, churches, and sports and entertainment facilities. The commercial investments are of types that pay their way in the short term, and the local government expenditure is covered by normal rates or taxes. The initial expenditure on land and primary development takes a longer period to fructify, which is why it is suited to public rather than private enterprise. But the experience of the first dozen or so towns shows that they are a sound public investment. Taken together, the first 12 New Towns in England and Wales had a surplus revenue after an average period of development of about 10 or 11 years, having covered all interest and repayment charges from the start. By 1971 the surplus revenue on these towns had reached over £2½ million a year. Under the acts this profit goes to the British Treasury; there is naturally a claim by the people of the towns that some of it should be used for their benefit. There is still a deficit on the accounts of the New Towns in Scotland and on those of the later towns, which may take longer to pay their way at the higher rates of interest they have to cover. But the subsidies on housing in all the towns are much lower than they would be on the multistory flats in cities that would be the alternative to the dispersal policy.

Industrially and commercially the New Towns are a success. Up to 1971 more than 1,770 new factories had been established in them, and over 780 office businesses, and they employed over 675,000 workers of all grades, the great majority of whom are housed within short distances. As the New Towns mature, they become more self-contained, and the proportion of occupied persons traveling daily to the nearby big city declines. In the case of Welwyn Garden City, for instance, the percentage of commuters dropped from about 15 percent in 1939 to about 6½ percent in 1966. There is, of course, some interchange of employment with neighboring towns and villages, tending to a pattern of regional clusters of towns as suggested by Ebenezer Howard in his chapter "Social Cities." By the skillful placing and resolute reservation of greenbelts or stretches of open country, it is practicable to plan "new cities" of considerable populations, with urban units of the order of 40,000 to 100,000, with quite short access for daily resort, and with rapid communications for less frequent journeys. In this way the evils or inconveniences of large, continuous built-up areas can be avoided.

Much thought and experiment has been devoted to the planning of the new towns, their residential standards and layouts, and their architectural design and landscaping. Since each town has its own technical staff and employs many architects and consultants for sections of its development subject to overall planning and design control, the towns differ considerably and together exhibit an immense variety in character—visually, economically, and socially. Some of their experiments are undoubtedly open to criticism, but they are all vastly more healthy and pleasant than the industrial towns of the past and the great cities of today, to which very few of their inhabitants return.

The problems raised by the overgrowth of cities, their excessive density, residential squalor, divorce from "nature," depersonalization, and (politically most obsessive) traffic congestion, are worldwide and worsening. Increasing interest is being taken in the British initiative for the creation of New Towns as a necessary element in state planning policies, and many countries are studying it and adapting its principles to their own circumstances and political systems. British experience indicates that governmental promotion and finance is essential for the right siting, assembly of land, and construction of the groundwork of new urban settlements; but free-enterprise states have been reluctant to accept this conclusion. Even in the United States, however, legislation for the federal encouragement of "new communities" has been passed in the 1960s, and there is growing recognition that the financing of the initial groundwork, being a long-term enterprise, is conveniently a governmental function, compatible with the commercial provision of building development within New Towns. In most of the world's states, whether "advanced" or "developing," the urgent necessity of putting a stop to urban overconcentration is now understood, and the creation of New Towns has begun or is seriously entertained. There is a flood of literature on the subject, of which only a few examples are named below.

BIBLIOGRAPHY: New Towns (Reith) Committee, Interim and Final Reports, H.M.S.O., London, 1945–1946; F. J. Osborn and A. Whittick, *The New Towns: The Answer to Megalopolis,* Leonard Hill, London, 1963, McGraw-Hill, New York, 1964, second edition, 1969; Annual Reports of New Towns Development Corporations and of the Commission for New Towns, H.M.S.O., London, 1948 to date; Lloyd Rodwin, *The British New Towns Policy,* Harvard University Press, Cambridge, Mass., 1956; Jean Viet, (ed.), *Les Villes Nouvelles,* (annotated bibliography in French and English), Unesco, 1960; R. Rosner, *Neue Städte in England,* Munich, 1962; Robin H. Best, *Land for New Towns,* London, 1964; International Federation for Housing and Planning, Report of 1963 Arnhem Conference, *Bigger Cities or More Cities?* The Hague, 1964; J. Riboud, *Developpement Urbain,* Paris, 1965; W. L. Creese, *The Search for Environment; Garden City Movement Before and After,* New Haven, 1966; Clarence Stein, *Toward New Towns for America,* Cambridge, Mass., 1966; *Planning of Metropolitan Areas and New Towns,* reports of symposia, Stockholm, 1961 and Moscow, 1964), United Nations, New York, 1967; M. Beresford, *New Towns of the Middle Ages,* London, 1967; Donald Canty (ed.), *The New City,* Report of National Committee on Urban Growth Policy, Urban America, Inc., New York and London, 1969; Frank Schaffer, *The New Town Story,* with introduction by Lord Silkin, London, 1970; Central Office of Information, *The New Towns of Britain* (official booklet), H.M.S.O., London, 1972; Town and Country Planning Association, *New Towns: the British Experience,* Charles Knight & Co. Ltd., London, 1972.

—FREDERIC J. OSBORN

NEW ZEALAND

Legislation and Administration   The legal basis for urban and regional planning throughout New Zealand is the Town and Country Planning Act of 1953 and amendments, together with the Regulations of 1960. Under the act, the Minister of Works is responsible for its overall administration and for all actions on behalf of government in stating the requirements of government works to be included in regional and district planning schemes.

The act requires district schemes to be prepared by all territorial local authorities and provides for regional schemes to be prepared by regional planning authorities set up specifically for that purpose. The crown, with the exception of housing under the housing act, is not bound by the provisions of planning schemes.

District Schemes   Each local authority (there are 246 local authorities for a population of less than 3 million) has a statutory responsibility to prepare and administer a district scheme for its area, including the hearing and determining of all applications and objections arising from the formulation and administration of the scheme. The general purpose of a district scheme is given as development and redevelopment of an area so as to "promote and safeguard the health, safety and convenience, and the economic and general welfare of its inhabitants, and the amenities of every part of the area." Regulating the use of land by zoning (together with appropriate requirements as to density, bulk, and location) is the principal means of achieving these aims, except where financial commitment is accepted by a public authority when the land in question is also designated for the particular purpose.

Public participation is provided for at each stage in the preparation and administration of schemes. Suggestions for inclusions in a scheme are invited, and there are rights of objection and appeal against a scheme and against decisions arising out of administration of a scheme. Objections are heard and dealt with by the local authority itself, but appeals are decided by an appeal board, an independent tribunal consisting of four members, the chairman being a magistrate.

District schemes have been effective in preventing the intrusion of incompatible land uses into already developed areas and in establishing minimum acceptable standards of subdivision, servicing, and engineering in developing areas. Where they have been inadequate is in not providing positive guidance to development, which takes place piecemeal, usually with little idea as to what the ultimate pattern will be.

Regional Schemes The initiative for the creation of a regional planning authority lies with adjoining local authorities, and for this reason district schemes have invariably preceded regional schemes. Also the legislative provisions for district schemes are much more specific than for regional ones, the result being that whereas district schemes are relatively uniform throughout the country, regional schemes have varied considerably in their approach.

The act states as the general purpose of regional schemes conservation and economic development by means of classification of lands, and coordination of such public improvements, utilities, services, and amenities as relate to more than one constituent local authority area. The scheme is to guide councils in the preparation of district schemes as well as public authorities and the private sector generally.

So far six regional planning authorities have been formed: the main metropolitan areas of Auckland, Wellington, Christchurch, and Dunedin, together with Whangarei and Marlborough. In 1965, a multifunction Auckland Regional Authority was formed with responsibility—in addition to regional planning—for public transport, the international airport, main sewer drainage and water supply, regional reserves, and regional roads. Recently a government-appointed commission reviewed local government in New Zealand and recommended the creation of a similar Wellington Regional Authority (along with amalgamation of local authorities into fewer and larger units). This would appear to be the pattern for the future, at least in predominantly metropolitan regions.

Dunedin's was the first regional scheme. Its provisions were so detailed as to make it virtually a large district scheme, an approach subsequently ruled invalid by the appeal board. At the other end of the scale in both time and approach is Auckland's, which is basically a policy framework designed to regulate decision making rather than a single decision or series of decisions in itself.

There are no direct rights of objection and appeal by an individual to a regional scheme, right of approval being the prerogative of local authorities (both territorial and special purpose). Here too, in the event of disagreement, the appeal board is the final arbiter.

Professional Practice   With the statutory obligation to prepare district and regional schemes, with the requirement that district schemes be prepared for every local authority area in New Zealand by 1971, and with the growing complexity of planning and administration, the balance of professional practice has been changing from the private to the public sector. Earlier most qualified planners were practicing architects, engineers, or surveyors with a British planning qualification. They were supplemented by people working in planning, usually in the larger local authority offices, who had qualified through the external town planning examinations of the Town Planning Institute of Great Britain. In recent years the main source of trained people has been the town planning department at Auckland University. In addition, many people and firms have regarded themselves as planners and have acted in that capacity by virtue of their training in a related discipline, but this practice is on the decline.

Planners in private practice function as consultants to three main groups: to those local authorities who may lack the staff resources necessary to prepare district schemes and reports on various matters such as commercial and community centers; to developers and industrialists in the sphere of market research and feasibility studies; and to the public generally in district-scheme objection and appeal procedures. Design of subdivisions has traditionally been the province of the surveyor, who is licensed by the state and has a duty to ensure a high standard of technical accuracy in his work.

In the public sector a variety of work, depending on the particular agency, is involved. Central government is concerned with examining district and regional schemes, ensuring that requirements of government departments are coordinated and included in district and regional schemes, and with making population projections and resource surveys. Besides the Town and Country Planning Branch of the Ministry of Works, planners are employed also in the Housing Division of that same Ministry, where the work involves the design and layout of state housing areas within the terms of reference set by government.

At the regional level planners are involved in resource and conservation studies, land-use and transportation studies, monitoring of data and trends, and coordination between local authorities. This may be within the context of regional plan formulation or in district-scheme objection and appeal procedures on matters of regional significance.

At the local authority level, planning activity usually centers around district-scheme formulation and administration, including the collection and analysis of survey data. Larger urban local authorities may also be involved in development proposals, urban renewal, and central area and transportation studies.

Although the act mentions economic and social planning, little of this has been done for various reasons, one being the shortage of economists and sociologists working in this field. In both the public and the private sectors, there is scope for a variety of disciplines and backgrounds in addition to planning itself, and, as in most other countries, there is a shortage of qualified planners.

Education and Training Formal education in town planning in New Zealand is of relatively recent origin, dating only from 1957 when a department of town planning was established within the faculty of architecture at the University of Auckland. Until that time people wishing to obtain a qualification had either to go overseas and qualify or take the external examinations of the Town Planning Institute of Great Britain. This latter course was made even more difficult than usual because conditions and planning in Britain were and are very different from those in New Zealand.

When the first professor of town planning arrived to take up the chair, the number of professionally qualified town planners was quite inadequate to put into effect in a few years the intention of the act, which was to produce district schemes for all local authority areas. In these circumstances, the immediate need was judged to be a shorter course that would give a basic understanding and training in fundamentals to a greater number of students drawn from all parts of the country rather than a more academic course requiring full-time attendance for at least 2 years of postgraduate study. The present postgraduate course for the diploma in town planning consists of 1 year's full-time study followed by the presentation of a dissertation. It is also possible to do this course part time. A masters course was commenced in 1971 consisting of 2 years of full-time postgraduate study and thesis.

There is no course in traffic engineering in New Zealand, the nearest being at the University of New South Wales in Australia.

Institutions The Town and Country Planning Institute of New Zealand was incorporated in 1952 as a branch of the British Town Planning Institute and became autonomous in 1969. Its secretariat is domiciled in Wellington, and annual conferences are held at different centers each year. No official branches have as yet been formed, the main means of communication being a newsletter and the *Town Planning Quarterly,* a lively and topical magazine edited in Auckland. In addition, informal planning groups meet in various centers, the largest and most active being in Auckland. Members include students and people from related professions working in planning.

Other professional bodies whose activities frequently overlap into the planning field are the Institution of Engineers, the Institute of Surveyors, and the Institute of Architects.

The civic trust movement is active in Christchurch and Auckland. It is based on the British movement but oriented more to watchdog activities than to conservation, the latter function being more the concern of the Historic Places Trust.

The Urban Development Association is a Wellington organization whose aims are primarily educational and propagandist. It holds annual conferences in Wellington and publishes a magazine entitled *Town and Countryside*. It has the same type of widely representative membership as civic trust organizations have in other centers.

Geographical and Climatic Conditions   New Zealand consists of three main islands, North, South, and Stewart, separated by relatively narrow straits. It is elongated, extending over 1,000 miles (1,600 kilometers) north to south and only 280 miles (448 kilometers) east to west at its widest point. A main chain of mountains extends the length of the South Island and a great deal of the North, and it has considerable influence on climate and communications. Indeed, the mountainous nature of the country is one of its most striking characteristics. The North Island contains many volcanic cones, some active, and associated with this volcanic activity are many hot springs and geysers. The South Island is even more mountainous but has fewer signs of recent volcanic activity. Parts of the country are particularly prone to earthquakes; a major one occurred in 1931, and 255 deaths resulted.

Important factors which influence climate are the position of New Zealand in the midst of a vast ocean and the shape and topography of the country itself. The first factor ensures an "island" climate with frequent variations and high average rainfall, while the latter is responsible for sharper climatic contrasts from east to west than from north to south. A pleasant feature of the climate is the high proportion of sunshine during the winter months. Snow, except on the mountains, is rare.

The population is about 2.8 million, of whom approximately 222,000 are of Maori or part Maori blood. In addition there is a large Polynesian population centered mainly in Auckland, making New Zealand's largest city also the largest concentration of Polynesian population in the world.

Traditions of Planning to the End of the Nineteenth Century   Town planning in New Zealand dates back to the 1840s, with the laying out of towns to accommodate the influx of settlers. The plans bear witness to a tradition that goes back much further—to the early colonial planning of North America and to England, from whence the early settlers originated. There was, too, an indigenous tradition, that of the Maori, whose villages and pas (fortified villages) give evidence of considerable ability to organize the physical pattern of settlement as an expression of function and tribal organization.

The New Zealand Company was associated with the settlement of six towns between 1840 and 1850; Wellington, Wanganui, New Plymouth, Nelson, Christchurch, and Dunedin. All sites were carefully chosen, but the plans were done under pressure—as the surveyors responsible were closely followed by settlers—which is why in some instances the regular gridiron plans usually adopted were imposed on unsuitable topography. Other features were the use of squares, octagons, and radial roads to give relief from the gridiron, and the provision of town belts, many of which were later compromised through shortsighted expediency. Auckland was designed

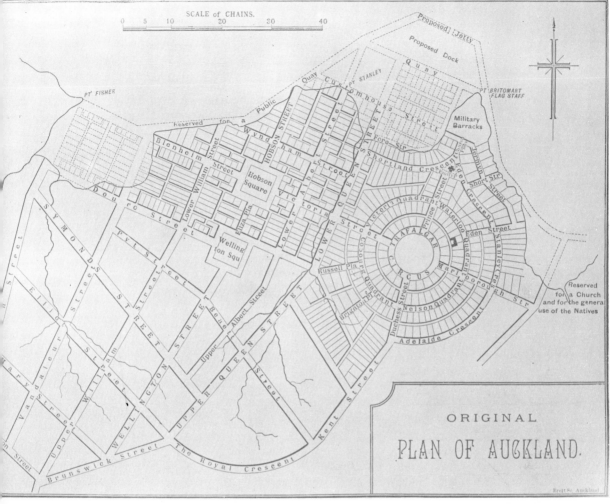

Original plan of Auckland (1840) by Felton Mathew. (Auckland Public Library Photograph Collection.)

with more regard to topography, but the attempt was not altogether successful and much of the original plan was later discarded.

The two decades between 1850 and 1870 saw the incorporation in sundry legislation of many measures of a town planning nature, but it was not until 1875 that specific town planning legislation was passed, and this was virtually limited to the extension of towns on crown land. It was not until 1926 that the first really important step was made toward comprehensive town planning.

Twentieth-century Planning

New Towns and Communities New towns generally arise as a response to one of two situations. First, as a result of unsatisfactory conditions in an existing city—such as overcrowding, poor hygiene, and traffic congestion; and second as a result of the growth of new industries based on raw materials located some distance from any existing town.

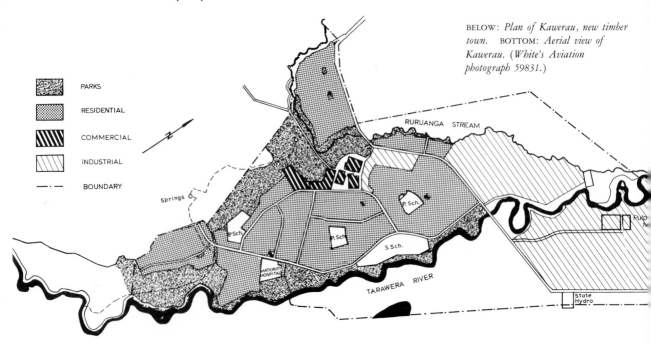

BELOW: *Plan of Kawerau, new timber town.*   BOTTOM: *Aerial view of Kawerau. (White's Aviation photograph 59831.)*

PARKS

RESIDENTIAL

COMMERCIAL

INDUSTRIAL

BOUNDARY

RURUANGA   STREAM

Springs

P. Sch.

P. Sch.

P. Sch.

S. Sch.

MATERNITY HOSPITAL

TARAWERA   RIVER

Pulp

State Hydro

There are no new towns in New Zealand as a result of the first situation, and this is not surprising, as cities in New Zealand are little more than 120 years old, the largest having a population of only 600,000. Also, New Zealand has always been basically an agricultural country—it is only in the last 20 years that more emphasis has been placed on industrial development—whereas the unsatisfactory conditions in older countries have often been legacies from the industrial revolution.

As regards the second situation, new towns have been created in association with the development of the pulp and paper industry, a rapidly growing one based on the exotic pine forests of the central volcanic plateau of the North Island. Tokoroa and Kawerau are new timber towns, generally well laid out, with adequate social facilities ensured by progressive industrial management.

More recently, Turangi has been developed in association with the Tongariro hydroelectric power-generation scheme, and an extension to Waiuku houses employees from the nearby steel mill. The latter is a recently established industry based on extensive deposits of iron sands on the west coast of New Zealand.

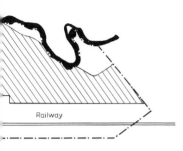

Railway

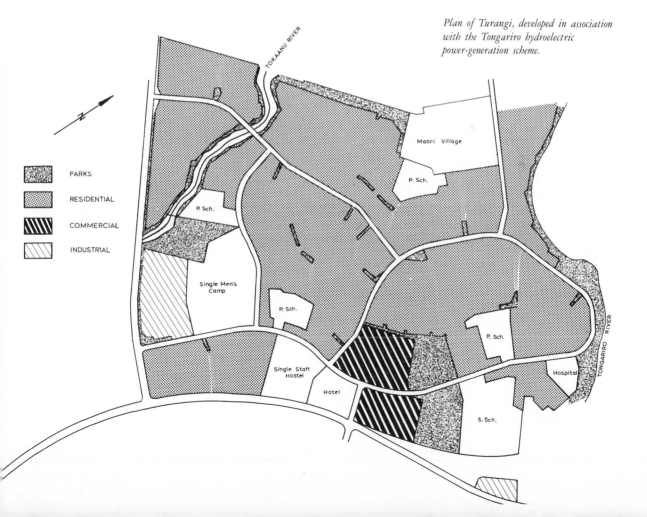

Plan of Turangi, developed in association with the Tongariro hydroelectric power-generation scheme.

PARKS

RESIDENTIAL

COMMERCIAL

INDUSTRIAL

ABOVE: *Aerial view of Turangi.* (*White's Aviation photograph 66387.*) RIGHT: *Typical low-density suburban development.* RIGHT TOP: *Urban renewal, Nairn Street, Wellington.* (*Architects: Burren and Keene.*)

City and Town Extensions Growth of urban areas has in general been either by low-density peripheral accretion or through the activities of the State Housing Division of the Ministry of Works.

The former is a result of the New Zealander's traditional demand for his own house and plot (usually around $\frac{1}{5}$ acre), the relatively small-scale operation of developers, and the development procedures normally followed. The legislation under which subdivision has been carried out has ensured high engineering standards, and in the main development has been fully serviced. The resultant suburbs are spacious and hygienic, but at the same time they tend to be monotonous due to lack of variation in street width and detail and because of the sameness of the housing type—until recently 85 to 90 percent of New Zealand housing was single-unit.

State housing suburbs have been comprehensively planned and have usually provided a greater range of housing than private development. The State Housing Division was set up in 1933 to meet a critical housing shortage, and the housing and planning was of a very high standard for its time. Since then, however, limitations to the operations of the division have meant that they provide basic housing units for the lowest socioeconomic section of the community. Therefore provision of many personal and community amenities is dependent on private enterprise and the initiative of the residents themselves. A commission of inquiry has now recommended the establishment of a national housing authority.

Urban Renewal Just as with new towns and the general absence of the sort of unsatisfactory conditions that give rise to them, so with urban renewal, particularly as concerns housing. Where unsatisfactory conditions have arisen, the need has often been no more than better enforcement of the Health Act, some encouragement toward renovation, and—in limited

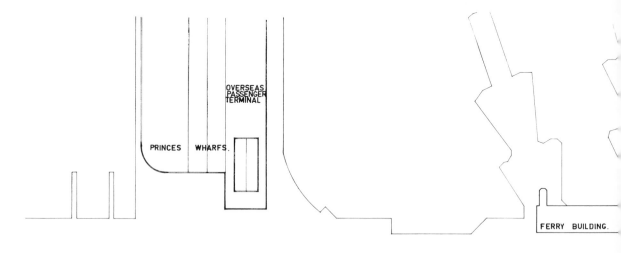

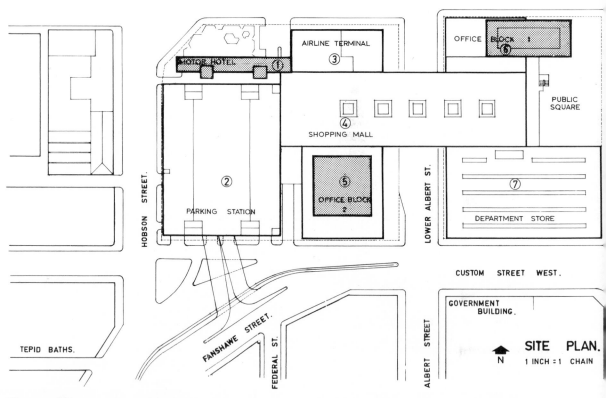

OVERSEAS
PASSENGER
TERMINAL

PRINCES WHARFS.

FERRY BUILDING.

QUAY STREET.

AIRLINE TERMINAL
③

MOTOR HOTEL ①

OFFICE BLOCK 1
⑥

PUBLIC
SQUARE

④
SHOPPING MALL

HOBSON STREET.

②
PARKING STATION

⑤
OFFICE BLOCK 2

LOWER ALBERT ST.

⑦
DEPARTMENT STORE

CUSTOM STREET WEST.

GOVERNMENT
BUILDING.

TEPID BATHS.

FANSHAWE STREET.

FEDERAL ST.

ALBERT STREET

▲
N

SITE PLAN.
1 INCH = 1 CHAIN

① MOTOR HOTEL
  13 STOREYS
  200 SUITES

② PARKING STATION
  6 STOREYS
  1600 CARS

③ AIRLINE TERMINAL
  2 STOREYS

④ SHOPPING MALL
  2 STOREYS

⑤ OFFICE BLOCK 2
  30 STOREYS

⑥ OFFICE BLOCK 1
  20 STOREYS

⑦ DEPARTMENT STORE
  3 STOREYS

Plan of redevelopment of downtown Auckland on reclaimed land.

areas—some clearance and redevelopment. Tardiness in applying these measures has often reflected the weakness of local government and the desire for more grandiose solutions, a desire not backed by the financial resources necessary to carry out the task.

New Zealand is a timber country and most of its housing is light timber construction, capable of almost endless renovation and adaptation. Nevertheless, the age of some housing, together with narrow sections inherited from earlier days of subdivision, means that increasingly, in the future, attention will need to be given to urban renewal.

In the 1940s the State Housing Division built some multistory apartment blocks in inner-city areas and later some low-rise apartments, some of which replaced previous obsolete structures.

In recent years most urban renewal housing schemes have been carried out by the local authorities. Of these, Freemans Bay in Auckland, Nairn Street in Wellington, and Airdale Court in Christchurch are probably the best-known examples.

Central area renewal of shops and offices has generally occurred piecemeal as a result of market forces unassisted by the public sector. In Auckland however, a major redevelopment project—the Downtown Scheme—is being built on reclaimed land owned by the Harbour Board and until recently the site of older two- to five-story office buildings. As a result of an in-

Redevelopment of downtown Auckland on reclaimed land. The large blocks in the center are an imposed model. (Architects: Peddle, Thorp, and Walker.)

ternational competition in 1964, the area is being redeveloped for offices, shops, a department store, an airline terminal, a trade center, a motor hotel, extensive parking, and a new public square.

New Zealand was colonized to a considerable extent by people dissatisfied with the conditions they had left. They sought a new life, and planning played a significant part by ensuring well-laid-out towns with a sense of order and by providing the security of a larger piece of land on which a single-family home could be built. With the passage of time, ideals of order progressively gave way to speculation, expediency, and laissez-faire.

Public dissatisfaction with the formless spread of the more rapidly growing cities and public concern with the environment generally, both physical and social, is paralleled by a feeling among many professionals that the aims and methods of existing planning legislation and practice are in need of review.

BIBLIOGRAPHY: D. E. Barry Martin, *The Development of Town Planning Legislation in New Zealand,* Technical Books Ltd., Wellington, N.Z., 1956; K. Robinson, *The Law of Town and Country Planning,* 2d ed., Butterworths, Wellington, N.Z., 1966; A. H. McLintock (ed.), "Towns and Cities, Growth of," in *An Encyclopaedia of New Zealand* vol. III, R. E. Owen, Government Printer, Wellington, N.Z., 1966, p. 415; "Town and Country Planning," *New Zealand Official Year Book,* R. E. Owen, Government Printer, Wellington, N.Z., 1971, p. 57; N. J. Burren and M. L. Curtis, *A Businessman's Guide to Town Planning,* Mobil Oil, N.Z. Ltd., Wellington, N.Z., 1969.

—DAVID GROVE

NOISE   Noise is one form of environmental pollution (*q.v.*) and is so considered by many governments. Its control is the subject of legislation in many countries. The protection of residential areas from noise and its general minimization are among the tasks of planning.

The principal sources of noise from which people suffer are (1) aircraft, (2) road transport, (3) rail transport, (4) industry of various kinds, (5) sport, and (6) the more intimate noises in residential areas—such as the noises made by animals, children at play, radio and television sets, and those who practice on musical instruments.

Noises from aircraft and road transport probably cause the greatest nuisance. Steps are being taken internationally to reduce aircraft noise and, in 1966, an international conference was held to discuss ways and means of minimizing such noise and to formulate international regulations and standards. The noise nuisance to resident populations is also being increasingly considered in the siting of airports. Until the Second World War, proximity to large centers of population and ease of access for travelers were the major considerations in siting civil airports; the noise nuisance to nearby residents did not appear to influence the choice of sites. Since 1950, however, this nuisance has been increasingly considered, and some of the strong objections to the proposed sites for new airports have been based on the threat of environmental noise pollution.

In the case of new airports, there is a strong body of opinion in favor of choosing sites away from built-up areas, either in sparsely populated areas or on the coast. Airports should be rapidly accessible from main centers of population, but this is less a matter of distance than speed of transit, and in the future it will be possible to arrange for very rapid rail transport from city centers to airports well away from built-up areas. This consideration would also apply to the people who are employed at an airport. In relating airports to built-up areas, the direction of runways is an important consideration. If these are, for example, east-west, then built-up areas would, with advantage, be at least 6 miles away east and west. To the north and south, however, they would have to be only 3 miles away to minimize the noise nuisance from aircraft. Vertical takeoff, if it becomes general, will affect these planning considerations in the siting of airports, but as this has been discussed with little result for at least 20 years, it is probable that the long runway will remain a consideration in planning for a considerable time.

With regard to protection from the noise of road and rail traffic and from industry, much can be done by good planning, although it is a matter that, up to the Second World War, was largely ignored except in the wealthier residential areas. It could be suggested from this standpoint that houses should not be built on arterial or main roads, or, if they are, that they should be sited well back, with service roads. They should not be built very near to railway lines, and certainly not near to goods yards, factories, large markets, distributing centers, or large professional sports grounds. That these have become all mixed up in the congested areas of conurbations is one of the regrettable results of a lack of planning in the past.

In modern neighborhood and residential precinct planning the minimization of noise is important. In some well-planned residential neighborhoods, there is a main road encircling the area but no through roads—only a series of culs-de-sac and footways. This system conduces to peace and quiet. The houses on the periphery near the main road do not face onto it but are well away and abut endwise.

As regards the more intimate noises of animals, children shouting, radios, television sets, and musical instruments, the minimization of such noises is chiefly a matter of sound insulation in the structure of dwellings and of local regulations and control. Such matters are of greater concern to the architect and structural engineer than to the urban planner. They pose greater problems in areas of high-density development, with large apartment blocks, than in low-density developments consisting of two- or three-story family dwellings with gardens or yards.

—Arnold Whittick

NORWAY

Assumptions for Physical Planning Integrated planning, from land use to social and cultural life in the community, has several definite stages. The urban region as a total system has subsystems; e.g., land use, technical infrastructure, economics, politics, and culture. As a technician the physical planner takes his cues from policies on housing, education, transport, and other related services.

The physical plan is a coordination of site demands from the differing needs of society. The question is whether these demands can be combined into a pattern that in itself creates environmental values. This should be the main task for the physical planner.

The regional plan and the master plan for a large community comprehend the general aspects of land use and amenities related to landscape, topography, and climate; and long-range decisions concerning development structure and preservation of natural resources should guide the planner.

The more localized plan must be a framework helping to shape good environment for living, working, recreation, and education; and in order to achieve this it is essential to ensure that building and traffic areas are arranged in such a way that the effects of dangerous traffic, noise, smell, and water pollution are reduced or eliminated.

At the next stage the physical planner is an adviser to those responsible for the actual building projects. For instance, in residential areas he might offer suggestions on the grouping and form of dwellings, schools, shopping centers, and children's institutions. Only at this moment is the physical environment produced and the result of housing, educational, and traffic policies shown in material form.

In Norway the physical environment, climate, landscape, topography, and vegetation play a larger role in settlement and urbanization than in many other countries.

Geographical and Climatic Conditions   The area of Norway is about 125,000 square miles (324,000 square kilometers). The southernmost point of the country is on the 57th parallel, the northernmost point on the 71st. The polar circle is on the 66th parallel.

The average height above sea level is more than 1,640 feet (500 meters), while that of Europe as a whole is about 1,000 feet (300 meters). This is due more to the absence of broad lowlands than the presence of high mountains. The largest agricultural plains are in the southeast around the Oslo Fjord and around the large lakes Tyrifjord and Mjösa north of Oslo. There are also fairly extensive plains around the Trondheim Fjord and near Stavanger.

From ancient times human settlements have been established along the seacoast, on islands, and by the fjords. Practically the whole coast is sheltered by large and small islands, and there are channels for navigation between them from south to north, even for large vessels. Good harbors can be found everywhere. Because of the Gulf Stream these waters are not frozen even in winter, and tide differences are small. Along the coast, communication is possible at all times, while the winter snow and the mountain barriers make communication difficult inland.

The development of towns has been strongly determined by these conditions. The most favorable position is where the fjord meets the valley with its agricultural land and surrounding forests, thus connecting both land and sea routes. In such places the larger regional and national centers have developed.

Until late into the nineteenth century the inland tracks between settlements were very primitive and suitable only for travelers on foot or on horseback. In winter, sleighs and skis could be used, and for this reason markets took place during the winter inland, especially in the southeast. At the coast markets were held in the summer because communication by sea was then more practical.

Town Planning up to 1940 The first town in Norway was probably Nidaros, now Trondheim, situated on the fjord north of the southern mainland and founded before the year 1000. By 1100, other towns were established: Oslo, Tunsberg, Bergen, Stavanger, and Hamar. All these towns except Hamar were situated on fjords and most of them on river estuaries where market-places were already in existence. They were often also sacrificial centers of the old Nordic religion. The first towns grew up as large marketplaces and later, when they became residences of kings and bishops, they received the status of towns. Stavanger and Hamar however, were founded and planned as cathedral towns, and cathedrals were also built in Oslo, Bergen, and Trondheim.

The towns did not have strong fortifications, but the castles of kings were always fortified, some being situated on strategic hills outside the towns.

In the year 1624 Oslo was destroyed by fire. The king of Denmark and Norway decided to build a new town on a new site behind the Akershus Castle, $1\frac{1}{4}$ miles (2 kilometers) west of the old town. The plan was a gridiron system of streets surrounded by fortifications and moats in the north, west, and east, and with the castle to the south.

In the latter part of the seventeenth century the first suburbs grew up outside the towns and were later assimilated. In Oslo the walls and moats were superseded. In 1769 there were 7,500 inhabitants inside the borders and less than 3,000 people in new suburbs outside them.

Railways in Norway were not developed to any degree before the end of the nineteenth century, and at the turn of the century suburban lines and trolley cars were introduced. The railways precipitated the influx of people from the country to the towns, and the trolleys and suburban lines made way for the beginning of suburbanization.

In the year 1900 the population of Oslo (Christiania) was 227,000; in 1914, 250,000; and in 1944, only 260,000. After the First World War most of the increase took place outside the town, and in the neighboring rural district the population rose by more than 100,000 in the same period.

From the First World War to the latter part of the 1920s, several large housing and renewal projects were built inside the confines of the towns. The housing development was under municipal management, and several interesting town quarters from this period can be seen in Oslo, Bergen, and Trondheim.

After the First World War great interest in town planning and housing arose among professional people, but there was little response from the citizens or the authorities.

Oslo got a comprehensive master plan in 1929, and in 1934, together with its two largest neighboring rural districts, prepared a master plan with land-use zones and main traffic systems. The so-called "tour ways" or ski tracks, sections of parkland with pedestrian paths leading from the central built-up area to the large nature reservations outside, were among the original features of this plan.

During the 1930s Norway became a modern industrial society. Her merchant fleet was one of the largest in the world. Products of the fish, timber, and chemical industries were exported all over the world. Norwegians were the pioneers of the antarctic whaling expeditions. Electric power for domestic and industrial use was generated by water resources. The standard of living rose and, together with this, came increased demands for improved equipment and goods, housing, and services. Wider national and local planning, cooperative housing, and municipal activity came to be elements of a new and democratic development of the nation.

Today there are four times as many people in Norway as in 1814, and they still live mostly in the same areas. Even so there are less than 4 million inhabitants in an area of 125,000 square miles (324,000 square kilometers), giving an average of 28 people per square mile (11 per square kilometer). This figure is misleading because the majority of the people live in fairly densely populated areas which are separated by vast uninhabited regions.

Town Planning after 1945

Legislation and Administration   Planning and building laws up to 1965 were not very satisfactory as regards planning. They did not provide powers to enforce plans for the entire country. The laws were revised in 1965, and now provide for land-use plans for all towns and rural districts. These plans not only designate development areas but also forest and agricultural areas.

The State Department of Local Affairs and Works is the highest authority on planning. A special section controls the local plans that must be confirmed by the department.

Another section in the department is responsible for national and regional planning through its central technical staff and staff attached to the county administration.

Local authorities may collaborate on a regional plan, and the state may decide that two or several municipalities ought to prepare a regional plan. Regional commissions are established when the region is defined.

Regional plans, and master plans for a municipal area, must be submitted by the local council and by the county administration to the state department for approval. Regions have been defined throughout the country, and regional commissions have been established according to the planning and building laws of 1965. Before this the larger towns and their surrounding districts had worked on regional planning through appointed regional commissions staffed by volunteers.

Master plans in towns and rural districts as well as local outline plans and schemes are prepared by the local authorities and passed by planning

commissions and municipal councils. The towns and the larger rural districts have planning offices, and they also engage private consultants to prepare plans.

Most of the income tax is assigned to the local authority which is responsible for the implementation of the plans. Roads, water supply, sewers, electricity, etc., as well as schools, social institutions, hospitals, playgrounds, and playing fields are also the responsibility of the municipality.

Public housing is financed by the State Housing Bank, and the sites must be prepared by the local authority. This constitutes half the production per year; the rest is financed privately.

All schemes have to be controlled by the municipal planning office and they must follow the official outline plan. The planning commission is elected by the local council.

The master plan in each municipality, urban or rural, constitutes the law of land use. No one is permitted to develop land otherwise than as designated in the master plan. This general rule is accepted by all the political parties in the municipal councils.

Education and Training   Town planners in Norway are recruited on the whole from the architectural profession, although some are also civil engineers (building and construction).

Architects and civil engineers receive their education at the Technical College in Trondheim, and courses in town planning are included in the curriculum. These courses have recently been extended, but they remain only part of the total curriculum.

The new profession of traffic engineering has been introduced recently and is now combined with town planning at the Technical College.

The Oslo School of Architecture, which was founded in 1945, acquired in 1967 the status of an architectural college and gives a similar education for architects as that given in Trondheim.

There are no separate professional schools for town planners. Education and training in Norway have been acquired mostly in municipal planning departments but also in state offices and in private consulting firms.

Some short town planning courses have been arranged for persons entering that profession by the state department dealing with town planning.

The Nordic Institute for Town and Country Planning was incorporated in 1968 in Stockholm to give advanced planning education. Candidates are drawn from the five Nordic countries, and in order to be selected applicants must have some professional experience. Three extensive courses of 1 month's duration are given each year.

Institutions The larger planning offices constitute comparatively strong concentrations of professional planners in the towns. The Norwegian Housing and Planning Association, whose members are interested persons of all professions, is the national body connected with the International Federation for Housing and Planning. The National Institution of Civil Engineers has special groups for planners and traffic engineers.

Some years ago an Institute for Town Planning and Regional Research was established under the Boards of Technical and Scientific Research. This institute can be employed by municipalities for analysis and preparation of comprehensive plans in different fields.

Oslo and the Oslo Region Oslo is the capital of both the country and its largest region, Östlandet, or the Eastern Country. The population here is half of the total for Norway and the land constitutes less than a third of Norway's total area. There are today 1.9 million inhabitants, while it is estimated that in the year 2000 about 2.5 million will be living here, which means an increase of 600,000.

The Oslo city region, consisting of the city itself and the 10 surrounding communities, has today about 700,000 inhabitants, and it is estimated the population will reach 1.2 million in 30 years.

These 11 municipalities have an area of about 600 square miles (1,500 square kilometers), while the development zones according to the plans are only 155 square miles (400 square kilometers). Large, comprehensive agricultural and forest areas will be retained.

The forested hills form a vast recreation area in summer and winter, and the coastline and islands in the fjord offer opportunities for open-air life and pastimes.

The plan for the Oslo city region forms three ribbons or linear belts in three directions from the main center, namely southwest along the west

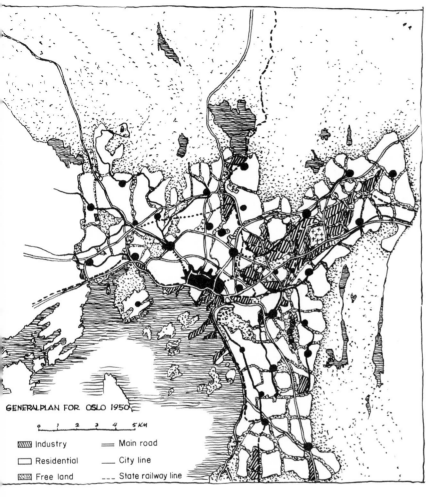

GENERALPLAN FOR OSLO 1950

0   1   2   3   4   5 KM

▨ Industry   ═ Main road

☐ Residential   ── City line

▩ Free land   --- State railway line

Oslo master plan. Land use, traffic lines, main center, and local centers.

side of the fjord, east-northeast inland, and south along the east side of the fjord. The ribbons are narrow, about 2½ miles (4 kilometers) wide, and so make the open recreation land easily accessible—the hills and forests on one side and the fjord coast and islands on the other.

In the central part—the downtown area and the densely built-up areas around it—the plan proposes to maintain, not augment, the number of jobs available; but it is intended to make the activities in the center more city-oriented. If one regards the city region as a balanced system, a population increase of 400,000 in the next 30 years will provide about 175,000 new jobs. Provision must be made for these mostly in new satellite towns outside the city area, one in the south, one in the east, and one in the southwest.

In the central part of the city the resident population must be maintained or increased. This can be done only by costly renewal work in existing residential areas. The central town can then house over 200,000 people, and the rest of the actual city outside this up to 400,000.

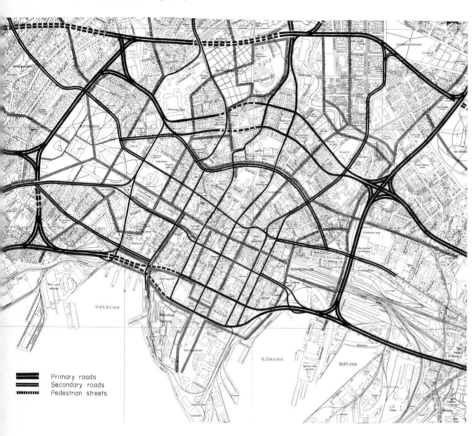

Oslo. Main center. Differentiation of streets.

Primary roads
Secondary roads
Pedestrian streets

The city council of Oslo and the joint working committee of Oslo and the surrounding couny of Akershus have agreed to these regional development principles, presented in the planning alternative called "maximum balance." This alternative is calculated to give the least traffic flow.

The traffic system has been integrated into the land-use pattern. According to calculations it may be assumed that up to 80 percent of the morning rush to the center can be dealt with by public transport, which includes the city's suburban and underground railway, the local lines of the state railways, and the bus routes. The main road network will consist of two main lines from the south; two main lines from the east; and two, possibly three, main lines from the southwest. The lower roads are joined to the ring road system around the downtown area, while the main upper roads are tied together by a city motor road north of the center. Connected with the ring roads around the center a number of garages are planned for long-term parking, to take in all about 20,000 cars. There is also long-term parking space near the suburban rail stations. Inside the center there will be restrictions on private-car use, and no long-term parking will be allowed.

This road system has a double purpose. On the one hand the function of the city as a place of work demands goods delivery, access for clients and customers, and occupational driving. On the other hand the vehicular traffic will be channeled to the main roads to make it possible to differentiate the street network within large enclaves, such as the different parts of the commercial center and the residential and other districts. Pedestrian streets can be established in and from the downtown area through the different districts to the open spaces with their pedestrian lanes and tracks.

This pattern for the city region of Oslo and Akershus will make room for 1.2 million inhabitants and about 500,000 jobs.

Olso traffic system. State railways, city suburban railway, and major roads.

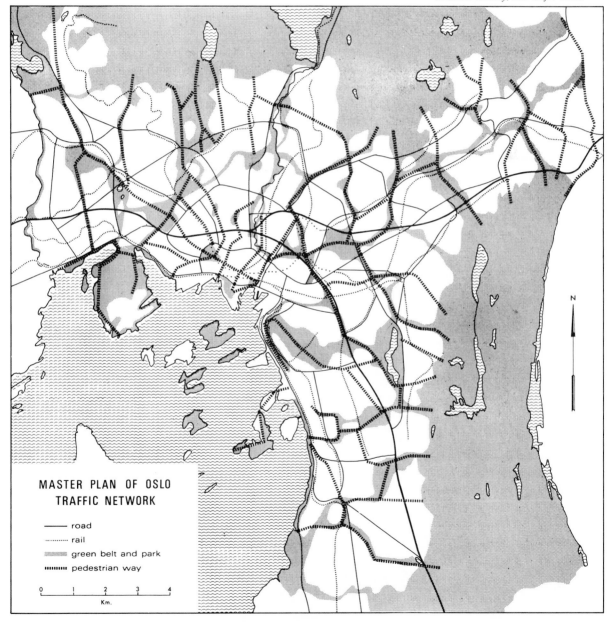

MASTER PLAN OF OSLO
TRAFFIC NETWORK

——— road

·········· rail

▓▓▓▓ green belt and park

▪▪▪▪▪▪ pedestrian way

0   1   2   3   4
Km.

In 1964 the voluntary regional committee for the Oslo region issued a report pointing out some alternatives for development. These alternatives were used in a transport analysis undertaken by the Oslo city planning office, and a report presented to the building commission in 1965 recommended the "maximum balance" alternative. The principle has now been formally accepted by the city council.

Another report was published in 1969 concerning the general development of the total Eastern Country region. In accordance with national policy, the aim of the report is to control growth in the Oslo area and to attract inhabitants to secondary town regions in the Eastern Country. Three main centers of growth are indicated: one far south on the west side of the Oslo Fjord, another south on the east side of the fjord, and a third inland by the great Lake Mjösa north of Oslo.

In fact there is no contradiction between the Oslo city region plan and the principles laid down for the larger region. The city region plan is an optimum plan not bound to a certain future year, and likewise the plans for the development of the surrounding secondary city regions are also optimum plans. Should the filling out of the Oslo area be delayed 15 years because the other centers have been successfully developed, it will not be without benefit to the Eastern Country as a whole.

The Stavanger Region   Excerpts from a report published by the local authorities in the region follow:

> In January 1968, Rogaland had a population of 160,000 roughly 7 percent of the total population of Norway; Oslo and Akershus are the only two counties with larger populations. Statistics show that the increase in population during the 20th century was larger in Rogaland than in Norway as a whole. Settlement is fairly highly concentrated, as many as two-thirds of the inhabitants of the county now live in towns and other urban areas. Scattered settlement is declining fairly rapidly.
>
> A forecast based on the tendencies of population development during the 1960s shows that the county will presumably have a total population of about 360,000 in 1990. This figure stipulates a very much stronger growth in Rogaland than elsewhere in Norway.
>
> The strong increase in population is naturally the result of a corresponding growth in industry, so that an increasing working population is able to find employment. The industry of Rogaland is varied and is expanding. The county can account for a fairly large share of Norway's entire production in the fields of agriculture, fishing, manufacturing, and shipping.
>
> The whole of Jæren must be considered as one unit, but the regional perspectives may indicate a certain distribution of roles between the municipalities.
>
> Leading urban development into channels which will result in the least possible conflict with agricultural interests is an accepted aim of regional planning. One must accept a steady development of the small towns served by the railway as service centers and, to some extent, as employment centers for their hinterland, but beyond a certain point of balance other areas for

Stavanger. Plan of center, 1960.

ØSTRE HAVN

VÅGEN

BREIAVATNET

CENTRAL STAVANGER

▬▬ PRINCIPAL TRAFFIC STREETS

▐▐▐ FEEDER AND PARKING STREETS

●●● PEDESTRIAN STREETS

○○○ PEDESTRIAN SUBWAY

▦ MULTI-LEVEL OR UNDERGROUND
CAR PARKS

■ BUILDINGS ERRECTED AFTER THE WAR

urban growth must be sought. Here one must consider whether it would not be best, from the point of view of agriculture, to direct urban development from the north towards the south by developing the Forus industrial area. A further aim is the development of a southern industrial center in the eastern parts of Klepp, where a marked industrialization is already under way, and where any conflict with agricultural interests will be less serious. This could form the basis for a plan which would, in the future, lead urban development eastwards and inland off the plain of Jæren, thus strengthening the development of eastern Jæren. The center of Stavanger should be able to continue as a big shopping center, and should not need to change character. Investigations show that it is possible to increase the shopping area of the city center, so that it can also in future serve as center for the much larger city which will gradually grow up. Most of the dwelling houses in the center have disappeared, and many small shops and tradesmen's premises are gradually being replaced by concerns more appropriate to the center of a city of 80,000, whose population will probably be something like 120,000 by the year 2000.

These changed plans, which gradually took shape, aimed at a traffic belt encircling the old city center, while the area within the belt was largely to retain the structure of the old center. The work of the municipality was now in principle limited to the outer traffic zone and the necessary parking arrangements, while the renewal of buildings within the actual center was, in principle, presumed to be carried out gradually by the owners of the properties there, even though the cooperation of the city authorities would also be required.

Outside the center and the traffic belt the most important of the new office buildings and institutions are located. Thus the center of the city is undergoing a certain amount of zoning, the primary center for shopping and the subsidiary zones containing parking lots, office buildings, and institutions.

The suggested regional plan for northern Jæren, far more detailed than such plans usually are, has also in part served as a general plan for the development of Stavanger. A general master plan, largely based on the regional plan, has been drawn up. Moreover, the long-term programs for housing are in part drawn up as total development programs, so that they form part of a complete general plan.

The Ministry of Local Government and Labour has initiated the preparation of consecutive five-year programs for housing in many of the municipalities of Norway. Investments connected with the social institutions necessary in conjunction with housing schemes are also included in these five-year programs. The first covered the period 1966–1971. All the municipalities of the Jæren region have prepared such programs.

The municipality of Stavanger has prepared five-year plans for the development and building of housing schemes, schools, social institutions, churches, cemeteries, cultural institutions, parks, sports grounds, and sites for industry.

Bergen   The city region of Bergen consists of the city itself and the Bergen Peninsula, with its five municipalities and Asköy to the west. The population in 1969 was nearly 190,000, and it is estimated it will be 250,000 in 2000.

Although the port of Bergen and its position on the coast has made the town an important trade center during the last 900 years, its mountainous surroundings and consequently difficult land communications hinder further urban settlement and expansion. The city region must therefore be

Bergen. Plan of center.

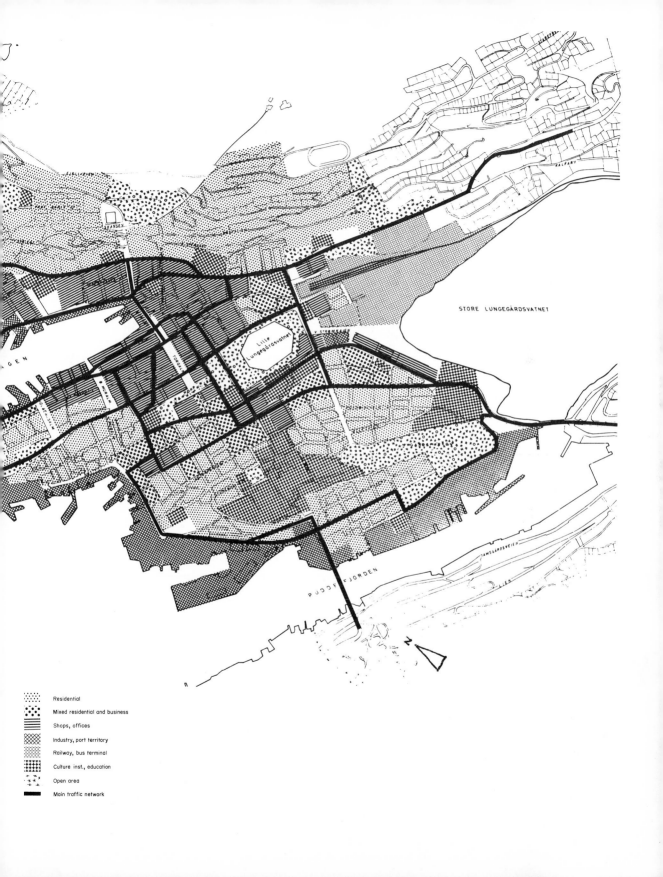

STORE LUNGEGÅRDSVATNET

Lille
Lungegårdsvatnet

PUDDEFJORDEN

Residential
Mixed residential and business
Shops, offices
Industry, port territory
Railway, bus terminal
Culture inst., education
Open area
Main traffic network

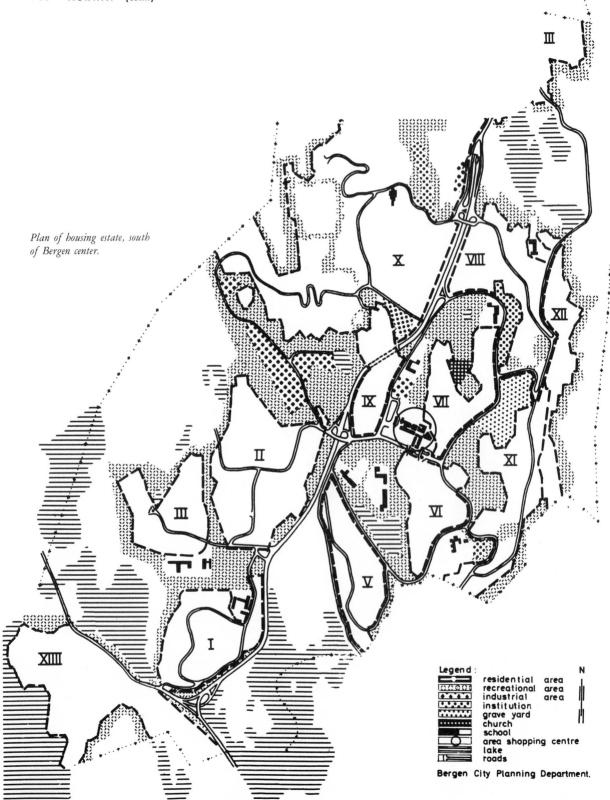

Plan of housing estate, south of Bergen center.

Legend :

	residential　area
	recreational　area
	industrial　area
	institution
	grave yard
	church
	school
	area shopping centre
	lake
	roads

N

Bergen City Planning Department.

compactly developed, and as distances are not great the necessity of establishing satellite centers or towns does not have to be considered, only that of secondary or tertiary local centers. The topography and landscape give scope for large and varied recreation areas, and the town itself must be preserved and developed as a major center with its attractive site and its historical monuments.

The Trondheim Area Trondheim, geographically in the middle of Norway, was founded by a Viking king as a capital and has kept its position as a provincial center. The main planning problem for the city region has been to decide on one or two directions for expansion and development and to find the appropriate place for satellite centers or towns in each sector. The city region today has a population of 127,000, and it is estimated that this will rise to 190,000 at the end of the century.

Trondheim. View of center.

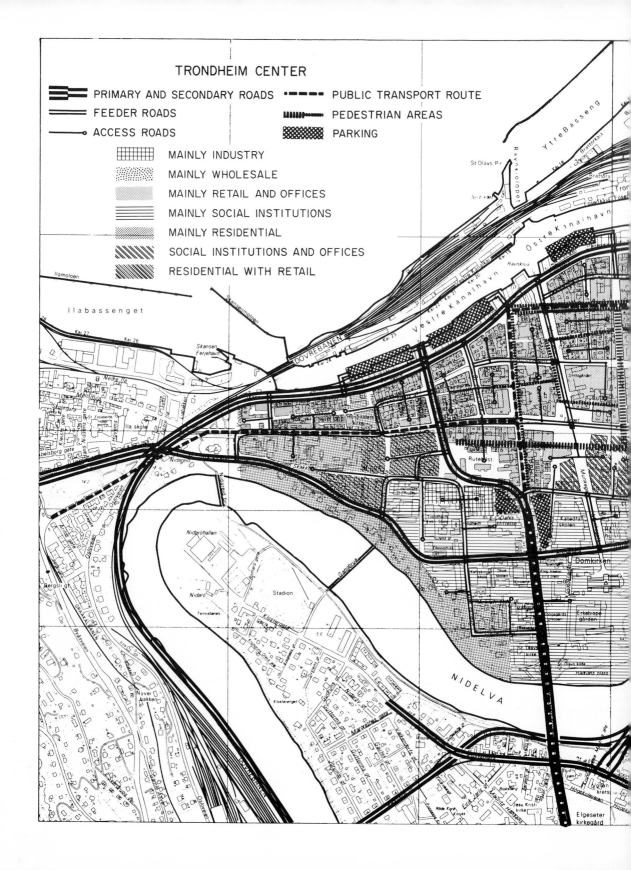

TRONDHEIM CENTER

- ▤ PRIMARY AND SECONDARY ROADS
- ▤ FEEDER ROADS
- ⊶ ACCESS ROADS
- ▦ MAINLY INDUSTRY
- ▦ MAINLY WHOLESALE
- ▦ MAINLY RETAIL AND OFFICES
- ▤ MAINLY SOCIAL INSTITUTIONS
- ▤ MAINLY RESIDENTIAL
- ▨ SOCIAL INSTITUTIONS AND OFFICES
- ▨ RESIDENTIAL WITH RETAIL
- --- PUBLIC TRANSPORT ROUTE
- ▥ PEDESTRIAN AREAS
- ▦ PARKING

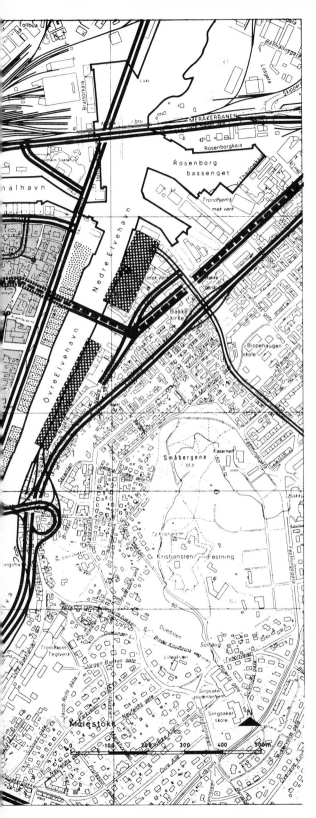

Trondheim. Plan of center. Land use and street differentiation.

Northern Norway   After the Second World War the state government passed laws for merging the smaller units and creating comparatively well-populated municipalities. Some of these new communities have become fairly large areas. There are towns with surface areas of about 800 square miles (2,000 square kilometers) but with populations of only about 20,000, which shows that only a very small part of the area is inhabited.

The plans for the war-damaged towns and villages were partly prepared under the occupation and partly just after the war. In their general form and technique these plans are similar to the plans generally accepted before the war. One may call them well designed if somewhat conventional plans of the prewar type. However, the important aspect of these plans was that they were based on master plans which assigned land for proper use, both present and future, and established a comprehensive traffic system. They made a good framework for schemes and projects and for the realization of housing, workplaces and institutions of an up-to-date standard.

The main city in the north of Norway, Tromsö, was not damaged by war and no master plan was made in the immediate postwar period. Now that the city has merged with surrounding districts, it has an area of more than 1,100 square miles (2,650 square kilometers). Only one-tenth of this area is habitable. The central town has an area of about 9 square miles (23 square kilometers) and a population of 22,000. Fifteen thousand inhabitants live in the outskirts. The total number is expected to rise from 37,000 in 1970 to 90,000 by the end of the century.

Tromsö. New bridge and church.

A new university is to be established here and the role as a provincial capital will be duly strengthened. A new master or regional plan will be based on an analysis of development possibilities.

The municipal planning commission has engaged two state institutes for research planning in this connection. Public participation has been aimed at from the start, and the attitude to development problems has been analyzed by interviewing different representative groups, among them the city council. This two-way method of obtaining information has met with much interest.

Preliminary outline plans for alternative development patterns have been put forward for discussion at meetings with the city council, youth organizations, and other assemblies, and this first phase of planning, started in 1968, was completed in 1971.

BIBLIOGRAPHY: *Oslo Master Plans,* 1929, 1950, 1960; *Master Plan for Oslo, Aker, Bærum,* published by the joint communities (merger between Oslo and Aker in 1948), 1934; *The Bergen Peninsula and Askôy, Proposal for a Master Plan,* City of Bergen, 1957; *Settlement Plan, Lower Telemark* (The Skien-Porsgrunn region), State Department of Housing, 1961; *Stavanger in the Melting Pot,* Urban Renewal of Stavanger, 1962; *Proposal for a Regional Plan for the Oslo Area,* Regional Planning Commission, 1963; *Transport Analysis of the Oslo Area,* City of Oslo, 1965; *Regional Plan for the Stavanger Area,* City of Stavanger, 1966; *Regional Plan for the Trondheim Area,* City of Trondheim, 1967; *Proposed Land Use Plan for Oslo and Akershus,* joint committee of the City of Oslo and the County of Akershus, 1968.

—ERIK ROLFSEN

NUCLEAR ENERGY AND NUCLEAR POWER STATIONS (*See* ELECTRICAL POWER GENERATION AND TRANSMISSION.)

O

OBLIQUE PROJECTION (*See* PROJECTION.)

OLMSTED, FREDERICK LAW (1822–1903)   Born in Connecticut but debarred from entering Yale College in 1837 by an eye affliction, Olmsted's chief education came from extensive travels by carriage with his family. At sixteen he had made four journeys of a thousand miles, and he continued these travels for the next 30 years, voyaging to China in 1843, making exploratory journeys to England and the Continent, to the southern states on horseback as far as Texas and Louisiana, and to California in 1854. His evenhanded account of life in the South under slavery, published in three books from 1857 to 1860, made a profound impression, and they are now historic classics. Meanwhile he spent $2\frac{1}{2}$ years studying engineering, and another half-dozen years practicing farming and rural landscaping. This direct, firsthand experience of landscapes and cities was the foundation of Olmsted's many important innovations in landscape architecture, park design, and city planning. His first professional job came, in partnership with Calvert Vaux, through their collaboration on a prizewinning design for New York City's Central Park. This was followed by a series of similar commissions, from Fairmount Park in Philadelphia to the Golden Gate Park in California. While in

California, he explored the Yosemite and enlisted public support for setting apart this picturesque rocky landscape as a state reservation: the first of a series of national wilderness areas so reserved. As a park planner he was adept in making use of difficult sites, like the series of strip parks along the eastern escarpment of Manhattan Island, or Riverside Drive itself, or the Back Bay Fens of Boston.

Olmsted's greatest innovation, important both for park and city design, was made in Central Park and never fully appreciated, even by Olmsted himself. This consisted in effecting an almost complete separation between the various means of circulation: pedestrian walks, bridle paths, vehicular roads, and a sunken east-west transverse for commercial vehicles. This was the first systematic use of the overpass now common in highway planning. In 1869, in his plan for Riverside, Illinois, Olmsted increased the dimensions of the residential blocks and reduced the number of needless crossroads; and he went further in providing more garden space without extra cost in his later plans for Roland Park and Guildford, near Baltimore, where he employed large blocks with culs-de-sac. As highway planner Olmsted carried further the design of French boulevards and parkways by proposing that special lanes be provided for electric rapid transit. Though he was influenced at the beginning by the naturalistic English landscape school, particularly Repton and Uvedale Price, even the design for Central Park has strong formal elements; and his layout for the Chicago World's Fair of 1893 was a masterly example of firm geometric organization.

After 1870 Olmsted dominated the planning scene. From 1875 on, when office records were kept, he laid out 37 public pleasure grounds, 12 suburban developments, the grounds of 11 public buildings and hospitals, 13 colleges, 4 large schools, 4 railroad stations, and 12 considerable private estates. One of the finest examples of Olmsted's work is the original design of Stanford University, consisting of a series of arcaded quadrangles, with the university quarter separated from the town of Palo Alto by a greenbelt a mile wide but connected by a wide palm-lined drive to the railroad station. In his too-little-known report on the landscaping of Stanford, Olmsted showed his mastery of ecology; for he pointed out that in the dry, "Mediterranean" climate of California, grassy collegiate lawns in the British fashion would be inappropriate, as well as costly in upkeep, and that the paved open spaces in Spanish and Italian style, with occasional oases of trees and flowers, would be more appropriate. Here, as in so many other places, Olmsted's ecological approach not only was ahead of his own generation, but is still ahead of many architects and planners who have ignored or flouted his many vital innovations. Olmsted's most important colleague and successor was Charles Eliot, Jr., who carried further Olmsted's Boston park plans and who proposed to create park strips on a regional scale along the northern Massachusetts coast; but some of his essential insights were rediscovered a generation later by Stein and Wright in their plan for Radburn and by Benton MacKaye in his Townless Highway and his plan for the Bay Circuit of parks and highways around metropolitan Boston (1929?). Olmsted's influence might possibly have been greater if, like Stein, he had made a systematic critical summary of his work; but the brief tract that he brought out in 1870, *Public Parks and the Enlargement of Towns,* though it introduced the new idea of a park system proceeding from the neighborhood square to the wider rural environment, came before his most important work was accomplished; and even now, a century later, a comprehensive study of his work has yet to be published. Though Olmsted was properly regarded by his contemporaries as the outstanding artist that he was, his full measure has still to be taken and the lessons of his remarkable education have still to be applied in the curricula of contemporary schools of landscape architecture and town planning.

BIBLIOGRAPHY: Frederick Law Olmsted, *Public Parks and the Enlargement of Towns,* American Social Science Association, 1870; F. L. Olmsted Jr. and Theodora Kimball (eds.), *Frederick Law Olmsted,* Landscape Architect, 1822–1902, Boston: 1922, 1928 (two vols.); *Walks and Talks of an American Farmer in England,* New York, 1952, reprinted, Ann Arbor, Mich, 1967; Albert Fein, (ed.), *Landscape into Cityscape: Frederick Law Olmsted, Plans for a Greater New York City,* Ithaca, N.Y., 1968.

—LEWIS MUMFORD

OPEN SPACE IN URBAN AREAS In the context of urban planning, "open space" is a comprehensive term for a wide variety of open areas on which nothing has been built. A useful broad classification employed by Garrett Eckbo (see bibliography) indicates the two principal uses of open space as passive space and as playgrounds. Passive space is the park or garden, landscaped as beautifully as possible and intended for peaceful relaxation, for meditating and reflection, for quiet conversation, and for strolling. Sometimes mixed with the trees, shrubs, and lawns are monuments, fountains, and sculpture, which engender the contemplative spirit. Cemeteries (*q.v.*), some of which are very beautiful, are included in this category of open space. Playgrounds are for more active recreation and include playing fields, baseball diamonds, tennis courts, and other play areas as well as swimming pools and children's play areas.

Parks (*q.v.*), often extensive, forming passive space, figure conspicuously in the large cities of the United States and Europe and are variously located in relation to the city. In some cities the gardens and parks are concentrically arranged, as in Vienna and a few American cities. Elsewhere, the park areas are located mainly in one region of the city. In London, Paris, and Berlin, for example, they are mainly in the western districts. Playgrounds sometimes form small subordinate areas within these large city parks, but playing fields are usually more widely dispersed in the localities where they are required.

Many of the municipal parks in the United States—of about 10 or 20 acres (4 or 8 hectares)—are multipurpose and provide for a wide range of varied recreational activities. Such a park will include a passive or quiet area, often with a picnic space adjoining; swimming facilities and an outdoor gymnasium; areas for games including a baseball diamond and tennis courts; and two children's playgrounds, one for school-age children and a tot lot. Often there is a community building with a refreshment section.

The desirable proportion of open space to built-up areas has been variously assessed. Sir Patrick Abercrombie in his plan for the County of London, 1943, suggested 4 acres (1.6 hectares) per thousand population, which he recognized was less than the 7 acres (2.8 hectares) per thousand population suggested by many authorities, but the 4 acres was suggested on the understanding that the balance of another 3 acres (1.2 hectares) would be provided outside the county area, on the periphery. The London Playing Field Association put the requirement much higher, at 10 acres (4 hectares) per thousand population, which is the same as the standard given by the American Institute of Park Executives. This institute suggests also that in the acquisition of open land for urban areas calculations should be based not on present population but on the likely population 40 or 50 years hence. It is, therefore, wise in making provision for urban space in newly developed areas to acquire much more land than is needed for the immediate future so as to have a reserve.

Open space in most cities and towns is generally both public and private, and the question arises to what extent the latter could be included in a calculation of open-space–population ratio. It would depend on the access afforded to the private open space. Often playing fields are owned by firms and associations who use them only occasionally, and if the public is given frequent access then this space would rationally be included in an open-space ratio. But if it were strictly private, then it would not be so included, although it would still be a useful amenity.

The golden rule in developing new areas is to be liberal in the provision of open space of all kinds with a view to probable future populations. (*See also* PARKS.)

BIBLIOGRAPHY: Patrick Abercrombie and J. H. Forshaw, *The County of London Plan*, Macmillan, London, 1943, chapter 3 and appendix 2; Patrick Abercrombie, *Greater London Plan 1944*, H.M.S.O., London, 1945, chapter 7 and appendix 19; Garrett Eckbo, *Urban Landscape Design*, McGraw-Hill Book Company, New York, 1964.

—ARNOLD WHITTICK

ORGANIC PLANNING   (*See* THEORIES AND IDEALS OF PLANNING.)

ORIENTATION

"The Orient" meaning "the East," "orientation" logically means turning toward the east or to the rising sun. A church is sited with the altar toward the east for religious reasons. In planning and building generally, the term means layout according to the points of the compass. Orientation is important in the siting of buildings and in the planning of streets and urban spaces for climatic reasons and to take full advantage of the sunlight.

OSBORN, Sir FREDERIC JAMES (1885–   )

British writer on planning and proponent of a state policy of great-city decongestion, greenbelts, and New Towns (*q.q.v.*).

Osborn was born in London on May 26, 1885, and, after working in a housing organization in that city, was appointed in 1912 to manage a cottage-building society in Letchworth. In this position he became an enthusiastic proponent of the garden city principle. In 1917 he joined

Sir Frederic J. Osborn.

Ebenezer Howard (*q.v.*) and two others (C. B. Purdom and W. G. Taylor) in forming the National Garden Cities Committee to advocate the building of New Towns as part of the postwar process of industrial, agricultural, and social reconstruction. For this group he wrote a short book entitled *New Towns after the War* (1918), which was followed by the promotion of the Welwyn Garden City project by Howard, by whom he was appointed an estate manager (1919–1936). He was also clerk of the Parish and Urban District Councils (1921–30) and for over 50 years was active in the town's development and social life.

In 1936 he became financial director of a radio company in Welwyn, and in the same year he became honorary secretary of the Garden Cities Association (now Town and Country Planning Association), of which he was successively chairman of executive (1948–1961), editor of its influential journal (1951–1965), and president (1970). In the course of the association's vigorous campaign he wrote many pamphlets and articles, lectured, broadcasted, organized conferences, drafted policy statements, and gave evidence to government inquiries, notably to the Royal Commission on the Distribution of the Population, whose report (1940) proved to be the turning point in British planning policy.

As adviser to Lord Reith, Minister of Works and Buildings (1940–1942), and to the postwar reconstruction committees of the political parties, Osborn had much influence on the general acceptance of the New Towns policy. As a member of the New Towns Committee from 1945 to 1946, he made valuable contributions to its reports. In 1942 he revised *New Towns after the War,* the preface to which contains an interesting letter from George Bernard Shaw. From 1944 to 1966 he was honorary treasurer and a member of the Bureau of the International Federation for Housing and Planning of which, in 1966, he was elected a vice-president.

The long campaign of the TCPA culminated in the New Towns Act of 1946 (*q.v.*), a measure that began a profound change in planning thought and practice all over the world. Osborn continued his advocacy by tours between 1947 and 1970 in many countries, including the United States, Canada, the U.S.S.R., and Japan, giving hundreds of addresses to congresses, universities, municipalities, and other institutions.

His influence was due to his special experience in garden city development, his realistic grip on economic and political processes, his deep concern for the human importance of a good urban environment in touch with nature, and his ability to write and speak interestingly and persuasively.

His many honors include a Knighthood in 1956, the Silver Medal of the American Society of Planning Officials (1960), The Gold Medal of the British Town Planning Institute (1963), and the Howard Medal of the Town and Country Planning Association (1968). He was an honorary member of the American Institute of Planners (1948) and of the British Town Planning Institute (1948) and corresponding member of the Akademic für Raumferschung und Landesplanung, Hanover (1967).

BIBLIOGRAPHY: Frederic J. Osborn, *New Towns after the War*, J. M. Dent, London, 1918, 1942, "Transport, Town Development and Territorial Planning of Industry," New Fabian Research Bureau tract, 1934, *The Planning of Greater London* (foreword by Sir Raymond Unwin), 1938, *Green-Belt Cities: The British Contribution*, Faber & Faber, Ltd., London, 1946 and Adams & Dart, 1965, *Can Man Plan? and Other Verses*, George G. Harrap, 1959, *The New Towns: Answer to Megalopolis* (with Arnold Whittick), Leonard Hill, London, 1963 and 1969, *Genesis of Welwyn Garden City*, 1970, editorials and planning commentaries in *Town and Country Planning Journal*, 1936–1969.

—ARNOLD WHITTICK

OVERCROWDING A term that generally refers to living conditions in dwelling houses and is usually based on the number of persons occupying rooms. What constitutes overcrowding is, to some extent, a matter of opinion and varies with traditional habits, conditions, and ways of life. What, for example, would be regarded as overcrowding in London would probably not be so regarded in Hong Kong. Yet some standards of occupancy have been formulated in legislation which, however, can be followed only as means permit. For example, in England maximum standards of occupation of dwelling houses is given in the Housing Act of 1935 as 1 room, 2 persons; 2 rooms, 3 persons; 3 rooms, 5 persons; 4 rooms, 7.5 persons, and 5 rooms, 10 persons—with an additional 2 persons for each room in excess of 5. A child over one year until the age of ten is half a person in these calculations. Anything in excess of these standards is overcrowding. A case in which persons of opposite sex who are not husband and wife occupy one room is also regarded as an instance of overcrowding. Standard sizes of rooms are indicated. For 2 persons, a room must not be less than 110 square feet (10.2 square meters); for $1\frac{1}{2}$ persons (one adult, one child), not less than 90 square feet (8.4 square meters); and for 1 person, not less than 70 square feet (6.5 square meters). The purpose of the rooms is not specified. Thus, in the case of a three-bedroom house (which constitutes the majority in England) with two other rooms (living and dining), 10 occupants would not constitute overcrowding, although this could mean parents in one bedroom, four daughters in another, and four sons in another. This would make such standards unsatisfactory, but in England, as in most countries, overcrowding is such that even in 1973 the minimum standards outlined cannot at present be followed.

Overcrowding is sometimes confused with high densities of population, but it is obvious that in some conditions there may be overcrowding at 50 persons to the acre (123 per hectare) and spacious living in luxury apartment houses at 200 persons to the acre (494 per hectare).

OVERSPILL The excess population, resulting from the redevelopment to improved standards of an urban area, which has to be reaccommodated elsewhere.

OWEN, ROBERT (1771–1858) British social reformer. Owen was a successful textile manufacturer deeply concerned for the living standards, edu-

Portrait of Robert Owen. (By Sam Bough, in the National Portrait Gallery, London.)

cation, and environment of the working classes, with whom he attained great popularity as a pioneer of the trade union movement and the retail cooperative movement. He made notable advances in housing, welfare, and education in his factory "village" of New Lanark, Glasgow (1799–1828), which became world famous. On the basis of this experiment he advocated, in *A New View of Society* (1813), *Report to the County of Lanark* (1820), and other writings, a general theory of the distribution of the population in cooperative agricultural-industrial communities of 300 to 2000 persons on sites of 150 to 2,000 acres (60 to 800 hectares). The people were to be housed in buildings of quadrangular form, with private bedrooms overlooking gardens and with common kitchens and dining rooms. Church and schools were to be inside the squares and factory buildings just outside. Owenite communities were actually started at Orbisten (Lanarkshire, 1825), New Harmony (Indiana, 1825), Ralahine (Ireland, 1831), and Tytherley (Hampshire, 1838), but all failed. Their pattern—associated with Owen's condemnation of "courts, alleys, lanes and streets . . . as destructive to almost all the comforts of human life"—cannot be said to have had much influence on modern planning, though it was imitated in hundreds of other socialistic communities of the early nineteenth century. But Owen's writings, like those of his contemporary F. M. C. Fourier (1772–1837) and their many followers, have historical and sociological interest.

BIBLIOGRAPHY: Autobiography 1857; J. Podmore, *Life of Robert Owen,* 1906; Margaret Cole, *Robert Owen of New Lanark.,* 1953.

—FREDERIC J. OSBORN

P

PAKISTAN AND BANGLADESH With the termination of British rule in India in 1947, the country was divided into the two sovereign states of India and Pakistan. The latter country consisted of two areas, West and East Pakistan, separated by the large territory of India—a distance of over 1,000 miles. Early in 1972 conflict resulted in East Pakistan becoming the separate state of Bangladesh.

This article on Pakistan was written before the events of 1972 and is concerned with urban planning and development in its various aspects in both West and East Pakistan up to the end of 1971. In view of the events of 1972, however, it has been necessary to make some adjustments, and where appropriate the name of Bangladesh is substituted for East Pakistan.

Although the areas now constituting Pakistan and Bangladesh have a brief political history, they have been cradles of old and dynamic civilizations. They thus have a rich history and traditions of town building and housing. The precise methods of city planning and building in the Indus Valley as well as the high level of development enjoyed by the cities of Dacca and Lahore during the Mughal period bear witness to this fact. In the first quarter of the seventeenth century, the Mughal empire already showed signs of collapse and the great cities of Lahore and Dacca began to decline. During the British rule of the Indo-Pakistan subcontinent, the old cities were ignored and new settlements called "cantonments" were planned and built on the outskirts of some of the large cities. The cantonments were essentially meant for housing the armed forces, but special areas were reserved for native civilians on the one hand and British officers on the other. Such areas were called the "civil lines" within each cantonment. Pakistani cities thus contain curious records of Hindu, Muslim, and British civilizations.

It is estimated that today the population of Pakistan and Bangladesh and their future projections are as follows:

	1970	1975
West Pakistan	62 million	72 million
Bangladesh	74 million	86 million

In 1961, Pakistan's total population was 94 million (51 million in East Pakistan and 43 million in West Pakistan).

Pakistan has a total area of approximately 310,000 square miles (802,900 square kilometers), and Bangladesh has 55,000 square miles (142,450 square kilometers). Climatically, Pakistan is in a hot, arid zone, while Bangladesh is a part of the hot, humid zone.

Today (1972) Pakistan consists of four provinces. The map of the administrative regions of Pakistan illustrates these details. In late 1958, Pakistan had a new revolutionary government which adopted a presidential form of government and abandoned the parliamentary form.

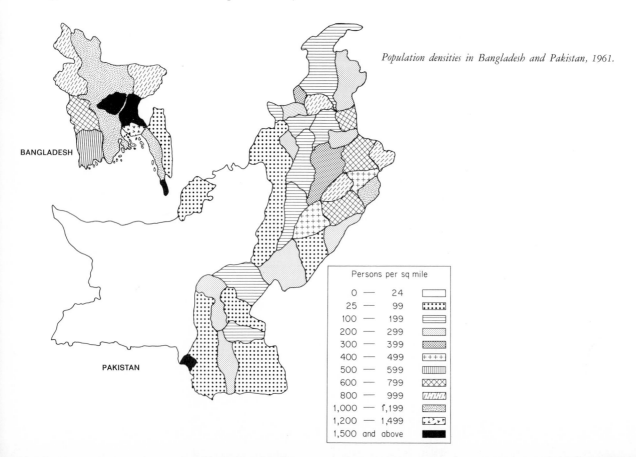

Population densities in Bangladesh and Pakistan, 1961.

BANGLADESH

PAKISTAN

Persons per sq mile	
0 — 24	
25 — 99	
100 — 199	
200 — 299	
300 — 399	
400 — 499	
500 — 599	
600 — 799	
800 — 999	
1,000 — 1,199	
1,200 — 1,499	
1,500 and above	

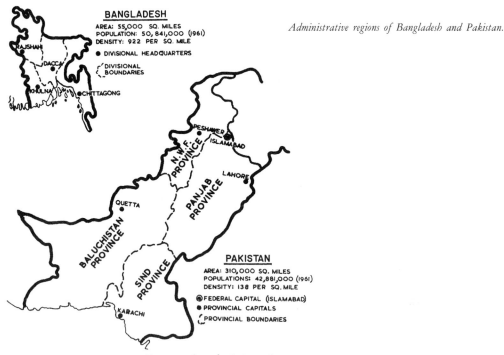

Administrative regions of Bangladesh and Pakistan.

Legislation, Administration, and Institutions For purely administrative purposes, Pakistan is divided into villages and urban areas which form a part of a district, the districts are then grouped into divisions, and divisions into provinces. The provinces are then responsible to the central government. The provincial and central governments consist of various departments and ministries, etc.

Pakistan now has 15 years of experience in national and provincial economic planning and about 7 or 8 years of experience in the urban and metropolitan planning of a few large urban areas. It also has some experience of regional planning and development for agriculture, industry, and water and power development. Large urban areas of Pakistan, for planning and development purposes, are under the control of autonomous bodies called improvement trusts and development authorities. In other urban areas, the municipalities also try to perform the planning and development functions in their own limited and haphazard fashion.

As per the 1961 census and in June 1970, the general details of Pakistan's population were as follows:

Urban areas (1961 census) 313
Villages (1961 census). 37,061
Municipalities. 87
Improvement trusts and development authorities 21

and of Bangladesh's population:

Urban areas (1961 census) 78
Villages (1961 census). 64,729

Pakistan's urban population has been growing dramatically, and the past growth as well as future projections are shown in the chart of urban growth in Bangladesh and Pakistan.

The history of Pakistan and Bangladesh can be divided into five periods: independence and formative period from 1947 to 1955, and four five-year plans from 1955 to 1975.

The people and governments of Pakistan and Bangladesh are now implementing the Fourth Five-year Plan (1970–1975).

Rapid population growth, especially in urban areas, has caused serious problems in keeping up the supply of essential goods and services.

Although the nation of Pakistan is new, its cities are old. This has posed serious problems of readjustment as well as planning. The nation has not been able to afford to abandon the old towns altogether and, like Taxila and Moenjodaro, to found new cities immediately in conformity with the new spirit of Muslim renaissance. The enormous mass of refugees seeking shelter in already overcrowded cities has aggravated the problem. From 1947 to 1955 and during the First (1955–1960) and Second (1960–1965) Five-year Plan periods, the government and the people were fully occupied with the settlement of displaced and homeless families, planning for economic development and industrialization, and rationalizing and improving the national, provincial, regional, and local government networks.

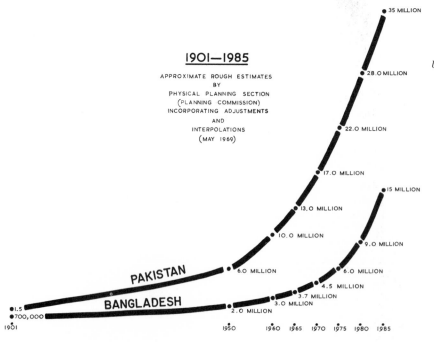

1901—1985

APPROXIMATE ROUGH ESTIMATES
BY
PHYSICAL PLANNING SECTION
(PLANNING COMMISSION)
INCORPORATING ADJUSTMENTS
AND
INTERPOLATIONS
(MAY 1969)

Urban growth in Bangladesh and Pakistan

Urbanization in Pakistan (including Bangladesh) can be divided into three phases: the period of the Mughals, of the British, and of post-independence. In the first phase there was a harmonious balance between the urban and the rural, and during the Mughal part of the second phase there were glorious cities and balanced development. The British part of the second phase was marked by the evolution of the cantonment and the civil lines and a general decay of the old city. The last or post-independence phase is marked by rapid urban growth and the evolution of large slums side by side with poorly planned but expensively built, fashionable colonies for the upper-middle class and the wealthy. There is an acute scarcity of community facilities and utilities and an outdated and overloaded urban transport system. The third phase is also marked by a new development: a widening of the socioeconomic and technological gap between the urban and the rural areas of Pakistan and Bangladesh.

The government and the planners were naturally somewhat puzzled by this phenomenon, as, during this period, the country did make substantial economic progress and the rate of economic growth, especially during the second plan period, was considered to be not only substantial but praiseworthy. However, somehow the growth of services and facilities did not keep pace with this remarkable economic growth, and as a result the physical environment has progressively deteriorated.

The principal cause of the deterioration of the physical environment is the lack of coordination and integration of economic planning with physical and social planning. Establishment of an economic activity—a factory, for instance—entails parallel investment in public utilities, roads, transport facilities, houses, sanitation, schools, and hospitals. In many cases, all these investments are not coordinated by a physical plan and the total requirements are underestimated; hence the physical environment starts to deteriorate.

At the conclusion of the first two plans (1965), the National Planning Commission and the government realized that it was not possible to solve the problem of urban development by an isolated public works approach. It was felt that economic planning had to be made more comprehensive in order to deal with the problem of social welfare. The government had realized that although the per capita and national income were increasing, it was not certain whether the per capita and national welfare were also increasing. In the case of developing nations like Pakistan and Bangladesh, it is possible to evolve minimum standards of per capita welfare in terms of food intake, shelter, water and sanitation, health, and clothing. It was also realized that, with the accelerated tempo of economic development as well as abnormal population growth, the rate of urbanization would be accelerated; therefore it was essential to have a national program for urban development as well as clear-cut policies for shaping future urban growth. The Planning Commission realized that it was necessary to broaden the base of economic planning and to integrate national planning efforts with regional and urban development.

After the experience of the First (1955–1960) and Second (1960–1965) Five-year Plans, the National Planning Commission became convinced that physical and social planning should be integrated with national economic planning. Therefore, education, manpower, and social welfare sectors were strengthened. A National Manpower and Education Commission has been established, and a separate Physical Planning Section has been set up within the National Planning Commission. These steps paved the way for launching some careful experiments for regional palnning. The United Nations and the United Nations Special Fund, the Dutch and the West German Research Institutions, the Royal Swedish Government, and several other international and national research and planning organizations welcomed these pioneering steps taken by the Pakistan National Planning Commission and offered technical, professional, and financial assistance. The National Planning Commission fully appreciated these kind offers but felt that before accepting them it must establish an appropriate foundation and framework on the national level for launching carefully designed pilot projects. It was decided that the National Planning Commission should exercise function No. IV of its charter and launch a few pilot projects for testing various approaches to regional planning as a part of national planning programs.

Three such projects were launched; the details of these are given at the end of this article. These three projects will be carried into the Fourth Five-year Plan on a high-priority basis. They are expected to be completed during the fourth plan period and will thus provide the much-needed experience, methodology, and techniques for regional development planning as a part of national planning. Once these have been clarified and established, regional planning will be pursued and developed on a more systematic basis during the fifth and subsequent plan periods. The projects are being executed by the provincial governments with close technical, professional, and policy guidance from the National Planning Commission.

As mentioned earlier, on the local level Pakistan and Bangladesh have the municipality, the improvement trust, and the development authority. These report to the provincial departments of local government. These, in turn, are supervised by the provincial planning and development boards (which are responsible for provincial economic planning as well), which have special sections for physical planning and development and for housing. In many cases, the provincial town planning departments are still located in the public works departments and not in the departments of local bodies, which is confusing. At the central government level six different ministries deal with physical planning and housing; while the National Planning Commission, located in the Secretariats of the President of Pakistan and Prime Minister of Bangladesh, tries to coordinate their work along with the provincial work and needs in the physical planning and housing sectors. This coordination is supervised by specialists in the field of physical planning, housing, regional and urban development, and other related professions.

At the time of independence and in the period following, events have exposed the great weaknesses from which the economic structure of

Pakistan and Bangladesh suffered. The vulnerability of the economy posed a serious challenge. The political and administrative elite as well as the commercial community were therefore conscious from the outset that the national economy could not be left to take care of itself. It was widely felt that efforts would be needed to break the stagnation of the economy and to create conditions for its rapid and balanced progress.

The evolution of the planning machinery can be divided into three phases. The first phase covers the period between 1947 and 1953. In the immediate postindependence period, before economic and administrative chaos had been fully overcome, the government began to think about economic priorities, programming, and coordination. A Development Board, a Planning Advisory Board, and an Economic Committee of the Cabinet were set up in 1948. The following year saw the formation of the Ministry of Economic Affairs for the purpose of interministerial economic coordination. The first formal exercise in planning was carried out by the Development Board when it produced the Six-year Development Plan (1951–1957) envisaging an outlay of 2,600 million rupees (4.75 Pakistani rupees = 1 United States dollar), of which 1,200 million rupees were to be financed externally and the rest raised internally. This Six-year Plan was framed at the instance of the Consultative Committee of the Colombo Plan (for cooperative economic development of South and Southeast Asia). It was incorporated in the Colombo Plan and adopted by the Pakistan government in November, 1950. This plan was in fact little more than an assorted set of different projects, each considered essential in its own right. It made provision for a flexible program, and quite a few changes were made in it. This, however, does not detract from the significance of the projects which the plan embodied. As against the modest outlay of 2,600 million rupees envisaged over a period of 6 years, actual expenditure in the first 5 years exceeded 3,000 million rupees.

The Six-year Plan was formulated at a time when the country possessed no prior experience of planning and when its authors were severely handicapped owing to the lack of essential data in regard to the availability of human, physical, and financial resources. The government set up autonomous administrative machinery comprising an Economic Council, a Planning Commission, and a number of subcommissions replacing the Development Board, the Planning Advisory Board, and the Economic Committee of the Cabinet. But none of the constituents of the planning organization was quite equal to the task. Besides, the period which the plan covered was one of much economic uncertainty. This was caused by the Korean War boom and the subsequent recession. Thus, whatever development took place, it did not follow the course charted by the plan.

The second phase in the evolution of the planning machinery began with the creation in July 1953 of the National Planning Board, later renamed the Planning Commission, which lasted a little over 5 years. Involved were the terms of an assessment of the resources which could be made available over the 5-year period beginning in April 1954 (later changed to April

1955); the preparation of a national plan of development; the making of proposals regarding the administrative machinery with a view to assuring the successful implementation of the plan; and the formulation of any other recommendations deemed essential to the success of the plan.

After delays in the formulation and finalization of the First Five-year Plan (1955–1960), it was published in draft form in May 1956, for eliciting public opinion and as a basis for discussions with the provincial government and the central ministries. The board later revised the plan in the light of these discussions and the comments that had been made and submitted it for the consideration of the National Economic Council (NEC) in February 1957. The NEC recorded general approval of its targets and programs in April 1957, 2 years after the plan period began.

The plan offered an incisive analysis of the problems of economic growth in the circumstances obtaining in the country, defined the concept of balanced growth for the first time, and contained excellent suggestions for adapting the administrative machinery to the needs of development and for carrying out vital institutional improvements. Also, the National Planning Board continued to offer advice on policy matters to implementing agencies during the plan period. Unfortunately, however, the plan's promise could not be fulfilled because there was no firm governmental commitment to its execution.

The third phase in the evolution of planning organization and procedures began with the change of political regime in October 1958. The revolutionary government showed a keen awareness of the need for bringing about such changes, in the planning machinery in particular and the administration in general, as would hasten the process of development.

A series of changes were introduced with the aim of raising the status of the planning agency, institutionalizing the planning process, and integrating the national plan's prescriptions and targets into the administration's practice. The President became the chairman of the Planning Commission; and the deputy chairman, the operational chief, was given the ex-officio status of a minister. The Planning Commission was constituted into a division in the President's Secretariat. As part of the attempt to build the development process into the working of the administration, planning departments were organized in the provinces and planning cells set up in ministries and departments. The Planning Commission is now represented on all high-level decision-making organs and bodies like the National Economic Council; the Executive Committee of the National Economic Council; the Central Development Working Party, which scrutinizes the public sector; and the Foreign Exchange Control Committee. The Industrial Investment Schedule for the private sector and the Annual Development Program, which is a part of the budget, are formulated within the framework of the Five-year Plan.

The main functions of the Planning Commission are (1) formulation of the Five-year Plan; (2) formulation of the Annual Development Program within the framework of the Five-year Plan; (3) planning for the private sector; (4) evaluation of progress; and (5) advising on development policies.

The formulation of the Five-year Plan is a fairly elaborate process. The Planning Commission evaluates the past performance of the economy and prescribes tentative targets in overall terms for national income saving, investment, taxes, and imports and exports.

The Annual Development Program is a crucial component of the planning process. It embraces projects which have been approved by the normal machinery of the government after the due scrutiny at various levels—technical, financial, and organizational. After the Annual Development Program as proposed by the Planning Commission is approved by the NEC, it is incorporated into the annual budget. It goes without saying that the Finance Ministry has an important say in the determination of the size of the Annual Development Program because of the responsibility it bears for the mobilization of resources.

With the introduction of the annual plan, the process of planning has moved to a new stage in its evolution.

Pakistan is now implementing its Fourth Five-year Plan (1970–1975). The Planning history follows the historical periods already given.

The Five-year Plans are generally made within the framework of a broad Perspective Plan (1965–1985).

This Perspective Plan underlines the need for placing increasing reliance upon the country's own resources and energies and for reducing dependence on external assistance. By the end of the Fourth Plan the country will be required to finance 80 percent of the development effort out of its own resources.

Major Achievements Looked at realistically, physical welfare, facilities, and services have not kept pace with recent dynamic and noteworthy economic growth. The present deteriorated living conditions in Pakistan are not necessarily due to neglect by the government, but are due more to the government's preoccupation with tasks which it considered more urgent and to which it assigned a higher priority. The first and second plans, for example, had to be devoted to the settlement of large numbers of displaced Muslim families from India who were squatting throughout the urban areas. Besides this gigantic task, the plans also aimed at creating the most essential institutional and organizational framework which could at least provide some semblance of the much-needed local and provincial governmental network for this sector. Some urgent water, sewerage, and drainage schemes were also taken up, and an unsuccessful effort was made to launch building and housing research and to initiate regional and urban planning.

With the settlement of the displaced families and the development of a crude institutional and organizational framework, the third plan then tried to initiate the first modest program both on a *curative* and a *preventive* basis. Unfortunately, this had to be abandoned very soon due to sudden war with India, and in 1965 to 1966 the sectoral program was reduced to the provision of only those bare essentials which could not be curtailed at any cost. This reduced, hard-core physical planning program of 2,470 million rupees is now completed and it is estimated that by June 1970 the program was executed at a cost of 2,000 million rupees, thus creating a shortage of 470 million rupees (i.e., approximately 20 percent). This shortage is not due to any lack of capacity or faulty planning or programming, but rather to nonrelease or badly timed release of resources or by lowering of the sectoral priority by the provincial governments at the time of preparation of the annual development program and budgets.

While reviewing the program by executing agencies, the central government seems to have performed the best (102 percent achievement in financial terms), with East Pakistan coming next (80 percent achievement in financial terms) and West Pakistan showing the poorest results (only 68 percent achievement in financial terms). West Pakistan's poor record is due to the fact that the provincial government has not yet been able to develop the much-needed institutions and organizational framework for physical planning and housing and, in spite of heroic prodding and leadership provided by the West Pakistan Planning Board, these problems still remain to be solved.

The present legislation on physical planning is not conducive to regional planning and development. Most of it consists of scattered acts and orders. There are at least 23 various acts and orders which relate to physical planning. It is necessary that appropriate legislation for physical planning on regional and local levels be enacted at an early date.

One of the main reasons for the dilapidated conditions of Pakistani towns is the absence of any modern planning legislation. During the time of the British rule, although significant developments were made in England for bringing out strong planning legislation, no systematic effort was made to introduce up-to-date laws for improvement of towns in prepartition India. Only a few acts with restricted jurisdiction were passed to solve immediate problems. After partition, this was not considered especially important, as there were other more urgent and immediate problems. However, a few laws were enacted on a provincial basis.

The first law to provide a base for town planning was the Sind Town Improvement Act of 1915, which applied to the entire Sind, including Karachi, and had provisions relating to the preparation of town planning schemes for some portions of the city. This was followed by the Punjab Town Improvement Act of 1922, with provision for improvement trusts for the preparation of development schemes and general improvement schemes for specified portions of various towns. There were similar acts in Bengal, which were later taken over by the government of East Pakistan (Bangladesh). No provision existed in these acts for the preparation of schemes or plans for towns as a whole. The Karachi Development Authority Order of 1957 was, however, an exception where—besides provisions for improvement schemes—special provisions for land acquisition, the preparation of a master plan, establishment of a building research center, and the sponsoring of cooperative societies were also included. It was not until the enactment of the Municipal Administration Ordinance of 1960 that preparation of comprehensive master plans for the city as a whole and their implementation by the municipalities was suggested. With the enactment of the Punjab Town Improvement Act, certain provisions of municipal administration relating to planning were transferred to improvement trusts. One of the major flaws in these two acts is that they are restricted to municipal limits and have no control outside these limits. This encourages the haphazard establishment of industries outside municipal limits to avoid various restrictions and municipal taxes. To control the haphazard growth of industries, a new industries ordinance has been passed.

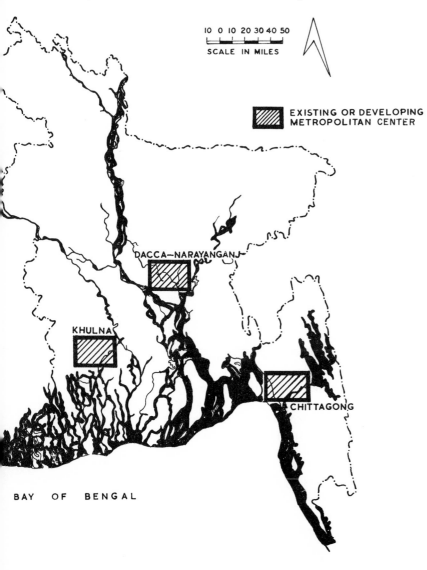

Developing metropolitan centers in Bangladesh (1961 census). (Planning Commission—Physical Planning and Housing Section.)

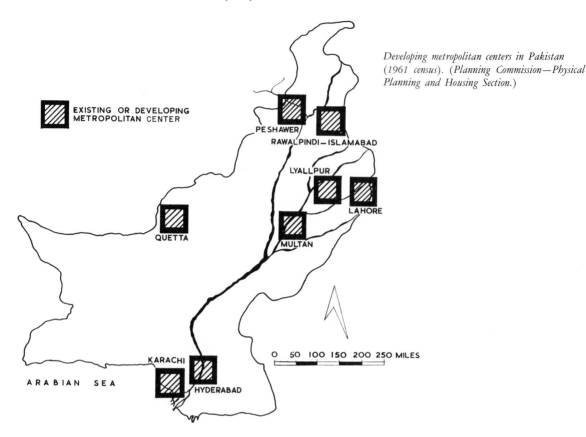

Developing metropolitan centers in Pakistan (1961 census). (Planning Commission—Physical Planning and Housing Section.)

The Capital Development Authority Ordinance of 1960, an ordinance to cover the construction of the new capital at Islamabad, has jurisdiction over a vast new federal area, much beyond the municipal limits, having special provisions for land-use control and land acquisition over the entire territory. This new ordinance is perhaps the most modern urban planning and development ordinance. However, it has not been used as a model elsewhere in the country.

The situation was only slightly better in East Pakistan. The Town Improvement Act of 1953 provided for the development and improvement of the towns of Dacca and Narayangonj and also for the establishment of the Dacca Improvement Trust and the Chittagong and Khulna Planning and Development Institutions. This was different from the similar enactments in West Pakistan as it provided for the preparation of master plans having jurisdictions beyond the municipal limits as well. The East Bengal Building Construction Act of 1952, which provided for building and land-use control over all of East Pakistan and included provisions for demolition in case of default, proved to be an effective instrument for the implementation of master plans in Dacca and Chittagong.

The central legislation, called the Municipal Administration Ordinance of 1960, was also effective in East Pakistan, which made it obligatory for the municipalities to prepare master plans. Under the East Pakistan Municipal Committee (town planning) Rules of 1968, made under this ordinance, all municipalities in the province except those of Dacca, Narayangonj, Chittagong, and Khulna were asked to prepare master plans of their respective areas under the general guidance of the Urban Development Directorate and within a specified time. These rules elaborate the details to be catered for in the master plans and the procedure for their approval. Separate ordinances were passed to provide for the preparation of comprehensive master plans and the creation of development authorities for their implementation in Chittagong and Khulna: the Chittagong Development Authority Ordinance of 1959 and the Khulna Development Authority Ordinance of 1961. None of these existing laws, however, provide for planning on a broader regional basis. The government of East Pakistan drafted The East Pakistan Town and Country Planning Act of 1969 to provide for physical planning and housing for which approval by the provincial government was pending at the time that East Pakistan became Bangladesh.

To summarize, there is scattered, old-fashioned legislation for building control and some local physical planning. There is no legislation on the regional, provincial, and national levels for national and provincial physical planning or regional and urban development as a part of the national and provincial economic development plans.

In terms of institutional development, planning is done by the respective units of the national and provincial planning commission and boards, but implementation is weak due to the absence of provincial departments of physical planning or regional and urban development as well as the continuation of old-fashioned institutions and procedures at the local level—such as improvement trusts and development authorities—which in some cases are being further proliferated by the creation of separate autonomous authorities or bodies for water and sewerage, transport, and other services.

Dacca Improvement Trust Building and surrounding area.

Education, Training, and Professional Practice   Facilities for the training architects and city and regional planners were not established in Pakistan until 1965. There are now faculties of architecture and town planning in the newly established universities of engineering and technology at Dacca and Lahore. Both faculties are well advanced in their architectural training programs, but their programs for urban planning are still in an infant stage. One or two groups of architects have been graduated from the faculty at Dacca and one group has come from the Lahore faculty. The planning program at Dacca began in 1970, while the Lahore faculty has been able to produce two groups of planners. However, the absorption of planners has been rather slow due to the nonavailability of jobs. Architects had the same fate in the public sector, and most of them have joined various consulting firms in the private sector or have set up their own practices.

In spite of this, the total number of architects and urban and regional planners available in Pakistan is extremely low compared with needs. Many Pakistanis proceed abroad to Europe, the United Kingdom, the United States, Canada, and Australia for education, training, and research in urban and regional planning and architecture. Both architects and urban planners have formed their own professional institutes, called the Pakistan Institute of Architects and the Pakistan Institute of City and Regional Planning.

Pakistan has no system or legislation for the registration of professional architects and planners, and accordingly the professional practice, the consulting firms, and the government agencies continue to utilize draftsmen, civil engineers, and men of related practical experience for these highly professional tasks. This naturally damages the quality of work. The government has to rely therefore on foreign experts and consultants, and it may continue to do so until highly skilled and experienced Pakistanis are available in large number.

The National Planning Commission is participating in a worldwide program of research and training in regional development launched by the United Nations. As a part of this program, special research and training centers for regional and urban development may be established in the coming 5 to 10 years in both Pakistan and Bangladesh.

Traditions of planning to the end of the Nineteenth Century and to the Beginning of the Third Five-year Plan (1965) Pakistan has an old tradition of building well-planned towns and cities. The remains of the Indus Valley civilization of about 5,000 years ago indicate a mastery of precise town planning. During the Mughal period, cities like Dacca and Lahore reached a high level of development. However, since the mid-twentieth century the problem of facilities, services, and housing has assumed a very different character, and it has to be tackled after more than two centuries of lost initiative.

The housing problems in Pakistan consist of the following:

1. A population increase of roughly 3 million every year.
2. An urban growth proceeding at twice the rate of the overall population increase.

3. A big carryover of shortage in urban housing: of 540,000 in 1947, 600,00 in 1960, 950,000 in 1965, and an estimated 1.2 million in 1970.

4. Inflow of Muslim migrants from India in a regular stream, rising rapidly in times of crisis such as 1947 to 1948, 1951, 1955, 1961, and 1964 to 1965. By 1951, the refugees numbered 10 percent of the total population of Pakistan. The total number of such immigrants up to December 1966 was 10.5 million, nearly equal to the population of Australia.

Low income and high production costs add to the difficulty of keeping pace with these aggravating factors, which impinge mainly on urban areas. As mentioned earlier, until 1965, the government could not take up any significant town planning scheme. All sections of government were fully occupied with the most urgent tasks of refugee rehabilitation and provision of essential urban infrastructure to large metropolitan areas. Some planned villages and new towns (marketing centers) were built in desert reclamation and agricultural development schemes.

Twentieth-century Planning   As mentioned earlier, a crude organizational framework in the shape of improvement trusts and development authorities has been rationalized. A number of housing colonies for low-income urban slum dwellers and refugees from India have been built. These are generally called "satellite towns" but are actually just dormitory communities. A few master plans have also been prepared but not well implemented. (Khulna, Chittagong, and Dacca do have master plans which were, however, outdated by the early seventies. A master plan has also been prepared for Lahore, but it has been shelved due to lack of legislative and institutional support.) Some more marketing centers and villages have been planned and built in the agricultural development and reclamation regions. As regards new towns, the government planned and is building a new federal capital at Islamabad and a smaller capital is being built at Dacca (Bangladesh). Besides a number of new community as well as commercial buildings have been built, in addition to schemes for low-cost and middle-income housing. This has provided Pakistan and Pakistanis with new building, architectural, and planning experience. Some hasty and ill-planned large-scale slum-clearance projects were also taken up at Karachi, Lahore, Dacca, and Chittagong. These were not very successful and the National Planning Commission, the University of Karachi, the Netherlands Universities Foundation for International Co-operation, and a Dutch University have formed a sort of research consortium to carry out in-depth studies of urban slums for their improvement and if necessary a planned and harmonious clearance. The project became operative in 1970. Dutch and Pakistani social scientists, planners, and other professionals are working together in this policy-oriented research work. As regards urban design and building styles, so far Pakistan has not evolved any distinctive style of its own. Some of the illustrations show these developments. In the case of regional and urban planning, the national pilot projects now under way will provide new techniques and methodology for systematic regional and urban development as a part of national planning.

Old slum area, Karachi (Pakistan).

Slum clearance and rehousing in Dacca (Bangladesh).

Once these have been clarified and established, regional planning can be pursued and developed on a more systematic basis during the fifth and subsequent plan periods. The projects are being executed by both the provincial governments under close technical, professional, and policy level guidance of the National Planning Commission.

Regional planning is not new to Pakistan, for several projects of this kind have been carried out since 1947 and even earlier. However, they were single-sector oriented, either for agriculture, or water and power, or transport, or industrial development. The national pilot projects are an experiment and exercise for multisector regional planning and are to serve as a laboratory for this comprehensive approach.

In order to provide an appropriate framework at the central level, a high-level committee has been set up with Dr. Khalid Shibli as its member/secretary. More details can be obtained from him. (Visiting Professor of International, Regional and Urban Development, GSPIA, University of Pittsburgh, Pittsburgh, Pa. 15213 U.S.A.)

Location and Planning of Cities in Bangladesh

National Pilot Project No. 1. Bangladesh has a very colorful history. Although today it is very poor and densely populated, this was not always the case. During the Muslim rule and earlier, it enjoyed a high level of prosperity and was noted for its balanced development. With the advent of British rule, the whole province was deindustrialized and was converted into a raw-material base for foreign exploitation. Since independence, the people and the governments of Pakistan and, later, Bangladesh have made efforts to develop the province.

Bangladesh has only three large urban centers: Dacca, Chittagong, and Khulna. As its physical infrastructure is not very well developed, most of the development efforts have tended to concentrate around these three metropolitan centers. Northern parts of the state are undeveloped and have a rather low per capita income, lower than the provincial average.

The pilot project launched in cooperation with the United Nations and the United Nations Special Fund has the following objectives:

1. To conduct research and prepare an outline of physical development for the entire province within the framework of national and provincial economic plans

2. Within the outline physical plan, to identify potential areas, centers, or sites for industrial development

3. To plan these areas, sites, or centers as New Towns

4. To prepare detailed plans for one or two of these New Towns and develop these to act as countermagnets to Dacca, Chittagong, and Khulna

5. To provide a broad yardstick for guiding the physical development of the state within the framework of economic development policies

6. To provide policy-level guidance (upon request) for the general growth and development of Dacca, Chittagong, and Khulna

The Project is fully operative. The United Nations have obtained the services of a senior physical planner and he is guiding the project as chief adviser/project manager. A vast amount of data has been collected and analyzed, and this will soon be synthesized into an outline physical development plan. All the related state departments and other agencies which are responsible for developmental planning are represented on an Urban Development Council, of which the provincial additional chief secretary (development) is the chairman.

Regional Development Plan for Peshawar Valley

National Pilot Project No. 2. Very few regions in the world have a history and background as complex and interesting as that of the Peshawar Valley. It has been the home of the ancient Gandhara culture, and it is the location of the great Tarbela Dam over the mighty Indus River.

The region is in a state of underdevelopment, and the population of the valley and the Peshawar Division (of which the valley is a part) have a per capita income which is much lower than the provincial average. Any planning for the valley must consider the larger planning region, that is, the Peshawar Division. The planning region covers an area of 28,000 square miles (72,520 square kilometers) and had a population of 6.4 million people in 1961. The valley itself is spread over an area of 2,800 square miles (7,252 square kilometers) and had a population of 2 million people in 1961.

The planning region contains important minerals, timber, building materials, and water-power resources as well as plenty of fruit, agricultural products, and many cottage industries. The human resource, however, is not yet highly skilled or well educated. The physical infrastructure is not well developed. The region contains a large, completed water and power project called the Warsak Dam, and new world-famous project called the Tarbela Dam is now under construction on the Indus River. The present national pilot project has the following objectives:

1. To remove interregional economic disparity
2. To promote balanced development of the valley and lessen the gap between the villages and urban areas
3. To provide a broad, flexible, generalized physical development plan for the whole of the planning region
4. To introduce systematic physical planning through coordination of investments
5. To explore the possibilities of planned, self-sufficient marketing and service centers

The project is now fully operative and the provincial government is going ahead with essential work under close technical and policy-level guidance of the National Planning Commission. All related provincial and central government units and agencies have been involved. The commissioner of the Peshawar Division has been appointed as project director. The project is thus a modest effort to revive the development of this valley and surrounding region by a systematic and scientific regional development policy. A substantial amount of work has been completed. The Royal Netherlands government has provided some technical assistance and some advisory and technical training facilities.

Development Plan for Karachi Metropolitan Region

National Pilot Project No. 3. The vast land of Pakistan, rich in history,

LEFT: *Low income apartment blocks, Karachi.* ABOVE: *Middle income houses, Islamabad (Pakistan).*

has seen the rise and fall of many great empires. Excavations at Harappa, Moenjodaro, and Kot Diji have brought to light evidences of an advanced civilization existing in this region. In 712 A.D. the Arab General Mohammad Bin Qasim landed near the present site of Karachi. Gradually the Muslims took root in the soil and influenced the life of the land by their culture, traditions, and faith. Later developments during the British period, based on regional geography and trade, lent a powerful influence to the expansion of this small fishing village. By 1859, ideas and programs for the development of Karachi as a harbor were taking shape. Within the next few years the population grew dramatically and the value of trade increased from 12 million rupees in 1843 to 90 million rupees in 1885. In 1947 Karachi became the capital of Pakistan, and this further accelerated its development. Although Islamabad is now the capital, Karachi still remains the financial, commercial, and industrial center of the nation. It is the hub of the nation's economic life and the largest metropolitan center of the country. Its heterogeneous population represents almost all the cultural and linguistic groups of Pakistan. Thus Karachi is more of a national and international center than a purely provincial metropolis. The metropolitan boundaries extend all over Karachi Division and it is futile to limit these to municipal or development authority limits. Unfortunately, over the years, the metropolitan area has become a fertile ground for administrative and bureaucratic confusion and chaos. Several national, provincial, regional, and local government organizations compete with each other for planning and development. No agency has any control or guidance over the economic forces which are responsible for the growth and expansion of the metropolis. Several functions are not coordinated, and some functions are not provided for at all.

Unfortunately, Karachi does not have a development plan to guide the growth and development of the approximately 3 million people who live in this region. The National Planning Commission and the West Pakistan Planning Board became conscious of this urgent need, and with the help of the United Nations and the United Nations Special Fund, National Pilot Project No. 3 has been launched. The Commission's purpose is to prepare a development plan for the Karachi metropolitan region and to provide something more than a simple physical or land-use plan. The project aims to analyze the socioeconomic base of the region and proposes to guide the development not by stopping or decelerating the growth but by guiding it into desirable directions. Thus the effort will be to integrate physical planning with social and economic planning. How to plan and guide the growth of this dynamic national metropolis, how to govern this heterogeneous society with myriads of problems and potentialities, is the complex and challenging task of this national pilot project.

The United Nations have now appointed a senior physical planner as chief adviser/project manager, and a separate project office has been established at Karachi. Some background information and data have been collected. The United Nations have granted a $750,000 subcontract to a consortium of American and Czechoslovakian regional planners to prepare the Plan, and work is in progress.   —KHALID SHIBLI

PALEOTECHNIC   A term coined by Patrick Geddes, following Lubbock's designation of the epochs of prehistoric archaeology, to describe the earlier and ruder elements of the industrial age.[1] The paleotechnic era is the age of the collieries, of steam engines, of the early railways, and of the expanding and crowded industrial towns.

PALLADIO, ANDREA (1518–1580)   Italian architect who, both through his buildings and his writings, has exercised a powerful influence on European architecture and, to a lesser extent, on town planning. Through the influence of Georgian England he may also be said to be the distant ancestor of the American "Colonial" style of architecture.

The Palladian style spread from Italy to France and reached England early in the seventeenth century. It was a revival of the severe dignity and allegedly perfect proportions of Roman architecture, though tending to be more decorative in detail.

From his birthplace, Vicenza, Palladio was summoned to Rome to collaborate in work on St. Peter's. He then succeeded Sansovino as architect in chief to Venice. It was there and at Vicenza that his main work in architecture and town development was achieved.

Famous for his architectural innovations, Palladio made a less significant contribution to town planning. He followed the standard pattern that, with a few notable exceptions, prevailed throughout the long period of the Renaissance, that of displaying the building in all its magnificence. This was the first consideration, with such elements as the straight primary street

---

[1] Patrick Geddes, *Cities in Evolution,* Williams & Norgate, Ltd., London, 1915.

with a terminal feature, the "place," and the Chessboard Plan being the main components of planning proper.

The Church of S. Giorgio Maggiore at Venice, splendidly placed on an island and on the very edge of the lagoon, is a characteristic example of Palladio's work.

While in Rome, Palladio carefully studied and measured the buildings of antiquity, drawings of which are included in his classic work: *I Quattri Libri dell'Architectura*. An annotated edition was published in England by his principal English disciple, Inigo Jones (*q.v.*).

—WILFRED SALTER

PARK, ROBERT E. (1864–1944) One of the founders of what has become known as the "Chicago school" of sociology, was a pioneer in many fields. His name is usually coupled with that of Ernest W. Burgess, with whom he wrote the highly successful, highly readable, and still relevant textbook *Introduction to the Science of Sociology.*

Starting his professional life as a reporter for daily newspapers, Park never lost the newsman's instinct for the dramatic in the commonplace, the significant detail, the human-interest story. With John Dewey, William James, and George Simmel as his intellectual mentors, he remained faithful, throughout his long career, to their humanist tenets. After taking his Ph.D. at Heidelberg in 1904 with a dissertation on the mass and the public, he taught philosophy at Harvard, traveled extensively in the South, and was an active speaker, writer, and worker in the cause of racial equality.

In 1914, at the age of fifty, Park joined the department of sociology at the University of Chicago, where he remained until his retirement in 1929. Many of his pupils were to become prominent names in the field of urban sociology, among them E. Franklin Frazier, Louis Wirth, and Everett C. Hughes.

His writings on the city and on human ecology (a term and a field he helped to establish) are of special interest to city and town planners. In these, as well as in the course on ecology which he introduced, one of his chief interests was the spatial correlates of social phenomena. Later works on the ghetto (by Louis Wirth), the metropolitan community (by Robert D. McKenzie), juvenile delinquency as a function of locale (by Clifford Shaw), and on urban subareas and subgroups (by Harvey W. Zorbaugh and Frederic Thrasher) were inspired by his pioneering venture.

It has been said that "probably no other man has so deeply influenced the direction taken by American empirical sociology as Robert Ezra Park" (Ralph H. Turner, 1967). He used, and urged others to do likewise, the city as a "social laboratory" for the study of social behavior since in "making the city man has remade himself." For it is in the city that "all the secret ambitions and all the suppressed desires find somewhere an expression. The city magnified, spreads out, and advertises human nature in all its various manifestations. . . . It is this . . . that makes it of all places the one in which to discover the secrets of human hearts, and to study human nature and society" (Turner 1967). Looking at his essays 50 years later is both an enjoyable and an intellectually profitable experience.

BIBLIOGRAPHY: Robert E. Park, *Collected Papers,* vol. 2, "Human Communities, the City and Human Ecology," 1916–1939; Robert E. Park and E. W. Burgess, *Introduction to the Science of Sociology,* Chicago, 1921; Ralph H. Turner (ed.), "Introduction," in Robert E. Park, *On Social Control and Collective Behavior,* Phoenix Books, The University of Chicago Press, Chicago, 1967, p. ix.   —SUZANNE KELLER

PARKS   There are basically three main types of parks:

1. A large area with woodland and pasture attached to a country house
2. An open area of land in a town designed for public use
3. An area of countryside kept for public benefit

Large areas of woodland were used in the early centuries for hunting parks, but it was in the eighteenth century that the English landscape school was at its height. During this period many landscaped parks were designed by William Kent, whose most famous are Rousham and Stowe, and Lancelot "Capability" Brown, who created numerous informal parks, the finest of which is Blenheim.

The parks included belts of trees to contain views within the site or to accentuate distant views or features, a serpentine lake or artificial stream, and lawn sweeping up to the house. Many of these parks are now open to the public and provide recreational activities other than hunting.

The provision of public open spaces within crowded towns where people could find rest and quiet, rich color, and recreational pursuits was primarily a Victorian idea. Early development was due to Humphry Repton, whose aim was to provide "the happy medium betwixt the wildness of nature and the stiffness of art; and convenience, comfort, neatness and everything that conduces to the purposes of habitation with elegance."

Excellent examples include Regents Park (1812), Battersea Park (1845), and Birkenhead Park (1847). Repton's ideas influenced America, and Frederick Law Olmsted's design for Central Park, New York, commenced in 1858. The overall design was one of lawns, trees, paths, lakes, playing areas, and flower gardens. There were also smaller divisions of varying attractions, and provision for activities including strolling, sitting, boating, and ball games. Modern parks follow many of these principles and often are linked as part of an urban open space system.

Large areas of countryside set aside for public benefit are called "national parks." These may be state-owned and controlled by a special service, or ownership may rest with individuals or authorities, with administration by joint planning boards.

These parks are areas of great beauty and landscape significance. Activities vary according to the particular area, but they may include mountaineering, walking, swimming, boating, camping, and picnicking.

Smaller areas of countryside of not less than 25 acres (10 hectares) have been designated as "country parks." Their purpose is to provide or improve opportunities for the public enjoyment with or without charge. Their facilities generally include parking, conveniences, and supervisory service.

—WENDY POWELL

PARKWAY   Definition in the *United States Manual* 41-6454 is "A scenic highway for non-commercial traffic with full or partial control of access and usually within a park or ribbon of parklike development."

There are many good examples of parkways in America. The term "parkway" originated in the United States with Frederick Law Olmsted's designs.

A scenic highway is a road with curves and gradients which are designed for specific motoring speeds. The road linking points together follows the natural lines of the existing contours of the landscape, gently curving with any undulations and avoiding excessively long, straight stretches which are monotonous for drivers as well as deep cuttings and high embankments which are expensive to construct. The road is aligned in the most harmonious position bearing in mind considerations of contours, woods, coast, hills and valleys, and other features. The road provides the most pleasant possible driving conditions both practically and visually.

The park may comprise existing wooded and parkland areas between and alongside the roads or it may be designed and planted to create the surroundings for the road.

Accommodation for recreational activities including parking, picnicking, walking, camping, and swimming may be provided within the park, or the road itself may give pleasant access to similar facilities.

—WENDY POWELL

PATIO   A Spanish term denoting the inner court—open to the sky—of a house. The "patio house" has been increasingly introduced in modern housing both in Europe and America. The expression is fairly loosely used and is applied to design where the house—or series of houses—is built around an open square, either on three or four sides, in the former the fourth side being a fence or wall. Among the advantages of patio housing are seclusion, privacy, and compactness. Many ingenious designs have been introduced.

PAXTON, Sir JOSEPH (1801–1865)   British horticulturist, landscape architect, and engineer born at Milton Bryant, Bedfordshire, in 1801; the son of a farmer. At fifteen he became a gardener at Battlesden, and in 1823 he worked at the Horticultural Society's gardens in Chiswick. In 1826 the sixth Duke of Devonshire asked him to become head gardener at Chatsworth, his home in Derbyshire. There he created a garden so full of interesting features that it became the most celebrated in England.

Paxton was basically a horticulturalist, but he had a great capacity for observation and experimentation. He was part realist, part romantic, and his gay and imaginative designs for the different elements at Chatsworth were much admired. His versatility was illustrated by the inclusion of an arboretum of 40 acres (16.2 hectares) and the planting of over 1,600 trees, the designing and building of water basins and cascades, and the creation of the superb Emperor Fountain. In 1840 the Great Conservatory, 277 feet (84.5 meters) long, 123 feet (37.5 meters) wide, and 67 feet (20.4 meters) high, was built to his design to house many of the tropical plants brought back by the plant hunters. He built a number of other structures of iron, glass, and wood, including a circular glass house specially designed for Victoria Regia, the giant water lily which was introduced in 1847.

Paxton showed interest in designing public gardens and wrote articles in *The Horticultural Register* in 1831 and *The Gardener's Magazine* proposing subscription gardens under a "Garden Company."

His first park design was Prince's Park in Liverpool, built in 1842. Birkenhead Park, where work began in 1844, was the most significant of Paxton's urban parks. Here, 125 acres (50.6 hectares) were set aside for public use. There was a general emphasis on views, and the main features were two large lakes. Frederick Law Olmsted visited Birkenhead Park in 1850 and was greatly impressed and influenced by the layout. Other urban open spaces that Paxton designed included Coventry Cemetery (1845) and the Peoples Park in Halifax (1855).

With the Lily House at Chatsworth, Paxton achieved technical competence in working with a prefabricated system of construction using glass and iron. He made use of this experience in designing his most famous work, the building for the Great Exhibition of 1851 in Hyde Park. The efficiency and well-ordered, detailed design of the building were unequaled for architectural originality. It was disassembled and re-erected with some alterations at Sydenham in 1853, made possible by its standardized, prefabricated method of construction. It became famous as the Crystal Palace.

Paxton was influenced by the technical skill of the railway age, particularly by the use of iron to facilitate the design of elegant structures.

He has been described as a typical Victorian, being a successful man in many fields including engineering, architecture, landscape architecture, and legislation (he became a Member of Parliament in 1851).

BIBLIOGRAPHY: G. F. Chadwick, *The Works of Sir Joseph Paxton,* The Architectural Press, London, 1961.

—WENDY POWELL

PEDESTRIAN WAY   (*See* SIDEWALK and PEDESTRIANIZATION.)

PEDESTRIANIZATION

North America has found out to its cost that it is possible to do too much for the motor car. Europe has begun to make the same discovery to its even greater cost, for with its long tradition of civilized town life and its smaller scale, in many cases totally unsuited to twentieth-century traffic, it has, perhaps, even more to lose.

The United States and Canada, prosperous countries with grid-planned cities and ample land, have found themselves unable to keep pace with the demand for more and yet more car space. Indeed, it has become clear that a version of Parkinson's law operates and that traffic proliferates to fill the road space available. In this situation there is little doubt that the quality of life which can be enjoyed in existing town and city centers has suffered from the now familiar effects of motor traffic: noise, fumes, visual intrusion, and danger. The function which has probably been affected to the greatest degree is that of shopping, a civilized pleasure that our parents took completely for granted. No longer, in the traditional traffic-filled city-center street, is the shopper able to enjoy what is an essentially gregarious activity.

In addition, because of the proliferation of motor vehicles in the confined spaces and streets of city centers, restrictive measures have to be taken by the highway authorities, usually under pressure, to improve the flow of traffic. These measures inevitably must include restrictions on curbside parking and usually have the effect of reducing untrammeled access to the city or town center. In turn this has, in many places, the effect of inhibiting to some extent the commercial efficiency of shops and other business activities. Coupled with the increasingly unpleasant environmental conditions in traffic-dominated city centers, there is little doubt that this spelled potential decline in many central areas and helped to promote the idea of the out-of-town center, especially in North America. It was argued that the basic requirements for shopping, convenience, safety, efficiency, and good environment could best be met by the development of shopping centers well away from traffic-congested areas but easily accessible by an affluent motor-borne society. There is no doubt that the suburban center, with its virtually unlimited land area, gave the designer the opportunity to produce a theoretically perfect solution. Car parking on a gigantic scale and increasingly sophisticated design principles, giving excellent conditions for shopping, combined to assure the commercial success of the more advanced North American examples. Use of the department store and the supermarket as shopping generators, simple but civilized layouts, and—latterly—the creation of air-conditioned, enclosed malls with surface car parking at the perimeter have become practically standard practice.

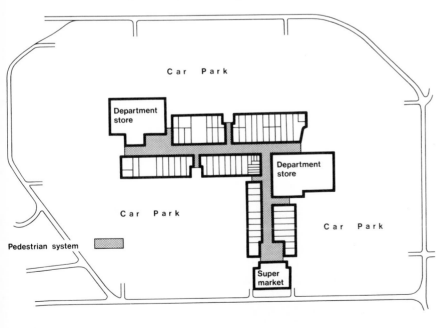

Yorkdale Shopping Centre near Toronto, Canada. A development of the early 1960s, Yorkdale has an enclosed mall configuration with three major shopping magnets. The total area of building covers about 20 acres (8.10 hectares) and the car park area some 60 acres (24.30 hectares).

The development of large and successful out-of-town and suburban centers had a very damaging effect on traditional downtown shopping areas and, indeed, in many North American cities this induced decline forced the authorities into major and expensive redevelopment schemes intended to improve the attractiveness of their central areas by providing a better environment for the pedestrian and easier access, latterly by the installation of sophisticated public transport systems.

In Britain, in particular, the development of new shopping areas has generally followed more conservative lines, due in part to the usually more limited opportunities for large-scale development or redevelopment. A significant exception has been, however, the New Towns, and in particular the New Town of Stevenage (L. G. Vincent, architect/planner). Owing a great deal to the influence of the Lijnbaan Centre in Rotterdam (Bakema & Broek), and the Coventry city center (Gibson & Ling), the precinct at Stevenage successfully exploited the idea of a relatively intimate and compact shopping area of simple repetitive design facing inward onto foot streets and pedestrian squares. Shopping became safe and pleasant; the center became a meeting place for the town. Car parking and servicing are placed

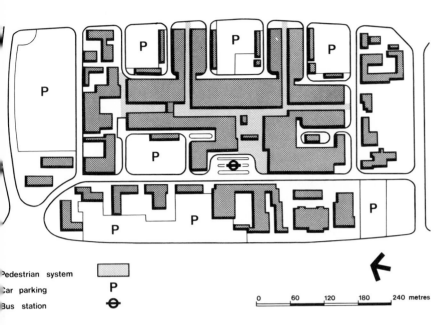

Pedestrian system

Car parking   P

Bus station

0   60   120   180   240 metres

Stevenage Town Centre. Stevenage was the first of the British New Towns to have an exclusively pedestrian center.

behind the shops, and probably the only environmental disadvantage of the town center occurs through this arrangement in that the main pedestrian approach to the shops is via these parking and servicing areas, traditionally somewhat untidy and depressing.

The Stevenage town center has, however, set new and very high standards for a traffic-free town center, and there is little doubt that it is in many ways responsible for the fact that pedestrian/vehicle segregation is by now usually standard practice.

A unique approach to shopping-center design has occurred in Cumbernauld New Town, near Glasgow, where the town center has been designed virtually as one building complex. Spanning the main central-spine road and the main car-park area, the enclosed town center at first-floor level (second-floor for North American readers) is approached by pedestrian bridges and ramps from the surrounding housing areas and by escalator, elevator, and staircase from the car parks. Servicing to the shops takes place at mezzanine levels with town-center maisonettes and flats placed at upper levels above the main shopping area. This approach, owing something to the abortive London County Council design for Hook New Town in 1961 by Shankland, then employed by the LCC, was conceived by Geoffrey

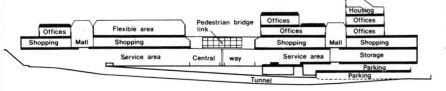

Cumbernauld New Town, Scotland. Cross section showing access, car parking, and service area with the main shopping floors linked across the town-center road.

Copcutt of the Cumbernauld team led by Hugh Wilson. It was subsequently developed by Wilson's successor, Dudley Leaker.

It seems unlikely that this comparatively elaborate model will be repeated widely; problems of economy and flexibility would seem to imply that New Town and redevelopment centers will remain predominantly monolevel designs, although the trend toward enclosing shopping areas will probably continue.

The painful North American experience whereby the development of out-of-town centers has led to the dereliction and redevelopment of traditional downtown shopping areas—was carefully studied in Europe in the 1950s, particularly in West Germany. It was felt that it would be unlikely that whole city centers could be redeveloped on the multilevel basis considered necessary to successfully separate pedestrians and vehicles in motorized central areas. The worldwide shortage of capital and the desire to retain historic buildings and picturesque districts led to an approach which is aptly described by Buchanan in *Traffic in Towns* as "environmental management." As the traditional downtown center has a complicated pattern of pedestrian and vehicle movements, overlaid with servicing problems for shops that often have rear-access facilities, a policy of traffic restraint was followed.

Essen, in West Germany, virtually the capital of the thickly populated Ruhr, demonstrates a characteristically European approach to environmental management. An important industrial center with a population of 725,000 and a regional shopping center, Essen was heavily bombed during the Second World War and lost about 85 percent of its central-area buildings. This devastating destruction allowed some reorganization of traffic routes, al-

LEFT: *Essen, West Germany. City Center Plan.* ABOVE: *Kettwiger Strasse, Essen. Semimature trees and shrub boxes help to create a civilized environment for shopping.* (*Werbegemeinschaft, Essen.*)

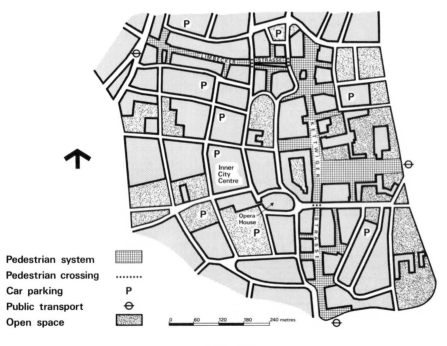

Pedestrian system
Pedestrian crossing
Car parking   P
Public transport
Open space

though the majority of the new buildings were erected in the prewar street pattern in the haste to rebuild the city.

An inner ring road circles the compact core of the city, the tramway system following its route at present. Multistory and surface car parks have been established in the four corners of the central zone with a present capacity of 8,000 car spaces and giving a maximum walk of 3 to 4 minutes to the pedestrianized shopping area. As a result of severe traffic congestion and a campaign by the Chamber of Commerce and the Werbegemeinschaft (a promotional and publicity organization), the main shopping street, Kettwiger Strasse, was closed to traffic between the hours of 10 A.M. and 7 P.M. in 1952. Although initially opposing the closure, the shopkeepers found that they soon gained increases in turnover from the improved environment of this important shopping street. The city authorities were then pressed to repave the street, which had retained the old pattern of street surface and sidewalks. Completed in 1960 and partly paid for by the shopkeepers on a street-frontage basis, the paving of Kettwiger Strasse also included landscaping with shrubs and semimature trees, showcases for rental, and seats donated by individual organizations and by the city authorities. The project also encouraged sidewalk cafes, and these have been provided in one or two places. Normally, servicing vehicles must clear the street by 10 A.M., but a strictly limited number of special permits allows essential vehicles (about four per day) to enter the area during the closed period.

After 7 P.M. and before 10 A.M. the following day, only service vehicles enter the street; it is not open to general traffic. A second street, Limbecker Strasse, and several smaller thoroughfares have been treated in a similar manner, but these areas already had rear service streets. There is little doubt that the exclusion of traffic in a large part of the central area has resulted in the creation of civilized conditions in the heart of the city, and this has, in turn, ensured that Essen will remain the main shopping town of the Ruhr. Thus environmental improvement is firmly equated with commercial benefit. This method of traffic restraint has become the pattern by which over 150 towns and cities in continental Europe have achieved foot streets during the last few years.

Norwich has a population of 160,000 and is in many ways one of the foremost historic cities in England. There a similar approach in environmental management, almost unique in Britain, is being conducted in order to reduce the impact of modern traffic on a sensitive city center and to improve the city's role as a regional shopping center serving a rural hinterland of nearly 500,000 people.

The interaction of traffic congestion and economic pressure threaten the very existence of the historic center. The Draft Urban Plan, produced by the Norwich City Planning Department, provides a general strategy for the next 30 years, during which car ownership will practically double—to 0.4 cars per person. It is a framework within which the city can continue to develop as a regional center while preserving its unique and historic character and enhancing the quality of everyday life for its citizens. These aims will

Norwich, England. The ring-and-loop system proposed for the city center provides for large traffic-free areas with restricted servicing periods. The creation of a foot street in London Street was the first stage in this process.

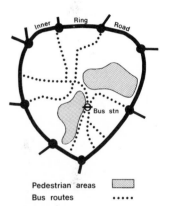

Pedestrian areas
Bus routes ·····

Routes open to all traffic
Service routes permanently open
Restricted servicing areas
Short stay car parks •

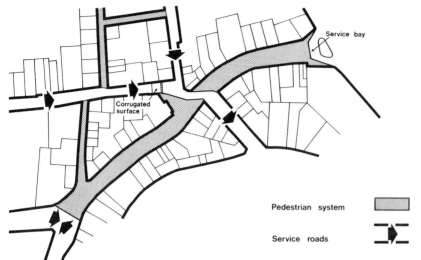

Norwich, London Street plan. The streets surrounding the converted foot street are for service traffic only and are now relatively quiet. Few of the buildings in London Street have rear-access facilities.

Service bay

Corrugated surface

Pedestrian system

Service roads

London Street, Norwich. Before July 1967, the street carried about 600 vehicles per hour. Environmental conditions were poor, there was an element of danger (see woman with stroller at left of picture), and there was evidence of some commercial decline. (City Planning Officer, Norwich.)

be met by creating a large pedestrian precinct in the central area, encouraging residential development to replace outworn industry within the old city, and by conserving the cathedral area and other historic zones. The central-area road pattern will be the ring-and-loop system. Private car penetration of the central area is confined to loop roads, not permitting cross-center movements. The loops provide access to car parks with a total ultimate provision of eight thousand short-stay spaces (forty thousand per day) to cater to shopping and business demand. Long-stay car parks are provided

London Street, Norwich. After its conversion to a foot street, the environment of London Street was improved, pedestrian traffic increased, and 30 out of 32 shops reported a considerable improvement in trading. Textured and patterned paving, seats, trees, and shrub boxes all helped to emphasize the new role of the street; it became an open-air living room. (City Planning Officer, Norwich.)

London Street, Norwich. Servicing traffic is permitted to cross London Street at one point and, in order that its speed should respect the new role of the street, a special roughened section of paving has been laid. This "sleeping policeman" effects an immediate speed reduction. (City Planning Officer, Norwich.)

outside the central area. Public transport is given one advantage in that buses can cross the city center adjacent to the traffic-free areas. The first stage in creating these areas was achieved with the closure of three streets, including London Street, in July 1967. Acting as a shortcut for traffic crossing the central area and containing some of the better shops in the city with practically no facilities for rear servicing, London Street carried about six hundred vehicles per hour.

An experimental closure took place in July 1967 and was immediately successful. Pedestrian traffic increased considerably and shopping turnover increased by up to 25 percent. Due to the particular layout of the area, the street was closed completely and servicing took place by trolleying goods from bays established at the ends and in the center. This foot street was made permanent in 1968 and was repaved early in 1969, the first shopping street in Britain of any significance to be so converted. Semimature trees, shrub boxes, seats, and an outdoor cafe have all helped to consolidate the new role of London Street.

The creation of a civilized environment for shopping is within the grasp of most towns and cities prepared to apply some element of order to traffic movement in their central areas. Convenient parking and good public transport facilities are also obvious and necessary ingredients to the widespread success of pedestrianization, but the main requirement must be the desire to improve the quality of life. Just as conservation of man's natural environment is fast becoming a matter of concern, the management of his urban environment is now a pressing problem in most of the world's cities and towns. The car must be put firmly in its place: a place not of master but of servant—a most useful and, indeed, indispensable servant. Foot streets demonstrate that this can be done now, in many places, without major alteration to the urban fabric and with immeasurable improvement to the enjoyment of part of our lives.

BIBLIOGRAPHY: London County Council, *The Planning of a New Town*, LCC, 1961; C. D. Buchanan, *Traffic in Towns*, HMSO, 1963; Paul Ritter, *Planning for Man and Motor*, Pergamon Press, New York, 1963; Institute for Center Planning, *By Center Menneske*, Danish Architects' Institute, 1965; P. H. Bendtsen, *Town & Traffic in the Motor Age*, Danish Technical Press, Copenhagen, 1967; A. A. Wood, *Foot Streets in Four Cities*, Norwich Corporation, 1967; Capital and Counties Prop Co. Ltd., *Shopping for Pleasure*, 1969; A. A. Wood, *London Street, The Creation of a Foot Street*, Norwich Corporation, 1969.   —ALFRED A. WOOD

PEPLER, Sir GEORGE LIONEL (1882–1959)   British town planner, born in Croydon. Trained as a surveyor and in practice from 1905, he was one of the first to specialize in the layout of housing estates and villages under the influence of the garden city (*q.v.*) movement. In 1914 he entered the government administration as chief technical planning officer, and he retained that position under various titles till 1946. Himself an enthusiast for town planning, he coupled administration with advocacy and had great influence in persuading local authorities and public opinion to accept it as a governmental function and to exercise planning powers, which were then largely optional. He took a leading part in developing the policy and machinery for the major Town and Country Planning Act of 1947, under which all land in Great Britain came under planning control.

Pepler was one of the founders of the Town Planning Institute in 1913; honorary secretary from then till his death; president, 1919 to 1920 and 1949 to 1950; and first goldmedallist, 1955. He was active in the International Federation for Housing and Planning (*q.v.*) from 1913, revived it (with the help of his wife) after the disruption of the 1939 to 1945 war, and served as its president from 1935 to 1938 and 1947 to 1952. He was president of the Town and Country Planning Summer School from 1943 to 1959 and a member of many government committees and national associations concerned with aspects of planning and land use. He was knighted in 1948. He prepared many local and regional plans and papers for conferences and learned societies; and though he published no books, he was a major contributor to modern international thought and practice on town planning. He died at Weymouth in 1959.   —FREDERIC J. OSBORN

PERGOLA   A passageway with a roof of trellis work on which climbing plants are trained to grow. Sometimes the trellis roof is channel-shaped.

PERRET, AUGUSTE (1874–1955)   Architect, engineer, and planner. Born in Brussels, he had his first architectural training at the École des Beaux-Arts in Paris, which he left before completing his examinations. He was one of the first architects to realize the potentialities of ferroconcrete. His apartment block (1903) in the Rue Franklin in Paris was an astonishing building for its time and represented a highly significant departure from traditional building methods.

The warehouses at Casablanca (1915), steel workshops at Montataire (1920), and aircraft hangars at Marseilles (1950) are considered to be the most free expressions of Perret's structural genius. His early interest in the standardization and industrialization of building components has been of considerable influence, and he will also be remembered as the sometime mentor of Le Corbusier.

As a town planner, Perret's significant contribution was the reconstruction of Le Havre after its destruction in World War II. He replanned this town on monumental lines, using reinforced concrete extensively and drawing on all his experience of the past. The result, unsoftened by compromise, has a grandeur and hugeness which, while difficult to appreciate, is yet impressive. When the trees have grown and the place becomes more venerable, it will be interesting to see whether it will become merely shoddy or if it will take on the patina of grace, mellowness, and solid, lived-in urbanity of towns of the past. It is of interest to compare the plan of Le Havre with that of the Cité Industrielle (1901–1904) by Tony Garnier. Le Havre possesses a classical spirit despite its rather crudely cubic appearance, and the strong axes of the French masters of the baroque are detectable in Perret's work. Perret was clearly seeking after balance, symmetry, and order to redress the tendency to anarchic informalism. Strongly axial plans express a longing for order and reason, and it is not surprising that Le Havre was built in unstable postwar France by an old and experienced architect.

Perret, like Le Corbusier, was essentially a classicist in his work as a town planner. The strong axes and the monumentality reveal a search after permanence in a world of shifting tides. Some would regard this formal approach and monumentality as being the antithesis of what society needs, namely, impermanent structures for easy change. However, man needs

Pergola in a British military cemetery, southern Ital.

recognizable objects in his environment which are permanent and which make a strong impact on the memory. Perret tried to give to the modern town this strong imagery and recognizable form and to bring back to town planning something of the classic calm and poise of the past. Time will tell just how successful he was.

BIBLIOGRAPHY: Paul Jamot, *A. et G. Perret et l'architecture du béton armé*, Paris and Brussels, 1927; E. Rogers, *Auguste Perret*, Il Balcone, Milan, 1955; Gerd Hatje (ed.), *Encyclopaedia of Modern Architecture*, Thames and Hudson, London, 1963. —JAMES STEVENS CURL

PERSPECTIVE RENDERINGS   A perspective rendering of an object, a building, or of an imagined urban scene is one drawn in accordance with strict mathematical principles which take into account the apparent reduction in size of an object as the distance between it and the observer increases. Although a pictorial representation which is almost photographic in effect can be achieved, distortion does result if, for example, too wide an angle of vision is selected. The angle between the left and right extremities of the subject should not exceed 60 degrees. A greater angle, that is, the selection of too close a viewpoint, will cause too sharp a convergence of the parallel edges of the subject; while a narrower angle, that is, too distant a viewpoint, will give a dull, flat result. The impression will also be distorted

Perspective of a scheme for flatted factories. (By Johannes Schreiner, Dipl. Arch., F.R.I.B.A.) Perspectives simulating oblique aerial views are excellent for illustrating planning schemes as this and the perspectives shown on pages 807 and 808 demonstrate.

An imagined redevelopment of an old urban area seen from the air. (By Johannes Schreiner, Dipl. Arch., F.R.I.B.A.)

if the vertical angle between the eye level and the highest point of the subject or between eye level and the lowest point exceeds 45 degrees.

If the observer's eye level is taken to be coincident with the ground level of the subject, say a building, that ground level will appear as a straight line on the drawing. In the more usual level view, the eye is taken to be 5 feet 6 inches (1.67 meters) above ground, in which case the ground-level line of the building will appear to recede on the drawing, that is, to converge with the roof lines. The eye level selected may be below the ground level of the building or above the roof level, in which case all three sets of dimensions will be shown to converge. This is called a "three-point perspective," each set of parallel edges when extended meeting at what is called

Aerial view of a scheme by Johannes Schreiner for a world university situated on the coast.

a "vanishing point." Most commonly, perspectives are "two point," the verticals being taken to be normal to the line of vision that is parallel to the plane of the drawing. "One-point" perspectives are sometimes used, for instance, to illustrate a street facade receding from the viewpoint of the observer.

Taking the example of a two-point perspective, the first stage is the drawing of a plan, and this and the marking of heights from the ground line on the drawing—along what is called the "height line"—are the only scaled measurements of the subject used.

The selection of a viewpoint follows. This should avoid distortion effects and ensure that the finished drawing is well composed and illustrates the features required to be shown. Normally, one facade of a building is emphasized, and then the nearest angle of the building will be well to one side of the "line of vision" which runs from the viewpoint bisecting the angle of vision. Poor composition usually results if the nearest corner is on the line of vision.

The next important stage is the drawing of a "picture plane" at right angles to the line of vision and arranged on the paper in relation to the plan according to the size of perspective view desired. On this line vanishing points are found by drawing lines from the viewpoint parallel to the sides of the plan. The eye-level line and ground lines are then drawn parallel to the picture plane and the positions of vertical features are found by projection to the picture plane line and thence to the ground line. The scaled dimensions on the height line and connections thereto radiating from the vanishing points, enable the perspective view to be built up.

The completed perspective view can be transferred to a separate sheet and then rendered with color washes or monochrome treatment and embellished with other detail to complete the artistic or photographic effect desired.
                                                                    —H. E. SPARROW

PHILIPPINES   (*See* ASIA, SOUTHEAST, DEVELOPING COUNTRIES.)

PHILOSOPHIES OF PLANNING   (*See* THEORIES AND IDEALS OF PLANNING.)

PHOTOGRAPHY AND ITS USE IN URBAN AND REGIONAL PLANNING   The usefulness of photography as a planning tool has been underestimated in town planning textbooks. This technique should not be used only once, during aerial surveys, but also at two other stages in the planning process. If this process is defined as an integrative one, then it may not only be described as cyclical but may be divided roughly into four main phases:
  1. The preparatory process
  2. The basic planning design process
  3. The design development and realization process
  4. The feedback and restart process
Photography in its various forms is relevant to the three latter phases.

Because it is a visual technique, photography is subject to obvious and inherent constraints. The use of photography may be crudely separated into those areas where *objectivity* may be achieved as opposed to those where *subjectivity* may dominate. The simple and direct technical recording of geographical locations at one point in time is achieved in accurate aerial photography. Given the scientific safeguard of limited spatial parameters, this may give a high degree of objective and accurate representation. However, in selective eye-level still photography and in television, subjectivity is likely to be more marked. The intended or incidental bias of the photographer may give rise to widely differing interpretations of extractions from the observed world. Photography may thus be seen as a tool that offers a range which extends from the scientific recording of information through to techniques with markedly artistic, subjective, and interpretive elements.

The aim of this article is to define, summarily, some of these photographic techniques in relation to such factors as well as to the various stages in the planning process.

Aerial Photography The best-established technical use of photography in relation to planning, especially in the developing countries, is in the field of aerial photography. The primary uses of this field are for the aerial survey of regions and of extensive sites, for purposes of mapmaking, land classification, data recording, and interpretation for selected criteria. Work may be either to survey existing physical situations or it may be policy-oriented, selecting areas and features for conservation or amelioration or areas and resources suitable for development. Lewis Keeble usefully differentiates four categories:

1. *Aerial verticals,* which give paired overlapping shots that show three-dimensional relief when read together through a stereoscope.

2. *Aerial mosaics,* which are based on a series of fixed runs and printed out in relation to a series of coordinates, such as the National Grid Squares in Britain.

3. *Oblique aerials,* which give panoramic views or aerial shots of specific urban or rural sites in a way that is more readily understood by laymen.

4. *Anaglyphs,* which are obtained from a little-used color stereoscopic technique of overlapping blue and red photographs of the same area. The increasing use of anaglyphs is commended by Keeble.

The accuracy of the first two techniques is high. With supplementary ground-pegging aids, verticals may give contour intervals of 10 or 20 feet (3 or 6 meters) generally, but in a survey of delta areas in Pakistan (with little variation of site level) an accuracy of up to 5-foot (1.5-meter) intervals has been recorded. The use of aerial surveys in planning has increased notably since 1950. An impressive example is the work done at Brasília. There, Donald Belcher and Associates of Ithaca, New York, in association with Geotecnica and Geocarga of Brazil, carried out exhaustive aerial site surveys and analyses in connection with the location of the new capital city. Aspects covered by the study included topography, water supply, forest location, building material sources, hydraulic power potential, nature of subsoil, and character of scenery. Site work supplemented the basic aerial studies.

Aerial Archaeology In North Africa, Central America, and the Near East, much work has been done in the field of archaeological interpretation from aerial photography—slight traces that are not apparent on the ground often being definable from the air. Such work is not only of great academic interest but may have considerable practical planning significance for:

1. Aiding the discovery, exploration, and uncovering of major historic sites of cultural importance and interest to tourists

2. Defining such areas and aiding their conservation and protection against inadvertent and inappropriate development

Aerial mosaic of a north Italian town.

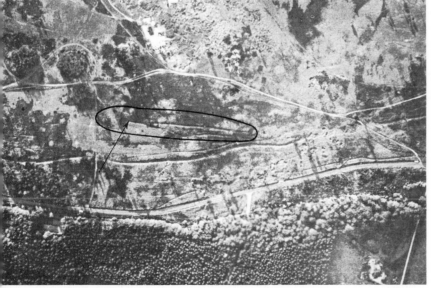

Aerial view of Ashdown Forest, Sussex, England. An example of how a Roman road was discovered by aerial photography. The road is almost parallel with the modern road. The photograph reveals a road of triple form, the central part—18 feet wide—raised and metaled, with side space left unmetaled. The thick dark mark which straggles across the Roman road is a medieval hollow way worn as much as 6 feet deep in places by the passage of pack-horse traffic. It obliterates part of the Roman road. (Aerofilms and Aero Pictorial, Ltd.)

An oblique air view from the sea of Kemp Town, Brighton, which gives an excellent three-dimensional impression—the plan and elevations both being clearly defined. (Aerofilms, Ltd.)

3. Helping the process of regional development by indicating past and present water resources, preferred site climate, and local soils advantages—based on ancient testing of areas by nomadic populations prior to choosing sites for early urban settlements

Infra-red Photography At the other end of the time scale, the space program and defense investments of the United States are producing some very helpful by-products. Infra-red air photography has been used primarily for military purposes. Its civil uses include differentiation of natural and man-made elements, definition of stages of building in a process of urbanization, estimating the extent of blight affecting economic crops in agricultural resource regions, or recording the spread of pollutants in water or on land. Geological mapping from the air may be aided by infra-red photography. The potential of this wide field of study has yet to be assessed.

An oblique air view of the center of the New Town of Hemel Hempstead. (Aerofilms, Ltd.)

Black-and-white Still Photography In comparison, there is already a wide range of apparent uses for black-and-white still photography in planning, and this includes:

1. *Purposive surveys* of physically extensive areas or indicative studies of physical, social, or economic conditions complementing statistical data surveys. Additionally, special factors, such as peak-hour traffic conditions or conflicts between vehicular and pedestrian movements, can be explained best in photographs when needed for committee or general publication purposes.

2. *Environmental records* of an exact nature, recording detailed architectural and/or landscape character, become increasingly important as the international movement for urban (as well as rural) conservation grows. The 1969

to 1970 Comprehensive Photographic Survey of the buildings in the New Town of Edinburgh is a good example of this use of photography.

3. *Special studies*—for example, on the social use of outdoor pedestrian areas in towns (such as the studies by Jan Gael of the Stroget in Copenhagen)—can be extended and sped up if photographs of pedestrian distributions are taken from rooftop level. The effects of factors such as weather and time of day may be added by the use of time-lapse photography.

4. *Time-lapse photography,* a technique whereby photographs of the same object, location, or area are taken automatically at fixed time intervals. It is well established as a method in relation to subjects concerned with growth and change (e.g., biology, horticulture, etc.), but its application to town planning is in its infancy. Its use would be a natural development of the field of progress photography, a technique used frequently to record the phased development of building sites on the scale of housing quarters, university campuses, etc. Progress photography in aerial coverage is a useful monitoring system on the rate and impact of new development, site infilling, and progress of redevelopment.

5. *Emergency planning.* Another field of application is where sudden calamities—such as an earthquake, blitz, tidal wave, or hurricane—have occurred and rapid overall appraisal from the ground or the air is needed. In such circumstances, photographic reconnaissance is one of the accepted tools of emergency physical planning.

6. *Multiple-alternative planning.* In the preparation of urban structure plans, photography may help to speed up the work process. If, for instance, alternative system trajectories are to be modeled, as suggested by McLoughlin, then one quick means of recording physical alternatives is the rapid photographing of a series of manually adjusted locations of fixed-quantity units of land use on base maps. A more sophisticated development of such techniques is the linking of a computerized planning data bank to a cathode ray tube, as undertaken in the model program for New Town development at University College, London.

Color Still Photography This can be expensive, but the extra costs may be justified in terms of savings in time and labor costs in some studies. To take one example in the developing field of recreation resource planning analyses, important low-level aerial photographic work may be done with the use of helicopters. A good control situation may be achieved, almost at one point in time and with other constants, when relative densities of recreation use on beaches and on selected stretches of countryside may be plotted in color, relating this to the extent of land resource and the mapped ease or difficulty of site access. Color greatly sharpens the definition in such cases.

Motion Picture and Television Photography This may be used in several stages of the planning process. First, in relation to townscape and route-design analysis, the preliminary work in Britain and America to date (i.e., Cullen, Nairn, Lynch, Appleyard) is concerned with the sensory responses of the moving observer and has been illustrated by static means. Traffic engineering departments (e.g., that at Birmingham University, England) already use, as a design aid, mounted mobile cameras for alternative test runs of possible highway routes on scaled models of landscapes. In traffic management, television control systems are widely used. Analogously, motion picture photography could be used as a planning technique of mobile design and management as well as of analyses.

Conventional film making for the cinema is geared to specific types of audience. The making of planning films and the demonstration and explanation of environmental problems and possibilities is a growing activity of national government information services in many countries as well as of specific planning agencies. Special sessions of film juries of the Council of Cultural Co-operation of the Council of Europe and the preparation of planning film catalogs by bodies like the Royal Town Planning Institute in England are indicative of this changing emphasis.

As opposed to film making for publicity or one-way information transfer, the growth of the international movement for public participation in planning—or two-way communication—and the idea exchange on planning matters provides a great challenge not only to motion picture production but for television, reaching as it does into so many homes, schools, workplaces, etc. Goals programs in the United States and public participation reports in Britain now need much more sophisticated use of motion pictures and television.

The potential planning use of many other forms of photography, not even discussed, is considerable. In terms of current professional practice and town planning education, we are only now starting to view these wide and distant horizons.

BIBLIOGRAPHY: Jan Gael, *Stroget;* Max Gruenwald and Cia Impressora Ipsis., *Brasília—* E. A. Gutkind, *Our World from the Air,* Chatto & Windus, Ltd., London, 1952; American Society of Photogrammetry, *Manual of Photogrammetry,* 2d ed., Washington, D.C., 1952; *Historia, Urbanismo, Arquitetura, Construcao,* Uma Edicao Acropole, pp. 256–257, 1960; Kevin Lynch, *Image of the City,* M.I.T. Press, Cambridge, Mass., 1960; G. Cullen, *Townscape,* The Architectural Press, 1961; Kevin Lynch and D. Appleyard, *View from the Road,* M.I.T. Press, Cambridge, Mass., 1964; *Town Planning Institute Film Catalogue,* London, 1966; Council for Cultural Co-operation, Council of Europe, *Report on Viewing and Selection of Films on the Cultural Theme "Historic Towns: Future Planning Schemes,"* Strasbourg, November 1969; Lewis Keeble, *Principles and Practice of Town and Country Planning,* 4th ed., The Estates Gazette Ltd., London, 1969; Ministry of Housing and Local Government et al., Skeffington Report, *People and Planning,* HMSO, London, 1969; Anthony S. Travis, "Ends and Means: Planning for a Changing Society," *Town Planning Review,* vol. 40, no. 2, July 1969; *Edinburgh New Town Survey,* 1969–1970; J. Kozlowski, *Towards an Integrated Planning Process,* Report of the Edinburgh Conference on Analytical Techniques in the Urban and Regional Planning Process: Threshold Analysis, Optimisation, Planning Research Unit, Edinburgh, May 1970.

—ANTHONY S. TRAVIS

PIAZZA   (*See* PLACE.)

PICTURESQUE   An urban or rural scene that possesses the features or materials for an attractive picture may be called "picturesque." The picturesque is a subjective creation and is composed by the percipient, who selects from his surroundings a scene which in his mind would make a good picture. The selection, which is sometimes partly subconscious, is often based on the rectangle because of the influence of the customary picture shape.

The formal relations that make a good composition in a painting are different from those that make a good urban design. This is because, in the former, the masses are translated to a flat surface, whereas in urban design the masses are three-dimensional and emanate largely from a plan. Thus the picturesque is more often the result of accidental effects than of pre-meditated design. Indeed, scenes both urban and rural are often considered to be increasingly picturesque when the effects of time are apparent and when there are elements of decay.[1] Ruins are often very picturesque, especially when they are partly overgrown, as some of the water colors of Turner make apparent. The contribution of the accidental to the picturesque provides an argument for those who believe that urban design should be given the utmost freedom and should not be subject to any rigid aesthetic control. (*See also* AESTHETICS.)

PIECEMEAL DEVELOPMENT   Development that has taken place in a haphazard or sporadic fashion in small, unrelated areas. Piecemeal development is, in a sense, the opposite of comprehensive development except that, in addition to being carried out in small quantities, the usage commonly implies that it is visually as well as physically unrelated to its surroundings.

Although piecemeal development is most often the result of a *lack* of planning, it can also occur where development plans have been prepared and there is a system for the control of development but where that control is weak. It can occur in the form of mixed or single land uses. The ribbons of service stations, motels, restaurants, and used-car lots on the approach roads to many towns in the United States are examples of piecemeal development in mixed uses.

Piecemeal development in single uses is often exemplified by small areas of housing, on the fringe of a town, jutting out into the surrounding agricultural land and often conforming to the former field boundaries.

—DAVID HALL

PIPELINE TRANSPORT   Among the systems of transport that are likely to be developed further in the future and of which the planner should take full consideration is a system of piping. Such systems are already employed extensively in the United States and Europe for the conveyance of water, oil, and gas; while coal, mineral ores, and lime are also pumped as slurries. Although the transport of food and other goods in long, torpedo-shaped containers carried by liquids in pipes is still in the experimental stage, there are prospects of considerable developments.

A pipeline system for countries, and ultimately for the whole world on a basis of international cooperation, has been likened to the circulatory system of arteries and veins in the human body. These blood vessels are

[1] See Sir Uvedale Price, *Essays in the Picturesque,* 1794.

under cover and, in the healthy body, function imperceptibly, and essential goods could be transported by an elaborate pipeline system with little disturbance of the surface other than at assembly and distribution points. Such a system, once installed, would have considerable advantages over other methods, especially over heavy long-distance transport by road.

PLACE   The term is derived from the Greek πλατύs, meaning "flat, wide, broad," and came to be applied in France as denoting any extensive urban space of whatever shape, including a very broad street. The term is also used in Britain, together with "square" and "circus." In Italy it is called *piazza;* in Spain, *plaza;* in Germany, *platz;* in Sweden, *plats;* in the Netherlands, *plaats;* in Denmark, *plads;* and in Portugal, *praca.* Some planners consider that it would be an advantage if one term were used internationally, and several planners in the United States prefer the Spanish *plaza.*

PLACE, SENSE OF   The sense of place is a widely shared personal, subjective experience that has become, to some extent, a minor purpose among some planners. The recollection of a particularly agreeable place in the urban scene, which is treasured in memory and to which there is a desire to return, partially describes it. The experience can be likened to the recollection of a passage of music which gives particular pleasure and arouses a wish to hear it again. The creation of such places can become a conscious purpose in planning, involving a study of the elements that compose them; but as these elements are so often accidental and mingled with time and the picturesque, they tend to elude analysis. Examples of such places are the intimate Italian piazza enclosed by a time-softened stately architecture, or an English village green surrounded by picturesque cottages and elm trees, pub and church. Efforts have been made in the layout of modern housing estates to inculcate something of the charm of the latter with varying results. Progressive architects and planners consider that such pleasing effect can be created in the modern idioms of construction, and the old examples are valuable in giving ideas of massing and spacing and the particular formal relations which characterize them. Some modern *Platzen* in the rebuilt centers of German cities succeed, for some people, in providing aesthetic, pleasurable recollections. (*See also* AESTHETICS.)   —ARNOLD WHITTICK

PLANNING INQUIRY (BRITISH)   A form of tribunal where evidence is heard by an appointed inspector or inspectors who report and assess the merits of a dispute between a public authority and a private person or persons. The inspector may have the power to give a decision or may be empowered only to recommend a course of action to the appropriate minister of central government. Planning inquiries are held in connection with compulsory purchase of land, objections to a development plan, designation order of a site for a New Town or, more commonly, an appeal to the Minister of Housing and Local Government against an adverse planning decision or failure by a local planning authority to reach a decision in respect of a planning application.

Disputed planning decisions comprise appeals against the following: a refusal of permission for development or an onerous planning condition, a tree preservation order, failure to grant a consent for alterations or demolition of a building of architectural merit, or refusal to consent to an application to display an advertisement.

Specific rules (planning inquiry rules) have been formulated to ensure that proceedings are fair and impartial. After lodging an appeal, an appellant is entitled to be supplied with a statement amplifying the local planning authority's decision and all plans and documents placed on public deposit for inspection. The public are notified by advertisement on the site. At least 42 days' notice of the inquiry must be given to the appellant and other persons directly affected. The following persons may be heard at the inquiry:

1. The appellant (may be legally represented)

2. The local planning authority (represented by legal and technical officers)

3. Landowners, agricultural tenants, members of the public who may object or support the proposal

The appellant has the right to begin and finally reply after evidence has been given by the other parties. The site may be inspected either before or after the inquiry, but an inspection is obligatory and the parties most concerned with the proposal are entitled to be present. In many cases the inspector is enabled to decide the case himself and his decision is communicated to all parties in writing. In major cases the inspector reports with a recommendation to the minister, who then decides. Generally, if the appellant or other parties are aggrieved by the decision of the inspector or the minister, there is no other form of appeal except on a point of law to the High Court. The procedure in respect of other types of inquiry is similar but in many cases less formal. The public inquiry system is an established feature of the British planning system and has a high reputation for impartiality. As planning matters are mainly determined by the local elected representative, a central government inspector is accepted as an impartial arbitrator who is technically qualified to assess the facts. Only a small proportion of adverse planning decisions are pressed to appeal.

Planning Inquiry Commission   The Town and Country Planning Act of 1971 has empowered the central government to set up an inquiry commission for development which raises questions of national or regional importance, e.g., international airports or nuclear power stations. The inspector, in such cases, will be replaced by a team of investigators. An inquiry must be held by the assessors and a report and recommendation made to a minister of central government.   —L. W. A. RENDELL

PLANS, PREPARATION OF   In the process of preparing a comprehensive or general plan, certain basic steps are normally followed regardless of the geographic scale of the project. These steps include (1) designing the planning process; (2) establishing goals and objectives; (3) data collection, analysis and forecasting; and (4) plan formulation. The particular elements included in the process, the depth of research and detail undertaken, and the form of the final plans vary considerably depending on whether one is concerned with a neighborhood, city, county, region, or state.

Changing Scope of the Plan   In the United States, the process of plan preparation and the form of the plan itself have been much influenced by the federal government's urban planning assistance program originally authorized by the United States Housing Act of 1954. The guidelines established by the Department of Housing and Urban Development (HUD) and its predecessor, the Housing and Home Finance Agency, have significantly determined the form and content of the comprehensive plans of thousands of cities and towns in the United States. The plans under this program have been basically physical or land-use plans. The major element of the plan document is a map variously called "land-use plan," "comprehensive plan," or "master plan."

Recently, especially in some of the larger cities, comprehensive plans have begun to emphasize social, economic, and environmental factors. Therefore, the studies and background reports which precede preparation of the plan have varied from the more traditional form. While planners continue to inventory and to analyze the physical characteristics of the community, some recently published plans discuss the nature and incidence of poverty, the provision of health care, air and water pollution, preservation of the natural environment, housing conditions, racial and ethnic characteristics, child care services, and crime prevention, among others. Revised HUD guidelines also reflect the changing scope of the plan.

Process of Plan Preparation

Work Programming   A schedule of the steps to be followed is the first step in the planning process. The schedule, or work program (sometimes called "the plan for planning"), describes the sequence of steps, the time limit within which each is to be completed, the product of each step, and the staff and other resources required. Flow diagrams are often used to illustrate the sequence to be followed and to ensure that all essential elements are included. Some planning agencies have attempted to refine further this process by utilizing such techniques as Program Evaluation and Review Technique (PERT) or Critical Path Method (CPM) [1] (see illustration). The key element of these devices is the network diagram which permits the agency to maintain greater control over the individual components. Such control becomes particularly important when computers are used to test and evaluate alternative land-use and transportation plans.

Formulating Goals   The second phase in the plan preparation process is the establishment of goals, objectives, and policies of the plan. The inclusion

---

[1] K. G. Lockyer, *An Introduction to Critical Path Analysis,* Sir Isaac Pitman & Sons, Ltd., London, 1964.

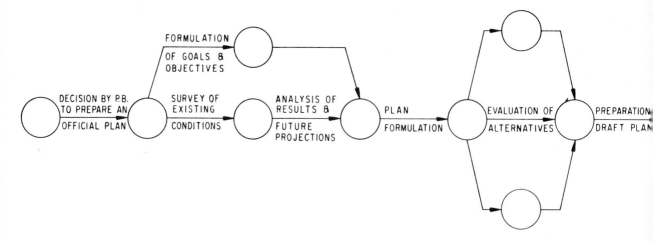

of this phase is a relatively recent development; most plans completed as recently as 10 years ago omitted any mention of the underlying goals upon which the plan was based.[1] Recently, however, goals and policies have been included in increasing numbers of plans. Some cities have produced so-called "policies plans," which are collections of specific objectives, generally in text rather than in map form. Those produced for the city of Chicago[2] and the Twin Cities area of Minnesota[3] are examples. In some communities, the policies plan has replaced the more traditional comprehensive plan. Formulating goals and policies can take many forms, but most communities have used this phase as an opportunity to elicit the assistance of lay citizens' groups in the planning process. Among cities in which such groups have been formed are Dallas, Texas; Tucson, Arizona; and San Jose, California.[4]

Data Collection, Analysis, and Forecasting Following the goals formulation phase, or concurrent with it, is the collection and analysis of data about the area. The result of this phase is a description of conditions as they currently exist in the form of text, maps, charts, tables, and other illustrations normally included in the final plan document. While it is not universally accepted, F. Stuart Chapin, in his *Urban Land Use Planning*, suggests a possible framework for organizing the collection and analysis of data on existing conditions for land-use planning under the following headings: the urban economy, employment studies, population studies, the study of urban activity systems, urban land studies, transportation, and land use. Social welfare studies are more frequently being added to this list. While

[1] Formulating community goals as part of the comprehensive planning process was recommended as early as the 1930s by the U.S. National Resources Planning Board and in 1943 in *Action for Cities* (see bibliography).

[2] *Basic Policies for the Comprehensive Plan of Chicago,* The Department of City Planning, Chicago, 1964.

[3] *Twin Cities Area Metropolitan Development Guide,* Report no. 5, The Joint Program, St. Paul, Minnesota, 1968.

[4] Franklyn H. Beal, "Defining Development Objectives," in Goodman and Freund, pp. 327–348 (see bibliography).

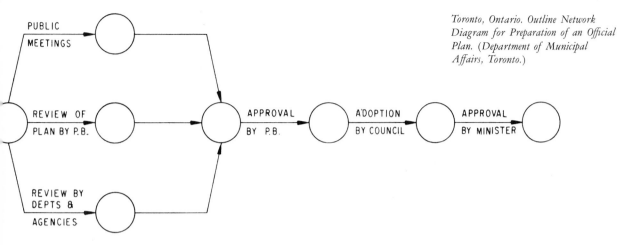

Toronto, Ontario. Outline Network Diagram for Preparation of an Official Plan. (Department of Municipal Affairs, Toronto.)

this framework is applied most readily to the preparation of plans for urban areas, it can be modified somewhat to fit the special needs of both smaller and larger areas.

Economic Studies. Urban-area economic studies include collection and analysis of data on the production, distribution, and consumption systems, including not only manufacturing, agriculture, and extraction of earth products but also trade, finance, transport, government, and other services.[1] Input-output or economic base analysis aids in understanding the economic systems in the urban area, to assist in evaluating the strength of the economy, and to forecast future activity. A forecast of future economic activity provides a foundation on which to base forecasts of future employment and population. Employment studies also provide data for estimating land requirements for industry and commerce.

Population Studies. These are divided into two parts: (1) estimates of the current population and (2) forecasts of future population. In most countries, the periodic census provides an accurate count of the number and characteristics of the population and a basis for estimating the population between census years. Such estimates are made by calculating births and deaths and in and out migration (called "fertility, mortality, and mobility").

Accurate forecasts of future populations necessitate making assumptions about characteristics of the area. Since these assumptions are necessarily judgmental—even though based on detailed knowledge—population projections are never truly "scientific." Perhaps the most satisfactory forecast technique is the "cohort survival method" which, in its simplest form, adjusts the figures from the previous census forward by age and sex groups by 5- or 10-year periods. As additional variables are introduced, this method becomes highly complex and, for large areas, requires the use of computers. Other methods include the migration and natural increase method, proration

[1]Wilbur R. Thompson, *A Preface to Urban Economics,* The Johns Hopkins Press, Baltimore, 1965.

of forecasts for larger areas, estimates based on employment forecasts, and various mathematical and graphic methods.[1]

Urban Activity Systems Studies. The introduction of studies of activity systems is an attempt at applying some of the techniques of the behavioral sciences into the planning process. Activity systems, as defined by Chapin, are the "behavior patterns of individuals, families, institutions, and firms which occur in spatial patterns. . . ."[2] Since such studies describe how the elements of these components relate to each other and to the other components, they require a knowledge of the activities of individuals and families (e.g., shopping, child-raising, recreation), institutions (e.g., education, police protection, health services), and firms (e.g., processing, distribution, services), and their interrelationships. A basic understanding of these systems helps to determine the spatial distribution and arrangement of physical facilities; the kinds of social, health, religious, and other services needed in different locations; and special programs which may have to be devised to meet the needs of particular individuals, families, groups, institutions, or firms.

Land-use Studies. Depending on geographic area, the land-use studies could include some or all of the following: physiographic features, geology, climatology; existing land use; suitability of vacant land; hydrology and flood potential; structural and environmental quality; land value; and aesthetics. The land-use survey may be quite general, using only four or five categories, or highly specific, with hundreds of different categories[3] (see illustration). Conducting the survey is a detailed and exacting chore which usually requires extensive field investigation. However, high-resolution aerial photographs analyzed by trained interpreters can minimize the amount of fieldwork with little loss in accuracy.

Included within the survey of structural and environmental quality are detailed investigations of housing conditions. The United States government now requires a housing element as part of the comprehensive plan, with particular attention paid to the needs of low-income and minority groups.

Transportation Studies. Also part of this phase is the transportation study, with particular attention to its land-use relationships. Such studies usually include an origin and destination survey to provide data on the traffic generation rates of different land uses, evaluation of capacities of each part of the transportation system, and existing transportation deficiencies. Transportation studies in the United States normally are conducted by metropolitan or regional agencies.[4]

Social Welfare Studies. With planners' concerns having been broadened in recent years to include social as well as physical and economic factors in planning, many planning agencies are making social welfare studies. Such

[1] See Chapin, *Urban Land Use Planning*, pp. 181–220; Henry Hightower, "Population Studies," in Goodman and Freund, pp. 51–75 (see bibliography).

[2] F. Stuart Chapin, *Urban Land Use Planning*, p. 224 (see bibliography).

[3] *Standard Land Use Coding Manual*, Urban Renewal Administration, Housing and Home Finance Agency and Bureau of Public Roads, U.S. Department of Commerce, 1965.

[4] Roger L. Creighton, *Urban Transportation Planning*, University of Illinois Press, Urbana, Ill., 1970.

Figure 3.—Example: Describing and Coding Activities

Standard Land Use Coding Manual, 1965. (Urban Renewal Administration, Housing and Home Finance Agency, and Bureau of Public Roads, U.S. Department of Commerce, pp. 20–21.)

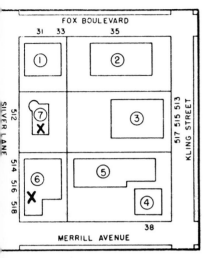

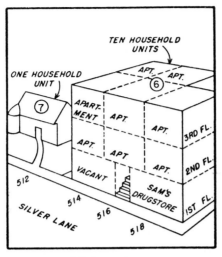

A—Block **Plan**   3B—Parcel **Schematic**

No.	Street Name	Building No.	Floor	Description of Activity	Auxiliary?	Activity Ownership	Residential Structure Type	No. of Household Units	Activity Code	Auxiliary Code	Ownership Code	Structure Code	No. of Household Units
1	2	3	4	5	6	7	8	9	5'	6'	7'	8'	9'
18	SILVER LANE	6	1	SAM'S DRUG STORE	—	PRIVATE	—	—	5910	0	20	—	—
16	SILVER LANE	6	2,3	HOUSEHOLD UNITS	—	PRIVATE	WALK-UP APART.	10	1100	0	20	31	10
14	SILVER LANE	6	1	VACANT FLOOR AREA	—	—	.	—	9400	0	—	—	—
12	SILVER LANE	7	1	HOUSEHOLD UNITS	—	PRIVATE	SINGLE UNIT—DETACHED	1	1100	0	20	11	01

3C—Example of Land Use Entries on a Field Listing **Form**

studies may include social pathology indices based on health, education, standard of living, crime and delinquency, family structure, and other elements. Analyses of these indices suggest areas of the planning district in need of greatest attention by public and private agencies.[1]

[1] Bernard J. Frieden and Robert Morris (eds.), *Urban Planning and Social Policy,* Basic Books, Inc., New York, 1968.

Ecological Studies. With increasing attention being given to environmental quality, some planning organizations, especially on the metropolitan-area level, are preparing ecological studies. These include not only environmental studies of forests, surface and subsurface water, marshlands, features of unique visual quality, steep slopes, etc., but also the natural processes they support. Some planners are advocating preparing plans based on natural processes, a process called "environmental determinism."[1]

The volume of data collected during this phase often necessitates the use of automated data processing and information storage systems. The relatively easy access of many planning agencies to automated equipment has permitted more extensive and intensive analysis of the data, in particular the relationships between the various elements.[2]

Plan Formulation   The final step is the formulation of the plan which, based on the previously adopted goals and objectives, describes in graphic and textual form the kind of community desired in the future. Traditionally, the major element has been the future land-use map showing the amount, location, and arrangement of the various land uses. On the regional or metropolitan-area level, such a map may be general, providing a framework, or it may represent a concept of urban form to guide local governmental units and private developers. For a small city, part of a large city, or a new community, the map may be quite detailed, allocating land uses to specific blocks and showing boundaries of such proposed major land users as industrial parks, airports, shopping centers, and parks (see illustration).

Other elements of the plan usually are prepared as separate projects and later combined to eliminate conflicts and to "optimize" the goals of the plan. Among such elements are:

Open Space and Recreation. Current open-space plans place less emphasis on quantitative standards (*x* acres per 1,000 population) than on the quality of the space in terms of fulfilling recreation needs, location with respect to population concentrations, variety of spaces and facilities, preservation of ecologically important areas, protection of urban areas from such dangers as flooding and erosion, and, to a lesser degree, giving form and structure to the urban area. Because of a critical open-space shortage in most urbanized areas, many open-space plans place much emphasis on methods of keeping land open.

Community Facilities and Services. A major element of the plan deals with the facilities which should be provided by the government: schools, police and fire stations, libraries, health centers, water, sewer and other utility systems, and refuse disposal. Some planning agencies are preparing plans for public *services* as well as facilities and are becoming involved in educational curricula, crime prevention, environmental health, health needs of poor people, pollution abatement, and social welfare systems.

[1] Ian L. McHarg, *Design with Nature* (see bibliography).
[2] Willard B. Hansen, "Quantitative Methods in Urban Planning," in Goodman and Freund, pp. 227–294 (see bibliography).

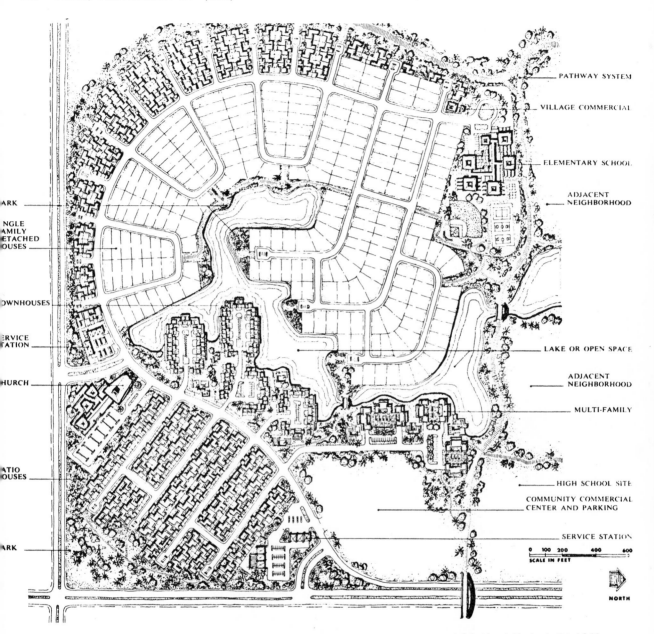

PATHWAY SYSTEM

VILLAGE COMMERCIAL

ELEMENTARY SCHOOL

ADJACENT NEIGHBORHOOD

LAKE OR OPEN SPACE

ADJACENT NEIGHBORHOOD

MULTI-FAMILY

HIGH SCHOOL SITE

COMMUNITY COMMERCIAL CENTER AND PARKING

SERVICE STATION

0 100 200 400 600
SCALE IN FEET

NORTH

ARK

NGLE AMILY ETACHED OUSES

OWNHOUSES

ERVICE TATION

HURCH

ATIO OUSES

ARK

A lakeside neighborhood, (Litchfield Park Properties, Inc., From Farmland to City, Litchfield Park, Arizona, p. 12.)

Transportation. The transportation element of the plan is based on a projected need for a variety of transportation facilities based on land use, density, and the interaction of activity systems. In particular, this element deals with the appropriate mix of private and public transportation facilities and their location with respect to major traffic generators such as employment, shopping, educational centers, and residential areas. Transportation plans may also include elements relating to intercity travel such as airports, heliports, railroads, and ports, with attention paid to changes in transportation technology and its effect on transportation facilities.

Design. Some plans include urban design or appearance elements. Attempts are made to define good appearance in relation to the design and layout of the area, the relationship of appearance to mental and physical health and the overall "quality of life," and specific techniques for improving community appearance.[1]

Because of the policy basis of current comprehensive planning, consultation with decision makers on the one hand and the general citizenry on the other is maintained throughout the plan formulation stage. Citizen participation will significantly increase the likelihood that the plans will reflect the view of those responsible for their implementation and will be accepted by those affected by the plans.

As each of the sections is completed, it may be necessary to refer back to previously completed reports and make revisions based on new information and recommendations. This process of preparing reports, feedback, reevaluation, and revision generally produces several possible plans. The alternatives are then evaluated, in consultation with other government officials and private citizens, before a final selection is made. The final plan may be published as a single document or in separate volumes. The plan is revised and refined periodically as conditions change.

Implementation Following completion of all the elements of the plan, special attention is focused on implementation tools, including the capital improvements program, zoning ordinance, subdivision regulations, official map, building and housing code, and urban renewal. Other devices include tax policy, government reorganization, public land purchase, incentives, and various specialized tools to deal with particular elements. Utilization of the full range of implementation devices greatly increases the likelihood that the recommendations of the plan will be achieved.

BIBLIOGRAPHY: American Municipal Association, American Society of Planning Officials, International City Managers' Association, *Action for Cities: A Guide for Community Planning,* Public Administration Service, Chicago, 1943; T. J. Kent, *The Urban General Plan,* Chandler Publishing Co., San Francisco, 1964; Chapin, F. Stuart, *Urban Land Use Planning,* 2d ed., University of Illinois Press, Urbana, Ill., 1965; Melville C. Branch, *Planning: Aspects and Applications,* John Wiley & Sons, Inc., New York, 1966; H. Wentworth Eldredge (ed.), *Taming Megalopolis,* Frederick A. Praeger, Inc., New York, 1967; F. Stuart Chapin, *Selected References on Urban Planning Concepts and Methods,* Department of City and Regional Planning, University of North Carolina, Chapel Hill, N.C., 1968; William I. Goodman and Eric G. Freund (eds.), *Principles and Practice of Urban Planning,* International City Management Association, Washington, 1968; Doris B. Holleb, *Social and Economic Information for Urban Planning,* The Center for Urban Studies, University of Chicago Press, Chicago, 1969; Lewis Keeble, *Principles and Practice of Town and Country Planning,* 4th ed., Estates Gazette, London, 1969; Ian L. McHarg, *Design with Nature,* Natural History Press, Garden City, N.Y., 1969; Melville C. Branch, *Comprehensive Urban Planning—A Selective Annotated Bibliography with Related Materials,* Sage Publications, Beverly Hills, Calif., 1970.

—MICHAEL J. MESHENBERG

[1] *Checklist for Cities: A Guide for Local Action in Improving the Design of Our Cities'* The Committee on Urban Design, The American Institute of Architects, Washington, 1968.

PLATO (428–348 B.C.) Influenced by his great teacher Socrates all his life, Plato in his turn influenced Western thought with his dialectic philosophy as no other thinker has before or since.

The span of his life coincides with the crucial period of his native city, Athens. During these years the Athenian democracy degenerated and finally dissolved, and with it the form of city-state prevalent in the Greek world for three centuries. These painful historical experiences led Plato (as well as other Greek thinkers) to seek a new, more stable, and just form of government. Within the frame of this ideal Platonic state will be found the few but very interesting theories of the philosopher for the external form (the ekistic form, as we would say today) which the ideal city should possess.

Plato's theories, to be found in the dialogues *Critias, Republic,* and *Laws,* form a mixture of pure philosophic and political deontology with elements of the Hippocratic hygiene and the Hippodamian method. (From the Hippodamian method Plato borrows not so much the advanced street layout of the Milesian town builder as the division of the city and the citizens into classes and into relative ekistic zones.)

The basis for the foundation of the Platonic city is the selection of the correct location from the point of view of winds, water, and natural resources in order to secure the physical and mental health of the citizens (*Laws* 747D). For practical and aesthetic reasons the area should be forested (*Critias* 111B–D). Coastal areas were rejected as unsuitable; instead, an inland site at a distance of 80 stadia (approximately 8.7 miles or 14 kilometers) from the sea was suggested so that intercourse between citizens and foreigners could be avoided and the unfavorable psychological and moral consequences resulting from trading and naval activities could be neutralized (*Laws* 704B–705A).

Calculations based on mathematical mysticism established that the population of the ideal city-state would be 5,040 citizens (*Laws* 737E). The city and the arable land were each to be divided into twelve areas. On an elevated site in the center of the city-state would be the walled acropolis with the temples of Hestia, Zeus, and Athena and the houses of the highest magistrates. The land was to be divided into 5,040 lots and every lot had two parts, one of which was near the city and the other near the borderline (*Laws* 745B–E). The administrative and other public buildings were to be located in the area around the agora. The sanctuaries were also to be placed around the agora, though some would also be on the heights surrounding the city (*Laws* 778C–D).

To ensure the health and vigilance of the citizens, a kind of unwalled city was specified—a city which was to be secured by the construction of a system of uniform houses positioned so as to enclose the city and give it the shape of an enormous residence (*Laws* 778E).

Any type of transaction or commerce was to be performed outside the city (*Laws* 847C–D). The structural form of the city-state would remain unchanged and unaffected by the whims of the private citizens (*Laws* 779C).

BIBLIOGRAPHY: R. Martin, *L'Urbanisme dans la Grèce Antique,* Paris, 1956, pp. 18–21.

—DEM MARONITIS

PLAYGROUND, CHILDREN'S The provision of children's playgrounds has become, since the Second World War, an increasingly important feature in the planning of residential areas, especially those of medium or high density where private gardens are small or nonexistent. The number of such playgrounds in relation to dwellings has increased with the realization of their social importance, and in an enlightened community no extensive residential area would be planned without some provision of this kind. The progress in this matter can be illustrated by the small provision for playgrounds in the plans for the first generation of British New Towns (1946–1952) and the much more liberal provision of them in the second generation (1961–1970).

Certain types of plan facilitate the provision of childrens playgrounds more than others. Such playgrounds should, for instance, be well away from through roads used by fairly fast traffic, and every house should have one within a quarter of a mile (one-half kilometer). Thus residential areas consisting mainly of houses lining roads, which were common up to the middle of the present century, do not facilitate the introduction of children's playgrounds. They have occasionally been introduced at the backs of houses in areas at the ends of the yard or gardens, but this has not been very common. With the liberal introduction of culs-de-sac, it was possible to run off children's playgrounds or link them with the ends, but again this has been done very occasionally. More often, the cul-de-sac itself became the children's playground, but this is unsatisfactory because adequate facilities are not possible. It is very makeshift, and its use in this way is often disturbing to some of the residents in the cul-de-sac.

Children's playgrounds have most satisfactorily been provided when large parts of residential areas are pedestrian precincts, as in the case of the second generation of the British New Towns. In these, sidewalks traverse the whole residential district. They broaden here and there into small open spaces, sometimes paved, sometimes lawns, sometimes graced with trees and flowerbeds. In many instances, these intimate spaces are utilized as children's playgrounds. In conformity with the play impulses of children, which are directed to physical development, to the joy of physical extension, of running about, jumping, crawling, turning over, etc., to the joy in fantasy, imitation, and adventure, the playgrounds are of a varied character. Many have curious assemblages of objects: concrete blocks of various shapes and sizes, old tree trunks, boulders, debris like wall units and large sections of piping from building sites—anything over which children can climb with little risk of injury. They are within easy distance of the children's homes and well away from road traffic. Examples of such playgrounds are to be found in the newer residential areas of the United States.

Such pedestrian ways and spaces with children's playgrounds among two- and three-story family dwellings with small yards or gardens are in medium-density areas of about ten to eighteen dwellings to the acre (twenty-five to forty-four per hectare). Higher-density areas, of about twenty to thirty dwellings or more to the acre (fifty to seventy-five per hectare), would be partly apartment buildings from three to eight stories in height. It is an advantage if such developments are well away from main roads, with gardens—parts of which can be utilized as children's playgrounds—between and around apartment blocks.

Children's playgrounds often form part of urban recreational parks, which in the United States are of increasing variety. They provide for a wide range of play activities including separate play areas, sometimes called tot lots, for the preschool child and others for the school-age child (*see* OPEN SPACE). A wide variety of objects and devices are provided, such as fantastic sculptures, tunnels, climbing towers, walls, and other structures tempting to the adventurer, while some larger play areas include bridges and miniature cars.

BIBLIOGRAPHY: Garrett Eckbo, *Urban Landscape Design,* McGraw-Hill Book Company, New York, 1964; *Town & Country Planning,* special issue on children and planning, vol. 36, nos. 10–11, London, Oct.–Nov., 1968.   —ARNOLD WHITTICK

PLAYING FIELDS   (*See* OPEN SPACE IN URBAN AREAS.)

PLAZA   (*See* PLACE.)

PLOT RATIO   A term used in British planning to denote the ratio of the total floor area of a building to the area of the site it occupies. Thus if the site is 20,000 square feet (1,860 square meters) and the total area of all the floors is 50,000 square feet (4,600 square meters), then the plot ratio is 2.5. It is similar to the floor-space index (*see* FLOOR SPACE STANDARDS) except that in this, half the widths of minor roads are included in the site area calculation, whereas in the plot ratio these are excluded.

POLAND

Legislation and Administration   Poland is a country of comparatively long traditions in physical planning. As early as 1928 the first Building Act, which formed the basis for official town planning, was passed. In its revised form in 1936, the concept of regional planning was introduced. The Ministry of Internal Affairs was responsible for the preparation and approval of regional and town planning schemes. Practical work in regional planning and survey was carried out in several regional planning offices covering nearly half of the country's area within the prewar boundaries, whereas urban plans were prepared within the town-planning "workshops" in bigger communities and by private consulting firms. Some years before World War II, a bureau was established to prepare concepts for the national investment plan. This body was attached to the Deputy Prime Minister's Office.

After World War II, activity in the field of environmental planning was organized within the framework of the socialist system of planned economy in the People's Poland. The legislative basis for this was the Decree on Physical Planning of 1946. Physical planning was organized on three levels: national, regional, and local. The responsible central authority was the Central Office for Physical Planning, a division of the Ministry of Reconstruction. Regional plans were prepared for each of the 14 voivodships (regions) by the regional offices, whereas local planning was carried on in major communities and for the smaller towns within the region. This hierarchy of physical planning offices was independent of the economic planning agencies for which the Central Planning Office was at first responsible.

In 1949 the whole system of planning was reformed. The State Commission for Economic Planning was set up. It dealt also with national and regional physical planning; and local planning was passed to the new Ministry of Building. Thus the previous structure was split in two. The national plan became the physical aspect of the plan for the development of national economy, and regional plans were prepared only for areas characterized by more intensive growth and investment processes. Such an arrangement created a gap between the regional and local level of planning. Town planning offices working since 1953 under the general direction of the Committee for Town Planning and Architecture were practically deprived of guidelines prepared at the regional and national level.

Since 1957, however, a revival of comprehensive physical planning occurred. Studies for regional plans were made in all voivodships (regions), and a wide network of town planning offices began to be organized. At first, 22 voivodship town planning offices—17 voivodships and 5 major metropolitan areas—were established. But soon the process of decentralization began. In 1969 there were town planning offices for all the 70 major cities and all the 314 *powiats* (counties).

In 1961 a new Physical Planning Act was passed which constitutes a comprehensive legislative basis for the whole of physical planning. The physical national plan prepared by the Planning Commission of the Council of Ministers is to constitute an integral part of the Plan for the Development of the National Economy. It also provides machinery for the coordination of regional plans prepared by regional planning offices incorporated in the economic planning commissions on the voivodship level. The voivodship town planning offices, once more under the supervision of the Ministry of Building, are entrusted with the preparation of more important projects and are, at the same time, guiding and coordinating agencies on local planning. The chief architects for a county or voivodship, included among the members of the Presidium of the People's Councils, are responsible for the activities of the town planning offices.

Professional Practice and Methods Professional town planning practice in Poland is carried on by state agencies in which about 2,500 persons are employed as specialized professional staff. The projects are prepared by teams composed of architects, geographers, economists, sociologists, engineers, and other necessary specialists.

The comprehensive legal basis and hierarchical organization of town planning agencies made possible comparatively uniform planning techniques. According to the Physical Planning Act, two kinds of urban plans are prepared: (1) The master plan for separate communities to scales of 1:5,000 and 1:10,000. In case of a conurbation, town planning schemes are first prepared to a scale of 1:25,000 for the whole area. (2) The detailed plan for structural parts of a town to scales of 1:1,000 and 1:2,000.

For rural areas plans are prepared which show the network of settlements within a county. On this basis plans to a scale of 1:2,000 are prepared for each rural community.

Long-term urban plans are prepared as (1) long-range expansion studies for periods longer than the so-called "prospective" period of development of the national economy; (2) long-term plans for a period of 20 years, to match economic plans; and (3) interim studies of the type of "action area plans" for a period corresponding to the 5-year economic plans.

The planning process consists of the following phases: survey based on physical phenomena; cartographical registration of land uses, built-up areas, infrastructure, physiographical features, land ownership, and other related data such as population, economic development, and living standards; specialized physiographical, demographic, and prognosis studies, and studies of expansion and of possible reconstruction of various built-up areas; of communications, traffic, and transportation and other infrastructural systems; and also of sociological and historic aspects. On the basis of these studies different variants of spatial planning are conceived, always within the framework of the program set up for the town on the general guidelines from the regional planning level. After an optimization procedure, the most efficient variant is chosen to be elaborated in the form of a project. Preparation is uniform in the matter of legends, contents of the written report, and tables containing the quantitative approach.

Projects are discussed in detail with all the investors concerned and are subject to open discussion with representatives of the public. Detailed plans are shown to private landowners to get their reactions and comments. The project is approved by the proper people's councils after consulting the people's councils at lower levels. Before approval, major projects have to be accepted by the Ministry of Building as far as the professional level of preparation is concerned. Projects for major metropolitan areas must be approved by the Prime Minister's Council.

The standardized form in which urban plans are to be presented does not mean that the methods of planning are stiffly uniform. Quite the reverse; there is a constant evolution of planning methods and techniques. In 1950, the first step was the elaboration of so-called "town planning standards" which constitute machinery establishing norms for per capita surfaces, volume, and other parameters in all kinds of accommodation and community facilities. At first, up to 1953, the master plans were prepared for the conventional period of 25 years; but the method of stage plans has since been developed. These consisted in matching the phases of implementation within the 5-year periods of economic plans. The new procedure gave way to the incorporation of various specialists and a more economic approach toward urban planning. The calculation of the so-called "economic efficiency" of investments has been applied to town planning problems. In the early sixties the extension of the economic planning period up to 20 years and the introduction of long-range studies confronted town planners with the problem of how to proceed with such studies, for, being unlimited in time, they cannot be satisfactorily related to planning programs. The so-called "threshold analysis" has been developed, allowing for expansion studies based on costs of developing urban land. Such an analysis became an important component in the preparation of plans even for limited periods of time. The quantified form of this analysis also created a common platform for discussion between planners at the regional and local levels.

Recent developments have two goals: the first is the introduction of mathematical and statistical methods in selecting the best spatial solutions; the second is an attempt to influence the implementation processes. The urban plan is conceived not only as a "picture" of future development but also as a steering process in time. Actually, techniques of the PERT type are experimented with to ensure a harmonious implementation of the plan.

Institutions, Professional and Research Professional practice carried on by town planning offices is supported by research work performed in several research institutes. The main center for urban planning research is the Institute for Town Planning and Architecture controlled by the Ministry of Building. This institute deals with the following research problems: principles of expansion of the urban network and factors affecting spatial structures of agglomerations, cities, towns, and rural settlements; models of urban structures, including mathematical ones; methods of economic evaluation of plans and other studies for the rationalization of urban planning; town planning standards; and the legal basis for physical planning.

In addition, town planning practice is also supported by the activity of other research institutes such as the Physical Planning Institute at the Technical University of Warsaw and the Housing Institute. There are also links with the Committee for Regional Planning and Space Economy at the Polish Academy of Sciences, which concentrates mainly on problems of national physical planning.

The Polish Town Planners Society, a professional institution, was founded in 1923. In 1970 it had about 1,300 members who represented all the regions of the country and many various disciplines and specialties involved in physical planning.

Education and Training Town planners in Poland are recruited from various university faculties. Architect-town planners, constituting the majority, are trained in the architectural departments of technical universities in Warsaw, Cracow, Wroclaw, Gdańsk, and Szczecin. However their curricula do not provide for specialization in physical planning. Engineers are trained in other faculties of these technical universities, whereas such specialists as geographers, economists, and sociologists are the graduates of other university faculties.

For the purpose of specialization in physical planning, various postgraduate courses have been organized. Such a course for graduates of various departments has been offered at the Warsaw Technical University since 1946.

In the late fifties, five postgraduate courses were created in major technical universities, and in addition a postgraduate course for regional planners has been established at the Central School for Planning and Statistics in Warsaw.

For the purposes of training the professional staff, seminars, organized by the Ministry of Building and by research institutes, are held periodically. The chairs of town planning in all architectural departments carry out the research and train the scientific workers.

All this, however, is not sufficient in relation to needs. This is why a reform of the education system stressing the need for the specialization in physical planning is being considered by the Polish Town Planners Society.

Geographical Conditions, Economic Development, and Urbanization Processes
Poland lies in the northeastern part of Central Europe on the Baltic Sea. It occupies a compact area of about 120,000 square miles (about 312,000 square kilometers).

Poland is a lowland country. Land, mostly plains, up to about 985 feet (300 meters) above sea level occupies 91.3 percent of the country's area, whereas mountains rising above 3,280 feet (1,000 meters) constitute barely 0.1 percent. Polish territory is divided into several geographic zones stretching from east to west, among them the glacial-lake land in the north, the alluvial plains of the Vistula and Odra Valleys in the central part, and the mountainous areas of the Sudeten and Carpathian ranges along the southern frontier, rising in the Tatra Mountains up to almost 8,200 feet (2,500 meters).

The climate is transitional, from the continental climate of Eastern Europe to the oceanic climate of Western Europe.

One-quarter of the country's area is covered by forests. The soils, especially on the plains, are fairly good for agriculture. As far as mineral resources are concerned, very rich deposits of hard coal, which serves as the main fuel source for Polish industries, have been exploited for centuries in Upper Silesia, as have deposits of iron, zinc, and lead ores. Recently, thanks to geological research, rich layers of sulfur, copper, salt, lignite, and natural gas have been discovered, forming a basis for many new industries.

The population of Poland in 1970 was about 32 million and in 1946 only about 24 million. The rate of natural increase, very high in the postwar years, has recently fallen to about 8 percent.

Before World War II, Poland was agriculturally rather backward and industrially underdeveloped. In 1931 about 60 percent of the total population earned its livelihood in agriculture, which in 1938 provided 44.9 percent of the national income.

During the period of World War II, 6 million persons were killed and war losses amounted to 40 percent of the national wealth. Since the end of the war, within a period of 25 years, Poland has become an industrialized country with a complete change in its employment structure. Only 38.7 percent of the total population is employed in agriculture compared with 61.3 percent in industry and the tertiary sector; only 20.7 percent of the total national income is provided by agriculture. The average annual growth of industrial production from 1947 to 1962 amounted to 16.5 percent, and the per capita national income was doubled in the years 1950 to 1965.

Rapid industrialization was accompanied by considerable urbanization. The urban population, which in 1931 amounted to 27.4 percent, grew in 1950 to 39 percent, in 1960 to 48.8 percent, and in 1966 to over 50 percent of the total population. In 1965, of the total urban population of 15.7 million, 6.5 million were living in the nine largest agglomerations: 1.75 million in the Upper Silesian conurbation, 0.58 million in Cracow, 0.56 million in the conurbation on the Gdańsk Gulf, 0.49 million in Poznań, 0.47 million in Wroclaw, 0.35 million in Szezecin, 0.27 million in Bydgoszcz, and 0.22 million in Lublin. These data show that the urban population, according to the "rank and size" rule, is very evenly distributed. This can be seen even more clearly from the table on page 842.

Traditions of Planning to the End of the Ninteenth Century   The earliest settlements in Polish territory date from 2000 B.C., in the Neolithic Age. In the period of Lusatian culture, 1300 to 400 B.C., occurs the well-known marsh settlement in Biskupin which was discovered and studied in the years 1934 to 1939 and 1946 to 1947. It was one of the defensive settlements laid out on the lake island, surrounded by a breakwater and walls of wooden construction with a very regular plan, composed of one-family houses for about 1,500 people.

The recent large-scale archeological investigations revealed an unexpectedly high level of settlement characteristic of the Slav population in the territory between the Bug and Odra Rivers in the period between the eighth and thirteenth centuries A.D. The evolution consisted here in constructing the first of the *grody* (fortified burghs) around which the additional settlements—military, working-class, and commercial suburbs—clustered. These "grapelike" agglomerations are typical of the early stage in the development of the Polish state founded in 966. Poznań is a good example of such a form of settlement.

The whole urban network was already fully crystallized prior to the fifteenth century. These medieval towns are still visible in the majority of contemporary Polish towns. Chelmno represents a typical medieval pattern of a town of about 2,000 inhabitants, whereas Cracow, the previous capital of Poland, shows a more highly developed form.

In the period of the Renaissance, until the middle of the seventeenth century, there was a strong Italian influence in the shaping of towns. This may be seen in Zamość, which is one of the finest examples of Renaissance city planning and architecture in Europe. This period is also characterized by two trends: (1) the tendency to spontaneous suburban growth outside the city walls, and (2) the siting of aristocratic residences on the outskirts of towns.

Already toward the end of the sixteenth century, Polish cities began to show symptoms of economic regression which worsened throughout the seventeenth and eighteenth centuries. This was caused by the policy of the aristocracy, by the continuous wars with Turkey and Russia, and by the

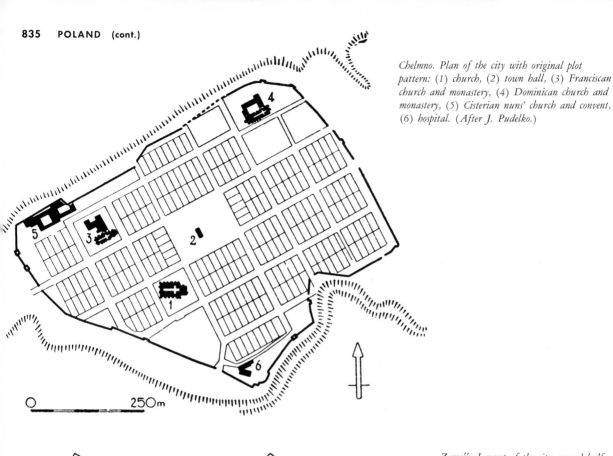

Chelmno. Plan of the city with original plot pattern: (1) church, (2) town hall, (3) Franciscan church and monastery, (4) Dominican church and monastery, (5) Cisterian nuns' church and convent, (6) hospital. (After J. Pudelko.)

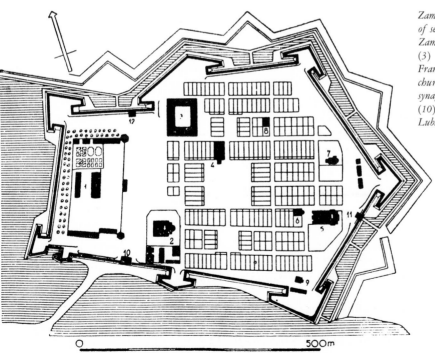

Zamość. Layout of the city, second half of seventeenth century: (1) Jan Zamoyski's Palace, (2) collegiate church, (3) Academy, (4) town hall, (5) Franciscan church, (6) Franciscan nuns' church, (7) Armenian church, (8) synagogue, (9) Greek catholic church, (10) Gate, (11) Lwow Gate, (12) Lublin Gate. (After W. Kalinowski.)

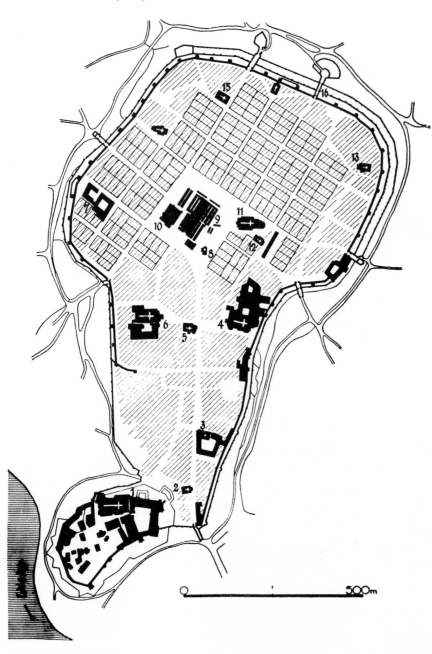

Cracow. Plan of the medieval city, founded in 1257: (1) Wawel Hill with castle and cathedral—oldest structures date from tenth century; (2) St. Giles' church; (3) St. Andrew's 1090; (4) Dominican church and monastery; (5) All Saints' church; (6) Franciscan church; (7) Collegium Maius, fifteenth century; (8) St. Adalbert's, 1100; (9) Drapers' Hall and stalls, fourteenth century; (10) town hall, fourteenth century; (11) Church of Virgin Mary, 1250; (12) St. Barbara's, fourteenth to fifteenth century; (13) Church of the Holy Cross, fourteenth century; (14) St. John's; (15) St. Mark's, thirteenth century; (16) St. Florian's Gate, 1300, and barbican. (After W. Grabski.)

Swedish invasions in 1655 to 1656 and 1705 to 1709. The political conditions worsened, and in 1795 the Polish territory was finally partitioned between Germany, Austria, and Russia.

In spite of this decay, there were remarkable periods of good planning. The first, at the end of the seventeenth century, was characterized by the creation of large-scale royal and aristocratic architectural designs like the

"Saxon Axis" in Warsaw. The second occurred during the reign of Stanislaus Augustus, 1764 to 1795, the last Polish king, when many excellent construction and reconstruction projects in Warsaw and other cities were undertaken; for example, the Royal Bath Palace and Park in Warsaw. At the end of the eighteenth century many town improvements took place thanks to the so-called commission of "Boni Ordinis." Also, the pre-industrial period 1815 to 1830 should be mentioned, with industrial developments along the Kamienna Valley (iron works) and around Lodz (textile industries). All these show a tendency toward regular neoclassical patterns.

Twentieth-century Planning   After World War I (1918), when the Polish state was reestablished, two most successful planning schemes were the construction of a modern port and town at Gdynia and the Central Industrial District, whose advanced implementation, however, was stopped by World War II.

The first planning task in the People's Poland, after the Second World War (1945), was the reconstruction of urban areas, industrial plants, and towns destroyed during the war as well as by the demolitions of the Nazi invaders. It is worthwhile to emphasize that during this first period most of the medieval nuclei of the towns were reconstructed in accordance with the historic design. The reconstruction of the Warsaw's Old City is the

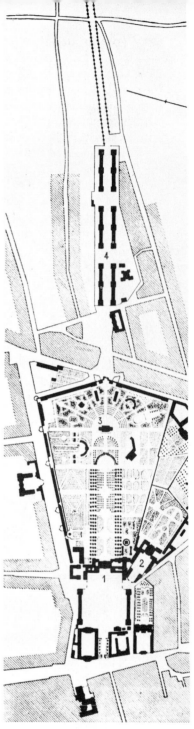

ABOVE: *Warsaw. Augustus II's Axis: (1) Palace of King Augustus II, (2) Palace of Minister H. Brühl, (3) Grand Salon, (4) barracks. (After Z. Bieniecki.)* LEFT: *Warsaw. The rebuilt "Old Town."*

most notable example. All the houses and churches have been rebuilt in their original form, but the conditions of dwellings were improved by sanitation and modern equipment. Alongside this reconstruction, a new east-west thoroughfare connecting the two sides of the Vistula River was built, with an underpass beneath the old city.

Within the period 1950 to 1955, great efforts were made to decentralize the Upper Silesian Industrial District and to create new industrial centers based on other natural resources. In this connection about 25 new towns were built or major expansions carried out. The best example is the town of Nowe Tychy (New Tychy) located about 10 miles (16 kilometers) to the south of the Upper Silesian Coal Basin. The master plan provides for

RIGHT: *Gdańsk-Gdynia. Conurbation. Present state. City and regional planning in Poland, 1966. (After J. Fisher.)*

Nowe Tychy. New Town. Master plan: (1) high-density development, (2) mid-density development, (3) open development, (4) industrial land, (5) forests, (6) open spaces. (Authors: K. Weychert and A. Adamczewska.)

■ 1   ▨ 2   ▧ 3   ▥ 4   ▨ 5   ☐ 6

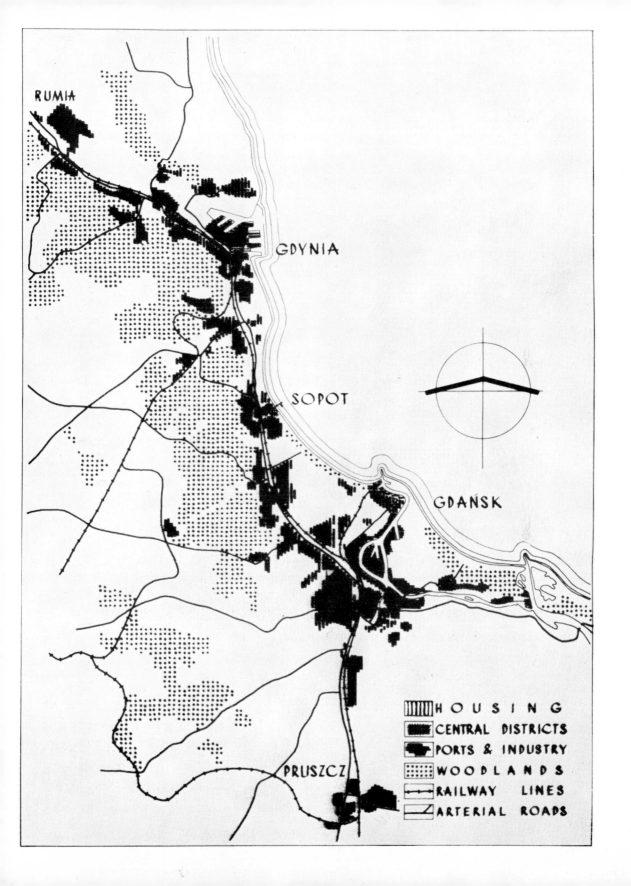

RUMIA

GDYNIA

SOPOT

GDAŃSK

PRUSZCZ

HOUSING
CENTRAL DISTRICTS
PORTS & INDUSTRY
WOODLANDS
RAILWAY LINES
ARTERIAL ROADS

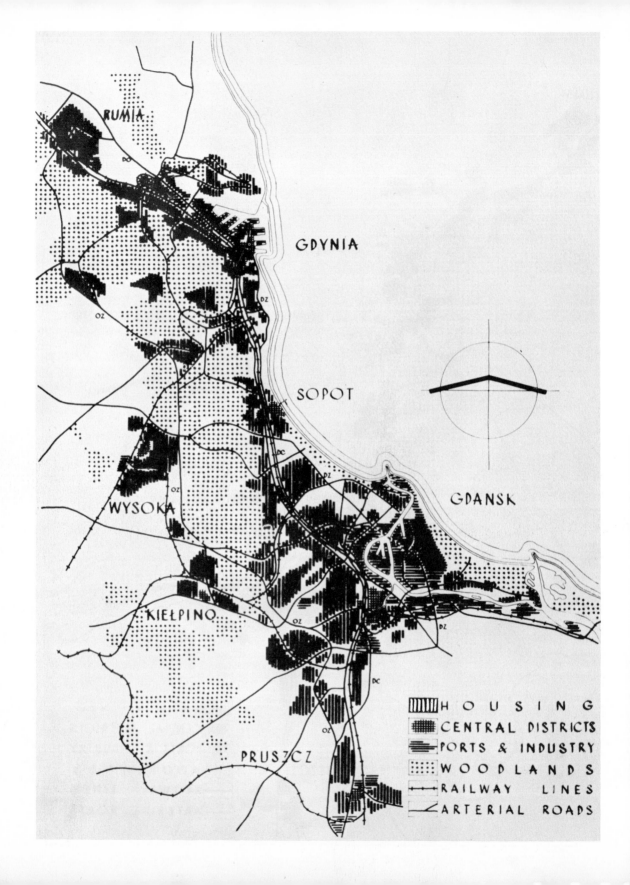

RUMIA

GDYNIA

SOPOT

GDANSK

WYSOKA

KIEŁPINO

PRUSZCZ

|||| HOUSING
CENTRAL DISTRICTS
PORTS & INDUSTRY
WOODLANDS
RAILWAY LINES
ARTERIAL ROADS

120,000 inhabitants, of whom 70,000 are already accommodated. The housing pattern follows the rule of modern residential units with all service facilities. The town center encompasses all the central services and urban amenities.

The commonest development in Poland is the extension of existing towns. The urban population increase of 9 million had to be accomodated in new districts and housing projects. Industries grouped into industrial parks had to be built, the range of services enlarged, and open green spaces created. For all these the infrastructural networks had to be provided. This is why, for all the 900 towns, master plans had to be prepared which are now revised every 5 years. The increase of urban population had to be accommodated in conformity with the development of industrial and urban centers. Some selected towns are extended in a major way whereas in others the populations are to be kept fairly static. To illustrate the main tendencies, the plan for the Gdańsk Bay conurbation is shown here. The comparison of the three stages gives the scale of expansion that is foreseen.

Since stress was being laid on the expansion of towns, there was not enough time or money for major renewal programs. It is only in more recent years that this action has been taken. Large-scale renewal is taking place at present in the central areas of Warsaw and Katowice (Upper Silesia), but schemes for the renewal of all the major town centers are being prepared.

OPPOSITE PAGE: *Gdańsk-Gdynia. Conurbation. Long-term plan. (After J. Fisher.)*

Warsaw. Part of the central area.

TOWNS AND URBAN SETTLEMENTS IN POLAND
ACCORDING TO RANK AND SIZE
(*Statistical Year-Book,* 1966.)

Size, thousands	1950		1965	
	Number of towns	Population, thousands	Number of towns	Population, thousands
Total	706	9,605	891	15,681
Up to 5,000 inhabitants	393	1,066	369	1,123
5–10	159	1,113	245	1,741
10–20	76	1,034	151	2,089
20–50	50	1,523	78	2,330
50–100	12	832	25	1,633
100–200	10	1,415	13	1,956
200–500	4	1,180	7	2,292
Above 500	2	1,434	3	2,517
Rural population		15,224		15,870

According to the official forecast, the total population of Poland will reach about 37.5 million in 1985, with an urban population of 23 million. These figures show, roughly, the tasks confronting town planning in Poland.

BIBLIOGRAPHY: B. Malisz, *Ekonomika ksztaltowania miast* (*Economics of Town Planning*), Polish Academy of Sciences, Committee for Space Economy and Regional Planning Studies, vol. IV, 1963; B. Malisz, "Zarys teorii ksztaltowania ukladow osadniczych" ("Theory Outline of Shaping Settlement Systems"), *Arkady,* Warsaw, 1966, French edition: *Formation des Systèmes d'habitat,* Dunod, Paris, 1972; J. Fisher (ed.), *City and Regional Planning in Poland,* Cornell University Press, 1966; W. Kalinowski, *City Development in Poland up to Mid-19th Century,* Institute for Town Planning and Architecture, vol. 108, Warsaw, 1966; *Directory of National Bodies Concerned with Urban and Regional Research,* United Nations, 1968; "Wspolczesna urbanistyka polska" ("Contemporary Town Planning in Poland"), *Arkady,* Warsaw 1972.
—BOLESLAW MALISZ

POPULATION GROWTH AND DISTRIBUTION   To be aware of population trends throughout the world and in one's own country and area in particular, and to have some notion of what is likely to be, according to reliable calculations, the future growth of population, constitutes essential background information for the planner. In the preface to the United Nations' *The Future Growth of World Populations,*[1] it is stated that, "if a plan for social and economic development is to have any chance of realistic implementation, it requires a parallel assessment of the dynamics of population growth."

A glance at world population and its distribution will demonstrate some of the problems which will confront planners in the future. Even now, in some urban areas, the population has increased so rapidly in the period since the Second World War that some planners have confessed their inability to cope with the increase, as some of the articles in this encyclopedia make apparent.

[1] United Nations, *The Future Growth of World Populations,* New York, 1958.

The history of man (apart from speculations from scanty remains about the period of his life on this earth) does not go further back than 10,000 years, and in that time it has taken until 1850 for the world population to reach 1,000 million. Since the beginning of the century, however, when the population had risen to 1,500 million, the population has grown very rapidly, to 2,500 million by 1950 and about 3,600 million by 1970, while it is estimated that, at the present growth rate, the population will be between 4,880 and 6,900 million in the year 2000.[1] The reason for this tremendous rise is not an increase in fertility rate, for that is steadily declining in almost every country in the world, but the almost universal decrease in the mortality rate. This decrease, however, is by no means consistent throughout the world, and mortality rates are still high in many Asian countries. This is the reason why, in these countries, population does not increase at a more rapid rate than in some countries where fertility is lower.

Population forecasts have sometimes been fairly accurate and sometimes very inaccurate, but methods of projection are, with experience, continually being improved. The population forecasts of P. K. Whelpton for the United States[2] proved to be fairly accurate, whereas several estimates for the United Kingdom made during the thirties, including those of G. G. Leybourne, and the official estimates of the Registrars General proved to be rather inaccurate.

In population projections a very large number of factors have to be taken into consideration for any country or area: whether fertility and mortality rates will decline, increase, or remain constant, and how these rates will be affected by such uncertain factors as the numerical relations of the sexes, the prevalence of birth control and the effect of religious influence on this, and the effects of economic prosperity and depressions, war, and epidemics of disease or famine. In some parts of the world these last are still likely to be factors. A comprehensive consideration of all known factors is unlikely to lead to the miscalculations made in Europe during the thirties, but there may still be factors as yet unknown.

Distribution The distribution of world population is very uneven. About half the population lives on only about 5 percent of the land surface of the earth, and 80 percent of the population lives between 20 and 60 degrees north latitude—although this area includes large tracts of uninhabitable country. Until the industrial revolution began to have an effect on the distribution of population, it was determined chiefly by geographical, cultural, social, and economic factors. The geographical factors include climatic conditions (mainly atmospheric temperature, precipitation, and geological conditions such as land forms) and the presence of minerals, fuels, and soils for agriculture and forestry. Proximity to the sea was also an influence. Related to the cultural and social factors are the centers of man's early settlements. Population would tend to spread from these, and its degree

[1] *Ibid.*
[2] *Population of the United States, 1925 to 1975,* 1928.

of extension would depend later on the degrees of economic and social organization that had been achieved. The processes of survival would later become distribution in response to economic opportunities.

With the industrial revolution that began in the late eighteenth and early nineteenth centuries in Western Europe there began the movement toward greater urban concentrations of population and migrations from rural to urban areas. It was accelerating a movement that had already begun with the growth of towns and cities for the purposes of trade, administration, culture, and social life. The areas in which the sources of power and raw materials were located became new centers of population, and new industrial cities grew at a tremendous rate in the 150 years from 1820 to 1970—first in England, then in northwestern Europe, later still in North and South America, until, finally, the process spread throughout the world. The financial administration of industry from the centers of cities and the great growth in the number of clerical workers has also increased concentrations. Among the consequences of the worldwide migration from rural to urban areas, which began in the nineteenth century, were overcrowding and bad living conditions in the centers of the great industrial cities. One of the purposes of planning has been to reverse this trend in order to achieve better distribution of industry and population and better living conditions. Efforts in this direction were made throughout the nineteenth century, and one culmination was the *Report of the British Royal Commission on the Distribution of the Industrial Population,*[1] which reviewed the social, economic, and strategic disadvantages of the existing distribution and recommended remedies. The report contributed to a policy of dispersal, partly by means of New Towns, that was subsequently adopted by the British government but which, in the opinion of many, has not gone far enough. This report and British policy has had considerable influence throughout the Western world.

Migration   One of the factors in the trends affecting distribution of population, for which the planner is called upon to provide, is migration, both external and internal—a migration over which he has no control. Governments sometimes meet this problem by resorting to induced migration, such as a dispersal policy. Migration can be broadly defined, for planning purposes, as a change of residence of substantial duration. (Movements of travelers for pleasure and business are logically considered under tourism and communication.) The reasons for migrations from one country to another are mainly economic, but climatic and social factors may also play a part. For instance, a person may migrate, with his family, for the sake of a better job; or in the case of women, the motive may be marriage and better social conditions. The economic prospects in the United States were, of course, the main reason for the tremendous migration from Europe, but there were other factors as well, such as dissatisfaction with life in Europe and a spirit of adventure coupled with curiosity. These motives are common among young, single persons.

[1] London, 1940.

Internal migrations are also mainly economic; people will go where the best jobs are, although climatic and social considerations have some influence. Sometimes there are forced economic migrations, like those that occurred during the Depression of 1929 to 1935, when people left the worst areas of industrial unemployment and moved to the more stable areas. An example of this in Great Britain was the movement from Scotland, South Wales, South Lancashire, and Tyneside to Birmingham, London, and the South East.

Any migrations which are so rapid as to make adequate planning provision for them difficult, provide a reason for planning measures which will counteract such movements. This can be done more easily with internal migrations than with those that are external. The latter occasionally provoke some control of immigration. To counteract migrations from depressed economic areas to those with more stability, the policy generally is to try to revive depressed areas by means of financial inducements to industry and the introduction of new industries to replace those that are declining. (*See* INDUSTRY, DISTRIBUTION OF.)

BIBLIOGRAPHY: An important source of information about population trends throughout the world with details of each country is contained in the *Demographic Yearbook of the United Nations,* New York, 1949–1970. Each issue has a special topic, as follows: General demography, 1948 and 1953; Natality statistics 1949–1950, 1954, 1959, 1965, and 1969; Mortality statistics 1951, 1957, 1961, 1966, and 1967; Population distribution, 1952; Population census statistics 1955, 1962, 1963, and 1964; Ethnic and economic characteristics of population, 1956; Marriage and divorce statistics, 1958 and 1968; Population trends, 1960. The United Nations has also published two useful studies of population: *The Determinants and Consequences of Population Trends—A Summary of the Findings of Studies on the Relationships Between Population Changes and Economic and Social Conditions,* New York, 1953; and *The Future Growth of World Populations,* New York, 1958. A. M. Carr-Saunders, *World Population—Past Growth and Present Trends,* Frank Cass, London, 1964; John I. Clarke, *Population Geography,* Pergamon Press, London, 1965; Peter Hall, *The World Cities,* McGraw-Hill Book Company, New York, 1966; Alfred Sauvy, *Théorie Générale de la Population,* Presses Universitaires de France, Paris, 1966 (English translation by Christophe Campos, *General Theory of Population,* Weidenfeld and Nicolson, London, 1969. Among journals are *Population Studies,* quarterly London School of Economics and the *Journal of the American Statistical Association,* Washington.
—ARNOLD WHITTICK

PORTS (*See* TRANSPORT.)

POWER STATIONS (*See* ELECTRIC POWER GENERATION AND TRANSMISSION.)

PRECINCT AND PRECINCT PLANNING The term "precinct" means an area enclosed by a boundary—either real, imaginary, or legally defined; it also designates, more vaguely, the immediate surrounding of a religious or other building. In the United States, "precinct" also means a particular area patrolled by police.

The precinct is an important element in modern urban planning. Its purpose is to seclude an area for a particular purpose such as a shopping, university, or civic precinct, or to protect an area from undesirable intrusions, such as through traffic, with parts exclusively for pedestrians.

Precinct planning was an important feature of Sir Patrick Abercrombie's plan for the County of London (1943) which, if not fully implemented, has had considerable influence on subsequent planning. In this work the precinct system of planning was adopted "to provide quiet areas for all social activity away from the noise, dust, and danger of the main traffic roads (paragraph 199, vi).

The pedestrian precinct has become a feature of the centers of New Towns and of extensions of existing towns; and in many cases (Bracknell, East Kilbride, Corby, and Cwmbran are examples), where the original plan provided for a central through road, this has been changed to a pedestrian area. In many old cities of Europe central streets and squares have been similarly converted to pedestrian precincts. (*See* PEDESTRIANIZATION *and* SHOPPING CENTERS.)   —ARNOLD WHITTICK

PRESERVATION AND PLANNED CHANGE When any large-scale urban development is proposed, or there is a need for urban renewal, or for new traffic routes in old and historic areas, there is often a conflict of values. The question that arises is whether the historic area with buildings of architectural merit should be sacrificed in order to serve the needs of the new developments or whether another scheme, saving something of the historic area, should be prepared. When there is a proposal to demolish a historic building of architectural merit because of a new traffic route or because of an urban renewal scheme, there is a storm of protest, with varying results. Sometimes the scheme is adopted and the historic buildings of architectural distinction are demolished, sometimes the preservationists win and another scheme is adopted, and sometimes there is a compromise.

The matter is, of course, a question of relative values and of knowing when to hold on and when to let go. Can any principles be formulated for the guidance of planners and planning authorities? It is probably impossible to do this to satisfy all interests because every case is different and must be judged largely on its own special merits, yet it is possible to suggest certain broad general considerations which might contribute to the formulation of principles.

If the claim is for the preservation of a building, a group of buildings, or an urban ensemble on the grounds of architectural merit, then the claim will be very strong if the subject is unique, or the best, or one of the best of its kind. If, however, the example is one of many others that are similar, the claim is much weaker. If the former case is one of considerable magnitude, then the development proposals would necessarily have to be very important and not admit of alternatives if they are to succeed and a demolition is to take place. If unique historical interest is coupled with architectural merit, as it sometimes is, then this strengthens the case for preservation.

Several other factors strengthen the case for preservation. Much support will be gained if the buildings are in very good condition and in good repair, if they continue to serve some useful purpose or could be adapted to do so, and if they are part of and contribute to a good urban environment. If, on the other hand, the buildings are in a poor and derelict condition, are not used, and stand in an area that is almost a slum, then obviously claims for preservation will be much weaker. Yet, even here, in the case of a unique structure, proposed demolition and development sometimes serve to call attention to a historically unique structure and prompt measures for preservation which could provide arguments for changing the character of a development. Sometimes preservation suggests an amendment that actually improves a given scheme. This and other forms of compromise often involve a happy blending of the old and new which is an urban asset. In such cases it is not necessary for the new development to be an imitation in form and style of the old buildings; the new can be wholly in the modern idiom provided there is a harmony of general forms and scale with the old.

In many countries, areas of special architectural and historic interest are designated as conservation areas which are determined by planning authorities. In Great Britain for example, the Town and Country Planning Act of 1962 and the Civic Amenities Act of 1967 make provision for measures of preservation, so that, when necessary development is proposed, such areas are given special consideration.

An interesting and recent example of the conflict of the claims for preservation and of development is the Vieux Carre of New Orleans, the original French colonial town founded in 1718 and one of the most important historic urban areas in the United States. It was built on the classical chessboard pattern with a central square (now Jackson Square) open on one side to the Mississippi River. Now, as the middle of a large sprawling city, it is inevitably subject to pressures for commercial development, and the claims of preservation and development are both strong. Among the consequences of the threat to the Vieux Carre by forces of disruptive change are the reports that have been prepared on this subject. These reports are based on the most extensive analyses of physical, social, economic, legal, and administrative factors ever undertaken for a historic district in the United States (report with seven supplementary volumes by the Bureau of Governmental Research of New Orleans with Marcou, O'Leary & Associates, planning and design consultants).

Among the important development proposals is that made in 1966 by the Louisiana Department of Highways for a riverfront expressway. This is to be part of an outer belt system of expressways around the central area of New Orleans and is to provide major access for traffic to the central area. Along the riverfront it is proposed as an elevated structure over the railway and will thus, in the words of the report, "raise a highly prominent visual barrier clearly alien to the character of Jackson Square across its entire open end, and will have a severely deleterious impact on Jackson Square's physical and environmental unity." The Bureau of Governmental Research of New Orleans considered that the expressway should be at ground level. The Louisiana Department of Highways examined alternative methods but could not find any satisfactory solution other than the elevated highway. This example illustrates the difficult problems confronting those who have to make a choice or compromise between preservation and planned change.

BIBLIOGRAPHY: British Ministry of Housing and Local Government, *Historic towns—Preservation and Change,* H.M.S.O., London, 1967; Bureau of Governmental Research, New Orleans, Louisiana, *Plan and Program for the Preservation of the Vieux Carré,* and seven supplementary volumes on the legal, administrative, economic, social, and aesthetic aspects, New Orleans, 1968.   —ARNOLD WHITTICK

PRIVACY   In residential areas, privacy includes both a desirable degree of seclusion—visual privacy—and peace and quiet, which means protection from noise (*q.v.*). Visual privacy means a fair degree of protection for the occupants of a house from being seen from outside and from neighboring buildings. Much can be done by site planning. What is generally considered to be desirable privacy is, of course, much more easily achieved in low- than in high-density development. When houses, whether they are two-story dwellings or apartment buildings, are fairly close together, privacy is difficult. It has been calculated that if houses on either side of a street are only 50 feet (15 meters) apart with facing windows, their occupants can easily see into one another's rooms. There is, therefore, a feeling of discomfort, and protection is sought in curtains that will darken the interiors somewhat. But if the distance is 80 feet (24 meters) or more, then the occupants are generally more comfortable. With parallel apartment buildings with a definite density of so many dwellings to the acre, say thirty, privacy is more likely to be secured with apartment buildings of eight stories than of three stories, because the latter would be much closer together whereas the former would permit a much greater space between the blocks.

In fairly high-density development in residential areas that are mainly pedestrian, with walkways between the houses, it is necessary, if a fair degree of privacy is to be secured, to avoid placing windows on either side of the walkway facing each other. Many ingenious methods of site planning have been employed to ensure the maximum degree of privacy in high-density precincts. One method is to turn the houses inward onto a court or small garden, with the walls of the houses adjoining the walkway completely blank. It is important in such siting that the garden or court side should be so oriented as to get a desirable degree of sunlight, a consideration that would, of course, vary with the latitude. There are many other ingenious ways of siting for privacy which can be seen in some of the best housing developments, especially since 1960, in both the United States and Europe.

PROCESSIONAL WAY   Religion and religious observances played an important part in the life of ancient cities, and frequently included in religious festivals was the procession, which generally terminated at a temple or other sacred edifice. The processional way to serve this purpose formed a principal feature of many ancient and primitive communities. The ancient Egyptian sacred avenue, lined with sphinxes or sacred animals, served the purpose of the religious procession, and the ancient British city of Avebury was approached by sacred avenues. Periodic religious festivals which included processions took place in ancient Greece, the best known being the Panathenaic procession at Athens, which was part of the 5-yearly festival in honor of Athena. The Panathenaic procession, after entering the city, went diagonally across the agora, on to the Propylea at the entrance to the Acropolis, and finally to the Parthenon, the famous sculptured frieze of which depicts this procession. The Panathenaic way does not appear to have been straight.[1] In later Greek cities, planned under the influence of the regular Hippodomian system, processional ways generally reverted to the Egyptian (or Mesopotamian?) prototype and became straight. This tradition was followed in Roman cities and was revived during the Renaissance. Most of the capital cities of Europe and America that were built or much enlarged and planned during the Renaissance and the extended period of its influence (1400–1900) embodied features of geometrical planning, including the handsome processional way with its terminal feature. Its religious significance, however, was lost, and instead of being lined with sacred sculptures it was lined with trees (Paris, Berlin). The terminal feature is either a magnificent building (e.g., the Capitol in Washington), a triumphal arch (as in Paris or Berlin), or some other impressive monumental structure. The descendant of the processional way in the form generally of a handsome central avenue with a terminal feature still appears in much modern planning and can be seen even in New Towns. —ARNOLD WHITTICK

PROJECTION Projection, in plan work, is the representation of a three-dimensional object on a plane. The various forms of projection are not only useful for illustrating the detail of individual buildings but also for illustrating the effect in three dimensions which it is desired to achieve in a plan—for example, in the design of a neighborhood center. The central projection, or perspective drawing, which attempts a true pictorial appearance, is dealt with under PERSPECTIVE RENDERINGS. There are various other forms of projection which combine an approximation to a pictorial representation with the possibility of principal lines being shown to scale or which consist of a drawing of different faces or elevations of the object or building concerned. The following notes are on the forms of projection most commonly used.

In oblique projection, the third dimension is expressed by drawing parallel oblique lines, usually at an angle of 30 or 45 degrees to the horizontal, from the front elevation of the subject, this being at right angles to the line of sight. The oblique lines may be of half the scale used for the vertical and horizontal dimensions of the front view in order to minimize the distorting effect this form of projection gives. Such projections can make it possible to illustrate some structural details more clearly, but only certain dimensions can be scaled off.

An axonometric projection is a pictorial view based on a true plan of the subject drawn with its sides at an angle to the horizontal, usually 45 and 45 degrees or 30 and 60 degrees. The verticals are drawn to the same scale as the plan and the lines in each dimension are drawn parallel. Again

[1] See Edmund N. Bacon, *Design of City,* Thames & Hudson, London, 1967, pp. 52–57.

there is some distortion. For example, while a circle on the side elevation of a flat-roofed building so illustrated will appear as an ellipse, one on the roof will still be shown as a true circle. As with an oblique projection, an axonometric projection is useful to illustrate structural detail, but only certain dimensions can be measured from the drawing.

A view similar to an axonometric projection but one in which the subject is shown with an equal foreshortening of its dimensions is called an isometric projection. Such a projection is not based on a true plan, for the dimensions of length and breadth are both drawn at 30 degrees to the horizontal. Thus a square plan will appear as a rhombus and circles would appear as ellipses on both plan and elevations. All lines in any one dimension are drawn parallel and the same scale is used throughout. Often a direct scale is used instead of the foreshortened or isometric scale. Such a projection is very useful for giving a detailed picture of structure.

A multiview projection is made up of a number of views of an object on planes which are normally at right angles to one another, as appear, for example, on an architectural drawing showing plan, front, and side elevations of a building. The views are so arranged that the draftsman can project the dimensions from the plan to the front elevation and from the plan and front elevation to the side elevations, e.g., the plan appearing above the front elevation, which is flanked on the right by the end elevation to the right and on the left by the end elevation to the left.

—H. E. Sparrow

PUBLIC PARTICIPATION IN PLANNING   One of the most constructive of recent influences on planning in Britain and North America, public or "citizen" participation may be defined as the means by which members of the community are able to take part in the shaping of policies and plans that will affect the environment in which they live. The demand for participation stems from a growing concern that the decisions which determine the quality of life in a community should reflect the wishes of those who live there rather than represent purely technical solutions imposed from outside.

This concept of participation implies that people should have access to the choices and proposals open to a planning authority and should be able to put forward ideas and comment at every stage in the planning process, from the initial identification of social objectives to the detailed implementation of plans.

Methods of inviting participation have been pioneered in the United States by large city planning departments and by organizations such as the New York Regional Plan Association and the San Francisco Planning and Urban Renewal Association. In Britain, they have been adopted by cities such as Coventry and Liverpool. These methods include local meetings, public debate, discussions with community and special-interest groups, exhibitions, information and inquiry centers, press-radio-television coverage, nontechnical summaries of proposals, civic affairs leaflets, home visits, local involvement in surveys, and ideas competitions. The range of methods adopted and the emphasis placed on particular methods will vary with each authority as it judges what will produce the best response.

Recent legislation in Britain (Town and Country Planning Act, 1968) requires planning authorities to ensure that people have an opportunity to voice their opinions before an authority is committed to a line of policy; in July 1969, an official Committee on Public Participation in Planning reported on the means of securing effective participation at the formative stage in the making of development plans.[1] The committee recommended that a planning authority, while maintaining a continuous pattern of participation, should intensify its efforts at two key stages in the planning process: when inviting comment on the choices open to the community and when presenting a statement of preferred proposals. It also advocated the creation of "community forums," in which local interest groups could discuss issues among themselves and with the authority, and the appointment of "community development officers" who would seek to engage the interest of "nonjoiners" in the community. It stressed the importance of feeding back the results of participation so that people feel their interest is worthwhile.

Public education about the purpose of planning and procedures is seen as an essential element in the stimulation of informed participation, especially if an authority is to gain accurate soundings of local opinion rather than simply the more vocal representations of articulate pressure groups. In Britain, civic societies have tended to be "middle class" in character and to be most active in areas where there are environmental qualities to conserve. In United States cities, public participation is becoming geared to the problems of inarticulate, underprivileged, and minority groups: it has acquired a harder, more abrasive edge, which is reflected in the recent influence of advocacy planning and the formation of neighborhood action groups with their demands for "people power." The Architects Renewal Committee in Harlem (ARCH), for instance, is one advocacy agency that has embarked on a program of community education in ghetto schools to increase local awareness of the processes and politics of urban growth. In Britain, planners and teachers are starting to collaborate on the introduction of environmental appreciation and other relevant studies into the curriculum of primary and secondary schools. The participation effort is now tending to broaden into the wider field of community action programs, both in the United States and in other countries.

Participation techniques have developed most widely at local and regional levels; they are considered not to be generally effective on national planning issues except where local pressure groups can exert influence on national or state legislatures. Whatever the scale of participation in an authority, it is recognized that the elected council members stand at the heart of the activity and that much of the success of participation depends on the strength of the links that they provide between the authority and the people

[1]Committee on Public Participation in Planning, *People and Planning*, H.M.S.O., London, 1969.

they represent and on their willingness to open up major decisions to public discussion. The planning profession, in its turn, is now training its members in the techniques of public participation.

Concern has been expressed in some quarters about certain aspects of public participation: about the cost, in terms both of its financial implications and of its demands on the time and services of local authority members and staff, and about the possibility that it might hinder the planning process if ill-informed disputation between the authority and the public were encouraged. It has to be accepted that participation, in its fullest sense, will exact a price from society in resources and time; if the community places a value on the expression of its opinions and the reconciliation of its various interests, it must be prepared to pay that price.

BIBLIOGRAPHY: Community Planning Association of Canada, *The Citizen's Role in Community Planning,* Ottawa, 1967; Ministry of Housing and Local Government, *People and Planning,* report of the Committee on Public Participation in Planning, London, HMSO, 1969; P. Robshaw, *Public Participation in Urban Planning,* Ditchley Foundation, England, 1969; *Journal of the American Institute of Planners,* **25,** July 1969; Judith V. May, *Citizen Participation: A Review of the Literature,* Exchange bibliography 210 & 211, Monticello, Illinois, Council of Planning Librarians, 1971; D. F. Mazziotti, *Advocacy Planning—Toward the Development of Theory and Strategy,* Exchange bibliography 241, Monticello, Illinois, Council of Planning Librarians, 1971.   —HAROLD LEWIS

PUBLIC RELATIONS Planning, by virtue of the impact of its processes on society, touches on issues to which people are intensely sensitive and which easily become inflamed when communications between planners and the public are poor. Planning procedures may seem tortuous and protracted; strategies and policies may be framed in terms that are intelligible only to the expert. The planning authority is then seen as an inhuman technocracy, indifferent to opinion and unresponsive to protest. Within the context of representative government, planning is one area in which the need to create and maintain a good relationship with the public is self-evident.

Communications are the essential element in this relationship; they are the bridge that forms the framework for participation and allows the interchange of attitudes and ideas. "Public relations" is a general term which embraces the set of activities involved in the communication of policies and operations. Publicity is only part of these activities, and a great deal of public relations work is done at the grass roots level of common sense and courtesy in personal contacts.

In 1971, for England and Wales, 18 of the 58 administrative counties, 33 of the 79 county boroughs, 27 of the 32 London boroughs, and the Greater London Council employed public relations officers, press and publicity officers, or information officers to coordinate their communications activities. Planning is treated as one aspect of the authority's responsibilities. The methods employed by public relations staff in local government include the production of information sheets (*News from the Town Hall*), leaflets, and brochures; liaison with the press and other media; information and inquiry centers; community service schemes; press conferences, exhibitions, and meetings; and the stimulation of interest in special facilities and features of the locality. Cities such as Philadelphia in the United States and Liverpool and Manchester in the United Kingdom have set up permanent planning exhibitions combined with information offices where local residents and visitors to the city can gain an up-to-date picture of the progress of development. In many United States cities, publicity for planning proposals and concern about urban problems are channeled through citizens' groups, which seek to exert pressure on political and property interests.

Other councils place public relations in the hands of each department, implementing a program of activities on public relations in planning which is drawn up by the planning office itself. Firms of public relations consultants are employed by some authorities.

In Britain, the Royal Town Planning Institute, through its headquarters and regional branches, and the Town and Country Planning Association undertake public relations for the planning profession. They emphasize the need for the planner, particularly when talking to news media, to communicate his purpose and ideas in simple, nontechnical language. They also stress the importance of helpful person-to-person contact between the planner and the citizen and the critical need for an authority to base its proposals on an appropriate measure of public involvement. In this sense, public relations techniques are part of the broader mechanism of public participation (*q.v.*).

—HAROLD LEWIS

Q

QUARRIES   (*See* EXTRACTIVE INDUSTRIES.)

QUASI-SATELLITE   A name given to small communities around London, planned to meet urgent housing needs, which were built a little beyond the suburban area. They are called "quasi" because they are not complete towns (with industrial and commercial employment near the residential area as in a complete satellite) but are rather dormitory areas, and they have been much criticized as unsatisfactory developments.

QUASI-SATELLITE TOWN   (*See* SATELLITE TOWNS.)

R

RADIAL PLAN   A development of radiating roads from a city center, with urban accretions along the roads. It is a plan that results from natural, uncontrolled, haphazard growth, but it often forms the basis of good planning if combined with concentric or ring roads, in which case the spider-web plan evolves. Another variation is the star-shaped plan with green wedges between the urban areas which diminish outwards.

RADIO COMMUNICATION   (*See* COMMUNICATIONS.)

RAIL TRANSPORT   (*See* TRANSPORT and METROPOLITAN RAILWAYS.)

RAMP   An inclined plane—footway or roadway—connecting two levels. A common use of ramps in modern urban planning is for road or railroad underpasses and overpasses. Ramps have advantages over stairways for such purposes as they are easier for old people to negotiate and more convenient for the transit of baby carriages or perambulators. More space is required for their construction than for stairways, and they are generally a little more costly. Sometimes both ramps and stairways are provided.

REAL ESTATE   The term generally employed in the United States for landed property, which includes any immovable developments on the land. The term "real property" was traditionally used in England for immovable property, such as lands and buildings, as distinct from movable property. The terms for real estate in French, Italian, and Spanish carry this meaning: *propiété immobilière, proprietà immobiliare,* and *propiedad immobiliaria.*

RECLAMATION   In connection with land use, "reclamation" means, in its widest sense, the recovery or conversion of land mainly for agricultural purposes but occasionally also for construction purposes. It includes (1) the recovery of arid or semiarid land by irrigation and drainage; (2) the recovery of land from the sea, lakes, and rivers; and (3) the recovery of derelict land, mainly after mining and quarrying.

Operations to transform barren land into fertile soil have been among the greatest and most valuable tasks of civil engineering since the irrigation schemes of ancient Egypt. The most extensive operations of this kind in the twentieth century have involved the reclamation by irrigation of the arid and semiarid lands in the western United States, following the Reclamation Act of 1902, conducted by the United States Bureau of Reclamation. The work involved the construction of vast dams and reservoirs, while a very valuable auxiliary of such undertakings was the utilization of the water power for electricity generation. Among the most recent large-scale operations is the Missouri River Basin project, which involves the irrigation of about 9,500 square miles (24,600 square kilometers). Other vast irrigation operations of the mid-twentieth century are the Snowy Mountains scheme in southeastern Australia (begun in 1949 and due for completion in 1975) to irrigate about 10,000 square miles (25,900 square kilometers), involving the construction of nine large dams and many smaller ones, about 100 miles (160 kilometers) of tunnelling, and 80 miles (130 kilometers) of aqueducts high in the mountains. Another vast operation is the Indus Basin Scheme in Pakistan begun in 1962 for the maintenance of life and food production in an area of about 51,000 square miles (132,000 square kilometers), of which about 39,000 square miles (101,000 square kilometers) is for agricultural irrigation and flood protection. The construction work involves large reservoirs, dams and barrages, and link canals. Auxiliary to this vast irrigation scheme is the provision of hydroelectric developments on a considerable scale. (*See also* AGRICULTURAL LAND USE, IRRIGATION AND LAND USE, and DRAINAGE AND LAND USE.)

Reclamation of land from the sea, lakes, and rivers has continued for centuries in various parts of the world, among the most notable and interesting being the operations in the Netherlands, the Fenn district in England, and several areas in the United States. As a result of the work of reclamation in the Netherlands in the last 300 years, the map of that country in 1971 is very different from that in the seventeenth century. During the eighteenth and nineteenth centuries much of the area of North Holland was reclaimed; during the twentieth century a large part of the Zuyder Zee is being reclaimed. The latter, since the construction of the enclosing dam 22 miles (35 kilometers) across, is called the Ijsselmeer. The process of reclamation has continued, so that ultimately only a very small part of the former Zuyder Zee will remain.

Reclamation of derelict land and of land after mining and quarrying is considered in the article on extractive industries.　—ARNOLD WHITTICK

RECREATION, PROVISION FOR　In its widest sense, recreation is the process whereby individuals and communities renew and refresh themselves by pleasant occupations, amusements, and entertainments both physical and mental after work or study. This is regarded as essential to the well-being of civilized society. It is therefore one of the functions of planned development in urban renewal, in the extensions of cities, and in the provision of new communities. Beyond home pursuits, recreation involves the provision of theaters, cinemas, concert halls, art galleries, museums, and of open spaces for passive enjoyment and for games and many other kindred pastimes. Recreation, study, and work often overlap, and some people find the best recreation in the study of interesting subjects either linked with or totally different from their work.

One of the criticisms of much modern planning development of new communities is that insufficient provision is made for recreational facilities or that they are very late in coming. Among the reasons for this is that such provision is often left to commercial enterprise, which likes to be sure of a good return for investment and is reluctant to take risks in a new community. Where, however, these facilities would normally be provided in whole or part by the local government, premises for recreation must necessarily have a low priority compared with the provision of houses, shops, industrial offices, and educational buildings, yet the criticism is often made that once these essentials have been provided there is far too much time lag in the provision of recreational facilities, some of which are cultural. Some contend that this provides an argument for the state provision of these facilities, as occurs to some extent in several countries, or that such provision by commercial enterprise should receive some measure of state support or subsidy at least in the early stages of the enterprise. Whatever the method of providing these amenities, the claims of good recreational facilities as an enrichment of life are increasingly being recognized. Among the planning factors contributing to the success of recreational facilities are ease of access, especially by public transport; the good quality and facilities in the actual premises; and the standard of the entertainment. (*See also* OPEN SPACE IN URBAN AREAS.)　—ARNOLD WHITTICK

REFUSE COLLECTION AND DISPOSAL　In the past too little consideration was given to the problem of refuse collection in the layout of housing estates. The need for a layout that would allow a collection vehicle to approach to within not more than 50 yards (48 meters) of the back door of each house and to turn without completely blocking the roadway was not always understood. More recently, houses have been designed with special compartments adjoining the front door to accommodate the garbage cans.

The economics of refuse collection are largely dependent on the length of haul from the center of the estate to the point of dispersal, and this is a factor to be taken into account in the planning of an area.

Methods of refuse disposal vary widely—from crude dumping, controlled dumping, and disposal at sea to incineration and pulverization. The degree of salvage of salable products of household refuse also varies greatly.

There are now very few places in Great Britain where crude dumping is possible, i.e., where the length of haul is reasonably short, yet the dump is sufficiently distant from dwellings. Controlled dumping is much more usual. Standards of control exist in many countries, and these standards are frequently imposed as a condition of planning permission. The cost of disposal by controlled dumping varies greatly depending on the extent to which the regulations are observed.

If proper control is exercised, there is generally little cause for complaint by nearby residents—though complaints are almost invariably received—and many lowlying areas have been successfully turned into playing fields by this method.

It is not satisfactory to dump house refuse onto waterlogged land or flooded gravel pits without taking special, expensive precautions.

Sites suitable for controlled dumping are becoming scarce and in many areas other, more expensive, methods have to be adopted. Disposal at sea is unsatisfactory and uneconomical, partly because of the pollution of the sea, partly because of the indestructability of plastics, and partly because in rough weather it is impossible for vessels to operate, with the result that large quantities of refuse lie rotting ashore for considerable periods.

When most dwellings were heated by coal, house refuse consisted largely of ashes. Its incineration produced clinker, which could be used for road making.

Today, refuse consists mainly of paper and plastics, and the product of incineration is dust. Attempts have been made to mix this dust with sewage sludge so as to produce a manure, but generally this is not a commercial proposition. Neither is the pulverization of refuse. The product of pulverization is usually an innocuous material suitable for filling lowlying land but of doubtful value as a fertilizer.

Salvage arrangements vary from the hand picking of paper, rags, and bottles to highly sophisticated plants using magnets and other devices for the mechanical extraction of metals and other salable products; but the economics of such installations are dependent on the market price of these commodities, which fluctuates within wide limits.

For the city planner, the siting of refuse dumps or disposal plants is a difficult problem. A solution should be found at a very early stage in the preparation of the plan; it certainly should not be left to take care of itself.

The use of sink waste grinders, or the Garchey system which provides for the water-borne removal of house refuse—used chiefly in France and to a limited extent in blocks of flats in Great Britain—is convenient to the housewife, as she just deposits the refuse into an aperture in the sink.

Crushing systems used in apartments in the United States are similarly convenient. Both slightly reduce the cost of refuse collection, but they tend to add slightly to the cost of sewage disposal.

BIBLIOGRAPHY: F. L. Stirrup, *Public Cleansing: Refuse Disposal*, Pergamon Press; American Public Works Association, *Refuse Collection Practice;* Frank Flintoff, "Municipal Cleansing Practice," *Contractors Record and Municipal Engineering.*

—JOHN G. JEFFERSON

RELIGIOUS INFLUENCES IN PLANNING   Many of the traditional patterns of city planning and the forms of ideal cities are due, in part, to the influence of religion and the supernatural, which the rationalizing tendencies of the mid-twentieth century do not always sufficiently comprehend. We often accept and incorporate the forms for aesthetic reasons without always being aware of the meaning which they originally had. An awareness of the original meaning of urban forms will sometimes conduce to their intelligent application.

The conception of the universe common in primitive and ancient times affected the design of cities. There is ample evidence that the sky was thought of as a great dome above the flat earth, with the sun moving round the dome in the day and the moon by night. There were, of course, many variations of this conception. One was that the sky was supported on earth by columns at the four corners, others thought of the sky as supported on a mountain where the gods dwelt. The Sumerian gods dwelt on the summit of a lofty mountain, the gods of the Greeks dwelt on Mount Olympus, and God communicated with Moses at the summit of Mount Sinai. Buildings for worship were thus erected on the tops of mountains, and when there were no mountains, these were built, which is the probable origin of the ziggurat in Mesopotamia, a religious structure surmounted by a temple. The Greek acropolis surmounted by a temple was one expression of the idea, and religious worship with temples as central features may have been one of the initial primary reasons for hill towns, with defense a subsequent reason.

In ancient Egypt the great temples and tomb structures, sometimes identical, were the most important buildings in cities, and these were approached by avenues lined with sphinxes for the religious processions. This is the earliest known example of the avenue with a terminal feature, an arrangement which has been a characteristic of city planning ever since. It is essentially religious in purpose. The religious processional way occurred in various forms in Greek cities, the most famous being the Panathenaic Way, which moved diagonally across the agora and on to the Propylea of the Acropolis to the Parthenon, where dwelt the goddess Athena.

A monumental terminal feature often employed in city planning is the triumphal arch, which can be seen in most capital cities and which almost certainly originated, like the dome, as a representation of the arch of the sky and thus as a symbol of the universe. This similitude is apparent in several twentieth-century examples, such as the All-India Arch at Delhi by Lutyens.

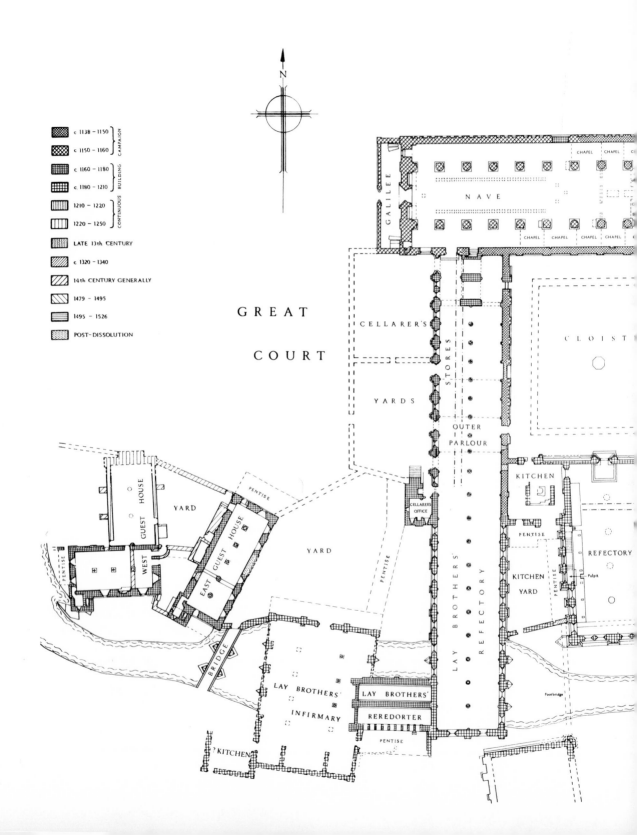

N

c 1138 – 1150 ⎤
c 1150 – 1160 ⎦ CAMPAIGN
c 1160 – 1180 ⎤ CONTINUOUS BUILDING
c 1180 – 1210 ⎦
1210 – 1220 ⎤ CONTINUOUS
1220 – 1250 ⎦
LATE 13th CENTURY
c 1320 – 1340
14th CENTURY GENERALLY
1479 – 1495
1495 – 1526
POST-DISSOLUTION

GREAT

COURT

NAVE

GALILEE

CHAPEL CHAPEL C

CHAPEL CHAPEL CHAPEL CHAPEL

CELLARER'S

STORES

YARDS

CLOIST

OUTER
PARLOUR

KITCHEN

CELLARERS
OFFICE

PENTISE

WEST GUEST HOUSE

YARD

EAST GUEST HOUSE

PENTISE

YARD

PENTISE

REFECTORY

PENTISE

PULPIT

KITCHEN
YARD

LAY BROTHERS' REFECTORY

PENTISE

BRIDGE

LAY BROTHERS'
INFIRMARY

LAY BROTHERS'
REREDORTER

Footbridge

? KITCHEN

PENTISE

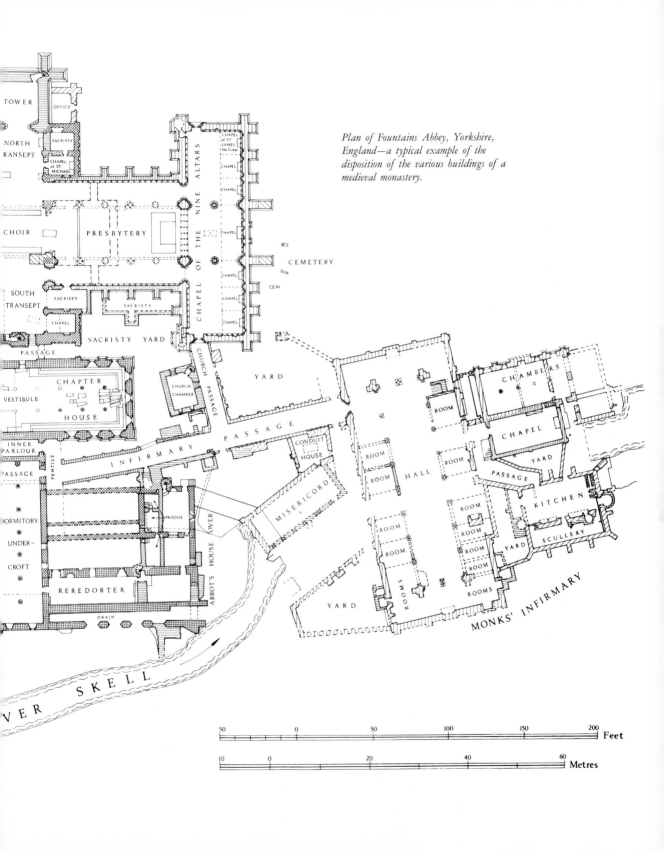

Plan of Fountains Abbey, Yorkshire, England—a typical example of the disposition of the various buildings of a medieval monastery.

TOWER

OFFICE

NORTH TRANSEPT

SACRISTY

CHAPEL of ST MICHAEL

CHAPEL of ST JAMES the Great

CHAPEL

CHAPEL

CHOIR

PRESBYTERY

CHAPEL OF THE NINE ALTARS

CHAPEL

CEMETERY

SOUTH TRANSEPT

SACRISTY

SACRISTY

CHAPEL

CHAPEL

SACRISTY YARD

PASSAGE

CHURCH PASSAGE

YARD

CHAPTER HOUSE

CHURCH CHAMBER

VESTIBULE

CHAMBERS

ROOM

CHAPEL YARD

INFIRMARY PASSAGE

ROOM

INNER PARLOUR

CONDUIT HOUSE

PASSAGE

ROOM

PASSAGE

PENTISE

HALL

KITCHEN

MISERICORD

ROOM

DORMITORY

OVEN

ROOM

ROOM

SCULLERY

PRISONS

ROOM

YARD

UNDER-CROFT

ABBOT'S HOUSE

ROOM

ROOM

ROOMS

REREDORTER

ROOMS

ROOMS

YARD

MONKS' INFIRMARY

DRAIN

RIVER SKELL

| 50 | 0 | 50 | 100 | 150 | 200 Feet |

| 10 | 0 | 20 | 40 | 60 Metres |

In the many conceptions of an ideal city by architects and planners of the Italian Renaissance, the circle or square or a combination of the two, sometimes called "the mandala" (the Hindu word for circle and an oriental symbol of order, unity, and wholeness), was a common basis, and it was chosen for religious reasons. God was conceived as the center around which all else revolves. It was felt that the perfect geometric figures, like the circle or square, were expressions of divine harmony, and that churches and cities should be built in conformity. Thus we find that many of the theoretic plans of cities that were made during the Renaissance were based on these regular geometric figures. A further support for the sacredness of the circle is the symbolic solar dance which originated the circular form of the orchestra. And the circle or square as the basic diagrammatic form of a city has persisted. It was strongly apparent in the nineteenth century, culminating in Ebenezer Howard's circular garden city. These geometric forms may have been considered by their authors as the most logical and convenient for city plans with a center, but some modern writers suggest that religious tradition, present perhaps, only on a subconscious level in the planner's mind, may have had some degree of influence on these plans.

Christianity and the monastic orders were the chief cultural influences in the early Middle Ages and were perhaps the chief agents in maintaining civilization through some of the dark periods of history. The group of monastic buildings, or complex as we might say today, was often an elaborate disposition of parts in the center of a settlement or community and consisted of a church, cloisters, chapter house, refectory, dormitory, school, infirmary, guest houses, bakehouses, garden and orchard, cemetery, mill, brewery, fishponds, and other structures necessary for community living. The remains of several monastic communities, such as Fountains Abbey in Yorkshire, are sufficient as a basis for reconstruction of the original.

It will be seen that here is the nucleus of a small town, and that although the central parts are formal and symbolic—like the church, with its cross plan and adjoining cloisters—the remainder, although following a roughly similar pattern, is more functionally planned according to convenience and according to the exigencies of the site, which was often near a river because of the supply of water and fish.

This formal planning in the center and more irregular, functional planning in the disposition of the surrounding buildings is a characteristic of the planning of medieval and many modern towns. It suggests the respective roles in planning of formality and symbolism and of more functional irregularity. Another important religious element in urban design is the creation of a sense of space. This is a religious purpose in the design of the interiors of cathedrals, and the same intention is sometimes apparent in the external effect. A supreme dual example is the spacious interior of St. Peter's, Rome, and the vast piazza in front recently enhanced by the Via della Conciliazione leading to it.

BIBLIOGRAPHY: Rudolf Wittkower, *Architectural Principles in the Age of Humanism*, Alec Tiranti, London, 1952 (originally published in 1949 as vol. 19 of the *Studies of the Warburg Institute*);

Banister Fletcher, *A History of Architecture on the Comparative Method*, 17th ed., revised by R. A. Cordingly, Athlone Press, London, 1961; Edmund N. Bacon, *Design of Cities*, Thames and Hudson, London, 1967; Charles Jencks and George Baird (eds.), *Meaning in Architecture*, especially Françoise Choay, "Urbanism and Semiology," Barrie & Rockliff, The Cresset Press, London, 1969.

—ARNOLD WHITTICK

RENAISSANCE PLANNING   The growth of individualism coincides with the development of the Renaissance. In Italy, there were numbers of classical buildings from a great past. Their destruction does not stem so much from the times of the invading barbarians or from the Middle Ages, but from a spate of building in *Renaissance* times. Thousands of columns and buildings were burnt to provide quicklime for the new projects. The discovery of ancient statues, such as the Apollo Belvedere and the Laocoön, gave new impetus to the Renaissance imagination. The pagan writers were studied anew, as it was decided this could be done in safety now that the true religion was established.

The Black Death and the reemergence of astrology were responsible for the Bill of 1484, which gave the official seal and recognition to the existence of witchcraft. A new tyrant-materialist class arose, and the great merchant-bankers even took over the papacy, making it a political force again. Names like Sforza, Borgia, and Este of Ferrara were famed in commerce and in ecclesiastical matters. Their rise to power was partly helped by the Italian Nationalists, for it was felt that if the source of all foreign intervention were removed, Italy could become united. It was from all-powerful persons in church and in state that the basic forms of Renaissance planning stem.

The design of towns in the Europe of the Renaissance period changed slowly at first from that conceived in the medieval spirit. At the beginning, the rise of secular power was expressed by the building of individual palaces within the *form* of the city, as in Florence. New emphasis, however, was placed on values based on the aesthetic of the classical period, since the formality and grandeur of antique design seemed lavish enough to suggest the ambition and egocentricity of the new aristocracy.

Rich and powerful men extended their patronage to artists, just as once the church had fulfilled this function. Artists and architects were brought in to embellish buildings within the *framework* of the medieval city, so the early phase might be described as *façadism* in terms of architecture.

With the widespread use of gunpowder, however, the corset of a wall around the medieval town became useless, so it was logical that towns should spread. The rivalries of groups of merchant-bankers had the opposite effect, for they desired the towns they controlled to be proof against even guns. The result was the development of massive new-style fortifications with earthworks, bastions, and artillery-resistant walls, making the towns secure once more. These new fortifications were enormously expensive to construct, and consequently they could not be moved outward. As the towns grew, therefore, terrible overcrowding occurred. Continental towns developed apartment living, while in England the same problem did not arise,

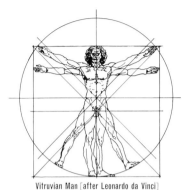

Vitruvian Man [after Leonardo da Vinci]

Note the mandala forms of square and circle and their relationship with the navel and genitals

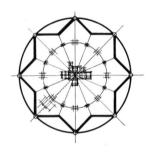

Sforzinda [after Antonio Filarete]

Vitruvian Ideal City.

Mandala forms.

due to the internal unification, the natural defense of the sea, and a lack of an urban tradition.

A phenomenon of Renaissance times was the rediscovery of ideal concepts in city design. These cities were conceived in the minds of individuals as entities: the static, unchanging *città ideale*. Basically, the ideal city consisted of a polygon with enormous star-shaped fortifications and a central core. The Renaissance designers froze the elements of a city into a formal pattern, rather like the crystal formations of a snowflake or a mandala, with streets which radiated from the center. The *città ideale* was also expressive of a longing for Utopia, conceived as perfection and remaining as such, and the symbolic creation of a city on which man imposed his own ideals of order and heroic dimensions while accentuating the egocentric nature of the period. Such designs emerged around the middle of the fifteenth century from the imaginations of Alberti, Filarete, and Martini, and it is in Alberti's works that we find designs for fortresses for tyrants. Alberti was keen on conformity and proposed that the nobility should be segregated from the vulgar in his scheme of things. He insisted that the plutocracy should have residences magnificent enough for their station. Ideas such as the development of a spiral street form were considered by Martini and others, partly to create interest and partly to resist cannon fire.

Both Michelangelo and Dürer designed highly complex bastions and fortifications which had a lasting effect on subsequent design. Many town fortifications were not removed until halfway through the nineteenth century. Other utopians, such as Scamozzi and Vasari, planned ideal cities within polygonal fortifications, but on traditional grid patterns. One *città ideale*, Palma Nova, was actually built as a Venetian fortress town in 1593. The plan was a nonagon with 18 radial streets and a central tower recalling Sforzinda. Palma Nova reflects the political climate of its day: the regular patterning, the conventional rules, the geometric perfection, and the disproportionately large fortifications, a source of enormous capital expenditure initially and for upkeep. The town symbolizes centralization, the problems of external threat, and the growth of specialization in the form of a standing army.

In the late-sixteenth and early-seventeenth centuries, unsettled times made defense a major consideration, and more land and capital were consumed by the fortifications. The exorbitant expense of standing armies and huge defenses made the citizens of towns more and more dependent on the financiers, aristocrats, princes, and kings. The resulting concentration of power gave birth to the nation states, whose heads challenged the power of the church and, in some cases, as in England, broke with Rome entirely. Almost overnight, English towns lost hundreds of chantry chapels, shrines, and monuments, and the great monastic foundations were dissolved. The confiscated wealth was distributed to the secular nobility in order to buy their allegiance.

Instead of the churches dominating the skyline of the towns and their

Ideal City [after Lorini]

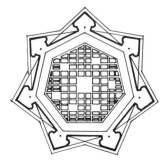
Ideal City [after Cataneo]

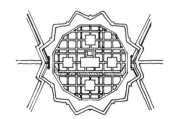
Ideal City [after Scamozzi]

Ideal cities (mandala variants).

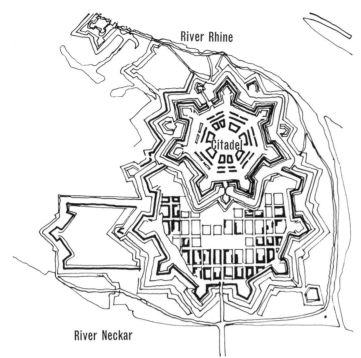

Seventeenth-century plans.

River Rhine

Citadel

River Neckar

MANNHEIM IN THE 17th CENTURY

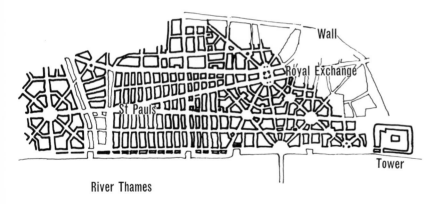

Wall

Royal Exchange

St Pauls

Tower

River Thames

WREN'S PLAN FOR LONDON 1666

very plans, as of old, the new dominants, palaces of the rulers, appeared. The centralization of power in the hands of a king or a prince created the grandiose egocentricity of Versailles, where all roads lead to the center of the palace and the town itself is completely dominated by it. Karlsruhe, too, is a shattering symbol of how much power rested in the hands of a secular ruler.

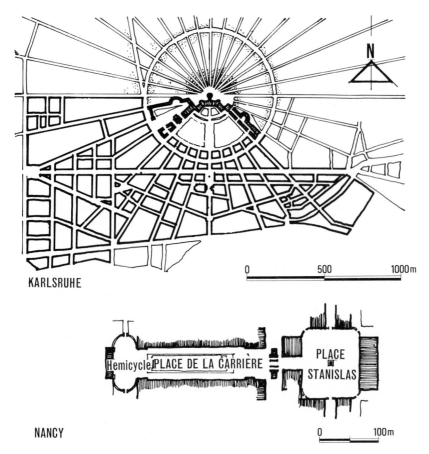

Diagrammatic plans of Karlsruhe and Nancy.

KARLSRUHE

0   500   1000m

Hemicycle PLACE DE LA CARRIÈRE

PLACE
STANISLAS

NANCY

0   100m

The regular, planned towns of the Renaissance, where the palace or the walls were the dominants, express their origins and the *Zeitgeist* in which they were created. They are also symbolic of that longing for order, for patterns, and for static, earthbound grandeur. The Middle Ages had defied gravity in its buildings and had attempted to reach up to the heavens with forests of pinnacles and spires. The Renaissance glorified man, especially the "super man," and God was replaced by the heroic dimensions of Renaissance reality.

BIBLIOGRAPHY: Jacob Burckhardt, *The Civilisation of the Renaissance in Italy,* S. G. C. Middlemore (trans.), Phaidon Press, Ltd., Vienna and George Allen & Unwin, Ltd., London, 1937; Arthur Korn, *History Builds the Town,* Lund Humphries, London, 1953; Cecil Stewart, *A Prospect of Cities,* Longmans, Green & Co., Ltd., London, 1952; Helen Rosenau, *The Ideal City in its Architectural Evolution,* Routledge & Kegan Paul, Ltd., London, 1959; James Stevens Curl, *European Cities and Society,* Leonard Hill, London, 1970.

—JAMES STEVENS CURL

RESEARCH   Information in its natural state, unprocessed and undisciplined by research techniques, is difficult to use and assimilate. It expands to fill as much time as it is given, it wanders into irrelevancy, and it repeats itself. To defend his budget against this tendency in his subject, the researcher must tame his data with carefully exercised controls.

Every researcher shares this need, but control over data is especially important to the economic consultant involved in urban and regional planning. The data he gathers is intended to serve the planners as a tool in making decisions. The planning team requires facts on which to base projections, opinions, and decisions; and it needs precisely those facts which illuminate the nature and relative desirability of alternative solutions. The researcher, therefore, must do more than simply accumulate facts; he must also select, analyze, interpret, and present them so that his research serves as a base for action.

This short article describes, first, the types of information which the researcher will encounter in urban and regional planning and, second, the rules of the research process which will assist him to achieve the purposes of the planning study.

Secondary Data The collection of secondary, or published, data is critical in almost all economic and planning studies. It is done early in the study to take advantage of existing studies (thus avoiding duplication of effort), to acquaint the researcher with new analytical techniques which may be developing in his field, and to provide background information on the study. Secondary data are important, clearly, not only for the knowledge they provide but also in the way they shape the researcher's approach to his study and prepare him for further work on the assignment.

The types of secondary data most often used in urban and regional planning are:
- Population trends and projections
- Population characteristics, such as age, income, occupation, and race
- Employment trends and projections, especially in different types of employment
- Land-use inventory data, showing square footages devoted to different specific types of uses
- Property value data
- Retail sales data

These items of information reveal what the planner has to work with, what he may have to work with in the future, and what is needed to achieve a workable, livable plan for the town or area under consideration.

The researcher must use caution in dealing with secondary data, however, for the following reasons:
- Data may not be up to date. In the United States, census data are collected every 10 years;[1] other sources are similarly passed by time. Many secondary sources, therefore, must be updated and supplemented to be useful in planning.

---

[1] In the United Kingdom it is also collected every 10 years, the last census having been taken in 1971. A sample census of one in ten households was taken in 1966. The practice of making such an intercensal survey may be continued in the future.—Editor.

- Data collection procedures vary. Sales tax information, for instance, may be kept well, sketchily, or not at all, depending on the law and the initiative of public officials.

- The source may be biased. Projections developed by a chamber of commerce or other promotional agency may reflect more hope than accuracy; a planning department's figures tend to be more realistic.

Secondary data, because of the caveats noted above, can be very misleading in the hands of an untrained and uncritical analyst. While such data must be at the researcher's disposal (preferably in a good public or company library), he must carefully weigh its value, analyze its meaning, and perhaps substantiate it with primary research.

Primary Data Primary, or original, research is essential to almost every planning study. By their nature, primary data are pertinent to specific problems; they are current; and often they constitute the only information available on certain issues or questions. On the other hand, they present their own problems.

Primary data are more expensive to get than secondary data. The methods of collection affect the accuracy of the results: poorly structured samples or questionnaires may result in faulty information. Moreover, it is always tempting to extract more from a survey than is statistically valid. On balance, however, the benefits of primary research justify (and demand) its use.

There are four chief methods of collecting primary data:

- Field surveys of physical facilities. These may include land-use inventories, measurements of the square footage of commercial facilities, and housing surveys.

- Field interviews with businessmen, government officials, real estate developers and brokers, tax assessors, financial institutions, etc. These are often the only sources of current, directly pertinent information; but they must be watched carefully for bias.

- Other interviews. Personal interviews are the best method, especially for getting in-depth information; but they are also the most expensive type of interview. Telephone interviews are less expensive than personal interviews, but the indirectness lowers the certainty of the response and even deters communications. Mail questionnaires are low in price but subject to bias and plagued by low response.

- Panel discussions. While panels of interested discussants do not produce statistically reliable data, they are excellent reflectors of community attitudes and interactions on subjects of concern.

There are also specialized techniques used in certain kinds of study. License-plate surveys are useful for retail trade analyses. In appraisals, real estate transactions may be analyzed.

The Research Process Most research assignments have three roughly sequential phases: (1) data collection, (2) analysis and interpretation, and (3) development of conclusions for presentation. Interpretation and conclusions would require far too broad a discussion to fit the scope of this article, since they involve many intangibles such as judgment, experience, and intuition. Data collection, however, is basic to a research study (although it is unproductive without the other two phases), and it has rules which can be simply set forth to aid the researcher in his task. These rules, of course, are rules of thumb, which vary according to the scope of the study, its purpose, and its budget. However, they have generally proved useful, and with some adaptations should serve a researcher well whatever his assignment.

Rule 1: The final purpose of the study should always be kept in mind. Research should always serve the object of the study. Interesting facts will always surround the pertinent facts; but if they do not bear on the purpose of the study, they should be simply marked up in memory as a useful source and not worked over as they arise. For instance, if one were working to produce a general land-use plan, one's concern would probably be with determining *ranges* of projections for population and land use rather than with attempting to pinpoint the figures exactly, as one would have to do for a specific facility.

Rule 2: Good work should not be duplicated. Governmental bodies often have large staffs whose job is to develop such statistics as population figures and projections. If such figures are available for the study area, it is folly for a research worker and his staff to duplicate their work. If there is confidence in their validity, existing figures should be used to develop *ranges* of projections and to translate these into meaningful projections of demand and into alternatives for future planning decisions.

Rule 3: A study should be structured as early as possible. It is helpful to formulate an outline of the study early in the research effort to assist in directing the work straight at the object, in developing the probable conclusions, and in deciding what areas need the most research. As a framework, this outline provides perspective on the entire effort. In building this structure, three subrules are helpful:

- Not more than one-third of the study effort and budget should be spent on data collection.
- The entire one-third should not be used at the start. As the study proceeds, gaps that need to be filled and points that need further research support or clarification will be found. A nest egg of time should be set aside and be used thriftily throughout the study.
- The report should be started about halfway through the study. As the fields of data were plowed, burrs of information, which can now be removed, will have clung to research workers. An early start in writing the report will also highlight the gaps and weak places in it, and it is at this point that the nest egg will prove of value.

Rule 4: Insights and ideas should be shared. A planning study is almost always a team effort, and teammates will have valuable insights into the research effort. Individual results and ideas should be exposed to the scrutiny of the team in "brainstorming" sessions. This may be painful, but it is useful. To work in a vacuum is to lose perspective and go into "data withdrawal," the symptoms of which are an obsessive concern with the facts as an end rather than a means.

Attention to these rules keeps the researcher flexible, selective, purposeful, and within his budget—an important thing to an economist.

—JOHN W. McMAHAN

RESERVOIR (*See* WATER SUPPLY and ELECTRIC POWER GENERATION AND TRANSMISSION.)

RIBBON DEVELOPMENT Urban spread along main roads, especially those leading to a city. The practice of building on either side of a main transport route has been common since the Middle Ages, and many villages and towns have arisen in this way. In modern times cities have spread partly in this manner. The provision of houses along a main artery to a city near principal bus routes is a natural form of dormitory development, and, although there are obvious advantages to residents, especially in the matter of transport, it is attended by many disadvantages. There is little residential quiet and seclusion for housing facing noisy traffic routes—which are dangerous, especially for children. The houses are often at greater distances from shopping centers and schools than they would probably be with concentric planning, there is a stretching of services which is uneconomic, and such development is usually unsatisfactory aesthetically. The many disadvantages prompted legislation in Great Britain to control development of this kind. (The Restriction of Ribbon Development Act, 1935.)

Building along transport routes is related to one form of the linear city, but if this is well planned, a more satisfactory, less haphazard relation of the main traffic route and buildings is secured and a degree of seclusion of residential areas is obtained in relation to nodal points and centers on the main route.

ROAD TRANSPORT (*See* TRANSPORT.)

ROMAN PLANNING (*See* ANCIENT PLANNING, ROMAN EMPIRE.)

ROMANIA

Geographical and Climatic Conditions Romania is situated in southeastern Europe, north of the Balkan Peninsula, and it has natural boundaries over two-thirds of its perimeter of almost 2,000 miles (3,153 kilometers). It is a harmonious geographical unit, with varied topography over a comparatively small surface of 94,500 square miles (237,000 square kilometers). The Carpathian Mountains, with altitudes of 2,600 to 8,200 feet (800 to 2,500 meters), border the Transylvanian Plateau of 1,640 to 1,970 feet (500 to 600 meters) located in the center of the country. Hilly areas of 656 to 2,600 feet (200 to 800 meters) lie to the south and east, followed by the lowlands (under 656 feet or 200 meters) of Moldavia and Muntenia.

Mountains constitute 37 percent of the country's area, are covered with forests, and are rich in minerals; hills and plateaus, representing 30 percent of the surface, are covered with orchards and vineyards and supply the country's oil; while plains make up the remaining 33 percent of the surface and provide fertile soil for agriculture. The pyramidal disposition of the territory, varied geographical character, and location at 45 degrees north latitude (equidistant from the polar circle and the equator) and 25 degrees east longitude (between the Atlantic Ocean and the European continental steppe) ensures a certain diversity of climate, which is, however, mainly temperate—continental.

Air circulation patterns are important in local variations of the climate: cold winter winds reach the eastern and southeastern parts of the country; in spring and autumn, warm winds bring a Mediterranean influence in the western part.

The four seasons are of equal duration. The average temperature varies from 77 to 86°F (25 to 30°C) in summer and from 14 to 5°F (−10 to −15°C) in winter. The annual average temperature is about 50°F (10°C). The variations of temperature are large in the flatlands and decrease toward the mountains. The yearly average duration of sunshine is between 2,000 and 2,500 hours, i.e., about a half the maximum. The rainfall and snowfall are moderate (between 16 and 40 inches—400 and 1,000 millimeters—in the plains and the mountains respectively). It usually rains in autumn and spring, and in winter it snows abundantly. The Carpathian curve constitutes a zone of 8 degrees on Beaufort's seismic scale.

The geographical conditions of Romania account for the importance traditionally given to life in the open air and for the basic occupations of the population.

Planning to the Middle of the Twentieth Century The ancient autochthonous peoples of Romania, the Gets and Dacians, erected a number of fortified towns and strongholds during the last centuries preceding the Christian era. Extensive clusters of such localities, like Gradistea-Muncelului, Costeti, Blidaru, and Sarmiegetua were discovered in the central mountainous area of the country. Beginning in the sixth century B.C., Greek colonists founded, on the shore of Pontus Euxinus (the Black Sea), a number of cities such as Callatis, Tomis, and Histria, which were centers of intense activity and trade with the natives.

The Roman occupation, about 100 A.D., brought with it intense town-building activity. Towns, Roman camps, and strongholds were erected and linked by a network of roads. Among the noteworthy localities of that period are Napoca (now Cluj), Apulum (now Alba Iulia), Potaissa, Porolissum, and Drobeta (now the port Turnu-Severin) on the Danube.

In the period from the Roman Empire to the twelfth century, the scarce information available confirms the decline or disappearance of some localities such as Histria or Sarmisegetuza. Others, such as Dinogetia, situated in secluded places which were therefore easier to defend, escaped the inroads of migratory peoples and disappeared only as a result of the shifting of economic interests.

After 1,000 A.D. mention is made of the first autochthonous Romanian feudal states. They grouped together later on and created the three Romanian principalities: Moldavia, Wallachia (Muntenia), and Transylvania. These principalities practically correspond to the three major geographical and geological subdivisions of the country.

The Romanian states led a separate existence for a long time, which accounts for some local differences among the three major provinces, although the character of the country is basically homogeneous.

In Moldavia and Wallachia, lying east and south of the Carpathian range, town life developed under more difficult conditions than in Transylvania, since these provinces were more exposed to wars. The boroughs and towns, especially those situated in the hilly areas, were small, with sparce clusters of buildings surrounded by palisades and moats. Usually they played a role in trade, transportation, navigation (e.g., Brăila, Giurgiu), or in administration and held the residences of the princes (e.g., Suceava, Iaşi, Tîrgovişte, Bucharest), which were settled in strongholds or fortified courts, as in Curtea-de-Argeş and Roman. Later, important artisans' centers developed around these nuclei.

Regulations, existing since the sixteenth century, established the alignment of the streets and marked the limits of the town perimeter. The street vistas as well as the general appearance of the localities were the result of continuous creative efforts, exhibiting predominantly horizontal lines and skylines varied by many church towers and abundant vegetation.

Transylvania, surrounded by the Carpathian Mountains, enjoyed greater economic stability, which was due also to its closer, more frequent relations with the rest of Europe. Influences in town building appeared when various groups of Western European migrants settled there. Some medieval towns in Transylvania outgrew the old Roman localities but preserved some elements of the street pattern, e.g., Cluj (ancient Napoca) and Alba-Iulia (Apulum). In other towns a functional pattern was developed in response to circulation requirements (e.g., Sighişoara, Braşov).

Inhabited by tradesmen and free artisans organized in guilds, these towns were usually protected by complex systems of defense structures.

Toward the end of the feudal period, in Wallachia, Moldavia, and especially in Transylvania, the fortifications were built in French or Austrian style (e.g., Timişoara, Arad, Giurgiu). Later, the growth of the towns resulting from the industrial development and expansion of trade led to the dismantling of the fortifications.

The nineteenth century brought important changes. The general rules concerning the planning, growth, and administration of towns were issued in 1832. At the same time, especially in Wallachia, an intense period of new-town building began. Turnu-Măgurele was founded in 1836, Olteniţa in 1852, and later Turnu-Severin and others. Usually, the new towns had a gridiron street pattern, sometimes unsuited to a settlement's functions, which were directed toward a central nucleus.

Interesting plans were prepared in 1836 and 1855 for the expansion of the towns of Brăila and Focşani. New urban legislation was issued in 1864;

this was amended in 1884 and remained in force until the First World War. In 1859, the state of Romania was created through the unification of Wallachia and Moldavia. After 1870, important works were started in Romania's capital, Bucharest. New boulevards were laid out, several town squares were replanned, parks were built, and the course of the Dîmboviţa River was regulated.

Before the First World War, similar developments occurred in other major towns of the country, largely as a result of the rapid growth of industry. These activities accelerated, especially after 1918, when Transylvania joined Romania and the unification of the country was completed.

Cooperative associations were created in order to house the growing urban population. A number of low-cost housing complexes were thus built, the Floreasca district in Bucharest being the best example of this kind of development. Nevertheless, the number and scale of the town planning achievements during the period between the two world wars remained relatively small.

During the same period, valuable theoretical studies were published by Alexandru Davidescu, an engineer and professor of town planning at the Bucharest Polytechnic School, and also by Cincinat Sfinţescu, former vice-president of the International Federation of Housing and Planning (headquarters in The Hague) and professor of town planning at the Bucharest Academy of Architecture.

The latter is known for his theory on "superurbanism" and his proposals concerning planning of Black Sea health resorts and other Romanian tourist zones. His development plan for Bucharest, prepared from 1914 to 1916, preceded the Bucharest Pilot Plan. This important and complex project was prepared in the 1930s by a team which included architects Duiliu Marcu and G. M. Cantacuzino, engineer T. Rădulescu, and others.

Legislation and Administration Radical socioeconomic transformations have taken place in Romania since approximately 1945. At present over 40 percent of the 20 million inhabitants live in urban localities. The census of March 15, 1966 showed that of a total of 19,105,056 inhabitants, the urban population amounted to 38.2 percent.

Administratively, the area of the Socialist Republic of Romania is divided into 39 territorial units or districts averaging 2,300 square miles (6,000 square kilometers) and 400,000 inhabitants. Bucharest, the capital city of Romania, including its surrounding territory, is a separate administrative unit. The other localities of the country have been classified into three categories according to their importance. The first category is represented by settlements each having a population of over 5,000 and consisting of 247 municipalities and towns. Bucharest has a population of about 1.5 million; 12 towns have populations ranging between 100,000 and 200,000; 7 towns have from 50,000 to 100,000 inhabitants; 41 towns have from 20,000 to 50,000 inhabitants; and 68 towns have from 10,000 to 20,000 inhabitants. Urban localities are uniformly distributed: there are no large areas without settlements, thus new towns are seldom built in Romania. The second category of settlements consists of 2,706 communes. Each commune contains four to five villages and has a total population of 4,000 to 5,000 inhabitants. The third category consists of villages which amount to a total of 13,149 units.

The rural localities are numerous and relatively small. This raises problems concerning their planning, equipment, and gradual regrouping within the framework of the administrative districts and communes.

The main governmental bodies of the country are the Great National Assembly—the highest legislative forum—and the people's councils, which are the organs of the local authorities. The State Council supervises the implementation of the laws and decisions adopted by the Great National Assembly. The organs of the state administration are the Council of Ministers, which is the supreme executive body; the Ministries and the State Committees, which are the central executive bodies; and the executive committees of the people's councils, which carry on the local executive activities.

The legislation, which has a complex structure and is constantly being brought up to date, comprises the following categories (in accordance with the importance and competence of the corresponding legislative bodies): laws enacted by the Great National Assembly; decrees issued by the State Council; decisions adopted by the Council of Ministers; technical and methodological directives of the central executive bodies; and also state standards.

The main enactment in physical planning was adopted by the Council of Ministers in 1966, specifying the central and local organs responsible for physical planning activities. This also includes the basic dispositions relating to the preparation, review, and approval of the studies and projects in this field. Within the framework of the central executive bodies, the State Committee for Local Economy and Administration (CSEAL) directs and coordinates the people's councils executive committees at the district, municipality, town, commune, and village levels. These executive committees supervise the actual implementation of the measures dealing with physical planning and the development of the territories and localities. They operate through their technical departments and technical scientific councils. The State Committee for Planning (CSP), which directs the economic planning activities in the country, is responsible, through its Section for Constructions, for investments of state funds in the housing construction sector, and for municipal and town equipment. It is also concerned with major regional, urban, and rural physical planning activities.

The practical responsibility for physical planning at the district, municipality, and town levels is invested in the respective local chief architects.

The technical, methodological, and substantive instructions for physical planning projects were prepared by the State Committee for Building, Architecture, and Planning (CSCAS), which is now merged with CSEAL. Compulsory prescriptions regarding various aspects of the physical planning of the territories and localities are also contained in different normative decisions of other technical bodies.

For instance, the Ministries of Education, Public Health, and Foreign Trade, the State Committee for Culture and Arts, and the Central Union of Handicraft Cooperatives prepare instructions dealing with the organization and functioning of the sociocultural and service facilities. The Superior Council of Agriculture prepares instructions with regard to the use of agricultural land. The Ministry of Electric Power, the Ministry of Transport, and other state departments make regulations for the use of urban technical equipment. Regulations for protection against fire are included in a standard document issued by a specialized department within the Ministry of Internal Affairs.

Property is of different types: state property, managed by the institutions or enterprises which use it; property of public organizations; and private property in the case of individual or cooperative dwellings. The legal status of the vacant plots in private property within the city or town perimeter and on which building is possible is determined by a law promulgated in 1968, according to which speculation on such lands is prohibited.

Expropriation in the public interest of vacant or occupied land is accomplished through decrees issued by the State Council. When land is acquired in this way (e.g., by the local people's councils or industrial enterprises) displaced persons must be compensated or provided with adequate dwellings.

Professional Practice The practice of town planning comprises study, research, and the preparation of city planning projects. These tasks are carried out by central or regional design institutes which may either be specialized or cover a broad range of activities.

The Institute for Research and Design in Building, Architecture, and Planning located in Bucharest (ISCAS) and the Design Institute of Bucharest (IPB) are both of a complex type and possess specialized units for regional, urban, and rural physical planning.

The 39 regional design offices existing in the important towns of the country each include at least one physical planning unit dealing with physical and town planning activities.

The above-mentioned design institutes prepare studies and plans of great complexity. When necessary, they may obtain the collaboration of some specialized design offices (e.g., in topography, geotechnics, hydrotechnics, electric power, communal services, transportation, or telecommunications).

Different design institutes that specialize in design and planning for various types of industrial activities participate in the preparation of regional, urban, and rural development plans. They may also prepare layouts for industrial zones whenever they deal with the creation or extension of important industrial areas.

The different possible types of physical planning projects are established by a specific decision of the Council of Ministers and by the instructions and regulations regarding the implementation of this decision. The different types of physical planning projects being prepared in Romania are the following:

- Regional studies and plans. Usually these projects are elaborated for a territory or a zone having certain common features and a predominant specific character: industrial, agricultural, and/or tourist. In other cases, these studies and plans can deal with the surrounding territory of a town taking into account the existing complex of economic and social interactions. Such exercises can also deal with the territory of a commune, which usually includes a number of villages.

- Master plans of cities, towns, health resorts, and villages.
- Site plans for certain areas of the localities such as urban central districts, areas under urban renewal, new residential districts and complexes, sport and amusement complexes, open spaces and traffic schemes, industrial zones, and civic centers in the communes.
- Layouts for areas of reduced dimensions.

In addition to the above-mentioned projects, the town planning professional activities include the preparation of research studies on specific or comprehensive subjects.

Projects are brought up to date periodically. The design and research institutes in the field of regional urban, and rural planning can get the necessary information from official central sources (Central Board of Statistics and ministries dealing with industrial activities) and from the local sections of the above agencies and institutions.

During the preparation of the studies and plans, the planner is expected to ask various state institutions for reviews of the project and for professional advice.

In the international field, Romania participates in the planning activities of corresponding international organizations or agencies such as the UN, the COMECON, the IUA, and the IFHP.

Training and Education   Urban planning education started in Romania at the beginning of the twentieth century. The first lectures were delivered at the Polytechnic School of Bucharest by engineer Alexandru Davidescu. Later on, this study was introduced also at the Academy of Architecture. Here, immediately after the First World War, a town planning chair was created which was occupied by engineer Cincinat Sfințescu, who did his best to spread this new science. The curriculum included lectures on town planning, municipal administration, and town legislation as well as practical activities. Summary lectures on town planning were also delivered at the Faculty of Law of the Bucharest University, at the Superior School of the Corps of Engineer Officers, and at the Superior School of State Science.

After the Second World War, town planning education in Romania continued in the Institute of Architecture of Bucharest, a university establishment with chairs for each of the main branches of building and planning activities. The town planning chair, the importance and scope of which have recently been much increased, was created for the teaching of physical and town planning so as to contribute to the formation of a special type of professional, the future architect-town planner. This town planning department offers an introductory and general town planning course, another course in the history of town planning, a course in town aesthetics and the art of landscaping, and a course in municipal works and equipment. During their last 3 years, students attend courses in regional and complex development planning and thus obtain additional knowledge in sociology, urban traffic, and economic problems. The practical aspect of teaching includes town planning design, exercises in town planning problems, and seminars. From 1970, Architecture and City Planning departments were established at the Polytechnic Institutes of Cluj, Iaşi and Timişoara. During the last year, a diploma project on a physical planning subject is prepared individually by each student under the direction of a professor. The diploma projects must bring solutions to real problems, which are usually studied at the same time by the town planning design and research institutes of the country.

During the preparation of their diploma projects, the students start specializing in the field of physical planning, working on a part-time basis in the urban or rural planning units of the design and research institutes.

The preparation of a thesis for a master's or doctor's degree in town planning has become an important form of specialization. Other kinds of specialized education in town planning, such as lectures, symposiums, debates, and discussions, are organized by the Union of Architects and by the Institute of Architecture. There are also high schools for architecture and building where comprehensive training is given, including urban planning courses and design exercises as well as related theoretical courses.

Lectures on town planning are also delivered in some universities that have links with architecture and town planning, including the institutes of construction in Bucharest, Cluj, and Timisoara and the law faculty and department of sociology at the University of Bucharest.

Institutions Some professional, educational, and public relations institutions in town planning in Romania, have long traditions, others are newer. They are either under the guidance of the central state agencies or they are autonomous. They cooperate in order to make urban planning more generally understood.

The most important is the Union of Architects, a national chapter of the IUA founded in 1952, with its headquarters in Bucharest. It replaced and continued the activities of an old professional union that had functioned since the end of the nineteenth century. The Union of Architects is organized in sections dealing with different specific problems, one of these being urban planning. The union organizes exhibitions, professional contests, and debates, and it establishes contacts with similar institutions abroad. At the same time, it is concerned with disseminating architectural and town planning information among the population. It also issues the magazine *Arhitectura*.

The Union of Architects has local chapters in the major design institutes as well as in 39 important cities of the country. Some related problems are dealt with by CNIT, the Romanian National Professional Union of Engineers and Technicians, whose constitution is similar to that of the Union of Architects. The Centre of Documentation in Building, Architecture and Planning (CDCAS) deals with the gathering and dissemination of specific technical information and its popularization through exhibitions, films, lectures, and publications. It publishes information bulletins and abstracts and has a large technical library, a film library, and an important collection of photos as well as photographic studios. The center is in close contact with many specialized institutions and centers abroad. The Institute of Technical Documentation (IDT) is more complex, but it, too, deals with town planning problems. It issues general information publications, organizes educational and special-subject exhibitions, and maintains relations with corresponding institutions abroad.

The Second Half of the Twentieth Century   The period following the Second World War witnessed an important urban planning effort which can be subdivided into three periods. The first occurs in the years 1944 to 1949, when the old design and building systems persisted. The few town planning activities were carried on mainly by private design offices, and priority was given to reconstruction of industrial enterprises and of national road and transportation systems. A number of residential quarters were built, still under the influence of the rationalistic ideas prevailing in urban planning before the Second World War.

The 1949 to 1956 period started with the creation of the first state design and building enterprises. During this period a formalistic tendency with archaic overtones predominated in urban planning and architecture. The disappearance of this tendency marked the end of this period. During this period, town blocks were the major examples of planning. An important positive element in the development of urban planning at that time was the adoption of a decision by the Council of Ministers regarding the socialist reconstruction of towns. As a result of this decision, urban planning was given considerable weight in the national economy.

The period starting in 1956 was marked by a return to contemporary urban planning principles and by the first important planning achievements. The idea of complex town planning units started to be implemented. National planning legislation became better adapted to the specific realities of the situation. A law promulgated in 1966 dealt with the assistance offered by the state for the construction of privately owned dwellings; another law, adopted in 1967, concerned the rational use of urban territory and regulated the use of agricultural land for other purposes. Another law, adopted in 1968, provided for the diversification of dwellings and for better upkeep of publicly owned houses.

As a result of the important efforts made by the state at present, all urban localities have master plans which are periodically brought up to date. The problems relating to physical regional planning are necessarily approached from a realistic standpoint, taking into account the broad context of economic, social, and administrative aspects. Important regional planning studies and projects have been prepared; some deal with problems at the national level. The link between economic and physical planning has become a permanent objective.

Although the building of New Towns is done only in special instances, there are some well-planned new localities. The few New Towns which appeared after the Second World War were usually built in close connection with the existing or proposed new industrial units. The New Town of Victoria, which was started in 1955, is such an example. It was built close to an important group of chemical industries. Victoria was planned as a garden city, with two-storied buildings along winding streets, having a density of 125 inhabitants per acre (308 per hectare). Another new town was started in 1952 in Moldavia, close to a zone of chemical industries located in the Trotu Valley. This town, called Gheorghe Gheorghiu-Dej, was built on the site where the small village of Oneşti stood and has now reached a population of more than 80,000 inhabitants. It is composed of neighborhood units with a polynuclear center; the buildings are very varied, ranging from 1 to 10 or more stories. Planners made sure that there would be plenty of open spaces leading to the surrounding countryside.

The building of a giant hydroelectric power station on the Danube, at the Iron Gates (Porţile de Fier) gave rise to the problem of removing the town and port of Orşova to a place located above the new level of the Danube. On this occasion a new approach to combine state cooperative and private investments was tested. The new town of Orşova is now under construction.

Part of the master plan of the New Town of Gheorghe Gheorghiu-Dej. The layout reflects various recent tendencies in Romanian contemporary urban planning. The neighborhood units are limited in size. The hospital is located at the northern limit of the city, which is planned to grow toward the south, around the central town area currently under construction on the southern edge of the plan.

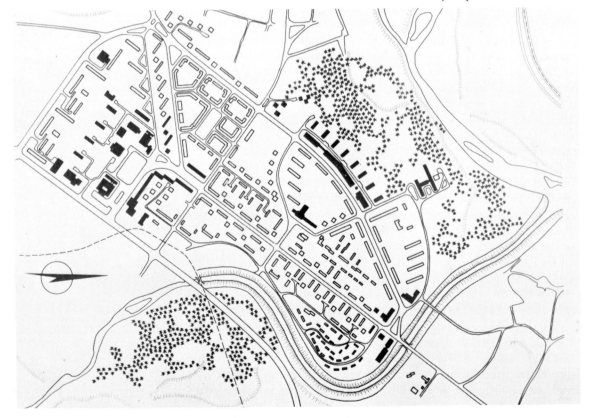

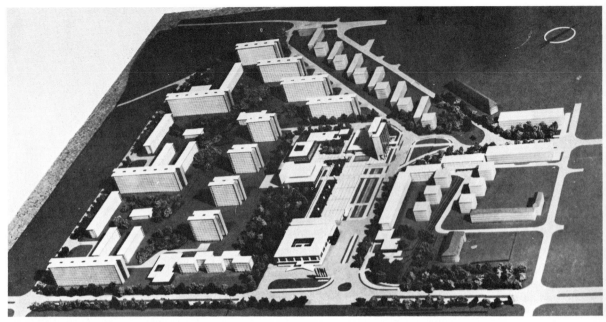

The New Town of Gheorghe Gheorghiu-Dej. Proposals for the administrative center. The high-rise building is an existing hotel. The other important construction at the other end of the esplanade is a cultural complex with an entertainment hall. The city will develop concentrically around this center.

Other new localities, with fewer inhabitants, were created near mining works (e.g., Motru and Bălan), or in the neighborhood of metallurgical industries (e.g., Oţelul Roşu). As a rule, the location of the new towns was established on the basis of a judicious analysis of economic, social, and functional criteria. New town planning principles were adopted for town structure, location of working zones, and sociocultural services.

There have been three main categories of urban construction. In the first of these belong existing towns which were developed or expanded. This happened first with many small localities which grew rapidly, usually because of industrial development. In the second group belong those medium and large cities where the existing houses were good enough to preserve and where the existing urban structure had to be maintained. Finally in the third category, are cities which were very extensively reconstructed, since neither the buildings nor their structure justified a conservationist attitude.

In the first category we may mention Hunedoara, whose expansion was based on the growth of its metal works. The town engaged the attention of urban planning specialists for a long time. A workers' quarter was built as early as 1948. A study for a physical planning project for the Hunedoara district was prepared in 1950, and in 1954 a plan for the Hunedoara-Deva-Simeria-Călan microregion was produced. The development plans dealt with an increase from 30,000 to 100,000 inhabitants.

Baia-Mare, an ancient mining settlement situated in the northern part of the country, represents another type of development where new residential quarters were built in the neighborhood of the old center, which had been

LEFT: *The new center of the town of Piatra-Neamț.* BELOW: *Mamaia. The new health resort on the Black Sea.*

preserved in good condition. The link between the new and the old parts was ensured by expansion of the existing central zone.

Piatra-Neamț is an example of a town with a fundamental reorganization of its structure, especially of its central area.

In all cases a common principle in contemporary Romanian town planning is applied. The new urban zones are organized in complex planning units separated by major transportation arteries or by natural elements.

Development of the health resorts on the Black Sea shore, such as Mamaia and Mangalia-Nord, also occurred along the same lines. Mamaia, placed on what was previously a strip of desert land between the sea and an inland lake, has a composition of tall buildings which give it a certain air of monumentality. Mangalia-Nord has a more lively composition, favored by the sort of topography and vegetation which create a more intimate atmosphere.

Bucharest, the capital of the country, is a singular example. Here the expansion of the city took place after the Second World War mainly through building on the free territories remaining between built-up zones stretching along the access roads to the city. This activity developed on a larger scale since the 1960s, when the first complexes of low-cost houses were erected. After 1956, when new town planning principles were applied, the physical planning organization of Bucharest was carried out in town districts comprising from 100,000 to 200,000 inhabitants, town quarters of from 40,000 to 50,000 inhabitants, neighborhood units accommodating from 4,000 to 12,000 people, and groups of dwellings having less than 1,500

Bucharest. Aerial view of the central area of the city with the new Conference Hall of the Palace of the Republic.

inhabitants. Each such structural unit has a center and sociocultural institutions and services which follow a preestablished hierarchy and have a capacity calculated according to existing state standards. Two large new town quarters of Bucharest, that of Titan in the east and Drumul Taberei in the west, were set up according to this principle. Although these residential quarters apply the same town planning principles, they exhibit two different solutions, both as to their planning layout and the size and shape of the buildings.

Urban reconstruction has frequently been imposed in Romania either by war damage or by the unsatisfactory state of existing dwellings. The needs created by the systematic redevelopment of towns gradually produced a definite methodology for urban reconstruction activities. These activities usually began modestly through the bridging of gaps between buildings situated along the major thoroughfares of the towns. At a later stage the whole architectural framework of some thoroughfares was restructured (e.g., in Bucharest—Calea Griviţei and Şoseaua Giurgiului; in Piteşti—Calea Bucureştilor; in Craiova—Calea Unirii).

At the same time, the problem of restructuring some central zones or central squares arose. Plans for these areas were obtained mainly through national design contests. This was the case at Iaşi for Piaţa Unirii and Piaţa Podul Roşu, at Ploeşti for the group of central squares, at Bacău for the central area, at Galaţi for the town center on the Danube, at Deva and Suceava for their centers, and in Bucharest for Piaţa—Palatului Republicii, Piaţa Chibrit, and Piaţa Gării de Nord.

The center of the city of Iaşi, with the new hotel.

The center of the town of Deva.

City of Galaţi. The scale model of the residential quarters Ţiglina I and II, recently built. A major avenue leading to the main industry divides the residential quarters. The southern area is a large neighborhood unit extending to the Danube. An open space follows a natural depression and represents a link between the social and commercial center and the exterior open spaces, providing a dramatic view toward the river. The northern part consists of two neighborhood units and a sociocommercial center. All town-planning units have their schools, kindergartens and shops. The adjacent sport complex is planned for the whole city.

From the functional point of view, these central areas can serve as civic centers, road intersections, or recreation plazas. Their planning is adapted to the configuration of the landscape, as was the case especially in Galaţi and Bucharest; it can also assure a link with existing historical elements, as in Suceava, Deva, and Piatra Neamţ. These new central complexes are

City of Galaţi. The new residential area Ţiglina.

given an individual character through the presence of important horizontal or vertical elements and volumes, and they become nuclei of an active urban life since the buildings surrounding these central areas have different uses (administrative, commercial, cultural, or residential).

Organizing urban areas in complex town planning units meant a great step forward in urban planning. The advantages of this method resided primarily in its elasticity, which allowed its adaptation to towns of any size, pattern, or architectural style. Based mainly on the neighborhood unit concept, this principle makes it possible to build clusters of dwellings of

The center of Ploieşti with the main food market of the city.

an optimal size and to endow them with adequate social and cultural services. The new residential districts of Suceava, Ploieşti, and Tîrgul Mureş provide good examples of this principle.

Among the town districts which were rebuilt or built completely anew, the largest are located in Bucharest (Titan, Drumul Taberii Pajura, Berceni), Galaţi (Tiglina I and II), Iaşi (Tataraşi), and Cluj (Gheorghieni and Grigorescu).

A special category of urban reconstruction is represented by the studies devoted to the replanning of historical zones (e.g., Braşov, Tîrgovişte, Sibiu, etc.).

Braşov. The medieval center of the city.

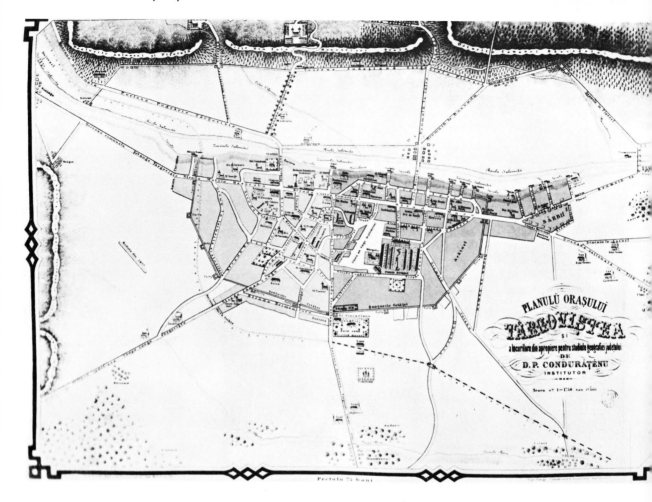

As a general principle the design of new or reconstructed complex units in town planning is done in stages determined by economic, functional, and social criteria. After careful individual analysis, it is decided to what extent the pattern of streets is to be retained and which buildings are still in good enough condition or important enough to be preserved. In essence, Romanian town planning activities carefully introduce new elements into an existing, built-up environment with its own individual style.

A consistent aim is the preservation of the traditional appearance of Romanian localities. A conscientious and carefully planned effort is being made to create new urban structures in line with the requirements of contemporary life while at the same time preserving the traditional environment.

Conclusion The problems and tasks of urban planning in Romania result from the economic and social changes which have occurred in recent decades. The planning of the national economy, the scientific exploitation of natural

Plan of Tîrgovişte (end of the nineteenth century). The former capital of Wallachia still preserves its fortified walls, which represent its limit. The river Ialomiţa completes the perimeter. The city is compact and well structured, resembling somewhat the "ideal" cities of the Rennaissance.

resources, and the active industrialization of the country, accompanied by a social policy aiming at the welfare of the population, have produced an important growth in the urban population, and also made necessary the study of the territorial distribution of economic and social activities. The important role of physical planning at the national, regional, and local levels is now officially recognized. In this context, urban planning plays a major role among those activities as it is a satisfactory means of restructuring and relocating the main residential and industrial zones.

The existing housing stock, which is insufficient and inadequate, is being substantially increased. The state is the main builder, since it erects out of its Centralized Investment Fund almost 40 percent of the country's total housing. In 1967, this production represented a ratio of 6.6 apartments built per 1,000 persons. The vast scale of building by industrial methods was a response to the existing large demand and has influenced urban planning. Newly adopted urban planning legislation established the necessary administrative framework for implementing national and local policy in urban planning. A recent reform of the administrative division of the country created better conditions for the physical planning of urban and rural settlements. The existence of central guiding and control organizations helps to coordinate and stimulate design and execution. Some problems still remain to be solved, especially those relating to the theoretical aspects of research in architecture and town planning.

Romanian urban planning seeks to achieve a new quality, the significance of which may already be noted in some new urban designs and theoretical studies. These refer to specific methods of settling the population into the territory; i.e., obtaining an optimal relationship between the labor and dwelling functions and between urban and rural neighboring settlements. The studies also deal with the redistribution of urban functions through organization of complex urban planning units where the coexistence of dwellings and industrial units is applied as a general principle. The research effort is also directed toward establishing a new interpretation of the relationship between the dwelling and related functions. As a general rule special attention is paid to the continuous adjustment of urban planning in Romania to national, regional, and local realities.

BIBLIOGRAPHY: Cincinat Sfințescu, *Urbanistica generală* (*General Town Planning*), Bucharest, 1933 (with a summary in French), *Urbanistica specială* (*Specialized Town Planning*), Bucharest, *Locuința urbană 1959–1961* (*The Urban Dwelling*), Editura Tehnică, Bucharest, 1962; Radu Laurian, *Probleme de estetica orașelor* (*Problems of Town Aesthetics*), Editura Tehnică, Bucharest, 1963, *Locuința, urbană*, 1961–1964 (*The Urban Dwelling*), Editura Tehnică, Bucharest, 1964; *Urbanismul* (*Town Planning*), Editura Tehnică, Bucharest, 1965; Grigore Ionescu, *Istoria arhitecturii in România* (*History of Romanian Architecture*), vols. I and II, Editura Academiei, Bucharest, 1963–1965 (with a summary in French); Gustav Gusti, *Arhitectura in România* (*Architecture in Romania*), Editura Meridiane, Bucharest, 1965 (album with English, French, German, and Russian captions); Gheorghe Curinschi, *Centrele istorice ale orașelor* (The Historic Centers of Towns), Editura Tehnică, Bucharest, 1967 (with summaries in English, French, and Russian); Gheorghe Hussar, *Iași—arhitectura nouă* (*Jassy—New Architecture*), Editura Meridiane, Bucharest, 1967; Victor Sebestyen, *Galați—Arhitectura nouă* (*Galați—New Architecture*), Editura Meridiane, Bucharest, 1967; Romeo Rău and Dan Mihuță, *Unități urbanistice complexe* (*Complex Town Planning Units*), Editura Tehnică, Bucharest, 1969; Grigore Ionescu, Dinu Teodorescu, and Petre Derer, *Arhitectura in România în perioada 1944–1969* (*The Architecture in Romania in the Period 1944–1969*), Editura Academiei, Bucharest, 1969.

The illustrations are by courtesy of the Romanian Union of Architects; the Documentation Centre for Building, Architecture and Planning (CDCAS); the Institute for Research and Design in Building, Architecture, and Planning (ISART); Editura Enciclopediie Romana; "Casa Scînteii," and the Romanian Press Agency (AGERPRES).

—GHEORGHE PAVLU, CIRUS SPIRIDE, MAURICIU SILIANU
PETRE DERER, A. BUDISTEANU

ROOSEVELT, FRANKLIN DELANO (1882–1945)   Thirty-second President of the United States (1933–1945). He was born to wealth at Hyde Park, New York, on January 30, 1882, and educated at Harvard and the Columbia University Law School. In 1912 he was elected to the New York State Legislature and later served as Undersecretary of the Navy. Stricken by poliomyelitis in 1922, he made a slow recovery and remained partially paralyzed. He was Governor of New York from 1928 to 1932, and in the latter year ran for the Presidency of the United States, eventually winning an unprecedented four terms in office. As President during the Depression of the thirties, F.D.R. sponsored a break with the long tradition of laissez-faire; and, under the New Deal, the federal government assumed responsibility for a broad range of social and economic developments. Certain New Deal programs have remained in effect or served as models for later action. Among these are mortgage financing, community public improvement projects, and federally financed public housing. Two projects that were abortive but which still attract controversy were Rexford Tugwell's greenbelt communities, only three of which were actually constructed, and a committee which served from 1934 under several names before—as the National Resources Planning Board—being dissolved in 1943. This committee produced some valuable studies but was largely unsuccessful in its principal functions of promoting state and local planning and providing the federal framework to coordinate such activity. Roosevelt and his motivations remain subjects of dispute among historians, who are concerned with distinguishing between politically expedient actions and those representing convictions. However, there can be little question that F.D.R. was sincerely interested in establishing regional planning as national policy. Influenced by his uncle Frederick Delano, a businessman turned planner, he supported programs of conservation and resource development and viewed the Tennessee Valley Authority as one of his administration's most important and successful accomplishments. It was during the New Deal period that the federal government first became involved in the problems of the American cities—problems formerly viewed, for all practical purposes, as the exclusive concern of local government.

BIBLIOGRAPHY: Paul K. Conkin, *Tomorrow a New World,* Cornell University Press, Ithaca, New York, 1959.   —STANLEY BUDER

ROSSETTI, BIAGIO (1465?–1516)   Italian architect and planner notable as the author of the plan for the city of Ferrara, made in 1492 and completed in 1567, probably the first systematic city plan of the Renaissance.

Duke Ercole I of Ferrara decided to enlarge the medieval city by extending it to the north, so as to enhance its importance, and he engaged Biagio

Rossetti to prepare a plan and to design several new palazzi. The Addizione Erculea, as it was called, planned by Rossetti north of the existing fortified wall, more than doubled the area of Ferrara. Rossetti's plan consisted of two wide axial streets crossing at right angles, one north-south and the other east-west. At the intersection of these wide streets four palazzi designed by Rossetti were built. The wall that divided the old and new cities became another wide street. The remainder of the plan was based on the Greek and Roman gridiron layout of streets, but the whole scheme was essentially functional, with the fortified walls following the contours and the important parts of the city—palazzi, piazzas, and gates—conveniently linked by the streets. The plan is notable as a serious attempt to adapt a classical system to the convenience of the city inhabitants.

BIBLIOGRAPHY: Bruno Zevi, *Biagio Rossetti, architetto ferranese il primo urbanista moderno europeo,* 1960; Paul D. Spreiregen, *Urban Design: The Architecture of Towns and Cities,* McGraw-Hill Book Company, New York, 1965; E. A. Gutkind, *International History of City Development:* Urban Development in Southern Europe: Italy and Greece, vol. IV, 1969, The Free Press, New York.   —ARNOLD WHITTICK

RUSKIN, JOHN (1819–1900)   English social reformer, writer on art, architecture, and political economy, and among the first to perceive the complementary relation of town and country. He was born in London on February 8, 1819.

Appalled by urban ugliness and sprawl, legacies of the industrial revolution that were menacing the countryside, he also clearly discerned the extent to which people were debased by poverty and the squalor of their surroundings. The Guild of St. George, which he founded in 1882, was intended to embrace social, economic, and planning reforms and was a vehicle for many of Ruskin's ideological fantasies. The schemes proposed never materialized.

Nevertheless, so great was Ruskin's fame and so powerful were his advocacies that he awakened Victorian England to a realization of the complex of social evils of which uncontrolled development is a symptom and a symbol. Ruskin was not a practical planner, but more than any man of his time he may be said to have prepared the way for the realistic pioneers and for practical idealists such as Ebenezer Howard. To them Ruskin was a great inspiration. It is significant that Ebenezer Howard gave a quotation from Ruskin's *Sesame and Lilies* at the head of the first chapter of his *Garden Cities of Tomorrow,* in which the principles of the garden city are proposed, especially in the matters of a limitation of size and the greenbelt. Sir Frederic Osborn, commenting on this in his *Green-Belt Cities,* says that "Ruskin's picture of the ideal town is very close to Howard's physical conception."

BIBLIOGRAPHY: Ruskin's criticisms of and ideas on society and living conditions are scattered throughout his numerous books but will be found particularly in *Unto this Last,* 1862, *Sesame and Lilies,* 1865, *The Crown of Wild Olive,* 1866, *Fors Clavigera,* 1871–1874, *Munera Pulveris,* 1872, and *Arrows of the Chace,* 1880. The principal biography of Ruskin is by W. G. Collingwood (2 vols., 1893, 2d ed., 1900). Other good biographies are those of J. A. Hobson (1899) and Frederick Harrison (1902). More recent are those by Derrick Leon, *Ruskin the Great Victorian,* Routledge & Kegan Paul, Ltd., London, 1949; and James S. Dearden, *Facets of Ruskin,* London, 1970.   —WILFRED SALTER

S

SAARINEN, GOTTLIEB ELIEL (1873–1950)   Architect and planner, born on August 20, 1873, at Rantasalmi, Finland. In his early years of practice from 1896 to 1905, Saarinen worked in partnership with Herman Gesellius and Armas Lindgren, and together they were responsible for some of the most notable Finnish architecture at the beginning of the century.

Saarinen developed his planning principles from Camillo Sitte's theories and the British garden city idea, the most important projects incorporating these being his scrupulously worked out town plan for the Munkkiniemi-Haaga area (1910–1915) and the first master plan for Greater Helsinki, based on the decentralization principle (1918).

Saarinen also worked on the Budapest town plan (1911–1912), won second prize with his entry for the Canberra, Australia, city plan (1912), and won an international competition for the Tallinn, Estonia, town plan (1913).

In 1922 Saarinen won second prize in the Chicago *Tribune* Tower competition, a project that was never implemented. He accepted several commissions in the United States and moved there with his family in 1923. From 1924 onward he held a professorship at the University of Michigan. He prepared schemes for the monumental and business centers of the Chicago lake front (1923) and Detroit river front (1924).

Eliel Saarinen (1873–1950).
(Museum of Finnish Architecture.)

From 1925, Saarinen was involved with the Cranbrook Foundation, a teaching and arts center. He died at Cranbrook, Michigan, on July 1, 1950.

BIBLIOGRAPHY: Eliel Saarinen, *Munkkiniemi-Haaga ja Suur-Helsinki*, Helsinki, 1915; Eliel Saarinen, *The City, Its Growth, Its Decay, Its Future*, New York, 1945; Albert Christ-Janer, *Eliel Saarinen*, Chicago, 1948.   —RAIJA-LIISA HEINONEN

SAINT-SIMON, C. R. DE ROUVROY, Count of (1760–1825) French utopian socialist, philosopher, and author. His system of society was based on the concept that the working classes should overthrow the existing ruling orders and that, since all society rested on industry, the workers should be in control. These ideas were enshrined in his *Du système industriel* (1821), the *Catéchisme des industriels* (1823–1824), and *Nouveau Christianisme* (1825). After his death, his theories were expounded by disciples. A plan for Paris to take the form of a man appeared in 1832, and large-scale proposals were made with emphasis on the uplifting moral value of public works, the key being power in the hands of the workers.

In the history of city planning, the Count of Saint-Simon is of interest as an originator of ideas. His followers evolved the usual "revolutionary" notions involving free love, the overthrow of existing orders, and the forming of a new community in which uniforms were to be worn. His utopian ideas took root in widely varying forms with Buonarroti, Cabet, Fourier, Godin, and others, but never with the same public-spirited enthusiasm. His approach was very different from that of the English reformers and utopians, and he foresaw the scale of values from which the ideals of a later French socialism were to come. As a child of the *ancien régime* himself and as a man of privilege, he was imbued with the ideas of Voltaire and the other great writers of the eighteenth century. He joins the pantheon of utopians of the nineteenth century, and if anything concrete can be associated with him, it is Flachat's project for the Grandes Halles in 1849—a project which epitomizes the scale of nineteenth-century industrialization and the requirements of social change.

BIBLIOGRAPHY: Helen Rosenau, *The Ideal City in its Architectural Evolution*, Routledge and Kegan Paul, Ltd., London, 1959; Leonardo Benevolo, *The Origins of Modern Town Planning*, Judith Lantry, tr., Routledge and Kegan Paul, Ltd., London, 1967; James Stevens Curl, *European Cities and Society*, Leonard Hill Books, London, 1970.
                                    —JAMES STEVENS CURL

SATELLITE TOWNS Term first applied (1918) by garden city advocates of New Towns which were thought of as mainly self-contained and separated by greenbelts from major cities, but economically and culturally related to them. Subsequently the term was sometimes used for large-scale city fringe developments more intelligibly named "industrial suburbs." The term "quasi-satellites" was applied by the London County Council about 1930 to some of its suburban housing projects of a purely dormitory character.

Satellite towns are often planned to implement a policy of decentralization from a large city in preference to suburban development, the eight satellite towns planned round London in the post Second World War period being a conspicuous example. They were initially called "satellite towns" following Abercrombie's Greater London Plan of 1944, but they were subsequently officially called "New Towns." (*See* DECENTRALIZATION AND DISPERSAL and NEW TOWNS.)

SCALE   The choice of a scale, being the ratio which a measurement on a plan bears to the actual dimension of the subject illustrated, will depend on a number of factors such as the amount of detail that is required to be shown, the size of the subject, and the size of drawing which is convenient. When planning survey results or planning proposals are to be plotted on printed land maps, similar considerations apply, but thought has also to be given to the effect of map preparation and reproduction on the printed detail of the base map—detail which it may be desired to retain. A series of standard scales is in common use and it is obviously desirable to use one of these.

The term "scale" as applied to the appearance of a building describes a quality of the relationship between dimensions of the building and its components and the modest range of dimensions and distances implied by the size of a human being and by his physical limitations, that is, the "human scale." That quality may, for example, be intimate, monumental, or perhaps overpowering. If, in the design of a building, there is not a clear reference to the human scale, if, for example, it is not almost instinctively apparent that the main entrance is one and a half times a man's height, the building is said to be deficient in sense of scale. Often objects of familiar size in the setting of a building will provide a point of reference for this purpose.

In a town setting made up of a broad boulevard flanked by tall office blocks, the human scale would not be reflected as it would be in a village square or a narrow pedestrian shopping mall formed by two-story buildings. Large buildings can, however, be provided with human scale in their relationship to their environs. The tall office tower can be designed to rise from a base block of modest height.

Buildings must also be in scale with their surroundings and other buildings. A large block which might be impressive in a wide landscape setting could be overwhelming in a locality of small houses. There are, of course, situations where a dominant building is acceptable as a point of emphasis or as a means of adding variety to the urban scene. The relationship of the size of buildings to their surroundings and in particular to the open spaces on which they front is of prime importance in town design. The height of buildings around a town square or place must be harmoniously related to the dimensions and character of the square so as to give a satisfying sense of enclosure. These considerations of scale can also be applied to the town as a whole. A residential neighborhood all parts of which can conveniently be visited on foot has a human scale unlike the business areas of the city, where the needs of traffic prevail over those of the pedestrian.

—H. E. SPARROW

SCHOOLS (*See* EDUCATIONAL BUILDINGS.)

SCOTLAND (*See* UNITED KINGDOM.)

SEGREGATION OF PEDESTRIAN AND VEHICULAR TRAFFIC (*See* PEDESTRIANIZA-
TION.)

SCULPTURE In addition to public monuments (*q.v.*) in appropriate places
in cities and towns, sculpture is often introduced to provide decorative items
of interest in the urban scene, and increasingly so, as can be seen in some
of the new urban areas in Germany, Great Britain, the Netherlands, Scandinavia, and the United States. Professor S. D. Adshead once referred to
"monumental memorials as the jewels in a monumental town plan."[1] This
could be said with equal or more justification of the sculpture introduced
with some felicity in several new urban areas of the 1950s and 1960s.
Residential and shopping districts in Scandinavian cities often include pieces
of sculpture, which are sometimes set among shrubs or trees. A very good
example of the introduction of works of sculpture is in the large new center
of rebuilt Rotterdam. In addition to the larger commemorative sculptures,
there are smaller works along the Lijnbaan and other places. Examples
include the drummer boy by Adrie Block, the bears at play by Anne
Grimdalen, a girl reading by H. Noorlander, and Mister John by L. O.
Wenckebach in the Coolsingel, which is intended to express the typical
Dutchman, hard-headed and contemplative but with a sense of humor. These
and other works, in addition to providing decorative focal points, add
considerably to the interest of the urban scene.

If the subjects of sculpture in residential or shopping areas are animals
or if the pieces are abstract designs with a tactile appeal, they are usually
attractive to children, who often climb and play on them. This is as it
should be, and sculptures could usefully be conceived with this in mind.
This approach is far better than that which provides sculptures with a "do
not touch" intention, possibly surrounded by a railing. Sculptural works,
therefore, are best executed in hard, resistant materials like granite, hard
stone, and concrete. Bronze sculptures should be substantially cast.

—ARNOLD WHITTICK

SEMEIOLOGY From the Greek word *semeion*, meaning "sign." The modern
science of semeiology is concerned with the meanings of signs and forms
that appear and are employed in all social activities. This science, which
emanates largely from the studies and theories of F. de Saussure, was initially
concerned with language, but it has gradually been extended to all the arts
including architecture and urban design. In these arts it is thus concerned
with the meanings of the forms employed. Many of the traditional patterns
and forms in city planning which were originally employed with a definite
purpose and had a distinct symbolical significance have lost their meanings
with time, although the designs are still used. It is the purpose of semeiology

[1] *Journal of the Town Planning Institute,* vol. 3, no. 5, London, 1917.

to restore these meanings so that, when traditional forms are perpetuated in architecture and city planning, they are employed with a fuller understanding and intelligence.

BIBLIOGRAPHY: Charles Jencks and George Baird, eds., *Meaning in Architecture,* Barrie and Rockliff, The Cresset Press, London, 1969 (the first part, "Semiology and Architecture," includes a chapter entitled "Urbanism and Semiology" by Francoise Choay).

SEMIDETACHED HOUSES Two houses which are structurally joined and divided by a party wall are called "semidetached." Such twin houses are very popular in estate development and are generally preferred to terrace houses (*q.v.*).

SERVICE INDUSTRY Industry devoted to the repair, servicing, and maintenance of goods as distinct from industry concerned with their manufacture. The distinction is made clear by the example of the automobile. After it has been manufactured and delivered to the customer, it generally requires periodic maintenance, servicing, and occasional repairs, and these are performed by a service industry, usually the local garage and its repair shops. Service industry covers the maintenance and repair of electrical apparatus of all kinds, of motor vehicles and cycles, of carts, baby carriages, perambulators, trailers and caravans, boots and shoes, furniture and clothing. It covers tailoring and dressmaking, laundries, the small-scale builder concerned with house maintenance and decorating, and several others. Whereas manufacturing industries are located at least a short distance away from residential areas, service industries, which are on a much smaller scale, are generally located within the residential areas they exist to serve, either at neighborhood, town, or city centers. In planning new settlements or communities, it is a good practice to provide sites for service industries, otherwise they are apt to be located in a haphazard manner and to become nuisances.

SERVICE ROAD In the planning of shopping centers with exclusively pedestrian ways and squares, provision has to be made for the delivery of goods at the rear of shops, and this is done by service roads. If the pedestrian center is all on one level, the service roads for the shops are usually branches from a ring road that encircles the center. When the center is on two or more levels, the servicing of shops is often done by a road or roads on the lowest level.

SEWERAGE AND SEWAGE DISPOSAL In the past it was common practice for the foul water and surface water from domestic premises to be combined in a single drainage system. This was cheaper for the householder, but it meant that the main sewerage system had to be capable of carrying large volumes of storm water, and the disposal works had to be designed accordingly—storm-water tanks and storm overflows being provided. In times of heavy rain, quantities of untreated sewage—albeit considerably diluted—passed into the streams or rivers. Today it is more usual to provide separate systems of drains and sewers (1) for surface water and (2) for sewage, and to design the disposal works, broadly speaking, on the basis of the dry-weather flow with some allowance for infiltration. This is more expensive for the householder, and it involves the authorities in providing a separate storm-water sewerage system; but the dangers of pollution are reduced.

Sewage treatment generally involves screening, sedimentation, filtration, and the disposal of settled sludge either in digestion tanks or on drying beds. It is the latter which may give rise to complaints of smell.

Standards of purification of sewage effluents were laid down by the British Royal Commission on Sewage Disposal and these standards are generally adopted in Great Britain.

The River Authorities are responsible for ensuring that proper standards are maintained, as regards not only effluents from sewage disposal but also the trade effluents from industrial concerns.

In the past, the sewage from coastal towns was conveyed, after rough screening, through outfall pipes into deep water; but this practice has given rise to serious complaints of pollution of bathing beaches. This method can be improved by macerating the crude sewage, but even this does not overcome the dangers of pollution and injury to fish. Residents on the coast usually press for full treatment, though this is, of course, much more expensive.

In regional planning, it is necessary to consider the relative advantages of a number of small disposal works compared with a main plant (which is usually more efficient) served by one or more large trunk sewers. Such consideration will involve questions of pumping versus gravity flow and whether or not a site for a large works can be provided without serious damage to amenity.

The effects of the increased runoff of storm water due to building or other development and the consequent risk of flooding are dealt with under DRAINAGE AND LAND USE.

BIBLIOGRAPHY: Peter C. G. Isaac, *Public Health Engineering,* E.V.F.N. Spon, 1953; L. B. Escritt, *Sewerage and Sewage Disposal,* C. R. Books Ltd., 1965; A. L. Downing, "Treatment and Disposal of Sewage Sludge," *Journal Inst. Mun. Eng.* vol. 94, no. 3, 1967; P. H. Steel, "The Bristol Regional Foul Drainage Scheme," *Journal Inst. C. E.,* vol. 38, December, 1967.
—JOHN G. JEFFERSON

SHOPPING CENTERS In the 1950s, in the first flush of enthusiasm after the war, planners and developers busied themselves with reconstructing the bombed shopping centers of Europe or building the new-style regional centers on other continents. In so doing, some new concepts were introduced in shopping center location, especially in America, and in shopping center design, as in the pedestrian precincts in Rotterdam and Coventry. While planning for pedestrian malls is now worldwide, Europe has been hesitant to accept the concept of regional, out-of-town centers, preferring to re-develop or improve existing centers. The recently completed Mander Centre at Wolverhampton is a good example of such a redevelopment scheme; and the Kettwiger Strasse, Essen, which was closed to traffic in 1952 and repaved in 1960, is a good example of an improvement scheme. Europe,

ABOVE: *The freestanding American regional center—shopping by car.*
BELOW: *Kettwiger Strasse, Essen, West Germany. Closed to traffic in 1952 and repaved in 1960. Kettwiger Strasse, Essen, is the most important thoroughfare in this large Ruhr city. There has been a massive increase in turnover in the shops since this was carried out. Public transport and lavish car parking are provided within about 4 minutes' walk of the majority of the foot streets in the system. (Werbegemeinschaft, Essen.)* RIGHT: *Rotterdam. Lijnbaan pedestrian shopping street.*

of course, has not experienced the massive population drift to the fringes of urban areas that has occurred in the United States, and demand has, therefore, been different.

In more recent times progress has been made in the development of location theory. Model building has been the subject of much analytical effort. The growing understanding of possible mathematical formulations that help to explain locational motivations is clearly important to planners and developers.

Progress has also been made in designing shopping centers that separate the pedestrian and the automobile on the vertical as well as the horizontal plane while providing accessibility for both public and private transport. Out of this design effort the shopping center is emerging as a new kind of environment that increasingly is seen as a leisure center as well as a functional retailing center.

Mander Shopping Center,
Wolverhampton, England.

But what of the problems that still face planners? Traffic congestion increasingly destroys the environment of central business districts. Urbanization continues as populations increase. In the quest for better mathematical relationships, the motivations of the actual shoppers—except insofar as they conform to those of the average person—may well be overlooked. It is important that an attempt be made to visualize the changing lifestyles of different social, ethnic, cultural, and age groups so that planning will be for the future rather than just to solve the problems arising from a past way of living. Problems still arise from lack of knowledge of the physical world. Because of this, solutions to the pedestrian-vehicle conflict that, on the drawing board, had the excitement and stimulus of new building shapes and building relationships have sometimes proved disappointing in actual practice. For example, it has happened that the shape of a project has so intensified the prevailing winds that its drawing-board pleasantness has been blown away.

The shopping node(s) in urban planning today may be seen as:

1. The regional central place—a highly specialized center accessible by both public and private transport (but in Europe, at least, with the emphasis on public provision).

2. The urban central place or places—major general-purpose centers that may, in a large city, be the "out-of-town" centers as well as the downtown; in smaller urban areas it will be simply "the central area." Accessibility will be largely by private transport and sometimes (especially to the centers of towns) by combinations of public and private transport. The present tendency to plan for multinucleated urban areas within a city region will result in a variety of such centers serving a large urban mass.

3. The local or community center—the focal point for a small community, providing convenience goods and local services but where choice and variety is limited.

There are other ways in which this categorization can be described, but essentially the structure of shopping centers is based on small groups providing day-to-day necessities, larger groups providing wider choice and comparison shopping, and the largest groups of all providing the most specialized facilities and sited at the focal point for the largest possible market. A typical hierarchy is shown in the plan for the new city of Milton Keynes, England, by Llewelyn-Davis Weeks Forestier-Walker and Bor.

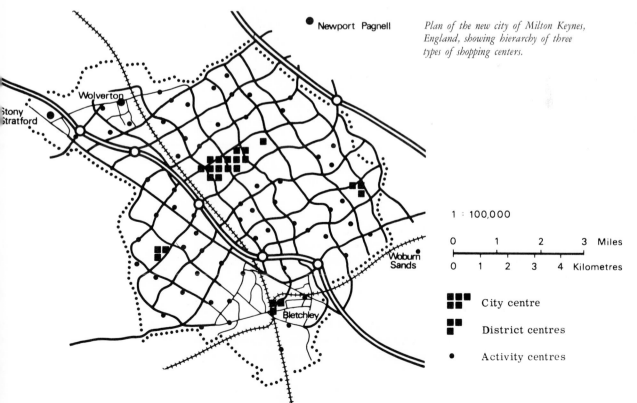

Plan of the new city of Milton Keynes, England, showing hierarchy of three types of shopping centers.

1 : 100,000

| 0 | | 1 | | 2 | | 3 Miles |

| 0 | 1 | 2 | 3 | 4 Kilometres |

▪▪▪
▪▪▪   City centre
▪▪

▪▪
▪   District centres

•   Activity centres

Perhaps facilities ordered in this form will continue to serve the mass of the people in the way they want. Yet, even now, there are some who do not react to a situation in accordance with the average stereotype. Consider one or two cases that may act as pointers. Carnaby Street in London is now world famous. But could the planner foresee such a development? Even more important, could he then foresee that further teen-age provision would blossom forth in King's Road, Chelsea? Clearly the answer is no—there is no way of foreseeing that the need itself exists, let alone where it is likely to be met. Surveys done for retailing seldom indicate the ways of thinking of the teen-agers, yet these young people are an increasingly important part of the market.

More is known about the middle mass of society, but what, for instance, does one envisage as the role of the viewphone (a combined television-telephone)? To what extent will deep freezing change shopping habits? Perhaps both are in line with the development of even larger supermarkets and the land-hungry, car-submerged centers that are being built today. Yet this same middle mass will sometimes be interested in exercising real choice for special durables and may be happy to use public transport to visit the specialized city center. Perhaps, also, a family will want to make an adventure out of a shopping trip—to an historic town that specializes in antique furniture or silver or paintings, for example. Perhaps such discriminating adventures will grow in popularity as affluence and mobility and leisure increase. But again, this middle mass of society is not uniform in aspirations, age structure, or habits. The housewife with young children may not have the use of the family car and may enjoy the outing to the local shop. The elderly, too, may actually prefer the nearby local shop to the big and impersonal shopping center. In spite of economic arguments to the contrary, there may still be a place for the "corner shop" and its local, social satisfactions.

Then there are the varied immigrant groups in many cities. Shops selling special foods and articles are required on a scale that few contemplated a decade ago.

It is the planner's job to provide the framework within which retailers can meet these changing needs without giving rise to other problems. Planners, therefore, must understand more about the real needs of people—social and physical as well as economic—so that planning designs can accommodate a variety of satisfactions rather than give rise to the monotonous regularity that has tended to be produced in recent years. That this monotony has not been all-pervading has been due less to designers' knowledge than to the actions of a public that will satisfy its desires whatever the physical framework may be. Planning solutions must be flexible enough to accommodate the unforeseen changes that are bound to occur.

New, well-designed shopping centers may provide much more comfort and convenience for shoppers (as illustrated by the town center of Stevenage); some may even have character. But new centers are not appropriate everywhere and there is, in Europe especially, a great treasury of historic

Pedestrian shopping precinct, Southend, England.

town centers. Many of these—historic and ordinary—centers could be made very much more attractive to people if streets were closed to moving traffic and repaved in materials designed for pedestrian movement and pleasantness. A recent example of this is at Southend.

BIBLIOGRAPHY: J. Ross McKeever, *Shopping Centers: Principles and Policies,* Urban Land Institute, Technical Bulletin no. 20, The Institute, Washington, D.C., 1953; J. Ross McKeever, *Shopping Centers Restudied,* Urban Land Institute, Technical Bulletin no. 30, The Institute, Washington, D.C., 1957; Wilfred Burns, *British Shopping Centres: New Trends in Layout and Distribution,* Leonard Hill, 1959; Richard Grant Thomson, *A Study of Shopping Centers,* Graduate School of Business Administration, University of California Press, Berkeley, 1961; James S. Hornbeck (ed.), *Stores and Shopping Centers,* McGraw-Hill Book Company, New York, 1962; Multiple Shops Federation, *The Planning of Shopping Centres,* The Federation, 1963; Edinburgh Architectural Association, Town Planning and Amenity Committee, *Shopping and the Future,* The Association, Edinburgh, 1965; Multiple Shops Federation, *Shopping Centres in North-West Europe,* The Federation, 1967; Gillian M. Pain, *Planning and the Shopkeeper,* Barrie and Rockliff, 1967; Town Planning Institute, West Midlands Branch, *Predicting Shopping Requirements,* The Institute, 1967; R. K. Cox, *Retail Site Management,* Business Books Ltd., 1968; M. Cordey Hayes, *Retail Location Models,* Centre for Environmental Studies, Working Paper 16, C.E.S., 1968; Multiple Shops Federation, *Standards for Service Areas in Shopping Centres,* The Federation, 1968; Colin Seymour Jones, *Regional Shopping Centres: their Location, Planning and Design,* Business Books, Ltd., 1969.

—WILFRED BURNS

SIDEWALK A way provided exclusively for pedestrians at the side of a road or street. In Great Britain this is called a "footway" or "pavement," and the term most usually given to a narrow path in country or urban regions is "footpath." Other variations have been used by modern planners, such as "pedestrian way" and "walkway," the latter term being often given to an elevated footway. Another term is "footstreet," sometimes employed for a vehicular street that has been changed to a pedestrian way.

SINGAPORE (*See* ASIA, SOUTHEAST, DEVELOPING COUNTRIES.)

SINGLE-PURPOSE PLANNING The prevalance of single-purpose planning, which concentrates primarily on one service or interest and gives inadequate consideration to other local, regional, and national interests, is one of the major defects in planning throughout the world. It is seen primarily in the field of transport, where plans for one form of transport are prepared with insufficient reference to other interests or even to other forms of transport. Plans are often prepared in this isolated manner—the examples are legion—for each specific kind of transport; air, rail, road, and water, with wholly inadequate reference to other and generally related forms. The siting of airports is often discussed, as in Great Britain, without a national plan for air transport.

Single-purpose planning and its bad effects can only be overcome by national planning (*q.v.*) in which all services and interests are comprehended and to which all plans for specific services can be related. To form a picture of where people are likely to live and work is an essential preliminary to all transport plans. As Erich Mendelsohn (*q.v.*) said, "isolated planning by one-track experts must be replaced by an all-round plan." It is possible that the plan by the expert in a particular service may amend and modify the all-round plan, but that all-round plan should exist before the work of experts in a particular field is begun and it should continue to exist in a flexible form after the periodic completions of the specialized plans.

SITTE, CAMILLO (1843–1903)   Architect and planner, son of an architect, born and died in Vienna.

During his practice Sitte designed various buildings, mainly churches, in historic styles. In 1875 he became director of the Technical College in Salzburg. He was so successful that he was asked to set up such a school in Vienna. He did so and served as its director until his death.

Sitte, a man of universal education, was a brilliant writer and lecturer and was interested in music, painting, and medicine.

In 1893 he published the book which made him famous: *City Planning According to Artistic Principles.* Afterward he produced town plans for various Austrian cities. His practical work shows that he did not regard city planning as merely a formal problem—a fact that might be gathered from the title of his book.

Today it is not easy to understand at first sight the revolutionary effect of Sitte's book, which was translated into several languages. It treats mainly of the functions and proportions of town squares and the siting of monuments and churches. The historic examples that he gives serve to demonstrate

Camillo Sitte.

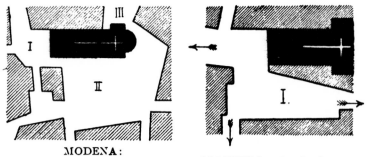

MODENA:
I. Piazza delle Legna.
II. Piazza Grande.
III. Piazza Torre.

MANTUA: S. Andrea.
I. Piazza d'Erbe.

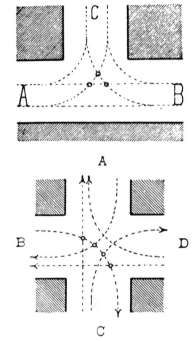

LEFT: *These figures show Sitte's concern about the interrelation or interplay between public buildings (e.g., churches) and open spaces. (Sitte, City Planning According to Artistic Principles.)*
BELOW: *These figures demonstrate the advantages of a T-crossing. They stand as proof that Sitte regarded town planning not only as a work of art, but as a very practical task as well. (Sitte, City Planning According to Artistic Principles.)*

that town planning ought to be regarded as a creative art. Sitte declared expressly that "modern life and modern building technique do not allow of copying old towns."

Sitte was the first to articulate an expert protest against the monotonous, two-dimensional "regulations" (gridiron subdivisions) of his time, which aimed only at maximum land exploitation. He founded his criticism on human considerations as well as on functional and practical arguments. It was his opinion that town planning ought to be based on fundamental research and on development programs. It is regrettable that he did not live to write the second book which he intended to publish under the title *City Planning According to Economic and Social Principles.*

BIBLIOGRAPHY: Camillo Sitte. *Der Städte-Bau nach seinen künstlerischen Grundsätzen,* Verlag von Carl Grabner, Wien, 1889, reprint edited by R. Wurzer, Georg Prachner Verlag, Wien, 1965.

Translations:
L'Art de bâtir les villes, Notes et Réflexions d'un Architecte traduites et complétées par Camille Martin, Genf, Paris, 1902; P. A. Mamatov and I. I. Vul'fert. *Gorodskoe stroitel'stvo s tochki zreniia ego khudozhestvennykh printsipov,* Moscow, 1925; Emilio Canosa, *Construcción de ciudades según principios artísticos por Camillo Sitte,* Barcelona, 1926; Charles T. Stewart, *The Art of Buildings Cities: City Building According to Its Artistic Fundamentals by Camillo Sitte,* New York, 1945; Luigi Dodi, *L'Arte di construire la città,* Milano, 1953. George R. Collins and Christine Casemann-Collins, *City Planning According to Artistic Principles by Camillo Sitte,* New York and London, 1965.

Publications about Camillo Sitte:
George R. Collins and Christiane Collins, *Camillo Sitte and the Birth of Modern City Planning,* London and New York, 1965; Rudolf Wurzer, *Camillo Sitte—Lebenslauf und Werk,* in Berichte zur Raumforschung und Raumplanung, 12, Jahrgang 1968, Heft 4, Springer Verlag, Wien, New York.   —GEORG CONDITT

SIZE OF CITIES, TOWNS, AND SETTLEMENTS

The best size of city or town has frequently been a subject of discussion among planners. Such discussions are valuable because they have as their purpose the best urban conditions for civilized life; and the size of an urban concentration can have a considerable effect on these.

Consideration of the subject falls naturally into the two categories of (1) the sizes of existing cities and towns and whether continued growth should be encouraged or the reverse, and (2) the planning of entirely new cities and towns and the major planned extensions of small existing communities. Discussion of the former is inevitably concerned with the capital city of a country, region, or state and of large commercial concentrations. Cities like New York, Tokyo, London, Moscow, Paris, Chicago, and Buenos Aires have grown to a tremendous size. (Their metropolitan regions encompass populations between 7 and 15 millions.) The reason for the tremendous increases during the present century is the great growth of population throughout the world (*see* POPULATION GROWTH AND DISTRIBUTION), the migration during the century from rural to urban areas, and the increasing proportion of the population of each country concentrating in the large metropolitan cities. The reason for the last is that capital cities generally act as magnets because they are the seats of government and they are the main centers of administration, of a country's institutions, and of the nation's commercial and cultural life.

Many planners and sociologists consider that these great cities have become too large for the well-being of peoples and that the disadvantages, especially those resulting from the pressures on space, greatly outweigh the advantages. The problem is how to counteract the forces that lead to the continued growth of cities, and how to apply those measures and policies, like planned decentralization, that are recommended.

In the planning of entirely new cities and towns and the major extensions of existing settlements, the question of the best maximum size for a city is important. A formula that has had much influence is the relevant part of Ebenezer Howard's definition of a garden city as a town designed for healthy living and industry, of a size that makes possible a full measure of social life, but not larger, and surrounded by a rural belt. The principle of a city surrounded by a greenbelt is widely accepted, but the question on which agreement is less easy to reach is the size of town necessary for a full measure of social life. In that "full measure of social life" would be included adequate shopping for all needs, a diversity of industry, and a full range of educational, sports, recreational, and cultural facilities. It would be necessary to provide for these purposes facilities for the various kinds of sports and games, libraries, a cinema, a concert hall and theatre, an exhibition gallery, and meeting halls. A further consideration is the size which conduces to the most economical provision of essential services.

In planning for satellite towns round London in 1944 Patrick Abercrombie put the size of each at 60,000, but the general feeling among later planners would be to put the figure a little higher, nearer to 80,000 or 100,000, because it is felt that a city or town much smaller could not provide and support the recreational and cultural facilities necessary for a full life.

Ebenezer Howard—writing, it must be remembered, at the beginning of the century—suggested a population of 32,000, but with growth he envisaged a cluster of cities, with a central city of a population of 58,000, all linked by a rapid transit system. The tendency more recently would be rather to double these totals, but the principle remains. The value of such a conception is that each city is kept to a small, intimate size surrounded by a greenbelt, thus securing proximity of town and country, while what one city in the cluster cannot provide in the way of educational, shopping, recreational, or cultural facilities can be provided by another in the cluster. The whole thus corresponds to a planned metropolitan region. This itself would with advantage be limited in size if great pressures on space with all their disadvantages are to be avoided.

BIBLIOGRAPHY: Lewis Mumford, *The Culture of Cities*, Martin Secker & Warburg, Ltd., London, 1938; Frederic J. Osborn and Arnold Whittick, *The New Towns, The Answer to Megalopolis*, Leonard Hill Books, London, 1963 and 1969 (especially chaps. 2, 3, and 5: "The Functions and Failings of Towns," "Some Data on Town Growth," and "Town Growth and Governmental Intervention"); Peter Hall, *The World City*, McGraw-Hill Book Company, New York, 1966 (valuable for the growth of capital cities).

—ARNOLD WHITTICK

SLUMS AND SLUM CLEARANCE   No precise definition is given in dictionaries of the term "slum," which is of comparatively modern origin (1812), possibly as a contraction of "slump," meaning to fall or sink in a swamp or muddy place. A slum is usually understood to be an area of overcrowded, squalid, closely built, and unhygienic housing. Urban slums arose in great numbers during the growth of industrial cities and towns in the nineteenth century, so that few great industrial cities established for a hundred years or more are without their slum areas.

One of the purposes of urban planning is to clear these slums and replace them with modern hygienic housing. Slum areas usually have a high-density population, and it is not always possible to rehouse the existing population in the same area while also maintaining acceptable living conditions. Therefore slum clearance often involves a policy of decentralization or dispersal (*q.v.*).

SMOKE CONTROL   (*See* AIR POLLUTION AND CLEAN AIR.)

SOCIAL ENGINEERING   A term sometimes employed to denote activities directed toward the improvement of societies according to social theories and precepts—ideas based on the potentialities of social behavior and development as these are interpreted. The idea emanates from the social theories of the American sociologist Lester Frank Ward (1841–1913).

SOCIAL GROUP   A collection of people linked by social ties which give a sense of belonging and social relationship to members through awareness of shared interests or experience.

Charles Cooley was the first to make the valuable distinction of primary groups as small groups which are relatively permanent and characterized by face-to-face contact of an informal and unspecific nature between members (e.g., the family—the most important and pervasive social group; a "gang" or group of friends).

Later the term "secondary group" was used for larger aggregates of people who come together for specific purposes (pressure groups, clubs, associations, religious groups, and trade unions are examples).

BIBLIOGRAPHY: Charles H. Cooley, *Social Organization,* New York, 1929; George Homans, *The Human Group,* Harcourt, Brace & World, New York.

—GILLIAN PITT

SOCIAL NEEDS AND OBJECTIVES IN PLANNING The question of what the objectives of urban planning should be and whose needs are to be satisfied has a number of separate components deserving special consideration. One of these may be labeled the "playing God versus your humble servant" dilemma. Planners view themselves in somewhat contradictory fashion as they oscillate between omnipotent paternalism and humble submission to the people's will. Take, for instance, the not unusual case where a particular group rejects the new buildings designed for it, cares little about hygiene, and is indifferent to parks and playgrounds—preferring instead the excitement, disorder, and inconvenience of crooked streets and crowded neighborhoods. Should planners provide what the people want (which may not be good for them) or should they impose their own preferences on them? Can a good community be prescribed? If so, then in which way are we planning for people? Is planning *for* people possible without planning *with* them? These questions have all assumed greater relevance and urgency as the rule by experts has come to be questioned along with so many other articles of faith.

Then there is the matter of standards. What is a good building, a safe street, a productive community, a creative setting? If we look seriously at this question we are forced to admit that most of our standards are inadequate, arbitrary, and outmoded. Far from discrediting them, however, these flaws only increase the rigidity with which, out of desperation rather than malice, they are professed and applied.

And finally we come to the knotty problem of human needs and priorities. Why does a family need a house or a garden? What yardsticks are there for determining what men need and want? In one study of a small city in England (Mogey 1956) it was discovered that dissatisfaction with housing increased in proportion to the adequacy of the accommodations. The more one has the more one needs. How then can needs be determined?

There are some basic or primary needs that must be satisfied for everyone. These are relatively easy to determine since most of them refer to what one might call the "prehuman" needs of our species. Another way to designate these is as basic versus derived, primary, or secondary; or as elastic and inelastic needs. Basic needs include consideration for air, water, food, movement, and shelter. These have a biological referent but are not without social content in the sense that there are socially structured perceptions and modes of satisfaction of them. In principle any food may assuage hunger, but in fact only food that is considered socially acceptable will actually do so. Nonetheless, compared to other types of needs, these are fairly clear cut, absolute, and universal.

Derived or secondary needs include all the desires and preferences added to these and merging with them. Here we are in the familiar, if elusive, realm of taste, judgments, ambitions, and desires. It is true that while one will physically die without water but not without one's favorite pub or restaurant, nevertheless the missing pub or familiar street may so depress the spirit that it may be likened to a form of dying. Derived needs differ from the more basic ones in being definitely culture bound. They cannot, therefore, be ascertained a priori or assumed but must be assessed by observing people in their own settings.

Needs may also be positive or negative. Karl Menninger has suggested that planners tend to stress the positive needs and ignore the negative ones (*Delos Symposion,* 1967). This bit of self-deception does not, unfortunately, alter our species' propensity for madness or mayhem.

And finally there are individual and social needs, with different groups differing also on this. Teen-agers, infants, working adults, the aged, and the sick—all constitute, for certain purposes, unique subuniverses.

Planners, as indeed most people, tend to individualize needs, whereas it would often serve them better if they learned to discern the collective, the average, the aggregate configuration of desires. This makes some compulsion inevitable, which may be why they tend to avoid the collective perspective. A street network cannot be equally accessible to all; a single dwelling will reflect one's share of communal resources; services must be estimated on the basis of average capacities and requirements. In other words, there are important respects in which each individual must be considered in his average aspect.

Many questions still need to be investigated. For example, in view of limited and scarce resources, should settlements be geared to all or to special groups? What are the indispensable demands of each segment of the population? Above all, since people differ in what matters to them most, the priority of values and varying configurations of needs based upon these clearly need attention.

The question of greatest interest to planners is of course how all of this can be translated into spatial terms, or rather which of the stipulated needs take a spatial form. It is clear that the need for neighbors does but that for friends does not.

Two primary social dimensions linking human needs with spatial arrangements are the social class divisions of a population and the course of the individual life cycle from birth to death. There is a spatial as well as a social language of rank, and planners can no more afford to be ignorant of this than of a settlement's climate, topography, or natural resources. Planners may have to plan for inequality and against mixing different social groups even though this offends their democratic principles. And they must pay close attention to the changing family if they wish to anticipate different phases of the life cycle. No standard formula exists and no standard package is possible.

In sum, there is much we need to learn in both disciplines—urban planning and sociology—particularly in their spheres of intersection. Above all we must be open minded to the respective contributions of each discipline. For whether we build mansions or huts, villages or megalopolises, we must keep in mind that we are building for many kinds of humans.

BIBLIOGRAPHY: Jean Gottmann, *Megalopolis,* New York, 1961; L. B. Holland (ed.), *Who Designs America?* Anchor Books, Doubleday & Company, Inc., Garden City, New York, 1965; J. Mogey, *Family and Neighborhood,* 1965; Gerald Breese, *Urbanization in Newly Developing Countries,* Prentice-Hall, Inc., Englewood Cliffs, N.J., 1966; *Delos Symposion,* Athens Center of EKISTICS, Athens, Greece, 1967; Suzanne Keller, *The Urban Neighborhood,* Random House, Inc., New York, 1967; J. Gans, *People & Plans,* Basic Books, Inc., Publishers, New York, 1968. —SUZANNE KELLER

SOCIAL STRUCTURE The social structure is the whole complex of relationships which forms the social framework of people's lives. The study of social structure involves the analysis of the social institutions, groups, and relationships in society; ideas, attitudes, and beliefs and their interaction and interrelation. The social structure of a society is determined by the composition and distribution of the population (age, sex, geography, and race); the political, economic, and educational systems; family and kinship patterns; religious organizations and beliefs; lawbreaking and law enforcement; the media of communication; patterns of urban development; and other aspects of social life such as the provision for leisure.

Many sociologists consider that the concept of structure suggests a too rigid and static view of society that does not make adequate provision for the continuous processes of change which are such a vital aspect of modern society. Certainly the term was developed by social anthropologists primarily concerned with the study of simpler cultures that change slowly (e.g., Radcliffe Brown). Today some prefer to consider societies as social systems, thereby implying a more fluid form. However, the concept of social structure is widely used in the study of modern societies; and if it is seen as a snapshot of a society, with the network of relationships caught at one point in an ever-changing pattern, the concept can be valid and useful.

BIBLIOGRAPHY: T. Parsons, *The Social System,* The Free Press, Glencoe, Ill., 1951; R. K. Merton, *Social Theory and Social Structure,* The Free Press of Glencoe, Inc., New York, 1957. —GILLIAN PITT

SOCIOLOGY It is curious that sociology and urban planning, each concerned in its particular way with the collective or corporate organization of men's activities, should still have little more than nodding acquaintance with one another. This despite the fact, as their practitioners would tend to agree, that the two fields are closely connected in life and hence should be so in theory.

Sociology, today as in the past, attempts to develop and systematize an understanding of how collectivities function, flourish, and perish. If its earliest impulse was to *reform,* its later one was also to *inform* and thereby make visible to men the nature of their longings, habits, and crimes.

Urban planning is concerned with the nature, structure, and functioning of human collectivities in physical space. It seeks to understand how these get organized into more or less enduring settlements and why they change. Like sociology, urban planning in its many versions is an offshoot of crisis and turmoil in human affairs, most recently, the growing incapacity of human beings to master the space in which they live. The symptoms of this crisis are distressingly familiar: bulging cities, overloaded arteries of transport and communication, mass migration propelling rural and small-town residents into a metropolitan existence whose pressures and requirements they only dimly understand. Everywhere there is growth without plan, movement without seeming purpose, variety without genuine choice. Cities are crippled by the distortions and imbalances of a machine-dominated age. Shelter is insufficient and inadequate as to volume, comforts, and beauty. And so far the remedies have largely been piecemeal. This is true in planning as well as in all the other specialized disciplines dealing with some facet of human behavior. Each is able, singlehandedly, to take things apart, but not to put them back together again. In theory space can, of course, be considered apart from the people who use it, but in life the two are inextricably intertwined.

Thus almost any proposition in urban planning has implications for where people live, work, and play. In turn, documented findings about human groups, social status, and life styles, accumulated over the past hundred years, would seem to be directly relevant to the planners' concerns. Why, then, do the two disciplines rarely meet, and if they do, why do they barely pause to speak?

The reason has to do less with indifference than with professionally engendered limitations. City planners, for example, are trained to consider community organization primarily as spatial and physical entities composed of shapes, distances, road linkages, and built-up surfaces. These are tangible, concrete, and comforting. Implicit in this approach is the notion that once one designs a proper container for human activities, the rest will somehow take care of itself. Hence when town planners are exposed to information about social life or human behavior, this is adjunct to their main assumptions and expertise.

Social scientists, on the other hand, have blind spots of their own. Their training virtually omits considerations of the spatial-physical features of social organization or includes them in peripheral and therefore superficial fashion. Hence many of their propositions about class, reference groups, work patterns, social movements, and individual value systems exclude systematic consideration of the settings in which these occur. There are some notable exceptions of course, including the social ecologists who worked at the University of Chicago in the twenties and thirties, for example, or the psychological ecologists, social historians, and more recently a few of the new breed of urban planners who are explicitly trying to close the gap (Herbert Gans at M.I.T., William Michelson at Toronto, Peter Wilmott in London). Sociology and related disciplines are also of course relatively new fields. There is much that we still do not know, and what we do know often cannot be stated in a form most useful to planners. To give just one example, take the matter of physical proximity and social relationships. Planners are by and large convinced that such proximity, if properly designed, is conducive to friendships. In this they ignore the role played by such well-documented sociological factors as social distance, group prejudice, and mobility strivings. All these may intervene so as to subvert the planners' good intentions. If socially incompatible groups are forced into unwanted physical proximity, not friendship but hostility in various forms—as refusal to cooperate in community projects, high rates of out movement, actual conflict between adjacent parties—may be the outcome. Yet one is hard put to find consideration of social distance in human communities in the planners' proposals.

Another difficulty lies in what we may call "the sociomorphic fallacy," or the idea that because we are all human we instinctively know what people should want, irrespective of local tradition and circumstance. Such "human-centrism," ignoring a vast body of accumulated information, is clearly untenable. Yet we continually find decisions about densities, circulation patterns, and community centers made on the basis of someone's projections of his own limited and often unique experiences.

None of this would matter if we managed, by some good fortune, to stumble on right solutions. But we are not doing so—which is precisely why the current cry is for the human factor to be put back into planning. Good towns are for people; and we must know a great deal more about people, as individuals and as aggregates, before we will be able to build the kinds of communities they need and desire.

The problem is not entirely an intellectual one. One can learn only so much from books. The union of sociology and urban planning will not take place unless planning firms hire sociologists as they now hire draftsmen, surveyors, and engineers, thus permitting these planners to become sensitive to the real problems they must confront, on the spot and in the heat of deadlines and concrete assignments.[1] As a member of such a team the sociologist cannot remain aloof, since he will have to feel some responsibility for the outcome to which he has contributed. Likewise the planners will then cease to think of sociology as jargon or statistics having little relevance for them. Both will be enriched by a new intellectual dimension in their perception of the world, and so will the human communities they will jointly help build.

In conclusion, some mention should be made of the sociological methods which planners might profitably draw upon. A number of useful techniques for classifying, assessing, and analyzing human behavior now exist to deal with many aspects of group life. Opinion and attitude surveys, if properly applied, can tell us much about a community's receptivity to various facets of a plan or design. Estimated rates of social, geographical, and residential mobility, expected growth or decline of population, consumer preferences for shelter and mode of transportation, all are indispensable to the estimates that planners must make. In this case, as in so many others, two heads and two disciplines may once again prove better than one.

---

[1] In Great Britain planning teams sometimes include a sociologist.—Editor.

BIBLIOGRAPHY: Jean Gottmann, *Megalopolis,* New York, 1961; L. B. Holland, (ed.), *Who Designs America?* Anchor Books, Doubleday & Company, Inc., Garden City, N. Y., 1965; J. Mogey, *Family and Neighborhood,* 1965; Gerald Breese, *Urbanization in Newly Developing Countries,* Prentice Hall, Inc., Englewood Cliffs, N.J., 1966; *Delos Symposion,* Athens Center of EKISTICS, Athens, Greece, 1967; Suzanne Keller, *The Urban Neighborhood,* Random House, Inc., New York, 1967; J. Gans, *People & Plans,* Basic Books, Inc., Publishers, New York, 1968.   —SUZANNE KELLER

SOIL CLASSIFICATION FOR AGRICULTURAL AND URBAN USES   There are thousands of different kinds of soil. Some soils are wet, some are steep, some are rocky, some are sandy and droughty, and some are clayey and difficult to work or manipulate. Some are well suited for growing crops, others are not. Some have good bearing qualities for roads, houses, and other structures; others have poor bearing qualities. Soil surveys provide the basic data needed for determining soil suitability for both agricultural, and urban uses.

A soil scientist studies and observes soils both in the laboratory and in the field. He makes soil analyses, mineralogical analyses, and numerous other studies. With his knowledge of soil genesis and behavior, he classifies the different kinds of soils and records their boundaries on a map.

Soil scientists prepare many different kinds of interpretations from a soil map. The basic principle for each of these interpretations, whether for city planners, engineers, sanitarians, farmers, woodland managers, or ranchers, is evaluating the soil properties of each kind of soil for each different use. The soils are then rated according to their suitability or limitations for each use.

The land capability classification is one of a number of interpretations made primarily for farming. Among features considered are slope, erosion, soil texture, depth, wetness, flood hazard, and other permanent soil properties that limit land use or impose risk of damage. Individual kinds of soil are grouped into eight broad classes on the basis of these features. These classes can be further subdivided into subclasses and units for greater specificity in interpretation. In this classification the soils are rated primarily on the basis of their capability to produce common cultivated crops and pasture crops without deterioration over long periods of time. The risk of soil damage or the limitations in use of soil increase as the class number increases from I to VIII. Soils in Classes I, II, and III are suitable for regular cultivation, with increasing limitations and hazards to soil use. Soils in Class IV can be cultivated but have very severe limitations. Soils in Classes V through VIII are limited in use and generally are not suited to cultivation without major modifications. Soils in Classes V and VI respond favorably to management, whereas soils in Classes VII and VIII do not. Soils in Class VIII are usually reserved for recreation, wildlife, or water supply.

Soil maps can also help urban users, such as community planners, local officials, land developers, and engineers, to plan uses that are compatible with the soil. Soil maps help make the best choices among alternative uses. A soil map can be interpreted to show both the soils that are favorable and those that are unfavorable for roads, pipelines, private dwellings, septic-tank filter fields, commercial areas, schools, parks, golf courses, and other urban facilities. For ease of understanding and using soil maps, interpretive soil groupings have been developed that place all soils into three classes. These classes are used to express relative degrees of hazard, risk, or limitation for essentially undisturbed soils. Ratings of slight, moderate, and severe limitations are used as follows:

- *Slight limitations:* Soils with properties that are favorable for an intended use. Soil limitations are minor and can be easily overcome.
- *Moderate limitations:* Soils with properties that are moderately favorable for an intended use. The limitations can be overcome or modified by special planning and design and by good management.
- *Severe limitations:* Soils with properties that are unfavorable for an intended use. Limitations are difficult and costly to modify or overcome.

Other interpretations are often made from soil maps. Realtors, credit agencies, land appraisers, and tax assessors find soil maps helpful in determining the value of land. Maps can be interpreted to show the capacity of different kinds of soil to produce different kinds of plants. Soil scientists and foresters determine the rate of growth of different species of trees on the different kinds of soil. With this information, predictions can be made of the amounts of wood crops that can be produced in a specific area.

More and more people are finding that soil maps are useful for many different purposes. The cost of making soil surveys is small in comparison with the benefits that can be derived from their use.

BIBLIOGRAPHY: U.S. Department of Agriculture, Soil Conservation Service, *Soil Conservation,* 29:97–120, 1963; 32:1–24, 1966; 32:73–96, 1966; 33:217–240, 1968; 34:1–24, 1968; 34:121–144, 1969; A. A. Klingebiel, "Bases for Urban Development: Air, Soil, Water," *Planning,* American Social Planning Office, 1963, pp. 40–47; L. J. Bartelli, A. A. Klingebiel, J. B. Baird, and M. R. Heddleson (eds.), *Soil Surveys and Land Use Planning,* Soil Science Society of America and American Society of Agronomy, 1966; William H. Bender, *Soils Suitable for Septic Tank Filter Fields,* U.S. Department of Agriculture, AB 243, 1967; A. A. Klingebiel, *Know the Soil You Build On,* U.S. Department of Agriculture, AB 320, 1967; Charles E. Kellogg, "Fit Suburbia to Its Soils," *Soil, Water, and Suburbia,* U.S. Department of Agriculture and U.S. Department of Housing and Urban Development, 1968, pp. 67–71, "A Forward Look at Soil Use in the United States," *J. Soil and Water Conserv.,* 23:127–130, 1968.

—ALBERT A. KLINGEBIEL AND ERLING D. SOLBERG

SOUTH AFRICA

Legislation and Administration   Modern town planning in South Africa dates from the early thirties of this century when Parliament, in terms of paragraph (1)(a) of section thirteen of the Financial Relations Act, transferred responsibility for the planning and control of urban development to the four provinces of The Cape of Good Hope, Orange Free State, Transvaal, and Natal. Each provincial council in due course approved a townships and town-planning ordinance; and although all were closely modeled on the lines of the British planning acts of 1909, 1925, and 1932, there have always been significant variations from the parent acts and from one to the other.

Delegation of responsibility to the provinces has been beneficial in most respects, particularly by decentralizing certain aspects of government (very necessary in such a vast and sparsely populated country) and by encouraging regional differences of approach, but there have been drawbacks too. Delegation did not go so far as to empower the provinces to control departments of government which all too often have ignored important objectives and provisions of planning schemes. More recently, this built-in conflict of interest in planning between central and provincial government has moved into a wider area. Central government, through its departments of community development and planning and acting in terms of the Physical Planning and Utilization of Resources Act of 1967, has been stepping actively into regional, urban, and even local planning. This has occurred in the course of implementing its policy of separate development and takes the form of promoting or preventing settlement or economic activity in many parts of the country previously under the full control of local planning authorities. Delegated powers could possibly be withdrawn and a three-tiered system with ultimate control at the center instituted in its place.

The emphasis of early planning legislation and practice was mainly on introducing control over the rapid growth of towns. The objectives were twofold: first, to prevent limitless peripheral sprawl caused by the subdivision of contiguous farmland into "townships" and, secondly, to secure both acceptable standards of layout and land for public purposes (roads, open spaces, schools, and other buildings) associated with the townships. This latter purpose was achieved as part of the conditions of approval of the subdivision. No plot could be sold or land developed until land designated for public purposes had been transferred free of charge to the local authority; basic services such as access, water supply, and drainage installed; and sometimes in addition or in lieu thereof a monetary endowment paid. These arrangements have proved not only effective in protecting the public interest but also acceptable to the developer who merely passes the costs on to the purchaser.

In the early years of applying the ordinances, town planning of settlements as a whole was a secondary consideration to the major interest in township development. Only a limited number of larger towns were required to prepare town planning schemes. However, since 1945, the weight of interest has shifted toward the overall planning of towns and cities which are now large and mature enough to be suffering the same difficulties found in modern urban complexes the world over. Most towns of any consequence have town planning schemes in operation, either fully approved or under the interim controls for those "in course of preparation." Indeed, many authorities have discovered so many advantages to be gained from postponing approval—such as encountering less trouble in amending the provisional scheme or delaying, perhaps totally avoiding, the payment of compensation for injurious affection in all but the most extreme cases of hardship—that they are in no haste to acquire the doubtful prestige of an approved scheme.

The controls which schemes have applied to each parcel of land have been specific rather than indicative; and in terms of defined use and density zoning they have been reinforced, where considered desirable, by height and coverage limitations as well as front, side, and rear building lines. It is noteworthy that the enabling legislation gives the planning authority virtually unfettered discretion to determine how and to what extent urban land may be developed and to impose any reasonable restrictions or conditions without incurring the liability to pay compensation except where an existing use or structure has to be removed or a portion of land expropriated. There are also provisions to tax betterment arising out of the operation of schemes or to require the transfer of land or the provision of public amenities in lieu thereof. Some ingenious devices have been applied in this connection both in the Transvaal and the Cape Province.

The administration of town planning falls under the control of the administrator in each province. He is advised both by his own administrative and professional staffs and by a township board. Local authorities have their own planning departments to prepare and administer local schemes and, in the three major city regions of the Witwatersrand, Cape Town, and Durban, also to engage in joint schemes of a subregional kind. The provinces are the approving and arbitrating authorities, but they also have positive powers to step in to prepare or amend local schemes (the stick) or to subsidize or carry out urgently needed development (the carrot).

Professional Practice Before the Second World War, South Africa relied for professional skill mainly on advice from abroad. Town planning then fell (and for the most part still falls) under the jurisdiction of the town or city engineer, and he often persuaded his council to employ a consultant to prepare the scheme which his department's building survey section would later administer. Of all the consultants who visited the country at that time, the one to have exercised the greatest influence by establishing the first professional standards was F. Longstreth-Thompson, P.P.T.P.I., who set up an active practice in Johannesburg under the local direction of Colonel Peter James Bowling. Thompson and Bowling prepared planning schemes up and down the country as well as a great many township plans, while also advising the Townships Board of the Transvaal on general policy and particular cases.

Since the war, all the cities and most of the larger towns have set up their own planning departments. These, together with the provincial and government planning departments, carry most of the professional burden.

Yet there is a small but significant role for the independent consultant. There are several firms able to offer a professional planning service, but usually as an adjunct to their main professional activity in architecture, engineering, surveying, or academic life. One very experienced planner has stated that so far there has not really been enough work to support more than one consulting firm fully engaged in planning.

Visiting consultants from Europe and America are still occasionally called in either as "ginger" men with fresh ideas or on some prestigious project arising outside the routine tasks of the established department. But the growing strength and self-sufficiency of the local profession set against the inevitable difficulties and limitations experienced in importing occasional advice, however distinguished, will no doubt lead to a decline in the role of the overseas consultant in South Africa. Indeed, South Africa has already started to export some of its native planning skill to neighboring, less developed African territories, and, given better international relations, this trend could develop fruitfully.

Education and Training   Practically all of the older generation of planners practicing in South Africa qualified either by taking the final examination of the Royal Town Planning Institute or by attending courses overseas, especially those in England recognized by the RTPI. In 1946, the first planning course was set up in South Africa in the department of architecture in the University of the Witwatersrand, Johannesburg. It started in a modest way on a 2-year part-time basis; but, in 1948, it was extended to 3 part-time years and gained recognition by the RTPI. The first chair of planning was held by E. W. N. Mallows and, under his direction, an independent department of town and regional planning was established. In 1965, the first 4-year undergraduate course in the country was set up, and it flourished alongside the part-time postgraduate course, both continuing to enjoy RTPI recognition.

There are also well-established postgraduate planning courses in the universities of Natal and Pretoria and some tentative but encouraging beginnings in the universities of Cape Town and Stellenbosch. Each year, however, a handful of candidates still presents itself for the TPI intermediate and final examinations. Most of these persons are employed in planning authority offices and trying by study in their spare time to equip themselves for full professional status.

As has happened elsewhere, the identification and development of town planning as an independent academic study is now well advanced in South Africa. The emphasis is shifting away from the aesthetic or technical aspects of development toward the long-term objectives of settlement policy. Here objective social trends and official political attitudes often come into conflict, especially in the important emerging field of regional planning. In this rapidly expanding and changing society, some strange yet interesting innovations in planning theory might be expected.

Institutions   The emergence of the South African Institute of Town and Regional Planners to its present position of strength as the representative body of the profession has not been without teething troubles and anxiety. Interest in town planning was first attracted by the propaganda work of pioneers such as the late Professor G. E. Pearse, who held the first chair of architecture in the University of the Witwatersrand, and their lead was followed mainly by other architects but also by some engineers and social scientists. Short-lived yet active pressure groups, composed of professional planners and amateurs, operated in several centers usually called into being by some urgent local issue.

Professional organization and representation was conducted satisfactorily for many years through the Southern Africa Branch of the Royal Town Planning Institute. To those in the branch, there seemed no great urgency to create an independent South African institute until suddenly a rival body, appealing for support particularly on national grounds, came on the scene.

Negotiations were precipitated and swiftly led to an amalgamation of the rivals and to the establishment, in 1957, of what is now known as the South African Institute of Town and Regional Planners. This institute is affiliated with the RTPI, thus preserving long-standing and valued links as well as broadly equivalent standards of entry to professional membership.

Educational facilities for planning in South Africa are to be found exclusively in the universities, which have long enjoyed a virtual monopoly of most branches of advanced higher education in the arts and humanities, sciences, technologies, and professions. Courses are still fairly small (the maximum intake in 1970 in the biggest department in the University of the Witwatersrand was set at 15 into the full-time undergraduate course and 25 into the part-time postgraduate course) and suffer from a shortage of staff qualified or otherwise able to give full-time attention to planning education. It is this factor which appears to be holding back development against the pressures for expansion.

Geographical and Climatic Conditions   South Africa is a vast, as yet thinly populated subtropical country, lying roughly between the tropic of Capricorn and 35 degrees south latitude. It is blessed generally by an extremely pleasant climate varying in character quite considerably from region to region. Practically all of the country is well suited to occupation by fair-skinned Western Europeans and this partly explains why, to date, it has developed more rapidly under the influence of Western civilization than any other part of Africa. Rainfall, in most parts concentrated in one season, varies greatly in quantity from one region to another. Some parts have over 50 inches (127 centimeters) of rain per annum while, at the other extreme, desert regions may have to wait years for a reasonable fall. In addition, rain falls unpredictably and erratically; sometimes severe drought prevails over several years, and at other times destructive floods and storms cause havoc.

The physical structure of the country is dominated by the great escarpment of the Drakensberg range of mountains, whose foothills start some 50 to 75 miles (80 to 120 kilometers) from the east coast, and by other great ranges which run parallel to the south coast. To the west and north respectively, guarded by the mountain ranges, lies a high plateau, 2,000 to 6,000 feet (610 to 1,830 meters) above sea level, tilting slowly toward the Kalahari Desert on the west coast. The coastal fringes from east to southwest are well watered and fertile, ranging from subtropical summer rainfall conditions in Natal, through perennial rain forest in the Knysna district in the south, to the winter-rainfall Mediterranean climate of the Southwest Cape. Most of the interior receives less than 30 inches (76 centimeters) of rain a year, usually in the summer months.

The topsoil is generally thin and, by comparison with Europe, poor in quality. Agriculture is thus a hazardous occupation though conducted on a vast, extensive scale in the dry interior. However, the country is practically self-sufficient agriculturally and exports large quantities of farm produce such as fruit, wool, meat, and products from man-made forests. There are superb fishing grounds around the coast, and the fishing industry is well developed, exporting its canned products all over the world.

South Africa's greatest asset is probably its mineral wealth. In addition to being the world's largest producer of gold and diamonds, it also has extensive deposits of iron, coal, manganese, uranium, platinum, copper, asbestos, limestone, marble, and clay—indeed almost every resource a modern industrial state could wish to have. Even oil and natural gas have been discovered. What the country lacks most is a sufficient, reliable supply of water, especially in the form of perennial streams and navigable rivers. A great deal of the rain that falls is lost in a very high and rapid runoff, which incidentally causes a great soil erosion problem; that which is impounded suffers high evaporation in the long sunny spells.

Distances between the major centers of population are great, and transportation from coastal ports to inland cities is difficult and costly because of the rugged, mountainous escarpment. The development of air services has dramatically shrunk distances and daily business commuting by air from Johannesburg to Durban (over 300 miles or 482 kilometers as the crow flies) is commonplace.

Physically, this is a country of scenic variety and beauty, offering distant views of great splendor—sometimes harsh in the contrasts of bright sunlight and deep shadow, sometimes flamboyant in sunrise and sunset, sometimes menacing under the black clouds of a gathering tropical storm. More than anything else, its cool, crystal-clear, starry nights are unforgettably lovely.

Traditions of Planning to the End of the Nineteenth Century   European occupation of South Africa began in 1652 when Jan van Riebeck arrived at the Cape of Good Hope with a small band of settlers. Their assignment was to provide a watering and victualing station for the ships of the Dutch East India Company passing around the Cape on their way to the Far East. Thus there is no more a medieval tradition of town building in South Africa than in the United States or Australia.

Towns were laid out in typically colonial style, the land being divided into simple rectangular blocks by a grid of streets. Every so often, open spaces would be set aside for public assembly, the drilling of the local militia, or to provide a setting for important religious or secular buildings. In the best examples, dullness was avoided by subtle orientation of the grid relative to dominating natural features (such as the shoreline of Table Bay and the great backdrop of Table Mountain in Cape Town) and the stressing of one axis more than the other by varying the widths of streets, the main ones being 100 feet (30 meters) or more wide.

Cape Town in the eighteenth century was a delightful and elegant model of the best in young colonial towns. Plans of the town at that time show a fascinating juxtaposition of the main elements around the dominating axis of the Heerengracht (now Adderley Street), tracing the most dramatic prospect from the shore to Table Mountain. Facing the mountain, on the left of the Heerengracht, were the Grand Parade terminated by the Castle and the Barracks debouching onto the Parade through its own square, and,

Cape Town—old central area viewed from the foreshore. Table Mountain in background to left, Lion's Head to right. (South African Embassy, London.)

further up, the Groote Kerk (Great Church) with its associated Church Square. On the right of the Heerengracht was a compact gridiron of streets, those at right angles substantially narrower than those parallel to the Heerengracht, providing rectangular blocks divided up for the houses of the burghers; and in the center was a single large square used for the "green" market and overlooked by the Town House. The Heerengracht terminated at the gates to the Company Gardens, where the vegetables and other fresh produce were grown and onto which the Governor's Residence faced. Buildings were almost uniformly two-storied, flat-roofed, plastered and whitewashed, with shuttered teak windows and elegant entrance doorways. Dappled shadow cast by oak and other trees modulated brilliant sunlit walls, deep cast shadows, and clear blue skies.

Although Cape Town has preserved all the important elements enumerated despite its growth into a large modern city, it is necessary to go to the small town of Stellenbosch, some 40 miles (64 kilometers) inland, to recapture an impression of the mother city in its eighteenth-century heyday. Stellenbosch is justly famous for its beauty, compounded of many well-preserved examples of Cape Dutch architecture, grand oak-lined avenues, and generous open spaces, all set before an inspiring mountain background.

Other settlements of historic note are Grahamstown, established by the British settlers of 1820, showing, in the island siting of the Cathedral in the widened main street related to what was the marketing and shopping heart of the village, something of the character of a small English provincial town: Kimberley, a curious petrified imprint of the outward-fanning paths

Johannesburg central area with railway station in foreground. (South African Embassy, London.)

of speculator diggers on their different ways from the mining camp to their diamond claims; Pretoria, a generously laid out grid of large rectangular blocks served by wide jacaranda-lined roads on the east-west axis of a sheltered valley, with its dominant church square at the center of the grid; and Johannesburg, perched on the top of a watershed, laid out mainly on a grid of blocks 200 feet (61 meters) square, and punctuated by occasional modest open spaces all too quickly occupied and covered by public buildings. It is said that Paul Kruger, the President of the Transvaal Republic, amended his surveyor's original, more generous plans so as to provide double as many corner sites for bars and bawdy houses to batten on the *uitlanders* (foreigners) attracted by the gold discoveries.

Twentieth-century Planning

New Towns and Communities South Africa's pioneer New Town effort in the present century was Pinelands, a dormitory town some 6 miles (9.5 kilometers) from the center of Cape Town. It was inspired by the English garden city movement (its main street is called Howard Drive) and had an informal, low-density layout. Architectural control originally specified that all houses were to be covered by thatch, but the terrible frequency of fire spread by high southeast winds in the dry summer months has caused this limited exercise in visual coherence to be abandoned. Although still enjoying the status of an independent municipality, Pinelands is really no more than a suburb of greater Cape Town.

During the dark years of the Second World War, it was decided to establish a large new steelworks near Vereeniging on the Vaal River. Its urgent purpose was to manufacture steel plate for the repair of allied shipping calling at South African ports. Dr. H. J. van der Bijl, the Director of ISCOR (The Iron and Steel Corporation), decided to use this opportunity to establish a planned new industrial town for an ultimate population of 200,000 rather than to attach the steelworks to some existing settlement. He set up a planning department for the purpose. Thus Vanderbijlpark came into being, and over a period of nearly 30 years has reached about the halfway mark toward its population goal. Van der Bijl's dream of a town of many varied industries with resources of resident skilled labor drawn from white and black neighborhoods equally accessible to places of employment has not been fully realized. First of all, the new town was not far enough away from neighboring Vereeniging to allow it to develop true self-sufficiency; secondly, ISCOR and associated companies have dominated the employment market to such an extent that Vanderbijlpark is very much a company town; thirdly, the government is now busily "eradicating" the existing African (Bantu) townships both in Vanderbijlpark and neighboring Vereeniging and constructing in their place a new concentrated African town, called Sebokeng, some 10 miles away. In Vanderbijlpark the first residential areas were planned as low-density neighborhoods, each with a population of about 2,500 persons, grouped around a primary school, major open space, and local shops in a manner reminiscent of Raymond Unwin and Clarence Stein, overlaid by local South African tradition and convention. Because of the competition from Vereeniging, the town center took nearly 20 years to get started and still does not exactly flourish.

BELOW: *New Town of Vanderbijlpark, Transvaal. Aerial view of residential neighborhood round the town center. (South African Embassy, London.)* RIGHT, ABOVE: *Town center, Vanderbijlpark (1970). (South African Embassy, London.)* RIGHT, BELOW: *Pedestrian square, town center, shopping area, Vanderbijlpark (1970). (South African Embassy, London.)*

Sasolburg, Orange Free State—a New Town based on conversion of coal to oil. (South African Embassy, London.)

On tne Orange Free State side of the Vaal River, the New Town of Sasolburg was established (planned by Max Kirchofer) around a government-sponsored enterprise to convert coal into oil. Sasolburg follows the Vanderbijlpark neighborhood model in principle, but the town structure as a whole is more convincing as a long-term strategy and the layout of individual neighborhoods is more advanced technically.

The new towns of the Orange Free State goldfields are generally undistinguished, the largest, Welkom, being probably the worst. Sited on expanding clay, wickedly destructive of conventionally constructed buildings, this town boasts a wide, long, dead-straight racing track called Stateway tearing through the town center. This out-of-scale boulevard, aided and abetted by a badly placed central park, effectively dislocates the functioning of the component parts of the central business area. The new civic center complex, with its tall clock tower anchoring its position on the featureless Stateway, has bridged one of the gaps while providing this twentieth-century mining camp with unexpectedly lavish cultural facilities in a highly civilized architectural environment.

For sheer scale, the enormous nonwhite townships must be mentioned. Some distance from each major city, extensive areas have been developed with thousands of single-storied bungalows or semidetached houses constructed to a small range of standard plans. Densities are low, space standards minimally adequate, finishes and equipment basic but frugal, yet capable of being improved or added to. Community buildings and facilities and the quality of roads, parks, and lighting are all greatly inferior to those in the white residential areas, though the Indian townships near Durban and the colored townships near Cape Town are significantly superior to their African counterparts. Nevertheless, and especially compared with the scandalously inadequate and unhygienic slums which they have replaced, these nonwhite townships must be regarded objectively as an outstanding and speedy achievement in mass housing.

Recent government policy aimed at developing the Bantu "homelands" has directed a good deal of attention to the so-called "border areas," that is to say, where the homelands abut areas reserved for white settlement. Here the government is encouraging the development of industries on the white side of the border to which African workers in new townships on the other side would commute daily. By this device, the policy of separate development is fostered. Thus areas near East London, Kingwilliamstown, Durban, and Pretoria are developing rapidly, while further growth in the traditionally strong industrial centers of the Witwatersrand, Cape Town, and Port Elizabeth is being restrained.

Possibly the most exciting regional scheme recently considered is the development of the Tugela Basin in Natal, to the north of Durban. The Natal Town and Regional Planning Commission had examined the great potential of this valley for intensive urban and rural settlement for many years, but recently the need for a second major port in Natal triggered development. Richard's Bay, some 100 miles up the east coast from Durban, is the site of the port which will be linked by rail to Durban and then on through Vryheid to the Witwatersrand. The former head of the Natal Planning Commission, Mr. E. Thorrington-Smith, was appointed consultant for the planning of Richard's Bay.

City and Town Extensions   Most of the larger towns and cities of South Africa enjoy a rapid rate of growth which is accommodated either by very extensive peripheral expansion or by the redevelopment of older single-family housing into luxury apartments built at greatly increased densities.

Peripheral expansion at low density for the white community has been made possible by the ubiquitous motorcar, and among the nonwhites by dependence upon public transport in crowded electric trams or diesel buses. Both forms of transport have imposed severe strain on existing facilities, and major investments in urban freeways and new suburban rail services continue. Cape Town's freeway system is vast, and renowned not only for its comprehensiveness but for its many engineering and landscaping successes.

On the Witwatersrand in particular, but in Cape Town and in Durban as well, the city-regional or conurbation scale has been reached. Johannesburg is the hub of the cross-shaped Witwatersrand complex, which spreads some 25 miles both to the east and to the west, 30 miles to the south to Vereeniging and Vanderbijlpark, and it is spreading so rapidly to the north that the gap separating it from Pretoria some 36 miles away will soon be closed. This city-region is the industrial and business heart of the country, but it is entirely dependent upon water impounded in the Vaal River which is purified and then pumped up to Johannesburg. The supply, it is predicted, will rapidly fail to meet increased demand. This factor above all others has forced the government to begin an attack on strategic planning issues on a regional scale. Plans for this region include restriction on industrial growth plus ambitious if long-range projects for pumping water across or through the Drakensberg watershed from the Tugela Basin on the Natal side into the Vaal system.

Strategic plans for the city regions of Cape Town and Durban are also being drawn up. The Durban plan, being prepared by the Natal Town and Regional Planning Commission, deals with a T shaped settlement pattern stretching westward from Durban some 45 miles inland to Pietermaritzburg and 20 miles or so both north and south along the coast. Cape Town itself, a linear city wrapped around the lower slopes of the Table Mountain range, is absorbing a number of independent towns and villages to the east and north spreading across the Cape Flats. It is still the most beautiful city in the country, lavishly endowed by nature and blessed by a fine early tradition of city building, but suffering lately from the conflict between traditional values and their aggressive modern counterparts. Some environmental crimes have already been committed in the name of progress, and it will require public vigilance and determined planning control to prevent more and worse abuses.

Urban Renewal   Urban renewal is basically of two kinds; either carried out piecemeal by private enterprise or initiated by major comprehensive projects commissioned for or prepared by the planning authority.

Town planning has encouraged private redevelopment by setting use and density controls at an attractively profitable level. Sometimes this is reinforced by levying a site rate on the full *potential* use of the site as indicated by the planning scheme rather than on the *existing* use. In a young, developing country, obsolete structures are demolished without the restraining influence of a reference to sentiment or tradition. Johannesburg, which will be 100 years old only in 1986, has been rebuilt four or five times in some parts of its central area.

The ebullient real estate market, together with civic pride in American-like growth created by the private sector, for a long time concealed the lag in the provision of a matching infrastructure of services and amenities by the public sector. In the middle fifties, the excessive "permissiveness' of use and density zoning began to be questioned, and attention became directed to the dormant betterment provisions of the planning ordinances. Analogies were drawn between the endowments claimed as a condition of township approval and betterment which might be claimed as a condition of redevelopment approval. The first experiments to exploit these possibilities in the ordinances were conducted in the Cape Province, where the setting of two levels of density zoning was suggested, the first or permitted range

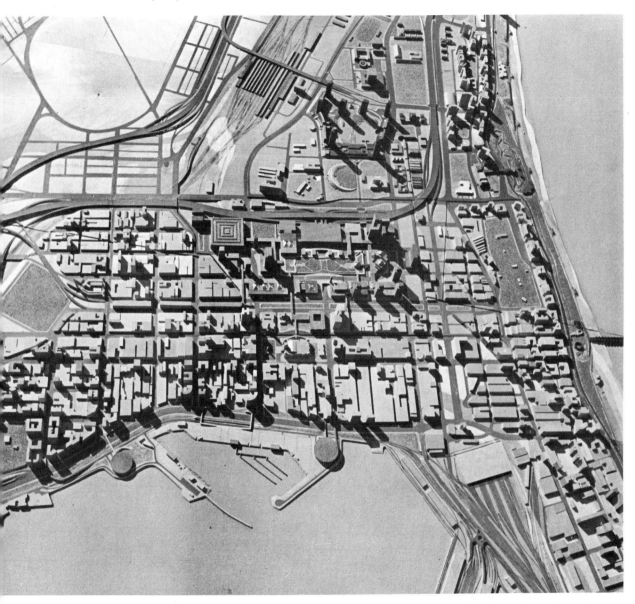

Model of proposed central area of Durban, Natal. (South African Embassy, London.)

to be allowed free but the second or optional range to be subject to a development charge pro rata to the increased density utilized. These ideas have been formalized in Amending Ordinance No. 25, 1969. The Transvaal, under pressure from the Johannesburg City Planning Department, has also legalized betterment when upward rezoning of existing approved schemes took place. Fifty percent of the increase in the assessed market value of sites which results, is claimed and willingly paid. The only disadvantage of this admirable idea is that existing zoning is already excessive in some parts and betterment can be obtained only by allowing even greater site exploitation. Johannesburg also operates a "bonus bulk" scheme whereby extra accommodation may be built or height limitations exceeded in exchange for the creation of public open spaces, widened sidewalks, and other amenities. In the huge Carlton Centre project, 2 acres of open space were transferred free of charge to the city.

Four major central-area renewal projects have been designed and partly implemented since the Second World War. The first was the scheme for the Cape Town Foreshore, a large tract of land immediately adjacent to the central business district reclaimed from Table Bay in the course of constructing the new Duncan Dock in 1938. An ambitious and monumental plan befitting the status of the mother city and the gateway to South Africa was drawn up by a special planning office (under R. H. Kantorowich, with the French planner E. E. Beaudouin acting as consultant) advising a joint committee of the council and the Railways and Harbour Administration. This plan was unanimously and enthusiastically accepted, and ever since incessantly and sometimes unconstructively argued about and reconsidered. However, many of the features of the 1947 plan are now implemented on the ground, and they generally impress by their breadth of scale and treatment. Some, such as the Maritime Terminal, have never been built because of changing modes of intercontinental transport (the effective gateway to South Africa is now Jan Smuts Airport near Johannesburg), and others, such as the proposed Civic Centre, have drifted inconclusively from their originally conceived location, only finding a firm resting place very recently.

Professor W. G. Holford (now Lord Holford) travelled out to his native South Africa in 1949 to advise the Pretoria Planning Department on a broad scheme for the development of the central business area and its relationship to a major development of government offices leading up to Sir Herbert Baker's famous Union Buildings. He returned in 1965 to Durban with Professor R. H. Kantorowich of the University of Manchester. There they acted as joint consultants for a major development scheme for the central area. A full investigation into the regional and national setting of this uniquely varied central-city area—simultaneously major port, industrial zone, regional business and shopping center, and national holiday and recreational ground—was backed by a full transport study. An opportunity for far-reaching change in the existing pattern of development was provided by a decision to remove and relocate the main railway station and associated yards, workshops, and installations, the land thus released becoming available for civic and commercial use. The report was published in December 1968, when the plan was adopted for implementation by the City Council.

In the late fifties, Johannesburg acquired a large area of poorly developed land to the north of the crowded central business district and held an international competition for the design of a new civic center and municipal office complex. The first prize was won by a team of architects led by Monte Bryer, who produced an outstandingly imaginative design which, after some unfortunate delays, is now being built. Planning in Johannesburg, as in most South African towns and cities, falls within the city engineer's department. Here Mr. A. Marsh leads a forward planning branch comprising town planners, traffic engineers, and statisticians, who for some years have been conducting basic land use and transport studies and have recently produced a transportation plan which, if adopted, should provide the framework for land-use/transport development in the future.

Port Elizabeth, the last of the major cities, has commissioned planning studies for the extensive reconstruction of its obsolete town hall, the latest from professors E. W. N. Mallows and J. Beinart. Although essentially the same advice was offered in each case, so far no implementation has been put in hand. Perhaps this may be explained by a reluctance to proceed until some solution to the growing congestion of the central business district as a whole can be discovered. It is most unfortunately confined to a narrow strip of land between the sea and a precipitous rise of several hundred feet. Reclamation from Algoa Bay on the Cape Town Foreshore model would seem to be an essential prerequisite.

—R. H. KANTOROWICH

SPACE   Urban design, like architecture, is partly an art of enclosing space; and the proportion or area of space in relation to building, the relationship of voids to solids, often greatly contributes to the success or failure of an urban development.

The magnificence of many of the much-admired cities of Europe and America is due, in some degree, to the effective enclosing of space, so that the spectator is more aware of space and is more sensible of its exhilarating effect by the enclosure than he would be otherwise. Well-known examples are the Piazza San Petro in Rome, the Place de la Concorde and the Champ de Mars in Paris, and the large area of Princes Street and gardens with the surroundings of Calton Hill and the Castle, part natural, part designed, at Edinburgh. This stimulation of the sense of space can be more intimate, as in the pleasure of a well-proportioned hall or large room or in the smaller piazzas of some of the north Italian towns like Lucca.

The appreciation of the value of space in urban design is important, and it may sometimes involve resistance to utilitarian impulse. In Italy, in the smaller towns like Lucca and Todi, the piazzas are kept open, with perhaps a fountain or monument at one side or corner. They are kept as valuable urban spaces because they have been traditionally used for various recreational, civic, and religious purposes, because the aesthetic result is pleasureable, and because it is satisfactory to keep them so despite the fact that their practical usefulness has decreased.

In some countries the utilitarian feeling is so strong that the preservation of urban spaces, as spaces, is difficult. There is always the impulse to put something in the space—monuments, kiosks, trees—often destroying the effect of the space. The London squares are famous, but there is little possibility in summer of enjoying the feeling of a certain calculated space surrounded by architecture because they are mostly occupied by tall plane trees which blot out much. Smaller trees, more in scale with the size of the space and with the architecture, would be more harmonious. One of the very few urban spaces in London that remains a space is the Horse Guards Parade, where space and the surrounding architecture can be enjoyed. This is because the space is occasionally used for military parades and ceremonies, but if it were not so used there would be a serious risk that the utilitarian impulse would quickly diminish it.

Several of the British New Towns have central squares which could also be valuable central spaces and be used for a variety of purposes, but the utilitarian temptation has not been resisted. This has resulted in the placing of so much urban furniture and foliage in these squares as to destroy the effect of space. The splendid open piazzas of Italian cities could be emulated more often with advantage.

The beauty of so many of the fine cities of the world is due in no small measure to the use of space in a manner that makes a particular setting at once serene and stimulating.   —ARNOLD WHITTICK

SPAIN

Legislation and Administration   The basic planning law in Spain is the Land-use Policy and Urban Planning Act of 1956. It deals basically with (1) land planning, (2) land-use policies, (3) realization of plans, and (4) control of planning and building operations by the central authorities. The first chapter of the act establishes that physical plans can be provincial (or regional) and municipal (limited to the boundaries of the municipality). Municipal planning has three stages:

(1) The drafting of a general or master urban plan dealing with the main pattern and with the zoning of a relatively large area, normally a whole city or town.

(2) The drafting of partial or particularized plans for developing a sector or part of a general plan. A partial plan must be part of a previously approved general plan.

(3) Implementation—the actual execution of a plan, in whole or in part.

Special plans are concerned with a specific aspect, as the protection of landscape, the protection of the cultural heritage, or drainage in a limited area.

The second chapter of the act deals with urban and rural land policies. The land of the entire country is classified under one of the three following headings: "urban land," "urban reservation land," and "rural land."

Under "urban land" are included not only the city areas, or urbanized zones, but also areas that are expected to be urbanized in the near future. These are areas for which there is a duly approved partial plan.

Areas that are intended for eventual urbanization are classified as "urban reservation land." There is no partial plan for land of this type, but it *is* included in a general or master plan.

All the remaining areas of the country are considered rural. Building on them, with some exceptions, is limited in volume to one cubic meter for every five square meters of the property.

The third chapter is related to the execution of urban plans. Actual physical planning can be performed directly by the central government agencies, by municipal or regional authorities, or by private initiative. Most frequently, public initiative comes from the *ayuntamientos* or municipalities. Private initiative in partial planning (not in the execution of plans) can be exercised when the property of the promoters is more than 60 percent of the whole area to be planned. In all cases, plans must be submitted to the public for a term of 30 days.

All regional and urban plans in municipalities of more than 50,000 inhabitants must be definitively approved by the central government authorities. In other cases they must be approved by regional planning boards that are appointed by the central government. The act also provides for various systems of cooperation between private agencies and municipalities for the realization of the plans.

The fourth chapter, which is the most controversial of the act, establishes the principle that the owner of land included in a sector designated as urban land has not only the right but the obligation to build on it according to the plans. If he does not build, any other citizen or public or private agency has the right to ask for its expropriation under condition of building on it within a certain time. The direct aim or object of this principle is evidently to increase the supply of land available for building purposes, thus bringing about a reduction in prices. This part of the act has not so far been applied and the purpose of the law has not been fulfilled. There has been a complete failure to prevent urban land speculation.

The last (fifth, sixth, and seventh) chapters are specially concerned with the financing of investments relating to physical planning (public aid, fiscal exemptions to stimulate the urbanization process), administrative organization, and legal technicalities.

Administration According to the law, the central government has full responsibility for regional planning, and local authorities (municipalities) have responsibility for urban planning under the control of the central government.

The chief authority in the control of planning and the execution of plans is the Ministry of Housing, which works through the General Directorate for Town Planning and the Town Planning Authority. The latter operates particularly in three different fields: residential building, industrial building, and building to relieve the overcrowding in Madrid.

Professional Practice and Educational Training Planning is mainly done by specialized architects and to a lesser degree by specialized engineers. Legally, an urban plan cannot be approved if it has not been prepared by a qualified architect or engineer. The present trend is to have plans prepared by teams composed of architects, engineers, sociologists, economists, and lawyers.

In all the high schools of architecture there is specialization in town planning. In Spain, secondary education, called *bachillerato* (as in the French *baccalaureat*), begins at 10 years of age and consists of 4 years of *bachillerato inferior,* 2 of *bachillerato superior,* and 1 year of pre-university. The student generally completes this course at the age of 16 or 17. The teaching of architecture normally begins with 2 years of preparatory school and 5 of specialization. Pupils can then obtain a master's degree. For a doctorate, they must submit a thesis. Parliament has discussed a new act to change the system.

Until a few years ago, all schools of architecture and engineering and all universities were owned by the state or central government. In the last few years, however, several autonomous universities with their own schools of architecture and city planning have been created.

Institutions Among professional bodies there are the Colegio Oficial de Arquitectos and the Colegio Oficial de Ingenieros, with subdivisions for such specialities as civil engineering, industrial engineering, and so forth. These are organized as guilds or professional unions on a regional basis. The Colegio Oficial de Arquitectos is connected with the UIA (International Union of Architects). There is also a public opinion institution for town and country planning propaganda—the Federacion Nacional de Urbanismo y de la Vivienda, connected with the FIHUAT (International Federation of Housing and Planning).

Traditions of Planning to the Civil War, 1936–1939 Spain is a country with an old planning tradition which is not only interesting as a subject of study but survives in the economic and social structure of today. It provides an attraction for tourism, which is the chief industry of the country.

The stages of the planning tradition in Spain follow the same lines as in southern Europe, with two points of difference. The first is the importation, through Moslem domination from the eighth to the thirteenth centuries, of the characteristic style of the cities of the Near East. The second is the importation from the American countries of a characteristic type of city, through one of the greatest social Utopias, the "Leyes de Indias" that served as a norm in the foundation of many cities of Mexico and of central South America. These laws, up to the sixteenth century, anticipated by 300 years the later theories that came after the industrial revolution, especially the principle of new cities in new places. They included detailed prescriptions for the selection of sites for new towns, taking into account such circumstances as climate, health, water supply, drainage and sewerage, and communications. At the same time they led to modern ideas of fundamental zoning, setting apart certain areas of the city for dwellings, administration, hospitals, and recreation. These cities were based on a pattern of straight streets, the width and the size of the blocks being established by law.

The Medieval Spanish City The centers of many Spanish cities still retain the old medieval pattern, more or less transformed. In many cases most of the old buildings are still preserved, creating a pleasing aesthetic effect

Medieval Spanish city of Cáceres.

in the urban landscape. The pattern of these urban areas has the greatest irregularity, but when it is analyzed one discovers the characteristics of a clear organism, in relation, of course, to medieval standards. These central areas, reflecting the old Spanish city with its medieval pattern, have become totally inadequate for modern transport. During the period between 1850 and 1950, an attempt was made to solve the traffic problems of these areas by means of demolition and the opening of new traffic ways, but this method has proved that instead of resolving the problem it has helped to aggravate it.

In more recent years, planning theories and practice in relation to these cities changed. The trend now is to retain the old center with its old, typical style as a neutralized nucleus for the traffic. The site can thus be preserved with all its historical and artistic value as a city of the past. These old centers with a characteristic style of their own, with a minimum of traffic, and with their particular commercial, cultural, and administrative functions constitute a focus of attraction for tourists. The ideal pattern is that of enclosing the ancient city with a main traffic street with several parking spaces all along it, thus avoiding the use of vehicles in the central areas. The application of this principle is not easy, since the land in these zones commands high prices and becomes the object of speculation, with a trend to increase the areas for new building.

Urban Planning after the Industrial Revolution The industrial revolution in Spain arrived very late. The nineteenth century was a period of decadence, and industrialization began only in the 1890's, not in Madrid but in other Spanish cities, such as Barcelona and Bilbao. In the later decades of the century the bigger cities grew beyond their ancient ramparts, and an act governing the extension and remodeling of major cities became necessary (Ley de Reforma y Ensanche de Grandes Poblaciones).

An important event in the urban planning of Spain and also of Europe was the extension plan for the city of Barcelona. This plan, which still governs the shape of the city, is usually called the Cerda plan, from the name of its planner. It is an interesting example of urban planning, not only for its pattern but for the arrangement of the buildings and the balance between buildings and open spaces. This Cerda plan consists fundamentally of a square block of 110 by 110 yards (100 by 100 meters), chamfered at the angles, with streets 22 yards (20 meters) wide. These blocks were built only on two of its sides, leaving a central green space in private ownership. But years later, as a result of the increase in land values, the remaining areas were built up as well (see illustration).

Another important event in planning—more of an ideal than an actual achievement—was the Ciudad Lineal (Linear City) of Madrid, planned by Arturo Soria about 1880. Up to that moment cities throughout the world had been conceived on a concentric plan. Arturo Soria planned and created a new city, near Madrid, developed on a linear pattern along tramways. This linear city was a practical success for a short time. Afterwards, absorbed by the explosively expanding modern city, it disappeared completely. But the idea was proposed many years after in other countries, especially in the U.S.S.R. With the English garden city, it constitutes one of the most interesting ideas in the revolution that urban planning experienced at the end of the nineteenth century.

Twentieth Century   The years between 1900 and the Spanish Civil War (1936–1939) were years in which there was a lack of orientation in Spanish cities, which expanded rapidly on the basis of the Law Governing the Extension and Remodeling of Major Cities (Ley de Reforma y Ensanche de Grandes Poblaciones), which was a base of purely physical planning—a plan for a new city was equivalent to a pattern of streets—without regard to social and economic considerations.

Planning since the Civil War, 1939–1970   Among the interesting developments that have arisen since the Civil War are the *poligono* developments around Madrid and the small towns or communities in underdeveloped land.

The word *poligono* (or polygon) is conventionally used by Spanish planners to designate totally new urban areas, either residential (containing one or more neighborhood units) or industrial. The *poligonos* around Madrid were created in an unsuccessful effort to absorb the overspill caused by the city's rapid growth.

There is only one special case where the full responsibility for rural and urban planning belongs to a department other than the Ministry of Housing. This is the National Institute for Colonization,[1] an autonomous agency

[1] The word "colonization" is used in the sense of total land development, as, for instance in the case of the Tennessee Valley Authority in the United States.

Cerda plan, Barcelona, Middle-
nineteenth-century development. The
blocks were originally open at the sides,
with central gardens.

directly under the Ministry of Agriculture. This agency was created immediately after the civil war to regulate the agricultural and industrial development of the former latifundium of almost desert land, dry and uncultivated
areas in the regions generally comprising the provinces of Jaen (Plan Jaen),
Badajoz (Plan Badajoz), Huesca-Zaragoza (Plan de Los Monegros), Córdoba,
Cadiz, and Ciudad Real. This plan includes the construction of dams and
irrigation systems, the subdivision of the land into parcels, and the building
of small towns with balanced, mainly agricultural economies. There were
294 of these new towns created and built between 1939 and 1969. Each
new town or village normally has a population of 1,500 inhabitants with
the necessary schools, churches and social centers.

The planning, remodeling, and rebuilding of historic sites and ancient
cities and monuments are under the control of the Ministry of Education
and Sciences through the General Directorate for Fine Arts and the General
Commissariat to Safeguard the National Artistic Heritage.

Spanish planning legislation can be considered adequate and up to date
despite the fact that it is some 16 years old. In these 16 years, the Land-use

Policy and Urban Planning Act of 1956 has proved its effectiveness in many respects, although it has also shown some inadequacies. This has not been the fault of the act but of the opposition of pressure groups, especially those relating to land speculation, which are interested more in a laissez-faire policy than in disciplined methods of planning.

New *poligonos* must be considered as an effort to provide dwellings, not only for millions of people who have, as a consequence of the Civil War, been living in slum areas, but for the increasingly growing population of the following decades. The *poligonos* can be criticized from the point of view of environment, lack of vegetation, social organization, and inadequate social facilities. In the last years, these deficiencies have gradually been remedied.

The same lack of environmental quality is initially evident in the new small towns, in spite of good architectural design. These towns, however, were built in desert zones, and such impressions during their construction, before the planting of trees, were premature. The increasing industrialization of the country in recent years has eliminated this type of rural planning, which has been an important and partially successful experiment.

Planning for Tourism   The importance of Spain as a tourist resort of recent years is well known. The number of tourists coming to Spain increased from 450,000 in 1950 to 21,682,000 in 1969. This number represents almost 17 percent of total worldwide tourism, involving some 128 million people. The principal reasons for this attraction are the beaches; the climate and landscapes; the old towns, villages, and monumental cities; ancient isolated monuments; and surviving elements of folklore. The total number of beds in the hotels in 1969 was 465,400, not including camping facilities and apartments.

OPPOSITE PAGE: ABOVE, Neighborhood unit of Algallarin, Córdoba. BELOW, Neighborhood unit of Cinco-Casas, Ciudad Real.

Planning for tourism—the island of Majorca where, in the course of urban development, the landscape beauty has been preserved.

The consequence of this development has been the creation of many new towns all along the coastal zones, almost without interruption. The rapidity of the phenomenon has led to a lack of quality in the urban patterns of the majority of these new towns, and the destruction, on a large scale, of natural values and landscapes. This is regrettable, as these values constitute the most attractive and important elements of the environment.

Until the last few years, there have been no natural reservations on the coast. Not one of the national parks existing in Spain is located on the coast, where they are most necessary. In spite of this, among the hundreds of buildings spoiling the beauty of Spanish beaches, several *urbanizaciones* can be pointed to as remarkably good examples of environmental planning.

BIBLIOGRAPHY: The most important architectural journals published in Spain which deal extensively with urban planning are *Arquitectura* (Madrid), *Temas de Arquitectura* (Madrid), and *Cuadernos de Arquitectura* (Barcelona). For the administrative and legal aspects of town and country planning the two reviews *Cinencia Urbana* and *Ciudad y Territorio,* published by the Instituto e Estudios de Administracion Local, are important.

—GABRIEL ALOMAR

ABOVE, LEFT: *Benidorm—an unsatisfactory development for tourism, showing urban disorder and the destruction of natural values.* ABOVE, RIGHT: *Industrial development on the outskirts of Malaga, 1960 to 1964.* RIGHT, ABOVE: *Development of Puebla del Rio, a satellite town of Seville, 1960 to 1964.* RIGHT, BELOW: *Extension of the northwest coast town of La Coruña, 1960 to 1964.*

SPENCER, HERBERT (1820–1903)　English philosopher and pioneering sociologist. Born in Derby (England), Spencer received an unorthodox education at home and at the age of seventeen began work in the expanding field of railway engineering and technology. This experience influenced his approach to the study of biology and sociology; and it was through his work in civil engineering, where he achieved considerable success, that he developed his interest in geology and biology. He also began to write on social, political, and economic questions, which led to his appointment, in 1848, as subeditor of *The Economist*. Later, when circumstances permitted, he gave up this position to devote himself to scholarship; and in 1860 he published a prospectus for *Synthetic Philosophy*, which became his major work, surveying the fields of biology, psychology, sociology, and ethics from an evolutionary viewpoint.

He wanted to integrate the sciences of biology and sociology, and his close analogy between social and biological organisms led his work into disrepute. This rejection included much of great value in his work; and although Spencer's direct influence was small, his indirect influence has been considerable.

Spencer's main contribution was his scientific approach to the study of society and his conception of society as a self-regulating organism which should be studied by considering the contribution of the parts to the whole, emphasizing their interaction and interrelation. As an evolutionist, he was primarily concerned with the growing complexity, accompanied by increasing integration, heterogeneity and definition, of evolving social structures. He also drew attention to the conditioning effect of environment on social institutions.

As philosopher, sociologist, and scientist, Spencer was in the forefront of intellectual development in Europe in the late nineteenth century. His approach to the study of society strongly influenced his younger contemporary Durkheim and, through him, trends in sociological thought and the development of social anthropology. Spencer's *Study of Society* made a strong impression in America where it became the textbook for the first course in sociology in the United States at Yale.

BIBLIOGRAPHY: Herbert Spencer, *The Study of Society,* University of Michigan Press, Ann Arbor, Mich., 1873, *The Principles of Sociology,* Appleton Century Crofts, New York, 1876–1896 (3 vols.); Jay Rumney, *Herbert Spencer's Sociology,* Atherton Press, New York, 1965.

—GILLIAN PITT

STEIN, CLARENCE S. (1882–　　)　Pioneering American town planner. Though Clarence Stein chose architecture as a profession after studying at Columbia University and the École des Beaux Arts, his work as architect gave way to his increasing absorption in the social problems of housing and community planning. His first introduction to planning came when, as chief designer for Bertram Goodhue, he planned a new mining community at Tyrone, New Mexico. After 1920 he was chairman of the new-formed Committee on Community Planning of the American Institute of Architects, and under the editorship of C. H. Whitaker he edited the community

Clarence S. Stein

planning section of its journal. Stein became an early American advocate of Howard's concept of the garden city and was strongly influenced by both the ideas and the work of Raymond Unwin and Barry Parker in Letchworth Garden City, Hampstead Garden Suburb, and Unwin's war housing schemes. Through his organizing skill and social insight Stein became the leader in the movement for better housing for the lower income groups, and he served as chairman of the New York State Housing and Regional Planning Commission. The 1926 report of this commission opened the way for government-aided housing (then an innovation in the United States), for the TVA, and for state and national planning surveys under President Franklin D. Roosevelt. In 1923 Stein took the lead in founding the Regional Planning Association of America, a small but influential group; and as architect and planner with Henry Wright he pioneered with new layouts and house types in Sunnyside Gardens, Chatham Village, and Radburn. Like Howard, Stein believed not in abstract models but in practical experiments on a small scale for trying out new ideas in community development: the research required to execute such projects he regarded as a prelude to action, not a substitute for it. As one of the planners of Radburn, Stein held fast, in all his later planning, to the main principles of that plan, with its separation of pedestrian from vehicular traffic, with its neighborhood organization of school, playground, and market, and with the ample internal green provided by the superblock. Stein served as consultant for two of the best examples of community planning in the thirties, Greenbelt, Maryland and Baldwin Hills Village, Los Angeles; and in 1951 he acted as chief planning consultant for Alcan's new town, Kitimat, in British Columbia. More than any other planner in America, he kept alive the idea of New Towns at a period when Howard's garden city concept had fallen into disrepute as "romantic," "impracticable," or "old-fashioned." Far from abandoning his advocacy, he reenforced it in an extensive review of his own experience in community planning entitled *Towards New Towns for America;* and he has lived to see this pioneering justified by a series of New Towns projects.

BIBLIOGRAPHY: Clarence S. Stein, "Dinosaur Cities," *Survey Graphic,* May 1925 (regional planning number), "Housing in the United States," *Encyclopedia Britannica,* 14th ed., (under Social Architecture), "An Outline for Community Housing Procedure," *Architectural Forum,* 1932; Clarence S. Stein and Catherine K. Bauer, "Store Building and Neighborhood Shopping Centers," *Architectural Record,* February 1934; Roy Lubove, *Community Planning in the Nineteen-Twenties,* Pittsburgh, 1964; Clarence S. Stein, *New Towns for America,* New York and London, 1951 (paperback), Cambridge, Mass., 1966.

—LEWIS MUMFORD

STORY (British: storey)   The stage in the height of a building marked by the floor level. The term probably originated from the painted or other representation of a story along the external horizontal bands between windows, common from the fifteenth to the eighteenth centuries, of which many remain in central Europe. Some particularly good examples are in the Swiss village of Stein am Rhein.

If this derivation is correct, "story," as used in the United States, is the correct spelling. "Storey" may have been first used in Britain to differentiate it from the other meanings of the term, or it may be due to a supposed derivation from the French *estorer,* meaning to build or to store.

STRUCTURE PLAN   A plan for a county or large or important urban area, formulating policy and general proposals. A structure plan relates to the social, economic, and physical system of an area so far as they are subject to planning control or influence. It is the planning framework for an area, including the distribution of populations, the activities and relationships between them, the patterns of land use, and the developments the activities create, together with the network of communications and the system of utility services. It is prepared by a local planning authority in cooperation with neighboring authorities and performs the following functions:

1. Interpreting national and regional policies
2. Establishing aims, policies, and general proposals
3. Providing a framework for local plans
4. Indicating action areas
5. Providing guidance for development control
6. Providing a basis for coordinating decisions between different levels of public authority
7. Bringing the main planning issues before central government and the public

The structure plan comprises a written statement, supported by fuller arguments in the report of survey, giving current policies and proposals together with an examination of resources likely to be available for carrying out the plan. It must contain or be accompanied by such diagrams, illustrations, and descriptive matter as the local planning authority thinks appropriate. It is to be submitted to central government after appropriate publicity, and it may be approved, modified, or rejected after a public inquiry. The plan may be altered at any time after approval, but a similar procedure as previously described must be followed. (*See* DEVELOPMENT PLAN.)

—L. W. A. RENDELL

SUBTOPIA   A compound of "suburbia" and "utopia" coined by Ian Nairn to denote or describe the less attractive characteristics of urban sprawl by means of suburbs—especially the lower-density, untidy developments on the outskirts, with badly designed street furniture, billboards, parking lots, and gas stations.

BIBLIOGRAPHY: Ian Nairn, *Outrage,* Architectural Press, London, 1955, *Counter Attack,* Architectural Press, London, 1957.

SUBURBS AND SUBURBAN GROWTH   Suburbs are the compactly developed and developing areas surrounding the central city in a metropolitan area. These areas are distinguished from the central city by their more homogeneous socioeconomic and physical character, although they are seldom as unvaried as they are pictured in much current literature. There is normally no identifiable boundary between city and suburb; in fact, in Europe the definition of the term tends to include far more urban areas than it does in the United States. But whatever the definition, the city merges gradually into the suburb without an appreciable break in physical aspect.

The Character of the Suburbs Suburbs take a number of forms as a function of their age, their location with respect to the central city, the cultural context within which they developed, and other circumstances. The most typical types now existing in North America and Europe can be characterized as "old suburbs," "new suburbs," and former independent communities.

Old suburbs are those built before the widespread use of the automobile and the prosperity which now allows individual home ownership by a substantial proportion of the population. These areas are generally located immediately adjacent to the central city; examples are Brooklyn and the Bronx in the New York area and suburban communities within London's greenbelt. They contain a relatively broad range of land uses and a mixture of single-family and multifamily housing at densities of 10 to 30 dwelling units to the acre (25 to 75 per hectare), with the highest densities near the old transit lines connecting them with the central city. Their residents are, on the average, older and at the same time more varied in income, social class, and ethnic background than those of the newer areas. Old suburbs generally include very little vacant land and in many cases are now experiencing declines in population.

The new suburbs are a phenomenon of the period following the Second World War. They are developed at much lower densities than the transit-oriented communities which grew before that war. In the United States, where the effects of high rates of automobile ownership and high personal income are reinforced by those of a relative abundance of land and where government policies and mortgage-insurance programs encourage private ownership of detached houses, densities are very low; those of three dwelling units and less to the acre are common. Densities in Europe, particularly in France, are considerably higher than this, but they are lower than in prewar areas and they are diminishing with new growth.

Nonresidential facilities also are less dense in the new suburbs, primarily to provide parking space for automobiles: the parking space at shopping centers in the United States is often five times as great as the space provided for commercial floor areas. The residents of these outer suburbs tend to be younger, with a predominance of working-age adults and school-age children, and far less diverse in age, income, and cultural background than those in the cities and older suburban areas.

Suburban communities which grew as independent towns and then were enveloped in the suburban spread of a large metropolitan city tend, like the central cities themselves, to have a greater mixture of commercial, industrial, residential, and institutional activities than those areas which developed as subsidiary parts of a larger urban complex. Housing types are mixed, as in the prewar residential suburbs, and their residents tend to be correspondingly varied in age, income, and social class.

New Brunswick, New Jersey, a former independent community now a suburb of New York City, developed at an average density of 30 dwellings to the acre (75 per hectare). (Photograph: Louis B. Schlivek; Regional Plan Association.)

Vienna. Suburban sprawl in the Vienna Woods. (Polizeilichtbildstelle, Wien.)

Levittown, Pennsylvania, a post-Second World War "new suburb" with a density of about three dwelling units to the acre (7.5 per hectare). (Photograph: Louis B. Schlivek; Regional Plan Association.)

Suburban Growth   The rapid growth of metropolitan areas throughout the world is one of the most significant and widely publicized phenomena since the second World War. Quite naturally, most of this growth has taken place in suburban areas, since land is scarce and expensive in the cities and relatively abundant and inexpensive in the suburbs. Illustrative of the scale of suburban growth is the fact that while the population in all standard metropolitan statistical areas in the United States (those with central-city populations of more than 50,000) grew by more than 23 million persons from 1950 to 1960, nearly 18 million, 76 percent of the total, occurred in the suburbs. In the Washington, D.C. metropolitan area the population of the central city grew by only 6,000 persons from 1950 to 1966 while the suburbs grew by over a million in the same period. European suburbs have experienced similarly rapid growth: population increases in London's

"Outer Ring" amounted to 40 percent of the net increase of the entire British population from 1951 to 1961, the population of the Seine-Banlieue in the Paris region increased by over half a million from 1954 to 1962, and the suburbs of Holland's Randstad cities grew by more than 20 percent from 1951 to 1963 while the cities themselves grew by only 13 percent.

Suburban growth has also included marked increases in economic activity. Large manufacturing plants have occupied suburban sites for many years, but more recently there has been a strong shift by other types of economic activity—many of them traditionally oriented to the city center—to more peripheral locations. These activities, which include book publishers, corporation headquarters, large and diversified retail stores, and a number of former downtown manufacturing firms, have moved to suburban areas. Outward shifts have occurred in reaction to central-area congestion and physical decay and to take advantage of cheaper land and the proximity of a more prosperous and better educated population, both as labor force and consumer market. In the period from 1952 to 1966, only one-eighth of the New York region's employment increase was in the central city; in the St. Louis region the city lost 50,000 jobs while its suburbs gained nearly 200,000. From 1952 to 1961 employment in the London conurbation grew by only 44,200 while that in the outer metropolitan region grew by 95,200.

Suburban growth can be seen as the series of phases through which a particular location passes as development proceeds from open land to mature urban development. In the United States, where land is plentiful and government controls are of limited effect, the characteristic sequence is first from open land or agriculture to a scattering of detached houses at very low densities. The current tendency is for housing to be built in "developments" or "subdivisions," each containing from four or five to hundreds of individual houses; increasingly such a development may contain or consist entirely of row houses or low-density apartments, even in outlying locations. The next phase is a filling in, as land costs rise, of land left unused in the first phase with higher-density housing and nonresidential uses. In a further phase, older buildings begin to decline and some rebuilding, in even higher densities, takes place. Finally, population declines and grows older as younger families move outward.

This suburban sequence is somewhat different in England and continental Europe, where land controls are more effective and where somewhat lower automobile ownership, the more limited availability of land, and different government housing policies have resulted in less sprawl and the more complete utilization of land resources.

The destiny of the suburbs, particularly in the United States, appears to be an extension of current trends. Government efforts to decentralize population and economic activity will have a limited effect on the growth of large metropolitan areas and therefore on that of the suburbs. The increase in the population of metropolitan areas in the United States between 1960 and 1985 has been estimated at 73 million persons; an increase of 58 million persons is expected in suburban areas. The diversion of more than a fraction of this increase to new towns or cities is unlikely in the next 15 years. The suburbs will accommodate this enormous increase through a combination of outward extension and increased density in the already settled areas in a manner very much the same as the prevailing one.

In Britain, experience since 1945 indicates essentially the same prospect. Even with public policy favoring dispersal from metropolitan areas, nearly two-thirds of population growth in this period has been in suburban areas. It seems unlikely that this trend can be altered substantially in the nearer future.

BIBLIOGRAPHY: Most current literature on suburbs and suburban growth is concerned with the sociology, psychology, and politics of the postwar suburb in the United States. This literature is too voluminous to cite here. A classic which describes early suburban growth is: Harlan Paul Douglass, *The Suburban Trend,* New York, 1925; and a good general reference work is: Dobriner (ed.), *The Suburban Community,* New York, 1958.

The most balanced considerations of the physical form and growth of suburbs are found in treatments of the metropolitan area as a whole. Examples of these treatments are the following: Patrick Abercrombie, *Greater London Plan 1944,* HMSO, London, 1945; Jean Gottmann, *Megalopolis,* The M.I.T. Press, Cambridge, Mass., 1961; Raymond Vernon, *Metropolis 1985,* Anchor Books, Doubleday & Company, Inc., Garden City, N.Y., 1963; Ministry of Housing and Local Government, *The Southeast Study, 1961–1981,* HMSO, London, 1964; Peter Hall, *The World Cities,* McGraw Hill Book Company, New York, 1966; Patricia Hodge and Philip Houser, *The Challenge of America's Metropolitan Population Outlook—1960 to 1985,* U.S. Government Printing Office, 1968.   —ARTHUR H. FAWCETT, JR.

SURVEY   In its relation to town and country or city and regional planning, "survey" might be defined as the process by which the information necessary for the preparation of a plan is ascertained.

Practice in Great Britain with regard to surveys provides a useful example. All statutory plans are based on maps prepared by the Ordnance Survey. These are published on scales varying from 1:250,000 to 1:2,500, and parts of some urban areas are covered by maps to a scale of 1:1,250.

Up to 1939 surveys of unmapped areas and revisions of the ordnance sheets were carried out by geodetic methods—i.e., theodolite or chain surveys and contours were obtained by dumpy level or tachymeter. Now such work (including contouring) is done mainly by aerial survey, which is usually less costly and sufficiently accurate for most planning purposes. However, site plans of building projects which need to be drawn to a scale of 1:500 or larger usually involve measurements on the ground.

The requirements of the British government in relation to surveys which must accompany all development plans are set out in *Development Plans—A Manual on Form and Content.*[1]

The following subjects are referred to:

a. Population. The total at significant stages and its composition by age, sex, and household size; recent trends; estimates of future changes (1) by natural growth and (2) by migration and the factors on which such estimates are based

[1] H.M.S.O., London, 1970.

b. Employment and Income. The total economically active population at significant stages and its composition by age and sex; its occupational structure and estimates of future changes

c. Resources. The income of the authorities in the area from rates, block grants etc., their capital investment program, the private investment in recent years, and other resources, e.g., land, raw materials, and labor force

d. Housing. An analysis of the existing situation and estimates of future needs

e. Industry and Commerce. An analysis of the existing situation, recent trends and commitments, and an estimate of future needs

f. Transportation. An analysis of the network and pattern of travel, journey to work, problems of the central area, parking, servicing industry, impact on environment, accidents, etc.; aggregated desire lines and assignment to existing network; current use of public transport; estimates of future growth

g. Shopping. An analysis of floor space, turnover by trade and centers, accessibility of centers and their prosperity; estimates of future changes and needs

h. Education. A survey of the existing situation, recent trends and commitments; estimates of future changes and needs

Similar information is also required in relation to (*j*) other social or community services; (*k*) recreation and leisure; (*l*) conservation, townscape, and landscape; (*m*) utility services; and (*n*) minerals.

The information required under (*a*) and (*b*) can usually be obtained from the Registrar General and the Board of Trade and from the records maintained by the local authorities—e.g., the medical officer of health and the director of social services.

Information under (*c*), (*d*), (*h*), and (*j*) is also generally available in the offices of the local authorities, but the requirements under (*f*), transportation, invariably demand a special survey.

By the use of computers, the technique of transportation surveys has improved very greatly in recent years. The first studies of this kind were developed in Detroit, Chicago, and other cities in the United States in the early 1950s; the first major study in Great Britain was the London Traffic Survey commissioned in 1961. The process has three main elements: (1) surveys of existing conditions, (2) forecasts of growth in the area of the study, and (3) estimates of the future travel demand. The last makes use of quantitative techniques of trip generation and distribution, model choice, and the assignment of traffic to transport facilities.

The collection of the necessary data is a formidable task involving traffic counts, questionnaires, house-to-house visits etc.; but the identification of the generalized relationship between traffic, land use, and population has led to the development of synthetic models of traffic behavior, and this has resulted in a lessening of the demands for survey data.

Information on (*f*), shopping, has become an essential requirement in relation to all schemes for central area redevelopment. These must now be accompanied by a detailed survey and analysis of the shopping and office potential, proving the justification of the scheme from an economic standpoint. No longer is it sufficient to base such proposals on wishful thinking.

The importance of surveys for (*k*), recreation and leisure, and (*l*), conservation, townscape and landscape, is now generally recognized, and today it is no longer sufficient for plans merely to impose restrictions aimed at the preservation of the countryside and of buildings of historic or architectural interest; they must now contain positive proposals based on a study of what is required to meet future demands.

There is need to provide for recreational facilities of a very wide variety, and the popularity of certain sports and pastimes changes over the years. It is therefore necessary to make detailed studies of existing facilities, likely demand, and future possibilities on land, on water, and in the air.

Similarly, in the areas of towns and villages of historic or architectural interest, it is no longer sufficient merely to make building preservation orders; development plans must include measures for the conservation and improvement of such areas, and the studies commissioned in respect to a number of historic towns in Great Britain and the United States are examples of an enlightened approach to this problem. (*See also* PLANS, PREPARATION OF.)

BIBLIOGRAPHY: Colin Buchanan, *Traffic in Towns,* H.M.S.O., London, 1963; Heather Bliss, "Local Changes in Shopping Potential," *Journal T.P.I.,* vol. 51, 1965; J. R. Meyer, J. F. Kain, and M. Wohl, *The Urban Transportation Problem,* Harvard University Press, 1965; C. L. Case, "A Critical Appraisal of Transportation Surveys," *Journal Inst. Mun. Eng.,* vol. 93, no. 11, 1966; J. M. Simmie, "Electronic Data Processing Applied to Town Planning," *Journal T.P.I.,* vol. 53, 1967; Tim Rhodes and Roy Whitaker, "Forecasting Shopping Demands," *Journal T.P.I.,* vol. 53, 1967; R. L. Cooke, "An analysis of the Age Structure of Immigrants to New and Expanding Towns," *Journal T.P.I.,* vol. 54, no. 91, 1968; J. M. Simmie, "Social Survey Method in Town Planning," *Journal T.P.I.,* vol. 54, 1968; A. M. Voorhees, "Land-Use/Transportation Studies," *Journal T.P.I.,* vol. 54, 1968.   —JOHN G. JEFFERSON

SURVEYOR   The total planning process, from concepts—both physical and economic—to the realization of a plan in terms of land utilization and physical building, involves many skills. Surveying embraces many skills which contribute to the planning process and which have not in the past been sufficiently recognized or, for the most part, efficiently or fully utilized. The surveyor's skills are, however, wholly related to the use and development of land and hence are directly or indirectly concerned with planning.

The land surveyor produces one of the basic tools of the planner, maps; the land agent is concerned with the quality of land, its suitability for agriculture and forestry, and with the management of land for this purpose. The valuation surveyor assesses the suitability of land and buildings for particular purposes in terms of monetary value and is directly involved in negotiation for acquisition and disposal, while the estate management surveyor is concerned with maintaining and enhancing the value of land and buildings to ensure a proper return from investment. The mining surveyor, the quantity surveyor, and the building surveyor all have contributions to make.

The planning processes have, over the last 50 years, moved toward a significant change in the realization that planning is more than a matter of civic design or arbitrary allocation of land for particular purposes. It has become increasingly recognized as an instrument of resource allocation in terms of the use of land and the investment of money in its development.

The surveyor has, therefore, an increasingly important role to play in planning by maintaining the bridge between planning as an exercise in design and the economist's approach. In other words, he can help to create a more effective synthesis of economic, financial, and physical planning.

One of the major omissions in the present range of technical skills is the ability to translate technical data into discussions that have to be held by people who are not themselves technically trained.

The experienced surveyor in planning is particularly well equipped to assist in this field because he is, by his training, always conscious of the basic characteristics of land and its use and of the fact that, in the end, it is a matter of dealing with people and their property.

In the past, a plan which could be shown to be physically feasible and politically or socially acceptable was considered to be *the solution*. As planning schemes become more complex, it is not now sufficient to provide *a* solution. The planner must be able to show that it is *the* optimal solution in that, regarded as an investment, whether in social terms or in strictly financial terms, the proposals give the "best value for money."

The skills required in this field are the ability to comprehend the problem in the wider field, to establish the relative values of design and social and financial objectives and the relative cost of constraints, and hence to understand how best to trade off the fulfillment of the objectives against cost of the constraints.

These are the traditional skills of the surveyor in which he combines his ability as a measurer and estimator with the particular responsibility of identifying the interplay and relationship of the economic and financial forces involved.

In Great Britain, the surveyor acts as a member of the multidisciplinary planning team, but his contribution becomes greater as the activities move from strategic planning to local plans and their implementation.

More emphasis is now being placed on the need to demonstrate that plans are both viable and socially acceptable, and it is of significance that the British Town and Country Planning Act of 1968 requires planning authorities to take into account not only the physical but also the economic characteristics of their area and, further, to have regard to the resources available for development. It seems apparent, therefore, that the prudent planner will increasingly avail himself of the skills of the planning surveyor.

—K. CLEMENS

SWEDEN

Legislation and Administration   Regulations relating to town planning are laid down in the 1947 and 1959 building and planning acts. Other legislation governing land use and urban development include the 1917 Expropriation Act, the 1917 Real Estate Formation Act, the 1943 Public Highways Act, the 1964 Nature Preservation Act, and the 1969 Environmental Preservation Act. A new Estate Formation Act came into force in 1972. Proposals have been tabled for a new Expropriation Act and a new Highways Act, the government having appointed a commission with the task of working out new planning legislation.

A basic feature of the Building and Planning Act is that all development requiring public highways and mains supplies shall comply with plans that have been worked out and approved by the municipal authorities.

The main features of land use and the communications system in a municipality are shown in a master plan.

If overall planning is needed for an area lying in more than one municipality, the municipalities concerned are required to form a regional planning association and to provide a regional plan. This must be approved by the regional planning authority and ratified by the government.

As an immediate basis for development, detailed plans (town plans) are prepared, indicating in detail the size and position of the buildings and the road system. Such plans must be ratified by the county administration or the government. This process has certain legal implications: the plan restricts prospective builders, and the municipality has the right to purchase certain land, but it is also responsible for purchasing land not intended for building.

Before a plan can be approved and ratified it must be presented for public inspection for a specified time.

In a directive to the government committee concerned with new building and planning legislation, a system of plans is outlined in which the general plans are accorded greater importance. The future existence of a national physical plan has been assumed and the preparatory work for this has been begun at the Ministry of Physical Planning and Local Government. Greater emphasis will be placed on regional planning. The local master plan will be coordinated with economic and social planning and it must also be ratified by the government. In return, the municipalities will have complete authority over the detailed development planning, and ratification of the resulting plans by the central government authorities will no longer be necessary.

It should be stressed that the decision on which areas are to be developed lies with the municipalities. A private landowner has no right to develop his land for building without the municipality's approval.

Other legal prescriptions of fundamental importance in the control by municipalities of urban development are the following:

> Land judged to be suitable for agriculture cannot be disposed for other purposes without special permission (the 1965 Agricultural Land Acquisition Act).
>
> The local government has wide powers for the expropriation of land required for urban development and housing (the Building and Planning Act; the Expropriation Act).
>
> Subject to certain conditions, the municipalities possess the option on all property put up for sale (the 1967 Option on Real Estate Act).

A further point of significance for land-use planning is that in common law any person has the right of access to another's land so long as he does no damage and does not approach too close to private dwellings.

In each municipality there is a building committee that is responsible for the local physical planning. Sometimes, however, the preparation of a master plan is the direct responsibility of the local government.

Municipal boundary reform is at present being carried through, its purpose is to combine groups of small municipalities into larger and more powerful units. Each must, in principle, comprise at least one town or urban place together with the surrounding area. The distinction between urban and rural municipalities will be abolished. By January 1, 1974, the total number of municipalities in the country will have been reduced to about 250.

A small number of regional planning associations have been formed. For the Stockholm Region special legislation has been introduced. Here, certain functions that would otherwise be the concern of the municipalities have been delegated to local government or the county council, which is responsible also for the regional planning.

Town planning is under the supervision of the state, the responsible bodies being the Ministry of Physical Planning and Local Government, the National Planning Board, the County Administration, and the county architects.

Town planning in Sweden is concerned primarily with the expansion and renewal of existing towns and urban areas. Only a few New Towns have been created in connection with the development of large industrial complexes.

Most local governments draw up 5-year housing programs, indicating the annual housing production. These are coordinated with the physical master plans which show the land areas for urban development and those where renewal is to be carried out within specified periods. The detailed preparation of town plans for a particular area is so scheduled that the area can be ready in accordance with the program. (It is calculated that for Stockholm at least 7 years is required for preparing the plans and providing the infrastructure for a major new residental area.)

In the case of an extensive new housing project, there is usually an additional stage between the overall land-use plan (the master plan) and the detailed development plan for which ratification is legally required.

This interposed plan—the "land disposal plan"—indicates the general physical design of the planning area. This plan is not mentioned in the legislation.

The municipal authority is responsible for the development of the entire infrastructure (mains services, highways, and open spaces) within new development areas and also for ensuring that land is available for building.

If, as sometimes happens, large developers purchase land, the developer and the municipality may enter into a town planning agreement which regulates the distribution of financial responsibility. The same arrangement is common in the case of major industrial expansion projects, but it is more usual for the municipality to acquire in advance all the land in a large development area. Then, after the plans have been prepared, the sites are sold or leased (the practice varies between municipalities) for housing or industrial development.

It is usual for agreements to be concluded with major developers on the basis of the master plan or the land disposal plan (where there is one) before the detailed planning work has begun. This is then arranged by the municipality in consultation with the developers and their architects. Otherwise the detailed planning is entrusted entirely to the developers (though under the supervision of the local government) so that it can be integrated with the housing program.

Professional Practice Most of the larger municipalities have their own town planning office with permanent planning staff; smaller municipalities rely on planning consultants. Not infrequently the municipalities have planning offices for general planning work but use consultants for more extensive projects or in connection with matters calling for special knowledge—for instance, traffic planning and socioeconomic studies. The regional planning bodies usually have their own offices. Consulting firms may be highly specialized, or they may deal with all aspects of physical planning and meet the need for comprehensive basic investigations.

In some parts of the country, particularly in the coastal regions and around the larger towns, there are extensive areas where the urban population has summer and weekend houses; here too, there is a need for town planning, and this is the responsibility of the municipalities. On the other hand, these do not as a rule concern themselves with the development of the recreational housing areas, which is managed by private entrepreneurs.

General regulations specifying the content of the town plans are contained in the building and planning acts. The National Planning Board prepares certain standards and rules relating to quality. Standard recommendations are also issued by other government bodies—for instance the Housing Board (God Bostad)—and in some cases by special government commissions (for instance, those on playgrounds for children and protection against traffic noise). There are also standards; one such is Planstandard 65, produced by the City of Stockholm Planning Office.

Regressive or less expansive municipalities often have no current master plans. Where plans exist they may cover the whole municipal region or only the central place and the area of expansion. The reason for this lies in Sweden's low population density. Originally, the master plan was, like the regional plan, purely a land-use plan, generally with a time perspective of 15 to 25 years. Today, it sometimes indicates a tentative timetable for development, and there may be a supplementary municipal investment plan for the first 5- or 10-year period. The master plan is invariably based on demographic and economic investigations, and the requirements as to quality and content are increasing all the time. In many quarters attempts are being made to develop such descriptive investigations into coordinated socioeconomic planning in the municipalities and to integrate this with the physical planning.

Physical regional planning is so rare that it is difficult to speak of a developed practice. In the Stockholm region the trend is roughly the same as that described above for municipal planning. In other regions the problem is complicated because regional bodies of the central government have important responsibilities in the socioeconomic field, while the physical planning is managed by municipal associations, which have executive functions. There are no legal requirements concerning competence for planning, nor is there any professional organization that accords authorization. Town planners do not constitute a distinct professional group; architects, civil engineers, and surveyors are traditionally found on town planning staffs. In detailed development planning, architects are now the most prominent. In master and regional planning, geographers and economists are being engaged to an increasing extent, as are architects and technologists.

Education and Training   Until quite recently there was in Sweden no special course of training for physical planners or city planners. At the university schools of technology in Stockholm, Göteborg, and Lund, the students training as architects, traffic engineers, or surveyors receive some instruction in town planning, with emphasis on solving practical planning problems. Since 1969, students in Stockholm have been able, for the last 18 months of a 4-year course, to choose to specialize in town and regional planning. In this way the theoretical training can also be extended. At the University of Umeå, the curriculum in cultural geography is centered on problems associated with physical planning. There is less concern with practical exercises than at the schools of technology.

In 1968, the Nordic Institute for Studies in Urban and Regional Planning was founded in Stockholm. It serves Denmark, Finland, Norway, and Sweden, and is intended for the postgraduate education of those engaged in physical planning, with emphasis on collaboration between representatives of different professions. Prospective applicants must have practical experience, as well as a degree obtained at a university or school of technology. The institute collaborates with the School of Architecture at the Academy of Art, where architects who have qualified at the institutes of technology can take advanced courses in the arts. Technological research and development work having a bearing on town planning—in connection with, for instance, construction and transport technology—are carried on for the most part independently of town planning, as is sociological research. It is only in more recent years that the departments of town planning have been conducting their own research, and now postgraduate training for this is available. Research is also conducted at some of the larger planning offices.

The need that every planner has of keeping up with progress in the field, acquiring new knowledge, and making the acquaintance of new methods is met to a large extent through a large number of courses and seminars arranged at the Royal Institute of Technology in Stockholm and by various professional organizations such as the Swedish Association of Technologists and the Swedish Association for Municipal Civil Engineering.

Institutions   Research in the subjects that provide basic data for town planning is conducted by many institutions, and particularly at the departments of geography and sociology at the universities of Göteborg, Lund, Stockholm, and Umeå and the Institute of Economic Research at the Stockholm School of Economics. The National Institute of Building Research has a separate department for planning subjects. Government grants for research are made available by the National Building Research Council and the National Sociological Research Council.

Population and housing censuses and the production of current statistics for the country are organized by the Central Office of Statistics. Regional analyses and the collation of statistical data are performed by the County Administrative Boards.

Professional organizations concerned with planning and with the dissemination of information include the Swedish Society for Town and Country Planning, the Swedish Association of Technologists and the associated Swedish Association of Architects, and the Swedish Association for Municipal Civil Engineering.

Publications dealing with the field of town planning include *Plan* (published by the Swedish Society for Town and Country Planning) *Stadsbyggnad* (published by the Association for Municipal Civil Engineering) and *Architecture* (the organ for the Swedish Association of Architects).

Geographical and Climatic Conditions   Sweden has an area of roughly 173,750 square miles (450,000 square kilometers). Over 8 percent of the area is covered by about 80,000 lakes. Approximately 55 percent of the land is forested, and 30 percent is highland. About 7 percent is cultivated, but this figure is decreasing as unprofitable agricultural enterprises are closed down and the land is taken over for forestry. Towns and urban areas account for less than 1 percent of the land area.

The north-south extent of the country is 994 miles (1,600 kilometers), and the greatest breadth is about 310 miles (500 kilometers). The northwestern part is highland with mountains, forest, and moorland. The northeast is lowland. The more urbanized southern third of the country is also largely lowland, but the terrain is broken; the bedrock there is usually primary rock, and the cover, where there is such, consists of loose soil strata.

The topography of the metropolitan areas of Stockholm and Göteborg is also very broken, with areas of bare rock separated by depressions with unstabilized clays. Urban development therefore requires extensive excavation work and reinforcement measures. It is further complicated in the Stockholm area by the numerous expanses of water. In the southernmost part of Sweden, including the Malmö region, quite different geological conditions obtain. Here are broad plains only rarely relieved by lakes. The soil types are quite stabilized and provide an ideal foundation for building.

Sweden lies at the same latitude as Alaska and southern Greenland, but the Gulf Stream Drift endows the country with a comparatively mild climate. The north-south climatic range is considerable, however: the mean temperature at Kiruna, the most northerly town, is 54°F (12.8°C) in July and 10°F (− 12°C) in February, while the corresponding span for Stockholm is 64°F (17.8°C) and 27°F (− 3.1°C), and for Malmö in the southernmost part of the country 64°F (18°C) and 32°F (0°C). The frost-free depth required for construction work is 2.2 yards (2 meters) in northern Sweden and 0.9 yard (0.8 meter) in the south.

The precipitation is moderate. The water resources for the whole country are adequate. The northern part of the country has a high snowfall, a factor of which account must be taken in highway design.

While the wind conditions vary considerably with the season and geographical location, southerly to southwesterly winds prevail.

Demographic and Socioeconomic Background   The population of Sweden in 1970, was approximately 8 million. The mean rate of increase for 1960 to 1970 was 0.75 percent per annum. The mean population density for the whole country is about 50 inhabitants per square mile (about 19.5 per square kilometer) of land area. More than 80 percent of the population lives in the southernmost third of the country and the population density in 1965 varied from about 7.5 inhabitants per square mile (about 3 per square kilometer) in the northernmost county to 358 (138) in the south and about 460 (178) in the Stockholm region. In 1965 about 66 percent of the population was living in towns having a population of more than 2,000, and about 30 percent in the three metropolitan regions of Stockholm, Göteborg, and Malmö. The population of Stockholm in 1970 was about 1.4 million, and the rate of growth was about 1.7 percent per annum. Urbanization is proceeding at a high rate.

Of the total population of Sweden in 1965, about 21 percent were under 15 years of age, about 66 percent between 15 and 64, and about 13 percent over 64. The mean expectation of life is about 74 years. The higher age groups are increasing rapidly in relative size. The gainfully employed constitute about 44 percent of the total population. In 1965, about 10 percent were engaged in agriculture and forestry, about 44 percent in industry— about 10 percent of these in the building and construction industries—and 46 percent in the "third sector." The corresponding figures for 1950 were 20, 41, and 39 percent.

The gross national product in 1969 was about Sw kr 147 milliard (about £ 12 milliard or $28 billion). Of this sum about 32 percent went to investments—about 15 percent to new investments in buildings and works—about 17 percent to public consumption, and about 50 percent to private consumption. The rate of growth in recent years has been about 3.5 percent per annum.

The per capita gross national product is higher in Sweden than in other European countries. The difference in income between the various population groups is probably smaller than in most other countries of Western Europe. The annual housing output, about 100,000 dwellings (1969), is the highest per capita value in Europe. Of the 1969 housing production, about 30 percent consisted of one-family houses and about 70 percent of multifamily houses. Sweden's figure of 260 private cars per 1,000 inhabitants (at the beginning of 1969) was the highest in Europe.

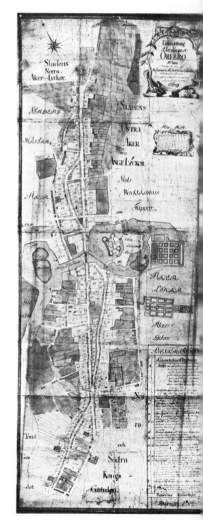

Plan of the old Swedish town of Örebro. Note the concentration of development along the main road.

Aerial view of Stockholm.

Traditions of Planning to the End of the Nineteenth Century The oldest towns in Sweden date from the Middle Ages; they were commercial centers and episcopal sees. Only in old Visby is there a preponderance of buildings from that era, and they are mostly ruins. Most towns were built of wood and were often ravaged by fire. The mediaeval road system still survives in some, while others have been modified in accordance with later town plans, usually with a strict gridiron pattern. Gamla Stan in Stockholm today has retained more features from the Middle Ages than have other Swedish towns; the present buildings are, however, mostly from the seventeenth and eighteenth century.

During the 1600s several new towns were founded by royal decree. From that time stems the provision for town plans to be ratified by the King in Council (the government). The seventeenth-century towns are all built on the gridiron pattern; an example is Göteborg, whose oldest quarter was built on the Dutch pattern, with an internal system of canals and surrounded with strong fortifications.

The beginning of the nineteenth century saw the introduction of a period when new towns were established and older ones remodeled. The gridiron pattern was again dominant, but the streets were now wider. To reduce the risk of fire, an attempt was made to introduce tree-planted strips.

The early 1860s saw the beginning of industrialization in Sweden. Some of the existing towns expanded rapidly and new urban areas and industrial complexes grew up, often around railway junctions. Swedish heavy industry grew up for the most part at isolated places in the extensively forested rural areas. In the larger towns, densely built blocks of flats were erected on the continental pattern. In the new communities, the development was of a sparse and open character.

Within the jurisdiction of the existing towns, new districts were planned outside the old ones. The town layout was, to begin with, on the gridiron basis, with superimposed diagonal and stellate places in the image of Paris and Vienna. A familiar example is the 1866 town plan for Stockholm.

The development outside the town boundaries and around the industrial complexes in the rural areas usually did not conform to a town plan, the pattern being determined largely by the existing structure of land ownership. Such development has since been adapted and reorganized according to subsequent town plans.

How densely and how high one was allowed to build was regulated in the respective periods by general directives. The town plan ratified by the King in Council specified only which land should be allocated for building sites, where one might build, which land should be for streets or other public places, and in which areas the local authority should be responsible for works and maintenance. There were no regulations governing the purpose for which building land might be used, and there was nothing to prevent housing and industry being mixed in the same area.

In only a few special instances were plans formulated to meet express aesthetic aims—one such case is the district around the Royal Palace in Stockholm. It was mainly during the eighteenth century that such interests were asserted.

Twentieth Century Around the turn of the century new hygienic and aesthetic demands in urban development began to be recognized, and special rules governing the mode of use and developmental design were incorporated in the formal town plans.

The differentiation of the economy and the separation of residential and working areas were reflected in the town plans. Separate industrial areas were provided. Villa districts grew up which in some measure reflected an English influence; early examples are the residential suburbs of Djursholm and Saltsjöbaden outside Stockholm, which came into being about 1890. The elaborate style of many town plans of this period and of the first decades of the twentieth century reflect stimuli from abroad, such as, for example, the ideas of Camillo Sitte. Göteborg has many examples of districts planned in this vein.

Around the 1930s, inspiration derived mainly from the urban construction of the 1920s in Germany, which was combined with new trends in social policy in Sweden. The pattern of closed town blocks was replaced with one of houses arranged in parallel rows. Most Swedish towns bear traces of this phase of development.

About 1945 the English concept of the neighborhood was incorporated in the Swedish town planning ideology. The development of the large and middle-sized towns has since been designed on the bases of catchment areas for retail trade and schools.

At the same time a less formal layout was aimed at. The first plans for urban districts with consistent separation of pedestrian and vehicular traffic were also conceived at this time.

In the forties, master plans were adopted to a greater extent; examples are those for Skövde (1949) and Stockholm (1952). The former was a pioneer work for method. In 1946, a regional plan was produced for the Göteborg region.

In the last two decades, the principles introduced in the thirties and forties have been further developed, but new production methods have favored a stricter design. Interest has shifted from the neighborhood toward larger functional units. With the increase in motor traffic, it has become still more important to exclude it entirely from the residential areas. At the same time the need for a rational approach to public transport has become more pressing, and this is reflected in the layout of the built-up areas in relation to the bus and underground routes. In the production of master and regional plans, care of natural resources and measures against pollution of air, water, and noise have assumed increasing importance.

A few examples will illustrate the stage reached in Swedish town planning.

New Towns and Communities The large number of small and scattered communities present a greater problem than do the metropolitan areas, and there is therefore no general desire to found new towns. In a few cases special conditions arising out of the location of industry have justified the building of a new urban center; an example is Märsta, situated 25 miles (40 kilometers) north of Stockholm. Planned for a population of 40,000 to 50,000 inhabitants, its construction was begun in 1960. (The population in 1969 was about 18,000.) The town is situated on four hills around a central valley, with the town center and parks leading down to lake Mälar.

City and Town Extensions In the metropolitan regions, the problems entailed by urban expansion are somewhat different from those in smaller towns. Greater Stockholm and the town of Örebro represent these two types.

Greater Stockholm accounts for about one-fifth of the housing production in Sweden. The development work in the region is carried out on the basis of a regional plan. The newly developed areas in Greater Stockholm are, as a rule, composed of units each with its local service center and themselves arranged around a somewhat larger center. The Vällingby group, which lies within the boundary of the city of Stockholm, is the earliest example of consistently realized urban expansion along these lines. Four residential

Master plan of Märsta by the
Stockholm Regional Planning Office.

Key:

Residential area: houses for
several families

Residential area: low-rise houses
for several families, terrace houses

Residential area: semi-detached houses,
chain houses, detached houses

Center: district center and
sub-centers

Employment area: offices

Employment area: industry

Parks and leisure-time
avenues

Schools, churches, etc.

Fringe parking

Water

Long-distance roads

Primary roads

Other regional roads

Secondary roads

Feeder roads

Ramps

Railways

Bus routes

Separate network of main walkways

Critical aircraft noise boundary
according to 1956 report

Plan boundary

0   100   200   300   400   500   600   700   800   900   1000 m

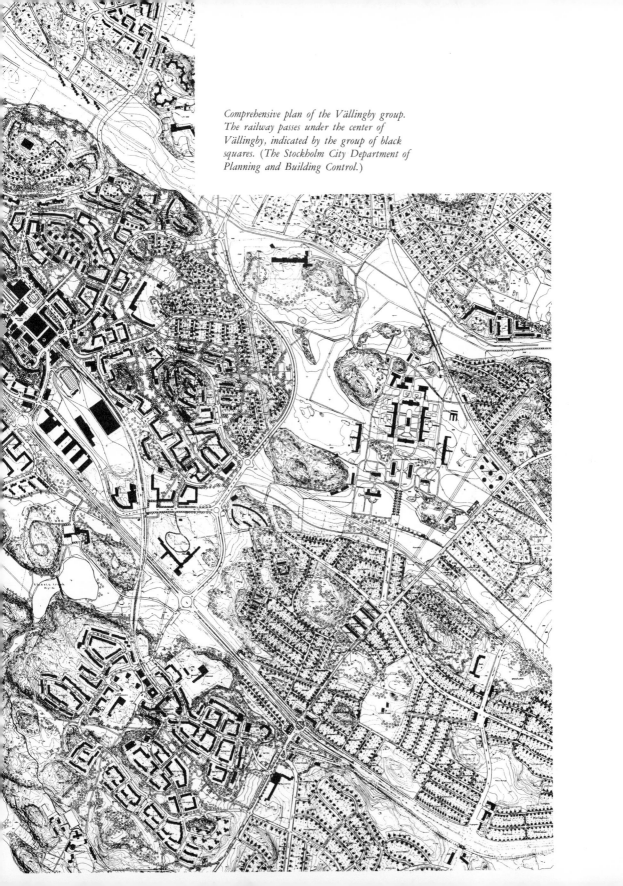

Comprehensive plan of the Vällingby group.
The railway passes under the center of
Vällingby, indicated by the group of black
squares. (The Stockholm City Department of
Planning and Building Control.)

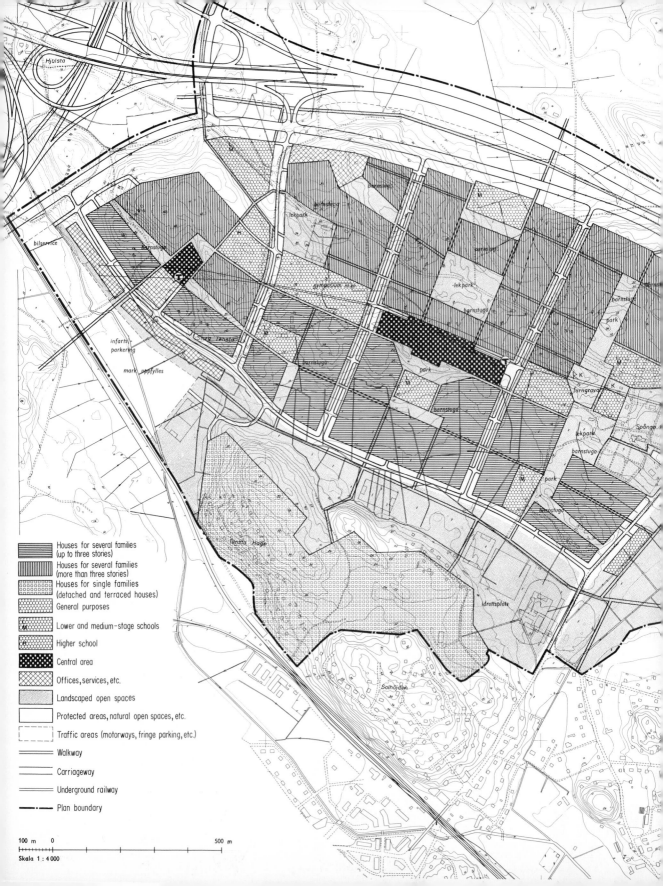

	Houses for several families (up to three stories)
	Houses for several families (more than three stories)
	Houses for single families (detached and terraced houses)
	General purposes
M	Lower and medium-stage schools
H	Higher school
	Central area
	Offices, services, etc.
	Landscaped open spaces
	Protected areas, natural open spaces, etc.
	Traffic areas (motorways, fringe parking, etc.)

Walkway

Carriageway

Underground railway

Plan boundary

100 m   0   500 m

Skala 1 : 4 000

Comprehensive plan of Rinkeby and Tensta. (The Stockholm City Department of Planning and Building Control.)

Aerial view of the center of Vällingby. (Photograph: Oscar Bladh.)

Aerial view of the Grindtorp in Täby. (Photograph: Oscar Bladh.)

View of Vivalla, Örebro.

View of Vivalla, Örebro.

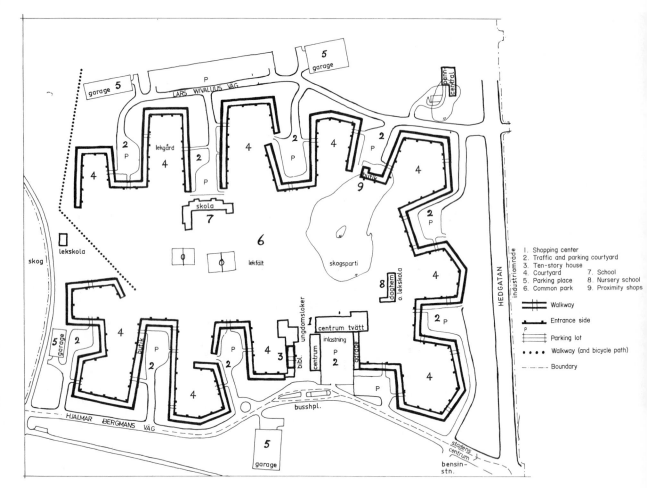

*Plan of Baronbackarna, Örebro, 1955. The area comprises 1200
dwellings. The built-up area consists of apartment houses of three to four
stories, forming courtyards opening out into a large common park with
hills and trees. The street with the parking facilities, on the outside of the
area, is connected with the courtyards by porches. All entrances face the
courtyard. No motor traffic is admitted to the shopping center facing the
residential area, the transport of goods taking place from the outside to
a traffic and parking courtyard. A ten-story house with small flats
within the center is planned. In a number of houses, flats for disabled
persons are on the ground floor.*

*Certain experimental flats have a number of smaller rooms to the same
floor area, according to the principle that each child should have a
separate bedroom. This has meant doing away with the small dining
room, meals having to be taken in the living room. The different uses of
the latter have thus been increased and, since it is now an inbetween
room, a new appelation of "all-purpose room" has been introduced.
Parking requirements have been estimated in the town plan at one
parking place per two flats. (White Office of Architects, A. B.)*

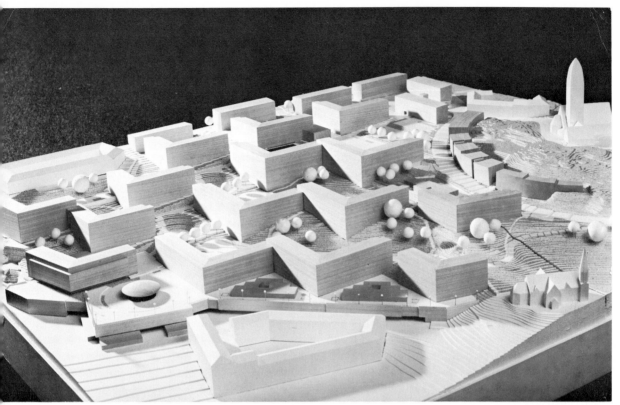

Model of Stigberget, Göteburg.

districts, each with 10,000 to 20,000 inhabitants, together with a small industrial estate form the major unit, centered on Vällingby itself. The four districts are grouped around a large common and are linked to each other and to central Stockholm by an underground line. The latest example of this pattern is provided by the districts of Rinkeby and Tensta, which are also located within the city of Stockholm and are planned for a total population of 30,000. An architectonically more expressive variation on the same theme is the service center and associated residential area for some 15,000 inhabitants in the suburb of Täby.

Örebro had a population of about 90,000 at the end of 1969 and the town has been expanded according to a plan based on neighborhood units. Baronbackarna built, in the mid-fifties for a population of some 3,500, is a classic example of a residential area with complete traffic differentiation. It consists entirely of three-story blocks of flats. Vivalla is the most recent contribution, it being finished in 1970. Its population of some 8,000 is accommodated in two-story blocks of flats, which were designed for construction on cheap and rational lines.

Urban Renewal   Since Swedish urban development is relatively young and there has been an urgent need for new housing, little emphasis has been placed on the renewal of older residential districts. On the other hand, the change in the functions of the urban core in many Swedish towns has demanded radical remodeling of large areas.

Göteborg is the only Swedish town where there has been renewal of extensive residential districts as a single project. One example is Stigberget, a steep slope toward the north, which was originally covered with wooden houses from the nineteenth century and now accommodates a population of some 3,000. Complete traffic separation has been achieved, most of the motor traffic being placed underground. The scheme was carried out at the end of the sixties.

The most radical remodeling of an urban core is that which has been proceeding for the last couple of decades in Stockholm. The latest version of the renewal plan is that of 1967.   —C. F. AHLBERG AND GÖSTA CARLESTAM

SWITZERLAND

Legislation and Administration   Before 1970 Switzerland had no overall planning legislation, and the position was that all powers concerned with physical planning rested with the 22 cantons, the legislation and administration of which are very different. The federal government (Bundesrat) could only indirectly influence physical planning as, for example, by planning and paying for the national roads, subsidizing the main roads, operating and extending the national railways, by legislation for the protection of country amenities and landscape, and by improving farming methods.

In September 1969, the Swiss constitution was broadened to include several new provisions, among which are:

1. Provision for the preparation of decrees by the federal government for the cantons, decrees by which principles of physical and environmental planning are followed so as to ensure the best utilization of land in the national interest

2. Provisions to assist and coordinate the plans of the cantons and to work with them

These measures are directed to fulfilling the needs of the country in regional and communal planning.

Legislation for these purposes is being prepared, and it may be expected that within 2 or 3 years these important measures will be put into operation. In most of the cantons regulations are now in operation for the protection of the landscape and amenities, for health, for zoning, for aesthetic and functional standards of urban development, for clean air and water, for the control and improvement of public services, for expropriation in the public interest, and for agricultural improvements.

Several regional plans which provide the necessary guidance for the cantons have been legally fixed. In accordance with the federal character of Switzerland, the autonomy of the communities, and the democratic administration, the cantons have delegated the preparation of plans to the communities, especially the larger ones like the towns, which have made some large and detailed proposals. These comprise general outline plans and the ensuing statutory plans, which include, for instance, the division of the areas into zones with different densities and different degrees of smoke control. These zone plans can prohibit the erection of buildings on particular sites if such buildings are considered to be against the public interest.

In such cases the consequent diminished value of the site has to be indemnified. The building rules, contained in the communal zone plan, give the necessary details insofar as they are not established by cantonal laws.

In spite of the differences of legislation in the cantons, a far-reaching uniformity of planning administration has been achieved in recent years. The administration provides plans for landscaping, zoning, transport, utility services for public buildings and installations, and for the stages of their implementation.

Professional Practice Planners can work in the following categories: as employees of the administrations of the cantons, of the larger towns, or, of the federal government; as private consultants or as their assistants for a public or private corporation; or as collaborators with the Institute for Communal, Regional and National Planning at the Federal Institute of Technology (ETH).

Since 1960 prospects for the profession of planner have much improved. Private planning consultants are now commissioned by public corporations to prepare plans on a large scale. Until recently there were no conditions or standards for the planners, but now the federal government requires that for any scheme to get state subsidy it is necessary for the person mainly responsible to be a qualified planner, and there are specific conditions for such qualifications. For the responsible chief in the preparation of regional plans the qualifications are much higher than for community plans, and these qualifications must usually include evidence of a basic academic study of architecture, building, engineering, geography, forestry, sociology, law or economics, and proof of a good knowledge of regional planning or special training in environmental (national) planning. It may be assumed that in the future there will be standards of qualification throughout Switzerland for those who wish to work as planners.

Education and Training Different departments of the Federal Institute of Technology are concerned with the introduction of physical planning. Interdisciplinary postgraduate studies in spatial planning started in 1967 and are essential for the planning qualifications, which are equivalent to a master of arts or science degree from a British university.

The postgraduate study extends for 2 years and terminates with an examination. The responsible body for these studies is the Kuratorium, which consists of representatives concerned in a variety of ways with physical and environmental planning. The studies are arranged by the Institute for Communal, Regional and National Planning. Training is extending rapidly in many fields.

Institutions Among the important planning institutions in Switzerland is the Institute for Communal, Regional and National Planning at the Federal Institute of Technology in Zurich (ORL-Institute ETHZ). It was founded in 1961, and in 1969 there were 80 permanent collaborators, 60 of whom were academicians with different basic training backgrounds. The main tasks of the institute are research on matters of urban order, physical planning, and environmental design; the provision of a 2-year postgraduate course in physical and environmental planning (since 1967) and other advanced courses of different kinds. Another institution is a private society called Schweizerische Vereinigung für Landesplanung (VLP) in Zurich. It was founded in 1943 and the members consist of the cantons, private enterprise firms, and individuals. The main purpose of the society is to give general help in physical and environmental planning and to inform the public about problems, methods, and solutions. Many cantons and the bigger towns have their own planning departments.

Geographical Conditions and Population   The total area of Switzerland is approximately 16,000 square miles (41,000 square kilometers) about 25 percent of which is forests, about 30 percent is suitable for urban development and farming, and about 45 percent consists of mountains, streams, lakes, and mountainous pastureland. The population increased from about 2.4 million in 1850 to 3.3 million in 1900, 4.7 million in 1950, 5.4 million in 1960, and 6.2 million in 1970. Thus the increase between 1950 and 1960 was about 15 percent and that from 1960 to 1970 about 13 percent. These formidable increases are due mainly to immigration from foreign countries.

Switzerland is a country of mixed population which in 1960 comprised 69 percent German speaking, 19 percent French, 10 percent Italian, 1 percent Romansh, and 1 percent of other people. The greatest concentrations of population (1969) are as follows:

City	Population
Zurich	671,500
Basel	364,800
Geneva	307,500
Berne	258,000
Lausanne	215,900

Switzerland is a highly industrialized country. The income per person is—together with Sweden—the highest in Europe. The quality of housing is remarkable. The annual production of apartments and single-family houses is about 40,000 to 50,000 units.

Traditions of Planning to the End of the Nineteenth Century   The federal political organization of Switzerland is based on linguistic, cultural, and topographical differences. The four languages—German, French, Italian, and Romansh—show the union of different cultures. This variety arises from Switzerland's geographical situation in the middle of Europe, through which important travel routes have run for centuries.

The ideas which have always provided the basis for Switzerland's evolution are influenced by two circumstances: by the cultures of the different parts of Switzerland and by the personal freedom and consequent sense of responsibility characteristic of the Swiss. These are shown in the autonomy of

Old city of Berne.

Zurich and its lake.

*Landscape in the midlands
(Halluylersee).*

*Landscape in the mountains
(Engadin).*

the communities, especially in all matters concerned with building developments, and in Switzerland's liberal economy. All forms of domination by individuals or small groups are discouraged. This may be the reason why, in Swiss towns, monumental edifices and squares do not exist.

Switzerland lacks raw materials, she does not adjoin the seas, and in very few places is there intensive farming. In the first half of the nineteenth century there was a rapid industrial development, with concentration on goods with low transport costs. Thus, there is little heavy industry. Despite the absence of federal planning laws or administration, orderly physical development occurred, marked by the absence of urban concentrations, slums, and similar unsatisfactory developments. A close network of railways and roads was constructed and operated, including the north-south crossing of Switzerland via the St. Gotthard tunnel, and colossal investments were made to improve large swamp areas such as Lindtebene. In several larger towns there were considerable large-scale building projects such as that at Zurich, where there was complete modification of the areas close to the old city, between the central station and the lake, including the modification of the whole bank.

Toward the end of the nineteenth century it was felt that planning on a large scale was necessary for the development of the bigger cities in the interest of the inhabitants. Cantons that included growing towns introduced legislation with planning administration, such as the enactments of the canton of Zurich of April 23, 1893.

Twentieth-century Planning   By the twentieth century the need for physical planning became more and more obvious, but the necessity for comprehensive overall planning has been generally recognized only recently. This is demonstrated by the many preoccupations of different administrative departments, which are subdivided into bureaus such as housing, traffic, utility services, protection of landscape and country areas, and colonization.

The following chronology of events is significant:
- 1905—Foundation of the Swiss Federation for Preservation of Beauty Spots.
- 1906—Foundation of the Swiss Federation for the Protection of Natural Amenities.
- 1915—International competition for a master plan for Zurich and its suburbs. This was the first competition for a comprehensive replanning of a large urban area.
- 1920—Publication by H. Bernhard, agronomist, geographer, and lecturer at Zurich University, of a program for the initiation of development and the necessary federal legislation. Vital points in the overall planning of Switzerland were specified.
- 1929—Publication by H. Bernoulli and C. Martin of *City Planning in Switzerland,* in which the development of urban areas is seen from the standpoint of the architect.
- 1932—A. Meili, the architect, becomes the foremost promoter of planning for the country. Three years later the Confederation of Swiss

Architects and the Association of Swiss Engineers and Architects approached the Bundesrat requesting that physical and environmental planning be promoted by the Bund to determine the areas that required planning schemes. The engineers and architects established working grounds to prepare practical and theoretical schemes.

- 1942—Foundation of a Center for Communal, Regional and National Planning at the Federal Institute of Technology, initiated by the geographer Professor Dr. H. Gutersohn. (president of the Swiss Society for Physical and Environmental planning, 1953–1962). The center was ultimately joined to the Institute of Geography.

- 1943—Foundation of the Swiss Society for Physical and Environmental Planning. In the same year the finalization of the building laws of the canton of Zurich made it possible to prepare and implement comprehensive plans for large areas.

- Beginning in 1945 there were growing activities by the communities to plan their areas. Many zone plans and building orders were made. Since 1950 there have been increasing efforts to prepare and implement comprehensive plans for larger areas. From 1958 onward there have been numerous revisions and supplements to cantonal building and planning laws.

- 1961—Foundation of the Institute for Communal, Regional and National Planning of the Federal Institute of Technology.

- 1967—The Bundesrat asks the previously mentioned institute to prepare different possible comprehensive studies for the whole of Switzerland.

- 1969—Incorporation in the Swiss Constitution of the laws regarding physical and environmental planning of the Bund.

Methods Until 1960 planning was much influenced by methods of architectural practice and building technology. As an outgrowth of more comprehensive knowledge of the social, economic, and political developments, the scope of planning was widened, leading to changes in the theoretical basis. Research into the best methods of procedure is being carried out. The present stage in the application of the new methods is given in the directions by the Institute for Communal, Regional and National Planning. These methods are continually being extended and reviewed. The English words "physical and environmental planning" are not a satisfactory translation for *Raumplanung,* and there may consequently be some misunderstanding about methods. *Raumplanung* includes all processes and activities which influence—and are influenced by—the environment. The total area—urbanized and nonurbanized—is the object of *Raumplanung.*

Important Problems Most of the really useful areas in Switzerland are highly developed. How much of the remaining useful areas of the midlands should be allocated for new settlements? The answer depends on the fixing of the agricultural zones and the protection of water and of recreational areas.

As half of Switzerland is alpine, one is faced with the question of what planning is appropriate to these mountain regions. The answer to this question depends on several factors such as tourism, the diminishing farming in the mountains, the social changes in the lives of the inhabitants, and military defense. What are the buildings and scenery to be protected and the best methods to employ? What will be the probable extensions of urban regions in the future? What, in the field of communication, will be the probable transportation policy in the future? What are the likely preferences of people in the matter of physical environment, both aesthetically and functionally? How can available funds, both from public and private sources, best be utilized in providing the buildings and infrastructures that are needed?

To achieve these purposes two further questions arise: how can it be assured that the knowledge and talents of those who will be responsible for these plans will be adequate? And how can the people best be informed?

Examples   Among the early notable examples of planning in Switzerland during the twentieth century was a master plan of Zurich and its surroundings (1915–1918), which was the subject of a competition, the first in Switzerland, for the comprehensive replanning of a large urban area (see illustration).

In 1960 a scheme was prepared for a community along the border of the protected zone surrounding the lake of Greifensee, and the purpose and value of the zone had to be protected. In this scheme (see illustration) the physical and economic development were integrated as a unit, and it is a typical example of cooperation between the state and private developers.

Another interesting housing scheme (1952–1960) consisted of tower blocks in the residential and artisan quarter of Carouge, blocks which were designed to fit into the original street grid of the old town with the result that, although following the concepts of modern town planning, they

BELOW LEFT: *Indication of the extent of the Master Plan of Zurich (1915–1918).*   BELOW RIGHT: *Scheme (1960) for a community near Greifensee.*

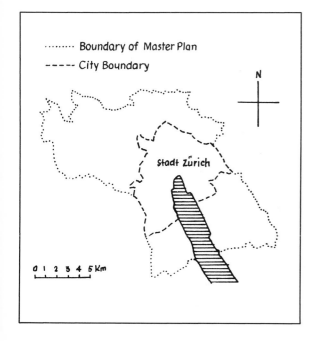

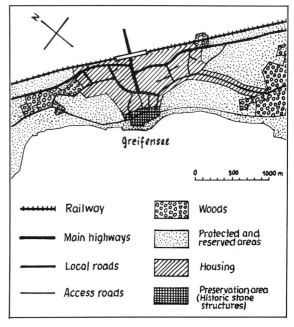

Scheme at Gruzefeld, Winterthur, for 370 dwellings in five long blocks (1965–1968) by C. Paillard and P. Leeman.

harmonize with the historical setting. In building these tower blocks an attempt was made to create the best possible conditions for the inhabitants with provision for their recreation and leisure.

A housing scheme at Gruzefeld, Winterthur, interesting for the designs of its 370 dwellings built in 1965 to 1968, consisted of five long blocks which varied from 2 to 12 stories in height (see illustration). The wide variety of house plans was based on the sequence of living room, kitchen, balcony, bathroom. The dwellings or apartments are staggered laterally by half a story in height.

In the Cité du Lignon-Aire in the canton of Genf, a new residential quarter was built in 1962 to 1970 from plans of Addor, Juillard, Bolliger, and Payot. It comprised an area of 280,000 square meters (334,880 square yards), of which 80,000 square meters (95,680 square yards) was set aside for churches, schools, sports, and playgrounds (see illustration).

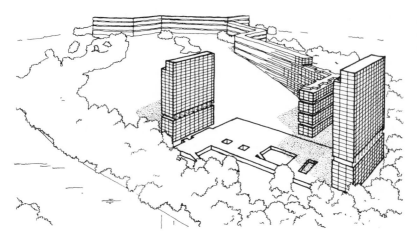

New residential quarter (1962–1970) in Cité du Lignon, Aire, (Architects: Addor, Juillard, Bolliger, and Payot.)

The built-up area includes a covered passage crossing the entire site. The buildings, in the form of slab blocks, are 12 to 30 stories in height, and the dwellings, except for those that form the terminals of the blocks, are uniform in design. Only two apartments are accessible from each landing, which contributes to privacy. The construction is of reinforced concrete with slab floors and prefabricated, insulated walls.

A housing scheme on the western edge of Berne (1966–1969) by E. Helfer and H. and G. Reinhardt was designed to accord with a pleasing landscape involving the preservation of the small river—the Gabelbach. The problem thus presented was solved by concentrating the 862 flats in only three large blocks. The community center, the school, hall, swimming pool, restaurant, and garages link the three massive structures and offer points of encounter for the inhabitants.

Among notable recent planning enterprises is the housing area of Jolieville on the periphery of Zurich. It is for about 2,450 dwellings and is designed by Litz, Huber, and Schnitter on very modern, functional lines in which the principal objects have been to create an urban environment, to mix different types and forms of housing, and to use economical methods of construction. A main highway crosses the area, and it was necessary to minimize the disturbing influence and noise of this by the layout of the buildings as seen in the model illustrated.

Model of housing area of Jolieville on the periphery of Zurich. (Architects: Litz, Huber, and Schnitter.)

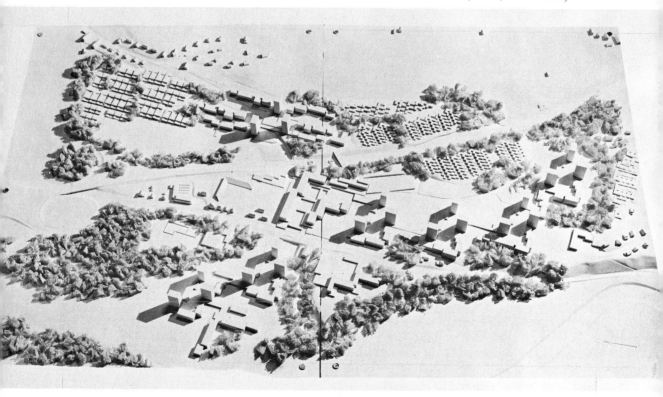

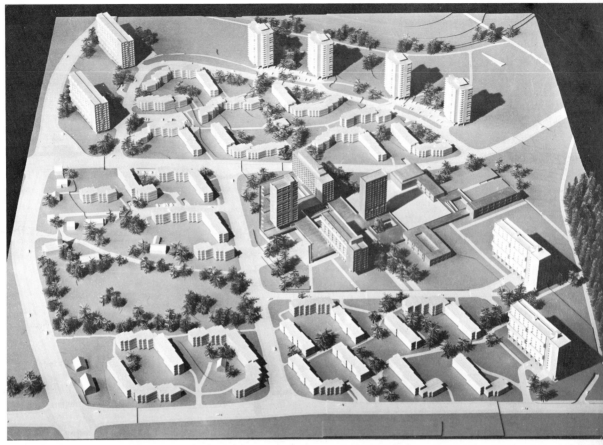

Also commenced in 1969 is a residential unit of 1,700 dwellings, in Affoltern on the periphery of Zurich, consisting of four-story blocks of apartments and higher tower and slab blocks. The area has its own center, with shops and commercial buildings, churches, and provision for recreation, sport, and leisure pursuits (see illustration).

A particularly interesting project is that for the center of the old historical town of Baden in the canton of Aargau. The town authority wanted to maintain, and indeed increase, its importance relative to Zurich, yet at the same time it wanted to preserve the historical character of the center. The problem thus posed was resolved in a project that occupied 10 years, from 1958 to 1968, with full public participation. A comprehensive development plan has been prepared taking into consideration all aspects—social, economic, aesthetic, and transport—and it was decided that implementation, which began in 1969, should take place slowly, step by step.

In a small yet progressive country like Switzerland, with many interesting and beautiful old cities and towns, the problem of combining preservation of the historical and the beautiful with modern developments will increasingly exercise the ingenuity of planners.

Model of residential area of Affoltern, Zurich. (Architects: Chief Architect, Zurich, Dubois, Escher and Weilenmann, Nrehus, de Stoutz, and Adam.)

BIBLIOGRAPHY: International competition for a comprehensive plan for the region of Zurich, 1915–1918; G. Fischer, National Income after Cantons, 1950–1965; Swiss statistical year book, 1969; Directives for Local, Regional, and National Planning, Institute for Local, Regional, and National Planning, Federal Institute of Technology, Zurich; Federal Swiss housing statistics; Periodicals: *PLAN,* Swiss magazine for National, Regional, and Local Planning; DISP, Information for Local, Regional, and National Planning, Institute for Local, Regional, and National Planning, Federal Institute of. Technology, Zurich; *Schweizerische Bauzeitung,* weekly magazine for architecture and housing; *Werk,* Swiss monthly journal for architecture and applied arts; Information und Dokumentationsstelle, Institute for Local, Regional, and National Planning, Federal Institute of Technology, Zurich.

—J. MAURER

SYMBOLIC MOTIFS IN PLANNING   (*See* RELIGIOUS INFLUENCES IN PLANNING.)

SYSTEMS APPROACH   A process for investigation and problem solving based on the application of scientific methods of research, experimentation, and logical analysis. Instead of fragmented, compartmentalized analysis, emphasis is placed on a holistic view of complex organization, focusing on inter-relations and interactions among parts from which emerge the properties of the whole. A system, broadly defined, is a set of elements in mutual interaction.

The systems approach provides a rational means for dealing with problems of choice under uncertainty through explicit procedures capable of duplication by others and generally modifiable in the light of new information. It involves a variety of techniques and activities for analyzing, designing, and managing systems. These include operations research, systems analysis, systems engineering, systems management, and the Planning-Program-ming-Budgeting System (PPBS). In recent decades the systems approach has been extensively applied in the American defense and aerospace fields. It is now beginning to be utilized to help solve social problems and improve urban conditions.

The problem-solving process used in the systems approach requires bounding the problem (or system) and defining objectives, devising alterna-tives for meeting these objectives, evaluating the alternatives in terms of their probable consequences, and designing and implementing a chosen course of action. Analysis of a system begins with formulation of hypotheses to explain system behavior. Models representing the system in abstract form are used to formalize and make specific the hypotheses. Through observation and experimentation, the model is tested and modifications are made to bring it into correspondence with the real world system. The model can be manipulated to simulate the effects of various actions upon components of the real world system, as in a laboratory experiment.

Computer technology has greatly increased the operational utility of models that require processing large amounts of data. Computer simula-tions together with operational games and scenarios are among the principal types of models. Where quantitative analysis is not feasible, as is often the case in urban affairs, for instance, scenarios may be appropriate. A scenario is a verbal simulation of the interaction of actors and issues in an unfolding

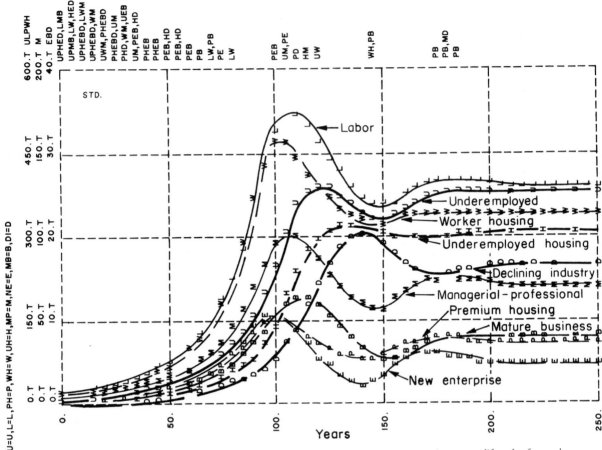

sequence of interconnected activities and events. Its use permits viewing the future as a dynamic whole to understand the various implications of alternative decisions.

The systems approach is a recent innovation. Operations research was first developed during World War II by British and later by American scientists to improve existing weapon systems and solve tactical problems. After the war, systems analysis evolved in the United States as a means for managing the revolution in weapons technology marked by the rapid introduction of nuclear power, guided missiles, electronic computers, and other advances. Systems analysis has become a key military tool for policy planning, resource allocation, and general problem solving.

The systems approach has its theoretical origins in the "general systems theory" initially formulated shortly before World War II by Ludwig von Bertalanffy. Subsequent development and parallel efforts in cybernetics, information theory, decision theory, relational mathematics, and game theory have demonstrated that concepts of wholeness, organization, and teleology are amenable to scientific study.

A 250-year life cycle of an urban area generated by computer in accordance with a simulation model of urban growth, starting with almost empty land and developing over a period of 100 years. By that time that land area has become filled, new construction decreases, and the urban system stagnates into a high level of underemployed housing and declining industry. The economic mix becomes unfavorable with too high a ratio of underemployed to skilled labor. The percentage of housing in the underemployed-housing class, and of industry in the declining-industry category is too high. These changes occur as a result of the aging of structures and the consequent change of activity occurring in them. In the growth phase, industry has a high intensity, and employment per unit of industrial land

Systems can be classified into several broad categories. Natural systems can be distinguished from man-made systems. Open systems, which include all forms of social organization, can be differentiated from closed ones, which do not interact with their environments. Open systems import, transform, and export materials, energies, or information with their environments through transactions, exchanging system outputs for new inputs. In social organizations, like urban areas, interrelations among system components are based on the transmission of information. Information processing is thus central to understanding the growth and evolution of cities. An open system utilizes information feedback to adapt to environmental change and is capable of elaborating or changing its structure to modify the functioning of the system relative to its environment.

The Planning-Programming-Budgeting System (PPBS) represents the application of the systems approach to management problems and, therefore, has particular relevance to urban planning and local government. In PPBS, alternative programs are compared on the basis of their predicted performance relative to cost and the actual performance of ongoing programs is subject to more or less continuous evaluation in terms of the intended objectives. PPBS was first extensively used in the U.S. Department of Defense and is now being extended to other federal agencies and to a number of American cities, counties, and states.

The systems approach is also currently being adapted from military practice to such civilian activities as regional highway planning, water resource development, and management information systems. Many of these efforts have suffered from difficulties in dealing with multiagency jurisdictions and a diversity of user groups. Critics maintain that inadequate attention has been paid in many civil systems studies to political and social considerations which strongly affect the feasibility and desirability of recommendations.

Fundamental differences exist in theory between defense systems and the emerging field of urban systems that have not been generally recognized in practice. In defense systems, a rational model is employed using a closed system of logic which conceptually minimizes uncertainty and conflict. However, coping with uncertainty and conflict is a critical problem in open systems like urban areas. In urban systems, knowledge regarding cause-effect relationships is largely insufficient and the outcomes of purposive activity are determined, in part, by actions within and outside the system that are not subject to centralized control. The human factor introduces a reactive and unpredictable element leading to conflict over both the system's ends and means. Interdependence between the system and its environment creates uncertainty regarding the effects of such basic factors as technological and social change on the system's functioning.

Relative certainty about goals and cause-effect relationships allows electronic computers to substitute for much human decision-making in programs such as the landing of a man on the moon. But where uncertainty and conflict pertaining to facts and values are widespread, as in urban

area is high. At the same time housing is constructed for those engaged in the expanding industry, the residential population is economically successful, and the population density is low per unit of residential land area. The type of construction determines and freezes the ratio of industrial to housing area. Then, as the structures age, the industrial vitality declines, new industries start elsewhere, and employment per unit of industrial land declines. But the opposite happens to population as housing ages. Rental costs decline and the kind of occupancy shifts to those people whose economic circumstances force more crowded population density per unit of residential land. In short, starting from a balance between industry and people at the end of the growth phase, employment declines while population rises until an equilibrium is reached in which the economic condition of the area falls far enough to limit further growth in population. (Jay W. Forrester, Urban Dynamics.)

systems, current systems thinking asserts the need for human judgment capable of achieving compromise among the competing interests of a pluralistic society.

Public policies in urban areas often generate unexpected and unintended results, while the intended results are not achieved. Because of the problem of determining the effects of causal action within urban systems, *effectiveness* in producing the desired outcome is the essential criterion of performance rather than *efficiency*, obtaining the result at least cost. Efficiency is concerned mainly with internal system operation and is inadequate for measuring transactions between the system and its environment. Emphasis on efficiency also obscures the purpose of organizational action and its consequences on the larger society.

The complexity of the characteristics of urban systems is the primary obstacle to effective planning. Long time delays between causes and effects, and their multiplicity, make it difficult to separate symptoms of problems from actual causal agents. Unintended but harmful consequences of corrective action frequently exceed the benefits, particularly when judged in terms of long-run system behavior rather than expediency. Expediency, however, serves pressing requirements for political accommodation while the benefits of the long-run view accrue mainly to the voteless unborn.

Modern systems research supports the view that institutional reform to change the system's internal structure, which generates the undesirable conditions in the first place, is potentially more effective than externally imposed corrective programs, especially in overcoming political expediency inherent in such programs. The urban system resists externally imposed corrective actions with compensating counteractions. Unless corrective efforts are directed to the critical influence points and reach relevant impact thresholds to affect the aggregate functioning of the system, they become neutralized by countervailing, internal adjustments. Structural changes need to be designed to promote self-generated, self-sustained improvements through the system's own functioning.

Deteriorated housing in the urban ghettos of the United States, for example, is a highly visible physical symptom of limited social and economic opportunities available to Negroes and other groups. Urban renewal and other externally imposed programs dealing with the physical symptoms have had little impact on ghetto conditions. From a systems viewpoint the urban system will continue functioning through the operation of the real estate market, taxation, racial segregation, and other practices to furnish incentives and supports for perpetuating ghettos until the system's structure itself is altered to provide all groups with access to the nation's available opportunities. The systems approach is a major new tool in promoting innovations to improve the planning and management process and adapt the structure of the urban system to change.

BIBLIOGRAPHY: Ludwig von Bertalanffy and Anatol Rapoport (eds.), *General Systems: Yearbook of the Society for General Systems Research,* vol. 1, 1956; Norbert Wiener, *Cybernetics,* 2d ed., M.I.T. Press, Cambridge, Mass., 1961; David Novick (ed.), *Program Budgeting, Program Analysis and the Federal Budget,* Harvard University Press, Cambridge, Mass., 1965; California

State Department of Finance, *The Four Aerospace Contracts, A Review of the California Experience,* System Development Corp., Santa Monica, Calif., 1966; John S. Gilmore, John J. Ryan, and William S. Gould, *Defense Systems Resources in the Civil Sector,* U.S. Government Printing Office, 1967; James D. Thompson, *Organizations in Action,* McGraw-Hill Book Company, New York, 1967; U.S. Department of Housing and Urban Development, *Science and the City,* 1967; Walter Buckley (ed.), *Modern Systems Research for the Behavioral Scientist,* Aldine Publishing Company, Chicago, 1968; Jay W. Forrester, *Urban Dynamics,* M.I.T. Press, Cambridge, Mass., 1969; J. Brian McLoughlin, *Urban and Regional Planning, A System Approach,* Faber and Faber, London, 1969.

—JEREMIAH D. O'LEARY, JR.

T

TERMINOLOGY AND TRANSLATIONS   As planning advances, new technical terms continuously come into use and older words and phrases acquire specialized meanings, not always completely standardized. Even within a single language usages vary. For example, what is commonly called a "flat" in England is in the United States an "apartment," a "garden" is a "yard," "semidetached" is "semiattached," "compulsory acquisition" is "condemnation," and "town planning" is more usually "city planning." As between languages, differences of laws and practices give rise to many expressions that are not exactly translatable in simple terms. Thus for international discussion glossaries are necessary, but new terms proliferate so rapidly that these soon become incomplete. One of the earliest was Gaston Bardet's *Petit Glossaire de l'Urbaniste* in six languages (French, English, German, Italian, Portuguese, and Spanish), published in Paris in 1946. This and the fuller *Glossary of Technical Terms used in Housing and Planning,* in five languages, by H. J. Spiwak (IFHP, 1951), remain very useful but need supplementation.

—FREDERIC J. OSBORN

TERRACE   A raised level space or platform supported by wall of masonry in a garden or park, or an extension from a building, often used as a promenade and provided with seats. Terrace houses are rows of houses joined together by party walls.

THAILAND   (*See* ASIA, SOUTHEAST, DEVELOPING COUNTRIES.)

THEORIES AND IDEALS OF PLANNING   The archetypal town plan is that indicated by the ancient Egyptian hieroglyph for a city: a cross contained within an oval or a circle. The cross expresses the magnetic function of the city as a center of organized power whose original core was the citadel, or "little city," the seat of the palace, the temple, and the granary. The circle, originally a protective wall, indicates the function of the city as a container, within whose sacred limits a common way of life and a common system of law and order promote the interaction of a diversity of occupations, talents, and regional backgrounds, thus breaking down the isolation and noncommunication of smaller primary groups, the tribe or village.

In its more intimate aspects, the structure of the city derives from the Neolithic agricultural village; but in its dynamic aspect, as a control and a communications center, the core of the city is the citadel. Though the original composition of magnet and container has undergone many changes, the functions they represent can still be detected, as symbols if not visible structures, in every existing city. Thus the once-solid walls of ancient cities are now represented by political boundary lines, by greenbelts, and even by multilaned ring roads or freeways—latter-day versions of the Ringstrasse of Vienna which replaced its ancient walls. The integration of the static and the dynamic functions of the city in a visually impressive structure that gives due weight to all its essential organs, economic, political, and cultural, may be said to constitute the art of town planning.

From the dual origin of the city, the two main types of plan derive: the abstract, geometric type, predetermined by public authority and capable of execution within a limited time; and the organic type, representing a purposeful organization of functions and spatial structures over a considerable portion of time and requiring the prolonged cooperation of institutions and groups. Organic plans are, by nature, never completed, and until they reach maturity they rarely exhibit the formal perfection that is possible under centralized direction wielding sufficient political and economic power. Theorists of planning, who often refuse to recognize the second type as planning at all, show that they have not understood or accepted the social complexity of the city and have given too large a role to those limited, often superficial operations whose formal plans and coordinated structures can be built within a single generation by a central authority. Moreover, they may overlook the disorder that often remains hidden behind imposing facades—as the overcrowded and degraded tenements of nineteenth-century Berlin were hidden behind seemingly spacious and elegant middle-class street fronts.

Since the sixteenth century one may divide the modes of planning cities further into five main categories: the authoritarian (formal or geometric), the utilitarian, the romantic, the utopian, and the technocratic. While all these types, often under pressures outside the town planner's control, contain characteristics that transcend these categories, the study of historic cities has given rise to a more organic conception of the planning function, partly formulated by Patrick Geddes, which has still to be fully embodied in any actual New Town plan. Many features in modern plans can be traced back to the earliest remains of the city in Jericho, Sumer, or the royal Egyptian mortuary cities—witness the long 20- or 25-foot (6- or 7.5-meter) building lot, which has remained standard for four thousand years despite the dark interiors such narrow fronts produce—while some of the most "advanced" technocratic plans, like Buckminster Fuller's city in the form of a single pyramid, utilize advanced technology to achieve the obsolete dreams of Bronze Age monarchs bent on imposing total control.

Authoritarian Planning Geometric planning had its heyday from the sixteenth century onward in planning done under priestly dictators and absolute monarchs seeking to create an urban setting that would emphasize their newly gained powers at the expense of such corporate institutions as the monastery and the guild, which they either diminished or displaced. The long straight street, the uniform blockfront, the wide rond-point or open plaza terminating in a monument or obelisk characterized this mode when first introduced by Sixtus V. Both the population and the buildings were subject to politically centralized requirements. Every avenue became a parade ground. When introduced in the cluttered and dilapidated quarters of medieval towns, such planning often enhanced the remaining sound structures. But where the same principles were applied to the city as a whole, as in the "ideal" geometric plans for political capitals like Karlsruhe or Versailles, Washington or Brasília, the plan became a truly functional setting only for the government, the army, and the bureaucracy. The design of such cities can only be maintained by stringent legal regulations; and in the long run it must be modified, openly or covertly, as in the rebuilding of Nash's Regent Street. By ignoring the social and economic needs of the townspeople, such plans, however elegant and orderly, too often have embalmed a corpse.

The fault of the authoritarian plan lay, not necessarily in its geometry, but in the false assumptions of centralized power which ignored the important "village" functions of neighborhood, market, and workshop. Geometric order itself, nevertheless, is a property of natural forms, as in crystals, snowflakes, and flower petals, and may clarify and perfect organic plans. The introduction of formal squares into the new quarters of Paris, London, Bath, and Edinburgh was a functional improvement in residential planning for the upper middle classes: so, too, the rond-point and long diagonal avenues first embodied in ideal Renaissance city plans, as in Wren's plan for the city of London, were intelligently used by L'Enfant in his plan for Washington to establish important public buildings in commanding positions that reflected the constitutional "separation of powers" between the executive, the legislative, and the judiciary. The same process of cutting through disorder and establishing a larger unity was Haussmann's notable achievement in nineteenth-century Paris; and his parks and boulevards, following through earlier improvements like the Seine Embankment and

Air view of Bath, England, showing Crescent and Circus. (Aerofilms Limited.)

the Rue de Rivoli, gave Paris both an aesthetic unity and a human richness that only a few other great cities, like Peking, possess.

Though authoritarian planning tends to neglect those essential functions of the city that do not submit to its relentless geometric schemes, the gift of public open space, whether as park, boulevard, or garden, is one of the permanent contributions of this mode. Perhaps the most functional application of geometric planning remains that of seventeenth-century Amsterdam which, beginning with an organic core formed by shipping and fishing on the Amstel, first created a formal development on one side, with an overcrowded working-class quarter, and then followed through with a more patrician quarter that turned the lopsided development into a spacious, nearly symmetrical one. As a result Amsterdam remained one of the most lively and functionally efficient cities in Europe, until its temporizing authorities submitted to the massive disruption of the motorcar. Meanwhile, the most imposing example of baroque (authoritarian) planning, the starlike fortifications perfected by Vauban, turned out to be only an ephemeral contribution to geometric planning, though happily salvaged in many towns, like Middleburg and Cracow, by being turned into a girdle of triangular greens.

The basic element in geometric planning is the square or rectangular block, with the streets and avenues composed by assembling and extending such blocks. Towns composed entirely on a rectangular system are not, as has often been erroneously supposed, an American invention, but one of the most ancient modes, whose orientation according to the points of the compass indicates its early religious basis. The simplicity and orderliness of this layout makes it extremely useful when a town must be built to order in a limited time—whether it be a sixth-century B.C. Milesian colonization town; a Roman military settlement, like Timgad; a medieval Prussian frontier fortress; a Provençal town, like Montpazier; an eighteenth-century colonial town, like Savannah, Georgia; or a nineteenth-century land speculator's subdivision, planned for quick sale. Most town extensions from the eighteenth century onward, until romantic principles prevailed in suburban layouts, were by rectangular blocks and long straight avenues of indefinite length.

On level land the checkerboard or gridiron plan has many advantages as long as open spaces are provided as a setting for major public buildings—as anciently in Pompeii, more recently in Philadelphia and New Haven—though where this is not done the impossibility of a frontal approach, with sufficient space to assemble large numbers, is both a functional and an aesthetic weakness. The disrepute into which the gridiron plan fell derives from lapses not inherent in the form itself. One was the fact that rectangular units do not conform economically or aesthetically to irregular topography, nor do they respect climatic conditions or geographic situation. The other is that automatic extensions by this method raised costs by increasing the number and area of unnecessary streets, whose paving and servicing throw a heavy burden upon the municipality, forcing it to provide transportation facilities, water, sewage disposal, and schools before the whole area is ready for development.

Utilitarian Planning Thus geometric planning, when reduced to standard repeating units (the urban block and narrow building lot), deteriorates into commercial-utilitarian planning based on maximizing pecuniary returns from sale and rent. Such utilitarian planning proceeded from expedience, not theory. But the larger number of new towns or town extensions during the last three centuries have conformed to its ideal of providing the municipal facilities for opening land to the largest possible population to be housed with a minimal allowance of parks, playground spaces, or meeting spaces, and maximal opportunities for private investment.

On paper, gridiron plans show strict, if limited, order, but when carried out in three dimensions, through building, the result is unduly monotonous, if not confused. The ultimate destiny of most such neighborhood planning is a blighted area; while for efficient planning of industrial facilities, the subdivision into uniform blocks is irrelevant and often positively obstructive. Originally a product of laissez faire economics, which assumed that order and purpose would emerge from the dynamics of unrestricted private competition, utilitarian planning has been carried out, on a day-to-day basis, by the municipal engineer, the land developer, the transportation expert, the commercial builder, and the real estate investor, with no thought for public welfare or municipal economy. On such terms planning was reduced to a commercial or industrial "happening."

Apart from its lack of functional differentiation between civic, commercial, industrial, and domestic functions and between neighborhoods, precincts, and quarters, utilitarian planning concentrates on increasing its mechanical facilities to accommodate an expanding local population at whatever sacrifice of other essential social functions. This single-minded subservience to utilitarian and industrial demands leads to the misuse and malfunctioning of the whole environment, often sacrificing central urban sites to functions better satisfied on peripheral urban land. The sewage and industrial waste poured into the neighboring waters destroy vital recreation space: similarly the marshaling yards of the railroad era and the parking lots of the automobile era preempt valuable urban space in the heart of the city, space which would not have been sacrificed if more adequate criteria than pecuniary profit had governed the planning of transportation systems. The result of utilitarian planning, even in cities that were once more adequately designed, has been to produce muddled, inefficient urban conglomerations, congested, unsanitary, destitute of public open spaces, and so lacking in domestic amenities that this condition has brought about an increasing exodus to the suburbs.

The attempt to regulate utilitarian planning and to superimpose a coherent pattern upon its random structure was responsible for a series of municipal regulations, established earliest in Germany, leading to the control of land uses through limitations of height and density of building, zoning into specialized quarters, and housing ordinances designed to prevent congestion and overbuilding, like those laid down for the English bylaw streets. This effort to plan wholesale by legislation suppressed not only disorder but also diversity: it produced monotonous residential areas without neighborhood identity or convenient local markets, business areas with land too high in price to accommodate a sufficient number of eating places and other local services, and zoned districts, as in New York, so favorable to congestion that buildings high enough to accommodate a population of 30 million in the existing area would be permissible. The final price of accepting the utilitarian ideal in city planning has been to undermine the city even as a useful place for doing business.

Romantic Planning At the moment utilitarian practice became supreme, a revolt against its underlying philosophy took shape in the romantic movement. Negatively, this revolt rejected a conception of life that made human development subservient to either political absolutism or mechanical invention. Positively, romanticism attempted to restore essential human values excluded from the industrial and bureaucratic complex. These life values

Air view of the center of Hampstead Garden Suburb. (Aerofilms Limited.)

were associated with a more rural environment whose sunlight, clear air, open spaces, and vegetation were favorable to child rearing and domestic health. Likewise, romanticism sought to restore historic continuity to urban forms and institutions as against the ruthless iconoclasm that was destroying, for private profit, an essential part of the historic heritage. The fresh appreciation of the natural landscape resulted in a distaste for formal geometric patterns. Thus the English landscape park, as formulated by Repton and Uvedale Price, became the ideal form in which the romantic urban plan would be set.

The earliest example of romantic suburban planning was in fact supplied by the urban park, or rather by the new cemetery; for Mt. Auburn Cemetery, in Cambridge, Massachusetts, was one of the first urban areas to be laid out on these principles. The chief American exponent, Frederick Law Olmsted (*q.v.*), likewise began here in his design for Central Park, New York (1856), and he followed this through with his suburban plan for Riverside, Illinois, in 1869. By abandoning repetitive blocks and unbroken street fronts and creating far larger units with freer outlines, by designing roads to conform in width and paving to population and traffic density, by following contours instead of grading the land, the romantic planner reduced the costs of development and was able to afford more space for gardens, thus beating the utilitarian planner at his own financial game. Many of Olmsted's innovations in Guildford and Roland Park, Maryland, were independently applied by Raymond Unwin and Barry Parker in Letchworth Garden City and later, more systematically, in Hampstead Garden Suburb. The latter remains in many ways the classic expression of the romantic suburb.

The other innovation in urban design derived from the romantic movement is the superblock, a layout not attributable to any identifiable planner, but spontaneously introduced in the Boston area, in Cambridge and Longwood, around the middle of the nineteenth century, and possibly preceded by Ladbroke Grove in London. The superblock not merely greatly enlarged the dimensions of the usual rectangular block but, instead of placing houses only at the perimeter, grouped them in culs-de-sac and clusters. The effect was not merely to diminish the capital outlay for needless traffic streets but to increase the area for gardens and ensure greater privacy and quiet. In an effort to adapt a modern town plan to the motorcar without being dominated by it, Wright and Stein reintroduced the superblock in the Radburn plan, using the cul-de-sac more uniformly; but perhaps the best example of this layout is Baldwin Hills Village, Los Angeles.

The historic side of the romantic movement was developed in theory by Camillo Sitte in his classic work entitled *The Art of Building Cities.* Sitte's examination of the medieval and Renaissance city demonstrated, by contrast, the aesthetic failure of the more rigid kind of geometric planning, with its overemphasis on symmetry, uniformity, and centralization. Sitte showed by specific examples of town squares that a readiness to accept asymmetry and irregularity in the placing of public monuments increased their aesthetic effectiveness; likewise that short vistas, broken by buildings, were aesthetically and socially more attractive than the windy perspectives of the baroque avenue, framed by uniform buildings, and designed to increase the speed of wheeled vehicles and the machinelike precision of marching soldiers. Sitte's work contributed to the recognition that diversified neighborhood units—markets, squares, green open spaces—rather than uniform avenues and blocks alone, were the basic units in planning. These principles were elaborated by Unwin, not merely in his book, *Town Planning in Practice,* (1909) but in his own planning.

Utopian Planning Utopian town planning, first exemplified in Thomas More's classic utopia, exhibits elements of all three types, authoritarian, utilitarian, romantic; but as an expression of centralized political authority, geometric formalism tends to dominate, with one notable exception in the Amana villages in Iowa. Despite his own humane views, More in his description of Amaurot, the capital of Utopia, emphasizes its regularity and uniformity and says that he who has seen one utopian city has seen them all. Nevertheless, More adopted a medieval parish organization for his neighborhood unit and made it a center of civic as well as domestic life. Later utopian planners, even when laying out small units—like Owen's ideal scheme, partly embodied in New Lanark—preferred austere quadrangles and made no more allowance for changing needs and changing styles of life than they did for individual preferences. Yet in some degree urban colonization schemes often had a utopian underpinning, from the planning of Savannah, Georgia, to that of Melbourne, with its large surrounding greenbelt; and Walter Burley Griffin's plan for the capital of Australia, Canberra, in attempting to apply the generous scale of suburban planning to a forthcoming metropolis, suggested that the worsening of conditions in central metropolitan areas had in fact turned the suburb itself into a popular latter-day utopia. Frank Lloyd Wright's scheme for Broadacre City, with its reservation for every family of from 1 to 3 acres of land set within a rigid grid of lots and roads, used planning deliberately as a means of urban dissolution: an approach seconded by E. A. Gutkind. Thus this conception of the ideal town, Eutopia, carried to the extreme, would ultimately become Outopia, or No Place.

A characteristic utopian readiness to make use of both technical and social innovations showed itself in James Silk Buckingham's conception of Victoria and in Richardson's ideal town of Hygeia. The first of these schemes, along with Kropotkin's *Fields, Factories and Workshops,* had an influence on the most successful application of utopian urban thought, that of Ebenezer Howard's project for the garden city. Though in its actual execution in Letchworth utopian experiment was minimized and conventional romantic-geometric components prevailed, Howard's special distinction was to conceive the town as an organic entity, integrating in its layout both urban and rural facilities and boasting the special organic characteristic not alone of fostering growth but of reproduction on another site, elsewhere, once the original town had become big enough to support all the necessary institutions of urban life. Howard's abstract scheme for the garden city was the first to do justice, at least in outline and intention, to every aspect of urban life, with its social and economic diversity, its inclusiveness, its magnetic attractions, its widening of interests and intensification of activities. In theory, Howard transcended the limitations of authoritarian, utilitarian, and romantic planning; and to that extent he introduced the conception of organic planning. Though Howard's explanatory diagrams were not in any sense town plans, they in fact provided for later features, like the pedestrian shopping mall and the neighborhood unit, that were not fully developed until the post-1947 New Towns were designed.

Before discussing further the ideals of organic planning, one must not overlook a mechanical by-product of utopian theory—the technocratic plan. The technocratic utopia was first brought into literary existence in Bulwer-Lytton's *The Coming Race.* The inhabitants of this utopia lived underground and utilized energy of nuclear potency for both work and destruction. The many current variations of this kind of utopia rest on the complete assemblage of all human functions and activities in a vast megastructure in which every detail of life is subject to absolute regimentation and bureaucratic control. Both H. G. Wells and E. M. Forster anticipated these technocratic plans and presciently demonstrated that, so far from ensuring a better life, they threatened to defeat anything that could be called a human existence.

The many variants of the technocratic plan all center exclusively upon technological invention in construction method, materials, or plan, varying from the organization of the city on a linear pattern along a spinal transportation artery, forming a series of continuous horizontal zones on either side, to the creation of a simple vertical structure a hundred or two hundred stories high. The most popular and influential form of the technocratic ideal was that of Le Corbusier, as set forth almost half a century ago in the Voisin plan and, with later variations, in *The City of the Future,* first published in 1924 as *Urbanisme.* The whole fabric of urban life, with its great diversity of needs, interests, activities, and purposes, was bureaucratically organized by Le Corbusier in the form of a central core of office buildings 60 stories high, widely separated, and served by multiple elevated and underground transportation routes leading to similarly regimented apartment houses. So admirably did Le Corbusier's planning ideals fit in with the contemporary processes of urban real estate speculation, bureaucratic administration, and large-scale engineering construction, that some variant of his city of the future was widely accepted for a whole generation as the only feasible mode for urban rehabilitation—despite the growing volume of protest against the dehumanized environment that resulted.

Technocratic Planning   Technocratic planning only carries to an ultimate conclusion the one-sided process that has been going on for the last century, of multiplying the number of urban mechanical services and utilities. Such planning brings about mounting costs of providing water from distant sources, of sewage and garbage disposal systems, paved streets, rapid transportation systems, tunnels, bridges, multilaned highways, garages, and parking lots—costs that absorb capital once available for the city as a work of art. The technocratic ideal aims ultimately at making every urban activity a function of the machine. In theory technocratic planning assumes that all human problems are open to a technological solution and that all human needs can be met by the ceaseless invention of mechanical or electronic devices for simulating them, satisfying them, or diverting them into other channels. Projects for great urban megastructures, under water, underground, or towering a mile high in the air, maximize totalitarian control and remove the possibility of any choices except those offered by the humanly underdimensioned technocratic system. The basic unit for the technocratic city is the prison cell: its chief contemporary model, the underground missile control center.

At the opposite extreme to this technocratic absolutism is the equally technocratic dispersal of the city into households, shopping centers, and self-sufficient industrial or commercial enclaves, without any coherent physical pattern or political unity: the urban nonentity fashionably termed "megalopolis." Though by intention this loose urbanoid tissue represents an effort to escape the regimentation and social corruption of the disorganized city, the necessary residual urban functions, including planning, must be performed by a centralized authority, which thereby extends and reenforces the very system from which this urban scattering seeks to escape. Either mode of technocratic planning, if widely adopted, would spell the end of the city and thereby permanently banish the art of town planning.

Organic Planning We come now to organic planning, whose positive proposals have sprung partly from a richer knowledge of the urban past, neglected even when available in the nineteenth century, and from a better sociological understanding of the nature of the city, as not only a "work of art" or an "act of the prince" but as the focal point in the development and expression of a many-sided culture whose natural setting and whose fields, factories, and workshops make essential contributions to its higher life. Unlike the other modes of planning described, organic plans cannot be reduced to any single type or confined to any single historic moment. "Organic" means not only well organized and capable of limited growth but also in dynamic balance, with a place for the full complement of urban organs. Not only must organic planning seek a structural answer to every function of the city, but it must express, as fully as possible both in the surface plan and the design of the buildings, the needs and the ideal purposes of the community, conserving past forms that are still serviceable while preparing to accommodate future needs. As noted, Ebenezer Howard's concept of the garden city was the first diagrammatic exposition of such an organic form; and not its least contribution to organic planning was the provision for further orderly growth, as in any organism, by colonization after the limits of acceptable growth had been reached.

The principles of organic planning have never been satisfactorily formulated, partly because they embody complexities incapable of expression on

Pedestrian precinct, Coventry.

a purely two-dimensional plan, even when accompanied by designs for three-dimensional structures, since the fourth dimension, time, is usually left out of account. One of the best examples of organic planning with a sufficient appreciation of time was the postwar planning for Manchester, under City Surveyor R. Nicholas. The replanning of specific areas was outlined in a series of stages, providing for the conservation, demolition, and replacement as required of both buildings and streets. Barry Parker, in his earlier plan for Wythenshawe (1927), gave similar recognition to the role of time in organic planning by deliberately leaving unallotted sites for future uses not yet foreseeable. The essential nature of organic planning reveals itself best, therefore, in historic cities, especially those like Lübeck or Siena, where there existed, during the centuries when the town took form, a working consensus and a common way of life which gave unity to both its private and public structures, often under the guidance of a municipal official, the city architect.

If the problem of formal planning is to allow for historic traditions, economic functions, and geographic features which would disturb the geometric regularity or symmetry of the plan, that of organic planning is to achieve intelligible order and social coherence without bowing to merely accidental features of no consequence or to traditional forms that have become useless or meaningless. Perhaps the most illuminating example of truly organic planning from the standpoint of both functional adequacy and aesthetic appeal is that of Venice, notably in the Piazza San Marco. This site, originally the orchard of a monastery, was turned into an open public space; while the site once occupied by a meat market became the Piazetta. Successive generations, starting with the Byzantine cathedral, followed by the Gothic ducal palace, gradually enclosed the square with a variety of new buildings, each conforming to the needs and the style of its period, yet subtly merging into the unity of the square. No single generation, no single mind, no single architect or planner, could have forecast or designed the final result, the living whole which both records and transcends the historic process.

Not by accident, the best conscious theorist of organic planning was by profession a biologist, Patrick Geddes. In his reports on Dunfermline and Indore and in many briefer reports on Indian cities unfortunately not generally accessible, he showed how much richer the texture of a city became when all its functions—civic, religious, domestic, and economic—were tactfully embraced and further integrated in a design. Unlike purely formal plans stamped with current clichés, organic plans cannot be made to order or put into instant execution. Hence organic planning requires an intimate knowledge of urban culture, a constant reappraisal of human needs, purposes, and means, and a cooperative participation, reenforced with critical judgment by the community, while new plans are under formulation. If modern technology releases working time for such joint civic enterprises, organic planning may replace utilitarian, bureaucratic, and technocratic planning as the new order of the day.

BIBLIOGRAPHY: Leone Battista Alberti, *Ten Books on Architecture,* 1485, London, 1955; Camillo Sitte, *Der Staedtebau,* 1899, New York, 1935; Ebenezer Howard, *Garden Cities of Tomorrow,* 1902, London, 1946; Patrick Geddes, *City Development,* Edinburgh, 1904; Daniel H. Burnham and E. H. Bennett, *Plan of Chicago,* Chicago, 1909; Raymond Unwin, *Town Planning in Practice,* 1909, London, 1932; Patrick Geddes, *Cities in Evolution,* 1915, London, 1968; Werner Heggeman and Elbert Peets, *The American Vitruvius,* New York, 1922; Pierre Lavedan, *Histoire de l'Urbanisme,* 3 vols., 1926–1952; F. L. Olmsted, Jr. and Theodora Kimball, *Frederick Law Olmsted,* New York, 1928; Marcel Poete, *Introduction a l'urbanisme,* Paris, 1929; LeCorbusier, *The City of the Future,* New York, 1930; A. Soria y Mata, *Le Ciudad Lineal,* Madrid, 1931; Frank Lloyd Wright, *The Disappearing City,* New York, 1932; Gaston Bardet, *Pierre sur Pierre,* Paris, 1946; F. J. Osborn, *Greenbelt Cities,* London, 1946; J. Tyrwhitt (ed.), *Patrick Geddes in India,* London, 1947; James Silk Buckingham, *National Evils and Practical Remedies,* London, 1949; Clarence Stein, *New Towns for America,* New York, 1951; Frederick Gibberd, *Town Design,* New York, 1953; E. A. Gutkind, *The Expanding Environment,* London, 1953; Lewis Mumford, *The City in History,* Secker & Warburg, New York, 1961; Ernst Egli, *Geschitchte des Staedtebauss,* 3 vols., Zurich, 1959–1967. —LEWIS MUMFORD

THRESHOLD ANALYSIS The differentiation of geographical space results in the fact that in the growth of a city or town there occur at some stages limitations or barriers to expansion. In the theory of threshold analysis these limitations are called thresholds of development. The thresholds can be classified as *physical,* which are created by natural features of land (such as hilly land, seashores, marshy land, or rivers to be crossed) or by existing land-use patterns (land already developed for other than urban purposes); *technological* which occurs in the extension of existing or construction of new and technical infrastructure systems (such as water supply, sewerage, transportation network) and *structural,* when the proposed expansion demands reconstruction of some structural units of a town (for instance the town center).

All these thresholds can be overcome—that is new inhabitants can be accommodated—but only by means of a considerable input of capital which often remains "frozen" for long periods of time. The analysis consists in comparing costs and respective population numbers of all relevant alternatives of possible town expansion. It aims at the choice of this alternative which involves the least costs of overcoming a series of successive threshold limitations.

Criticisms of this analysis have been made on the ground that different categories of thresholds are likely to overlap, and that in this analysis only the costs of expansion are considered leaving out the benefits. Both these points hardly affect the validity of the analysis because overlapping thresholds also result in higher costs, and because in this preliminary stage of planning only the successive adaptation of land is decided, leaving free choice for the program and pattern of development.

The threshold analysis was first developed in Poland by Boleslaw Malisz in 1963. It has been widely employed in several countries and has proved to be a relatively simple and useful method. (*See also* POLAND.) Recently this analysis has been developed by the author for regional planning purposes.

BIBLIOGRAPHY: J. Kozlowski and J. T. Hughes, "Urban Threshold Theory and Analysis," *Journal of the Town Planning Institute,* vol. 53, no. 2, London, 1967, "Threshold Analysis an

Economic Tool for Town and Regional Planning," *Urban Studies,* vol. 5, no. 2, London, 1968; Boleslaw Malisz, "Implications of Threshold Theory for Urban and Regional Planning," *Journal of the Town Planning Institute,* vol. 55, no. 3, London, 1969, "Validity of Urban Threshold Analysis—But What For?," *Journal of the Town Planning Institute,* vol. 56, no. 8, London, 1970.   —BOLESLAW MALISZ

TOURISM, PLANNING FOR   The great increase of tourism in the mid-twentieth century means that in many countries it represents a major industry, and many new settlements and towns have been and are being planned and built in answer to growing demands, especially in coastal regions. Among the most important of these are in the countries that surround the Mediterranean: Spain, France, Italy, Yugoslavia, Greece, Turkey, and the countries of North Africa. The reasons for their popularity are that the climate of the Mediterranean is pleasant, the countries surrounding it offer beautiful scenery and attractive sea bathing, and the region is rich in the remains of past civilizations.

In some of the Mediterranean countries many settlements and towns have been built or extended primarily in answer to the needs of the tourist. These have been variously planned and developed. Some accord well with their surroundings and fit well into the natural landscape, but others have not been satisfactorily developed and have evoked the criticism that they spoil the natural beauties of the region and its coastline. It would appear to be a matter of enlightened commercial self-interest that such areas be planned and built to accord as much as possible with the distinctive beauties of each environment, as such harmony itself constitutes one of the attractions for the tourist. In the development of any region designed to attract the tourist, an overall plan that gives due regard to aesthetic and natural landscape values and to which separate commercial developments must conform is very much to be desired in itself and for the sake of the interests of such regions.

TOWN   An urban settlement generally with a population of not less than about three thousand persons, below which, in England, it is usually termed a "village." In the United States, when a village or town exceeds five thousand population, it usually becomes a city. "Town" is the adjective most commonly used for urban planning in Great Britain, as "city" is in the United States. The use of "town" in this context was established by the first Town Planning Act of 1909, which was followed by the Town Planning Review founded at Liverpool University in 1910, followed by the Town Planning Conference in London in the same year, and the foundation of the Town Planning Institute in 1914.

TOWN-COUNTRY MAGNET   The term used by Ebenezer Howard to explain the genesis of his idea of a garden city. Howard argued that the causes which draw people into cities may all be summed up as "attractions," and that the remedy lies in presenting greater attractions elsewhere. "Each city," he says, "may be regarded as a magnet, and the remedy is to provide a greater magnet." He then speaks of the country magnet, and says:

> But neither the town magnet nor the country magnet represents the full plan and purpose of nature. Human society and the beauty of nature are meant to be enjoyed together. The two magnets must be made one. . . . town and country must be married, and out of this joyous union will spring a new hope, a new life, a new civilization.

A first step can be taken by the construction of the town-country magnet which Howard adumbrates in his plan for a garden city, an idea that in principle subsequently materialized in Letchworth (1902), Welwyn Garden City (1920), and the New Towns of Great Britain (1946–1970).[1] (*See* GARDEN CITY.)

TRAILER (*See* MOBILE HOME.)

TRAILER CAMPS, SITING OF (*See* MOBILE HOME PARKS.)

TRANSPORT

Accessibility and Land Use The history of urban settlements has been one of almost continuous development and change. Throughout this history the need to maintain good accessibility has been an important force in determining the location of settlements and the form and internal layout of the individual towns and cities. Innovations in transport technology have had, at times, a marked impact on both the settlement pattern and the city structure. In the nineteenth century, for example, the railways not only opened up whole new areas of North America to human settlement but also facilitated the rapid growth of London's suburbs. But perhaps the greatest and most widespread changes have been brought about by the motor vehicle, particularly the private automobile. New highways, parking garages, and other traffic facilities have proliferated within the city, and new patterns of accessibility have begun to change the land-use patterns. New pressures for urban sprawl have been unleashed, making nonsense of the old boundaries between town and country and allowing the rapid development of new life-styles in urban and rural populations virtually the whole world over.

Although transport in all its forms will account for anything between 10 and 20 percent of a developed country's gross national product and is likely to be an important force in the national and urban economy, transport is not an end in itself. Rather, it is a means of reducing the friction of distance within and between urban areas and between nations; a means of permitting land-use activities (people, firms, and institutions) to be separately located while still maintaining the linkages of economic and social inter-

[1]The explanation by Ebenezer Howard of the town-country magnet is given in his introduction to his book *To-Morrow: A Peaceful Path to Real Reform,* 1898; second edition title changed to *Garden Cities of Tomorrow,* 1902. Third edition, with a long historical preface by Frederic J. Osborn and an introduction by Lewis Mumford entitled "The Garden City Idea and Modern Planning," published by Faber & Faber, Ltd., London, 1946.

dependence between them. The economic cost of transport is therefore often a major consideration in the selection of a location. Economists have long since recognized the fundamental relationships between transport, accessibility, and the use of land. Formal theory is generally held to have begun with Von Thünen[1] and developed via Weberian location theory[2] into central place theory through Christaller[3] and Lösch[4] and into regional science through the influence of Isard.[5] However, the first major attempt to demonstrate in a pragmatic way the pervasiveness of these relationships within the city and their importance to the traffic engineer and the city planner was by Mitchell and Rapkin[6] in 1954. Their main contribution was a restatement of the principle that movement within the urban area is a function of the use of land. They identified and classified the basic characteristics of trip making and movement and commended a basic terminology including terms such as "establishments," "work-based trips," "home-based trips," "linkage," and many others which have subsequently been adopted in transportation planning.

Accessibility can be regarded as a measure of the extent to which the effects of the physical separation between any two places is modified by the existence of a mode of transport connecting those places and its availability and cost for a specific journey purpose. Location and urban economists have observed that it has been the specialization of urban activities that has made communication between them necessary, and thus ease of communication is important. Where that communication is through the medium of the physical movement of goods and people, establishments have chosen locations by reference to the spatial distribution of those others with which they interact. In this way a retail store which needs to maximize the number of contacts with potential customers will tend to locate in the most accessible position in relation to this market. For large retail outlets, this position has traditionally been at the center of the town where transportation routes converge, but now it is increasingly at some suburban or out-of-town location where better parking facilities and the relative absence of traffic congestion make it more accessible to the private motorist. This example illustrates that accessibility is mode-dependent, so that when distance or spatial separation is overcome by means of traffic using urban streets, accessibility depends on "the degree of freedom for vehicles to circulate and to penetrate to individual destinations and stop, and park on arrival."[7]

Transportation Planning Because good accessibility is generally necessary for the efficient and effective functioning of urban activities and institutions,

[1]J. H. Von Thünen, *Der isolierte Staat in Beziehung auf Landwirtschaft und Nationalökonomie,* Hamburg, 1875.
[2]A. Weber, *Über den Standort der Industrien,* Tübingen, 1909.
[3]W. Christaller *Die zentralen Orte in Süddeutschland,* Jena, 1933. English translation by Carlisle W. Bask in *Central Places in Southern Germany,* Prentice-Hall Inc., New Jersey, 1966.
[4]A. Lösch, *The Economics of Location,* New Haven, 1954.
[5]W. Isard, *Location and Space Economy,* New York, 1956.
[6]R. B. Mitchell and C. Rapkin, *Urban traffic: A Function of Land Use,* New York, 1954.
[7]C. D. Buchanan et al., *Traffic in Towns,* London, 1963, p. 220.

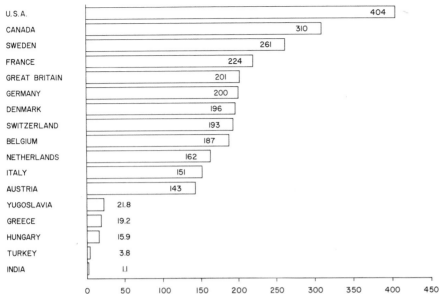

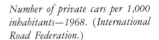

Number of private cars per 1,000 inhabitants—1968. (International Road Federation.)

society sets a high premium on the provision of better transportation facilities. In the twentieth century, with the increasing urbanization of Western Europe and North America and the enormous growth in the number of motor vehicles (see illustration), increasing attention has had to be given to maintaining accessibility within urban areas by reducing traffic congestion and upgrading and extending the highway network.

As a consequence, a whole new transportation planning process has been evolved in the last 30 years; it has been a movement which gathered momentum as the nature of the relationships between movement and land use became better understood, as the need to forecast future movement demands became clearer, and as the development of computing science made feasible the use of analytical techniques handling large amounts of data.

The Evolution of Study Methods   Traffic studies were being carried out in urban areas of the United States as early as 1885 when regular counts of the volume of traffic passing along the streets were used to formulate traffic regulations. Subsequently, the early years of the twentieth century saw a good deal of attention focused on improving the interurban and farm-to-market roads and emphasis swung to gathering rural rather than urban traffic data. This trend continued throughout the 1930s, fostered in the United States by the Federal Aid Highway Act of 1934 which permitted the expenditure of up to 1.5 percent of the federal aid given to any state for the purpose of conducting traffic surveys and making plans. About this time, the conducting of roadside interviews was begun to elicit information about the origins and destinations of traffic. The information was used principally to establish a need for bypass roads for the urban areas. By the 1940s it was generally recognized that considerable improvement to the urban highway networks was required, and the 1944 Federal Aid Highway Act provided funds for certain urban highway projects. Roadside interview techniques were extended to survey the origin-destination characteristics of traffic in urban areas, and later they were adapted to gain information about the population's travel behavior at source—i.e., at the place of employment or at the home. These home-interview and origin-destination survey procedures were standardized and codified by the Bureau of Public Roads.[1] During the 1940s and early 1950s several hundred home-interview origin-destination surveys were carried out using systematic samples of urban residents. Barkley[2] and Schmidt and Campbell[3] provide extensive bibliographies and summaries. These surveys provided data on the amount and direction of movement of goods, people, and vehicles within and between urban areas. Although a few attempts were made to predict future movement demands from these surveys, it was not until the commencement of the Detroit Metropolitan Area Transportation Study in 1953 that forecasts were made on an analytical basis which related traffic to urban land uses.

The transportation studies of the 1950s still used data derived from conventional home-interview surveys; but in the analysis, the surveyed travel characteristics were related to characteristics of population and land-use activities, and, assuming the relationships to be stable over time, a forecast of land-use and population changes was used to produce forecasts of future patterns of travel behavior. The forecasts of travel demand between all origin and destination zones of the study area and by different modes of transport were then used to devise alternative plans for improving both highway and public transport facilities. The alternatives were evaluated and final transportation plans produced using cost-benefit criteria; the best of the alternatives being that which showed the highest savings in travel and other costs to the users of the transportation facilities compared with the costs needed to construct and maintain the facilities.

From these beginnings, pioneered by the Detroit and Chicago transportation studies, these types of analytical methods were subsequently used to prepare transportation plans for most of the major metropolitan areas of North America during the late 1950s and early 1960s and had begun to be used in Western Europe by the early 1960s (The London Transportation Study began early in 1962).

In the United States the importance of these urban transportation planning studies was formally acknowledged in the 1962 Federal Aid Highway Act which sought to secure proper coordination of long-term highway planning with other transportation developments and with land-use plans. This act set July 1, 1965, as the date after which no highway project for an urban area with a population exceeding 50,000 would qualify for federal aid unless the proposal had been formulated within a continuing, comprehensive transportation planning process carried on cooperatively by states and by local communities. Additional federal aid had been provided by the

[1] Bureau of Public Roads, *Procedures for the Metropolitan Area Traffic Studies,* Washington, D.C., 1946.
[2] R. E. Barkley, "Origin-Destination Surveys and Traffic Volume Studies," *Highway Research Board Bibliography No. 11,* p. 3, Washington, D.C., 1951.
[3] R. E. Schmidt and M. E. Campbell, *Highway Traffic Estimation,* Saugatuck, 1956.

Housing and Home Finance Agency in 1961 to enable planning agencies to finance the land-use surveys required in these studies. By September 1965, there were some 195 comprehensive transportation studies under way in 224 urbanized areas of the United States.[1]

In Britain, the publication in 1963 of the report "Traffic in Towns"[2] emphasized the need to develop a much closer relationship between land-use planning and transportation planning. At the same time transportation studies modeled on the North American pattern were being initiated in the major conurbations with financial support from the Ministry of Transport. Formal recognition of the need to relate transportation plans to urban plans was provided in the Town and Country Planning Act of 1968, whereby certain local planning authorities were required to prepare urban structure plans (replacing the old style development plans). The new structure plans will set down the long-term policies for the development of land and for traffic and the environment.

In recent years transportation studies have become broader in scope and the methods used in them have become more refined. One major development, initiated in the Penn-Jersey Study in the mid-1960s, was the new emphasis given to producing better land-use forecasts. Attempts were made to forecast the different land-use patterns that would emerge as a consequence of different policies with regard to the timing and location of new transportation facilities. The development of urban land-use models was stimulated in the 1960s by the growing awareness that the validity of movement forecasts produced in the transportation planning process was utterly dependent on the quality of the forecast land-use patterns. The Northeast Corridor Transportation Study (United States) has also been developing models to forecast the response of the spatial distribution of economic and demographic activity to changes in transport facilities.[3] This study has also tried to take account of the way in which political attitudes could affect the implementation of different transportation plans. In general, pressures have been mounting in recent years to permit more effective public participation in the goal-formulation and decision-making phases of the transportation planning process.

Transportation Planning Models   At the heart of the transportation planning process is a set of analytical and predictive models used to estimate, for each zone of the study area, the total number of arrivals and departures (trip generation or trip-end estimation); the other zones to which these trips are going or have come from (trip distribution); the mode of transport used (modal split); and the route taken (trip assignment). These models are used sequentially, as illustrated, and require as input some independently derived forecasts of future land use, population, employment, and other activities. The comprehensive land-use transportation study requires the

The transportation planning process.

[1] R. A. Moyer, Comprehensive Urban Transportation Study Methods, *Proceedings of the American Society of Civil Engineers,* vol. 91, p. 65, HW2, 1965.

[2] C. D. Buchanan, et al., *Traffic in Towns,* London, 1963.

[3] S. H. Putman, "Developing and Testing an Intra-regional model," *Regional Studies,* vol. 4, no. 4, 1970.

collection, storage, and analysis of what are often very extensive sets of land-use and travel data. These data are employed in the forecasting models and, because of the sheer number and complexity of calculations involved, developments in transportation planning techniques over the past 20 years have been very closely linked to developments in computer hardware and software.

Trip generation models   Because it is impossible to forecast directly the number of trips emanating from each zone of the study area, models have been formulated using the principle that travel is an orderly phenomenon, and that if the amount of travel produced or generated by each zone can be related to some measure of the characteristics of the land-use activities of that zone, then it should be possible to forecast changes in future travel via changes in future land use.

In the Detroit study, where this approach was developed, trip production rates were defined for each type of major land-use category—the number of trips produced and attracted varying with the zone location and the land area devoted to each use.

This simple type of analysis was quickly replaced in later studies by multiple linear regression analysis, a standard statistical technique which permits the systematic explanation of the relationships between the quantity of trips produced and attracted and significant characteristics of the land-use activities that generate them. The result is a predictive equation of the general form

$$Y = a + b_1 X_1 + b_2 X_2, \ldots, b_n X_n \qquad (1)$$

where Y, the dependent variable, will be the number of trips attracted to, or originating from, the zone. Generally this is for a particular journey purpose, and often it is further stratified into trips that are home-based and those that are not. $X_1, X_2, \ldots, X_n$, the independent variables, are characteristics of land uses and socio economic activities such as population, car ownership rate, average household income, and numbers of persons employed. In these equations, a is the regression constant and b the regression coefficient.

A technique now widely used is that of cross-classification analysis. It enables use to be made of more detailed relationships between household characteristics and trip making and is better suited to handling the nonlinear relationships and the discrete variables. (The use of zonal averages for regression analysis can give unreal figures, such as a car ownership rate of 1.3 cars per household or household size of 3.6 persons.)

The method of cross classifying data for home-based trip generations suggested by Wootton and Pick,[1] based on experience from the London Transportation Study (1962) and the West Midlands Transportation Study (1967), uses 108 categories of household type defined by three car-ownership levels, six types of household structure (using the number of residents and

[1]J. H. Wootton and G. W. Pick, "A Model for Trips Generated by Households," *Journal of Transport Economics & Policy*, vol. 1, no. 2, 1967.

the number of persons employed), and six household income levels. Average trip-making rates have been calculated for each of the 108 categories, for six different journey purposes, by three different modes of travel. The relative merits of these models are discussed in a Bureau of Public Roads manual.[1]

Trip distribution   This is a process where the trips produced by each origin zone (denoted by subscript i) are allocated among all the available destination zones (subscript j). In the earlier transportation studies relatively simple growth-factor methods were employed in which the forecast number of trips between a particular pair of zones (T_{ij}) was based on the surveyed number of trips (t_{ij}) but modified by a factor (E) representing the way in which the total number of future trips generated by these zones was going to change in relation to the present totals. Thus

$$T_{ij} = t_{ij}\, E \qquad (2)$$

Four principal variants of the growth-factor method have been developed: uniform factor, average factor, Fratar, and Detroit, each differing in the way in which the factor E is defined and handled in the computational methods.

One of the major disadvantages of these methods was that they could not accommodate radical changes in forecast land-use patterns. It was to overcome this deficiency that the synthetic (or analogous) distribution models were developed. The most common of these is the gravity model.

Formulated analogously to Newtonian laws of gravity, the model was originally used to describe population migration and retail location[2] and was developed for use in transportation planning by Voorhees.[3] The model states that for a particular type of journey (for example, work or shopping trips), the number of trips that will be attracted to a possible destination zone will be in direct proportion to some measure of the attractiveness of the zone (for example the number of job opportunities or the number of shops in that zone), but that the attractiveness will diminish as the spatial separation between origin and destination increases.

The general equation for the gravity model is given as:

$$T_{ij} = A_i B_j O_i D_j f(d_{ij}) \qquad (3)$$

Where T_{ij} = number of trips from zone i to zone j
$\qquad d_{ij}$ = travel time or distance between zone i and zone j
$\qquad O_i$ = number of trips generated in zone i
$\qquad D_j$ = number of trips attracted to zone j
$\qquad A_i$ and B_j are solved iteratively.

Before it can be used in a transportation study to predict future trip patterns, the model has to be calibrated so that it can describe the observed effect that spatial separation of zones exerts on the existing origin-destination matrix of the particular study area. The calibration thus is an attempt to

[1]Bureau of Public Roads, *Guidelines for Trip Generation Analysis*, Washington, D.C., 1967.
[2]W. J. Reilley, *The Law of Retail Gravitation*, New York, 1931.
[3]A. M. Voorhees, "A general Theory of Traffic Movement," *Proceedings Institute of Traffic Engineers*, 1955.

find a value for the term $f(d_{ij})$ which appears to explain the observed travel pattern. The early gravity models used a simple inverse exponential function of the distance between i and j, but by 1963 the Bureau of Public Roads had recommended the use of empirically derived travel-time factors for each journey purpose and for trips originating from different sectors of the study area. This practice was widely adopted, the model then sometimes being referred to as a trip interactance model.

The entropy-maximizing model has provided a new theoretical basis for the gravity model using concepts derived from statistical mechanics rather than Newtonian physics. The model defines the trip distribution pattern that is most likely to occur within the constraints of a given set of trip attractions and generations and set of interzonal travel costs and assuming that there is a fixed total expenditure on transport within the study area at any point in time.[1] This form of model was tried in the Southeast Lancashire and Northeast Cheshire (SELNEC) transportation study using a generalized cost of travel as perceived by car owners and by captive public transport users for different modes of transport.[2]

The general form of the model is expressed as

$$T_{ij}^{kn} = A_i^n B_j O_i^n D_j e^{-\beta n} c_{ij}^k \qquad (4)$$

where in this case k is the type of mode, n the class of person (car owner, or not), and c_{ij}^k the interzonal travel cost by each mode.

A second major type of synthetic distribution model is the opportunity model. Developed by Schneider for the Chicago Area Transportation Study, it was subsequently used in other major studies in North America. The model expresses the probability of a trip finding an acceptable destination in a particular zone as a function of the total possible trip destinations in all other zones nearer to zone i than is zone j. This model differs from the gravity model in that it is not concerned with actual values of distance or travel cost between zones, only with relative locations of destination zones. Mathematically this can be expressed as:

$$T_{ij} = P_i [e - ^{LT} - e^{-L(T+T_j)}] \qquad (5)$$

where T_{ij} = number of trips originating in zone i with destination in zone j

P_i = trip origins in zone i

T = sum of trip destinations nearer to zone i than zone j is

T_j = total trip destinations in zone j

L = a measure of the probability that a random destination will satisfy the needs of a particular trip. It is an empirically derived function which describes the rate of trip decay with increasing length of trip.

[1] A. G. Wilson, "The Use of Entropy Maximising Methods in the Theory of Trip Distribution, Mode Split and Route Split, *Journal of Transport Economics and Policy,* vol. 3, no. 1, 1969.

[2] A. G. Wilson, A. F. Hawkins, G. J. Hill and D. J. Wagon, "Calibration and Testing of the SELNEC Transport Model," *Regional Studies,* vol. 3, 1969.

Modal split   Modal split models have been largely concerned with estimating how the future number of trips will "split" between the use of the private car and use of public transport, either through the exercise of choice or because the trip maker is "captive" to one mode (someone with no car available can be regarded as a captive public transport user).

The early modal split models were formulated as simple diversion curves which described the proportion of travelers using a particular mode in terms of characteristics of the person making the trip, the journey purpose, and the land use and location of the origin and destination.

As it became clearer that the choice of travel mode was not as simple to model as the early diversion curves implied, the number of factors included in the models was extended to include other characteristics of the trip and the different modes of transport available to the traveler, such as total journey time, time spent waiting, and the perceived cost of travel. Concomitantly techniques of analysis were refined, sets of diversion curves being aggregated and handled by means of multiple regression analysis. More recently, statistical techniques such as discriminant analysis[1] have been used as a means of analyzing the modal behavior of individual travelers rather than dealing with aggregated zonal data.

The Bureau of Public Roads has classified modal split models into "trip-end" and "trip-interchange" models; a distinction based on the position the model occupies in the transportation planning process.[2] Trip-end models are applied prior to the trip distribution phase, while trip-interchange models are applied subsequent to it.

Trip assignment   The purpose of the assignment model is to select the route that will most likely be taken in traveling between a given origin and destination.

Again, early developments of assignment models were in the form of diversion curves, but subsequently the Chicago study adopted a technique developed by Moore,[3] who had used mathematical graph theory to devise a routine for selecting the shortest route through a network.

The shortest-route procedures developed for the Chicago study were developed by the U.S. Bureau of Public Roads as an "all-or-nothing" assignment process. The model is based on the assumption that travelers wish to minimize their travel time, travel cost, or journey distance, and the routine selects a minimum-time path by systematically searching among all available paths and from a description of the network stored in the computer accumulating the sum of travel times by each. Having defined the shortest paths between every origin and every destination, the flows

[1] D. A. Quarmby, "Travel Mode for Journey to Work," *Journal of Transport Economics and Policy*, vol. 1, no. 3, 1967.

[2] M. J. Fertal, et al., *Modal Split: Documentation of Nine Methods for Estimating Transit Usage*, U.S. Bureau of Public Roads, 1966.

[3] E. F. Moore, "The Shortest Path through a Maze," *Proceedings*, International Symposium on the Theory of Switching, Harvard, 1957.

between these zones are loaded onto the network and total flows on each link of the network can be calculated.

A more realistic expression of the way in which traffic behaves on a highway network is afforded by "capacity restrained" assignments. These routines simulate the speed-flow relationships governing highway capacity (as flow increases, average speed falls). As successive increments of the origin-destination matrix are loaded onto each link in the network, new travel times are calculated for those links (an incremental increase in volume giving an incremental lengthening of travel time over that link) and new shortest paths are determined. This process is repeated in successive iterations until all trips have been assigned. Other variants of these two basic routines have been developed.

Criteria other than minimum journey time have been successfully used in assignments: travel cost or a combined function of travel time and distance, for example.

Transportation Plans and Policies The transportation planning models are required simply to provide the planner with a forecast of future demands for travel both within and between urban areas. The end purpose of the process is to enable the planning agencies to formulate plans and policies which, within overall budgetary and other planning constraints, should attempt to balance the supply of transportation facilities with the demand.

What the nature of the plans and policies for any particular area will be will largely depend on the particular planning objectives formulated for that area. In the immediate postwar period, simple objectives, such as the elimination of traffic congestion, led to narrowly conceived plans for building more roads. By the late 1950s and early 1960s, however, criticism was mounting in the United States over the large investments (largely through federal aid) in massive urban freeway projects while other urban transportation facilities were suffering from capital starvation. Following the lead given by the early major comprehensive transportation studies, Mitchell[1] set down a series of principles which were to guide the subsequent scope and content of transportation plans and policies. They are summarized as follows:

1. A new highway or public transport facility cannot be planned in isolation from the rest of the system. Each improvement must be viewed as part of the whole system, and the effect of each project on the rest of the system must be evaluated.

2. Highway and public transport facilities cannot be planned in isolation from each other. A plan should provide for each mode of transportation to do that part of the job for which it is best fitted.

3. Transportation planning must be metropolitan in scope. Studies ought to embrace the whole urban region, and as travelers pay little heed to

[1]R. B. Mitchell, "Transportation Problems and their Solution," *Proceedings American Philosophical Society,* vol. 106, no. 3, 1962.

municipal boundaries, plans and policies must be formulated to cover a broad area without being confined within such boundaries.

4. Transportation planning cannot be separated from urban land-use planning. First, the future location and density of residential and commercial areas, of industry and recreation will determine the amount and direction of travel in the city. Second, the new transport system will establish new patterns of accessibility and exert a strong influence on where new activities will be located and on the rate of change in older areas.

Buchanan also made an important contribution in laying down principles which ought to be adhered to in preparing transportation plans. In brief, they are as follows:

1. Meaningful transportation planning can be carried out only in the overall context of urban land-use planning.

2. Plans for different modes of transport—private and public, passenger and freight, and intracity as well as intercity—must be coordinated.

3. Depending on the population and density of the urban area, there is an absolute limit to the amount of traffic that the city can physically accommodate. To the extent that the demand for the use of the private car exceeds this limit, traffic will somehow have to be restrained.

4. For a given budget for investment in roads, the more accessibility is provided for, the more is the quality of the urban environment likely to be degraded.

5. Public transport will have to continue to play an important role in accommodating urban-area movement demands, especially in the large cities.

It is now widely accepted that urban transportation plans and policies ought to be part of a comprehensive and strategic set of policies concerning all aspects of urban development. The selection of a particular plan ought to be made by evaluating, for each alternative, the total benefits accruing to all sectors of the community and comparing these with the public, private, and social costs involved.

In formulating policies and plans, there is as yet no hard and fast formula which can be applied to the planning objectives and the financial, political, physical, and technical constraints operating within a particular city to yield the optimal planning solution. In the meantime, it appears that the choice as to what proportion of the total transportation investment should be for the benefit of the private car and what proportion should be assigned to the development of public transport depends upon the size, density, and layout of the city, upon what type of transport systems are already operated, whether new systems are being contemplated, and what value is placed on the nontransport impacts that each type of transportation facility will have on the rest of the urban area. In large, high-density cities, rapid-transit schemes appear to be necessary as accessibility by private car is likely to remain at a low level, especially within and near the central business district. This is borne out by the fact that many West European cities are currently engaged in upgrading and extending their rapid-transit facilities. In smaller cities and in those with low residential densities, trip-end densities are not high enough to make conventional rapid-transit systems financially viable. Here it appears that more emphasis will have to be given to improving facilities for the private vehicle, with public transport operated as some kind of bus system.

Difficulties in making a choice between these ranges arise largely because the private car affords its user advantages of comfort, convenience, and flexibility that are not available to the user of public transport. However, these benefits are achieved at the expense of increasing public and social costs such as the disruption of urban communities caused by the building of major urban freeways, atmospheric and noise pollution, and the cost of road accidents. Only in exceptional circumstances can public transport offer service comparable to that enjoyed by the private motorist, but—provided that it can be operated on an acceptable financial basis—it imposes few public and social costs. Principally for this reason, there has recently been a resurgence of interest in ways of revitalizing public transport in the major cities of Europe and North America.

In the United Kingdom, an attempt to achieve a better coordination of public transport services within major urban areas was promoted by the 1968 Transport Act. This legislation created passenger transport authorities with a new unified responsibility for planning and managing public transport services as part of wider planning policies for the future development of the urban areas they served. In the United States, the Urban Mass Transportation Act of 1964 empowered a federally sponsored project to "study and prepare a program of research, development and demonstration of new systems of urban transportation that will carry people and goods within metropolitan areas, speedily, safely, without polluting the air, and in a manner that will contribute to sound city planning." A number of "demonstration projects" were subsequently undertaken, and with the stimulus of this enactment there has been a good deal of research into technological innovations which would provide public transport systems with better levels of service and greater operational or economic flexibility.

Technological solutions to present-day transport problems have always appealed strongly to the popular imagination, but past innovations in transport technology have tended to be marginal and evolutionary rather than dramatic and revolutionary. However, the "new system study" carried out by the Department of Housing and Urban Development examined nearly three hundred projects with immediate application possibilities. Their evaluation studies indicated that the following new public transport systems at least showed promise:

Dial-a-bus A demand-actuated type of bus system in which the potential passenger would perhaps telephone a central control to indicate his wish to use the service, the request being fed to a computer which would then schedule and direct buses to specific pickup points and destinations in response to the calls received.

Dual-mode and Automated Systems The principle here is that in the vicinity of the origins and destinations of the passengers a public transport mode needs the flexibility of the motor vehicle to pick up and set down passengers along conventional streets, but in the midportion of the journey, say between the suburb and central area, a rail system or automatic guideway would give advantages of high speed, high capacity, and safe operation. Vehicles could be either large or small, publicly operated or privately owned and operated, depending on the particular system envisaged.

New Systems for Major Activity Centers   These would include such systems as continuously moving belts and capsule transit systems, some on guideways and others perhaps suspended above city streets.

BIBLIOGRAPHY:
Works dealing with the overall process and the techniques involved in transportation planning.
B. V. Martin, F. W. Memmott and A. J. Bone, *Principles and Techniques of Predicting Future Demand for Urban Transportation*, M.I.T. Research Report no. 38, 1961; R. M. Zettel and R. Carll, *Summary Review of Major Metropolitan Area Transportation Studies in the U.S.*, I.T.T.E., Berkeley, 1962; W. Y. Oi and P. W. Schuldiner, *An Analysis of Urban Travel Demand*, Northwestern University Press, Evanston, Ill., 1962; *Traffic Assignment Manual*, U.S. Bureau of Public Roads, 1964; *Calibrating and Testing a Gravity Model for Any Size Urban Area*, U.S. Bureau of Public Roads, 1965; *Modal Split: Documentation of Nine Methods for Estimating Transit Usage*, U.S. Bureau of Public Roads, 1966; K. R. Overgaard, *Traffic Estimation in Urban Transportation Planning*, Civil Engineering and Building Construction series no. 37, Acta Polytechnica Scandinavia, 1966; *Guidelines for Trip Generation Analysis*, U.S. Bureau of Public Roads, 1967; A. G. Wilson, D. Bayliss, A. J. Blackburn and B. G. Hutchinson, *New Directions in Strategic Transportation Planning*, Centre for Environmental Studies, W.P. 36, London, 1969; M. J. Bruton, *An Introduction to Transportation Planning*, Hutchinson Publishing Group, Ltd., London, 1970; R. L. Creighton, *Urban Transportation Planning*, University of Illinois Press, Evanston, Ill., 1970.

Works dealing primarily with issues and policies in urban transportation.
R. B. Mitchell and C. Rapkin, *Urban Traffic: A Function of Land Use*, Columbia University Press, New York, 1954; C. D. Buchanan et al., *Traffic in Towns*, H.M.S.O., London, 1963; J. R. Meyer, J. F. Kain, and M. Wohl, *The Urban Transportation Problem*, Harvard University Press, Cambridge, Mass., 1965; *Tomorrow's Transportation*, U.S. Department of Housing and Urban Development, 1968; *Transportation Systems for Major Activity Centers*, O.E.C.D., Paris, 1970.

Reports from some of the major transportation studies.
Detroit Transportation Study, Final Report, 1955–1956, 3 vols.; *Chicago Area Transportation Study, Final Report*, 1959–1962, 3 vols.; *Penn-Jersey Transportation Study*, 1965; *London Transportation Study*, 1965–1969, 3 vols.; *Merseyside Area Land Use Transportation Study, Final Report*, 1969, 2 vols.   —David Briggs

TREES IN URBAN AREAS   The introduction of some degree of verdancy into urban areas has been a feature of city planning from the seventeenth century onward. Among early notable examples are the tree-lined streets of Paris and the garden squares of London. Later, as cities became larger and private gardens became smaller, parks, public gardens, and small green areas between buildings were introduced. When the desired verdant character was achieved, the result was refreshing and decorative.

Trees are the most conspicuous factors in giving this character. They can often afford much delight in an urban scene, especially in spring, whether it is a street in Jerez (southern Spain) lined with orange trees, a street in Rome lined with Judas trees or umbrella pines, or the Parkway in Welwyn

Harmans Water neighborhood, Bracknell, England.

Parkway in Spring, Welwyn Garden City, England.

ABOVE: *Water gardens, Spokane, Washington. Here can be seen the effect of trees against modern architecture, which, combined with the water, make a very attractive scene.* LEFT: *Center of Stevenage, England. Trees with light foliage seen in relation to a modern square.*

Garden City, which is partly lined with cherry trees. As these examples indicate, the selection of trees for cities is controlled to some extent by climate, and generally, although not always, the choice would be different in the southern and northern regions of Europe and the United States. A large number of trees, however, are suitable in many latitudes and in both sheltered and exposed positions, making the choice of trees for urban areas fairly extensive. The export and import of trees among many countries has continued for three centuries, and many trees have thrived in their new habitats. At least a dozen of the familiar trees in Britain (and many more that are less familiar) were imported from the United States from the seventeenth century onward, and many were imported from other parts of the world.

A few general warnings can be given and a few principles suggested in the selection of trees. (There is a considerable number of books on the subject to give guidance to the planner. Some of these are given in the bibliography.)

Information on root systems of various trees, on diseases, on potential size, and on density and character of foliage is essential for intelligent tree planting in cities. Many studies of root systems in relation to soils have been made—as, for example, the study of 31 species growing in fargo clay in North Dakota, which yielded the information that the roots of most trees are confined to the upper 4 feet of soil. Among root hazards are the damage to road surfaces, drains, and foundations caused by some systems. For example, poplars have often been planted along roadsides, and in some cases, where the soil is a shrinkable clay, this has resulted in damage of the kind mentioned. Disease is another hazard. In Buffalo, New York, a large number of trees had to be removed because of Dutch elm disease, and the same has occurred in southern England. Another disease to which some trees are particularly susceptible is fireblight. Heavy autumn leaf falls from some trees, such as plane and sycamore, are apt to make road surfaces and sidewalks slippery. These and many other hazards are necessary considerations in the selection of trees for urban planting.

An important aesthetic consideration is the relation of trees to buildings. In a street or square, trees are of great decorative value. They complement buildings and enhance their appearance, especially if these are architecturally distinctive. They should not be so large or have such dense foliage as to blot out the surrounding buildings. This has occurred with large plane trees in the London squares. A typical example is Bedford Square, the distinctive Georgian architecture of which can be seen and appreciated only at a satisfactory distance in the winter, because in summer the dense foliage of the immense plane trees blots out the architectural surroundings. A better relation of trees and architecture is exemplified by Jackson Square in the old center of New Orleans, where there is a sprinkling of smaller trees allowing generous glimpses of the distinctive architectural setting (*see illustration to* AESTHETICS). Instead of using only large trees with dense foliage in the squares and along the streets of cities (the plane tree grows to 90 feet), it would be better to think more in terms of a larger number of medium- or smaller-size trees, or, if larger trees are desired for very broad avenues between buildings, then those with light foliage, like acacia, could be used with good effect. Sometimes, however, in the case of some tall forest trees like conifers, the foliage in the full-grown trees is concentrated toward the top and surrounding buildings of not more than three stories can be clearly seen between the trunks, an effect that is often obtained in new residential areas where old trees have been retained.

Flowering trees are often planted along the roadside because of the rich, colorful effect in the spring, but unless the tree is otherwise attractive and suitable it is questionable whether such a selection should be made just for a fortnight each year. An example is the Japanese cherry which blooms in great profusion for a fortnight or three weeks in spring but for the rest of the year is not among the most decorative of trees and cannot compare with, say, the silver birch or mountain ash. A more rewarding flowering tree is the crab apple, especially the *Malus lemoinei* which has a pleasing shape, bright crimson flowers, and coppery foliage.

Many trees that line roadways, like poplars and limes, have been subjected to severe pruning with not very satisfactory results. Pollarded trees often look ugly. For urban planting it is best to select trees with thought of the space for their maximum growth, so that their natural shapes can be preserved. Medium-sized or small varieties have advantages in this respect. It is best to select kinds that do not need pruning, but if this is sometimes unavoidable, it should be done with restraint so as to preserve as much as possible the natural shape of the tree.

Among the felicitous effects in the urban scene are trees in conjunction with buildings and water. This often creates effects that appear accidental but are usually carefully designed. Among the notable examples are the town hall trees and water at Hilversum (Netherlands), the water gardens in the town center at Hemel Hempstead (England), and the water garden at Spokane, Washington. Trees and modern architecture, which is often severe and plain, often appear to good advantage when seen together. When, for example, light foliage is silhouetted against the large plain wall of a modern building, the trees provide the decoration that the building lacks. In this way they complement each other.

BIBLIOGRAPHY: Association for Planning and Regional Reconstruction, *Trees for Town & Country,* Lund Humphries, London, 1949; Ronald J. Morling, *Trees: Including Preservation, Planting Law, Highways,* Estates Gazette, London, 1954, 2d ed., 1963; Ministry of Housing and Local Government, *Trees in Town & City,* H.M.S.O., London, 1958; Garrett Eckbo, *Urban Landscape Design,* McGraw-Hill Book Company, New York, 1964; Robert Zion, *Trees for Architecture and the Landscape,* D. Van Nostrand Company, Princeton, N.J., 1970.

—ARNOLD WHITTICK

TURKEY

Legislation and Administration   The present City Planning Laws in Turkey were put into force in 1957. They took the place of the Municipal Construction and Roads Laws which had been in force for almost 25 years, while before that Building Laws dating from the Ottoman Empire had been in operation.

The new legislation has been prepared in the light of previous experience and developments in other countries. For example, in the Building Laws of the Ottoman Empire no mention was made of development plans. In the Municipal Construction and Roads Law that followed, planning and zoning standards were nearly the same for each municipality, and in the present legislation these standards have been left as bylaws and regulations allowing for some degree of flexibility. Existing laws necessitate a building permit and an occupation permit after the building is completed. The control of construction is the responsibility and under the authority of the municipalities.

Local administration in Turkey is divided into three groups: village administration, provincial administration, and municipalities. In 1969 there were about 35,000 village and 67 provincial administrations with 1,283 municipalities. A commune of less than 2,000 inhabitants is a village and one of more than 2,000 a municipality. Each grade of local administration has its special laws, and only municipalities are responsible for the preparation and application of development plans.

The number of municipalities in the last 20 years has increased from approximately 600 to 1,300, with an annual increase of about 35. The reason for this increase is that a large amount of municipal income is provided by the state in accordance with the Municipal Incomes Act of 1948. A percentage of state revenues such as income tax and customs duties is allocated to the Bank of Provinces (İller Bankası) and 80 percent of this is distributed amongst the municipalities according to their populations. Municipalities having less than 50,000 population receive financial and technical assistance from the remaining 20 percent. Since villages are not entitled to receive such aid, municipal administrations are in a more advantageous position by comparison. This explains why neighboring villages choose to combine and form municipalities.

According to present Town Planning Legislation (Imar Kanunu) all municipalities should first prepare a current land-use map and have it approved. Municipalities having more than 5,000 inhabitants are also required to have development and sewage plans, while those below 5,000 should have a road map, as designated by the municipal council. The municipal council can decide to have a development and sewage plan prepared, and since a majority of small municipalities do this, the number not having road plans has become negligible.

There are many laws, other than Town Planning Legislation, dealing with the rights and responsibilities of municipalities; the most important being the Municipal Act of 1930 and the Municipal Revenues Act of 1948, while in the Constitution there are articles relating to municipalities and local administrations. The necessity to provide local administrations with sources of income proportionate to their functions is clearly stated in the Constitution.

The planning activities of municipalities is under the control of the Ministry of Town Planning (İmar ve İskan Bakanlığı). The first Ministry of Town Planning—founded in 1923—was abolished a year later and a new one came, after 34 years, in 1958.

The Real Estate Credit Bank (Emlak ve Kredi Bankası) and the Bank of Provinces, previously connected to the Ministries of Finance and Interior Affairs respectively, are now part of the Ministry of Town Planning. The former bank distributes housing credit while the latter gives credit and technical assistance to local administrations. More than 95 percent of the functions of the Bank of Provinces are concerned with municipalities. Also connected to the Ministry of Town Planning is the Land Office (arsa ofisi), founded in 1969, which has important responsibilities toward meeting the

LEFT: *Nursery School in Atakoy with apartment blocks in the distance.*
BELOW: *General view of Atakoy—a housing development along the European part of the coast of Marmara in Istanbul, built by the Real Estate Credit Bank.*

land requirements of municipalities. The General Directorate of Land and Resettlement (Toprak ve İskan Genel Müdürlüğü), which was a part of the Ministry, has now been transferred to the Ministry of Village Affairs, founded in 1964. The Ministry of Town Planning has aimed at reaching the municipalities more efficiently through its eight newly established regional directorates. These are also responsible for taking the necessary precautions against disasters such as earthquakes, fire, and flood.

The Ministry of Interior Affairs has administrative control of local administrations, approves the budgets, and supervises municipal functions other than planning. The General Directorate of Local Administrations is connected with this Ministry. The State Planning Office (Devlet Planlama Teşkilatı), founded in 1960, also has the important function of supervising municipal investments.

Only municipalities among the local administrations in Turkey are planning authorities. This authority is vested in persons who have the main legal authority, including, since 1963, the mayor, who is elected by the people. The standing committee of municipalities is formed of members of the municipal council and department heads; the majority being the latter. Municipal councils are authorized to form special committees when necessary, including the development committee, especially during the period when budgets are prepared.

Survey A municipality that decides to have a development plan must conduct a survey beforehand. The method for the survey is given in a regulation adopted in 1969. A committee called the Development Commission was responsible for the preparation of surveys until 1969. There have been successful Development Commission reports presented by large municipalities in the last 15 to 20 years. The report prepared for the 1952 International İzmir Development Plan Competition was published in Turkish; while that for Ankara was published in Turkish, English, German, and French in 1954. The survey reports of large cities such as Erzurum, Sivas, and Konya have also been prepared and published in Turkish.

Design The design stage is initiated by the Ministry of Town Planning after approval of the survey. It can be given to a single planner or town planning office, or a competition may be held—on a national or international scale. Another alternative is that the Bank of Provinces undertakes the work through its own planners. The bank can also assist municipalities financially and technically in such matters as announcing competitions or by giving the work of survey and design to a contractor. The plan has to receive the approval of the Ministry after it has been accepted by the Municipal Council, and the same procedure has to be followed for amendments. The plans have to be made public, and some municipalities organize exhibitions for this purpose.

Up to 1969, development plans were prepared for a period of 30 years, but the new regulation has reduced this to 20 years.

Implementation Municipalities have legally to prepare 4-year programs for the application of their development plans, but these programs—which are not effective enough in the process of realization—are neglected by most municipalities due to the lack of supervision.

The Bank of Provinces is the most effective agency in the implementation of plans as well as in the surveying and design processes. It assists municipalities both financially and technically; starting from the preparation of current land-use maps up to the determination of the infrastructure and superstructure designated in the plans. Each municipality is eligible to receive credit for water supply systems, sewage disposal, electrical installations, construction of slaughterhouses, and other municipal activities. (The nominal capital of the bank is around $120 million, and more than half of this amount has been collected through the 5 percent share from the revenues of the municipalities and provincial administrations.)

Places having less than 50,000 population are donated a certain sum from the municipalities fund of the bank for the preparation of current land-use maps and development plans. The credit given to these municipalities is without interest for a term of 20 years. All this however, has to receive the approval of the Ministry of Town Planning.

The planning offices of the bank give technical assistance to municipalities in the preparation, implementation, and supervision of projects. Most of this work is carried out in the 15 regional directorates. The bank also organizes periodic in-service training courses mostly for the personnel of the smaller municipalities. There are also funds under the control of the Ministry of Interior Affairs, most of which go to small municipalities in the form of grants.

Professional Practice   Those employed in city planning can be divided into three groups: (1) government officials working in the various departments of the central administration, (2) officials in the local administration, (3) those practicing privately. This is not a strict separation however. It is common for a government official to enter planning competitions in his free time, alone or in a group. University members also have the same rights.

The largest number of planners is employed by the Ministry of Town Planning. After development plans are completed and when alterations are made, they have to receive the approval of the General Directorate of Planning and Development connected to the Ministry.

The Bank of Provinces—connected to the Ministry—is also a central organization employing planners. It plays an important role in preparing the development plans of small municipalities through its own personnel, assisting the survey work of large municipalities, and arranging competitions.

There is little opportunity for planners in local administrations. None may be employed by the small municipalities. Some of the medium-size municipalities give planning work to the engineers and architects they employ. A few large municipalities such as Ankara, Istanbul, and Izmir have their own planning departments. The chamber of Turkish Architects protested strongly, some years ago, when a lawyer was appointed director of the planning department in Istanbul. The answer was that planning involved teamwork and the coordinator does not necessarily have to be a designer.

In private practice there is not sufficient specialization and teamwork because, for many years, civil engineering, architecture, and town planning could be carried out by the same person. Only a few architectural firms turned to planning. These are located in Ankara in order to be near the Ministry and the Bank of Provinces. The remaining firms engage in planning work with their architectural practice.

These facts clearly indicate why planners have not been able to form a separate association. There are almost fifty planners today (having B.C.P. or M.C.P. degrees) and they are trying to organize an independent association of planners.

The inadequacies seen in some work indicates clearly that there are shortcomings in the education of planners. Education by itself, in schools specializing in architecture, engineering, and fine arts, is not enough for successful town planning. Planning graduates of the Middle East Technical University in Ankara are still too few to change the situation. The natural outcome is that certain architects concentrate more on planning practice after small-scale experiments to test their qualifications. The Bank of Provinces makes great contributions in this area because its offices have been a medium for the training of planners for the last 30 years.

Foreign planners, mostly German, have contributed in the last 40 years by winning competitions, working in government offices or large municipalities (such as Ankara, Istanbul, and Izmir), by teaching in universities, or by acting as adjudicators.

Education and Training Planning was taught in the Academy of Fine Arts and the Engineering School in Istanbul before the Second World War, but these were courses in physical planning, taking almost no account of the socioeconomic aspects. A planning course with emphasis on the socioeconomic factors was started in 1938 in the School of Political Sciences in Ankara. Professor Ernst Reuter was the first lecturer, and he continued in this capacity until his return to Germany in November, 1946. (He died in 1953 while serving as mayor of West Berlin.)

After the Second World War the Engineering School became a technical university; but the planning course in its newly established faculty of architecture remained the same. The Academy of Fine Arts continued planning education in a similar manner. The School of Political Sciences became one of the faculties of the University of Ankara in 1950, and planning courses stress socioeconomic aspects as before. Physical planning is taught by the faculty of architecture of the new technical university in Trabzon and in some dozen private colleges of engineering and architecture.

The planning department of the faculty of architecture of the Middle East Technical University in Ankara, established in 1961, is the first and only place which gives bachelor's and master's degrees in city planning. The faculty also has departments of regional planning and restoration. Both physical and socioeconomic aspects of planning are taught in this school. Master's degree programs are open to administrators, sociologists, historians, geographers, economists, and law school graduates as well as architects. This reflects the modern concept of planning as teamwork.

View looking south of the Middle East Technical University, Ankara. On the left is the library and on the right the Faculty of Architecture. (Architects: Altug and Behruz Cinici.)

The curriculum of the regional planning department is based on socio-economic factors such as urbanization, population movements, problems of metropolitan areas, and disparities between regions or between the village and the town.

The restoration department contributes greatly to the preservation and evaluation of historical monuments. It has inaugurated an international campaign for the preservation of the monuments in Elâziz (Eastern Anatolia) which will be flooded by the $300-million Keban Hydroelectric Project.

Institutions   The 50 planners in Turkey have only recently made their first attempt to organize their own association. The Town and Country Planning Institute established in the faculty of political sciences in 1953 carries out work other than physical planning. An association was formed in 1965 to support the studies of the Institute. Turkish and foreign professionals working in the fields of urbanization, land speculation, housing, community development, and regional planning as well as politicians and people interested in these subjects come together during the annual Town and Country Planning Week organized by the Institute where the problems of the country and developments outside Turkey can be discussed and debated.

A similar institute was set up in 1967 in the faculty of architecture of the Technical University of Istanbul. This faculty and The Union of the Turkish Chambers of Architects organize conferences on various aspects of planning. The bulletins of the chamber are means of directing public opinion toward existing problems.

The Association of Turkish Municipalities was founded 30 years ago. It has published a monthly review for the past 30 years and occasionally organizes regional seminars.

There are thousands of amenity and development societies in almost all the towns and cities. They make themselves felt as pressure groups from time to time, pointing out certain problems of their towns or cities, and they exert great pressure during the elections.

The Istanbul Regional Planning Association tries to reach public opinion and political organs by organizing periodical conferences. A society against air pollution was established in 1968 in Ankara.

Geographical and Climatic Conditions   Turkey, lying between 36 and 42 degrees north latitude and 26 and 45 degrees east longitude, is a large land mass (301,380 square miles or 780,576 square kilometers) that is partly in Europe (9,160 square miles or 23,623 square kilometers) and partly in Asia (292,220 square miles or 756,953 square kilometers).

The Anatolian peninsula, a solid and rugged mass of land about 930 miles (1,500 kilometers) long and 372 miles (600 kilometers) wide, thrusts out of Asia into Turkish Thrace, forming a practically impassable mountain barrier between the Black Sea and Mediterranean basin. It is interrupted only by the narrow and easily controlled natural passageway of the straits (Bosphorus and Dardanelles). This has resulted in a sharp isolation and differentiation of the two cultural realms in the north and south of Turkey.

New Gediz built by the Turkish government for a population of 10,000 on a new site after the old town was destroyed by an earthquake in March 1970. It was completed at the end of 1970 in the short time of 9 months.

Turkey as a whole is included in the recent folded zone which runs in the east-west direction from Europe to southeastern Asia, between two ancient plateaus on the north and south. Perhaps the most outstanding general feature of the country is that it is an area that has recently been warped upward, forming a high threshold between the basins of subsidence of the Black Sea and the Eastern Mediterranean. Indeed, the mean altitude of the country (3,600 feet or 1,100 meters) is about 8,200 feet (2,500 meters) higher than the floor of the adjacent seas (mean depths of the Black Sea and the Eastern Mediterranean are respectively 4,265 feet or 1,300 meters and 4,921 feet or 1,500 meters). The difference between the marginal mountains and the basin floor is even greater and in places exceeds 16,400 feet (5,000 meters). The altitude of the country increases eastward to an average of 6,560 feet (2,000 meters) in eastern Anatolia, where even many depressions lie at more than 6,560 feet (2,000 meters).

Turkey is situated in the subtropical transition zone between the tropical climates to the south and the polar air masses and temperate climates to the north. The climatic conditions of the country are determined by the seasonal changes which result from the interaction of these two climatic regions.

Four types of climate can be distinguished in Turkey:

1. *The Mediterranean* (in the south and west), with hot or mild dry summers and rainy winters

2. *The Black Sea* (in the north), with warm summers, mild winters, and sufficient precipitation at all seasons

3. *The continental* (in the northeast), with fairly warm summers but very cold winters and sufficient precipitation at all seasons

4. *The semiarid* (in the interior and southeast), with cold winters and hot, dry summers

The regions of concentrated settlements derive their names from the nearest sea: Marmara, Aegean, Black Sea, and Mediterranean. In these regions the population centers are situated on low plains.

Approximately one-seventh of Turkey is deprived of exterior drainage. The most extensive and compact interior basin, which owes its origin mainly to the semiarid character of the climate, is situated in the heart of central Anatolia. The rest of the country is drained to the surrounding seas and, in the northeast, to the Caspian.

Traditions in Planning   The Turkish Republic is rich in remnants of civilizations going as far back as the Hittites. The best known are the cities founded or developed by the Greeks, Byzantines, Romans, Seljuks, and Ottomans.

Planned studies in the modern sense, conducted on a city scale by a city administration, are quite recent in Turkey. The first community administration of the Ottoman Empire was established first in Istanbul in the middle of the nineteenth century. Such administration, which spread with time to other places, was concerned with such local services as hygiene, sanitation, lighting, water supply, and the control of the price and quality of food and of markets rather than with town planning.

In earlier times, local services were mostly in the form of endowments. The basic idea behind them was to serve communities and to fulfill divine commands. These endowments provided the following:

1. Aqueducts, canals, fountains, wells for the water supply of towns and villages

2. Sanitary services: the cleaning of roads and squares, baths, laundries, and public lavatories

3. Health services: hospitals, mental institutions, special places for the control and treatment of infectious diseases, and spas

4. Social services: kitchens, homes for the poor and aged, wayside inns, assistance in cases of death, accident, or sickness

5. Cultural services: schools, libraries, and assembly halls

6. Public works: roads, bridges, closed markets, lodging for state employees, official and religious buildings

One cannot say that these services were distributed equally in all cities. They lost their effectiveness, as did other institutions, with the decline of the Ottoman Empire.

The Ottoman Buildings Law, which was still in force in the first quarter of the twentieth century, did not mention city planning. The law enabled construction to proceed without municipal supervision once a building permit was issued.

The imaret (*külliye*), a complex of schools, hospitals, kitchens, libraries, bazaars, and lodgings around a mosque situated on a hill crowning a city—is an important city planning accomplishment of the Ottoman period. Imarets were built by the sultans, viziers, commanders, or other rich people. One can still come across them on most of the hills of Istanbul.

These social and cultural institutions were neglected with time mostly because such sources of income as farms, bazaars, and inns were outside the territories of the declining empire. The General Directorate of Endowments has recently taken important steps toward the maintenance and restoration of these imarets and other historic monuments.

Twentieth Century In 1973 the Turkish Republic was 50 years old. City planning achievements during this period have been mentioned partly under "Legislation and Administration."

This is a period of urbanization and organized studies. In the early years of the Republic there were five cities with populations over 50,000. In 1972 there were 40. In 1927, the year of the first modern census, 6.2 percent of the people lived in cities with over 100,000 population. This figure became 18.5 percent in 1965. Istanbul and Ankara have both shown rapid expansion. The population of Ankara, which was about 20,000 after the First World War, reached 1,400,000 in 1973. As there are good and bad examples of Turkish city planning in Ankara, it will be worthwhile to consider its recent history.

The Directorate of Development (İmar Müdürlüğü) was established in Ankara by special legislation in 1928. The experiences of this directorate have greatly influenced the preparation of succeeding legislation related to zoning, and replotting was first applied in Ankara. For a period of 6 years, until 1936, the directorate was the sole authority to certify the development plans prepared by other municipalities as set forth in the Municipality Act of 1930. It organized the competition for the Ankara city plan in 1928, which was won by a German, Prof. Dr. Herrmann Jansen, who supervised the implementation of his plan as a consultant until 1939.

The administration at that time calculated that the population of Ankara would be 300,000 in 50 years. Jansen planned accordingly over an area of approximately 3,706 acres (1,500 hectares). In 1939 the development area was increased eleven-fold to 40,770 acres (16,500 hectares) without any serious studies or surveys.

The hasty decision taken by the government in 1939 to increase the development area was a great boon to land speculators. Fifteen years later, in 1954, a new international competition was announced to overcome the resulting defects, and the winners were two Turkish town planners. The need for a new plan is felt greatly, as the scattered growth outside the development boundaries indicates. The population, predicted to be 300,000 in 1978, was already 900,000 in 1965 and 1,400,000 in 1973.

A law passed in 1925 authorized the administration of Ankara to expropriate about $1\frac{1}{2}$ square miles (4 square kilometers) of land at the legal value (i.e., fifteen times the value registered in 1915) although it was argued in Parliament that paying the legal value instead of the market price was against the Constitution. This is the only instance of such a decision in the planning history of the Republic.

Yenisehir-Yenimahalle A question brought up in Parliament during the discussion of the above law in 1925 was whether to redevelop old Ankara

Panoramic view of Yenimahalle, a modern development in the northwest area of Ankara.

KEY TO THE PANORAMIC VIEW OF YENIMAHALLE-ANKARA:

T.V. STATION (on the top of the hill)

① A NEW DISTRICT	② HOUSING	③ YENI MAHALLE	④ MUSHROOM	⑤ HOUSING
← →			← →	→
SCHOOLS	SCHOOLS	YENI MAHALLE ←	YENI MAHALLE	YENI MAHALLE →

or to build an adjacent new city. The advocates of the first proposal pointed out the opportunity to renew the old city, two-thirds of which was destroyed by fire in 1915. The second group believed that city planning principles could be applied with greater success on cheaply expropriated land, and this was the decision accepted.

The Yenişehir (new city) of Ankara with its modern housing, work and amusement places, embassies, ministries, and Parliament was thus built according to Jansen's plan, mainly on cheap land provided through the law of 1925.

Urban Renewal There has not been any major, large-scale urban renewal in Turkey other than the design and rebuilding of commercial zones in Ankara and Istanbul. Recently, however, especially in Ankara, higher and larger structures having stores, cinemas, and other commercial facilities on the ground floors and in the basements are replacing 15- to 20-year-old buildings which occupy expensive lots but bring little rent. This sort of disorderly urban renewal is spreading rapidly to other cities, destroying all

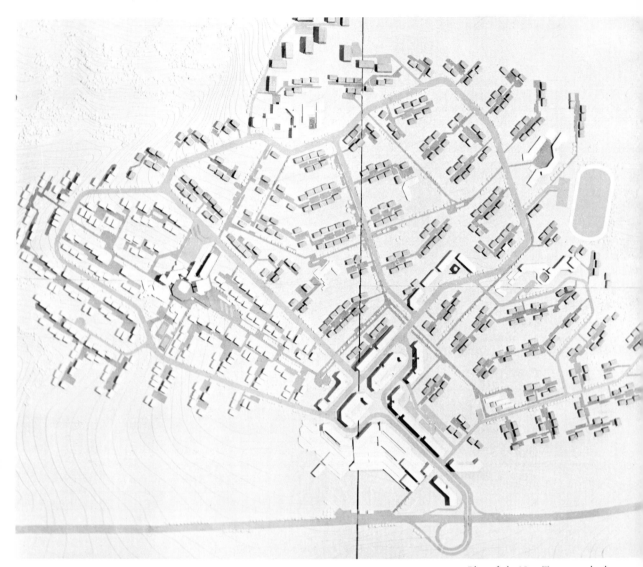

principles of density and serving only to make the landlords richer. The constant change in building regulations and the new law enabling apartment ownership have catalyzed this movement as well as land speculation.

Housing Modern housing and the mushroom areas (the new slums of underdeveloped countries) exist side by side in Ankara. Although Jansen advised strongly in his report that priority should be given to the construction of workers' housing and that land speculation should be prevented, neither suggestion was followed. Therefore the masses who came to Ankara had to build their own houses, since they could not afford to live even in the ancient dwellings of the old city. In 1970 more than 60 percent of the population lived in mushroom houses, mostly on state-owned land.

Plan of the New Town or suburban settlement of OR-AN for a population of 30,000, about 10 kilometres from the center of Ankara, on a site of about 100 hectares (247 acres) divided into four neighborhoods each with a population of about 7,000 in 1,750 dwelling units. Building started in 1970 and the town will be completed by 1978. The first stage of 800 dwellings was completed in 1971.

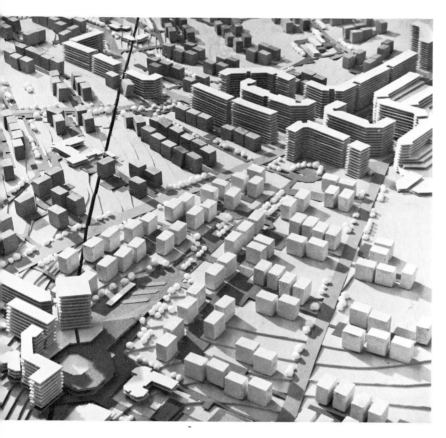

Model of OR-AN (Ankara) showing town center (bottom left corner) and apartment blocks.

Model of multilevel center of the New Town of OR-AN (Ankara). The 16-story tower block holds the chimney of the district heating system.

These shacks are constructed from scrap material and—since they are illegal—they have to be finished quickly (sometimes in a single night). They have been tolerated for social and political reasons, and therefore new districts sprout up each year. The city is now surrounded by these slum districts instead of a greenbelt.

Yenimahalle (new neighborhood), northwest of Ankara, is an example of successful public housing. It was started in 1949, and more than 3,000 houses were built in the following 4 to 5 years, because of cheap land, while suitable credit was provided and construction was compulsory. The number of apartments (flats) in each house varies between one and four.

Regional Planning Development in Ankara is important from the viewpoint of regional planning. When Ankara was made the capital of the Turkish Republic in 1923, many found it difficult to understand how Istanbul, capital of the Byzantine Empire for 1,000 years and of the Ottoman Empire for almost 500 years, could be changed. The shift to Ankara resulted from the decision made by Atatürk, the founder of modern Turkey, to go to the center of the Anatolian peninsula, neglected for centuries, and to try to solve the problems of the country there. Many underdeveloped countries suffer from being tied to a single center. Ankara has appeared as a second center and has developed rapidly. In fact, Ankara has already approached or perhaps surpassed the optimal city size for Turkey, and for this reason new centers must be developed in eastern Turkey in accordance with the rules of regional planning. For example, today there are three universities in Ankara, whereas the Trabzon and Erzurum universities are meeting great problems in their slow development. It is also necessary to secure an even distribution of education, health, cultural institutions, and economic activities according to the principles of regional planning. When Atatürk proclaimed Ankara as the capital, the term "regional planning" did not exist. Modern technology now provides the means whereby the principles of regional planning can be comprehensively and imaginatively applied.

BIBLIOGRAPHY: O. Nuri Ergin, *Türkiye'de Şehirciliğin Tarihi İnkişafı,* İstanbul, 1936; *Komün Bilgisinin Esas Meseleleri,* İstanbul Üniversitesi Hukuk ve Iktisat Fakülteleri Yayını, İstanbul, 1936; C. Esad Arseven, *Şehircilik (Urbanizm),* Devlet Basımevi, İstanbul, 1937; Ernst Reuter, *Komün Bilgisi-Şehirciliğe Giriş,* Siyasal Bilgiler Okulu Yayını, Ankara, 1940; Ernst Egli, *Şehirciliğin ve Memleket Planlamasının Esasları,* Türkiye ve Orta Doğu Amme İdaresi Enstitüsü Yayını, Ankara, 1957; *İskân ve Şehircilik Haftası Konferansları,* vols. I–IX, Ankara Ü. Siyasal Bilgiler Fakültesi Yayınları, Ankara, 1955–1969; Safa Erkün, *İmar Hukuku Prensipleri,* Halk Basımevi, İstanbul, 1950; Cevat Geray, *Şehir Planlamasının Başlıca Tatbik Vasıtaları,* Ankara Üniversitesi Siyasal Bilgiler Fakültesi Yayını, Ankara, 1961; Ruşen Keleş, *Şehir ve Bölge Plânlaması Bakımından Şehirleşme Hareketleri,* Ankara Ü. Siyasal Bilgiler Fakültesi Yayını, Ankara, 1961; Sirri Erinç and Sami Güngör, *Some Documents Concerning the Geography of Turkey,* Milli Eğitim Basimevi İst., 1962 (English and French): Gündüz Özdeş, *Şehirciliğe Giriş ve Toplum Mikyası,* İstanbul Teknik Üniversitesi Mimarlık Fakültesi Yayını, İstanbul, 1962; Fehmi Yavuz, *Şehircilik,* Ankara Üniversitesi Siyasal Bilgiler Fakültesi Yayını, Ankara, 1962; Tekin Aydın, *Anadolu'da İnsan Toplulukları ve Yerleşme İlkeleri,* İstanbul Teknik Ü. Mimarlık F. Yayını, İstanbul, 1963; *II. İmar Kongresi,* İmar ve İskân Bakanlığı Yayını, Ankara, 1963; *Şehircilik Konferansları (1962–1963),* İstanbul Teknik Üniversitesi Mimarlık Fakültesi Yayını, İstanbul 1964; K. Ahmet Aru, *Yayalar Taşıtlar,* İstanbul Teknik Ü. Mimarlık Fakültesi Yayını, İstanbul, 1965; Ali Tanoğlu, *Nüfus ve Yerleşme,* İstanbul Üniversitesi Coğrafya Enstitüsü Yayını, İstanbul, 1966; Mümtaz Soysal, *Local Government in Turkey,* Türkiye ve Orta Doğu Amme İdaresi Enstitüsü Yayını, Ankara, 1967; *İstanbul Bölge Kalkınma Kongresi,*

İstanbul, 1967; Erol Tümertekin, *Türkiye'de İç Göçler—Internal Migrations in Turkey,* İstanbul Üniversitesi Coğrafya Enstitüsü Yayını, İstanbul, 1968 (Turkish and English); *Büyük Belediyelerde Şehirleşme Sorunları Konferansı,* Türk Belediyecilik Derneği Yayını, Ankara, 1968.

—FEHMI YAVUZ

TWILIGHT AREA   An area, commonly adjacent to or even surrounding a city center, where the need for redevelopment is considerable, where buildings are in poor condition and decrepit in appearance, and where the whole environment is run down and deteriorating. Site values in such areas are usually very high, but there is not yet the demand on the central area as a whole for these fringe areas to be profitably redeveloped. Thus twilight areas are areas of transition (hence their name). They may formerly have been areas of predominantly mixed *or* single uses, but as twilight areas they most often contain mixed uses for which buildings have been adapted, often temporarily. Because of the phenomenon of towns often growing in concentric rings from the center, the twilight ring moves out from the center as the town grows.

The residential parts of such areas are usually characterized by overcrowding, inadequate conversions of houses to flats, a lack of basic sanitary or cooking facilities, and structural defects. They are consequently areas where social problems are particularly acute.

BIBLIOGRAPHY: Lewis Keeble, *Principles and Practice of Town and Country Planning,* Estates Gazette Ltd., London, 1969 (includes comprehensive bibliography).

—DAVID HALL

U

UNITED KINGDOM OF GREAT BRITAIN AND NORTHERN IRELAND

Legislation and Administration Of the four countries that make up the United Kingdom of Great Britain and Northern Ireland, England and Wales are governed by the same planning laws passed by Parliament at Westminster; Scotland is governed by similar laws adjusted to the different circumstances of the Scottish legal system, also passed by the Westminster Parliament; and Northern Ireland's laws though separately enacted are similar in content.

The purpose of planning legislation is the same in each country though administration differs marginally to suit local circumstances. The descriptions of legislation and administration given below refer to England unless stated otherwise.

The purpose of town and country planning in Britain, as expressed in the COI reference pamphlet,[1] is "...to provide pleasant surroundings for people to live and work in. The land of Britain is one of the most densely populated areas in the world: it is, therefore, important to preserve a balance between the competing claims made on the land by homes, industry, transport and leisure."

[1]Central Office of Information, ref. pamphlet no. 9: *Town & Country Planning in Britain,* HMSO, November 1967.

1030

The principal laws governing building and the development of land are those which are concerned with town and country planning, new towns, housing, transport, distribution of industry, the countryside, and civic amenities. A number of acts governing the use of land and the distribution of resources were passed soon after the Second World War; many of these have been substantially revised in the last 2 or 3 years to bring legislation into line with the demands of new situations. Britain is more densely populated and wealthier and its people have more cars and more leisure time than was forecast in the 1940s, so that the nature of demand for the use of land has changed considerably. The Town and Country Planning Act of 1968 is an outstanding example of this revision. Its provisions are now included in the consolidating Town and Country Planning Act of 1971 and will be described in more detail below.

It will be best to give a brief description of the system of planning administration before describing the provisions of the planning acts.

The Administrative System

The Part Played by the Central Government. It is the duty of the Secretary of State for the Environment, as the member of the Government responsible to Parliament, to see that planning legislation is carried out in both the spirit and the letter of the law in England and Wales. He is expected to ensure consistency and continuity in planning decisions and policies. He is also responsible for housing, transport, recreation, local government administration and finance, for a number of public services provided by local government, and for new towns. His department has executive power in England only, the Welsh Office takes over in Wales. In Scotland, the Scottish Development Department, under the Secretary of State for Scotland, has similar responsibilities, as does the Ministry of Development in Northern Ireland.

To achieve coordination the department[1] works with other government departments and with local authorities to devise policies and to check and coordinate planning proposals both on a national scale and locally. If there is a dispute over planning decisions, whether over proposals for the future or over current development, the Secretary of State takes the final decision except on points of law. One of the department's most important tasks is writing the "regulations" and "directions" which fill in the legislative and administrative details as to how and when planning legislation should come into force. The department also issues circulars and bulletins offering guidance on methods of dealing with planning problems; it runs a research team and will, if necessary, take over regional planning tasks: for example, in 1969 to 1970 a specially recruited team worked on a policy for the southeast region, and this was published as the "Strategic Plan for the South East."

The other central government departments principally involved in landuse planning are those concerned with the coordination, use, and development of economic and social resources at national and regional levels; with

---

[1]All references to "the Secretary of State" and "the department" refer to the Secretary of State for, and the Department of, the Environment.

measures to promote and control the location of industrial and office expansion in an attempt to encourage growth in the less fortunate parts of the country; with the production and use of power resources; with agriculture; and with defense installations. In recent years there has been much reorganization of central government administration. Several "giant" departments have been formed from groups of Ministries with related tasks. The Department of the Environment and the Department of Trade and Industry are examples. There have also been some devolutions of responsibility to regional offices in these and other departments.[1] This has strengthened regional departmental administration but has not, of course, established any regional policymaking or executive unit in English government.[2]

The Part Played by Local Authorities. In Britain, local authorities play a very large part in the administration of many public services affecting everyday life, not least in town and country planning. Each local authority is controlled by a locally elected council and staffed by officers in local government service. Their duty is to implement, in the light of local circumstances, the provisions for public well-being enacted by Parliament.

Local Government before and after 1974. In England, one of the three systems of local government operates according to the type of area. These will continue until April 1, 1974, when a new system will come into operation which has been enacted in the Local Government Act, 1972. Far-reaching changes will be introduced especially in planning. Both systems are outlined below; however, the reader will appreciate that many details of the new system will be worked out only as the new local authorities take over, following their election in 1973 and the transfer of all powers in 1974.

An unique situation exists in Greater London. After the London Government Act of 1963, a two-tier system was established with the Greater London Council as the top tier authority[3] and 32 London boroughs and the Corporation of the City of London as the second tier. The Greater London Council is responsible for the overall development plan establishing, in cooperation with the second-tier authorities, the major policies on land-use communications, housing, shopping, and open space. Detailed development plans are the responsibility of the second-tier authorities, as is development control, only the largest issues and those of strategic importance being referred to the Greater London Council. The Local Government Act, 1972, does not alter the substance of the London Government

---

[1]See DOE circular 48/72 "Decentralization of the DOE's Administrative Work on Planning Matters."

[2]Nonelected Regional Economic Planning Councils have operated in an advisory capacity since 1964 and have become increasingly concerned in land-use planning. There are eight in England: Scotland, Wales, and Northern Ireland each count as one. A Royal Commission on Local Government Reform, reporting in 1969, advised that (among other radical reforms) elected provincial councils should be set up, and these would have a regional planning function. This proposal was not taken up.

[3]The Greater London Council covers an area of some 620 square miles (160,000 hectares) with a resident population of some 8 million.

Act, 1963: the Greater London Council and the London Boroughs are marginally affected by the latest reform.

Outside Greater London most large towns and some historic cities before 1974 constituted county boroughs. These were single-tier authorities handling all local-authority business; it followed that a county borough was a local planning authority. Over the rest of the country a two- and three-tier system operated. The councils of administrative counties[1] formed the top tier and dealt with countywide services, including planning. Urban and rural district councils—the second tier—provided more localized services (including housing) and, in rural districts only, parish councils formed a third and still more localized unit. County councils were required to delegate some planning decisions to districts with 60,000 people or more, and some in practice also delegated decisions to others though retaining responsibility for countywide planning policies and for decisions on the more important development proposals. District authorities and, usually, parish councils were consulted on development plan proposals.

The system of local government in England, by which planning was administered, was established by the end of the nineteenth century and operated until 1974. The great increase in population, the growth of conurbations and large towns, with economic and technological changes, combined to make the old pattern unsuited to mid-twentieth-century conditions. Many county and county borough areas were too small and too poor in terms of financial, land, and labor resources to tackle the problems of reconstruction or development of their economic, physical, and social environment. The object of local government reorganization was to establish areas which are big enough and wealthy enough to administer local government services adequately.

In recent years the nature of local government activity has been changing. Services such as gas and electricity are now supplied by nationalized industries. The government is in the process of reorganizing water and sewerage on a comprehensive basis and from April 1974 these services are administered by new regional water authorities, not by local authorities, and many public health functions have transferred to new regional and local health authorities. While these services have reorganized on a regional and national basis, local authorities have become increasingly involved in government activities concerned with the quality of life. Planning and social services are notable examples.

Local authorities have also become more anxious to coordinate their activities—to match policies in economic, physical, and social spheres to agreed objectives, and corporate planning techniques have been introduced. It is hoped that reorganization in 1974 will afford new opportunities for management reform[2] and corporate planning. However, taking into account

---

[1] Administrative counties are not always coterminous with geographical countries.

[2] Under the former system only county and county boroughs were local planning authorities; by no means all district councils engage trained planning staff.

the new service authorities and the division of responsibilities between new local authorities outlined below, it is clear that each of the new organizations will be responsible for only a part of the total government activity at local level and much cooperation is needed to achieve coordinated action and planning for the whole community. The introduction of corporate planning techniques in the new authorities will undoubtedly have a great deal of influence on the formation of policies for structure and local plans.

The Local Government Act of 1972 established a dual authority system of counties and districts everywhere. Six metropolitan counties are established in the conurbations centered on Newcastle-on-Tyne, Liverpool, Manchester, Leeds, Sheffield–Doncaster, and Birmingham. In these areas metropolitan counties have responsibility for highways and transport, for structure planning, and strategic planning control decisions. Each has some reserve housing powers to deal with overspill for example. The counties are the authorities for police, fire, and ambulance services. The metropolitan districts have responsibility for all other local government services including local planning and most development control. Elsewhere county councils (for convenience called shire counties) undertake the same services as metropolitan counties but in addition run the education and social services. County districts again undertake all the more local services and the local aspects of county services.

Under this new system all county and district councils are planning authorities. The counties are responsible for structure plans and all strategic development control decisions: the districts make local plans, unless special arrangements to the contrary are made, and they handle most development control and the great majority of work on local subjects such as conservation. The effect of the Act of 1972 is to treble the number of planning authorities.[1] Clearly, considerable efforts are needed to overcome the problems of shortage of trained staff and to coordinate policy-making and day-to-day decisions on development. The Act provides that a Development Plan Scheme shall be worked out by county and district establishing each authority's responsibilities as regards local plans and establishing a method for consultation.

Expanded Towns. Local authorities sometimes cooperate with each other, with the consent of the Minister, under the powers conferred by the Town Development Act of 1952 to arrange for industry and workers to move out of congested areas to towns which need new development. The Greater London Council is particularly active with such schemes and has made agreements with over 20 towns, some as far as 150 miles away.

New Towns. Special administrative arrangements have been made for the building of New Towns in Britain in the postwar period. The preliminary work on siting and land requirements is often commissioned from private consultants. Before a draft order for compulsory acquisition of land is published, the Ministry consults with the local authorities in the area,

---

[1] See "The New Local Authorities, Management and Structure," Baines Report, HMSO, 1972.

statutory contractors, landowners, and any other interested bodies. If there are objections to the draft order, a public inquiry is held before an order is confirmed. A development corporation is set up to prepare a master plan and to build and manage the New Town. The corporation is wholly financed from national funds. It is responsible for most building operations, but the local authority plays a large part in creating the New Town since it provides services such as education, welfare, public transport, police and fire services, and sometimes main drainage. Statutory services (water, gas, electricity) are provided by the usual suppliers.[1] It was originally intended that the New Towns should be taken over by local authorities on completion, but this has not proved feasible. Instead a New Towns Commission has been set up to supervise the final, slower stages of growth.[2] Its purpose is "to maintain and enhance the substantial assets of land and property that have been built up . . . while paying attention to the purpose for which the town was developed and to the needs and wishes of the people living there."[3]

The Development Plan Under the Town and Country Planning Act, 1962,[4] all local planning authorities are obliged to make careful surveys of their area and to estimate the needs over the next 20 years for housing, schools, industry, shopping, and roads. The authority is then to draw up proposals as to how these needs should be met in terms of land allocations, taking into account all they can discover by consultation with public and private organizations of the development likely to be needed. The proposals are shown on a map (the notation is specified) at a scale of 6 inches to the mile (about 10 centimeters to the kilometer) in county boroughs and 1 inch to the mile (about 1.5 centimeters to the kilometer) in county areas; county plans are supplemented by more detailed "town" maps for the urban areas within them. Town maps also show proposals for any areas of comprehensive development where special powers for land acquisition may be sought.

The development plan must be supported by a written statement which outlines the main proposals and by a program map showing when, during a 20-year period, they are expected to be implemented. The program is usually divided into 5-year periods, and the authority should revise its plan every 5 years.

When surveys, forecasts, and consultations are complete, the authority issues a draft plan (the same procedures operate on revision) which is made available for public inspection. Various prescribed notices are published in local papers and the London Gazette and a period of time is allowed to elapse so that people may consider the proposals. If there are objections,

---

[1]Electricity and gas are supplied throughout Britain by national public corporations. Water is supplied by a variety of local government and other public agencies.
[2]Crawley, Hatfield, Hemel Hempstead, and Welwyn Garden City were the first New Towns to be taken over by the commission.
[3]*Op. cit.* (COI reference pamphlet no. 9).
[4]This act is now the principal act: it consolidates planning legislation from 1947 to 1962. Its provisions regarding development plans remain in force until the Minister directs a local authority to initiate those of the 1968 act described below.

a public inquiry is held by an inspector—a civil servant and qualified planner—who hears and considers the objections and reports to the Minister. The Minister, in due course, decides whether or not to approve the plan and what if any modifications should be made. Once his seal is set upon a development plan, all development which departs substantially from it must be open to objection from the public; people whose interests are affected may demand a public inquiry into the departure. This does not, however, imply that permission for any development in accordance with the plan will automatically be granted. The local authority may refuse permission despite its provisions if they see good reasons for doing so.

Development Control   Planning permission for all but relatively minor development must be obtained from the local authority. The meaning of development is fairly rigorously defined and covers almost all physical change or substantial change of use of property and land.[1]

The local authority may grant permission, with or without conditions, as to how development should be carried out or the proposals modified. Under provisions of the 1968 act, permissions are valid for only a limited period.

If the authority refuses permission, the applicant may appeal to the Minister. The case may be argued in writing, but if either the applicant or the authority wish, a public inquiry is held by a Ministry inspector. Since January 1969, inspectors have been empowered to decide disputes in certain cases, such as small-scale residential development, and it is hoped that the types of inquiry which they will decide without reference to the Minister will be increased. In all other cases the inspector reports to the Minister, whose decision is final and may only be challenged on a point of law through normal legal channels.

Planning permission may be revoked or modified by the local authority in certain circumstances and with due compensation to the developer. Should development take place without planning permission, the authority has power to enforce a decision against the development and to insist on its being undone.

The Town and Country Planning Act, 1968   The Town and Country Planning Act of 1968, now the Act of 1971, was mentioned earlier as an example of recent legislation which has revised law and administration to meet needs that were unforeseen in the 1940s.

Essentially, devolution of responsibility to local planning authorities and public participation in planning decisions are the key themes of the new procedures. Measures are also introduced to speed up administrative procedures, particularly to avoid the long delays which have occurred in approving development plans and in deciding appeals.

Under the act, a two-tier system for making and approving development plans is gradually being introduced, first into groups of larger authorities covering the major provincial conurbations. Meanwhile the "old" system will continue to operate in other parts of the country, though development

---

[1]See the current General Development Order and Use Classes Order.

plans will be revised only with the agreement of the Secretary of State. Under the new system, the overall plan is known as the "structure plan" and shows the framework for future development; it will continue to be approved by the Secretary of State. Local plans, filling in the details, are largely the responsibility of the district authority.

The structure plan consists of a written document explaining policies for the future development in broad terms and illustrated by diagrams, *not* maps. Like the development plan, it is supported by surveys and forecasts, though these put heavier emphasis on the land requirements of the local economy and transport networks. The program for development is outlined and the costs of implementation related to estimated resources. It is not necessarily defined in 5-year periods but is as realistic as possible for each type of development (for example, it may be easier to relate needs to resources over time for housing than for open space). The structure plan does not show comprehensive development areas; instead it indicates where action area plans (see below) may be made, and these may cover comprehensive development proposals. New and simpler provisions for compulsory acquisition of land are made in the act.

The procedure for making and approving structure plans is very similar to that for the development plan except that the people in the area are encouraged to take part in drawing up policies right from the beginning. The local authority advertises that it is about to make a plan and gives people an opportunity to say what they think it should contain before the draft is produced. They have the same right as before to object to proposals in the draft plan. The Town and Country Planning (Amendment) Act, 1972, however, enables the Secretary of State to amend the form of the Public Inquiry into objections so as to expedite the proceedings.

Local plans are made largely at the discretion of the local planning authority. Provided that the Secretary of State is satisfied that the public is fully informed and can comment on the early stages of plan making and that the local plan conforms to an approved structure plan, the Secretary of State takes no further part in the process. The local plan progresses through publication, objection, and inquiry stages as usual, though in this case the local authority may appoint the inspector and its decision on his report is final. A resolution by the council to adopt the plan will bring it into effect. Local plans may be many and various. They may cover one aspect of policy over all or part of the authority's area, or they may cover all aspects in only one part of it. The most important type is probably the action area plan which shows details of impending development in a degree of detail sufficient for a developer's brief.

In all cases, local plans consist of a map with an Ordnance Survey[1] base supported by a written statement. The map is the more important document.

---

[1]The Ordnance Survey of Britain is the independent government cartographic department. It produces very accurate maps to a variety of scales. The most widely used are $\frac{1}{1250}$ in cities and either one inch or 6 inches to one mile (either 10 or 1.5 centimeters to the kilometer—approximately) in rural areas. Maps are revised according to the rate of change in land use as between one area and another.

No specific time limits are set on revision for either structure or local plans; it is possible to update them as necessary.

BIBLIOGRAPHY: Report of the Planning Advisory Group. *The Future of Development Plans,* HMSO, London, 1965; D. Heap, Outline of Planning Law, 5th ed., Sweet & Maxwell, London, 1969; *Town and Country Planning CMD* 3333, HMSO, 1969; *The Development Plan Manual,* Department of the Environment, HMSO, 1970; Central Office of Information pamphlets: *1—Local Government in Britain; 9—Town and Country Planning in Britain; 40—The Central Government in Britain,* HMSO, 1970; Department of the Environment Circular 44/71, "Town and Country Planning Act 1968," Part 1—*The Town and Country Planning (Structure and Local Plans) Regulations, 1971;* S. Ade Smith, *Constitutional and Administrative Law,* Penguin Education, London, 1971; J. K. Friend and N. Jessop, *Local Government and Strategic Choice,* Tavistock, 1971; Department of the Environment Circular, *Public Participation,* 1972; J. B. Cullingworth, *Town and Country Planning in Britain,* Town & Country Hall Series 8, Allen & Unwin. London, 1972.   —D. A. DENNIER

Professional Practice   The practice of town planning in Britain is divided between those in local government employment (the majority); those in central government service or New Town corporations; and those engaged in some form of private practice. There are about 4,600 members of the Royal Town Planning Institute, but all figures for those engaged in practice are approximate, since some members of the RTPI do not practice planning and an unknown but growing number of practitioners are not members of the RTPI.

Planners who are local government officers are employed by counties and districts to carry out the duties imposed on these local authorities by the Town and Country Planning Acts, which are broadly the same throughout Great Britain and Northern Ireland.

The work varies greatly in complexity between the largest and smallest authorities, but it is the same in its general nature. Surveys are made of the resources and needs of the area, of existing land uses and communications, and the quality of existing developments. Outline proposals are then made for meeting needs over a period of time, and these, including the probable benefits, costs, objections, and timing, are then discussed with interested public and private organizations of all kinds. Revised proposals are then submitted to the Secretary of State and are approved subject to desirable changes. Detailed programs are then prepared for the first stages of intended works, and these are published and objections heard. Progress is reviewed from time to time. Guidance of current building development forms a large and vital part of the work, as proposed developments may be in conflict with long-term aims of the planning authority.

Those engaged on this work are necessarily drawn from a number of professional and academic disciplines. Statistical surveys and forecasts are mainly undertaken by economists and geographers, and detailed development plans and guidance of current development are the concern of architects, engineers, and lawyers. An increasing proportion of the professional grades hold a town planning qualification, often in addition to another professional or academic qualification. It is now customary for men and women to enter local planning services as planning assistants at about 23 years of age. Promotion thereafter is dependent on merit and experience. The chief planning officers of large authorities have great responsibilities and are well paid.

Central government employs a far smaller number of men and women of similar training. Some of these are engaged on research or the production of advisory publications on planning subjects. The majority are in the big Department of the Environment and examine and advise on plans submitted by local planning authorities and discuss them with other government departments and public corporations concerned such as the Department of Trade and Industry.

Those engaged in private practice of regional and town planning are relatively few in number and tend to be flexibly organized to meet a varying demand. Approximately 15 percent of the members of the Royal Town Planning Institute are engaged in private practice within the United Kingdom. Private practitioners fall into two main groups. A few larger firms combine regional and town planning, and sometimes traffic planning, with the practice of architecture, and they use the latter to support the former. Commissions for one type of work may lead to a commission for the other. The remaining practitioners are drawn from several disciplines and usually offer some special skill: economic or social or cost-benefit studies, or traffic, architectural, or landscape design. Both the large and small firms tend to recruit or regroup according to the work on offer, and both draw on university staffs for assistance in specialist fields.

A large growth in the numbers of practitioners in Britain is frequently forecast, and numbers are growing. There have been two significant features of the growth in the past decade. The first is the increase in the number of different skills engaged in regional and town planning and associated activities, including almost all the social and analytical sciences. Secondly, growth has been concentrated in public service, central or local. Accurate figures are unobtainable for private practitioners because of the number of firms that combine town planning with some other activity, but it is unlikely that the number of qualified persons engaged full time in private practice has grown in recent years.   —H. MYLES WRIGHT

Education and Training   The education of planners in Britain is guided by the Royal Town Planning Institute. The institute governs and conducts examinations for candidates, and its syllabus serves as framework for certain approved university courses which qualify for exemption from these examinations. The first examination syllabus was published in 1916 and amended in 1919 in time for the first examination in 1920. In 1930 a joint examination board, including representatives of the Royal Institute of British Architects, the Institution of Municipal Engineers, and the Institution of Chartered Surveyors, was set up to coordinate planning examinations. In 1931 this board issued a syllabus for an intermediate examination which was open to candidates who had no other professional qualifications. This marked the beginning of the growth of a town planning discipline in its own right.

During the Second World War, there was a great upsurge of interest in planning in Britain which culminated in the Town and Country Planning Act of 1947. To meet the demand for planners which resulted from this act, a committee under the chairmanship of Sir George Schuster was appointed by the Minister of Town and Country Planning "to report what qualifications are necessary or desirable for persons engaged in Town and Country Planning." This committee concluded that planning required various specialized skills and suggested that the basis for membership of the Town Planning Institute should be substantially widened to include holders of degrees in subjects such as geography and economics.

During the 1950s there was a steady growth in the number of people entering the institute. An increasingly large number entered through schools of planning which awarded degrees or diplomas recognized as giving exemption from the final examination. These schools offered two main types of courses: 4- or 5-year undergraduate courses for entrants straight from school, and 3-year part-time or 2-year full-time postgraduate courses for graduates in allied disciplines. The first schools to be recognized by the institute were the department of civic design at the University of Liverpool (established in 1909), the department of town and country planning at the University of London (1914), and the department of town and country planning at the University of Newcastle (1932). In 1968 there were 12 schools of planning in Great Britain and 5 overseas recognized by the institute for exemption from its examinations; in addition, there were a number of recently established schools which can be expected to seek official recognition in the next few years.

In the 1960s there has been a further great upsurge of interest in planning, and this is reflected in the growing number of courses given by university departments other than those directly concerned with town planning. These relate mainly to specialized aspects of the subject, such as transport studies, urban design, and economic and regional planning, and are not recognized by the Royal Town Planning Institute as affording exemption from its examinations. —F. I. Masser

Institutions A large number of institutions are associated with regional and town planning in Britain. These may be very broadly divided into professional, research or educational, and propagandist.

The central professional body is the Royal Town Planning Institute (RTPI), founded in 1914 and having a membership of 4,600 plus 4,000 student members. Other professions concerned with the development of land also have a close interest in town planning: e.g., the Royal Institute of British Architects, the Institution of Civil Engineers, the Royal Institution of Chartered Surveyors, the Institution of Municipal Engineers, and the Institute of Landscape Architects. Members of the RTPI may also be members of one of these bodies. Some barristers and solicitors are also legal members of the RTPI. The annual Town and Country Planning Summer School is closely associated with the RTPI and discusses a broad range of subjects. It is attended by planners from many countries, elected members of local authorities, and other interested persons.

Government institutions interested in aspects of town planning include (in addition to the ministries mentioned in the next paragraph) the Building Research Station, Road Research Laboratory, Commission for the New Towns, Countryside Commission, and the Land Commission.

Research bearing on regional and town planning is conducted by many organizations, including sections of government departments. The main supervising Ministry in planning is the Department of the Environment, which looks after town and country planning, housing, local government, and transport. The Department of Trade and Industry is concerned with regional economic planning. Others interested include the broad-based research societies like PEP (Political and Economic Planning) and the Dartington Amenity Research Trust; the recently established Centre for Environmental Studies and the Regional Studies Association; and many university departments. The scope of research bearing on town planning has greatly widened in the past decade and now interests university departments of architecture, economics, sociology, geography, traffic and transport, building science, and others.

Education for town planning (see above) has become increasingly centered in universities or institutions likely to become universities. Fourteen institutions in Britain offer courses which exempt graduates from examination of the Royal Town Planning Institute, and up to 20 other courses are concerned with subjects closely associated with regional or town planning.

Numerous societies exist to encourage public interest in town planning and related subjects. Some of these exist to promote general interest and review most aspects of the subject. Others have narrower objectives. The Town and Country Planning Association is among the most influential of the societies that promote a general interest and its journal reviews a wide range of problems and solutions. The Civic Trust concentrates more on actual improvements—the preservation and conservation of parts of towns. The National Housing and Town Planning Council, Nature Conservancy, the CPRE (Council for the Preservation of Rural England), the Institute of Transport, British Road Federation, Inland Waterways Association, and many other bodies including civic societies in a number of cities have specialized or local interests indicated by their titles. There are also a large number of societies, mainly with academic membership, which bring together persons interested in regional, urban, or land-use studies.

—H. Myles Wright

Traditions of Planning—The Structure of Britain The era of architectural town planning was initiated in Britain by Inigo Jones's layout for Covent Garden, London, and found its most comprehensive expression in Wren's unrealized plan for London after the Great Fire of 1666. The postwar reconstruction of London demonstrated the inadequacy of the purely architectural approach, which had become increasingly evident during the interwar years. Increasing mobility, the accelerating rate of economic growth, and social change with its attendant problems of the distribution and movement of population in relation to the location of industry required a scientific expertise beyond the competence of the architect or engineer, who had hitherto played the predominant role in planning. The 1947 Town Planning Act, with its emphasis on the use of land, added a new dimension which transformed planning thought and practice—a transformation that made the Beaux Arts interpretation of planning history which was concerned only with planned cities quite inadequate in this decade. In short, the task of the planning historian is now to explain *how the land came to be used* as it is *used* today.

Geographical and Climatic Conditions Geologically, Britain is divided into two parts by a line drawn from Teesmouth to Exmouth. Approximately north and west lies the Highland Zone, made up of the older, harder rocks of the Paleozoic Age. These give rise to the mountainous areas, which reach over 3,000 feet (about 900 meters) in the northwest of England and Wales and over 4,000 feet (about 1,200 meters) in Scotland. The rivers are often shallow, fast-flowing, and broken rapids. The Lowland Zone to the south and east is made up of the softer rocks of the Mesozoic and Cainozoic formations. These have weathered to undulating forms averaging only a few hundred feet in height; rivers wide, deep, and slow-moving give access to the interior from the Humber, the Wash, the Thames, and Southampton Water.

The prevailing southwest winds give a much heavier precipitation of rain in the Highland Zone, varying between 40 inches (100 centimeters) and over 100 inches (254 centimeters), compared with the lowland zone, which varies between 18 inches (45 centimeters) on parts of the east coast and 40 inches (100 centimeters) on the edge of the Paleozoic outcrop. In the northern half of Britain, summers are cool, with mild winters in the west and cold winters in the east. In the south the summers are warm, with mild winters in the west, but cold winters in the east.

Natural Vegetation The better-drained soils of the Lowland Zone, such as chalk, limestone, sands, and gravels, support associations of heaths, oak-woods, ashwoods, or beechwoods; whereas the heavier soils, such as clays, carry the damp oakwood which formed such an effective barrier to communications in early times. In Roman and early medieval times, Britain was heavily wooded with large areas of undrained fens, marshlands, and mosses.

Historical Perspective An appreciation of this physical differentiation can assist in understanding the initial location and subsequent growth of settlements. The more accessible Lowland Zone was easily overrun, whereas in the Highland Zone invasion was difficult and resistance protracted. In the former, invading cultures were "infused," and in the latter "absorbed." Each fresh invasion tended to divorce its predecessors from the stimulus of the Continent.

The Roman Occupation of Britain The peopling of Britain had been in progress for thousands of years before the Roman invasion in 43 A.D., and continued

RIGHT: Britain's Structure. *Halder MacKinder (1907) and Cyril Fox (1932) called attention to the historical significance of the structural and climatic differentiation between the Highland and Lowland Zones of Britain. The concept was latent in F. Haverfield and G. Macdonald (1924). Fox's interpretation has been contested, qualified, supplemented, and amended. The significance of loams and gravels was stressed by S. W. Wooldridge and D. L. Linton (1933), and H. J. Fleure (1948) directed attention to the development of the 'fall zones' at the base of the Pennines and the Cambrian Massif during the Industrial Revolution. The concept has been further developed by E. G. Bowen (1944), R. G. Collingwood (1937), and E. E. Evans (1964). (Making use of inter alia Cyril Fox, The Personality of Britain, Cardiff, 1947, Map B, and S. W. Wooldridge, The Anglo Saxon Settlement, in H. C. Darby's An Historical Geography of England before 1800, Cambridge, 1936, Fig. 14.)*

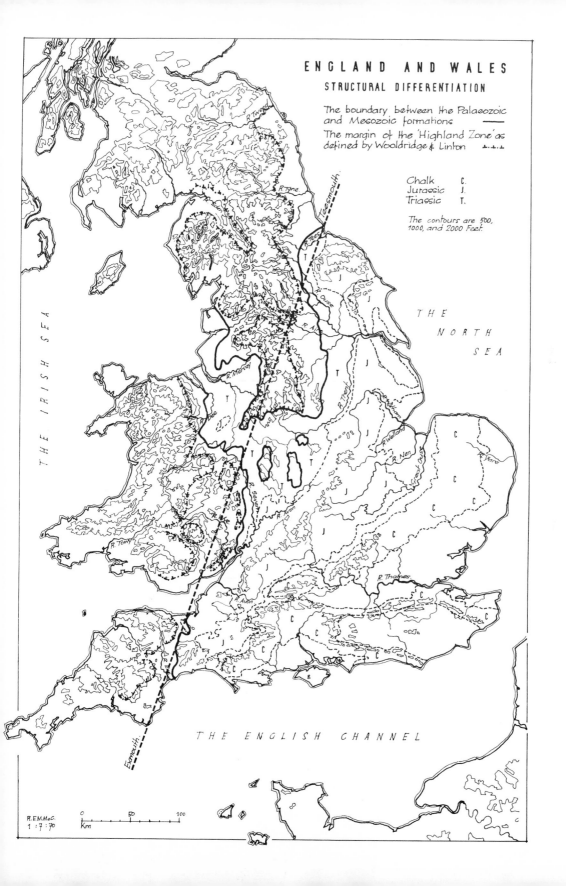

ENGLAND AND WALES
STRUCTURAL DIFFERENTIATION

The boundary between the Palaeozoic
and Mesozoic formations ———

The margin of the 'Highland Zone' as
defined by Wooldridge & Linton ┴┴┴

Chalk   C.
Jurassic   J.
Triassic   T.

The contours are 500,
1000, and 2000 Feet.

THE NORTH SEA

THE IRISH SEA

THE ENGLISH CHANNEL

R.EM.McC.
1:7:70

0   50   100
Km

ENGLAND AND WALES

NATURAL VEGATION ABOUT 500 A.D.

Open Forest
Dense Forest
Fenlands.

Shaded areas indicate the probable
extent of the Royal Forests during
the Middle Ages.

THE NORTH SEA

THE IRISH SEA

THE ENGLISH CHANNEL

Teesmouth

Exmouth

R.E.M.Mc
24:7:70.

0   50   100
Km.

LEFT: *Natural Vegetation of England. In Roman and Saxon times when man had much less control over his environment, the areas of "damp" oakwood on the heavy clays, fenlands, marshes, and waterways presented effective barriers to movement and occupation. The Antonine itinerary, a third-century road book, directed travellers from London to Chichester to go by Silchester and Winchester. Similar detours were recommended for the roads from London to York and Chester to Carlisle. The damp oak forest masked the Midland Gap between the Pennines and the Cambrian Massif. The hatched areas indicate the extent of the Royal Forests, which had become quite extensive by the fifteenth century. The Royal Forests came under a separate law, which was regarded as an expression of the Royal will.*

ABOVE: *Isca Silurum (Caerleon). One of the three legionary fortresses located at the boundary of the Highland Zone, it covered approximately 50 acres with four gateways, and small lookout towers at 150-foot intervals for sentries. The fortress consisted of the legionary headquarters, the commander's house, stores and magazines, barracks, and stables. Outside was the amphitheater. A legion consisted of about 5,000 men. (Reconstruction by Alan Sorrell, H. V. Nash-Williams.* The Roman Legion Fortress at Caerleon, Monmouthshire, *Cardiff, 1946, pl. III.)*

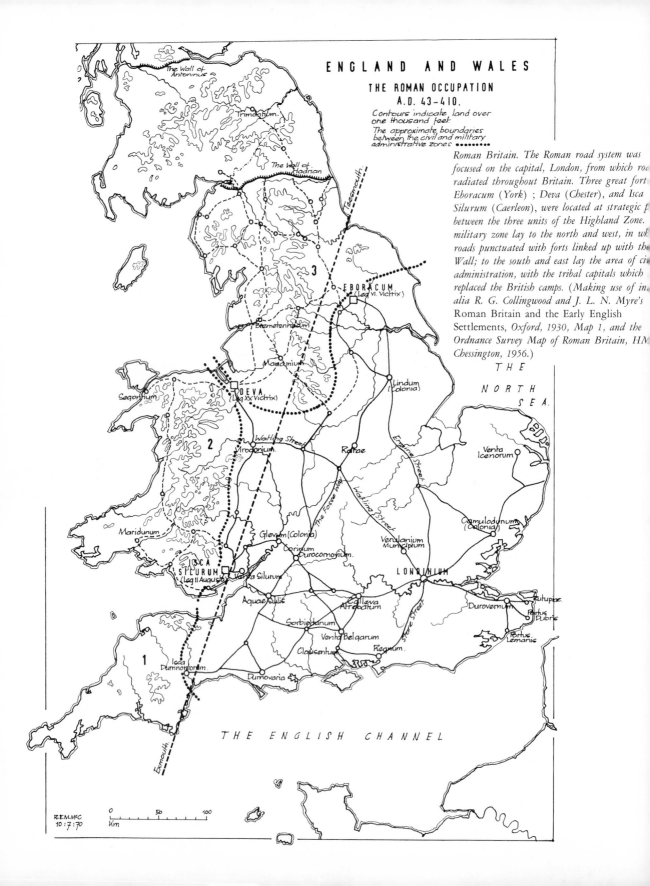

ENGLAND AND WALES

THE ROMAN OCCUPATION
A.D. 43–410.

Contours indicate land over
one thousand feet.
The approximate boundaries
between the civil and military
administrative zones ●●●●●●●●

*Roman Britain. The Roman road system was
focused on the capital, London, from which road
radiated throughout Britain. Three great fort
Eboracum (York) ; Deva (Chester), and Isca
Silurum (Caerleon), were located at strategic p
between the three units of the Highland Zone.
military zone lay to the north and west, in wh
roads punctuated with forts linked up with the
Wall; to the south and east lay the area of ci
administration, with the tribal capitals which
replaced the British camps. (Making use of in
alia R. G. Collingwood and J. L. N. Myre's
Roman Britain and the Early English
Settlements, Oxford, 1930, Map 1, and the
Ordnance Survey Map of Roman Britain, HM
Chessington, 1956.)*

THE
NORTH
SEA.

THE ENGLISH CHANNEL

The Wall of Antoninus

Trimontium

The Wall of Hadrian

Tinomouth

3

EBORACUM
(Leg.VI.Victrix)

Bremetennacum

Mancunium

DEVA
(Leg XX Victrix)

Segontium

Lindum
(Colonia)

2

Watling Street

Vriconium

Ratae

The Fosse Way

Watling Street

Ermine Street

Venta
Icenorum

Maridunum

Glevum (Colonia)

Corinium

Durocornovium

Verulanium
Municipium

Camulodunum
(Colonia)

ISCA
SILURUM
(Leg II Augusta)

Venta Silurum

LONDINIUM

Aquae Sulis

Calleva
Atrebatum

Durovernum

Rutupiae

Portus
Dubris

Gorbiodunum

Venta Belgarum

Stone Street

Portus
Lemanis

1

Isca
Dumnoniorum

Clausentum

Regnum

Dumnovaria

Exmouth

R.E.M.MɛC
10:7:70

0   50   100
km

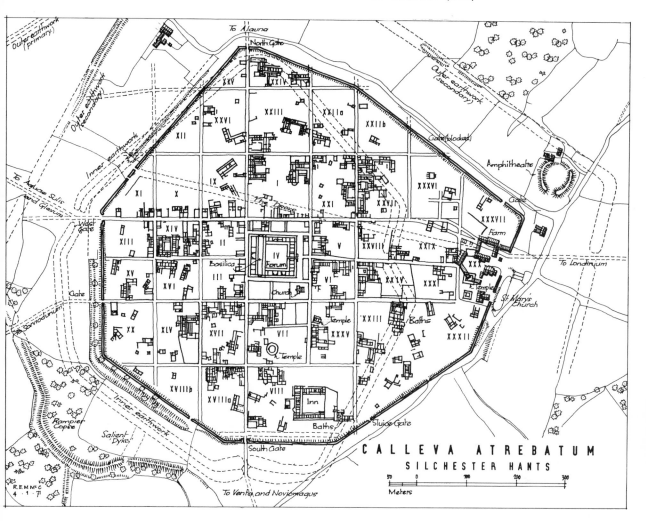

C A L L E V A   A T R E B A T U M
SILCHESTER HANTS

for over 500 years after the evacuation in the fifth century. In a few years the Romans overran the Lowland Zone and planted settlements at Colchester, Verulanium, and London. London was made the capital, and it was the center from which the road system radiated throughout Britain. Three legionary fortresses, York, Chester, and Caerleon, were located at key points on the edge of the Highland Zone. From these, military roads protected by forts led through the passes and joined the Wall. In the south and east were the tribal capitals, such as Winchester and Silchester. Unlike the military settlements, these were laid out on a gridiron plan with a forum at the center. Rural society, based on the valla, flourished in the south and east, especially during the fourth century, when urban centers were declining. The population was probably just over a million. London may have had 15,000 inhabitants, and a small settlement such as Silchester only 2,000 inhabitants. The Romans developed trade and industry. Six years after the

Calleva Atrebatum (Silchester). The capital of the Atrebates, one of the Roman settlements which did not survive. It was laid out on a gridiron plan. The original orientation was altered, and the later alignment cut through the portico of the public baths. The population has been variously estimated between 2,000 and 5,000. The walls were not related to the grid. (Based on B. C. Boon, Blegic and Roman Silchester, Excavations of Silchester with an Excursus on the Early History of Silchester, Archaeologia, cii, 1969, 1–81.)

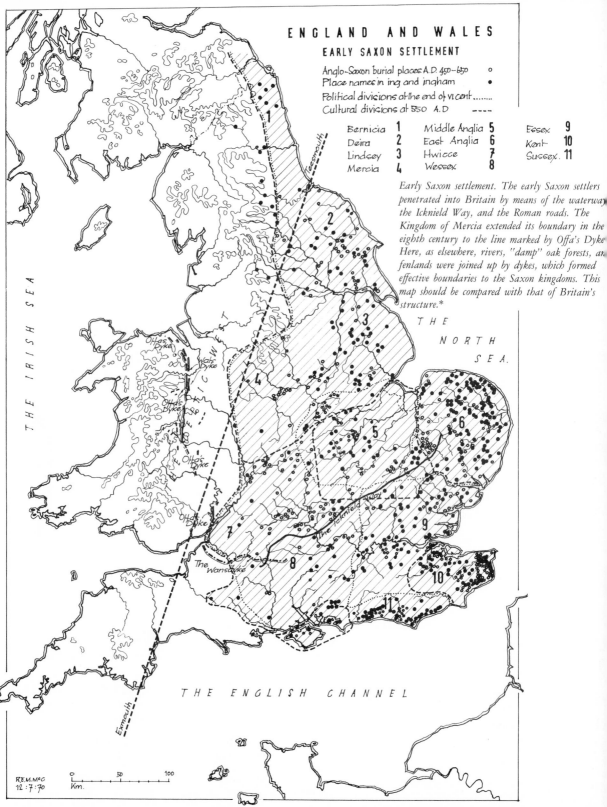

ENGLAND AND WALES
EARLY SAXON SETTLEMENT

Anglo-Saxon burial places A.D. 450–650   o
Place names in ing and ingham   •
Political divisions at the end of vi cent ....
Cultural divisions at 550 A.D   -----

Bernicia 1	Middle Anglia 5	Essex 9
Deira 2	East Anglia 6	Kent 10
Lindsey 3	Hwicce 7	Sussex 11
Mercia 4	Wessex 8	

*Early Saxon settlement. The early Saxon settlers penetrated into Britain by means of the waterway the Icknield Way, and the Roman roads. The Kingdom of Mercia extended its boundary in the eighth century to the line marked by Offa's Dyke. Here, as elsewhere, rivers, "damp" oak forests, and fenlands were joined up by dykes, which formed effective boundaries to the Saxon kingdoms. This map should be compared with that of Britain's structure.**

THE IRISH SEA

THE NORTH SEA.

THE ENGLISH CHANNEL

Offa's Dyke
Wat's Dyke
Offa's Dyke
Offa's Dyke
Offa's Dyke
The Wansdyke
The Icknield Way
Tees mouth
Exmouth

R.E.M.MᶜᶜC
12:7:70
Km.
0   50   100

(Making use of inter alia, E. T. Leeds, The Archaelogy of the Anglo-Saxon Settlement, Oxford, 1913, Figs. 1 and 4.)

invasion they were working the lead deposits in the Mendips, those of Flintshire in 74 A.D., and those of Yorkshire in 81 A.D. They established a thriving pottery industry, Castor ware becoming quite celebrated.

Anglo-Saxon Settlements Anglo-Saxons penetrated the Lowland Zone along the waterways, the Roman roads, and the Icknield Way. In the southeast, settlements were on the lines of communication, and elsewhere they were off the lines of communication as in Lincolnshire, where the Roman road forms the boundary between the parishes with spring-line settlements on either side. The early progress of settlement can be traced from the distribution of pagan cemeteries and place names ending in "ing," "ingham," "ton," and "ley." The damp forests and undrained lands formed effective boundaries between tribal groups. The Saxons had quickly occupied the Lowland Zone, but it was 200 years before they had settlements on the west coast, and it was not until the thirteenth century that their descendants were able to subdue the Highland Zone. Domesday Book shows that by the eleventh century England had become a land of "vills," whose distribution largely corresponds to that of the English village today.

Settlements off the line of communication. In Kent Saxon settlements were located on the lines of communication, whereas in less settled areas further north they were off the lines of communication. The map shows settlements in Cambridgeshire off the line of communication. They are located some distance on either side of the Icknield Way, which forms the boundary between the two parishes, and also on either side of the Roman road which crosses the Icknield Way. In a similar manner, settlements are located on the spring line along both sides of the Roman road leading from Lincoln to the Wash. (After J. Jones, A Human Geography of Cambridgeshire, *London, 1924, Fig. 8.)*

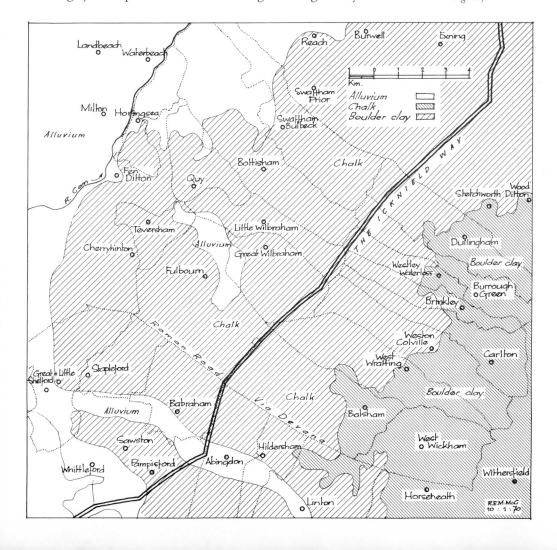

The Manor and the Open Field System Agricultural economy was based on manorial institutions, under which a community of dependent cultivators held land in return for services to the lord of the manor. The arable lands, consisting of two or more open fields made up of individually owned strips, were collectively cultivated on a 3-year crop rotation. One-third of the land was left fallow each year to recover its fertility. There were many variations in the general system, as in East Anglia and Kent, which in the west the Celtic system prevailed.

Medieval Towns Urban origins in Britain is a complex subject, and it is unlikely that any single explanation will be found to be of more than limited application. The evidence suggest that all the Roman towns except Exeter were abandoned and later reoccupied: important exceptions are Wroxeter, Caistor, and Silchester. The essential prerequisite for urban growth was the acquisition of a charter which conferred the right of electing officers and controlling the trade of the town.

Planned towns usually show traces of rectilinear form in their layout. Oxford, probably laid out by King Edward in the tenth century, shows such a form, as do Ludlow and Bury St. Edmunds, both of which were built in the eleventh century by the Normans. The most active period of town planning in England was about the beginning of the thirteenth century, toward the end of which, the activity was extended to Wales. In 1220, Bishop le Poer moved his cathedral from Old Sarum to the banks of the Avon, where he laid out a new town on a gridiron plan. The most impressive builder of towns was Edward I (1272–1307). In 1288 he replaced old Winchelsea with a new settlement laid out in checkerboard form. He restored Berwick upon Tweed and extended the port of Kingston upon Hull. After he had crushed Welsh resistance, he planned a number of settlements in North Wales, the most spectacular being Caernarvon and Conway (1283). (*See illustrations to* EDWARD I.)

Population Distribution The poll tax returns (1377) show that most of the population was located in the Lowland Zone, with the greatest concentration in East Anglia and the east Midlands. The total population was about 2 million. London may have reached 30,000; York, 11,000; Bristol, 10,000; and Coventry, 7,000.

Medieval Roads Although the Roman road system had fallen into decay, Watling Street, Ermine Street, and Fosse Way, together with the Icknield Way, were the four roads that enjoyed the king's peace as late as the eleventh century. Gough's fourteenth-century map shows that London had fully reestablished its dominant position as the focal point of the road system given to it by the Romans. Fosse Way still survives as part of the road between Bristol and Doncaster. It is noticeable, however, that the Highland Zone was not as well served as in Roman times. The discovery of England really began in the sixteenth century when John Leland published his itinerary. The chroniclers, such as Holinshed and the great Camden, and mapmakers such as Norden, Saxton, and Speed, described and portrayed the extent and wonder of the realm that was England.

A three-year crop rotation. In early medieval times the Open Field system, with its dispersed strips of land, farmed on a three-crop rotation, with the sharing of manpower and equipment, was an effective method of winning land from scrub and forest, and of establishing a viable agricultural economy. However, before the end of the Middle Ages the Open Field system had outlived its usefulness. The scattered units were wasteful in time and labor and inhibited progress. The introduction of root crops, legumes, and clovers eliminated the necessity for fallow, thus appreciably increasing the area under crops. These gains were consolidated by the Enclosure Movement, which made possible better drainage and the specialized cultivation of plants and breeding of livestock. On the other hand, these revolutionary changes inflicted great hardships on the poorer landowners and resulted in a change in the social structure of the rural population. (Based on H. C. Darby, An Historical Geography of England and Wales to 1800, Cambridge, 1936, p. 192.)

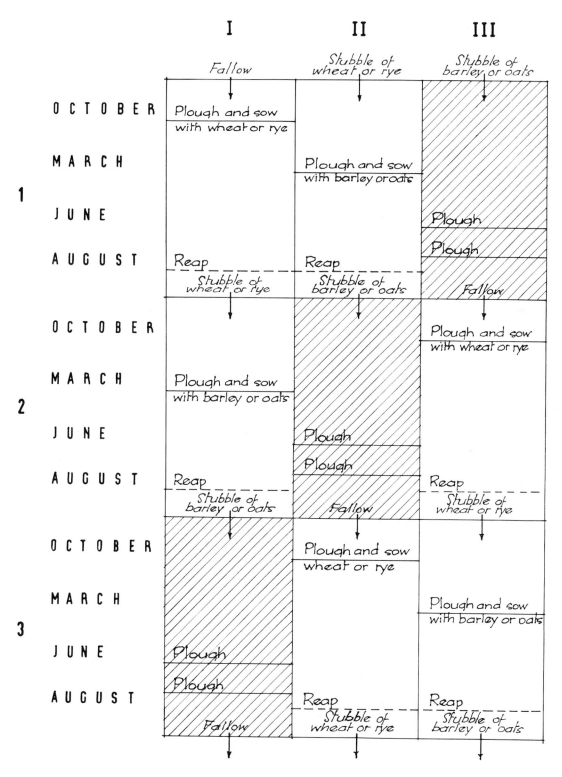

Dissolution of the Monasteries, and the Great Estates Under the acts of 1536 and 1539 the monasteries, their revenues, and their lands passed to the Crown and subsequently to the lay lords, who either adapted them as dwellings or used them for building materials for the great mansions which were then replacing the obsolete castles. Many were erected at this time: Cowdray (1492–1548), Compton Wyngates (1450–1512), Longleat (1550–1580), and Montacute (1580–1601).

Gardens were laid out in a formal manner with terraces, walls, piers, and topiary work as Canons Ashby. The influence of André Le Nôtre (1613–1700) became evident in the introduction of vistas and formal pools, as at Wrest Park and Badminton. It was William Kent (1684–1748) "who leapt the fence and saw all nature was a garden." At Stowe he introduced encircling belts of trees, tree clumps, and irregular pools, elements which were later developed by Lancelot "Capability" Brown (1715–1783), whose greatest work was the landscaping of Blenheim. His successor, Humphrey Repton (1752–1818), coined the term "landscape architect." The replanning of the great estates often necessitated the resiting of the village, as at Castle Howard, Nuneham Courtenay, and Milton Abbas. The charm of the English village is partly due to its intimate scale, derived from low ceiling heights, and the use of local materials which gives to each area its unique character.

The grandeur and horror experienced by travelers crossing the Alps during the "grand tour" helped them to appreciate the paintings of Salvator Rosa (1615–1673). The acquisition of his paintings and those of Claude Lorraine (1600–1682) played an important part in inculcating a new attitude to landscape. The writings of Edmund Burke in 1750 and those of Uvedale Price (1747–1829) and Richard Payne Knight (1750–1824) helped to develop the concept of the "picturesque" which preceded the romantic age. The Rev. William Gilpin (1724–1804) in his writings and paintings and later Wordsworth (1770–1850) called attention to the outstanding beauty of Lakeland, which eventually became England's largest national park.

The observations on landscape during the seventeenth and eighteenth centuries by travelers such as Defoe (1660–1731), Pepys (1632–1704), and Cobbett (1762–1835) were as far removed from the rapturous enjoyment of nature reflected in Irish, Welsh, and Latin literature of the early Middle Ages as the terror-haunted forests of Beowulf (eighth century ?). Even Johnson (1709–1784), gazing on the 600-foot escarpment of Hawkstone, remarked on "the awfulness of its shades, the horror of its precipices." The gradual rediscovery of the wonder of nature can be traced from Chaucer (1340?–1400) to Wordsworth (1770?–1850) through Thompson, Dyer, Collins, and Gray. In 1716 Shaftesbury in the *Moralist* had directed attention beyond the formal garden to the everlasting hills. Addison (1672–1719) anticipated Kent in claiming "all nature as a garden." Although the picturesque was essentially a "composed" landscape, it played a contributory part in inculcating an appreciation of the scenery of the highland zone. As early as 1750, Killarney was called "an enchanted place," and in 1770 Joseph Craddock traveled in Wales for "the purpose of enjoying scenery." Mean-

OPPOSITE PAGE: *Population Distribution in the Middle Ages. The replacement of the forged Diploma by the Anglo Saxon venacular Writ is evidence of the gradual development of a competent Saxon administration. This made it possible for the illiterate Norman Conqueror to institute the Domesday Inquest. That it was a Geld Book has been seriously contested. There can be little doubt that it was intended to legalize the spoilation of lands and act as the title deeds of the new nobility. Estimates of population distribution based on these returns suggest that the most heavily populated areas were in the center of the Lowland Zone, with the greatest concentration in Norfolk and Suffolk. Although the population had increased by the fifteenth century, the relative distribution had not substantially changed apart from a marked increase in Leicestershire and Northamptonshire. (After An Historical Geography of England before 1800, edited by H. C. Darby, Cambridge, 1936, Fig. 30.)*

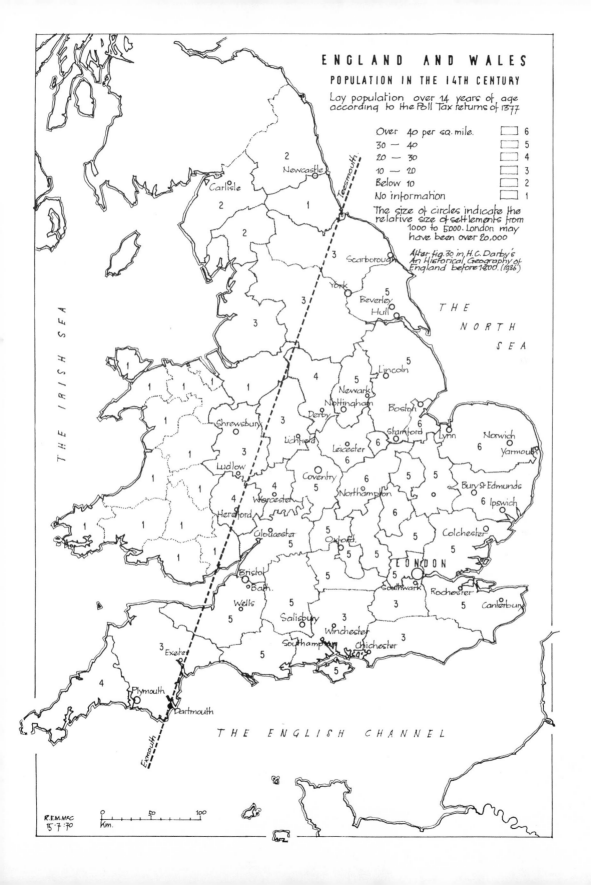

ENGLAND AND WALES

POPULATION IN THE 14TH CENTURY

Lay population over 14 years of age
according to the Poll Tax returns of 1377

Over 40 per sq. mile.		6
30 — 40		5
20 — 30		4
10 — 20		3
Below 10		2
No information		1

The size of circles indicate the
relative size of settlements from
1000 to 5000. London may
have been over 20,000

After fig. 30 in, H.C. Darby's
An Historical Geography of
England before 1800. (1936)

THE IRISH SEA

THE NORTH SEA

THE ENGLISH CHANNEL

Newcastle 2
Carlisle 2
2
1
2
3 Scarborough
York 5
Beverley
Hull
3
3
THE
1 NORTH
1 SEA
1 4
3 5 Lincoln 5
Newark
Shrewsbury Nottingham 5 Boston
Derby 6
3 Stamford Lynn
Lichfield 6 Norwich 6
Ludlow Leicester 6 Yarmouth
3 Coventry 5
4 Worcester 6 Northampton 5 Bury St Edmunds
4 5 6 Ipswich
Hereford
Gloucester 5 5 Colchester
1 Oxford 5
1 Bristol 5 LONDON
Bath 5 Southwark 5
Wells 3 3 Rochester
5 Salisbury Canterbury 5
5 Winchester 3
Southampton Chichester 3
3 Exeter 5
4 5
Plymouth
Dartmouth

R.E.M.McC
15·7·70

Km. 0   50   100

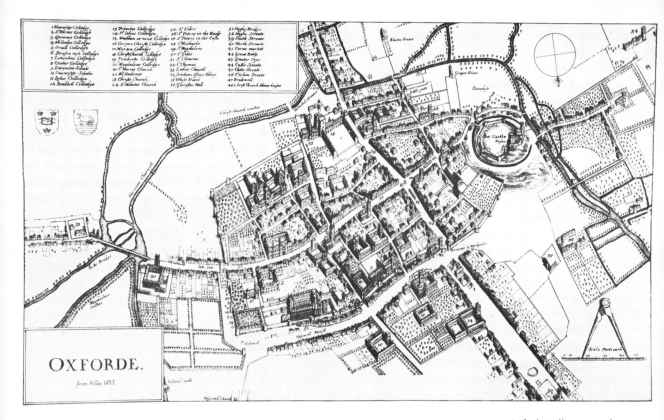

OXFORDE.

from Hollar, 1643.

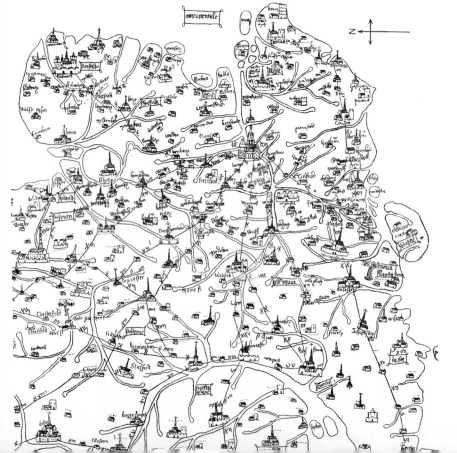

ABOVE: *Oxford. Hollar's map of Oxford 1643 in which the early gridiron layout is still visible. It is possible that King Edward, who had a manor of eight virgates of arable land, turned them into building lots in 912.*

LEFT: *Roads in medieval Britain. The roads in this illustration can be compared with those shown on the maps of Roman Britain and roads in the seventeenth century. Travel during the Middle Ages was difficult and dangerous. The Statute of Winchester (1285), enacted by Edward I, contains this significant clause: "Highways leading from one market town to another shall be enlarged, whereas bushes, woods or dykes be so that there be neither dyke nor bush whereby a man may lurk to do hurt within 200 feet of one side and 200 feet on the other side of the way." The Paston Letters, the correspondence of a Norfolk family in the fifteenth century, conveys a vivid picture of the hazardous nature of travel through a land disected by forest and fen.*

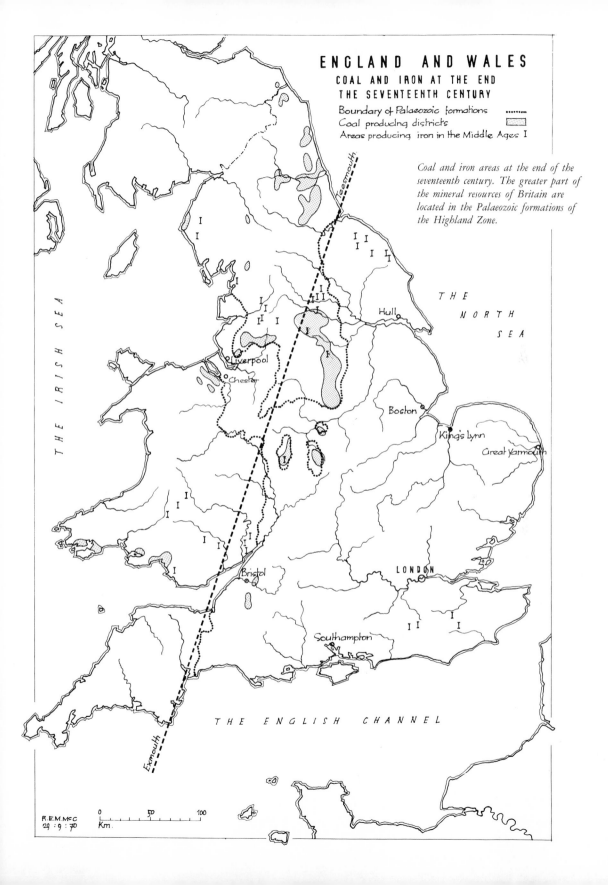

ENGLAND AND WALES
COAL AND IRON AT THE END
THE SEVENTEENTH CENTURY

Boundary of Palaeozoic formations ....
Coal producing districts
Areas producing iron in the Middle Ages I

Coal and iron areas at the end of the seventeenth century. The greater part of the mineral resources of Britain are located in the Palaeozoic formations of the Highland Zone.

THE NORTH SEA

THE IRISH SEA

Teesmouth

Hull

Liverpool

Chester

Boston

King's Lynn

Great Yarmouth

LONDON

Bristol

Southampton

THE ENGLISH CHANNEL

Exmouth

R.E.M. Mc C
29 : 9 : 70

0   50   100
Km.

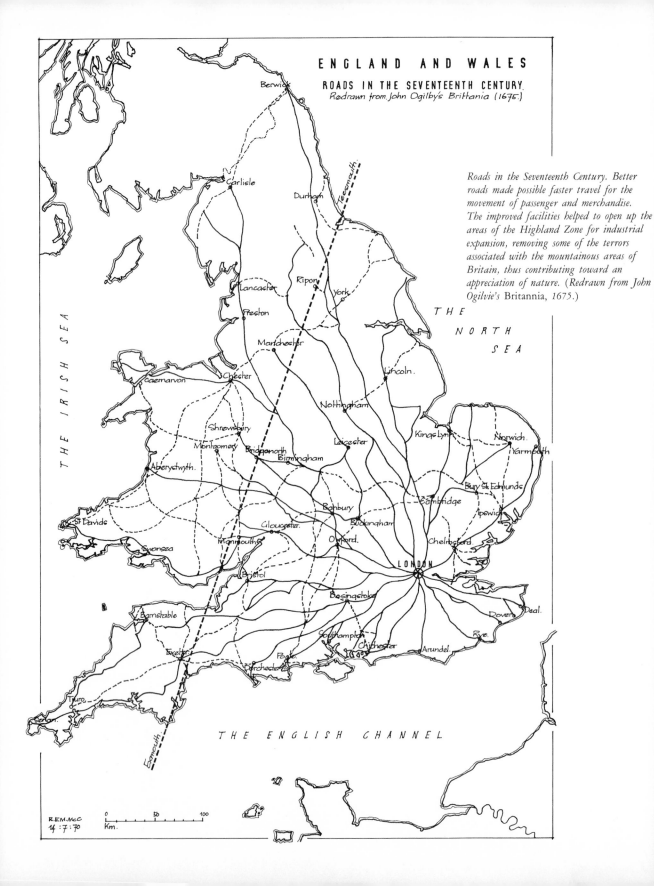

ENGLAND AND WALES

ROADS IN THE SEVENTEENTH CENTURY.

Redrawn from John Ogilby's Brittania (1675.)

Roads in the Seventeenth Century. Better roads made possible faster travel for the movement of passenger and merchandise. The improved facilities helped to open up the areas of the Highland Zone for industrial expansion, removing some of the terrors associated with the mountainous areas of Britain, thus contributing toward an appreciation of nature. (Redrawn from John Ogilvie's Britannia, 1675.)

THE IRISH SEA

THE NORTH SEA

THE ENGLISH CHANNEL

Berwick
Carlisle
Durham
Teesmouth
Lancaster
Ripon
York
Preston
Manchester
Lincoln
Chester
Caernarvon
Nottingham
Shrewsbury
Leicester
Kings Lynn
Norwich
Montgomery
Bridgenorth
Birmingham
Yarmouth
Aberystwyth
Bury St Edmunds
St Davids
Banbury
Cambridge
Ipswich
Swansea
Gloucester
Buckingham
Monmouth
Oxford
Chelmsford
Bristol
LONDON
Basingstoke
Barnstable
Dover
Deal
Southampton
Rye
Exeter
Chichester
Arundel
Poole
Dorchester
Truro
Seaton
Exmouth

R.E.M.McC
14:7:70

0   50   100
Km.

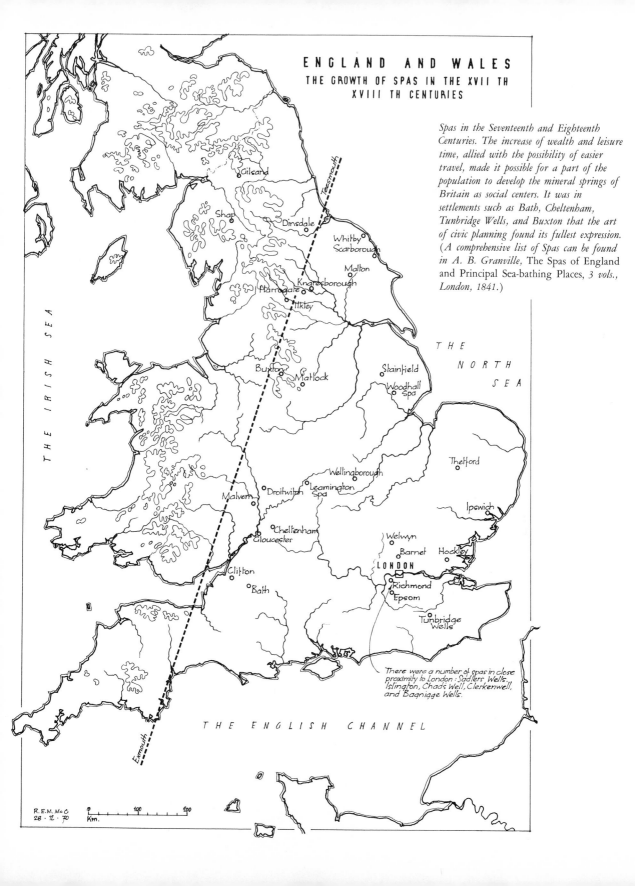

ENGLAND AND WALES
THE GROWTH OF SPAS IN THE XVII TH XVIII TH CENTURIES

Spas in the Seventeenth and Eighteenth Centuries. The increase of wealth and leisure time, allied with the possibility of easier travel, made it possible for a part of the population to develop the mineral springs of Britain as social centers. It was in settlements such as Bath, Cheltenham, Tunbridge Wells, and Buxton that the art of civic planning found its fullest expression. (A comprehensive list of Spas can be found in A. B. Granville, The Spas of England and Principal Sea-bathing Places, 3 vols., London, 1841.)

THE IRISH SEA

THE NORTH SEA

THE ENGLISH CHANNEL

Gilsland
Shap
Dinsdale
Whitby
Scarborough
Malton
Knaresborough
Harrogate
Ilkley
Buxton
Matlock
Stainfield
Woodhall Spa
Thetford
Wellingborough
Leamington Spa
Droitwich
Malvern
Ipswich
Cheltenham
Gloucester
Welwyn
Barnet
Hockley
LONDON
Clifton
Richmond
Epsom
Bath
Tunbridge Wells

There were a number of spas in close proximity to London: Sadlers Wells, Islington, Chads Well, Clerkenwell, and Bagnigge Wells.

Teesmouth

Exmouth

R. E. M. McC
28 · 12 · 70

0   100   200
Km.

while Pennant, Gilpin, and Gray were extolling the beauties of Lakeland. The growing enthusiasm for mountain scenery is reflected in Ann Radcliffe's *The Mysteries of Udolpho* (1794).

Architectural Town Planning   Town planning in the Middle Ages was based on the gridiron, which is the simplest way of laying out plots and may or may not be civic design. Indeed, it was not until English architects became acquainted with the work of Italian or French architects that fresh forms were introduced. In 1618 Inigo Jones laid out Covent Garden in the Italian manner with the church on the axis.

Between 1609 and 1641 the citizens of London carried through the great regional project known as the Londonderry Plantation. The plan of Londonderry recalls the piazza element in Scamozzi.

The most important proposals for the rebuilding of London after the Great Fire in 1666 were put forward by Valentine, Newcourt, Evelyn, and Wren. Wren's plan (*see* WREN) ignored the contours and the previous street pattern and replaced the docks with an esplanade. It has been cogently argued that the plan was economically impracticable and administratively impossible. Yet there can be little doubt that he could have—if he had been given the chance to work up his *esquisse*—made London the finest city in the world. The Rebuilding Act (1667), which laid down the heights of buildings in relation to street widths, resulted in London's being converted from a timber city to one mainly of brick.

A number of London squares were built in the seventeenth and eighteenth centuries: Leicester Square (1635), Bloomsbury Square (1665), Soho Square (1681), St. James Square (1684), and Grosvenor Square (1725). In the latter, for the first time, the architect, Edward Shepherd, treated the houses on one side of the square *as a single composition* in the Palladian manner.

John Wood (1704–1754) and his son were largely responsible for the planning of Bath. In 1729 he built Queens Square, treating the houses on each side of the square as a single composition, similar to Grosvenor Square, which he had seen while working in London. The Circus, laid out in 1760, recalls his engraving of Branham Park, with its avenues intersecting at a *rond-point*. The Crescent was added in 1769. (*See* WOOD *and* THEORIES AND IDEALS OF PLANNING *for illustrations.*)

The elements of civic architecture developed by the Woods—the terrace, the square, the circus, and the crescent—were used by others. John Carr laid out the Crescent in Buxton between 1779 and 1781. Craig's ambitious plan for the "new town" of Edinburgh (1767) was realized only in part. John Dance carried Wood's ideas a little further by introducing a double crescent in his proposals for the Camden Estate in 1791.

The most exciting application of these elements was provided in John Nash's proposals for Regent's Park. His first report (1812) showed an imaginative use of terraces, the crescent, the circus, and formal and informal pools. The building of Carlton House Terrace, Regent Street, Park Crescent, and the Regent Park Terraces was the most ambitious project ever realized in London. Unfortunately the vicissitudes of time have not dealt kindly with Nash's great work.

RIGHT: *Lowther Westmorland. A rural settlement, probably designed by James Adam, which makes use of the square and the circus. It was built during the second half of the eighteenth century.*

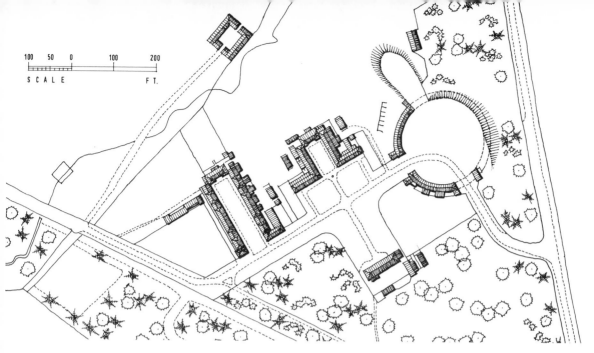

100 50 0   100   200

S C A L E   F T.

The Canal

The Market

Church

Quinquette

Military
Barracks

The Canal

MARYLEBONE PARK
PLAN IN THE FIRST REPORT 1812
After John Summerson's John Nash, Architect to George IV page 113

R.E.M M°C
6 1 7

Marylebone Park, by John Nash. Architectural town planning in which the architect has integrated in an admirable manner, the square, the circus, and the crescent; elements first introduced by the Woods at Bath. The landscape treatments probably reflect the influence of Humphrey Repton, with whom Nash was once associated. (Redrawn from John Summerson, John Nash: Architect to King George IV, *London, 1935, p. 13.)*

The Reclamation of Waste Lands and the Enclosures At the end of the sixteenth century, there were still more than 10 million acres (4 million hectares) of heath and moor in England and Wales, and even as late as the seventeenth century there were 100,000 acres (40,500 hectares) of waste in Lancashire and over 250,000 acres (100,000 hectares) in Yorkshire.

The enclosure movement had been in progress since at least the fifteenth century and it had gained considerable impetus by the time of George III. Some 5 million acres (about 2,023,400 hectares) were enclosed. The procedure was simplified by the Act of 1801. The appearance of the land changed from open "champagne" country to small plots bounded by stone walls or hedges so typical of Britain today. The changes facilitated the advances in livestock breeding and the introduction of a new rotation of crops in which the fallow was eliminated by the introduction of turnips and clovers. The new ideas were propagated by Arthur Young (1741–1820).

The draining of the Fens between the seventeenth and nineteenth centuries, and also draining of the Lancashire mosses, made available for agriculture some of the most productive agricultural soil in Britain.

The Industrial Revolution and the Growth of Population Between the sixteenth and nineteenth centuries, England was transformed from being a largely rural society, in which even towns had their common fields, to an urban society in which the majority of the population lived in towns. Increased food production, advances in medicine, and better sanitation had contributed to a reduction of the death rate from 35.8 percent in 1740 to 21.1 percent in 1820, although there had been no appreciable increase in the birth rate. In 1700 the population was about $5\frac{1}{2}$ million; in 1801, nine million; and in 1871, about $16\frac{1}{2}$ million. The greatest concentration of population was now in the Highland Zone and the "fall zones" at the base of the Pennines. The census figures for 1801, 1881, and 1851 show the rate of growth: Leeds, 53,000, 123,000, 172,000; Bradford, 13,000, 44,000, 104,000; Oldham, 22,000, 51,000, 72,000; and Blackburn, 12,000, 27,000, and 65,000. It is significant that in 1851 over half the population of these towns were migrants.

The introduction of turnpikes enabled the construction of more serviceable roads and the use of faster coaches, which considerably reduced traveling time. A comparison of John Ogilvie's road atlas (1675) with that of Daniel Patterson (1771) indicates the extent of improvement in road provision. The widening and joining of navigable rivers and the development of the canal system linked the industrial areas with London. The opening of the Stockton and Darlington railway in 1825 presaged the "railway age," which provided rapid transport throughout the country.

Inventions in spinning and weaving revolutionized the cotton and wool industries, leading to a rapid expansion of the factory system and the growth of industrial settlements in the fall zones of the Pennines and South Wales. The Davey lamp, the Newcomen pump, and the application of steam power made possible the exploitation of the mineral wealth of the Highland Zone, which had just been opened up by the revolution in transportation. The introduction of coke in smelting at Coalbrookdale began the transformation of the iron industry and considerably increased the output of iron and steel.

RIGHT: *Population distribution at the beginning of the nineteenth century. The greatest concentration of the population in medieval times has been in the areas associated with the woollen trade, which was the staple industry of England. The technological advances of the eighteenth and nineteenth centuries saw the growth of new industrial centers in the "fall zones" on either side of the Pennines, and in Wales near the sources of power and of raw materials. This resulted in a relatively greater concentration of population north and west of the Tees/Exemouth line, especially in Lancashire, Yorkshire, and Durham.* (An Historical Geography of England and Wales to 1800, *edited by H. C. Darby, Cambridge, 1936, Fig. 84.*)

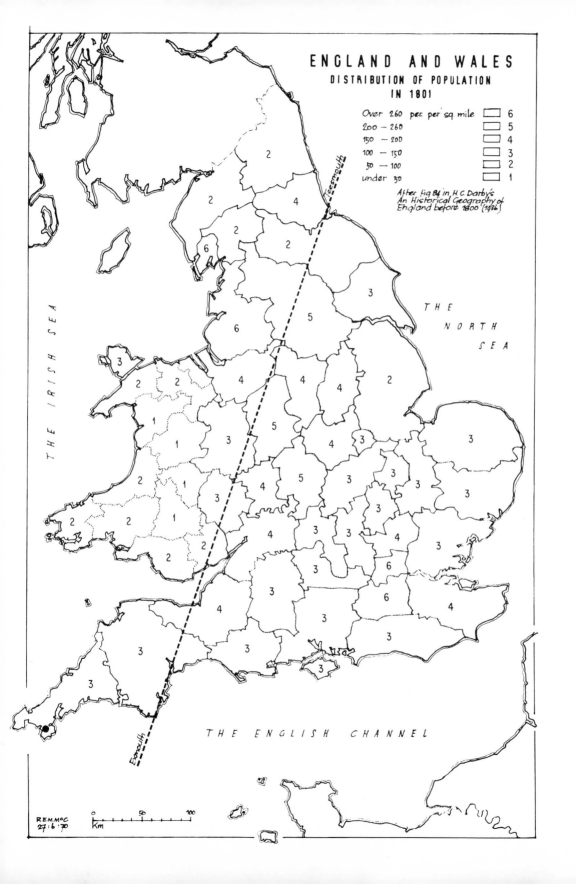

ENGLAND AND WALES
DISTRIBUTION OF POPULATION
IN 1801

Over 260 per. per sq. mile	6
200 — 260	5
150 — 200	4
100 — 150	3
50 — 100	2
under 50	1

After fig 84 in H.C. Darby's
An Historical Geography of
England before 1800 (1936)

THE IRISH SEA

THE NORTH SEA

THE ENGLISH CHANNEL

Teesmouth

Exmouth

R.E.M.McC
27:6:'70

0   50   100
Km

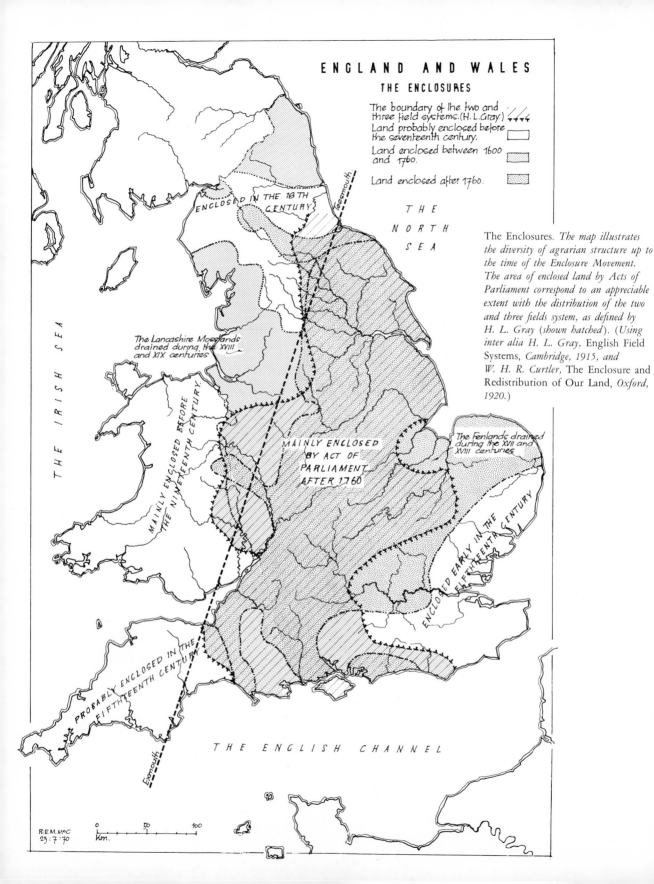

ENGLAND AND WALES
THE ENCLOSURES

The boundary of the two and three field systems. (H. L. Gray.)
Land probably enclosed before the seventeenth century.
Land enclosed between 1600 and 1760.
Land enclosed after 1760.

THE NORTH SEA

The Enclosures. *The map illustrates the diversity of agrarian structure up to the time of the Enclosure Movement. The area of enclosed land by Acts of Parliament correspond to an appreciable extent with the distribution of the two and three fields system, as defined by H. L. Gray (shown hatched). (Using inter alia H. L. Gray,* English Field Systems, *Cambridge, 1915, and W. H. R. Curtler,* The Enclosure and Redistribution of Our Land, *Oxford, 1920.)*

ENCLOSED IN THE 18TH CENTURY

Teesmouth

The Lancashire Mosslands drained during the XVIII and XIX centuries

THE IRISH SEA

MAINLY ENCLOSED BEFORE THE NINETEENTH CENTURY

MAINLY ENCLOSED BY ACT OF PARLIAMENT AFTER 1760

The Fenlands drained during the XVII and XVIII centuries

ENCLOSED EARLY IN THE EIGHTEENTH CENTURY

PROBABLY ENCLOSED IN THE FIFTEENTH CENTURY

Exmouth

THE ENGLISH CHANNEL

R.E.M.M.cC
23.7.70

0   50   100
km.

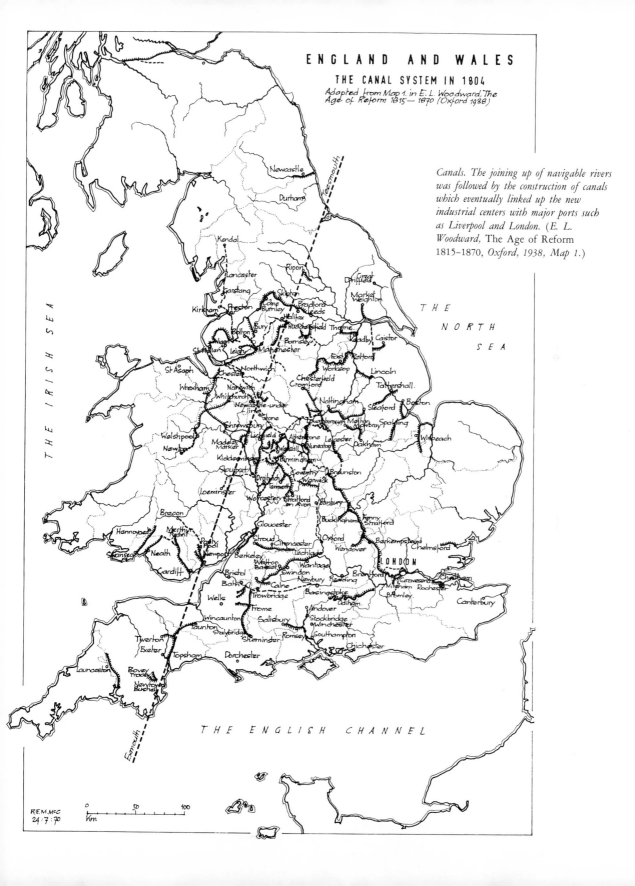

ENGLAND AND WALES
THE CANAL SYSTEM IN 1804
Adapted from Map 1, in E. L. Woodward, The
Age of Reform 1815 — 1870 (Oxford 1938)

Canals. The joining up of navigable rivers was followed by the construction of canals which eventually linked up the new industrial centers with major ports such as Liverpool and London. (E. L. Woodward, The Age of Reform 1815–1870, Oxford, 1938, Map 1.)

THE IRISH SEA

THE NORTH SEA

THE ENGLISH CHANNEL

R.E.M.MᶜC
24:7:70

Km

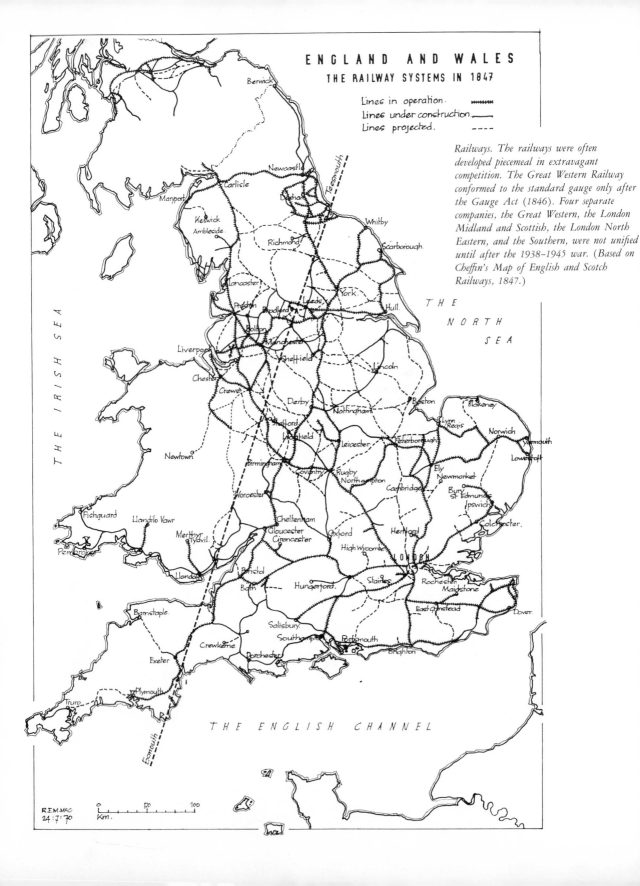

ENGLAND AND WALES
THE RAILWAY SYSTEMS IN 1847

Lines in operation. +++++++
Lines under construction. ———
Lines projected. -----

Railways. The railways were often developed piecemeal in extravagant competition. The Great Western Railway conformed to the standard gauge only after the Gauge Act (1846). Four separate companies, the Great Western, the London Midland and Scottish, the London North Eastern, and the Southern, were not unified until after the 1938–1945 war. (Based on Cheffin's Map of English and Scotch Railways, 1847.)

THE IRISH SEA

THE NORTH SEA

THE ENGLISH CHANNEL

R.E.M. M⁵⁰
24:7:70

0   50   100
Km.

Berwick
Newcastle
Carlisle
Maryport
Durham
Keswick
Ambleside
Whitby
Richmond
Scarborough.
Lancaster
York.
Preston
Leeds
Bradford
Hull.
Bolton
Liverpool
Manchester
Sheffield
Chester
Lincoln
Crewe
Derby
Boston
Stafford
Nottingham
Blakeney
Lichfield
Lynn Regis
Leicester
Peterborough
Norwich
Newtown
Birmingham
Yarmouth
Coventry
Lowestoft
Rugby
Ely
Northampton
Newmarket
Worcester
Cambridge
Bury St Edmunds
Ipswich
Fishguard
Cheltenham
Colchester.
Llandilo Vawr
Gloucester
Oxford
Hertford
Merthyr Tydvil.
Cirencester
Pembroke
High Wycombe
LONDON
Llandaff
Bristol
Rochester
Bath
Staines
Maidstone
Barnstaple.
Hungerford
East Grinstead
Salisbury.
Dover.
Crewkerne
Southampton
Portsmouth
Exeter
Dorchester
Brighton
Plymouth
Truro
Teesmouth
Exmouth

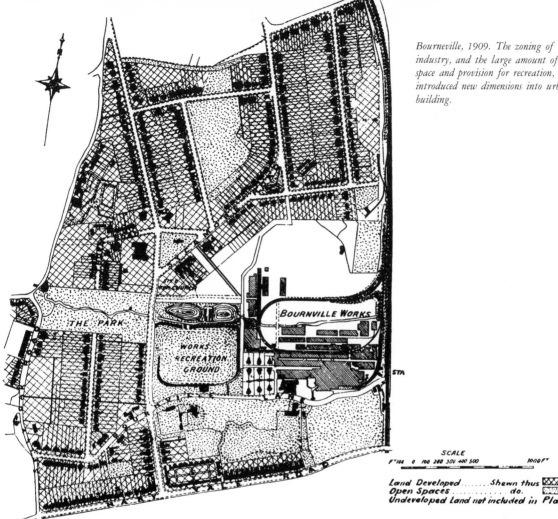

THE PARK

BOURNVILLE WORKS

WORKS RECREATION GROUND

STA.

SCALE

F¹¹⁰⁰ 0 100 200 300 400 500   1000 FT

		Acres
Land Developed........Shewn thus	▨	102
Open Spaces............. do.	▨	16
Undeveloped Land not included in Plan		407
		525

Towns in the Nineteenth Century Apart from exceptions such as the "Iron-masters" plan for Middlesbrough, the majority of industrial settlements expanded with little if any thought for adequate standards in housing or the location of industry. Some attempts were made to ameliorate these bad conditions: Robert Owen (1771–1858) provided at New Lanark a better standard of living and working, and in 1851 Titus Salt founded Saltaire, with much improved conditions for his workers.

Public conscience was awakened and found its expression in the Towns Improvement Act (1847) and the Public Health Act (1848), the first of several which culminated in the Public Health Act of 1875. From this resulted the bylaw planning so typical of northern towns such as Preston and Leeds. Meanwhile, squalid pit villages were rising in the mining areas.

In 1876 Norman Shaw laid out the first garden suburb at Bedford Park. In 1888, W. H. Lever transferred his factory from Warrington to a site of 56 acres (23 hectares) on the west bank of the Mersey, 32 acres (13 hectares) being reserved for housing. In 1917 the death rate in Port Sunlight was 9.7 compared with 14.3 for the country. In 1909 George Cadbury, inspired by the Quaker indistrial village at Bessbrook in Ulster, built a new settlement for his workers at Bourneville near Birmingham.

Birkenhead was laid out in the nineteenth century with a magnificent public square as the focal point of a gridiron plan, to which was added a public park which was laid out by Paxton. This can be compared with Belfast, another gridiron plan with a central square, in which was located the Linen Hall, the symbol of the rising prosperity of the linen industry. Fleming's map of Glasgow shows the early expansion in a number of unrelated gridiron layouts. Decimus Burton's plan for Fleetwood is similar in character.

In 1898 Ebenezer Howard published *Tomorrow: a Peaceful Path to Real Reform* and reissued in 1902 as *Garden Cities of Tomorrow*, envisaging a model city of 32,000 inhabitants on a site of 6,000 acres (2,400 hectares), of which 1,000 (405) would be devoted to housing and the remainder to a greenbelt.

Belfast. Plan illustrating the various stages in the growth of Belfast. At 4 can be seen the gridiron layout of the early linen magnates with the Linen Hall at the center. A dotted line indicates the boundary of the city just after the middle of the nineteenth century. (Map by E. E. Evans. Belfast: The Site and the City, Ulster Journal, Arch. VII, 1944, pp. 5–29, Fig. 2.)

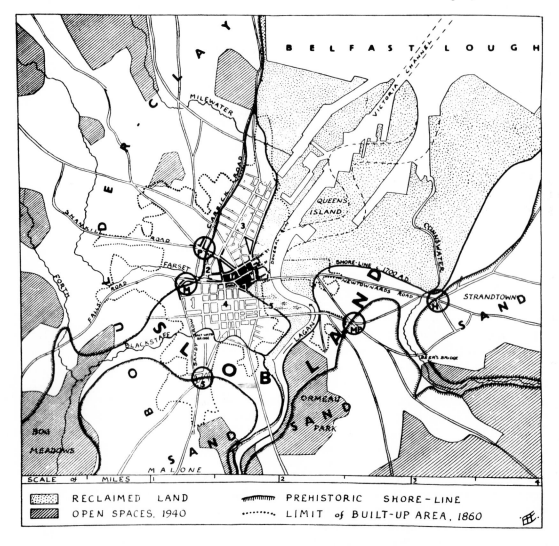

RECLAIMED LAND

OPEN SPACES, 1940

PREHISTORIC SHORE-LINE

LIMIT of BUILT-UP AREA, 1860

Hampstead Garden Suburb, 1906. Layout by Raymond Unwin and Barry Parker in association with Sir Edwin Lutyens. An intriguing blend of Beaux Arts axial planning with the crow's foot, and the informal layout recommended by Camillo Sitte. The dominant element is off the axis, but is balanced by the subtle relationship between the smaller church and the adjacent housing. (Aerofilms, London)

The book provoked considerable discussion, as a result of which a Garden City Association was formed. In 1903 a site for a New Town was purchased at Letchworth for a population of 20,000. Of the site, 1,250 acres (500 hectares) were reserved for the town and 2,500 (1,000) for the greenbelts. The architects were Barry Parker and Raymond Unwin. Raymond Unwin was also associated with Edwin Lutyens on the layout of Hampstead Garden Suburb in 1907.

Raymond Unwin expressed his ideas in *Town Planning in Practice* (1909), in which he advocated the "informal" layout recommended in Camillo Sitte's *Der Stadte-Bau nach seinen Künstlerischen Grundsätzen* (1889).

Population in the Nineteenth Century The invention of the combustion engine and the development of the motor vehicle at the turn of the century was destined to become a major factor in transforming urban and rural life in Britain. The increased mobility, coupled with the availability of electrical power for industry, made possible the movement of industry and population from the industrial areas of the Highland Zone and the fall zones to the London area. Tramways, suburban railways, and the motor vehicle played a vital role in the lateral expansion of cities, just as iron construction and the increasing use of the elevator made possible their vertical expansion. In 1871 the population of Liverpool was nearly 500,000, Glasgow was about 400,000, Leeds and Birmingham over 250,000. In Greater London, however,

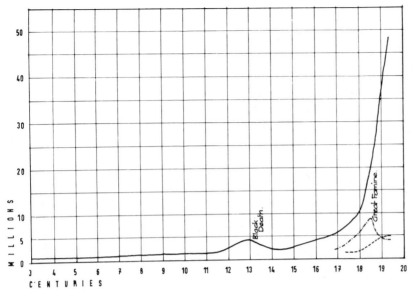

Population growth. Population figures before the second half of the nineteenth century are at best inspired guesses. It is not possible to say how many died of the Black Death; some areas escaped lightly, while others were decimated. The increase in population after the eighteenth century was due to a number of factors, such as better food, better sanitation, and preventative, as well as curative, medicine.

between 1857 and 1871, the population increased 45 percent from 2,681,000 to 3,886,000. The increase in population raised problems of water supply and sewage disposal necessitating the acquisition of large tracts of land outside the towns' boundaries for catchment areas, reservoirs, sewage farms, and other social needs.

Town Planning Legislation The John Burn's Town Planning Act of 1909 empowered local authorities to prepare plans for the proper layout of land, the provision of adequate sanitation, and the protection of amenity.

In the same year the Lever chair at the University of Liverpool was endowed by the family who had built Port Sunlight. The "Department of Civic Design," as it was called, published the *Town Planning Review* in 1910.

At the Town Planning Exhibition in 1910 at Burlington House, Patrick Geddes called attention to the sociological implications of regional and town planning and stressed, for the first time, that planning should be preceded by a systematic survey.

In 1914 the Town Planning Institute was founded.

In retrospect, it will be seen from this very short and necessarily unqualified and undocumented outline, that the evolution of the landscape, and the growth of settlements from early historic times in Britain, is essentially the story of man's conquest of his environment: how innovations in agrarian methods resulting in the elimination of the fallow made possible more effective utilization of the soil; how advances in technology made available fresh sources of energy and power, which could be applied in the extraction of hitherto inaccessible mineral wealth; and how methods of manufacture became more productive. These advances, in conjunction with increasing accessibility made possible by the revolution in the means of transportation, contributed toward the opening up of the Highland Zone and the "fall zones," not only for the extraction of mineral resources and the development of industry, with its consequent migrations and concentrations of population, but also for the physical recreation and spiritual enrichment of the mind. Thus, since Roman times man has adapted and molded the *use of the land* in Britain to meet his changing physiological, sociological, and spiritual needs.

BIBLIOGRAPHY:
Physical Environment
S. W. Wooldridge and D. L. Linton, "Loam Terrains in South-East England and Their Relation to Early Settlement, *Antiquity VII,* 1933, pp. 397–310; Cyril Fox, *The Personality of Britain: Its Influence on Inhabitant and Invader,* 4th ed., Cardiff, 1947; H. J. Fleure, "Some Aspects of European Civilization," Fraser Lecture, 1947, Oxford, 1948; A. G. Tansley, *Britain's Green Mantle: Its Past, Present and Future,* London, 1949; E. E. Evans, "The Atlantic Ends of Europe," British Association for Science Lecture, 1958, in *Advancement for Science No. 58,* 1958, "Prehistoric Geography," in *The British Isles: a Systematic Geography,* edited by G. J. W. Watson and J. B. Sissons, London, 1964.

History
J. L. B. and B. Hammond, *The Bleak Age,* London, 1917; F. W. Maitland, *The Constitutional History of England,* Cambridge, 1919; Carl Stephenson, *Borough and Town, A Study of Urban Origins in England,* Cambridge, Mass. 1933; V. H. Galbraith, "The Literacy of the Medieval English Kings, The Raleigh Lecture on History," *The Proceedings of the British Academy,* vol. 21, 1935, pp. 1–40; F. M. Stenton, "The Road System of Medieval England," *Econ. Hist. Rev.* VII, 1936, pp. 1–21; Ian Richmond, *Roman Britain,* London, 1940; F. M. Powicke, *Medieval England 1066–1455,* Oxford, 1942; Helen M. Cam, *Liberties and Communities in Medieval England,* Collected studies in Local Administration and Topography, Cambridge, 1944; T. S. Ashton, *The Industrial Revolution 1760–1830,* Oxford, 1948; V. H. Galbraith, *Studies in Public Records,* London, 1949; T. P. F. Lazlitt, *The World We Have Lost,* London, 1965.

Landscape, Settlement, and Planning
H. C. Darby, *The Draining of the Fens,* Cambridge, 1940; John Summerson, *The Heavenly Mansions,* London, 1949; W. G. Hoskins, *The Making of the English Landscape,* London, 1955; W. J. Hipple, *The Beautiful, The Sublime and The Picturesque in the Eighteenth Century. British Aesthetic Theory,* Carbondale, 1957; Patrick Abercrombie, *Town and Country Planning* (revised by D. Rigby Childs), London, 1958.

NOTE: Comprehensive lists of original sources and secondary works on English history are given in "English Historical Documents," vol. I–XIII, edited by H. C. Douglas (London, 1955, in progress) and Handbook of Dates for students of English History, edited by C. R. Cheney (London, 1945).

—R. E. M. McCaughan

Twentieth Century Planning action is determined by current legislation, and current legislation by the objectives of the day. As objectives change, so does legislation and the area over which the planner can act.

The goal of planning activity in Britain throughout the present century has remained substantially the same: to provide a good living and working environment for as many people as possible. But the interpretation of this goal in terms of objectives has varied as a deeper understanding has evolved of what constitutes a "good environment" and as new factors working against the goal came to be recognized. This reformulation of objectives can be viewed as a series of gradually merging streams, some of which have their source in the nineteenth century.

1900 to the 1940s
Garden City Movement. Public opinion was influenced by the work of the reformers, in particular those associated with the garden city movement, who in turn drew lessons from the paternalistic settlements of the nineteenth

century. Reference has already been made to Ebenezer Howard's influence in the founding of the first garden city in 1903.

From the paternalistic settlements and garden cities, there emerged many of the working tools of urban design; e.g., the master plan, reservation of sites for community buildings, a pattern of open spaces, and the definition of the edge of a town by a greenbelt.

The implementation of Howard's ideas by Parker and Unwin had a side effect in the garden suburbs which began to appear in existing towns and which set the pattern for suburban living to the present day. The New Town planned and built as a whole was still generally beyond the reformers' reach.

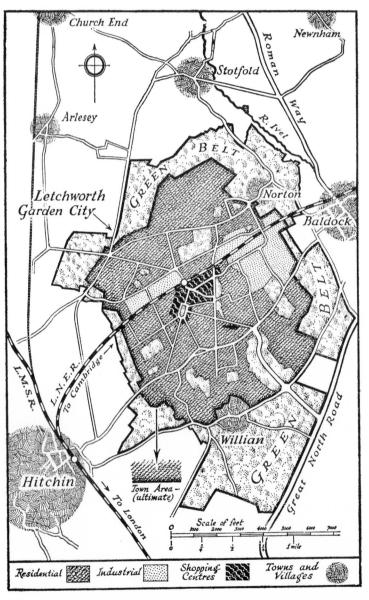

Letchworth, 1903. Plan by Raymond Unwin and Barry Parker. The layout is informal, and extensive landscaping formed an important element. Housing areas of different maximum densities were defined and minimum standards formulated to guide the layout of these areas. (Garden Cities of Tomorrow, Faber and Faber, 1946.)

Regulative Measures. The bylaws evolved in the preceding century continued to be applied until 1909. The Housing and Town Planning Act of that year indicates a slight widening of objectives. Bylaws were still a major regulative device, but in addition an attempt was made to achieve the orderly development of vacant land in and around towns. This act produced very few planning schemes, but one, that for Ruislip-Northwood, indicates the influence of Letchworth and Hampstead Garden Suburb and itself was an influence on the drafting of the 1947 Town and Country Planning Act.

Civic Design Projects. Until the Second World War, most large towns and cities continued to apply the palliative measures of the nineteenth century. New streets such as Kingsway in London were built, their design based on Beaux Arts principles. A small number of civic building groups such as Southampton Civic Centre were also planned. But these projects did little to overcome the intensifying problems of the large urban areas, which continued to increase rapidly in size.

Geddes and Regionalism. These problems had been restated by Geddes in the early part of this century, and he pressed for surveys and a fuller understanding of the urban regions he called "conurbations." He stressed that a plan should evolve from the existing structure of a town or city and that, to achieve this, comprehensive surveys were necessary. His work laid the foundation for a systematic approach to the preparation of plans, and the first result was the appearance of the planning report consisting of a comprehensive array of maps, diagrams, and plans based on detailed surveys. His work on the conurbations formed part of the growing interest in regionalism. The objectives of regionalism have been threefold: the reform of local government, the achievement of regional planning and development, and the achieving of administrative decentralization. Regionalism as a topic created much interest in the early part of the century and many regional plans were produced, for example, the Cambridge Regional Plan of 1934.

American Influence. The work being carried out in America in the 1920s and 1930s made an initial impact on British planning in the interwar period. Particularly influential was the work of Perry relating to the neighborhood. His concept, and its development as "Radburn planning" by Stein and Wright, was of even greater significance after the Second World War.

Linear Planning. Linear planning as proposed by Soria y Mata in Spain was of international interest, and eventually, in 1933, an English linear city association was formed by Freese and Drury. But the linear city movement did not have the strength or popular appeal of the garden city in Britain and the idea of linear urban forms was not applied until the MARS plan for London in 1942 and in much more recent New Town proposals.

Continental Reformers. Another major influence was the work of other continental reformers such as Gropius and Le Corbusier. But again their work did not gain popular support in Britain until after the Second World War. The ideas contained in, for example, La Ville Radieuse (1922) were taken up in later plans for the New Towns, and the transportation aspects were developed by Alker Tripp (1942) and Buchanan (1963).

In the late 1920s the concept of the satellite town emerged from the studies then being made, in particular the regional studies. One of the satellite towns that was built was Wythenshawe near Manchester, and to a great extent it synthesizes the ideas then current.

The major synthesis is, however, found in the Scott and Barlow reports and in the plans for London. The Barlow commission was concerned with the decentralization and dispersal of industry and industrial population. The Scott committee was concerned with the problem of development in rural areas and its effect on agriculture and rural amenities.

In terms of land-use planning, the County of London Plan (1943) and the Greater London Plan (1944) draw together all the varying streams of thought that had developed up to that time. The former, by Abercrombie and Forshaw, was for a major city region and was a very detailed study and analysis of urban problems. It suggested that communities which had been absorbed by London's growth should be reidentified, and the major road network and open spaces proposed were designed to achieve this. It also introduced the concept of the precinct based on the work of Alker Tripp. Abercrombie in his Greater London Plan made proposals for the location of overspill population in satellite suburbs, in existing towns beyond a greenbelt, and in New Towns for which sites were suggested.

1940s to the 1960s During and at the end of the Second World War, it seemed that both major political parties believed that control and guidance were necessary to improve the physical environment. In 1945 there was a four-point plan: special help, based on regional studies, for areas of decline; planned renovation of big cities largely within their prewar boundaries; overspill from big cities to new towns 30 or 40 miles (48 to 64 kilometers) away; and a holding operation elsewhere by means of county development plans.

In 1951 a change in government produced a change in objectives. From 1946 to 1950, 14 New Towns had been designated. From 1951 to 1960 only one further town, Cumbernauld in Scotland, was designated. The emphasis changed from New Town development to the expansion of small existing towns, the Town Development Act being passed in 1952. The regional approach was also abandoned in this period, and planning in general was reduced to a regulative minimum. It was in the 1950s that many of the large-scale commercial urban renewal schemes got under way.

The 1960s saw a return to the policies of the immediate postwar period. To date (1973), 15 New Towns have been designated since 1961 and plans for four others have been prepared. Economic planning regions were drawn up in 1965, based to a large extent on those established by the Ministry of Town and Country Planning in 1946. Legislation relating to the conservation and use of the countryside was extended and improved. The possibility of rehabilitating older housing areas was seen, and the problems of historic towns were given serious thought.

In the 1960s, the civic society movement had developed rapidly and the two principal effects of this were (1) that laymen became increasingly aware of their environment and (2) that there were mounting demands for participation by the public in the formulation of planning objectives. The latter is reflected in the provisions for consultation included in the 1968 Town Planning Act.

This period, and to a lesser extent the preceding decade, also witnessed major changes in the planning profession. Disciplines which had hitherto been considered peripheral to or outside land-use planning became closely associated with it and introduced new analytical and predictive techniques. Many of these techniques had been developed in America, and American attitudes to planning were imported together with the techniques. The greater precision that the use of these methods makes possible is best seen in some of the subregional studies carried out in the 1960s.

Examples of the main types of urban plan produced since the end of the Second World War are described below.

New Towns. In terms of urban form, three distinct groups of New Towns can be distinguished: the towns designated between 1946 and 1950 make up the first group; Cumbernauld (1955), the abortive proposal for Hook (1960), and Skelmersdale (1961) the second group; the remaining New Towns constituting the third. This third group can be further subdivided.

Most of the first group of New Towns (e.g., Harlow—see illustration)

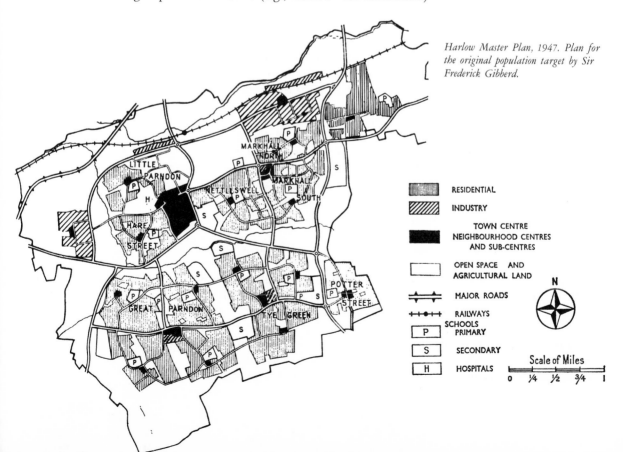

Harlow Master Plan, 1947. Plan for the original population target by Sir Frederick Gibberd.

	RESIDENTIAL
	INDUSTRY
	TOWN CENTRE NEIGHBOURHOOD CENTRES AND SUB-CENTRES
	OPEN SPACE AND AGRICULTURAL LAND
	MAJOR ROADS
	RAILWAYS
	SCHOOLS
P	PRIMARY
S	SECONDARY
H	HOSPITALS

N

Scale of Miles
0   ¼   ½   ¾   1

had target populations of between 50,000 and 80,000 and were located on largely virgin sites. Their form derived primarily from the garden city and the neighborhood concept and was based on studies carried out by the Ministry of Town and Country Planning and design standards assembled by the Reith committee. The target population was considered to be also the *maximum* population, and the towns were to be balanced communities. Residential densities of 30 persons per acre (75 per hectare) and densities of 50 workers per acre (125 per hectare) in industrial areas were planned. Generous open-space standards were applied and it was thought that car ownership would not be more than one car to about ten people.

The two principal influences on the second group of towns (e.g., Hook—see illustration) were increasing awareness of the effects of the growth in vehicle ownership and a reaction against the low-density form of the first group of towns. The first group was criticized for lack of cohesion and sense of place. To overcome this, the idea of the neighborhood was largely abandoned and higher residential densities were adopted so that most of the population would be within walking distance of the town center. The resulting form was more compact and therefore visually more cohesive. The predicted rise in vehicle ownership had two principal effects on the form of these plans: (1) it implied that pedestrian/vehicle segregation was essential if a safe and satisfying environment was to be achieved (influenced by the work of Stein and Wright), and (2) it made necessary the provision of substantial road systems, leading to the idea of a hierarchy of roads (a further development of the ideas of Le Corbusier, Alker Tripp, and Abercrombie).

There are two major characteristics that the third group have in common: the emphasis given to provision for movement and a conceptual approach to urban form that could be termed "cellular." The Buchanan Report (1963) had a major impact on this group of New Towns and also on the planning of existing urban areas. The concept of a hierarchy of roads and its parallel concept of environmental areas were now firmly established. Forms appropriate for efficient and economically viable public transport systems have also been examined in many of these plans, leading to a renewed interest in linear forms. The concept of the environmental area and a partial return to the neighborhood idea has produced in these plans a cellular structuring of the urban area, the residential component being variously termed (e.g., "village," "district").

From this common basis, various urban forms have been developed, dependent partly on the specific site characteristics and partly on the choice of emphasis as between private and public transport (see illustration of Washington). A further major difference within this group is the population to be accommodated. All these towns were planned taking account of the regional context, but the larger ones (for example, Central Lancashire, planned for 500,000) were intended to perform a new and special function. They were intended to relieve congestion in the conurbations not only by accommodating overspill population but also by becoming themselves major

RIGHT: *Plan of a New Town at Hook, in Hampshire, England, proposed by the London County Council (now Greater London Council) in 1956.*

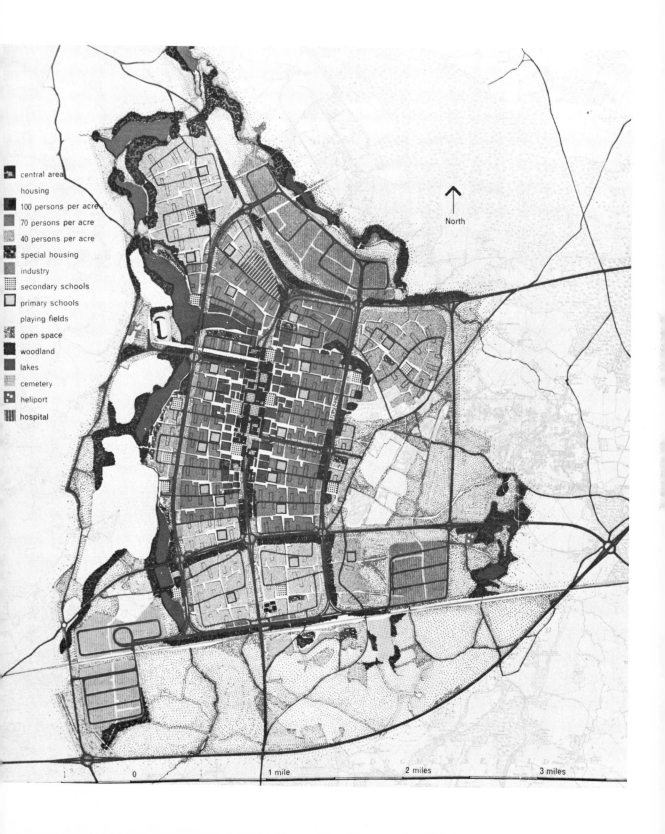

central area

housing

100 persons per acre

70 persons per acre

40 persons per acre

special housing

industry

secondary schools

primary schools

playing fields

open space

woodland

lakes

cemetery

heliport

hospital

North

0   1 mile   2 miles   3 miles

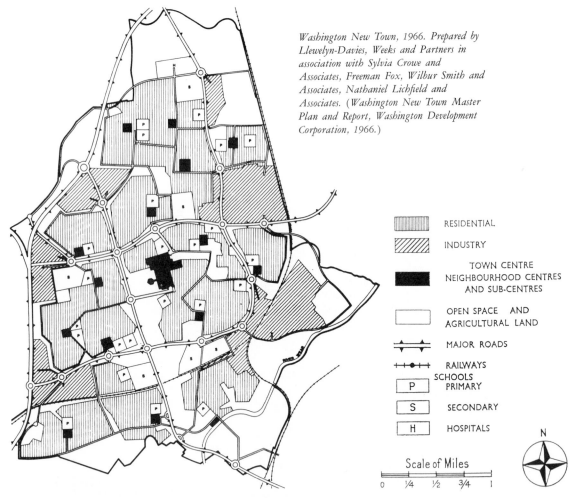

Washington New Town, 1966. Prepared by Llewelyn-Davies, Weeks and Partners in association with Sylvia Crowe and Associates, Freeman Fox, Wilbur Smith and Associates, Nathaniel Lichfield and Associates. (Washington New Town Master Plan and Report, Washington Development Corporation, 1966.)

RESIDENTIAL

INDUSTRY

TOWN CENTRE
NEIGHBOURHOOD CENTRES
AND SUB-CENTRES

OPEN SPACE AND
AGRICULTURAL LAND

MAJOR ROADS

RAILWAYS

SCHOOLS
P   PRIMARY

S   SECONDARY

H   HOSPITALS

Scale of Miles
0   ¼   ½   ¾   1

N

new centers within the region. Another important difference between preceding New Towns and this group is that many of them are based on substantial existing settlements.

Expanded Towns. Since the Town Development Act of 1952, about fifty town development schemes have been agreed, and it is likely that many more will follow. This form of development is seen as an advantage to the exporting authority (in that it offers some relief to the problem of overcrowding) and to the receiving authorities, many of whom are small country towns in danger of decline or stagnation. Employment as well as population is exported. Development takes place by agreement between the exporting and receiving authorities, and the government gives financial support. The county councils of the receiving areas also often give financial and technical assistance.

Subregional Studies. A large number of subregional studies were carried out in the 1960s, and similar plans will be required for the new counties under the new Local Government Act of October 1972. The subregional studies so far published (1970) have either been prepared in association with New Town proposals (e.g., Livingston), by a group of authorities (e.g., Merseyside Area Land Use and Transportation Study), or by a central government department (e.g., Severnside).

Urban Local Authorities. Since the Second World War, plans have been prepared for all existing towns and cities. Many of these plans are now seriously inadequate in the light of the lessons learned in New Town design and in terms of studies such as the Buchanan Report[1] and recent legislation.

Local authority boundaries have been found to be a serious restriction in many cases, and the new Local Government Act of October 1972 making major changes in local authority areas is the result of pressures for a more logical system of local government and land-use planning.[2]

There are a number of plans for major cities which illustrate the application of current thinking, for example, Liverpool, Newcastle upon Tyne, and Coventry. They also illustrate the form of plan envisaged in the 1968 Town and Country Planning Act.

A special type of plan for existing urban areas has resulted from the conservation studies commissioned by the government. Four ancient cities, York, Chester, Bath, and Chichester, were examined by planning consultants with the intention not only of providing a plan for each of these cities but also of drawing up guidelines for the study of towns with similar problems.

BIBLIOGRAPHY: Ebenezer Howard, *Garden Cities of Tomorrow,* Faber & Faber, Ltd., London, 1902 and 1906; Ministry of Works and Planning, *Report of the Royal Commission on the Distribution of the Industrial Population* (Barlow Report), HMSO, London, 1940; Ministry of Works and Planning, *Report of the Committee on Land Utilisation in Rural Areas* (Scott Report), Command Report 6378, HMSO, London, 1942; Department of Civic Design, University of Liverpool (eds.), *Land Use in an Urban Environment,* Liverpool University Press, 1961; London County Council, *The Planning of a New Town* (Hook), Alec Tiranti, 1961; Report of the Steering Group and Working Group, *Traffic in Towns* (Buchanan Report), HMSO, London, 1963; J. B. Cullingworth, *Town and Country Planning in England and Wales,* George Allen & Unwin Ltd., London, 1964; W. Ashworth, *The Genesis of Modern British Town Planning,* Routledge & Kegan Paul, Ltd., London, 1965; B. Smith, *Regionalism in England, Its Nature and Purpose, 1905–1965,* The Acton Society Trust, 1965; Colin Buchanan and Partners in association with Economic Consultants Limited, *South Hampshire Study,* HMSO, 1966; J. B. McLoughlin, (director), *Leicester and Leicestershire Sub-Regional Planning Study,* Leicester City Council and Leicestershire County Council, 1969 (2 vols); F. J. Osborn and Arnold Whittick, *The New Towns,* second edition, Leonard Hill, London, M.I.T. Press, Boston, 1969.

—DON FIELD

Twentieth Century—Urban Renewal A desirable process of urban renewal is one in which the rate of change and adaptation of the urban fabric is such as to permit the replacement of individual parts to proceed without disruption of the whole. Implicit in such a process is that the rate of change is gradual, keeping pace with fully established changes in social demands.

Two major factors may disrupt this process:

1. A halt in the usual rate of replacement of outworn parts of the fabric, e.g., by war, and the consequent diversion of resources.

---

[1] *Traffic in Towns,* Ministry of Transport, HMSO, 1963.
[2] *Royal Commission on Local Government in England 1966–69,* Command Report 4040 June 1969.

2. Sudden changes in social demands and practices; e.g., a rapid rise in the standard of living, changes in income and expenditure patterns, greater mobility among the populace, increased car ownership and usage. Such factors can render components of the urban fabric functionally obsolete or inadequate, often long before they are physically outworn.

Both factors were operative in the urban areas of Great Britain in the postwar period. The problems were in part exacerbated by war damage, in part relieved by the opportunities for change which such areas presented. For inherent in the problems of renewal are those of fragmented land ownerships and the organizations and fiscal agencies through which funds are channeled in order that urban renewal programs may be effected.

Agencies for Urban Renewal Most urban renewal projects in the first half of this century were fragmentary, small in scale, and speculative in nature. Where significant contributions were made, in town planning terms, the development was usually comprehensive and the agencies responsible either philanthropic or local authorities with a statutory obligation; e.g., for slum clearance and rehousing or road construction. It is true that some progress was made in strengthening the theory and technique that now forms the basis for comprehensive design, but during this early period most of the building which took place occurred haphazardly in time and location, with little cooperation between neighboring developers whose basic motivations were largely irreconcilable.

It was obvious in 1945 that individual landowners and entrepreneurs could not command adequate resources, nor achieve the necessary degree of coordination, which would be essential if the decaying, blitzed, and obsolete sectors of most urban areas were to be restructured to meet the demands of the postwar period. The power to gather together and clear adequate parcels of land for comprehensive redevelopment was therefore vested in the local authorities through the provisions for compulsory acquisition laid down in successive planning acts. But the enormous capital costs of reconstruction were beyond the means of most public authorities and private enterprise had to be allowed, indeed encouraged, to play its part in the renewal process. Therefore, although in general the guidance of urban renewal was the responsibility of the county boroughs (i.e., the large cities) and they received central government subsidies to supplement local taxes, the range of those urban facilities for which they were responsible and in which they invested public money was limited. Accommodation for commercial and trading activities where a risk element existed had (other than in exceptional cases) been provided through a variety of agencies which administer private investment capital; e.g., land and property development companies, insurance companies, building societies, and trustees of pension funds. (In an age of fluctuating monetary values, investment in real property—i.e., land and building—is seen as a secure hedge against losses due to inflation.)

While the 1950s will be remembered as a period of conflict between the broad aims and objectives of planning for the common good and the property speculators who rose rapidly from obscurity to wealth, the 1960s have seen a stabilizing of the situation as development companies switched from short-term, rapid-turnover policies to long-term investment and more sophisticated management techniques.

Specialized agencies such as development companies bring with them a level of expertise and realism in analyzing the economic aspects of urban redevelopment, for designing and organizing large-scale constructional programs, and for estate management, which is beyond that to be found in local government. It follows therefore that some of the most successful recent exercises in large-scale urban renewal in the United Kingdom are those which have been undertaken in formal partnership between local authorities and private enterprise on an equity-sharing basis or sliding scale of ground rents as and when the development becomes profitable.

Urban renewal projects (as distinct from town expansion schemes) can be conveniently divided into three main periods: up to 1914, 1919 to 1939, and 1945 to 1972. (The two world wars form obvious break points.)

1900 to 1914 In the period up to 1914 economic and social forces continued to encourage compact arrangement of buildings. Production and employment around 1909 were closely tied to railways and the city center, thus placing a premium on central positions. The higher value of such places dictated intense forms of development and the use of cramped sites, but it was an uncoordinated plot-by-plot development that took place.

The physical form of development, street patterns and widths, the space around buildings, and (indirectly) the building density, were regulated by local bylaws that were intended to maintain minimum conditions of health, safety, and amenity. The regulations were simple and their implementation was straightforward, so much so that extreme monotony was engendered in such sectors as housing (see illustration of by-law housing in Scotswood

By-law housing at Scotswood on Tyne. The area was laid out after 1900, at over 40 dwellings per acre. (Land Use in an Urban Environment, p. 192, Fig. 5 or C.S./NZ 2164 S.E., and Aero Pictorial.)

on Tyne). The influence of "civic design" did not extend to this kind of development but was virtually limited to monumental layouts around important buildings (e.g., St. John's Garden, St. George's Hall, Liverpool) and improvement schemes such as Kingsway, London (see illustration).

1914 to 1939 Because of the great changes which took place in transport (public and private), this phase was more notable as a period of urban expansion rather than renewal. Land on the edges of towns and along the main radial routes was both available and cheap and, to the expanding middle classes, suburban living seemed to hold out the promise of an amalgam of urban and country qualities—especially in the provision of "homes fit for heroes." The 1930s proved to be a period of reaction in which informed public opinion was most concerned with the inability of the local authorities to restrict this urban sprawl; but it was also a period

Kingsway, London. This street-improvement scheme, completed by 1905, provided an opportunity for a better arrangement of the new offices. Building density and site coverage were greatly reduced as a result of wider streets, and new development followed an overall design. But liability to noise from traffic and poor facilities for loading and servicing were disadvantages that were reincorporated into the new scheme. (Land Use in an Urban Environment, p. 203, Fig. 13 or O.S./T.Q. 3080 N.E., and Aero Pictorial.)

when six or seven monumental civic centers were built; for example, Southampton Civic Center.

Within the cities concentration of floor space in favored localities continued to be profitable, but the controls exercised by the planning authorities, under "interim control of development" and indirect regulation by means of "model clauses" (governing building height and site coverage), were negative in character. For the most part the terms of the clauses had an inflexibility in common with the bylaws or, where one was in force, with the local building act.

Shops in the centers of towns became fewer and larger in size, and there was an extension of chain stores backed by heavy capital investment. The few central schemes which were to any extent designed as a unified whole, such as the Regent Street Quadrant and Headrow at Leeds (see illustrations), were greatly outnumbered by the construction of new shopping centers at road junctions and along the main streets of new suburbs; for example, at Southgate, London (see illustration). In the inner areas of large cities the replacement of slum areas with local authority housing resulted in a new type of development. In London, Liverpool, and Leeds, for example, blocks of flats at densities of 200 to 300 persons per acre (500 to 750 per hectare) were built.

The Quadrant, Regent Street, London. This shopping street was redeveloped to comply with a comprehensive design by Sir Reginald Blomfield. The high building density and site coverage generate a heavy load of traffic, especially loading and service traffic, but the plan did not make adequate provision for service roads. (Aero Pictorial & Regent St. Assoc. and O.S./London sheet VII. 72.)

The Headrow, Leeds. A street improvement carried out in the early 1930s, which allowed improved grouping and enlargement of building sites and some uniformity of appearance. But it remains a dual-purpose, shopping and traffic street, with poor rear access. (Aero Pictorial.)

Suburban shopping center at Southgate, London. Some provision has been made for loading and service vehicles and for parking, but the shops are placed at a main traffic junction though near to the underground station. (Aero Pictorial.)

1945 to 1972 The postwar period falls into subdivisions which largely reflect the philosophies of the political parties concurrently in power:

1. The immediate postwar period, a time of understandable austerity, shortage of labor and material, and strict control of building licences

2. The period 1952 to 1960, in which public investment flagged, to be replaced by a rush of private speculation

3. The period 1961 to 1972, which saw a stabilization in the management and affairs of the private development agencies and later a resurgence of interest and participation by local authorities in urban renewal problems

In the first phase, local authority housing and the building of the New Towns took precedence over other forms of development. Resources were scarce and therefore closely controlled, thus suppressing building by and for the private sector. Nevertheless a number of renewal programs were begun which displayed the major requirements of a coordinated environment; e.g., the Lansbury neighborhood scheme in London and the first stage of the Coventry town center scheme. The extensive war damage in the center of Coventry enabled the city to go ahead rapidly—other cities were compelled to proceed in piecemeal fashion rather than comprehensively.

The second phase (after 1951) began with a relapse toward pre-1939 layouts as regards scale of operation and design. This was particularly evident in the many office-building projects in London and other central areas, where the existing roads were incapable of supporting the new transport demands. Later, when the success of centers such as those at Stevenage and Coventry had been noted, a considerable number of developments (either publicly sponsored but privately financed or wholly privately organized) got under way; e.g., shopping and office centers at Birmingham, Bradford and Sheffield; Piccadilly scheme in Manchester; the Elephant and Castle in London; and the Barbican scheme in London. An example of good comprehensive planning in the housing field at this time (1953–1963) was that built at Golden Lane by the City of London. An even larger project which embodied similar principles was the Park Hill residential complex by the Sheffield Corporation (1957–1962). This is notable for the intelligent use made of a steeply sloping site and the overall residential density of 192 persons per acre (480 per hectare) net. Densities of up to 138 persons per acre (345 per hectare) were achieved in other schemes, such as at the Canada Estate, Southwark, by the Greater London Council. An example of comprehensive urban renewal on a wider canvas yet is illustrated in the plan published in 1965 for the central area of Liverpool. At this scale progress will inevitably be slow and many changes can be expected to the forms of development illustrated as individual projects crystallize nearer to their time of execution.

The major political parties in the United Kingdom now agree fundamentally on the need to integrate fully all decisions regarding major urban renewal projects with the overall planning policies operative at regional, subregional, county, and district level. The comprehensive nature of the planning system now operative reflects this awareness, and future progress is likely to be limited only by the need to conserve resources at a time of national economic stringency.

That a better balance is necessary between investment in communications, in redevelopment, rehabilitation and overspill projects has led to a more rational ordering of priorities. The techniques of comprehensive design—that is, the integration of activities achieved in multiuse, multilevel urban development; the solutions to the problems of servicing and the segregation of incompatible traffic flows, vehicles, and pedestrians; the awareness of the microclimatic problems created and the need to achieve a balance in the reconciliation of social goals and private economic aims—are now almost universally understood if not always achieved in practice. Above all is the apparent awakening to the fact that planning and building must meet the needs of the people rather than merely create grandiose urban settings. Parallel to this, the methods of management and implementation have reached a much more sophisticated level.

It is likely in the coming age of higher per capita incomes, greater individual mobility (in terms of private car ownership, choice of residential locations, and jobs), and the forecast increase in leisure time, that the process of renewal in the older urban centers will be relatively slower than the growth of more dispersed, low-rise, and lower-density housing developments, satellite shopping centers, and places of employment.

BIBLIOGRAPHY: Raymond Unwin, *Town Planning in Practice,* Fisher & Unwin, London, 1909; C. H. Holden and W. G. Holford, *The City of London—A Record of Destruction & Survival,* Architectural Press, London, 1947; Department of Civic Design, University of Liverpool (eds.), *Land Use in an Urban Environment,* Liverpool University Press, 1961; *Ten Years of Housing in Sheffield, 1953–1963,* Sheffield City Architects Department and City of Sheffield Housing Development Committee, 1962; *Liverpool City Centre Plan,* City Centre Planning Group, C&BC of Liverpool, 1965; David Lewis (ed.), "The Pedestrian in the City" *Architects' Year Book.* vol. 11, Elek Books, London, 1965; P. Johnson-Marshall, *Rebuilding Cities,* Edinburgh University Press, 1966; *City of Coventry Review Plan, 1966,* Coventry City Council, 1967; Ministry of Housing and Local Government handbooks (HMSO): *Design and Layout of Roads in Built-Up Areas,* 1946, *Redevelopment of Central Areas,* 1947, *Housing Manual,* 1949, *Design in Town and Village,* 1953, *Flats and Houses,* 1958, *Homes for To-day and Tomorrow,* 1961; Ministry of Housing and Local Government, Planning Bulletins (HMSO): *Town Centres: Approach to Renewal,* 1962, *Residential Areas: High Densities,* 1962, *Town Centres: Cost and Control of Development,* 1963, *Town Centres: Current Practice,* 1963, *Parking in Town Centres,* 1965; Ministry of Housing and Local Government publications, (HMSO): Viscount Esher, *York: A Study in Conservation* 1969, Donald W. Insall & Associates, *Chester: A Study in Conservation,* 1969, Colin Buchanan and Partners, *Bath: A Study in Conservation,* 1969, G. S. Burrows, *Chichester: A Study in Conservation* 1969.

—E. W. CHANDLER

UNITED NATIONS CENTER FOR HOUSING, BUILDING, AND PLANNING The United Nations' interest in urban development and housing is as old as the organization itself. The involvement of the international community can be traced to the United Nations Relief and Rehabilitation Administration (UNRRA), created before the United Nations to deal with the reconstruction of Europe after the Second World War. Because of this, housing and urban developments were identified as important areas of concern. From this emerged a small unit in the United Nations Secretariat to deal with housing. This unit became the nucleus of the Center for

Housing, Building, and Planning created by the Economic and Social Council of the United Nations in 1962.

The Center for Housing, Building, and Planning is, within the United Nations system of organizations, the focal point for matters pertaining to urbanization, housing, and building. Its responsibilities are related to the analysis and evaluation of world problems and trends in human environmental development, promotion and coordination of research, development of comprehensive concepts and policies, and servicing United Nations bodies in regard to environment development.

The purpose of the Center is the "improvement of man's physical environment in pursuit of the social, economic and cultural goals of society," as stated in Article 55 of the United Nations Charter. The Center throughout its work emphasizes the development and expansion of the organizational, financial, and personal resources that countries require to institutionalize planning and to develop the strategies, formulation, and implementation of planning schemes.

The rapid population growth coupled with the massive transfer of populations from rural to urban areas is resulting, for most countries in the developing world, in a number of acute problems which, according to the center's findings, are aggravated by (1) lack of comprehensive policies on the ways in which these populations are to be accommodated, (2) weak administrative and financial institutions, (3) lack of experienced trained personnel, and (4) lack of experience in putting policies and programs into effect.

The work of the Center reflects the priorities indicated by member states and, in particular, takes into account the needs of developing countries. In the broadest sense, these requirements have been conceived in answer to the most pressing needs of the human environment. These needs are:

1. The comprehensive development of human settlements
2. The development of housing as one of the basic functions of human settlements
3. The development of building technology as a means of meeting the massive demand for housing

These requirements are met by the following means:

Technical Cooperation The Center is responsible for projects in housing, building, and planning under the United Nations Technical Cooperation Program and, as such, is the substantive unit serving the Office of Technical Cooperation for all technical assistance projects within the Center's professional competence. The Center works in liaison with the regional economic commissions, the World Food Program, the specialized agencies, and with nongovernmental organizations and other appropriate bodies.

The Center's technical cooperation activities take the form of substantive backstopping of technical assistance experts, seminars, study tours, conferences, and pilot projects as well as the technical review of requirements for projects to be financed from the United Nations regular program of technical assistance and the United Nations Development Program. The work includes the evaluation of member states' requests for technical assistance; active participation in the cooperative effort of the United Nations family to provide staff, fellowships, and equipment in projects meeting these requests; and technical supervision of such projects, including periodic evaluation of programs (or projects) of technical cooperation in the urban and housing fields.

Three examples will serve to illustrate the scope of this work in urban development. In 1963, the United Nations was requested by the government of Yugoslavia to assist in the preparation of a plan for the ancient city of Skopje, then a city of 200,000 which had been devastated by an earthquake in July 1963. After 2 years of intensive efforts and the application of new techniques and methodologies, the plan was prepared, and it is currently under implementation. Work of a similar nature is proceeding in Singapore and Karachi, the object of which will be to establish a satisfactory basis for the future development of these large cities.

In regional planning, the center has been called upon by several countries to impart a physical dimension to economic development plans. In Korea, for example, the regional implications of macroeconomic targets in the third 5-year plan will be examined with physical and social factors in mind. Thus it will be a question not only of whether a particular locality is economically suitable for the location of a new industrial or infrastructure project but also of what the effect of this location will be on the cities' total physical and social environment.

A third type of project concerns assistance in the establishment of institutions capable of undertaking research and studies on all aspects of urbanization phenomena: proposing policies for coping with these phenomena, preparing plans for town and city development, and developing housing schemes.

Such projects have been initiated in Afghanistan (where a Central Authority for Housing and Town Planning is now in existence) and in Taiwan.

At the end of 1969, there were 19 projects in the field of housing, building, and planning financed under the Special Fund component of the United Nations Development Program at a total cost of $44,293,432 (including governing council earmarkings and government counterpart contributions). Of these 19 projects, 12 involve some aspect of urban development.

Short-term assistance under the technical assistance program of both the United Nations and the United Nations Development Program in the field of urban and regional planning has accounted for a major portion of the center's activities in the overall field of housing, building, and planning. During 1968, of the 138 experts providing technical assistance to requesting governments, 70 were in the field of urban and regional planning.

Pilot and Demonstration Projects The Center's technical cooperation, research, and development activities are brought together in a concerted effort to test and demonstrate effective development strategies for critical problem areas and particularly for problems resulting from rural-urban migration, rural underdevelopment, and uncontrolled urban growth in the most rapidly urbanizing countries. The center prepares guidelines for these projects; investigates the needs and potential resources for their operational and research support by the United Nations family and other bodies; and provides guidance for the technical assistance provided by the United Nations to member states in planning, implementing, and evaluating pilot and demonstration projects.

The complex nature of the subjects of these projects requires an especially close coordination of the center's sectoral activities with those of a wide range of United Nations and other agencies in order to help establish a comprehensive development strategy for these problem areas.

Dissemination and Exchange of Information and Experience The Center helps to ensure that information and experience obtained in the operational and research activities of both member states and the United Nations in the field of housing, building, and planning shall be distributed and exchanged among the many bodies and institutions needing it for development purposes throughout the world. For this purpose the center initiates and supports seminars and other meetings at national, regional, and interregional levels; it also has a program of publication which covers research studies and other information in its field of interest and presently publishes a periodic bulletin for the dissemination of up-to-date information for the benefit of developing countries.

Research The Center's activities related to research have been of a very pragmatic nature and of limited scope, and while greater involvement of the Center is envisaged, its role in this field has primarily been to promote and coordinate research. Its own research activities will continue to be in applied research geared to feed the needs of developing countries and to satisfy its own needs for the purposes of orienting and guiding the United Nations technical cooperation programs in these fields.

Since the resources available to the center are very limited, the center has concentrated its efforts on the more urgent problems, limiting them to certain key specific problems and topics.

Based on the center's experience and the requirements of member states, seven fields of interest have been selected for the purpose of research. The first field of interest concerns the overall strategy of comprehensive development; the next three concern the social, economic, and physical elements that must be coordinated in planning for comprehensive development; the last three fields of interest concern the legislative, institutional, and training means by which comprehensive development plans are implemented.

In the *field of methodology for comprehensive planning and development of the human environment,* particular emphasis is placed on the interdependence of physical planning with economic and social planning at national, regional, and local levels.

In this field, work will be undertaken on the methods and techniques of comprehensive physical development of human settlements and the protection of the physical environment.

These studies will cover methods for integrating economic and physical planning, regional physical planning, and urban planning; they will review man-made changes in the physical environment; and they will establish environmental standards for urban and regional planning, land use, densities, provision of services and community facilities (residential, industrial, and recreational), and urban traffic and transportation. The development of an international terminology and international symbology for the preparation of plans will also be studied.

Within the same basic field of interest the center is involved in the improvement of rural settlements. Its work is related to physical, economic, social, and administrative improvements in settlement planning of existing villages and to the development of improved building materials and methods, to management techniques, to the fostering of community organizations, and to employment promotion and other measures for raising the social and economic levels of rural living.

As a result of the center's involvement in assisting countries in the reconstruction of regions or cities which have been faced with disasters, the center has also undertaken the preparation of *standards for planning and construction to guide governments in disaster-prone areas* in adopting appropriate local building codes and town planning regulations to minimize the effects of earthquakes, hurricanes, volcanic eruptions, and floods.

In the *social field,* special emphasis is placed on the interaction between evolving social needs, demands, and preferences on the one hand and the functional and physical organization of the settlement on the other.

Study in the area aims at providing the missing inputs in social aspects— inputs which must be taken into consideration in the formulation of policies and programs on housing and urban development.

The *economics of urban development* is another of the Center's main fields of interest and one in which the Center will undertake and promote studies as well as to participate. It will concern itself with the economic implications of development under varying degrees of urbanization, industrialization, and scale of undertaking. This would include studies on the costs and benefits of various patterns of urbanization as a means of guiding the formulation of policies of population distribution and the resulting patterns of human settlements. The Center, as a first step, organized a seminar which was held in Denmark in mid-1970 in cooperation with the Danish Government.

The Center has also actively engaged in the study of the *methods and ways of financing housing development* aiming at assisting developing countries to: (1) identify their capital requirements to meet planned and expected programs for housing and community facilities and for the construction and building-materials industry; (2) provide the systems and institutions to mobilize and manage the necessary investment funds; (3) develop guidelines for the efficient allocation and management of both capital and recurrent expenditures in this sector; (4) analyze capital requirements for housing and related activities in selected developing countries; (5) estimate the potential flow of capital to the housing sector from existing sources, both public and private; and (6) recommend steps to increase the flow of funds to this sector and to improve efficiency in budgeting and financial management.

In the field of *physical and functional components of human settlements,* three main areas are being considered: (1) housing development; (2) the rehabilitation of slum and squatter settlements; and (3) building technologies and materials for the rapidly growing housing needs of the world's population.

Research work on the problems of housing development are related to *policies, programming, and administration in housing development* and to the formulation of guidelines for the design of low-cost housing and community facilities. An attempt is being made to formulate improved criteria for the construction of housing and community facilities in low-income areas taking into account climatic, cultural, social, and economic conditions. In this connection the Center, under its technical cooperation program, conducted an international competition on high-density, low-rise developments for a pilot project in Lima, Perú.

The rehabilitation of squatter settlements and slum areas has high priority in the Center's activities and, in addition to the assistance that will be given in the execution of pilot programs in a number of countries, the Center is conducting a study on rural-urban migration and low-income settlement in the rapidly urbanizing regions, particularly for the programs undertaken in developing countries on a pilot and demonstration basis, with the assistance of the United Nations family, donor governments, and other bodies.

In the area of *building technologies and building materials,* the center is actively engaged in the improvement and development of building technologies based on locally available materials. The Center will consider improved construction techniques, building materials, and tools based on traditional methods and local raw materials and will disseminate knowledge obtained. It is also active in the industrialization of building. A study on this subject will review the adoption of industrial processes for the production of housing units and components and will evaluate their degree of applicability in developing countries.   —A. CIBOROWSKI

UNITED STATES OF AMERICA
Legislation

Early Settlements In the first several hundred years of the settlement of what was to become the United States, little existed in the way of town planning legislation or codification that would qualify in the sense of creative long-range intention, conception, and implementation or of immediate-current serious control. Some of this did take place by way of enlightened custom and common understanding. What did take place needs to be included here as a backdrop to late nineteenth- and twentieth-century attitudes, since the early patterns affected later developments in legislation, administration, and implementation.

The formal legal position in the colonization and settlement period was generally limited to terms and definitions under which areas were granted to settlers by the various European states. The main interest was to set up permanent outposts which would pragmatically validate the territorial claims of England, Spain, France, and the Netherlands and to develop sources of revenue for the mother country (later, after independence, for state and federal government). The physical-social setup and its effects, beneficial or otherwise, on the people were of no primary interest in themselves and did not appear to any substantial degree in the terms of the grants or subsequently in any legislative form, whether in colonial times or after independence. An exception was the Spanish law of the Indies, covering towns and surrounding lands, site selection, and street layout. Its effects, however, appear to have been limited to a few settlements, as indeed the Spanish influence in North America was very limited.

Such meritorious prototypes as were created give no evidence of being the product of any broad legislation. It is true that the Town Planning Act passed in Virginia in 1691 helped to produce the cities of Annapolis and Williamsburg. But most towns were rather the product of folk memory and the way people had lived or were living in the old country and in desired adaptations, such as the New England towns; or they resulted from a single person's vision of excellence, based in part on some admired example (e.g., Oglethorpe's Savannah influenced by London's open spaces; Penn's Philadelphia). In the latter situation, the rules were singular to the specific case, not the application to a local situation of generally accepted principles and laws or standards of urban planning. In New England, a more general pattern is evident, and principles evolved whose creative manifestations are still partially visible. There were two basic approaches: (1) the arrangement built around a generous central green—which served as both meeting place and parade ground—with church and town hall adjoining (New Haven is a pure and well-known example), and (2) the approach that is based on the principle and practice of "hiving off" (i.e., when a certain size had been reached, there was no further expansion). Once the town had reached its maximum size, subsequent population settled elsewhere, either nearby or as far away as Ohio. This principle was later submerged and there followed indefinite expansion in place.

For some two centuries, to the end of the nineteenth century, the dominant ethos or nonethos in city building was supplied by the incredibly fast settlement of the vast country. So intense and widespread were the threefold urge and drive to open up the practically free and inexhaustible land, to get away from the settled areas, and to make fortunes out of land speculation, that there was no demand for any control or legislation requiring creative planning. Only the crudest surveys, quick engineering plats, were required; the land grants contained only minimal conditions, requirements, or constraints. Physical standards for sanitation, water supply, and paved roads were nonexistent. As this speculation was a sort of national game at which many played and everyone thought he could play, the hardships and the crudities were fairly cheerfully borne for the prospect of immediate or future wealth.

This spirit of mobility and of national eagerness first spread west of the

Alleghenies when the dangers to settlement there were somewhat eased at the end of the eighteenth century. It was at various times prodded forward or renewed by physical-technological events such as canal development, the discovery of gold, the opening of the railways. The floods of immigration by the oppressed of Europe had several reinforcing effects. They provided more and more people who explosively pushed the front ranks forward to open the west. Many of them stayed at or near the Eastern seaboard, so that the demand for land and for any kind of shelter multiplied rapidly there. The speculative waves, which for a long time had not developed in these older areas, now caught on heavily, both in land and in production of the crudest kind of shelter with very low standards cheerfully borne by those who expected to profit by their forbearance. In the East, the hordes of new immigrants passively accepted the exploitation partly because they had come from European misery and were used to miserable standards and partly because they too expected to rise above these conditions quickly, perhaps themselves to take part in the local game.

This is a very brief résumé of the powerful dynamics that prevailed up to the third quarter of the nineteenth century. During this long period there *were* some examples of creditable city building; one even splendid. Such achievements were, however, certainly small in number. They will be noted in the section entitled "Traditions of Planning to the End of the Nineteenth Century." However, even in the few cases of early excellence, the rapid growth of these towns much beyond any early expectation during this crudely hectic period largely diluted their quality. In the growth areas of the cities, which were much larger than the original nuclei, such early amenities of functional and architectural foci and setting as the essential character of open spaces did not become part of the speculative expansionist urge and surges. This was the case in Savannah and Philadelphia. Even in cities that were planned liberally and with imagination, the original planned open spaces themselves were crowded into and built on. Among many examples is Louisville, Kentucky, where the original open strips that were provided and the original open park area along the river were built on.

This brief summary has been given as a basis for several important points:

1. To explain why in this long period of helter-skelter-development there was no genuine city building movement or legislative framework requiring it. The dominant mood and dynamics of the era experienced no need for other than the prevalent crude forms of development.[1]

[1] There were elements of fervent dissatisfaction with the dominant crassness. This produced many new "intentional" or utopian communities, or what John W. Reps calls "Cities of Zion." A dissident leaven with generally religious and egalitarian ideals and impulses expressed itself in both physical plans and social arrangements of these communities; often they were designed to accommodate special forms and ethics of industrial production. Generally they were products of the eighteenth and early nineteenth century, and some are still flourishing physically. Their total subsequent influence in any general way is small, but it is still substantial in local regions such as parts of Pennsylvania and North Carolina. Salt Lake City is the most substantial remaining example. A number of the present hippy attempts at new communities may be cited as exemplars of the same spirit, though of course not yet showing anything comparably mature, organized, determined, and physically or productively significant.

2. To note that later the coming of the railroads not only opened the western hinterlands but also made it possible to live in suburbs while working in the cities. Middle-class families, finding no urge to battle the inferiorities of the city or to push for orderly planning, settled in the suburbs: a fateful decision for the cities of the United States.

When legislative action finally seemed essential, it was for a long time remedial rather than fully creative.

Impulses toward City Planning, 1893–1933   The first widespread impulse toward urban planning arose from the Chicago World's Fair and its "White City" in 1893. There, millions of people were exposed to an orderly, articulated plan with generous open spaces, regular cornice lines, trees, canals, and other bodies of water. This was not an adventurous foray pointing a way into the future. But the experience created or filled the need for order, for distinction, for elegance, for comprehensibility. It seemed to indicate how the city could be replanned. A wave of enthusiasm for civic planning and beautification swept the country. In a number of cities the business elite, distrusting the city government and "politics" generally, privately employed prominent architects and engineers to draw up improvement programs. The banner was "the city beautiful."

Not based on reality, with practically no earnest support from or understanding of the people and their living and working requirements, dealing mainly with civic centers, and supported only by the mandate of the elite group—who, however, were not ready to furnish the funding that Haussmann, the great exemplar, had received from Napoleon III—only one or two cities such as Washington and Chicago experienced any flowering. In Philadelphia, the elegance of the Benjamin Franklin Parkway is fragmentary evidence. It was indeed a false dawn. The "city beautiful" fell into perhaps excessive discredit and abandonment. Even the comprehensive and deeper efforts such as "Boston-1915," launched in 1909 (intended to get into full swing by 1915), left scarcely a trace. These impulses came to life again in connection with urban renewal more than half a century later.

There was a good deal of excitement when the first National Conference on City Planning was held in 1909, with well-known names of the period (John Nolan, Frederick Law Olmsted, Jr., Frederick Adams, Frederic Delano, and others) active then and later in discussions and alarums. This conference ultimately produced the Regional Plan Association of New York, a citizen-foundation group, which issued an important document and plan in the late 1920s.

In the next 25 years there was a great deal of city planning—serious but still ineffectual—whose elements were land use and control by zoning, streets, transportation, recreation, and city centers. That is, planning largely in terms of physical considerations. By 1927, at the nineteenth annual conference on city planning, it was noted that 176 cities with a total population of 25 million—that is, generally the smaller cities—had city plans, 390 cities had planning commissions, and 525 had zoning ordinances. This period was characterized also by "comprehensive planning," which did not generally concern itself with the local districts—that is, the areas where the people lived—as entities. Neither did the planning have serious socioeconomic study at its base, nor housing and community—though this latter was brought into limited focus at the end of the period by the Regional Plan Association. Basic or organic city planning had its real conception, and later, birth, in the 1930s in reaction to the slum and its wretched housing and living conditions, evoking the deep outrage, missionary convictions, and eloquence of the social workers and the settlement houses. They saw and felt the devastating effects of the miserable shelter in the squalid environment. Beginning at the end of the nineteenth century, their aim was improvement of the inferior shelter at rents that could be afforded. The names of Jacob Riis, Lawrence Veiller, Mary Simkhovitch, and others are identified with this phase. Some decades later, they were joined and endowed with a broader view by a few design-planning thinkers and professionals such as Stein, Henry Wright, Mumford, Bauer, and Ackerman. They saw the need for new housing, new community—in short drastic creative action. Their view was that just regulatory action had definite limits and involved many obstacles—so that actual performance had been almost negligible. They felt that existing aims and methods were inadequate.

In 1933 Franklin Roosevelt's New Deal with its adventurous tempo, social concern, and alertness to identify new opportunities to increase employment came together with these two forces. A group of which the writer was a member drafted the early outlines of limited-dividend housing and large-scale public housing community. The work at this stage was ad hoc until, in 1937, Congress passed legislation setting up the United States Housing Authority. This was a momentous move just on the face of it, but it was even more significant because of the seeds it contained, the sprouting effects plus and minus.

First, there were the needs or requirements of community planning that kept empirically becoming more insistent, that empirically had to be met as they were felt.

Second, it will be seen from the succession of legislation since, that much or most of the pressure for planning-development came from the social-oriented group and their humane insistence on housing-community; much less pressure came from the planners, who for a long time maintained themselves as purist professionals "above the melee." Federal legislation from then till now has been an intermingling if not interweaving of housing, social and economic content, and physical-aesthetic intent and direction. For a long time the principal input and ingredient was housing, in spite of some lip service to planning-development in legislative preambles and presidential oratory. Thus while the input of the socially concerned supplied the needed dedication and determination, their limitations and preoccupations stamped a character and content on the program and, for a substantial period, inevitably stood in the way of realization of larger planning purposes.

Third, the frequent legislation, though broadening and deepening, has in each case come about more in response to specific defects in previous experience than in the form of creative leaps forward. This was the case until 1969. However, subsequently there have been several drastic leaps, as will be seen at the end of the section on Federal Legislation.

The following does not include all the federal legislation nor all the provisions of any one act. It is an attempt to present the character of this legislation, selections of outstanding, significant elements composing the mosaic of urban planning progress. As so frequently in United States history, much of the leavening and of the specific content of national legislation, especially in its early stages, came from the experiments and experience of single states (notably, New York State); but these remained limited in actual achievement and isolated in impact until the national body took active hold. Also, as major tax revenue in the United States is national, through the income tax, the major funds for implementing planning-development must come from the federal treasury. Therefore, although there is still occasional leavening from the states, in this short account it is logical to follow the federal level, with several creative exceptions and additions to be noted later.

Federal Legislation   This then is, in this context, a representative annotated listing of major federal legislation:

The Tennessee Valley Authority Act, 1933. This was the earliest example of federal legislation in the United States for planning in its modern sense. However, for reasons to be explained, comments on it appear later in a different context.

The United States Housing Act, 1937.[1] This created the United States Housing Authority, a federal agency, to provide loans and annual subsidies to local (municipal and county) housing authorities for slum clearance and low-rent housing. It succeeded the ad hoc mechanism which, since 1933, had operated as a minor branch of the Public Works Administration. This legislation was entirely directed to housing. It will be seen that, as time went on, legislation took on more community and urban planning aspects and ultimately concerned itself with planning on metropolitan and regional levels.[2]

---

[1] Unless otherwise noted, the legislation referred to is at the federal level, by Congress.

[2] Previous to this Public Housing Act, the first New Deal emergency measure in housing, the National Housing Act of 1934 created the Federal Housing Administration (FHA) whose main function was to insure mortgage loans so as to pump funds of the then frightened money market into housing construction and thus to increase employment.

These two acts, both strictly housing acts, had profound effects on planning-development. The FHA did succeed in its objective of reviving employment. But, entirely guided by the underlying customs and practices of the current commercial home builder, it concentrated for a number of years altogether on single middle-class houses in large tracts in outlying areas, completely ignoring the major part of the cities. This accentuated and accelerated flight to the suburbs and their stratified and minority-exclusive character. While these subdivision developments were somewhat better laid out than theretofore, the larger town planning considerations and relationships were ignored and the total effect was stratified sprawl.

Until the major act of 1949 there was no significant planning legislation. Much "war housing" was authorized and built hastily to supply shelter for war workers who had migrated from rural areas, without much thought of urban planning.

The Housing Act of 1949. The ringing tones of this act's groundbreaking statement of purpose provides for "the realization as soon as feasible of a decent home and a suitable living environment for every American family, thus contributing to the development of and redevelopment of communities and to the advancement of growth, wealth, and security of the nation;" and Title I provided that "the Administrator shall encourage the operations of such local public agencies as are established on a state or regional or unified metropolitan basis . . . to contribute effectively toward the solution of community development or redevelopment problems on a state or regional or unified metropolitan basis." This act authorized federal assistance for slum clearance and community development and urban redevelopment: the first provision for what is now known as "urban renewal." One of the conditions for its capital grants required that the development should conform to a general plan of the locality: urban renewal could be thought of as the action arm of city planning, which has only very partially and unevenly fulfilled that function.

The Housing Act of 1954. The term "urban renewal" was substituted for "urban redevelopment" in this act, which was of very great significance in this context. It made two notable provisions:

It developed the concept of the "Workable Program for Community Improvement" for meeting its overall problems of slums and urban blight as prerequisite to urban renewal and housing assistance. The seven requisites of the program included, among others, land-use plan, thoroughfare plan, community facilities plan, public improvements program, and zoning ordinance.

In the way of direct planning encouragement to localities, the important Section 701 established the Urban Planning Assistance Program. Planning grants were authorized to states, and through the states to local governments to facilitate comprehensive planning for urban development, to the extent of one-half the costs of planning consultants and/or planning staffs for cities

---

In the Housing Act of 1937, there was a serious flaw of a social and planning character. *Slum clearance* was the important goal, and only so much new housing was to be created as slum dwelling units were first demolished. This approach had two grave defects. First, *additional* supply of good new housing was and is the crux of city rebuilding and family well-being, and slum clearance is socially effective only when demolition follows, rather than precedes, new housing. Second, vacant land is much cheaper than slum land and buildings; hence subsidy required per unit is much less. But to the social workers, the slum was sentimentally the devil. And to the powerful real estate lobby, it was highly desirable not to increase housing supply. At the time, Lewis Mumford, Henry Wright, and the writer urgently presented the viewpoint noted above, in articles and otherwise, but to no avail. Only now, over 30 years later, is this alternate approach just *starting* to become operative policy. But tremendous damage has been done, and the larger city planning has been distorted.

under 50,000 population.[1] Grants were authorized also for planning work in metropolitan and regional areas. This constituted the first direct recognition of urban planning.

The original authorization for urban renewal in the 1949 act limited it to areas predominantly residential in character before redevelopment or after. The Housing Act of 1954 permitted 10 percent of federal capital grants to be used for nonresidential projects. This limit was raised in three subsequent acts, reaching 35 percent in 1965.

The Housing Act of 1959. In this act provision was made for community renewal programs for entire cities, the purpose being to study and schedule the renewal process as a long-range matter—that is, beyond immediate projects. The act authorized grants up to two-thirds of cost to assist communities in analyzing urban blight on a communitywide scale.

The Housing Act of 1961. This act included extension of planning grants to localities under Section 701 to cover transportation facilities. It also raised the federal portion of planning grants to two-thirds of the amount allotted, and raised from $20 million to $75 million grants included for demonstration projects in mass transportation.

The purpose of Title VII is to provide grants to states and local bodies to obtain open land for recreation, conservation, and scenic and historic purposes in urban or urbanized areas. The area to be acquired must be important to the execution of a comprehensive plan (metropolitan).

The Federal-Aid Highway Act of 1962. This act established the requirement for metropolitan areawide transportation planning. Note that here we are, again, inching in on metropolitan planning. Such requirements or inducements toward metropolitan planning are seen to characterize, increasingly, much of the legislation. But local compliance varies greatly, from minimal compliance to effective overall planning.

The Civil Rights Act of 1964. Title VI of this act provides that no person in the United States shall on the ground of race, color, or national origin be excluded from participation in, be denied the benefits of, or be subjected to discrimination under any program of activity receiving federal financial assistance.

It applies to all newly constructed housing provided in urban renewal areas. It also covers all newly constructed housing under the college housing and senior citizens direct loan programs. It applies to all low-rent public housing both new and existing. However, Title VI does not apply to the FHA mortgage insurance program (unless rent supplements are involved) or to the Veterans Administration mortgage guarantee program.

This act is noted to show how closely the deep issues of race and minority pervade and cut across all planning, housing, and development; and to show that even in this basic legislation there are exceptions.

The Urban Mass Transportation Act of 1964. This represents a very consid-

---

[1] Since enactment in 1954, 5,500 localities and 200 metropolitan and regional areas have participated in this 701 planning program.

erable expansion of provisions of the housing acts of 1961 and 1962. It is noted here as an example of the piecemeal character of planning legislation. It took effect only 3 years after the first act, two years after the 1962 act, and was followed in 1966 by amendments.

The Appalachian Regional Development Act of 1965. This act established the Appalachian Regional Commission. The main intention was to assist this economically depressed region: to promote economic development by joining federal and state action on a regional basis. The plans developed under this act include some for new towns and some for joining small towns to form more viable centers.

The Housing and Urban Development Act of 1965. This act established the Cabinet-level Department of Housing and Urban Development. The elevation to Cabinet level signalized the new importance of these areas. The change in name from Housing and Home Finance Agency (1947) to Housing and Urban Development (1965) marks the accumulating importance over the years of planning-development considerations and grants.

Urban planning assistance grants were increased to $230 million in 1965 (Section 701 of the 1954 act). They include planning grants to be made to metropolitan areas or to regions—indicating serious recognition of the reality that, in the age of the automobile, city planning as such within the political boundaries of a municipality is confined within almost purely imaginary lines and that urban planning must be in the context of region.

The open space land program was enlarged and made to include urban beautification.

Section 704 authorized grants to state and local governments equal to interest payments for up to 5 years on advance acquisition of land for public facilities.

This act included authorization to the Federal Housing Administration to insure mortgages which finance the acquisition of land and installation of water and sewage facilities for new communities. No single mortgage can exceed $10 million (or 50 percent of land cost, or 90 percent of development cost).

The Demonstration Cities and Metropolitan Development Act of 1966. Title I of this act provided for grants to demonstration cities (later called "model cities") to deal with the many-sided, coordinated reconstruction of an area containing at least 10 percent of the population of a city receiving funds.

To qualify for assistance, a model cities program must be designed (1) to renew entire slum neighborhoods by combined use of physical and social development programs; (2) to increase substantially the supply of standard housing of low and moderate cost; (3) to make marked progress in reducing social and educational disadvantages, ill health, underemployment, and enforced idleness; and (4) to contribute to a well-balanced city.

The city must also indicate that (1) the projects and activities which are part of the program will be initiated reasonably soon; (2) adequate local resources to carry out these projects and activities are or will be available; (3) the fullest utilization possible will be made of private initiative and enterprise; (4) a relocation plan exists that will adequately serve those displaced; and (5) the program is consistent with comprehensive planning in the entire urban and metropolitan areas.

Title II of this act authorizes supplementary grants to states and local public bodies carrying out federally aided development projects which have an impact on the growth of metropolitan areas. The supplemental grant, which is designed to encourage and assist communities in making comprehensive metropolitan planning and programming more effective, may not exceed 20 percent of the eligible project cost.

Broadening the provision of the 1965 act, FHA is authorized to insure mortgages financing cost of land and development to include new communities (New Towns); up to $25 million is permitted for a single mortgage; the maximum total outstanding is $250 million.

The act also requires that applications for federal assistance in carrying out these projects be submitted to a metropolitanwide planning agency.

The Housing Act of 1968. This act amends Section 704 of the 1965 act and provides for loans for advance acquisition of land for *any* public purpose and for longer periods. It allows up to $50 million in a single operation and up to $250 million in total loan guarantees to start new communities.

Section 404 states that new community development projects are eligible for assistance only if the secretary determines that (1) the proposed new community will be economically feasible and will contribute to the orderly development of the area of which it is a part; (2) there is a practicable plan (and time schedule) for financing the land acquisition and development costs and for the improvement and marketing of the land which, giving consideration to the purposes of the title and the special problems involved, represents an acceptable financial risk to the United States; (3) there is a sound internal development plan for the new community that meets state and local requirements, provides for a proper balance of housing for families of low and moderate income, and provides satisfactory supporting facilities for its future residents; and (4) the internal development plan is consistent with planning for the area in which the new community is situated.

Subsequent Legislation and Action Several important developments occurred in the early seventies. The National Environmental Policy Act set up the National Council on Environmental Policy and subsequently the U.S. Environmental Protection Agency: ecological landmarks. The Housing and Urban Development Act of 1970, Title VII, The Urban Growth and New Community Development Act defines new policy and provides increases in funding programs—a leap to catch up with arrears. On January 5, 1973, the President unexpectedly announced a moratorium on many housing and urban renewal programs, stating that results of 30-odd years were incorrigibly bad. A new approach was to be announced September 7. This was not forthcoming by September 19, 1973.

However, the direction of the President's thinking was disclosed in the Administration's Better Communities Bill, before Congress in 1973, making block grants to states and localities, with minimal conditions for compliance, on the thesis that the localities best know their needs. Others felt that national standards were necessary, to overcome existing local economic and social inequality that might otherwise be perpetuated. Finally, in late 1973 Congress debated for the first time in history an Act covering National Land Use Policy. This was a beginning.

Administration and Implementation While the foregoing indicates a formidable record of intention and progress, in performance it is a great deal less impressive because of conditions at the federal level—as well as at the state and local levels, which in a federal system of government are really the levels of performance. This is gravely worsened by the moratorium.

At the federal level, two major points need to be observed. First, the program and the funds authorized in legislation, while themselves already small in proportion to need, are almost invariably cut very severely in the subsequent stage of actual fund appropriation. Legislation in this field is largely an expression of intention in response to outside pressures. Actual appropriation of funds is much lower, so that the programs, whose scale so greatly determines their effectiveness, are often token or marginal. The rate of actual availability of funds and resources is so inadequate that environmental deterioration proceeds far faster than the assignment of funds to city rebuilding, to regional development, or to new towns.

Second, the multiplicity of powerful federal administrative agencies to whom the various types of projects under the legislation are assigned makes for confusion and delay. They are, among others, the departments of Housing and Urban Development; of Health, Education and Welfare; of Commerce; of Transportation; and numerous subagencies within them such as the Economic Development Administration in the Department of Commerce and the independent Office of Economic Opportunity—which are two out of dozens.

The President's Executive Order of December 29, 1967 underlined the troubled situation that had arisen from the extension of policies and programs without, however, appreciably unraveling administration:

> . . . prescribing arrangements for coordination of the activities of regional commissions and activities of the Federal Government relating to regional economic development and establishing the Federal Advisory Council on Regional Economic Development" establishes a framework for closer coordination of Federal participation in regional programs and for evaluation of programs within the framework of the existing statutory authorization. Although reported in the press as markedly changing the relative roles of Federal and State governments in the establishment and operation of regional commissions, the Commission finds no significant intergovernmental implications in the change.[1]

Local Implementation and the Effect of Zoning In the federal system of the United States, the power of the federal government, though heavily on the increase for a half-century or more, is still limited, so that in many ways

[1]Quotation from *Urban and Rural America: Policies for Future Growth*, Advisory Commission on Intergovernmental Relations, Washington, D.C., April 1968, p. 134.

the last word as to administration-implementation lies with the state and city.

For instance, federal legislation has tended toward metropolitan planning—development which is the logical move from town or city planning in view of modern communications and transportation developments, which have made urban legal boundaries essentially obsolete. It is beyond the constitutional power of the federal government to impose effective metropolitan planning-development, but inducements have been legislated to this end. Degrees of acceptance vary around the country. The generally one-class (middle-class) white suburbs object to this legislation as interfering with their serenity or pseudoserenity and out of fear of racial and economic integration which could result from the influence or predominance of the major central city. The increasing minority populations of the cities are wary of it because they see the possibility of fairly soon becoming the dominant majority in a number of cities and of losing potential political power or control in a truly metropolitan situation.

Another major obstacle to the implementation of creative planning on the local level is the existence of zoning. First formalized into law in New York City in 1916, zoning became immensely popular and has been almost universally adopted. It prescribes allowable land uses in different districts so as to avoid an arbitrary mixture of, say, unpleasant industry, residences, and automobile service stations. It also governs building heights and density of coverage.

Initially zoning was enacted and accepted with enthusiasm because it appeared to be the way to ensure an orderly city, the ending of the anarchic use and mix-up of land uses that had characterized the noncontrol of preceding urban history, and it also seemed to support the businessman's desire for stable and increasing land prices. However, its stabilizing influence has frequently turned into stagnation, its often excessive density restrictions have prevented the building of apartment houses in single-family areas (while on the other hand permitting areas of very dense office building development), and it has thus produced or buttressed racial and economic class segregation against those who cannot afford large-lot homes.

To counter this latter aspect, an experiment has been initiated. The New York State Urban Development Corporation, established in 1968 by the state legislature, is a public organization endowed with the authority to build and to disregard local zoning. It is to be seen to what extent it will exercise this potential cutter of the Gordian knot. There are several other signs that suggest innovative modification of the zoning tyranny (such as "cluster zoning" and large-development zoning)—a tyranny which is, in this and its other effects, harmful to creative planning-development. Zoning has become and still is a powerful negative influence, readily subject to manipulation, which erodes its residual merits.

The phenomenon of diminishing actuality and scale from initial big policy statements to shrunken actual impact and effectuation locally may be set out as diagramatically as follows:

STATEMENTS   OF   PURPOSE
(Presidential Eloquence — Congressional Preambles)
||
Provisions in Actual Congressional Legislation.
||
Reconsideration and Actual Funding
||
Federal Multi-Agencies
||
Local
City-Region

This quantitative dilution or diminution, accentuated by the time involved in the processes just diagrammed, means great danger of "too little
and too late"; so that, once the process has run its course into the final
actions, the ills to have been cured have often expanded and have both
changed their nature and become more severe.

Finally, on the local administrative side, since about 1960 there has been
the growing recognition in city government that the compartmentalization
of city departments is a handicap as programs proliferate. In a number of
cities, city planning, urban renewal, housing development, and building
regulation are being put under one control.

Some Other Significant Developments during This Period This legislative and
administrative survey shows the sequence of city planning and associated
fields from the modern beginnings to 1970. However, there have been
individual policies and events of moment whose import or contribution
to the total picture is not in all cases clear. Some appear not to have been
in the mainstream, not to have been begetters of future progeny, yet they
need to be recorded—if only to prompt the question why they did not
take root.

Three of those to be recorded had their origin in the adventurous days
of the New Deal, which was receptive to new ideas; two preceded the New
Deal.

The Regional Plan of New York and Environs. This was an ambitious and
influential effort, a nongovernmental citizen operation (already briefly noted)
which appeared at the end of the 1920s. Financed by Russell Sage Foundation, it preceded by over 20 years the earliest governmental recognition of
metropolitan-regional planning. Its even more definite contribution was its
promulgation of the self-contained neighborhood (and superblock) concept
of Clarence Arthur Perry. It still flourishes and is promulgating its Second
Regional Plan.

The National Resources Planning Board. This existed from 1934 to 1943
and employed the best planners of the time in making studies and reports
of distinction. In 1937 it produced the notable report entitled *Our Cities:
Their Role in the National Economy.* The board was established by President
Roosevelt with no authorizing legislation. It did not command any serious
public lobbying pressure and never succeeded in gaining a foothold in
Congress. Public planning was then quite unacceptable to dominant American opinion—as it still is in very considerable degree. Perhaps that is why

the legislative sequence noted finally reached some planning formulations: as was explained above, such planning as has been authorized over the years came in piecemeal as adjunct to other purposes and has even yet not achieved a national policy synthesis.

Greenbelt Towns. In another New Deal effort, the attempt was made to create what were called *"greenbelt towns"* outside of Washington, Milwaukee, and Cincinnati under the federal government's Resettlement Administration. In 1935 three, of self-contained character like the English New Towns, got under way in strategic locations on ample sites. Here again, the work was done by Presidential order without specific congressional legislation, in response to a combination of stimuli: making work for the unemployed and providing low-rent housing. The intention was to plan them on the emerging principles of relative self-containment, separation of pedestrian and vehicular traffic, and unpierced residential superblock districts. Specifically, they had been launched through the conviction and persuasiveness of a brain truster, Rexford Guy Tugwell, and a small number of planners with a vision but no mass support. After the first superblock of 750 or so houses had been built (1,500 in one of the towns, Greenbelt) and the Second World War had intervened, the New Deal impulse had evaporated, the large unbuilt acreage was sold off to private interests, and the embryo towns remained fragments in a sea of speculative development. Thus this operation which could well have been as seminal as Letchworth and Welwyn in England expired with scarcely a ripple of effect on the country's thought and outlook.[1]

The impulse for the greenbelt towns came from two sources. First, from the British examples of Letchworth and Welwyn Garden City (which later flowered into the New Towns movement in Britain) via a very few enthusiastic planners who had seen and studied them and had also studied Ebenezer Howard's *Garden Cities of Tomorrow.* (*See* HOWARD, EBENEZER.)

Radburn, New Jersey, was the other parent. It was a New Town effort in 1929 by the private developer Alexander Bing. He had given Clarence Stein and Henry Wright the opportunity to develop their theories of twentieth-century living. While the proposed town developed only two superblocks before the Great Depression stopped the operation, the area that was completed was large enough to furnish a living illustration or dramatization of certain principles:

1. Separation of vehicular and pedestrian circulation.
2. Through traffic on the periphery of superblocks, not piercing them.
3. Internal park area in each superblock, with easy safe access from every home. This was a neighborhood core which had important social effects and implications.[2] It gave physical form to the Perry conception.

---

[1]For an account of these interesting fragments 30 years later, see Albert Mayer, *The Greenbelt Towns Revisited,* a study made for the National Association of Housing and Redevelopment Officials. It appeared in abbreviated form in *Journal of Housing,* January–April 1967. Published in full as monograph in October 1968.

[2]Clarence S. Stein, *New Towns for America,* M.I.T. Press, Cambridge, Mass., 1967.

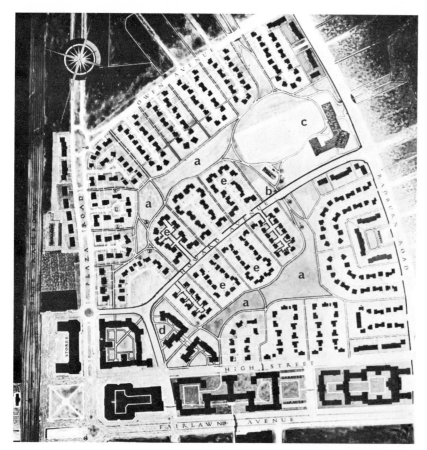

LEFT: *Radburn, New Jersey, "the town for the motor age." Although builder Alexander Bing was forced to leave it incomplete in 1929, its technical, land-use, and social conceptions have had world-wide impact. Basic concept: no piercing of superblock by traffic. By Clarence Stein and Henry Wright. The superblock neighborhood: (a) internal block parts in each superblock, (b) pedestrian underpass between blocks, (c) elementary school and playground, (d) community center, management, shops, (e) typical culs-de-sac.   BELOW: Radburn, New Jersey. Underpass between blocks, completing separation of pedestrians from vehicles—freedom and safety for children. (Gretchen Van Tassel, Kensington, Virginia.)*

The Radburn idea got a further tryout in the greenbelt towns (especially in Greenbelt, Maryland, near Washington) which, as noted, were likewise abortive and not of much influence at the time. This Radburn idea was soon very influential in Europe, especially in Swedish and British town designs; only later, in fact not until the late 1950s and 1960s, did its influence permeate the United States.

The Tennessee Valley Authority. The TVA was set up in the early days of the New Deal, fathered by Senator George Norris and a small group of imaginative thinkers. Authorized in the legislation of 1933, it was one of the really great planning-development concepts and achievements in the history of the United States or of any country. It provided for regional resource development in a poverty-stricken area, both exhausted and under-developed—the watershed of the Tennessee River, an area of 40,000 square miles (about 100,000 square kilometers). In action it included creation of hydroelectric power, river navigation, resource conservation, introduction of improved crops and fertilizers, important industries attracted by ample low-cost power, a small new town, education and reanimation of the people's outlook, and close work with them.

In short, as an imaginative, integrated concept brought to fruition, it continues to flourish on an increasing scale with unexhausted inventiveness. It includes actual town development and is a prototype in the sense of dealing with total enhanced living. Its relevance here is that the total town-regional concepts, that are only now being recognized as indispensable, have there had a continuous history of 35 years. An influential model in many countries since, it has never been repeated in the United States and has had little demonstrable overall influence here. Recently TVA has come under ecological attack on the ground of purchase of coal produced by strip mining, and of inadequate land restoration.

Professional Practice—Evolution at Progressively Sharpening Tempo   When town planning or city planning first became recognized, at the end of the nineteenth century and in the first years of the twentieth, as a desirable endeavor, a sacred tenet was the conception of impartiality. The professional planner and the city planning commission were supposed to be quite neutral, to be above class or political bias. There was prevalent an image of one correct plan of physical development and land use to be discovered amid the confusion, a plan that would produce an orderly physical environment and provide equally for everyone—in short, a plan that would constitute one optimum, comprehensive answer.

As part of this ethos, the planning commission evolved. This body was independent to the extent, for example, that its members, generally non-professional, were appointed for overlapping terms, so that there was continuity, nonremovability, and very considerable independence from mayor or council. The professional arm of this commission was at the beginning an itinerant planning consultant or firm which was employed to make a plan of definite, more or less once-and-for-all nature which was then left to the city. Such a consultant would make plans for a number of cities as clients. He might or might not be called on to return and restudy and update his plan.

At the next stage there was an employed planning staff whose members themselves made the plan, usually under or with such a consultant. But still the plan was considered an absolute. The professional planner was sufficiently expert to come up with the right plan—in other words, the reigning image was that there was one right plan, and that it generally stayed right with time. At that stage of events all the most eminent professionals were the independent consultants. The municipal staff planner was distinctly lower in prestige with the public and the profession.

This "one right plan" concept and planning aloofness were coeval with the period when plans were rarely executed. For one thing, the executive departments of the city (highways, health, water supply, and others), whether they had been consulted or not, did not feel themselves committed and in execution went their own way. But when the exigencies or anarchies of city growth and of private development dynamics began to call for real application of the plan, it became obvious that there was no real enforcement power behind it; its "independence" meant that the mayor or city executive body had no commitment and perhaps no full understanding. The plan itself was often not really up to date.

Two important devices then came into being. One was the concept of the capital budget, usually a long- and a short-term one—a 5-year tentative budget and a 1-year immediate actual budget, both drawn up as accompaniments of the planning. This was a very powerful instrument indeed, for all departments had to appear to make their pleas for funds. The planning authority would then allocate available capital funds among them, a total invariably much less than the total of requests. After public hearings, these figures were generally adopted by the governing body with no very serious changes.

The second change has been in many cases[1] the substitution, for the "independent" planning commission, of a planning department under the city executive—a department which became an increasingly important arm of vital city decisions.

With these accessions of real power and immediacy, many eminent professional planners who had hitherto been the consultants now became interested in the public municipal planning positions. For example, Edmund Bacon in Philadelphia and Charles Blessing in Detroit have devoted their distinguished careers almost entirely to a single city. Likewise the federal government, which has been and is the seat of power which is buttressed by the disposition of funds, has attracted important professionals. Thus members of the planning profession in public employment exceed the numbers in private consulting practice and in quality stand up very well indeed. There is, however, considerable interchangeability: the man (much less often, woman) who has gained an important reputation in government service may become a consultant practitioner; and to a lesser extent vice versa.

While these developments were taking place, city planning was also changing, deepening, broadening, diversifying. From the initial scope and purpose of orderly physical and spatial development, utilities and transit systems, and some architectural awareness or emphasis, there came the input of social, economic, and even psychological thinking and specialists. The planner became more and more the orchestrator of these and other disciplines. Often he was no longer the architect or engineer as originally, but came from other disciplines, such as that of management. Also, the institution of the public hearing, originally a more or less superficial and orderly proceeding, became much more spirited and raucous. Organized opposition groups turned out in large numbers. Thus, planning had come a long way from its imputed detachment. The planner had to be prepared both by way of his prepared material and in his personal attitude to defend, to amend. He began to be in the thick of things.

This state of affairs has been only a transient stopping point on a road.

---

[1]In so large and diverse a country as the United States, there are many variants in these and other matters; so here again, in this relatively brief presentation, the fully interested reader must go to the reference material and, indeed, beyond.

The oppositions at that stage were well organized and determined, but they were generally on the same plane of semidetachment. It was not yet a passionate situation.

In the last dozen years, beginning about 1960 and increasingly so since, a quite different, more intense, even passionate participation by people from the localities in the city has built up. This was part of the general ferment of the sixties. Encouraged by the newly set up federal Office of Economic Opportunity early in the decade, taking at its face value the 1966 Model Cities Act as to community participation, and distrusting "city hall"—the municipal establishment—the localities in cities have increasingly asserted themselves. They increasingly object to plans in which they feel they have not been fully consulted, in which they have not participated in a sufficiently decisive way in terms of formulation and then of control. This trend has led to many intense confrontations and impasses, for not infrequently local people would rather prevent the action and physical development than agree to planning-development they do not consider to be genuinely their own. In some cases this local insistence has successfully remolded plans which are now going forward. In others there is much delay and sometimes stalemate.

A striking example is this: For years, successive planners and administrations in New York City had pushed the idea of a lower Manhattan expressway to carry vehicular traffic across from New Jersey to Long Island without causing delays and mixups with local traffic, but these planners were always faced with the protests of local residents and small businesses who were to be displaced. Finally, the local groups mustered so much strength that the plan has been finally abandoned.

The crux of the question now is not the issue of consulting the localities, of having them participate, but of who is to have the last word. Whatever is and will be the net effect on actual development—that is, the quantity, rate, and content of production or execution of development—two points are to be observed:

First, the internal "suburbanization" or Balkanization of the city, especially the large city. There are numerous situations and subjects where the interest of the total city as an entity must be overriding. There must be limits on the independence of the locality if the city is not to fall apart. In short, while the planning and development should be on a two-tier basis with subjects clearly demarcated (as, for example, in the case of the London boroughs vis-a-vis the Greater London Council), there is danger of an anarchic independence, such as bedevils the metropolitan situation because of the separatist suburbs. This is one question in the new or emerging planning.

Another question is this: Who *is* the locality or community? In cities which are multiracial or multiethnic, there are two needs: (1) the demarcation of local boundaries (which of course does much to determine who is in control of a locality); and (2)—presently lacking—the establishment of democratic political procedures that will enable local elected officials to arrive at final decisions. Even the most devoted efforts by planners to achieve consensus often have only ephemeral results.

These matters are now very much in flux. The intensities and varieties of experience that have accumulated make it suitable or urgent to try to produce relationships that are more than ad hoc and opportunistic.

Two particular points must be added to what has been called "confrontation" so as to give a true impression of the atmosphere. Not infrequently this goes so far that determined "confronters" prevent or break up important meetings. And it must always be borne in mind by anyone not familiar with the American scene that the questions of racial and ethnic minorities permeate all planning, social processes, and decisions.

The planner is increasingly in the arena. The senior planners who endeavor to develop acceptable citywide plans need to and do acquire closer understanding of the predilections and requirements of localities; and they must handle very tense situations with skill. Their staff planners spend much more time in the field, tuned in as closely as they can contrive to local opinion and acting as informal emissaries.

A quite recent development in the profession is what is called "advocate planning"—or it might almost equally well be called "adversary planning." These planners represent the dissident groups, which the local groups frequently or usually are. Frequently these planners give their time, or most of it, free of charge. Sometimes the local groups receive funds for planning from philanthropic foundations who wish to promote particular experiments. Sometimes the city itself provides moderate funding. While leading planners sometimes operate at this level as a service, usually the advocate planner is in the early years of his practice and builds up a tough, belligerent stance—which is at the opposite pole from where planning started in its early above-the-struggle ideals or assumptions. These advocate planners serve to give the local groups a standing in the current controversies that they could not otherwise command.

In any event the planners—both local advocate planners and planners at broader levels—are in the very midst of this time of change. They might well be playing both a stronger and a more understanding role themselves, supplying more of the needed combination of loyal client representation and of intercementation. It is peculiarly part of the planner's trust to catalyze the future.

In this discussion, the "city beautiful" concept has been left far behind, as it was in actuality in our cities generally. When planning came to include in its constituent ingredients the gamut of sociology, economics, health, education, and other fields, these elements of social substance and planners with those specific disciplines, came to predominate. Along with this trend, considerations of overall form and aesthetics tended to fade into the background.

A recognition of the importance of form returned with the rise of urban redevelopment in the 1950s. This aspect will be considered at greater length under "Urban Renewal."

Briefly, in individual, limited areas of urban renewal, eminent architects have attempted an amalgam of architectural creation and urban thought and scale with some excellent limited results. More recently, there has been recognition of and emphasis on urban design in a more extended sense. In some cities, notably New York, there is a municipal staff devoted to this. These efforts are architectural-aesthetic while taking account also of the more "scientific" aspects—such as psychological and mental health effects on people—and also of space characteristics and relationships. There is now a growing professional or semiscientific literature.

In the area of the planning and development of New Towns the criteria discussed in these paragraphs are seen in an altogether different light. This matter will be considered below, under "New Towns."

Education and Training   The first degree in planning was offered at Harvard University in 1923. By 1945 there were nine more universities offering degrees. By 1969, there was a total of 60.[1] Thus, at the end of the first 22 years there was a total of 10; and by the end of the next 24 years 50 more—or, about six times as many. There is another way of looking at the situation. In the first 31 years, 27 institutions offered degrees. Then came the 1954 Housing Act, which included the famous Section 701, offering planning grants to states and localities. In the next 14 years, through 1969, 33 new degree courses were offered.

Most (not all) of these degrees are at the graduate level and are strictly professional: urban and regional planning, public administration (specialization in planning or related fields), government (with urban and regional planning as a field). Some are described as "community planning," which indicates strong social emphasis, though no doubt all now do have increasing social content. There are (1969) only six degrees in urban design and three in environmental design.

There are many undergraduate degrees variously described as, for example, majors in urban studies or in urban life. These have particular interest because they are frequently taken by those who may not make a career of planning but who, as citizens, will take major interest in urban problems. It is of course in the degree of citizens' interest and the priority they place on it that the future lies. An index of growing interest and concern are the adult education evening courses in planning and urbanization, which continue to multiply. From this point of view, too, the sensitizing of children to an awareness of environment and its crucial importance, in secondary school and even before, is critically important but only rarely under way.

There are proliferating in the United States, community or 2-year colleges. These offer both lay adult education in urban planning-development and urban life, and vocational courses for paraprofessionals. By the middle of 1969, there were already thirteen 2-year colleges offering certificates as urban development assistant (and the like).

[1]For listing of the institutions and degrees, see *Colleges and Universities Offering Degree Programs in Planning and Related Fields,* American Institute of Planners, published annually.

One final matter may be noted. There has been, within a very few years, an almost unbelievable growth and intensity of concern in and identification with the subject of ecology. Outrage at various forms of pollution, of erosion and destruction of the natural environment and their rapid increase, this subject—the relation of man and of all organisms to each other and to the environment—has become an absorbing concern for scientists and laymen alike; incipiently, subject of legislation. But in most planning schools—except the schools of landscape architecture and a few institutions such as the University of California's School of Environmental Design, combining planning, architecture, and landscape architecture—the subject has not yet completely (as of 1969) been incorporated into the curriculum. Undoubtedly it will.

It is not easy to separate education and training. The government at various levels in the United States, but particularly at the federal level, offers a number of fellowships for students to be trained at various universities, especially in planning administration. There are also opportunities available, generally for a period of 1 year, for actual in-service experience.

Institutions (Professional, Educational, and Propagandist)   There is an abundance of research in the United States. Most planning schools in universities have some research in progress. There are a large number of research institutions, national and regional, some connected with universities but not fully part of them, some independent. Some idea of the wide range and subject matter is suggested by these few:
- Brookings Institute, Washington, D.C. (National.)
- Resources for the Future Inc., Washington, D.C. (Includes studies of land, ecology, and urban studies.)
- Harvard–Massachusetts Institute of Technology Joint Center for Urban Studies, Cambridge, Massachusetts
- Southwest Urban Policy Institute, Memphis, Tennessee
- Northwest Economic Research Institute, Minneapolis, Minnesota
- University of Pennsylvania, Philadelphia (Noted especially for its work in "regional science" and the application of computers to urban planning.)
- National Urban Coalition, Washington, D.C. (An action group that also does much specific research.)
- Regional Plan Association of New York (This is another example of an action agency that does much research. This is a common combination in the United States. Most of the professional and propagandist institutions are doing research.)
- Rand Corporation (Typical and best known of the "think tanks," a species which originated in space and defense work.)

Much of this research is financed by the federal government and by foundations. The Ford Foundation contributes both across the board and for urban social investigation. Specifically and notably, it finances studies as well as action research concerning race and minority in urban planning and living, a much-needed undertaking in the United States. Other foundations are in this field also, but to a lesser extent.

The Advisory Committee on Inter-governmental Relations is noted especially; it is unique in that it is a research arm of the U.S. Congress. In spite of its narrower title, it publishes studies on subjects like national urban policy.

The only purely professional organization—in that it has definite educational and achievement standards for membership—is the American Institute of Planners.[1]

The other national and local associations are either practitioner-based,[2] generally with membership open to anyone interested, or citizen-propagandist. Most of the latter are concerned with urban planning and development, originating from and still with main emphasis on housing.

It should be noted that they are activist and immensely helpful in lobbying measures through Congress and legislatures and often effective as watchdogs in seeing or trying to see that the legislation is really implemented and carried out. And perhaps they are a step or two ahead of current political thinking, policy making, and legislation. But in general they do not create, think through, introduce, support, or propagandize ideas and undertakings appreciably ahead of their time. By contrast, The Town and Country Planning Association in England started its New Towns work long before it was really known to the public, made it a public issue, and was largely responsible for its great subsequent progress. It may be noted, too, that the two examples of legislation breaking quite new ground in planning—The Tennessee Valley Authority Act and Section 701—do not appear to have been proposed or strongly supported by any planning organization but rather by an individual or individuals in strategic positions.

There are innumerable local-based citizen pressure groups in housing-planning; a half-dozen or so on the national level, some with a number of local chapters. Two of the organizations not only have strength of their own but act as secretariat and leader for thirty or forty other national organizations whose major interest is in another field; acting really as their informed alerters on legislative issues and marshaling their joint influence. These are the National Housing Conference and the National Committee against Discrimination in Housing, whose concerns embrace also a number of planning issues.

One organization, The National Urban Coalition, formed in 1967, has given evidence and promise of being ahead in anticipating and pushing for more drastic measures, and their accomplishment nationally and locally, than is characteristic of the older groups.

Geographic and Climatic Conditions, Pollution, Ecology   While there are considerable variations in climate over the country, their influence is seen in

[1] Planners for Equal Opportunity is a small dissident group, radical in outlook, with less rigorous professional standards.

[2] In planning, this is the American Society of Planning Officials. In housing-planning there is the National Association of Housing and Redevelopment Officials. A new militant organization, National Black Planning Network, in March 1970 heavily attacked ASPO, as, among other things, "disseminating racist planning practices" and asked that "ASPO raise $5 million to promote the development of minority causes." A small group, its action here is cited as an example of the climate of confrontation.

house types, layouts, and materials rather than in any urban planning characteristics.

Direct geographic effects are not readily traceable. "Accidentally geographic" were the cotton plantations in the South, with their self-contained character, their manor houses, slave quarters, warehouses, and primitive factories. These plantations were urban-rural in character. While they and the form of economy that they embodied were flourishing, they hampered or made less appropriate the development of large cities such as the North knew. However, with radical changes in the Southern economy, their influence is now largely touristic and no longer relates to nor influences city plans.

One might well have expected that other geographic-climatic influences would be discernible, but these can hardly be identified. There does not appear to be, for example, avoidance of city building in areas subject to hurricanes or to earthquakes; nor do such dangers appear to have marked influence on city plans.

Substantial portions of cities have been built in flood plains; thus they have periodically been damaged or destroyed and then rebuilt on the same sites. Houses have not infrequently been built on unstable slopes and have slid off into the ocean. Street directions do not seem to have been influenced by direction and severity of winds.

Our knowledge of the effects of climate and of microclimate has increased, and the latter has enabled us to make beneficial use of even slight slopes or undulations. Yet in general we need to be—and we are—really less sensitive than ever, because air conditioning can massively take care of whatever situation is produced. Indeed, it is becoming customary to enclose and air-condition areas of the environment such as shopping centers so as to be quite independent of climate there. This trend is to be carried considerably further, into other areas, in the proposed experimental city in Minnesota. For economy, the air-conditioning engineers are exercising some marginal influence in the placing of buildings to absorb the least sun load.

Related elements have recently, belatedly, claimed attention with startling sharpness and penetration, the more so because of long inattention. The negative manifestations are air pollution, water pollution, noise pollution, solid wastes in quantity beyond what we have been able to devise disposal of. On the creative side, the subject of ecology—harmonious adjustment of the human-urban to the total organic and inorganic environment—is becoming an essential element in planning.

Traditions of Planning to the End of the Nineteenth Century The subject has already been covered to a degree in the discussion of early settlements at the beginning of this article. It was noted that there was some early planning, later engulfed in a sea of population pressure, early expansionist technical advances in transportation, and resultant pressure of the speculative impulse.

The one city that almost fully lived up to its early plan, and maintained its quality, is Washington. This was a grand plan whose strength and character were not bent or broken. The essentials of its elegance and serenity,

the proportions of street widths and of the dimensions of squares and circles to the uniform building height lines have never been violated, thus giving full scope to the drama and nobility of the two high symbols: the Capitol and Washington Monument. Luckily this has all been retained. Unluckily it never became a tradition in the cities of the United States.

Other major American cities are an anarchic jumble of competitive skyscrapers, actual and hoped for: New York-ness rather than Washington-ness. Other originally planned cities such as Boston, Savannah, Philadelphia, and New Haven, with their commons and open spaces, have retained in varying degrees their original central character but did not retain with expansion those proportionate recurrences and locations of openness and foci that would have permeated the city as a whole with the original character and intent.

ABOVE: *Washington, D.C. The five monuments—(a) Capitol, (b) White House, (c) Washington Monument, (d) Lincoln Memorial, (e) Jefferson Memorial—are at the ends and intersection of the two central axes. Traffic problems at intersections of diagonals with the gridiron pattern are dealt with by depressing the diagonal through-artery at the crossing. Uniform maximum height of buildings lends serenity and permits the monuments to dominate visibly from almost anywhere. (Aero Service, Philadelphia.)* RIGHT: *New Haven, seventeenth century. Original plan showing the center green. (Art Library, Yale University, New Haven.)*

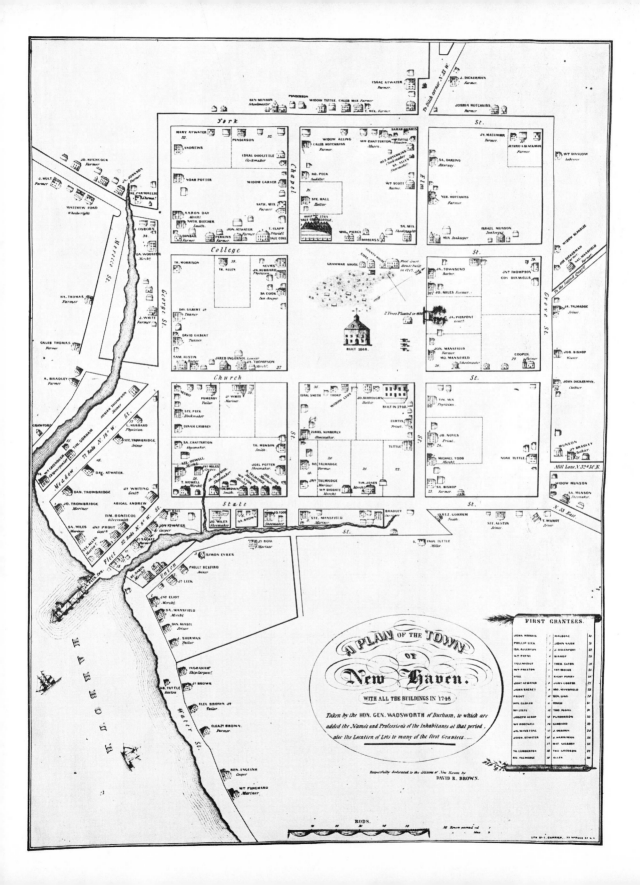

A PLAN OF THE TOWN
OF
New Haven.
WITH ALL THE BUILDINGS IN 1748

Taken by the HON. GEN. WADSWORTH of Durham, to which are
added the Names and Professions of the Inhabitants at that period
also the Location of Lots to many of the first Grantees.

Respectfully dedicated to the Citizens of New Haven by
DAVID R. BROWN.

LEFT: *New Haven, 1961. The green. Still virtually intact after 300 years. On the upper side is Yale University. On the two streets bordering the green are now office buildings, shops, and hotels. (New York Airways.)* BELOW: *Philadelphia. William Penn's nucleus plan (1682). The five open squares are no more than $\frac{1}{2}$ mile ($\frac{4}{5}$ kilometer) from any point. The central square was and is City Hall. (Philadelphia City Planning Commission; Lawrence Williams, Photographer, Upper Darby, Pennsylvania.)*

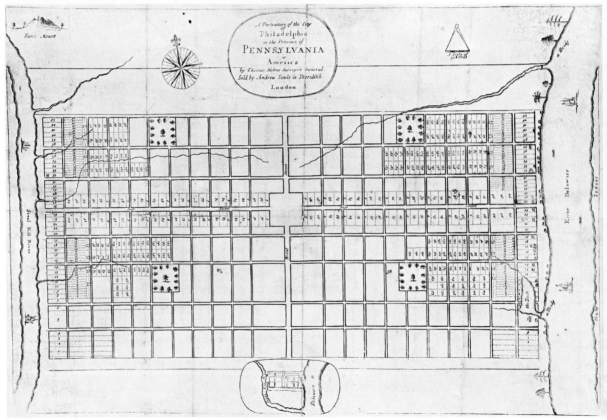

During the period there were industrial towns built by their own dominant industry, mostly of a mephitic character. But early, in the city of Lowell,
Massachusetts, and others patterned on it, there was for a time a planned
character that expressed the social qualities of the people. With growth,
this special character disappeared. Pullman, Illinois, in the latter part of the
nineteenth century, was thoughtfully planned, with civic and recreational
elements. However, in the face of the paternalistic and feudal attitude of
the Pullman Company, characteristic generally of the "company town," and
the notoriously bitter strike at the end of the century, the concept of the
employer-industrial town came into disrepute.

The "city beautiful," contemporary legacy of the 1893 World's Fair, has
been discussed at the beginning of this article. Burnham's plan for Chicago,
though by no means fully carried out, remains a great exemplar of this
era and impulse.

The major positive contribution of the nineteenth century to urbanism
has been the great central park, a large, romantic, naturalistic oasis generally
near the center of the city. Though by no means equivalent, because on
much larger scale, this ranks with the early commons as a high physical-
spiritual point in the urban scene. Surprisingly part of the Zeitgeist, which
was otherwise so very utilitarian, the great creative figure in the movement,
in design and in expressive eloquence, was Frederick L. Olmsted. Central
Park in Manhattan and Prospect Park in Brooklyn are the best known;
others are in St. Louis, San Francisco, Boston, Hartford, and Trenton;
and a large number elsewhere.

*Present-day Central Park, New York
City. (New York Park Department.)*

Twentieth-century Planning   It has been explained that in the early years of the twentieth century city planning experienced a lively boom, but on a physical and somewhat generalized and superficial basis. The significant change in planning came in the 1930s, in the ferment of the early days of Roosevelt's New Deal, though the seminal examples of Sunnyside and Radburn (and Forest Hills) date from a somewhat earlier period. The significant changes—injection of social-economic content of housing and community concepts, and to an extent of ecological considerations—began in the twenties, particularly in New York State.[1] These found partially fertile soil in the New Deal.

It seems well to make this last section of this history and analysis representative of the recent past, the present, and the emerging present-future. The notable examples are taken roughly in the order of their major chronological appearance as types, though individual efforts may have been made previously:

- City and town extensions: quantitatively now spent
- Suburbs: quantitatively vast recent and current expansion, generally without distinction
- Urban renewal: in midpassage
- Model cities or demonstration cities: off to a tenuous start
- New Towns and communities: working up to some volume
- Adumbrations of metropolitan and regional planning and development

City and Town Extensions   Three kinds of city and town extensions may be distinguished:

First, those settled as distinct suburbs, originally separated by some distance and open space from the city, with their own municipal governments. The open spaces between these inner suburbs and the city have since been covered by sprawl. Physically, these suburbs may be considered to have become city "extensions," but in social, economic, and governmental terms they are quite separate and separatist.

Second, the sprawl which has expanded outward from the central urban area, more or less concentrically but most densely along road and railroad lines and which is generally amorphous in form—what Henry Wright called "urbanoid."

---

[1] Specifically in two developments, both under New York Governor Alfred E. Smith, which produced:

The State Housing Board, the highly significant prototype for housing in the United States. Its influence became strong within a few years after it started to operate.

The Commission of Housing and Regional Planning, of which Clarence Stein was the creative director. Henry Wright was the gifted author of its report (1926), strongly advocating state planning. Its then original total approach, penetrating historic analysis, forward penetration, and climatic-topographic, urban-rural, projective technical analyses were unfortunately ahead of their time and had no immediate influence. However, the document *Change, Challenge, and Response: A Development Policy for New York State*, issued by New York State's Office for Regional Development in 1964 (the first such), pays tribute to this earlier report.

Other states have later and recently begun to perform pioneering or prototype roles—notably California, Massachusetts, and New Jersey.

Third, the separate enclaves which originally developed at or near the edge of the city and are now some distance back from it—that is, engulfed or surrounded by the expanded city but retaining some or much of the original homogeneity and architectural-landscaping distinguishability. Both the suburbs and these enclaves are middle class. While a number of cities have such enclaves, the total number is comparatively small; they are far less numerous than suburbs. Both are generally characterized by romantic layouts and curvilinear streets, in contrast to the general gridiron of the city. Examples of enclaves are Forest Hills and Riverdale in New York City, Roland Park in Baltimore, the J. C. Nichols development in Kansas City, and Chatham Village in Pittsburgh.

Neither the suburbs nor these enclaves offer the kind or pattern of urban-metropolitan solution of the entities of Vallingby and Farsta, the satellites or districts at the edge of Stockholm which have a good deal of local office-industrial employment, residents of a broad range of incomes, varied patterns of densities and heights of residential quarters, important civic subcenters, and shopping centers. The resemblance of the enclaves is rather to the original Hampstead Garden Suburb in London. They are islands of refreshment but not prototypes that have led with any frequency to others.

Urban Renewal (and Demonstration or Model Cities) This movement was originally conceived as more effectively dealing with slums and housing in terms of complete living (act of 1949). By the innovative use of the right of eminent domain to assemble large sites and of public subsidy for the write-down of land prices, the intention was and continues to be to attract investment mainly by private enterprise. In a very short time, the cities changed the focus of the effort, and the federal acts were continually amended to authorize larger and larger percentages to be nonresidential. The cities' influence on the effort went further, so that urban renewal largely encompassed transformation of decayed or decaying central areas, whether residential or not, into more or less glamorous or spectacular civic-cultural-commercial areas. Urban renewal now comprises three aspects:

1. The central "spectacular" just noted, which has constituted the bulk of the operations. This is in part a reemergence of the "city beautiful." Also there has been considerable residential construction in these same central areas, generally for upper- and middle-income people with no or few children.

2. Residential buildings, sometimes communities, within the city but not so close to the center. These have been largely middle income.

3. Low-cost public or otherwise subsidized housing: rarely in the center, sometimes in association with the previous category. The amount so far has not been major and varies from city to city.

The following effects may be discerned:

Use of eminent domain has permitted assemblage for suitably large-scale enterprises. The publicly subsidized write-down of land prices in city center urban renewal probably is not necessary, because the reuse usually takes the form of office buildings and costly apartment houses at considerable density.

The write-down is probably more of a windfall for the entrepreneur than a necessity in the central areas.

The central renewals all show spectacularly higher tax assessments and payments than the prerenewal structures. This is emphasized by proponents and by city officials, though it appears that this would happen with or without the inducements of urban renewal. There is a basic profitable market for such developments.

The workable program and city wide community renewal, noted above at several points in the list of federal legislation as a requirement of urban renewal, is a plus factor. These aspects must receive attention and involve quickening citizen understanding and participation. However, this is by no means an action mechanism but something like a promissory note without a definite due date.

Urban renewal was found to involve physical change and upgrading without, in many or most cases, improving the quality of total living and livelihood, especially of lower-income people. This state of affairs produced the Demonstration Cities Act of 1966 (see "Federal Legislation," above). Cities' proposals under it have been comprehensive and ingenious. As the earliest approved ones are just getting under way in the field, the quality of results is not yet known.

The significance of urban renewal to date might be summarized as follows: The revival and enhancement of city centers has produced some distinguished architecture, an urban spiritual revival, and renewed confidence and pride in the city—though the average 12-year chaos from demolition of the old to completion of the new ensemble has somewhat dampened this spirit. New legislation for minimizing this period has been haltingly put in motion. This renewal of pride and faith exists to very varying degrees, being most felt in influential circles. However, such cases as Charles Center in Baltimore, the central renewals in New Haven and Hartford, and the City Hall area in Boston probably affect all classes.

On the other hand, to the poor and the minorities, central urban renewal is seen and felt as callous displacement, the breaking up of communities, seriously inadequate provision of relocation housing, and a time gap of inconvenience and uncertainty. There is probably a sharp feeling that the poor, who were chiefly living in the destroyed areas, are as usual the ones at whose expense the renewed city heart is being achieved. It seems imperative that their part in the form of good housing in good neighborhoods—the original declared purpose in the "Magna Charta" of 1949—must be stepped up sharply, and that *their* subcenters of housing and local excellence must have much higher priority. One effect of this sharp protest has been less emphasis on demolition and somewhat more rehabilitation in place, of the substandard quarters.

The illustrations cover a range of types of notable urban renewal projects completed to date, in the categories noted.

City centers (largely nonresidential): Charles Center, Baltimore; City Hall area, Boston; Constitution Plaza, Hartford

Baltimore's Charles Center. Notable theater by John Johanson. Central urban renewals are more notable for single distinguished buildings and pedestrian-functional solutions than for total architectural ensemble. (M. E. Warren, Annapolis, Maryland.)

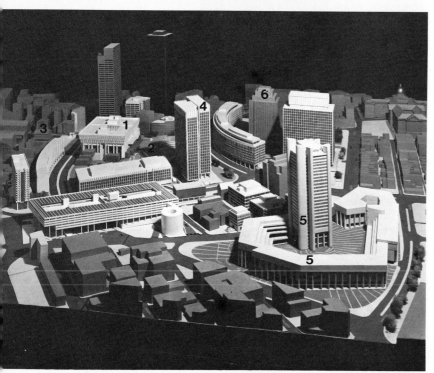

Boston's Government Center. While respecting the historic character of Old Boston, this federally aided urban renewal project in the heart of the city (Master plan by I. M. Pei) revitalized the core, with state and federal office facilities and notably the new City Hall, as well as private office buildings. The major government construction encouraged massive private investment in the same area. (1) New City Hall (architects: Kallman McKinnell and Knowles), (2) City Hall Square, (3) Faneuil Hall, (4) Federal Office Building, (5) State Service Center (architect: Paul Rudolph), (6) Suffolk County Court House. (George Zimberg, Cambridge, Massachusetts.)

ABOVE: *Hartford's Constitution Plaza. Upper (pedestrian) level. Note the serenity, which is in contrast to the roaring traffic below and around. (Jim Hughes, Christian Science Monitor.)* LEFT: *San Francisco. Local urban renewal. Sponsored by International Longshoremen's Union Pension Fund, this is a cooperative residential project of refreshing design with moderate carrying charges. Interracial—approximately 55 percent white, 25 percent Negro, 10 percent Chinese, 10 percent Japanese. (Architects: Marquis & Stoller; Richard F. Conrat, San Francisco)*

Urban but not in city centers (largely residential): San Francisco (middle income); New Haven (middle and low income); Baltimore (low income—rehabilitation); New York (high income)

New Haven, Dixwell Avenue Project. LEFT: *Before slum clearance, 1962. (Carl J. Muller, New Haven.)* RIGHT: *Local renewal by demolition and replacement. Low-rent Florence Virtue Homes, 1965. This neighborhood renewal supplies new dwelling units at rentals that can be afforded by the previous inhabitants of the slum. (Charles R. Schulze, New Haven.)*

Baltimore-Harlem Park. LEFT: *Before urban renewal. Substandard dwellings and backyard jungle.* RIGHT: *Renewal by rehabilitation, nondisplacement. Buildings are reconditioned; there are common open areas. (Baltimore Renewal and Housing Authority.)*

New Communities: Towns and Cities These may be identified in three categories:

1. Privately developed, by the principal industry in connection with its operation, early-twentieth century. Examples are Gary, Indiana; Kohler, Wisconsin; Kingsport, Tennessee.

2. Sponsored by the federal government (New Deal and World War II). Examples are Norris, Tennessee; Hanford, Washington; Oak Ridge, Tennessee; and the greenbelt towns.

3. Privately developed since World War II or currently being developed. Examples are Park Forest, Illinois (in Chicago metropolitan area); Reston, Virginia and Columbia, Maryland (in Washington metropolitan area); Litchfield Park, Arizona (near Phoenix); El Dorado, California (near Sacramento); Irvine, California (one of several near Los Angeles); experimental city MXC in Minnesota (in no metropolitan orbit); Lysander, New York (near Syracuse); Amherst, New York (near Buffalo).

In the first two categories, the examples named constitute a large proportion in their class. In the category since the war, these are only a small proportion of those in varying stages of progress. The first two categories will be considered only briefly; the third category will be discussed at greater length.

In the first two categories, the greenbelt towns have already been discussed in another context. In those of the first category the planning was reasonably competent and the original and further development in growth was reasonably faithful to the planning, but no new ground was broken in any seminal sense, as may be said of Letchworth and Welwyn in England. They did not start any movement. The impulse for an industry to create its own town was at an end.

The towns created by the federal government were, except Norris,

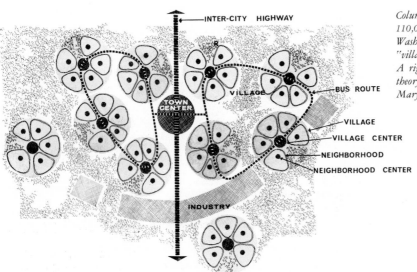

Columbia. New City (*ultimate population, 110,000*) *between Baltimore and Washington. New Town diagram showing "villages," neighborhoods, circulation plan. A rigorous application of the neighborhood theory. (The Rouse Co., Baltimore, Maryland.)*

for the very special purposes of atomic energy and atom bomb development. They were sold off later to private interests, as the greenbelt towns had been. Thus, these towns also had no significance as forerunners of a new town-development policy.

Norris, Tennessee, has remained a small town of some 5,000 inhabitants. It is mentioned because it was part of the TVA regional-and-resources development. TVA is now planning the town of Tellico, expected to reach a population of some 35,000. It is integrally linked with imminent dam and lake development and is planned to become a subregional center of recreation in the natural outdoors as well as a center of culture. In spite of the small populations so far involved, this situation deserves attention because of its potential as an exemplar or forerunner of overall urban-regional resource-ecological linkage.

It appears to be a growing national intention to develop New Towns and cities as one answer to the expected population growth of some 100 million in 30 years and through them to develop a better urban life than by the expansion of large cities. It is intended to do this through private enterprise.

These towns are intended to have populations varying from some 15,000 (Lysander, near Syracuse, New York), through 125,000 (Columbia, near Washington, D.C.), up to 250,000 (the Minnesota city of MXC). In the recent publication entitled *The New City*, by the eminent National Committee on Urban Growth Policy, large numbers of new towns are recommended, among them 10 of ultimate population of 1 million.

As contrasted with a suburb or a large residential subdivision, a New Town is intended to be relatively self-contained for employment, and for commercial and recreational opportunities, so that commuting and other daily forms of time-consuming travel are eliminated or minimized. As a result, traffic is reduced and money saved. New Towns are intended to be integrated ethnically, and to have a representative economic or income cross section. Federal help to New Towns is predicated on this policy of economic and ethnic integration.

The best of the New Towns show imaginative planning, ingenious systems of traffic separation and pedestrian safety, and an eagerness to introduce the best and most advanced educational programs. The best, again—such as Columbia—have marshaled teams of consultants not only to study and advise in their own specialties but to think of policy, program, and implementation jointly; to cross-fertilize. In Columbia and MXC in Minnesota, some new institutions, applications, and combinations seem to be emerging. Several, such as Reston and Columbia, are succeeding in attracting industry and office employment so as to achieve a reasonable minimum of commuting. Of course, this quality of endeavor and input ranges downward to some communities that are not New Towns in the recognized sense at all.

However, there are some limitations that appear inherent in the choice of private enterprise as the main or only instrument as compared with government development corporations and public authorities. These limitations all stem from the fact that private enterprise must operate at a profit competitive with other sources of possible income for its investments; also, it cannot afford to have its funds tied up too long.

The question of attracting sufficient varied enterprises for local employment to achieve some balance and minimize long journeys to work out of town is important. In the seller's market for housing that currently characterizes the United States, there is almost no limit to the sale of and profit in housing. It may not be profitable to wait for industry. Park Forest, the first of the crop of New Towns after the war, has no industry and little office employment, though it had originally reserved land for it. This condition may remedy itself in time, when major employers discover the advantages of New Towns—as they have in England.

With economic and racial integration, the private entrepreneur may in good faith wish to live up to requirements desirable from the national viewpoint. But that is not nearly enough. With building costs high, it may be difficult or impossible to come down far enough to accommodate low-income people. Prime motivation to private enterprise to undertake a New Town is profit on land. So the initial advantage of low land cost soon disappears. And minorities, aside from being generally low-income people, are known to be reluctant to move from central-city situations, where they feel at home, to new areas where they must make their way socially. Thus, unless the goal of integration has a very high priority and the developer can "wait it out," these integrations do not take place. This is just what is happening presently in new cities, so that their possible function to help to even out the imbalances in the cities is not eventuating. However, there is a late development in Columbia New City. The Interfaith Union has built 300 homes for those of low and middle income on six different sites. They state their intention of doing more. This is still not lowest-income housing, but it is potentially significant.

Another way in which New Towns can contribute to the national well-being is in connection with the strong national trend for the already very populous metropolitan areas to absorb higher and higher portions of the nation's people by immigration, and even more so because, with so much of the population there now, natural increase takes place most heavily there. With air, water, and noise pollution and solid waste problems, as well as exacerbated and interacting ground and air traffic, a large proportion of the New Towns should be located in the relatively empty regions (90 percent or more in area) of the country. This can take place because, with twentieth-century communications, transportation, and diffusion of culture, most industry need not be tied down by market or natural resources. But the quickest and surest return for private enterprise is in the already crowded metropolitan areas. Thus with private enterprise, the distribution of people in metropolitan areas will become less inconvenient and more rational; but the problem of basic overdevelopment remains. The New Towns are almost all in the metropolitan orbits of major metropolises, although there is one in Minnesota and there are one or two elsewhere. But there are none in "new regions."

Summarizing, New Towns by private enterprise may well produce places that are better arranged internally, with fresh and updated solutions to the problems that stand in the way of good living. But under the present auspices, they are unlikely to help bring about optimum national and regional configurations or to ameliorate basic social arrangements and ethnic distribution.

Adumbrations of Metropolitan-Regional Planning and Development It needs little demonstration to make a very strong case for planning and development on a metropolitan scale. The motorcar has obliterated urban boundaries. Air and water pollution—and solutions for them—likewise know no political boundaries. Economy and adequacy point to the logic of unified water, sewage, and drainage systems. Industries and corporate offices continue to move out of the central city into and beyond suburbs, with suburban exclusionism forcing workers to remain in the central city and commute at high cost. The central city is disadvantaged by loss of the tax base of wealthy people who work there but live elsewhere.

That is, creative and effective planning speaks powerfully for a metropolitan basis. This has made some progress, especially in what may be called the nonhuman fields such as water supply and distribution, road and transit systems. But in the human-social situation—in land use (who can live next to whom for example), in zoning, in housing—under the banner of home rule—there has been and is massive resistance from the suburbs. In these aspects there is little in the way of effective planning-development; and it appears that short of metropolitan *government,* with power to formulate and *enforce* (such as flourishes notably in Greater London and Toronto, in the form of "federal" two-tier government, with spelled-out spheres of local and regional jurisdiction; and to a substantial extent in Miami, Jacksonville, and Nashville in the United States), creative and inclusive metropolitan planning *and* development cannot be a vital reality.

Varying partial approaches do exist in something like one hundred of the over two hundred metropolitan areas. There are official single-function or several-function metropolitanwide agencies like the San Francisco area's BART (Bay Area Rapid Transit) and the Port of New York Authority (including mainly bridges, airports, and bus terminals). These carry out, with authority, their assigned functions. There are influential voluntary citizen groups, the major prototype of which is the Regional Plan Association in the New York area. There are public bodies authorized by statute, with members including officials from constituent communities, but with no legal enforcement power. Among these may be noted the Northeastern Illinois Metropolitan Planning Commission (Chicago area) and the Baltimore Regional Planning Council, with its concept and pattern of metrotown centers.

One of the best situations, which by that very token reveals the current weaknesses, is that of the Washington Area Council of Governments. It

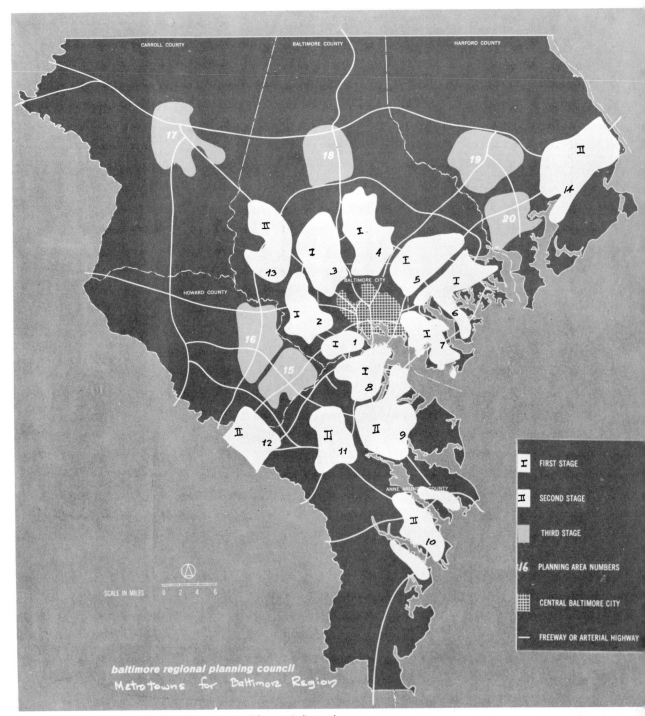

Baltimore: Metrotowns for the Baltimore region. The map indicates three stages: 1970, 1980, 1990. However, as in all metropolitan plans, these orderly indications are not attainable without much more stringent governmental controls, especially over land use, than are available. (Baltimore Regional Planning Council.)

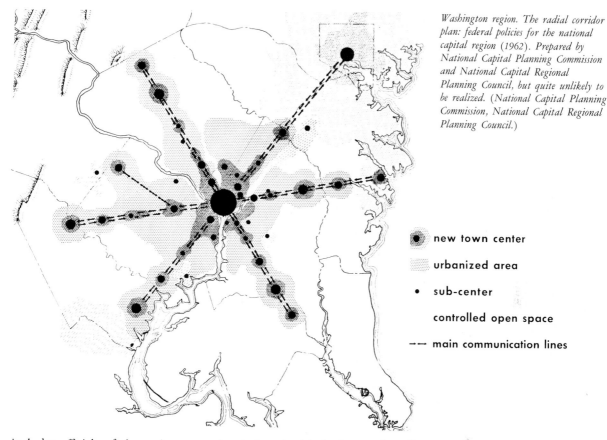

Washington region. The radial corridor plan: federal policies for the national capital region (1962). Prepared by National Capital Planning Commission and National Capital Regional Planning Council, but quite unlikely to be realized. (National Capital Planning Commission, National Capital Regional Planning Council.)

- new town center
- urbanized area
- sub-center
- controlled open space
- main communication lines

includes officials of the various counties, it has sizeable budget and staff, it is active and influential in the "nonhuman" fields, and it is beginning to be so in the field of crime prevention. But by its own showing and in the review in the annual report for 1969, its quite sensible regional plan for the year 2000 as formulated in 1960 (see illustration) is now almost unrecognizable. Land-use control is local, not regional; the famous green wedges separating the wide spokes of development have been the subjects of speculation and have been heavily and haphazardly built on. Something will be rescued, but not much.

It has been noted that the suburbs have been opposed to metropolitan government. More recently, it appears that the central city may now be opposed also, or that it soon will be. In some of the major cities, due to heavy rural immigration and relative birth rate, the minority or nonwhite population may soon outnumber the white. There is growing disinclination among them now to give up this imminent or potential dominance of the city, for if they did they would again become a minority in the total metropolitan area.

But there are also counter-counter tendencies toward metropolitan government. Rising crime, particularly in the suburbs, is much more difficult to cope with in the presently divided jurisdictions. The alarming increase in the use of drugs in both suburb and city is only feebly coped with in the fragmented situation. These problems begin to fall into the human realm.

Thus there are tendencies evident both toward and against the fruition of an effective metropolitan area. But it is not at all clear that in general it will get beyond the advisory stage, the voluntary stage, the stage of effectively dealing with mainly nonhuman elements. Like so much else today in planning-development, and indeed so much in American life, things are sharply in flux. One cannot clearly discern or conscientiously predict; one can simply present the current scene, the issues, and the forces at work.

BIBLIOGRAPHY:
The whole subject and content of urban planning have been changing radically in the last decades, and at an accelerating rate. For reasons indicated in the article, these changes affect the tempo, substance, and issues within the city; and it is no longer possible to treat the city adequately within its borders. It must be considered also a major node within a region and indeed in a national pattern. While these new and changing elements have been indicated, it has not been possible to handle them altogether adequately in the uniformly prescribed framework. This bibliography is included, of course, for the normal reason: to give the reader the opportunity to extend and deepen his understanding of the matters discussed. But in addition, references are introduced which by their very titles are a sort of shorthand to emphasize emerging subjects which, to have been adequately handled in the text, would have taken up a prohibitive amount of space.

Also, because in the present state of flux in the United States and the fluctuating balance or imbalance of forces the future is by no means predictable, it may be particularly useful for the reader to be able to keep up with these developing factors. The most viable measure is to refer to current and recurring sources such as periodicals, professional societies, and organizations which issue monthly or quarterly journals and often annual reports and reviews. Therefore, journals and annual reports of representative character are included. Melville C. Branch, *Comprehensive Urban Planning*, Sage Publications, Beverly Hills (a selective annotated bibliography); *Housing and Planning Reference*, Library of Department of Housing and Urban Renewal (HUD), Washington, D.C.

The National Destiny—the City's Place in It
Goals for Americans—Programs for Action in the Sixties, Report of the President's Commission on National Goals, Prentice-Hall, Inc., Englewood Cliffs, N.J., 1960; Charles Abrams, *The City is the Frontier*, Harper & Row, Publishers, Incorporated, New York, 1965; Albert Mayer, *The Urgent Future. People. Housing. City. Region*, McGraw-Hill Book Company, New York, 1967; Lewis Mumford, *The Urban Prospect*, Harcourt Brace & World, Inc., New York, 1968; William R. Ewald, Jr. (ed.), *Environment for Man*, Indiana University Press, Bloomington, Indiana, 1968.

City Planning—Building
Our Cities, Their Role in the National Economy, National Resources Committee (Urbanism), Washington, D.C., 1937; Lewis Mumford, *The City in History*, Harcourt Brace & World, Inc., New York, 1961; Martin Meyerson & Associates, *Housing, People and Cities*, McGraw-Hill Book Company, New York, 1962; John W. Reps, *The Making of Urban America*, Princeton University Press, Princeton, 1965; Julius G. Fabos and Weinmayr Milde, *Frederick Law Olmstead, Sr.*, University of Massachusetts Press, Amherst, 1968; Mel Scott, *American City Planning* (since 1890), University of California Press, Berkeley, 1969; National Commission on Urban Problems (Douglas Commission), *Building the American City*, Frederick A. Praeger, Inc., New York, 1969.

City Space, Design, Effects
Serge Chermayeff and Christopher Alexander, *Community and Privacy—Toward a New Architecture of Humanism*, Doubleday & Company, Inc., Garden City, N.Y.; Lowdon Wingo (ed.), *Cities and Space*, The Johns Hopkins Press, Baltimore, 1963; Paul Spreiregen, *Urban Design*, McGraw-Hill Book Company, New York, 1965; Arthur B. Gallion and Simon Eisner, *The Urban Pattern. City Planning and Design*, 2d ed., D. Van Nostrand Company, Inc., Princeton, 1966; Edward T. Hall, *The Hidden Dimension*, Doubleday & Company, Inc., Garden City, N.Y., 1966; Vincent Scully, *American Architecture and Urbanism*, Frederick A. Praeger, Inc., New York, 1969.

Conservation, Pollution, Population, Ecology
Fairfield Osborn, *Our Plundered Planet,* Little, Brown and Company, Boston, 1948; Philip M. Hauser (ed.), *The Population Dilemma,* Prentice-Hall, Englewood Cliffs, N.J., 1963; *Restoring the Quality of our Environment,* President's Science Advisory Committee, report of the Environment Pollution Panel, Washington, D.C., November 1965; Barry Commoner, *Science and Survival,* The Viking Press, Inc., New York, 1967; Ian McHarg, *Design with Nature,* The Natural History Press, Garden City, Long Island, 1969.

Education for Planners
Harvey S. Perloff, *Education for Planning: City, State, and Regional,* The Johns Hopkins Press, Baltimore, 1957.

Metropolitan and Multicounty Nonmetropolitan
Governmental Structure, Organization and Planning in Metro Areas, Advisory Commission on Inter-Governmental Relations, Washington, D.C., 1961; *A Plan for the Year 2000,* National Capital Planning Commission, National Capital Regional Planning Council, Washington, D.C., 1961; James L. Sundquist and David W. Davis, *Making Federalism Work,* The Brookings Institution, Washington, D.C., 1961; Metropolitan reports and technical bulletins, 1960–1965 (a pattern emerges June 1962; stages and measures February 1963); *Metropolitan and Economic Disparities: Implications for Inter-Governmental Relations in Central Cities and Suburbs,* Advisory Commission on Inter-Governmental Relations, Washington, D.C., 1965; Royce Hansen, *Metropolitan Councils of Governments for Advisory Council of Inter-governmental Relations,* Washington, D.C., 1966; Stanley Scott and John C. Bollens, *Governing a Metropolitan Region: The San Francisco Bay Area,* Institute of Governmental Studies, University of California Press, Berkeley, 1968; Amos H. Hawley, *The Metropolitan Community: Its People and Government,* Sage Publications, Beverly Hills, 1969; "Metrotowns for the Baltimore Region," Maryland State Planning Department; "Metrotowns for the Baltimore Region," Baltimore Regional Planning Council; Mid-Hudson Pattern for Progress, New Palt, New York; *The Changing Region,* The Metropolitan Washington Council of Governments.

New Towns and Cities
"Columbia, Maryland: Master Plan, Village Plans," *House & Home,* New York, 1964; Clarence S. Stein, *Toward New Towns for America,* The M.I.T. Press, Cambridge, 1966; Donald Canty (ed.), *The New City. Urban America,* National Committee on Urban Growth Policy, Frederick A. Praeger, Inc., New York, 1969; "Litchfield Park, Arizona: Master Plan, Village and Neighborhood Plans and Details," Litchfield Park Properties.

State; Region
Henry Wright, *Commission of Housing and Regional Planning New York State Report, 1926,* Clarence Stein, chairman; Clarence Lewis, *The Tennessee Valley Authority: A National Experiment in Regionalism,* American University Press, Washington, D.C., 1938; *Change, Challenge and Response. A Development Policy for New York State,* Office of Regional Development, Albany, 1964; Melvin R. Levin, *Community and Regional Planning,* Frederick A. Praeger, Inc., New York, 1968; Maynard H. Hufschmidt (ed.), *Regional Planning: Challenge and Prospects,* Frederick A. Praeger, Inc., New York, 1969; J. Brian McLoughlin, *Urban and Regional Planning: A Systems Approach,* Frederick A. Praeger, Inc., New York, 1969.

Transportation
Lewis Mumford, *The Highway and the City,* Harcourt Brace & World, Inc., New York, 1963; Lyle C. Fitch & Associates, *Urban Transportation and Public Policy,* Chandler Publishing Company, San Francisco, 1964; Oscar Ornati, *Transportation Needs of the Poor,* Frederick A. Praeger, Inc., New York, 1970; Edwin T. Haefele (ed.), *Transportation and National Goals,* the Brookings Institution, Washington, D.C.

Urban Renewal, Model Cities
Coleman Woodbury (ed.), *The Future of Cities and Urban Redevelopment, Urban Redevelopment Problems and Practices,* University of Chicago, Chicago, 1953; James Q. Wilson (ed.), *Urban Renewal—The Record and the Controversy,* The M.I.T. Press, Cambridge, 1966; Marshall Kaplan, Gans, Kahn, *The Model Cities Program,* Frederick A. Praeger, Inc., New York.

Emerging and Critically Sharpening Dimensions of Planning-development
National Advisory Committee on Social Disorders, *Urban America and the Urban Coalition,* Kerner Riot Commission Report, Frederick A. Praeger, Inc., New York, 1968; National Advisory Committee on Social Disorders, *Urban America and the Urban Coalition. One Year Later,* (an assessment of the nation's response to the report of the National Commission on Social Disorders), Frederick A. Praeger, Inc., New York, 1969.

Journals, Annual Reports, and Reviews of Representative Character

Advisory Commission on Inter-Governmental Relations (appointed to advise U.S. Congress, it has since issued a series of important studies and recommendations on urban, rural, metropolitan, and regional matters that go far beyond what its title would suggest) American Academy of Arts and Sciences, Boston (journal *Daedalus,* which has included special numbers—e.g., "The Future Metropolis (Symposium)," Winter 1961)

American Academy of Political and Social Science, Philadelphia (bimonthly *Annals;* monographs and symposia on urban and urban-related topics)

American City Magazine (monthly), New York

American Institute of Architects, Washington, D.C. (monthly journal)

American Institute of Planners, Washington, D.C. (bimonthly journal; monthly newsletter; special publication, "Environment for Man")

American Journal of Sociology (bimonthly), University of Chicago Press, Chicago

American Public Health Association, New York, (*American Journal of Public Health* (monthly); urban studies)

American Society of Landscape Architects, Louisville, Ky. (*Landscape Architecture* (quarterly)—regional and land planning, design, and construction)

American Society of Planning Officials, Chicago (monthly newsletter; annual *Planning—* selected papers from the national planning conference)

Appalachian Regional Commission, Washington, D.C. (monthly *Appalachia;* annual reports)
Architectural Forum (monthly), New York

California Tomorrow, Sacramento, (*Cry California* (quarterly)—urban questions, superhighways, conservation, pollution)

Environment Monthly, New York

Environment & Behavior (quarterly), Sage Publications, Beverly Hills

Ford Foundation, New York (annual reports; special brief reports on representative specific projects financed by them, many of them on urban and related subjects)

Housing and Urban Development, Department of, Washington, D.C.

Joint Center for Urban Studies of the Massachusetts Institute of Technology and Harvard University, Cambridge (a "flow of studies"; annual reports)

National Association of Housing and Redevelopment Officials, Washington, D.C. (*Journal of Housing*)

National Municipal League, New York (*National Civic Review*)

National Urban Coalition (formerly Urban America), Washington, D.C. (bimonthly *City;* monthly supplement *Chronicle*)

Population Council, New York (periodicals and studies)

Resources for the Future, Washington, D.C. (*Resources* every 4 months; annual report and review, with bibliography of their own publications—regional and urban studies, land use and management, quality of the environment)

Urban Affairs Quarterly, Sage Publications, Beverly Hills

Urban Land Institute, Washington, D.C. (monthly *Urban Land;* technical bulletins of able special studies from the point of view of private developers)

—ALBERT MAYER

UNIVERSITY CAMPUS OR CITY   Universities of the modern world (from the early Italian of the tenth to twelfth centuries and the University of Paris founded in the twelfth century, followed by those of Oxford and Cambridge in the same century) were initially single college buildings situated near the centers of the medieval cities. Other colleges were gradually founded, and the early universities grew with the cities. This process occurred in Europe up to the beginning of the twentieth century. In the early centuries the additional colleges were located fairly near the city centers, as at Oxford and Cambridge; but later, with the more rapid growth of cities, the new colleges were further flung, a process which occurred to a marked degree with the universities of Rome and London, so that the various colleges and faculties were scattered in various districts and students often had to travel from one part of the city to another to attend lectures necessary for their courses of study. The universities of Rome and London have both been replanned. The new University City of Rome was built between 1933 and 1936 under the control of Marcello Piacentini. The various buildings, mostly of neoclassical design, of the schools and faculties are grouped around a large, gardenlike piazza with a central avenue. The new campus of the University of London, designed by Charles Holden with a similar classical monumentality, was built between 1930 and 1965 on a long rectangular site involving, for the purpose, the demolition of one of the pleasant London squares. The plan of the complex of buildings was based on a long central spine with the buildings of the various faculties and colleges branching from it. As a university campus, Rome's has obvious advantages over that of London, being far more of a self-contained precinct.

The enclosed court was a distinguishing feature of the earlier universities, the series of three courts of St. John's College, Cambridge (1511), being a classical example. This type of planning still influenced the plans for the universities of Rome and London, and it has also influenced some later plans. It influenced the planning of many college buildings during the colonial period of North America, but since the beginning of the nineteenth century it has largely been abandoned, although with some exceptions, such as Princeton. What is usually considered the first university campus plan in the United States was that prepared in 1813 by Joseph Jacques Ramée for Union College, in Schenectady, New York, which, symmetrically planned on a spacious plot, comprises a central library flanked by curved colonnades and buildings opposite a circular domed structure commemorating Eliphalet Nott, the first president of the College. This central group is further flanked by two L-shaped college buildings. The whole is set among woodlands and gardens. Thomas Jefferson's plan (1825) for the University of Virginia departed somewhat from European traditions. Around a central rectangular space with lawns and trees were a series of small buildings or pavilions on the long sides, with palatial buildings at either end. Other buildings were gradually added, set symmetrically in spacious formal gardens.

By the mid-twentieth century many of the universities of the United States had become very large, of the dimensions of small cities, several with more than thirty thousand students. This has created problems of space, although in many cases there was a fairly generous allocation of land with provision for considerable expansion.

The developments and plans for the grouping of university buildings in the United States in the 1960s appear to follow the pattern of a central plaza around which are grouped the buildings most likely to be generally used by all students, such as the library, the various halls, auditorium and theater, student union, and dining rooms. Health centers of various kinds, specialist schools and faculties, and students' quarters are more toward the periphery. The central areas are pedestrian, with minor roads on the outskirts. In the central plaza of the student center of the University of California (Berkeley), the paved pedestrian area has a car park underneath, and it is immediately enclosed by the university auditorium and theater, the classroom building, and the student union, while occupying part of the plaza is a one-story dining hall. The development plan for the University of Pennsylvania has a similar central plaza, with libraries, college hall, and humanities building immediately surrounding it. Sports facilities and health centers are toward the periphery.

Essentials in university campus planning are the requirements of the various departments and the relative space each should occupy in relation to the function of the university. Generous space should be allowed for future requirements, many of which cannot always be foreseen. This is often a provision wisely made in the United States, but it is much more difficult to make in the small, densely populated countries of Europe.

In siting a new university, one of the major questions is always whether an adequate area can be found in or near the center of a town or city, or whether it should be a little outside in the open country. There are advantages and disadvantages in both. Among the advantages of the former is that both students and townspeople could benefit by mixing, and the townspeople can more easily benefit from facilities provided by a university like public lectures, exhibitions, and social events. If the university is sited in open country some miles away, there is the risk of remoteness and isolation, which some, however, might regard as an advantage. Also space for playing fields adjacent to the university is more likely to be secured outside the town or city. This was a determining factor in siting many of the new universities in the United Kingdom, where 26 have been founded between 1948 and 1973. To provide for playing fields adjacent to the university buildings, it was necessary to find sites of 200 acres, which was possible only outside the cities or towns. Examples are Sussex (1961), East Anglia (1963), York (1963), Lancaster (1964), Essex (1964), Warwick (1965), and Kent (1965).

Whether the new university is to be of the collegiate or unitary type will necessarily determine the layout and grouping of the buildings. Both types have been almost equally adopted in the new British universities.

BIBLIOGRAPHY: Richard P. Dober, *Campus Planning*, Reinhold Publishing Corporation, New York, 1963; Harlan D. Bareither and Jerry L. Schillinger, *University Space Planning—Translating the Educational Program of a University into Physical Facility Requirements*, University of Illinois Press, Urbana, Ill., 1968; Nicholas Bullock, Peter Dickens, and Philip Stedman, *A Theoretical Basis for University Planning*, Land Use and Built Form Studies Report no. 1, Cambridge, Eng., 1969; Tony Birks, *Building the New Universities*. David and Charles, Newton Abbot, 1972.

—ARNOLD WHITTICK

UNWIN, Sir RAYMOND (1863–1940) British architect and town planner, born at Whiston near Rotherham. Trained in both engineering and architecture, he did not practice the latter until he entered partnership, in 1896, with Barry Parker (1867–1947). In 1901 he published with Parker *The Art of Building a Home,* a book reflecting the influence of Ebenezer Howard's garden city concept (*q.v.*) in addition to the social and aesthetic idealism of William Morris and the arts and crafts movement. In the same year the partners planned New Earswick, near York, for the Rowntree Village Trust, and in 1903 they began the first garden city at Letchworth in Hertfordshire, one of the most significant and influential planning ventures of the century. Its open layout, varied grouping of houses with gardens, and lavish planting and landscaping were characteristic of Unwin and Parker's architectural and planning aesthetics. Their later work at Hampstead Garden Suburb, begun in 1907, carried their principles to greater perfection in a plan that is generally regarded as a masterpiece of suburban planning and that has had immense international influence on urban design.

In addition to his practical work, Unwin was a tireless thinker, writer, and propagandist for planning. His *Town Planning in Practice* (1909) was a closely argued and richly illustrated practical textbook to a new discipline; *Nothing Gained by Overcrowding* (1912) demonstrated the social and aesthetic merits of garden city housing at moderate densities as against conventional layouts of the past. The first British planning act of 1909 was much influenced by Unwin's ideas and practice, as was the important Report of the Tudor Walters Committee on Housing (1918).

After lecturing at Birmingham University from 1911 to 1914, Unwin was appointed Chief Planning Inspector to the Local Government Board, the first of many influential official posts which included that of director of housing to the Ministry of Munitions (1916–1918) and chief architect to the Ministry of Health, where he produced the Ministry's seminal *Housing Manual* of 1918. As chief technical adviser to the Greater London Planning Committee from 1929 to 1933, he developed regional concepts which anticipated in principle Abercrombie's London County and Greater London plans of 1943 and 1944.

Unwin paid many visits to America as university lecturer and planning consultant. The report of his study of low-cost housing in 1934 for the National Association of Housing Officials influenced Roosevelt's New Deal planning legislation in 1935. He was president of the TPI in 1915 to 1916, of the RIBA from 1931 to 1933, and of the IFHP from 1928 to 1931. Among his many honors he received the Royal Gold Medal of the RIBA, the Howard Memorial Medal, honorary degrees from several foreign universities, and knighthood in 1932. He died in Connecticut in 1940.

Unwin's early association with William Morris was reflected in the ideals behind his own work. His great respect for the past and his understanding of modern needs inspired the character of his architecture and planning. He valued craftsmanship very highly, and he brought to his own work, whether in the minutiae of a cottage or the wide scope of a regional plan, an intense attention to detail, materials, and design. He had a strong feeling for community life and a desire for beauty in all things, which led him always to plan for a good environment for all classes of people. And to these ideals he added great technical and organizing ability, an instinct for good design, and perceptive social insight.

BIBLIOGRAPHY: Walter L. Creese, *The Search for Environment,* Yale University Press, 1966, *The Legacy of Raymond Unwin,* MIT Press, 1966.

—FREDERIC J. OSBORN

URBAN RENEWAL   *(See articles on countries.)*

URBAN SOCIOLOGY   In some respects the term "urban" sociology is redundant in highly urbanized societies where "urban" and "social" are effectively coterminous. This was not the case when this subdiscipline of sociology first emerged to describe the distinctive urban centers taking shape in what was then still largely a rural world.

The field of urban sociology, though born in Europe, developed most rapidly in the United States. In essence, its aim was to describe and document the impact of urban concentrations on social behavior. Many of the early studies necessarily contrasted urban phenomena with rural ones, while later studies concentrated on the impact of different urban scales.

The conceptual underpinnings of the field stem largely from German and French writings, in particular from the famous Gemeinschaft-Gesellschaft typology of Toennies which led to the concept of the rural-urban continuum and other dichotomies. These conceptual typologies soon proved to be oversimplified as the phenomena to which they referred turned out to be multidimensional and continuously variable rather than dichotomous. Much work has grown out of these initial efforts at classification, refining them considerably. Sjoberg's discussion of different types of cities in preindustrial and industrial eras, Duncan and Reiss's work on different sized settlements, and efforts at ascertaining optimal sized cities, densities, and distances are prominent examples.

Part of the American contribution to urban sociology is known as the "ecological" school which flourished at the University of Chicago in the middle decades of the century. Chiefly associated with the names of Park and Burgess, its principal luminaries, it also nourished a number of other major talents and was for a long time the chief center of empirical research in the United States. We owe some of the best field studies of ghettoes and ethnic groups to this school. Its conceptual contributions were more limited, however. Chief among these are Burgess's concentric zone hypothesis, the invasion-succession process in cities, and the concept of natural area. Critics of the assumptions and contributions of this school generally address themselves to the questionable attempts to graft the concepts and techniques of plant and animal ecology to the human sphere.

With the rise of the Third World and its special problems and needs in recent years, it was necessary to supplement what had threatened to become a rather ethnocentric view of the urbanization process based on the Western experience by information from other parts of the world. One significant difference between these two worlds is that in the West urbanization and industrialization were locked into each other more or less directly and explicitly. In currently developing societies, however, these two processes are not so nearly geared to each other. Propelled into cities by the population explosion and starvation on the land, urban immigrants are often little more than displaced rural refugees.

A major strain running through Western and especially American studies of the city is a moralistic one, as evidenced by attempts either to vilify, or, far less often, to idealize the city. While it indeed appears true that property crimes, alcoholism, psychoses, and suicide are higher in cities, it is not at all clear whether the city is the cause of these deviations or whether these merely reflect its differential attraction for actual or potential deviants. To this date we still do not possess sufficient information to answer this question.

Urbanism has many facets and some of these may be conducive to dissensus and deviancy as conventionally defined. Anonymity, diversity, rapid change, culture conflict, all have been found greater in urban areas and all these may be linked to the lessened social restraints which deviancy implies. Greater diversity means greater multiplicity of standards and fewer moral absolutes, more varied "definitions of the situation" as well as greater opportunities for "differential association" and for meeting like-minded others, whether criminal or conformist.

Town planners should become familiar with the major findings and concepts of urban sociology as well as with the direction which such studies are currently taking. As cities become more specialized not only within but among themselves, specialized concepts are needed to do justice to them. There is no single form of the city and each must be placed in a conceptual and empirical context which will make planning more meaningful and appropriate.

BIBLIOGRAPHY: A. F. Weber, *The Growth of Cities in the 19th Century,* New York, 1899; Ernest W. Burgess, "The Growth of the City: An Introduction to a Research Project"; Robert E. Park and E. W. Burgess, *Introduction to the Science of Sociology,* Chicago, 1921; P. A. Sorokin and C. Z. Zimmerman, *Principles of Rural-Urban Sociology,* New York, 1929; Louis Wirth, "Urbanism as a Way of Life," *American Journal of Sociology,* vol. 44, July 1938; O. D. Duncan and A. J. Reiss, *Social Characteristics of Urban and Rural Communities,* New York, 1956; Richard Dewey, "The Rural-Urban Continuum: Real but Relatively Unimportant," *American Journal of Sociology,* vol. 66, no. 1, July 1960; Gideon Sjoberg, *The Preindustrial City,* The Free Press of Glencoe, Inc., New York, 1960; C. A. Moser and Wolf Scott, *British Towns, a Statistical Study of their Social and Economic Differences,* London, 1961; George A. Theodorsen (ed.), *Studies in Human Ecology,* Row, Peterson & Company, Evanston, Ill., 1961; Hans Blumenfield, *The Modern Metropolis,* The M.I.T. Press, Cambridge, Mass., 1967.

—SUZANNE KELLER

UNION OF SOVIET SOCIALIST REPUBLICS

Legislation and Administration The chief institution for planning and coordinating capital construction in the Soviet Union is the State Planning Committee (Gosplan) of the U.S.S.R. Council of Ministers. Every ministry in charge of a particular industry—acting on the basis of a long-term development program—submits to the State Planning Committee its suggestions, based on corresponding technical and economic indices, on expansion of productive capacity through construction and reconstruction. The U.S.S.R. State Planning Committee drafts a national plan of capital construction, settles problems involving material and technical supplies, and coordinates the use of the productive capacities of building organizations.

The size and structure of houses in Soviet towns are based mostly on the general town development plans which are approved at sessions of the local soviets of Working People's Deputies.

The draft program of capital construction of major projects—intended, as a rule, for a period of 5 years—is discussed by the U.S.S.R. Supreme Soviet, amended, and promulgated as a law. Plans for the next year are drawn up on the basis of the 5-year plan.

Capital investments in projects envisaged in the plan are drawn from the state budget of the U.S.S.R. and of the Union Republics. Construction is financed by the state through the U.S.S.R. Bank for Capital Investments (Stroibank) and its provincial branches in accordance with outlays envisaged by the summary financial estimate.

In the Soviet Union, industrial construction is carried out by specialized ministries directing building projects for particular industries. These are, for example, the Ministry of Transport Building, the Ministry for Building, Chemical Industry Enterprises, etc. According to the volume and specialization of construction, a ministry incorporates several central boards (glavks) which are in charge of practical construction work. Town building is carried out by large industrial organizations—trusts—specializing in specific types of work. In large cities with a fairly wide range of housing construction, such trusts are integrated under a special central board. The latter is subordinate to the city soviet.

Before commencing construction work, the client—a town or city soviet or an industrial ministry—signs a contract with a building organization. The trusts and central boards, carrying out such orders, work out annual programs subject to approval by a superior body. Such a program is based on a number of documents: the annual list of building projects in a given town, blueprints and financial estimates, and decisions of higher bodies on the commencement of construction work on a given project. On the basis of these documents, the U.S.S.R. Bank for Capital Investments provides the funds required for the preparatory and other stages of construction.

The results of the activities of any building organization in the U.S.S.R. are assessed by a comparison of planned and actual construction costs. If the prime cost is less than planned, the building organization is allowed to use the money saved for its own development and to provide material incentives to personnel.

Ministries are represented at building sites by the project directorates, whose functions include control of the quality and timely fulfillment of work assignments and of the delivery and distribution of equipment and building materials. The directorate confirms the completion of definite stages in construction in accordance with documents submitted by the building organization and accepted by the bank for payment to be remitted to the account of the building organization.

In the sphere of city and town building, quality control is exercised by the state agency of architectural and building inspection, a division of the executive of the town soviet.

Control over the correct operation and good working order of hoisting machinery and over the observance by building-trades employees of appropriate rules is exercised throughout the Soviet Union by a special inspection agency of the U.S.S.R. State Committee for Construction, subordinated to the U.S.S.R. Council of Ministers. In the Soviet Union, great importance is attached to the protection of the country's natural wealth. No draft project is given legal force unless it is approved by the State Sanitary Inspection Agency of the U.S.S.R. Ministry of Health, which keeps an eye on the observance of the sanitary rules relating to construction and designing.

In addition to control by the state sanitary inspection agency, designs are approved only after they have been sanctioned by the State Fire-fighting Inspection Agency of the U.S.S.R. Ministry of the Interior and the building workers' trade unions. Moreover, the technical indices of the design must be higher than those of similar earlier designs.

Permission for construction is issued only when specialists employed on the building site have proved that they are suitably qualified by specialized education and many years' experience in construction to direct building operations. The control inspection agency accepts a signed obligation from the construction superintendent—the immediate supervisor of building in a given project—and only then does it issue a permit for building to proceed.

Through the whole period of construction, a log is kept to indicate operatives, jobs and blueprints, characteristics of materials, and structural elements. A completed project is accepted by a commission made up of representatives of the contracting parties, the town or city soviet, inspectors of the sanitary and fire-fighting services, and a representative of the trade union of a particular branch of the building trade. All the accounts documents related to the project are kept, after its commissioning, within the state control system.

The legislative body outlining technical policy in the field of construction is the State Committee for Construction (Gosstroi) of the U.S.S.R., with its subordinate committees in the Union Republics pursuing a definite technical policy.

The U.S.S.R. State Committee for Construction incorporates the State Committee for Industrial Construction and the State Committee for Civil Construction and Architecture (Gosgrazhdanstroi). Both these committees have under their jurisdiction a number of design and research institutes which carry out directly, and jointly with the State Committees for Construction of the Union Republics, technical policy in designing, estimating, and scientific research.

Uniformity of technical policy is ensured by the use of standard documents valid throughout the Soviet Union; taken together, they constitute what are known as the "building regulations."

Professional Practice An architect in the Soviet Union is an employee of a state organization for design or administration. Naturally, he may take part in the architectural contests quite popular in Russia. At a state studio, groups of designers and architects work under his direction. He directs their activities on the basis of his experience, personal skill, and knowledge of the merits of his colleagues.

The chief of a studio is usually promoted from among the ranks of these groups. A few studios are integrated into design associations or institutes subordinated to the State Committee for Civil Construction and Architecture of the U.S.S.R. (Gosgrazhdanstroi), and, in the Union Republics, to the State Committees for Construction. In the biggest cities, some design institutes serve only the building organizations and, like the latter, are subordinated to the city soviet. Soviet ministries directing building industries have their own design associations working on industrial projects. These associations maintain branches close to the building sites.

Every studio and every member of its staff has authorship design rights, the right of expert examination, of drawing up and calculating a project, and of control over its implementation.

In practice, this works out in the following way: a group of designers draw up a sketch design corresponding to the assignment in volume and detail. This is followed by discussion, the introduction of amendments, and approval by the directorate of the design institute. In further work on the project, account is necessarily taken of the requirements of standard documents and the tendencies of technical policy, which are expressed in particular in the application of novel ideas, designs, and calculations. A completed project is finally approved at the design institute and is forwarded for expert examination to the architectural and design department of the town or city soviet or to a leading design institute of the State Committee for Construction in the given republic. When standard projects are to be approved for serial production, expert examination is carried out by the State Committees for Construction of the Union Republics and the State Committee for Civil Construction and Architecture (Gosgrazhdanstroi) of the U.S.S.R. Designs produced by the institutes of a building ministry are subjected to expert examination within the ministry as well as to a simultaneous examination at other institutes.

During expert examination, the project is considered in comprehensive detail and an evaluation of the rationality and quality of the volumetric layout and design is made. Special attention is paid to the strict observance of fire-fighting and sanitary-hygienic standards. A project cannot be recommended unless it is approved by these services. A project which has been approved by the experts is then forwarded to the client.

Control over all elements of the realization of the project on location is exercised. The authors are also obliged to examine the structures erected, to evaluate their conformity to the design, and to introduce on the spot the required amendments in individual details of the design. Therefore, in estimating the total tentative cost of construction, the studios make provision for expenses of supervision by the authors of the design.

In case of any violation of building regulations (for instance, replacement of structures without the authors' consent), or in case of unsatisfactory work that could impair the service characteristics of structures, the authors have the right to impose a moratorium on further building operations.

In each of the above-mentioned organizations, a specialist works in the sphere of research and development and also introduces their results into building. In this way every specialist deals with the various aspects of the building process.

Education and Training   In the Soviet Union specialists in planning and construction are trained at architectural and structural engineering institutes. However, the demand for them is so great that, at the majority of polytechnic and industrial institutes which train engineers for a number of industries, special departments have been set up to train structural engineers. The latter are trained for the most part in those specialties which correspond to the local industry of the district where the institute is situated.

There are academies of art and industrial art schools in the capitals of Union Republics, in Moscow, Leningrad, and Kharkov. They train sculptors, specialists in monumental-decorative and applied decorative and industrial art, and interior and equipment designers.

Soviet structural engineering, polytechnic, and industrial institutes have specialized departments in industrial and civil construction; town building; sewerage, water supply, and ventilation; structural technology; mechanics; road building; and hydroengineering. In each of these departments tuition is given in narrower specialities in from two to six fields. Construction specialists are also trained at the institutes of motor transport, railway transport, communications, and water-borne transport.

The basic principle in training construction specialists in the U.S.S.R. is reliance on the latest scientific and technological achievements—in creative ideas and their realization in practice. Therefore, in the training process, problems of architecture and building technology are not opposed; much attention is paid to the relationship between architectural design and the solution of structural problems. At the same time, a narrow specialization is not aimed at in the curricula. Experience shows that the best specialists come from among students with a wide general training who develop their leanings independently in the course of studies. For specialization in the final stage of training, students are offered a free choice of themes for their annual and diploma designs as well as opportunities for work under the guidance of instructors at students' scientific societies.

The training of specialists in architecture includes general technical study and work on independent assignments, design or theoretical research, and specialization and concentration in a limited number of special subjects. At the final level of tuition, specialized assignments are given in the subject chosen. There is also a year of design and practical work at an organization (practice before receiving a diploma) providing opportunities to handle practical problems.

The choice of theme for a diploma design is influenced mostly by the student's work in the period of practice prior to receiving a diploma. Therefore, the diploma design is based on the realistic figures of a specific assignment required for designing and building work. In many cases the diploma work serves the purposes of scientific research.

At the Moscow Institute of Architecture, during the third curricular course, a design has to be made for a settlement with 4,000 residents; during the fourth course, for a town 40,000 residents—including a detailed layout of a neighborhood, indicating solutions for all town-building problems. During the fifth course, the layout of a large city with 200,000 residents is required, including the design of the central quarter of a city and a design for the reconstruction of a part of a city.

The training of architects for industrial construction differs from that given to future town builders in the character of specialization and the solution of design problems by senior undergraduates.

In training engineers to work on building sites for translating architectural designs into structures as well as in the field of scientific research and the mechanization of construction, the opposite task is performed: the training is intended to produce a specialist with a knowledge of engineering and economics in a specific special subject which is chosen at a senior course, but one who also has a wider outlook in the related fields of building science and practice and a general grounding in the aesthetic principles of design.

Generally the training of engineers is less specialized, so that they may be of service in the ramified Soviet economy. For instance, a structural engineer holding a diploma knows how to calculate ferroconcrete structures, can handle geodetic instruments, can calculate and organize construction at several levels, and is a specialist in residential and industrial buildings. This makes it possible for him to be placed—in case of a shortage of specialists—in any section of the building trade: directly on the construction site, at designing or surveying, in research organizations, or at any level in the direction and design of construction.

Specialists are distributed upon graduation according to requests filed by various organizations and departments of ministries. At the same time, the graduate's domicile, specialization indicated in the diploma, and personal preferences are also taken into consideration.

Graduates who have displayed an ability for research are able to go on to postgraduate courses or to scientific research centers at the recommendation of corresponding departments of the institute. Postgraduate training lasts from 3 to 4 years.

Information Services In the Soviet Union, the provision of information services in the sphere of construction is considered an important task of the government. To improve the efficiency of the information service, it has been organized at several levels: there are information departments in all the principal divisions of the directing bodies—from the U.S.S.R. State Committee for Construction and building ministries to design institutes and local building organizations. Numerous specialized journals, thematic collected reports on individual problems of construction, periodicals, and other publications are issued to promote the exchange of experience in organizing building work directly on the construction site.

The task of Soviet information services as a whole is the promotion of scientific and technological progress, increasing the efficiency of production, scientific research and designing, the quick utilization of scientific and technological achievements, and the summing up and dissemination of advanced methods of scientific organization of work and management of construction.

The directing body which shapes technical policy in the building industry—the U.S.S.R. State Committee for Construction—directs the operation of all information services covering advanced foreign and domestic experience. In addition, it publishes a journal containing its decisions, information on new materials, approved design documents and financial estimates, reports on new directives, and the repeal of earlier ones.

Every building ministry, either national or republican, and all large territorial building organizations (for instance, those of Moscow, Leningrad, Kiev, and Kharkov) have their own information organs. The principal direction of these is information on specific problems of building work characteristic of a given industry.

In areas where construction is carried out by several ministries or departments, there is an interdepartmental scientific and technical information center. In this way, any organization is in a position to use materials of its own and also those of the interdepartmental service.

Every building organization of the trust type has its own department (or section) of technical information.

With the information services brought closer to the productive sphere, more and more space is taken up by reports and decisions relating to specific problems involved in construction work. The role of disseminating information at building sites is played by what are known as scientific and technical aid centers (orgstrois) serving large territorial building organizations, or central boards (glavks). As a rule, Soviet building ministries also have central scientific and technical aid centers to which the local branches are subordinate.

In addition to providing information through brochures and technical leaflets, the scientific and technical aid centers give direct technical assistance to building organizations: their specialists instruct workers of a subordinate building organization, helping them to learn advanced methods of work, how to use new materials, and how to make and apply various contrivances and implements. These specialists also popularize effective methods of organizing construction at advanced schools for specialized central boards.

Soviet periodical journals publish information on construction, in its aspect of a specific branch of applied science. The central information services of the building industry publish thematic collections of reports and surveys on individual problems, brochures, technical leaflets, and items of a purely practical character with descriptions of actual solutions.

An important role in the propagation of information is played by the Scientific and Technical Society of the building industry, a Soviet public organization, which has branch offices in every building organization. Membership in this society is voluntary and is open to all who are willing to contribute their knowledge to scientific and technological progress.

The society sponsors seminars, conferences, and symposia for the exchange of experience. At these gatherings research workers, designers, engineering and technical personnel, and operatives of building organizations are widely represented.

Geographical and Climatic Conditions   In the Soviet Union urban development is carried out in areas which differ widely in climatic conditions. More than 90 percent of the total volume of construction in Russia is based on standard designs, which increases the effectiveness of capital investments, ensures a larger volume of building in a shorter time, and helps to reduce construction costs. Therefore, improvements in design and building necessarily involve changes in standard designs while also taking account of local natural, climatic, topographical, material, and technical conditions of construction as well as local and national traditions.

For a more correct and complete account of the natural and climatic conditions of construction, the principal standard directive document—SNIP—divides the Soviet territory into four climatic regions consisting of fifteen climatic districts.

In every climatic region and district, the details are given of mean monthly temperature of the air in January and July and relative air humidity in July; average wind speed in the winter; characteristics of climate and weather; estimated winter and summer temperatures; natural geological features.

The first climatic region, which includes the whole of Siberia, is subdivided into five districts. The mean temperatures in these districts in January vary from 7°F (-14°C) to -26°F(-32°C); in July, from 31°F (0°C) to 69°F (21°C). The climate is rigorous or cold and wintry, the estimated winter temperatures being within the range of -26°F (-32°C) to -85°F (-65°C). Throughout the territory permanent frost areas are to be found; in individual localities earthquakes of 7 points are a regular occurrence. The number of months during which there are comfortable temperatures is not more than three annually.

The second climatic region includes the seacoast of the west, northwest and east, and the center and north of the European part of the U.S.S.R. The climate ranges from cold and wintry to temperate. The mean temperature in January ranges between 24 and 7°F (-4 and -14°C); in July, between 45 and 69°F (8 and 21°C); the estimated winter temperatures are from -5 and -27°F (-20 and -32°C). The region is subdivided into three districts. The number of months during which there are comfortable temperatures is not more than four annually.

The southern Ukraine and the regions south of the middle reaches of the Volga, Kazakhstan, and the foothills of the Caucasus are included in the third region, which is subdivided into three districts. The climate varies from continental to warm. The mean temperatures in January range between 35 and −5°F (2 and −20°C); in July, from between 69 and 76°F (21 and 25°C). The estimated winter temperatures are between 20 and −45°F (−6 and −42°C); the summer temperatures are between 35 and 85°F (2 and 30°C). The number of comfortable months is up to five annually.

The fourth climatic region, subdivided into four districts, includes Central Asia, the Transcaucasian Republics, and the Black Sea littoral. The mean temperatures in January are 4 and 42°F (−15 and 6°C); in July, from 71°F (22°C) up. The estimated summer temperatures are 76 and 103°F (25 and 40°C); the winter temperatures range from 31 to −27°F (0 to −32°C).

The features peculiar to a particular climate zone are reflected above all in the architecture and layout of buildings. For example, the first climatic zone is characterized by self-contained compositions that afford protection against snowdrifts, strong winds, and frosts. Not infrequently, whole housing estates and even small townlets are designed to be covered by one roof, uniting apartment houses, schools, child welfare centers, shops, etc.

The fourth climatic zone is provided with pavilion-type compositions in which functionally close groups of premises are designed within separate buildings connected by light, unheated passages. Such compositions make possible the convenient adaptation of architecture to the natural surroundings and the distribution of architectural complexes on an intricate mountainous relief. The characteristic features of the fourth climatic zone are reflected in other elements of building design, such as sun-protection arrangements (sunshields, canopies, collapsible screens), green backyards, and loggias.

The features peculiar to the second and third climatic zones, with their temperate climate, afford the architect and planner a wide choice of compositions. Sectional and centralized compositions are often used in these zones.

When designing dwelling houses, it is considered expedient to develop for various groups of climatic districts specialized types of standard designs, taking into account local conditions as regards construction, residential comfort, and national traditions. For this purpose a series of standard designs is proposed for each republic, since many of the Soviet constituent republics extend through two or more climatic districts.

In the designing and building district of each republic, it is planned to use a few series of designs differing in structural and technical characteristics and wall materials. Variants of serial designs are to be worked out for specific conditions of construction.

By agreement between the designing and building districts within a republic, a common series of standard designs may be developed, or a republic may use the series of designs produced by another republic for analogous building conditions.

For towns with an annual volume of construction of at least 548,600 square yards (500,000 square meters) of floor space or those of special economic, historical, and cultural importance, special series of standard designs for apartment complexes may be developed.

For urban residential areas with a volume of construction of at least 54,860 to 109,720 square yards (50,000 to 100,000 square meters) of floor space, variants of architectural designs are produced to be applied in a given town, making the maximum use of local products.

Certain types of dwelling are based on the current climate zoning of Soviet territory for building. Standard requirements in the planning of an individual town or housing estate are met on the basis of the calculation of the principal factors of the microclimate and their interconnection in town building.

Among the methods in use is that of complex climatology, including a physicogeographical description of districts, the microclimatic zoning of town territory, and the relationship of landscape to climate. The importance of climatic differences in the area under examination is determined in accordance with hygiene and building regulations.

In each individual case this method makes it possible to select the healthiest areas for housing estates and to distribute functional zones in conformity with hygienic requirements. It also reveals individual areas that require their microclimate to be improved by means of special measures such as planting greenery on slopes, providing wind barriers of trees and houses, and creating areas of water.

Traditions of Planning and Architecture to the End of the Nineteenth and the Beginning of the Twentieth Centuries   The mid-nineteenth century in Russia was a period of further aggravation of the crisis of the feudal-serfdom system. The peasant reform of 1861 marked the country's resolute turn to the path of capitalist development.

The contradictions of Russia's social development in that period produced different effects on architecture.

First, the development of industry, trade, transport, and the resulting growth of cities brought into being new types of buildings: big factory buildings, buildings of large commercial companies and offices, railway terminals, hotels, town halls, special educational institutions, and tenements, relegating to the background the formerly predominant types—palaces and landlords' mansions.

Second, the need for building new types of structures, like wide-span bridges and factory and plant buildings, along with the growth of the iron and steel industry, contributed to the development of new building technology, in particular a wide use of ferrous metals—pig iron and rolled steel. In view of the introduction of ferrous metals into certain fields of construction (and, from the late nineteenth century, of ferroconcrete), a number of new construction types and architectural forms came into being.

Third, the development of Russian architecture of the nineteenth and early twentieth centuries was increasingly influenced by the tastes and views of the rising bourgeoisie.

At the turn of the twentieth century, when Russia was drawn into the world imperialist system, modern-style architecture, opposing the past by the affected novelty of its forms, began to coexist with the eclecticism of restoration.

Architects either borrowed from the past for their forms or, if they did not, their stilted modernistic forms bore no connection with the general composition of the building and structural materials. There was a deep divergence between both aspects of architecture—utilitarian and artistic: buildings of novel design were often based on obsolete compositional schemes, while the elements made of new building materials were ornamented with details borrowed from the past and designed initially in another material.

When building housing estates in large cities, the chief concern of the building company was to derive as much profit as possible from every plot of land. The occupants of houses had to live in poorly lit and ventilated rooms, with windows opening onto deep and narrow backyards resembling wells.

In spite of the new building designs and the achievements of construction technology, the development of capitalism in Russia from the mid-nineteenth century onward was accompanied by the degradation of the artistic aspect of architecture, which was strikingly manifest in the field of urban building. Building companies sought not so much to make the architecture of a building conform to its surroundings as to make it conspicuous; so, under these conditions, any architectural harmony of the layout of streets and squares was out of the question. Only in a few cases were architects capable of blending their designs into the existing architectural ensembles, as seen, perhaps more often than anywhere else, in St. Petersburg (now Leningrad), where the traditional austere and uniform architecture of streets and squares dominated the buildings erected in the late nineteenth and early twentieth centuries.

Not less characteristic of the towns of capitalist Russia was the sharp growth of contrasts between the relatively well-appointed central quarters and the extremely ugly factory belts with their often primitive conditions. Chaotic construction in the central quarters resulted in a tangled layout of areas within housing estates divided into narrow, enclosed backyards without any greenery, dark, and poorly ventilated.

Even in New Towns, springing up at that time in Eastern Siberia and the Far East, nothing of any architectural value was built: a standard plan was used for the central quarters of towns, and they lacked cohesion, looking motley and built at random.

In capitalist Russia, architecture was not influenced by great artistic ideals and its development was therefore lopsided. New types of buildings—for industry and trade—were designed successfully from an engineering and a utility point of view. Artistic problems were not posed at all or they were solved by purely decorative means, almost disregarding the purpose and general composition of the buildings. Therefore, the opportunities inherent in the new methods of general composition of buildings and connected with their designation were not adequately realized and used in practice by architects of that period.

Planning New Towns During the Soviet period, more than eight-hundred New Towns have appeared in the U.S.S.R. To give an idea of how Soviet architects plan a New Town, the design of a town for 175,000 residents made by the Central Research and Design Institute of Town Planning can be cited.

The task of producing an experimental design of a New Town is defined as follows: construction of industrial districts with a clustered distribution of industrial enterprises; formation of residential districts on the basis of their division into housing estates and neighborhoods; differentiation of streets and thoroughfares according to traffic speed and types; rational organization of cultural and everyday services for the population, and formation of town centers for public use.

In the opinion of Soviet specialists, the planned structure of a town cannot be considered without regard to its long-range development; therefore, the designs provide for reserve possibilities and the potential development of the town structure.

A new layout, in contrast to past practice, must take into account the fact that no town, large or small, should be considered in isolation. Towns have growing economic, cultural, and other external connections which must be allowed for when planning town size, distribution of industrial and residential districts, and the character of buildings.

Technicoeconomic Indices. The basic principle determining the size of a New Town is the full and rational use of manpower. In the U.S.S.R. a new method has been devised for estimating population size. The age structure of the population of a New Town is analyzed, together with the structure of manpower and the possibility of its increase through migration and natural population growth as well as through maximum involvement of the nonworking able-bodied population in social production.

Account of the specific features of the age structure of the population in a New Town (prevalence of young people, small families, and absence of pensioners in the early stages of construction; and stabilization of the age structure in the later periods) and planning a balance of labor, including women, make it possible to establish the maximum size of the labor force with full employment of the entire able-bodied population.

Special investigations have shown that in New Towns it becomes necessary to widen the sphere of employment in order to draw into socially useful work women and other members of the family, as well as those population groups that are unable for different reasons to work in the town's basic industries. The share of enterprises set up for this purpose in respect of numbers employed should be not less than 25 to 30 percent of the town's total industry. In New Towns, account is also taken of the growing use of manpower in services: at present up to 20 percent of the labor force

Plan and scale model for development north of Murinsky Creek, Leningrad.

is employed in services, whereas in the coming 25 to 30 years this proportion will grow to 40 percent.

Sanitary-Hygienic Indices. In the opinion of workers of the Central Research and Design Institute of Town Planning, the cardinal problem of the structure of a New Town—the purity of the air and the water supply as well as of the soil—depends on the unsolved problems of the disposal of harmful waste and requires the earliest possible solution on a scientific and industrial level. This, however, does not lessen the urgency of measures for pollution control by organizing sanitary protection zones to reduce to a minimum the health hazards of industrial wastes.

One experimental design includes, in addition to technological measures, the following specific planning requirements:

Where enterprises are to be located in three or more consecutive rows in relation to the residential zone, it is prohibited to set up among them enterprises listed as first-category health hazards.

When it is necessary to set up such first-category enterprises together in one complex with other enterprises, their consecutive arrangement must be in two rows or an additional sanitary protection zone should be provided within the limits of the industrial district itself, to widen the space between the industrial and residential zones. The latter condition, as optimal, is envisaged in the present project.

In the project, analysis of the climate at the construction site of a New Town is carried out by the new method of complex climatology developed at the Institute of Geography of the U.S.S.R. Academy of Sciences. Account is taken not only of the condition of the terrestrial layers of the atmosphere but also of the microclimatic conditions of the underlying surface.

The Town Structure. The principles of providing the best possible conditions for work, everyday living, and the leisure of the town's residents are expressed in the experimental project, above all, by a division of the town into three functional zones: the first zone is a large industrial district with an area of some 3,000 acres (2,000 hectares); the second zone is a compact residential area with mostly multistoried apartment complexes (most of which have nine stories and some sixteen) as well as with a certain number of four-storied houses; and the third zone is a complete suburban recreation area with a large forest, a water reservoir, and an area of mountainous country.

Location and Layout of an Industrial District. The experimental design of the layout of an industrial district uses the principles of clustered distribution of enterprises worked out at the Central Research and Design Institute of Town Planning, with cooperation in production and auxiliary services and using minimal territory; provision of the shortest transport connections; cultural and everyday services for the working people with provision of public centers; conditions for scientific research and personnel training in the place of production, and the setting up of scientific and technical centers.

The experimental design of the general layout has demonstrated that the

LEFT: *Model of town center of Ivanovo.* BELOW: *Barnaul. Outline plan showing a compact city arrangement.*

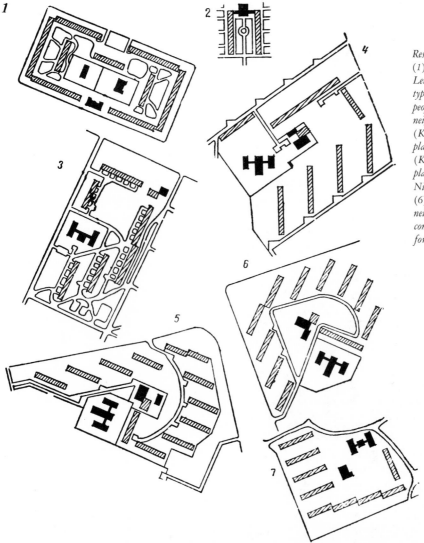

Residential neighborhood plans:
(1) Neighborhood 7 in the area of the Leningrad Square (Kiev) (2) Standard-type plan of a residential complex for 500 people (3) Residential complex in the neighborhood north of Brovarsky Highway (Kiev) (4) Residential complex in the plan for neighborhood 3 for Bereznyaki (Kiev) (5) Residential complex in the plan for neighborhood 8 for Nikolsky-Borshchagovka (Kiev) (6) Residential complex in the plan for neighborhood 9 (Kiev) (7) Residential complex in the plan for a neighborhood for the town of Kalush

compact arrangement of enterprises (compared with a beltlike disposition) yields better technicoeconomic indices. The area is reduced by 25 percent, the coefficient of utilization of territory increased by 12 percent, and length of railways is reduced by 20 percent.

Cultural and Everyday Services and the Public Center. The problem of cultural and everyday services is approached in such a way as to provide coordinated services in three zones—industrial, residential, and recreation—to test the graded service system worked out theoretically, specifying at the same time the composition and methods of arrangement of specialized common town centers: medical, educational, sports, and child welfare.

The Routes and Means of Transport. The basic principle of planning for city traffic and transport is to ensure a minimum loss of time in commuting from home to distant enterprises. An experimental design of the transport connections has reduced commuting time to less than 30 minutes on the average (from home to factory) and to 40 minutes at most. To achieve this result the project suggests the following:

The use of a scheme of through connections cutting down commuting time by 5 minutes on the average

A compact layout of the industrial district (with two trunk routes and a circular traffic scheme) and a compact layout of the residential zone

The use of conventional (in traffic speed) types of transport (bus, tram) with stops at 428-yard (400-meter) intervals

Distribution of buildings in a way that takes accessibility into account

Calculations for the experimental project have shown that these measures ensure a rational organization of the transportation services in New Towns with populations of up to 150,000 to 200,000 with an average length of travel of $1\frac{1}{4}$ miles (2 kilometers) within town limits and a distance of 3 to 4 miles (5 to 6 kilometers) to the industrial district. In towns with 300,000 to 350,000 and more residents, with an increase of the total length of travel within town limits to 2 to $2\frac{1}{2}$ miles ($3\frac{1}{2}$ to 4 kilometers) and more, it is more expedient to increase the intervals between stops to 850 to 1,070 yards (800 to 1,000 meters). Moreover, if the distance to the industrial district is more than 6 to 9 miles (10 to 15 kilometers), it is necessary to use faster means of transport.

Architectural Style and Landscape Architecture. Experimental work on the architectural aspects of New Towns is being carried out in the following principal directions:

Improving the standard of industrial architecture

Designing the ensemble of the public center and modern public buildings

Working out the compositional building methods in conditions of standard mass-scale housing construction in different situations

Emphasis on greenery and on areas of water

Greenery. Experimental work has revealed the following conditions necessary for a rational planting of greenery:

The laying out of town and district parks according to a regular plan within a distance no more than 880 yards (800 meters) from housing estates

The laying out of district parks on large areas of 62 to 74 acres (25 to 30 hectares) to increase the functional and hygienic effects on health of green plantings

Engineering equipment. Scientific studies have proved the expediency of a combined industrial and municipal water supply that subsequently separates into two systems. Water intended for industrial purposes is partially cleaned, water for municipal uses is cleaned thoroughly. This principle is used in the experimental project because the separation of the water supply saves up to 20 percent of capital investment and cuts down maintenance costs considerably.

The principle of complex distribution of industry accepted in the experi-

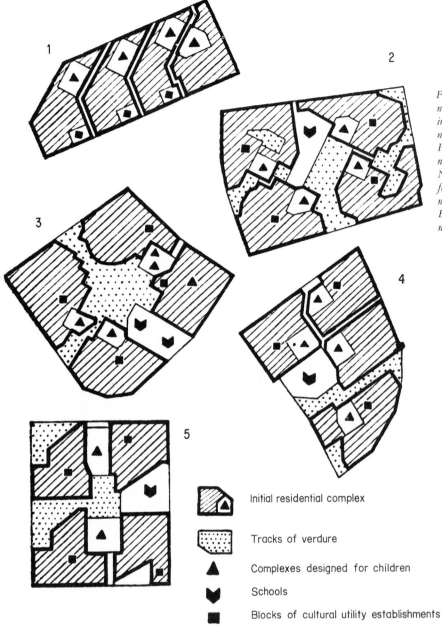

Functional arrangement of neighborhoods with complete organization of initial residential complexes. (1) The neighborhood 2 north of Brovarsky Highway (Kiev) (2) Plan for neighborhood 8; the residential area, Nikolsky-Borshchagovka (Kiev) (3) Plan for neighborhood 11 (Kiev) (4) Plan for neighborhood 3; the residential area, Bereznyaki (Kiev) (5) Plan for the neighborhood 4 (Kiev)

Initial residential complex

Tracks of verdure

▲ Complexes designed for children

♥ Schools

■ Blocks of cultural utility establishments

mental project enables the use of one large heating plant to supply all the needs of industry and towns, while the single-tube system of heat supply is the most economical, theoretically.

The use of a common sewerage system is unacceptable from the economic and sanitary point of view; therefore, a separate system is used in the experimental project. The project suggests two variants of waste disposal:

either at a refuse processing plant for compost production or at a refuse burning plant for heat supply to the town.

Reconstruction of Towns In the Soviet Union the reconstruction of large cities is connected with the problems of migration, provision of favorable conditions for the modernization and development of industry, renewal of city housing and the city structure, improvement of the services for the population, rational utilization of city land, and increasing economic efficiency in the construction and maintenance of housing. Soviet specialists adhere to the principle that the reconstruction of towns is a continuous process.

In their opinion there should be in reconstruction a limitation of the growth of large cities and a regulation of the distribution of the population in the city itself and in the agglomeration of towns formed on its basis. There should also be improvement of the layout of existing, and the organization of new, industrial districts; the creation of sanitary projection zones; the expulsion from towns of industrial enterprises posing health hazards; the replacement of small, unremunerative enterprises by large ones and the improvement of their distribution; the closing down of warehouses situated near residential areas and along the riverside; the closure or transfer to another locality of railway branches crossing residential districts; the reconstruction and development of the common city center; the reconstruction of old, small-sized housing areas, consisting of dilapidated buildings unfit for habitation, by building in their place well-appointed multistoried apartment complexes; the demolition of apartment houses unfavorably situated from a sanitary point of view; capital repairs to and the reconstruction of buildings of considerable material and cultural value; the development and reorganization of the system of cultural and everyday services, setting up local public centers in residential districts and neighborhoods; the expansion of the green area, the laying out of new parks, gardens, public gardens, and boulevards; the widening and straightening of thoroughfares; building of new thoroughfares, motorways for fast traffic and continuous traffic ways, overpasses at busy crossings, and pedestrian tunnels; building new (and reconstruction of existing) bridges and overpasses; building embankments and arranging parking lots; improving transport connections with the suburban zone; the transfer beyond city limits of large marshalling and maintenance yards of railways and airfields; the development and modernizing of water supply networks and structures, sewerage systems, gas and electric power supply, and heat supply; implementation of measures required for the engineering preparation of territories and town sanitation; protection of historical and architectural monuments; and the organization of a suburban zone with recreation areas.

At the initial stage, reconstruction is mostly carried out on individual city thoroughfares, measures are taken to improve the cultural and everyday services for the population in the old city quarters where more greenery is planted, better amenities and engineering equipment are provided, and areas of ramshackle houses of little value are reconstructed. The most urgent is the task of reconstructing the biggest cities with over a million residents (Moscow, Gorky, Kuibyshev, Novosibirsk, Kiev, Baku, Kharkov, Sverdlovsk), as well as cities with limited territory and unsatisfactory housing.

In the opinion of Soviet specialists, long-range development plans for reconstructed cities should be based on a strict limitation of the growth of cities with a population of over 500,000. Therefore, it is forbidden to build new industrial enterprises there (except those for service needs), while reconstruction of existing enterprises is carried out without attracting manpower from other towns and regions of the country.

With regard to the distribution of population in reconstructed towns, it is expedient to ensure that the average time taken in travel to the principal places of work should not be more than 30 minutes and to the town center not more than 60 minutes.

In the reconstruction of large cities, Soviet planners strive to preserve the existing industrial districts in which the overwhelming majority of industrial workers are concentrated. The building of large new industrial districts in large cities is prohibited; it is permitted to form only small new districts for the food, light, and other consumer industries.

A major problem in urban reconstruction is the reduction of the health hazards posed by industrial enterprises to the surrounding residential districts.

In the industrial districts of reconstructed towns, the area under industry and related establishments should represent no more than 50 to 60 percent of the total district area.

Highly important is the formation, within the limits of residential areas, of large planned districts with auxiliary public centers of townwide significance. Such districts may vary in size, but a population of 100,000 to 250,000 is considered an optimum. It would be sensible to set up the center of a planned district near a river or another area of water and in the immediate vicinity of large tracts of greenery.

Planned town districts where employment opportunities are available to most of the residents at nearby industrial enterprises should preferably be organized as industrial-residential districts with the following prerequisites:

That size be limited by the employment capacity of industrial enterprises and the town size itself as well as the existing cultural and everyday town services and the possibility of incorporating sufficient green recreation areas

That residential areas be provided, as far as possible, within walking distance from factory areas

That convenient connections be available between all parts of the residential district and the industrial enterprises

That the public center of a town district be located in relation to travel routes from home to work

That the cultural and everyday services of housing and industrial areas be combined in a cooperative (within a range of not more than 1,650 yards or 1,500 meters)—that is, if the industry is not separated from housing by a wide sanitary protection zone

Multistoried blocks of flats built in Russia before 1917, in which the

Master plan for neighborhood D-18, Zhirmunai District, Vilnius. (1) Five-story four-section large-panel house (2) Six-section house (3) Eight-section house (4) Nine-story house for small families (5) Boiler room (6) Kindergarten-nursery for 280 children (7) House-management office (8) School for 1,712 pupils (9) Shop (10) Public and commercial center (11) Cloth-making establishment

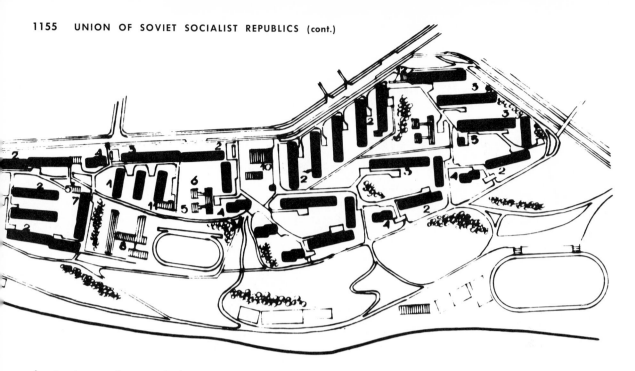

density in certain cases is between 3,800 to 4,800 square yards per acre (8,000 to 10,000 square meters per hectare) net, require successive reequipment, complex capital repairs, and partial reconstruction.[1]

The decisive factor determining the need for comprehensive capital repair of housing in the U.S.S.R. is the state of the main walls and foundations, whose material decay should not exceed 30 percent, and of the house as a whole, which should not require more than 60 percent reconstruction. Loss of dwelling space when planning the repair and modernization of housing should not exceed 15 percent as a rule, exclusive of loss due to total or partial demolition.

The economic effects of housing reconstruction are determined in the first stage of construction by a comparison of the cost per square meter

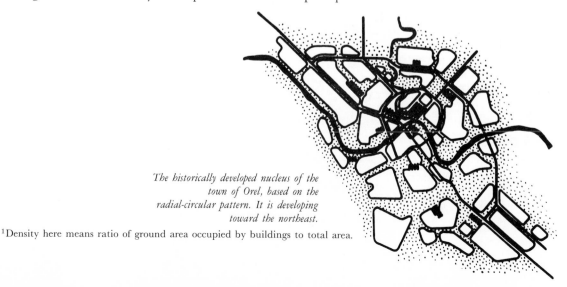

The historically developed nucleus of the town of Orel, based on the radial-circular pattern. It is developing toward the northeast.

[1]Density here means ratio of ground area occupied by buildings to total area.

The Novye Kuzminki development in Moscow.

Medvedkovo, a new development in Moscow.

of new housing in reconstructed quarters as opposed to new quarters on vacant territory. Moreover, besides the basic construction costs, the following costs are taken into account:

Costs of building in vacant territory (engineering preparation and provision of engineering and transport communications).

Costs of demolishing old housing (structures seriously delapidated to the extent of over 60 percent are not included in these costs).

Savings from the use of existing engineering communications, amenities, and greenery, as well as building for cultural and everyday services.

Savings from intensified rates of building in reconstructed quarters, permitting a reduction of the vacant area needed by the town; all costs are calculated according to the average cost of equipment and the level of amenities per hectare of town territory.

The long-range economic effects of reconstruction are determined by an increased density of gross housing in residential areas, on the principle that in large cities this index should not be less than 644 square yards per acre or 1,500 square meters per hectare (in isolated cases not less than 572 square yards per acre or 1,300 square meters per hectare) and not larger than 750 to 800 square yards per acre (1,700 to 1,800 square meters per hectare).

In the view of Soviet specialists, neighborhood green areas for various purposes should constitute up to 53 percent of the total area and up to 50 percent of the total residential area.

When solving architectural problems from the aesthetic standpoint in

The Rusanovka development in Kiev's Darnitza suburb.

reconstructed towns, the chief emphasis is laid on remodeling existing buildings by an addition of new elements on whole ensembles and on preserving valuable historical and architectural relics.

An important means of improving the aesthetic aspect of town buildings and creating a well-balanced architectural composition is the system of public centers which are regarded as of dominating importance. In contrast to earlier epochs, a characteristic feature of a modern Soviet town should be a uniform distribution of public centers in neighborhoods, residential and industrial districts, and public recreation areas. This principle must be reflected in the compositional layout of the town in general and of its common center in particular.

To ensure high architectural standards of building in reconstructed town districts, new construction should be carried out not by the selective erection of new buildings amid old housing but by building a whole complex of houses—a neighborhood or a housing estate. At the same time, new housing should be in logical and spatial harmony with the environment and the principal elements of the composition of a given district—the existing thoroughfare, a garden, a public garden, or a preserved public building.

When reconstructing the network of streets and roads in large cities, account is taken of increasing traffic intensity due to the growing fleet of passenger cars as well as the development of the most up-to-date city transport services.

High-speed roads should be built mostly on new routes to relieve congestion on existing thoroughfares. Road network density should be of the order of 20 percent. The width of area adjoining high-speed roads, including protective greenbelts, should be equal to 110 to 130 yards (100 to 120 meters) if vacant territory in conditions of new construction is available.

In large cities, one of the key problems in the initial stage of construction is the reduction of building costs and increasing the efficiency of utilization of residential areas in housing estates and neighborhoods. In view of this, the building of tall houses is encouraged in large cities with a historically formed layout.

BIBLIOGRAPHY: A. I. Stanislavsky, *Planning and Building of Small City Centers,* Gosstroiizdat, Kiev, Ukrainian S.S.R., 1960; N. V. Baranov, *Modern Town Building: Main Problems,* Gosstroiizdat, 1962; A. Y. Stramentov and M. S. Finelson, *City Traffic,* Gosstroiizdat, 1963; N. V. Baranov, *Composition of City Centers,* Gosstroiizdat, Moscow, 1964; L. S. Zalesskaya, *Course in Landscape Architecture,* Moscow, 1964; V. A. Lavrov, *The City and Its Public Center,* Stroiizdat, Moscow, 1964; "Sociology in the USSR," *"Mysl,"* Moscow, 1966; V. G. Davidovich, *The Settling of Industrial Areas of Moscow,* Gosstroiizdat, 1966; G. A. Gradov, *The City and Its Everyday Life,* Stroiizdat, Moscow, 1968.

—VYACHESLAV K. STEPANOV

UTOPIA AND UTOPIAN PLANNING The name "utopia"—nowhere land—comes from the famous book by Sir Thomas More (1478–1535), first published in Latin in 1516, portraying in fictional form "the best state of a commonwealth." Thomas More acknowledged as a classic predecessor Plato's *Republic,* and his work has had many imitators with varying ingredients of idealism, satire, and constructive sagacity. Though the adjective "utopian," as commonly used, carries an implication of impossibility or unreality, the literature of utopias has had much valuable influence on sociological thought and political policy.

There are two broad types of utopias, not always clearly distinguished by historians of the subject: those that describe imaginable societies of the future, to be desired or dreaded or simply predicted; and those that propose immediate practical action by founding new communities of an "ideal" character. The latter may be conveniently labeled "community projects" rather than utopias, but in many studies they come under the same heading.

Notable examples of true utopias, after Plato's and More's, are *Christianopolis* (J. V. Andreae, 1619), *New Atlantis* (Francis Bacon, 1624), *Oceana* (James Harrington, 1656), *City of the Sun* (T. Campanella, 1637), *Voyage in Icaria* (E. Cabet, 1845), *Looking Backward* (E. Bellamy, 1888), *News from Nowhere* (William Morris, 1890), and *A Modern Utopia* (H. G. Wells, 1905). Many others are mentioned in the books listed below.

In the other class, projects and actual experiments are innumerable, especially in the eighteenth and nineteenth centuries when impulses to migration and revulsion against urban industrialism were at their peak. Their motivation varied widely, from socialist ideologies, egalitarianism, belief in cooperation, escape from religious persecution, and the hope of new ways of life to philanthropic efforts to settle the unemployed or to advance human happiness, goodness, or (in Carlyle's sense) blessedness. Most of the projects were undertaken by voluntary groups, but very many were sponsored by European governments in their American colonies and by the new colonial governments themselves.

Of special interest in the town planning context are the communities promoted by Robert Owen (1771–1858, *q.v.*), by the followers of his contemporary F. M. C. Fourier (1772–1837, *q.v.*), and by others, which involved community buildings in agricultural surroundings, setting a physical pattern for later projects. In general these paternalistic and voluntary cooperative communities failed or had very short lives. The most viable proved to be those founded by religious bodies, with a quasimonastic discipline that held their members together. Important as the community projects are as evidence of the aspirations of people frustrated by their environmental and economic circumstances, it cannot be said that they have had much direct influence on the forms or principles of modern town planning—even on the garden city or New Towns movements (*q.q.v.*), though there is some coincidence of impulse.

BIBLIOGRAPHY: M. Kaufmann, *Utopias,* Kegan Paul, London, 1879; Henry Morley, *Ideal Commonwealth,* Routledge, London, 1885; Lewis Mumford, *The Story of Utopias,* New York, 1922; Karl Mannheim, *Ideology and Utopia,* Kegan Paul, London, 1936; P. and P. Goodman, *Communitas,* Random House, 1947; W.H.G. Armytage, *Heavens Below,* Routledge, London, 1961; David Riesman, "Some Observations on Community Plans and Utopia", in *Individualism Reconsidered,* Free Press, New York, 1954.

—FREDERIC J. OSBORN

V

VIETNAM (*See* ASIA, SOUTHEAST, DEVELOPING COUNTRIES.)

VITRUVIUS (Marcus Vitruvius Pollio), Roman military engineer and master builder of the first century A.D., in the reign of Augustus.

Through his architectural treatise *De Architectura,* Vitruvius exercised a potent influence on architects and planners of the Italian Renaissance since the fifteenth century and consequently—though with ever diminishing authority—on the architecture and town development of a considerable part of the world down to present times.

De Architectura was based in the main on Greek authorities and deals with architectural style, water engineering, aqueducts, and planning generally. Much of Vitruvius's work was carried out in Africa.

Early Renaissance architects, notably Palladio, imaginatively adapted Vitruvian principles to the requirements of their own age; but in the hands of the later classical school they tended to harden into rigid formulas, accepted without question and resulting in designs that were stereotyped and lifeless.

In the opinion of many authorities, it was as an inevitable reaction to this that the baroque phase of architectural development originated in Rome in the seventeenth century and later spread throughout Europe.

Historically, however, Vitruvius remains an important figure in the evolution of architecture and planning, and his treatise has been translated into many languages.

Much of the first book (Chapters 4–6) of *De Architectura* is devoted to the siting and building of a city. Vitruvius made several recommendations on the choice of a site, in which he gives first attention to health. He recommends a site that is high, in a climate neither hot nor cold, but temperate and without marshes unless it is near the sea and above sea level, so that it can be drained. He refers to the necessity of good water supply, the availability of good food, and easy means of transport to the city by good roads or rivers. He also discusses the layout of streets and the siting of dwellings and public buildings, and he remarks that in street planning winds should be excluded or minimized as much as possible, a consideration that is not always observed in siting new towns in the twentieth century.

BIBLIOGRAPHY: The accepted edition of Vitruvius is that of Valentine Rose based on the Lindisfarne manuscript, 2d ed., Leipzig, 1899. English translations are by Newton, London, 1791; Gwilt, London, 1826 (reprinted 1860 and 1874); Morris Hicky Morgan, Harvard University Press, Cambridge, Mass., 1914; and F. Granger, Heinemann Educational Books, Ltd., Loeb Classics, London, 1931.

—WILFRED SALTER

W

WAGNER, OTTO (1841–1918) Born in Vienna where he also died, Otto Wagner received his academic training at the Technical University in Vienna, at the Royal Academy in Berlin, and at the Academy of Fine Arts in Vienna, where he was to become professor from 1894 to 1912. Having won his first architectural competition (with many others to follow) in 1863, he established himself as an independent architect and building contractor. He soon freed himself from eclecticism, developing a unique style of his own. He planned and built churches, hospitals, department stores, office buildings, apartment houses, and villas, making bold use of new building materials like reinforced concrete, steel, and glass.

In 1893 he won the first prize in the international competition for the General Regulation Plan of Vienna. The motto of this plan was typical for Wagner: "Art's only master is necessity." The plan included farsighted arrangements for interurban traffic.

The technological conditions of that time required that the transport pattern for goods should radiate from the numerous railway stations within the city. The railway lines, which were also to serve for passenger transport, were to be embedded in wide avenues. Wagner also suggested some large-scale urban solutions for public squares and for the siting of public buildings, but he tended to plan most areas however, according to a rather monotonous gridiron pattern.

Otto Wagner

Design of a city extension: aerial view of the district center. (Wagner, Die-Großstadt.)

Wagner developed and elaborated his ideas on town planning in his book entitled *A Study of the Large City* (1911). For Vienna he envisaged an unlimited concentric growth and wide ring roads. Each sector was to comprise the necessary public buildings and green spaces, leaving only 50 percent of the land for private construction of blocks of apartments.

Wagner's progressive ideas were not adopted by the municipal administration. He was, however, appointed chief artistic adviser for hydraulic constructions and for the new interurban railway lines within Vienna in 1894. In this capacity he achieved his biggest success, combining his talents both as architect and as town planner.

BIBLIOGRAPHY: Otto Wagner, *Erläuterungs-Bericht zum Entwurfe für den General-Regulierungs-Plan über das gesamte Gemeindegebiet von Wien mit dem Kennworte: 'Artis sola domina necessitas,'* Wien, 1893; Joseph August Lux, *Die Wagner-Schule 1902*, Wien, Leipzig, 1903; Otto Wagner, *Die Broßstadt: Eine Studie über diere von Otto Wagner*, Wien, Verlag von Anton Schroll u. Komp., 1911; Joseph August Lux, *Otto Wagner*, München, Delphin-Verlag, 1914; Heinz Geretsegger and Max Peintner, *Otto Wagner 1841–1918: Unbegrenzte Großstadt, Beginn der modernen Architektur,* Salzburg, Residenzverlag, 1964.

—GEORG CONDITT

WALES (*See* UNITED KINGDOM.)

WASTE DISPOSAL (*See* REFUSE AND REFUSE DISPOSAL.)

WATER Areas of water as refreshing and decorative features in the urban scene have a place in the collage of the city designer. Cities, towns, and monastic settlements have been sited on rivers or by the sea since ancient and medieval times for the purposes of water supply, power, transport, and food.

The river on which a city is situated has generally been utilized in part as an amenity in a wide variety of ways, but in addition areas of water have been created for decorative and recreational purposes as attractive items in much new urban development. A spectacular modern example is the large Lake Burley Griffin, created for Canberra, the capital city of Australia. Artificial lakes have generally been created in fairly close proximity of water, either by utilizing an existing river by damming, as in the case of Canberra, or by draining marshy or waterlogged development sites by means of sumps which serve a utilitarian purpose while at same time being designed as decorative and amenity features.

The combination of buildings, sheets of water, and trees can add much to the beauties of the urban scene. The United States and Europe both provide many good modern examples. The Netherlands particularly offers many examples of the use of sheets of water in felicitous relation to buildings and trees.

Another aquatic feature that has served to beautify the city scene is the well or fountain that was commonly found in ancient and medieval market-places. It has survived as an attractive decorative feature in many squares and may be seen in the piazzas of some new urban developments.

WATER SUPPLY   Water is supplied from underground sources by means of wells and from rivers and streams by means of storage reservoirs. In either case, it is necessary for the planning authority to restrict land uses which may tend to pollute the source of supply. This particularly applies in chalk areas.

It is also necessary to consider the feasibility of increasing the supply of water to serve the future population of the area; this is an important aspect of the regional plan.

Proposals to create an impounding reservoir by flooding a valley in an area of high landscape value invariably prompts opposition; but service reservoirs, pumping stations, and purification works can usually be located in proximity to residential areas without adversely affecting amenity.

In most countries the consumption of water per head of population rises sharply with extensive urban development. This causes problems and necessarily influences the siting of the new settlements, towns, and city extensions.

Opinion differs on the extent to which storage reservoirs may be used for recreation such as fishing and sailing, thus providing useful amenities.

BIBLIOGRAPHY: J. W. Henderson, "Planning and Engineering," *Journal of the Town Planning Institute,* vol. 37, no. 2, 1950; Peter C. G. Isaac, *Public Health Engineering,* E. & F.N. Spon, 1953; S. J. Asher, *Water Supply and Main Drainage,* Crosby Lockwood, 1961; H. Speight, "The Water Resources Act—Purpose, Pattern and Possible effects," *Journal Institute of Municipal Engineering,* vol. 94, no. 8, 1967.   —JOHN G. JEFFERSON

WATER TRANSPORT   (*See* TRANSPORT *and* HARBORS AND DOCKS.)

WEBER, ADNA   (1870–1967)   American statistician who, in the 1890s, pioneered in the systematic study of urbanization. Born and raised in upstate New York, he studied mathematics at Cornell University after receiving a Ph.B. in 1894. Columbia University awarded him a Ph.D. in 1898, and his doctoral dissertation, *The Growth of Cities in the Nineteenth Century,* was published the following year. This work is generally accepted as a classic effort to chart the causes and consequences of the rise of nineteenth-century urban-industrial societies. It includes extensive tables, graphs, and statistics on a wide variety of social and demographic topics. Despite the fact that Weber's research was inevitably flawed by the crudeness and inaccuracy of the national records relied on for raw data, his study remains of value due to the author's considerable skill and insight. Cornell University Press republished the book in 1965, and this edition contains bibliographic material and a brief biographical essay. Until blindness forced formal retirement in 1923, Weber was employed by various New York State agencies as a statistician.

—Stanley Buder

WELLS, H. G. (HERBERT GEORGE) (1866–1946)   English writer of great versatility whose works included science fiction, novels of realistic human comedy and of social and political criticism, works of scientific and sociological prediction, and (in collaboration with specialists), educational books on history, biology, industry, and social welfare. His idealistic prescriptions for the future, notably *A Modern Utopia* (1905) and *New Worlds for Old* (1908), had great influence on the rising socialist and labor movement.

Of special interest to town planners is his chapter in *Anticipations* (1902), entitled "The Probable Diffusion of Great Cities," a brilliant forecast of the effects of rapid transport, economic change, and scientific discovery on urban development—not altogether correct, but showing an appreciation of the human desire for houses with gardens in delightful country surroundings. He joined Howard's Garden City Association and was for a time a vice-president. But he took little if any part in the advocacy of governmental planning control. With all his powers of imaginative foresight, he was too impatient with politicians to attempt to influence legislation directly.

Nevertheless, his inexhaustible fecundity of ideas and a literary style that made him readable both to academics and the masses placed him among the most profound influences on modern thought and social policy.

—Frederic J. Osborn

WOOD, JOHN, THE ELDER (1704–1754)   With his son John Wood the Younger (*q.v.*), Wood replanned the city of Bath—an imaginative project which not only retains its interest as a major aesthetic achievement but continues to exemplify principles of planning that are abidingly valid.

One of the most ancient and historic of English cities, Bath in the eighteenth century, largely under the auspices of Richard Nash, better known as Beau Nash, was also one of the most fashionable on account of the medicinal value of the waters from its hot springs. The Woods put into practice the taste for Roman grandeur prevailing in England at the time with the influence of the Italian Renaissance. Their work comprises the interrelated group of Queen's Square, the Circus, and the Crescent, and it is particularly notable for the success with which it illustrates the aesthetic principle of variety within unity.

—Wilfred Salter

WOOD, JOHN, THE YOUNGER (1727–1782) After the death of his father, he continued the work and contributed many important designs of his own. He completed the building of the Circus, and was responsible for the architectural design of the Royal Crescent, the culminating glory of Bath which was completed in 1767. Writing of it in *Town & Country Planning* (Oxford University Press, 1959), Sir Patrick Abercrombie remarks:

> The Royal Crescent, in which domesticity reaches a truly monumental but restrained grandeur, is an example of aristocratic and architectural result obtained without pressure on the part of landlord or architect; the uniformity of external effect (for the house plans vary) was obtained as a result of a common inclination towards restraint of individualism.

A significant contribution of the Woods to both planning and architectural design lay in their sensitive combination of straight with curvilinear vistas. The Woods set the theme of classical formal planning at Bath for several later architects, of which the most notable was Thomas Baldwin, who designed part of the layout south of the river Avon including Laura Place and the magnificent Great Pulteney Street.

BIBLIOGRAPHY: Reginald Blomfield, *A History of Renaissance Architecture in England, 1500–1800,* G. Bell & Sons, Ltd., London, 1897; Walter Ison, *"The Georgian Buildings of Bath from 1700 to 1830,* Faber & Faber, Ltd., London, 1948; Bryan Little, *Bath Portrait,* Burleigh Press, Bristol, 1961.

—WILFRED SALTER

WORLD TOWN-PLANNING DAY Organizacion Internacional del Dia Mondial del Urbanismo was founded in 1949 by Professor Carlos Maria della Paolera of the University of Buenos Aires. Each year, on November 8, planners and planning bodies are asked to send telegrams or postal greetings to a leading planner in a particular country, designated by the international organization as president of the local committee for that country, who is also asked to arrange celebrations (meetings, lectures, exhibitions, press articles, other publications, etc.) on or about November 8 to publicize developments in planning at home and in other countries. The address of the organization is: Director, OIDMU, Ombu 2905, Suc. 25, Buenos Aires, Argentina.

The well-known symbol of World Town-Planning Day was designed by Professor della Paolera in 1934.

BIBLIOGRAPHY: F. J. Osborn, *World Town-Planning Day: Aide-Memoire for Speakers and Writers,* 1969.

WREN, Sir CHRISTOPHER (1632–1723) England's most famous architect, was born at East Knoyle in Wiltshire on October 20, 1632. His early life was spent chiefly in the study of astronomy, of which he became professor at Oxford in 1662. Shortly before the great fire of London in 1666, he turned to architecture. The great fire provided Wren with his opportunities. It destroyed 436 acres of buildings, including St. Paul's Cathedral, 87 churches,

Portrait of Sir Christopher Wren by Sir Godfrey Kneller, 1711 (National Portrait Gallery, London.)

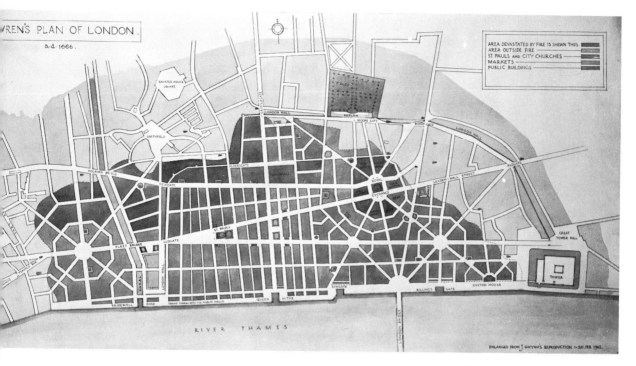

Wren's plan for London after the great fire of 1666.

44 halls of city companies, and 13,200 houses. Seven plans were made for rebuilding the city—by Peter Mills, the city surveyor, and by John Evelyn, Robert Hooke, Valentine Knight, Richard Newcourt (who made two plans), and Christopher Wren. The plan of the first mentioned has not survived. Wren's plan received the commendation of Charles II; it is the most comprehensive and satisfactory of those that were prepared. It has been studied and admired by succeeding generations of planners.

Evelyn's plan has many features in common with Wren's, and it is difficult to decide whether the two were made completely independently or as the result of mutual influence. None of the plans was adopted, mainly because of the trouble in obtaining the necessary collaboration of property owners, the legal difficulties, and the cost.

Wren's plan (see illustration) is on formal, classical Renaissance lines with long straight streets, an adaptation of the gridiron plan in one part, and a series of piazzas with radiating streets linked by concentric roads all ingeniously contrived with a view to their practical application and the minimization of sharp angles for building blocks. The chief focal points are a circular piazza at the west end, from which eight streets radiate linked by an octagonal road; a large triangular space ascending and widening to St. Paul's Cathedral at the east end; the Royal Exchange in the middle of a large piazza which forms the main center from which ten streets radiate, one of which to the south extends to the semicircular space at the head of London Bridge. A broad quay was planned along the river, with numerous transverse streets making approach to it easy and convenient. Sir Reginald Blomfield said of this plan that it "would have made the City of London one of the most beautiful in the world."

The middle period of Wren's long life was devoted mainly to designing and building St. Paul's Cathedral and numerous city churches, but a little later he designed a considerable number of secular buildings, among them hospitals at Chelsea and Greenwich which gave some scope for his talents as a planner. The buildings are spaciously laid out on classical, symmetrical lines. The scheme at Greenwich had been begun with The Queen's House by Inigo Jones and the "King Charles Block" of the Hospital by John Webb, and on the basis of the existing theme Wren created a magnificent group with colonnaded and domed buildings symmetrically flanking courts opening to the river, with the rising ground of Greenwich Park forming a background.

After a few years of peaceful retirement Wren died at Hampton Court on February 25, 1723.

BIBLIOGRAPHY: Christopher Wren, Jr., and Stephen Wren, *Parentalia,* London, 1750; Sir Reginal Blomfield, *A History of Renaissance Architecture in England,* G. Bell, & Sons, Ltd., London, 1897, 2 vols.; Wren Society, *Miscellaneous Designs—Plans for Rebuilding,* London, vol. XII of a 20-volume work; Martin S. Briggs, *Wren the Incomparable,* George Allen & Unwin, Ltd., London, 1953.   —ARNOLD WHITTICK

WRIGHT, FRANK LLOYD (1869–1959)   The most famous American architect of the twentieth century, born in a rural district near the town of Spring Green, Wisconsin, on June 8, 1869. Here he spent his early years, a fact which is not without significance, as a love of the country in all its moods and manifestations was a ruling passion of his life and dominated his work both as architect and planner. Many of his greatest achievements were in the field of domestic architecture. He designed a very large number of houses, some of them of considerable size, and a principal aim in his designs was to integrate his buildings with their natural surroundings. He said that a house should not be *on* a hill but *of* a hill, and that it should be difficult to discern where the house ends and the garden begins. This was an expression of his philosophy that building is an extension of the creative process of nature and that all design should conform to the principles of organic growth and unity.

These ideas influenced Wright's work as a planner. He insisted that people should have the country near at hand to enjoy. Thus his plans always meant very low-density development and a generous measure of open space and gardens between the houses.

Among his early schemes for a housing layout was his "quadruple block," which was a compact design of four houses grouped in the center of an acre plot so as to obtain the maximum area of surrounding land. Wright was to reproduce this idea in several later plans, such as the projects for the towns of Bitter Root (1910) and Broadacre City (1930).

In 1927 he prepared a scheme for the considerable sized settlement of San-Marcas-in-the-Desert, near Chandler, Arizona, which comprised much ingenious stepped development and planning in a hotel and houses.

The project for Broadacre City was for a development occupying about 4 square miles. In this plan Wright combined family houses at low density, many on 1-acre plots, several apartment blocks, agricultural units, a steel cathedral, and a planetarium. Several of these structures represented earlier projects which he included in this city plan. A later project was for the Florida Southern College campus on the edge of a lake, with a large orange plantation as a central feature. The scheme included a central chapel of unusual design, a water dome, an arboretum and laboratories, a museum, studios, an open-air theater, and a swimming pool all spaciously disposed among the orange groves.

None of these large-scale projects was ever completely implemented, and very little urban planning by this great architect actually materialized. Yet in his insistence on organic unity and on the integration of buildings with their natural surroundings, so eloquently manifested in his many houses from the palatial residence to the cottage, he exercised a great influence on architects, urban planners, and landscape architects. He died on April 9, 1959, shortly after completing two ambitious projects, one for an opera house and surroundings in Baghdad, and the other for the Marin County civic center, the long, superimposed arcades of which were significantly described by Vincent Scully, Jr., as almost like Roman aqueducts stretching out to grasp the rounded hills above the automobile traffic which rushes and flows below them.

BIBLIOGRAPHY: Henry-Russell Hitchcock, *In the Nature of Materials, 1887–1941: The Buildings of Frank Lloyd Wright,* Duell, Sloan & Pearce, Inc., New York, 1942; Grant C. Manson, *Frank Lloyd Wright to 1910: The First Golden Age,* New York, 1958; Vincent Scully, Jr., *Frank Lloyd Wright,* George Braziller, Inc., New York, and Mayflower Publishing Co., London, 1960.
—ARNOLD WHITTICK

WRIGHT, HENRY (1878–1936) Born in Kansas, Wright studied architecture at the University of Pennsylvania, but he settled in St. Louis as a landscape architect and there developed a special skill as site planner for subdivisions, by preference on difficult or almost unusable sites, such as Forest Ridge near Forest Park. As planner, Wright developed further the innovations of Olmsted and Unwin, diminishing the amount of space wasted on unnecessary or excessively wide streets and roads, and using this saving to provide more useful open spaces for gardens and playgrounds. After serving as planner for the United States Shipping Board's wartime housing (1917–1918), Wright came to New York to take part, during the next decade, in the new low-cost housing program of the City Housing Corporation. This association led to his active membership in the Regional Planning Association of America and his service as chief planning consultant on the New York State Housing and Regional Planning Commission. The final report of this commission, a plan for the State of New York which brought to a head 3 years of research, bears the unmistakable stamp of Wright's mind and style, down to the actual drawings for a new distribution of the urban population, on a unified but decentralized (postmetropolitan) basis. In his collaboration with Stein (*q.v.*), Wright's contribution was mainly in planning; and though he helped to develop the Radburn plan, he never

Henry Wright.

committed himself to any single program or solution, however successful, but kept on inventing new openings and trying new combinations like the veteran chess player he was. Sojourning in Germany in 1932, Wright came in contact with the best current housing, that of Ernst May in Römerstadt and Werner Moser in Neubuehl (Zurich). In 1933, as cofounder of the Housing Study Guild, Wright gave fresh direction to a younger generation of architects and planners whom he gathered about him, first at his own private summer school, then when visiting professor in various universities. Unfortunately his influence, apart from his book *Re-Housing Urban America* (1935), was cut short by his death. Wright's experimental open-mindedness, his skill in quantitative cost analysis, his ability to bring together specialists in many different fields, and not least his vivid sense of communal, family, and personal needs, placed him apart from more rigid, fashionable theorists with their neat geometric solutions. Henry Wright's site plan for Chatham Village, Pittsburgh, in its very freedom from mechanistic clichés, remains one of the timeless masterpieces of contemporary urban design.

BIBLIOGRAPHY: *Final Report,* New York State Housing and Regional Planning Commission, New York, 1926 (Though not put in final form by Wright, the main ideas and the actual illustration of the phases of development are by him. See Mumford, *The Culture of Cities,* Plate 22.); Henry Wright, "Cottage and Tenement in the U.S.A.," *Papers of the International Housing and Town Planning Congress,* Vienna, 1926, "The Autobiography of Another Idea," *Western Architect,* September 1930, *Re-housing Urban America,* New York, 1935; *Dictionary of American Biography,* vol. XXII, Supplement 2, New York, 1958; Roy Lubove, *Community Planning in the Nineteen-Twenties,* Pittsburgh, 1964.

—LEWIS MUMFORD

WURSTER, CATHERINE BAUER (1905–1964)   American writer on housing and city planning. Her book *Modern Housing* (1934), written after a tour in Europe, was notable for its literary quality as well as its integration of the subject with urban sociology, the distribution of population, and the decentralization of industry. Thereafter, in many articles, as lecturer at Harvard, Wisconsin, Cornell, and California universities—as well as adviser to the United States Government and the United Nations—she had considerable influence on United States housing and planning policy. In 1940 she married William W. Wurster, sometime dean of architecture at the University of California. A book of essays in her memory, *Shaping an Urban Future* (MIT Press, Cambridge, Mass., 1969), contains a bibliography of her writings.

YUGOSLAVIA

Legislation and Administration   Before World War II Yugoslavia was one of the less developed states with great social and economic differences between various regions and with a centralized government. Town planning legislation before 1918 was based on Austro-Hungarian and Serbian laws. The influence of Western, especially German, planning theories began about 1932, when an enactment obliged all towns to examine and revise development plans. A few years later a building act was passed which contained progressive provisions for that period, corresponding with contemporary theories of planning. The first urban programs, preliminary sketches, and development plans with the necessary regulations to ensure their implementation were elaborated at that time.

Today, Yugoslavia is a federal socialist republic, composed of the national socialistic republics of Bosnia and Herzegovina, Crna Gora (Montenegro), Croatia, Macedonia, Slovenia, and Serbia as well as the autonomous socialist countries Kosovo and Vojvodina, with a total population of 18.5 million inhabitants.

The federal assembly and the federal government are concerned mainly with the protection of the Constitution, with basic legislation, and with urgent administration especially important for the state, such as national defense and foreign affairs. Town planning is the concern of the communities and municipalities which prepare, pass, and implement all town and country planning schemes for their territories.

The federal Assembly exercises its authority in town and regional planning through its commission composed of members of Parliament, deputies of professional organizations, and public workers. Its function is to assure the coordination of laws and prescriptions concerning spatial planning in a wider sense, to provide and regulate transport, agriculture, and the location of industry. Its main task is to prepare conditions for a national spatial plan.

At the national level there are secretariats for town planning, housing, and municipal engineering, which include urban inspectorates. Administrative departments for planning in the communities and municipalities are concerned with the control and execution of planning policy.

The autonomy of the municipalities and public control is confirmed by the councils for planning, composed of professional people, local representatives, experts, and politicians. Final decisions are given by municipal assemblies.

The first legislative town planning document after the 1939 to 1945 war was the federal regulation, issued in 1947, concerning the general urban plan. Municipalities were required to prepare plans for the spatial structure. This law was based on the experiences of the U.S.S.R. and of the Western states. Although it was progressive at that time, it could not be brought into practice because of a shortage of trained experts, weak public support, and also because of the unfavorable economic situation.

Among other federal laws, that providing for the nationalization of built-up areas in towns should be considered. According to this law, all built-up areas and building plots must be sold to the municipality and prepared for eventual development. By these means land speculation is theoretically prevented and development made possible.

Another very important law is concerned with the preparation and use of urban land. According to it the occupation of building plots is permitted only when the land is equipped with all municipal utilities such as water supply, sewerage, electricity, gas, and heating. In developed regions this is not difficult. But in the past there were many mistakes made in satisfying these requirements, and insufficiently equipped residential and central areas remain to be completed.

In general, legislation provides three degrees of planning:

1. The urban program for the territory of the whole administrative community or municipality, which has to be prepared following the regional analysis, with a forecast for future development

2. The long-range urban plan in a restricted sense for settlements, towns, and central villages, industrial settlements and holiday resorts and for special areas which hold prospects for development

3. The short-range detailed development plans for urbanized areas which have to be built up within 5 to 10 years

Legislation in regional spatial planning is in force at republican levels. In some socialistic republics, for example in Slovenia, the revision and amendment of the regional spatial plan has been continuing for several years.

Professional Practice Planning practice in a wide sense can be divided into the following categories:

1. Town and spatial planning, based on the enactments of the Republic, comprehends the preparation of regional plans for territories of the republics, economic-geographic units, and recreational areas. It also includes the preparation of urban programs for the territories of metropolitan areas and rural communities. The communities are basic units of authority and administration. They are relatively large, with populations ranging from 5,000 to 100,000. In some bigger towns the connection between the municipal authorities and the local population is established by local communities as neighborhood units, with only local competencies. Similar local bodies exist in villages.

Town and regional planning is assigned to special institutions, organized by national, municipal, or communal authorities, including the Federal Planning Institute in Belgrade, 64 planning agencies, and various institutes or offices.

2. Urban design is practiced by the same organizations, or in architectural and engineering bureaus, which are equipped with experts for traffic, municipal engineering, and landscaping. Development plans for central or residental areas are generally secured by public competition.

3. The execution and control of urban plans is by municipal and communal authorities. In smaller communities which have not enough experts, this task may be assigned to one of the nearest planning offices.

4. Research institutes for planning exist in Belgrade, Zagreb, Sarajevo, and Ljubljana, some being independent, self-governing institutions and some being attached to universities. They are financed partly by federal and national funds and they are concerned with practical phases of planning, including architecture, transport, water economy, and tourism.

In recent years collaboration with foreign planning and research bodies has become more extensive. The International measures for the reconstruction of Skoplje, destroyed by an earthquake in 1963, should be mentioned as an example. The help of foreign experts on this project, especially those from Poland, Greece, and Japan, has been very precious. The same results are expected from the action for the South Adriatic Project, which is assisted in a similar way by the OUN. Among special forms of international collaboration are the American-Yugoslav project for urban and regional planning studies, which was founded by an agreement between the National Town Planning Institute of Slovenia and Cornell, later Wayne, university of the United States and partly assisted by the Ford Foundation. This has now extended its activities to many Yugoslav towns and regions and will grow into an international planning center.

Education and Training and Planning Institutions In the first years of the new

Yugoslavia there was no question who must and who has the right to occupy himself with town planning. In the beginning, as is well known, this was the field of architecture. The term "urbanist" was identical with "architect who is practicing town planning." Before World War II, urbanism had been taught at the departments or faculties for architecture in the universities of Belgrade, Zagreb, and Ljubljana. After the war the number of faculties and graduated architects increased, so that the number is now sufficient. However, the lecture programs in many schools of architecture are too much based on design and too little on planning, and it has become evident that the collaboration of experts in other scientific branches was not sufficiently considered. The faculties where such specialists should be trained have not yet shown enough interest in spatial planning in their programs. However, in the department of municipal engineering and geodesy in the University of Ljubljana, the faculty for traffic engineering in Belgrade, and the urban department of the faculty for architecture in Sarajevo, urban and regional planning are included in the lecture programs.

In order to promote an interdisciplinary approach to planning, some faculties organize temporary postgraduate courses for improving knowledge of towns and regional planning. Through such programs, graduate students of various backgrounds can obtain master's or specialist's degrees. The number of doctorates in urbanism is still very modest.

Yugoslavia is one of the countries where there are no official regulations specifying who is qualified to carry out town and regional planning. While it is strictly prescribed which schools and diplomas are necessary for obtaining the authorization to design a bridge, a house, and a road, for instance, town, regional, and development plans, which are more important and far-reaching, can be carried out by small local planning agencies without the desirable specialists. Here can be seen the drawbacks of decentralization. Fortunately, this paradoxical situation will soon be improved.

It is necessary to establish an organization for the management and protection of the professional side of planning, like the American Institute of Planners or the Royal Town Planning Institute in the United Kingdom, which could take care of the systematic training of planners and could regulate their professional role.

The urbanists' societies in Yugoslavia played a very important role in the years when town planning was not included as a department in government and local bodies. In some republics, districts, and communities, town planning was attached to public works, or to social welfare and public health, or to industry. For that reason professional planners employed in planning agencies or offices searched for an organization where they could discuss current questions of urbanism, exchange their experiences, and improve their professional knowledge. Since 1949 annual or biennial conferences of urbanists have been organized, 15 having so far been held. The first urbanists' societies were founded in 1954, and in 1955 the Yugoslav Town Planning Federation was organized. It is composed of 12 republican and municipal societies and is incorporated into the International Federation for Housing and Planning.

Generally, membership of professional organizations in Yugoslavia is based on qualifications obtained in different faculties and high schools. There are associations of architects, of civil engineers, of geographers, and of economists, The Yugoslav Town Planning Federation includes those concerned with planning: architects, municipal engineers, and other specialists, governmental and municipal planning officers, members of Parliament and of public bodies, planning agencies, and research institutes.

Owing to the very intense daily activity of local associations and of the Yugoslav Town Planning Federation, the public began to understand and to accept modern planning ideas. Step by step the necessary laws were introduced, state secretariats for planning were nominated, spatial planning was accepted as a national task, and the whole planning procedure was adapted to the general principles of democracy and self-government.

Geographical and Climatic Conditions   Yugoslavia is situated in the southeastern part of Europe generally called "the Balkans." Its topographical character is threefold: on the northeastern side are big areas of the Pannonian lowland belonging to the Danubian river basin; along the southwestern border lies a narrow, 496-mile-long (800-kilometers) strip of the Adriatic coast with Istria, Dalmatia, and the South Adriatic; and between these topographical formations are large mountains—the southern Alps and the Dinar Mountains—which extend from the Austrian to the Albanian borders. The extensive areas of the Dinar Mountains are less suitable for settlement and traffic. There are also different climatic conditions in Yugoslavia—a mild climate in the middle and the south Adriatic, and the continental climate in the Pannonian lowland and in the Dinar areas. The alpine regions are well known for their quantities of atmospheric precipitation. Because of frequent snowfall, the higher areas are very suitable for winter sports.

This topographical structure has influenced the development of the transport network. As is well known, an important travel route between Central Europe and the East passes through Yugoslavia. The main communications follow the currents of large rivers: the Sava, Danube, Morava, and Vardar. To this longitudinal backbone are connected roads and railroads of national importance, penetrating along river courses in the interior of the Dinar masses and connecting the Pannonian lowland with the Adriatic coast. Many of these communications have been provided in the last 20 years. Among them, the Adriatic main road, which runs along the coast from Trieste to the Alvanian border, is of special importance.

Land use in Yugoslavia is firmly connected with its topographical character. The valleys of big rivers are at the same time very highly developed agriculturally, while the central areas are very rich in minerals.

Yugoslavia has a population of 20.5 million, with an average density of 80.3 inhabitants per square kilometer (209 per square mile). Only 34.9

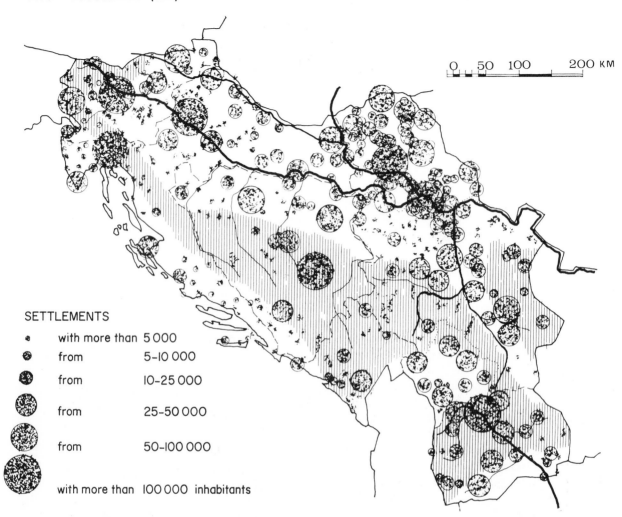

SETTLEMENTS

●	with more than	5 000
◉	from	5–10 000
◉	from	10–25 000
◉	from	25–50 000
◉	from	50–100 000
◉	with more than	100 000 inhabitants

0   50   100   200 KM

Urbanization. The hatched areas show the Southern Alps and the Dinar and Rodop mountain chains.

percent of the total population live in towns with over 5,000 inhabitants and only 13.5 percent in towns with over 100,000 inhabitants. It is not a country of big towns, but the social and professional structures are changing very fast.

It is significant that only one-third of the nonagricultural population live in towns with over 20,000 inhabitants. This means that two-thirds of the people employed in industry and professions live in villages and smaller settlements—which emphasizes their importance.

Traditions of Planning to the End of the Nineteenth Century Owing to its geographical position, Yugoslavia was firmly connected with three cultural spheres which influenced its architecture and planning; namely, the cultures of Central Europe, of the Mediterranean, and of the Orient. Their presence can be followed until the beginning of industrialization, which by degrees advanced from west to east.

The medieval towns on the north and west of Yugoslavia belong to the Central European cultural circle. Some of the towns of these territories formed their characteristic architectural images in the baroque period, among them some larger towns, such as Ljubljana and Zagreb.

In the Mediterranean region of Yugoslavia, which extends along the Adriatic coast, there exist a great number of coastal towns, where—due to their stone construction—medieval buildings are still preserved. The later development in the Renaissance and baroque periods has given to these towns an added charm, which can be seen, for example, in Dubrovnik.

The rural and urban settlements in the eastern and southeastern regions of Yugoslavia, some of them belonging to the Turkish Empire until the middle of the nineteenth century, still show in their general scheme, especially in their central areas, the strong influence of Oriental town design. This can be seen in Skoplje, Sarajevo, and Prizren. Planning ideas from that period show traits very similar to modern principles of land use; for example, the centralization of commercial and public life around the *tsharshiya* (Turkish bazaar) and the well-organized residental units (*mahala's*), all connected by a characteristic transport network divided into traffic and pedestrian streets.

Dubrovnik. A characteristic example of Mediterranean town planning.

Twentieth Century

New Towns and Communities The population structure of Yugoslav towns shows certain specific features. Only the capital, Belgrade, had attained 1 million population. Zagreb has 566,000, and only five towns exceed a population of 100,000. There are, consequently, no problems of overspill. The Yugoslav new towns were founded for other reasons characteristic of a developing country.

Intensive industrialization began in Yugoslavia about 1950, with a strong emphasis on the improvement of less developed regions. Because the existing—almost primitive—villages and country towns were not suitable to receive the necessary labor of new industrial and mining enterprises, it became urgent to build new workers' settlements.

Many of them never attained the necessary size of a normal neighborhood unit and remained incomplete and isolated housing groups without connection with the next country town. Some, however, due to their favorable sites, traffic conditions, and other advantages of location, developed into complete new towns, as, for example, Železnik near Belgrade, Velenje in Slovenia, and some small new towns in Bosnia and Herzegovina. Velenje obtained a reputation for its architectural and urban qualities. It was founded as the center of a coal district 37 miles (60 kilometers) northwest of Ljubljana, with very exact boundaries of built-up land bordered by coal reserves. The site is comparatively flat, with hills on the northern and southern sides. In the south, at the foot of the castle hill, the old village Velenje is situated. The northern part of the plain was built up during the first years after the liberation, mostly with individual houses. In the next building periods emphasis was given to blocks of apartments and to the

Velenje New Town. Panoramic view. In the foreground the main place, or square; on the left the community center.

development of the town center, with the necessary civic, cultural, commercial, and educational services for the whole district. The recent tendency to build detached houses caused some change in the general conception of the town plan, and a large area in the northern part is now built up with houses and bungalows. In 1970 the size was 10,000, and it is planned to reach 30,000 in 1980.

The pattern of the town has been subjected to some criticism. Conditions of planning were not very favorable, especially because of the time factor. Some criticism is directed at the main central place, which is large and monumental but not sufficiently equipped with shops, cafeterias, and other necessary premises. Nevertheless, because of specific conditions of its growth, Velenje is a kind of display of Yugloslav architecture, of both the modest and the most luxurious achievements. It represents what is typical and progressive in Yugoslav architecture and planning.

City and Town Extensions The territorial extension of towns is, in Yugoslavia as almost everywhere, the commonest way to provide for the increasing population. Opportunities to extend towns on a large scale are rare. One successful solution is New Belgrade, the new residental and administrative center of the Yugoslav capital.

Town extension. Master plan of New Belgrade; (1) residential areas, (2) central areas and isolated public buildings, (3) services, (4) industry, (5) green spaces.

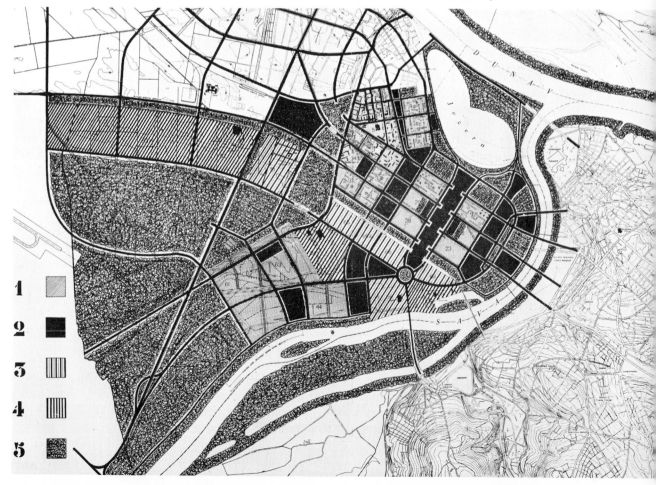

Town extension. Community center in New Belgrade.

In 1945 the Yugoslav federal government concluded that the territory of Belgrade was too small for the increasing population and for the needs of new governmental institutions. Therefore, in collaboration with municipal authorities, it was decided to occupy the large sandy area on the left bank of the Sava River over which pass the communications with the western part of the state. The Sava River was for centuries the border between the eastern and western civilizations, between Serbia and Austria. The new plan had to symbolize the unification of all Yugoslav territories.

The principal scheme for New Belgrade aims to connect Belgrade with the town of Zemun, 6 miles (10 kilometers) away. It seems to be a little rigid and unnecessarily monumental, with its main axis between the railway station and the palace of the federal government and with large, regularly designed green spaces. Some people see in this scheme the ancestor of Brasília. However, this conception makes possible construction in stages and also the disposition of a modern traffic network with sufficient capacities for future needs. The size of residential buildings seems to be beyond the human scale, but the designers try to make some interior places more attractive and intimate. New Belgrade is planned for a population of 200,000. It exceeded 50,000 in 1972.

Urban Renewal   In Yugoslav towns urban renewal is undertaken for different reasons. Beside the usual historical motives, such as demolition of city walls, widening of streets, improvement of railway junctions, or the repair of buildings damaged by war, urban renewal becomes necessary because of the increasing concentration of population and because of growing space needs of individuals and communities. It is especially urgent in cases where the central areas are not used on a rational basis and where the floor space index is unsufficient. This argument is characteristic of developing countries, where the increasing population is not followed by adequate spatial improvements.

The reconstruction of Skoplje is taking place for completely different reasons. The capital of the socialist republic of Macedonia, Skoplje, was ruined to such a degree in the big earthquake of July 26, 1963, that rebuilding on an entirely new site, far away from the existing one, was seriously contemplated. But seismic research has shown that the old site is as safe as any other in that part of the country.

Thus, during the rescue operations, the first new houses were being erected. Then, in only a few months after the disaster, big new housing estates, mostly one-family houses, were constructed on free ground. They

Urban renewal. Master plan for Skopje, 1981. The areas of low density are already developed. These are new settlements of prefabricated houses, erected immediately after the earthquake.

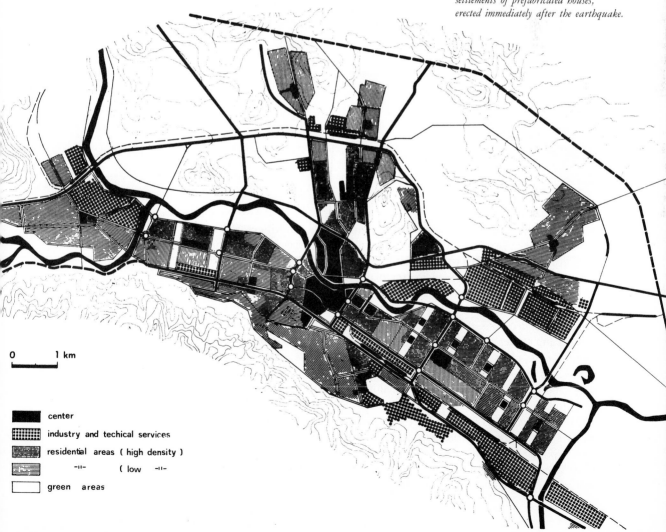

0   1 km

- ◼️ center
- ▦ industry and techical services
- ▓ residential areas (high density)
- ▤   -"-   (low   -"-)
- ☐ green areas

Urban renewal. Results of the international competition. (First prize: Kenzo Tange.)

were put together entirely of prefabricated elements on the fringes of the ruined city. The construction was financed by other Yugoslav republics and by many other countries as a part of their help to Skoplje. Before the disaster the city already had an approved master plan which, however, had to be dropped. Preparations for a new master plan for Skoplje and its region were started soon after the earthquake. The first—undoubtedly very justified—reconstruction decisions determined to a considerable extent the future directions and conceptions of the development of the city and defined many elements of the plan. For that reason, the length of the agglomeration is now over 12 miles (20 kilometers). In the prefabricated villages there are about 15,000 dwellings with 60,000 inhabitants—nearly one-third of the total population of Skoplje.

All urban documents for Skoplje, by its planning agency and by groups of experts from many countries, especially Poland and Greece, were guided and controlled by the International Consultative Board nominated by the O.U.N. Special Fund. Reconstruction works were organized by a special Direction for City Reconstruction.

Special attention was given to the renewal of Skoplje's central area. For this reason an international competition was organized in 1965. The winners were Kenzo Tange from Tokyo and Miščević and Wenzler from Zagreb. The definitive plan was elaborated by both working groups in collaboration with the Municipal Planning Agency.

The population of Skoplje is 200,000 and is planned to reach 350,000 in 1981.

BIBLIOGRAPHY: "Yugoslav Planning," special Issue of *Arhitektura-urbanizam,* Belgrade, 1965; Nikola Dobrović, *Urbanizam kroz vekove—Jugoslavija,* Belgrade, 1950; Saša Sedlar, "A Yugoslav New Town," *Town and Country Planning,* London, March 1961; Adolf Ciborowski, "Some Problems in Connection with the Rebuilding and Development of Skopje," *Your Aid to Skopje,* Skoplje, October-December 1964; Saša Sedlar, "Planning Achievements in Yugoslavia," *Official Architecture and Planning.* London, 11/1965; *Skopje Master Plan,* Report prepared for the United Nations as executing agency for the UN Special Fund, vol. 5, Skoplje, 1966; Saša Sedlar, "Problemi urbanistici della ricostruzione di Skopje," *Umana,* Trieste, 5–6/1966; Municipal Town Planning Office, Belgrade, *Novi Beograd,* Belgrade, 1967; Saša Sedlar, *Städtebau in Jugoslawien,* Zentralinstitut für Städtebau an der T.U., Berlin, 13/1967; Igor Vrišer, *Landesplanung in Jugoslawien,* Plan, Zürich, 12/1965; Vladimir Mušič, "Problems of Regional Planning in Yugoslavia," *The New Atlantic,* Milano, 1969; Boris Gaberščik, "Jugoslawien—Raumordnung und Raumplanung," *Handwörterbuch der Raumforschung und Raumordnung,* Hannover, 1970.

—SAŠA SEDLAR

Z

ZIGGURAT An ancient Babylonian and Assyrian structure like a stepped pyramid, with a temple at the top and approached by a processional way. In every important city there was at least one ziggurat. The ziggurats were probably, originally, imitations of mountains where it was thought that the gods dwelt. (*See* ANCIENT PLANNING: MESOPOTAMIA.)

The romantic notion of building ziggurats has occurred to modern architects and planners as a means of providing a dominating feature in the townscape. The term "ziggurat architecture" is used in connection with building that has some resemblance to the stepped pyramid, although the term is rather loosely applied.

ZONING AND ZONING LAWS Zoning is the division of a community into zones or districts according to present and potential use of properties for the purpose of controlling and directing the use and development of those properties. It is concerned primarily with the use of land and buildings, the height and bulk of buildings, the proportion of a lot which buildings may cover, and the density of population of a given area. As an instrument of plan implementation, zoning deals principally with the use and development of privately owned land and buildings rather than with public land, buildings, and facilities.

Zoning became widespread in the United States before the advent of community planning. The first ordinance that districted an entire community was enacted in New York City in 1916. By 1930, several hundred localities had followed suit and had established their own ordinances. Zoning ordinances typically subdivide the city or town into districts, in each of which specified uses are authorized and building height, bulk, and setback requirements are imposed.

Under British Planning Acts, no provision is made for the regulatory provisions of the zoning ordinance. Instead, the local planning authority, not having any detailed rules, studies each application on its merits, "having regard to the development plan." The legislative body is thus not expected to make decisions on potential application in advance by general rules, which is the function of the zoning ordinance.

The division of the community into zones is necessary in order to provide special regulations for different sections of the community in accordance with the planned development of each particular section. Although zoning regulations vary according to the uses established for each type of zone, regulations within a given zone or the same kinds of zone must be uniform. Thus, zoning contemplates different regulations to effectuate different land uses in different zones, but it seeks to avoid discrimination in the application of those regulations to the use of property similarly situated within a given zone or in the same kind of zone.

Zoning attempts to group together those uses which are most compatible. It has among its purposes (1) conserving the value of its property, (2) assuring orderly community growth, and (3) safeguarding the general public welfare. It seeks to preserve the planned character of the neighborhood by excluding uses and structures which are prejudicial to the restricted purposes of the area and to achieve the gradual elimination of existing nonconforming uses. At the same time, zoning legislation is designed to protect the owners of nonconforming property from unreasonable hardship occasioned by the compulsory elimination of nonconforming uses. By guiding community growth along orderly lines, zoning helps to minimize the demands for school facilities, utilities, streets, policing, fire protection, and other facilities and services, in particular before the city is prepared to provide these.

The objective of zoning legislation is to establish regulations which provide locations for all essential uses of land and buildings and to ensure that each use is located in the most appropriate place. While zoning helps to exclude nuisances which would tend to create blight in a particular district, it is not solely a means of nuisance control. Legitimate business operations which may be undesirable in one location may represent appropriate land use in some other area.

—TREVOR WHITTLEY

index